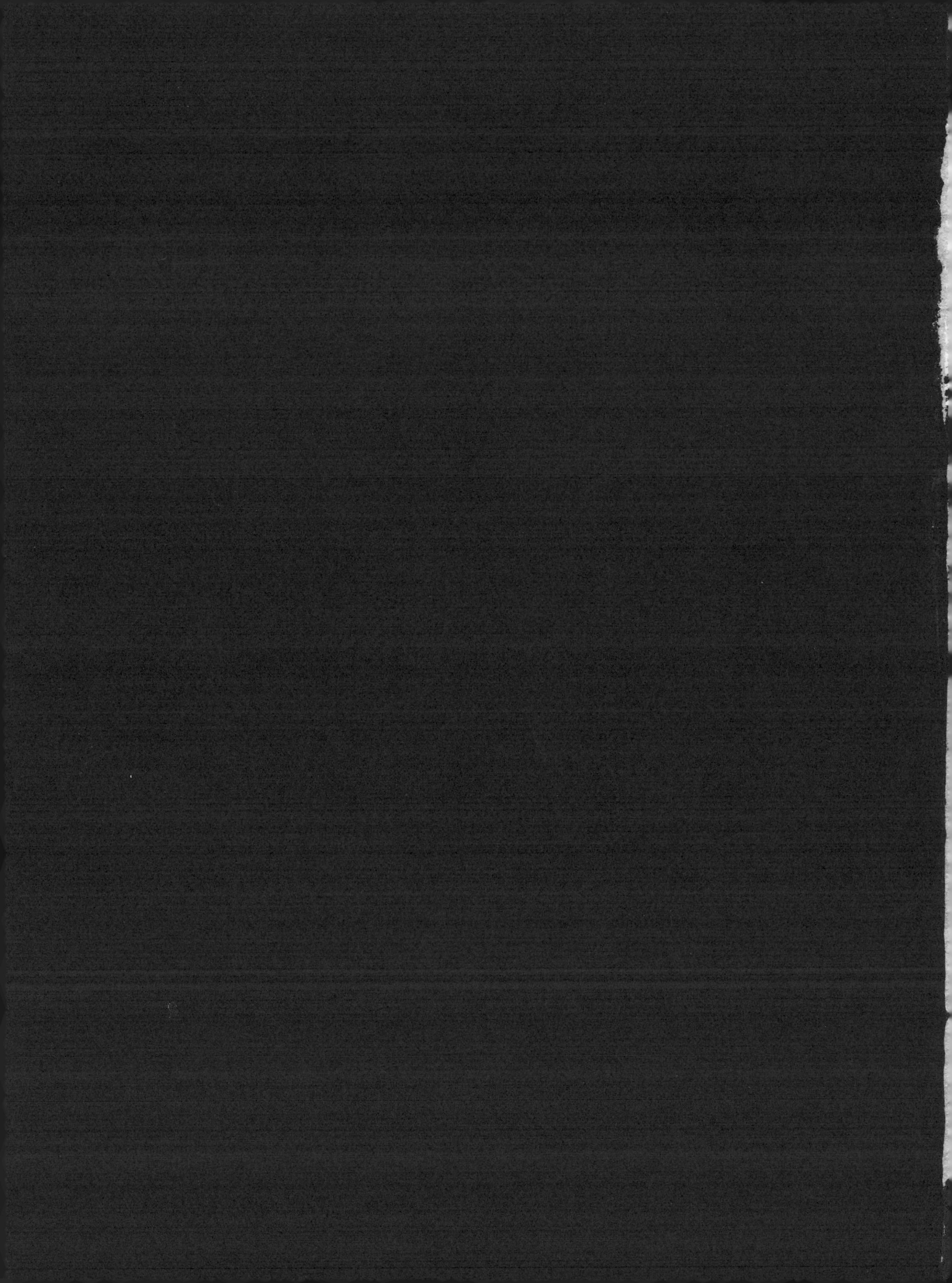

U.I.S.P.P.
Mesolithic Commission

THE
MESOLITHIC IN EUROPE

PAPERS PRESENTED AT THE THIRD INTERNATIONAL SYMPOSIUM
EDINBURGH 1985

Edited by

Clive Bonsall
Department of Archaeology, University of Edinburgh

JOHN DONALD PUBLISHERS LTD
EDINBURGH

ISBN 0 85976 205 X

Phototypesetting by Outline Edinburgh
Upmake by EMS Edinburgh
Printed in Great Britain by Bell and Bain Ltd,
Glasgow

Contents

Contributors

N. Arts
Instituut voor Prae- en Protohistorie,
Universiteit van Amsterdam, Singel 453,
1012 WP Amsterdam, The Netherlands.

E. Avellino
Antropologia, Dipartimento di Biologia Animale e
dell'Uomo, Città Universitaria, Piazzale Aldo
Moro, I-00185 Roma, Italy.

P.G. Bahn
428 Anlaby Road, Hull HU3 6QP,
United Kingdom.

S. Bang-Andersen
Arkeologisk Museum i Stavanger, Boks 478,
N-4001 Stavanger, Norway.

I. Barandiarán
Department of Prehistory and Archaeology,
University of the Basque Country, Vitoria,
Spain.

J. Bárta
Archeologický Ústav, Slovenská Akadémia
Vied, 949 21 Nitra-Hrad, Czechoslovakia.

R.N.E. Barton
Historic Buildings and Monuments Commission for
England, Fortress House, 23 Savile Row,
London W1X 2HE, United Kingdom.

P. Biagi
Dipartimento di Scienze Storiche Archeologiche e
Orientalistiche, Università di Venezia,
Palazzo Bernardo S. Polo 1977/A, I-30125 Venezia,
Italy.

A. Bietti
Antropologia, Dipartimento di Biologia Animale e
dell'Uomo, Città Universitaria, Piazzale Aldo
Moro, I-00185 Roma, Italy.

C. Bonsall
Department of Archaeology, University of
Edinburgh, 16–20 George Square,
Edinburgh EH8 9JZ, United Kingdom.

V. Boroneanţ
Association Internationale d'Etudes du Sud-Est
Européen, 47 Chaussée Kiseleff,
71268 Bucarest, Romania.

E. Brinch Petersen
Institut for Forhistorisk og Klassisk Arkæologi,
Københavns Universitet, Vandkunsten 5,
DK-1467 København K, Denmark.

G.M. Burov
Department of Ancient and Mediaeval History,
State University of Simferopol', 4 Yaltinskaya
Street, 333036 Simferopol', U.S.S.R.

A. Cava
Department of Prehistory and Archaeology,
University of the Basque Country, Vitoria,
Spain.

J.C. Chapman
Department of Archaeology, The University,
Newcastle upon Tyne NE1 7RU, United Kingdom.

J. Cherry
9 Kent Lea, Kendal, Cumbria LA9 6ED,
United Kingdom.

G.A. Clark
Department of Anthropology, Arizona State
University, Tempe, Arizona 85287-2402, U.S.A.

D. Coggins
Bowes Museum and Art Gallery, Newgate, Barnard
Castle, Co. Durham DH12 8NP, United Kingdom.

T. Constandse-Westermann
Instituut voor Prae- en Protohistorie,
Universiteit van Amsterdam, Singel 453,
1012 WP Amsterdam, The Netherlands.

J. Coularou
Centre d'Anthropologie des Sociétés Rurales,
CNRS et EHESS, 56 rue du Taur,
F-31000 Toulouse, France.

S. Coulson
Universitetets Oldsaksamling, Frederiks gate 2,
N-0164 Oslo 1, Norway.

A. David
Historic Buildings and Monuments Commission for
England, Fortress House, 23 Savile Row,
London W1X 2HE, United Kingdom.

M.R. Deith
Subdepartment of Quaternary Research,
University of Cambridge, Godwin Laboratory,
Free School Lane, Cambridge CB2 3RS,
United Kingdom.

L. Domańska
Katedra Archeologii, Uniwersytetu Łódzkiego,
Plac Wolności 14, 91-415 Łódź, Poland.

J.V. Dumont
117 Linden Lane, Princeton, New Jersey 08540,
U.S.A.

K.J. Edwards
Department of Geography, University of
Birmingham, P.O. Box 363, Birmingham B15 2TT,
United Kingdom.

E. Engelstad
Tromsø Museum, Universitet i Tromsø,
N-9000 Tromsø, Norway.

J.A. Fernández-Tresguerres Velasco
Departamento de Historia y Artes, Universidad de
Oviedo, Spain.

A. Fischer
Skov- og Naturstyrelsen, 10. kontor, Slotsmarken
13, DK-2970 Hørsholm, Denmark.

I. Gatsov
Institute of Archaeology, Al. Stambolijsky
Square 1, Sofia 1000, Bulgaria.

D. Geddes
Centre d'Anthropologie des Sociétés Rurales,
CNRS et EHESS, 56 rue du Taur,
F-31000 Toulouse, France.

P.A. Gendel
2226 Nashville Avenue, New Orleans,
Louisiana 70115, U.S.A.

L. Giacopini
Antropologia, Dipartimento di Biologia Animale e
dell'Uomo, Città Universitaria, Piazzale Aldo
Moro, I-00185 Roma, Italy.

M.R. González Morales
Departamento de Ciencias Históricas,
Universidad de Santander, Edificio
Interfacultativo, Avenida de los Castros s/n,
39005 Santander, Spain.

B. Gramsch
Museum für Ur- und Frühgeschichte Potsdam,
Schloss Babelsberg, DDR-1591 Potsdam-
Babelsberg, German Democratic Republic.

C. Grigson
Odontological Museum, Royal College of Surgeons
of England, 35–43 Lincoln's Inn Fields,
London WC2A 3PN, United Kingdom.

O. Grøn
Langelands Museum, Jens Winthersvej 12,
DK-5900 Rudkøbing, Denmark.

J. Guilaine
Centre d'Anthropologie des Sociétés Rurales,
CNRS et EHESS, 56 rue du Taur,
F-31000 Toulouse, France.

J.B. Innes
Institute of Prehistoric Sciences and
Archaeology, University of Liverpool, William
Hartley North Building, Brownlow Street,
Liverpool L69 3BX, United Kingdom.

M. Jackes
Department of Anthropology, University of
Alberta, Edmonton T6G 2H4, Canada.

M. Jochim
Department of Anthropology, University of
California, Santa Barbara, California 93106,
U.S.A.

K. Kloss
Museum für Ur- und Frühgeschichte Potsdam,
Schloss Babelsberg, DDR-1591 Potsdam-
Babelsberg, German Democratic Republic.

M. Kobusiewicz
Zakład Archeologii Wielkopolski, Instytut
Historii Kultury Materialnej, Polska Akademia
Nauk, ul. Zwierzyniecka 20, 60-814 Poznań,
Poland.

S.K. Kozłowski
Instytut Archeologii, Uniwersytet Warszawski,
ul. Widok 10, 00-023 Warszawa, Poland.

K.L. Kvamme
Arizona State Museum, University of Arizona,
Tucson, Arizona 85721, U.S.A.

L. Larsson
Lunds Universitet Historiska Museet,
Kraftstorg 1, S-22350 Lund, Sweden.

T. Laurie
15 Pierremont Crescent, Darlington DL3 9PB,
United Kingdom.

O. Le Gall
Institut du Quaternaire, Université de
Bordeaux I, allées des Facultés,
F-3400 Talence, France.

A.J. Legge
Archaeological Laboratory, Centre for
Extra-Mural Studies, Birkbeck College,
University of London, 26 Russell Square,
London WC1B 5DQ, United Kingdom.

J.G. Lewthwaite
Department of Archaeological Sciences, The
University, Bradford BD7 1DP, United Kingdom.

A. Lo Pinto
Antropologia, Dipartimento di Biologia Animale e
dell'Uomo, Città Universitaria, Piazzale Aldo
Moro, I-00185 Roma, Italy.

D. Lubell
Department of Anthropology, University of
Alberta, Edmonton T6G 2H4, Canada.

R. Maggi
Museo Archeologico, Via Costaguta 4,
I-16043 Chiavari, Italy.

M. Martzluff
Institut d'Etudes Andorranes, Université de
Perpignan, Chemin de Passio Vella,
F-66000 Perpignan, France.

H. Matiskainen
Suomen Lasimuseo, Tehtaankatu 23,
11910 Riihimäki, Finland.

C. Meiklejohn
Department of Anthropology, University of
Winnipeg, Winnipeg, Manitoba R3B 2E9, Canada.

J.E. Morais Arnaud
Instituto de Arqueologia, Faculdade de Letras,
Universidade de Lisboa, 1699 Lisboa Codex,
Portugal.

A. Morrison
Department of Archaeology, 10 The Square,
University of Glasgow, Glasgow G12 8QQ,
United Kingdom.

R.R. Newell
Biologisch–Archaeologisch Instituut,
Universiteit van Groningen, Postraat 6,
9712 ER Groningen, The Netherlands.

R. Nisbet
Dipartimento di Antropologia ed Archeologia,
Via Accademia Albertina, Torino, Italy.

S.V. Oshibkina
Institute of Archaeology, Academy of Sciences of
the U.S.S.R., Ulyanova 19, Moscow 117036,
U.S.S.R.

S. Palmer
London Borough of Bromley Museum, Orpington,
Kent BR6 0HH, United Kingdom.

T.D. Price
Department of Anthropology, University of
Wisconsin-Madison, 1180 Observatory Drive,
Madison, Wisconsin 53706, U.S.A.

J. Roche
16 avenue du Bel-Air, F-75012 Paris, France.

P.A. Rowley-Conwy
147 Victoria Road, Cambridge CB4 3BU,
United Kingdom.

J-G. Rozoy
26 rue du Petit Bois, F-08000 Charleville,
France.

A. Saville
93 Church Road, Leckhampton, Cheltenham,
Gloucestershire GL53 0PF, United Kingdom.

R.T. Schadla-Hall
Leicestershire Museums, Art Galleries and
Records Service, 96 New Walk,
Leicester LE1 6TD, United Kingdom.

R. Schild
Instytut Historii Kultury Materialnej, Polska
Akademia Nauk, ul. Świerczewskiego 105,
00-140 Warszawa, Poland.

I.G. Simmons
Department of Geography, University of Durham,
Science Laboratories, South Road,
Durham DH1 3LE, United Kingdom.

B. Skar
Universitetets Oldsaksamling, Frederiks gate 2,
N-0164 Oslo 1, Norway.

C.A. Smith
Department of Archaeology, The University,
Newcastle upon Tyne NE1 7RU, United Kingdom.

D. Srejović
Odeljenje za Arheologiju, Filozofski Fakultet,
Čika Ljubina 18–20, 11000 Beograd, Yugoslavia.

D.G. Sutherland
2 London Street, Edinburgh EH3 6NA,
United Kingdom.

R.M. Tipping
Department of Archaeology, University of
Edinburgh, 16–20 George Square,
Edinburgh EH8 9JZ, United Kingdom.

R. Tringham
Department of Anthropology, University of
California, Berkeley, California 94720, U.S.A.

J. Turner
Department of Biological Sciences, University of Durham, Science Laboratories, South Road, Durham DH1 3LE, United Kingdom.

K. Valoch
Ústav Anthropos, Moravské Muzeum v Brně, náměstí 25. února 6, 659 37 Brno, Czechoslovakia.

P.M. Vermeersch
Laboratorium voor Prehistorie, Instituut voor Aardwetenschappen, Katholieke Universiteit te Leuven, Redingenstraat 16bis, B-3000 Leuven, Belgium.

M. Vicari
Antropologia, Dipartimento di Biologia Animale e dell'Uomo, Città Universitaria, Piazzale Aldo Moro, I-00185 Roma, Italy.

B.A. Voytek
Center for Russian and East European Studies, Stanford University, Stanford, California 94305-2024, U.S.A.

S. Welinder
Institutionen för Arkeologi, Gustavianum, S-75220 Uppsala, Sweden.

C.R. Wickham-Jones
Society of Antiquaries of Scotland, Royal Museum of Scotland, Queen Street, Edinburgh EH2 1JD, United Kingdom.

L. van Wijngaarden-Bakker
Instituut voor Prae- en Protohistorie, Universiteit van Amsterdam, Singel 453, 1012 WP Amsterdam, The Netherlands.

P.C. Woodman
Department of Archaeology, University College, Cork, Eire.

R. Young
Department of Archaeology, University of Leicester, University Road, Leicester LE1 7RH, United Kingdom.

I. Zagorska
Institute of History, Academy of Sciences LSSR, 19 Turgeneva Street, Riga 226524, U.S.S.R.

F. Zagorskis (d. 1986)
Institute of History, Academy of Sciences LSSR, 19 Turgeneva Street, Riga 226524, U.S.S.R.

M. Zvelebil
Department of Archaeology and Prehistory, The University, Sheffield S10 2TN, United Kingdom.

Preface

Since the first meeting in Warsaw in 1973, the International Mesolithic Symposium has been the major forum for debate and for the exchange of ideas and information amongst scholars interested in the early Postglacial settlement of Europe. It has in turn served to stimulate further research into what is increasingly viewed as a crucial period in the evolution of European society. This book is the outcome of the most recent of the Symposium meetings. As such, it reflects the breadth and intensity of current research and at the same time provides an insight into future trends and objectives. Much of the information contained in it has not previously been published or is being presented for the first time in English.

The Third International Mesolithic Symposium was held at the University of Edinburgh from 31 March to 6 April 1985. It was attended by 88 scholars from all over Europe, as well as from the United States and Canada. All but six of the papers presented at the Edinburgh meeting are published here; in most cases the authors have taken the opportunity to revise their texts in the light of our discussions in Edinburgh and to incorporate new data. A number of papers were originally presented in either French or German, and these have been translated into English for publication. Also included in the volume are four papers by authors who, for various reasons, were unable to attend the Symposium.

The organization of the Edinburgh meeting of the Mesolithic Symposium was made possible by financial support from the British Academy, the British Council, the Great Britain/East Europe Centre, and by grants from the Dean of the Faculty of Arts' Fund, the Faculty of Arts Research Fund and the Institute for Advanced Studies in the Humanities of the University of Edinburgh.

The editing and preparation for publication of the sixty-two papers which make up this volume proved to be a formidable, and at times daunting, task. That it has been accomplished, albeit four years after the Symposium took place, is due in no small part to help received from friends and colleagues. I am particularly grateful to Jenny Bradbury and Gilian Mackinnon who re-typed the authors' manuscripts onto disk, to Alice Jackson who handled the typesetting, to Gordon Thomas and Mairi Anna Birkeland who re-drew or modified many of the line illustrations, and to Dennis Halligan, Sheila Lithgow, Bob MacEwen, Joe Rock and Adele Watson, all of whom provided expert help in the latter stages of production of the book. Sigrid and Alex Morrison, Jane Murray, Ian Ralston and Marek Zvelebil undertook individual pieces of translation, while Brian Barron helped me to overcome my own shortcomings as a translator. Christopher Bergman, Alison Girdwood, Rosemary Lennon, Roger Mercer, Mark Newcomer, David and Francesca Ridgway, Donald Sutherland and Richard Tipping all gave advice and made many helpful suggestions which have been incorporated into the text.

My thanks also go to Stefan Kozłowski who conceived the idea of the International Mesolithic Symposium and in so doing has done much to further the cause of Mesolithic studies, to Doug Price without whose efforts and enthusiasm the Edinburgh meeting might never have taken place, and to Dennis Harding and Trevor Watkins of my own Department who helped to make the 1985 Symposium a happy and memorable occasion.

The final word must be reserved for the contributors who have shown immense patience and understanding in awaiting the publication of their work.

Clive Bonsall

Notes to Readers

Unless stated otherwise, dates quoted in this book are in radiocarbon years BP, according to the convention agreed at the International Radiocarbon Conference at Trondheim in 1985 (Mook 1986).

Where the term 'Postglacial' is used, this is a synonym for 'Holocene' or 'Flandrian' and refers to the period beginning *c.* 10,000 BP; 'post-glacial' refers to the period following deglaciation in any particular area, and thus has no particular chrono-stratigraphic significance.

Where references are made to Lateglacial and Holocene pollen zones, these follow the system adopted in the country concerned – in Britain the system proposed by Godwin, in Denmark that proposed by Jessen, etc.

Metric units are used throughout; where imperial equivalents are shown, these should be taken as approximate.

Altitudes are given in metres 'above sea level' or, for Great Britain and Ireland, in metres above their respective Ordnance Datums (O.D.); for a definition of British Ordnance Datum, see p. 203, note 2.

Reference

MOOK, W.G. (1986) Recommendations/Resolutions adopted by the Twelfth International Radiocarbon Conference. In R.R. Kra and M. Stuiver (eds), *Proceedings of the 12th International Radiocarbon Conference Trondheim, Norway, June 24–28, 1985* (=Radiocarbon, vol. 28, no. 2A & B). New Haven, American Journal of Science: 799.

The Environmental Basis of Mesolithic Settlement

Kenneth L. Kvamme and Michael A. Jochim

Abstract

Prehistoric site distributions comprise a data-set of potentially great value. Previous studies of Mesolithic site locations have isolated a number of environmental variables, such as elevation, soil type, proximity to water and availability of shelter and view, as important characteristics of site placement. Inferences about prehistoric behaviour based on such locational patterns, however, must examine the natural distribution of these environmental characteristics in the background as a whole. Only by knowing the range of potential camp sites can we begin to assess the nature and degree of selectivity of certain features by prehistoric peoples.

This paper presents and discusses one approach to the study of site locations which can evaluate this selectivity by comparing the distribution of known sites to a sample of randomly chosen locations in the environment. As a case study, the distribution of Mesolithic sites in a 940 km² region of southern Germany is analyzed. These sites show a significant selection for level ground, high local relief and wide views, but tend to be far from water, to face all cardinal directions, and to possess little natural shelter. Computer-generated maps of significant environmental variables are presented, together with a summary map projecting the locational pattern of known sites across the entire landscape of the study region. Such a map can be used to guide fieldwork in conjunction with various research questions. Interpretations of the patterns detected are offered and suggestions are made for future applications and modifications of this approach.

INTRODUCTION

Archaeological data ideally are representative of the complete range of site types and of material used by prehistoric populations in a particular area. Mesolithic data, however, consist largely of surface collections of stone artifacts gathered haphazardly over many decades. These data, in consequence, are: (i) not necessarily representative of the range of sites and activities in particular regions, but rather represent accidents of exposure in ploughed fields and the biases of collectors seeking such materials; and (ii) informative about prehistoric behaviour only to the extent that we understand the determinants of tool form and discard. Both site assemblages and the range of site types known are likely to be incomplete and indirect records of Mesolithic behaviour. In an attempt to augment this archaeological record and extract more information about the past, a number of archaeologists have examined site locations and distributions within broad regions.

A study of site locations has much justification. Even when artifact collections are incomplete, poor-ly documented or even lost, usually the location of findspots is recorded; it is available data. Moreover, site location is an important source of information, one which is often overlooked or undervalued. Even in the absence of organic remains as direct evidence of economic activities it may be possible to infer something about past economies from the pattern of site locations relative to environmental features of possible economic significance. This paper presents an approach to the study of such patterns which has great potential because it relies on robust techniques of pattern-seeking, allowing strong arguments about locational patterns in existing data and prediction of site locations based on such patterns.

PREVIOUS WORK

Site locations have been the focus of a number of studies of Mesolithic materials. One of the most explicit of such studies is that by Hahn (1983), who systematically examined the placement of Mesolithic sites in south-west Germany. Mesolithic rock-shelters in this area tend to be situated low in their valleys and to avoid northern exposures, with west and south east being the most common orientations. He suggested that solar insolation may have been a factor in the choice of orientation, while the importance of a view from these sites may have been minimal, given the presence of a dense floodplain forest in the low valleys. Hahn also observed that, by contrast, Mesolithic open-air sites tend to be high in elevation, mostly on ridge tops or prominences, often on sandy soils near water sources. The potential view from these locations is uncertain, given widespread forests. He emphasized the uniformity of these open-air site locations.

Vencl (1970), on the other hand, stressed the diversity of topographic situations of Mesolithic sites in Bohemia, with a slight preference for locations high above and somewhat distant from watercourses, on drier soils, and adjacent to two or more vegetational communities. He related this locational diversity to the mixed economy of the Mesolithic population.

Metzger-Krahe (1977) has given considerable attention to Mesolithic site locations on the lower Elbe in north Germany. In this region both valley floors and plateau tops were avoided, with mid-slope positions given preference. Sites are situated on sandy soils, often 300 m or more from water, most commonly on slopes facing south or south east. Confluences of streams are frequently nearby. Metzger-Krahe's interpretation of this pattern stresses the importance of dry soils, shelter from wind, solar insolation, and defensibility against enemies.

Mellars and Reinhardt (1978) examined the distribution of three Mesolithic artifact types in southern England, emphasizing the general importance of various dry soils and vegetation, and of proximity to major watercourses, despite differences in the distribution of each artifact type. Proximity to a diversity of habitats seems to be a common feature of sites. In an examination of the British upland Mesolithic, Simmons (1975) stressed site location on both ridges and flanks of hills, often close to water, although he suggested that blanket peat may be masking sites in lower elevations. Jacobi (1978) pointed out a similar pattern for north English Mesolithic sites, usually on ridges, hills and valley heads, and emphasized the potential view available from such locations, especially if burning of the vegetation was practised during Mesolithic times. Proximity of the tree line was also suggested by Jacobi as an important locational factor, as this would have increased the diversity of nearby resources.

All of these studies seek to learn something about the economy and lifeways of prehistoric populations from the pattern of choice indicated by the site distributions. They give attention to topography, soils and watercourses as these would affect the availability of food resources, raw materials, view, shelter, and adequate drainage at each location. While some emphasize the uniformity of patterning, others stress the diversity. While some give importance to the proximity of water, others deny its significance. Potential view from a site receives differing emphasis because of varying interpretations of forest cover as an obstacle. These differences may be real and suggestive of differing economic emphases among regions. They may, on the other hand, reflect biases by the site collectors and weaknesses in the locational analyses. It is this latter problem which is addressed here.

Two weaknesses appear to characterize many studies of prehistoric site location. The first is that the assessment of the importance of various locational features is largely subjective and imprecise. Except for certain quantitative measurements such as absolute elevation and distance to water, most variables are only qualitatively evaluated. These include factors such as degree of shelter, position on slope, and presence of a view. While these assessments may be largely correct in determining the relative importance of each among sites in one area, their imprecision hampers comparison among areas studied by different individuals. They also may not be easily replicable, so that studies by two different individuals of the same area might yield different interpretations. An objective, quantitative set of measurements is needed to facilitate replication and comparison.

The other weakness of such studies is the lack of attention given to the background environment. Without a knowledge of the range of potential site locations offered by an area, it is impossible to determine the nature and degree of selectivity practised by the prehistoric inhabitants. In a well-watered environment, all sites may appear to be close to water. What is needed is an approach which allows one to assess whether sites are closer to water than one would expect by chance alone, an approach which can truly evaluate the selective preference given to various locational characteristics (Kvamme 1985). Although Mellars and Reinhardt (1978) take the background environment into account by looking at differing site densities by soil type, most other studies ignore the range of environmental possibilities entirely.

To illustrate the necessity of a reference control group we might imagine a variable such as *distance to water* measured at known prehistoric site locations within a region. The distribution of these measurements might tend to show short distances to water, promoting the conclusion that water proximity is an important site locational factor. A question that must be asked, however, is – how far is water from *any* location within the area under study? If distance to water were measured at random points throughout the study region, these background control measurements might form a nearly identical distribution, forcing the conclusion that water generally is close to any location and that site proximity to water is not a significant locational factor in the area.

STUDY AREA AND DATA

The study area lies in southern West Germany in the state of Baden-Württemberg, about 20 km east of Stuttgart. The area encompassed by the study is approximately 940 km² and roughly corresponds to the region depicted by the 1:50,000 scale maps of Schwäbisch-Gmünd and Backnang. This region was selected because it contains a relative abundance of known Mesolithic sites, with some 170 having been discovered and recorded (*Fig. 1*). These site locations were gathered from *Fundberichte aus Schwaben*, a collection of regional archaeological reports that offer a verbal description of the site

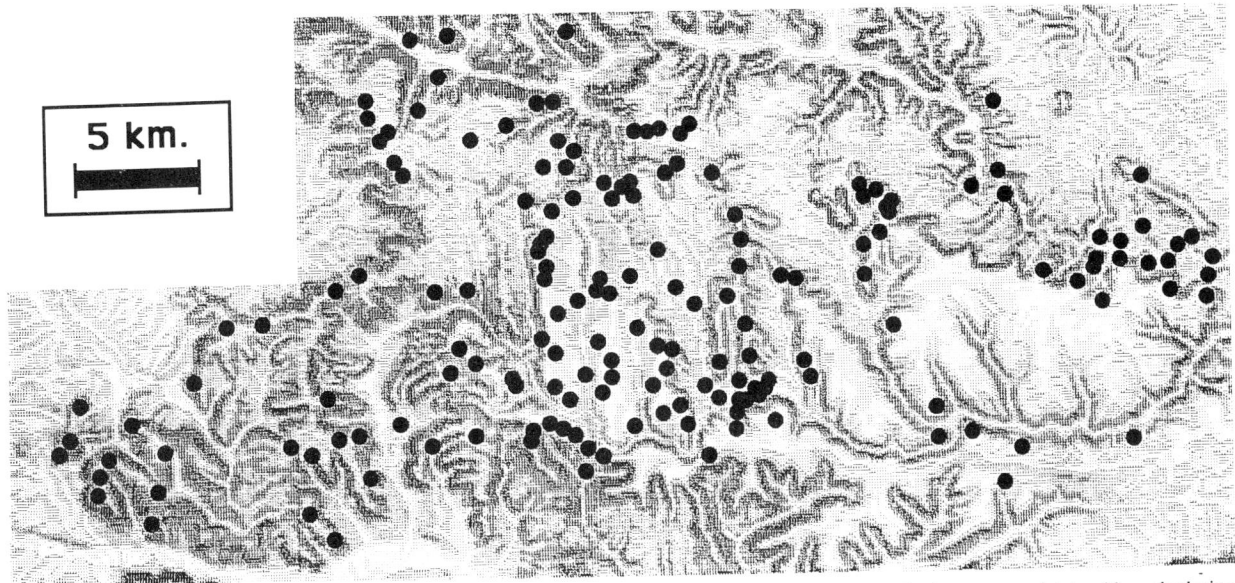

Figure 1   Computer image of the study region, with circles representing known Mesolithic sites. The image was obtained by calculating slope as percent grade every 100 m and shading the image by degree of slope. Steep locations are darkly shaded.

locations. The descriptions varied in quality but typically offered enough information for relatively accurate placement – for example, '400 m north of church, 80 m west of water tower, elevation 407.2 m'. It is recognized that verbal descriptions in some cases may not be precise, and this factor represents one possible source of error in this study.

Environmental variables

When investigating patterning in site locations it is important to attempt to develop quantitative measures of the phenomena under investigation. Nine environmental variables are defined here for study. These variables pertain to landform, water availability, view and shelter quality, all of which have been considered in the Mesolithic studies discussed.

Landform

The investigation of landform and its relationship with settlement patterning is probably the most common of practices in site location studies. Settlements typically are located on level surfaces where steep slopes do not interfere with day-to-day activities (Judge 1973; Williams *et al.* 1973). This concept is easily measured as *slope as percent grade*. The form or roughness of local terrain also has been investigated (Plog and Hill 1971; Hurlbett 1977), presumably because rough local terrain would increase energy and time expenditures in travel to and from a site (Ericson and Goldstein 1980). One measure of terrain roughness is *local relief* (Hammond 1964), the range in elevation within a predefined radius of a location under investigation. The arbitrary radius selected in this study is 600 metres. Large values of relief suggest rugged terrain while

low values suggest gentle terrain. *Elevation* is examined here because of the observed tendency for Mesolithic sites in many areas to be located on higher elevation ridge tops as opposed to lower elevation valley bottoms.

Water availability

Water is widely viewed as an important factor in settlement studies. Most often examined are distances to a variety of water sources such as permanent rivers, semi-permanent streams, lakes, springs, or streams of specified rank (e.g. Plog and Hill 1971; Roper 1979; Scholtz 1981). *Horizontal distance to nearest stream* and *vertical distance to nearest stream* are both examined here. Additionally, *horizontal distance to nearest Strahler third-order stream* (or greater) is investigated, since these larger streams might reflect more secure sources of water and more productive sources of riverine resources.

View

The importance of view to hunter-gatherers for surveillance of the surrounding terrain is widely emphasized, often linked to the need to watch for game animals or for other humans for social or defensive reasons (Judge 1973; Jochim 1976). A rough measure of *view* was introduced by Brown (1979) as the angle of surrounding terrain visible from a site (*Fig. 2A*). This measure has been used with success in a number of settlement studies (Larralde and Chandler 1981; Kvamme 1985).

Shelter

The importance of *shelter quality* of a location is often recognized in site location studies. In this study an interval-level measure of shelter is used that

3

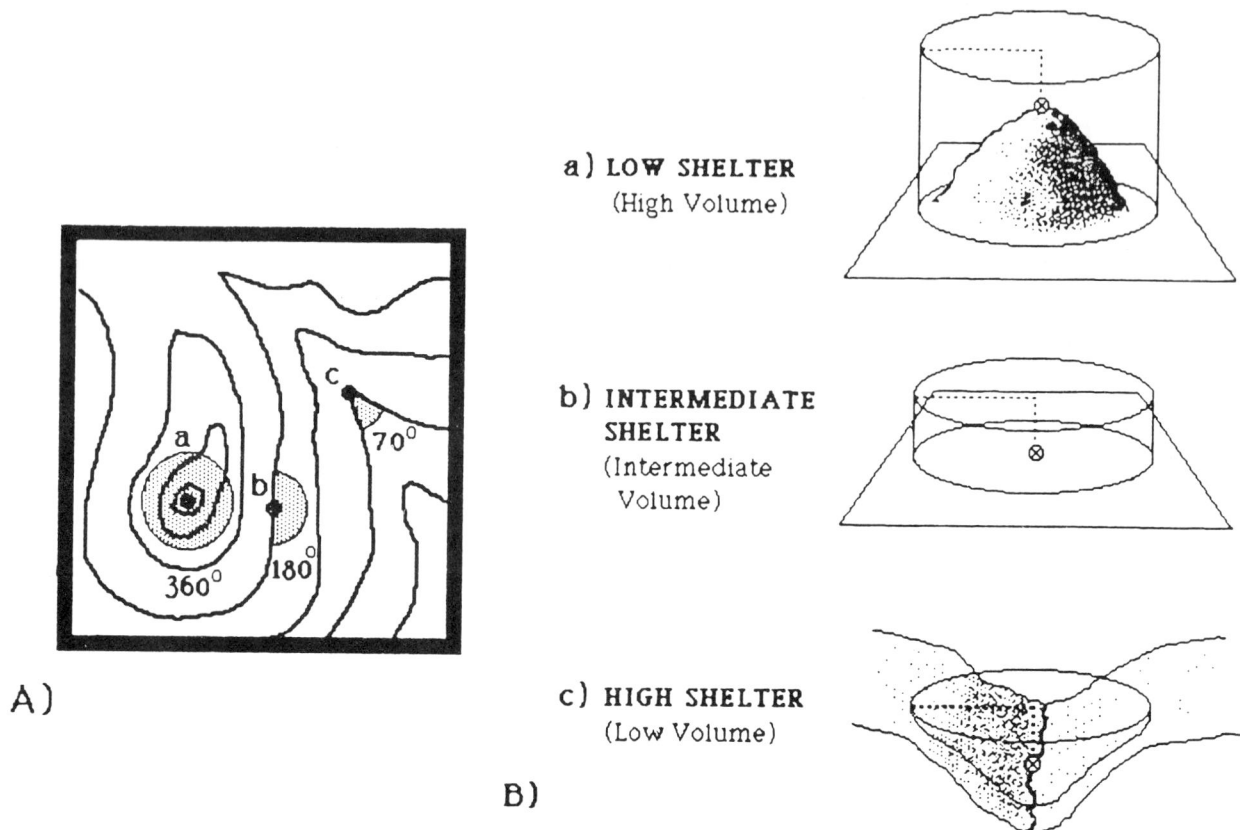

a) **LOW SHELTER**
(High Volume)

b) **INTERMEDIATE SHELTER**
(Intermediate Volume)

c) **HIGH SHELTER**
(Low Volume)

A)

B)

Figure 2   Measurement of certain variables used in this study. A) *View angle*. The hilltop (a) has the widest view, the ridge flank (b) has a narrower view, and the drainage bottom (c) has the narrowest view. B) *Shelter*. Cylinder volumes are inversely proportional to the shelter offered by a location. The hilltop (a) offers poor shelter and has a large volume; the level plain (b) offers intermediate shelter and has an average volume; and the valley bottom (c) is better sheltered and has a small volume.

examines how exposed a location is in terms of the shape of surrounding terrain. The measure is the volume of air above the ground surface encompassed by an imaginary cylinder with its top a constant height above the location (arbitrarily set at 100 m) and sides a constant radius from the location (arbitrarily set at 300 m). A large volume (e.g. surrounding a hilltop location) suggests an exposed location with little shelter while a small volume (e.g. surrounding a valley bottom location) suggests a relatively sheltered location (*Fig. 2B*). This measure of shelter quality might also be viewed simply as an index of hill-like or valley-like characteristics. It does not consider such factors as the direction of prevailing winds or forest cover.

The principle exposure or *aspect* of a site is often examined in settlement studies in terms of sheltering effects. A south-facing aspect, for example, might offer a winter camp greater warmth from the sun; an east-facing aspect might protect from westerly winds. Aspect is usually measured by noting the prominent direction of sloping terrain and recording the azimuth of the direction, which provides a measurement that ranges from 1° to 360°. A difficulty that this scale poses is that values near 1° and those near 360° both indicate approximate north, which can be a problem to most quantitative analysis techniques. By re-

scaling the compass scale, collapsing the west half of the compass over the east half such that every azimuth on the west half is given the azimuth of its mirror image on the east half, the difficulty can be resolved. This transformation allows the measurement of direction relative to north or south where 0° is north, 180° is south, and 90° is east or west. Other transformations are, of course, possible.

The computer database

In order to pursue the investigation a regional computer database was established. In more formal terms this database constitutes a 'Geographic Information System', a computer-based means for assembling, analyzing and storing varied forms of data corresponding to specific geographical areas, with the spatial locations of these areas forming the basis of the system (Tomlinson *et al.* 1976). The information on a topographic map, such as elevation contour and stream location data, can be electronically encoded and stored in computer-compatible form. Computer programs can then be applied to these data to derive secondary environmental information appropriate for archaeological settlement studies. For example, utilizing the inter-relationships between nearby points of known elevation that are encoded in the computer, the computer can

A

B

C

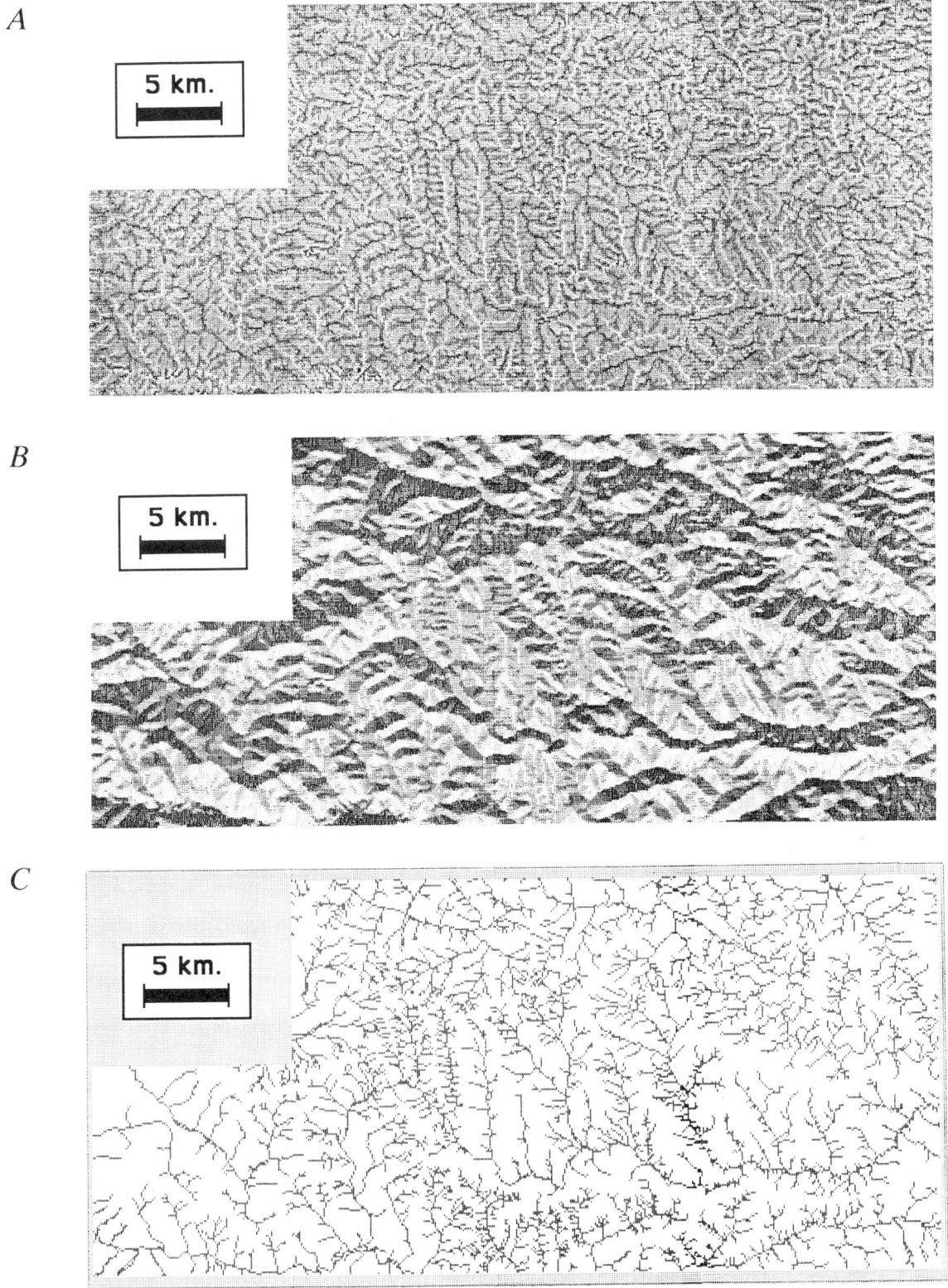

Figure 3   Computer mappings of variables. A) The view-angle surface tends to show ridge crests and hilltops (good views) with dark shading and the valley bottoms (poor views) with light shading. B) The aspect surface shows the prominent direction of sloping terrain. South-facing locations are lightly shaded and north-facing locations are dark. C) The network of watercourses.

estimate at any locus many of the variables discussed above. Moreover, the computer can repeat this process systematically at regular intervals (e.g. every 100 m) across a study region. In a similar fashion, electronically encoded stream location data can be used to compute horizontal and vertical distances from any specified water type across a map area. These computer programs and others have been described in greater detail by Kvamme (1983, 1986), and it is beyond the scope of this discussion to describe them here.

In the present study, the elevation contours and stream courses on the 1:50,000 scale maps of the project area were electronically digitized. A 100 m grid was superimposed over the entire region (approximately 84,000 grid cells) and in each cell (i.e. every 100 m) values for each of the nine environmental variables defined in this study were estimated by the computer. Additionally, the 170 cells representing the locations of the known Mesolithic sites were 'flagged' to represent the locations of the special site class of interest. Armed with this abundance of data (84,000 cells each with nine variables), we can compare environmental patterning exhibited by the known Mesolithic site locations (in the 170 flagged cells) against environmental patterning indicated by the same variables in the environment as a whole. Before doing so, however, it might be instructive first to examine some of the individual variable maps generated by the computer.

Standard computer cartographic techniques (Monmonier 1982) may be used to provide 'pictures' of the various analytical surfaces. The slope map was given in *Fig. 1* because this variable, when mapped, tends to illustrate quite well the terrain features of a region. In *Fig. 3A* the view-angle surface is portrayed with dark regions indicating wide angles of view and light regions showing narrow angles of view. Note that the mapping of this variable tends to delimit the ridge crest system as the dark lines (with wider views), while the drainage systems tend to be portrayed as lightly shaded lines (with restricted views). The surface for aspect, or orientation (*Fig. 3B*), on the other hand, portrays the prominent direction of sloping terrain and tends to illustrate features of the topography related to the drainage system. In this figure, light shading indicates south-facing terrain while dark shading represents north-facing terrain. The full hydrological system is illustrated in *Fig. 3C*, where only the stream courses are indicated. It should be noted that in all the cells without a stream course (the white portions of the map) a Euclidean distance to the nearest stream cell has been calculated by the computer and stored. Lack of space prohibits illustration of the other surfaces. The shelter surface is similar to the view-angle surface when mapped, but tends to show more subtle high and low points and tends to delimit plateau rims rather than ridge crests. The local relief surface is a cruder surface that tends to contrast level areas and high ridge tops and plateau rims.

RESULTS

Before examining the results of our investigation it is prudent first to sound a note of caution. The sample of 170 known Mesolithic sites is not a random sample of sites of this area. Most of the sites were discovered through the haphazard investigations of amateur archaeologists and, consequently, the sample might reflect to some degree locational biases resulting from where these archaeologists decided to look for sites, or places where sites were more visible. The site sample, therefore, may not be representative of the Mesolithic pattern of settlement in the study area. This possibility is discussed in greater detail below.

If we could argue that the site sample is representative, it would be tempting to use statistical inferential procedures to assess the significance of observed locational patterning with respect to the environmental variables. This approach has been undertaken in a number of studies in the western United States (Scholtz 1981; Kvamme 1985; Parker 1985). In these studies, however, regional random samples of prehistoric sites are obtained through the use of various probabilistic sampling designs (Mueller 1975). Environmental patterning exhibited by the site samples is then compared against a control sample of field inspected regions where sites are known to be absent (rather than a control group representing the whole environment at large), and statistical procedures such as Student's *t*-test are used to examine environmental differences between these distinct groups. In the present study we have one distinct group, known Mesolithic site locations, but the control group represents the environment at large, which includes both locations with no sites and locations with as yet undiscovered sites. It would seem that in statistically comparing the two groups, we would, in part, be comparing the class of suitable site locations against itself. This difficulty can be resolved to a major extent by recognizing that prehistoric sites are a relatively rare phenomenon. In the western United States where extensive archaeological survey has been conducted in hunter-gatherer contexts it has been discovered in many regions that the chance probability of prehistoric site occurrence at a particular location is of the order of about one percent and often less (e.g. Williams *et al.* 1973). Although no similar data on site density are available for the German Mesolithic, we might argue conservatively that the chance that a location (100 m grid cell) in our study region contains a Mesolithic site is somewhere between one and ten percent, and probably closer to the lower figure (note that the high figure of 10% would suggest a Mesolithic site in about one out of every ten grid cells or about one site in every 320 metre square, which seems unduly high). We can then infer that somewhere between 90% and 99% of our control group of background environment would constitute areas with no Mesolithic sites, thus forming a reasonably distinct class with little detrimental influence on the results of the analysis.

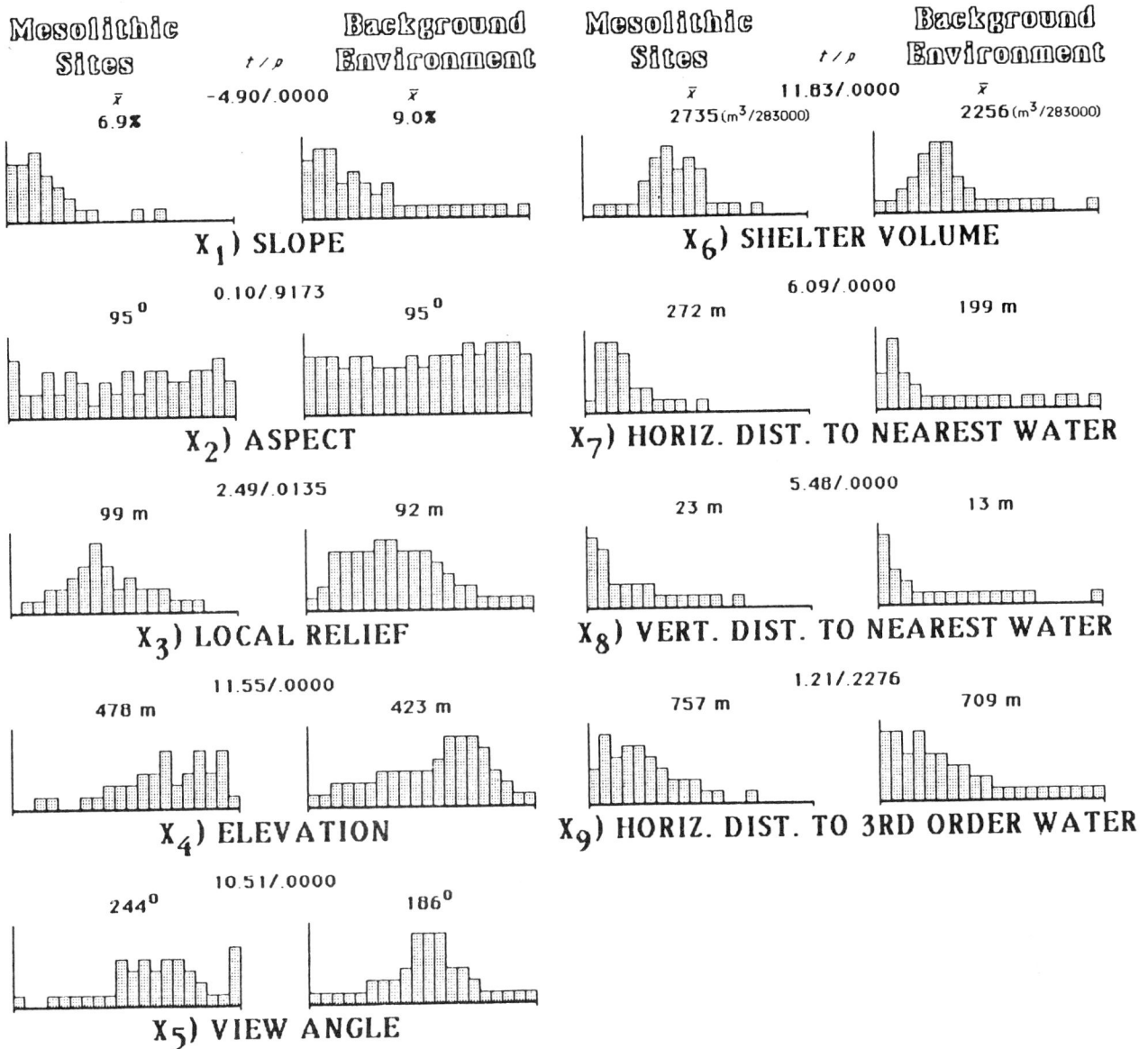

Figure 4   Histograms and descriptive statistics for the south German Mesolithic site locations and background environment.

Univariate analysis

The nine environmental variables measured at the 170 Mesolithic site locations are compared against the same variables measured at 3201 background locations obtained by selecting cells at the intersection of every fifth row (one-half kilometre) and every fifth column in the computer database. Histograms of these data for each variable and group, along with sample means, are given in *Fig. 4*. By comparing the shapes of the histograms, as well as differences in the mean values, it is apparent that strong locational patterning is present. Also given in *Fig. 4* are the results of a two-tailed *t*-test (modified to allow for unequal class variances) between the site and background groups. The results of this test should be viewed conservatively because: (i) the known Mesolithic sites may not constitute a representative sample; (ii) the control group may not represent an entirely distinct class; and (iii) the

observations in each group undoubtedly are spatially correlated to some extent (Cliff and Ord 1973), thus violating the assumption of statistical independence required by this test.

The Mesolithic sites, when compared to the background environment, have a tendency to occur on level ground as indicated by the variable *slope*, which is not very surprising given the steepness of much of the region. In terms of principal orientation, or *aspect*, however, there is little pattern in the site locations, with no strong preference to face any direction. The sites do have a tendency to be located in regions of greater local *relief* and a marked preference for high *elevation* locations. The combination of these latter factors immediately points to the high elevation ridge crests and the edges of broader plateau tops as the primary locus of site placement in this region, and this is largely borne out by the remaining variables. The sites possess a

7

distinct locational tendency for wider angles of *view* and high values for *shelter* quality, consistent with poorly-sheltered high points. Finally, all of the water-related variables show fairly substantial locational preferences to be rather far from water. This, too, undoubtedly reflects in part the tendency for sites to be located on ridge crests and plateau rims, which tend to be located far from drainages.

Settlement pattern modelling

A number of rather strong environmental differences were observed between the locations of the Mesolithic sites and background environment, suggesting substantial settlement patterning. If we now quantitatively abstract the entire pattern in all nine variables simultaneously, we obtain a mathematical model of the Mesolithic settlement pattern; with this model, the computer database and cartographic techniques can be used to provide a summary map or idealized 'picture' of the pattern of settlements.

The quantitative settlement pattern model was established by fitting a discriminant function to the Mesolithic site and background environment classes. The discriminant function is merely a linear combination of the original variables which has the characteristic of utilizing the differences on all variables together in order to maximize the separation between groups (Morrison 1976). It is possible to calculate a score for any location (based on the original nine variables) on the single resulting discriminant axis. Large positive scores suggest environmental characteristics similar to the locations with Mesolithic sites while large negative scores suggest environmental contexts very different from the Mesolithic site locations (i.e. more similar to the background environment class as a whole). A simple transformation can be used to re-scale the discriminant scores to range between 0 and 1, which can be interpreted as probabilities of membership in one of the two classes of location when appropriate statistical assumptions are met. In the present analysis, since we do not know if our Mesolithic sites constitute a representative sample, and since we do not know the relative density of Mesolithic sites in the background environment and hence, how distinct our two classes really are, we present the discriminant function and its mapping merely as a mathematical description of patterns in the data and make no pretence concerning probabilistic inference.

The discriminant function obtained through multiple logistic regression recently has come into favour among settlement pattern analysts because it is not based on the multivariate normal model, like the more traditional Fischer's Linear Discriminant Function (Morrison 1976). The Mesolithic site and background environmental data were subjected to the BMDP logistic regression program (Dixon *et al.* 1983) which yielded the following discriminant function:

$$L = -8.913 - .0814\,X_1 + .00239\,X_2 + .0110\,X_3 \\ + .0101\,X_4 + .00196\,X_5 + .00145\,X_6 \\ + .00153\,X_7 + .0149\,X_8 - .00120\,X_9$$

where the variables referred to by the X_i are given in *Fig. 4*. The resulting score, L, which ranges between plus and minus infinity, can be re-scaled to range between 0 and 1 through the logistic transformation: $p = 1 \div (1 + \exp(-L))$. After this transformation, locations that are found to yield values near 1.0 can be interpreted to possess environmental characteristics similar to those of the known sites, while locations yielding a value near 0 possess environmental measures unlike the known site sample.

Since the computer has calculated and stored all nine variables in each of the 84,000 cells which comprise the study area, it only remains to calculate the above equation for every cell, that is, to calculate the discriminant function and its transformed value 84,000 times. Computer cartographic techniques then may be used to lightly shade cells with a value near 0, to darkly shade cells with a value near 1, and to moderately shade cells with intermediate values. In so doing, we are mapping locations that possess characteristics similar to the Mesolithic site sample (darkly shaded regions) and locations whose environmental properties generally are dissimilar (lightly shaded regions). In other words, we obtain a picture of the extrapolated Mesolithic pattern of settlement in this part of southern Germany (*Fig. 5*).

By comparing this settlement pattern map to other images of the study area terrain it is readily apparent that the mapping of the extrapolated site location pattern closely agrees with the findings of the previous univariate analysis. The Mesolithic settlement pattern tends to conform to ridge tops or plateau rims which possess high relief and are far from drainages.

Interpretations

As suggested earlier, any patterns in this non-random sample of sites might reflect Mesolithic locational preferences, modern collector bias, or both. Two factors that would impose a bias on site discovery are geological processes and modern land use. Although the general patterns of landform and drainage in this area have not changed since the Mesolithic, alluvial deposition has occurred. The result of this process is that any sites in areas of deposition are likely to be deeply buried and not readily visible from surface materials. Hence, a bias toward locations higher than valley floors should be demonstrated in the sample. Another natural factor to consider is erosion; any sites along stretches of

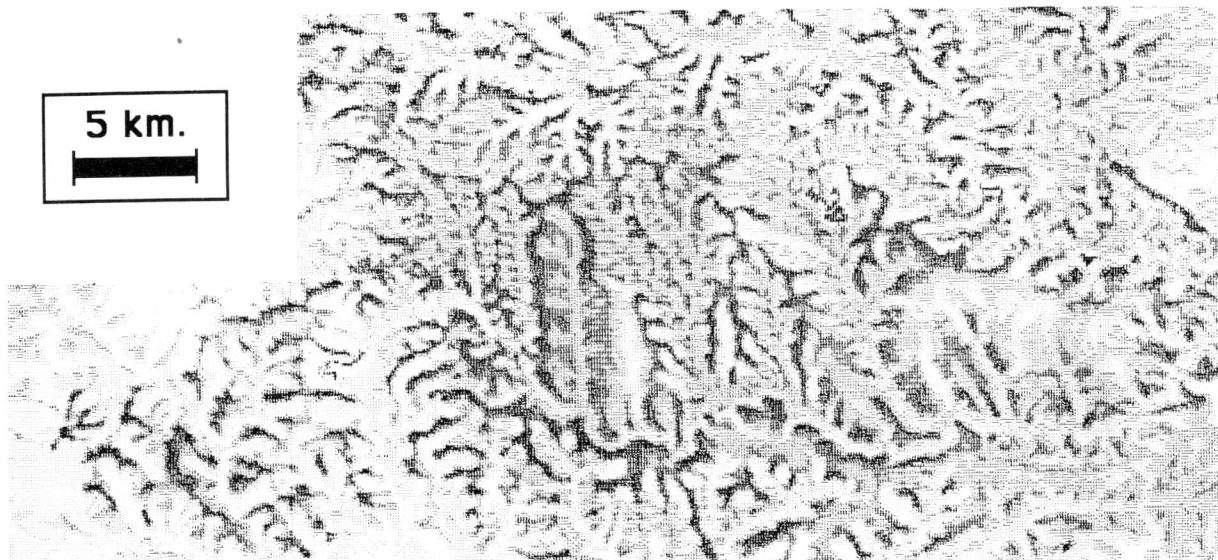

Figure 5   Computer image of the quantitative model of the Mesolithic pattern of settlement projected throughout the study area. Dark regions illustrate the settlement pattern.

streams where downcutting or meandering has occurred, or on steep slopes, would probably have been destroyed, thus imposing a bias toward locations away from steep slopes and stream edges. Both natural processes would cause the sample to under-represent possible sites on slopes and low on valley floors. In addition, modern uses of the land clearly affect visibility of sites. Forested areas would have the lowest visibility and ploughed fields the highest. Consequently, the sample is likely to be biased toward areas currently under cultivation: river terraces, gentle slopes, and broad plateaux.

The result of both sets of biases is that certain locations are probably excluded from examination by modern collectors: steep slopes, marshy valley floors and hilltops of very small area. The pattern of sites due to collector bias alone, then, should show a preference for river terraces, gentle slopes, and ridge and plateau tops. This is, indeed, a pattern similar to that demonstrated by the sites, but it is more inclusive. Sites tend not to be on river terraces or hill flanks, nor are they on all portions of plateaux, but rather on their edges. This more restricted distribution would appear to be the result of Mesolithic locational preferences.

Interpretations of the meaning of these preferences must take into account one other problem with the archaeological sample. It includes *all* reported sites in the study area, regardless of their function or season of occupation. Sites of different functions, such as residential base camps and short-term hunting camps, could have quite different locational requirements. Similarly, winter and summer camps could show different distributions reflecting seasonal changes in resources and climatic factors. The locational pattern of such a mixed group of sites is difficult to interpret. In part it represents a blending of characteristics specific to each site type

and season, weighted according to their proportional representation in the sample. Since the site types and their proportions are not currently known, it is not possible to separate these different specific patterns. In this study, for example, sites showed no tendency to face any direction. It may be, however, that winter residential camps in fact showed a tendency to face south, while sites of other seasons and functions had other characteristic orientations. The mixed sample would obscure these separate patterns.

In addition, and more importantly, the overall pattern reflects those characteristics common to all site types, the set of environmental features selected for all sets of activities. Interpretations of this pattern, as a result, should emphasize general advantages of such locations rather than those relevant to only certain seasons or specific activities. The dominant pattern in the sample is for sites to be located on ridge tops and plateau edges. Advantages of such locations may have included: (i) wide views, useful for spotting both game and strangers in any season; (ii) strong breezes, which would keep away insects and provide comfort in summers and reduce snow cover in winter; (iii) good drainage in all seasons; and (iv) light forests adapted to these exposed, dry situations and the various soils found there, which may have offered ease of hunting, movement and burning. The distance from water may reflect an unimportance of riverine resources, an avoidance of dense riverine forests, or simply the overriding importance of high elevations which happen to be far from water. The emphasis on very gentle slopes most likely represents a preference for performing any activities on level ground.

IMPLICATIONS AND POTENTIAL
Quantification

The approaches undertaken in this investigation

9

offer a number of assets to the study of prehistoric settlement patterning. The use of quantitative measures of various phenomena eliminates much of the vagueness and uncertainty often found in impressionistic descriptions of the same phenomena and provides a common 'currency' that may be replicated by other investigators. Such a practice encourages objectivity and precision in the description of our data. Importantly, the use of continuously measured data opens the doors for application of a wide range of more powerful modes of analysis, research designs, and computer applications. We hope that one outcome of this research will be to demonstrate that it is only through the use of background control measurements that reasonable arguments can be made concerning features of the environment that are related to the locations of sites. Finally, the use of computer-based Geographic Information Systems techniques offers a number of important benefits to regional archaeological research. The computer is able to provide vast numbers of measurements for many kinds of variables commonly (and not so commonly) investigated in settlement research. These data provide sound and ample evidence concerning the nature of the background environment, and cartographic techniques allow variables to be mapped, providing illustration of how various phenomena relate to the landscape. Its greatest potential, however, possibly lies in its ability to provide a summary 'picture' of prehistoric patterns of land use through application of complex mathematical settlement models.

Settlement theory

Settlement locations represent choices of particular spots on the landscape. These choices may be guided by a variety of different goals and they are constrained by the structure of the environment. From a review of ethnographic studies of hunter-gatherers it is possible to identify a number of common features of camp locations, including dry, level and clear ground and proximity to water, food, and raw material sources. Additional characteristics of varying importance are the degree of shelter from the elements, the availability of a view for game and strangers, and the accessibility of routes of travel and communication (Jochim 1976: 51–55). Climatic factors, economic activities, and patterns of social interaction will determine the relative importance of these various considerations. The structure of the environment will determine the feasibility of satisfying all requirements in particular locations.

If all desired environmental features are not found together, then compromises must be made in selecting camp locations. In many ethnographic situations such compromises show an interesting pattern: the most important economic factors are not necessarily the most important in determining specific camp spots. To cite one example, autumn caribou-hunting camps of the Nunamiut Eskimo of interior Alaska are often located along caribou migration routes, but next to fishing lakes, even though fish are generally of little importance at this time (Campbell 1968). One reason is that the caribou herd might not appear, or the hunt might fail, and fishing would be an important back-up activity. Similarly, the distribution of plant foods is often more important than that of animals in determining camp locations for many groups, regardless of the relative economic importance of the two types of foods. In general, it seems that camps are located close to more stationary foods, those for which much movement is not required during exploitation, so that reducing the travel costs to them by camping close by effectively minimizes their entire procurement costs.

Such ethnographic patterns are useful in suggesting the kinds of factors considered in camp locations and in cautioning us against simple inferences about the economic significance of various factors based on their importance in determining site locations. Yet, neither cross-cultural generalizations nor specific ethnographic patterns can be simply transferred to the past. Archaeological interpretations must allow for unique adaptations in the past and must be based on the specific patterns in the archaeological data.

Prehistoric populations selected certain locations for their camp sites and this pattern of selectivity can only be revealed by a comparison of site locations to the entire range of background environmental possibilities. The approach presented here provides one way of performing such a comparison. It objectively demonstrates the pattern of selectivity of various environmental factors, thereby providing a reliable set of archaeological data. Giving meaning to the pattern is another task and requires consideration of other archaeological data as well, such as site size, contents, and frequency of occupation.

This approach can also offer practical guides to fieldwork. By mathematically summarizing the locational pattern in a body of site data, it can project this pattern to other areas and map locations of varying degrees of conformity to the pattern. Locations most similar environmentally to known site locations may have a high probability of having prehistoric occupation. In other words, such areas of high settlement probability may be selectively surveyed if the research aim is to locate as many additional sites as possible. On the other hand, areas of low settlement probability might also be selectively surveyed to verify the absence of sites or to discover other site types that do not conform to the pattern and diversify the database.

DIRECTIONS FOR FUTURE RESEARCH

There are a number of ways in which this approach could be applied and modified for future work. First of all, new variables could be introduced to allow for a more meaningful examination of site location. Soil type in particular has been found to be important in known Mesolithic distributions and could be easily incorporated here. Vegetational communities could be reconstructed on the basis of soil, elevation and exposure, and used as another locational variable. The nature of soils and vegetation could be examined both at specific site locations and at varying distances from such locations. The combination of soils and vegetational communities, or their overall diversity within various distances of sites might also be profitably examined.

A second modification would be to create a site typology based on other data, such as size, artifact assemblages or faunal evidence of seasonality, and to evaluate the locational patterns of each type separately. Any locational differences among site types might help give meaning to the other differences observed. This approach is currently being used in the study area, in which it is possible to differentiate sites according to size and diversity of the stone tool assemblages. There appears to be some tendency for the largest and most diverse sites to show greater selectivity for level ground even further from water than other sites. This selectivity would make sense if, for example, these larger, more diverse sites represent base camps occupied for extended periods.

A third task for future research rests in putting the present investigation on a more rigorous quantitative footing. This could be accomplished through establishment of a regional survey based on principles of random sampling. A regional sample known to be representative would allow more rigorous statistical treatment and settlement pattern models whose predictive capabilities could be more reliably assessed (see Kvamme 1985).

A fourth application of this approach would be to use it to compare settlement patterns in different regions. Different patterns of Mesolithic site placement in two areas might reflect simply differences in topography and environment between the two. They might, on the other hand, reflect different patterns of selectivity by the prehistoric inhabitants. This approach could distinguish between the two possibilities and thus offer suggestions about economic differences between the two regions, to be followed up by other types of analysis.

Additionally, this approach can help investigations of culture change. The transition from Palaeolithic to Mesolithic, for example, involves changes in climate, vegetation, economy and, perhaps, social organization. The available evidence allows us to discuss changes in food resources and to suggest changes in patterns of settlement and mobility. By objectively comparing site locational patterns and the variance in these patterns for the two periods in the same area, this approach would allow us to confirm such inferences and to investigate more rigorously changes in how people organized themselves across the landscape. Finally, studies of the Neolithic and later periods, when permanent villages occur and it is possible to establish approximate contemporaneity, might include cultural factors such as distances to nearest neighbour villages, central places, or even prehistoric road networks in analyses, allowing an evaluation of the role of natural and cultural features in the placement of settlements.

Acknowledgements: We would like to thank JoAnn Christein, Anne Peebles and Katherine Heyman for their considerable effort and diligence in digitizing the topographic maps. Digitizing was accomplished through use of a Calcomp 9000 series digitizer. All computations were performed on a DEC Vax 11/780 computer using software written by the first author, unless otherwise specified. The computer maps were generated using a Diablo daisywheel printer programmed at 144 characters per square inch. *Figs. 2 & 4* were drafted and produced on an Apple Macintosh computer.

References

BROWN, K.L. (1979) Late prehistoric settlement patterns in southwestern Kansas. *Plains Anthropologist*, 43: 482–486.

CAMPBELL, J.M. (1968) Territoriality among ancient hunters: interpretations from ethnography and nature. In B. Meggars (ed.), *Anthropological Archeology in the Americas*. Washington, Anthropological Society of Washington: 1–21.

CLIFF, A.D. and ORD, J.K. (1973) *Spatial Autocorrelation*. London, Pion.

DIXON, W.J., BROWN, M.B., ENGLEMAN, L., FRANE, J.W., HILL, M.A. and JENNRICH, R.I. (1983) *BMDP Statistical Software*. Berkeley, University of California Press.

ERICSON, J.E. and GOLDSTEIN, R. (1980) Workspace: a new approach to the analysis of energy expenditure within site catchments. In F.J. Findlow and J.E. Ericson (eds), *Catchment Analysis: Essays on Prehistoric Resource Space* (Anthropology UCLA, 10). Los Angeles, University of California: 21–30.

HAHN, J. (1983) Die frühe Mittelsteinzeit. In H. Müller-Beck (ed.), *Urgeschichte in Baden Württemberg*. Stuttgart, Theiss Verlag: 363–392.

HAMMOND, E.H. (1964) Analysis of properties of land form geography: an application to broad-scale land form mapping. *Annals of the Association of American Geographers*, 54: 11–19.

HURLBETT, R.E. (1977) *Environmental Constraint and Settlement Predictability, Northwestern Colorado*. Denver (Colorado), Bureau of Land Management, Cultural Resource Series 3.

JACOBI, R.M. (1978) Northern England in the eighth millennium bc: an essay. In P.A. Mellars (ed.), *The Early Postglacial Settlement of Northern Europe*. London, Duckworth: 295–332.

JOCHIM, M.A. (1976) *Hunter-Gatherer Subsistence and Settlement: a Predictive Model*. New York, Academic Press.

JUDGE, W.J. (1973) *Paleoindian Occupation of the Central Rio Grande Valley, New Mexico*. Albuquerque, University of New Mexico Press.

KVAMME, K.L. (1983) Computer processing techniques for regional modeling of archaeological site locations. *Advances in Computer Archaeology*, 1: 26–52.

KVAMME, K.L. (1985) Determining empirical relationships between the natural environment and prehistoric site locations: a hunter-gatherer example. In C. Carr (ed.), *For Concordance in Archaeological Analysis: Bridging Data Structure, Quantitative Technique, and Theory*. Kansas City, Westport Publishers: 208–238.

KVAMME, K.L. (1986) The use of geographic information systems for modeling archaeological site distributions. In B.K. Opitz (ed.), *Geographic Information Systems in Government*, vol. 1. Hampton (Virginia), A. Deepak Publishing: 345–362.

11

LARRALDE, S.L. and CHANDLER, S.M. (1981) *Archaeological Inventory in the Seep Ridge Cultural Study Tract, Uinta County, Northeastern Utah, with a Regional Predictive Model for Site Location*. Salt Lake City (Utah), Bureau of Land Management, Cultural Resource Series 11.

MELLARS, P.A. and REINHARDT, S.C. (1978) Patterns of Mesolithic land-use in southern England: a geographical perspective. In P.A. Mellars (ed.), *The Early Postglacial Settlement of Northern Europe*. London, Duckworth: 243–294.

METZGER-KRAHE, F. (1977) *Mesolithikum an der Unterelbe* (Offa-Ergänzungs-Reihe, 2). Schleswig, Landesmuseum.

MONMONIER, M.S. (1982) *Computer Assisted Cartography: Principles and Prospects*. Englewood Cliffs (New Jersey), Prentice-Hall.

MORRISON, D.F. (1976) *Multivariate Statistical Methods* (2nd Edition). New York, McGraw-Hill.

MUELLER, J.W. (ed.) (1975) *Sampling in Archaeology*. Tucson, University of Arizona Press.

PARKER, S.C. (1985) Predictive modeling of site settlement systems using multivariate logistics. In C. Carr (ed.), *For Concordance in Archaeological Analysis: Bridging Data Structure, Quantitative Technique, and Theory*. Kansas City, Westport Publishers: 173–207.

PLOG, F.T. and HILL, J.N. (1971) Explaining variability in the distribution of prehistoric population aggregates. In G.J. Gumerman (ed.), *The Distribution of Prehistoric Population Aggregates*. Prescott (Arizona), Prescott College Anthropological Reports no. 1: 7–36.

ROPER, D.C. (1979) The method and theory of site catchment analysis: a review. In M.B. Schiffer (ed.), *Advances in Archaeological Method and Theory*, vol. 2. New York, Academic Press: 119–140.

SCHOLTZ, S.C. (1981) Location choice models in Sparta. In R. Lafferty, J.L. Otinger, S.C. Scholtz, W.F. Limp, B. Watkins and R.O. Jones, *Settlement Predictions in Sparta*. Fayetteville, University of Arkansas, Arkansas Archaeological Survey Research Series 14: 201–222.

SIMMONS, I.G. (1975) Towards an ecology of Mesolithic man in the uplands of Great Britain. *Journal of Archaeological Science*, 2: 1–15.

TOMLINSON, R.F., CALKINS, H.W. and MARBLE, D.F. (1976) *Computer Handling of Geographical Data: an Examination of Selected Information Systems*. Paris, UNESCO.

VENCL, S. (1970) Topografiká poloha Mesolitických sidlišt v Čechách. *Archeologické rozhledy*, 23: 169–187.

WILLIAMS, L., THOMAS, D.H. and BETTINGER, R.L. (1973) Notions to numbers: Great Basin settlements as polythetic sets. In C.L. Redman (ed.), *Research and Theory in Current Archaeology*. New York, John Wiley: 215–238.

The Revolution of the Bowmen in Europe

J-G. Rozoy

Abstract

The chronological limits of the Epipalaeolithic ('Mesolithic') – like those of all periods in prehistory – must be based on human achievements, such as industries and methods of production, and not on extrinsic geological phenomena. If the beginning of the period is defined by the end of glaciation, then circular reasoning is being employed (climatic change would have caused industrial change) and it becomes impossible to make comparisons between different natural regions.

Each of the major periods of prehistory has its own technical and social unity. This unity derives from the techniques used for the most important activity – in this context, the procurement of food. The basis of subsistence in the Epipalaeolithic was hunting with a bow (the technique of the bow and arrow is discussed). This technique is demonstrated by the microlithization of armatures. The large-scale and persistent use of sharp-pointed armatures weighing less than 5 g must serve to define and delimit this epoch. The geometric character of these pieces is of no significance.

Three major chronological subdivisions can be recognized based on diversification in the classes of armatures and their techniques. These factors suggest that a greater variety of hunting methods came to be used. The technical changes (which were gradual, inter-related and developed independently) occurred in a geographical mosaic, and this provides evidence for the multiplicity of centres of invention and the easy circulation of ideas.

From an economic viewpoint the Epipalaeolithic was definitely not evolving towards food production. Rather the reverse – it received this technique from outside contacts. On the other hand, in demographic, cultural and intellectual spheres, it achieved a slow maturation – substantial increases in population, detailed familiarity with the land, improved capacity for abstract thought, and the understanding of biological mechanisms. Indeed, these developments provided the starting point from which the spread of the Neolithic became possible (but not necessary).

The successive changes which marked the Epipalaeolithic occurred, on three occasions, each *shortly* before a change of climate; if cause and effect is to be perceived here, then it might seem that it was the inventions that caused the climatic change. It can also be suggested that these innovations were a response to constant pressure from the environment – and not just from its modifications – by a species that is particularly adaptable.

THE LIMITS OF THE PERIOD

In contrast to other divisions between prehistoric periods, which are well defined – sometimes too well defined, thus concealing continuity between them – the distinction between the Palaeolithic in its final stages and the 'Mesolithic' remains particularly obscure to many people. This is true not only for specialists in other periods, which is perhaps understandable, but also for most Mesolithic scholars. The contrived term 'Epipalaeolithic'[1] is often used to indicate the short interval of post-Magdalenian time

before the advent of 'true cultures with geometric microliths', and care is taken not to specify whether this 'Epipalaeolithic' should be assigned to one side of the dividing line or the other. In the end, since students must be given guidelines, the date of 10,000 BP is usually adopted; this has the advantage of being a 'round number'(!) and also refers to the bipartition of the Scandinavian ice sheet, the official end – such things have to be fixed – of the 'Würm' or 'Weichsel' Glaciation (neither its name nor its subdivisions are important, since only its closing stages are relevant in the present context). Thus one finds authors, some of them being most authoritative in this respect, stating that the Mesolithic is 'the period which follows the Ice Age and precedes the introduction of food production'.

A PREHISTORIC EPOCH IS DEFINED BY HUMAN ACTIVITIES

As I had occasion to recall in a recent issue of *Mesolithic Miscellany* (Rozoy 1984*a*), this definition of the Epipalaeolithic is fundamentally unsound, since it begins with a geological event, extrinsic to man (with very different consequences in different regions), and ends with a purely human advance. A prehistoric epoch must be defined by human activities. To draw the boundary between Palaeolithic and Mesolithic as corresponding to the end of glaciation immediately precludes all possibility of recording the same events in other climatic zones; what does 'the end of the Ice Age' mean in the Near East – a most sensitive area in this respect – or in the heart of Africa? It is by no means certain that the stages in the evolution of human society witnessed in Europe also occurred in the same way in India or Central America; what was done in three stages in Europe could have been done in four, five, or only two stages elsewhere. If we are to make comparisons, however, we must discount local circumstances in order to concentrate on the criteria of general applicability.

The most striking quality of general applicability possessed by mankind is his remarkable independence of widely varying environmental conditions.

What other animal or vegetable species could we refer to which finds a livelihood from the Poles to the Equator, as well in desert as amid swamp, in mountain or plain, fishing as much in fresh water as in the sea? – we could go on *ad infinitum*. Imagine trying to transport ants from Europe to the Amazon (where different species of ants live), reindeer to the Sahara, or wheat to the Tropics; wheat, reindeer and ants are all strictly conditioned by their environment and could not tolerate major variations.

Man lives in every part of this planet (and looks forward to conquering space), which is why C.J. Thomsen with his Three Age System (Stone, Bronze, Iron Ages) as early as 1836 (Thomsen 1836, 1837) and then G. de Mortillet (1869) based the prehistoric classification – which is still broadly in use – on products of human activity, as also did Sir John Lubbock (1865) in making the distinction between Palaeolithic and Neolithic. All our classifications are based on human activity, whether concerned with tool shapes, economy, or even social organization.

How, then, does it come about that intelligent people still accept ('for lack of something better') for the Palaeolithic/'Mesolithic' boundary alone a principle which would take us back to the 'Ages' of the cave bear, the mammoth and the reindeer in the ephemeral geological classification used by Lartet (Lartet and Christy 1865)? The reason is simple; it is not possible for them, as it was for Lubbock when considering the Palaeolithic and the Neolithic, to contrast the two epochs point by point, since they have had no success to date in relating the tools described (burins, scrapers, piercers and javelins, on the one hand, and Tardenois points, trapezes and notched blades, on the other) to the basic technical actions which produced them. A perfect example is the paper by Gilead (1984).

Some of the tools of the Upper Palaeolithic show similarities over the time-range from the Aurignacian to the Magdalenian (and the Pavlovian), to the extent that the same type-list can be used to describe assemblages, with only a few groups of tools being specific to particular periods (e.g. Solutrean tools – shouldered points, laurel leaves, etc.). Our purpose here is not to argue for or against the utility or efficiency of such lists of tool types, but merely to record that the Upper Palaeolithic toolkit can be described using just a single type-list. The same applies to the toolkits of the Middle Palaeolithic, on the one hand, and the 'Mesolithic' (or Epipalaeolithic – the word is unimportant) on the other. This provides evidence for the existence of a technical community and, beyond, a socio-cultural one. For the Upper Palaeolithic this unity was based on hunting in large groups with the spear and javelin.

Whether we have elucidated more or less completely the why and the wherefore of these facts for each period, or not, should not prevent us from retaining them; each of our great periods is based on technical and social unity. This is particularly clear for the Epipalaeolithic ('Mesolithic'), for it is a state of society whose basic technique is at least as well established as that of the Neolithic. The latter is based on arable cultivation and animal husbandry – although some hunting, with its own individual character, was still practised occasionally – and the very diverse forms of Neolithic industries do not prevent us from distinguishing the common basis. The common basis for the Epipalaeolithic ('Mesolithic') is also well established – hunting with a bow.

MICROLITHIC ARMATURES: EVIDENCE OF THE BOW AND ARROW

G. Schwantes (1923, 1952) sought to use the axe as the distinctive trait separating the Palaeolithic from the 'Mesolithic' – or, to be exact, the Palaeolithic from the Neolithic, since in 1923 the idea of the 'Mesolithic' was not generally accepted and cultures with microliths were assumed by many people to be early Neolithic. The use of the axe as a distinctive trait only *appears* to be an advance over the use of the phrase 'Postglacial', because the axe, although it is of course a tool, is strictly dependent on climate and the growth of forests. In any case, many cultures with microliths lack flint axes. This does not mean that the hunters in question did not know how to cut wood, for they had blades of bone which may have been used as axes (Rozoy 1978: 988–996). For a discussion of the criteria used to define the Palaeolithic/Epipalaeolithic boundary, see Rozoy (1978: 894–895).

We must focus our attention on the most important activity – namely, the procurement of food. There had been no appreciable deforestation which could have contributed to subsistence activities in the Epipalaeolithic. The essential item of equipment for the acquisition of food was the bow and arrow, involving the use of sharp-pointed microliths. The widespread distribution of microlithic armatures is much better established in Europe than that of the axe – with the exception of the great Russian loess plain where there is no stone, and where armatures, tiny ones, were made of bone. The proportion of armatures in Epipalaeolithic assemblages varies from *c.* 20% (Ardennian) to *c.* 60% (Tardenoisian), and is sometimes as high as 85% (the Causses group). This proportion is seldom less than 10% of the tools present, while the rare Magdalenian sites which have produced armatures (e.g. Gare de Couze) have only 3–5% at most. And so we find once more the high proportions of armatures (10–50%) that were known in the Solutrean, but the Solutrean pieces were much larger (*Fig. 3*).

Some odd myths concerning microlithic armatures must be dispelled once and for all. Firstly, there is

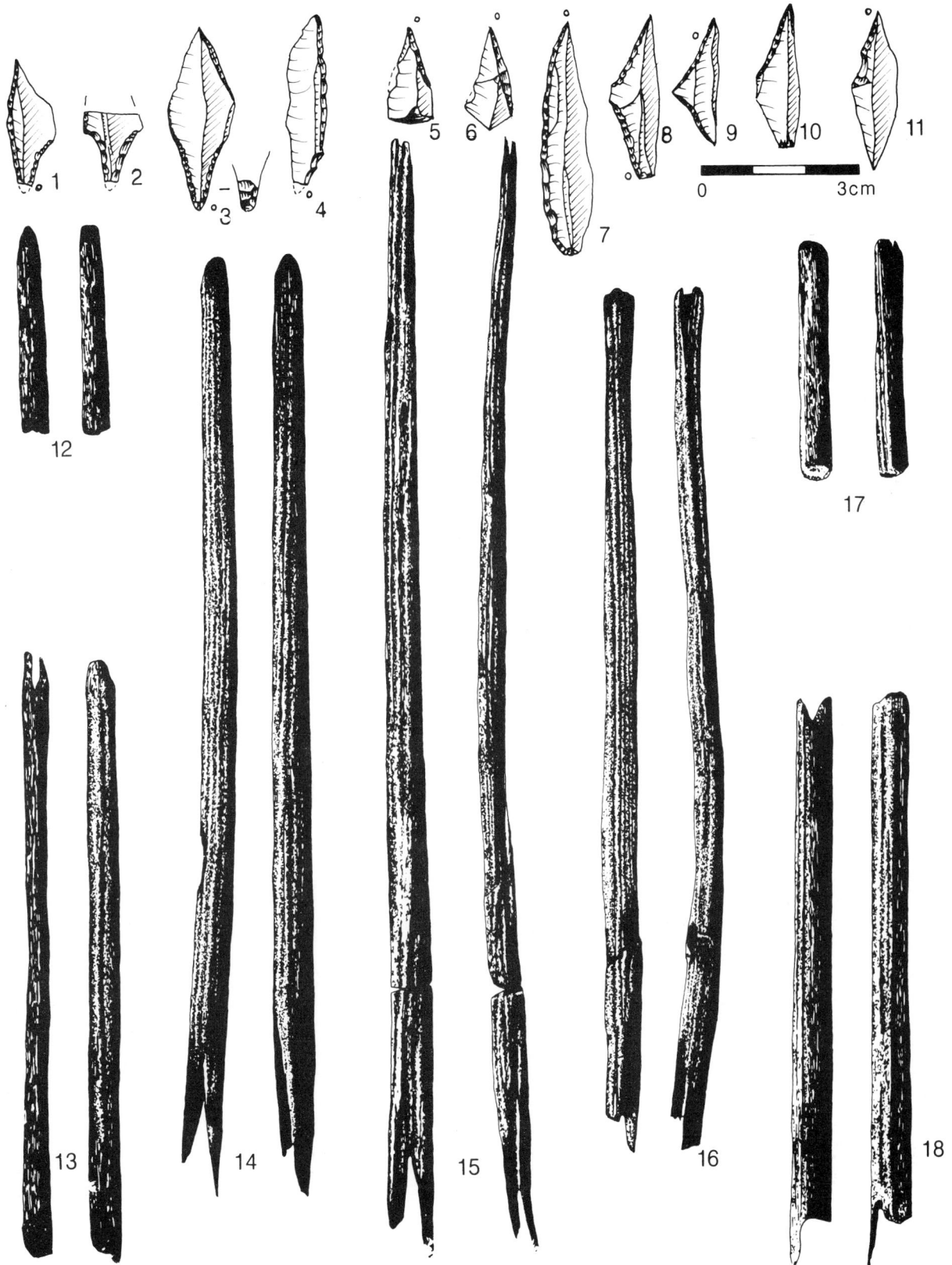

Figure 1 Ahrensburgian: armatures from Geldrop III–1 (Biologisch–Archeologisch Instituut, Groningen); arrows from Stellmoor (after Rust 1943). Microlithization is achieved during full glacial conditions.

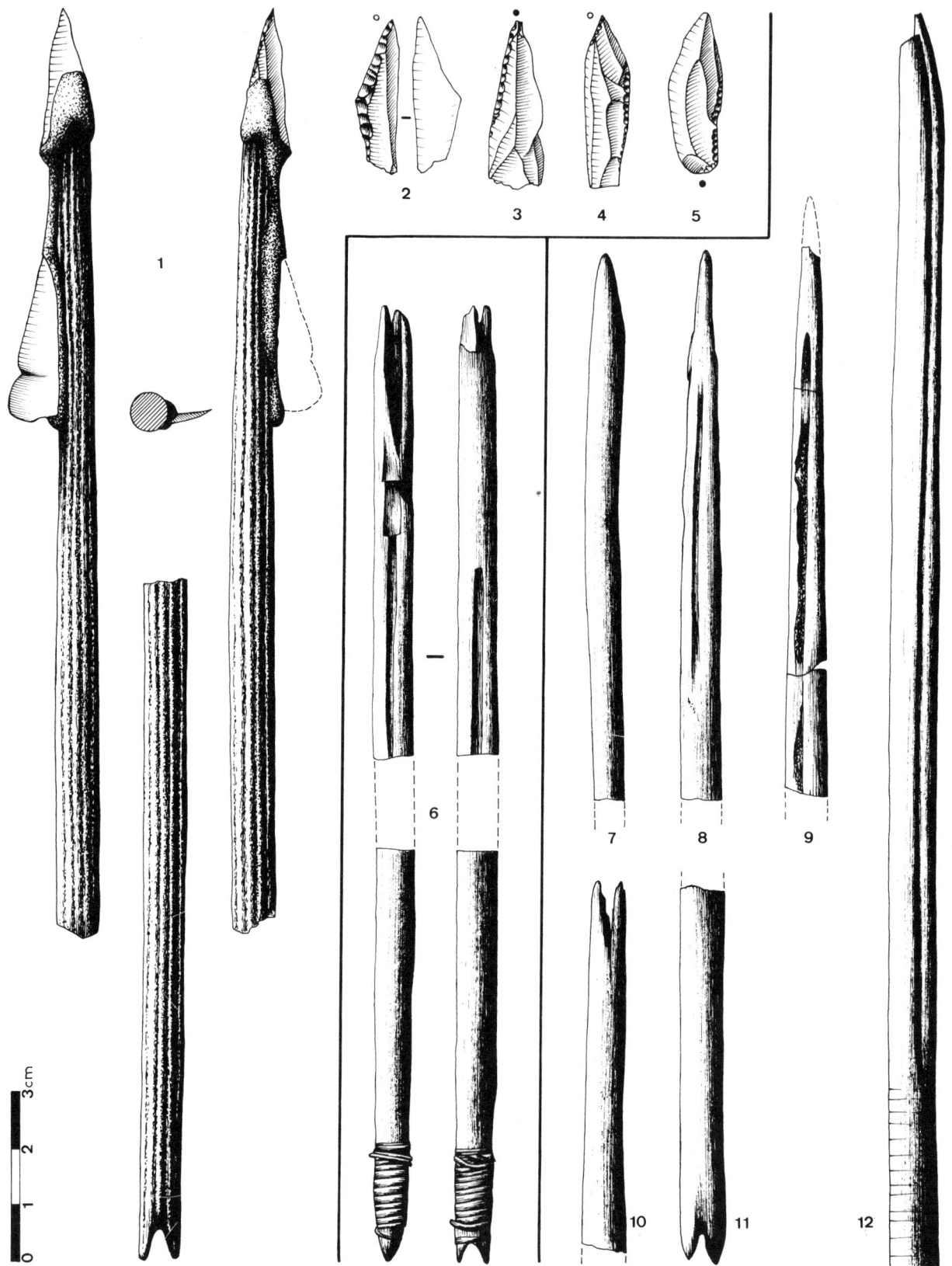

Figure 2 Arrows from the early and middle periods: Loshult (after Petersson 1951; Malmer 1968), Vinkelmose (after Troels-Smith 1961), Holmegaard (after Mathiassen 1948). There is no technical difference from the Ahrensburgian examples.

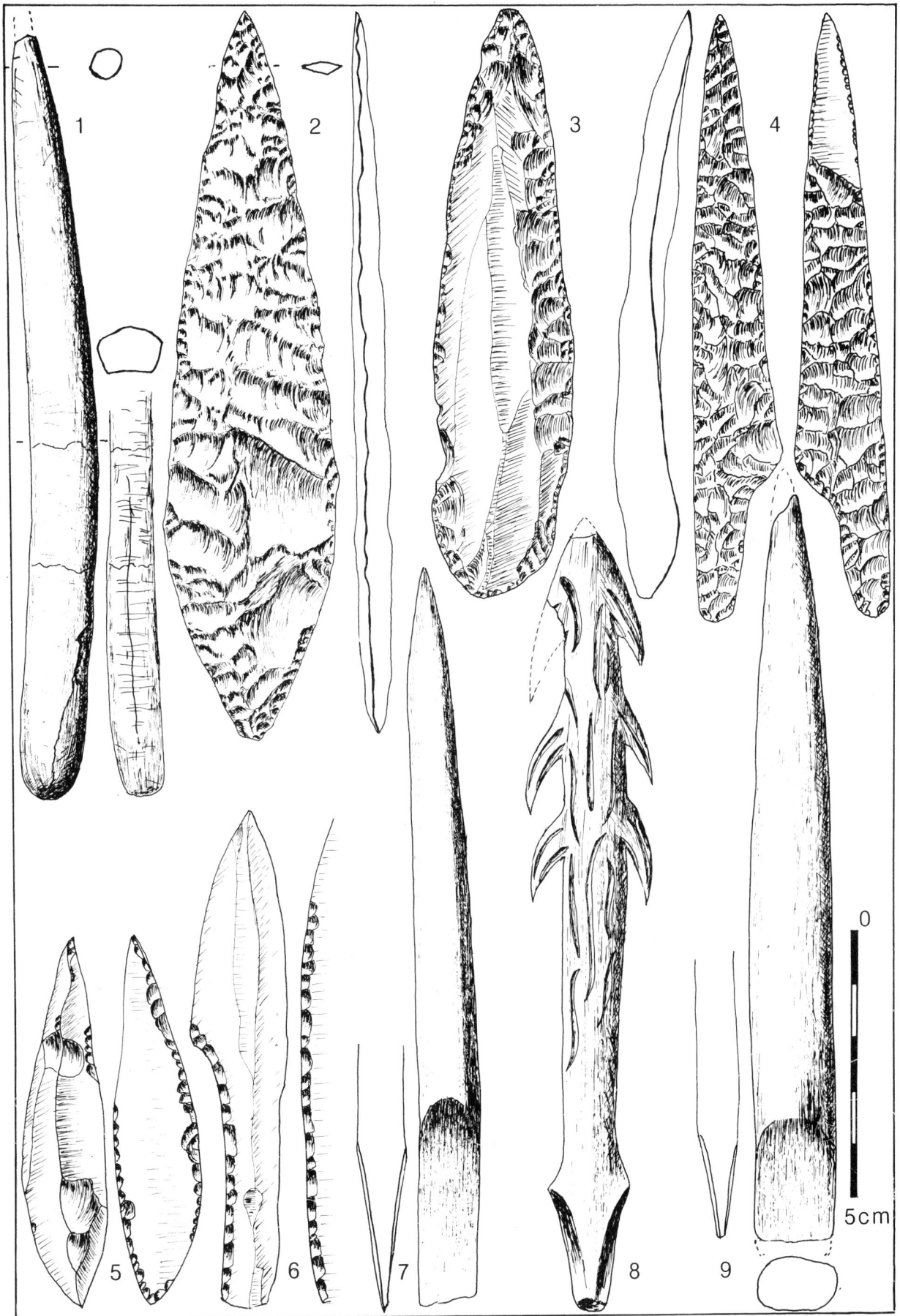

Figure 3 Upper Palaeolithic armatures: 1–4, Solutrean (after Smith 1966); 5–9, Magdalenian (after Sonneville-Bordes 1960). The dimensions are quite out of proportion with those of the Epipalaeolithic, and hence inconsistent with use as arrowheads.

their so-called 'geometric' character, something which has no chronological unity nor, more importantly, any technical significance. Non-geometric Tardenois points were made by the same methods as the scalene triangles or crescents which accompany them, and they were used for the same purposes. This applies also to the 'Sauveterre points' when compared to the little short scalenes from the Midi, and to the points with oblique truncations found everywhere – the simplest, even the basic, type. It is not the geometric character which is important, but the microlithization of the sharp-pointed armatures which began long before the appearance of the geometrics (Azilian points, Valorguian points, etc.).

Another well-worn expression is the term 'microlith' itself. Many tiny piercers or retouched bladelets are, in the strictest sense, 'micro-liths' – being less than 5 cm long and less than 4 mm thick. So, of course, are the backed bladelets that the Magdalenians used so extensively. What is significant – and most scholars realize it, however confusedly – is the concept of a *pointed* armature of low weight (less than 10 g and, in practice, usually less than 2 g).

The technique of oblique truncation on bladelets is the basis of nearly all European microlith production. Very sharp points can, of course, be made in other ways – by shaping the end of a bladelet (see, e.g., Rozoy 1978: pl. 5, nos. 4, 5), for example, or by adapting the technique of backing. Other methods were subsequently developed in the Neolithic, with transverse arrowheads and points shaped by surface retouch. Essentially, however, the very sharp points produced in the Mesolithic were obtained by the conjunction of an oblique truncation with an un-retouched cutting edge (*Fig. 1*). These elements both have their uses, as we shall see in the following sections.

It is worth recalling that the first appearance of this technique, as a systematic and generally adopted phenomenon, occurred in north Germany during Dryas III – in the Ahrensburgian. Rahir (1920) and Rust (1937, 1943) understood its importance well and rightly assigned the Ahrensburgian of Re-mouchamps and of Ahrensburg to the 'Mesolithic' – initially called 'Tardenoisian' throughout Europe. It is important to remember that over one hundred arrows were found at Ahrensburg (*Fig. 1*), some with the flint tang inserted into the wooden arrow-shaft (for a list of finds of hafted armatures, see Rozoy 1978: 956–968). Later Mesolithic arrows (*Fig. 2*) are no different.

DIFFERENCES FROM THE MAGDALENIAN

In terms of technique, Epipalaeolithic toolkits are distinguished (from those used throughout the 25,000-year tradition of the Upper Palaeolithic) by the use of numerous microlithic points made of flint, re-placing earlier types of points which were character-istically much larger, scarce, and made of antler (and for this reason necessitated burins for their prepar-ation). There was, of course, the Solutrean phase (Smith 1966) when carefully shaped stone points were used, but these were the same size as Aurignac-ian and Magdalenian antler points and were much heavier on account of the greater density of the material. Nevertheless, the essential difference in size remains. Palaeolithic points were much heavier, weighing more than 10 g and, in the majority of cases, more than 20 g (*Fig. 3*); exceptions are rare. It can also be observed that microlithic armatures could be produced much more quickly (in 10–20 seconds), which made it possible to produce them in large quantities. Spears are retained, but some arrows are lost.

THE TECHNIQUE OF THE BOW AND ARROW

The arrows recovered measure about 90 cm in length, with a diameter of one centimetre. They were fitted with points weighing 0.5–2.0 g, so that, together with a little mastic and fletching, the total weight would be 20–30 g; a heavier tip would have unbalanced them. An arrow travels at 100 km per hour, this initial high speed being the reason for its effectiveness ($\frac{1}{2}mv^2$). It is possible to shoot over distances of 100 or even 200 m, but in practice arrows are generally used over 20–50 m; beyond this, the force of penetration diminishes too much. An arrow is designed to shoot medium- and large-sized game, which it would pass through completely. The fundamental advantage of the bow is its precision. The role of the flint point is obviously to pierce the fur and hide of the animal; the armature is positioned so that its cutting edge hits the target obliquely and cuts the skin and organs it meets. Flint points are more efficient in this respect than steel points (Pope 1962). A second armature placed along the shaft, as on the Loshult arrow (*Fig. 2*), makes the cut wider and enlarges the wound not only in the skin, but in all the tissues pierced. They are thus not barbs, like those on Magdalenian harpoons, but lateral cutting edges. Epipalaeolithic groups whose assemblages contain a very high percentage of armatures probably used several of these cutting tools on each shaft. It is not impossible that some of the backed bladelets of the Upper Magdalenian were mounted in much the same way, but these would be parallel to the shaft; the shaft would also have been much larger, judging from the dimensions of the points mounted at the head, and the analogy is therefore of secondary importance.

Behind each armature (or each group of two or three armatures) we should imagine such an arrow, propelled by a bow 1.60 m long and able to penetrate and pass right through a bear at fifty metres. The Epipalaeolithic was essentially the era of hunting with a bow. Modern attempts to study the social evolution of the Epipalaeolithic (e.g. Constandse-Westermann, Newell and Meiklejohn 1984; Newell 1984) would be even more interesting if greater account were taken of its socio-technical basis (for more details, see Rozoy 1978: 956–968, 1008–1020).

THE THREE MAJOR PERIODS OF THE EPIPALAEOLITHIC IN EUROPE

In the very early period (twelfth and eleventh millennia BP) there was no uniformity; each culture adapted its traditional technique, in its own way, to include the new invention. This was a transitional period – in one area armatures were points with curved backs, in another points with straight backs, elsewhere points with truncated bases, or with a tang. Only the Ahrensburgian culture invented truncation on bladelets, while other cultures solved the problem in other ways. There was, however, one common characteristic: each regional group made only one class of armature at a time – Istres points in the Valorguian (*Fig. 4*), Tjonger points in the north,

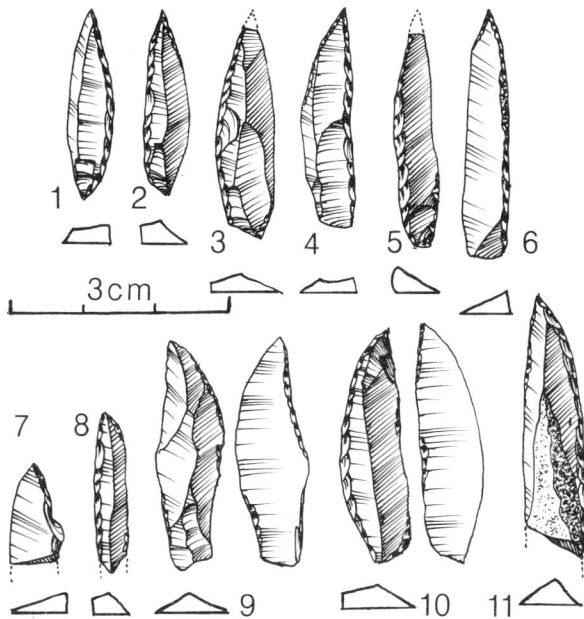

Figure 4 Valorguian armatures: 7–11, Cornille layer 12 (Lateglacial, proto-Valorguian); 1–6, Cornille layer 10a (Allerød). These form a single class of armatures that is already clearly microlithic.

the pre-Tardenoisian of Les Blanchères, etc. Only the Ahrensburgian, dated to Dryas III, used tanged points at the same time as simple points made by truncation, together with some triangles and atypical trapezes (*Fig. 1*).

In the early and middle periods (tenth and ninth millennia BP) oblique truncations on bladelets spread everywhere, although treated differently in different regions to produce either geometric or non-geometric armatures. More importantly, in each regional group two or more classes of armatures were in use at the same time (*Fig. 5*), and one class was only abandoned (gradually) when a third had become established. This diversity strongly suggests diversification of types of bows and arrows, although this cannot currently be proven.

In the recent and final periods (eighth and seventh millennia BP) trapezes made on more regular blades and bladelets were used, with diverse types occurring in different regions, and still with several classes in use at the same time (*Fig. 6*). Nothing is known of the nature of the intervening technical development – it must have been very important since it spread rapidly by 7850 BP – and it is difficult to pinpoint its origin geographically. In the southern two-thirds of France trapezes were made with retouch almost invariably on the left side (point upwards), thus following on the unvarying tradition of the middle period. In Belgium the point is retouched on the right side; in the Tardenoisian 75–80% of trapezes are retouched on the right side. This practice must have been acquired from an external source, since the earlier tradition used retouch on the left side, in accordance with the rest of France. In Belgium, however, from c. 8200 BP a regional variety of armatures was being made (the 'feuilles de gui' group) with retouch on the right (*Fig. 5*). It is probable, therefore, that this was the geographical origin of trapezes. The time-range over which trapezes existed alongside armatures of the middle period varies from region to region (*Fig. 7*).

Trapezes did not penetrate (or penetrated only slightly) some regions (e.g. Ardenne, Beaugency), where people adapted their traditional armatures but using ancillary techniques similar to those of their neighbours (e.g. style of retouch, flat inverse retouch, etc.).

The final period (seventh millennium BP) is characterized mainly by the use of flat inverse retouch, probably indicative of a new hafting method, and this was applied to quite different types of armature. Small transverse arrowheads (Montclus and Le Châtelet types – Rozoy 1978) appeared in the southern half of France.

THE SALIENT FEATURES OF THE CHANGES

The changes in armatures, as in the industries generally, occurred in a mosaic-like way (Chavaillon *et al.* 1978). These changes were *gradual*; for instance, the armatures of the middle period took more than a millennium to disappear after the invention of the trapeze. On the one hand these changes were *inter-related* within a single culture; on the other, they were *autonomous* from one culture

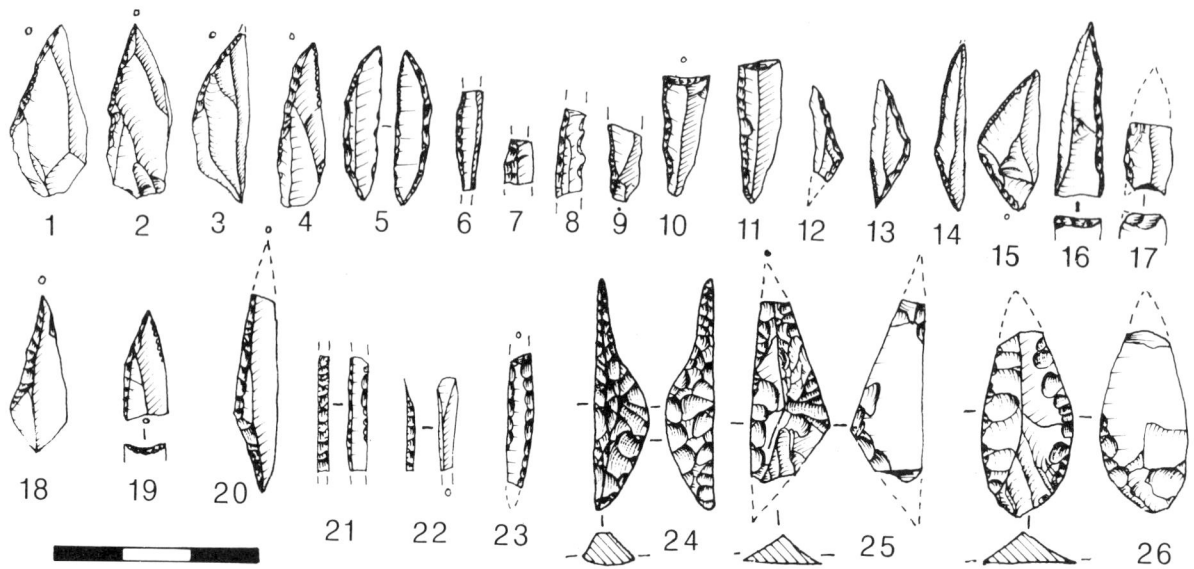

Figure 5 Armatures from the early and middle periods: 1–17, Roc-La-Tour II; 18–26, Oirschot V (B.A.I., Groningen). There are several classes of armatures at each site. Note the armatures with invasive retouch (24–26) which have the truncation on the right side as early as the middle period.

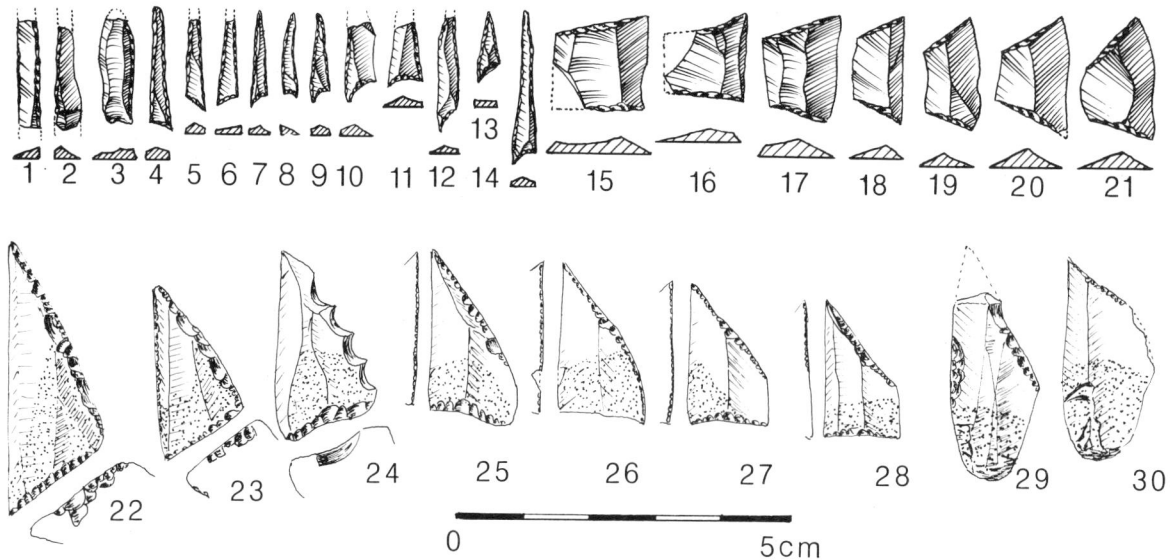

Figure 6 Armatures from the recent and final periods: 1–21, Montclus layer 16; 22–30, Allée Tortue X, Fère-en-Tardenois. Stippling indicates marks (of hafting?). In each group there are three main classes.

to another, and their diffusion around each centre of invention varied. Where diffusion was widespread, as in the case of oblique truncations in the early and middle periods and of trapezes in the recent and final periods, it led to the development of many variations, reflecting the personality of the groups using them.

The diffusion of inventions, which was sometimes very rapid, is evidence of the fundamental homogeneity of technical and cultural levels, and of the existence of a network of communications between regional groups.

THE RELATIONSHIP TO NEOLITHIZATION

It has often been postulated that this period re-presents a 'transition' (this is the etymological meaning of the term 'Mesolithic') towards the Neolithic. In a recently published work, Grahame Clark even speaks of a 'prelude' (Clark 1980). This point of view can be considered from at least three aspects, whether related or not: (i) technical progress towards food production, for example by specialization on a single animal species, systematic harvesting of wild cereals, and so forth; (ii) the objective preparation (obviously unplanned and unconscious) of a human setting favourable to the introduction of food production, in terms of population density and familiarity with the land; and (iii) subjective preparation (no less unplanned and unconscious) as a consequence of intellectual evolution. It is appropriate to examine these elements separately, without

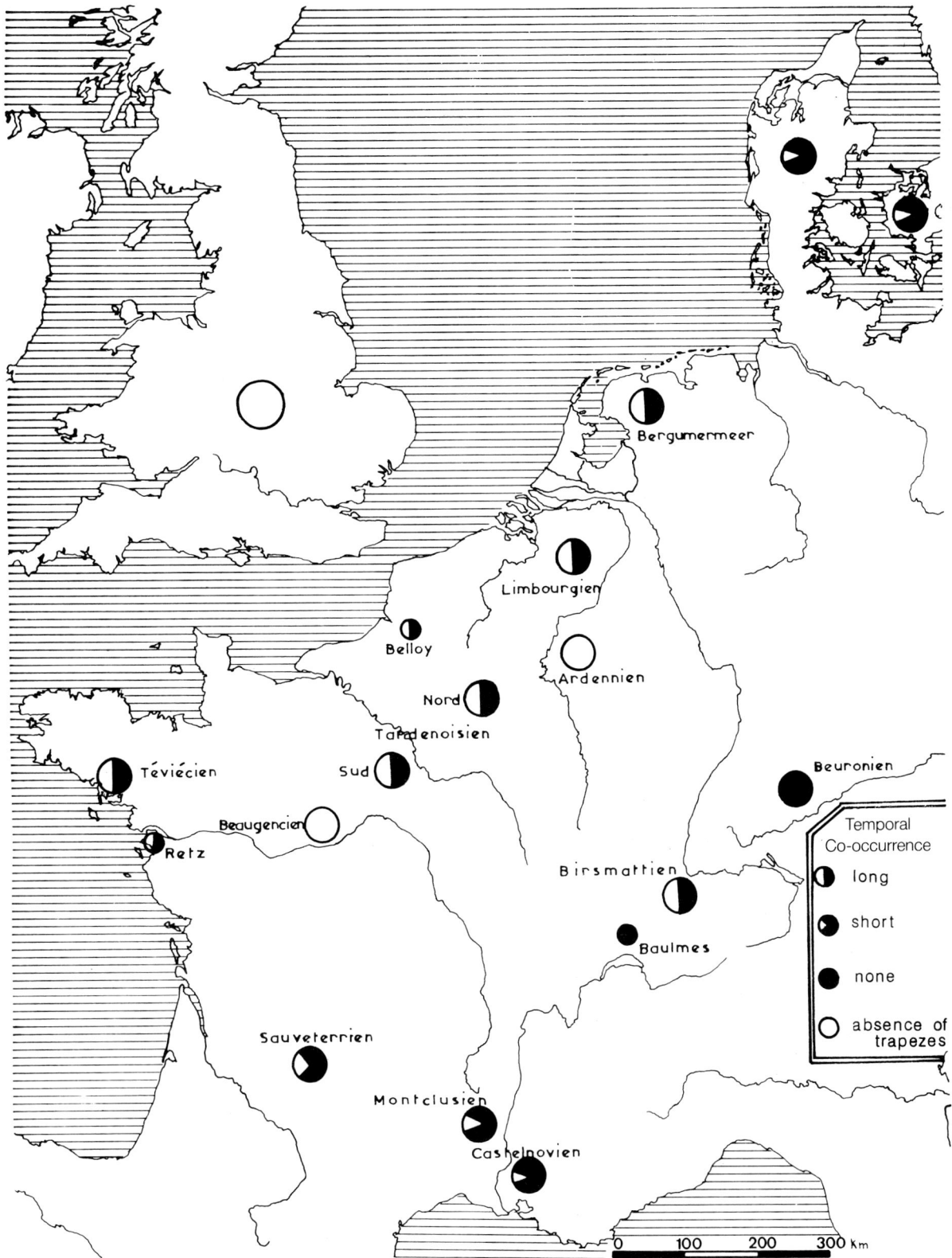

Figure 7 The co-existence of trapezes and armatures inherited from the middle period. This varies in different cultures, but the trapezes themselves can include several types (e.g. *Fig. 6*).

losing sight of their constant overlapping and inter-actions.

(a) Economic aspects

In Europe the Epipalaeolithic ('Mesolithic') reveals no signs whatsoever of movement towards food production. There was no specialization on a single species, rather the contrary. The Magdalenians, who relied on reindeer for 80% of their subsistence (at least at certain times and places, perhaps for ecological reasons) were far more specialized than Epipalaeolithic peoples. In the latter case, conversely,

21

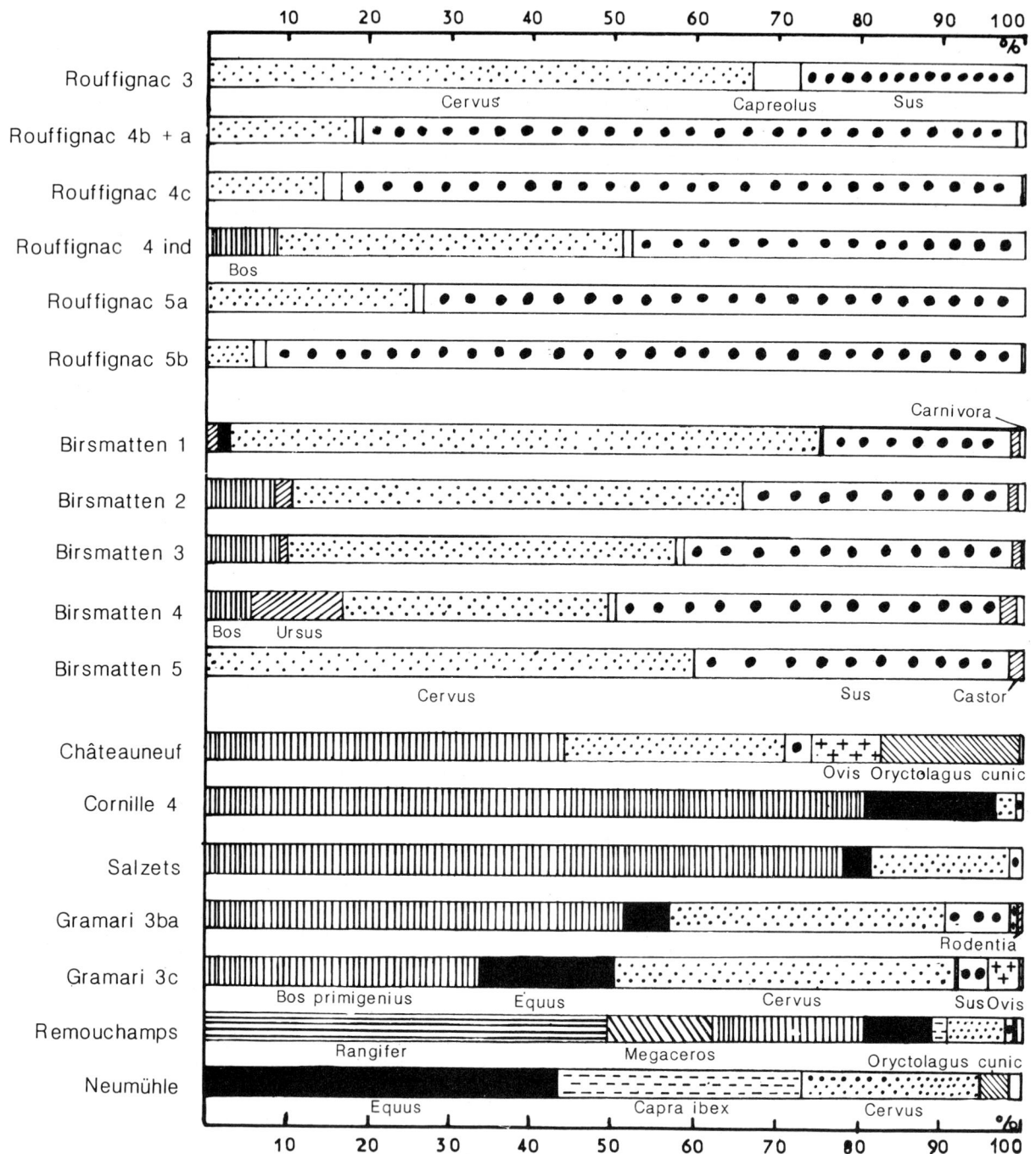

Figure 8 Proportion of animals killed (in terms of meat weight) at Epipalaeolithic sites. There are always at least two staple sources; these differ in different areas (even adjacent areas) and periods.

a clear and systematic diversification is perceived (*Fig. 8*), reflected in the variety of classes of armatures mounted at the tips of arrow-shafts.

Most of the traces of harvesting or of the domestication of animals which some people thought they had perceived in the Epipalaeolithic have, in the long term, been shown to derive from old or very insecure data; for example, the sheep at Téviec – represented by a single tooth which has since vanished (Péquart *et al.* 1937; Rozoy 1978: 787). Those which can be substantiated from recent research are all in the Mediterranean region. The sheep (*Ovis*) at Gazel and at Dourgne (Guilaine

1976a, 1976b, 1980) are contemporary with Neolithic cultures, from which the animals could have been stolen or perhaps borrowed. In any case, this concerns only the very end of the period. Some harvested plants (*Lens, Vicia, Pisum, Cicer*) are known from ninth millennium BP contexts at Font-bregoua and L'Abeurador (Guilaine 1980); but gathering is not cultivating, and in this instance did not continue.

No major deforestation, even on a local scale, took place before the middle of the Atlantic period – that is, before the intrusion of the Neolithic (this event took place earlier in the Mediterranean zone,

22

and precisely where the Cardial culture was in existence as early as 8000 BP). Sedentism has often been claimed to exist in the Epipalaeolithic, but this is very difficult to prove; it seems unlikely in most regions where there are numerous sites with only slight occupation debris. Traces of solid buildings are not found until the Neolithic, when they appear as early as its earliest stage (LBK) in the region under discussion. An exception could be claimed for coastal sites, but the coasts of this period are only known in a part of Denmark and in the north of the British Isles (Bonsall 1988), the rest now being submerged. For example, at the time of their occupation, Téviec (Péquart et al. 1937) and Hoëdic (Péquart and Péquart 1954) were several kilometres inland (Rozoy 1978: 779–796, pl. 198).

There is no serious evidence of a trend towards food production during the twelfth, eleventh, tenth or ninth millennia BP. As for the cultures with typical trapezes and notched blades, the evidence which does exist is confined to periods and regions where borrowing – whether of objects or practices – from Neolithic neighbours was possible and, therefore, likely.

Naturally, such conclusions cannot be extended to apply to the Earth as a whole. The transition certainly occurred somewhere and probably at many points, especially in the Near East. But it cannot be inferred from this that analogous processes occurred in Europe, even if the technical starting point (bow, arrows and microlithic armatures) was the same. Nor can the possibility be excluded that in other regions, in America for example, a direct transition from the Palaeolithic to the Neolithic took place, without the intervening period of the bowmen. Such problems must be investigated without any pre-conceptions.

(b) Demographic aspects

The situation is rather different. It is certainly an extremely delicate matter to attempt calculations of past populations from archaeological evidence. What-ever basis is considered – skeletal remains (Con-standse Westermann et al. 1984), faunal remains, or site distributions – it would be necessary, as Bordes et al. (1972) have stated, to revert to Biblical chronology – to compress the whole of the develop-ment of mankind into the period since 4004 BC – and this period would still be too long! Too little is preserved, still less brought to light, and of that only about one per cent is excavated. Thus at Fère-en-Tardenois (Allée Tortue), which is considered to be an extremely rich deposit, with some ten concent-rations of flint artifacts, we found some five thousand tools relating to occupation during the seventh millennium BP – that is, about five tools a year (or 50 for each decade). This does not imply a very large population, and certainly not even a tenth (or even a

hundredth) of the population that actually existed.

We are thus reduced to estimating populations from the nutritional capacity of the territory (Rozoy 1978: 1055–1060, 1105–1109), and to making com-parisons between periods in terms of the number and importance (based on numbers of tools) of sites known. Nonetheless, these, albeit approximate, comparisons give the following indications for the Epipalaeolithic:

a) The population had expanded to occupy the whole of the available land area, even areas which might be the size of a modern French 'canton' or even 'commune', in contrast to the Upper Mag-dalenian when the population was scattered in isolated islets (Rozoy 1985: map), with very large territories completely empty (Brittany, Champagne).

b) Sites were much smaller (both in area and in the number of tools), but occur in much greater numbers than in the Upper Magdalenian. This leads to the conclusion that social groups were more restricted in size (but with a larger number of primary groups) or that there was more mobility; probably both of these were true.

c) Cultural units were more restricted in size – about 100 km across compared to 500 km in the Magdalenian. Thus the composition of Upper Mag-dalenian toolkits is the same in Belgium and in the area to the south east of Paris (Rozoy 1984b, 1985, in press), the qualitative difference being at best the presence of 'zinken' in Belgium (even then not found at every site). In the Epipalaeolithic in the same region a number of cultural units can be distinguished: the Limburgian, the Ardennian group (which ought perhaps to be subdivided), the northern Tardenoisian, the southern Tardenoisian, the group from the Loing valley (Les Richoux, Les Champs Bertin – Pigeot 1973), the Beaugencian and, on the fringes, the groups from Belloy and from Luxemburg (Spier 1982), without counting those which have not yet been identified. There is a corresponding number of different assemblage types, each with its own style and special tools.

Population estimates suggest the strong probability that each cultural group contained roughly the same number of people (1000–3000 persons, including children) in both the Upper Palaeolithic and the Epipalaeolithic, but that the overall population showed a marked increase by a factor of between five and ten. On the other hand, the primary groups appear to have been smaller (15–20 people instead of 50–80 people), with greater individualism. Thus each of the regional Epipalaeolithic groups main-tained itself (with minor variations in boundaries) from millennium to millennium in the same territory, as can be seen in the persistence of certain technical details ('bordage', for example – see Rozoy 1967: 212, 1968: 336) peculiar to each region.

From this one can deduce not sedentism proper, but well-defined movements within a limited territory, of which the topographical detail would be well known and appreciated (Turnbull 1961, 1968). In other words, people were acquiring an exhaustive and intimate knowledge of the land, to a degree that was not possible in the final Palaeolithic. Moreover, the evident cultural unity indicates the existence of many close relationships between primary groups in an awareness of their regional unity. The rapid diffusion of inventions also points to the existence of good inter-cultural relations. The 'frontiers' of cultures were certainly easily penetrated, and socio-technical levels were absolutely equivalent.

All of these elements produced conditions that were, by their very nature, favourable to the subsequent diffusion of the Neolithic. Nevertheless, it is unlikely that any single element was an indispensable preliminary, and these conditions certainly did not in any way make the transition to food production necessary – a hunting way of life could have continued for a long time. In any case, this traditional mode of subsistence continued for several millennia alongside cultures in which food production was already well developed. Within France itself, nearly two thousand years passed between the Cardial neolithization along the Mediterranean littoral and the general spread of food production to the rest of the country. The evidence from Montclus (Rozoy 1978: 298–299, 1190) seems to show that, far from evolving inexorably towards cultivation and stock-breeding, Epipalaeolithic peoples preferred to sever contact with their neolithized cousins.

(c) Cultural and psychological aspects

The cultural and intellectual changes that occurred during the Epipalaeolithic, although very difficult to demonstrate, were perhaps the most important of all. Some of them derived from the sociological changes brought about by the use of the bow. Restricted group size encouraged the existence and autonomy of the nuclear family and probably made possible the greater role of individualism, initiative and responsibility. A more numerous overall population would have permitted greater social interaction. Life was more fulfilling and more easily assured.

Art, and non-utilitarian evidence in general, gives only a very broad indication of the intellectual levels attained by the whole population. First, there is the almost total disappearance of the figurative animal art of the Upper Palaeolithic. Modern research, and that of A. Leroi-Gourhan (1965) in particular, has clearly established that the naturalistic figures constituted symbols, and were not a basis for magic. It can be argued that these signs, or abstractions, which still took concrete form, had to be figurative in order to be understood. Towards the end of the Magdalenian phase abstract symbols multiplied,

sometimes associated systematically with particular naturalistic figures (e.g. Rozoy 1984b, 1985), and in the Epipalaeolithic only the abstract symbols survived. It could be argued, therefore, that sufficient numbers of Epipalaeolithic people were now able to grasp these abstractions. This would indicate an increase in the capacity for abstract thought amongst the general population. The grouping of the figures in scenes is an analogous indication, and the centring of these scenes on humans instead of animals is yet another.

Abstract thought is also seen in the *ability to count*. In the Upper Palaeolithic there is evidence of this in the form of sets of signs engraved on bone ('marques de chasse' or 'hunting tallies'), but very few of these convey a system which we can comprehend or even perceive. In this context, reference can be made to the 'churinga' from the grotte de la Roche at Lalinde, dated to the very end of the Palaeolithic (*Fig. 9*), on which there are alternating series of five horizontal and five vertical marks. There are five groups of each, but the last vertical group contains only four marks, and the aesthetic character of the whole, surrounded by other marks, casts doubt on the view that its primary purpose was for calculation. The engraver at least would have known how to count to five on his fingers. The common use of abstract numbers up to five is thus assured.

In the Ahrensburgian assemblage from Remouchamps (microlithic and 'Mesolithic', it must be stressed) there is a bone which is very similar to the hunting tallies, but the subtle organization of this piece is beyond our understanding, in spite of the bold hypothesis put forward by its finder (Dewez 1974a, 1974b). It was accompanied by another example with more systematic markings – groups of five cupmarks, arranged like the number 'five' on dominoes (*Fig. 9*). This piece seems therefore, and even more clearly than at Lalinde, to involve first-order notation, which was in itself a considerable advance, occurring around 11,000 BP. Nevertheless, there are no groups of 5×5 or 10×5. Therefore, second-order notation (i.e. groups of 5 or 10, counted as second-order units) is not attested, but it is possible that it was reached later. This cannot be taken further for lack of other evidence, but it does show continuity from the Magdalenian and the extent of progress in the capacity for abstract thought. There is little need to emphasize the importance of a system of numeration for the transition to food production.

At the same time we see the disappearance of female figurines centred upon maternity, or rather potential maternity – for Magdalenian outline drawings and statuettes, and even Gravettian statuettes, do not portray pregnancy, merely those parts of the female anatomy connected with reprod-

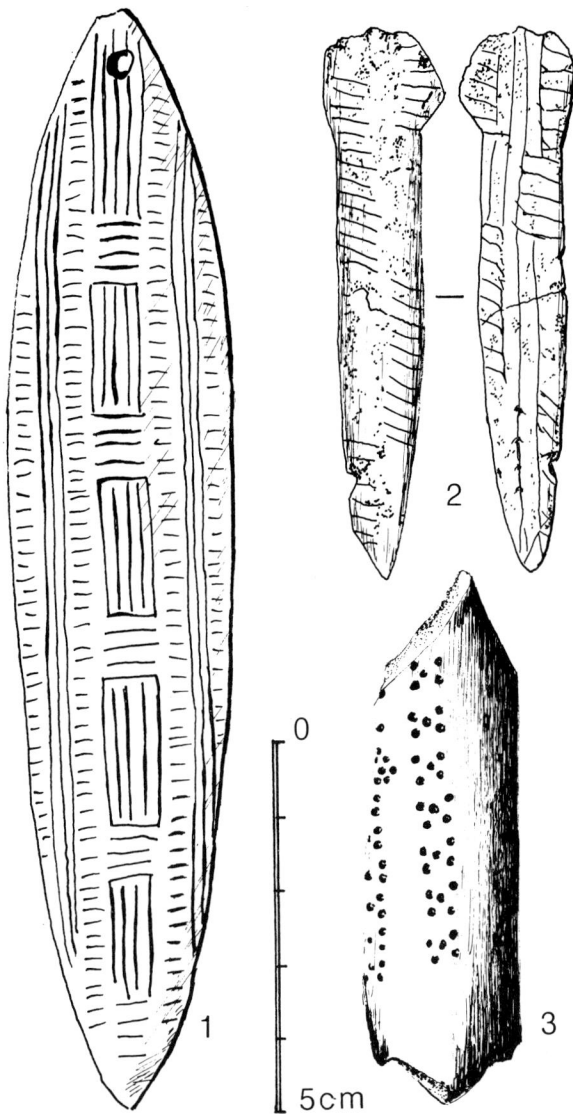

Figure 9 Rare examples of evidence of numeration: 1 – 'churinga' from Lalinde, final Magdalenian (slightly reduced, after Sonneville Bordes 1967); 2, 3 – engraved bones from Remouchamps (after Dewez 1974). First-order numeracy only is proven.

uction and childbirth. The Epipalaeolithic statuette from Gaban, for instance, is already realistic and complete. It is possible that this corresponds to an understanding of the process of procreation. Such an advance is clearly important in facilitating the transition to food production – to sow to obtain a harvest, to put the cow to the bull to obtain calves.

Relations to the Neolithic – summary

As we have seen, the 5000 years of the Epipalaeolithic, considered as a whole, constituted as a matter of objective fact a basis without which neolithization could not have taken place. This basis, sociological as much as intellectual, made the transition to food production *possible*. It did not make this *necessary* and, in temperate Europe, it did not include any technical element tending towards food production. In short, neolithization needed this social and intellectual basis which had developed slowly over more than 100,000 years during the Palaeolithic, not really reaching maturity until the Epipalaeolithic ('Mesolithic'). From this basis, food production made its appearance in those places with a favourable climate (the Near East, southern China, Central America), while less favourable regions followed the traditional way of life based on hunting. These regions then received the new techniques and attitudes from external sources and were able to adopt these easily since the necessary social and intellectual level had already been widely achieved.

CLIMATIC CHANGE AND SOCIO-TECHNICAL CHANGE

It is often stated that the technical changes that occurred in prehistoric societies, and in particular that which marked the beginning of the Epipalaeolithic, were the result of environmental change. This thesis appears so self-evident to many workers, that they confine themselves to formulating it without attempting any demonstration. For them, it is in a sense a postulate, a presupposition, an act of faith, even a ritual invocation. Underlying it, whether consciously or not, is for some people undoubtedly an unwillingness to accept any explanation for change other than a material one, with any doubts on this point being automatically denounced as spiritualism, even deism or creationism. Prehistoric cultures are thus described as being so many 'adaptations' to the environment or, above all, to changes in the environment. It is in fact a mis-use of the scholastic principle 'post hoc, ergo propter hoc'.

I have already pointed out the splendid circular reasoning which begins by defining the 'Mesolithic' as being Postglacial (disregarding the Ahrensburgian people and certain other groups who manufactured armatures of 1 g in weight), and then concludes that it was climatic change that caused changes in industries.

It goes without saying that we must applaud the desire of scientists to study nature (including man) exactly as it is, and – I would add – on the basis of the facts, all the facts, and nothing but the facts; and consequently without any presupposition – most particularly about causes and mechanisms. The facts are these ...

The technical basis of the Epipalaeolithic is characterized by certain essential changes. Firstly, there was the microlithization of armatures, which was gradual and lasted for more than a millennium. Its starting point was Palaeolithic armatures and techniques – even in the Ahrensburgian region, since microlithization began in the Tjongerian with curved backed points. This microlithization began as early as the end of Dryas II; it was already evident in some Magdalenian assemblages when various experiments were tried out (e.g. Gare de Couze –

25

Bordes and Fitte 1964; Rozoy 1978: pl. 85, 85b) and in which the Azilian point appears before the end of Dryas II. The process of microlithization continued through the Allerød and was only accomplished fully in Dryas III (La Borie del Rey – Coulonges 1963; Remouchamps, etc.). In the Valorguian, too, Istres points ('pointes fusiformes' – cf. Rozoy 1978: 275) which are roughly shaped in layer 12 at Cornille (*Fig. 4*), dating to the Lateglacial (Dryas II), are abundant in layer 10 which is dated to the Allerød (layer 11 is sterile). The glaciation had by no means ended, and in Dryas III it was still extremely cold; yet microlithization continued and became increasingly significant. It is evident, therefore, that this first technical change preceded climatic change (Dryas II to Allerød) and intensified with returning cold.

The second change marked the beginning of the early and middle periods. It consisted of the widespread adoption of the technique of oblique truncation on bladelets (with or without the microburin as a waste product, according to which group is considered) and, more importantly, the diversification of classes of armatures made easier by this technique, which allows for multiple combinations. Thus one truncation makes a simple point, two could make a scalene or a Tardenois point, and so forth (*Fig. 5*). It is this change which other authors see as marking the beginning of the 'Mesolithic proper'. On the whole these innovations, which were also introduced very gradually, correspond to the Pre-Boreal. However, as mentioned above, their invention goes back to the Ahrensburgian in Dryas III, where tanged points co-existed with points with oblique truncation, points with unilateral retouch, and a few triangles (*Fig. 1*; Rozoy 1978: 115–155). Once it had appeared here, the technique spread very widely. Again, technical innovation preceded climatic change.

The third major technical change was the introduction of typical trapezes and débitage in the 'Montbani' style. This is securely dated everywhere to *c.* 7800–7850 BP (*Fig. 6*) – yet the Atlantic period did not begin until *c.* 7500 BP.

So we can see that, three times, the changes in industries occurred before the changes in climate. *Once* may be chance, *twice* is a coincidence, but *three times* becomes a proof. Since it is out of the question to contest the principle of cause and effect ('post hoc, ergo propter hoc'), we are led to the following revolutionary conclusion: *changes in industries caused climatic changes (three times)!*

Such a conclusion may seem somewhat surprising if looked at only superficially; it has, nonetheless, some elements of merit – *it is just as solidly founded as the previous hypothesis, according to which climatic changes caused industrial change.*

Moreover, this conclusion has the subordinate advantage of actually conforming to facts. Its sociological and philosophical implications are considerable – mind over matter. But these considerations lie outside our present concerns, and the task of developing them must be left to others. Let us simply note in passing that popular wisdom has decided that atomic experiments have unsettled the weather (*Fig. 10*).

Figure 10 'They are upsetting the weather with their flint-chipping experiments' (after Faizant 1982). This opinion has as much scientific value as saying that changes in environment are the causes of changes in industries.

THE CONSTANT PRESSURE OF THE ENVIRONMENT

If we really wish (as we should) to study nature purely as it is, 'without any external addition', the very first consideration must be the constant pressure that the environment exerts on all its constituent parts, including the human species. It is not only environmental change which affects man, but rather the ever-present environment itself: there is the speed of running animals; there is the danger of wolves; there is cold, snow, floods which come with the thaw, permafrost, the shortage of game if spring comes too late, the inevitable 'plague' of mosquitoes when spring comes at last; there are females and young animals that are more wary than the males, the charge of bison when attacked, and so on. These are the stimuli for *continual* adaptation. Of course, increasing warmth was far from being a catastrophe. The reindeer departed, but red deer multiplied (to such an extent that roe deer were not hunted, or only occasionally). Wild boar also proliferated. Mammoth had disappeared, but there were more aurochs and more bison than ever (so long as the forest did not become too dense). Moreover, fuel for warmth was abundant, although there was less need of it.

Moreover, if a milder climate was the cause of technical change, it would have occurred tens of millennia earlier in the warm regions of the Earth; yet this did not happen. The same would be true of Europe at the beginning of each interglacial.

The question of whether modifications in animal species (morphological changes or behavioural changes, if such there were) were a response to climatic changes, must be left to the zoologists. It is well known, however, that the main characteristic of the human species is non-specialization, which gives rise to adaptability; and it is this trait, quite natural though it is, which sets our species apart.

The course of prehistory is marked out by inventions, some of considerable significance – stone throwing, the club, manufactured tools, fire, clothes, artificial shelter, bifacially flaked axes, the Levallois technique, bone-working, blade débitage, figurative art, the bow and arrow, the domestication of plants and animals, and so forth. These inventions were responses to permanent pressure from the environment, and their general spread depended on the ability of the whole population to exploit them according to the level of conceptual advance at the time. The bow and arrow were probably invented several times in different periods and regions (e.g. in the Spanish Solutrean of Parpalló). They could not spread and become the standard of that time until mental evolution (probably conditioned by its physical basis, i.e. the biology of the brain) was sufficiently advanced throughout the population as a whole. The driving force behind this evolution has not been provided just by changes in the environment (from which one could escape by moving, as animals did), but rather by the constant pressure exercised by the environment on a species that has been far more capable than all others of continual adaptation.

Note:

1. Elsewhere in this volume, the spelling 'Epi-Palaeolithic' has been adopted. At the author's request, the spelling used in this paper follows that (*Epipaléolithique*) in his previous publications (e.g. Rozoy 1978). (Ed.)

Acknowledgements: Both the author and the Editor would like to thank Jane Murray for producing the basic translation of the original French text. Brian Barron, Department of French, University of Edinburgh, gave assistance with the more difficult pieces of translation. The author would also like to express his gratitude to Clive Bonsall for his kindness and patience.

References

BONSALL, C. (1988) Morton and Lussa Wood: the case for early Flandrian settlement in Scotland. *Scottish Archaeological Review*, 5: 30–33.

BORDES, F. and FITTE, P. (1964) Microlithes du Magdalénien supérieur de la Gare de Couze, Dordogne. *Miscelanea en Homenaje al Abate Henri Breuil*. Barcelona, Instituto de Prehistoria y Arqueología: 259–267.

BORDES, F., RIGAUD, J.P. and SONNEVILLE-BORDES, D. DE (1972) Des buts, problèmes et limites de l'archéologie paléolithique. *Quaternaria*, 16: 15–34.

CHAVAILLON, J., CHAVAILLON, N., HOURS, F. and PIPERNO, M. (1978) Le début et la fin de l'Acheuléen à Melka-Kunturé: méthodologie pour l'étude des changements de civilisation. *Bulletin de la Société Préhistorique Française*: 105–115.

CLARK, J.G.D. (1980) *Mesolithic Prelude. The Palaeolithic–Neolithic Transition in Old World Prehistory*. Edinburgh, University Press.

CONSTANDSE-WESTERMANN, T.S., NEWELL, R.R. and MEIKLE-JOHN, C. (1984) Human biological background of population dynamics in the western European Mesolithic. *Proceedings of the Koninklijke Nedelandse Akademie van Wetenschappen*, B87: 139-223.

COULONGES, L. (1963) Magdalénien et Périgordien post-glaciaires. La grotte de la Borie del Rey (Lot et Garonne). *Gallia Préhistoire*, 6: 1–29

DEWEZ, M. *et al.* (1974a) Nouvelles recherches à la grotte de Remouchamps. *Bulletin de la Société Royale Belge d'Anthropologie et Préhistoire*, 85: 5–160.

DEWEZ, M. (1974b) New hypotheses concerning two engraved bones from la grotte de Remouchamps, Belgium. *World Archaeology*, 5(3): 337–345.

FAIZANT, J. (1982) Cartoon from 'Jours de France'.

GILEAD, I. (1984) Is the term 'Epipalaeolithic' relevant to Levantine prehistory? *Current Anthropology*, 25(2): 227–229.

GUILAINE, J. (1976a) Grotte Gazel. Le Mésolithique et le Néolithique. Abri de Dourgne II. *IXe Congres U.I.S.P.P. (Nice). Livret-Guide de l'Excursion C2 Provence et Languedoc Méditerranéen, Sites Paléolithiques et Néolithiques*: 279–284, 312–315.

GUILAINE, J. (1976b) Les civilisations néolithiques dans les Pyrénées. In J. Guilaine (ed.), *La Préhistoire Française*, tome 2. Paris, Centre National de la Recherche Scientifique: 326–327

GUILAINE, J. (1980) *Dossiers de l'Archéologie*, 44 (June 1980).

LARTET, E. and CHRISTY, H. (1865–1875) *Reliquiae Aquitanicae*. London, Williams and Norgate. Paris, Baillière.

LEROI-GOURHAN, A. (1965) *Préhistoire de l'Art Occidental*. Paris, Mazenod.

LUBBOCK, J. (1865) *Prehistoric Times as Illustrated by Ancient Remains and Customs of Modern Savages*. London, Williams and Norgate.

MALMER, M.P. (1968) Die Mikrolithen in dem Pfeilfund von Loshult. *Meddelanden från Lunds universitets historiska museum*, 1966–1968: 249–255.

MATHIASSEN, T. (1948) *Danske Oldsager. I. Ældre Stenalder*. Copenhagen, Nordisk Forlag.

MORTILLET, G. DE (1869) Essai d'une classification des cavernes et des stations sous abri, fondée sur le produit de l'industrie humaine. *Comptes Rendus de l'Académie des Sciences de Paris*, 1.3.68; and *Bulletin de la Société Géologique de France*, série 2, 26 (1868–1869): 583–587; and *Matériaux pour Servir a l'Histoire Primitive et Naturelle de l'Homme*, série 2, n° 3: 172–179.

NEWELL, R.R. (1984) On the Mesolithic contribution to the social evolution of western European society. In J. Bintliff (ed.), *European Social Evolution: Archaeological Perspectives*. Bradford, University of Bradford: 69–82.

PÉQUART, M., PÉQUART, ST-J., BOULE, M. and VALLOIS, H. (1937) *Téviec, Station-Nécropole Mésolithique du Morbihan* (Archives de l'Institut de Paléontologie Humaine, 18). Paris, Masson.

PÉQUART, M. and PÉQUART, ST-J. (1954) *Hoëdic. Deuxième Station-Nécropole du Mésolithique Côtier Armoricain*. Antwerp, De Sikkel.

PETERSSON, M. (1951) Mikrolithen als Pfeilspitzen. Ein Fund aus dem Lilla Loshult-Moor, Ksp. Loshult, Skåne. *Meddelanden från Lunds universitets historiska museum*, 1950–1951: 123–137

PIGEOT, N. (1973) Analyse typologique d'une série de 163 pointes du Tardenois. *Cahiers du Centre de Recherches Préhistoriques de l'Université de Paris 1 (U.E.R. Art et Archéologie)*, 1: 19–29.

POPE, S.T. (1962) *A Study of Bows and Arrows*. Berkeley, University of California Press.

RAHIR, E. (1920) L'habitat tardenoisien des grottes de Remouchamps, Chaleux et Montaigle. L'industrie tardenoisienne et son évolution en Belgique. *Bulletin de la Société Royale d'Anthropologie de Bruxelles*, 35: 31–91

ROZOY, J-G. (1967) Essai d'adaptation des méthodes statistiques à l'Epipaléolithique ('Mésolithique'). Liste-type provisoire et premiers résultats. *Bulletin de la Société Préhistorique Française*, 64: 209–226.

ROZOY, J-G. (1968) Typologie de l'Epipaléolithique ('Mésolithique') franco-belge, introduction. *Bulletin de la Société Préhistorique Française*, 65: 335–342.

ROZOY, J-G. (1978) *Les Derniers Chasseurs. L'Epipaléolithique en France et en Belgique. Essai de Synthèse* (Société archéologique champenoise, numéro spécial). Charleville, J-G. Rozoy.

ROZOY, J-G. (1984a) The age of red deer or of bowmen? *Mesolithic Miscellany*, 5(2): 14–16

ROZOY, J-G. (1984b) Le Magdalénien supérieur à gravures de Roc-La-Tour I. *Congrès de Nivelles (2e Congrès de l'Association des Cercles Francophones d'Histoire et d'Archéologie de Belgique, 1984)*, vol. 2: 122–132.

ROZOY, J-G. (1985) Deux modes de chasse sur le plateau ardennais. *Jagen und Sammeln. Festschrift für H.G. Bandi* (Jahrbuch des Bernischen Historischen Museums, 63/64, 1983–84). Berne, Stämpfli: 245–252.

ROZOY, J-G. (in press) Le Magdalénien supérieur de Roc-La-Tour I. *Helinium*.

RUST, A. (1937) *Das altsteinzeitliche Rentierjägerlager Meiendorf*. Neumünster, Karl Wachholtz.

RUST, A. (1943) *Die alt- und mittelsteinzeitlichen Funde von Stellmoor*. Neumünster, Karl Wachholtz.

SCHWANTES, G. (1923) Das Beil als Scheide zwischen Paläolithikum und Neolithikum. *Archiv für Anthropologie*, N.F. 20: 13–41.

SCHWANTES, G. (1952) Wann endete das Paläolithikum? *Zeitschrift für Morphologie und Anthropologie*, 44(1–2): 237–244.

SMITH, P. (1966) *Le Solutréen en France*. Bordeaux, Delmas.

SONNEVILLE-BORDES, D. DE (1960) *Le Paléolithique Supérieur en Périgord*. Bordeaux, Delmas.

SONNEVILLE-BORDES, D. DE (1967) *La Préhistoire Moderne*. Périgueux, Fanlac.

SPIER, F. (1982) Les stations épipaléolithiques–mésolithiques de la commune de Hespérange (Grand-Duché de Luxembourg). In A. Gob and F. Spier (eds), *Le Mésolithique entre Rhin et Meuse*. Luxembourg, Société Préhistorique Luxembourgeoise: 229–256).

THOMSEN, C.J. (1836) *Ledetraad til Nordisk Oldkyndighed*. Copenhagen, Det Kongelige nordiske oldskriftselskab.

THOMSEN, C.J. (1837) *Leitfaden zur nordische Althertumskunde*. Copenhagen, Det Kongelige nordiske oldskriftselskab.

TROELS-SMITH, J. (1961) Et Pileskraft fra Tidlig Maglemosetid. *Aarbøger for Nordisk Oldkyndighed og Historie*, 1961: 122–146.

TURNBULL, C.M. (1961) *Le Peuple de la Forêt*. Paris, Stock.

TURNBULL, C.M. (1968) The importance of flux in two hunting societies. In R.B. Lee and I. DeVore (eds), *Man the Hunter*. Chicago, Aldine: 132–137.

Hunting with Flint-Tipped Arrows: Results and Experiences from Practical Experiments

Anders Fischer

Abstract

A substantial number of flint points have been produced and used for various activities, including shooting at several kinds of animals. As a result, macro- and micro-wear traces diagnostic of the projectile point function are defined, the efficiency of the flint-tipped arrow is demonstrated, and an explanation of the rapid typological evolution of Stone Age flint points is developed.

INTRODUCTION

Among archaeologists dealing with the Upper Palaeolithic and the Mesolithic, the flint points have been the object of special attention for decades. However, this concern has concentrated almost exclusively on chronological aspects. Until recently, only minor interest was ever devoted to such questions as: how were the points produced; how were they used; if, as is generally supposed, they were used as tips for spears and arrows, how effective were these weapons; why did the morphological evolution of the points seemingly progress much more rapidly than that of all other groups of tools?

The present paper reports on a series of experiments designed to answer some of these questions. The experiments were carried out at the Lejre Research Centre. They were directed by Peter Vemming Hansen, Peter Rasmussen and the present author, and were carried out in close cooperation with the Danish Society of Bowhunters (Fischer, Vemming Hansen and Rasmussen 1984; Fischer 1985).

LABOUR COSTS OF FLINT POINT MANUFACTURE

During our experiments several hundred flint points were produced. We concentrated on two morphologically different types – late Palaeolithic tanged points of Brommian type and late Mesolithic transverse flint tips (*Figs. 1–3*). To ensure that our results were directly comparable to prehistoric situations, we tried to make true replicas – i.e. by using the same raw materials and, as far as we could ascertain, the same flaking techniques and working postures as used originally.

As part of the experiments a skilled flint knapper produced 100 Brommian points under carefully controlled conditions, allowing us to calculate the labour cost of this manufacturing process. The latter included detaching blades by direct percussion with soft hammerstones and retouching selected blades using hammerstones and a hardwood anvil. It took him 171 minutes to produce the blades required, and a further 77 minutes to do the retouching. Thus the entire process (excluding the procurement of flint and fabricators) lasted 4 hours and 8 minutes, or approximately 2½ minutes per point.

The replication of other late Palaeolithic and Mesolithic types of points takes roughly the same amount of time (cf. Beckhoff 1967: note 15). So, to Stone Age man, the manufacture of missile heads must have represented a relatively small labour investment by comparison with the production of the shafts of the weapons.

WEAR AND TEAR ON FLINT POINTS USED AS MISSILE HEADS

The main purpose of the experiments was the development of methods for identifying missile heads on the basis of marks caused by wear and tear. To this end, 153 replicas of prehistoric flint points were mounted on arrows and spears (*Fig. 1*) in ways similar to the original – as far as this can be ascertained from prehistoric finds. The points mounted on arrows were fired with bows, the power of which was comparable to that of finds from the Danish Mesolithic, i.e. 50–70 lbs. The targets for our spears and arrows included simulated hunting objects such as a boar, seven sheep, four pike, and several joints of prime quality Danish bacon. In addition, we shot at a number of objects which Stone Age hunters could have hit by mistake, such as trees, bushes, grass, and soil. Finally, several hundred points and blades were exposed to other activities such as cutting and stabbing, as well as to 'accidental' fracturing processes – for example, walking on them. These alternative ways of using and fracturing the flint artifacts were designed with the specific

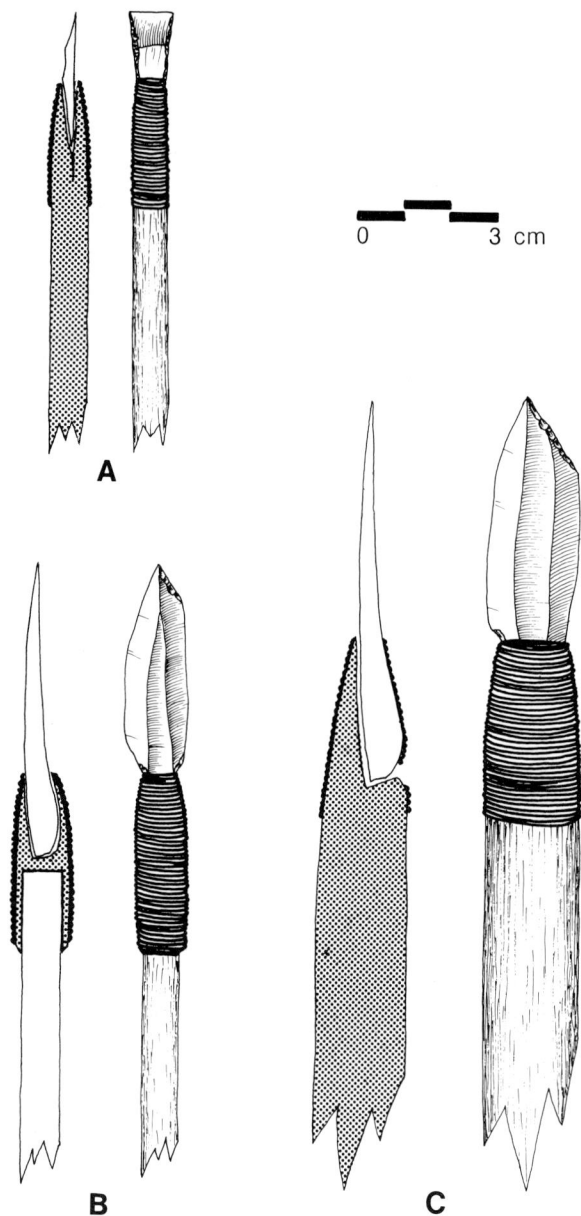

Figure 1 Hafting principles employed in the experiments. *A*: transverse flint tip mounted on an arrow-shaft. *B*: Brommian point mounted as the tip of an arrow. *C*: Brommian point fixed to a spear shaft. *Drawn by Peter Vemming Hansen.*

purpose of imitating the wear marks of the experimental missile heads.

The target shooting and other activities resulted in a wide spectrum of wear marks. When we classified them according to their shape, size and orientation, it turned out that some of them were to be found on the missile heads only (see Fischer *et al.* 1984, for further discussion and definitions). These included fractures visible to the naked eye (*Fig. 2*), as well as microscopic polish and striations (*Fig. 3*). The conditions under which these occurred seemed to be limited to use as missile heads, i.e. to the longitudinal direction of movement and the very short period of active contact with other material.

The macro-wear traces characterizing the pro-

jectile heads are all varieties of bending fractures (cf. Ho Ho Committee 1979) and are orientated perpendicular to the longitudinal axis of the points. They derive from pressures parallel to the direction of movement (e.g. from the ends) which develop when the missiles hit resisting material such as meat, bone or wood. Upon hitting the target, chips of flint are often separated from the projectile heads. When the missiles continue into the resisting material of the target these chips score the surface of the flint points, thus producing micro-polish and scratches parallel to the direction of movement (Fischer *et al.* 1984).

None of the points shows the types of micro-wear which characterize, for example, knives and scrapers used for the treatment of hide, meat, wood, etc. (Keeley 1980). The reason for this is undoubtely the very short period during which the missiles are in active contact with the target.

All the macro- and micro-wear marks described appear on all the types of experimentally used missile heads, irrespective of their size, shape, mounting method, type of weapon and target (cf. Barton and Bergman 1982: fig. 1; Moss and Newcomer 1982: fig. 8; Bergman and Newcomer 1983: fig. 2). We have termed these wear traces *diagnostic of the projectile point function*. On the basis of the few experiments conducted so far, however, we cannot forward any definite proof that they occur on missile heads only (cf. Olausson 1983: fig. 26). Attention should therefore be paid to the morphology and general state of preservation of any flint object before it is identified as a projectile point on the basis of these macro-fractures and micro-striations. Moreover, it must be taken into consideration that these features do not appear on all flint points used as missile heads. The experimental pieces indicate that the frequency of diagnostic macro- and micro-wear traces on arrowheads shot into large animals is approximately 40% and 60%, respectively (*Table 1*).

The applicability of the projectile diagnostication described has been tested on a selection of prehistoric flint assemblages from Denmark and northern Germany. The selection was purposely made so as to include a large number of Brommian points and transverse flint tips. Furthermore, all Danish finds of animal skeletons with associated flint points referable to a morphological type were examined.

The analyses, which covered 510 prehistoric flint points of widely differing ages, sizes and shapes, revealed examples of all the experimentally derived characteristics of projectile heads (*Table 2*). This not only applies to Brommian points (*Fig. 4*) and transverse flint tips (*Fig. 5*), but also to all other point types examined (see e.g. *Figs. 7–8*). The only exceptions are certain microliths (*Fig. 7*, nos. 6, 7, 10, 11) which would probably not be regarded as

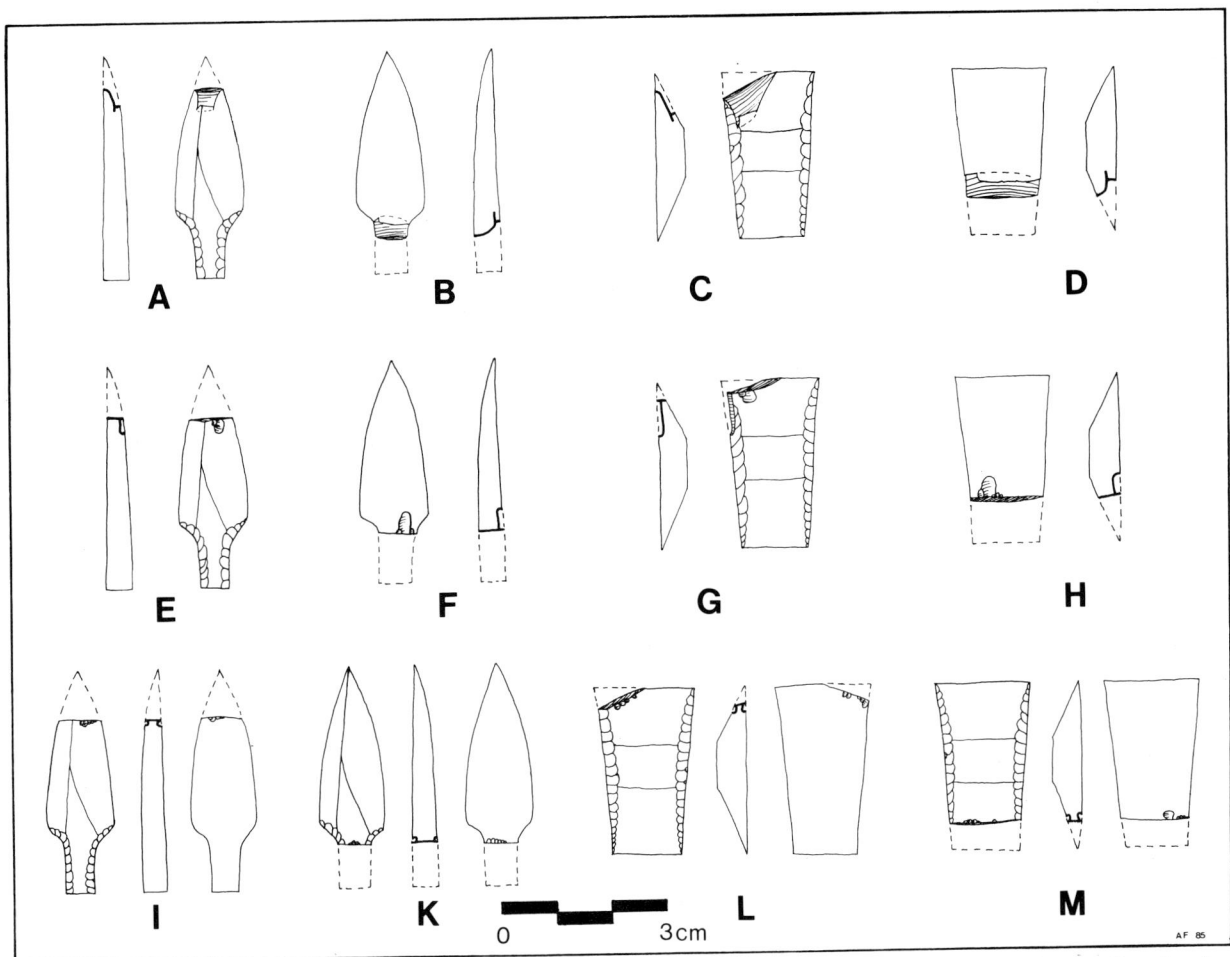

Figure 2 Idealized examples of Brommian points and transverse flint tips showing macro-fractures diagnostic of projectile points (not to scale). *A–D*: step-terminating bending fractures perpendicular to the longitudinal axis. *E–H*: large, unifacial spin-offs originating from a bending fracture (on the transverse flint tips, spin-offs more than 1 mm long are considered large enough; on the largest of the Brommian points a length of 6 mm is required). *I–M*: bifacial spin-offs irrespective of their length, originating from a bending fracture. *Drawn by Anders Fischer.*

missile heads in any case, but rather as barbs and marginal edges (cf. Becker 1945; Malmer 1968). Moreover, none of the points shows traces resulting from applications other than as projectile heads – that is, they do not display the types of microscopic polish known to appear when treating meat, hide, bone, wood, etc. (Keeley 1980).

Several of the prehistoric points examined undoubtedly served as missile tips. This applies to 21 flint artifacts found in the immediate vicinity of complete animal skeletons from Stellmoor upper level (Rust 1943: 191), Vig (Hartz and Winge 1906), and Prejlerup (Aaris-Sørensen 1984). It also applies to a flint point embedded in a bone found at the Kongemose site (Noe-Nygaard 1974; Fischer 1985). Thus the types of wear marks which on the basis of experiments are considered characteristic of projectile heads are numerous on Stone Age flint points, and they occur on flint artifacts which actually served as the tips of prehistoric arrows or spears.

Several of the sites listed in *Table 2* must have been genuine settlements. This is true of Meiendorf (Rust 1937), Bromme (Fischer and Sonne Nielsen, in press), Vejlebro layers 8 and 9 (Malmros 1975), Præstelyng (Troels-Smith 1981: note 4), and Muldbjerg (Troels-Smith 1960). These sites all contained extensive and varied toolkits and large quantities of flint waste. The same does not apply to Ommelshoved (Holm 1972) and Eskebjerg (Rasmussen 1970) which were probably special activity sites (Fischer 1976). The two water-deposited assemblages from Stellmoor cannot be grouped in any of these categories. More likely, they represent a refuse area and a storage place for meat and raw materials for tool production. The flint points of both layers probably all represent used arrowheads which were originally embedded in reindeer carcasses or mounted on arrows when deposited in the pond.

As will be apparent from *Table 2*, the corrected frequencies of diagnostic macro- and micro-wear traces on the flint points of the settlements analyzed are between 4% and 32%. The frequencies are considerably lower than the *c.* 40% and 60% respectively which, according to our experiments, occur on points shot into large animals. In most cases they are even lower than what might be

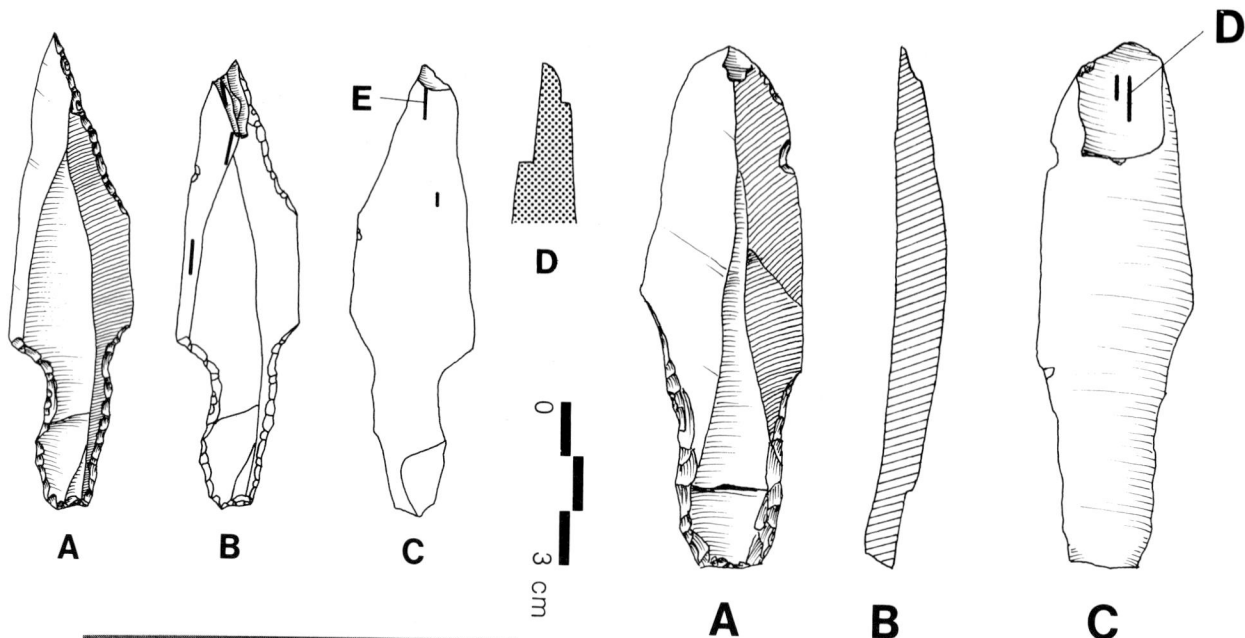

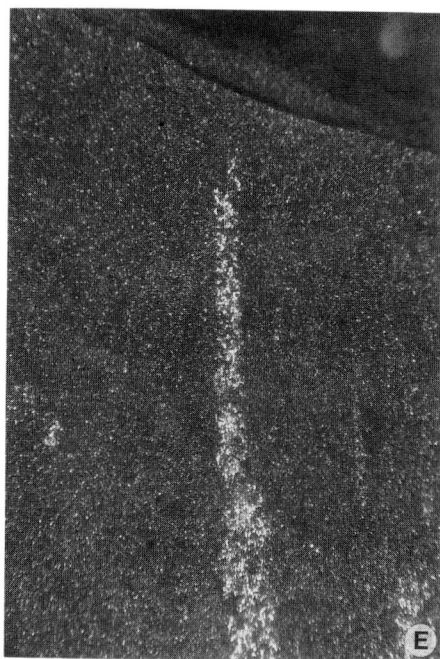

Figure 3 Experimental Brommian point shot into a boar where it cut a rib in two and wedged between two ribs on the opposite side of the chest. *A*: prior to use. *B, C*: after use with indications of macro- and micro-wear marks. The tip shows a step-terminating bending fracture originating on the dorsal surface, and running onto the ventral face. Spin-offs originate from the bending fracture and run up to 13 mm onto the dorsal side. Further, a number of small cone fractures can be seen. They originate from the edges and run obliquely towards the base of the point. *E*: photomicrograph of linear polish and striations orientated parallel to the longitudinal axis of the point (magnification=42×). *Drawing by Peter Vemming Hansen; photo by Peter Rasmussen.*

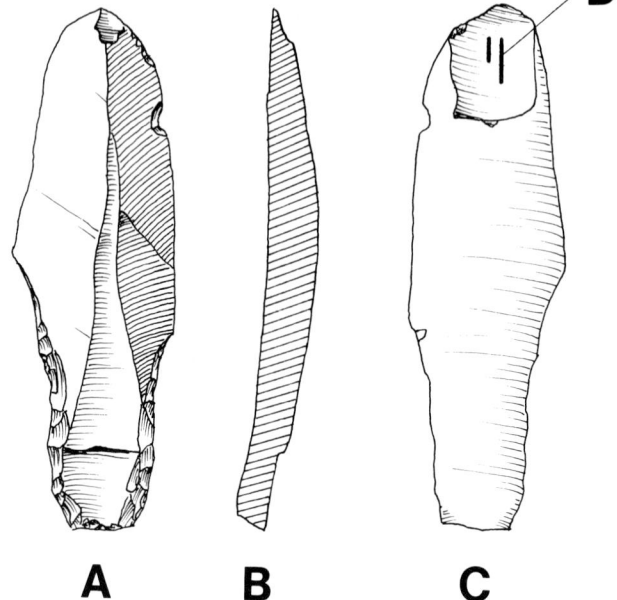

Figure 4 Example of a Lateglacial tanged point of Brommian type from Ommelshoved, showing macro- and micro-wear marks diagnostic of projectile points. Its tip has a step-terminating bending fracture from which bifacial spin-offs originate. The surface of the bending fracture has linear polish, orientated parallel to the longitudinal axis of the point (magnification=42×). *Drawing by Peter Vemming Hansen; photo by Peter Rasmussen.*

32

Table 1: Wear traces on projectile points from all the experimental shootings; the three experiments of greatest significance are shown in bold type

Point type	Mounted on	Shot into	Distance (m)	MACRO-WEAR TRACES			MICRO-WEAR TRACES		
				Number of examined points	Number of points with diagnostic macro-fractures	Frequency of points with diagnostic macro-fractures	Number of examined points	Number of points with diagnostic micro-wear traces	Frequency of points with diagnostic micro-wear traces
Brommian point	**Arrow**	**Whole boar**	**10**	**23**	**9**	**39%**	**23**	**14**	**57%**
	Spear	Whole boar	3–4	2	2	100%	0	–	–
	Spear	Boar head	1–3	6	3	50%	0	–	–
	Spear	Whole sheep	2	3	1	33%	0	–	–
	Arrow	Boned leg of boar	4	5	3	60%	5	1	20%
	Arrow	**Pork with bones**	**10**	**42**	**19**	**45%**	**12**	**8**	**66%**
	Arrow	Fish	1–3	10	1	10%	4	3	75%
	Arrow	Reed growth	–	4	0	0%	4	0	0%
	Arrow	Grass and soil	–	7	1	14%	5	1	20%
	Arrow	Willow bush	3	3	1	33%	3	1	33%
	Arrow	Birch trunk	4	5	3	60%	2	2	100%
Transverse arrowhead	**Arrow**	**Whole sheep**	**10**	**27**	**11**	**41%**	**27**	**18**	**66%**
	Arrow	Pork with bones	2–10	5	4	80%	0	–	–
	Arrow	Tree trunk	10	1	0	0%	0	–	–
Other point	Arrow	Pork with bones	4–5	5	2	40%	0	–	–

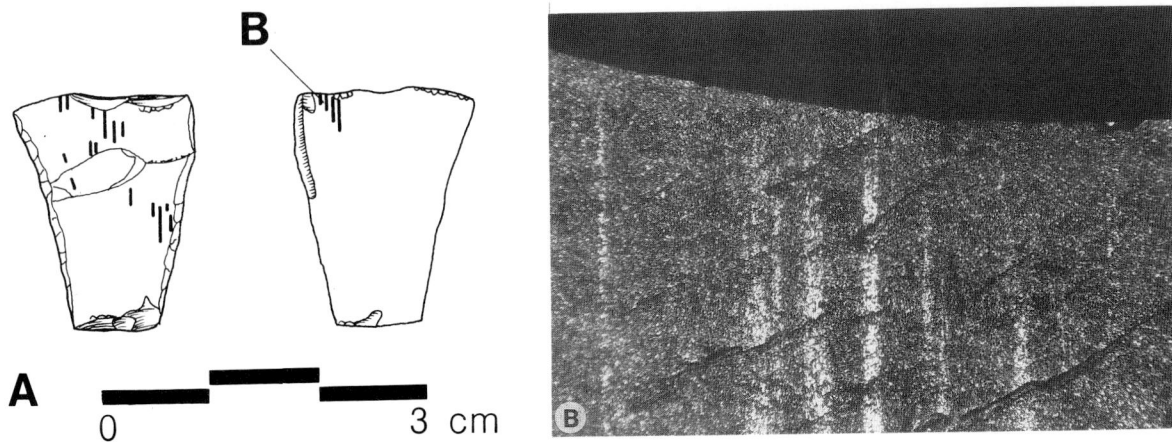

Figure 5   Transverse arrowhead with macro- and micro-wear traces from the early Neolithic site of Muldbjerg (*photomicrograph*: magnification=42×). The edge has several small cone fractures and two small bending fractures. From these bending fractures, several spin-offs originate, running along the ventral as well as the dorsal side. A spin-off, 8 mm long, runs like a burin blow along one of the retouched sides. The proximal end has a step-terminating bending fracture from which bifacial spin-offs originate. *Drawing by Peter Vemming Hansen; photo by Peter Rasmussen.*

Table 2: The results of the application of the macro- and micro-methods to prehistoric points (the frequency of projectile diagnostic wear is stated both in relation to the total number of points analyzed and in relation to those points whose preservation makes them suitable for the method concerned)

NAME OF SITE	SCIENTIFIC DATING Pollen zone ex. Jessen	Conventional C14 age BP	NUMBER OF AVAILABLE POINTS	RESULT OF MACRO-ANALYSIS Number of analyzed points	Number of points unsuitable for macro-analysis	Number of points with projectile diagnostic macro-fractures	Frequency of points with projectile diagnostic macro-fractures	Corrected frequency of points with projectile diagnostic macro-fractures	RESULT OF MICRO-ANALYSIS Number of analyzed points	Number of points unsuitable for micro-analysis	Number of points with projectile diagnostic micro-wear	Frequency of points with projectile diagnostic micro-wear	Corrected frequency of points with projectile diagnostic micro-wear
Meiendorf	I	12,400	75	50	0	14	28%	28%	–	–	–	–	–
Stellmoor, lower level	I	12,200	4	4	0	2	50%	50%	–	–	–	–	–
Ommelshoved			100	110	22	11	10%	13%	15	14	1	–	–
Eskebjerg			49	49	0	7	14%	14%	–	–	–	–	–
Bromme	II		65	65	18	4	6%	9%	61	61	–	–	–
Stellmoor, upper level	III	10,000	45	45	0	19	42%	42%	23	0	8	35%	35%
Vig, aurochs	IV		3	3	0	1	33%	33%	3	3	–	–	–
Prejlerup, aurochs	V	8,400	15	15	0	6	40%	40%	15	8	0	0%	0%
Kongemose, oblique point in a bone	VI	7,400	1	1	0	1	100%	100%	1	0	1	100%	100%
Vejlebro, level 8		5,500	24	24	0	5	21%	21%	–	–	–	–	–
Vejlebro, level 9		5,500	42	42	0	2	5%	5%	–	–	–	–	–
Præstelyng	VII	5,200	57	57	1	8	14%	14%	57	4	2	4%	4%
Maglelyng, transverse arrowhead in a bone	VIII		1	1	0	0	0%	0%	1	1	–	–	–
Muldbjerg	VIII	4,800	44	44	0	14	32%	32%	30	5	4	13%	16%
Σ	–	–	535	510	41	–	–	–	206	96	–	–	–

34

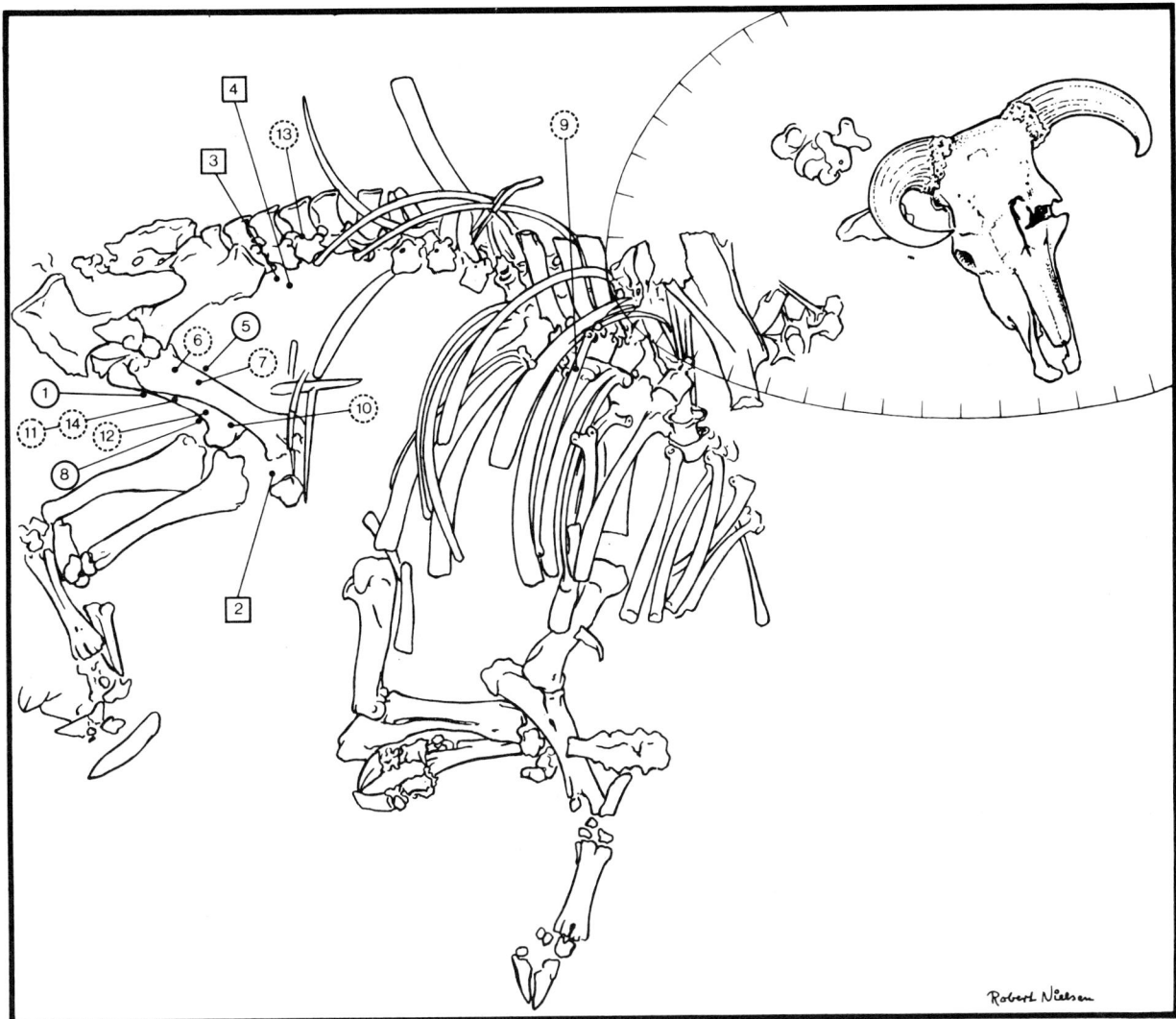

Figure 6   The aurochs from Prejlerup showing the positions of the flint points and a fragment of an arrow-shaft (after Aaris-Sørensen 1984). The positions of the missile heads show that the majority of the shots were fired obliquely from behind. This may be due to the hunters' fear of confronting the animal's horns. However, shooting from this direction would also give the hunters a chance of hitting the vital organs (the heart and lungs) without the risk of the arrows being stopped by the ribs. *Drawn by Robert Nielsen.*

expected from arrows which missed the target (cf. *Table 1*). On this basis it must be concluded that a considerable proportion of the points from the settlements and even from the special activity sites were hardly ever used for hunting.

The points included in *Table 2* are all finished and usable specimens. They show no positive evidence of functions other than as tips of missiles. Assuming that 40% of a population of used missile heads will show the macro-wear marks described, then 20–88% of the points from the examined settlements must be considered unused! Apparently, Stone Age flint knappers generally produced far more points than were actually needed. In this way they were always sure to have some of these quickly-produced specimens in stock, from among which they could select the ones best suited to their laboriously produced shafts and to the hunting expeditions ahead.

THE EFFICIENCY OF FLINT-TIPPED ARROWS

Shooting at simulated hunting targets gave us a clear impression of the efficiency of Stone Age arrows (*Fig. 9*). To explain these observations, I should first like to draw attention to the way a hunting arrow kills. It does so either by causing bleeding or, more rapidly, by penetrating the vital organs such as the central nervous system, the heart or the lungs, causing almost immediate death by stopping the admission of oxygen to the body.

Their fatal effect was most carefully documented in an experiment in which we shot arrows tipped with transverse flint points at three newly-killed and still warm sheep. The arrows were fired from a 50 lb bow. Its properties were not identical to those of the elm bows from the relevant period of the Danish Stone Age. However, experiments using replicas of

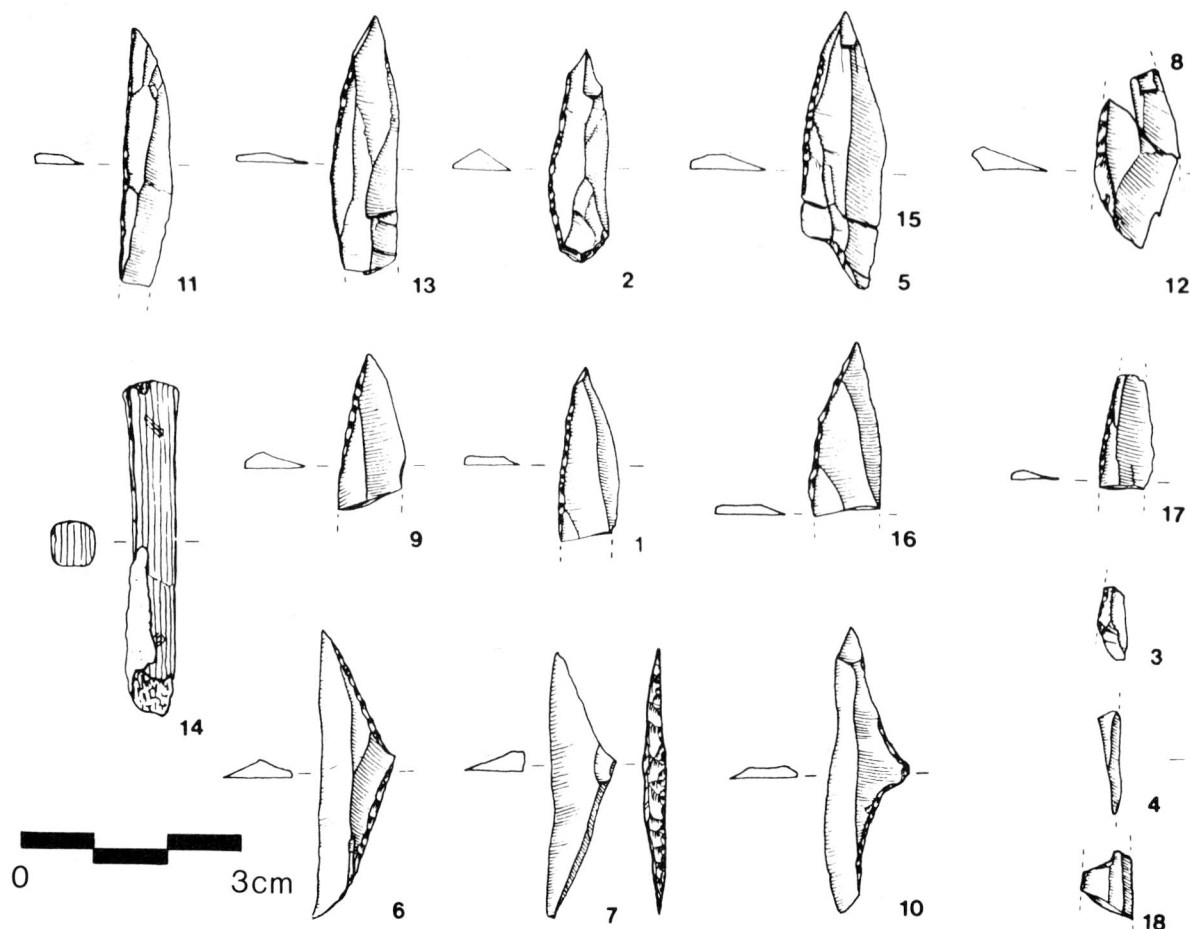

Figure 7   The microliths and a fragment of an arrow-shaft found in the immediate vicinity of the aurochs skeleton from Prejlerup (after Aaris-Sørensen 1984). Nos. 7 and 16 fit together. To judge from the texture of the flint, several of the others were probably also produced from the same flint nodule. Owing to surface alteration the flints are not fit for micro-wear analysis. However, the types of macro-fractures considered diagnostic of projectile heads may be seen in nos. 3, 4, 8/12, 9, 17 and 18. Nos. 1, 2, 5/ 15, 13 and 16, which are of the same morphological type and of which four show related macro-fractures, probably also served as arrowheads. No. 11 presumably served as a longitudinal edge, and nos. 6, 7 and 10 as a combination of barbs and longitudinal edges. *Drawn by Peter Vemming Hansen.*

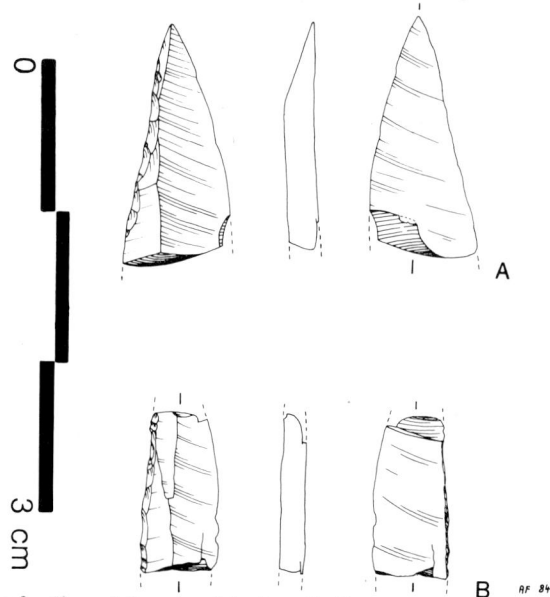

Figure 8   Two of the microliths from Prejlerup showing macro-wear marks diagnostic of projectile points. Both have step-terminating bending fractures perpendicular to their longitudinal axes. In addition, *A* has what may be a spin-off fracture originating from the bending fracture. *Drawn by Anders Fischer.*

Mesolithic longbows suggest that its effect on the arrows released was not significantly different from the effect of the original bows. A series of 16 arrows were fired from a distance of 10 metres. They struck the breast of the sheep perpendicular to the areas protected by ribs, with the following results:

a)   One arrow stopped in the shoulder blade on the side of penetration. To a Stone Age hunter it would have been a definite miss; it would have caused pain to the animal, but would not have been fatal.

b)   Three arrows passed through the rib cage and cut their way into the thoracic cavity. They would have caused death within a few seconds.

c)   Twelve arrows went through the rib cage of both sides of the animals, their tips being visible on the obverse side. Neither ribs, entrails, nor the approximately 10 cm thick layer of wool could stop them. Death would have been instantaneous.

From the large number of shootings at whole and still warm animals, it can be concluded that Stone Age arrows were extremely penetrative. The experi-

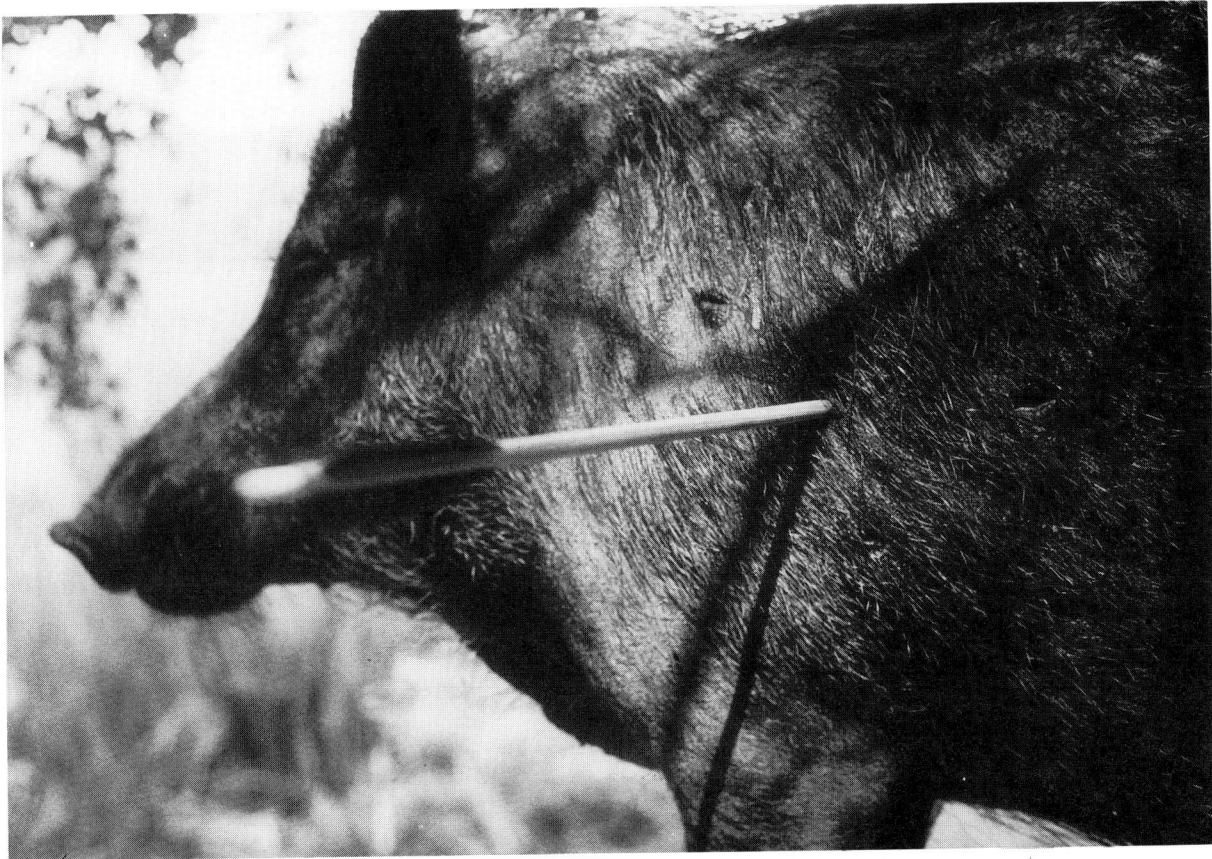

Figure 9 A 'fatal' shot – a boar hit by an arrow tipped with a Brommian point. *Photo by Henrik Christiansen.*

mental arrows often forced their way through the ribs of the sheep and even of the full-grown boar. In many cases, the shoulder blades of pigs were penetrated too. So, in the hands of skilled hunters able to get within close range of the prey, these weapons would have proved highly effective – they did not just cause pain and subsequent exhaustion to large game, thus preparing them to be killed by other weapons, as proposed by Møhl (1978: 21). Evidently, the ribs of the largest game hunted by Mesolithic man could afford protection against the arrows (cf. Hartz and Winge 1906: plate 1; Noe-Nygaard 1974: plate VIb, 1–8); but hits in between, or behind (cf. *Fig. 6*) the ribs would have given Stone Age man a good chance of killing a red deer, an elk or even an aurochs, with a single shot. In the case of roe deer and smaller game, almost any arrow hitting the chest of the animal would have caused instantaneous death.

CAUSES OF FLINT POINT EVOLUTION

For decades prehistorians have been aware of the chronological potential of the rapid morphological evolution of Stone Age flint points. To refine our chronologies we have classified these artifacts in terms of size, shape, manufacturing techniques, and so forth. When producing, hafting and using such points during the experiments, I learned to look at

them from quite another viewpoint – viz. with regard to their practical properties such as penetration qualities, directional stability, ease of mounting, and size of flint nodules needed to produce them. This in turn suggested some possible reasons for the typological evolution of the points (*Fig. 10*).

First of all, changes in the size of points from the Danish Stone Age may have been caused basically by variations in the supply of flint through time (Fischer 1985). Secondly, some of the morphological changes seem to represent the introduction of specific technical improvements. For instance, changing the base of the tanged point from the thick bulbar end to the thin distal end of the blades (cf. Fischer 1978: fig. 2) was obviously advantageous with regard to hafting. In the same way, the introduction of the microburin technique made it possible to produce a stable tip which was sharper than the retouched tips produced previously.

Behind the minor environmentally and technically determined adjustments to the flint points, I see a more general cause for their typological evolution. This point of view is based on the observations of modern bow-hunters. Their experience has led me to expect the ideal flint tip meant for bow-hunting to have the following characteristics: (i) optimum penetrative qualities; (ii) the capacity to produce the sharpest cut possible – that which would result in the heaviest bleeding; and (iii) being as symmetrical

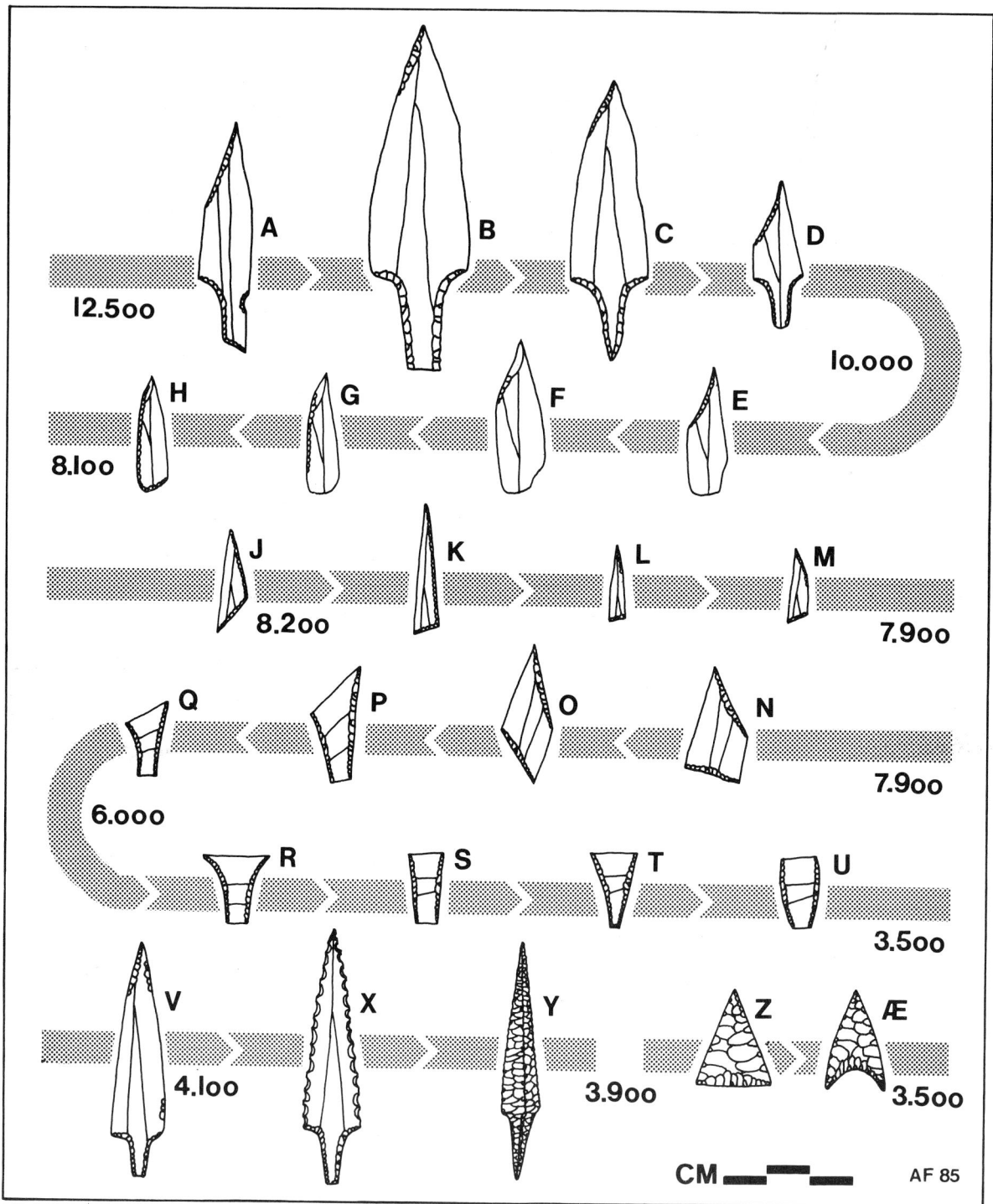

Figure 10 The evolution of flint points in the late Palaeolithic, Mesolithic and Neolithic of southern Scandinavia. The various types of points are tentatively grouped into five developmental sequences; radiocarbon dates are in years BP. *Drawn by Anders Fischer.*

along its longitudinal axis as possible, to ensure maximum directional stability of the arrow.

The evolution of Stone Age flint points can be viewed in terms of continuous adjustments aiming at the optimum interplay between these three functional demands. This, moreover, would explain the marked stagnation of the development of this group of implements from the time of the introduction of the straight-edged transverse arrowhead onwards. This type of missile tip was produced with only minor variations in shape for more than 2000 years – during the final part of the Mesolithic period and right through the otherwise highly innovative early, middle and late Neolithic periods.[1] This deceleration can be seen as the result of the discovery of an almost optimum interplay of the three demands. Only one other type of flint head can be considered closer to the optimum: the symmetrical, bifacially pressure-flaked point (cf. Pope 1923: 369). In Denmark this type was introduced in the late Neolithic and

38

remained in production, almost unaltered, into the Late Bronze Age (Strømberg 1954), thus outlasting the transverse arrowhead by nearly a millennium.

Thus, the well-known typological development of Stone Age flint points can be explained in purely practical terms. Moreover, considering the importance of a predictable and successful outcome for each arrow released by the hunter, it is hardly surprising that the evolution of missile heads appears to have progressed much faster than that of all other tool types of the period.

Note:

1. In the middle Neolithic period another group of flint points – blade points (Becker 1950) – were produced at the same time as transverse arrowheads. These points, as well as the bodkin-shaped bone points of the early and middle Neolithic, probably served as the tips of arrows for use in warfare as opposed to hunting (Fischer 1985; cf. Becker 1952; Vebæk 1957: fig. 3).

Acknowledgements: The author wishes to express his appreciation to Peter Vemming Hansen and Peter Rasmussen for pleasant and inspiring cooperation, and for their support during the writing of this paper. I should also like to thank Jonathan Sydenham for revising the English of the original draft of this paper, and to express my gratitude to Bo Madsen for producing most of the points used in the experiments. The micro-wear analyses were carried out by Peter Rasmussen. Søren Moses kindly placed information about his experiments on replicating Mesolithic long bows at my disposal.

References

AARIS-SØRENSEN, K. (ed.) (1984) *Uroksen fra Prejlerup. Et arkæologisk fund*. Copenhagen, Zoologisk Museum.

BARTON, R.N.E. and BERGMAN, C.A. (1982) Hunters at Hengistbury. Some evidence from experimental archaeology. *World Archaeology*, 14(2): 237–248.

BECKER, C.J. (1945) En 8000-aarig stenalderboplads i Holmegaards Mose. Forløbig meddelelse. *Fra Nationalmuseets Arbejdsmark*, 1945: 61–72.

BECKER, C.J. (1950) Den grubekeramiske kultur i Danmark. *Aarbøger for Nordisk Oldkyndighed og Historie*, 1950: 153–274.

BECKER, C.J. (1952) Skeletfundet fra Porsmose ved Næstved. *Fra Nationalmuseets Arbejdsmark*, 1952: 25–30.

BECKHOFF, K. (1967) Zur jungpaläolithischen Kerbspitze. *Die Kunde*, Neue Folge, 18: 8–15.

BERGMAN, C.A. and NEWCOMER, M.H. (1983) Flint arrowhead breakage: examples from Ksar Akil, Lebanon. *Journal of Field Archaeology*, 10: 238–243.

FISCHER, A. (1976) Senpalæolitisk bosætning i Danmark. *Kontaktstencil* (Turku), 12: 95–115.

FISCHER, A. (1978) På sporet af overgangen mellem palæoliticum og mesoliticum i Sydskandinavien. *Hikuin*, 4: 27–50, 150–153.

FISCHER, A. (1985) *Paa jagt med stenalder-vaaben*. Lejre, Historisk-arkæologisk Forsøgscenter.

FISCHER, A., VEMMING HANSEN, P. and RASMUSSEN, P. (1984) Macro and micro wear traces on lithic projectile points. Experimental results and prehistoric examples. *Journal of Danish Archaeology*, 3: 13–46.

FISCHER, A. and SONNE NIELSEN, F.O. (in press) Senistidens bopladser ved Bromme – en genbearbejdning af Westerby's og Mathiassen's fund. *Aarbøger for Nordisk Oldkyndighed og Historie*, 1986.

HARTZ, N. and WINGE, H. (1906) Om uroxen fra Vig, saaret og dræbt med Flintvaaben. *Aarbøger for Nordisk Oldkyndighed og Historie*, II Række, 21: 225–236, plate I.

HOLM, J. (1972) Istidsjægere på Ærø. *Fynske Minder*, 1972: 5–16.

HO HO COMMITTEE (1979) The Ho Ho Classification and Nomenclature Committee report. In B. Hayden (ed.), *Lithic Use-Wear Analysis*. New York, Academic Press: 133–135.

KEELEY, L.H. (1980) *Experimental Determination of Stone Tool Uses*. Chicago, University Press.

MALMER, M.P. (1968) Die mikrolithen in dem pfeil-fund von Loshult. *Meddelanden från Lunds universitets historiska museum*, 1966–1968: 249–255.

MALMROS, C. (1975) Vejlebro – en stenalderboplads ved Arrefjorden. *Nationalmuseets Arbejdsmark*, 1975: 99–117.

MOSS, E.H. and NEWCOMER, M.H. (1982) Reconstruction of tool use at Pincevent: microwear and experiments. In D. Cahen (ed.), *Tailler! Pour quoi faire: préhistoire et technologie lithique II. Recent progress in microwear studies. Studia Praehistorica Belgica*, 14(2): 289–312.

MØHL, U. (1978) Elsdyrskeletterne fra Skottemarke og Favrbo. *Aarbøger for Nordisk Oldkyndighed og Historie*, 1978: 5–32.

NOE-NYGAARD, N. (1974) Mesolithic hunting in Denmark illustrated by bone injuries caused by human weapons. *Journal of Archaeological Science*, 1: 217–248.

OLAUSSON, D.S. (1982) Lithic technological analysis of the thin-butted flint axe. *Acta Archaeologica*, 53: 1–87.

POPE, T.S. (1923) A study of bows and arrows. *University of California (Berkeley) Publications in American Archeology and Ethnology*, 13(9): 329–414, plates 45–64.

RASMUSSEN, J. (1970) Eskebjerg – en rensdyrjægerboplads paa Knudshoved Odde. *Aarbog for Historisk Samfund for Præstø Amt* (Næstved), 1969–70: 201–214.

RUST, A. (1937) *Das altsteinzeitliche Rentierjägerlager Meiendorf*. Neumünster, Karl Wachholtz.

RUST, A. (1943) *Die alt- und mittelsteinzeitlichen Funde von Stellmoor*. Neumünster, Karl Wachholtz.

STRØMBERG, M. (1954) Bronzezeitliche Wohnplätze in Schonen. *Meddelanden från Lunds universitets historiska museum*, 1954: 295–318.

TROELS-SMITH, J. (1960) *The Muldbjerg Dwelling Place: an Early Neolithic Archaeological Site in Aamosen Bog, West-Zealand, Denmark*. Washington D.C., Smithsonian Report for 1959, Publication 4413.

TROELS-SMITH, J. (1981) Naturwissenschaftliche Beitrage zur Pfalbauforschung. *Archäologie der Schweiz*, 4(3): 98–111.

VEBÆK, C.L. (1957) Et usædvanligt stenalders gravfund paa Djursland. *Fra Nationalmuseets Arbejdsmark*, 1957: 75–82.

The Analysis of Lithic Styles through Distributional Profiles of Variation: Examples from the Western European Mesolithic

Peter A. Gendel

Abstract

This paper explores a methodology for the analysis and interpretation of stylistic variation in lithic artifacts. Attention focuses on the spatial distribution of lithic styles, and examples are drawn from the western European Mesolithic. Recent ethnographic investigations have shown that different processes or behaviours, including social interaction and various types of information exchange, may determine the manner in which style in terms of material culture is distributed over space. Distinct types of spatial distributions, or 'profiles of variation', are associated with these various aspects of style and they may be characterized statistically and illustrated graphically. They may also be recovered in the archaeological record. The spatial distribution of several stylistic variables among microlithic types from Mesolithic sites in northern France, Belgium, and the southern Netherlands are examined in the light of these findings. Profiles of stylistic variation are determined by the correlation between stylistic similarities and geographic distances between Mesolithic sites. Both continuous (random to clinal) and discontinuous profiles of variation are shown to occur. Random distributions of stylistic variation are most frequent and occur throughout the Mesolithic. Discontinuous profiles of variation, which may signal the presence of socio-cultural boundaries, are extremely rare, and occur only during the late Mesolithic period.

INTRODUCTION

One of the more puzzling aspects of variation in lithic artifacts is that related to style. Simply, the identification of stylistic variation in stone tools may pose a number of problems. Nevertheless, chronological changes in lithic styles, such as the appearance, disappearance or modification of particular shapes, are known from the Mesolithic and within certain limits may serve as horizon markers. However, the manner in which the styles are distributed over space is poorly documented and the meaning of such distributions is even less evident. Despite the lack of such rigorous documentation and the absence of a coherent theory of style, several researchers have attempted to define the presence of distinct style zones in the European Mesolithic (Gramsch 1973; Newell 1973; Kozłowski 1975; Arora 1976; Rozoy 1978; Jacobi 1979; Kozłowski and Kozłowski 1979; Hinout 1980; Gob 1981; Decormeille and Hinout 1982; Gendel 1982). The possibility that such style zones reflect distinct regional human groups or social territories (Clark 1975) also has been considered. Re-analysis of some of the north-west European material (Gendel 1984) has shown the present

situation to be largely unsatisfactory. Previously defined style zones all too easily collapse under the weight of new evidence, and different scales of analysis produce conflicting results.

Information obtained from recent ethnographic investigations (e.g. Wiessner 1983) has demonstrated the complexity of behaviour underlying stylistic variation in material items. At the same time, these studies have begun to provide a framework with which to interpret stylistic variation in the archaeological record. The study of distributional profiles of stylistic variation is one method by which the archaeological data may be linked to the various patterns of behaviour responsible for stylistic variation. This methodology is discussed below and applied to data from the western European Mesolithic.

PROFILES OF STYLISTIC VARIATION

There can be little doubt that previous investigations into stylistic variation among lithic artifacts of the European Mesolithic, such as many of those studies cited above, have utilized an overly simplistic set of models and assumptions. In most such analyses, groups of sites are defined on the basis of similarities in certain aspects of lithic artifacts. Variation in artifact form and in the frequency of occurrence of certain types are common criteria with which to measure similarities between sites. If clusters of sites possessing certain stylistic similarities are also found to exhibit some geographic integrity, the existence of distinct socio-cultural groups is often hypothesized to explain this correlation. This model possesses a number of shortcomings, some of the less obvious of which I hope will become clear below. For the present, it is sufficient to note that only one dimension of style is recognized or capable of being illustrated by this model.

The origins of stylistic variation in artifacts appear to be complex and not necessarily capable of being understood by reference to a single explanatory framework (cf. Plog 1983). For example, it is possible that stylistic variation may result from or reflect the intensity of social interaction between

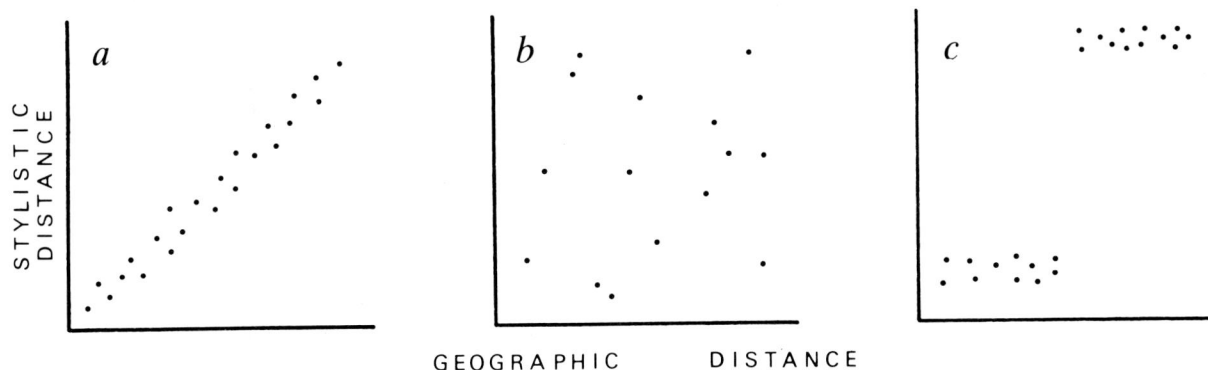

Figure 1 Idealized profiles of stylistic variation: *a* – clinal; *b* – random; *c* – discontinuous or discrete.

individuals or groups. In this case, choice or preference in formal variability is constrained in part through the learning process or through social proximity and contact (Whallon 1968; Voss 1977; Close 1978; Sackett 1982). If geographic distances between sites are used as a measure of social interaction (e.g. Plog 1976, 1980), similarity in style would be expected to vary inversely with the increasing distance between localities. The relationship is illustrated schematically in *Fig. 1a*. Clearly, if only the extremes of the total geographical distribution of localities were sampled, then stylistic differences would appear to be more discontinuous than would actually have been the case. Thus, sampling error alone may produce a spurious picture of the distribution of stylistic variation, a fact not readily accounted for in the traditional model outlined above.

Style has also been observed to function in the realm of information exchange (Braun 1977; Wobst 1977; Hodder 1979; Plog 1980; Wiessner 1983). Wiessner (1983) has shown that many different types of information may be conveyed using artifact styles. One type or aspect of style, termed 'assertive' style, conveys information about individual identity; it is a form of personal expression and it may be learned or acquired through contact or diffusion. Indeed, Wiessner has proposed that assertive styles may have:

> the potential to diffuse with acculturation and enculturation, providing a measure of inter-personal contact for archaeologists (1983: 258).

She predicts that assertive styles will have continuous spatial distributions, or 'profiles of variation', ranging from random to clinal. *Figs. 1a & 1b* show idealized representations of these possible distributional profiles. In fact, assertive styles may exhibit similar profiles of variation to those expected on the basis of the social interaction model outlined above.

Style may also be used to convey information regarding social group affiliation and identity and, in certain cases, may function in maintaining intergroup boundaries (Hodder 1979, 1982; Wiessner 1983). Indeed, differences in material items of two groups may be maintained in the presence of frequent social interaction between them (Hodder 1977). Stylistic variation related to language group membership was identified by Wiessner (1983) among Kalahari San projectile points. These 'emblemic' styles exhibit a different distributional profile of variation, one in which discrete breaks occur between homogeneous style units. An ideal distribution of this type is shown in *Fig. 1c*.

Some recent ethnographic and archaeological studies have shown that different profiles of variation may characterize individual formal attributes, even on the same artifact type. Again, the clearest example is described by Wiessner (1983) for Kalahari San projectile points. Among these points, the attributes of size and body shape variously carried information concerning linguistic group identity and individual identity, and had correspondingly distinct profiles of variation. Therefore, the evaluation of distributions of stylistic variation should focus initially upon individual stylistic attributes (cf. Plog 1983; Wiessner 1983; Gendel 1984). In contrast, most previous studies have worked with clusters of attributes, often from a variety of different artifact types.

Finally, some researchers have argued that certain categories of material items may be more likely to exhibit one or another aspect of stylistic variability. Wobst (1976) has suggested that information regarding social group affiliation should occur primarily among artifacts which function in ceremonial or ritual contexts, rather than among artifacts tied more directly to the subsistence quest. However, stylistic variation in projectile points among the Kalahari San conveyed such information because of their important role in a system of exchange which increased their visibility (Wiessner 1983). Similarly, ceramic exchange in the American Southwest may have increased the visibility of certain ceramic types and their suitability for carrying stylistic information regarding social group affiliation (Plog 1980). Both the function and the visibility of particular material items seem to be important factors which determine which aspect of style they are likely to be associated

41

with. Only crude generalizations of this sort are warranted given the current data. Moreover, an entirely different set of circumstances may indicate exactly *when* particular material items will be used to convey information about social group identity or individual identity, or when and to what extent they may reflect social interaction. These conditions are discussed at greater length by Gendel (1984).

In summary, stylistic variation in artifacts may result from a variety of processes or behaviours; some of these have been suggested above. Only in certain cases will style reflect the existence of distinct social groups or be used to maintain inter-group differences. Distinct spatial distributions of style, or profiles of stylistic variation, appear to provide one possible link between the archaeological record and the behaviour associated with these various aspects of style.

PROFILES OF STYLISTIC VARIATION IN THE WESTERN EUROPEAN MESOLITHIC

Methods

An attempt was made to characterize distributional profiles of stylistic variation in the western European Mesolithic. The data originate from over 80 Mesolithic sites in northern France, Belgium, and the southern Netherlands. Their locations are shown in *Fig. 2*. A more comprehensive discussion of the specific sites and of the stylistic data is given in Gendel (1984). Attempts to order Mesolithic assemblages in this region have resulted in a number of local chronological sequences in which anywhere from two to five periods of the Mesolithic have been suggested (Newell 1973; Rozoy 1978; Gob 1981; Gendel 1984). Three periods are recognized here: *early* Mesolithic (*c.* 10,000–8400 BP); *middle* Mesolithic (*c.* 8400–7700 BP); *late* Mesolithic (*c.* 7700–6000 BP).

Only the microlithic armatures (points and barbs) of the assemblages were analyzed. A series of metric and non-metric variables which describe the size, shape, and aspects of secondary preparation were recorded for each artifact. For each site, metric variables such as length, width, etc., were summarized by their means and standard deviations. Qualitative or non-metric variables, such as base shapes or the lateralization of asymmetric microliths, were expressed by the frequency of occurrence of each attribute state.

There are perhaps a number of ways in which to construct profiles of stylistic variation using these data. In this case the profiles are based upon correlations between geographic distances and stylistic differences between sites. The sites examined in this study are distributed primarily along a south west–north east axis (*Fig. 2*). Geographic transects

across the study area were generated through a principal components analysis of the site locations (*Fig. 3*). The first transect corresponds to the first principal component (Factor 1, SW–NE axis) and the second transect corresponds to the second principal component (Factor 2, SE–NW axis). The position of each site along the axes (or transects) corresponds to its factor score derived from the principal components analysis.

Corresponding stylistic data (variables having two or more attribute states) were treated using the same procedure. A principal components analysis was performed and the stylistic variation between sites reduced to two principal component axes. Stylistic 'distances' between sites are represented by their factor scores along the component axes. Correlations (product–moment coefficient) between the factor scores of the first two principal components of geographic distance and stylistic distance were then used to determine the profile of stylistic variation. A maximum of four correlations can be obtained for each analysis of a stylistic variable. These coefficients measure the relationship between stylistic variation and the geographic location of the sites. Scatter plots of the paired factor scores can be used to illustrate these distributional profiles and are useful in distinguishing between clinal and discontinuous distributions, both of which would be expected to yield high correlation coefficients. While the entire procedure may appear rather involved, particularly with respect to the relatively simple examples presented below, it becomes very practical when examining numerous attribute states, or in the case where several variables are considered simultaneously. A more comprehensive discussion of the methods can be found in Gendel (1984).

Analysis and results

The results of the analysis of the three stylistic variables are presented below and the distributional profiles of variation are illustrated. These variables represent only a small sample of those investigated for the Mesolithic assemblages under consideration. One simple variable, *lateralization*, having two attribute states (left, right) is examined below for three artifact types. The procedure follows that outlined above. For each of the three data-sets, a principal components analysis of the site locations was performed. Principal components analyses of the stylistic data (microlith lateralizations) were also carried out. Information pertaining to the three analyses of stylistic variation is given in *Table 1*.

Product–moment correlation coefficients were then obtained between the factor scores from the first two principal components of site locations and the factor scores from the first principal component of the stylistic data (microlith lateralization). Only

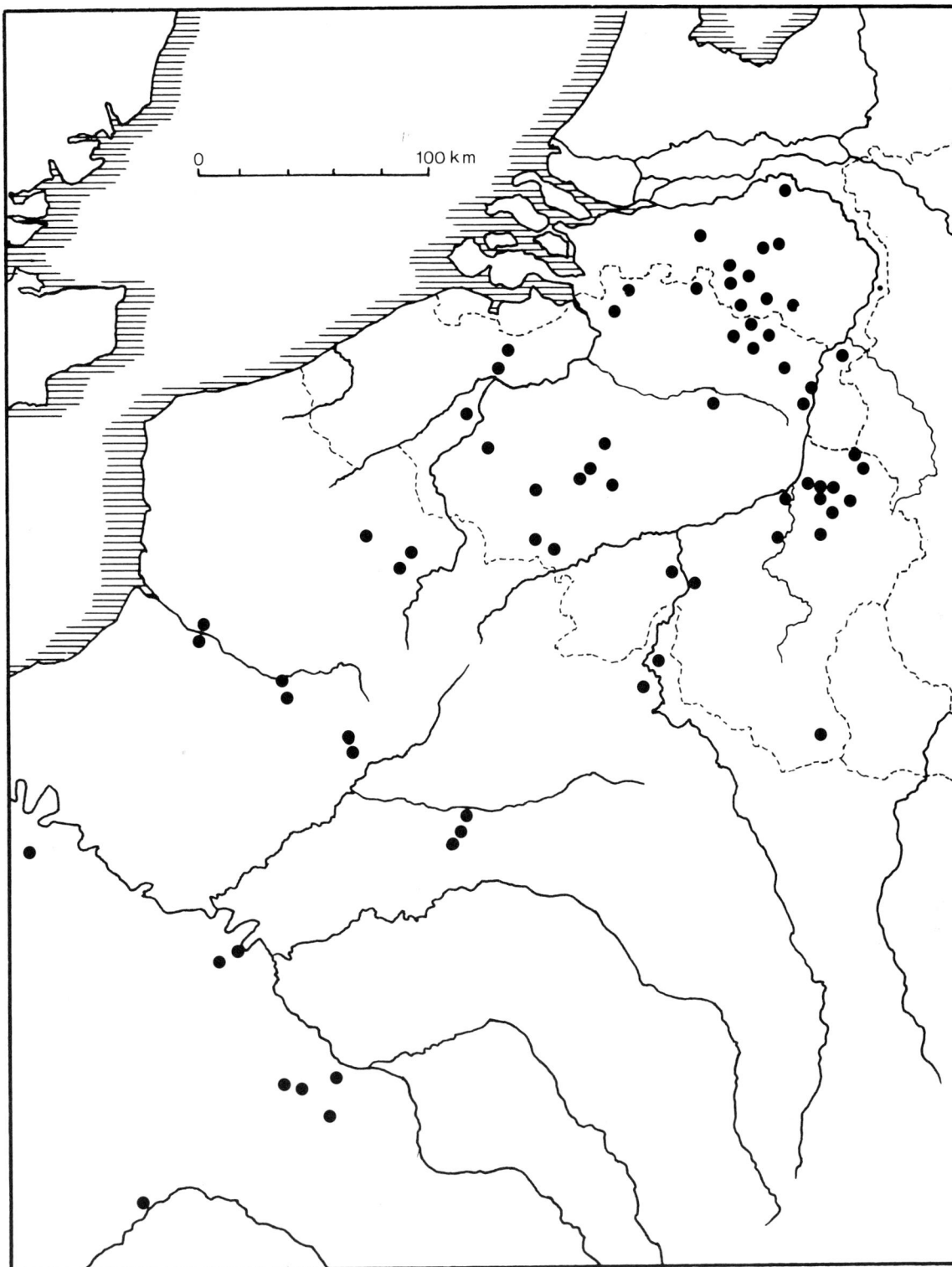

Figure 2   The location of Mesolithic sites investigated.

Table 1:   Summary information for the analysis of three stylistic
variables

Artifact type	Variable	No. of sites	Period
1. Scalene triangles	lateralization	14	Early Mesolithic
2. Points with unretouched base	lateralization	15	Middle Mesolithic
3. Right-angled and rhombic trapezes	lateralization	19	Late Mesolithic

the first principal component of the stylistic data was considered, since it explains 100% of the variance in each case. These correlations provide a statistical measure of the distributional profiles of stylistic variation and are given in *Table 2*.

The analysis of lateralizations among scalene triangles dating from the early Mesolithic period revealed random distributional profiles of stylistic variation. One such profile is illustrated in *Fig. 4*. One random and one clinal distribution profile were

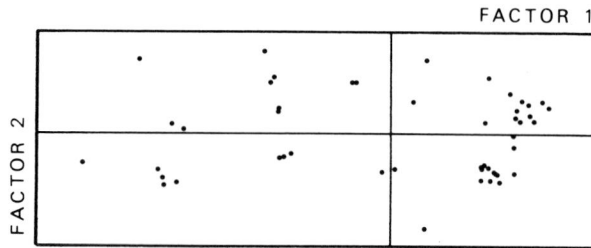

FACTOR 1

Figure 3 Principal components scatter diagram of site locations.

Table 2: Correlation coefficients for factor scores from the principal components analyses and inferred profiles of stylistic variation for three variables. Significant correlations are underlined: R – random; C – clinal; D – discontinuous

	A		B	
1.	.2074	R	.3023	R
2.	.7343	C	.2218	R
3.	.8084	D	.0220	R

Column A: First principal component (style) with first principal component (site location).

Column B: First principal component (style) with second principal component (site location).

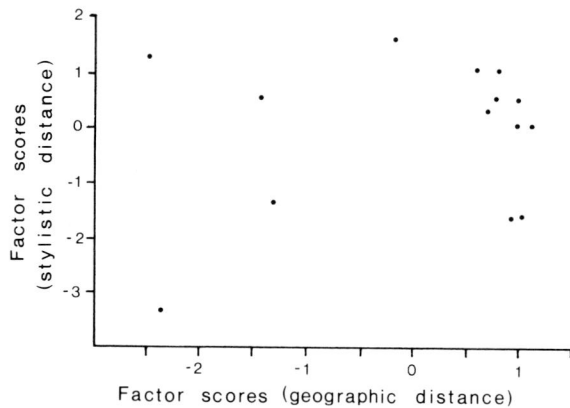

Figure 4 Scatter plot of factor scores of the first principal components for scalene triangle lateralization and site locations.

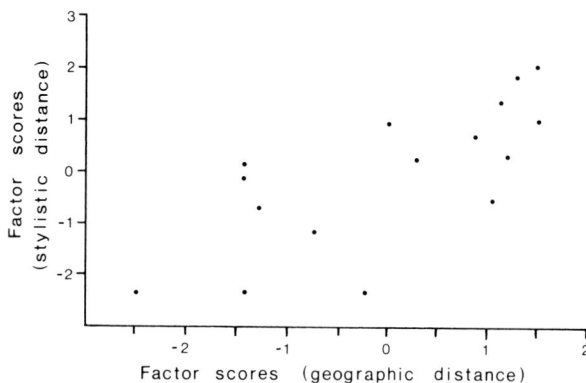

Figure 5 Scatter plot of factor scores of the first principal components for lateralizatons of points with unretouched base and site locations.

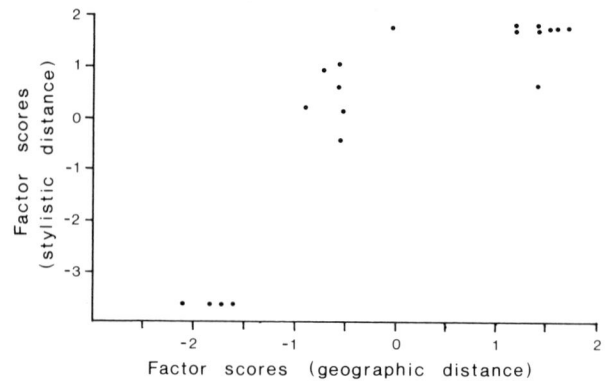

Figure 6 Scatter plot of factor scores of the first principal components for lateralizations of right-angled and rhombic trapezes and site locations.

determined to characterize the lateralization of the points with unretouched base dating from the middle Mesolithic period. The clinal profile of variation occurs along the SW–NE transect across the study area and is illustrated in *Fig. 5*. Finally, the analysis of lateralizations among right-angled and rhombic trapezes dating from the late Mesolithic period yielded one discontinuous distributional profile, or one in which a discrete break between fairly homogeneous style zones is present. This distributional profile is illustrated by the scatter plot in *Fig. 6*. In geographic terms, this boundary occurs approximately along the Seine river in northern France (*Fig. 7*).

In the analyses presented above, six distributional profiles of stylistic variation were generated. While stylistic variability generally was shown to be random across the study area, two profiles revealed statistically significant patterning along the SW–NE transect across the region. The three profiles given in *Figs. 4–6* exemplify the principal types of distributions that may be generated using the methodology.

DISCUSSION AND CONCLUSIONS

Although only a few examples were described, the presence of the various stylistic distributions suggests the existence of more than one source of stylistic variability among lithic artifacts in the western European Mesolithic. Random distributions appear to dominate the picture of lithic styles throughout most of the period. For the early and middle Mesolithic in this area, it was previously determined (Gendel 1984) that 60 or 64 stylistic distributions could be characterized as random, similar to those shown in *Fig. 4*. The remaining variables exhibited clinal distributional profiles. These types of distributions may reflect the operation of 'assertive' style, or simply the existence of a widely shared or easily replicated repertoire of formal variations.

Distributional profiles exhibiting true stylistic discontinuities, such as that shown in *Fig. 6*, are

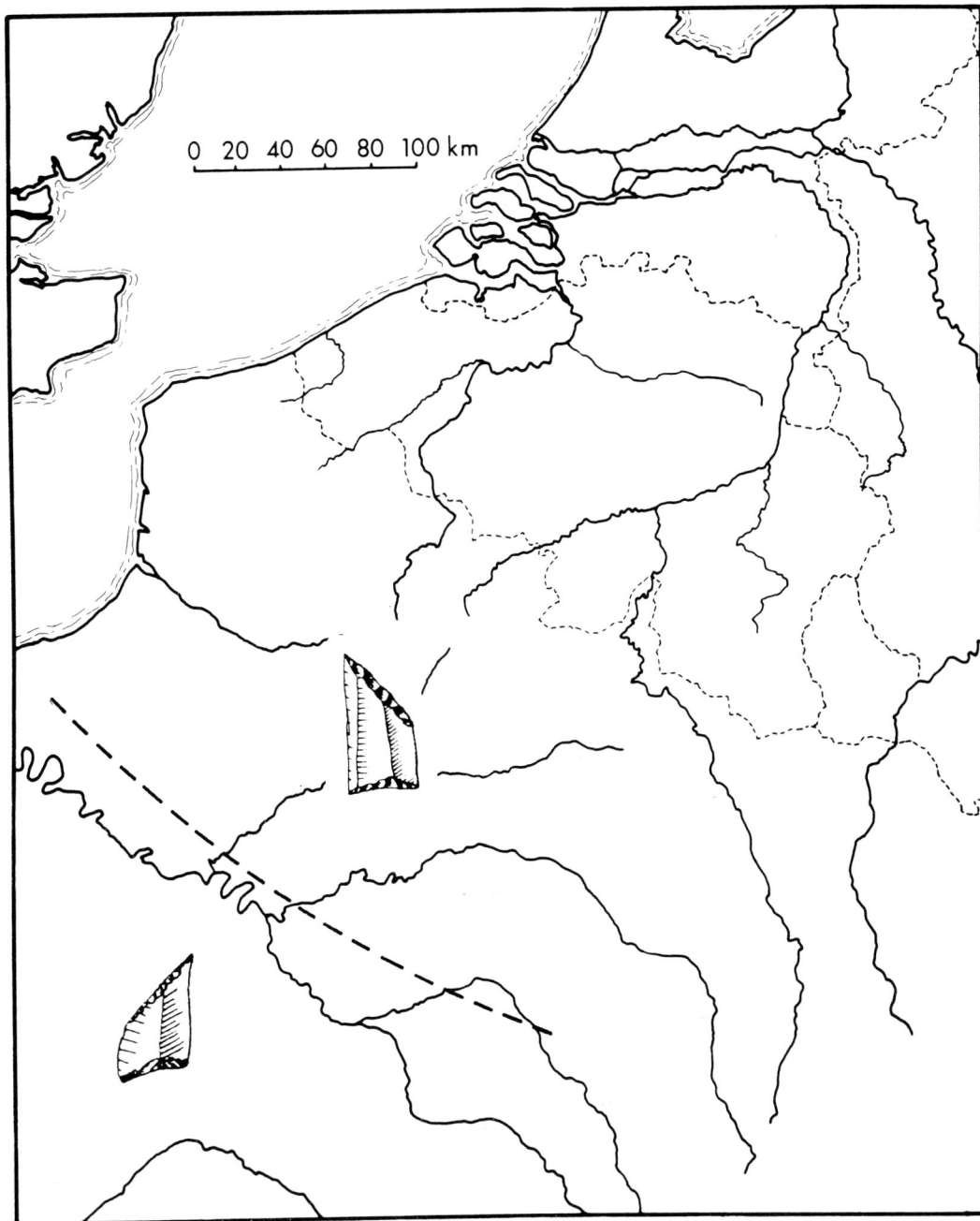

Figure 7 Approximate geographic boundary between left and right lateralization among right-angled and rhombic trapezes.

extremely rare and appear only during the late Mesolithic (Gendel 1984). Given the evidence for inter-regional connections and communications in the region, such as the spread of Montbani débitage and broad trapezes, these distributions may well reflect the existence of socio-cultural boundaries and the use of lithic styles in maintaining between-group differences. Indeed, the geographic discontinuity in trapeze lateralizations (*Fig. 7*) corresponds quite closely to the southern distributional limits of points with surface retouch (*Fig. 8*) and derived trapezes in north-west Europe (Gendel 1984). It is therefore possible that, for the late Mesolithic, portions of distinct hunter-gatherer social territories (Gendel 1984) or differentiated social network systems (Mad-

den 1983) become visible in the archaeological record. The conditions which led to the use of style in microlithic armatures in the process of boundary maintenance may have been absent during the earlier periods of the Mesolithic.

This brief presentation was designed to introduce the concept of distributional profiles of stylistic variation and to illustrate how they may be applied to the archaeological data. The method emphasizes the consideration, at least initially, of individual stylistic variables, rather than grouping together a number of attributes simultaneously (e.g. Jacobi 1979; Gendel 1982). At the same time, a regional approach to the archaeological record is suggested (cf. Plog 1980; Wiessner 1983). Clearly, such an

45

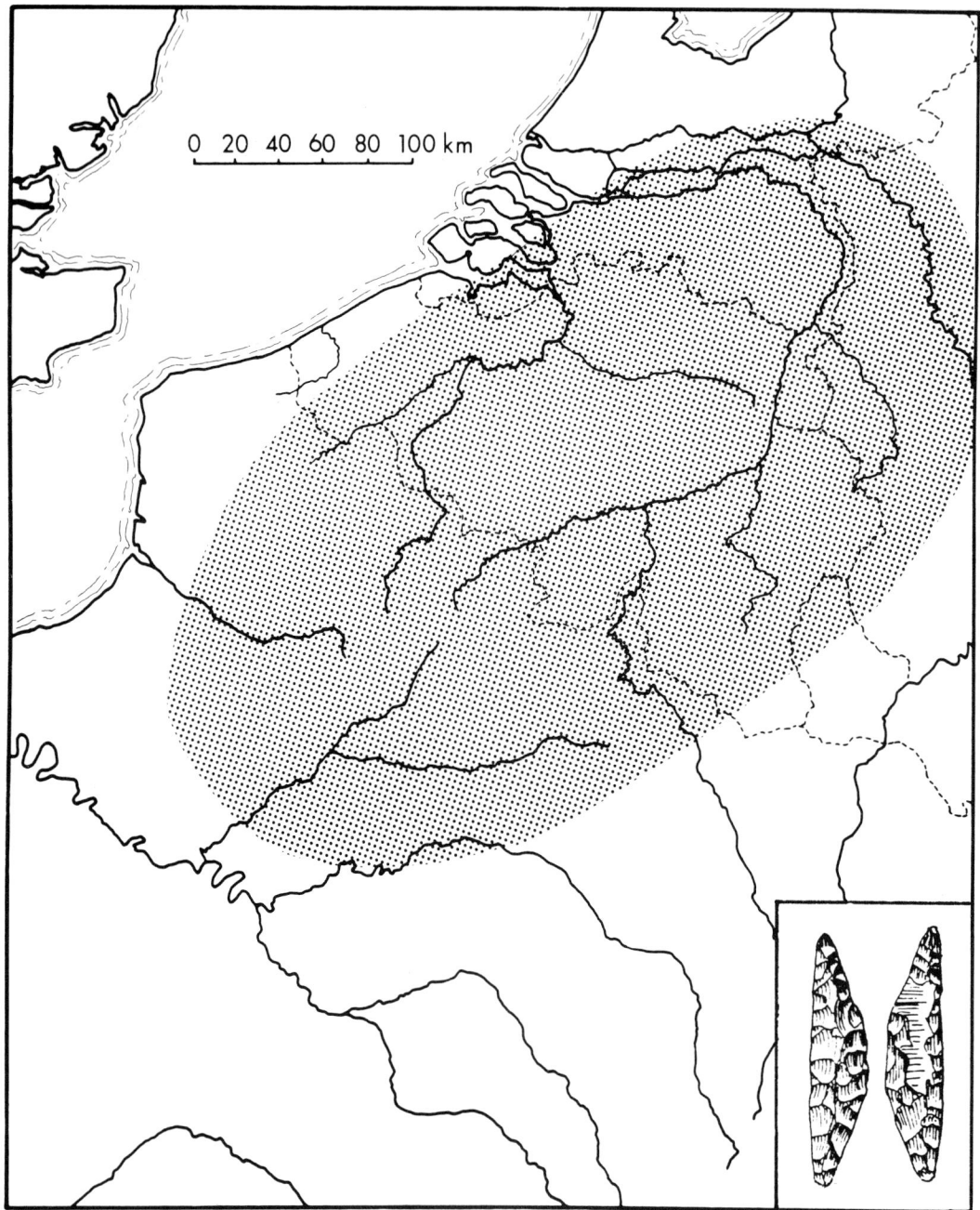

Figure 8   Distribution of points with surface retouch during the late Mesolithic.

approach requires a measure of chronological control and of relatively large and reliable archaeological site samples not everywhere present for the European Mesolithic. Indeed, one could desire improvements in these aspects of the data-set considered here. Hopefully, this potential will eventually exist in many areas.

References

ARORA, S.K. (1976) Die Mittelsteinzeit im westlichen Deutschland und in den Nachbargebieten. *Reinische Ausgrabungen*, 16: 1–68.

BRAUN, D.P. (1977) *Middle Woodland–(Early) Late Woodland Social Change in the Prehistoric Midwestern United States*. Ph.D. dissertation, University of Michigan. Ann Arbor, University Microfilms.

CLARK, J.G.D. (1975) *The Earlier Stone Age Settlement of Scandinavia*. Cambridge, University Press.

CLOSE, A.E. (1978) The identification of style in lithic artifacts. *World Archaeology*, 10: 223–237.

DECORMEILLE, A. and HINOUT, J. (1982) Mise en évidence des différentes cultures mésolithiques dans le Bassin Parisien par l'analyse des données. *Bulletin de la Société Préhistorique Française*, 79: 81–88.

GENDEL, P.A. (1982) An analysis of stylistic variation in some late Mesolithic assemblages from northwestern Europe. *Bulletin de la Société royale belge d'Anthropologie et de Préhistoire*, 93: 51–63

GENDEL, P.A. (1984) *Mesolithic Social Territories in Northwestern Europe*. Oxford, British Archaeological Reports (International Series) S218.

GOB, A. (1981) *Le Mésolithique dans le Bassin de l'Ourthe*. (Mémoire de la Société wallone de Palethnologie, 3). Liège, Presses Universitaires.

GRAMSCH, B. (1973) Das Mesolithikum in Mecklenburg und Brandenburg – zeitliche Gliederung und Formengruppen. In

S.K. Kozłowski (ed.), *The Mesolithic in Europe*. Warsaw, University Press: 209–235.

HINOUT, J. (1980) Trois cultures mésolithiques dans le Nord-Occidental européen. *Bulletin de la Société Préhistorique Française*, 77: 195–196.

HODDER, I. (1977) The distribution of material culture items in the Baringo district, western Kenya. *Man*, 12: 239–269.

HODDER, I. (1979) Economic and social stress and material patterning. *American Antiquity*, 44: 446–454.

HODDER, I. (1982) *Symbols in Action: Ethnoarchaeological Studies of Material Culture*. Cambridge, University Press.

JACOBI, R.M. (1979) Early Flandrian hunters in the south-west. *Proceedings of the Devon Archeological Society*, 37: 48–93.

KOZŁOWSKI, S.K. (1975) *Cultural Differentiation of Europe from 10th to 5th Millennium B.C.* Warsaw, University Press.

KOZŁOWSKI, J.K. and KOZŁOWSKI, S.K. (1979) *Upper Palaeolithic and Mesolithic in Europe. Taxonomy and Palaeohistory* (Prace Komisji Archeologicznej, 18). Wrocław, Polska Akademia Nauk.

MADDEN, M. (1983) Social network systems amongst hunter-gatherers considered within southern Norway. In G. Bailey (ed.), *Hunter-Gatherer Economy in Prehistory*. Cambridge, University Press: 191–200.

NEWELL, R.R. (1973) The Post-glacial adaptations of the indigenous population of the Northwest European Plain. In S.K. Kozłowski (ed.), *The Mesolithic in Europe*. Warsaw, University Press: 399–440.

PLOG, S. (1976) Measurement of prehistoric interaction between communities. In K.V. Flannery (ed.), *The Early Mesoamerican Village*. New York, Academic Press: 255–272.

PLOG, S. (1980) *Stylistic Variation in Prehistoric Ceramics: Design Variation in the American Southwest*. Cambridge, University Press.

PLOG, S. (1983) Analysis of style in artifacts. *Annual Review of Anthropology*, 12: 125–142.

ROZOY, J-G. (1978) *Les Derniers Chasseurs: l'Epipaléolithique en France et en Belgique* (Bulletin de la Société archéologique champenoise, numéro spécial). Charleville, J-G. Rozoy.

SACKETT, J. (1982) Approaches to style in lithic archaeology. *Journal of Anthropological Archaeology*, 1: 59–112.

VERMEERSCH, P.M. (1984) Du Paléolithique final au Mésolithique dans le nord de la Belgique. In D. Cahen and P. Haesaerts (eds), *Peuples Chasseurs de la Belgique Préhistorique dans leur Cadre Naturel*. Brussels, Institut royal des Sciences naturelles de Belgique: 181–193.

VOSS, J.A. (1977) The Barnes site: functional and stylistic variability in a small Paleo-Indian assemblage. *Midcontinental Journal of Archaeology*, 2: 253–305.

WHALLON, R.E., Jr (1968) Investigations of late prehistoric social organization in New York State. In S.R. Binford and L.R. Binford (eds), *New Perspectives in Archaeology*. Chicago, Aldine: 223–244.

WIESSNER, P. (1983) Style and social information in Kalahari San projectile points. *American Antiquity*, 48: 253–276.

WOBST, H.M. (1976) Locational relationships in Palaeolithic society. In R.H. Ward and K.M. Weiss (eds), *The Demographic Evolution of Human Populations*. London, Academic Press: 49–58.

WOBST, H.M. (1977) Stylistic behavior and information exchange. In C.E. Cleland (ed.), *Papers for the Director: Research Essays in Honour of James B. Griffin*. Ann Arbor, Museum of Anthropology (University of Michigan) Anthropological Papers 61: 317–342.

The Reconstruction of Mesolithic Diets

T. Douglas Price

Abstract

Current methods for the reconstruction of Mesolithic subsistence – the use of faunal and floral remains, studies of dentition and other skeletal attributes, and the development of predictive models – have not provided reliable information. Most theoretical statements exhibit a pronounced 'meat bias' toward terrestrial large game animals. To date, little is known about the importance of plant foods, shellfish, fish, or marine mammals in Mesolithic subsistence. The analysis of bone for elemental and isotopic composition, however, may provide a means of reconstructing the relative contribution of plants and animals to diet and of distinguishing marine from terrestrial components in subsistence. Future enhancements of these methods are likely to provide even more detailed information.

INTRODUCTION

The Mesolithic in north-west Europe extends from approximately 9500 to 5500 BP, and somewhat later in the north. This was a period of warmer temperatures compared to the preceding late Pleistocene and one characterized by increasingly abundant vegetation as birch, pine, and finally dense, mixed-oak forests covered the landscape. A variety of shrubs and herbaceous plants accompanied the spread of forests. Red deer, wild pig, roe deer, aurochs, and European elk became important game animals, replacing the reindeer in the area at the close of the Pleistocene. Numerous species of smaller mammals, birds, and fish also migrated into this former zone of glacial and periglacial environments. Rising sea levels reached the modern coastline around 7000 BP. From that point on most archaeological sites on the coast contain evidence for some reliance on marine resources such as seals, fish, and shellfish.

Clearly, a wide range of foods from the land, sea, and air were available to the Mesolithic hunter-gatherers. Subsistence activities appear to be greatly intensified through the period. Resource procurement becomes both more specialized and diversified – specialized in terms of the nature, technology, and organization of foraging, and diversified in terms of the numbers and kinds of species and habitats exploited. Certain resources, particularly nuts and shellfish, become much more visible in the Mesolithic but represent greater variety in the diet rather than a change in staple foods (e.g. Bailey 1978). These additions to the diet generally come from lower trophic levels in the food chain and require more complex processing techniques.

Statements regarding human subsistence in this period are made regularly by various authorities:

> The conclusion is irresistible that, while on coastal settlements the men of this time [late Mesolithic in south Scandinavia] depended primarily for meat and furs on land-mammals, they at the same time exploited the special opportunities offered by sea mammals ... as well as by sea-fish .... (Clark 1975: 192).

> The European Mesolithic aboriginals were neither predominantly hunters nor mammal meat consumers but largely gatherers, with a substantially vegetal diet whose abundant sources are difficult to appreciate in the *degraded* ecology of modern Europe (Clarke 1976: 451).

> There is no question of shellfish and land snails being 'emergency foods' in time of famine since their collecting needs much time .... a maximum contribution (95–100%) to the diet being made by the large species .... the contribution of fish can be estimated as anywhere between 25 and 75% of the total diet ... plant foods will only have made an occasional contribution (5%?) to the diet and then only at certain seasons (Rozoy 1978: 1162).

In spite of these pronouncements, there is little reliable information on the composition of diet. The evaluation of prehistoric subsistence in the Mesolithic has been at most subjective and impressionistic. Although the general categories of food available can be recognized and certain trends in the use of foodstuffs can be identified, it has been impossible to specify human diets.

In the following pages, I will consider the current archaeological evidence for diet and subsistence in the Mesolithic and discuss certain deficiencies in those data and perspectives. New methods involving the chemical analysis of prehistoric bone for the reconstruction of past diet will be the subject of the second portion of the paper. Some examples of the application of these methods to materials from southern Scandinavia will be presented.

CURRENT EVIDENCE FOR SUBSISTENCE

Past human subsistence is one of the most important areas of archaeological research. The quest for food directs and conditions many aspects of prehistoric human society, including group size and social organization, residence patterns and settlement location, tool manufacture and technology, and transportation. Information on past diet is essential to characterize the trophic position of prehistoric populations, the utilization of the environment, the determinants of site placement, the nature of subsistence activities, status differentiation, and the like.

Existing evidence for diet comes from a number of lines of research: faunal analysis (e.g. White 1953; Ziegler 1973; Lyman 1982; Parmalee 1985), palaeoethnobotany (e.g. Smith 1985), faecal studies (e.g. Callen 1963; Bryant 1974; Fry 1985), dental studies of wear and the frequency of caries (e.g. Molnar 1971; Perzigian 1977; Powell 1985; Rose, Condon and Goodman 1985), physical anthropology (e.g. Huss-Ashmore *et al*. 1982; Martin *et al*. 1985), ethnographic analogy (e.g. Leone and Palkovich 1985), and quantitative modelling (e.g. Higgs and Vita-Finzi 1972; Jochim 1976; Bettinger 1980; Keene 1981). Close consideration, however, reveals serious deficiencies in each of these methods.

The vast majority of archaeological sites from the Mesolithic period do *not* contain preserved organic materials or any trace of food remains. Only in unusual circumstances do conditions of soil pH and/or moisture provide for the preservation of plant and/or animal remains. Even in situations of excellent preservation, such remains were never sufficiently well discarded to provide an accurate picture of what was actually consumed (e.g. Carbone and Keel 1985).

Two important Mesolithic sites with outstanding preservation, Star Carr and Tybrind Vig, exemplify this point. The subsistence focus at Star Carr in north-eastern England, where a variety of floral and faunal remains were recovered, has been the source of significant controversy regarding both the activities and the diet of its inhabitants (e.g. Clark 1954, 1972; Wheeler 1978; Pitts 1979; Andresen *et al*. 1981; Price 1982). The importance of plants, fish, and even the relative contribution of large game to subsistence remain uncertain (see Legge and Rowley-Conwy, this volume).

The submerged site of Tybrind Vig on the west coast of the Danish island of Funen contains perhaps the best example of a preserved assemblage of artifacts and other materials from the Mesolithic in all Europe. Wood and twigs, sinew, bone, fish scales, and other organic materials have been recovered intact at the site (Andersen 1980). Evidence for subsistence activities is abundant. Items associated with fishing – hooks, bone points, leisters, weirs and traps, boats and paddles – are particularly common (Trolle-Lassen 1984). In addition, food remains in ceramic vessels at the site contain fish bones, scales, and residues from certain grasses. Bones from both large and small fish are common at the site and at least nine species are represented. Cod is most abundant. A concentration of cod crania in refuse areas at the site suggests fish-cleaning activities. Bones from terrestrial mammals are also common. Porpoise and seal bones are not abundant, perhaps as a result of butchering practices. Plant remains in the form of leaves, fruits, seeds, and shells are found at the site. Hazel-nut shells (and perhaps acorns) are particularly well represented. In spite of the distinctive evidence for fishing and the diversity of other remains, however, the archaeological evidence offers little indication of the relative contribution of these various classes of food to the diet. Tybrind Vig is an excellent example of how little we know about human subsistence in the Mesolithic.

The highly visible remains of certain foods – particularly animal bones, mollusc shells, and nut shells – bias archaeological interpretations in favour of these more durable categories. The fragile and ephemeral nature of many food remains renders them less visible and more briefly discussed in reconstructions of past diet. For many years, the *køkkenmøddinger* of Denmark were regarded as definitive evidence that shellfish were a major component of the diet. More recent data, however, suggest that molluscs were simply seasonal supplements to a subsistence pattern focused largely on marine fish and mammals. Extensive shellfish beds are found only under specific conditions of water depth, temperature, salinity, and current, and shell is absent or rare at many Mesolithic sites in southern Scandinavia.

Faecal matter is rarely preserved at archaeological sites in northern Europe. In any event, the analysis of such unusual remains provides information only on the foods consumed individually over a very brief period, not a long-term summary of group subsistence patterns.

Studies of stature and other skeletal indicators can provide information on the quality of the diet. For example, there appears to be a significant decline in human stature from the Upper Palaeolithic to the Neolithic (Frayer 1980; Key 1980; Meiklejohn *et al*. 1984) but little is known of the reasons for this decrease. Studies of dentition and caries have been used for a number of years as indicators of diet and nutrition (e.g. Christopherson and Pedersen 1939) but without clear resolution. Meiklejohn *et al*. (1984: 87) observe that rates of dental caries suggest marked dietary differences between the Mesolithic and Neolithic. Dental caries are less common in the Mesolithic, perhaps as a result of greater tooth wear, but specific causes are unknown.

Predictive models provide intriguing patterns for possible dietary and subsistence arrangements. Jochim (1976) utilized certain characteristics of various food sources, such as weight, density, mobility, and non-food value, to estimate their relative importance during the south German Mesolithic. Price (1978) applied this model with minor modifications to north-west Europe; *Fig. 1* is a graphic representation

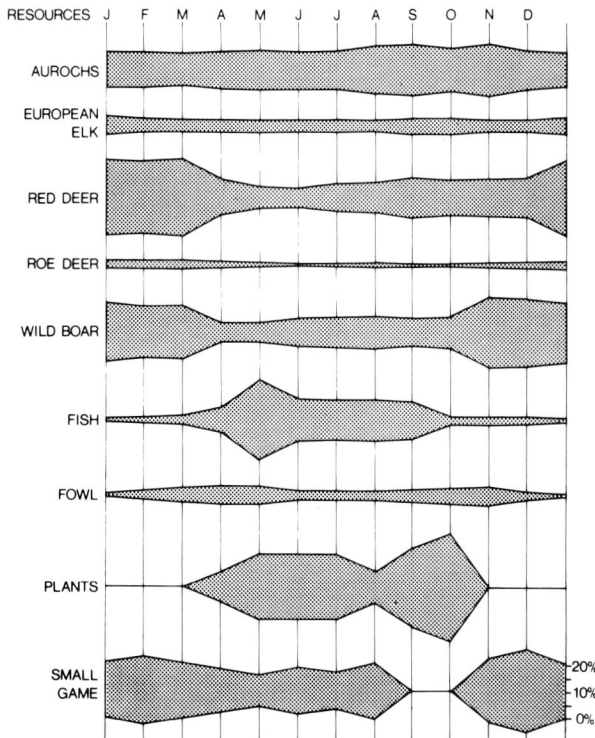

Figure 1   Predicted annual resource utilization of various food categories for the inland Mesolithic in north-west Europe. Original data from Price (1978).

of this predicted utilization of resources. Although such formulations appear precise, they are in fact based upon a variety of assumptions and missing data. The estimate in *Fig. 1*, for example, assumes that large game animals are the focus of subsistence. Marine creatures, fowl, fish, and plants are ignored or allowed to play only a minor role. Attributes such as density and mobility are difficult to measure for migratory marine species.

The utilization of plants, wildfowl and fish in the model is based simply on the *assumption* that their annual proportions in the diet are 15%, 5% and 10% respectively. A wide range of plants were at least available to Mesolithic hunter-gatherers. Birds and fish should have been present in large numbers. Small game utilization is assumed to take place when other resources do not provide sufficient return. These projections are dependent upon extant archaeological evidence for available food categories and exhibit a pronounced meat bias. Further, such

estimates are completely unverifiable given the present state of our knowledge. Thus, while predictive models may be informative, they do not provide reliable estimates of past diet.

THE CHEMICAL ANALYSIS OF BONE

We simply do not have much information about the composition of human diet in the Mesolithic. We need to know (i) the importance of plants in the diet and the species that were utilized, (ii) the significance of various coastal and marine resources, (iii) the differences between coastal and inland diets, and much more. Is the meat of large game animals in fact a major focus of the food quest? How important are hazel-nuts and/or acorns in the Mesolithic diet? Are there grasses, seeds, weeds, and other plant species that provide a significant portion of subsistence?

Table 1:   Plants of potential economic value in the Mesolithic of north-west Europe (see also Newell 1970; Clark 1972; Clarke 1976; Pitts 1978)

Scientific Name	Common Name	Product(s)
Corylus avellana	Hazel	nuts
Fagus sylvatica	Beech	nuts
Juglans regia	Walnut	nuts
Quercus sp.	Oak	acorns
Trapa natans	Water Chestnut	nuts
Potentilla anserina	Goose-tansy	roots
Stachys palustris	Hedge Nettle	roots
Nymphaea alba	White Water-lily	tubers/seeds
Alisma plantago-aquatica	Water Plantain	rhizomes
Menyanthes trifoliata	Bog Bean	rhizomes
Phragmites communis	Reed	rhizomes
Typha latifolia	Broadleaf Cattails	rhizomes
Atriplex sp.	Atriplex/Orache	seeds
Chenopodium sp.	Goosefoot	seeds
Gramineae sp.	Grasses	seeds
Nuphar lutreum	Water-lily	seeds
Polygonum sp.	Knotweed	seeds
Vicia sp.	Vetch	seeds/greens
Crataegus sp.	Hawthorn	leaves/fruit
Fragaria vesca	Wild Strawberry	leaves/fruit
Malus sp.	Crab Apple	fruit
Prunus avium	Wild Cherry	fruit
Pyrus sp.	Wild Pear	fruit
Ribes nigrum	Blackcurrant	fruit
Rosa sp.	Wild Rose	fruit
Sambucus nigra	Elderberry	fruit
Vaccinium sp.	Blueberry	fruit
Empetrum nigrum	Crowberry	leaves
Epilobium sp.	Willow Herb	leaves
Galeopsis tetrahit	Hemp/Nettle	leaves
Polygonum bistorta	Bistort	leaves
Rumex crispus	Curled Dock	leaves
Stellaria media	Chickweed/Starwort	leaves
Urtica dioica	Nettle	leaves

The potential for plant food utilization is enormous (*Table 1*). As David Clarke has pointed out:

> The temperate oak/hazel forests .... commonly yield 700–1000 litres of edible acorns for each mature oak

tree, half a tonne of hazel nuts a hectare, 20–25 tonnes of edible bracken root per square kilometre, 5,000–10,000 kilograms of fungi and 13–15 kilograms of blackberries a day in season. These figures themselves are dwarfed by the huge quantity of protein directly available in a wide range of edible herbaceous leaves and plants, consumed as cress, salad, spinach, and asparagus meals (1976: 458).

Fortunately, the chemical analysis of human bone may provide a means for obtaining reliable information on palaeonutrition (e.g. Sillen and Kavanagh 1982; Klepinger 1984; Gilbert 1985; Price, Schoeninger and Armelagos 1985). Both the *elemental* and *isotopic* composition of bone are of concern. These studies can provide information on marine versus terrestrial components in the diet, the importance of plants versus animals, the presence of certain types of plants, and more. In the future these techniques may also reveal the importance of specific classes of foods – such as nuts and shellfish – in the diet.

Isotopic analysis

Isotopic analysis of bone for dietary information to date has concentrated on carbon and nitrogen. While the amount of these *elements* in bone is under strict metabolic control, the ratio of stable *isotopes* ($^{13}C/^{12}C$ and $^{15}N/^{14}N$) in bone collagen reflects the ratio in diet. The interpretation of carbon isotopic ratios is relatively straightforward. Individual variability is due largely to diet because the natural reservoir of carbon isotopes is constant. Isotopic ratios in bone collagen do not appear to undergo diagenetic alteration (Price, Schoeninger and Armelagos 1985). Carbon isotope ratios are reported in terms of $\delta^{13}C$ values that generally become more positive along the continuum from plants, to herbivores, to carnivores in both marine and terrestrial regimes (Schoeninger and DeNiro 1984: 625).

Tauber (1981), Chisolm *et al.* (1982), and Schoeninger *et al.* (1983) have used carbon isotope ratios to distinguish marine from terrestrial organisms in human diet. The $^{13}C/^{12}C$ ratio in seawater bicarbonate is higher than in atmospheric carbon dioxide. This difference is also seen in the plants that inhabit the two regimes, as well as in the bone collagen of animals that feed on these plant species. In addition, many tropical grasses such as sorgum, millet, amaranth and maize (designated as C_4 species) utilize a photosynthetic pathway that efficiently metabolizes carbon dioxide by initial conversion to a 4-carbon compound which incorporates more available ^{13}C (Bender 1968; O'Leary 1981). C_3 plants, which are more common in temperate areas, produce a 3-carbon compound. The carbon isotope ratios in the bone collagen of animals feeding on 3- or 4-carbon plants reflect the isotopic differences in the two categories. This principle has been used by Vogel and Van der Merwe (1977), Bender *et al.* (1981), and others to study the introduction of corn into prehistoric North America. C_4 plants are essentially absent in Mesolithic northern Europe, however, and will not be involved further in this discussion.

Staple isotope ratios of nitrogen ($^{15}N/^{14}N$) in animal bone also reflect the ratio from diet. Three major classes of organisms can be distinguished using nitrogen isotopes: (i) nitrogen-fixing plants and the animals that feed on those plants; (ii) terrestrial food chains not involved in nitrogen-fixation; and (iii) marine foods not based on nitrogen-fixation. Freshwater systems may constitute another distinguishable class but are not yet well understood. Given this information, it should be possible to examine human bone to distinguish groups whose diets are based largely on leguminous plants, marine, or terrestrial (non-leguminous) foods (Price, Schoeninger and Armelagos 1985). To date, however, studies of nitrogen isotope ratios in archaeological material are rare (e.g. Farnsworth *et al.* 1984; Schoeninger *et al.* 1983).

Elemental analyses

Concern with the by-products from nuclear testing during the 1950s initiated intensive investigations of the relationship between bone chemistry and diet. Strontium 90, a harmful radioactive isotope produced by fission weapons tests, appeared in substantial quantities in milk and other foods and was deposited in the human skeleton. Studies of the movement of both the isotopes and the whole element through the food chain indicated that strontium was differentially distributed as a consequence of certain physiological and/or dietary processes. For example, the amount of strontium in vegetation varies by plant part and species. This information was used by Toots and Voorhies (1965) to distinguish browsing and grazing diets among fossil herbivores.

In animals, approximately 99% of all body strontium is deposited in bone tissue. Clear differences in bone strontium levels can be seen along the food chain. Herbivores incorporate in bone tissue only about 20–25% of the strontium from the plants they ingest. Carnivores both consume less strontium in their diets and discriminate metabolically against it. Thus, the bones of herbivores and carnivores can be distinguished by their strontium content. Omnivores fall between these two extremes, depending upon the amount of plant food in their diet. Human bone is completely remodelled over a period of 5–10 years so that chemical information on diet represents a composite view of nutrition.

Human strontium levels thus should reflect a composite strontium value from various foods, with marine animals and plants contributing higher levels of strontium and terrestrial animals providing only low amounts (*Fig. 2*). Other food sources such as shellfish and nuts have distinctive strontium levels (Katzenberg 1984). Rosenthal *et al.* (1970) report

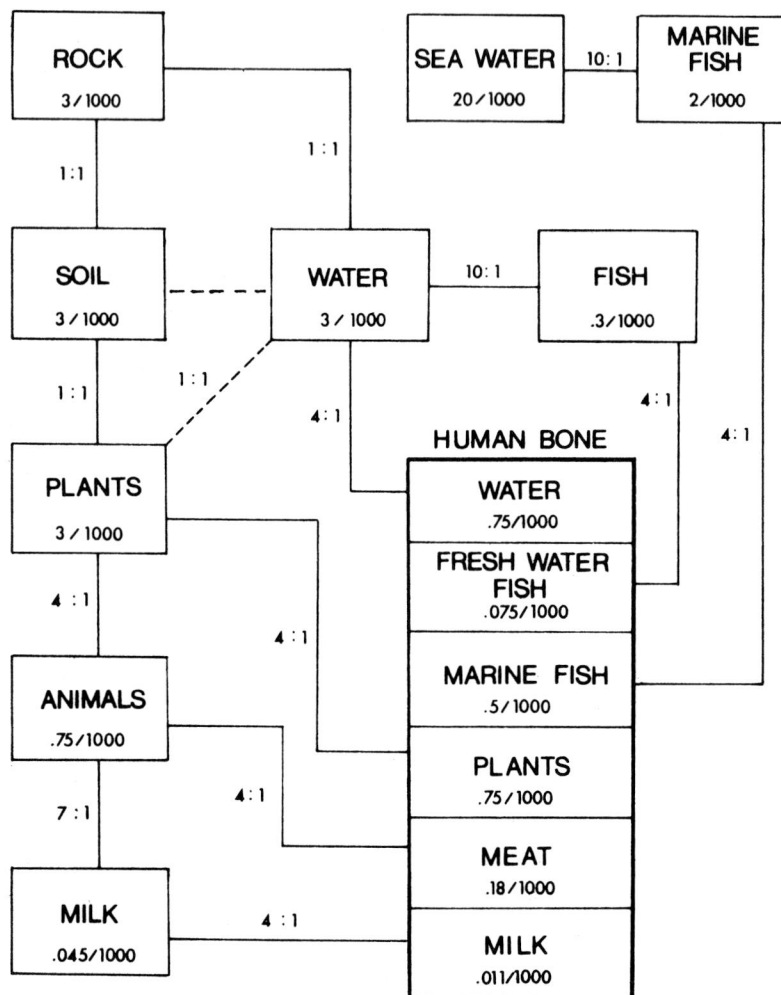

Figure 2 Hypothesized movement of strontium into human bone from various dietary sources (after Kavanagh 1979). Sr/Ca ratios (in boxes) and discrimination ratio (between boxes) are approximate. Sr/Ca levels are shown as parts strontium to 1000 parts calcium.

lower strontium levels in freshwater fish and shellfish compared to marine species. Marine fish and shellfish exhibit quite high levels of strontium due to the higher mineral content of ocean waters. Plants concentrate strontium in roots and lower leaves (Isermann 1981) and some types of nuts appear to exhibit high levels of strontium (Schroeder *et al.* 1972).

Brown (1973) first employed the principle of strontium flow in the food chain for the investigation of past *human* subsistence. Strontium analysis since has been used to examine the relative contribution of plants and animals to prehistoric diets (e.g. Price and Kavanagh 1981; Sillen 1981), marine versus terrestrial foods in subsistence (Connor and Slaughter 1984; Nelson *et al.* 1984), the transformation from hunting-gathering to agriculture (Sillen 1981; Schoeninger 1982), the relationship between status and diet (Lambert *et al.* 1979; Schoeninger 1979), and the age of weaning (Sillen and Smith 1984).

Strontium analysis is relatively straightforward. *Dietary* and *environmental* sources of strontium are

the major determinants of the amounts present in human bone. The nature of diet – e.g. the proportions of plants versus meat – affects the amount of strontium entering the blood stream and bone tissue. Local environmental levels of natural strontium determine the total amount of strontium available to the food chain.

Nevertheless, the method is still in an experimental stage and a number of questions remain to be resolved regarding other sources of variation. Two additional sources of variability require further discussion: *individual* differences and diagenesis. *Individual* variability within a population is relatively high, with a coefficient of variation ranging between 20% and 35% (Schoeninger 1979; Price, Schoeninger and Armelagos 1985). Sources for this variability include age, sex, and individual metabolism. Strontium levels in bone increase slightly with age (Sowden and Sitch 1957). Lambert *et al.* (1979) found that relative concentrations of strontium, sodium and zinc decreased in childhood, increased during adolescence, remained generally stable between the ages of 20 and 50, and showed a slight increase in individuals over 50. Tanaka *et al.* (1981) have reported a gradual increase in strontium levels with age. Because of high variation in strontium levels among sub-adults, most palaeodietary studies have concentrated on the bones of individuals older than eighteen years of age.

Sex-related differences within a population are not adequately documented. Early tests on modern bone samples indicated no differences (Turkian and Kulp 1956). Tanaka *et al.* (1981) reported very little difference between modern males and females in Japan. However, Snyder *et al.* (1964) recorded significant differences in a study of U.S. males and females between the ages of 20 and 59. Lambert *et al.* (1979) observed statistically higher strontium levels in males from the Late Woodland period in Illinois that were not noted among earlier Middle Woodland burials.

The effects of *diagenesis* – post-depositional chemical changes in bone – are not well understood. Studies of diagenetic effects are often vague and contradictory. Toots and Voorhies (1965), Parker and Toots (1970, 1980), and others have argued that no significant post-mortem changes in bone strontium levels occur. Sillen (1981), on the other hand, examined strontium concentrations in herbivore and carnivore bone from Aurignacian levels in Israel and observed no significant difference in bone strontium between the two classes of animals. The absence of expected difference was suggested to be due to the equilibrating effects of diagenesis.

Lambert *et al.* (1979, 1982, 1985) have considered the question of post-mortem alteration for a number of elements. Comparison of elemental concentrations in bone and adjacent soil indicated that the bone had been contaminated by iron, manganese, and potassium from the soil. Strontium, zinc, magnesium, calcium, sodium, and copper appeared to be less subject to contamination.

The question of diagenetic modification is far from resolved. Nevertheless, strontium levels in bone appear to be unaffected in some depositional contexts while dramatically changed in others (Price 1986). The condition of bone in the ground is clearly a function of soil acidity and reduction–oxidation conditions. White and Hannus (1983) have examined this relationship between bone-weathering and soils in detail. They conclude that the diagenesis of hydroxyapatite in bone is begun by acids, formed by the microbial decomposition of collagen, as protons replace calcium in hydroxyapatite. As collagen in the bone is depleted, continued diagenetic change in calcium levels is dependent upon soil conditions. If soils are acidic and protons are available, weathering may cease as calcium levels in the bone stabilize. Although calcium is more soluble, strontium also is

likely to be mobile under extreme conditions of diagenesis. Calcium and strontium may also be added to bone via calcium carbonate enrichment (Katzenberg 1984; Price 1988).

BONE CHEMISTRY STUDIES IN THE MESOLITHIC

The study of the chemical composition of human bone from the Mesolithic has only begun; analytical methods are new and experimental, relatively little human skeletal material has been recovered from this period, sources of strontium are not well defined. Nevertheless, the information that is available indicates the potential for such studies.

Isotopic analyses

The results of carbon isotope assays of several Mesolithic burials are presented in *Fig. 3*. The

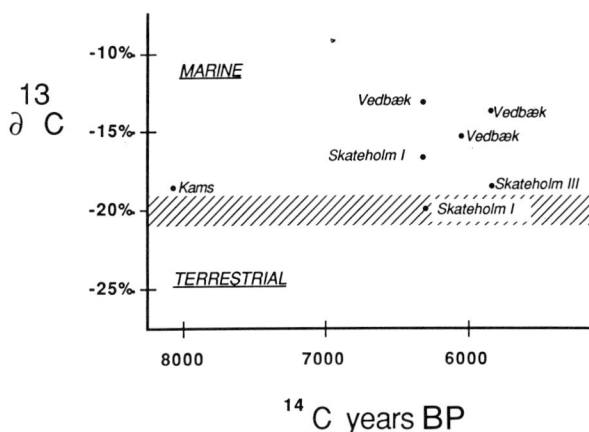

Figure 3 Carbon isotope ratios from Mesolithic burials in northern Europe. Data come from Tauber (1981), Trolle-Lassen (1984), and Håkansson (1982, 1983, 1984).

samples come largely from coastal sites, including the well-known cemetery at Vedbæk (Albrethsen and Brinch Petersen 1976). These results are discussed below in terms of marine and terrestrial diets. C_3 plants, and terrestrial animals consuming those plants, have $\delta^{13}C$ values ranging between $-22‰$ and $-30‰$. In sea water, the absorption of CO_2 and the formation of bicarbonate is responsible for the enrichment of the heavier isotopes. Marine plants, and the sea animals that depend on those plants, exhibit $\delta^{13}C$ values ranging between $-10‰$ and $18‰$ (Tauber 1981). Thus, values greater than *c.* 20‰ indicate a predominance of marine foods in the diet while lesser values are more closely related to the consumption of terrestrial plants and animals.

The $\delta^{13}C$ values from Vedbæk range from $-13.4‰$ to $-15.3‰$ and are close to values for historical Eskimo skeletal material (Tauber 1981). Greenland Eskimo utilized marine foods extensively, perhaps for as much as 70–90% of the diet, and a similar proportion of seafoods may have characterized the later Mesolithic diet.[1] Clearly, marine fish, seals, porpoise, whales, and molluscs contribute a major portion of the diet at Vedbæk. Assay of a dog from the Vedbæk area gave a $\delta^{13}C$ reading of $-14.7‰$, within the range of the humans and suggesting a very similar diet for the canine (Noe Nygaard 1983). Neolithic burials in Denmark show a sharp decline in carbon isotope ratios, indicative of a decrease in the importance of marine foods among these agriculturalists (Tauber 1981: 232). Nitrogen isotope analysis shows a less pronounced separation of Mesolithic and Neolithic populations (Schoeninger et al. 1983).

The skeletal materials from the Ertebølle sites at Skateholm in southern Sweden (Larsson 1984a; Persson and Persson 1984) provide similar results. Over sixty burials have been excavated at Skateholm I, making it the largest Mesolithic cemetery in Europe. Twenty-two graves were recovered from the nearby burial area at Skateholm II, while a single burial is preserved from the site of Skateholm III. Skateholm I dates from 6300 to 5600 BP; Skateholm II dates from 6600 to 5500 BP; Skateholm III is dated to c. 5850 BP. The $\delta^{13}C$ ratios from the human skeletal material at Skateholm I now available are $-16.8‰$ and $-20.1‰$ (Håkansson 1982, 1984). The single value from Skateholm III is $-18.6‰$. Samples from Skateholm II lack sufficient collagen to obtain a date or isotope ratio (Larsson, pers. comm.). The $\delta^{13}C$ values from Skateholm are lower than those from Vedbæk, reflecting either the lower mineral content of the Baltic or the predominance of freshwater fish at Skateholm, or both.

Carbon isotope analysis of a burial from Tybrind Vig provided a $\delta^{13}C$ ratio of $-15.7‰$, indicative of a predominantly marine component to the diet (Trolle-Lassen 1984). The importance of cod at Tybrind Vig is clearly reflected in this value. The Tybrind burial should be typical of late Mesolithic adaptations in marine coastal contexts. A single burial from the site of Kams on the Swedish island of Gotland in the Baltic has also been analyzed (Håkansson 1983; Larsson 1982). The Kams burial dates to c. 8000 BP. The $\delta^{13}C$ value for the Kams burial is $-18.0‰$, however, suggesting an important proportion of marine foods in the diet. This site is discussed again below.

Elemental analyses

The trace element analysis of some of these materials is underway.[2] Samples of both human and animal bone have been obtained from Mesolithic cemeteries at Skateholm and Vedbæk. In addition, analyses of the single burials from Tybrind Vig off the coast of western Funen, and from Kams on Gotland, are included in the following discussion.

The most detailed trace element analysis to date has been conducted for human and faunal remains from Skateholm. Human bone samples from both Skateholm I and Skateholm II, along with bone from red deer, seal, pike, marten, and wild cat from Skateholm I, have been analyzed by atomic emission spectrometry for nine elements: calcium, sodium, strontium, zinc, copper, manganese, aluminium, manganese, and iron. The results of the analyses, sample sizes, and descriptive statistics for calcium, strontium, and zinc concentrations in bone are presented in Table 2.

Table 2:   Elemental analysis of human and animal bone from Mesolithic northern Europe

Site	Species	Age/Sex	Ca%	Sr ppm	Zn ppm
Skateholm I					
	H. sapiens	Adult Female	35.09	749	226
	H. sapiens	Adult Female	36.88	431	195
	H. sapiens	Adult Male	35.48	795	185
	H. sapiens	Adult Female	36.89	506	195
	H. sapiens	Adult Female	37.30	543	175
	H. sapiens	Adult Male	36.85	428	202
	H. sapiens	Adult Female	35.72	603	604
	H. sapiens	Adult Female	31.65	678	277
	H. sapiens	Adult ?	31.17	513	447
	n=9	Mean	35.23	583	266
		Standard Deviation	2.29	133	158
		Coefficient of Variation	6.5%	23%	59%
	Cervus elaphus	Adult	32.09	819	443
	Cervus elaphus	Adult	26.02	942	234
	Cervus elaphus	Adult	31.78	1035	534
	Cervus elaphus	Adult	34.46	864	370
	Cervus elaphus	Adult	30.92	1081	469
	Cervus elaphus	Adult	31.68	1225	621
	n=6	Mean	31.16	994	444
		Standard Deviation	2.79	150	137
		Coefficient of Variation	8.9%	15%	31%

Site	Species	Age/Sex	Ca%	Sr ppm	Zn ppm
	Phocidae sp.	Adult	29.88	643	335
	Phocidae sp.	Adult	27.98	965	325
	Phocidae sp.	Adult	28.82	759	436
	n=3	Mean	28.29	789	365
		Standard Deviation	0.95	163	62
		Coefficient of Variation	3.4%	21%	17%
	Esox lucius	?	26.72	1137	344
	Esox lucius	?	29.92	1260	567
	Esox lucius	?	28.17	1062	447
	Esox lucius	?	28.48	1241	602
	Esox lucius	?	29.86	1356	609
	Esox lucius	?	28.03	1317	387
	n=6	Mean	28.53	1229	493
		Standard Deviation	1.21	111	115
		Coefficient of Variation	4.2%	9%	23%
	Martes martes	Adult	30.83	967	473
	Felis sylvestris	?	28.33	769	404
Skateholm II	*H. sapiens*	Adult Male	34.76	805	178
	H. sapiens	Adult Female	28.96	715	113
	H. sapiens	Adult Female(?)	30.14	780	195
	H. sapiens	Adult Male	31.60	832	277
	H. sapiens	Female	36.53	618	143
	H. sapiens	Adult Female	29.75	723	126
	H. sapiens	Adult Male	32.49	895	225
	H. sapiens	Adult Female	29.35	642	130
	H. sapiens	Adult Female	31.51	910	360
	n=9	Mean	31.68	769	194
		Standard Deviation	2.56	103	81.7
		Coefficient of Variation	8.1%	13%	42%
Kams	*H. sapiens*	Adult Female	38.01	124	150
Tybrind Vig	*H. sapiens*	Sub-adult	32.63	1306	241
	Cervus elaphus	Adult	37.07	1614	138
	Martes martes	Adult	38.05	1648	223
Maglemosegård	*Cervus elaphus*	?	37.06	1030	97
	Cervus elaphus	?	38.68	728	119
	Cervus elaphus	?	37.99	830	95
	Cervus elaphus	?	38.22	1274	113
	Cervus elaphus	?	38.73	788	101
	n=5	Mean	38.14	966	105
		Standard Deviation	0.68	241	11
		Coefficient of Variation	1.8%	25%	10%
	Phocidae sp.	?	34.36	1146	127
	Phocidae sp.	?	31.81	1262	170
	Phocidae sp.	?	35.59	911	128
	n=3	Mean	33.92	1106	140
		Standard Deviation	1.93	179	27
		Coefficient of Variation	5.7%	16%	19%

Several elements show differences in human bone at Skateholm I and II. This is particularly true of those elements that are susceptible to diagenesis. Iron, aluminium and manganese, for example, are much higher in the burials at Skateholm II, suggesting that these remains have been subject to more intense contamination. Bone calcium levels are lower at Skateholm II (31.7%) compared to Skateholm I (35.2%), also indicative of greater diagenetic activity at the older site and the absence of collagen at Skateholm I, noted above. Modern human bone ash contains approximately 37.0% calcium (Price 1986). The lower calcium levels at Skateholm II cause other elements to appear in higher concentrations. Thus, the unexpectedly higher values for strontium at Skateholm II are probably an artifact of reduced calcium content. The mean strontium values for humans at Skateholm I (583 ppm; $n = 9$) and at Skateholm II (769 ppm; $n = 9$) are significantly different at 0.05.[3] Correction for the lower calcium levels at Skateholm II makes the strontium values similar at the two sites.

Over 89 species have been identified to date from Skateholm. The percentages of roe deer and freshwater fish are higher at Skateholm II, compared to more abundant saltwater fish, seal, and wild boar at Skateholm I (Larsson 1984b). On the basis of the faunal evidence, marine species appear to be of greater importance in the diet at Skateholm I. Elemental analysis of the faunal remains is informative. Both red deer ($\bar{x} = 994$ ppm) and seal bone ($\bar{x} = 789$ ppm) are higher than the human bone strontium values from Skateholm I and II. Mean bone strontium in red deer (966 ppm) from Maglemosegård in nearby Denmark compares very well with the value for this species at Skateholm I. Seals, however, show much higher strontium levels (1106 ppm) at Maglemosegård. The higher values for seal at Maglemosegård are probably due to the greater mineral content of the waters of the Øresund compared to the Baltic. In addition, the data suggest that Baltic seals may have migrated only within the Baltic, while the seals of the Øresund at Maglemosegård moved out into the North Sea.

The human bone strontium levels at Skateholm are also lower than those for the carnivores, marten and wild cat, which produced values of 967 ppm and 769 ppm respectively. The relatively low bone strontium values in humans suggest a diet focused on low strontium foods, either terrestrial animals or fish.

Zinc values are higher at the younger site of Skateholm I and indicative of an increase in meat consumption (Gilbert 1975; Beck 1985). Zinc concentrations are higher in carnivores than in herbivores (Rheingold et al. 1983) as meat is a better source of zinc than plants (Klepinger 1984). Together, the change in zinc and strontium values suggests that meat may have been less important in the diet at the site of Skateholm II.

In sum, the elemental analysis of the Skateholm sites suggests that human diets were orientated more towards lower strontium foods such as terrestrial game or freshwater fish. The carbon isotope values from Skateholm I ($-16.8‰$ and $-20.1‰$) indicate a mixed diet incorporating both marine and terrestrial food sources. These values are likely to have been reduced by a higher $\delta^{13}C$ ratio in the waters of the Baltic. Combined with the analysis of the faunal remains from both sites, it would appear that the inhabitants of Mesolithic southern Sweden consumed a wide range of animals: marine and terrestrial species along with freshwater fish, in roughly equal proportions. The younger site of Skateholm I contains a higher proportion of saltwater fish and seal remains, although this is not reflected in human bone strontium. Evidence from the zinc content of the human samples suggests that the consumption of animal meat is lower at Skateholm I. The importance of plant food is unknown. The abundant strontium in marine foods may mask significant plant consumption.

Differences in bone strontium are also observed between adult males and females at both Skateholm I and II. Although sample sizes are small, the mean values for males at both sites (I = 612 ppm; II = 844 ppm) are higher than those for females (I = 585 ppm; II = 727 ppm). Studies of modern human populations have indicated that there is little difference between males and females in bone strontium content. Prehistoric samples, however, often show significant differences between the sexes (Price et al. 1986). These differences are probably related to both diet and reproductive status. Pregnant and lactating rats exhibit significantly higher bone strontium levels than either males or virgin females (Price et al. 1986). Thus, the unexpectedly higher bone strontium levels in the adult *males* from Skateholm suggest that there were pronounced differences in male and female diets. The most likely sources for high male strontium are marine foods.

The single human bone sample from Kams contains very low bone strontium levels, which is not surprising given the consumption of red meat and freshwater fish which might be expected at this site. The three samples from Tybrind Vig exhibit very high levels of bone strontium (human – 1306 ppm; red deer – 1614 ppm; marten – 1648 ppm), reflecting the coastal focus of the site and the fact that the mineral content of the waters of the Kattegat had increased by the end of the Mesolithic. The value for marten may indicate a diet emphasizing saltwater species.

CONCLUSIONS

Isotopic and elemental analysis are in an experimental stage as methods for the investigation of prehistoric diet. Analysis of human bone from Mesolithic sites in northern Europe provides some indications of the potential of the techniques. Carbon isotope analyses document the importance of marine resources in the diet. Elemental analyses of strontium and zinc document a complementary utilization of terrestrial resources. The relative contributions of freshwater fish and plants remain difficult to assess. Plant foods are not detectable in coastal populations. The abundance of strontium from marine species in the diet masks potentially significant plant foods. In order to determine the potential of plant foods in the diet, it will be necessary to analyze human remains from inland sites with a focus on terrestrial foods.

A number of other elements may become important as indicators of past conditions as more is learned regarding their physiological behaviour and depositional stability in bone. Barium (e.g. Elias *et al.* 1982), copper (Gilbert 1975), and magnesium (Klepinger 1984) have not yet been examined in depth. Barium resembles strontium in its passage through the food chain and is of use in distinguishing trophic levels in terrestrial and marine systems. Animals and certain seafoods are better sources of copper than plants (Gilbert 1975; Wessen *et al.* 1977). However, most copper in the body is bound to the organic matrix of bone (Bratter *et al.* 1976) and may not be a reliable post-mortem indicator of diet. Magnesium is generally found in higher concentration in plant foods (Alfrey and Butkus 1974) but the effects of diagenesis on this element are not yet clear. A number of ultratrace elements have yet to be considered. Through the investigation of these and other elements and isotopes in bone, the next decade may well provide the essential chemical keys to past human diets in the Mesolithic. In combination with the continued study of faunal assemblages, palaeoethnobotany and physical anthropology, bone chemistry brings the accurate interpretation of prehistoric subsistence closer to reality.

Notes:

1. Carbon isotope ratios in Mesolithic burials from the Muge basin of Portugal reflect a diet of approximately 50% marine foods (Lubell, Meiklejohn and Jackes, this volume).

2. Trace element analyses were carried out at the University of Wisconsin Laboratory of Archaeological Chemistry. Samples were cleaned manually with an air abrasive tool and ultrasonically in a bath of distilled/de-ionized water (see Brown and Keyser 1978). The bone was then oven-dried to constant weight, ashed at a temperature of 600 °C for approximately 8 hours, and ground to powder. 0.25 g of this powder was digested in a mixture of HNO_3 and $HClO_4$ for approximately 3 hours at a final temperature of *c.* 215 °C. Samples were then diluted to 50 ml with de-ionized water and introduced into an Inductively Coupled Plasma/Atomic Emission Spectrometer at the Soil and Plant Analysis Laboratory. Trace element concentrations are normally reported in parts per million (ppm) of dry bone ash weight. More common elements such as calcium are reported as a percentage by weight of dry bone ash.

3. Statistical comparison was done by means of an *F*-test, accepting a significance level of 0.05, after Lambert *et al.* (1982).

Acknowledgements: The research described in this paper is the result of the efforts of a number of individuals and institutions. Samples and information were provided by Lars Larsson, Søren Andersen and Erik Brinch Petersen; Lars also kindly commented on the manuscript. Discussions with Henrik Tauber were most useful and informative. Kim Aaris-Sørensen of the Zoological Museum of the University of Copenhagen provided the faunal samples from Vedbæk. Morten Melgård of the same institute identified the faunal remains from Skateholm. John Parsen of the Soil and Plant Analysis Laboratory of the University of Wisconsin carried out the analytical work. Funding was provided by the Wenner–Gren Foundation and the National Science Foundation (BNS-8119043). The assistance of all the above is gratefully acknowledged.

References

ALBRETHSEN, S.E. and BRINCH PETERSEN, E. (1976) Excavation of a Mesolithic cemetery at Vedbæk, Denmark. *Acta Archaeologica*, 47: 1–28.

ALFREY, A.C. and MILLER, N.L. (1974) Evaluation of body magnesium stores. *Journal of Laboratory Clinical Medicine*, 84: 153–162.

ANDERSEN, S.H. (1980) Tybrind Vig. Foreløbig meddelelse om en undersoisk stenalderboplads ved Lille Bælt. *Antikvariske studier*, 4: 7–22.

ANDRESEN, J.M., BYRD, B.F., ELSON, M.D., McGUIRE, R.H., MENDOZA, R.G., STASKI, E. and WHITE, J.P. (1981) The deer hunters: Star Carr reconsidered. *World Archaeology*, 13: 31–46

BAILEY, G.N. (1978) Shell middens as indicators of Postglacial economies: a territorial perspective. In P.A. Mellars (ed.), *The Early Postglacial Settlement of Northern Europe*. London, Duckworth: 37–63.

BECK, L. (1985) Bivariate analysis of trace elements in bone. *Journal of Human Evolution*, 14: 493–502.

BENDER, M.M. (1968) Mass spectrometric studies of carbon 13 variations in corn and other plants. *Radiocarbon*, 10: 468–472.

BENDER, M.M., BAERREIS, D.A. and STEVENTON, R.A. (1981) Further light on carbon isotopes and Hopewell agriculture. *American Antiquity*, 46: 346–353.

BETTINGER, R.L. (1980) Explanatory/predictive models of hunter-gatherer adaptation. In M.B. Schiffer (ed.), *Advances in Archaeological Method and Theory*, 3: 189–255.

BRATTER, P., GAWLIK, D., LAUSCH, J. and ROSICK, U. (1976) On the distribution of trace elements in human skeletons. *Proceedings of the 1976 International Conference on Modern Trends in Activation Analysis*, 1: 257–265. Munich.

BROWN, A.B. (1973) *Bone Strontium Content as a Dietary Indicator in Human Skeletal Populations*. Unpublished Ph.D. thesis, Department of Anthropology, University of Michigan, Ann Arbor.

BROWN, A.B. and KEYSER, H. (1978) Sample preparation for strontium analysis of ancient skeletal remains. *Contributions to Geology*, 16: 85–87. Laramie, Wyoming.

BRYANT, V.M., Jr (1974) The role of coprolite analysis in archaeology. *Bulletin of the Texas Archaeological Society*, 45: 1–28.

CALLEN, E.O. (1963) Diet as revealed by coprolites. In D. Brothwell and E.S. Higgs (eds), *Science in Archaeology*. London, Thames and Hudson: 186–193.

CARBONE, V.A. and KEEL, B.C. (1985) Preservation of plant and animal remains. In R.I. Gilbert, Jr and J.H. Mielke (eds), *The Analysis of Prehistoric Diets*. Orlando, Academic Press: 1–19.

CHISHOLM, B.S., NELSON, D.E. and SCHWARCZ, H.P. (1982) Stable carbon isotope ratios as a measure of marine versus terrestrial protein in ancient diets. *Science*, 216: 1131–1132.

CHRISTOPHERSON, K.M. and PEDERSEN, P.O. (1939) Investigation into dental conditions in the Neolithic period and in the Bronze Age in Denmark. *Dental Record*, 59: 575–585.

CLARK, J.G.D. (1954) *Excavations at Star Carr*. Cambridge, University Press.

CLARK, J.G.D. (1972) *Star Carr: a Case Study in Bioarchaeology*. Addison–Wesley Module in Anthropology no. 10. London, Cummings Publishing Company.

CLARK, J.G.D. (1975) *The Earlier Stone Age Settlement of Scandinavia*. Cambridge, University Press.

CLARKE, D.L. (1976) Mesolithic Europe: the economic basis. In G. de G. Sieveking, I.H. Longworth and K.E. Wilson (eds), *Problems in Economic and Social Archaeology*. London, Duckworth: 449–481.

CONNOR, M. and SLAUGHTER, D. (1984) Diachronic investigation of Eskimo diet utilizing trace element analysis. *Arctic Anthropology*, 21: 123–134.

ELIAS, R.W., HIRAO, Y. and PATTERSON, C.C. (1982) The circumvention of the natural biopurification of calcium along nutrient pathways by atmospheric inputs of industrial lead. *Geochimica et Cosmochimica Acta*, 46: 2561–2580.

FARNSWORTH, P., BRADY, J.E., DeNIRO, M.J. and MacNEISH, R.S. (1985) A re-evaluation of the isotopic and archaeological reconstructions of diet in the Tehuacan Valley. *American Antiquity*, 50: 102–116.

FRAYER, D.W. (1980) Sexual dimorphism in the late Pleistocene and Holocene of Europe. *Journal of Human Evolution*, 9: 399–415.

FRY, G.F. (1985) Analysis of fecal material. In R.I. Gilbert, Jr and J.H. Mielke (eds), *The Analysis of Prehistoric Diets*. Orlando, Academic Press: 127–154.

GILBERT, R.I., Jr (1975) *Trace Element Analysis of Three Skeletal Amerindian Populations at Dickson Mounds*. Unpublished Ph.D. thesis, Department of Anthropology, University of Massachusetts, Amherst.

GILBERT, R.I., Jr (1985) Stress, paleonutrition, and trace elements. In R.I. Gilbert, Jr and J.H. Mielke (eds), *The Analysis of Prehistoric Diets*. Orlando, Academic Press: 339–358.

HÅKANSSON, S. (1982) University of Lund Radiocarbon Dates XV. *Radiocarbon*, 24: 194–213.

HÅKANSSON, S. (1983) University of Lund Radiocarbon Dates XVI. *Radiocarbon*, 25: 875–891.

HÅKANSSON, S. (1984) University of Lund Radiocarbon Dates XVII. *Radiocarbon*, 26: 392–411.

HIGGS, E.S. and VITA-FINZI, C. (1972) Prehistoric economies: a territorial approach. In E.S. Higgs (ed.), *Papers in Economic Prehistory*. Cambridge, University Press: 27–36.

HUSS-ASHMORE, R.A., GOODMAN, A.H. and ARMELAGOS, G.J. (1982) Nutritional inference from paleopathology. In M.B. Schiffer (ed.), *Advances in Archaeological Method and Theory*, 5: 395–474.

ISERMANN, K. (1981) Uptake of stable strontium by plants and effects on plant growth. In S.C. Skoryna (ed.), *Handbook of Stable Strontium*. New York, Plenum

JOCHIM, M. (1976) *Hunter-Gatherer Subsistence and Settlement. A Predictive Model*. New York, Academic Press.

KATZENBERG, M.A. (1984) *Chemical Analysis of Prehistoric Human Bone from Five Temporally Distinct Populations in Southern Ontario* (Archaeological Survey of Canada, Paper 129). Ottawa, National Museum of Man, Mercury Series.

KAVANAGH, M. (1979) *Strontium in Bone as a Dietary Indicator*. Unpublished M.A. thesis, University of Wisconsin, Madison.

KEENE, A. (1981) *Prehistoric Foraging in a Temperate Forest: a Linear Programming Model*. New York, Academic Press.

KEY, P. (1980) Evolutionary trends in femoral sexual dimorphism from the Mesolithic to the late Middle Ages in Europe. *American Journal of Physical Anthropology*, 52: 244.

KLEPINGER, L.L. (1984) Nutritional assessment from bone. *Annual Reviews in Anthropology*, 13: 75–96.

LAMBERT, J.B., SZPUNAR, C.B. and BUIKSTRA, J.E. (1979) Chemical analysis of excavated human bone from Middle and Late Woodland sites. *Archaeometry*, 21: 115–129.

LAMBERT, J.B., VLASAK, S.M., THOMETZ, A.C. and BUIKSTRA, J.E. (1982) A comparative study of the chemical analysis of ribs and femurs in Woodland populations. *American Journal of Physical Anthropology*, 59: 289–294.

LAMBERT, J.B., SIMPSON, S.V., SZPUNAR, C.B. and BUIKSTRA, J.E. (1985) Bone diagenesis and dietary analysis. *Journal of Human Evolution*, 14: 477–482.

LARSSON, L. (1982) De aldsta gurarna. *Gotlandskt Arkiv 1982*: 7–14

LARSSON, L. (1984a) The Skateholm Project: a late Mesolithic settlement and cemetery complex at a southern Swedish Bay. *Meddelanden från Lunds universitets historiska museum* 1983–84: 5–38.

LARSSON, L. (1984b) Skateholmsprojektet. På spåren efter gravsedsförändringar, ceremoniplaster och tama rävar. *Limhamniana* 1984: 49–84.

LEONE, M.P. and PALKOVICH, A.M. (1985) Ethnographic inference and analogy in analyzing prehistoric diets. In R.I. Gilbert, Jr and J.H. Mielke (eds), *The Analysis of Prehistoric Diets*. Orlando, Academic Press: 423–431.

LYMAN, R.L. (1982) Archaeofaunas and subsistence studies. In M.B. Schiffer (ed.), *Advances in Archaeological Method and Theory*, 5: 331–393.

MARTIN, D.L., GOODMAN, A.H. and ARMELAGOS, G.J. (1985) Skeletal pathologies as indicators of quality and quantity of diet. In R.I. Gilbert, Jr and J.H. Mielke (eds), *The Analysis of Prehistoric Diets*. Orlando, Academic Press: 227–279.

MEIKLEJOHN, C., SCHENTAG, C., VENEMA, A. and KEY, P. (1984) Socioeconomic change and patterns of pathology and variation in the Mesolithic and Neolithic of western Europe: some suggestions. In M.N. Cohen and G.J. Armelagos (eds), *Paleopathology at the Origins of Agriculture*. Orlando, Academic Press: 75–100.

MOLNAR, S. (1971) Human tooth wear, tooth function and cultural variability. *American Journal of Physical Anthropology*, 34: 175–189.

NELSON, B., DeNIRO, M.J., SCHOENINGER, M.J. and DePAOLO, D.J. (1983) Strontium isotope evidence for diagenetic alteration of bone: consequences for diet reconstruction. *Bulletin of the Geological Society of America*, 95: 652.

NEWELL, R.R. (1970) *The Mesolithic Affinities and Typological Relations of the Dutch Bandkeramik Flint Industry*. Unpublished Ph.D thesis, University of London.

NOE-NYGAARD, N. (1983) The importance of aquatic resources to Mesolithic man at inland sites in Denmark. In C. Grigson and J. Clutton-Brock (eds), *Animals and Archaeology: 2. Shell Middens, Fishes and Birds*. Oxford, British Archaeological Reports (International Series) S183: 124–141.

O'LEARY, M.H. (1981) Carbon isotope fractionation in plants. *Phytochemistry*, 20: 553.

PARKER, R.B. and TOOTS, H. (1970) Minor elements in fossil bone. *Bulletin of the Geological Society of America*, 81: 925–932.

PARKER, R.B. and TOOTS, H. (1980) Trace elements in bones as paleobiological indicators. In A.K. Behrensmeyer and A.P. Hill (eds), *Fossils in the Making*. Chicago, University Press: 197–207.

PARMALEE, P.W. (1985) Identification and interpretation of archaeologically derived animal remains. In R.I. Gilbert, Jr and J.H. Mielke (eds), *The Analysis of Prehistoric Diets*. Orlando, Academic Press: 61–95.

PERSSON, O. and PERSSON, E. (1984) *Anthropological Report on the Mesolithic Graves from Skateholm, Southern Sweden. I. Excavation Seasons 1980–1982*. Lund, Institute of Archaeology Report Series no. 21.

PERZIGIAN, A.J. (1977) Teeth as tools for prehistoric studies. In R.L. Blakely (ed.), *Biocultural Adaptation in Prehistoric America*. Athens (Georgia), University of Georgia Press.

PITTS, M. (1979) Hides and antlers: a new look at the gatherer-hunter site of Star Carr. *World Archaeology*, 11: 32–42.

POWELL, M.L.(1985) The analysis of dental wear and caries for dietary reconstruction. In R.I. Gilbert, Jr and J.H. Mielke (eds), *The Analysis of Prehistoric Diets*. Orlando, Academic Press: 307–337.

PRICE, T.D. (1978) Mesolithic subsistence–settlement systems in the Netherlands. In P.A. Mellars (ed.), *The Early Postglacial Settlement of Northern Europe*. London, Duckworth: 81–113.

PRICE, T.D. (1982) Willow tales and dog smoke. *Quarterly Review of Archaeology*, 3(1): 4–7.

PRICE, T.D. and KAVANAGH, M. (1981) Bone composition and the reconstruction of diet: examples from the Midwestern United States. *Mid-continent Journal of Archaeology*, 7: 61–79.

PRICE, T.D., SCHOENINGER, M.J. and ARMELAGOS, G.J. (1985) Bone chemistry and past behavior: an overview. *Journal of Human Evolution*, 14: 419–448.

PRICE, T.D., SWICK, R.W. and CHASE, E.P. (1986) Bone chemistry and prehistoric diet: strontium studies of laboratory rats. *American Journal of Physical Anthropology*, 70: 365–375.

RHEINGOLD, A.L., HUES, S. and COHEN, M.N. (1983) Strontium and zinc content in bones as an indication of diet. *Journal of Chemical Education*, 60: 233–234.

ROSENTHAL, H.L., EVES, M.M. and COCHRAN, O.A. (1970) Common strontium of mineralized tissues from marine and sweet water animals. *Comparative Biochemistry and Physiology*, 32: 445–450.

ROSE, J.C., CONDON, K.W. and GOODMAN, A.H. (1985) Diet and dentition: developmental disturbances. In R.I. Gilbert, Jr and J.H. Mielke (eds), *The Analysis of Prehistoric Diets*. Orlando, Academic Press: 281–305.

ROZOY, J-G. (1978) *Les Derniers Chasseurs. L'Epipaléolithique en France et en Belgique* (Bulletin de la Société archéologique champenoise, numéro spécial). Charleville, J-G. Rozoy.

SCHOENINGER, M.J. (1979) *Dietary Reconstruction at Chalcatzingo, a Formative Period Site in Morelos, Mexico*. Ann Arbor, University of Michigan Museum of Anthropology, Technical Report 9.

SCHOENINGER, M.J. (1982) Diet and the evolution of modern human form in the Middle East. *American Journal of Physical Anthropology*, 51: 295–310.

SCHOENINGER, M.J., DeNIRO, M.J. and TAUBER, H. (1983) ^{15}N/^{14}N ratios of bone collagen reflect marine and terrestrial components of prehistoric human diet. *Science*, 220: 1381–1383.

SCHOENINGER, M.J. and DeNIRO, M.J. (1984) Nitrogen and carbon isotopic composition of bone collagen from marine and terrestrial animals. *Geochimica et Cosmochimica Acta*, 48: 625–639.

SCHROEDER, H.A., NASON, A.P. and TIPTON, I.H. (1972) Essential metals in man: strontium and barium. *Journal of Chronic Diseases*, 25: 491–517.

SILLEN, A. (1981) Strontium and diet at Hayonim Cave. *American Journal of Physical Anthropology*, 56: 131–137.

SILLEN, A. and KAVANAGH, M. (1982) Strontium and paleodietary research: a review. *Yearbook of Physical Anthropology*, 25: 67–90.

SILLEN, A. and SMITH, P. (1984) Weaning patterns are reflected in strontium–calcium ratios of juvenile skeletons. *Journal of Archaeological Science*, 11: 237–245.

SMITH, C.E., Jr (1985) Recovery and processing of plant remains. In R.I. Gilbert, Jr and J.H. Mielke (eds), *The Analysis of Prehistoric Diets*. Orlando, Academic Press: 97–125.

SNYDER, W.S., COOK, M.J., KARHUSEN, L.R., NASSET, E.S., HOWELLS, G.P. and TIPTON, I.H. (1964) *Report of the Task Group on Reference Man*. Oxford, Pergamon Press.

SOWDEN, E.M. and STITCH, S.R. (1957) Trace elements in human tissue. *Biochemistry Journal*, 67: 104–109.

TANAKA, G.I., KAWAMURA, H. and NOMURA, E. (1981) Reference Japanese Man – II: Distribution of strontium in the skeleton and in the mass of mineralized bone. *Health Physics*, 40: 601–614.

TAUBER, H. (1981) ^{13}C evidence for dietary habits of prehistoric man in Denmark. *Nature*, 292: 332–333.

TOOTS, H. and VOORHIES, M.R. (1965) Strontium in fossil bones and the reconstruction of food chains. *Science*, 149: 854–855.

TROLLE-LASSEN, T. (1984) A preliminary report on the archaeological and zoological evidence of fish exploitation from a submerged site in Mesolithic Denmark. In N. Desse-Berset (ed.), *2ᵉ Rencontres d'Archéoichtyologie*. Paris, Centre National de la Recherche Scientifique, Notes et Monographies Techniques no. 16: 133–143.

TUREKIAN, K.K. and KULP, J.L. (1956) Strontium content of human bone. *Science*, 124: 405–407.

VOGEL, J.C. and VAN DER MERWE, N.J. (1977) Isotopic evidence for early maize cultivation in New York State. *American Antiquity*, 42: 238–242.

WESSEN, G., RUDDY, F.H., GUSTAFSON, C.E. and IRWIN, H. (1977) Characterization of archaeological bone by neutron activation analysis. *Archaeometry*, 19: 200–205.

WHEELER, A. (1978) Why were there no fish remains at Star Carr? *Journal of Archaeological Science*, 5: 85–90.

WHITE, E.M. and HANNUS, L.A. (1983) Chemical weathering of bone in archaeological sites. *American Antiquity*, 48: 316–322.

WHITE, T.E. (1953) A method of calculating the dietary percentages of various food animals utilized by aboriginal peoples. *American Antiquity*, 18: 396–398.

ZIEGLER, A.C. (1973) *Inference from Prehistoric Faunal Remains*. Addison–Wesley Module in Anthropology no. 43. Reading (Massachussets), Addison–Wesley Publishing Company.

Bird-Foraging Patterns in the Mesolithic

Caroline Grigson

Abstract

Analysis of the abundance of various bird species in relation to their rank order reveals two main types of bird foraging, specialized and generalized.

The curves produced by plotting the logarithm of abundance against rank order for specialized foraging are steep and concentrated at the left of the graph; that is, numerous bird bones are present but they represent only a few species. The curves produced by generalized foraging are spread over many species and are gently concave. The concavity indicates a slight degree of preference for some of the species. A sharply concave curve suggests a dual foraging strategy, i.e. one that has both a specialized and a generalized component.

Specialized foraging involves the systematic exploitation of one, or a few, spatially concentrated species and is always markedly seasonal. One coastal site was so specialized that only a single species (whooper swan) was present. As the site contained only a few mammal bones it can be considered as a camp for the extraction of swans. Specialized bird foraging is not confined to coastal sites; one inland site seems to have been specialized for the procurement of white-tailed eagles, probably when they were breeding.

Generalized foraging involves a wider range of species which may, or may not, have been seasonally concentrated. It may sometimes have involved the systematically-organized wholesale slaughter of birds, but was probably usually opportunistic.

While both coastal and inland sites may have either specialized or generalized bird-catching strategies, some (so far identified only on the coast) have dual strategies, with a generalized as well as a specialized component, which may have been practised at different times of the year.

INTRODUCTION

Bird bones from prehistoric sites are a potential source of a great deal of information about past human behaviour. This is because birds have precise environmental requirements and behavioural traits that are characteristic for each species and vary greatly from one species to another. In order to procure birds, people have to make quite specific decisions involving modification of their own daily and annual behaviour patterns. Bird behaviour has been, and is being, extremely well studied, and so bird bones of known date and place that can be identified to taxon carry (unlike flints and potsherds) a great deal of *intrinsic* behavioural information, and if they can be analyzed in numerical terms their potential is enormous.

In spite of this, bird bones from European sites have mostly been studied only on a presence and absence basis and as seasonal indicators. Even when the bones are enumerated, analysts rarely comment on the significance of the numerical variations. Two important exceptions are the reports by Olsen (1967) on the bones from sites on the Varanger fjord in Norway, and by Møhl (1978) who showed that the Mesolithic site of Aggersund on the Limfjord in Denmark was a specialized camp site for the procurement of whooper swans.

In northern Europe bird populations can be divided into various types: resident species, summer visitors (usually breeding), winter visitors, and spring and autumn migrants, all living in particular habitats at particular times of the year. Obviously, care has to be taken when applying modern attributes of birds to the past; it is unlikely that the basic behaviour patterns have changed, but habitat changes (largely anthropogenic) and hunting pressures have led to the restriction of the range of a few species and to the extinction of a few others. Some birds have been introduced to new areas by man. Climatic change will also affect geographical distribution, but has been relatively minor since the Boreal period.

Apart from seasonal attributes many birds have quite specific environmental preferences, some species being confined to low shores, others to high rocky shores, woods, moorlands, wetlands, and so on. Many may occupy more than one habitat, and may breed in one type of habitat and then move to another in the winter. For example, many seabirds breed on inaccessible, high cliff faces but are pelagic for the rest of the year, some even out of sight of land. Whooper swans breed in swampy and marshy tundra in northernmost Scandinavia and Russia, but overwinter in Britain and in areas near the North Sea, the Baltic, the Adriatic, the Black Sea and the Caspian, mostly in sheltered coastal waters and estuaries. Many ducks breed in inland wetlands, but move, often only short distances, to the seashore in winter.

Another attribute which is important for human foraging strategies is that birds vary in their degree of gregariousness. Many sea birds breed in very dense colonies but are dispersed at other times of the year. Swans, geese and ducks tend to be solitary when breeding, but gregarious at all other times. Other factors, such as ease of access for people to areas used by birds, and the actual number of birds available, obviously affect the degree to which they are exploited. Some birds are more useful than others and selection will be made on the basis of size, palatability and general utility to the people concerned. Some species may be preyed upon chiefly for their eggs. Irrational factors may also influence the choice of species.

NUMBERS OF BONES AND NUMBERS OF SPECIES

When analyzing the bird bone identifications made by Bramwell (Bramwell and Grigson, forthcoming) from the late Atlantic Mesolithic middens on the island of Oronsay in the Inner Hebrides, I realized that different species were represented by very different numbers of bones. It became clear that they could be divided into two groups – one consisting of only a few species with a large number of bones per species, and the other consisting of many species – each represented by only a few bones. I then looked at behavioural characteristics of the species in the two groups and found that in the first they were highly seasonal and colonial at the time of year when they would have been present in the vicinity. Those in the second group were either less markedly seasonal or were resident, and, if colonial, were less so than those in the first group. I surmised that a specialized, systematic foraging strategy would be needed to procure the birds in the first group, and that those in the second group were obtained in a more random, generalized and opportunistic fashion.

I then tried to analyze the bird bone data from other Mesolithic sites in the same manner, to test whether the hypothesis of systematic and opportunistic foraging was tenable elsewhere. It quickly became apparent that, while all the data could be analyzed in those terms, the criteria employed were rather subjective and it was uncertain to what extent the types of distribution could be attributed to chance. What was needed was a more rigid mathematical analysis of the numbers of individuals per species, so that quantitative criteria for the recognition of those strategies could be established. Similar parameters are utilized in present-day ecological studies when faunas are analyzed in terms of the relationship between the numbers of individuals and the numbers of species to which they belong.

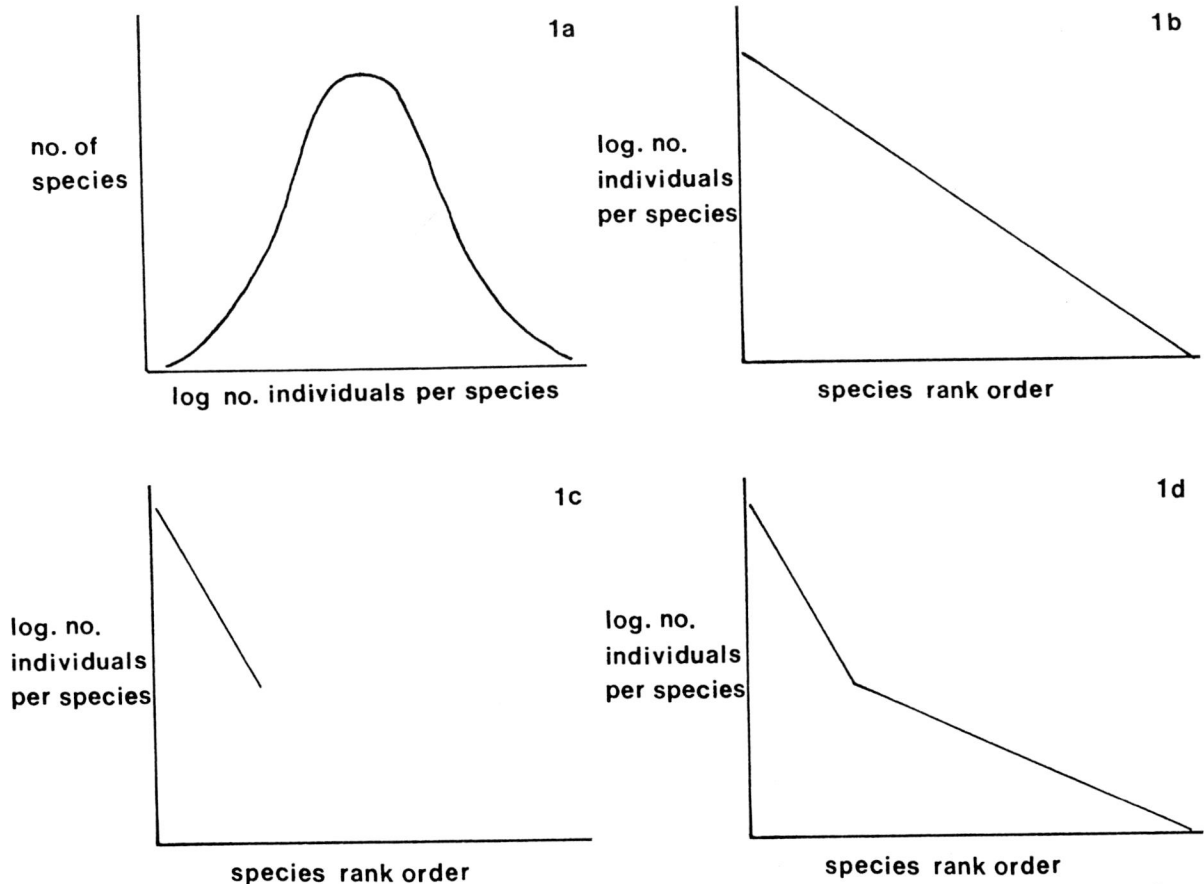

Figure 1   *a.* the log-normal curve produced by plotting the number of species in a fauna against logarithms of their frequencies; *b.* the log frequency of each species plotted against its rank order (the resulting line will be straight if the sample is random or generalized); *c.* the concentrated distribution produced by specialized extraction; *d.* the sharply concave curve produced by a combination of generalized and specialized extraction.

61

The analytical methods employed by ecologists have been usefully summarized by Southwood (1966).

In nature the abundance of species within a fauna (i.e. all the animals in a particular area or habitat) is usually normally distributed, and the same is true of random samples taken from that fauna, except that as samples are unlikely to contain rare species the curve may be truncated at the left. Small samples contain smaller numbers of species than large samples, but the increment of species added with increasing sample size is not arithmetically proportional to sample size; because of the differential abundance of each species larger and larger samples are needed for the addition of each rare species, and the distribution of the number of individuals per species follows a log-normal curve (Southwood 1966), as in *Fig. 1a*.

If the log of the number of individuals per species in such a sample is plotted against the rank order of the species, the resulting graph is frequently a straight line, as shown in *Fig. 1b* (cf. Southwood 1966: 351).

It would seem likely that an archaeological sample of animal remains (in this case of bird bones) would behave in the same way, provided that it was random. Indeed, one would expect a generalized sample to describe the same distribution as that in *Fig. 1b* with the numbers of bone finds plotted on a log scale on the *y*-axis. The assumption is that each bone find (i.e. each single bone or each spatially associated collection of bones) represents one individual bird in any open site known to have been occupied for more than a few days.

A specialized sample, that is one which concentrated on the extraction of only a few species, would be concentrated towards the left and would not contain any uncommon species (*Fig. 1c*).

If a sample comprised both a generalized and a specialized component, one would expect a sharply concave curve compounded of both elements (*Fig. 1d*).

I suggest that the random generalized pattern would be produced by opportunistic foraging, and the specialized pattern by systematic foraging. A strongly concave curve would indicate that both types of foraging were being practised.

The rest of this paper consists of analyses of bird bones from various sites in order to test whether the hypothesis of opportunistic and systematic foraging can be maintained and demonstrated on the samples available. The samples chosen are from inland and coastal sites of the Danish Mesolithic. Not only does Denmark have a large number of sites, but also the fauna of most of them has been published in numerical detail ever since, and beginning with, the pioneering work of Herluf Winge in the late nineteenth and early twentieth centuries.

COASTAL DENMARK

The coast of Denmark is a complicated interdigitation of land and sea which, with its many islands and islets, means that the coastline is very long compared to the terrestrial area. In northern Jutland this ratio was even greater during the marine transgressions of the Atlantic period (*Fig. 2A*). The coast is, and was, characterized by low-lying land and very shallow surrounding sea. This structural complexity of islets, swamps, salt marshes, coastal meadows, tidal flats, lagoons, and shallow water gives high organic productivity and differentiated foraging possibilities (Ferdinand 1980). Of course, people foraging on the shore can also use the adjacent terrestrial areas.

Danish coasts and islands have colonies of breeding seabirds, especially eider ducks, common gulls, herring gulls, various terns and, in the past, the now extinct great auk. Large flocks of waders, ducks, geese, swans, and coots pass the winter in sheltered coastal waters. Some of them breed in inland Denmark; others are winter visitors breeding elsewhere.

The only cliffs of any height in Denmark are on small islands near Bornholm, *c.* 130 km east of Zealand in the southern Baltic. They are the only places with colonies of the cliff-breeding seabirds, common guillemots and razorbills, which migrate out of the Baltic through the Øresund and the Kattegat into the North Sea in autumn, and return in late winter for breeding. The presence of their bones in the Ertebølle sites of eastern Zealand suggests that gannets may have done the same in the past.

All the surviving coastal sites of Mesolithic Denmark belong to the Atlantic period, as almost the entire Boreal coast was flooded in the subsequent marine transgressions and is too low to have been exposed by more recent regressions.

Foraging patterns can only be established for sites with a numerically adequate sample of bird bones whose numbers have been recorded species by species. These are Havnø, Klintesø, Ølby Lyng, Aggersund, and Ertebølle.

Havnø

In the Atlantic period Havnø (Madsen *et al.* 1900) was a small island at the north of the Mariager fjord in north-east Jutland (*Fig. 2A*). All the birds taken (Winge, in Madsen *et al.* 1900) were either winter or autumn visitors with a small number of resident species. *Fig. 3a* shows a clear concentration on velvet scoters and whooper swans, suggesting systematic exploitation, with a small number of other birds exploited in a generalized, opportunistic way. The dual nature of avian exploitation is shown by the strongly concave regression line. The seasonal differentiation is so strongly biased in favour of winter visitors that it is likely that this was purely a winter

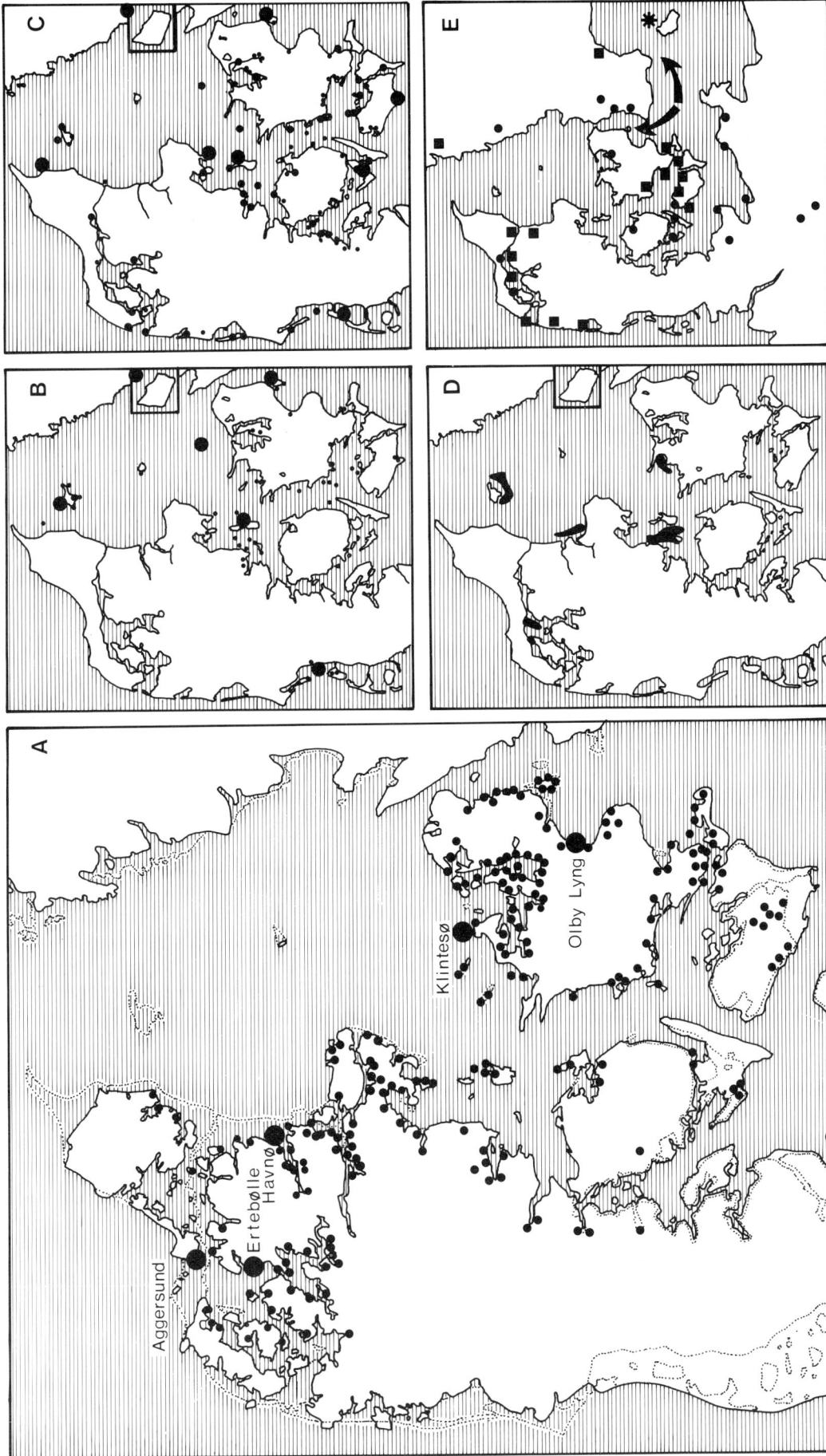

Figure 2 The geographical relationship between Ertebølle sites and modern areas of abundance of particular bird species in Denmark. *A*. the distribution of Ertebølle sites: *large dots* are sites with detailed bird bone reports; *small dots* are sites without; the *continuous line* marks the position of the maximum transgression of the sea in the Atlantic period; the *dotted line* marks the present shoreline. *B*. Eider duck (*Somateria mollissima*): *dots* indicate present breeding grounds; *large dots* are major breeding grounds. Klintesø was on a small islet, not far from the present eider breeding ground of Nekselø; it is likely that both eider ducks and the extinct great auk (*Alca impennis*) bred there and on the chain of islands that preceded Sjællands Odde immediately to the west of Klintesø. *C*. Herring gull (*Larus argentatus*): *dots* mark present breeding grounds (note the propinquity of Ertebølle to one of them). *D*. Velvet scoter (*Melanitta fusca*): moulting areas are shown in black (note the propinquity of Havnø and Ertebølle to two of them). *E*. Whooper swan (*Cygnus cygnus*): *dots* and *squares* mark present wintering grounds; and Guillemot (*Uria aalge*): the *asterisk* marks the breeding ground on an islet north of Bornholm – note the propinquity of Aggersund, Havnø and Ertebølle to two of the 14 areas designated as 'Areas of International Importance' for whooper swans (*black squares*). The site of Ølby Lyng is close to the migration routes of guillemots in and out of the Baltic (*arrow*). (*Source*: Ferdinand 1980)

63

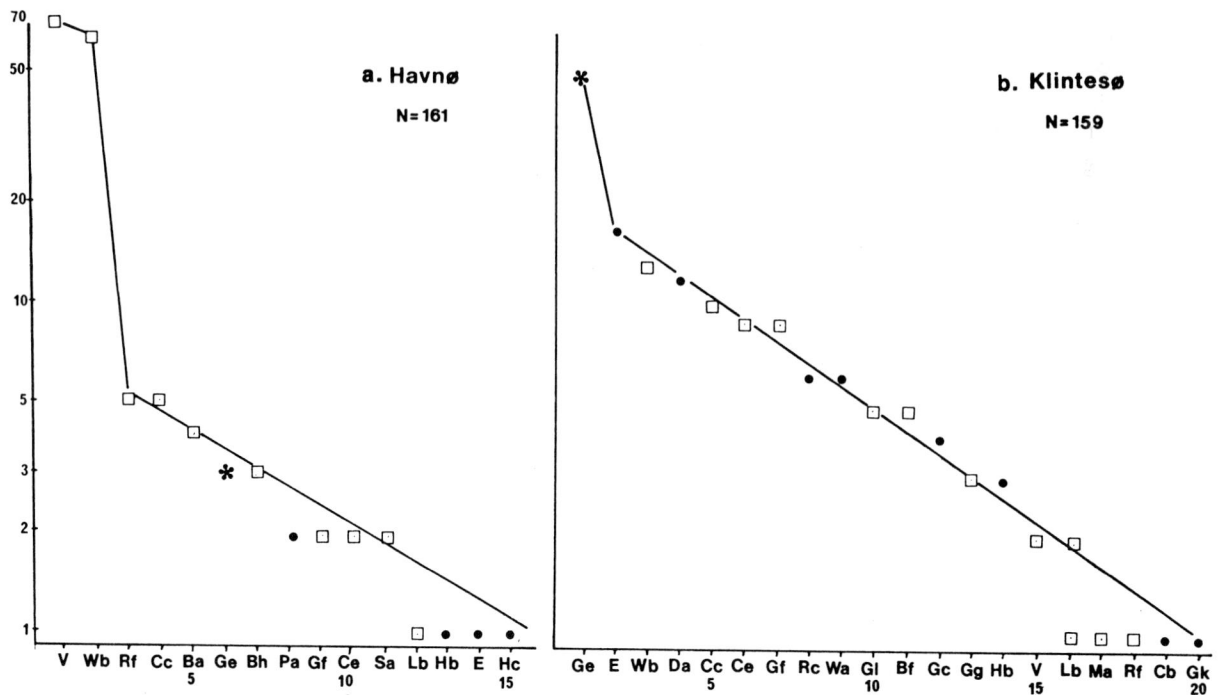

Figure 3   *a*. Havnø; *b*. Klintesø – log abundance of species against rank order (*source*: Winge, in Madsen *et al.* 1900). Both these coastal sites have a specialized as well as a generalized bird-foraging component. At Havnø both types of bird-catching activity seem to have taken place in autumn and winter with specialized foraging of velvet scoters and whooper swans. At Klintesø there is generalized activity in the winter coupled with specialized foraging for great auks in the summer. *Squares* denote species that are coastal in winter, as well as winter visitors; *dots* denote resident species. The letters on the *x*-axis are symbols for the names of birds (*Key*: see Appendix).

site with the resident birds also being taken in the winter.

Velvet scoters are not obvious targets for any hunting strategy. They visit Danish coastal waters in winter and, though gregarious, are not particularly numerous or concentrated. However, about 60,000 are present in Denmark during the moulting period (Ferdinand 1980) from late July to early October, and for 3–4 weeks during this time the birds are completely flightless (Cramp *et al.* 1977). When moulting in Denmark velvet scoters are confined to five small areas (*Fig. 2D*), one of which is the sea just to the west of Havnø (Joensen 1973; Ferdinand 1980) which supports about 20,000 of them; so it seems likely that velvet scoters would have been taken when moulting.

Between 5000 and 11,000 whooper swans winter annually in the Danish wetlands, mainly on coastal waters and on the Limfjord in Jutland (*Fig. 2E*). Most arrive in late October and leave by the end of March (Ferdinand 1980). They are gregarious except when nesting and, being large and conspicuous, would be an obvious target. Møhl (1978) suggests that they were hunted mainly for their skins, but they are also highly palatable and their wing feathers may have had many uses. The area around Havnø is one of fourteen in Denmark designated as 'Areas of International Importance' for whooper swans.

It is significant that even though eider ducks are the most common bird of the area (Ferdinand 1980), as moulters in late July to early October (Joensen

1974), they were scarcely preyed upon, only one bone of eider duck having been found at Havnø.

Bones of pig, roe deer, red deer and aurochs were found at Havnø, but the island was too small to have supported populations of terrestrial mammals (Rowley-Conwy 1983); so their carcasses must have been imported. The mammal bones were not well quantified, but the birds seem to have formed a significant proportion of the faunal remains. The mammal list also includes many grey seal (*Halichoerus grypus*) bones. Rowley-Conwy's map (1983: fig. 10.7) shows a string of barrier islands about 10 km east and seaward of the site, and it is likely that grey seals bred there in January and February as they used to do on the island of Anholt in the Kattegat (Møhl 1970*b*). Their presence was probably the main reason for the occupation of Havnø, with swans and scoters being obtained on the sea between the barrier islands and the site.

Klintesø

The site of Klintesø (Madsen *et al.* 1900) is on the north coast of Zealand, just to the east of a long, narrow peninsula – Sjællands Odde (*Fig. 2A*). In the Atlantic period the site was on the shore, close to an islet, and the peninsula itself was broken into a string of small islands.

The shape of the regression line (*Fig. 3b*) is very similar to those from Havnø and Ølby Lyng, its sharp concavity suggesting a dual specialized and generalized strategy for obtaining birds. In contrast

64

to those sites, however, the birds systematically exploited (certainly great auks and probably also eider ducks) would have been obtained in the summer when breeding, and indeed there are bones of juvenile great auks in the sample (Winge, in Madsen *et al.* 1900). Great auks have probably been extinct since the prehistoric period in Denmark, but would have nested on small islands around the coast.

In Denmark eider ducks also breed only on islands. The nearest breeding area today is at Nekselø (Ferdinand 1980) 25 km to the south west (*Fig. 2B*), and there is no doubt that eider would have bred on the Sjællands Odde when this was insulated. The presence of common seal (*Phoca vitulina*) bones (Møhl 1970*b*) suggests that the site was used in August and September (Joensen *et al.* 1976). Although the six resident species could have been exploited in the summer, the absence of other summer visitors and the presence of 13 winter species suggests that opportunistic foraging was confined to the winter, perhaps taking place at the same season as the exploitation of grey seals whose bones were present in the midden and which used to breed in Denmark in February and March.

Ølby Lyng

The site of Ølby Lyng (Møhl 1970*a*) is on the east coast of Zealand just to the south of the Øresund which joins the Baltic to the Kattegat and so to the North Sea (*Fig. 2A*). Animals moving in or out of the Baltic have to follow this route and marine mammals – harp seals (*Phoca groenlandica*), grey seals and probably porpoises – as well as guillemots were exploited from Ølby Lyng.

Of the 232 auk bones, only 15 were definitely of common guillemot (*Uria aalge*); the rest were probably of the same species, but razorbills (*Alca torda*), whose bones are often difficult to distinguish from those of the guillemot, may also have been present. Both species migrate out through the Øresund in autumn, returning in late winter to breed on islets near to Bornholm. The presence of 23 bones of gannet (*Sula bassana*), which is not found in the Baltic today, indicates that it may have bred there in the past.

Fig. 4a suggests that at Ølby Lyng there was intense systematic exploitation of guillemots and perhaps of gannets; this would have taken place

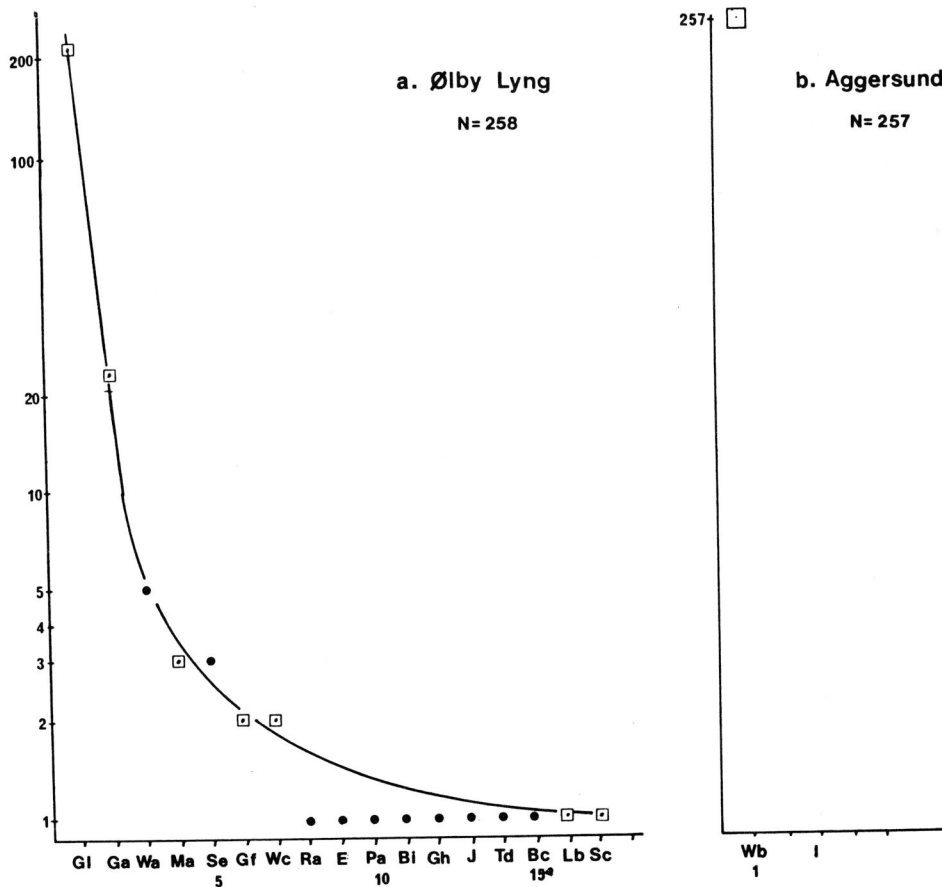

Figure 4   *a.* Ølby Lyng (*source*: Møhl 1970*a*); *b.* Aggersund (*source*: Møhl 1978) – log abundance of species against rank order. Ølby Lyng is a coastal site with a specialized as well as a generalized bird-foraging component; birding seems to have been confined to the winter with specialized foraging of guillemots and gannets. Aggersund is a highly specialized camp site for the extraction of a single species (whooper swan) which is only present in Denmark as a gregarious winter visitor. *Squares* denote species that are coastal in winter, as well as winter visitors; *dots* denote resident species. The letters on the *x*-axis are symbols for the names of birds (*Key*: see Appendix).

when the birds were migrating in or out of the Baltic in autumn or winter (*Fig. 2E*). In addition there was a more generalized opportunistic exploitation of other birds, some of which would only have been present in the area in the winter. With six winter visitors to one summer visitor it seems likely that the exploitation of the resident species was confined to the winter.

A significant number of the mammal bones were of seals, mostly grey, but including a few harp seals. Grey seals are easiest to obtain when breeding in February and March, which they did until recently in Denmark on the island of Saltholm not far to the north of Ølby Lyng. Harp seals are northern animals which migrate to the Arctic in the summer to breed on the ice and disperse to the south in the winter. They only rarely come as far south as the North Sea, but their quite common occurrence in Danish archaeological sites (Møhl 1970*b*) suggests that they might have bred in the Baltic in the past. Whether breeding in the Baltic or not, they are strongly migratory and would have had to pass through the

Øresund to travel from the North Sea to the Baltic and vice versa, and would most probably have been in Danish waters only in the winter. Thus, faunal exploitation at Ølby Lyng was strongly centred on breeding grey seals, and on harp seals and guillemots, when migrating in and out of the Baltic.

Aggersund

All the 257 bird bones found at Aggersund (Møhl 1978) are of whooper swans (*Fig. 4b*). Aggersund is on the northern side of the Limfjord in northern Jutland and in Atlantic times was on the south-west corner of an island (*Fig. 2A*). It is close to an 'Area of International Importance' for whooper swans (*Fig. 2E*; Ferdinand 1980) and the Limfjord here is known for sea ducks, including velvet scoters (*Fig. 2D*). It is uncertain whether the mammals were obtained locally, on what was then a large island, or whether their remains represent food stocks imported into the site; but as swan bones outnumber all the mammal remains together and as no other birds were represented, it is clear that the site was highly

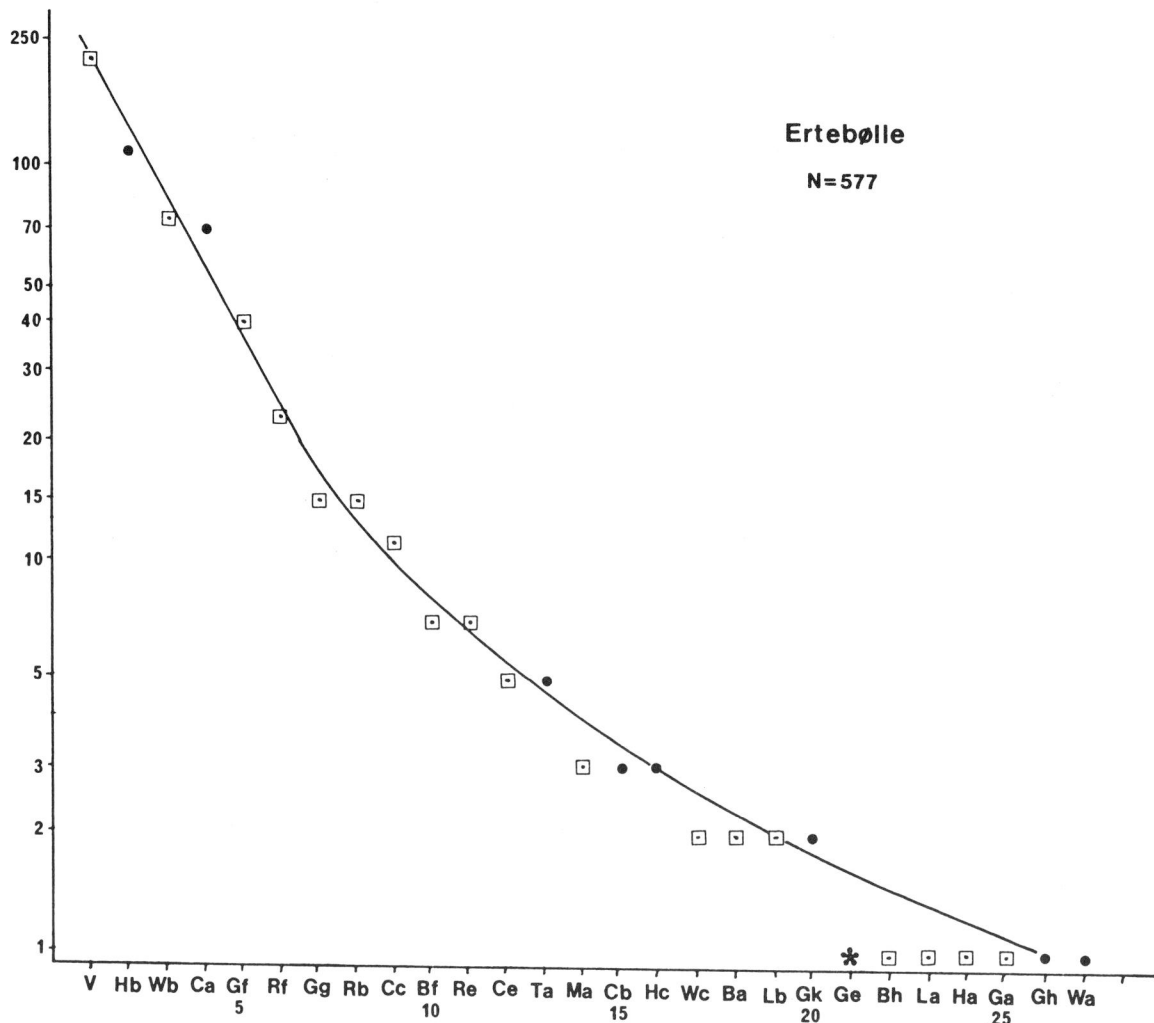

Figure 5 Ertebølle – log abundance of species against rank order (*source*: Winge, in Madsen *et al.* 1900). Bird foraging at this coastal site seems to have been generalized; the bird bones certainly indicate winter occupation, but birding in summer for nesting herring gulls cannot be excluded. *Squares* denote species that are coastal in winter, as well as winter visitors; *dots* denote resident species. The letters on the *x*-axis are symbols for the names of birds (*Key*: see Appendix).

specialized for the systematic exploitation of swans (Møhl 1978).

Ertebølle

Ertebølle (Madsen *et al.* 1900; Rowley-Conwy 1983) is a large midden a few kilometres south of Aggersund, on the edge of an inlet of the south side of the Limfjord (*Fig. 2A*). It has the largest number of identified bird bones (577 bones of 27 species). On a percentage basis one would suspect specialized extraction of velvet scoters and herring gulls, but the log plot (*Fig. 5*) shows that the regression line is a gentle, continuous curve that characterizes generalized foraging, in complete contrast to the specialized

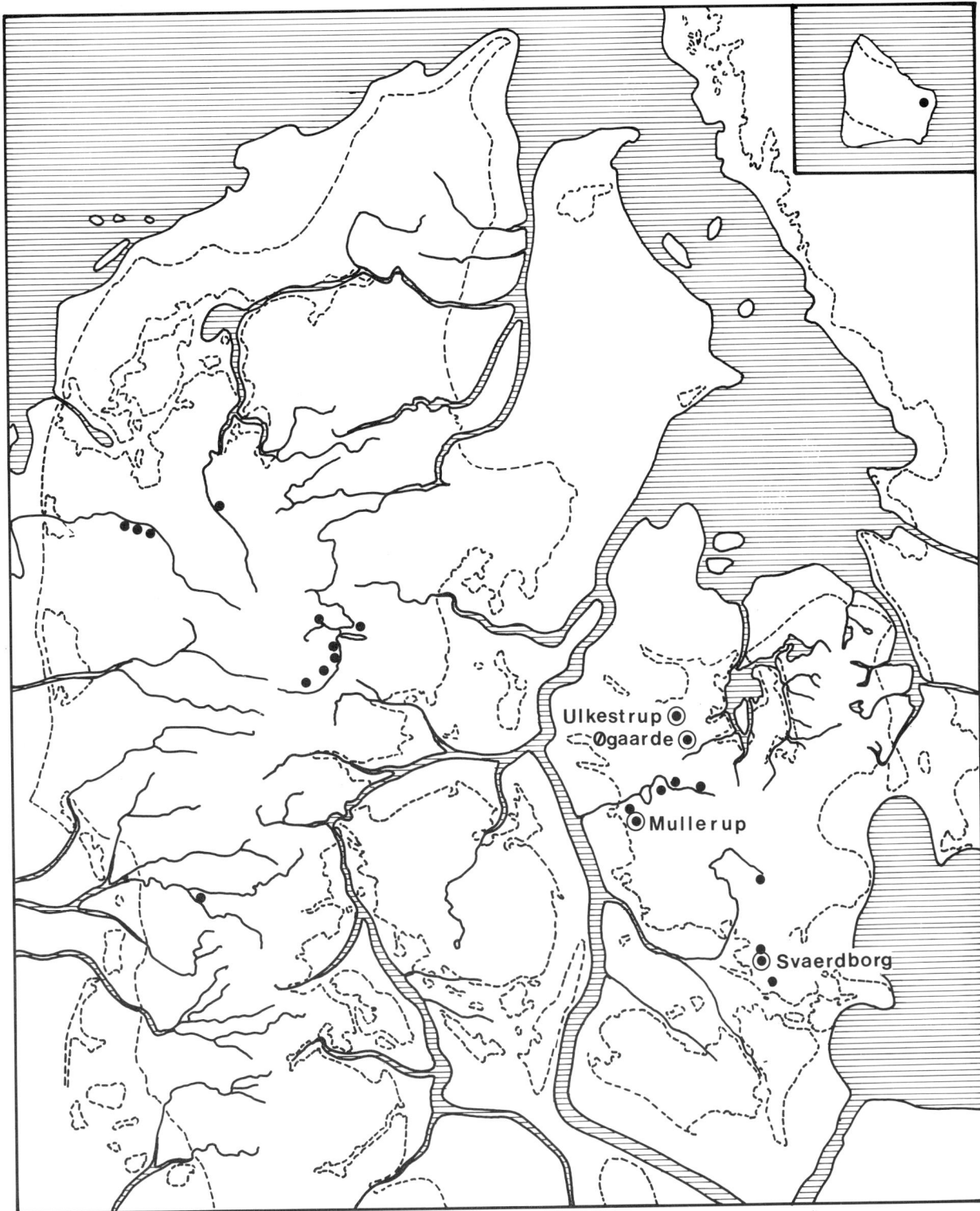

Figure 6   The distribution of Maglemosian sites in Denmark: *large dots* denote sites with detailed bone reports; *small dots* denote sites without. The *continuous line* marks the position of the coastline in the Boreal period; the *dotted line* is the present shore. After Brøndsted 1957.

systematic activity at Aggersund. Its concave nature suggests some preference for velvet scoters, herring gulls, whooper swans and capercaillies. Ertebølle is close to modern areas of abundance of scoters (*Fig. 2D*), gulls (*Fig. 2C*) and whooper swans (*Fig. 2E*). Velvet scoters and whooper swans would have been obtained in autumn or winter, but the main problem is whether or not the site was also utilized in the summer. Rowley-Conwy (1983) suggests that Ertebølle was a large base camp occupied all the year round, but there are almost no bones of summer-visiting birds to support this. However, herring gulls were taken in quite large numbers. They breed colonially on islets near to Ertebølle (Ferdinand 1980) and are more dispersed, but still present locally, outside the breeding season. It seems more likely that they would have been obtained in early summer than in winter, and the presence of much shed red deer antler could perhaps be taken as confirmation of summer occupation. Capercaillie would have been resident in the pine woods nearby and could have been obtained at any time of the year.

The significance of absolute numbers of bones on archaeological sites is very difficult to assess, as both the duration of occupation and the number of people who used the site are unknown. However, the large number of bird bones at Ertebølle and the fact that they were roughly equal in number to the bones of mammals suggests that birding was very important, and the birds may have been obtained, not on an opportunistic basis as one would expect from the generalized curve, but by some sort of large-scale, indiscriminate slaughter. As most of the species taken are aquatic birds that would have been living along the semi-estuarine flats of the Limfjord coast, it would have been practicable, for example, to have driven them into nets.

INLAND DENMARK

Although some inland sites are known from the Atlantic period, their fauna has not yet been published in detail; so, with one exception, the sites discussed here are from the Boreal period. The exception is Øgaarde, the occupation of which spans the entire Boreal and Atlantic periods ending at *c.* 4500 BP (E. Brinch Petersen, pers. comm.). All the sites are on the island of Zealand which, in the Boreal, was not an island but was attached to Scania; it was separated from the rest of Denmark and northern Germany only by a river draining the Ancylus Lake (Brøndsted 1957: 56; Clark 1975: 41; see *Fig. 6*).

In the Boreal period Zealand was covered by young, open, largely deciduous forest and had areas of swamp, bog and small lakes. In spite of local variations it was a far less varied environment than the coastline of the Atlantic period discussed above,

and it was one that could be considered to have been fine- rather than coarse-grained.

Many of the sites are situated on dry spots in bogs or beside lakes. There is stratigraphical evidence for winter flooding of some sites, and the bird remains usually indicate summer occupation (Clark 1975). Most seem to have been used for pike fishing as well as for procuring mammals. The sites with bird bone samples that are large enough to be analyzed in detail from the point of view of foraging patterns are Mullerup, Ulkestrup, Sværdborg I and Øgaarde.

Mullerup

Mullerup (Sarauw 1903) is in the Maglemose bog in western Zealand. It has high proportions of summer visitors and residents, includes the young of cormorants, kites and jays, and has very few bones of winter visitors (Winge 1903); it was undoubtedly a summer site. The gently concave regression line (*Fig. 7a*) indicates a generalized, opportunistic bird-foraging strategy. The two most numerous species are mute swan and mallard, both of which are resident and very common in Denmark today. There are many mute swan breeding sites in the Maglemose area and mallards breed all over inland Denmark (Ferdinand 1980). According to Joensen (1974) mute swans are common inland from April to September and mallards moult in the summer in most wetland habitats, usually in small flocks, but sometimes numbering several hundred, on large lakes and in densely-vegetated marshland.

Ulkestrup Lyng Øst

Ulkestrup is a lakeside site in the Aamose bog in western Zealand. Several factors, as well as bird bones, show that the site was occupied in the summer. It has a high proportion of summer visitors and breeding residents, and includes bones of the young of many species – garganeys, black kites, cormorants, bitterns, white-tailed eagles and coots (Richter 1982). Although the white-tailed eagle bred in Denmark in the last century, it is now only a winter visitor (Cramp *et al.* 1980). These finds and those at Sværdborg I (Winge 1919) prove its resident status in the Mesolithic.

The gently concave regression curve (*Fig. 7b*) is very similar to those at Mullerup and Sværdborg I, but here coots are the most numerous species, probably reflecting their natural abundance. Coots breed in the Aamose area today and are the second most abundant breeding bird of Denmark; in summer they live on all types of wetland, except the open sea (Ferdinand 1980), but in winter almost all coots move to areas of salt or brackish water (Joensen 1974).

Sværdborg I

The samples from the 1917 (Winge 1919) and 1943 (Aaris-Sørensen 1976) excavations are combined

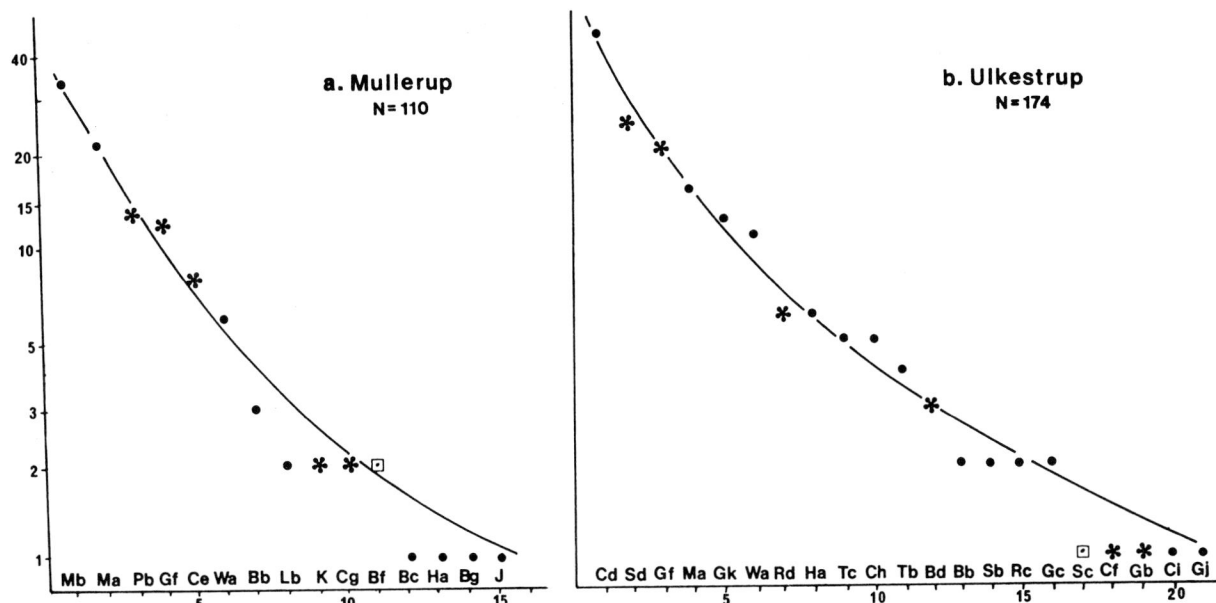

Figure 7   *a*. Mullerup (*source*: Winge 1903); *b*. Ulkestrup (*source*: Richter 1982) – log abundance of species against rank order. Bird foraging at both these inland sites seems to have been generalized. The *square* denotes the black-throated diver which is now a winter visitor, although it may have bred in Denmark in the past; *asterisks* denote summer visitors, as well as nesting species and others that spend the summer inland; *dots* denote resident species. The letters on the *x*-axis are symbols for the names of birds (*Key*: see Appendix).

here, but when considered separately the results are very similar.

The site is on a peninsula jutting into the Sværdborg bog in southern Zealand (Friis-Johansen

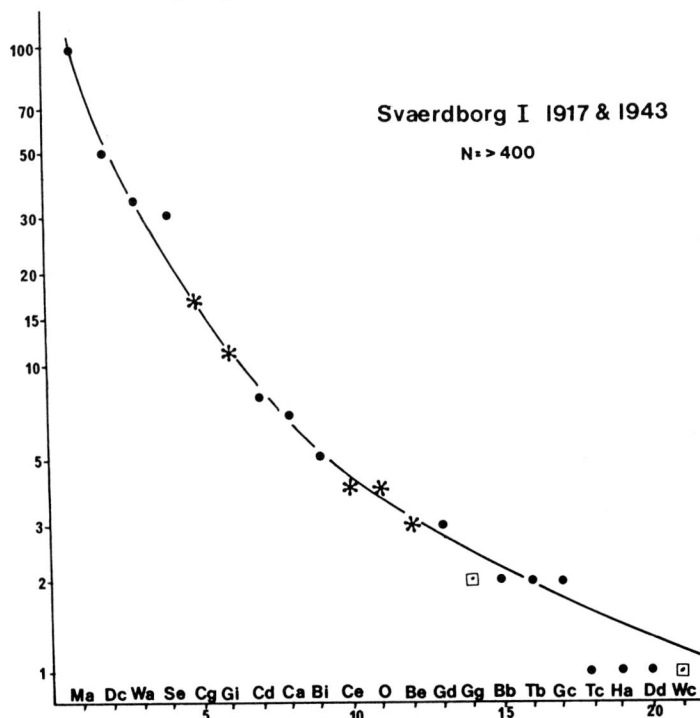

Figure 8   Sværdborg I – log abundance of species against rank order (*source*: Winge 1919; Aaris-Sørensen 1976). Bird foraging at this inland, summer site was generalized and very similar in pattern to that at Mullerup and Ulkestrup. The *squares* denote a winter visitor and a species that sometimes goes inland in winter; *asterisks* denote summer visitors as well as species that spend the summer inland; *dots* denote resident species. The letters on the *x*-axis are symbols for the names of birds (*Key*: see Appendix).

1919; Henriksen 1976). Many resident bird species are represented, but the high proportion of summer compared to winter visitors suggests utilization in the summer. The gently concave regression curve (*Fig. 8*) is similar to that at Mullerup and suggests a similar opportunistic bird-foraging strategy. There is a slight emphasis on mallard which reflects its status as the commonest duck and one of the most common breeding birds of Denmark (Aaris-Sørensen 1976; Ferdinand 1980). Bird bones formed only 5.7% of the total mammal and bird bone sample.

Øgaarde

Øgaarde is also in the Aamose bog (Mathiassen 1943). Although it is only a few kilometres away from Ulkestrup, its regression curve (*Fig. 9*) is completely different. Its steep slope and concentration to the left suggest a specialized, systematic foraging of one species (white-tailed eagle) with a very small opportunistic element, both probably taking place in the summer.

As already mentioned, white-tailed eagles were breeding birds in Zealand in the Mesolithic, and it is likely that these solitary or paired birds would have been easiest to procure when nesting in early summer. According to Clark (1948) they were probably valued primarily for the use of their pinion feathers for fletching arrows, but they are also highly palatable (Cott 1947).

Mammal bones far outnumber those of birds at Øgaarde (Degerbøl 1943); so it cannot be considered as a highly specialized extraction site for eagles in the way in which Aggersund was for swans (Møhl 1978).

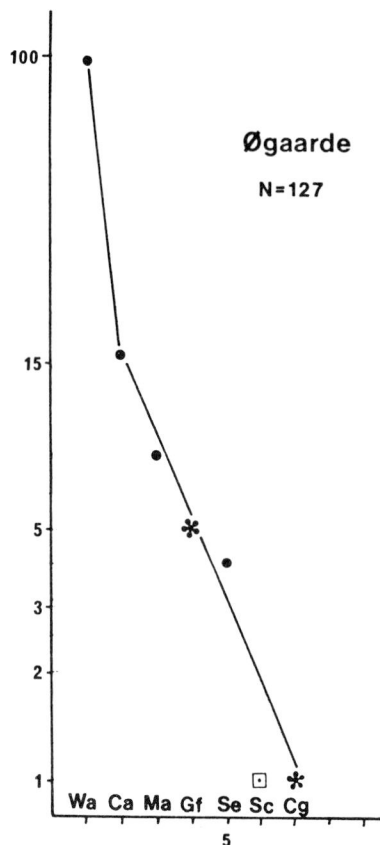

Figure 9 Øgaarde – log abundance of species against rank order (*source*: Degerbøl 1943). This was an inland, summer site with a specialized bird-foraging strategy that concentrated on white-tailed eagles, probably when they were nesting. The *square* denotes a winter visitor; *asterisks* denote summer visitors and those that go inland in summer; *dots* denote resident species. The letters on the *x*-axis are symbols for the names of birds (*Key*: see Appendix).

CONCLUSIONS

Specialized foraging

The high number of just a single species (whooper swan) at Aggersund shows that, as already suggested by Møhl (1978), avian foraging strategies can be very highly specialized. Indeed, Aggersund is best described as a camp for the seasonal extraction of whooper swans. Another site which is highly specialized is the inland site of Øgaarde in which white-tailed eagles (and just a few other species) were obtained in the summer. The other sites with a specialized component are all coastal, with velvet scoters and whooper swans in the autumn and winter at Havnø, great auks in the summer at Klintesø, and guillemots on winter passage at Ølby Lyng. All these species are gregarious at the time of the year when they would have been in the vicinity of the sites, but only great auks could be described as colonial. Great auks and white-tailed eagles seem to have been taken when breeding, velvet scoters when moulting, whooper swans in winter flocks, and guillemots in migratory flocks.

All these species, with the exception of white-tailed eagles, are highly seasonal. However, eagles are at their most vulnerable when breeding, and as their bones are numerous only in summer sites, their systematic exploitation was probably confined to the early summer.

Clearly, all these species would have been systematically exploited but, as argued below, a generalized exploitation policy could include a fairly organized, wholesale slaughter of birds (see below); so the term *specialized foraging* seems preferable.

Generalized foraging

Some coastal sites (such as Ertebølle) and some inland sites (such as Mullerup, Ulkestrup and Sværdborg I) can be shown to have had generalized strategies for obtaining birds. Most of the species at Ertebølle are winter visitors or residents, but nesting herring gulls might have been obtained there in the summer. While some birds, such as capercaillies, must have been obtained in nearby woodland, there are so many bird bones there of the species that would have lived along the semi-estuarine coastline, that wholesale slaughter, perhaps by driving into nets, can be envisaged. In that case, although the extraction pattern was clearly generalized, it cannot be described as opportunistic.

Mullerup, Ulkestrup and Sværdborg I are all summer sites. They all have birds from various habitats, and here the extraction pattern seems to be genuinely opportunistic. Many of the birds would have been taken when breeding, when they tend to be more dispersed than they are in the winter.

In all these generalized sites the regression curves of abundance against rank order are gently concave, suggesting that foraging may not have been entirely random and that there was deliberate, though not marked, preference for some species.

Mixed foraging

Havnø, Klintesø and Ølby Lyng have indicators of a generalized foraging strategy in addition to their specializations. At Havnø and Klintesø the birds in the generalized category are all (except for small numbers of great auk at Havnø) species that would have been caught along the coast in winter, but there are not enough to be sure whether this represents any form of wholesale slaughter. At Ølby Lyng the birds in the generalized category are from very varied habitats and probably represent a small element of truly opportunistic foraging.

Conclusions

The main distinctions in bird-foraging strategies seem to be: (i) specialized foraging, with the systematic exploitation of one, or a few, spatially concentrated species (this is always seasonal); (ii) generalized foraging of a wider range of species, which may or may not have been seasonally or spatially concentrated. Sometimes generalized foraging might have involved wholesale slaughter of birds in a particular environment and this would have to have been systematically organized, but sometimes it seems to have been genuinely opportunistic. Generalized foraging can be either seasonal or unseasonal.

Some sites may have had either specialized or generalized bird-catching strategies; others may have had both, sometimes at different seasons of the year. All the sites with dual strategies studied so far are coastal, but this may be a result of the small number of sites.

In the end, the type of information provided by the bird bones is not so much about the fauna of Mesolithic Denmark as about human behaviour. Analyses of this type provide information on the choices that people made in utilizing the environment to obtain food, in different places, at different times of the year.

If the implications of foraging analysis can be combined with information on the physical methods used to obtain birds, and if the degree of co-operation between people that these methods and strategies imply can be assessed, a great deal will have been learnt about human behaviour in the past.

Acknowledgements: I am most grateful to Erik Brinch Petersen for advice on archaeological aspects, to Peter Rowley-Conwy, Christian Ejlers, Kim Aaris-Sørensen and Ronnie Liljegren for help with the literature, and to Ulrik Møhl who has taught so many people so much about archaeozoology.

APPENDIX: Key for symbols used to indicate bird species in scattergrams (*Figs. 3–5, 7–9*). The species are listed in the alphabetical order of their common names. Danish common names have been translated with the help of Jørgensen (1958). Binomial nomenclature from Heinzel *et al.* (1974).

Ba	Bewick swan	*Cygnus bewickii*
Bb	bittern	*Botaurus stellaris*
Bc	black-headed gull	*Larus ridibundus*
Bd	black kite	*Milvus migrans*
Be	black stork	*Ciconia nigra*
Bf	black-throated diver	*Gavia arctica*
Bg	black woodpecker	*Dryocopus martius*
Bh	brent goose	*Branta bernicla*
Bi	buzzard	*Buteo buteo*
Ca	capercaillie	*Tetrao urogallus*
Cb	common gull	*Larus canus*
Cc	common scoter	*Melanitta nigra*
Cd	coot	*Fulica atra*
Ce	cormorant	*Phalacrocorax carbo*
Cf	corncrake	*Crex crex*
Cg	crane	*Grus grus*
Ch	crow	*Corvus corone*
Ci	curlew	*Numenius arquata*
Da	diving ducks – scaup	*Aythya marila*
	goldeneye	*Bucephala clangula*
		(Anatinae)
Dc	duck sp.	
Dd	dunlin	*Calidris alpina*
E	eider	*Somateria mollissima*
Ga	gannet	*Sula bassana*
Gb	garganey	*Anas querquedula*
Gc	goosander	*Mergus merganser*

Gd	goose sp.	(Anserinae)
Ge	great auk	*Alca impennis*
Gf	great crested grebe	*Podiceps cristatus*
Gg	greater black-backed gull	*Larus marinus*
Gh	great spotted woodpecker	*Dendrocopus major*
Gi	grebe sp.	*Podiceps sp.*
Gj	green woodpecker	*Picus viridis*
Gk	greylag goose	*Anser anser*
Gl	guillemot	*Uria aalge*
Ha	heron	*Ardea cinerea*
Hb	herring gull	*Larus argentatus*
Hc	hooded crow	*Corvus corone cornix*
J	jay	*Garrulus glandarius*
K	kite	*Milvus sp.*
La	little grebe	*Tachybaptus ruficollis*
Lb	long-tailed duck	*Clangula hyemalis*
Ma	mallard	*Anas platyrhynchos*
Mb	mute swan	*Cygnus olor*
O	osprey	*Pandion haliaetus*
Pa	?pelican	*Pelecanus crispus*
Pb	pintail	*Anas acuta*
Ra	raven	*Corvus corax*
Rb	razorbill	*Alca torda*
Rc	red-breasted merganser	*Mergus serrator*
Rd	red kite	*Milvus milvus*
Re	red-necked grebe	*Podiceps grisegena*
Rf	red-throated diver	*Gavia stellata*
Sa	scaup	*Aythya marila*
Sb	shoveller	*Anas clypeata*
Sc	smew	*Mergus albellus*
Sd	stork	*Ciconia sp.*
Se	swan sp.	*Cygnus sp.*
Ta	tawny owl	*Strix aluco*
Tb	teal	*Anas crecca*
Tc	tufted duck	*Aythya fuligula*
Td	thrush, etc.	*Turdus sp.*
V	velvet scoter	*Melanitta fusca*
Wa	white-tailed eagle	*Haliæetus albicilla*
Wb	whooper swan	*Cygnus cygnus*
Wc	wigeon	*Anas penelope*

References

AARIS-SØRENSEN, K. (1976) A zoological investigation of the bone material from Sværdborg I–1943. In B.B. Henriksen, *Sværdborg I (Excavations 1943–44). A Settlement of the Maglemose Culture* (Arkæologiske studier, 3). Copenhagen, Forhistorisk–Arkæologisk Institut: 137–148.

BRAMWELL, D. and GRIGSON, C. (forthcoming) *The bird bones of the Oronsay middens* (paper).

BRØNDSTED, J. (1957) *Danmarks oldtid. I. Stenalderen* (2nd edition). Copenhagen, Gyldendal.

CLARK, G. (1948) Fowling in prehistoric Europe. *Antiquity*, 22: 116–130.

CLARK, G. (1975) *The Earlier Stone Age Settlement of Scandinavia.* Cambridge, University Press.

COTT, H.B. (1947) The edibility of birds. *Proceedings of the Zoological Society of London*, 116: 371–524.

CRAMP, S. *et al.* (eds) (1977) *Handbook of the Birds of Europe, the Middle East and North Africa: the Birds of the Western Palearctic. Volume 1. Ostrich to Ducks.* Oxford, University Press.

CRAMP, S. *et al.* (eds) (1980) *Handbook of the Birds of Europe, the Middle East and North Africa: the Birds of the Western Palearctic. Volume 2. Hawks to Bustards.* Oxford, University Press.

DEGERBØL, M. (1943) Om dyrelivet i Aamosen i stenalderen. In T. Mathiassen, *Stenalderbopladser i Aamosen.* Copenhagen, Gyldendal: 165–206.

FERDINAND, L. (1980) *Fuglene i Landskabet.* Copenhagen, Dansk Ornitologisk Forening.

FRIIS-JOHANSEN, K. (1919) En boplads fra den ældre stenalder i Sværdborg Mose. *Aarbøger for Nordisk Oldkyndighed og Historie*, 1919: 106–235.

HEINZEL, H., FITTER, R. and PARSLOW, J. (1974) *The Birds of Britain and Europe.* London, Collins.

HENRIKSEN, B.B. (1976) *Sværdborg I (Excavations 1943–44). A Settlement of the Maglemose Culture* (Arkæologiske studier, 3). Copenhagen, Forhistorisk–Arkæologisk Institut.

JOENSEN, A.H. (1973) Moult migration and wing-feather. Moult of sea ducks in Denmark. *Danish Review of Game Biology*, vol. 8, no.4.

JOENSEN, A.H. (1974) Waterfowl populations in Denmark 1965–73. *Danish Review of Game Biology*, vol. 9, no. 1.

JOENSEN, A.H., SØNDERGAARD, N-O. and HANSEN, E.B. (1976) Occurrence of seals and seal-hunting in Denmark. *Danish Review of Game Biology*, vol. 10, no. 1.

JØRGENSEN, H.I. (1958) *Nomina Avium Europaearum*. Copenhagen, Munksgaard.

MADSEN, A.P. *et al.* (1900) *Affaldsdynger fra Stenalderen i Danmark*. Copenhagen, A.A. Reitzel. (especially contributions by Winge, pp. 81–89, 110–111, 129–132)

MATHIASSEN, T. (1943) *Stenalderbopladser i Aamosen*. Copenhagen, Gyldendal.

MØHL, U. (1970a) Oversigt over dyreknoglerne fra Ølby Lyng. En østjællandsk kystboplads med Ertebøllekultur. *Aarbøger for Nordisk Oldkyndighed og Historie*, 1970: 43–77.

MØHL, U. (1970b) Fangstdyrene ved de danske strand: den zoologiske baggrund for harpunerne. *Kuml*, 1970: 297–329.

MØHL, U. (1978) Aggersund-bopladsen zoologisk belyst. *Kuml*, 1978: 57–75.

OLSEN, H. (1967) Varanger-funnene IV. Osteologiske material. *Tromsø Museums Skrifter*, 7(4): 14–182.

RICHTER, J. (1982) Faunal remains from Ulkestrup Lyng Øst. A hunter's dwelling place. *Nordiske Fortidsminder*, 7: 141–177.

ROWLEY-CONWY, P. (1983) Sedentary hunters: the Ertebølle example. In G.N. Bailey (ed.), *Hunter-Gatherer Economy in Prehistory: a European Perspective*. Cambridge, University Press: 111–126.

SARAUW, G.F.L. (1903) En stenalders boplads i Maglemose ved Mullerup sammenholdt med beslægtede fund. *Aarbøger for Nordisk Oldkyndighed og Historie*, 1903: 148–315.

SOUTHWOOD, T.R.E. (1966) *Ecological Methods*. London, Chapman and Hall.

WINGE, H. (1903) Oversigt over knoglematerialet fra Mullerupbopladsen. *Aarbøger for Nordisk Oldkyndighed og Historie*, 1903: 194–198.

WINGE, H. (1919) Oversigt over knoglematerialt fra Sværdborgbopladsen. *Aarbøger for Nordisk Oldkyndighed og Historie*, 1919: 128–134.

Clams and Salmonberries: Interpreting Seasonality Data from Shells

Margaret R. Deith

Abstract

Examples of shellfish-gathering activities among several hunter-gatherer-fisher groups, mainly taken from the ethnographic record of the Northwest Coast Indians and Australian aborigines, demonstrate a wide range of roles for shellfish within the annual economic cycle. The implications of these variations for the archaeologist attempting to interpret seasonality data from shells are discussed. It is concluded that seasonality data in themselves can only inform on the time of year when shellfish were *collected* but that, in Mesolithic Europe, this is likely to be synonymous with the time when they were eaten. The use of shellfish as bait, whilst it does not affect the question of seasonality, has other implications for the archaeologist trying to assess the contribution of different foods to the diet. Finally, the role of shellfish cannot be seen in isolation; whether they were a resource to fall back on in lean times, a way of providing variety in the diet or a sign that a part of the group was engaged in ritual activities must be seen against the total background of annual socio-economic activities.

INTRODUCTION

We left the boat anchored and came ashore in the rubber dinghy, and dragged it up on the sand where it'd be safe. We didn't eat any clams or oysters because it was salmonberry and blackberry time, but we had potato salad and crab and smoked salmon and cold beer...

This cameo account of a day's blackberrying with grandmother, by an elderly Nootka woman reminiscing to her own granddaughter, reveals a glimpse of an ordered year in which different foods and different activities had their seasons, within a framework of culturally mediated traditions.

The seasonal factor in hunter-gatherer subsistence and settlement studies, especially in temperate zones like Mesolithic Europe, is clearly of major importance. Archaeologists naturally seek to understand the seasonal aspect of a site or the seasonal relationships within a group of sites. The presence of migratory species is a useful clue where such species are found. Inferences from the seasonal behaviour of animals or from shed antler may lead to some very different conclusions, however, as they have done most notably at Star Carr (Clark 1972; Legge and Rowley-Conwy, this volume). Direct seasonal analysis of the material from a site therefore appears to offer a less ambiguous approach. Shell midden sites are particularly conspicuous in the European Mesolithic, and shells which can be identified with

confidence as the remains of meals (and not decorative objects) provide a rich and plentiful source of analytical material. Techniques for the analysis of marine shell, such as oxygen-isotope analysis (Shackleton 1973) and growth-line analysis (Koike 1973), are now well established. Whilst not all species are responsive to any one technique, and a few respond to none, there are nevertheless many which produce reliable results (Deith 1985). Given such seasonal data, how are they to be interpreted? How should they be understood in terms of the human activities that produced the heaps of shells?

In this paper, I shall look at some examples of shellfish gathering in the ethnographic record, among different groups of present-day hunter-gatherer-fishers, to discover what kinds of traces would be left in the archaeological record from a variety of different behaviours. The aim is not to find ethnographic parallels and apply them to archaeological situations, but to consider the fundamental question of inference from this kind of archaeological evidence and to try to distinguish between what is valid and what is not valid. The examples come mainly from the Northwest Coast Indians and the Australian aborigines, whose shellfish-gathering activities have been most fully documented.

ETHNOGRAPHIC EXAMPLES

The ways in which shellfish are used by the Northwest Coast Indians are many and various, partly in response to different conditions encountered by different groups.

In the north, where the environment is particularly rich for hunters and fishers, and the diet is dominated by salmon, shellfish are used in the main to lend variety to the diet. Both the Nootka of Vancouver and the Tlingit of Alaska included in their diet such sea food as 'chitons, clams, scallops, limpets, snails, cockles, mussels, sea urchins, sea cucumbers, abalone, crab, octopus, seals and sea lions' (Olson and Hubbard 1984: 930). Olson and Hubbard (1984: 930) comment that most of these items were small and had little food value individually, 'necessitating their collection in considerable quantity'. At the same time, they augmented the basic diet of fish, giving it 'variety and superabundance'. The Nootka collected shellfish in the first quarter of their year (starting at the end of October/beginning of November), when they were in their winter villages and food getting was not a priority because they were living on stored food. Sporadic visits to the shore lent variety to a diet composed mainly of dried salmon. During this time of year, the outer beaches were not accessible because of winter storms, but shellfish were gathered from there in the spring and summer (Drucker 1951). The appearance of shells in archaeological deposits should not therefore be construed as an inevitable sign of hunger. In this case, it is the mark of a desire for variety. Both the absolute quantity of shell material and the way in which it is disposed through the deposits are significant in an archaeological context. That is, whether the shells are scattered or occur in large, pure lenses is some indication of whether their role in the diet of a prehistoric group was for variety or dictated by the economic necessities of annual or unexpected lean periods.

Even groups like the Nootka occasionally experienced periods of scarcity, however, and it was to counteract such lean times that shellfish were often more actively sought. At such times, people would collect the small mussels that can be found in sheltered coves, when the winter storms did not permit collection from the outer beaches. Times of scarcity were not very frequent among coastal groups in this area, however (Drucker 1951).

Some groups, whose times of scarcity were more predictable, organized for them as part of the regular cycle of activities. The Tlingit, for example, intensified their year-round, low level of exploitation during the period when the shellfish were in prime condition and then dried or smoked the meat for the lean period or for trading with inland groups (Oberg 1973). In this case, the period of most intensive exploitation (March and April) did not coincide with the late winter period of privation. This kind of dislocation would be difficult or impossible to recognize archaeologically. A similar pattern obtained among the Coast Yuki of northern California. Both molluscs and sea fish were dried and taken to the winter camp sites on the ridges in autumn, when the coastal sites were abandoned for the winter (Gifford 1939). The time for drying sea foods was July and August, a different time of year from that of the Tlingit, although the meat might well have been eaten at about the same time. The timing is clearly dependent on other activities in the seasonal round. In the case of the Tolowa of Oregon, for example, the timing of the period on the coast was determined by the movements of the salmon. Between the spring salmon run in the early summer and the fall salmon run in the late summer was the time when people left the river for the beach, for the shellfish and smelt and to hunt sea

lions (Drucker 1937). These were cured for storage, to add to the supplies of dried salmon caught in the autumn. That is, the scheduling of seasonal activities and movements was based on the seasonal abundance of the major resource. Some rivers, the larger ones, had two runs of salmon each year, in spring and late summer/autumn, but the smaller rivers and tributaries had only the late-season run:

> The spring runs provided abundant fresh salmon in the most excellent condition of the entire year (the late-season fish being of generally poor condition) at a time when stored provisions, generally including dried salmon and acorns, were dwindling or exhausted after a long winter of use. The spring salmon season may have been the most critical juncture in many native fishing economies, so great was the seasonal range from the previous fall abundance (which was largely dried and stored while the weather permitted) to the scarcity of good quality fish in the winter months (Swezey and Heizer 1984: 972).

Groups based on those rivers with a single salmon run were thus more dependent on acorn-gathering and hunting than those living on the major rivers. This fundamental difference in basic resources clearly affected seasonal settlement patterns. Compare, for example, the movements of the Tolowa, visiting the coast between salmon runs, with the Coast Yuki, spending six months in the hills and six months on the coast.

The correspondence between settlement on the coast and the exploitation of coastal resources, whether eaten at the time or preserved for the winter, has so far been seen to be a direct one. For the Coast Yuki, however, settlement and resource exploitation were not precisely aligned. For example, people started to make excursions to the beach in March from their winter quarters in the hills, to offset their food shortages. In April they started moving to the beach and building houses. After spending the summer on the beach, they started to look for acorns in the hills in September, while they were still resident on the coast, only moving out in October (Gifford 1939). The slight dislocation between residential movements and the exploitation of the shore suggests a possible small source of error, if the techniques for establishing seasonality are sufficiently fine-grained to pick up monthly differences.

Some inland groups made occasional trips to the coast, eating clams raw or boiling them and drying and packing quantities of them for the winter. Among these were Californian groups such as the Bear River people (Nomland 1938), the Wappo (Driver 1936) and the Yokut (Pilling 1950). The latter group travelled long distances on horseback once a year, leaving behind on the coast shell heaps of varying sizes, from a few centimetres to more than a metre deep. Such shell heaps, left by inland groups, might well be difficult to distinguish archaeologically from those left by groups of the Mission Indians, who later inhabited the coastal region and who tried to drive the visiting Yokut from their land.

The drying and storage of sea food is not a world-wide phenomenon, however, for a number of reasons. A 'collecting' way of life is conducive to the development of storage techniques, which are inappropriate for a 'foraging' one (see Binford 1980). In the case of the foraging Anbarra of northern Australia, behaviour which is economically appropriate is underlined by cultural attitudes. For example, they set great store by the freshness of the food they eat, and collect their shellfish daily (Meehan 1977). In fact, they will abandon food that is still perfectly edible, on the grounds that it is not absolutely fresh. Meehan draws attention to the importance of cultural factors in shellfish-gathering activities. The January rainy period, when there was a gap in the availability of other resources, was known as 'shellfish time'. Yet the site at which the highest frequency of shellfish gathering occurred was occupied in the dry season. Not only was it anomalous in this respect, but the main shell beds lay as much as 3 km away:

> There is a cultural explanation for this high frequency which overrides spatial and seasonal factors. The duration of my observations at Ngalidjibama coincided with the last few weeks of a Kunapipi ceremony, which culminated as usual on a full-moon night. During this time the population was increasing daily and the men in the secret camp, fully occupied with ritual preparations for the finale, had little time to hunt for food. The heavy responsibility for providing sustenance for everybody fell upon the mature women, who responded to the challenge in two ways – by preparing *Cycas media* bread and by collecting shellfish (Meehan 1982: 66).

It is a timely warning that economic activities cannot always be explained in wholly economic terms.

All these examples of the use of shellfish amongst hunter-gatherer-fisher groups concern shellfish as human food. One of the accounts (Oberg 1973) also mentions the use of clams as bait. The use of shellfish as bait in fishing communities is, in fact, documented in recent times in parts of Europe such as Scotland and Scandinavia (Fenton 1984). Indeed, Fenton mentions that eating shellfish is more of an English tradition than a Scottish one and that the majority of shellfish, especially mussels and limpets, were collected for use as bait. When mussels were not obtainable, limpets were used, either by being put directly on hooks or by being mashed and scattered in the water to attract the saithe. The efficiency of line fishing was ensured by a division of labour, whereby the women collected the shellfish and baited the hooks, while the men fished. One of the most interesting points made by Fenton is that the quantity of bait used was almost equivalent to the quantity of fish caught. He quotes the average annual catch of fish per boat at Eyemouth in Berwickshire, from 1885 to 1887, as varying between 41 and 43.5 tons, and the amount of bait between 37.5 and 38 tons (presumably this weight includes the shell). A large number of shells in a midden is thus no guarantee that people were in fact eating shellfish. They may have been converting them into other forms of protein which they found more palatable or which were culturally more acceptable. There is a nice distinction between the Scots and the English here.

GENERAL ARCHAEOLOGICAL IMPLICATIONS

It is clear from these accounts of shellfish gathering that the ways in which shellfish are used are multifarious. Seasonality of shellfish collection may not correspond with seasonality of shellfish consumption. The collection of shellfish may be an indication that there was a period of hardship during the year, either at the time of collection or at some other time, or that people were suffering from a surfeit of smoked salmon. The shell heaps on the coast might have been left by groups whose other sites were nearby. Thus, they might be part of a settlement system based on the nearest river system, or the residue of an inland group. There are some more general warnings here for the archaeologist:–

a) The calorie-counting approach is suspect, even without the complications of assessing such imponderables as plant food, since shells may not appear where the shellfish were eaten and vice versa. Indeed, they may not even be the remains of meals at all in sites where there are fish bones.

b) The optimal foraging approach would fail to appreciate that a low-status food might be gathered simply for variety, and interpret the appearance of shells in a deposit as a sign of either general hardship or of a seasonal trough in an otherwise productive environment. It would also fail to take into account cultural factors such as ceremonial obligations.

c) The assumption that the sites in an area have all been produced by the same group may be unwarranted. Thus the appearance of an occasional exotic artifact need not be an indication of long-distance trade (Pilling 1950).

Faced with just a few of the patterns of human behaviour that result in shell refuse, how far is it possible to interpret seasonality data in terms of the behaviour which generated it? The only indisputable information about the people who discarded the shells is that they were on the shore at the time(s) of the year indicated by the seasonality studies. No further inferences can be drawn *from these data alone*. They do not inform on when or where the shellfish were eaten, or why they were collected (for periods of hardship or to provide variety), or whether they were for direct or indirect consumption on sites where fish bones occur. This may seem remarkably little, but a distinction must be drawn between the information the data actually contain and what is inference.

MESOLITHIC EUROPE

Storage

The question of storage is clearly a crucial issue in the interpretation of seasonality data. Direct evidence is negligible and inconclusive in Mesolithic Europe. A suggestion that pottery found at the very late Mesolithic sites of the Pitted Ware culture in eastern Sweden might have been used for the storage of seal products (flesh, blubber and blood) is a rare indication of storage practices among hunter-gatherer groups in Europe (Welinder 1976). The only equivalent to the storage pits of the Jomon period in Japan (Akazawa 1986) is the set of pits round the back of the major structure at Mount Sandel in Ireland (Woodman 1985). Nevertheless, negative evidence is no guarantee that people were not storing food. Boxes, baskets and store houses would leave no permanent record, except for postholes, which are equivocal. Oberg (1973) paints a vivid picture of the Tlingit taking great quantities of clams and mussels from the islands off southern Alaska, drying and smoking them, then packing them in airtight boxes or hanging them in the roof.

The implication of this description is that a degree of sedentism, with substantial buildings, is a condition of food storage. Storage pits in Jomon sites are associated with house structures from the earliest times, indicating that stable residential patterns were established *in conjunction with the use of storage* (Aikens *et al.* 1986). Both Drucker (1937) and Driver (1936) refer to the winter quarters of the Tolowa in Oregon and the Wappo of southern California as 'towns', which they describe as 'permanent', in contrast to the temporary summer camps.

There are thus concomitants of storage, which may be more archaeologically visible than the storage system itself. Indeed, from his study of North American salmon economies, Schalk was led to the conclusion that the changes associated with the implementation of a storage strategy constituted an 'evolutionary threshold' (Schalk 1977: 231). The motive force for such change was demographic pressure, without which hunter-gatherers would tend towards generalized adaptations, involving a wide range of resources and little or no food storage (Schalk 1977). The use of storage techniques enlarges the carrying capacity of an area, alters the time of seasonal stress from the lean period to the time of intensive harvesting, both permits and demands a greater degree of sedentism, and sets a much higher value on efficient organization. It is associated with technological innovations – in the case of salmon for taking greater quantities of fish, for processing and for storing them – with decreasing mobility and with the reorganization of social systems. The greater need for efficiency favours more centralized control, increased complexity of labour organization, and task specialization

which, in turn, favours increased social differentiation (see Schalk 1977). Some of the effects of such a radical shift in perspective should be visible in the archaeological record.

Schalk has warned against generalizing, since the seasonal behaviour of the fish in different river systems and at different latitudes has a high degree of variability and the pressure on human groups varies according to the particular circumstances of their locality. This warning is also relevant to a consideration of different kinds of stored foods. Anadromous fish probably produce the most extreme pressures of any resource. At the other end of the spectrum, resources such as nuts and acorns, which require far less technology for either harvesting or storage, minimal task specialization and are not harmed by the loss of a few days or even weeks between harvesting and storing, exert less severe pressure on the labour force to organize the work speedily and efficiently. Whilst decreasing mobility is likely to be a correlate of storing any resources, where task specialization and precise timing are not so important, the corresponding pressure towards social differentiation is also reduced. Analysis of Jomon pit contents has shown that nuts and acorns were being stored at these sites (Makabe 1979; Otomasu 1984). Although storage techniques were employed from very early times (Initial Jomon, *c.* 7000–6000 BP), the major change in social organization, towards a more hierarchical structure, reached a peak in Middle Jomon times, following a long but gradual expansion in population (Aikens *et al.* 1986).

The precise concomitants of a storage technology thus vary according to the behaviour of the resource in any given situation. While there are certain features which are generally associated with storage, others are required only where efficient organization is at a premium and many different processes must be co-ordinated.

The kind of evidence which we should expect to find in association with storage is increasingly apparent in the later phases of the Mesolithic in Europe. Gradual population growth through the Mesolithic led to demographic pressure in some areas, mobility was curtailed and a degree of sedentism ensued. Groups which are considered to have had sedentary populations by the late Mesolithic include the Danish Ertebølle people (Rowley-Conwy 1981), the inhabitants of the Uzzo cave in Sicily (Tusa 1985) and Sarnate in Latvia (Zvelebil 1986), and the Asturian peoples of the coastal strip of northern Spain (Clark 1983), although the latter is somewhat contentious (Bailey 1983). Much more striking in its evidence of having passed the kind of evolutionary threshold referred to by Schalk, is the cemetery of Oleniy Ostrov in northern Russia. O'Shea and Zvelebil's analysis indicates that it was:

produced by a relatively large and stable population. It was a society with considerable internal differentiation, which included not only hereditary social positions, but also a complex economic system reflecting the incipient development of an institutionalized system of social inequality (1984: 35).

Shellfish storage

Indirect evidence for storage therefore exists in the kind of societies that developed through the Mesolithic. What of the storage of shellfish? It is significant that, in recent societies where shellfish were dried and stored, other resources, most notably salmon, were also stored. Thus the necessary organization was already in existence and did not need to be set up for what is essentially a secondary resource (see Meehan 1977).

When we consider the European situation, there are certain basic differences from the north-west coast of America where drying and smoking took place in the ethnographic past. In the first place, the European shellfish themselves are smaller, apart from the oyster, and would give smaller returns on the energy that would need to be invested. Secondly, Europeans are not handicapped by the Pacific winter storms that kept people away from the shore for long periods of time. Indeed, in some places, like Denmark, the harvest is more easily gathered in winter after a storm, when the subtidal bivalves are washed up on shore. There is thus a trade-off between gathering shellfish when they are in peak condition, usually in summer, for drying or smoking, and collecting them fresh in the winter.

The great oyster middens of the Ertebølle in Jutland represent a resource of a different order of magnitude, however. Rowley-Conwy believes that they accumulated as a result of 'heavy seasonal usage of oysters to plug a gap in the resource cycle' (Rowley-Conwy 1984: 306). Since the oyster is in good condition from February to April, when this gap is calculated to have occurred, and also at its most accessible because of low spring tides in the Litorina period in the Baltic (Rowley-Conwy 1984), there is no reason to suppose that there was any need for preserving shellfish in this instance.

In conclusion, then, the probability that shellfish were gathered in one season and eaten in another, during the Mesolithic in Europe, is low. It is reasonable to assume that seasonality data from shells can be taken at face value, and that shellfish were eaten at the time they were gathered.

Shellfish as bait

The question of whether shellfish were used as bait or for direct consumption is not necessarily an insuperable one, since there may well be indications in the shells themselves. It is easiest to remove the meat by cooking the shellfish. Cooking softens the flesh, mak-

ing it less effective as bait, because it breaks away from the hook (J. Morais Arnaud, pers. comm.). The easiest way of removing the flesh for bait is by smashing the shell. As a technique for preparing human food, this is less than ideal, since little bits of smashed shell adhere to the meat. Where midden shells have been systematically smashed, therefore, it is likely that the shellfish were used as bait. A good example is that of Franchthi cave in Greece, where broken shells of *Cerithium vulgatum* Bruguière occur throughout the Mesolithic deposits. These shells appear to have been broken in a systematic fashion (J.C. Shackleton, pers. comm.). Conversely, Morais Arnaud (pers. comm.) has found large numbers of bivalves with hinges still intact in the Mesolithic middens of the Sado estuary, Portugal. The much more careful treatment accorded to these shells suggests that they are the remains of human meals.

As far as the seasonality aspect is concerned, the use of shellfish as bait is not significant, since the shellfish would have been collected live for either purpose.

Seasonality data from shells

Once seasonality data have been collected, their implications for the interpretation of the site as a whole can be considered. Taken in conjunction with other evidence, they may make a substantial contribution to the way in which the settlement of a site or an area is perceived.

A case in point is that of the Mesolithic site of Morton in south-east Scotland. Here, the seasonality data demonstrated that shellfish had been collected at several different times of the year (Deith 1983). If this were the only piece of evidence, it would not have been legitimate to construe it as an indication of either permanent, year-round settlement or of limited visits to the site in different seasons. The site report, however, records quite emphatically that the settlement consists of numbers of small camp sites, occupied for brief periods of only a few days at a time by a very small group of people (Coles 1971). The contribution made by the seasonality data was, in fact, to prompt new questions about the site. Why would a small group of people visit Morton at different times of the year? What resources do not have a seasonally restricted availability? The organic remains from the site indicated a wide range of resource utilization, militating against any interpretation of the settlement's function in terms of a specialized camp for the exploitation of any one specific food resource. The explanation that Morton was a procurement site for flint and other raw materials, however, fits most of the evidence. A second function, that of fishing for cod, encompasses the remainder (Deith 1986). Whether the shellfish were being eaten by the people or used for bait is not material to the issues of why or when they were there. Here, the seasonal data have led to inferences about site function, which emerges from a consideration of all the evidence from the site, including both organic and lithic remains.

A second way in which seasonality data may be used is in testing hypotheses of settlement. Along the northern coastal strip of Spain, there are many Asturian (Mesolithic) sites with shells. In some places, there are clusters of sites that are so close together as to allow little in the nature of individual territories in the classic 'site catchment analysis' sense. How did such clusters of sites function, assuming them to be synchronous? Bailey (1983) has suggested that the sites might have been used sequentially so that, as the shellfish were used up along one stretch of shoreline, the people moved to the next virgin expanse. If a single group was moving in this way, the seasonality of shellfish gathering would be different for each site within the cluster. An alternative hypothesis is that different families within the band were apportioned a share of the shore. Such an arrangement existed in Labrador in recent times, where stress conditions arising from the movements of game resulted in the breaking up of a communal hunting band into family units (Speck and Eiseley 1942). In this case, the seasonality would be the same for each site within the cluster. Other hypotheses could also be constructed to account for the clustering of sites in northern Spain. Such hypotheses are open to falsification by the seasonal analysis of shells, although the validation of any particular hypothesis is a more difficult proposition.

CONCLUSIONS

The ethnographic record indicates that shellfish gathering is an integral part of the structured fabric of society. To a great extent, the seasonal role of shellfish depends upon the seasonality of other, primary resources, because it is the scheduling of these resources that establishes the broad outline of seasonal activities. Within that broad outline, however, there is scope for considerable cultural variation in how shellfish are used.

Certain aspects of shellfish collection may be difficult for the archaeologist to retrieve. Shells indicate *when* people were on the coast though not necessarily the full extent of their stay. They do not indicate *why* they were there. The affluent Nootka, bored with their staple diet of smoked salmon, are a far cry from the inhabitants of Tierra del Fuego, whose miserable existence so horrified Darwin (1889). Neither the role of shellfish nor its usage can be directly inferred from the shell data alone. These data do, however, provide an unequivocal baseline from which questions of seasonality of settlement, site function or functional relationships between sites can be viewed. Shells do, in fact, contain a great deal of information, much of it only indirectly concerning

the people who left the midden accumulations. How this information is handled determines the validity or otherwise of the conclusions that are reached.

Acknowledgements: I wish to thank José Morais Arnaud, Peter Rowley-Conwy, Judith Shackleton, Graham Southgate, and Carol Thomas for their helpful comments on the manuscript of this paper at different stages in its evolution.

References

AIKENS, C.M., AMES, K.M. and SANGER, D. (1986) Affluent collectors at the edges of Eurasia and North America: some comparisons and observations on the evolution of society among north-temperate coastal hunter-gatherers. In T. Akazawa and C.M. Aikens (eds), *Prehistoric Hunter-Gatherers in Japan*. Tokyo, University Press: 3–26.

AKAZAWA, T. (1986) Regional variation in procurement systems of Jomon hunter-gatherers. In T. Akazawa and C.M. Aikens (eds), *Prehistoric Hunter-Gatherers in Japan*. Tokyo, University Press: 73–89.

BAILEY, G.N. (1983) Economic change in late Pleistocene Cantabria. In G. Bailey (ed.), *Hunter-Gatherer Economy in Prehistory*. Cambridge, University Press: 148–164.

BINFORD, L.R. (1980) Willow smoke and dogs' tails: hunter-gatherer settlement systems and archaeological site formation. *American Antiquity*, 45: 4–20.

CLARK, G.A. (1983) Boreal phase settlement/subsistence models for Cantabrian Spain. In G. Bailey (ed.), *Hunter-Gatherer Economy in Prehistory*. Cambridge, University Press: 96–110.

CLARK, J.G.D. (1972) *Star Carr: a Case Study in Bioarchaeology*. Addison–Wesley Module in Anthropology, no. 10. London, Cummings Publishing Company.

COLES, J.M. (1971) The early settlement of Scotland: excavations at Morton, Fife. *Proceedings of the Prehistoric Society*, 37: 284–366.

DEITH, M.R. (1983) Molluscan calendars: the use of growth-line analysis to establish seasonality of shellfish collection at the Mesolithic site of Morton, Fife. *Journal of Archaeological Science*, 10: 423–440.

DEITH, M.R. (1985) Seasonality from shells: an evaluation of two techniques for seasonal dating of marine molluscs. In N.R.J. Fieller, D.D. Gilbertson and N.G.A. Ralph (eds), *Palaeobiological Investigations: Research Design, Methods and Data Analysis*. Oxford, British Archaeological Reports (International Series) S266: 119–130.

DEITH, M.R. (1986) Subsistence strategies at a Mesolithic camp site: evidence from stable isotope analysis of shells. *Journal of Archaeological Science*, 13: 61–78.

DRIVER, H.E. (1936) Wappo ethnography. *University of California Publications in American Archaeology and Ethnology*, 36: 179–220.

DRUCKER, P. (1937) The Tolowa and their southwest Oregon kin. *University of California Publications in American Archaeology and Ethnology*, 36: 221–300.

DRUCKER, P. (1951) *The Northern and Central Nootkan Tribes*. Washington, Smithsonian Institution, Bureau of American Ethnology, Bulletin 144.

FENTON, A. (1984) Notes on shellfish as food and bait in Scotland. In B. Gunda (ed.), *Fishing Culture of the World*. Budapest, Akadémiai Kiadó: 121–142.

GIFFORD, E.W. (1939) The Coast Yuki. *Anthropos*, 34: 292–375.

KOIKE, H. (1973) Daily growth lines of the clam, *Meretrix lusoria* – a basic study for the estimation of prehistoric seasonal gathering. *Journal of the Anthropological Society of Nippon*, 81: 122–138.

MAKABE, Y. (1979) Prehistoric diet. In H. Otsuka, M. Tozawa and M. Sahara (eds), *Japanese Archaeology* (vol. 3). Tokyo, Yuhikaku: 231–253.

MEEHAN, B. (1977) Man does not live by calories alone: the role of shellfish in a coastal cuisine. In J. Allen, J. Golson and R. Jones (eds), *Sunda and Sahul*. London, Academic Press: 493–531.

MEEHAN, B. (1982) *Shell Bed to Shell Midden*. Canberra, Australian Institute of Aboriginal Studies.

NOMLAND, G.A. (1938) Bear River ethnography. *University of California Anthropological Records*, 2: 91–126.

OBERG, K. (1973) *The Social Economy of the Tlingit Indians*. Seattle, University of Washington, American Ethnological Society, Monograph 55.

OLSON, W.M. and HUBBARD, L.T. Jr (1984) Fishing: the key to Tlingit culture. In B. Gunda (ed.), *Fishing Culture of the World*. Budapest, Akadémiai Kiadó: 917–938.

O'SHEA, J. and ZVELEBIL, M. (1984) Oleneostrovski mogilnik: reconstructing the social and economic organization of prehistoric foragers in northern Russia. *Journal of Anthropological Archaeology*, 3: 1–40.

OTOMASU, S. (1984) Use and function of pits. In Kokugakuin University (ed.), *Nippon Shigaku Ronshu*, vol. 1. Tokyo, Yoshikawa Kobunkan: 32–57.

PILLING, A.R. (1950) The archaeological implications of an annual coastal visit for certain Yokut groups. *American Anthropologist*, 52: 438–440.

ROWLEY-CONWY, P. (1981) Mesolithic Danish bacon: permanent and temporary sites in the Danish Mesolithic. In A. Sheridan and G. Bailey (eds), *Economic Archaeology*. Oxford, British Archaeological Reports (International Series) S96: 51–55.

ROWLEY-CONWY, P. (1983) Sedentary hunters: the Ertebølle example. In G. Bailey (ed.), *Hunter-Gatherer Economy in Prehistory*. Cambridge, University Press: 111–130.

ROWLEY-CONWY, P. (1984) The laziness of the short-distance hunter: the origins of agriculture in western Denmark. *Journal of Anthropological Archaeology*, 3: 300–324.

SCHALK, R.F. (1977) The structure of an anadromous fish resource. In L.R. Binford (ed.), *For Theory Building in Archaeology*. New York. Academic Press: 207–249.

SHACKLETON, N.J. (1973) Oxygen isotope analysis as a means of determining season of occupation of prehistoric midden sites. *Archaeometry*, 15: 133–141.

SPECK, F.G. and EISELEY, L.C. (1942) Montagnais-Naskapi bands and family hunting districts of the central and southeastern Labrador Peninsula. *Proceedings of the American Philosophical Society*, 85: 215–242.

SWEZEY, S.L. and HEIZER, R.F. (1984) Ritual regulation ot anadromous fish resources in native California. In B. Gunda (ed.), *Fishing Culture of the World*. Budapest, Akadémiai Kiadó: 967–989.

TUSA, S. (1985) The beginning of farming communities in Sicily: the evidence of Uzzo cave. In C. Malone and S. Stoddart (eds), *Papers in Italian Archaeology IV. Part ii: Prehistory*. Oxford, British Archaeological Reports (International Series) S244: 61–82.

WELINDER, S. (1976) The economy of the Pitted Ware culture in eastern Sweden. *Meddelanden från Lunds universitets historiska museum 1975–1976*, New Series, 1: 20–30.

WOODMAN, P.C. (1985) Mobility in the Mesolithic of northwestern Europe: an alternative explanation. In T.D. Price and J.A. Brown (eds), *Prehistoric Hunter-Gatherers. The Emergence of Cultural Complexity*. Orlando, Academic Press: 325–339.

ZVELEBIL, M. (1986) Postglacial foraging in the forests of Europe. *Scientific American*, 254: 86–93.

Economic Intensification and Postglacial Hunter-Gatherers in North Temperate Europe

Marek Zvelebil

Abstract

The objective of this paper is to examine the evidence for economic intensification among Postglacial hunter-gatherers and to relate this process to the substitution of foraging by farming. Despite numerous studies on the subject, no objective measure of intensification has yet been developed. In this paper an attempt will be made to assess economic intensification in terms of the exploitation of preferred and sub-optimal resources. The status of resources will be ranked according to the net production as defined by McCullough (1970) and the net acquisition rate. This index of resource optimum will then be applied to bone assemblages in temperate Europe.

INTRODUCTION

Recent studies of Postglacial hunter-gatherers have emphasized the development of 'complex' (Rowley-Conwy 1983; Price and Brown 1985) or affluent societies (Koyama and Thomas 1981). These societies are said to be characterized by: (i) the intensified use of resources; (ii) the shift from residential to logistic mobility and towards more permanent settlement; and (iii) an increase in complexity of social organization. In the context of Postglacial Europe, and indeed in other parts of the world (Cohen 1977; Akazawa 1981), this apparent trend towards social and economic complexity has been interpreted as the beginning of a process leading to the transition to farming and as an early indication of crisis developing in the hunter-gatherer food procurement system. The key element of such interpretations rests in the archaeological evidence for intensification which plays, as Cohen (1977), Binford (1983) and many others have noted, a crucial role in the chain of events leading to the transition to farming. Yet, despite frequent references to the process of intensification, no objective measure of intensification has been developed.

The objective of the present contribution is to assess the concept of intensification and to trace the evidence for economic intensification among the Postglacial hunter-gatherers of north temperate Europe – and of the east Baltic in particular – and to relate it to the substitution of foraging by farming. I will first examine two ecological indicators of intensification, one based on the productivity, the other on the diversity of food resources, and will then go on to consider some cultural indicators of economic intensification. At the risk of reducing a complex issue to its broad essentials, *intensification* in this paper will be defined as maintaining or increasing food procurement through increased labour investment.

THE STUDY AREA

The data chosen for this study consist of 21 faunal assemblages from sites dating to the Stone, Bronze and early Iron Age in the east Baltic (*Fig. 1*), which were analyzed and published by Paaver (1965). The faunal samples range from several hundred to more than 17,000 bones. In describing the samples, Paaver grouped the assemblages into four categories according to their preservation. In order to introduce some measure of control over preservation bias, assemblages with poor preservation have been left out of the present analysis.

The Stone Age in the east Baltic is marked by the long persistence of hunter-gathering adaptations which, by mid-Holocene times, reached an unusual level of social and economic complexity in some coastal and lacustrine areas. Farming was introduced during the fourth millennium BP, but did not become the principal means of subsistence until the Iron Age. A concise description of the chronology and culture history of the area can be found in Sulimirski (1970) and in recent publications by Dolukhanov (1979, 1986; see also Kozłowski, this volume).

The sites used in the analysis were grouped into five periods:

Period 1: dates to the Boreal phase, 9500–7500 BP, and is characterized by early Mesolithic hunter-gatherer societies.

Period 2: dates to the Atlantic period, 7500–5000 BP, and is also characterized by Mesolithic hunter-gatherers.

Period 3: covers the early Sub-Boreal period, 5000–4000 BP. It is characterized by pottery-using hunter-gatherer communities, sometimes also known as the 'forest Neolithic'.

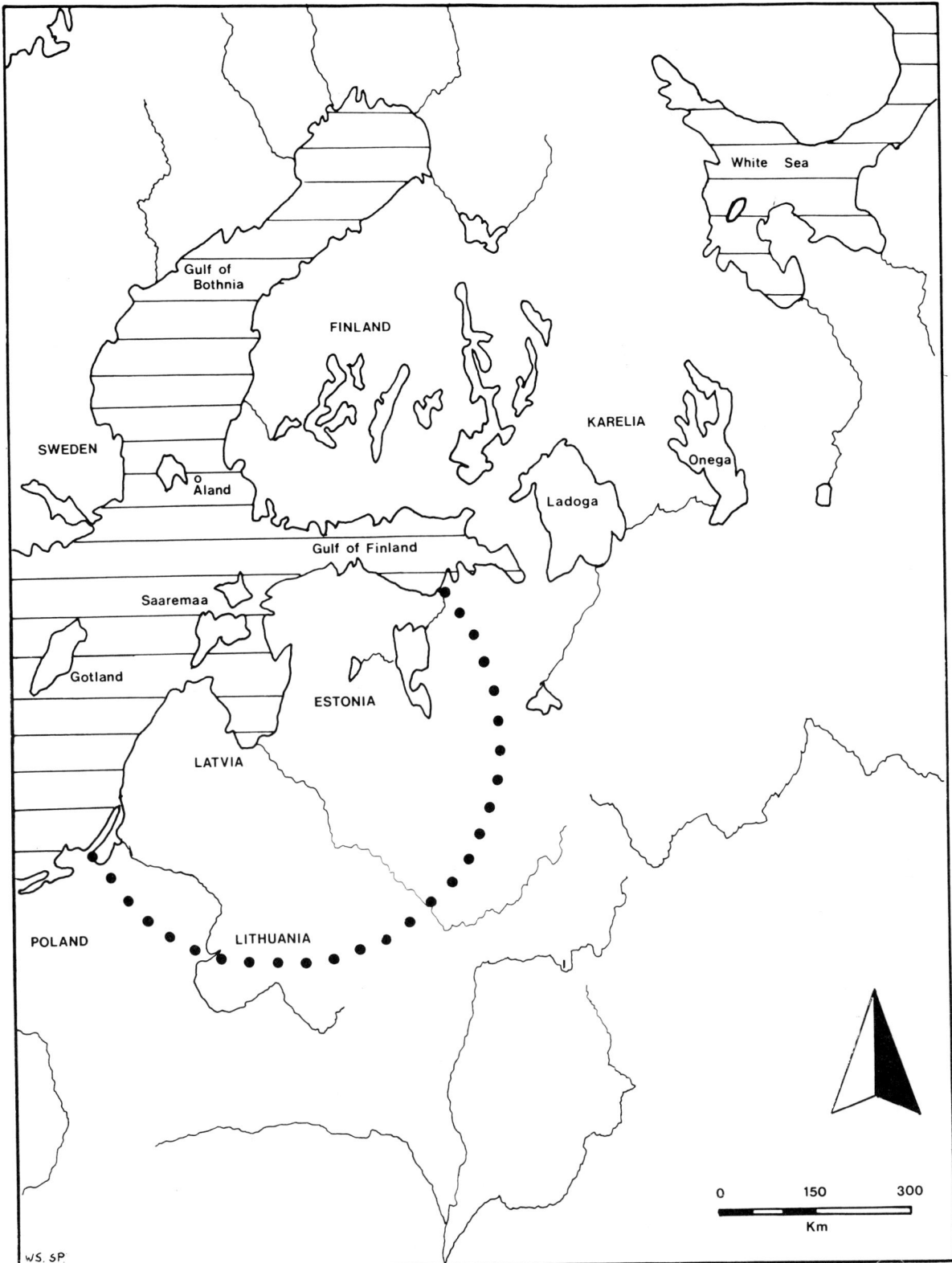

Figure 1   Map of north-east Europe, with the east Baltic area marked.

Period 4: covers the later Sub-Boreal period, 4000–3000 BP. Although the earliest elements of farming economy appear during this period, the culture and the economy remains essentially a hunting and gathering one.

Period 5: dates to the third millennium BP. It is characterized by bronze- and iron-using communities who relied primarily on farming.

NET PRODUCTIVITY AS A MEASURE OF INTENSIFICATION

Two ecological variables, size and diversity of resources, are commonly used to characterize the use of resources (Hardesty 1975, 1980; Jochim 1976; Winterhalder and Smith 1981; Zvelebil 1981; Clark and Yi 1983). Assuming that larger resources are always more productive than smaller ones, Cohen (1976), Hayden (1981), Binford (1983) and others have linked the shift from the use of large animals to small ones with population pressure, stress and increased labour costs.

There is, however, no *direct* relationship between animal size and its productivity. Rather, as McCullough has pointed out, resources can be divided into three groups: opportunist species, or *r*-strategists (low capacity to accumulate biomass, high capacity to reproduce), stable species, or *k*-strategists (high capacity to accumulate biomass, low capacity to reproduce), and the intermediate group where the capacity to reproduce and to accumulate biomass achieve a reasonable balance (McCullough 1970: 119–120).

As McCullough noted, it will be the resources with a balanced biomass:reproduction ratio which will have the highest net productivity within each trophic level and will, therefore, form the optimal long-term sources of energy. Such intermediate resources are usually medium-sized, ranging between 40 and 500 kg at the secondary production level. Labour costs associated with the procurement of these resources will usually be lower than for resources at either extreme of the range. This is due directly to the size of the resource, smaller ones

being more expensive to process than larger ones; but also to their aggregation and density patterns as well as their availability and predictability, all of which favour medium-sized resources (Winterhalder and Smith 1981). It follows, therefore, that deviation towards either end of the size range, small or large, will be likely to result in higher labour costs and lower sustained yield. It also follows that net productivity can serve as a broad indicator of labour costs of procurement, with costs increasing as the net productivity declines. Sub-optimality can be defined, then, by decreasing net productivity of resources, while intensification can be indexed by the increasing use of sub-optimal resources.

Returning to the east Baltic, resources were marked in order of their net productivities (*Table 2*). The resources make-up of faunal assemblages was then ordered along this dimension (*Fig. 2*). The emerging patterns indicate:

(i) There is no clear trend towards more intensive use of sub-optimal resources, although the reliability of the earlier sample (Periods 1 and 2) is clearly flawed by the small number of cases (*Table 1*). At first sight, the concentration on productive resources at Boreal sites such as Kunda (*Fig. 2a*) contrasts with a broader use of resources at sites dating to the Atlantic period, such as Narva (*Fig. 2b*). This difference, however, may be a result of sample bias owing to a small number of cases, or it may reflect a greater range of resources available in the east Baltic

Table 1: Niche-widths of faunal assemblages from Stone Age and early Iron Age settlements in the east Baltic

	Faunal Assemblage	Niche-width	
PERIOD 1	Kunda	2.42	9500–7500 BP
PERIOD 2	Narva	5.76	7500–5000 BP
PERIOD 3	Kääpa	4.71	5000–4000 BP
	Riigiküla 3	2.80	
	Riigiküla 2	2.34	
	Riigiküla 1	3.47	
	Akali	2.58	
	Kreichi (early layer)	4.01	
	Piestina	4.56	
	Range = 2.34–4.71		
PERIOD 4	Villa	3.88	4000–3000 BP
	Tamula	4.06	
	Loona	2.72	
	Naakamäe	2.14	
	Kreichi (late layer)	4.06	
	Leimaniški	2.45	
	Range = 2.14–4.06		
PERIOD 5	Ridala	3.84	3000–2000 BP
	Mukukalns	4.69	
	Petrašjunai	3.26	
	Asote	3.05	
	Aukštadvaris (hillfort)	4.52	
	Aukštadvaris (settlement)	2.96	
	Range = 2.96–4.69		

Table 2: Data on resource productivity used in the ranking of resources and in calculating the 'optimal niche width'

Rank	Species	Biomass (kg)		Edible Calories (meatweight as % of biomass × Calories/kg)		Density per km²		Productivity (% max cull)		Net Production (Kcal)
1.	Aurochs/Bison	687	×	0.5×2000=687,000	×	3.0	×	0.20	=	412,200
2.	Pig	190	×	0.6×4840=551,760	×	3.0	×	0.20	=	331,000
3.	Red deer	255	×	0.5×2000=255,000	×	4.0	×	0.20	=	204,000
4.	Elk	320	×	0.5×2000=320,000	×	1.0	×	0.20	=	64,000
5.	Horse	287	×	0.5×2000=287,000	×	1.0	×	0.20	=	57,400
6.	Fish	1	×	1.0×1000= 1000	×	500.0	×	0.10	=	50,000
7.	Seal (Ringed)	80	×	0.5×5000=200,000	×	2.0	×	0.10	=	40,000
8.	Hare	3.5	×	0.5×2000= 3500	×	50.0	×	0.20	=	35,000
9.	Roe deer	24	×	0.5×2000= 24,000	×	6.0	×	0.20	=	29,000
10.	Beaver	20	×	0.6×3000= 36,000	×	5.0	×	0.15	=	27,000
11.	Waterfowl	1	×	0.5×3000= 1500	×	20.0	×	0.50	=	15,000
12.	Bear, Fur game, Predators	range of values (see Zvelebil 1981)						0.10	=	2100

CALCULATION OF NICHE-WIDTH:

Species	Net Production	PI	(PI)²
Aurochs/Bison	412,000	0.324	0,105
Pig	331,000	0.260	0.068
Red deer	204,000	0.160	0.026
Elk	64,000	0.050	0.003
Horse	57,400	0.045	0.002
Fish	50,000	0.040	0.002
Seal	40,000	0.031	0.001
Hare	35,000	0.028	0.001
Roe Deer	29,000	0.023	0.001
Beaver	27,000	0.021	0.001
Waterfowl	15,000	0.012	0.000
Bear, fur, etc.	2100	0.002	0.000

Notes: Data on elk, fish, seal, hare, beaver, waterfowl, bear, fur game and predators were adopted from Zvelebil (1981: Appendix 3). Data on pig, red deer, horse and roe deer were adopted from Clark and Yi (1983) and from Jochim (1976). Data on aurochs and bison were adopted from Clark and Yi (1983), Lott (1974), and Fuller (1961) (the latter two on bison densities and productivity). In selecting biomass values, the larger size of mid-Holocene animals was taken into account (Paaver 1965). Caloric value of meat was estimated according to the proportion of fat. In selecting density values, minimal densities were selected for pig, red deer, roe deer and horse, since the east Baltic can be considered a marginal environment for these species. Low productivity figures were chosen, in order to account for predation and competition. Density of fish, seal and waterfowl was estimated taking into account the length of the shoreline and the surface area occupied by water (estimated at 10%). All figures are rough estimates with potentially a wide margin of error.

during the period of the Climatic Optimum (Paaver 1965). A deliberate policy of selection of sub-optimal resources cannot, therefore, be demonstrated.

(ii) In addition to sites with a generalized range of faunal remains, there is clear evidence for the emergence of specialized sites, such as Riigiküla (waterfowl), Loona (fish and seal) or Naakamäe (seal). These resources have a relatively low productivity when compared to ungulates and their specialized use contrasts with earlier Boreal patterns of resource use at sites such as Kunda, which were based on the exploitation of terrestrial game, such as cattle, elk and pig.

(iii) With the introduction of farming, a return can be observed to a more specialized use of highly productive resources, if domesticates are grouped together within the same productivity rank.

DIVERSITY AS A MEASURE OF INTENSIFICATION

Net productivity is merely one way of measuring resource use. Diversity is another. In ecology, the diversity of resources is commonly used to characterize niches of individual species. The same concept can be applied to human societies. In the present paper, one measure of diversity, *niche-width*, will be used. Introduced to anthropology by Hardesty (1975, 1980), niche-width expresses the comparative diversity of resources present in individual faunal assemblages or in assemblages that have been grouped at a regional scale, and is represented by the formula (Hardesty 1975):

$$\text{NICHE WIDTH} = 1/\sum_{1}^{n}(pi)^2$$

where p is the proportion of the total subsistence contributed by resource i, and n is the total number of resources used for subsistence. Values can range from 1 (highly specialized = low diversity) where only a single resource was exploited, to n (maximum diversity), n being the maximum number of resources that could be used. In the present case this would be 12, and a value of 12 would indicate that all twelve resources were used in equal proportions.

Niche-width has been used in a number of previous studies, in particular in the case of prehistoric hunter-gatherers in Cantabrian Spain (Clark and Yi 1983).

Following optimal foraging theory, Binford (1983) and other workers have suggested that in a situation of abundant resources, hunter-gatherer societies will select the most productive resources for exploitation. As the population increases or as optimal resources

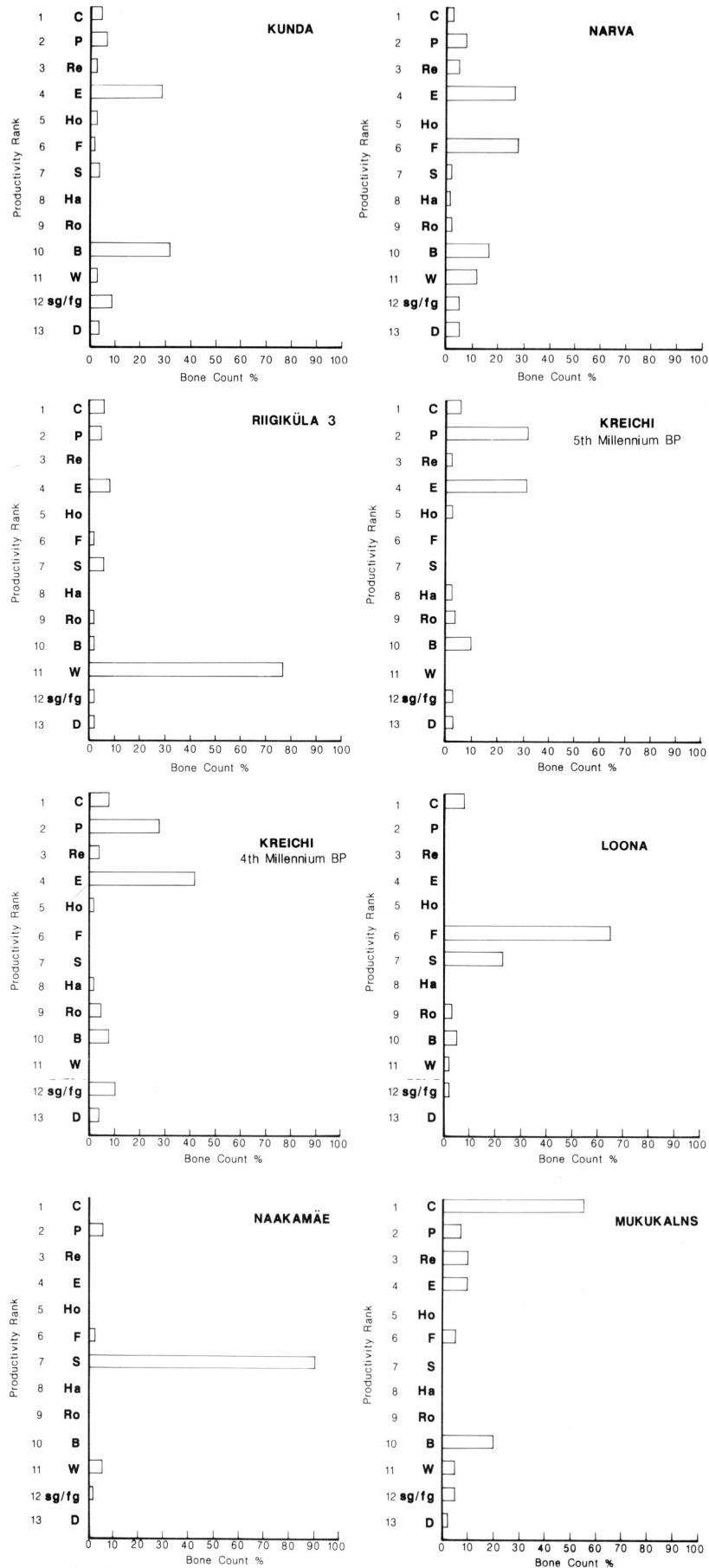

Figure 2 Diagram showing the use of resources at selected sites. Resources are ranked according to their productivity.

decline in number, more sub-optimal resources will be added to the range of species exploited, and the environment will become more *intensively* utilized. Increased diversity in the use of resources, as indicated by the niche-width, will therefore indicate economic intensification.

Increase in the range of resources used by Post-glacial as opposed to Lateglacial hunter-gatherers has been noted by many workers, most notably Flannery (1969), who termed this trend 'broad spectrum revolution'. Following ecological theory, 'broad spectrum' can be explained as an attempt to render the economic system more cost-effective in the situation of stress (Watts 1973: 34).

The application of the niche-width concept to the faunal assemblages in the east Baltic produced the following results (*Table 1*):

(i) There is no marked change in niche-width within hunter-gatherer economy during the Postglacial period, although small-scale changes may have been present but are difficult to assess using this method (see below).

(ii) There is a considerable variation between individual samples within Periods 3 and 4, with some assemblages reflecting broad resource use strategies; others, with narrow niche-width indicating specialization, have already been noted in the previous section. It would appear, therefore, that during the late Mesolithic, economic specialization complemented the broader use of resources.

(iii) Niche-width does not decline with the introduction of farming. This is in contrast to the results obtained by Clark and Yi (1983) in Cantabrian Spain, where niche-width declines to a low value, indicating specialization on domesticates as a consequence of the transition to farming. In the east Baltic, the niche-width value remains high because hunting and fishing continued to play an important role even after the adoption of farming, providing a broad economic base for the Iron Age societies of the third millennium BP and the first half of the second millennium BP.

The use of niche-width as an index of intensification has several drawbacks. First, diversification is not the only way to intensify. Specialization on a selected range of resources is, of course, another form of increasing production through increased labour investment. Yet it will result in a narrow niche-width, as in the case of Naakamäe or Loona. Taking the settlement pattern as a whole into account, it may be difficult to demonstrate intensification where both the diversified and specialized sites form a part of the same settlement–subsistence system. Rather, the niche-width of such sites may simply reflect the local availability of resources, thereby removing any element of choice in adopting resource use strategies. It will be only at a regional level that a variation in niche-width between individual economic systems can be properly evaluated.

This brings us to the second point. Both the diversification and the specialization of the niche are relative to the total range of resources in the environment. It follows that the total range of resources, expressed in terms of their net productivity, should be used as a standard against which the shifts in the actual resource use patterns could be evaluated. Such a standard is difficult to define, however, first because of the paucity of relevant figures on the productivity of potential food resources and, second, because of variation in what is perceived as potential food.

Third, an increase in a niche-width, and an inclusion of 'sub-optimal' resources in a resource use strategy does not necessarily indicate stress or a lack of more productive resources. Factors other than productivity play a part in the formation of a resource use strategy. Reduction of risk is one of the major considerations (Wiessner 1982; Torrence 1983, 1986; Cashdan 1985) and this may result in the extension of the niche-width beyond an optimal one, strictly from the point of view of resource productivity. It must be remembered, too, that resource productivity and risk reduction are related variables, and that they both are mediated by the technological competence and organizational structures of the human group in question.

Finally, variation in the availability of food resources over time further complicates the issue. In the east Baltic some of the more temperate resources, such as red deer, roe deer, horse, wild pig and cattle, declined towards the end of the Sub-Boreal period as colder climate and more boreal landscapes replaced temperate forests of the Climatic Optimum. This means that the changes observed in the niche-width can reflect either or both of two processes – changes in the natural environment and changes in the resource use strategies – thereby rendering the interpretation of the niche-width statistic far more difficult.

The use of a net productivity model (Zvelebil 1981) goes some way to meet these problems and represents an elaboration of the existing measures of intensification along the lines suggested above. The model combines the niche-width concept with the productivity indices used in the earlier section of this paper and provides a standard against which the fluctuations in the niche can be measured.

The model is based on the assumption that in the absence of stress and under a generalized resource use strategy, resources will be utilized in proportion to their productivities (*Fig. 3*). Such a strategy would have an 'optimal niche-width', composed of the proportional use of food resources available in a given environment. Since only a fraction of net productivity is utilized – in concrete cases within a

D

PRODUCTIVITY

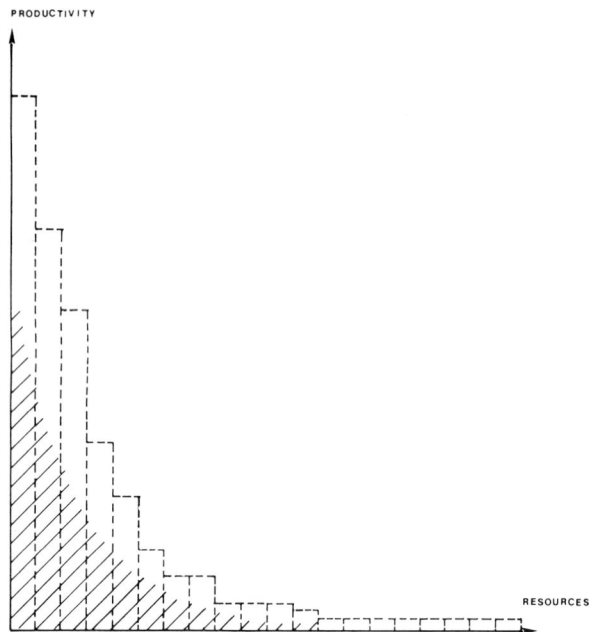

Figure 3 Productivity model of resource use. Shaded area denotes the proportion of the resource productivity likely to be used by human groups (after Zvelebil 1981).

10–50% range – resources with low productivity would be effectively ignored under the generalized resource use strategy (GRS). Deviations in niche-width from the hypothetical optimum established by the GRS could then be seen as indications of specialization or of diversification. With each change in the environment, a new GRS would apply and a new 'optimal niche-width' would be established. In summary, then, the 'optimal niche-width' of a non-selective, general resource use strategy will correspond to the natural niche-width of a given environment.

Let us apply this model, as a test case, to the period covered by the Atlantic and earlier Sub-Boreal phases, marked by the presence of temperate ungulates throughout the region. The data used in calculating the niche-width of the environment during this period (i.e. 'optimal niche-width' of a non-selective food procurement strategy) are summarized in *Table 2*. We obtain the following value: $NW = 4.76$. Comparing this standard with the niche-widths based on the faunal samples from archaeological sites, we can make the following observations:

(i) Since the total range of resources has been considered in calculating the 'optimal niche-width', this should be compared against the niche-width of a regional subsistence system, rather than individual sites, to allow for the local variation in resources. Even so, considering the range of niche-width values for each relevant time period (*Table 1*), it becomes clear that most of the sites had niches narrower than the hypothetical optimum; only at one site, Narva, do we find a niche-width broader than the optimum. This again indicates a tendency

towards specialization rather than 'broad spectrum' economy.

(ii) If the range of sites within Periods 3 and 4 is considered as representative of a complete subsistence–settlement system – and there is good artifactual evidence to support such a contention – the niche-width still ranges from specialized sites with a narrow width to more generalized sites with width values approaching the regional optimum. This underlines the fact that at a regional scale specialized and generalized strategies are not mutually exclusive, but can and probably did form part of the same economic system. In our case, local specialization on coastal resources was probably complemented by broader resource use strategies inland.

TECHNOLOGICAL DEVELOPMENT AS A MEASURE OF INTENSIFICATION

Ecological measures of intensification do not take into account many cultural and taphonomic variables which affect archaeological remains. In the present case, for instance, the taphonomic processes which were bound to introduce bias into faunal samples and the problems involved in reconstructing the total range of food resources, both those which were actually used and those which were potentially available, render niche-width and other ecological measures unconvincing as measures of intensification, unless supported by more direct evidence.

In my view, economic intensification can be measured more directly in terms of labour and commitment invested in individual food procurement activities. This includes technological investment, commitment in terms of settlement location, socio-economic organization and other cultural variables. The problems with this approach lie in devising operational measurements of intensification along these lines.

Labour investment can be selected as, potentially, the most comprehensive and quantifiable measure of intensification. Although precise data regarding the labour investment in the manufacture of various toolkits are lacking, several technological developments during the Mesolithic period in north temperate Europe suggest intensification. These include:

(i) The development of specialized toolkits dedicated to the procurement of specific resources, such as those for fishing, water-fowling or sealing.

(ii) The development of toolkits designed for the exploitation of a wide range of resources in rapid succession. Such toolkits must be flexible, capable of being redeployed on different resources, and reparable in the field, rather than at the base. Bleed (1986) characterized such technologies as maintainable. Microlith component technology represents, in my view, such a technological development among Postglacial hunter-gatherers.

(iii) The development of facilities for capture and storage of resources, such as pits, traps, weirs, etc. (for further discussion of the significance of the extensive use of facilities – see Testart 1982; Torrence 1983; Zvelebil 1984; Rowley-Conwy and Zvelebil, in press).

Because these forms of technology are expensive in terms of labour investment, their development represents a major commitment to the resources in question and such resources must provide a major contribution to the diet. In north temperate Europe, technological developments outlined above appear to have occurred simultaneously and they correspond to the two aspects of the Mesolithic economy observed in the faunal samples: one characterized by specialization on aquatic or littoral species, the other by a more generalized use of resources. This dual nature of Mesolithic economy provided a measure of stability for the Postglacial hunter-gatherers until one of its two aspects collapsed through the decline in resources, as in the east Baltic, Denmark and southern Finland (Zvelebil and Rowley-Conwy 1986).

CONCLUSIONS

1. As indicators of economic intensification, niche-width, net productivity and other ecological variables are useful only in conjunction with cultural evidence showing increased commitment to a procurement of a specific range of resources.

2. At a more general level, niche-width provides a good descriptive measure of the way in which the environment is utilized and, when used in combination with 'optimal niche-width', it forms an effective standard against which resource use patterns can be characterized and evaluated.

3. In the case of the east Baltic, economic intensification appears to have taken the path towards specialization on aquatic resources, rather than developing a 'broad spectrum' economy. This is especially the case in the fifth and fourth millennia BP, prior to the adoption of farming. Nevertheless, the overall economy of late Mesolithic groups, most likely combined both generalized and specialized resource use strategies.

4. As to the immediate causes of the transition to farming, two subsistence-related processes can be suggested as having played a major role:

(a) Late Mesolithic communities diversified to the point where the economy was no longer viable, due to low return on labour investment in sub-optimal resources. This was demonstrably not the case in the east Baltic, but was more likely to occur in more inland areas of continental Europe and western Asia.

(b) Late Mesolithic communities specialized in a narrow range of resources to the point where such strategies became vulnerable to minor fluctuations in their availability. Such over-dependence was advanced by competition with neighbouring farmers for space and resources, leading to excessive niche specialization and to the eventual collapse of the hunting economy. In their final phase, the hunter-gatherer communities in the east Baltic, the Pitted Ware culture in middle Sweden and the Ertebølle culture in southern Scandinavia were probably involved in this process. Nevertheless, the adoption of farming by these coastal, specialized hunter-gatherers took place later than the transition to farming among the groups practising 'broad spectrum' economy in the interior.

This leads me to suggest two hypotheses regarding the pattern of the transition to farming (cf. Akazawa 1986; Zvelebil 1986):

(i) Where specialized subsistence strategies became an important aspect of the economy, as in the east Baltic, Scandinavia or north-east Japan, transition to farming was delayed at least partly because of the technological investment in the existing economy.

(ii) Where diversification gained the upper hand, as in some interior areas of temperate Europe or in the Near East, the transition to farming occurred earlier, partly because of the more generalized nature of the microlith component technology.

Thus, contrary to the traditional wisdom, maritime economy does not pre-adapt hunting-gathering communities to the adoption of farming. Rather, it is this deviation from the balance between the specialized and the diversified elements of the Mesolithic economy which can be seen as the immediate cause of the transition.

References

AKAZAWA, T. (1981) Maritime adaptation of prehistoric hunter-gatherers and their transition to agriculture in Japan. In S. Koyama and D.H. Thomas (eds), *Affluent Foragers*. Osaka, National Museum of Ethnology: 213–260.

AKAZAWA, T. (1986) Hunter-gatherer adaptations in the transition to food production in Japan. In M. Zvelebil (ed.), *Hunters in Transition*. Cambridge, University Press: 151–166.

BINFORD, L.R. (1983) *In Pursuit of the Past. Decoding the Archaeological Record*. London, Thames and Hudson.

BLEED, P. (1986) The optimal design of hunting weapons: maintainability or reliability. *American Antiquity*, 51(4): 737–747.

CASHDAN, E.A. (1985) Coping with risk: reciprocity among the Basarwa of northern Botswana. *Man*, 20: 454–474.

CLARK, G.A. and YI, S. (1983) Niche-width variation in Cantabrian archaeofaunas: a diachronic study. In J. Clutton-Brock and C. Grigson (eds), *Animals and Archaeology: 1. Hunters and their Prey*. Oxford, British Archaeological Reports (International Series) S163: 183–208.

COHEN, M.N. (1977) *The Food Crisis in Prehistory*. Yale, University Press.

DOLUKHANOV, P. (1979) *Ecology and Economy in Neolithic Eastern Europe*. London, Duckworth.

DOLUKHANOV, P. (1986) The late Mesolithic and the transition to food production in eastern Europe. In M. Zvelebil (ed.), *Hunters in Transition*. Cambridge, University Press: 109–119.

FLANNERY, K.V. (1969) Origins and ecological effects of early domestication in Iran and the Near East. In P.J. Ucko and G.W. Dimbleby (eds), *The Domestication and Exploitation of Plants and Animals*. Chicago, Aldine: 73–100.

FULLER, W.A. (1961) Ecology and management of the American bison. In F. Bourlière (ed.), *Ecology and Management of Wild Grazing Animals in Temperate Zones*. Morges (Switzerland), IUCN: 286–304.

HARDESTY, D.L. (1975) The niche concept: suggestions for its use in human ecology. *Human Ecology*, 3: 71–85.

HARDESTY, D.L. (1980) The use of general ecological principles in archaeology. In M.B. Schiffer (ed.), *Advances in Archaeological Method and Theory*, 3. New York, Academic Press: 157–187.

HAYDEN, B. (1981) Research and development in the Stone Age: technological transitions among hunter-gatherers. *Current Anthropology*, 22(5): 519–548.

JOCHIM, M.A. (1976) *Hunter-Gatherer Subsistence and Settlement. A Predictive Model*. London, Academic Press.

KOYAMA, S. and THOMAS, D.H. (eds) (1981) *Affluent Foragers* (Senri Ethnological Studies, 9). Osaka, National Museum of Ethnology.

LOTT, D.F. (1974) Sexual and aggressive behaviour of adult male American bison. In V. Geist and F. Walther (eds), *The Behaviour of Ungulates and its Relation to Management*. Morges (Switzerland), IUCN: 382–394.

McCULLOUGH, D.R. (1970) Secondary productivity of birds and mammals. In E.D. Reiche (ed.), *Temperate Forest Ecosystems* (Ecological Studies, 1). Berlin, Springer-Verlag: 107–130.

PAAVER, K.C. (1965) *Formirovanye Teriofauny i Izmenchivost Mlekopytayushchikh Pribaltiki v Golotsene*. Tartu, Akademiya Nauk Estonskoi SSR. (German summary: *Die Enstehung der Säugetier-fauna und der Variabilität der Säugetiere des Ostbaltikums in Holozän*).

PRICE, T.D. and BROWN, J.A. (1985) *Prehistoric Hunter-Gatherers*. The Emergence of Cultural Complexity. New York, Academic Press.

ROWLEY-CONWY, P. (1983) Sedentary hunters: the Ertebølle example. In G. Bailey (ed.), *Hunter-Gatherer Economy in Prehistory*. Cambridge, University Press: 111–126.

ROWLEY-CONWY, P. and ZVELEBIL, M. (in press) Saving it for later: storage by prehistoric hunter-gatherers in Europe. In J. O'Shea and P. Halstead (eds), *Bad Year Economics*. Cambridge, University Press.

SULIMIRSKI, T. (1970) *Prehistoric Russia*. London, John Baker.

TESTART, A. (1982) The significance of food storage among hunter-gatherers: residence patterns, population densities, and social inequalities. *Current Anthropology*, 23(5): 523–537.

TORRENCE, R. (1983) Time budgeting and hunter-gatherer technology. In G.Bailey (ed.), *Hunter-Gatherer Economy in Prehistory*. Cambridge, University Press: 11–23.

TORRENCE, R. (1986) Hunter-gatherer technology and the management of risk. *Paper presented at the Fourth International Conference on Hunting and Gathering Societies, London, September 1986*.

WATTS, K.E.F. (1973) *Principles of Environmental Science*. New York, McGraw Hill.

WIESSNER, P. (1982) Risk, reciprocity and social influences on !Kung San economics. In E. Leacock and R. Lee (eds), *Politics and History in Band Societies*. Cambridge, University Press: 61–84.

WINTERHALDER, B. and SMITH, E.A. (eds) (1981) *Hunter-Gatherer Foraging Strategies*. Chicago, University Press.

ZVELEBIL, M. (1981) *From Forager to Farmer in the Boreal Zone*. Oxford, British Archaeological Reports (International Series) S115.

ZVELEBIL, M. (1984) Clues to recent human evolution from specialised technologies? *Nature*, 307: 314–315.

ZVELEBIL, M. (1986) Mesolithic societies and the transition to farming: problems of time, scale and organisation. In M. Zvelebil (ed.), *Hunters in Transition*. Cambridge, University Press: 167–188.

ZVELEBIL, M. and ROWLEY-CONWY, P. (1984) Transition to farming in northern Europe: a hunter-gatherer perspective. *Norwegian Archaeological Review*, 17(2): 104–128.

ZVELEBIL, M. and ROWLEY-CONWY, P. (1986) Foragers and farmers in Atlantic Europe. In M. Zvelebil (ed.), *Hunters in Transition*. Cambridge, University Press: 67–94.

The Formation of Homogeneous Occupation Units ('Kshemenitsas') in Open-Air Sandy Sites and its Significance for the Interpretation of Mesolithic Flint Assemblages

Romuald Schild

Abstract

Most of the open-air Mesolithic sites of the North European Plain occur as artifact concentrations which are often confined within an enclosed network of articulations. These are interpreted as homogeneous occupational units or 'entities', otherwise known as *kshemenitsas*. An understanding of the formation of these units should add a new dimension to our interpretation of the flint assemblages occurring in individual *kshemenitsas*, and also shine some light on the problems associated with the use of a site, the length and number of occupations, etc.

At the site of Całowanie in the Vistula valley, near Warsaw, three final Palaeolithic and at least three early Mesolithic occupational units in cut III are associated with both mineral and organic sediments. Precise dating of these units based on palynology and 17 radiocarbon determinations has permitted chronological evaluation of their formation.

INTRODUCTION

Most of the Mesolithic sites on the North European Plain occur within sandy deposits such as dunes, river terraces, glacial outwash plains, and so forth. As nearly all of the sites were formed after the deposition of the sands had ended, the Mesolithic occupation horizons invariably occur in the lower A- and upper B-horizons of Holocene podzol, podzolic, or brown sandy soils. Archaeological stratigraphy in these sandy sites is practically non-existent, and very often materials classified within different taxonomic entities occur mixed together, as well as with older, final Palaeolithic occupations or with even younger archaeological units – all of which post-date the deposition of the sands.

One of the key problems in the study of the north European Mesolithic concerns the homogeneity of assemblages occurring in such a stratigraphic context. Clearly, evaluation of the homogeneity of an assemblage is not only necessary for the construction of adequate taxonomic systems, it is also an important factor in any assessment of settlement pattern, horizontal distribution of occupation units, their chronological relationship, internal functional clustering, and the number and duration of occupations. Indeed, the question of whether a Mesolithic occurrence in a sandy site is a single homogeneous phenomenon, or represents many different instances of occupation, is fundamental to all research goals pertaining to the north European Mesolithic,

whether concerned with taxonomy, chronology, or settlement archaeology.

Already in the early years of this century, some prehistorians who collected from and excavated final Palaeolithic and Mesolithic dune and terrace sites observed that at some localities the lithic materials occurred in clusters several metres in diameter, while at other sites they formed more or less continuous spreads covering much larger areas. It was suggested that the discrete clusters represented homogeneous units and could, therefore, serve as the basis for sound taxonomic constructs. This view has been accepted by many European prehistorians and is still a basic proposition in studies of the north European Mesolithic.

The last two decades have brought about a remarkable expansion of interest in the study of horizontal patterning in Mesolithic assemblages occurring in the sandy lowlands of the North European Plain. Various techniques have been used to demonstrate homogeneity and/or behavioural dependence in the patterning of lithics at these sites, and to define individual occupational units (*kshemenitsas*).[1] Of these techniques, the construction of articulation networks (refits), wear trace analyses, and statistical methods of discrimination and/or clustering of the materials are considered to be the most informative and to yield the most reliable results.

In theory, the use of strict chronological controls to establish the precise length of occupations and to determine whether they were single or repeated, could serve as a test of hypotheses based on studies of the horizontal distribution of the lithics. However, conventional radiocarbon dating has proved to be unsuitable for this task. This is particularly true of the sandy sites of the North European Plain. The lack of stratigraphy, the subsurface character of sites – open to prehistoric and recent contamination – and the limitations of the method itself, are responsible for this situation. Charcoal samples collected at such subsurface Mesolithic sites are frequently mixed and have very often resulted from tree-falls, or from accidental or culturally-generated fires, which occurred throughout the Holocene. Sometimes, however, Mesolithic features – usually hearths – give reliable radiocarbon dates. These are rare, however, and never occur in series which permit the dating of several individual features in a single *kshemenitsa*, or even in the various *kshemenitsas* of the same site. Furthermore, the conventional radiocarbon method usually requires a sample composed of a large number of individual charcoal pieces. These not only derive from different trees or sections of the same tree, which can show different isotopic contents, but, more important, they may represent different instances of occupation. The radiocarbon dates obtained from such samples are simple means of all their isotopic components. A large series of dates obtained from individual pieces of charcoal from the same occupation unit, or from the various units of the same site, would be necessary in order to falsify or verify hypotheses resulting from distributional analyses. Today, such a task can be performed only by AMS or conventional radiocarbon dating using single, large pieces of wood, preferably pine cones or small branches. These, however, are not available at most of the sandy sites. Only localities where the cultural layer is sealed by later sediments are suitable for such

experiments. One such site is Całowanie, in the *voivodedom*[2] of Warsaw (Schild 1975).

THE MESOLITHIC PRESENCE AT CAŁOWANIE

Całowanie is a multi-level, multi-unit site in the Vistula valley, some 30 km upstream from Warsaw. The site is made up of an old river bar deposited in the early and middle Allerød, overlain by an early Younger Dryas dune. It lies in the middle of an elongated and slightly curved former channel of the Vistula river, which was abandoned during the early upper Allerød. The channel is filled with mineral and organic sediments deposited during the final Lateglacial and throughout the Holocene. Thick peat beds of Allerød to recent age form the main part of the fill. During eight field seasons (1963–69, 1983), 13 large cuts, 22 stratigraphic trenches and 10 peat trenches were excavated. Some 30 radiocarbon dates, as well as several pollen diagrams, permit relatively precise chronological placement of the cultural layers.

Counting from the base there are six cultural layers representing the final Palaeolithic (I–VI) and

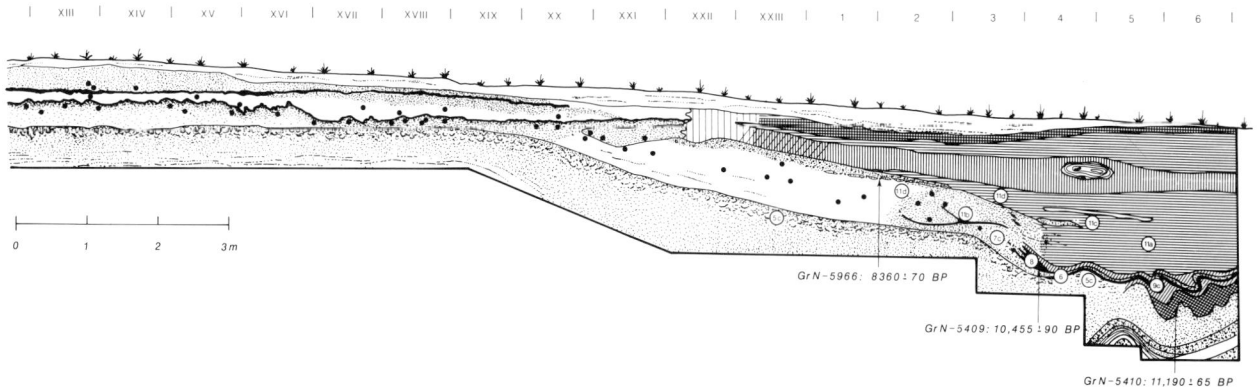

Figure 1 Cross-section through peat trench IX and the northern portion of cut III. *Key:* 5c – late Allerød soil; 6 – silt horizon, early Younger Dryas; 7c – aeolian sands, early Younger Dryas; 8 – thin horizons of silt and gyttja, grading into 9c, mid-Younger Dryas; 9b and 9c – gyttja and peat, late Younger Dryas and beginning of Pre-Boreal; 11a – peat bed, Pre-Boreal and Boreal; 11b – reworked beach sands with cultural material; 11c – sand lenses in the peat; 11d – lenses of culturally sterile sand. Cultural layers are indicated by Roman numerals. (after Schild 1975)

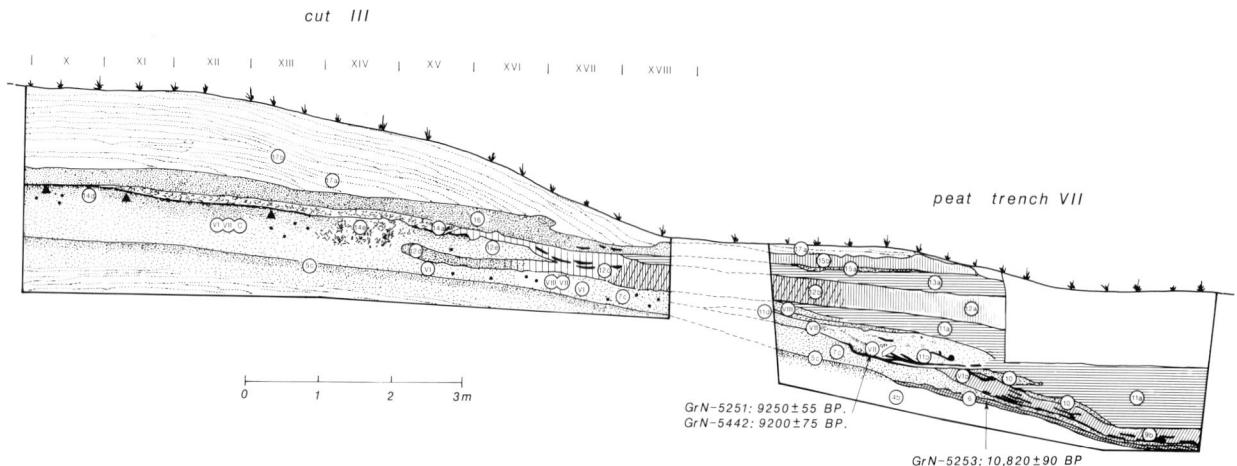

Figure 2 Cross-section through peat trench VII and the northern portion of cut III. For key see *Fig. 1*. (after Schild 1975)

90

dating between c. 11,600 BP and c. 9700 BP; these are succeeded by layers VII and VIII belonging to the early Mesolithic, Narvian complex (Komornica culture) and dated to the late Pre-Boreal and Boreal, between c. 9400 BP and c. 8300 BP. It is these two Mesolithic layers and the youngest final Palaeolithic layer (VI) which are of interest here.

The Masovian lithic assemblages of layer VI occur mixed with the early Mesolithic materials in the eluvial and illuvial horizons of the podzolic soil developed in the top of the early Younger Dryas dune. Both the Masovian and early Mesolithic occupations post-date the formation of the dune and were originally deposited over its surface. Only in the dune border zone, in the north-western part of the site – where the mineral sediments and fossil soils interdigitate with the organic deposits of the peat bog (*Figs. 1 & 2*) – could the upper three cultural layers be separated stratigraphically.

In the dune border zone, the Masovian materials of layer VI occur in the reworked dune sands of the beach which interdigitates with a sandy or silty gyttja grading into silty peat with sand admixture. The thin, basal horizon of this gyttja (level 8, base) gave a radiocarbon date of 10,455±90 BP (GrN-5409). A number of other dates on charcoal from the main bed of gyttja (level 9) place the end of this Masovian occupation around 9700 BP.

The early Mesolithic materials in the border zone occur in two sandy, reworked dune beds separated in places by a thin (less than 10 cm) layer of sterile sand (level 11d). The sandy cultural layers interdigitate with and/or grade laterally, toward the surrounding peat bog, into a thick body of peat (level 11a), rich in charcoal throughout. The lower of the cultural horizons (layer VII) is clearly dissect-

ed by several minor erosional surfaces and displays the characteristics of a seasonal, high water beach.

Three radiocarbon dates obtained in the early 1970s, combined with the palynological evidence (Dąbrowski 1981), suggested a late Pre-Boreal or early Boreal age for the Mesolithic layers (*Fig. 3*). Two samples of charcoal were collected from the earliest erosional surface of cultural layer VII (level 11b, base). These gave dates of 9250±55 BP (GrN-5251) and 9200±75 BP (GrN-5442). Another date of 8360±75 BP (GrN-5966) was obtained from a charcoal sample collected from layer VIII in the border zone (peat trench IX). It was assumed at that time that the radiocarbon dates indicated the age of the two major periods of Mesolithic occupation. It was also believed that the unstratified early Mesolithic materials in the adjacent cut III represented these same two occupations.

The excavations in cut III (765 m²) revealed the presence of rich early Mesolithic materials mixed with Masovian artifacts in the lower A- and the B-horizon of the podzolic soil. The Masovian, final Palaeolithic materials clustered into three large but thin concentrations, termed 'eastern', 'central' and 'western' (*Fig. 4*). Similarly, the much richer early Mesolithic artifacts seemed to form three large but overlapping clusters, designated I, II and III. Each of these contained smaller sub-concentrations (*Figs. 5 & 6*).

The intensity of the cultural debris in layer VIII of peat trench IX, near the westernmost concentration, seemed to indicate the association of this unit (III) with the younger Mesolithic occupation dated to the early middle Boreal. On the other hand, clusters I and II were the closest to peat trenches VII and VIII where the debris in cultural layer VII was the

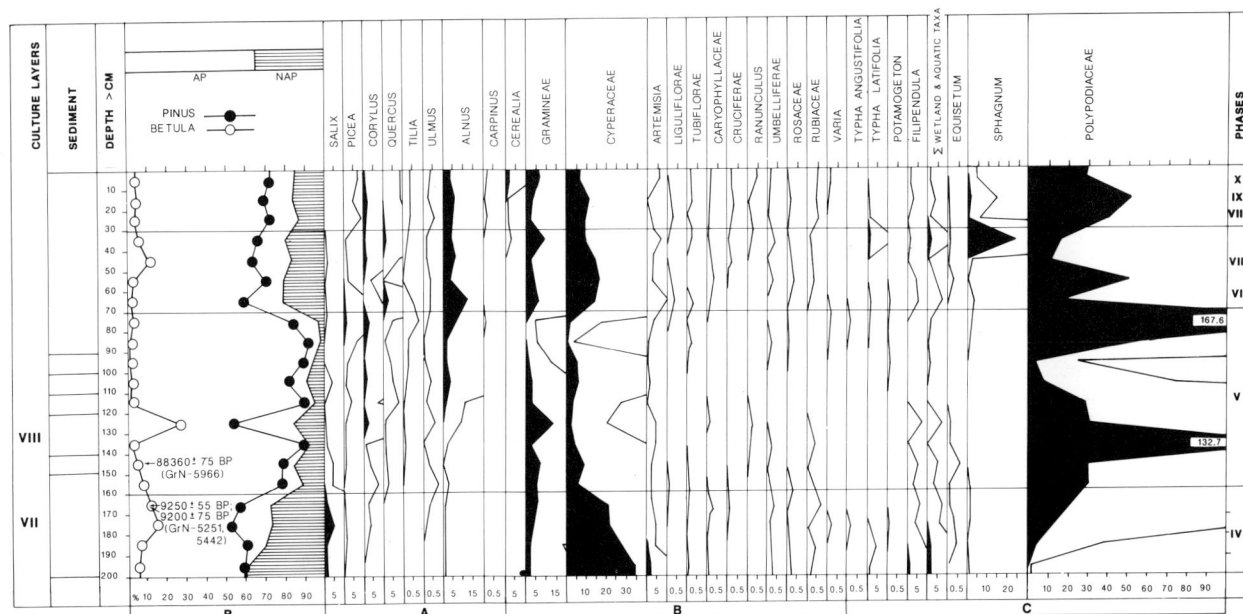

Figure 3   Pollen diagram Całowanie IV showing, projected from the beach zone, the positions of early radiocarbon dates from cultural layers VII and VIII, left column. (after Dąbrowski 1981)

91

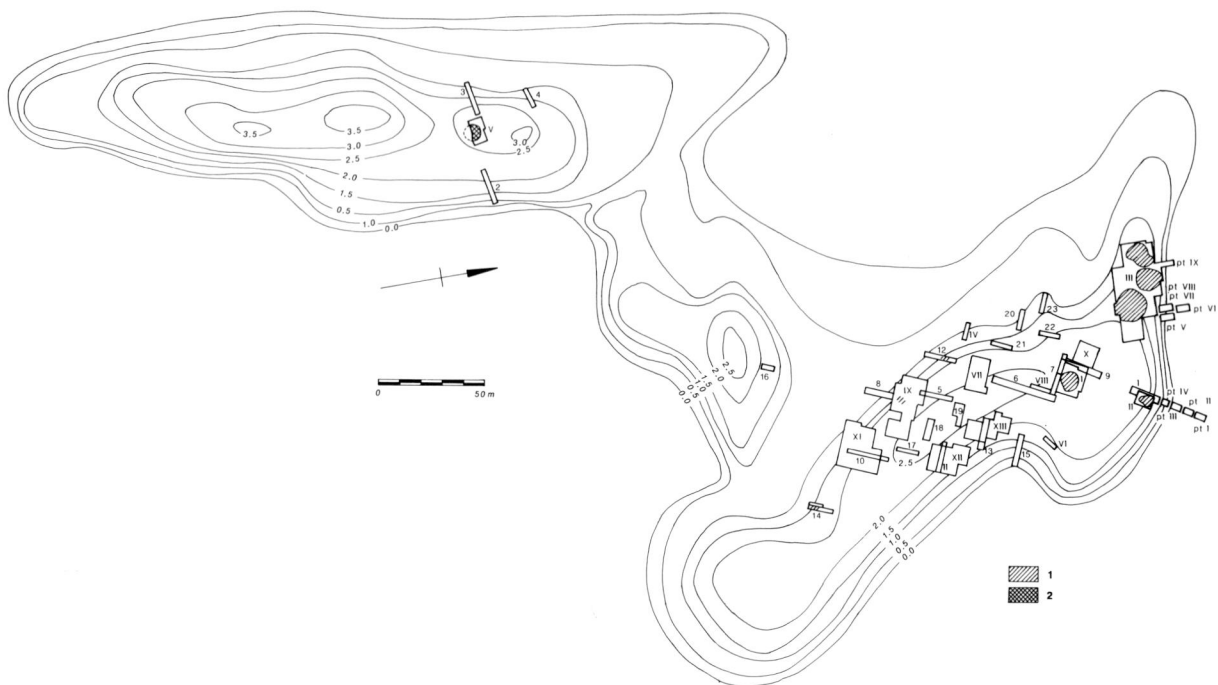

Figure 4 Island of Całowanie, layer VI: distribution of cultural occurrences during the post-dune phase of the Younger Dryas and early Pre-Boreal. *Key*: 1 – Masovian occupations; 2 – Grochale type units. (after Schild 1984)

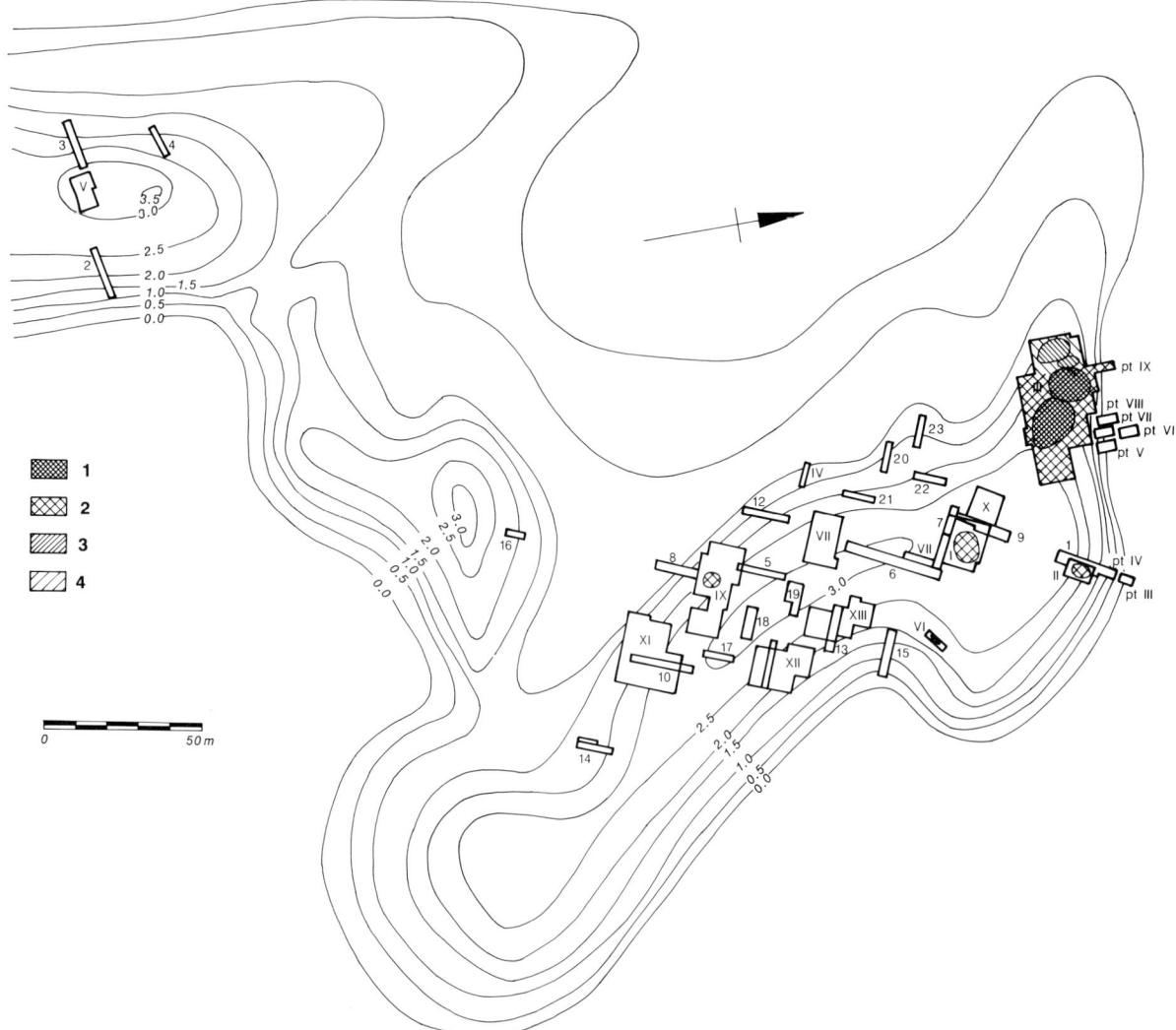

Figure 5 Island of Całowanie, layers VII and VIII: distribution of cultural occurrences during the late Pre-Boreal and first half of the Boreal. *Key*: 1 – dense scatter of artifacts of the presumed layer VII; 2 – thin scatters of artifacts of the presumed layer VII; 3 – dense scatters of artifacts of the presumed layer VIII; 4 – thin scatter of artifacts of the presumed layer VIII.

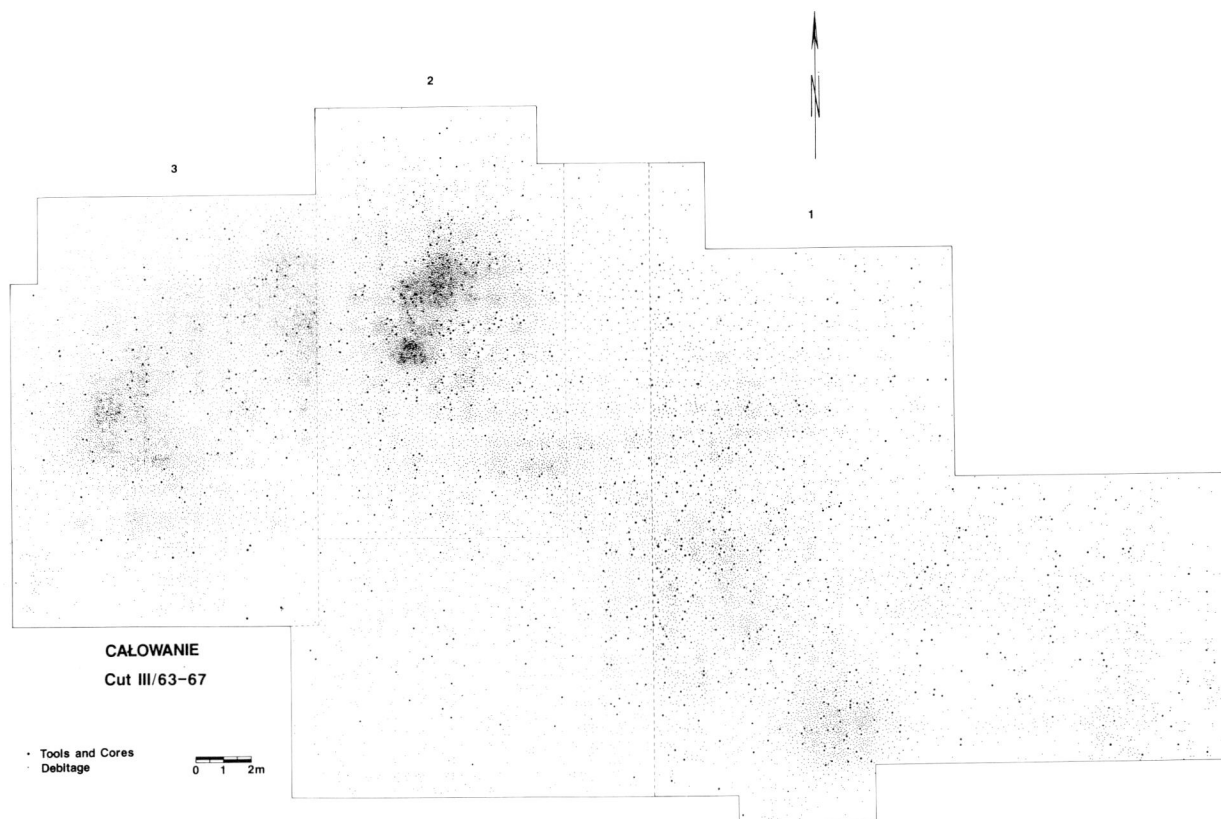

Figure 6 Cut III: unprocessed horizontal distribution of artifacts and arbitrary subdivision of assemblages (dotted lines). Tools and cores are shown by larger dots.

richest, and were therefore linked with the earliest late Pre-Boreal Mesolithic occupation. Several other cuts in the site failed to disclose any other important Mesolithic occupations (cf. *Fig. 5*).

Analysis of the horizontal distribution of the artifacts, together with radiocarbon dating, pollen analysis, and the stratigraphy in the dune border zone led to the conclusion that there were two periods of early Mesolithic occupations. It was believed that the earlier settlement was composed of two occupation units, perhaps belonging to the same camp, while the later settlement also included two, but much smaller, entities. Similarly, the radiocarbon dates and stratigraphy of the Masovian layer VI in the peat trenches adjacent to cut III indicated that there might be some variation in the age of the recorded *kshemenitsas*. This was the state of chronological and structural evaluation of the late Masovian and early Mesolithic settlements of Całowanie a decade ago.

Objections have since arisen to this simple, though attractive, picture of well-structured and well-dated settlements. Analyses of numerous final Palaeolithic and Mesolithic sites in Poland have shown that differences in the horizontal distribution of artifacts, as well as in their relative and absolute frequencies in a unit, can be of considerable magnitude. This suggested that the so-called *kshemenitsas* could also have been formed as a result of many occupational events of varying intensity, duration, and character. The site of Całowanie seemed to be

the best on which to test a hypothesis that some of the *kshemenitsas* could, in fact, have been formed during many episodes of occupation.

RETHINKING THE MESOLITHIC OCCUPATIONS AT CAŁOWANIE

In the 1983 season a new peat trench (X) was opened, only 50 cm west of peat trench VII. The aim of this new excavation was to recover another series of radiocarbon samples from the horizons known to be associated with cultural layers VI to VIII, in order to test the hypothesis of a multi-occupational character of the final Palaeolithic and early Mesolithic settlements in cut III. In addition, a third series of burnt pine branches and pine cones, excavated in previous seasons, was to be dated. It was assumed that the single burnt pine branches or cones would yield dates reflecting individual human occupation events in the area adjacent to the north-western border zone in cut III – the most complex Mesolithic settlement of the entire site.

Four new radiocarbon samples from the final Palaeolithic gyttja (level 9b) were dated (*Fig. 7*): one from the middle; one from the entire thickness of the horizon; and one from its very top. The dates from the middle and the top of the gyttja were measured on single pieces of charred pine branches. Another charred branch, recovered during a previous season from the Mesolithic beach zone, gave a final Palaeolithic date.

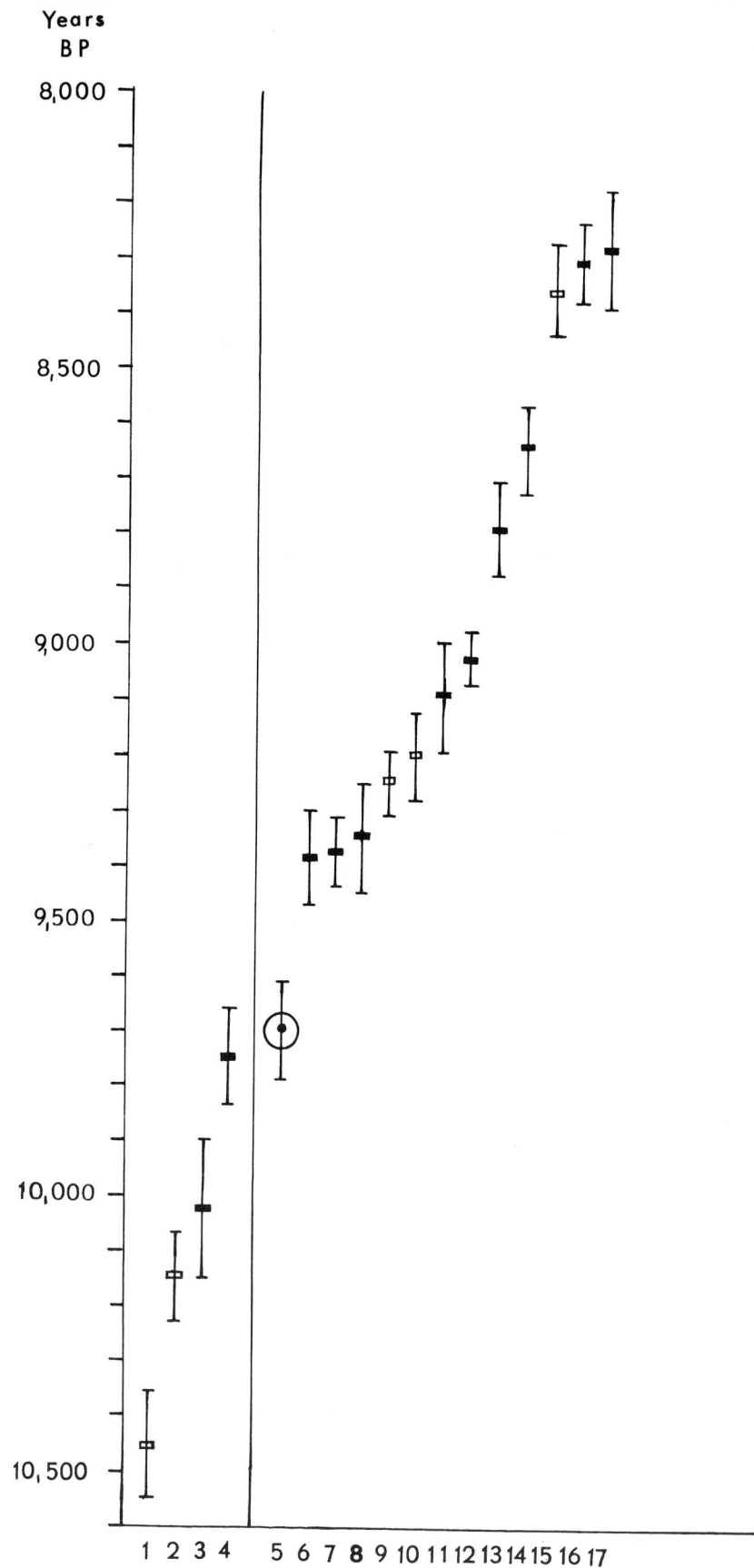

Figure 7 Radiocarbon dates from the late Masovian and early Mesolithic occupations in peat trenches VII, IX and X. Measurements on charred pine cones or branches are indicated by black boxes. *Late Masovian*: 1 – level 8, charcoal, GrN-5409; 2 – level 9b, whole thickness, charcoal, Gd-1648; 3 – level 9b, middle, burnt branch, Gd-2147; 4 – level 9b, top, burnt branch, Gd-1662; 5 – level 11b (secondary context), burnt branch, Gd-1717. *Early Mesolithic*: 6 – level 11b, burnt branch, Gd-1721; 7 – level 11b, burnt branch, Gd-1719; 8 – level 11b, burnt branch, Gd-2198; 9 – level 11b, base, charcoal, GrN-5251; 10 – level 11b, base, charcoal, GrN-5442; 11 – level 11b, burnt branch, Gd-2149; 12 – level 11b, burnt branch, Gd-3041; 13 – level 11b, burnt branch, Gd-1667; 14 – level 11b, burnt branch, Gd-1668; 15 – just above level 11d, charcoal, GrN-5966; 16 – level 11b, burnt branch, Gd-1670; 17 – level 11b, pine cone, Gd-2146.

WESTERN   C E N T R A L   E A S T E R N

20   40   60%   20   40   60%   20   40   60%

	WESTERN	CENTRAL	EASTERN
1	6	6	13
2	25	18	8
3	2	2	
4			
5	2		1
6	8	3	8
7		1	1
8	1		
9			
10		1	
11	8	13	14
	52	44	45

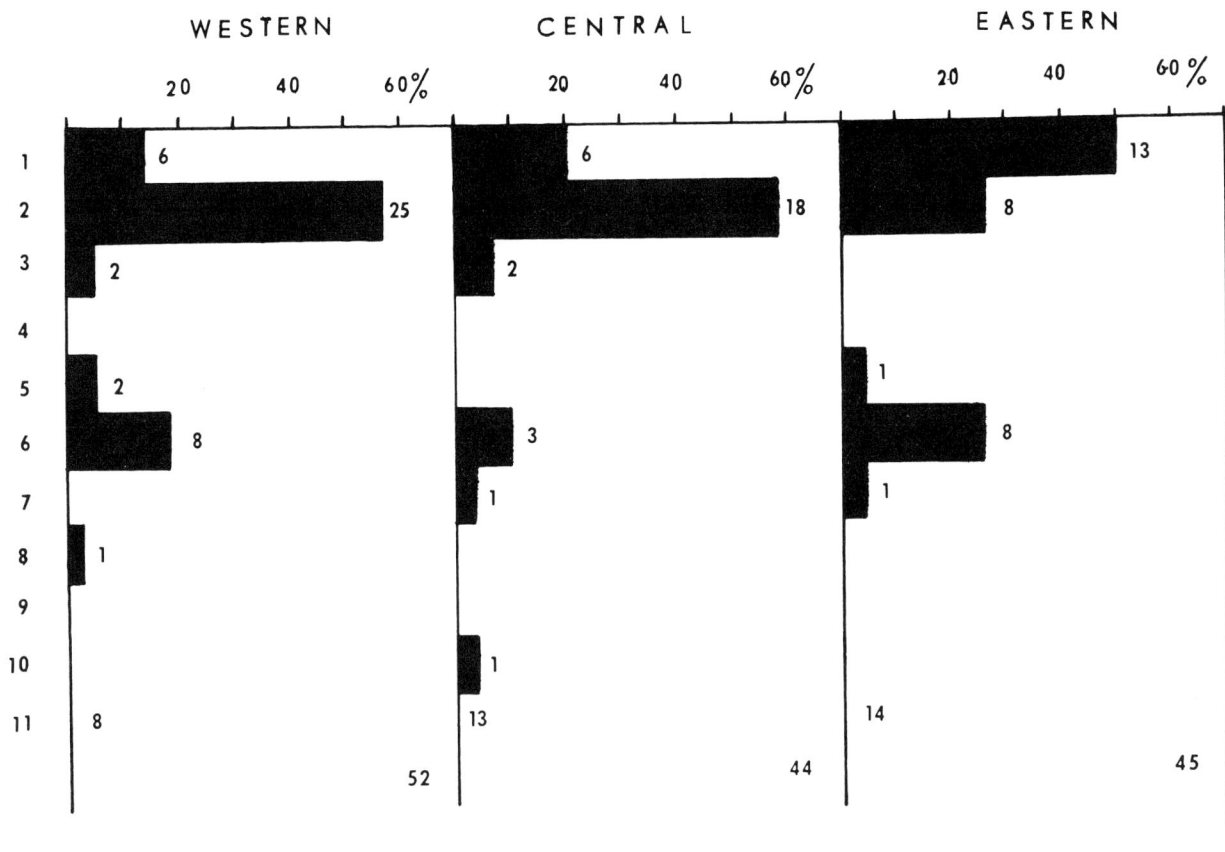

Figure 8 Całowanie, cut III, cultural layer VI, late Masovian. General tool composition: 1 – end-scrapers; 2 – burins; 3 – perforators; 4 – backed elements; 5 – truncations, regular; 6 – Masovian, willow-leaf points; 7 – Masovian, pendunculated points; 8 – Ahrensburgian points; 9 – micro-truncations and geometrics; 10 – miscellaneous and indeterminate.

Although some of the final Palaeolithic dates were measured on samples containing numerous charcoal pieces, the series of radiocarbon determinations obtained clearly indicates semi-continuous human presence from *c.* 10,500 BP to *c.* 9700 BP.

The new, large series of nine Mesolithic radiocarbon measurements yielded interesting results (*Fig. 7*). Most of the new dates were obtained from single, burnt pine branches and cones. They showed a statistically continuous (at the 2*s* level) human presence from *c.* 9400 BP to *c.* 8300 BP. Two of the dates obtained from single branches (Gd-1670 and Gd-2146) gave an age slightly younger than the previous youngest Mesolithic date from layer VIII (GrN-5966). The branches had been recovered during earlier campaigns from the upper section of the beach zone, where layers VII and VIII were not separated stratigraphically.

The analysis of the lithic assemblages from the separate artifact clusters, previously believed to represent individual occupations, is of considerable interest. First of all, the three final Palaeolithic assemblages are quite poor, each containing only 40–50 tools (*Fig. 8*). The differences in the general tool composition of the assemblages are not statistically significant (Kolmogorov–Smirnov test: $\alpha = 0.01$), suggesting that the occupations were of similar functional character. In contrast, the three Meso-

lithic assemblages are relatively rich, each containing over 100 tools, between 40 and 140 cores, and between 5000 and 6000 pieces of débitage. Again, the differences in general tool composition (*Fig. 9*) are not statistically significant ($\alpha = 0.01$).

The new radiocarbon dates suggest a radically different interpretation of the history of formation of the *kshemenitsas* in cut III of Całowanie. In the light of these dates, which mark periods of human presence, both the final Palaeolithic and early Mesolithic artifact aggregations can be regarded as having formed either during many instances of reoccupation or by two single, long-term habitations, of which the first lasted *c.* 800 years and the second over 1000 years. The latter hypothesis, however, seems very unlikely.

Why was this small, north-western part of the large dune island so frequently visited? The modern morphology of the island and the surrounding peat bog do not offer any clues in this respect. On the other hand, a reconstruction of the palaeomorphology of the entire, fossil Vistula channel and its bar and dune islands is of some relevance. The reconstruction has been based on a large number of auger soundings which yielded precise data concerning the depth of the peat bed, and thus about the morphology of the channel before the formation of the peat (*Fig. 10*). It is presumed that the depres-

Figure (chart columns I, II, III)

Row	I	II	III
1	65	38	18
2	16	4	4
3	10	5	5
4	37	35	20
5	8	11	7
6	5	8	
7	14	13	3
8	9	8	
9	1		
10	13	19	8
11		4	4
12	13	14	12
13	4	1	1
14	27	26	15
15			1
16	21	26	14
17	2	2	1
18	30	29	7
Total	275	243	120

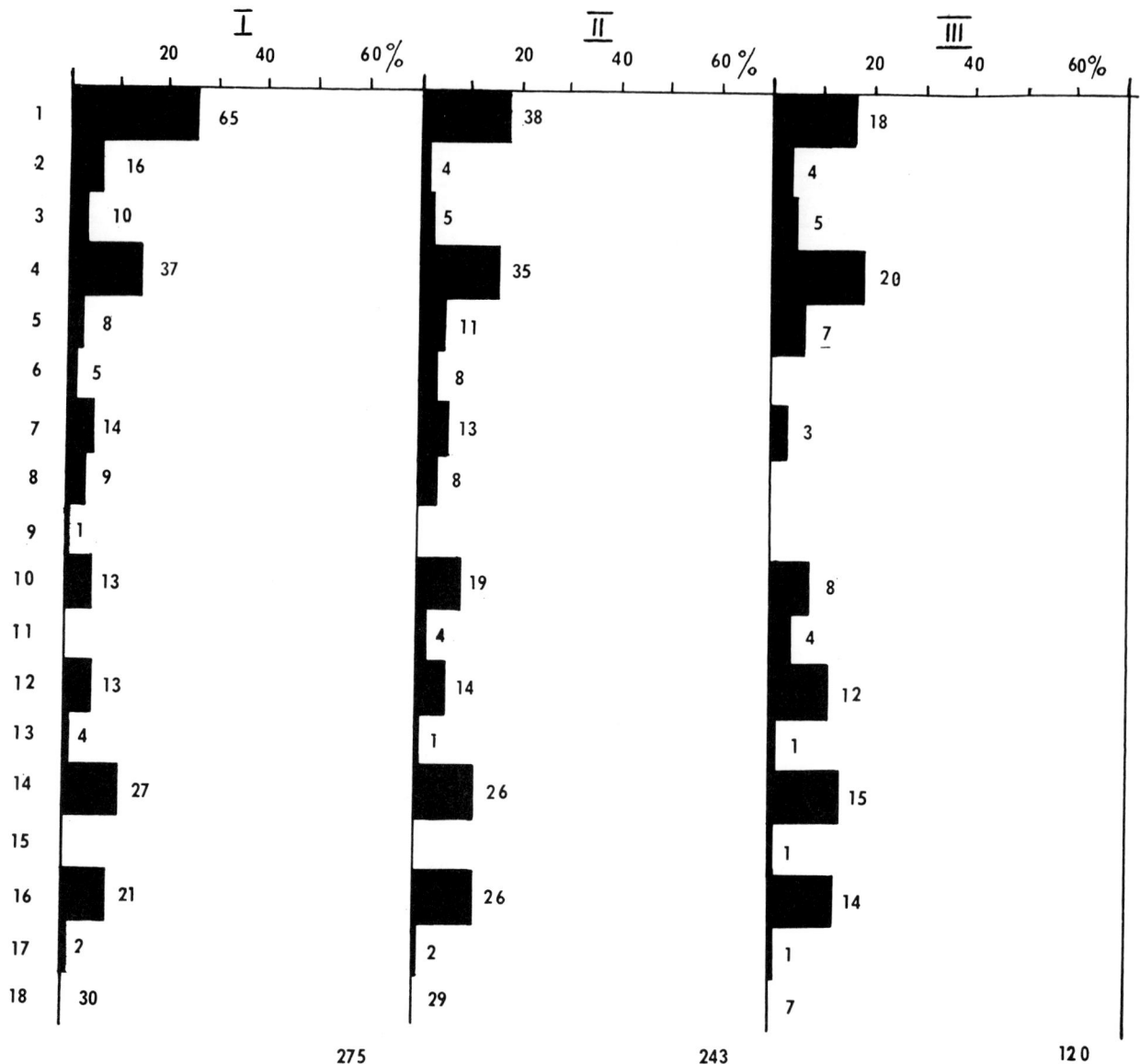

Figure 9 Całowanie, cut III, early Mesolithic. General tool composition: 1 – end-scrapers; 2 – burins; 3 – perforators; 4 – pointed, straight-backed bladelets; 5 – pointed, arch-backed bladelets; 6 – blunt-backed bladelets; 7 – micro-truncations; 8 – truncations, regular; 9 – double truncations; 10 – scalene triangles, wide-angled; 11 – scalene triangles, right-angled; 12 – isosceles triangles; 13 – shouldered backed bladelets; 14 – microlith fragments; 15 – trapezoids; 16 – microburins; 17 – flake axes; 18 – miscellaneous and indeterminate.

sions in the channel would have held larger bodies of water and, therefore, that areas on islands near these depressions would be more attractive for human occupation.

Pollen and radiocarbon evidence indicates that substantial beds of peat began to form in the late Allerød and almost certainly only in the lower, depressed section of the fossil channel (Dąbrowski 1981: pollen diagram I). Therefore, the morphology of the channel near the island recorded in the peat soundings was that of the late Younger Dryas and Pre-Boreal (Dąbrowski 1981: pollen diagram IV).

The thickness of the peat bed surrounding the island of Całowanie shows that the deepest section extends along the northern and eastern border zones of the island, and not just near its north-western portion. This observation was confirmed by the peat

trenches sunk into the peat bog just off the northern border zone. It thus became clear that the whole northern and eastern parts of the island were equally attractive for settlement, at least as far as water supply was concerned.

There are no obvious, natural, geomorphological features that would account for the repeated occupation of the island, which is less than 10,000 m² in area. There may, therefore, be a cultural explanation. It could be hypothesized that the repetition of human camps in the north-western part of the island was culturally generated, and that the same area was constantly reoccupied by the same groups of hunter gatherers, and their descendants, over a long period of time. The clustering of the lithic materials, in spite of such a long period of reoccupation, may even indicate the use of the very same spot, during every

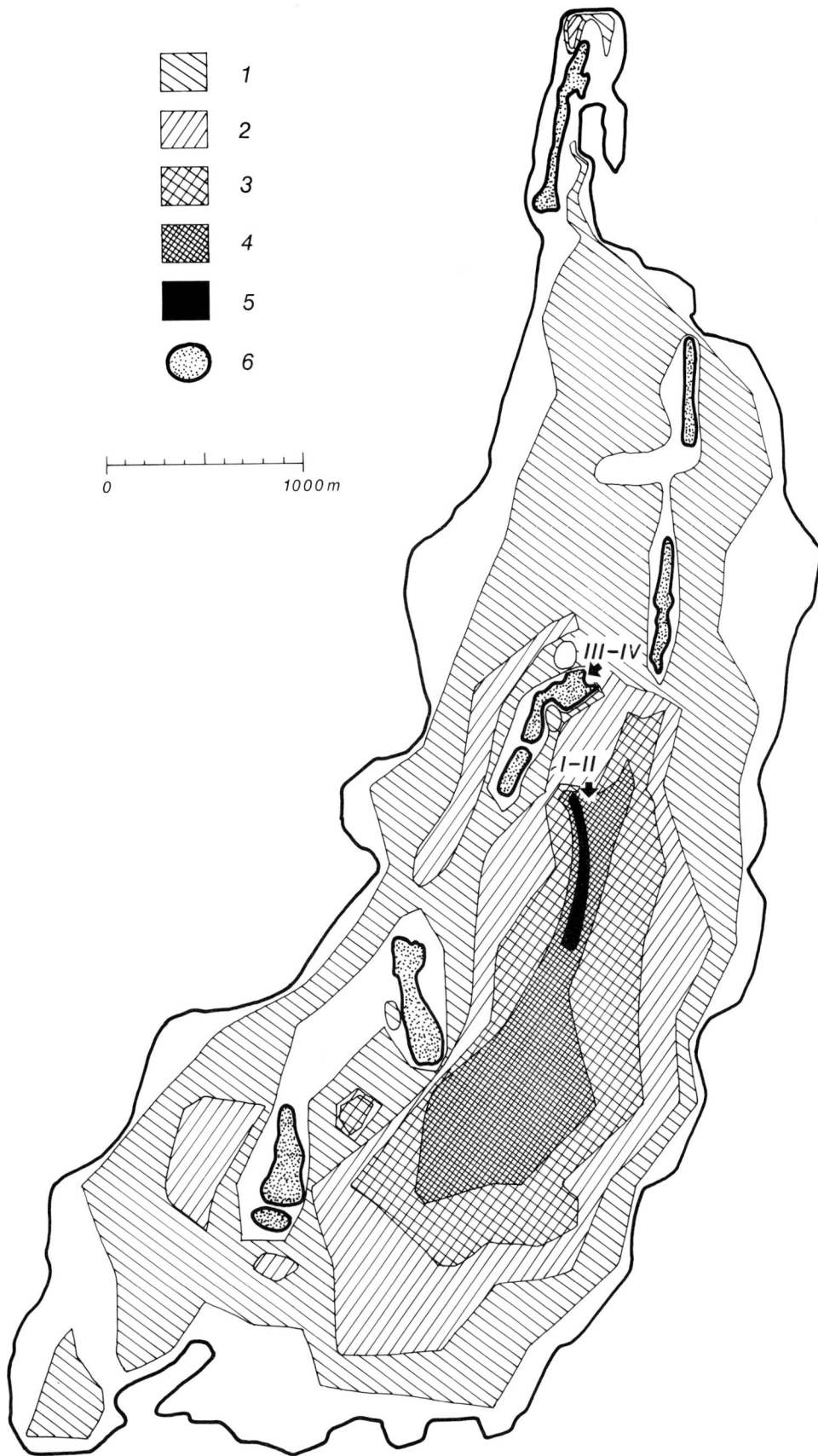

Figure 10 Distribution of peat in the Vistula palaeochannel near Całowanie: 1 – 0–1 metres; 2 – 1–2 metres; 3 – 2–3 metres; 4 – 3–4 metres; 5 – 4–5 metres; 6 – sand islands. Location of pollen diagrams is shown by arrows. Pollen diagrams III and IV are from peat trench IX. (after Dąbrowski 1981)

episode of occupation, by the same small social entities forming the group – possibly, nuclear families. Such phenomena are not rare among modern nomadic populations.

GENERAL CONCLUSIONS

This exercise in the chronological analysis of the occupation clusters at Całowanie adds several new dimensions to our present understanding of the formation of settlement units in subsurface, sandy sites of the North European Plain. These new observations also seem to be valid for all sites formed during a period characterized by a lack of sediment accumulation.

The example of Całowanie indicates that the formation of seemingly homogeneous occupation units could be a very complex process involving many periods of occupation, sometimes perhaps even hundreds. The possibility cannot be excluded that at some sites the individual instances of occupation of the same spot reflect regular visits to the area by the same group, probably during specific seasons of the year. Certainly, many of the rich *kshemenitsas* of the final Palaeolithic and Mesolithic could be reasonably suspected of having been formed during many episodes of occupation, an idea already expressed before re-examination of the final Palaeolithic and Mesolithic settlements at Całowanie was planned (Schild and Królik 1981).

The relative paucity of the final Palaeolithic inventories in cut III of Całowanie, in spite of the frequent reoccupation of the loci, is of considerable interest. It now seems obvious that the assemblages recovered were formed over several hundreds of years, indicating that the individual episodes of occupation each added only a very limited number of tools to the *kshemenitsas*. It is likely that this mode of assemblage formation partially reflects a specific raw material economy based on imported chocolate-coloured flint, and different from that employed during the early Mesolithic which commonly used local, erratic flint. On the other hand, it could be hypothesized that the individual episodes of occupation during the Younger Dryas and the Holocene were radically different in dur-ation, reflecting exploitation of quite different environments. The difference is perhaps equivalent to that observed among the site horizontal distribution patterns of the Allerød and Younger Dryas phases of the Lateglacial.

The probable complex history of the formation of at least some settlement units of the final Palaeolithic and Mesolithic cannot be disregarded by the taxonomist. It appears that the basic unit of classification used by taxonomists in the construction of space/time units – the assemblage – could, in fact, represent accumulations of artifacts formed over several hundreds of years, if not millennia. Furthermore, such assemblages could include a number of different functional uses of the site and, therefore, may never permit proper functional identification of the occupations that have made up the assemblage.

The complexity of the late Masovian and early Mesolithic assemblages at Całowanie cannot be regarded as unique on the North European Plain. The message conveyed by the chronology of the formation of the assemblages at Całowanie suggests that a multi-aspectual approach to final Palaeolithic and Mesolithic sites in the sandy lowlands not only permits a much better understanding of settlement use and environment exploitation, but is necessary for the proper construction of taxonomic systems based on lithic assemblages.

Notes:

1. Anglicized spelling of the Polish *krzemienica* (plural: *krzemienice*), meaning a discrete or tightly confined concentration of lithic artifacts. (Ed.)

2. The district administered by a *Voivode*. (Ed.)

References

DĄBROWSKI, M.J. (1981) Analiza pyłkowa torfowiska Całowanie (woj. warszawskie). *Archeologia Polski*, 26(2): 269–294.
SCHILD, R. (1975) Późny paleolit. In W. Chmielewski and W. Hensel (eds), *Prahistoria ziem polskich*, vol. 1. Wrocław, Ossolineum: 159–338.
SCHILD, R. (1984) Terminal Palaeolithic of the North European Plain: a review of lost chances, potential, and hopes. In F. Wendorf and A.E. Close (eds), *Advances in World Archaeology*, vol. 3. Orlando, Academic Press: 193–274.
SCHILD, R. and KRÓLIK, H. (1981) Rydno. A final Palaeolithic ochre mining complex. *Przegląd Archeologiczny*, 29: 53–100.

General Spatial Behaviour in Small Dwellings: a Preliminary Study in Ethnoarchaeology and Social Psychology

Ole Grøn

Abstract

On the basis of distribution patterns of artifacts repeated at a number of Maglemose sites – apparently inside the dwelling areas – a general discussion is presented of the organization of social space within the dwellings of hunter-gatherers. A number of general rules for such spatial structuring are postulated on the basis of cases drawn from anthropology and from social psychology. The archaeological usefulness of such spatial patterns is briefly discussed.

INTRODUCTION

During studies of the horizontal distribution of different artifact types at Maglemose sites of restricted size (maximum diameter of the main concentration – 10 m) and with typologically homogeneous material, it became clear that the microliths on a number of sites were distributed in a very characteristic bipartite pattern. In all these cases, it appeared that this pattern had a specific orientation in relation to the prehistoric lake shore (*Fig. 1*). In one case – the well-preserved rectangular hut floor from Ulkestrup I (measuring 6 × 4 m) – the bipartite pattern was found inside the hut area. On the basis of a number of anthropologically known cases, two assumptions were made: (i) that the two microlith concentrations represent working areas of fixed location in dwellings of uniform shape, size and interior organization; and (ii) that these dwellings had approximately the same orientation in relation to the adjacent lake shore.

Another series of sites revealed a different pattern in the horizontal distribution of microliths, showing only a single concentration. At Duvensee W.8 and, probably, Ulkestrup II this pattern is found inside huts of less than 15 m² – in the latter case apparently with the entrance orientated towards the shore, as in the larger huts (Grøn 1987a).

A study of the position of fireplaces inside the hut areas supported the initial impression that the two hut types had contained households consisting of one or two families, respectively. In three cases where remains of fireplaces were found associated with the smaller dwelling type, the existence of only one fireplace was indicated. With regard to the larger dwelling type, two fireplaces were indicated in

three out of four cases, where this could be studied. In each hut type, fireplaces seemed to have fixed locations. At Ulkestrup I, where two fireplaces could be expected, but only one was found during excavation; the fireplace occupied a central position closer to the water than the microliths. Whereas in the larger dwellings the fireplaces were placed in front of the microlith concentrations in relation to the lake shore, within the smaller ones they were placed beside them. This demonstrates that the bipartite patterns do not consist of two non-contemporaneous small units. Furthermore, it indicates that the organization of activities around the fireplaces was independent of the wind direction, and thus reflects an indoor situation. For a more detailed discussion of the dwellings of the Maglemose culture, see Grøn (1983, 1984, 1987a, 1987b, 1988).

ETHNOGRAPHIC EVIDENCE

Collection of anthropological data concerning the spatial behaviour of primitive cultures in their dwellings – especially hunter-gatherer societies – became a natural part of the study. The more information was compiled, the more it became evident that patterned behaviour in dwellings according to culture-specific rules was a universal phenomenon that had not been given sufficient attention in archaeological research.

In his book *Tents. Architecture of the Nomads*, Torvald Faegre writes:

> The space within the ordinary tent is not large and so must be carefully organized. This organization is always a reflection of social organization and determines where people are seated and where possessions are kept. There is always a division between the men's and women's sides of the tent. The line between the sides may be quite strict, as in Arab cultures where there is a dividing curtain and where no adult male but the husband ever enters the woman's side, or the line may be loose and people of both sexes may move about freely as with the Inuit. This division of the tent also constitutes a separation of the type of work for which each sex is responsible, so the looms, churns, and utensils are kept and used on the women's side while the saddles, harnesses, and weapons are kept on the men's side (1979: 7).

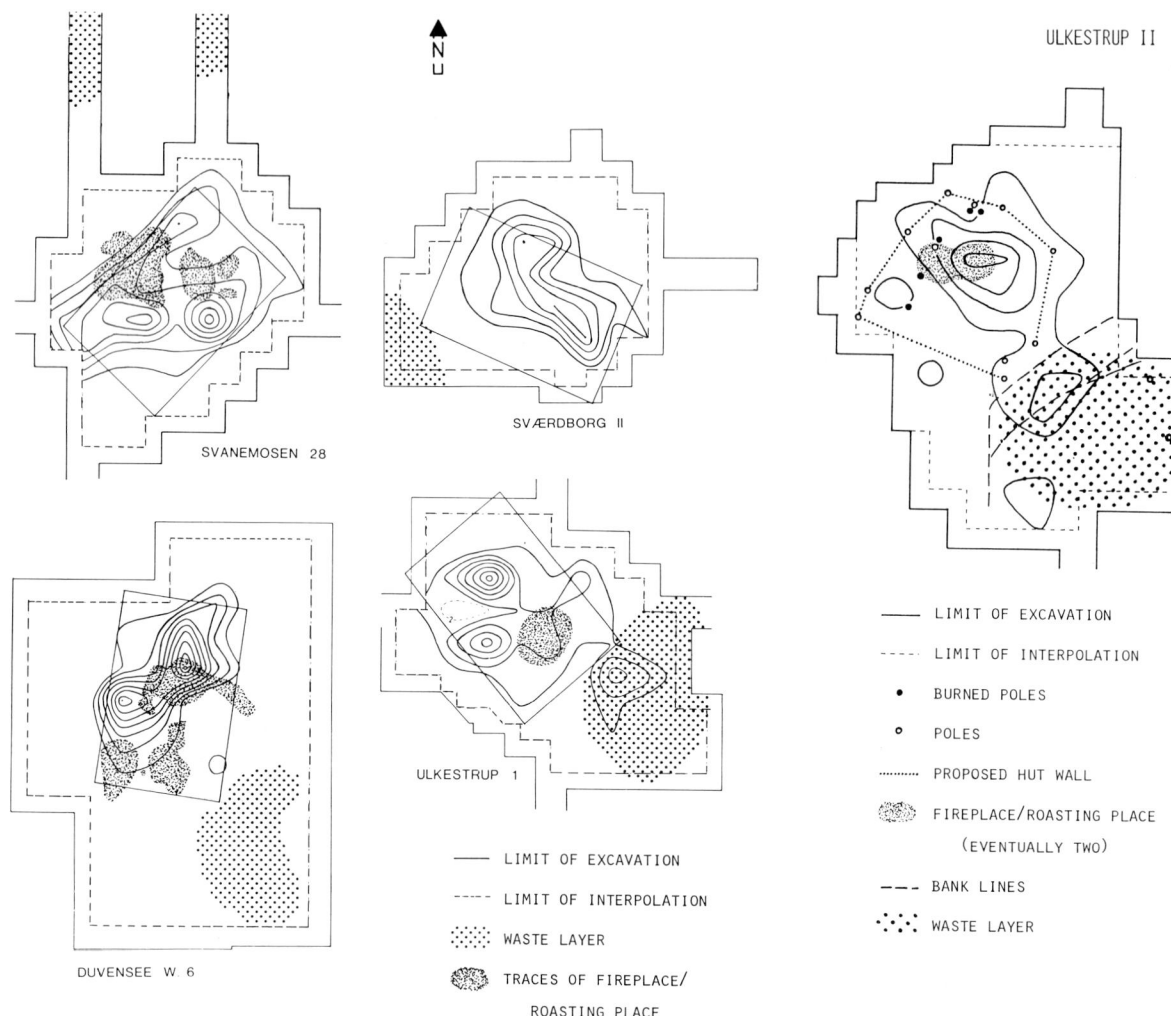

LIMIT OF EXCAVATION

---- LIMIT OF INTERPOLATION

• BURNED POLES

○ POLES

········· PROPOSED HUT WALL

FIREPLACE/ROASTING PLACE

(EVENTUALLY TWO)

— — BANK LINES

WASTE LAYER

SVANEMOSEN 28

SVÆRDBORG II

ULKESTRUP 1

LIMIT OF EXCAVATION

---- LIMIT OF INTERPOLATION

WASTE LAYER

TRACES OF FIREPLACE/

ROASTING PLACE

DUVENSEE W. 6

Figure 1 Distribution of microliths and locations of hearths and waste layers at five Maglemosian sites: Duvensee W.6, Svanemosen 28, Sværdborg II, Ulkestrup I and Ulkestrup II.

In his very important work *Das System der Raumeinteilung in den Behausungen der nordeuroasischen Völker*, Gustav Ränk writes:

> In einem übertragenen Sinne bedeutet die Raumordnung somit ein Abbild des gesamten gesellschaftlichen Aufbaus der betreffenden Völker im Kleinen, im welchem sich alle hier zu Tage tretenden Beziehungen zwischen den einzelnen Generationen, Altersklassen, Gesellschaftsschichten, Geschlechtern und die Arbeitsteilung zwischen diesen in konzentrierter Form wiederspiegeln. Da sich nun dieses Ordnungssystem sozusagen organisch auf wirtschaftlich-sozialer Grundlage ausgebildet hat, in Verbindung mit mannigfachen religiösen Vorstellungen, *so ist danit zugleich gesagt, dass es als eine Funktion des ökonomisch-sozialen und geistigen Lebens aufzufassen ist* (1951: 141).

Where hunter-gatherers are concerned, a worldwide geographical distribution of the habit of organizing social space inside dwellings can be documented. For the Tierra del Fuego tribes, the documentation is the detailed descriptions made by Father Martin Gusinde (1931). For the Indians of the Plains, numerous descriptions exist of the strict tepee etiquette (Morice 1910; Parker 1975; Faegre

1979), while one of the most interesting studies of organization of social space in dwellings of hunter-gatherers has been made by Adrian Tanner in his work on the forest Indians in the area around Lake Mistassini in Canada (Tanner 1979).

This is also well-documented for Eskimo societies. A uniform standard pattern is found, the wife having her place in the outermost part of the platform to the side where her cooking utensils are, next to her the smallest child, then the husband (being placed approximately in the centre), and after him the other children (Balikci 1970; Briggs 1970; David Damas, pers. comm.).

The northern Eurasian area (from the Lapps of northern Scandinavia to the Ainu of Sachlin) is covered by Ränk's publication, from which a general observation has already been quoted (Ränk 1951).

For Africa, there is some documentation of patterned behaviour in the huts of the pygmies (Gusinde 1956). With the bushmen studied by the Marshall family, it was observed that one side of the fireplace in front of the hut was regarded as the women's side and the other as the men's. If no screen was constructed, it was the custom to thrust two upright sticks into the ground to represent the entrance, so that the family might orientate itself (Marshall 1959: 354).

Organization of dwelling space among the Andaman islanders was not focused upon in either E.H. Man's or Radcliffe-Brown's studies. However, there are some indications that the single-family dwellings and the equally organized living areas of the single families in communal dwellings were divided into one part for the males (normally to the left?) and one for the females (normally to the right?) – not unlikely through the central fireplace. Since cooking for the single family was regarded as a female activity, and the food in all cases was stored to the right of the single-family fireplaces in a twelve-family communal hut described, and since right and left in other connections are regarded as feminine and masculine sides respectively, it seems likely that some division or sexual 'polarization' existed within these dwellings (Radcliffe-Brown 1964). This is clearly supported by a notion that unmarried women and men had to occupy opposite ends within single-family dwellings, whereas the married couples were placed in between (Man 1883: 108, note 1).

The habit of organizing the space inside the windbreaks is also documented for Australia (Tindale 1972, 1974).

It must be stressed that the habit of organizing the social space inside dwellings is by no means restricted to nomadic cultures. It is also found in a number of recent farming communities (e.g. Ränk 1949), and according to E.T. Hall is present in the organization of modern western houses (Hall 1969).

Thus culture-specific spatially structured behaviour inside dwellings must be regarded as a general human characteristic. From an archaeological point of view, this opens possibilities for analyzing the social structure of prehistoric households from the spatial distribution of artifacts and structural remains inside their dwellings. As mentioned, this has already been attempted on the sites of the Maglemose culture (Grøn 1983, 1987a).

In the anthropological record the pattern of behaviour in habitations tends to be less complicated the smaller the habitations are. This is probably due to the fact that in dwellings of restricted size, the inhabitants have to restrict their activities spatially. The same place, therefore, very often serves as sleeping, working and sitting space for one person. From an archaeological point of view, this tendency favours research on prehistoric nomadic cultures, which have obvious reasons for using dwellings of restricted size.

SPATIAL ORGANIZATION IN PREHISTORIC DWELLINGS

To understand how far the phenomenon concerned can be used for analysis of the social structure of prehistoric households, it is important to understand what factors are behind it and what function it might have. Regarding it as a cultural tradition which dispersed from a single place of origin, in the classic anthropological way, seems rather unproductive because of its world-wide distribution (even in regions that culturally have been isolated for a long time – e.g. Australia) and its connection with all kinds of economies. Rather, it has proved far more beneficial to look at the matter from a psychological point of view, as human spatial behaviour in dwellings to a large extent seems to be regulated by a number of basic psychological factors. Since the least complicated and, in relation to hunter-gatherers, most relevant dwelling type is the tent, hut, or house of restricted size consisting of one undivided room within which sleeping and eating are normally carried out, and to which access is obtained through one normally-used entrance, the following discussion will focus on this type.

From social psychology it is known that decreasing distance between individuals is correlated with increasing intimacy. If a number of individuals are to be placed within relatively restricted space, unnecessary tensions are avoided if the spatial distances between them are proportional to their 'distances' socially and personally (Hall 1969; McFeat 1974). Just such 'conflict damping' structuring of the occupation within the dwelling space can be observed with the anthropologically described placing patterns. One example is the organizational patterns of the Mistassini Cree, studied in detail by Adrian Tanner (1979). In the one-family dwelling (*Fig. 2*),

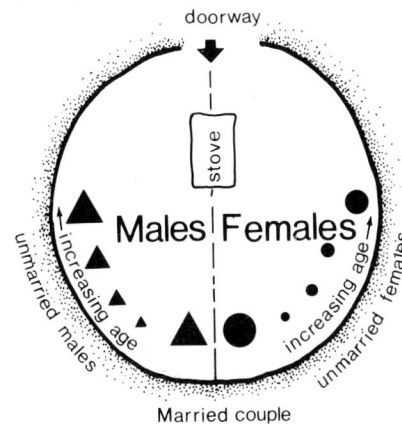

Figure 2 Location of individuals in a Mistassini one-family dwelling.

the parents are placed beside each other opposite the door. The unmarried females (daughters and women adopted by the family after having lost their spouses) sit after the mother in order of increasing age. In the same way the unmarried males are ordered symmetrically after the father. A man and a woman adopted by a family after having lost their spouses will be the two most 'unrelated' persons according to this pattern.

101

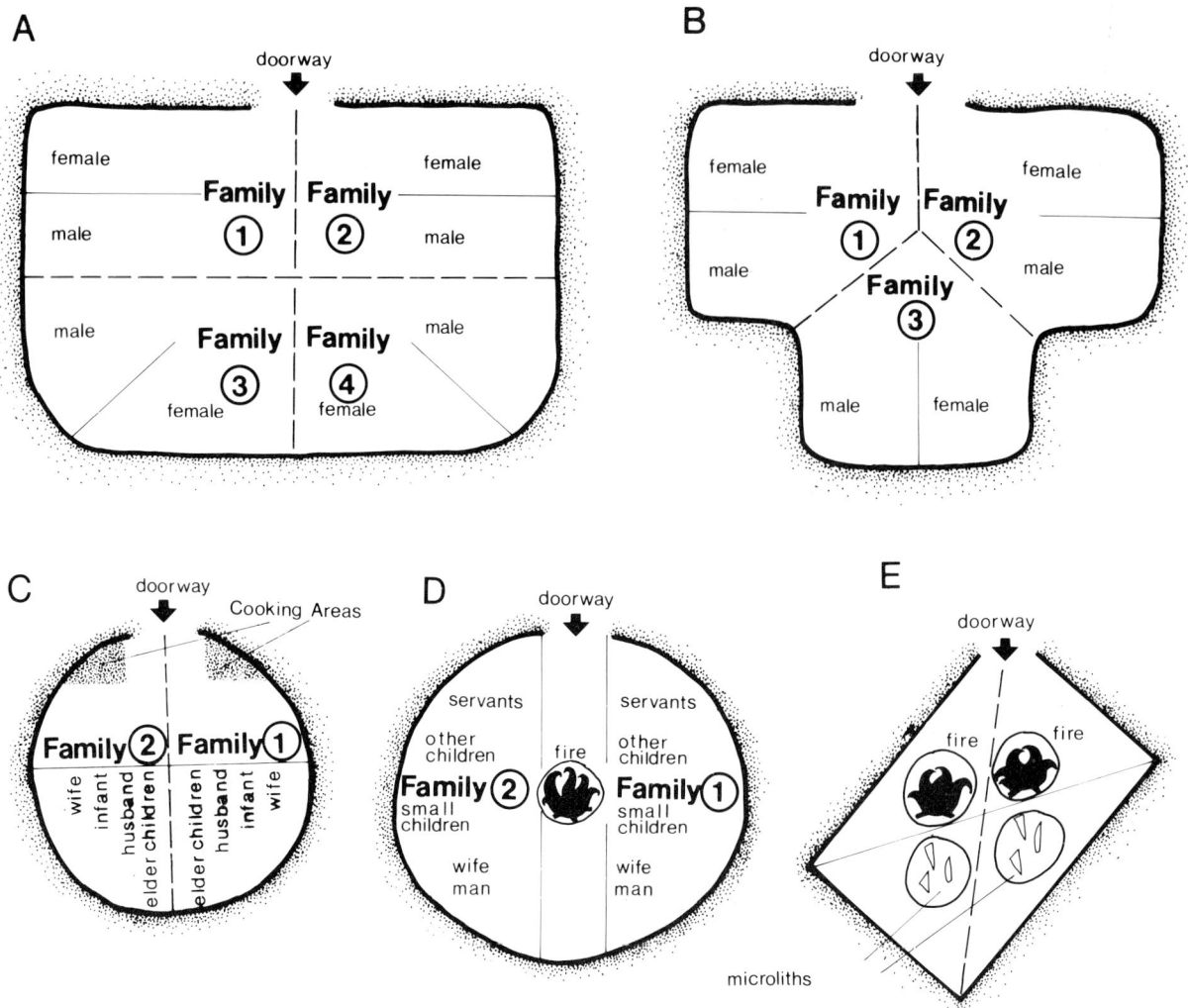

Figure 3 Organization of the dwelling space – with the Mistassini in four- (A) and three-family (B) communal dwellings; with the Eskimos in two-family (C) igloos; and with the Lapps in two-family tents (D). E shows the pattern suggested for dwellings interpreted as the two-family dwellings of the Maglemose culture.

One kind of conflict that considerable efforts are often made to avoid is internal sexual conflict in households consisting of two or more families. This is often reflected in the placing patterns. Amongst the Mistassini, the interior of communal dwellings is arranged like the interior of a number of separate dwellings, but in such a way that the two families nearest the entrance have their women placed by the door, while the males are placed nearer to the rear of the dwelling. The two following families are orientated so that the males are nearest the door (*Fig. 3*, A). A consequence of this is that persons from one family are placed nearest to persons of their own sex from the neighbouring families. If an uneven number of families occupy a communal dwelling, effort is made to mark the separation of the single families more clearly by the form of the dwelling (*Fig. 3*, B) (Tanner 1979). The Eskimos living in two-family huts use a symmetrical organization where the two women are placed at the outer ends of the sleeping platform, then come the smallest infants on each side, then the two men, and

in the middle the rest of the children (*Fig. 3*, C) (Briggs 1970; Jenness 1970; Boas 1972). The Lapps (among whom several groups until recently practised hunting and gathering) in their two-family dwellings are known to have used a similar symmetrical organization (*Fig. 3*, D; Ränk 1951; Vorren and Manker 1976). Conflict-damping structures of the kind discussed here also seem to be inherent in the organization pattern in the proposed two-family dwellings of the Maglemose culture (*Fig. 3*, E).

The fact that each individual has his or her own clearly defined place within the dwelling seems to have a conflict-damping effect in itself. Jean L. Briggs offers a rather interesting description of how she was able to withdraw from what was going on around her and, to a certain degree, isolate herself within the borders of her personal place defined by her status as daughter in the igloo of her 'adopted' Eskimo parents. The same phenomenon was observed with the Eskimo men by Binford (Briggs 1970; Binford 1983).

Together with the psychologists Ask Elklit and

102

Janne Albertsen, I have studied the same kind of 'invisible screen-effect' within an experimental reconstruction of a two-family Maglemose dwelling. The two families involved in the experiment had to stay inside their own part of the dwelling. Furthermore, the females had to stay inside the half near the entrance whereas the males had to stay inside the other half. Rather quickly – and much more clearly than expected – a polarization between the two families developed, the persons in the experiment only to a limited degree feeling involved in what was happening on the other side of the border. Even when one of the families was eating, whereas the other had no food prepared and was hungry and tired, the reactions from the latter – even from the children – were surprisingly limited!

In a few cases, a restricted use of real curtains seems to underline the character of the invisible borders around the personal areas of every individual. From the Kutchin there is a description of a dwelling six feet (1.83 m) high, with a maximum diameter of 12–13 feet (3.66–3.96 m), and designed to contain one or more families. The interior is divided into 'stalls' open to the central space (Fig. 4). These probably mark personal areas of single

Figure 4 Tent of the Kutchin with 'stalls' probably marking personal areas.

individuals able to withdraw into isolation (Morgan 1965). With the Lapps the habit was that at least the parents and the smaller children slept within little tents of canvas that in the night were hung from the sloping inner sides of the dwelling (Vorren and Manker 1976: 73).

According to E.T. Hall:

> Space perception is not only a matter of what can be perceived but what can be screened out. People brought up in different cultures learn as children, without ever knowing that they have done so, to screen out one type of information while paying close attention to another. Once set, these perceptual patterns apparently remain quite stable throughout life. The Japanese, for example, screen visually in a variety of ways but are perfectly content with paper walls as acoustic screens. Spending a night at a Japanese inn while a party is going on next door is a new sensory experience for the Westerner (1969: 44–45).

The character of the 'invisible' borders under discussion is such that they can function as effective 'filters' of visual and auditory involvement, but the moment communication is demanded and accepted, they can be ignored. Apparently, the openness and closedness are expressed and read by details in the attitudes and movements of the inhabitants (Briggs 1970; McFeat 1974).

In the context of small dwellings consisting of one room with a single normally-used entrance – the type under discussion here – another factor in all anthropologically described placing patterns known to the author is that the individuals are placed so that communication and eye-contact is possible between all of them. That is to say they are placed more or less in a circle, or one or more segments of a circle, facing a common centre. This may sound rather banal but, for an understanding of the spatial, communicative and non-communicative structures under discussion, it is important, and in the interpretation of spatial organization of prehistoric dwellings it may be an important fact to keep in mind.

The quotation from Faegre (1979) cited above suggests that there is normally a men's and a women's side in the kind of dwellings under discussion. In a number of cases it would be more correct to speak of a gradual sexual polarization of the dwelling space with no fixed borders as is known, for instance, among the Lapps (Ränk 1951; Vorren and Manker 1976).

There exist two main forms of widely distributed patterns of polarization. In one the feminine element is connected with the entrance area, while the masculine element is connected with the rear of the dwelling. This pattern has been discussed in great detail by Ränk and his pupil Paulson. Apparently, with this pattern the masculine–feminine polarization is very often coincident with a polarization between sacred and profane, respectively. In a number of cases, this pattern is also connected with the existence of a ritual door opposite the normally-used entrance (Ränk 1951; Paulson 1952).

With the other pattern, the sexual polarization is between the two sides of the dwelling, as with the one-family huts of the Mistassini, the Yamana Indians of Tierra del Fuego and, probably, the Maglemose culture (*Figs. 1 & 2*; Gusinde 1933). With this pattern, it also seems to be the rule that prestige increases with distance from the entrance.

According to Paulson (1952) the first pattern of sexual polarization is due to a rather well-developed patriarchy, whereas the second is found associated with a lesser degree of such. As a partial explanation of why the place opposite the door is generally connected with a maximum of prestige, he stresses the psychological aspects of the matter, stating:

> Most of us choose a comfortable corner place in the train and, I think, any one of us would prefer to sleep in a bed standing near the wall of the bedroom rather than in its middle (1952: 65).

From the defensive point of view, a position opposite and facing the entrance will clearly be the optimum, and so impose a certain feeling of security on the person occupying it.

That the organization of social space within the type of dwellings under discussion varies from culture to culture is probably due to culture-specific factors – for instance, as indicated above, the man–wife relation can be given different values in different cultures, and will therefore find different spatial expressions. Seen from an archaeological point of view, the factor of importance is that the organizational patterns are normally regulated by a set of general social-psychological factors. As a hypothesis, a number of these factors can be outlined:

1. The spatial distance between the individuals will be congruent with their distance socially.

2. In a household, the individuals will be placed so that communication and eye-contact is possible between all of them. This means that they will be placed more or less in a circle or on one or more segments of a circle, facing a common centre.

3. The place opposite the door has the greatest prestige value and as such is the most desirable.

4. The greater the status of a person, the more his or her wishes with regard to spatial position are taken into account.

With simple screens, access can be obtained from different directions. Though a specific entrance zone as focal point of access is absent, the focal point of prestige generally seems to be the most central point within the structures (Man 1883; Gusinde 1933; Radcliffe-Brown 1964). With the Pitjandjara of Australia, the children are placed beside the mother, who again is placed beside the father. With an increasing number of children, the place of the parents moves away from the centre of the structure which is constructed only to provide cover for the number of individuals present within the family.

With many bushmen, the huts are used only for storage and as shelter when it rains. Daily activities are carried out around a fireplace in front of the hut. Though at least some of these groups were observed to distinguish between a men's side and a women's side of the fireplace, this convention was rather loose and did not not prevent people from moving around the fire to avoid the smoke (Marshall 1959; Elizabeth M. Thomas, pers. comm.).

Because the organization of social space of the kind discussed here to a large extent seems to be based on general socio-psychological factors, which must be assumed to have remained unchanged for a considerable span of time, there can be little doubt that such organizational patterns were normal also with Mesolithic hunter-gatherers. From an archaeological viewpoint, therefore, the important question

is how they may be observed. In cases where actual remains of dwelling structures are not preserved, the crucial point will be whether it is possible to recognize the dwelling area and the position of the entrance in other ways.

In the study of distributional patterns on prehistoric sites, a generally accepted view is that physical borders (e.g. the walls of a dwelling) will be reflected in the distribution of the artifacts. At first sight this sounds reasonable, but one must be aware that many nomadic cultures living in dwellings of light construction (tents, bark huts, etc.) often do not regard the walls of their dwellings as borders of such consistency as do the archaeologists the walls of prehistoric dwellings. In fact, it is reported in the ethnographic literature that members of some nomadic cultures, when the weather is nice, roll up the sides of their tents or remove parts of the covering material from their huts (e.g. Morice 1910; Birket-Smith 1957; Rogers 1967; Faegre 1979). Thus, it is to be expected that the distribution of some artifacts (in ideal instances, specific types) will reflect the existence of the walls of the dwellings, whereas that of other artifacts will not. Such a phenomenon may be observable in the dwellings of the Maglemose culture (Grøn 1987a).

Another point that has been the object of some discussion is whether an area where artifacts – including waste from working processes – are concentrated can be regarded as the dwelling area. From an anthropological point of view, this is possible (e.g. Binford 1983). Floors made up of branches of the kind known from many primitive cultures, as well as the huts of the Maglemose culture, can 'absorb' considerable amounts of litter (Rogers 1967; Andersen, Jørgensen and Richter 1982). With regard to flint-working inside the dwellings, the crucial problem seems to be the flint pieces a few millimetres and less in size that spread like dust and cause much irritation. Because of this I am inclined to believe that flint-knapping, which must have been carried on inside the dwellings of the Maglemose culture, must have been executed just before the sites were left, the people carrying with them an amount of prepared raw material such as selected blades, microblades, and/or finished tools for the new site.

Concentrations of material on prehistoric sites may also represent outdoor activities or dumps. The individuals inside a dwelling are placed solely in accordance with a traditional conception of the dwelling space, whereas individuals outside the dwellings will normally choose to place themselves in some relation to the natural features there, such as trees (for shadow) and stones (for seats). It must therefore be expected that outdoor activities will not show one pattern repeatedly on a number of sites.

The constant rotation of people round outdoor fires to avoid the smoke must also be expected to give activities carried out in this situation a relatively blurred spatial configuration compared to indoor activities.

With regard to dumps, one should normally expect them to contain a rather random distribution of the different types of artifacts and litter. No repeated structuring should be expected from site to site. Nevertheless, deposition of litter in some anthropological cases is carried out in a ritual and spatially structured way (Adrian Tanner, pers. comm.). One must expect this to cause some difficult cases in spatial analysis.

For the analysis of spatial distribution patterns, a certain intensity of items is necessary. The sites of the Maglemose culture are often ideal for carrying out such analysis, the material representing one small typologically homogeneous site normally containing between 10,000 and 40,000 pieces of flint. Moreover, the numbers of tools are normally adequate for the purpose. In the context of the late Palaeolithic Bromme culture and the Hamburgian culture, repeated patterns in the flint distributions are discernible but, as the intensity of tools is often very low, the significance of their distributional patterns is low, and thus the sites are less suited to detailed analysis.

The size of the dwellings of nomadic people seems to be determined, amongst other things, by a balancing of the effort they are willing to invest in construction and/or transportation of a dwelling, the materials obtainable, and the demand for dwelling area of a size that will not cause unnecessary conflicts between the members of the individual households. As the spatial structures normally contain some culture-specific elements, it seems unlikely that there would be an *exact* general relation between the number of inhabitants and the size of a dwelling.

Where social anthropology is concerned mainly with studies of cultures through relatively restricted intervals of time, the method presented in this paper should make it possible in some cases to follow the development of group structure over periods of considerable length, and thus to gain an insight into the role of social structure as a dynamic adaptive mechanism. It is the present author's hope that in this way the social aspects of the change from Mesolithic to Neolithic in southern Scandinavia may be elucidated.

References

ANDERSEN, K., JØRGENSEN, S. and RICHTER, J. (1982) *Maglemose Hytterne ved Ulkestrup Lyng*. Copenhagen, Det Kongelige Nordiske Oldskriftselskab.

BALIKCI, A. (1970) *The Netsilik Eskimo*. Garden City (N.Y.), The Natural History Press.

BINFORD, L.R. (1983) *In Pursuit of the Past. Decoding the Archaeological Record*. London, Thames and Hudson.

BIRKET-SMITH, K. (1957) *Fjærne Folk. Kår og Kultur i seks Primitive Samfund*. Copenhagen, Jespersen og Pio.

BOAS, F. (1972) *The Central Eskimo*. Lincoln (Nebraska), University of Nebraska Press.

BRIGGS, J.L. (1970) *Never in Anger. Portrait of an Eskimo Family*. Cambridge (Massachussets), Harvard University Press.

FAEGRE, T. (1979) *Tents. Architecture of the Nomads*. London, John Murray.

GRØN, O. (1983) Social behaviour and settlement structure. Preliminary results of a distribution analysis on sites of the Maglemose culture. *Journal of Danish Archaeology*, 2: 32–42.

GRØN, O. (1984) Bostad och samhälle under mesolitisk tid. *Populär Arkeologi*, 2(3): 11–13.

GRØN, O. (1987a) Dwelling organization – a key to the understanding of social structure in Old Stone Age societies? An example from the Maglemose culture. In J.K. Kozłowski and S.K. Kozłowski (eds), *New in Stone Age Archaeology* (Archeologia Interregionalis). Warsaw–Kraków, Państwowe Wydawnictwo Naukowe: 63–82.

GRØN, O. (1987b) Seasonal variation in Maglemosian group size and structure. *Current Anthropology*, 28(3): 303–327.

GRØN, O. (1988) Anvendelse af socialpsykologi i den arkæologiske forskning. In T. Madsen (ed.), *Bag Moesgårds Maske: Kultur og samfund i fortid og nutid*. Aarhus, Universitetsforlag: 47–55.

GUSINDE, M. (1931) *Die Feuerland-Indianer*. Modling bei Wien, Anthropos-Bibliotek.

GUSINDE, M. (1956) *Die Twiden. Pygmäen und Pygmoide im tropischen Afrika* (Veröffentlichungen zum Archiv für Volkerkunde, 3). Vienna, Museum für Volkerkunde Wien.

HALL, E.T. (1969) *The Hidden Dimension*. New York, Anchor Books.

JENNESS, D. (1970) *The Life of the Copper Eskimos* (Report of the Canadian Arctic Expedition, 1913–1918, vol. 12, part A). New York, Johnson Reprint Corporation.

MAN, E.H. (1883) On the aboriginal inhabitants of the Andaman Islands. *Journal of the Anthropological Institute of Great Britain and Ireland*, 12: 69–175.

MARSHALL, L. (1959) Marriage among !Kung Bushmen. *Africa*, 29(4): 335–365.

McFEAT, T. (1974) *Small-Group Cultures*. New York, Pergamon Press.

MORGAN, L.H. (1965) *Houses and House-Life of the American Aborigines*. Chicago, University Press.

MORICE, F.A.G. (1910) The Great Déné Race. *Anthropos*, 4–5 (1909–1910): 113–142, 419–443, 643–653, 969–990.

PARKER, A.C. (1975) *The Indian How Book*. New York, Dover Publications.

PAULSON, I. (1952) The 'seat of honour' in aboriginal dwellings of the circumpolar zone, with special regard to the Indians of northern North America. In S. Tax (ed.), *Indian Tribes of Aboriginal America*. Selected Papers of the 29th International Congress of Americanists. Chicago, University Press.

RADCLIFFE-BROWN, A.R. (1964) *The Adaman Islanders*. New York, Free Press.

RANK, G. (1949–1951) *Das System der Raumeinteilung in den Behausungen der nordeuroasischen Völker*. Stockholm, Institutet för Folklivsforskning (vol. 1, 1949; vol. 2, 1951).

ROGERS, E.S. (1967) *The Material Culture of the Mistassini*. Ottawa, National Museum of Canada, Bulletin 218.

TANNER, A. (1979) *Bringing Home Animals. Religious Ideology and Mode of Production of the Mistassini Cree Hunters*. London, C. Hurst.

TINDALE, N.B. (1972) The Pitjandjara. In M.G. Bicchieri (ed.), *Hunters and Gatherers Today*. New York, Holt, Rinehart and Winston.

TINDALE, N.B. (1974) *Aboriginal Tribes of Australia. Their Terrain, Environmental Controls, Distribution, Limits and Proper Names*. Berkeley, University of California Press.

VORREN, Ø. and MANKER, E. (1976) *Samekulturen*. Tromsø, Universitetsforlaget.

Social and Biological Aspects of the Western European Mesolithic Population Structure: a Comparison with the Demography of North American Indians

Trinette S. Constandse-Westermann
and Raymond R. Newell

Abstract

In this paper several extant models of Upper Palaeolithic/Mesolithic demography and population structure are reviewed and compared. Thereafter, they are compared to demographic data from a large number of relevant, analogous North American pedestrian hunter-fisher-gatherer Indian societies. From the results of the statistical comparison, a more specific model of Mesolithic social structure, level of social organization, and demographic parameters is proposed

INTRODUCTION

In the most recent archaeological literature palaeo-demography is a subject of growing interest and relevance. Current issues are: absolute population numbers, population density and inherent problems of population structure, dynamics and growth, sex and age distribution within defined skeletal populations, reproduction rate and its causative mechanisms, population mortality profiles and related problems of health and nutrition, and life expectancy. Recently, several of these problems have been considered in relation to the western European Mesolithic (Constandse-Westermann and Newell 1984, Constandse-Westermann, Newell and Meiklejohn 1984; Newell and Constandse-Westermann 1986a).

In this contribution we shall proceed from the data presented in the last paper and compare our perception of the western European Mesolithic population structure with some other published models. These are: (i) the model proposed by Grahame Clark (1975: 13–15) for the late Palaeolithic and Mesolithic of Scandinavia, based largely on economic arguments; (ii) the model presented by Meiklejohn (1978) for the European late Palaeolithic and Mesolithic, based on some archaeological and ecological observations; (iii) the model proposed by Williams (1974) for hunter-fisher-gatherer societies, based on a study of the breeding structure in ethnographic hunter-fisher-gatherer populations and theoretical considerations; and (iv) the model for the Palaeolithic presented by Wobst in several consecutive publications (1974, 1975, 1976) which was largely based on computer simulation. All of these models proceeded from, and were inspired by, the pioneer-

ing work of J.B. Birdsell (1950, 1953, 1958, 1968, 1973).

A comparison of these models with the results obtained from our analysis of North American Indian demographic variables will proceed on six attributes: social structure, the spatial configuration of the structural units, population numbers, territorial extension, the derived variable population density, and biological population structure. The results of this comparison will lead to a new hypothesis of the development of western European social and biological structure. Before commencing that comparison, we will briefly summarize the main characteristics of each of the cited models.

THE EXTANT MODELS

Clark envisages a three-stage hierarchical spatial structure: the annual, the social, and the techno-territory. The size of the smallest unit, the annual territory, is dependent upon the size of the home base. In his conception, this is an area with a 5–10 km radius (one to two hours' walking distance), which may be circular or more irregular in form. The annual territory would contain several such areas, in view of seasonal migration patterns. From Clark's text we must conclude that he expects the breeding group to be contained within this annual territory.

The social territory is defined by Clark (1975) as:

> the total territory drawn upon for supplies ..... by a society, by virtue of its belonging to a larger social grouping (1975: 14).

It may contain 'many annual territories without necessarily involving the passage of individuals' (1975: 14) from one territory to another, but with a high degree of social interaction between them. It is the most extensive territory of which the 'ordinary individual' (1975: 22) would have been aware, all redistribution and display of idiosyncratic styles taking place within it. It would be based on common descent and/or allegiance to common political institutions. According to Clark, it would be occupied by the *band*.

The highest unit in the hierarchy would be

represented by the techno-territory, occupied by groups of bands 'lacking in all probability any formal association' (1975: 22). It would be characterized by substantial common elements of technology. Clark does not relate this territorial unit to a specific social structural unit, e.g. in the sense of Steward (1955), Fried (1967) and Service (1971).

In Meiklejohn's model a distinction is made between the late Palaeolithic and the Mesolithic. He claims that both periods would contain groups within the 'general size range reported for modern hunter-gatherers' and that they both show 'little evidence for permanence in their site occupation' (1978: 68). The late Palaeolithic would be characterized by large sites, representing group aggregation, occurring during a major portion of the year and at several places, each of them being inhabited during a specific stage of the annual round (1978: 60). The aggregation sites would have a social and an economic function, and would lead to high site visibility. The *apparent* year-round occupation of such sites would give an exaggerated impression of population numbers. However, Meiklejohn is not clear about the actual importance of such aggregation sites during the late Palaeolithic, because later in his paper he claims that they would be of short duration and not easy to document archaeologically (1978: 70–71). For these late Palaeolithic sites at least two hierarchical units are mentioned, although defined on the basis of different criteria. The larger unit would be the total breeding group, also called major group or macro-unit. Following Wobst (1974), Meiklejohn estimates that the minimum size of such a group would be 475 individuals. However, according to Meiklejohn, a population number of *c.* 1000 would be more likely. Population densities between 0.008 and 0.090 would then lead to territorial extensions of 24,000–60,000 km² for the minimum sized groups (475) and 50,000–125,000 km² for the larger units.[1] With low population densities there would be 8–12 such groups (1978: 70) in habitable western Europe north of the Mediterranean basin. However, taking into account the possibility of higher population densities, seasonal site occupation and the necessity for reserve resource areas in times of stress, Meiklejohn claims a wider range for this number, viz. 'between 4–6 and 20' (1978: 71). Each of these groups would contain a number of lower hierarchical units, i.e. locally defined bands, consisting of groups of closely inter-related extended families.

The transition to the Mesolithic would be characterized by shorter aggregation phases, having only social purposes. The population units would be smaller, but more evenly spread over the landscape and more densely packed. There would be 'incipient sedentism' (1978: 71). However, this latter conten-tion contradicts his earlier claim for little evidence of permanent site occupation.

Proceeding to the model designed by Williams, we find him testing six postulates relating to band structure. The first of these deals with territoriality in general. According to his postulates 2 to 6, the band is a patrilocal exogamous kinship unit, which has maximum autonomy with respect to resources, being based on a lineage system. Its optimal size is 'the minimal size in which marriage alliances can be maintained with all surrounding bands indefinitely' (1974: 27). According to Williams this latter postulate determines the population number which is contained within the band and some of its other quantitative parameters. In his model of approximately hexagonal packing, each band would be surrounded by five to six other bands. This number has indeed been established empirically in a study by Wilmsen (1973) and by ourselves (see below). An average number of 10–12 eligible women would guarantee two marriage alliances with every neighbouring band per generation, i.e. one alliance every 12–13 years. When we assume complete generational overlap, negotiations with all the neighbouring bands would be more or less continuous. Taking into account the number of children who grow up to a marriageable age, this would require about 10 households, or in total about 50 individuals, with a range of variation of 25 to 75. Moreover, Williams considers the band territory to have an optimal size when its radius is no more than 5 km, i.e. one hour's walking distance. This leads to a territorial extension of 78 km² and to an average population density of 0.64 (50÷78) individuals per km². Williams claims that at or under this density a structure of autonomous bands can be expected. In the populations which he studied, as well as in other hunter-fisher-gatherer societies, he found lower densities in most cases.

A number of bands together form a *connubium*, or endogamous group. Such a group would be a cultural and linguistic, rather than a political, entity. It would agglomerate annually for social (marriage arrangements) and ceremonial purposes. It would contain 7–17 bands and therefore its size would range between 210 (7×30) and 1275 (17×75) individuals. From Williams' data an optimal territory can be computed for the *connubium* of 546 (7×78) km² to 1326 (17×78) km² for closely-packed bands. As can be expected from the observed densities under 0.64 per km², Williams actually found larger territories in the ethnographic literature. However, the population numbers which he encountered were fairly close to his expectations.

The last model to be discussed is that of Wobst. This model is explicitly designed to represent Palaeolithic society. In many respects it leads to the same predictions as that of Williams. In his 1974 publication, Wobst also starts from the ethnographically based premiss of a larger endogamous hierarchical unit, which he calls the maximum band, containing a number of minimum bands, and from a hexagonal pattern of the structural units. The hexagonal pattern leads him to predict that the maximum band would contain between seven (one tier around a central band) and 19 (two tiers around a central band) minimum bands. By computer simulation he determines that the minimum size of a biologically self-perpetuating maximum band is a function of its mating system and inherent prohibitions and rules, its sex-ratio, and its mortality and fertility rates. Its maximum size would be the maximum number of individuals that can be integrated by cultural mechanisms. Therefore, the size of a maximum band is dependent upon its territorial extension, i.e. upon population density, which makes it difficult to estimate by simulation.

In those simulations Wobst starts from a minimum band size of 25 individuals based, again, on his ethnographic observations and on the work of Birdsell (1953, 1958, 1968). He claims that this starting point does not influence the simulation results. However, it does influence his evaluation of these results. In various runs Wobst obtains a mean minimum size range for the maximum band of 74.7 to 332.7 individuals. In view of the hexagonal packing of minimum bands of 25 individuals each, he translates this range into 175 (7×25) to 475 (19×25) individuals. From his 1975 publication it can be derived that the latter number is the more relevant. In a further publication (Wobst 1976), the territorial extension of the maximum band is studied on the basis of the ethnographically observed density figures of 0.500 to 0.005 per km^2, most figures being less than 0.050. These densities yield maximum band territories of 9500–95,000 km^2. On the basis of these territorial figures, Wobst then abandons the idea of maximum band endogamy (on which the population figure of 475 was initially based) and proposes instead a system of overlapping marriage networks.

THE NORTH AMERICAN INDIAN APPROXIMATION

From the above, the most obvious conclusion is the lack of consensus between the authors of the various models. This is demonstrated in *Table 1*, of which the first four columns summarize the foregoing.

The extant confusion became apparent when we reviewed these models in search of a starting point for our Mesolithic demographical and skeletal research. In order to find a satisfactory solution, we investigated the early post-contact observed demographic parameters of 256 North American Indian pedestrian hunter-fisher-gatherer dialectic tribes.[2,3]

This sample covers the range of latitude, temperature regime, relief, vegetation and fauna observed for western Europe during the Mesolithic period. In order to obtain mutually comparable demographic figures, we accepted actual population counts made at a similar moment in the historical development of each analogous society; that is, we took the earliest post-contact or initial rebound figure for each tribe (Catlin 1884; Krzywicki 1934; Thwaites 1959; Taylor 1963; Cook 1966, 1976; Dunn 1966; Denevan 1976; Ubelaker 1976, 1977; Thornton 1978, 1980). We judged this to be a better procedure than using pre-contact estimates which vary widely in the manner in which they are determined and, therefore, in their reliability (Merriam 1905; Mooney 1928; Kroeber 1939; Swanton 1952; Cook 1955, 1956; Taylor 1963; Dobyns 1966). We are aware that the figures determined in this way are still *minimum* figures. However, they will approximate more closely to the aboriginal situation than figures taken in a more recent context. Finally, we tested our Mesolithic archaeological and skeletal data against this ethnographic analogue. The results of this investigation are discussed extensively in two recent publications (Newell and Constandse-Westermann 1986a; Newell *et al.*, in press). The main conclusions are presented in the last two columns of *Table 1*.

The first issue which became clear during this investigation is that large differences exist in the degree of social complexity between the various recent hunter-fisher-gatherer societies. At least two levels of social organization are present, the band and the tribal level, with the chiefdom level a third possibility (see e.g. Steward 1955; Service 1971; Newell *et al.*, in press). The differences between the two levels which are most relevant to this paper are stated below.

A second point which needs explanation is that a three-fold hierarchical social structure exists at both the band and the tribal level of social organization. At both levels bands and dialectic tribes (Birdsell 1968) are present, although at the latter level the organizational focus shifts from the band to the dialectic tribe as the corporate entity. At the band level of social organization, the band is an active unit of social interaction in a milieu of equal and independent units which more or less passively form the dialectic tribe. At the tribal level the bands have become subordinate units in this greater cohesive entity.

However, still larger hierarchical structural units are present at both levels of social organization. These are the language families or language area networks. Hill (1978) described this spatial and linguistic unit as:

a major level of structural significance in the organization of human populations: areal units and network systems that go beyond the local group (1978: 3).

Table 1: Results of the investigation of North American Indian hunter-fisher-gatherer demography (Newell and Constandse-Westermann 1986a; Newell *et al.*, in press) compared to earlier models of hunter-fisher-gatherer population structure[1]

		CLARK (1975)	MEIKLEJOHN (1978)	WILLIAMS (1974)	WOBST (1974,1975,1976)	CONSTANDSE-WESTERMANN & NEWELL — Band level society	Tribal level society
SOCIAL STRUCTURE	Qual.	annual territories / "locally defined band"	"locally defined band"	band	minimum band	band	band
		social territories				dialectic tribe	dialectic tribe
		techno-territories / "breeding group" or "major" "macro unit"	"breeding group" or "major" "macro unit"	connubium	maximum band	language family	language family
	Quant.			7-17 bands per connubium	7-19 minimum bands per maximum band	number of bands per dialectic tribe — min 1.0 x̄ 3.9 max 15.0	
						number of dialectic tribes per language family — 0.5 5.5 61.2	
SPATIAL CONFIGURATION		circular or more irregular areas		hexagonal areas	hexagonal areas	number of contiguous bands 2.3 4.9 7.6	
						number of contiguous dialectic tribes ? ca 5.5 ?	
						number of contiguous language families -0.8 4.9 10.5	
POPULATION NUMBER			25/30-75	25		MIN 49 X̄ 302 MAX 1865	MIN 45 X̄ 323 MAX 2348
						148 1034 7242	89 773 6724
			475-1000	210-1275	175-475 (minimum 74.7-332.7)	158 2815 50,119	2535 13,111 67,298
TERRITORIAL EXTENSION IN KM²		P_x (78-314) for circular areas[2]		78	(500-5000)[3]	144 6060 255,228	13 278 5737
		"many times" annual territory				140 8191 478,564	40 987 24,635
		24,000-60,000 or 50,000-125,000		(546-1326)[3]	majority between 9500 and 95,000	298 15,475 801,309	5559 30,709 170,216
POPULATION DENSITY			.008-.090	.640 or lower	.500-.005 majority ≤ .050	.002 .101 5.043	.043 .839 16,460
BIOLOGICAL STRUCTURE		annual territories endogamous	band exogamous	band exogamous	band exogamous	band endogamy not possible	band endogamy not possible
						no endogamy in majority of dialectic tribes	endogamy present in majority of dialectic tribes
		major/macro unit endogamous		connubium endogamous	overlapping marriage networks	overlapping marriage networks within language families	overlapping marriage networks within language families

Notes:

1. The minimum and maximum figures given in the table are $\bar{x}-2s$ and $\bar{x}+2s$, respectively.
2. P = the number of structural poses in the annual round.
3. The data in brackets are derived from other figures in the same model.

At the band level of social organization, the language family is not an emically recognized or conscious unit of social cohesion. However, we may expect it to function *de facto* in the definition of the breeding population and the wider ranging systems of communication and mate exchange. Moreover, as Elsasser (1978) has indicated, the linguistic similarities within the language group are precisely those which set it off from neighbouring groups. While we cannot yet demonstrate our point, we predict that the shift of emphasis from the band to the tribal level of social organization will also have its consequence in the cohesion and effective integration of the language family.

There is a gradual transition between societies organized at the band level of social organization and those at the tribal level. This transition becomes apparent from the large overlap between the quantitative data presented in columns 5 and 6 in *Table 1*. Nevertheless, a number of significant differences between the two levels are apparent. This is shown in *Table 2*. The Mann–Whitney U-tests demonstrate that there are no significant differences between the population numbers of any of the three structural

Table 2: Mann–Whitney U-Tests of the demographic attributes of 256 analogous societies, partitioned according to level of social organization

	Band level	Tribal/ Chiefdom level		
	N	N	Z	p
Band/Clan areas	44	25	−5.474	p< .001
Band/Clan populations	91	22	−0.185	p=.853
Tribe areas	121	94	−6.743	p<.001
Tribe populations	99	94	−1.785	.077>p>.073
Language Family areas	14	5	U=20	p>.100
Language Family populations	14	5	U=13	p=.050
Tribe population densities	93	77	−6.225	p<.001

units, as partitioned according to level of social organization, i.e. the band and the tribal levels. However, the territorial extension of both the bands and the dialectic tribes does differ significantly. For the language families, this is not the case. As a consequence of these territorial differences, the population densities also show significantly different distributions between the band and the tribal level. The numbers of contiguous units to each structural unit have not yet been analyzed separately for the two levels of social organization. Our ongoing analysis predicts that these will be similar for both levels. The same is true for the numbers of bands per dialectic tribe and the numbers of tribes per language family.

The existence of at least two levels of social organization in hunter-fisher-gatherer societies has been insufficiently appreciated in all the models described above. This considerably limits their general applicability. The complexity of the social organization can be demonstrated to increase with increasing population density and, therefore, with time. When studying a specific archaeological period it is essential to proceed from the most relevant level(s) of social organization. One simple model is not sufficient to depict extant or past hunter-fisher-gatherer social structural variability. From our own investigation (Newell 1984; Van Holk and De Roller 1985; De Langen 1985; Newell and Constandse-Westermann 1986a; Newell et al., in press) it can be predicted that a gradual development from band to tribal level society took place during the final stages of the western European Mesolithic.

COMPARATIVE ASPECTS

Comparing our results with the extant models, two general points of agreement are apparent. Firstly, the hexagonal territorial structure, on which two of the models are based, is confirmed by the mean values of about six equivalent contiguous units for the bands, the dialectic tribes, and the language families. Secondly, we find that our observed pop-

ulation numbers for the three structural units show little variation between the band and the tribal level. Therefore, the existing differences in population density are closely related to differences in the territorial extension of the structural units. This is also at the basis of most other models.

In addition to these similarities, however, a careful study of Table 1 reveals a number of inconsistencies. In the first place, it is obvious that only two of the three ethnographically founded structural units are recognized in most models. The band and the dialectic tribe would coincide with Williams' band and connubium, with Wobst's minimum and maximum band, and probably also with Meiklejohn's 'locally defined band' and 'macrounit'. However, comparing the three structural units with Clark's three-fold territorial hierarchy, the correspondence is less clear. According to Clark, his social territory would contain the band. In this case the techno-territory would contain the dialectic tribe, and the language family would be absent. The annual territory would then correspond to a unit which forms only part of the band. Similar units have been defined as 'primary subsistence units' (Steward 1955) or 'task groups' (Helm 1968). However, these will probably not exist as separate entities within the band on a year-round basis (Newell and Constandse-Westermann 1986a; Newell et al., in press). In the following discussion we will use the names band, dialectic tribe and language family, referring to social structural units in all of the above models.

A second aspect of the social structure which merits our attention is the number of constituent units in each hierarchical category. Together these form the second highest structural unit, i.e. the number of bands per tribe and the number of tribes per language family. Starting from a hexagonal model and from a regular spatial distribution of the bands and the dialectic tribes, the number of bands per tribe has been estimated at 7–19. The actual ethnographic figures are considerably lower. Apparently, the regularity of the spatial distribution of the bands and the dialectic tribes is less strict than suggested by the models of Williams and Wobst. As has been stated above, there is no discrepancy with respect to the hexagonality of the spatial configuration of hunter-fisher-gatherer structural units.

The next attribute to be examined is population numbers. It is obvious that the population numbers of bands, tribes and language families, observed in the North American ethnographic context, are much more variable and considerably higher than has been currently hypothesized for hunter-fisher-gatherer societies. The number of 25 individuals for the band approaches the absolute observed minimum, while the ranges of variation as presented by Meiklejohn and by Williams for the dialectic tribe also cover only the lower part of the observed range, i.e. just up to or slightly above our observed mean values.

Four causes for this discrepancy can be cited. In the first instance all currently available models lean heavily on the data originally presented by Birdsell (1950, 1953, 1958, 1968, 1973). The fact that Birdsell's research was specifically designed to approach an absolute minimum situation has been insufficiently appreciated by his followers. It is explicitly stated in his 1950 publication that:

> Drift might be expected to operate throughout Australia, but its effects should be most marked in areas where the size of the effective breeding population is the smallest. ..... It is generally agreed that in populations which fluctuate markedly in size in a cyclical sense through time, the effective breeding size is nearer the lower limit of the population than its upper limit. ..... For these reasons the arid wastes of central Australia may be expected to show the effects of random genetic drift more clearly than other portions of the continent (1950: 261).

The above is confirmed by the procedure followed in his 1953 research, where Birdsell purposely omits 286 tribes from his sample of 409. Of these, 155 were rejected because they had access to marine and/or riverine resources, and therefore did not represent an absolute minimum situation. Similarly, three others were omitted because of their relatively advanced political systems.

Secondly, Meiklejohn, Williams and Wobst all make their calculations on the basis of the minimum number of individuals necessary to maintain a biologically viable unit. Williams starts his calculations from the band and computes the number of people needed to maintain sufficient contacts with the surrounding structural units on the basis of marriage alliances. Wobst, on the other hand, simulates the reproductive process and aims at the minimum group size needed for its long-term perpetuation, virtually biologically independent of other groups. Both approaches are obviously leading to minimum estimates.

Thirdly, we must realize that all ethnographic figures quoted in the above publications are heavily influenced by prolonged European contact. Most ethnographic data presented are from a relatively recent date. Although our data are also minimum data, they are from an earlier period and were recorded sooner after contact. Therefore, we expect them to be closer to their pre-contact values. Moreover, they are from an ecologically less marginal area than, for example, Australia. As such they may be expected to approximate better to the European Postglacial situation.

Finally, the wide range of variation in our data is to a certain extent a function of the historical processes of the rise (development) and/or decline (demise) of some of the structural units. Both the upper and the lower extremes of the distributions would not represent long-term viable situations. However, they are part of the observed ethnographic record.

Having explained the discrepancy in population numbers, we now move toward the territorial extension figures. Here, there is an even greater discrepancy between our results and those of earlier authors. The figure which we can derive from Clark's approach depends upon the number of structural poses occupied by each structural unit during its annual round. From our ethnographic data, an average number of 2.6 structural poses was derived from 159 dialectic tribes. This indicates that Clark's 'annual territory' would minimally range between 203 (2.6×78) km^2 and 816 (2.6×314) km^2. As stated already, from Williams' model we could calculate a minimum territorial extension of 546–1326 km^2 for the *connubium*, i.e. in a situation of close spatial packing of the bands. Wobst's density-derived territorial extension of the dialectic tribe would correspond to band territories of 500 ($9500 \div 19$) km^2 to 5000 ($95,000 \div 19$) km^2. None of the figures and/or ranges hypothesized for the band completely covers our observed range of variation. This is also the case for the observed tribal territories in band level societies. On the other hand, the range of the tribal territories in tribal level societies appears to be somewhat more restricted than most of the hypothesized ranges. It is also shifted toward smaller territories than are predicted in the earlier models.

Again, the discrepancies between the theoretical models and the ethnographic record can be explained. Firstly, the difference between band level societies and tribal level societies, which is particularly relevant to the territorial figures, has been neglected to date. This fact is bound to lead to anomalous results. In the second place, the observed upper territorial extremes also result from the fact that hunter-fisher-gatherers tend to display a non-uniform and non-exhaustive use of the landscape which is at their disposal (Birdsell 1958: 54, 1968: 230; Burch 1972, 1980, 1981; Sahlins 1972). Unused and temporarily uninhabited areas are always present. This causes the measured territories to be larger and the densities to be lower than in an otherwise similar, but fully packed, context. This non-exhaustive use of the available landscape is an inherent characteristic of all hunter-fisher-gatherer societies.

These two facts can also be viewed as causes for the discrepancy in the attribute population density, derived from the above two variables. The various theoretical models do not even approach the upper limit of the density distribution observed in our analogous North American band level societies. The observed densities in the societies functioning at the tribal level of social organization are far greater than those hypothesized to date.

THE BIOLOGICAL POPULATION STRUCTURE

The last aspect to be discussed is that of the biological structure of hunter-fisher-gatherer populations. There is not so much disagreement concerning the matter of band exogamy, which is a starting point for all the above authors, except for Clark who is explicit about endogamy within his 'annual territories'. However, the problem of dialectic tribe endogamy merits further consideration here.

The assumption that the dialectic tribe should be endogamous forms the basis for the other three models. Although Williams starts his computations at the band, and Wobst at the tribe, both paint the same picture of an endogamous dialectic tribe. Meiklejohn also uses this idea in his reasoning. Wobst, however, abandons that position at a later stage in his research, using instead arguments of distance between mates and the effort it would require to find a suitable mate within such a closed breeding network.

Because our research was designed to yield a firm basis for our human biological analysis of the skeletal remains of western Europe in the Mesolithic period, the question of endogamy was of prime importance. We therefore tested the demographic parameters of the social structural units, both at the band and the tribal level, against some theoretically and empirically based expectations concerning exogamous groups.

From a study by Adams and Kasakoff (1975), it became apparent that breeding groups displaying about 80% (70–90%) endogamy have rather narrow numerical and spatial parameters. This was observed throughout a number of societies with widely varying degrees of social complexity. In the large majority of these societies, 80% endogamy occurred in groups varying between 850 and 10,000 individuals. In addition to group size, the territorial constraints were such that 80% endogamy occurred mainly within areas whose radii extended up to c. 17 miles. This figure would pertain to societies lacking seasonal migration patterns.[4] With larger territorial extensions the geographical location of the individual within the territory would become so important that a system of overlapping breeding units (Sharp 1968; Wobst 1976) would occur.

In view of this uniformity and of the theoretical thrust of Adams and Kasakoff's argument, we have used these parameters to test the population numbers and territorial extensions of the North American Indian structural units for the potential realization of effective endogamy. Because Adams and Kasakoff's data were derived from sedentary populations, their territorial extension figures were multiplied by 2.6, to account for the average number of structural poses which characterize the seasonal migration patterns of our analogous societies (Newell *et al.*, in press). The results of these tests are presented in *Table 3*. They demonstrate that at the band level of social organization, endogamy is not possible for any of the structural units contained in that society; either the population numbers are too small, or the territorial extensions are too large. At the tribal level, i.e. at increasing population density, effective band endogamy will also not occur. However, the majority of the dialectic tribes will start to develop endogamous patterns at the transition of the band to

Table 3: Feasibility of the development of 80% endogamous groups, isomorphic with the various structural units, according to their demographic parameters

		Band level societies	Tribal level societies
BAND	Population numbers:	too small	too small
	Territorial extension:	too large	suitable
DIALECTIC TRIBE	Population numbers:	middle and upper part of range suitable	middle and upper part of range suitable
	Territorial extension:	too large	suitable
LANGUAGE FAMILY	Population numbers:	lower extreme of range suitable	lower extreme of range suitable
	Territorial extension:	too large	too large

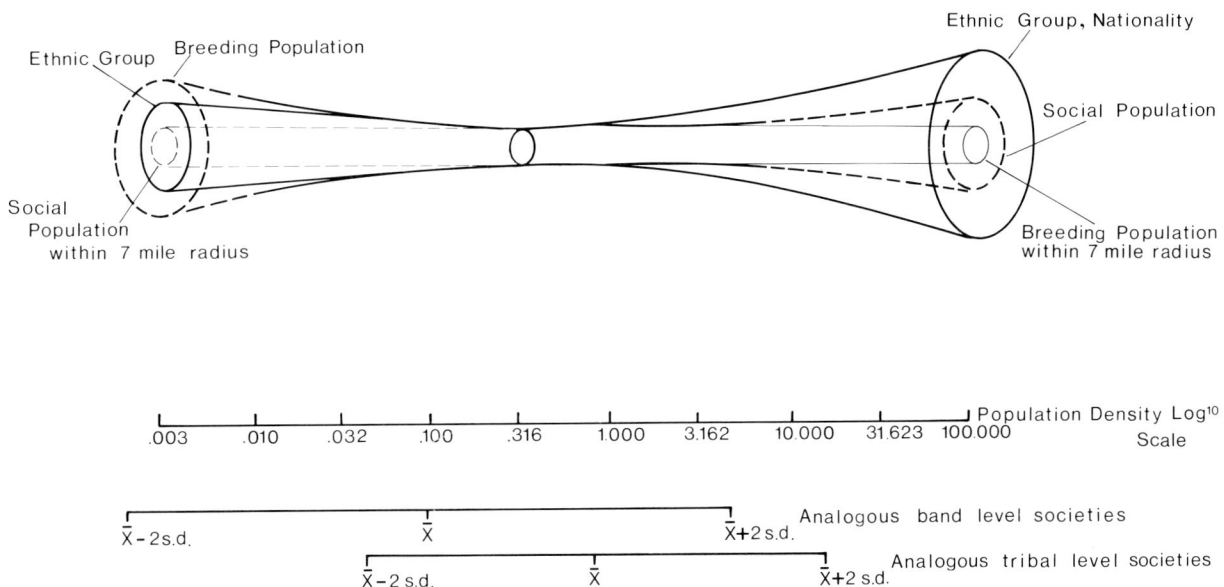

Figure 1 Heuristic transformation model of the relationship between social and biological units at varying population densities (0.003–100.000 inhabitants per km²; log¹⁰ scale). *Source*: Newell 1984; Newell and Constandse-Westermann 1986a.

the tribal level of social organization. At the tribal level the territories of the language families are still too large for the great majority to function as effective endogamous units.

The foregoing is depicted in our schematic transformation model (*Fig. 1*). On the left side of the figure, low population density is represented. The breeding population is not clearly bounded, hence the broken line. Closed marriage systems will not be visible. One may expect closed systems to become established only after the point at which the breeding population can coincide with the dialectic tribe, i.e. where the different sets of transformation lines cross. This is also the point at which band level societies achieve the tribal level of social organization (Steward 1955; Owen 1965; Service 1971; Newell 1984). Because the numerical parameters of the social populations show no directional change, it follows that only the territorial sizes of the dialectic tribes will vary with density. Because population growth and the concomitant increase in population density is non-linear relative to time, the model is based on a log¹⁰ scale, taking into account the exponential form of the population growth curve.

Unfortunately, space is lacking to demonstrate that all the results of our ongoing research point in the same direction. The reader is referred to our study of the spatial and chronological variation in the distribution of Mesolithic personal decorative ornaments (Newell *et al.*, in press), mortuary practices (De Langen 1985; Van Holk and De Roller 1985; Newell *et al.*, in preparation), Mesolithic population density (Newell and Constandse-Westermann 1986a), North American Indian and Mesolithic technology (Newell and Constandse-Westermann 1986b), stature (Constandse-Westermann *et al.* 1985, and work in progress), and our preliminary analysis of Mesolithic

cranial metric variation.

On the basis of all these results we have been able to establish that the western European Mesolithic is represented by the area to the left of, and somewhat through the middle of, our transformation model. Proceeding from a complete and critically assessed database (Newell, Constandse-Westermann and Meiklejohn 1979), we will use this transformation model as a starting point for our final analysis of the Mesolithic cranial and post-cranial metric attributes (Constandse-Westermann and Newell, in preparation).

CONCLUSIONS

A comparison of the results of our analysis of North American Indian hunter-fisher-gatherer demographic data with extant population models for hunter-fisher-gatherer societies leads to the following conclusions:

1. A combination of different points of departure is necessary for the establishment of an adequate model of western European late Palaeolithic and Mesolithic hunter-fisher-gatherer population structure. Considering the size of the breeding population as the only attribute for such an exercise is too limited. In previous theoretical models, socio-cultural factors have not been sufficiently accommodated, and analogous ranges of variation in demographic data have not been adequately observed.

2. In these previous models, premises have been combined which are relevant to widely divergent levels of social complexity. The assumption of very small bands refers only to the most simple forms of band level hunter-fisher-gatherer societies. On the other hand the assumption of endogamous dialectic tribes is relevant only to societies which are well on their way into the tribal level of social organization.

This discrepancy in the basic points of departure can never lead to a realistic representation of hunter-fisher-gatherer population structure.

Notes:

1. The 24,000 and 50,000 km² estimates are based on density figures of 0.020 per km².

2. Excluded from our analysis are those societies whose subsistence is based almost entirely on nut collecting (i.e. middle and southern California and the Great Basin).

3. Similar research on the Eskimo societies of the continent is in progress.

4. Seasonal migration was absent in all but one of Adams and Kasakoff's societies.

Acknowledgements: The issues discussed in this paper and the formulation presented are the result of perceived lacunae in current Mesolithic research and of stimulating discussions and debate with our students. The final product has gained in content and clarity through critical, but always constructive, review by our colleagues. To all of them we wish to express our heartfelt gratitude for their continuing support. This paper would not have been possible without the cooperation of Ms M.C. van Straaten and Mr F. Stelling, both of the Instituut voor Antropobiologie at Utrecht and Mr J. Dijkema of the Biologisch–Archaeologisch Instituut at Groningen. They performed part of the typing and drafting, respectively. The first author also profited from several travel grants from the Netherlands Organization for the Advancement of Pure Research (Z.W.O.) for the collection of data.

References

ADAMS, J.W. and KASAKOFF, A.B. (1975) Factors underlying endogamous group size. In M. Nag (ed.), *Population and Social Organization*. The Hague, Mouton: 147–174.

BIRDSELL, J.B. (1950) Some implications of the genetical concept of race in terms of spatial analysis. *Cold Spring Harbor Symposia on Quantitative Biology*, 15: 259–314.

BIRDSELL, J.B. (1953) Some environmental and cultural factors influencing the structuring of Australian aboriginal populations. *American Naturalist*, 87: 171–207.

BIRDSELL, J.B. (1958) On population structure in generalized hunting and collecting populations. *Evolution*, 12: 189–205.

BIRDSELL, J.B. (1968) Some predictions for the Pleistocene based on equilibrium systems among recent hunter-gatherers. In R.B. Lee and I. DeVore (eds), *Man the Hunter*. Chicago, Aldine: 229–240.

BIRDSELL, J.B. (1973) A basic demographic unit. *Current Anthropology*, 14: 337–357.

BURCH, E.S. (1972) The caribou/wild reindeer as a human resource. *American Antiquity*, 37: 339–368.

BURCH, E.S. (1980) Traditional Eskimo societies in northwest Alaska. In Y. Kotani and W.B. Workman (eds), *Alaska Native Culture and History* (Senri Ethnological Studies, 4). Osaka, National Museum of Ethnology: 253–304.

BURCH, E.S. (1981) *The Traditional Eskimo Hunters of Point Hope, Alaska: 1800–1875*. Barrow, The North Slope Borough.

CATLIN, G. (1884) (1973) *Letters and Notes on the Manners, Customs, and Conditions of the North American Indians*. New York, Dover Publications.

CLARK, J.G.D. (1975) *The Earlier Stone Age Settlement of Scandinavia*. Cambridge, University Press.

CONSTANDSE-WESTERMANN, T.S., BLOK, M.L. and NEWELL, R.R. (1985) Long bone length and stature in the western European Mesolithic. I. Methodological problems and solutions. *Journal of Human Evolution*, 14: 399–410.

CONSTANDSE-WESTERMANN, T.S. and NEWELL, R.R. (1984) Mesolithic trauma: demographical and chronological trends in western Europe. In G.T. Haneveld and W.R.K. Perizonius (eds), *Proceedings of the 4th European Meeting of the Paleopathology Association, Middelburg/Antwerpen 1982*. Utrecht, Elinkwyk B.V.: 70–76.

CONSTANDSE-WESTERMANN, T.S. and NEWELL, R.R. (in preparation) *The biological aspects of western European Mesolithic population structure by means of a metrical analysis of the skeletons* (paper).

CONSTANDSE-WESTERMANN, T.S., NEWELL, R.R. and MEIKLEJOHN, C. (1984) Human biological background of population dynamics in the western European Mesolithic. *Proceedings of the Koninklijke Nederlandse Akademie van Wetenschappen*, B87: 139–223.

COOK, S.F. (1955) The epidemic of 1830–1833 in California and Oregon. *University of California Publications in American Archaeology and Ethnology*, 43: 303–326.

COOK, S.F. (1956) The aboriginal population of the north coast of California. *Anthropological Records*, 16: 81–130.

COOK, S.F. (1966) Comment on Dobyns: An appraisal of techniques with a new hemispheric estimate. *Current Anthropology*, 7: 427–429.

COOK, S.F. (1976) *The Indian Population of New England in the Seventeenth Century*. Berkeley, University of California Press.

DE LANGEN, G.J. (1985) *Status and Rol in de Midden Steentijd*. Honours thesis Cultural Anthropology, Subfaculteit der Sociaal–Culturele Wetenschappen, Rijksuniversiteit Groningen.

DENEVAN, W.M. (ed.) (1976) *The Native Population of the Americas in 1492*. Madison, University of Wisconsin Press.

DOBYNS, H.F. (1966) An appraisal of techniques with a new hemispheric estimate. *Current Anthropology*, 7: 395–416, 440–444.

DUNN, F.L. (1966) Comment on Dobyns: An appraisal of techniques with a new hemispheric estimate. *Current Anthropology*, 7: 430–431.

ELSASSER, A.B. (1978) Mattole, Nongatl, Sinkyone, Lassik, and Wailaki. In R.F. Heizer (ed.), *Handbook of North American Indians. Volume 8: California*. Washington D.C., Smithsonian Institution: 190–204.

FRIED, M. (1967) *The Evolution of Political Society. An Essay in Political Anthropology*. New York, Random House.

HELM, J. (1968) The nature of Dogrib socio-territorial groups. In R.B. Lee and I. DeVore (eds), *Man the Hunter*. Chicago, Aldine: 118–125.

HILL, J.H. (1978) Language contact systems and human adaptations. *Journal of Anthropological Research*, 34: 1–26.

KROEBER, A.L. (1939) *Cultural and Natural Areas of Native North America* (University of California Publications in American Archaeology and Ethnology, 38). Berkeley, University of California Press.

KRZYWICKI, L. (1934) *Primitive Society and its Vital Statistics*. London, Macmillan.

MEIKLEJOHN, C. (1978) Ecological aspects of population size and growth in Late-glacial and early Postglacial north-western Europe. In P.A. Mellars (ed.), *The Early Postglacial Settlement of Northern Europe*. London, Duckworth: 65–79.

MERRIAM, C.H. (1905) The Indian population of California. *American Anthropologist*, 7: 594–606.

MOONEY, J. (1928) *The Aboriginal Population North of Mexico* (Smithsonian Institution Miscellaneous Collections, 80). Washington D.C., Smithsonian Institution.

NEWELL, R.R. (1984) On the Mesolithic contribution to the social evolution of western European society. In J. Bintliff (ed.), *European Social Evolution: Archaeological Perspectives*. Bradford, University of Bradford: 69–82.

NEWELL, R.R. and CONSTANDSE-WESTERMANN, T.S. (1986a) Testing an ethnographic analogue of Mesolithic social structure and the archaeological resolution of Mesolithic ethnic groups and breeding populations. *Proceedings of the Koninklijke Nederlandse Akademie van Wetenschappen*, B89: 243–310.

NEWELL, R.R. and CONSTANDSE-WESTERMANN, T.S. (1986b) Population growth, density and technology in the western European Mesolithic: lessons from analogous historical contexts. *Palaeohistoria*, 26: 1–18.

NEWELL, R.R., CONSTANDSE-WESTERMANN, T.S. and DE LANGEN, G.J. (in preparation) *The physical anthropology and burial ritual of the Mesolithic population of northern and western Europe* (paper).

114

NEWELL, R.R., CONSTANDSE-WESTERMANN, T.S. and MEIKLE-JOHN, C. (1979) The skeletal remains of Mesolithic man in western Europe: an evaluative catalogue. *Journal of Human Evolution*, 8: 1–228.

NEWELL, R.R., KIELMAN, D., CONSTANDSE-WESTERMANN, T.S., VAN GIJN, A. and VAN DER SANDEN, W.A.B. (in press) *An Inquiry into the Ethnic Resolution of Mesolithic Regional Groups: a Study of their Decorative Ornaments in Time and Space*. Leiden, E.J. Brill.

OWEN, R. (1965) The patrilocal band: a linguistically and culturally hybrid social unit. *American Anthropologist*, 67: 675–690.

SAHLINS, M. (1972) *Stone Age Economics*. Chicago, Aldine.

SERVICE, E. (1971) *Primitive Social Organization: an Evolutionary Perspective* (2nd edition). New York, Random House.

SHARP, L. (1968) Discussion on: Hunter social organization: some problems of method. In R.B. Lee and I. DeVore (eds), *Man the Hunter*. Chicago, Aldine: 158–161.

STEWARD, J.H. (1955) *Theory of Culture Change*. Urbana, University of Illinois Press.

SWANTON, J.R. (1952) (1976) *The Indian Tribes of North America* (Smithsonian Institution Bureau of American Ethnology, Bulletin 145). Washington D.C., U.S. Government Printing Office (Reprint: St Clair Shores, Michigan, Scholarly Press).

TAYLOR, H.C. (1963) Aboriginal populations of the lower Northwest Coast. *Pacific Northwest Quarterly*, 54: 158–165.

THORNTON, R. (1978) Implications of Catlin's American Indian population estimates for revision of Mooney's estimate. *American Journal of Physical Anthropology*, 49: 11–13.

THORNTON, R. (1980) Recent estimates of the prehistoric California Indian population. *Current Anthropology*, 21: 702–704.

THWAITES, R.G. (ed.) (1959) *The Jesuit Relations and Allied Documents 1610–1791* (73 volumes). New York, Pagent Book Company.

UBELAKER, D.H. (1976) The sources and methodology for Mooney's estimates of North American Indian populations. In W.M. Denevan (ed.), *The Native Population of the Americas in 1492*. Madison, University of Wisconsin Press: 243–292.

UBELAKER, D.H. (1977) Prehistoric New World population size: historical review and current appraisal of North American estimates. *American Journal of Physical Anthropology*, 45: 661–666.

VAN HOLK, A.F.L. and DE ROLLER, G.J. (1985) *Ethniciteit en Stijl in het Vroege Mesolithicum. Een Onderzoek naar Grafinventarissen*. Groningen, Rijksuniversiteit Subfaculteit Biologisch–Archaeologisch Instituut.

WILLIAMS, B.J. (1974) *A Model of Band Society* (Memoir of the Society for American Archaeology, 29). Washington D.C., Society for American Archaeology.

WILMSEN, E.N. (1973) Interaction, spacing behavior, and the organization of hunting bands. *Journal of Anthropological Research*, 29: 1–31.

WOBST, H.M. (1974) Boundary conditions for Palaeolithic social systems: a simulation approach. *American Antiquity*, 39: 147–178.

WOBST, H.M. (1975) The demography of finite populations and the origins of the incest taboo. *Memoirs of the Society for American Archaeology*, 30: 75–81.

WOBST, H.M. (1976) Locational relationships in Palaeolithic society. *Journal of Human Evolution*, 5: 49–58.

The Mesolithic of Munster: a Preliminary Assessment

Peter C. Woodman

Abstract

It had been presumed until recently that Ireland's southern province was first occupied late in prehistory, usually during the Neolithic but in some areas not before the Bronze Age. Recent work has shown that not only is there evidence for an early Neolithic presence, there was also a Mesolithic occupation of Munster. So far, most of the evidence for early Mesolithic settlement has come from the Blackwater valley in Co. Cork, while later Mesolithic material has been recovered at Ferriters Cove, Co. Kerry. This paper examines the problems of working in an area where not only was the Mesolithic lacking, various environmental factors were liable to inhibit discovery. It also examines the problems created by the discovery of a Mesolithic in Munster.

INTRODUCTION

In 1978 it was suggested that there were several obvious identifiable goals for research in the Irish Mesolithic (Woodman 1978). These included the problem of the chronological gap within the Irish Mesolithic as well as the need to verify the economic basis through the examination of sites outside the north east of Ireland. However, the most attainable goal was thought to be the question of the extent of occupation of Ireland during the Mesolithic. By 1978 it had been demonstrated through excavations at Lough Boora (Ryan 1981) that, even in the Irish early Mesolithic, the centre of Ireland had been visited by Mesolithic populations. Therefore, the apparent absence of Mesolithic material in the southern third of Ireland became even more anomalous.

If, for example, the assumption that the south-west peninsulas were not colonized until the beginning of the Bronze Age is put in a broader European context (De Valera and Ó Nualláin 1982), then this same assumption implies that quite accessible parts of Ireland were not occupied until nearly 4000 years after the Varanger fjord area, significantly north of the Arctic Circle, in Norway. This paper will examine the archaeological background to this perception of the prehistory of the province of Munster, the research strategies adopted in tackling this problem, and the first results of this programme of research.

HISTORICAL BACKGROUND

It has usually been assumed that the south of Ireland was only colonized at a late date, as there were no Neolithic monuments which could be confidently ascribed to the early Neolithic. There has been much discussion in recent years about the traditional chronological sequence of megalithic tombs in Ireland, in particular whether 'court tombs' should be given chronological primacy or whether some other forms (F. Lynch 1975), even simple passage graves, could not be seen as equally early (Burenhult 1984). As all these tomb types were either scarce or even lacking from many parts of Munster, it has been assumed that their absence could imply the virtual absence of any population in the early Neolithic. Therefore, if there was no early Neolithic and in some areas no Neolithic at all, then it seemed only reasonable to presume that it was unlikely that there would be any earlier, Mesolithic, populations present.

Recent research has begun to suggest that there may have been a more significant Neolithic presence than has hitherto been presumed. Dr A. Lynch (1981) has identified *Triticum* pollen grains at 5800 BP at Cashelkeelty in County Kerry and, although it would presumably date much later in the Neolithic, a Neolithic leaf-shaped piercing arrowhead was found on an adjacent excavation. An examination of the chronology of Irish prehistory through a radiocarbon dating programme being carried out by the Groningen laboratory (e.g. Brindley *et al.* 1983) has also begun to show that certain simple burial monuments – often termed Linkardstown cists – have a significantly greater antiquity in the Neolithic than was presumed. These are found in parts of Munster. Similarly, Molleson has managed to obtain a radiocarbon date from skeleton B, Kilgreany Cave, County Waterford, which shows that simple burials outside megalithic tombs could have existed early in the Neolithic. The occurrence of single burials at Lough Gur Site C early in the sequence of occupation (Ó Ríordáin 1954) would also seem to confirm that Neolithic settlement can be associated either with very simple monuments or non-megalithic burials.

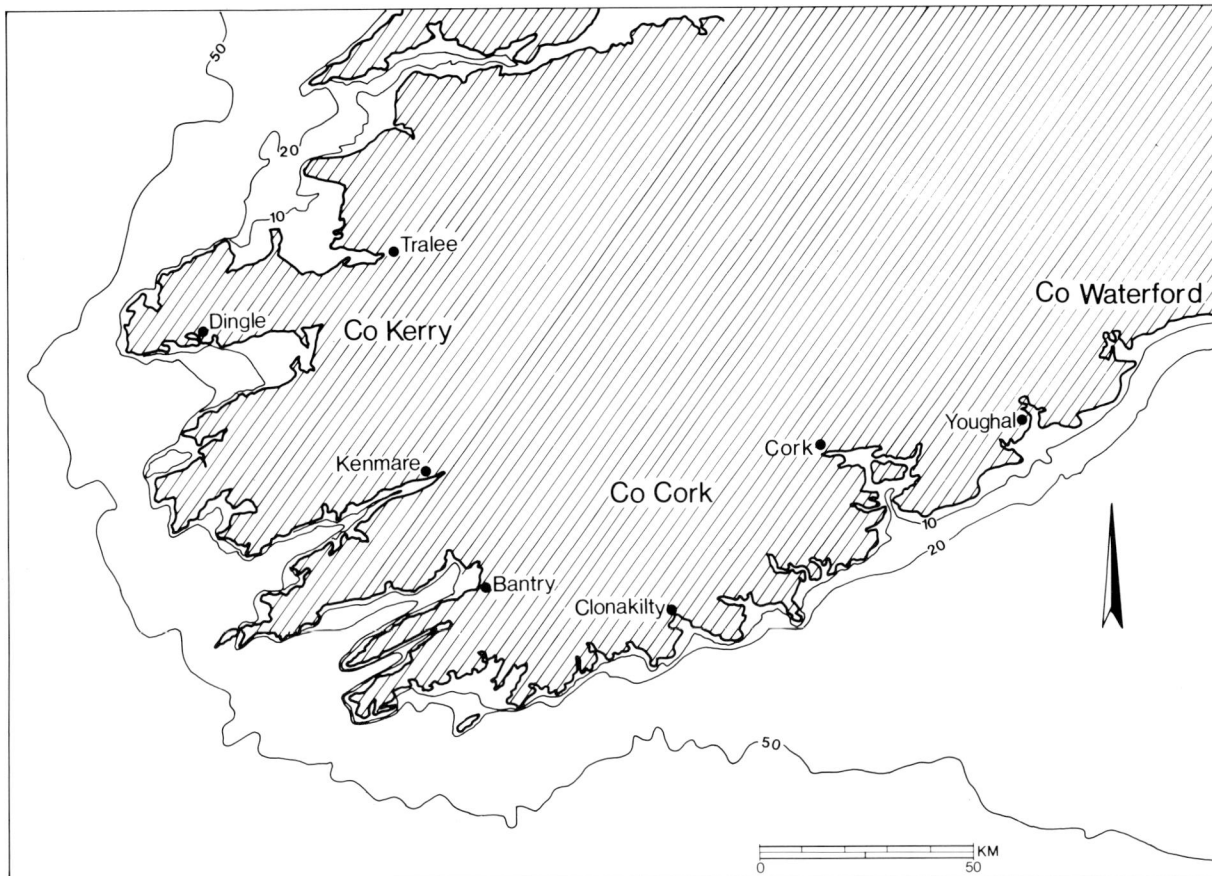

Figure 1 Submarine topography of south-west Ireland.

As can be seen from *Fig. 1*, a drop of 50 fathoms or nearly 100 m in relative sea level would expose a significant area of the south coast of Ireland. If there was any coastal Lateglacial occupation on the south coast, it would presumably be buried well out to sea. However, this same topography has often been regarded as an inhibiting factor in discovering Mesolithic settlement.

The south coast of Ireland has always been regarded as one of the classic drowned landscapes of Europe. In particular, the occurrence of a simple megalithic tomb in the inter-tidal zone of Cork harbour has been used to demonstrate the fact that the local relative sea level rose during the Neolithic or after it. While there is no doubt that the south east of Ireland, in particular, was not subject to isostatic uplift, there is no reason to believe that it is sinking like parts of southern England (Carter and Orford 1981; Devoy 1983). In fact, Devoy (1983) has suggested that with ice sheets covering the extreme south west of Ireland, it is possible that there may have been a limited amount of isostatic uplift in that area. In the Cork harbour area, Devoy (1983) has found evidence that there was a marine transgression at −12 m O.D. at *c.* 7500 BP. This implies that at the same date the sea was, relatively speaking, transgressing areas of land at present about 10 m lower than on the north-east coast of Ireland (Carter 1982). The

difference is, of course, explained by the incomplete isostatic recovery of north-east Ireland.

This later transgression in the south presents problems, but if early Mesolithic sites can be found on the north-east coast of Ireland when relative sea level was lower than today, then some sites should have survived in coastal locations in the south. In fact, the extensive erosion from longshore drift has probably removed and destroyed as many settlements as the marine transgressions.

The presumed scarcity of good raw materials for the manufacture of stone tools was a limiting factor in a different sense. The use of raw materials other than those traditionally recognized by archaeologists could create problems in the discovery and identification of sites, in particular the key role implicitly given to flint which was thought to be extremely scarce. However, flint can be found in some abundance in certain coastal areas and no coastal area in the south and south west of Ireland has been totally lacking in flint. Much of this flint may have been brought onshore by ice sheets which left tills such as Garryvoe till (Mitchell 1976; see below for further discussion).

RESEARCH STRATEGY

In setting out to ascertain if there was any evidence of Mesolithic settlement throughout the rest of

117

Ireland, several factors had to be taken into consideration.

The first and most obvious one which was to condition the research strategies adopted was the fact that there is no extensive tradition of amateur fieldwalkers and collectors in many parts of Ireland and, in particular, the southern third of the island. The work of the major nineteenth and early twentieth century collectors such as Knowles, Gray, and Hewson (Woodman 1978) had been mostly confined to the north east of Ireland, with a few holiday excursions to sand dune sites on the west coast. A more recent generation of collectors has concentrated on the east coast. Therefore, searches of the museum collections were to prove fruitless, and so a new programme of fieldwalking had to be initiated.

As a hundred-year lag in research cannot be overcome even in a decade, it was decided that specific areas would be chosen for research. Two fieldwalking projects were then initiated:

The Ballylough Project. In the Waterford harbour area, a project has been undertaken by Professor S. Green, University of South Carolina, Dr M. Zvelebil, University of Sheffield, and Professor J. Moore, City of New York University. The Ballylough Project has been centred on an area surrounding the major estuary of the Barrow and Suir where probable early Neolithic could be expected – on the basis of numerous megaliths – and where, owing to the large estuary, Mesolithic settlement might also be expected (Zvelebil *et al.* 1987).

County Cork. Here a fieldwalking project undertaken by the author and funded by the Royal Irish Academy Archaeological Research Fund, has concentrated on the Blackwater valley and the coast to the east of Cork harbour.

The regions were chosen with particular care to overcome two other factors which could inhibit discovery:

1. In the narrow estuaries, the change in relative sea level would not affect dramatically the local topography to the extent that all sites would be obscured by a rising sea level. Like the Bann valley, both Waterford harbour and the lower reaches of the Blackwater are fairly steep-sided, large valleys subject to flooding, so that some settlement at least would be expected to be placed above the valley floor, as at Mount Sandel. As a contrast, areas such as Cork harbour were ignored, as relatively small changes in sea level could inundate large areas of land.

2. The second inhibiting factor was the percentage of arable farming. Many parts of Ireland are given over exclusively to dairy and beef farming, and so there is often little arable farming. In particular, limestone areas are often preferred for permanent grasslands. Unfortunately, in many parts of Munster limestone is confined to the valley floors where Mesolithic settlement would be expected. Therefore, areas have to be found where, because of economic factors, arable farming overrode this natural tendency towards grassland. For this reason, two areas were selected. The portion of the Blackwater valley north of Cork harbour had, perhaps for historical reasons as well as the presence of a sugar beet factory, a much higher incidence of arable farming than is usual on limestone. Similarly, perhaps because of the demand for grain at the nearby distilleries, the east Cork coast had a high incidence of arable land.

Besides the fieldwalking programmes, the Department of Archaeology, University College Cork, has undertaken the examination of coastal shell middens in south-west Ireland in the hope that some of these might prove to be later Mesolithic in date. So far, excavations have concentrated on a series of shell middens at Ferriters Cove, Dingle peninsula, Co. Kerry. These excavations, although initially undertaken on the assumption that the site was Neolithic, are revealing occupation that is primarily late Mesolithic in date.

RESULTS

Early Mesolithic[1]

At the moment, we are proceeding on the assumption that the early Mesolithic can be defined at two levels. Firstly, any site which has produced microliths is presumed to date to the early Mesolithic which, in Ireland, is earlier than 8000 BP. At the moment, four sites containing microliths have been radiocarbon dated to earlier than 8000 BP (Woodman 1978), while all those which lack microliths and are characterized by a much heavier blade tradition (see below) have been dated to later than 8000 BP – at least eight sites. Other sites have yielded a blade industry produced by controlled percussion. Unfortunately, the same technique was used at Lough Gur in the Neolithic. The absence of Neolithic elements and the presence of anomalous backed and worked blades can be taken as a less certain indicator of an early Mesolithic presence. All the early Mesolithic sites occur in the Blackwater valley (*Fig. 2*).

The early Mesolithic of Munster can be summarized as follows (see also *Table 1*).

Kilcomer Lower, Co. Cork

This site is located on top of a 30 m high cliff at the confluence of the Blackwater and its tributary, the Awbeg. 90% of the material is confined to an area no more than 50 m in diameter. This is the only substantial early Mesolithic site to be discovered so far.

Figure 2 Distribution of early Mesolithic sites.

Known Early Mesolithic Material

Table 1: List of artifacts and retouched tools from early Mesolithic sites in Munster

	Kilcomer	Lefanta	Castleblagh
Cores	3	1	–
Decortical flakes	4	2	–
Flakes	18	5	1
Blades	28 (38)	4 (3)	3 (3)
Débitage	144	9	10
Microliths	9	–	1
Backed blades	1	1	–
Scrapers	–	2	–
Miscellaneous tools	1	1	1

(Bracketed numbers represent blade fragments)

While none of the short edges of scalene triangles have been discovered, several, such as *Fig. 3*, nos. 3–5, are probably fragments of scalene triangles. Others, such as *Fig. 3*, nos. 1–2, are obliquely trimmed while *Fig. 3*, nos. 6–8 are rods. *Fig. 3*, no. 9 could be a fragment of a larger backed blade. *Table 1* shows a remarkably low incidence of cores and decortical flakes. Blades and blade fragments are a dominant form of artifact. Much of the material has a deep white patina.

Castleblagh Td., Co. Cork

A small scatter of flint artifacts (19 in all) was recovered from a gravel ridge on the south side of the Blackwater. No specific concentration was found and only one microlith was recovered. Much of the material is heavily weathered and patinated.

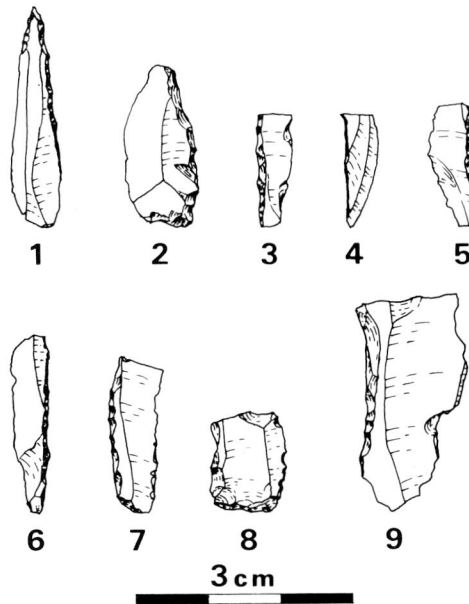

Figure 3 Microliths from Kilcomer Lower, Co. Cork.

Ballynamona Td., Co. Cork

A small scatter of blades was recovered adjacent to the Awbeg river. It is just possible that they came from an early Mesolithic site. Only 15 pieces have been recovered so far. This site is questionable.

Lefanta Td. (Cappoquin), Co. Waterford

An open scatter of artifacts (26 in all) found on a low ridge beside the Blackwater river. These came from an area 100 m across. Again a blade assemblage produced by controlled percussion which, though lacking in microliths, did produce a worked blade reminiscent of those found at Mount Sandel. Almost certainly this is an early Mesolithic assemblage (Woodman 1984).

Newport Td., Co. Waterford

Here a single, large, backed blade was recovered. This could either be seen as early Mesolithic or, conceivably, as Lateglacial in age (Woodman 1984). In spite of intensive examination of the area, no concentrations of lithic artifacts have been found.

Later Mesolithic

In comparison to the north of Ireland where later Mesolithic assemblages outnumber early Mesolithic assemblages by nearly 10:1, only two certain later assemblages have been found through surface collections (*Fig. 4*).

The Irish later Mesolithic is, of course, usually characterized as a heavy-bladed industry. It is often implied that its use of a direct percussion technique to produce large broad blades is a product of flint availability in north-east Ireland. Thus, while at one level we have accepted that a chronological primacy

119

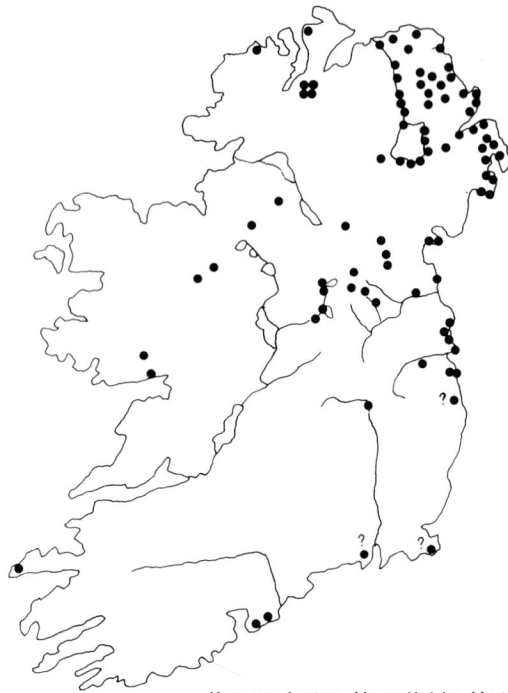

Known Later Mesolithic Material

Figure 4   Distribution of later Mesolithic material.

for the north-east corner no longer exists – now on both typological and distributional grounds – we still unconsciously presume that flint availability in the north east determines the methods of manufacture throughout the whole island. If either the nature of the resources changes or if they become scarce, can we, therefore, presume that later Mesolithic industries would remain in the same recognizable form? Before examining the evidence for a later Mesolithic in Munster, therefore, it might be worth considering how these industrial techniques evolved.

The Irish later Mesolithic can be characterized by a heavy blade, direct percussion technology resulting in a variable size of striking platform but usually a large, smooth platform. If it is to be described as Larnian, then the distinctive uniplane cores should be present in some numbers (Woodman 1978). The artifacts are usually made on large blades, the most common of which are the butt-trimmed forms such as the tanged and leaf-shaped 'Bann Flakes'. It would appear that at Newferry, in zones 8 and 7 main, the forms of retouched tools were already in existence and that relatively broad classic Larnian forms of flakes and blades only appeared at a later date (Woodman 1977). Similarly, at Cushendun, although distinct artifact types were missing, as at Newferry zone 8, there was a rather more elongated blade element stratified below the rational alder rise, i.e. before 7000 BP.

Besides the fact that the classic broad blade technology appeared later than the retouched tools with which this technology is associated, there is the fact that absence of flint has neither changed the technology nor the retouched tools. This can be seen

from the material recovered at sites such as Newferry where there is no flint available in the immediate vicinity (Woodman 1981). Even on the basis of what we know from the north Midlands where the raw material is chert, as at sites such as Lough Derravaragh (Mitchell 1972) and Moynagh Lough Crannog (Bradley 1983), the heavy blade assemblage existed along with retouched tools but without some of the characteristics of the Larnian industrial techniques, notably the uniplane core. This characteristic would be mostly appropriate when flint nodules are being used. For these reasons, we can presume that in Munster later Mesolithic material should occur in an archaeological context in a recognizable form.

Therefore, it is hardly surprising that some late Mesolithic assemblages have been found in Munster. These fall into two categories: two sites found through surface collection, and one through excavation. Surface collection has also produced two sites in east County Cork, both on the coast.

Gyleen, Co. Cork

This area has produced a scatter of struck stone tools found over several fields adjacent to a small river and the present coastline, where extensive erosion has taken place. In the corner formed by the coastal cliff and the river valley, a significant concentration of heavily patinated uniplane cores was found. In a gridded collection, these occurred more frequently in this one specific place than elsewhere in the immediate vicinity. A small bar form was also recovered. Nearby, two small 'Bann Flakes' were found (Woodman 1984). Unfortunately, this area was re-used on numerous occasions in later prehistory. Therefore, it is virtually impossible to sort out what is specifically later Mesolithic.

Dunpower, Co. Cork

Here a site was recovered when soil was inadvertently stripped from an area on top of a 30 m high cliff. While the Gyleen material was mixed, this cliff-top location would seem to have particularly suited a fishing community, as there was comparatively easy access to the shore for rock fishing immediately adjacent to the only source of fresh water in the vicinity. As can be seen from *Tables 2 & 3*, this is a classic later Mesolithic assemblage of Larnian type and, although flint was particularly scarce on this cliff-top location, the mean blade length of 5.5 cm equates favourably with that at sites such as Sutton, Co. Dublin, on the east coast of Ireland outside the Antrim coast.

Apart from these two sites, several locations under investigation by Zvelebil *et al.* (1987) in east Co. Waterford could be later Mesolithic, as could an assemblage found in east Co. Wexford. In particular,

Table 2: Breakdown of core types from selected later Mesolithic sites

	Single	Dual	Multiple Platform
Curran Point (Co. Antrim)	124	6	3
Rough Island Beach (Co. Down)	33	1	2
Sutton (Co. Dublin)	10	2	–
Dunpower (Co. Cork)	9	1	1

Table 3: Mean blade size from selected later Mesolithic sites

	Length	Breadth
Newferry 3, Zone 4 (Co. Antrim)	6.8	2.4
Bay Farm 1, Lower (Co. Antrim)	6.7	2.8
Curran Point (Co. Antrim)	6.3	2.6
Rough Island (Co. Down)	5.0	3.0
Sutton (Co. Dublin)	5.3	2.5
Dunpower (Co. Cork) – patinated	5.5	3.2

they have brought to light a large 'Bann Flake' of silicified siltstone found on the edge of Waterford harbour.

Ferriters Cove, Co. Kerry

Unlike the assemblages discussed so far, where the material was found through surface collection, this site has seen some preliminary excavation. Owing to the discovery of a plano-convex knife (*Fig. 5*, no. 1) adjacent to a shell midden in an eroding shoreline context (Vernon 1976), a rescue excavation was undertaken at Ferriters Cove at the western end of the Dingle peninsula (Woodman, Duggan and McCarthy 1984).

Three locations which seemed to be in particular danger were chosen for immediate attention. These have produced the following radiocarbon dates (we are indebted to the British Museum Research Laboratory for these dates):

Site 1: 5400±220 BP (BM-2227R)
5420±150 BP (BM-2227AR)

Site 2: 5750±140 BP (BM-2228R)
5850±130 BP (BM-2228AR)

Site 3: 5490±160 BP (BM-2229R)
5500±130 BP (BM-2229AR)

Several features were common to all these sites. They rested on a wave-cut platform which may initially have been created during the Last Interglacial but reworked in the Holocene. The commonest raw material used for stone tools was not flint, which did exist in small quantities, but rhyolite and a related series of volcanic ashes. These rock sources seem to have been of variable quality, but some exceptionally good quality stone-working has taken place (e.g. *Fig. 5*, nos. 3–4).

While the dates referred to earlier overlap with the suggested arrival of agriculture in this area, there is reason to believe that some of the sites at least might be later Mesolithic. It is significant that the plano-convex knife was found adjacent to Site 1 which produced the latest radiocarbon dates. In the area from which the charcoal was taken, a suspiciously narrow blade industry was found. Although this was in rhyolite, it was rather reminiscent of the narrow blade tradition which typifies so many Neolithic assemblages. At the other sites and even within a pit found at Site 1, a much heavier broad blade type of industry was found – e.g. *Fig. 5*, no. 4, which came from Site 1, feature 23. The only potentially diagnostic artifact to be found *in situ* at Site 2 is a large, leaf-shaped, sandstone flake which is reminiscent of a 'Bann Flake' (*Fig. 5*, no. 2). While the small polished axe found on Site 2 (*Fig 5*, no. 5) is rather reminiscent of those found at Newferry, Co. Antrim (Woodman 1977), it cannot be regarded as a later Mesolithic type-fossil.

The Irish later Mesolithic is not overly endowed with diagnostic artifacts other than 'Bann Flakes'. Therefore, it is not too surprising that there are few type-fossils at this site. What is significant in demonstrating that these sites belong to the later Mesolithic is that certain elements characteristic of the Neolithic are absent from Sites 2 and 3. Not only are there no distinctive Neolithic stone artifacts from these sites, no pottery occurs on them.

When the economic basis of these sites is examined, it would seem to be a purely hunter-gatherer economy. Owing to a geological freak, the soils in the vicinity of this site are not particularly acid, and so some animal bones have survived. These are red deer and pig. So far, no domesticates have been found. There would seem to have been extensive exploitation of marine resources. Concentrations of shellfish, in particular limpets, whelks and winkles, were found – usually each heap containing only one species. In one instance, several thousand winkles filled a pit. In the case of limpets, there may have been a deliberate selection of the smaller, more edible limpets found at low water mark (McCarthy, in preparation).

So far, work has only begun on the identification of the fish bones. However, a tentative list of species noted in *Table 4* is rather similar to those found on the contemporaneous Leinster shell middens (Woodman 1978).

While it is possible that this site was used for only a short season of the year – possibly autumn, on the

121

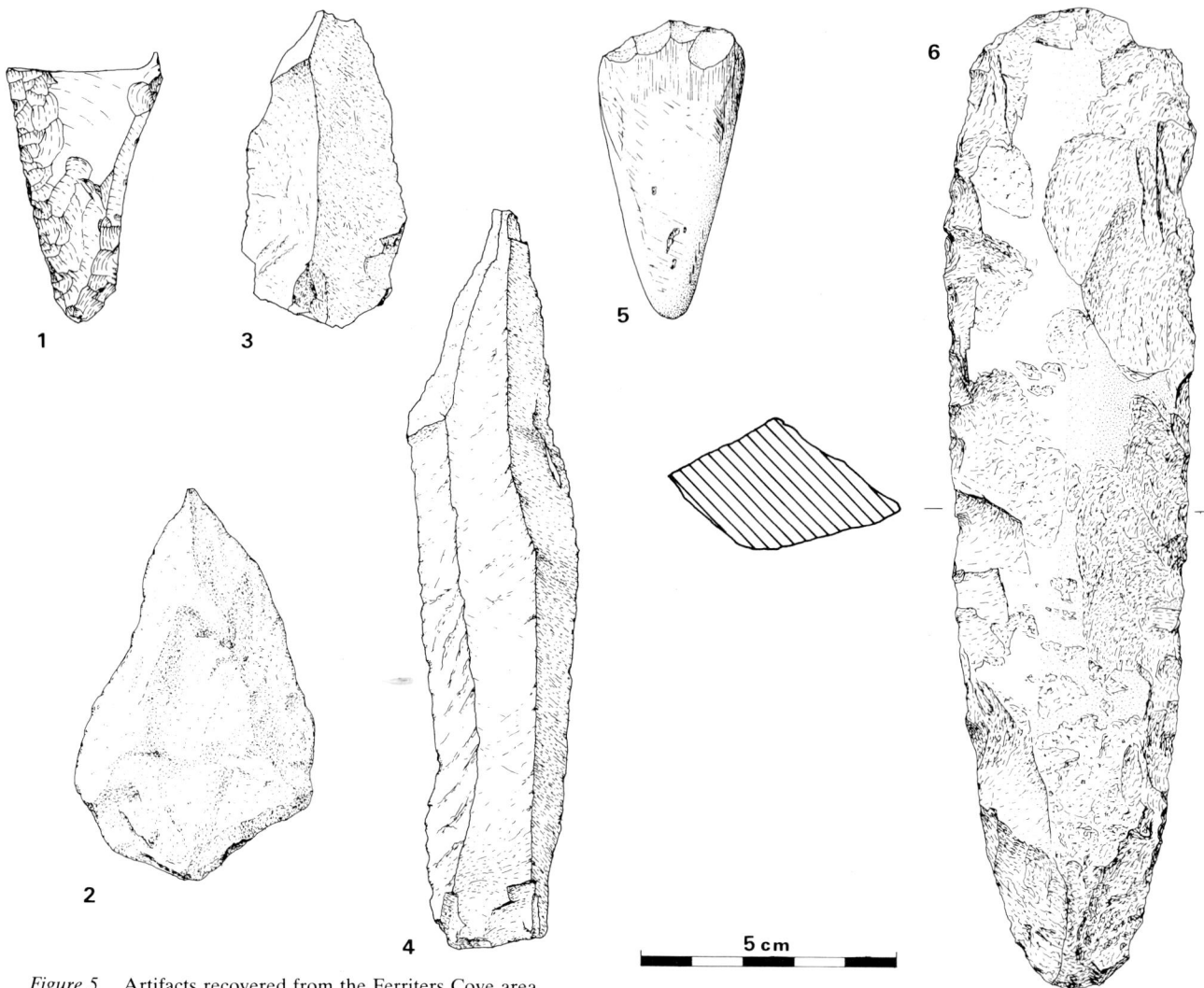

Figure 5   Artifacts recovered from the Ferriters Cove area.

Table 4:   Sea fish from later Mesolithic sites

	Ferriters Cove	Sutton	Dalkey	Rockmarshall
Sea fish (unspec.)		P		
Wrasse	C		R	
Mullet			R	P
Tope	P		P(?)	P(?)
Cod	P		R(?)	
Conger eel			P	
Sole				P(?)
Hake	P(?)			

C   Common   P   Present   R   Rare

basis of hazel-nut presence and on the growth rings of the mussel shells recovered – it seems to have had more than casual importance. The rhyolite sources were several miles away; in fact, an unfinished rhyolite axe (*Fig. 5*, no. 6) was recovered in recent years on the slopes of Clogher Head. Therefore, if rhyolite was being brought to the site, then the site would probably have been more than a simple specialist exploitation location.

In recent years, we have managed to demonstrate that all of Ireland was probably occupied for most of the Irish Mesolithic and, therefore, one goal noted in 1978 has been achieved. However, the simple discovery of some Mesolithic sites within the province has, of course, raised a new series of questions.

PROBLEMS

While the scarcity of excavated sites obviously creates a whole range of problems owing to the lack of a good database, there are already some other specific questions which must be tackled.

It is, of course, questionable whether the spots marked on the maps of Munster could be described as creating distribution maps. The initial field-walking survey in Co. Cork concentrated on the types of locations where it was known that Mesolithic sites occurred in the north east. Their riverine and coastal distribution in Co. Cork may, therefore, be totally artificial. The more systematic programme based on the Ballylough Project will give a more accurate picture of the types of environment exploited in Munster. It is quite possible that, without the large lakes on the Shannon system or Lough Neagh, a totally different economic strategy may emerge in Munster.

There is already one noticeable difference between the early and later Mesolithic. With the rise of at least 20 m in sea level since the early Mesolithic, the relative scarcity of early coastal sites is not surprising; but the absence of later Mesolithic material from the Blackwater valley, a rich salmon river, is rather striking. Even allowing for the lack of good raw materials in this area (see below), work in the north east (Griffiths and Woodman 1987) has shown that stone tools can be transported to preferred areas of settlement. Is there a genuine absence of inland later Mesolithic sites in this area or is it all buried in the river valleys? How much would be known of the later Mesolithic of the north east of Ireland if there had been no commercial exploitation of the Bann valley diatomite?

Besides the fact that the Blackwater early Mesolithic sites are quite small, the distribution of material (as seen in *Table 1*) suggests that they are rather transitory. This is also reflected in their use of raw material. This western end of the Blackwater valley has yet to produce any natural flint, even as erratics. The flint artifacts found at Kilcomer Lower contain an element of distinctive flint which has not yet been found elsewhere. So far as can be seen from *Fig. 6*, flint is mostly found as erratics from the movement onshore of ice sheets from the continental shelf. The absence of chert in any quantity on these early sites implies less contact with the limestone central plain of Ireland where chert can occur in abundance. We must presume that like the small concentrations of early Mesolithic material at Culbane, Glenone and other sites on the River Bann, all we have from the Blackwater are transitory inland sites. We can also presume, as in the north east at Mount Sandel and Portrush, that there would have been a significant presence on the coast. If, as is becoming clear from Ireland's early Mesolithic faunal remains (Van Wijngaarden-Bakker, this volume), non-migratory fish did not exist and red deer was not of importance, could there ever have been more than a transitory occupation of Ireland's interior?

The problems of raw materials are not confined to the early Mesolithic. The discovery of two rhyolite sources in Munster is, of course, of interest. While we know that the Kerry outcrops were in use at the end of the Mesolithic, so far the work of the Ballylough Project suggests that the Tramore outcrops would seem to have been used mostly in the Neolithic. How great an antiquity will the use of rhyolite have? The other problem will be the importance of these outcrops as sources of raw material. Already, occasional flakes of rhyolite have been identified from sites up to 80 km to the east and west of Tramore.

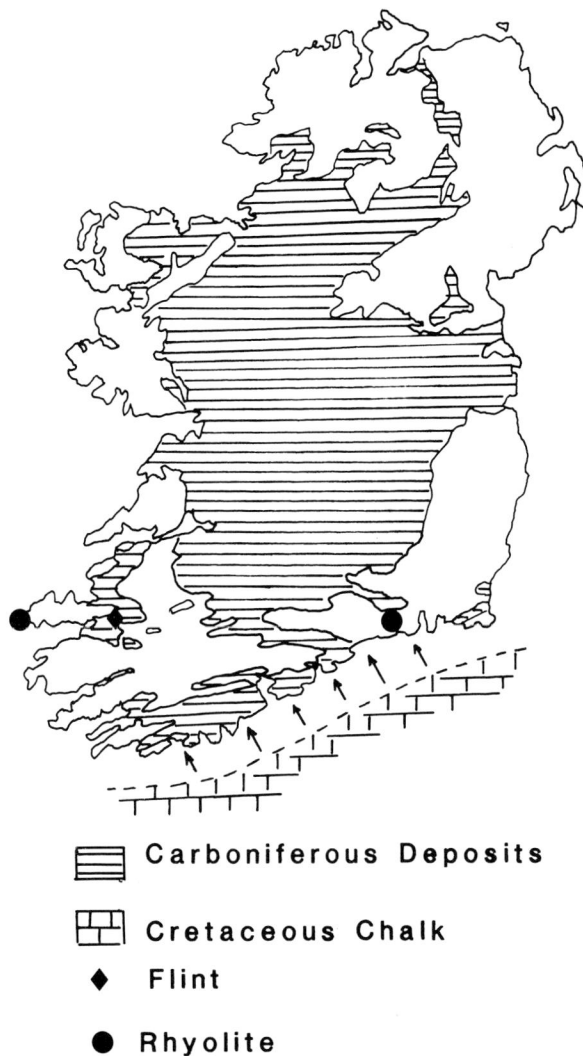

Figure 6 Distribution of lithic sources in southern Ireland.

THE BEGINNING OF THE NEOLITHIC

As noted in the historical introduction, the absence of early Neolithic monuments in many parts of Munster gave rise to what could be described as the 'Empty Landscape Philosophy' – that the reason for their dearth was that Munster was largely unoccupied. A. Lynch's work at Cashelkeelty (1981) and the discovery of indications of a substantial Mesolithic occupation in Munster has negated that theory. New models for the spread of agriculture are needed for this part of Ireland. In fact, there may be many regional differences, in particular between the south-west peninsulas and areas such as Waterford. The possibility of an Ertebølle-type situation existing in the south west, where hunter-gatherer communities survived for a significant period, must exist.

In summary, the identification of a Mesolithic occupation in Munster may have created more problems than it has solved.

Note:

1. *Figs. 2 & 4* are also up-dated distribution maps for the whole of Ireland.

123

References

BRADLEY, J. (1983) Excavations at Moynagh Lough, Co. Meath 1980–81: interim report. *Riocht na Midhe*, 7: 12–32.

BRINDLEY, A., LANTING, J.N. and MOOK, W.G. (1983) Radiocarbon dates from the Neolithic burials at Ballintruer More, Co. Wicklow, and Ardcrony, Co. Tipperary. *Journal of Irish Archaeology*, 1: 1–9.

BURENHULT, G. (1984) *The Archaeology of Carrowmore* (Theses and Papers in North-European Archaeology, 14). Stockholm, Institute of Archaeology.

CARTER, R.W.G. (1982) Sea level change in Northern Ireland. *Proceedings of the Geologists Association*, 93(1): 7–23.

CARTER, R.W.G. and ORFORD, J. (1981) *The South and East Coasts of Co. Wexford*. Coleraine, Irish Association for Quaternary Studies Field Guide no. 4.

DE VALERA, R. and Ó NUALLÁIN, S. (1982) *Survey of the Megalithic Tombs of Ireland*. Dublin, The Stationery Office.

DEVOY, R.J. (1983) Late Quaternary shorelines in Ireland: an assessment of their implications for isostatic land movement and relative sea level changes. In D. Smith and A.G. Dawson (eds), *Shorelines and Isostasy*. London, Institute of British Geographers: 227–254.

GRIFFITHS, D. and WOODMAN, P.C. (1987) Cretaceous chert sourcing in north east Ireland: preliminary results. In G. de G. Sieveking and M.H. Newcomer (eds), *The Human Uses of Flint and Chert*. Cambridge, University Press.

LYNCH, A. (1981) *Man and Environment in South-west Ireland, 4000 B.C.–A.D. 800. A Study of Man's Impact on the Development of Soil and Vegetation*. Oxford, British Archaeological Reports (British Series) 85.

LYNCH, F. (1975) Excavations at Carreg Samson megalithic tomb, Mathry, Pembrokeshire. *Archaeologia Cambrensis*, 124: 15–35.

MITCHELL, G.F. (1972) Some ultimate Larnian sites in Lake Derravaragh, Co. Westmeath. *Journal of the Royal Society of Antiquaries of Ireland*, 102: 160–173.

MITCHELL, G.F. (1976) *The Irish Landscape*. London, Collins.

Ó RÍORDÁIN, S.P. (1954) Lough Gur excavations: Neolithic and Bronze Age houses on Knockadoon. *Proceedings of the Royal Irish Academy*, 56: 297–459.

RYAN, M. (1981) Ireland's first inhabitants. *Ireland Today*, Dec. 1981: 13–16.

VERNON, P.D. (1976) A Neolithic scraper from Ferriters Cove, Dingle peninsula, Co. Kerry. *Journal of the Cork Historical and Archaeological Society*, 81: 118–119.

WOODMAN, P.C. (1977) Recent excavations at Newferry, Co. Antrim. *Proceedings of the Prehistoric Society*, 43: 155–199.

WOODMAN, P.C. (1978) *The Mesolithic in Ireland*. Oxford, British Archaeological Reports (British Series) 58.

WOODMAN, P.C. (1981) Problems of flint utilization within eastern Ireland. In F.H.G. Engelen (ed.), *Third International Symposium on Flint* (Staringia no. 6). Maastricht, Nederlandse Geologische Vereniging: 113–115.

WOODMAN, P.C. (1984) The early prehistory of Munster. *Journal of the Cork Historical and Archaeological Society*, 89: 1–11.

WOODMAN, P.C., DUGGAN, M. and McCARTHY, A. (1984) Excavations at Ferriters Cove. *Journal of the Kerry Archaeological and Historical Society*, 17: 4–9.

ZVELEBIL, M., MOORE, J.A., GREEN, S.W. and HENSON, D. (1987) Regional survey and analysis: a case study from southeast Ireland. In P. Rowley-Conwy, M. Zvelebil and H.P. Blankholm (eds), *Mesolithic Northwest Europe: Recent Trends*. Sheffield, University of Sheffield Department of Archaeology and Prehistory: 9–32.

Faunal Remains and the Irish Mesolithic

Louise H. van Wijngaarden-Bakker

Abstract

The *c.* 5000 faunal remains identified from the early Mesolithic sites of Lough Boora and Mount Sandel were found to consist almost exclusively of calcined bone fragments of small size. The taphonomic processes that may have acted on the bone assemblages are discussed, as well as the analysis of the mammal, bird, and fish bones. The zooarchaeological data are used for an estimation of the nature and the seasonality of both sites, with special reference to the possibility of food storage. The absence of red deer remains in the Irish early Mesolithic is briefly discussed.

INTRODUCTION

Of the more than 180 Mesolithic sites that are known from Ireland (Woodman 1978*a*), only a small number have produced animal remains (*Fig. 1*). Among them are both coastal and inland sites (*Table 1*). The *coastal* sites where animal remains have been pre-

Table 1: Main animal species recovered from the Mesolithic coastal and inland sites (data from Adams 1899; Allen 1937; Movius 1940, 1953; Stelfox 1940; Mitchell 1947, 1956; Jope 1960; Hatting 1968; Brinkhuizen 1977; Woodman 1985; Van Wijngaarden-Bakker 1986*a*, this volume)

Site	Type	Main species
Curran Point (Co. Antrim)	coastal	molluscs, whale
Cushendun (Co. Antrim)	coastal	wild boar, conger eel
Dalkey Island (Co. Dublin)	coastal	molluscs, whale, seal, birds, fish
Ferriters Cove (Co. Kerry)	coastal	molluscs, fish, red deer
Glenarm (Co. Antrim)	coastal	molluscs red deer
Ormeau Bridge (Belfast)	coastal	molluscs, red deer
Ringneill Quay (Co. Down)	coastal	molluscs, birds
Rockmarshall (Co. Louth)	coastal	molluscs, crustaceans, whale, mullet
Rough Island (Co. Down)	coastal	molluscs
Sutton (Co. Dublin)	coastal	molluscs, seafish, red deer, hare
Lough Boora (Co. Offaly)	inland	wild boar, pigeon, eel, salmonids
Mount Sandel (Co. Derry)	inland	wild boar, pigeon, ducks, salmonids
Newferry (Co. Derry)	inland	eel, salmonids

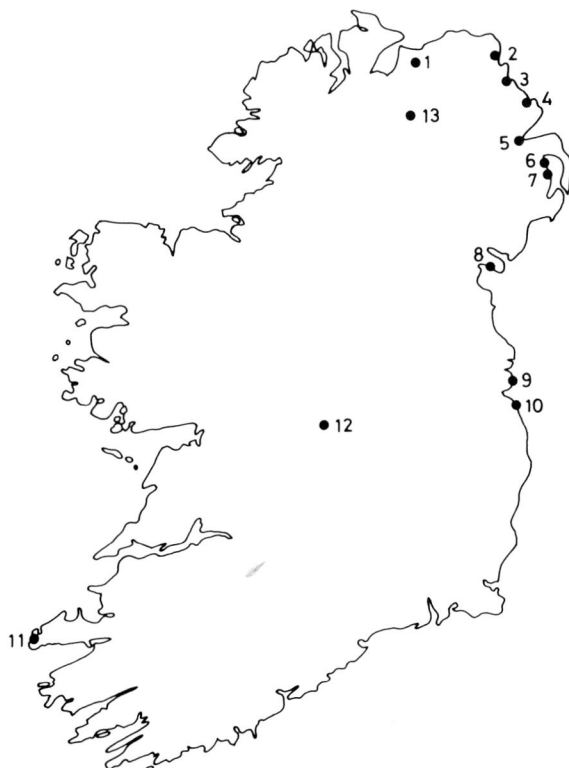

1 Mount Sandel (upper)
2 Cushendun
3 Glenarm
4 Curran Point
5 Ormeau Bridge
6 Rough Island
7 Ringneill Quay
8 Rockmarshall
9 Sutton
10 Dalkey Island
11 Ferriters Cove
12 Lough Boora
13 Newferry

Figure 1 Mesolithic sites with identified faunal remains.

served and identified share some common characteristics. All of these sites contain late Mesolithic[1] industries and their radiocarbon dates centre around 5500–5000 BP. The faunal remains from these sites consist mostly of small numbers of identifiable bones and of unquantified numbers of mollusc remains. Finally, at none of the sites was sieving of the excavated material carried out. Consequently the faunal data from these sites allow only some broad generalizations. The main conclusion is that coastal resources were exploited. Most of the sites are middens and there is some fairly good evidence for the exploitation of molluscs, crustaceans, seafish, birds, seals, and whales. With the exception of Ferriters Cove, where the animal remains have not yet been fully studied, each of the coastal sites has also yielded a number of bones of domestic animals. Deer, hare and wild boar are also present at some of the sites. The faunal evidence is too scant to allow further conclusions regarding the seasonality of occupation of the sites or their palaeoeconomy.

So far only three *inland* sites have produced identifiable animal remains: Newferry, Mount Sandel and Lough Boora. Of these Newferry yielded *c.* 100 fish vertebrae, mainly of eel (Brinkhuizen 1977). Unfortunately the finds cannot be incorporated with any certainty into the long radiocarbon sequence of the site which ranges between 6200 and 7000 BP. The two remaining sites, however, have each produced several thousands of animal bones. This paper will focus on the evidence from Mount Sandel and Lough Boora and will attempt to draw some conclusions, with the aid of the animal remains, on the nature and the seasonality of the two sites.

LOUGH BOORA AND MOUNT SANDEL: SITE LOCATION

In 1977 an early Mesolithic habitation site was discovered on the bed of Lough Boora, Co. Offaly. The site lies on a fossil lake shore, formerly sealed by peat and subsequently inundated by the modern lake. The site was revealed when the lake was drained and the peat harvested by the Irish Turf Board. The excavation produced nearly 200 microliths, about 400 blades, numerous cores and three polished stone axe-heads. The site is composed of several hearths and a chert-working area. Charcoal from the hearths has yielded four radiocarbon dates between 8980±360 BP and 8475±75 BP (Ryan 1980). The archaeological layer was very rich in burnt bone material of very small size and in burnt hazel-nuts.

The site of Mount Sandel (upper), Co. Derry lies on a bluff overlooking the River Bann. Excavation between 1973 and 1977 revealed a number of circular hut areas, numerous post- and stake-holes, and small and large pits. The industry is microlithic, dominated by scalene triangles and micro-rods. The site also produced over 1000 microblades and two polished stone axe-heads (Woodman 1978a, 1978b). Here again the archaeological layer was rich in burnt bone material and burnt hazel-nuts. The latter have been used for radiocarbon dating, producing five dates between 8960±70 BP and 8440±65 BP (Woodman 1978b).

TAPHONOMY

The faunal remains from Lough Boora and Mount Sandel consist almost exclusively of calcined bone fragments of a whitish to light-grey colour. Only at Lough Boora were a few heavily burnt (dark-brown to black) teeth recovered. Colour alone is insufficient to identify precisely the temperature to which a bone or tooth has been heated, but it can be used to deduce a range into which the temperature of heating falls. Experiments by Shipman *et al.* (1984) show that the whitish colour on bone and teeth appears at temperatures above *c.* 400 °C. During experimental heating of a carcass the bones calcined between 400 and 650 °C, which is precisely the temperature range of a normal camp fire (Tylecote 1962).

Decomposition of the organic component of bone probably occurs between 360 and 525 °C (Ubelaker 1978). Dehydration during heating causes extensive cracking and splitting of the bones. At Lough Boora and Mount Sandel a number of shaft fragments of mammal bones have been preserved, on which curved transverse fracture lines and irregular longitudinal splitting can be observed (*Fig. 2*). These

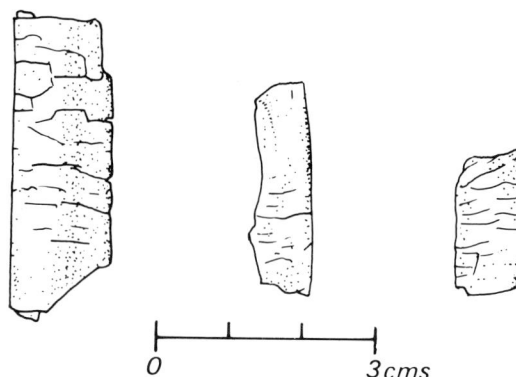

Figure 2   Lough Boora: transverse fracture lines on fragments of calcined long bones. *Drawn by Bob Donker* (IPP)

phenomena suggest that calcination took place when the bones were still fresh (Ubelaker 1978). The extensive warping of bone fragments that usually accompanies the transverse fracturing has not been found at either site. Since meat insulates bones from heating, the above observations suggest that the prolonged burning probably occurred after the meat was removed and was not part of the normal food preparation procedure. Rather, the available data suggest that the bones became calcined in the process of refuse disposal. The fact that the bones must have undergone extensive heating for a considerable time while in a fresh state might also suggest that they were deliberately discarded into the fire. Almost all of the mammal and bird bones were recovered from the hearth areas or their near vicinity. Refuse disposal may then have occurred at the place of preparation and consumption of the

126

meat; the bones constitute primary refuse in the terminology of Schiffer (1975).

At Lough Boora and Mount Sandel literally thousands of calcined fish vertebrae were recovered. Unfortunately, much less is known of the effect of heating on fish bones. Boiling fish is reported as rendering fish bones so soft that they will not survive in a recognizable form (Van Wijngaarden-Bakker 1986a). Prolonged roasting or smoking, however, would lead to the decomposition of the organic fraction of the fish bones and so to their preservation. Of course, further calcination may take place through disposal of the food refuse into the fire.

It must be borne in mind that the research on the animal bones from these two early Mesolithic sites is severely constrained by the fact that only calcined bones are available for study. It is not possible to assess how much of the food refuse was discarded at the sites without going through the process of prolonged burning and so has not been preserved.

LOUGH BOORA AND MOUNT SANDEL: THE ANIMAL REMAINS

At Lough Boora a total of 3028 identifiable animal remains were recovered of which 23% come from mammals, 8% from birds, and 69% from fish. At Mount Sandel 2192 fragments have been identified with 15% mammals, 4% birds and 81% fish remains. A detailed report on the faunal remains from Mount Sandel has been published elsewhere (Van Wijngaarden-Bakker 1986a) and these data will be used here for comparison with those now available from Lough Boora (*Table 2*).

Mammalia

Ireland has a restricted mammal fauna which consists of only 14 native species. Four of these have become extinct in prehistoric or historic times: wild boar, wild cat, brown bear, and wolf. The unbalanced Irish mammal fauna may be taken as evidence that the island was not populated through the normal Postglacial sequence, but that the immigrating species had to cross a sea water barrier in order to reach the island (Van Wijngaarden-Bakker 1986b). The restricted faunal composition of Ireland fits in well with the island colonization theory of MacArthur and Wilson (1967).

At Lough Boora and Mount Sandel 98% of the mammal remains come from wild boar (*Sus scrofa*). This species is known to be an excellent swimmer (IJseling and Scheygrond 1962) and its omnivorous habits and high reproduction rate make it a good colonizer. During the Boreal period, when birch–pine–hazel forests were gradually replaced by oak–elm forests, it may have spread quickly over the island.

At both sites all the skeletal elements of the wild

Table 2: List of species from Lough Boora and Mount Sandel (data from Van Wijngaarden-Bakker 1986a and this report)

Species	Lough Boora	Mount Sandel
MAMMALS		
Sus Scrofa (wild boar)	705	322 (6)
Lepus cf. *timidus* (hare)	–	6 (3)
Canis sp. (wolf/dog)	(4)	1
Felis silvestris (wild cat)	1	–
BIRDS		
Gavia stellata (red-thr. diver)	–	3
Anas platyrhynchos (mallard)	9	15
Anas cf. *crecca* (teal)	1	2
Anas penelope (wigeon)	–	2
Accipiter gentilis (goshawk)	–	6
Aquila/Haliaeetus (eagle)	–	2
Falco peregrinus (peregrine)	2	–
Tytonidae/Strigidae (owls)	2	–
Tetrao urogallus (capercaillie)	–	1
Lagopus/Lyrurus (grouse)	6	7
Fulica atra (coot)	–	1
Scolopacidae (snipe/woodcock)	–	8
Columba palumbus (wood pigeon)	191	24
Garrulus glandarius (jay)	28	–
Turdus sp. (thrush)	4	8
FISH		
Salmo salar (salmon)	–	894
Salmo trutta (trout)	709	568
Salmo sp. (salmonid)	–	43
Anguilla anguilla (eel)	1371	122
Dicentrarchus labrax (seabass)	–	144
Pleuronectidae (flatfish)	–	13

( )=identification uncertain

boar are present, but elements of the head and feet predominate. Among the foot bones there is a high proportion of phalanges. Epiphyseal fusion data for Lough Boora give c. 10% unfused phalanges, while at Mount Sandel c. 50% of the phalanges were found unfused. Epiphyseal fusion of the first and second phalanges of *Sus scrofa* takes place between 19 and 22 months (Van Wijngaarden-Bakker and Maliepaard 1982). As almost all the unfused phalanges from Mount Sandel approach adult size, these would come from animals nearly 1½ years old.

At Lough Boora there is evidence for young piglets through the presence of numerous fragments of unworn milk teeth. Also at Lough Boora were three fragments of canine teeth which could be attributed with certainty to adult female wild boars. Although the data should be handled with care in view of the taphonomic constraints, there are some indications for seasonality at both sites. On the basis of a birth period in May, there is evidence for winter killing at Mount Sandel and for summer killing at Lough Boora.

Bones of other mammals are very scarce; at Lough Boora there is one carnassial tooth from a wild cat (*Felis silvestris*) and at Mount Sandel there is evidence for the presence of hare (*Lepus* cf. *timidus* – 6 fragments). One proximal radius from Mount

127

Sandel has been attributed to *Canis* sp. Calcination of bones always results in shrinkage, and this may amount to between 4% and as much as 25% of the original size (Shipman *et al*. 1984). Consequently, in the case of Mount Sandel radius measurements of the bone will not allow distinction between dog and wolf. At Lough Boora four tooth fragments exhibit a distinctive cingulum and may also come from a canid. Here again further identification is not possible.

Noteworthy is the absence at both sites of bones of the red deer (*Cervus elaphus*), a species which usually holds a prominent place among the game animals of Mesolithic hunters in Europe.

Aves

The bird bones have been sorted and identified by Rik Maliepaard of the Albert Egges van Giffen Instituut voor Prae- en Protohistorie (IPP), University of Amsterdam. At Lough Boora the main species is the wood pigeon (*Columba palumbus*) which is present in 95% of the bird samples. The jay (*Garrulus glandarius*) comes in second place, and there are small numbers of bones of two duck species, the mallard and the teal. Six bones could be identified as coming from a grouse. Distinction between the bones of the red grouse (*Lagopus lagopus*) and the black grouse (*Lyrurus tetrix*) is difficult, especially when calcination has obliterated

most of the morphological and osteometric criteria. There is some slight evidence, however, that seems to point to the black grouse. The remaining bird bones come from a thrush, the peregrine, and some unspecified species of owl.

At Mount Sandel the main species is also the wood pigeon, but here nearly one-third of the bird bones consists of ducks and divers. Among them are mallard, teal, wigeon, and red-throated diver. These species together with the coot and snipe, bones of which have also been identified, nowadays immigrate in large numbers in autumn and winter (Deane 1954). The red-throated diver only occurs from October to April on the Irish coasts. A few bones of birds of prey were also recovered from Mount Sandel, among them bones of the now extinct goshawk and of an eagle. Grouse, either red or black, are also represented, together with the capercaillie.

The use of bird bones as seasonal indicators requires extreme caution. Migratory patterns of bird species are known to have altered significantly in historic and modern times (Schuz 1971). The absence of goose and swan bones from the two Irish early Mesolithic sites might well be attributable to different migration routes from those that are followed nowadays by these species. For resident species hunting is usually assumed to have taken

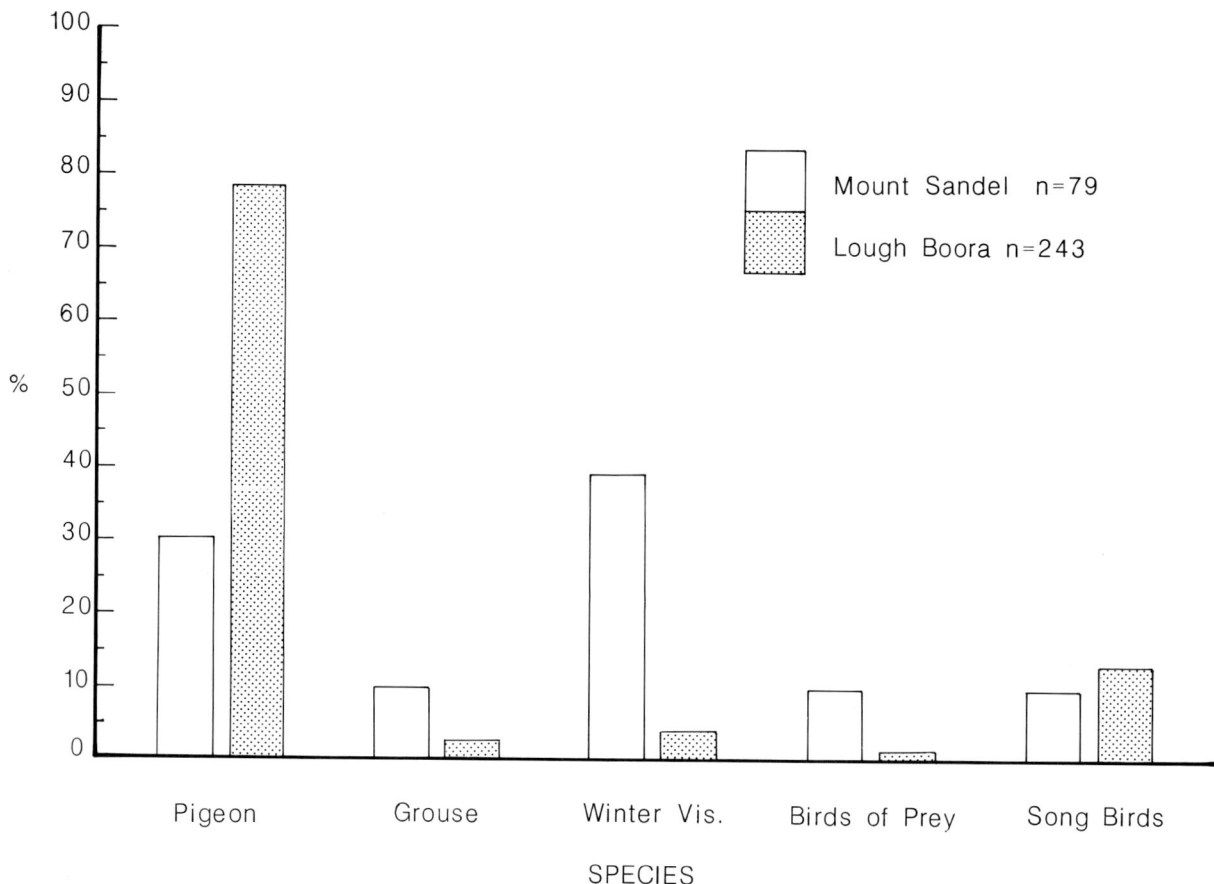

Figure 3   Relative frequency of bird species at Lough Boora and Mount Sandel.

128

place at the season of nesting and/or moulting; but opportunistic bird hunting should never be ruled out.

With the above considerations in mind, the data assembled in *Fig. 3* should be viewed critically. There seems to be some evidence for bird hunting during winter time at Mount Sandel. At Lough Boora there are no such indications.

Pisces

Ireland is dotted with lakes covering approximately 2500 km² and there are about 14,000 km of fish-bearing rivers (O'Reilly 1985). None of the fresh-water fish that nowadays constitute the main source of coarse fishing are original indigenous species. In fact, Ireland has no primary freshwater fish (Wheeler 1977) and the species that are now present such as pike, bream, rudd and roach have all been introduced in historic times. Their dates of introduction are mostly well documented (Van Wijngaarden-Bakker 1985).

For inland sites of the prehistoric period only migratory fish would have been available. Coastal sites could of course profit from the rich resources of the seas surrounding the island, the Irish Sea and the Atlantic ocean.

Large numbers of calcined fish vertebrae were noted by the excavators of Lough Boora and Mount Sandel. In the laboratory the sieving samples were found to contain, apart from numerous vertebrae, also small numbers of the cranial elements of the fish skeleton. Identification of the fish remains was done at the IPP by Marion Seeman and Pauline Vos-Kelk.

At Lough Boora only two species were found to be present. Of the *c.* 2000 identifiable fish remains, 77% come from eel (*Anguilla anguilla*) and the remaining 23% from salmonids. The salmonid remains (mainly vertebrae) are of a uniformly small size, which suggests the trout (*Salmo trutta*). Minimum numbers of individuals based on the atlas gave 43 eel and 21 salmonids. Apart from the identifiable fish remains from Lough Boora there are about 1500 small broken fragments which probably can also be attributed to the eel (M. Seeman, pers. comm.).

Among the *c.* 1800 fish remains from Mount Sandel salmonids are the dominant species. Among the salmonid vertebrae two size classes could be distinguished: large-sized vertebrae which have been attributed to the salmon (*Salmo salar*) and smaller vertebrae, in size range similar to those from Lough Boora, which have been attributed to the trout (Van Wijngaarden-Bakker 1986a). The remaining fish bones from Mount Sandel come from seabass (*Dicentrarchus labrax*) and flat fish.

Migratory fish can be very useful as seasonal indicators. Their migratory behaviour is so closely linked to their reproductive requirements that there is very little room for variation. Eel are katadromous fish that spend most of their lifetime in freshwater lakes and streams of western and central Europe. Upon reaching adulthood they migrate to the Sargasso Sea to spawn and to die. Eel runs are confined to the autumn months (Deelder 1984) with a maximum catch in October (Frost 1950). During their migration to sea adult eels may be caught in rivers with the aid of a weir system.

In their period of growth, eels require an environment of nutrient-rich waters with sufficient possibilities to hide in the form of muddy substrates, rocks, or heavy plant growth. The simplest way to catch immature eels in lakes is by way of individual spearing with the aid of a pronged eel fork (Went 1952). Examples of such gear are known from several parts of Europe and date back at least to the Mesolithic period (Wundsch 1962). A prerequisite for this method of catching is that the fish are visible in shallow and clear water. If this is not the case, either nets or baited lines may be used. Unfortunately, none of these methods needs leave any evidence in the archaeological record.

At low temperatures eels become passive, and from November to March they hibernate in the mud or under stones (Deelder 1984). During the Boreal period the climate was characterized by dry and frosty winters (Lamb 1977). In these conditions eels would undoubtedly go into hibernation. The presence of large numbers of eel bones at Lough Boora must inevitably have originated from fishing in the summer months. The site location leaves strong evidence that immature eels were caught locally in the lake. To test this hypothesis the incremental lines on the eel vertebrae have been analyzed by the Dutch Institute for Fisheries Research (Rijksinstituut voor Visserij onderzoek) at IJmuiden. However, the research failed to produce satisfactory results.

Present-day Lough Boora is connected by the River Little Brosna to the Shannon river system, a connection that presumably already existed during the occupation of the Mesolithic site. The Little Brosna has only a small catchment area, so that massive catches of mature eel on their run to sea are less likely.

The site location of Mount Sandel makes it highly probable that mature eels were caught there during their migration run in early autumn. The catchment area of the River Bann includes Lough Neagh, Ireland's largest lake. Present-day catches of mature eels at Toome on the River Bann are reported to be up to 240,000 kg/year (Tesch 1977).

The fairly small salmonid vertebrae from Lough Boora have been provisionally attributed to the brown trout. This species may attain a weight of 9–12 kilograms. Nowadays the brown trout is the commonest and most widely distributed of Irish freshwater fish. It is found in every river and stream, in all the large lakes, and even in the small lakes where there are spawning streams. Recent surveys have recorded densities as high as 64 kg/hectare of lake surface (O'Reilly 1985). Brown trout (*Salmo trutta*) perform downstream–upstream return migration entirely within freshwater. The young fish live in the nursery stream for one to four years before moving into the main river or lake where they spend most of their lives (Baker 1978).

Trout go through a period of reduced mobility during winter, but they do not go into actual hibernation. Consequently they are less suitable as seasonal indicators. During the summer months, however, catches will be most frequent, and under optimal foraging conditions (Winterhalder 1981) trout fishing will be concentrated at that time. Trout are strictly territorial and catching them will always be on an individual basis.

Contrary to the trout, the salmon is a distinctly anadromous species. It constitutes a highly predictable and productive resource (Schalk 1977). Atlantic salmon run into the Irish rivers from the end of April onwards, with the most massive runs in July and August. Spawning takes place in the upper reaches of rivers and streams. Most salmon die following this event and consequently do not return to sea. The temporally confined salmon runs make this species a most useful seasonal indicator. Its high proportion at Mount Sandel indicates summer occupation. The data from both sites have been assembled in *Fig. 4*.

SEASONALITY

The animal remains of Lough Boora and Mount Sandel have been found to contain seasonal indicators of two distinct types. The first type consists of the presence of seasonally available species. Migratory fish species have been found extremely useful for this type of evidence. Migration runs of katadromous eel and anadromous salmon are confined to restricted parts of the year. Moreover, the hibernating habit of the eel temporally restricts the fishing of immature specimens of this species.

In view of the more varied avian migration pattern, the use of bird remains as seasonal indicators must be viewed with caution. Among the bird remains from Lough Boora useful seasonal indicators could not be recorded, but at Mount Sandel the bird bone assemblage allows for some indication of seasonal occupation.

The second type of indicator consists of physiological data, in this case epiphyseal fusion and dental eruption data. The wild boar remains from both sites contain this type of evidence.

In general, whenever zooarchaeological data are used for seasonality studies, these data should not be treated separately from the site location data. Through the use of ethno-ecological analogues the evidence can often be strengthened or refined.

For the interpretation of the seasonality estimation, storage and transport of food resources that

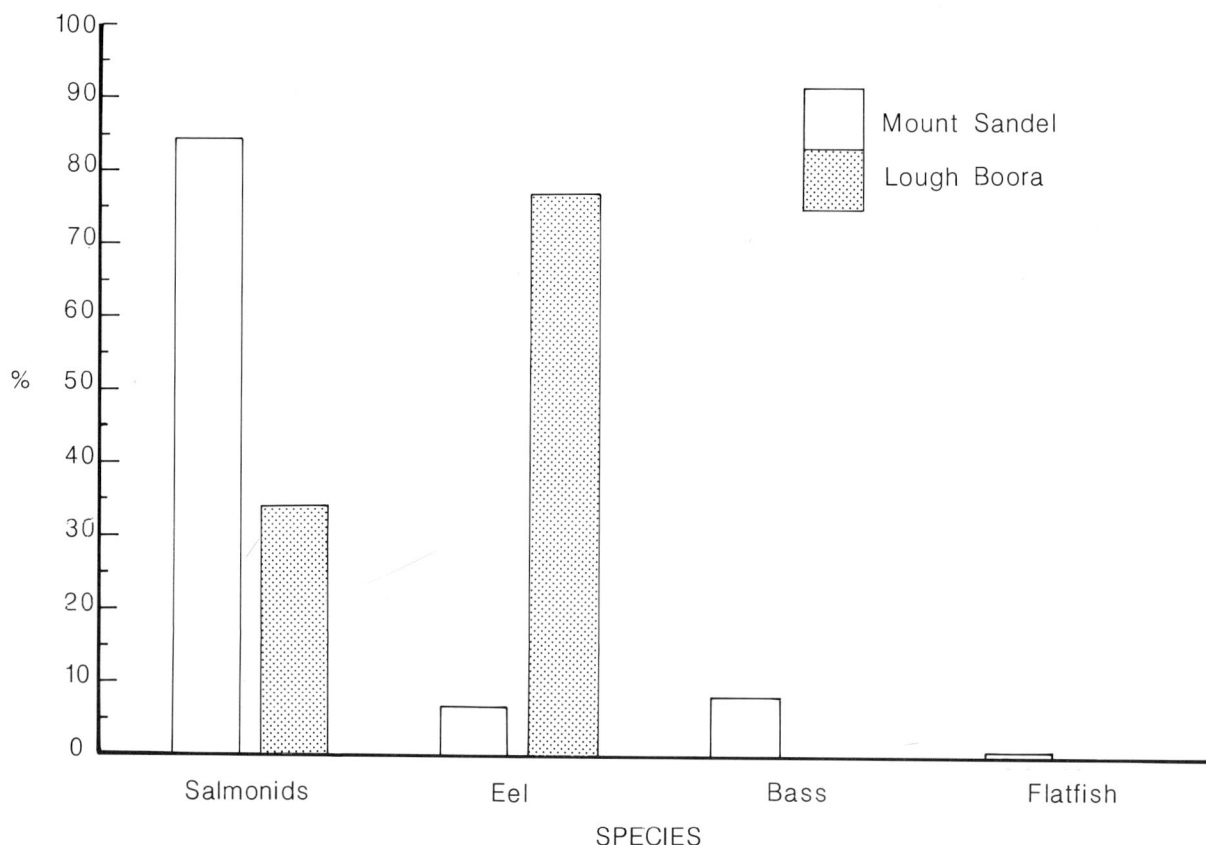

Figure 4 Relative frequency of fish bones at Lough Boora and Mount Sandel.

leave durable remains must always be considered (Monks 1981). Storage of resources is practised by many groups of hunter-gatherers and is determined by the presence of four conditions: the resource is (a) abundant and (b) seasonal, it can be (c) efficiently harvested and (d) stored (Testart 1982). For the Irish Mesolithic the first two conditions may be fulfilled by the annual runs of salmon and eel. The most efficient technique for a massive harvest of these species would be to build a weir system in a river. The stone axes that are characteristic of the Irish early Mesolithic show that the technology for heavy wood-working was available. The technique of storage through drying and/or smoking has also been available since the late Palaeolithic (Binford 1982; Van Wijngaarden-Bakker 1984). Actually, fish may have been the most widely stored food before the advent of intensive grain harvesting (Yesner 1983).

The presence of numerous eel and trout bones at Lough Boora, together with the site location on the bank of a shallow lake, suggests that fishing for trout and eel took place, presumably by a technique involving individual harvest. It seems unlikely that under these circumstances the conditions of resource abundance and mass harvest were met. Presumably storage was not carried out on any scale. In view of the small catchment area of the Little Brosna, it also seems unlikely that massive runs of mature eel occurred in the vicinity of the site. The only storable resource that was recovered are the numerous, burnt hazel-nuts.

In conclusion, the available data for Lough Boora may be summarized in the following model. The site is a summer camp where fishing for eel and trout was carried out as the main subsistence basis. Procurement of both species was probably carried out on an individual basis. A variety of other resources were also exploited. Wild boar was hunted and the presence of adult female animals and juveniles suggests that advantage was taken of the temporally and spatially restricted mobility of sows and their young. Birds were also hunted, most notably the wood pigeon. The occupation of the site may have continued into early autumn as evidenced by the numerous hazel-nuts. These nuts would have been collected in the immediate surroundings of the site, as hazel was already widespread over Ireland during the Boreal period. Transportation of heavy loads of this food resource seems unlikely in this case. Evidence for the exploitation of other vegetal resources, though expected (Clarke 1976), has not been forthcoming.

At Mount Sandel there is evidence for summer occupation during which the salmon runs could be exploited. The abundance and high seasonality of this resource might have led to some form of storage. Archaeological evidence for storage at the site can perhaps be found in the presence of large pits, which were not found at Lough Boora. A variety of other resources could have been exploited during the summer occupation: seabass and flatfish in the Bann estuary, birds, wild pigs and vegetal resources further inland. The presence of burnt hazel-nuts again suggests extension of the occupation into early autumn when eel runs could also be exploited. The epiphyseal fusion data of wild pig and the presence of some foetal bones can be taken as evidence for a winter occupation. The extremely heavily built hut foundations at the site might also be explained as evidence for a winter camp. During the winter young male wild boars usually have a restricted territorial mobility and at that time may have constituted the main prey of the hunters. In fact, the Mount Sandel site may have been occupied for the greater part of the year. The link between permanence of settlement and storage of food resources has repeatedly been put forward (Schalk 1977; Testart 1982; Yesner 1983). Mount Sandel may well fit these models.

THE ABSENCE OF RED DEER

The faunal assemblages from almost 98% of European Mesolithic sites have been found to contain red deer remains (Jarman 1972). The question arises whether the absence of red deer bones from the early Mesolithic sites of Lough Boora and Mount Sandel is genuine or a consequence of taphonomic constraints. At both sites the general refuse disposal pattern for c. 20 animal species resulted in the calcination of the skeletal remains. A differential disposal method for one species is perhaps less likely, but may not be ruled out.

However, Woodman (1978b) has already drawn attention to the scarcity of burins and scrapers at Mount Sandel and to the general absence of early Mesolithic sites in the Irish highlands. Moreover, Dumont (1986) noted virtually no traces of skin-, bone- or antler-working on the Mount Sandel artifacts that he used in his micro-wear study. The above data taken together rather suggest a genuine absence of red deer in the Irish early Mesolithic, i.e. during the Boreal period. In Atlantic times deer remains were recovered from several late Mesolithic sites (*Table 1*). On the now available evidence it seems that *Cervus elaphus* may have been a late immigrant to Ireland.

Deer carcasses may be put to many uses, but for each of these substitutes can easily be found. The faunal data of Lough Boora and Mount Sandel present evidence for a varied and balanced diet; bone and/or wood may be substituted for antler for toolmaking; vegetal fibres, birch bark, and skins of seals, birds or fish are useful substitutes for deer hides. It should be noted that, because of the bristle penetration through the skin and its high fat content, pigskin was unsuitable for use (Van Driel-Murray, pers. comm.). The technology for pigskin-working evolved only in the post-Mediaeval period, so that the use of hides of wild boar may be ruled out for the prehistoric period.

Seal skins approach deer skins in size and texture. The optimal time of procurement of the latter, late spring, would coincide with a generally low period in the subsistence cycle of hunter-gatherers in temperate climates. The dense settlement pattern of the Irish coastal areas (Woodman 1978a) might have arisen from a migration pattern in which annual visits to the coast for seal hunting constituted an important element.

Note:

1. The use of the terms *early* and *late* Mesolithic in this paper follows their usage by Woodman (1978b).

Acknowledgements: The author is most grateful to the excavators of Lough Boora and Mount Sandel, Michael Ryan and Peter Woodman, for the opportunity given to study the animal remains from their sites. Special thanks are due to Rik Maliepaard and Marion Seeman for their help with the identification of the bird and fish remains from Lough Boora. Willem Dekker helped with information on the ecology of the eel.

References

ADAMS, W. (1899) Prehistoric sites near Ormeau Bridge, Belfast. *Ulster Journal of Archaeology* (2nd series), 5: 5–8.

ALLEN, G.M. (1937) The animal remains from Glenarm. In H.L. Movius, 'A Stone Age site at Glenarm, Co. Antrim'. *Journal of the Royal Society of Antiquaries of Ireland*, 47: 216.

BAKER, R.R. (1978) *The Evolutionary Ecology of Animal Migration*. London, Hodder and Stoughton.

BINFORD, L.R. (1982) Comment on R. White, 'Rethinking the Middle/Upper Palaeolithic Transition'. *Current Anthropology*, 23: 177–181.

BRINKHUIZEN, D.C. (1977) The fish remains. In P.C. Woodman, 'Recent excavations at Newferry, Co. Antrim'. *Proceedings of the Prehistoric Society*, 43: 197.

CLARKE, D.L. (1976) Mesolithic Europe: the economic basis. In G. de G. Sieveking, I.H. Longworth and K.E. Wilson (eds), *Problems in Economic and Social Archaeology*. London, Duckworth: 449–481.

DEANE, C.D. (1954) *Handbook of the Birds of Northern Ireland*. Belfast, Belfast Museum and Art Gallery Bulletin vol. 1, no. 6.

DEELDER, C.L. (1984) Synopsis of biological data on the eel, *Anguilla anguilla* (Linnaeus 1758). *FAO Fisheries Synopsis*, 80, revision 1.

DUMONT, J.V. (1986) A preliminary report on the Mount Sandel microwear study. In P.C. Woodman, *Excavations at Mount Sandel 1973–77* (Northern Ireland Archaeological Monographs no. 2). Belfast, Her Majesty's Stationery Office: 61–70.

FROST, W.E. (1950) The eel fisheries of the River Bann, Northern Ireland, and observations on the age of silver eels. *Journal du Conseil International pour l'Exploration de la Mer*, 16: 358–383.

HATTING, T. (1968) Animal bones from the basal middens. In G.D. Liversage, 'Excavations at Dalkey Island, Co. Dublin, 1956–59'. *Proceedings of the Royal Irish Academy*, 66C: 172–174.

JARMAN, M.R. (1972) European deer economies and the advent of the Neolithic. In E.S. Higgs (ed.), *Papers in Economic Prehistory*. Cambridge, University Press: 125–147.

JOPE, M. (1960) The mollusca and animal bones from the excavations at Ringneill Quay. In N. Stephens and A.E.P. Collins, 'The Quaternary deposits at Ringneill Quay and Ardmillan, Co. Down'. *Proceedings of the Royal Irish Academy*, 61C: 65–77.

LAMB, H.H. (1977) *Climate. Present, Past and Future. 2. Climatic History and the Future*. London, Methuen.

MACARTHUR, R.H. and WILSON, H.T. (1967) *The Theory of Island Biogeography*. Princeton, University Press.

MITCHELL, G.F. (1947) An early kitchen-midden in County Louth. *Journal of the County Louth Archaeological Society*, 11: 169–174.

MITCHELL, G.F. (1956) An early kitchen-midden at Sutton, Co. Dublin. *Journal of the Royal Society of Antiquaries of Ireland*, 87: 1–26.

MONKS, G.G. (1981) Seasonality studies. In M.B. Schiffer (ed.), *Advances in Archaeological Method and Theory*, 4. New York, Academic Press: 177–240.

MOVIUS, H.L. (1940) An early post-glacial archaeological site at Cushendun, Co. Antrim. *Proceedings of the Royal Irish Academy*, 46C: 1–48.

MOVIUS, H.L. (1953) Curran Point, Larne, Co. Antrim, the type site of the Irish Mesolithic. *Proceedings of the Royal Irish Academy*, 56C: 1–95.

O'REILLY, P. (1985) Game fishing in Ireland. *Bulletin of the Department of Foreign Affairs*, 1015: 11–14.

RYAN, M. (1980) An early Mesolithic site in the Irish Midlands. *Antiquity*, 54: 46–47.

SCHALK, R.F. (1977) The structure of an anadromous fish resource. In L.R. Binford (ed.), *For Theory Building in Archaeology*. New York, Academic Press: 207–249.

SCHIFFER, M.B. (1975) *Behavioural Archaeology*. New York, Academic Press.

SCHUZ, E. (1971) *Grundrisz der Vogelzugskunde*. Berlin, P. Parey.

SHIPMAN, P., FOSTER, G. and SCHOENINGER, M. (1984) Burnt bones and teeth: an experimental study of color, morphology, crystal structure and shrinkage. *Journal of Archaeological Science*, 11: 307–325.

STELFOX, A.W. (1940) Report on the animal bones. In H.L. Movius, 'Report on a Stone Age excavation at Rough Island, Strangford Lough, Co. Down'. *Journal of the Royal Society of Antiquaries of Ireland*, 70: 142.

TESCH, F.W. (1977) *The Eel. Biology and Management of Anguillid Eels*. London, Chapman and Hall.

TESTART, A. (1982) The significance of food storage among hunter-gatherers: residence patterns, population densities, and social inequalities. *Current Anthropology*, 23: 523–537.

TYLECOTE, R.F. (1962) *Metallurgy in Archaeology*. London, Edward Arnold.

UBELAKER, D.H. (1978) *Human Skeletal Remains*. Washington, Taraxacum.

WENT, A.E.J. (1952) Irish fishing spears. *Journal of the Royal Society of Antiquaries of Ireland*, 82: 109–134.

WHEELER, A. (1977) The origin and distribution of the freshwater fishes of the British Isles. *Journal of Biogeography*, 4: 1–24.

WINTERHALDER, B. (1981) Optimal foraging strategies and hunter-gatherer research in anthropology: theory and models. In B. Winterhalder and E.A. Smith (eds), *Hunter-Gatherer Foraging Strategies*. Chicago, University Press: 13–35.

WOODMAN, P.C. (1978a) *The Mesolithic in Ireland*. Oxford, British Archaeological Reports (British Series) 58.

WOODMAN, P.C. (1978b) The chronology and economy of the Irish Mesolithic. In P. Mellars (ed.), *The Early Postglacial Settlement of Northern Europe*. London, Duckworth: 333–369.

WOODMAN, P.C. (1985) *Seeing is Believing. Problems of Archaeological Visibility*. Cork, University Press.

WUNDSCH, H.H. (1962) Noch einiges zum Gebrauch der 'Aalspeere' an der Ostseeküste der Deutschen Demokratischen Republik. *Deutsche Fischerei Zeitung Radebeul*, 9: 206–210.

VAN WIJNGAARDEN-BAKKER, L.H. (1984) Faunal analysis and historical record: meat preservation and the faunal remains at Smeerenburg, Spitsbergen. In C. Grigson and J. Clutton-Brock (eds), *Animals and Archaeology: 4. Husbandry in Europe*. Oxford, British Archaeological Reports (International Series) S227: 195–204.

VAN WIJNGAARDEN-BAKKER, L.H., (1985) Littletonian faunas. In K. Edwards and W. Warren (eds), *The Quaternary History of Ireland*. London, Academic Press: 221–249.

VAN WIJNGAARDEN-BAKKER, L.H. (1986a) The faunal remains. In P.C. Woodman, *Excavations at Mount Sandel 1973–77* (Northern Ireland Archaeological Monographs no. 2). Belfast, Her Majesty's Stationery Office: 71–76.

VAN WIJNGAARDEN-BAKKER, L.H. (1986b) The colonisation of islands – the mammalian evidence. *Journal of the Irish Biogeographical Society, Occasional Publication*, 1: 38–41.

VAN WIJNGAARDEN-BAKKER, L.H. and MALIEPAARD, C.H. (1982) Leeftijdsbepaling aan het skelet van het wilde zwijn *Sus scrofa* Linnaeus, 1758. *Lutra*, 25: 30–37.

IJSSELING, M.A. and SCHEYGROND, A. (1962) *Onze Zoogdieren*. Zutphen, Thieme.

YESNER, D.R. (1983) On food storage among hunter-gatherers. *Current Anthropology*, 24: 119–120.

The Early Post-Glacial Settlement of Scotland: a Review

Alex. Morrison and Clive Bonsall

Abstract

This paper summarizes the evidence relating to the chronology of early post-glacial (Lateglacial/early Flandrian) settlement in Scotland. It is suggested that a date of 8000/8500 BP can no longer be regarded as a *terminus post quem* for the earliest settlement following deglaciation. Typological and radiocarbon evidence is used to infer that the Mesolithic sequence is broadly equivalent to that established for southern Britain, with an *early* phase represented by sites with 'broad blade' microlithic assemblages dating to the early Flandrian before 9000 BP, and a *later* phase characterized by sites with 'narrow blade' microlithic assemblages. The persistence of the 'narrow blade' technology after 5200 BP cannot be demonstrated on present evidence. Earlier, Lateglacial, settlement can be inferred, but the evidence is largely circumstantial. The preponderance of surface sites is seen as a major obstacle to the development of a more refined chronology for early post-glacial settlement in Scotland.

INTRODUCTION

The utterly inhospitable conditions which prevailed during [the] earlier phases of the general deglaciation would be adverse to the immigration of late Upper Palaeolithic man into Scotland. This country was then girt by a high-level arctic sea, and riven by ice-laden, swollen estuaries and fjords. In the lowland areas it was cumbered by lakes of dead ice, flooded by icy torrents and piled by hummocked slush; its high grounds still fed great glaciers. That the conditions would be intolerable to man is also indicated by the scarcity of the remains of even the hardiest animals referable to the late stages of this interrupted spell of deglaciation. This fact is also shown by the character of the retreat deposits (Lacaille 1954: 309).

On the basis of the environmental evidence available to him thirty-five years ago, Lacaille painted this vivid picture of Lateglacial conditions in Scotland. His estimates put the earliest human occupation – his 'Early Larnian' culture – at about 7000 BP. This assessment of early post-glacial settlement, however, was based on fewer than one hundred sites, mostly chance surface finds and a very small number of excavations.

Since 1954 a greater body of evidence has become available. There is now a great deal of information relating to the environmental changes of the past 20,000 years (for summaries, see Price 1983; Lowe and Walker 1984; Sutherland 1984; Bowen *et al.* 1986); many more sites have been discovered by amateur and professional fieldworkers, particularly in inland areas; while the application of radiocarbon dating, though limited, has begun to provide the basis of a more secure chronology. In spite of these advances in knowledge of recent years, much of the evidence pertaining to the nature, chronology and extent of early post-glacial settlement in Scotland can be regarded as equivocal.

ENVIRONMENTAL BACKGROUND

At its maximum extent, *c.* 18,000–20,000 BP, the last (Late Devensian) ice sheet covered almost the whole of Scotland. Parts of Orkney, the Outer Hebrides, north-east Caithness and the Buchan peninsula probably remained ice-free (Sutherland 1984), but the climatic regime in these areas is likely to have been one of arctic severity with the average annual temperature less than −6 °C.

The events associated with deglaciation are not known in detail, but glacier ice had disappeared from the greater part of Scotland by *c.* 13,000 BP, and there is evidence for the beginning of organic sedimentation in lake basins at around this date.

The final stages of deglaciation coincided with a period of marked climatic improvement, known in Britain as the Lateglacial Interstadial, which lasted from *c.* 13,500 to 11,000 BP (Lowe and Walker 1984). The transition from an arctic to a temperate environment seems to have taken place very rapidly at some stage between 14,000 and 13,000 BP. Coleopteran evidence suggests that the thermal maximum was achieved around 13,000 BP, when summer temperatures similar to those of the present are indicated for Britain as a whole. Mean July temperature in southern Scotland reached 14–15 °C, *c.* 4–5 °C lower than in southern England, implying a more marked temperature gradient from north to south across Britain. Temperatures were maintained at about this level for around a thousand years. There then followed a general climatic decline until, around 11,000 BP, cold conditions were re-established in Scotland. The vegetation of the early part of the interstadial, before *c.* 13,000 BP, appears to have been dominated by grasses, sedges and herbaceous plants, with a high representation of disturbed or bare-ground taxa. This phase was succeeded by one in which the pollen of shrubs, such as juniper (*Juniperus*), willows (*Salix*), crowberry (*Empetrum*) and dwarf birch (*Betula nana*), became relatively more abundant. Macrofossil evidence indicates that tree birches eventually became widespread in Scotland, although to what extent these were able to form woodland (as in areas further south) is uncertain.

The succeeding cold phase, the Loch Lomond Stadial (*c.* 11,000–10,000 BP), was marked by renewed glacier activity. Ice accumulated to a thickness of 400–500 m over the western Highlands, the main ice mass covering an area of several hundred square kilometres at its maximum extent between 10,000 and 10,500 BP; there were smaller ice caps in the Grampian Highlands and on some of the islands of the Inner Hebrides, with outlying corrie and valley glaciers in other parts of the Highlands and in the Southern Uplands. Beyond the ice margins periglacial conditions were widespread, and there was a mainly open heath or tundra-like vegetation. Mean July temperatures ranged from 6–7 °C in the Highlands to 8–9 °C in south-west Scotland, although mean annual temperatures may have been well below 0 °C in many areas.

The fauna of Scotland during the Lateglacial period is only poorly documented. Records of large herbivores of definite or probable Lateglacial date include reindeer (*Rangifer tarandus*), elk (*Alces alces*), giant deer (*Megaloceros giganteus*) and red deer (*Cervus elaphus*); while remains of seal are known from coastal sediments.

The rapid climatic amelioration which marked the beginning of the Flandrian (Holocene) was followed by progressive afforestation. Birch woodland appears to have become widespread in Scotland between *c.* 9500 and 9200 BP, and as the forest changed in character and became more closed during the early to mid-Flandrian, open habitats probably became restricted to the higher mountain areas, to areas of shingle and blown sand along sea coasts, and to certain other areas where local topography or soils were unfavourable to tree growth.

Sea-level movements around the Scottish coastline during the Lateglacial and Flandrian were primarily a consequence of two factors: (i) the general eustatic rise of sea level between *c.* 18,000 and 6000 BP caused by melting of ice sheets and glaciers worldwide; and (ii) the glacio-isostatic recovery of northern Britain as a result of the removal of the weight of the Late Devensian ice sheet. The resulting pattern of sea-level change was complex, and varied according to geographical location. Around coasts in areas marginal to the Highlands (the main area of ice accumulation where isostatic downwarping and rebound were most marked) relative sea level during much of the Lateglacial and Flandrian was higher than at present. Thus, around coasts in these areas

(e.g. Inverness-shire, Argyll, the Firth of Clyde, the Forth and Tay valleys, and the Cromarty Firth) raised shoreline features of early to mid-Lateglacial age are preserved, although their archaeological potential has remained largely unexploited. Conversely, in areas that were peripheral to the former ice sheet and where, consequently, isostatic movements were less marked – Orkney, Shetland, the Outer Hebrides, Caithness, Buchan, parts of south-west Scotland, Berwickshire – sea level was below present sea level for much of the post-glacial period, so that evidence relating to Lateglacial/early Flandrian shorelines in these areas lies submerged beyond the present coastline.

EVIDENCE FOR LATEGLACIAL SETTLEMENT

The date of man's colonization (or recolonization) of Scotland following deglaciation is still very much a matter of argument. The earliest radiocarbon dates are in the second half of the ninth millennium BP and, on this evidence, many workers have supposed that Scotland was uninhabited throughout the Lateglacial and for almost 2000 years into the Flandrian. Advances in knowledge of the early post-glacial environment, however, suggest that for much of the Lateglacial period environmental conditions were not unfavourable to human occupation. Even during the Loch Lomond Stadial large areas of Scotland remained unglaciated and the tundra is known to have supported large mammals, including reindeer. Human activity in periglacial environments during the late Pleistocene is widely attested in Europe. Moreover, recent work in the southern Norwegian highlands suggests that areas that were ice-covered during the Last Glaciation were colonized by man within a few hundred years of deglaciation (Bang-Andersen, this volume), while the far north of Norway beyond the Arctic Circle is known to have been settled before 9000 BP (Engelstad, this volume). To accept a much later date for the earliest human presence in Scotland is to imply that the process of recolonization lagged far behind that in Scandinavia, even though deglaciation, making new land available for settlement, was achieved much earlier in northern Britain.

Lawson and Bonsall (1986*b*) identified a number of factors which could have inhibited the discovery or recognition of Lateglacial sites in Scotland. They observed:

a) that much of the evidence for Lateglacial occupation of England and Wales occurs in particular geological situations – sandy heathlands of pre-Flandrian origin (in the case of the majority of open-air sites) and outcrops of Carboniferous and Permian limestone (in the case of the majority of caves and rock-shelters) – and that similar contexts are of very much more limited occurrence in Scotland;

b) that there has been no major tradition of cave archaeology in Scotland;

c) that the pattern of fieldwork has tended to favour the discovery of Mesolithic (*vs* Upper Palaeolithic) sites, flint collectors having concentrated their efforts in coastal areas on raised shorelines of mid-Flandrian age, rather than on earlier shoreline features;

d) that a scarcity of good quality flint in Scotland may have led to a greater reliance on bone and antler as raw materials for toolmaking, which are much less likely to survive in the archaeological record; and

e) that the concomitant use of flint pebbles and materials such as quartz and chert for the manufacture of stone tools may have resulted in lithic assemblages which bear little morphological resemblance to the late Upper Palaeolithic blade industries characteristic of southern and central areas of Britain, and are thus not recognizably of Lateglacial age.

It follows from this last point that evidence of Lateglacial occupation may already exist in museum and private collections in Scotland, but has hitherto gone unrecognized. Amongst these collections, however, there is some material for which a Lateglacial date may be inferred.

The Creag nan Uamh caves

A Lateglacial date has sometimes been suggested for the earliest human use of caves in the Cambrian limestone of the Creag nan Uamh, in the Assynt district of north-west Scotland (*Fig. 1*) (Callander, Cree and Ritchie 1927; Movius 1942; Lawson and Bonsall 1986a, 1986b). In Reindeer Cave, one of three adjacent caves of similar size, fragmentary remains of at least 900 reindeer antlers were excavated in 1926–27 from a layer of thermoclastic scree in the entrance chamber of the cave and similar deposits infilling a vertical shaft at the rear of the chamber. A bulked sample of the antler fragments gave a radiocarbon date of 10,080±70 BP (SRR-1788). This date, and the presence of bones of arctic lemming (*Dicrostonyx torquatus*) and tundra vole (*Microtus gregalis*) in the same layer, suggest deposition in the later part of the Loch Lomond Stadial. Re-examination of the assemblage (Lawson

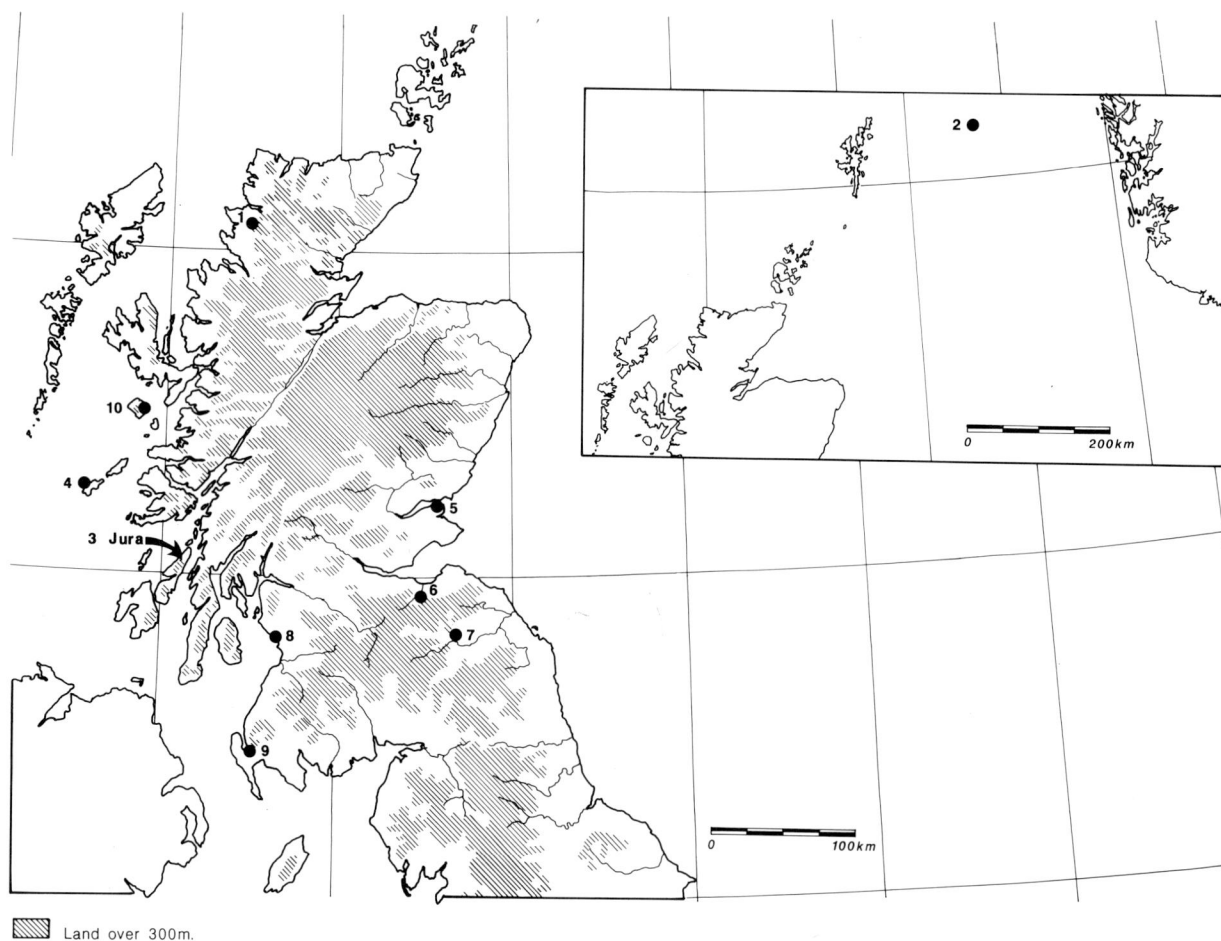

Land over 300m.

Figure 1   Principal sites and localities referred to in the text: 1 – Reindeer Cave, Assynt; 2 – flint scraper from vibrocore 60+01/46; 3 – Isle of Jura; 4 – Ballevullin, Isle of Tiree; 5 – Morton/Tentsmuir, Fife; 6 – Elginhaugh; 7 – Craigsford Mains, Tweed valley; 8 – Shewalton, Ayrshire; 9 – Auchrocher Moss, Wigtownshire.

136

and Bonsall 1986a; C. Bonsall, J. Rackham and N. Murray, unpublished data) indicates that the antlers are those of adult female and juvenile reindeer, were all naturally shed, and were complete when deposited in the cave, becoming fragmented through post-depositional processes.[1]

Lawson and Bonsall (1986a: 3–4) considered three hypotheses to explain the presence of such a large quantity of shed antlers within Reindeer Cave: (i) that reindeer had frequently entered the cave and shed their antlers there; (ii) that the antlers had been collected and brought into the cave by carnivores such as wolves; and (iii) that man was the agent responsible.

Given the absence of signs of gnawing of the antlers by either reindeer or large carnivores, and the fact that shed antlers were not found in the adjacent caves which would have been equally accessible to the animals, neither of the first two hypotheses was considered to offer an adequate explanation. For these reasons, and in view of the known importance of reindeer antler to Lateglacial hunter-gatherer groups as a raw material for tools and weapons, an anthropogenic explanation was considered more likely. This interpretation is strengthened by the presence of charcoal fragments in the layer containing the antlers (Callander et al. 1927: 171). In the absence of firm evidence of actual habitation of the cave, Lawson and Bonsall (1986a) suggested that the site had functioned primarily as a cache where shed antlers were stored. It was envisaged that this would have acted as a central reserve to which members of a hunting band could return at appropriate times in the annual round of subsistence activities in order to collect raw material for tool-making. Certain aspects of the evidence from Reindeer Cave must be regarded as equivocal, but if the interpretation proposed by Lawson and Bonsall is correct, then Reindeer Cave is probably one of a complex of sites in the Assynt area connected with late spring or early summer exploitation of mother-and-calf reindeer herds during the closing stages of the Lateglacial. The recognition of residential and kill sites associated with Lateglacial occupation of the area is only likely to be achieved through archaeological surveys of the kind recently undertaken in southern Norway (cf. Bang-Andersen 1987, this volume).

Lawson and Bonsall (1986a) mention several caves in south Wales and south-west England where substantial accumulations of shed antler have also been discovered. A more interesting parallel, however, is suggested by recent work at the Trou des Blaireaux, near Vaucelles in southern Belgium (Bellier and Cattelain 1983). Excavation of the earliest deposits within the cave (layer III) produced quantities of reindeer antler, remains of a 'cold'

fauna (including variable hare, arctic fox and lemming), and a single flint artifact – tentatively identified as a burin spall. Two radiocarbon dates, 13,790±150 BP (Lv-1314) and 13,850±335 BP (Lv-1309D), were obtained for the layer, indicating deposition shortly before the Lateglacial climatic amelioration. The antlers are all shed and are reported to be exclusively from young female reindeer.[2] They consist mainly of basal fragments or sections of the beam – antler tines and palmate sections being rare. Some fragments are reported to show signs of having been broken by bending, but no traces of gnawing by reindeer or other animals were iden.ified. The excavators suggest that the assemblage may be waste material from antler-working, parts such as the tines having been removed for use or processing elsewhere. The site is interpreted as a regular stopping place of hunters associated, at least in part, with the collection of the shed antler of female reindeer. Apart from the dates, the similarities to Reindeer Cave at Creag nan Uamh are striking and strengthen the suggestion of Lateglacial human activity at the latter site.

Other finds

The climatic improvement of the Lateglacial Interstadial has been used as part of an argument for possible human presence at the sites of Lussa Wood and Lussa Bay on the island of Jura (Fig. 2; Mercer 1979, 1980). It was suggested that Jura could have been occupied during the interstadial, 'at least in the summers and, with Eskimo-like adaptation, possibly in the winters too' (Mercer 1980: 348). The archaeological evidence for this presence is unfortunately very limited, being based on the discovery, in derived locations in gravels, of three supposed 'tanged points' in broken and rolled condition, and their possible affinities with late Upper Palaeolithic tanged point industries in southern England and mainland north-west Europe. This Lateglacial occupation is suggested as having been on the beach at a time of rising sea level, the sea having removed all but a few rolled stone tools. Judging from the published illustrations, only one of the three artifacts can be regarded as a tanged point (Mercer 1980: fig. 7, no. 29); the piece is broken in such a way, however, that the precise form of the tang cannot be discerned, thus making typological comparisons difficult. In the absence of a secure archaeological or geological context for these finds, the case for Lateglacial occupation of Jura, whilst plausible, cannot be proven.

Similar considerations apply to the interpretation of three 'tanged points' from Millfield Farm (Stronsay) and Brodgar (Mainland) on Orkney, and Ballevullin on the Hebridean island of Tiree – part of a collection of prehistoric material presented to the Hunterian Museum, Glasgow, in 1951 by A.

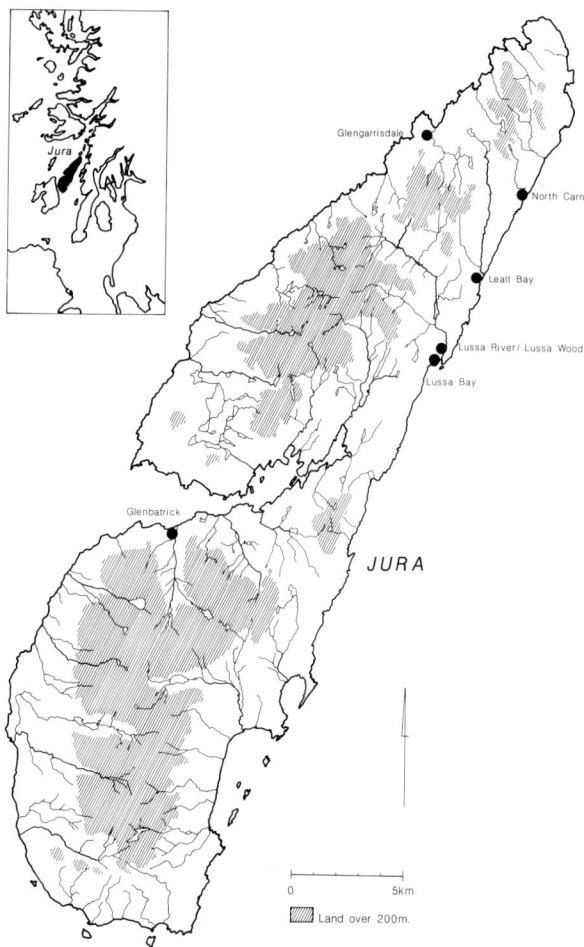

Figure 2 Isle of Jura: principal Mesolithic sites. The collections from Glenbatrick, Lussa Wood and Lussa Bay contain a significant early Mesolithic ('broad blade' microlithic) component.

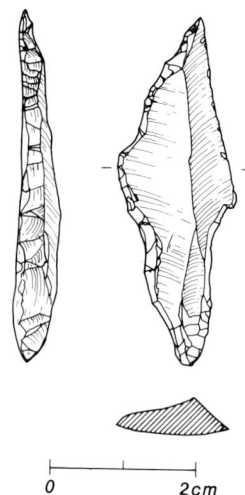

B.1951.2030

Figure 3 Ahrensburgian tanged point from Ballevullin, Isle of Tiree. *Drawn by G. Thomas*

Henderson Bishop.[3] They were described by Livens (1956); he suggested that the closest parallels for the Tiree and Stronsay points were amongst Upper Palaeolithic assemblages from mainland Europe, but observed (1956: 438) that all three artifacts were found 'in circumstances which make their post-Palaeolithic date unquestionable' – although in the case of the two Orkney points it was conceded that the exact findspots and circumstances of discovery were unknown.

The only one of the three artifacts which the present authors have had an opportunity of examining is that from Tiree (*Fig. 3*). The provenance is given as 'Red Mound, Ballevullin', and it is presumed to have been recovered in the course of Bishop's (unpublished) investigation of a site in the Ballevullin area in 1912. It is made on a flint blade, is 4.6 cm long, and has a maximum width of 1.6 cm. The tang is made on the proximal end of the blade by heavy abrupt retouch, while the point is formed by oblique truncation and is short in relation to the tang. As Livens observed (1956: 442), in terms of size, form and technique it conforms to the definition of an Ahrensburg point (cf. Taute 1968: 12–13) – a type

characteristic of final Palaeolithic sites in the central and western parts of the North European Plain dating to the period between *c.* 10,000 and 11,000 BP. Given the existence of sites in southern Britain which can be assigned to the Ahrensburgian techno-complex (Barton, this volume), a Lateglacial or very early Flandrian date for the Ballevullin find is not unlikely. Livens argued for a much later date on the basis of the proximity of the site to the present coastline and the existence within the Ballevullin area of raised marine features and blown sand deposits which, on evidence available at that time, were assumed to relate to marine transgression during the mid-Flandrian. Recent research, however, has shown that the coastal sediments and landforms of western Tiree were formed at more than one period (A.G. Dawson, in preparation). In the Ballevullin area raised shorelines of Lateglacial and Flandrian age occur at heights of up to *c.* 9 m O.D., and areas above that level have probably been dry land since deglaciation. The chronology of sand dune formation around the coasts of the Western Isles is uncertain; it is possible that blown sand deposits have been accumulating intermittently in these situations since the Lateglacial. Thus, assuming the provenance to have been correctly recorded, the only obstacle to accepting the Ballevullin tanged point as evidence of late Upper Palaeolithic occupation is the lack of precise information on the location of the find relative to former sea levels. Unfortunately, Bishop's field notes (kept in the Hunterian Museum) do not record the exact findspot of the tanged point or the precise location of the 'Red Mound'. However, at least some of the lithic and other material that he recovered from the

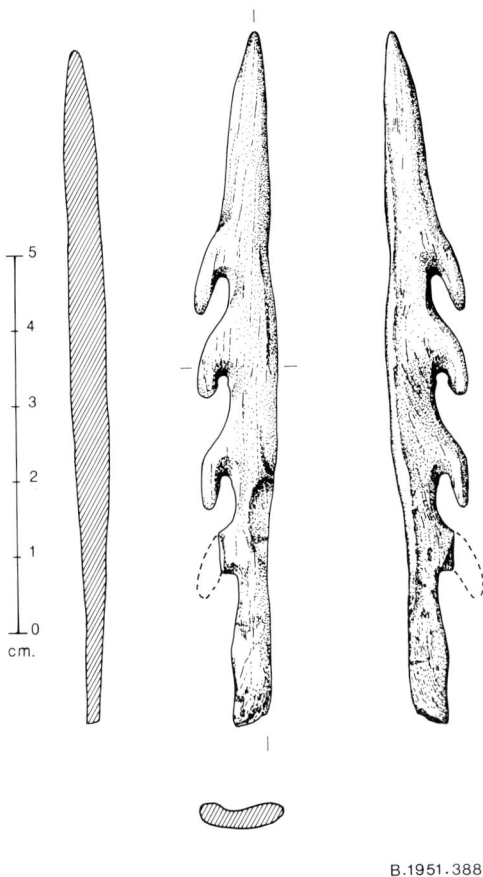

Figure 4   The 'Glenavon' barbed point. The lowermost barb has evidently been broken off since the piece was illustrated by Lacaille (1954). *Drawn by G. Thomas*

B.1951.388

Ballevullin area is known to have come from locations above 10 m O.D.

Another potentially early find is a uniserially-barbed bone point, supposedly from a peat moss at Glenavon (*Fig. 4*; Lacaille 1954). The county is usually given as Banffshire, but this is not definitely known. This piece is quite unlike the flat barbed points of 'Obanian' type from late Mesolithic sites around Oban bay and on the islands of Oronsay and Risga (Lacaille 1954: 196–245) in western Scotland. Its closest analogues appear to be with the uniserially-barbed points of 'Maglemosian' type, which occur mainly as isolated finds farther south in Britain and which, on the basis of conventional and AMS radiocarbon dating, have a time-range from *c.* 12,500 to 9000 BP. Lacaille himself (1954: 184–185) suggested that it was 'tempting to see in this Scottish example an illustration of the spread of the Baltic tradition'. Lacking a secure archaeological context, and information relating to the exact location of the find and the full circumstances of discovery, the Glenavon point can only be regarded as a *possible* indication of human occupation of Scotland before 9000 BP.

Firmer evidence for human activity in the north at this time is the find of a flint scraper, brought up in a sediment core from the bed of the North Sea

between the Shetland Islands and Norway, from a depth of −140 m (Long, Wickham-Jones and Ruckley 1986). The sands in which the artifact was contained are considered to have formed in littoral or near-shore conditions, and it is thought probable that the scraper was derived from a nearby land area and incorporated in Holocene sediments when the North Sea transgressed the region. Long *et al.* (1986: 59, fig. 17) suggest that low sea level corresponding to glacial maximum at *c.* 18,000 BP resulted in the exposure of large areas of the sea bed between the Scottish and Scandinavian ice sheets, and that these land areas were progressively transgressed as sea level subsequently rose. Evidence from the Norwegian sector (Rokoengen *et al.* 1982) indicates that substantial areas of land were still exposed in the northern part of the North Sea basin, between Shetland and Norway, during the Lateglacial Interstadial, although these are likely to have been transgressed by the beginning of the Holocene. The recovery of an undoubted flint artifact from this context appears to provide good evidence for human occupation of these former land areas at some stage before 10,000 BP. Although this evidence appears to indicate activity nearer the Norwegian coast than Scotland, palaeogeographic considerations make land connections to Shetland or further south in the North Sea basin more probable than to the Scandinavian peninsula. This fact must increase the likelihood of occupation of the Scottish mainland during the Lateglacial period.

EARLY FLANDRIAN SETTLEMENT

There are now several hundred confirmed and probable Mesolithic sites in Scotland, a notable advance being in the number of inland sites now recognized. However, a firm chronological framework for Mesolithic settlement has yet to be established.

An area of particular importance is the island of Jura (*Fig. 1*), where the excavations of the late John Mercer at Lussa Wood, Lussa River, Lussa Bay, Lealt Bay, North Carn, Glenbatrick Waterhole and Glengarrisdale (*Fig. 2*) have been a major contribution to knowledge of the Scottish Mesolithic (Mercer 1968, 1970*a*, 1970*b*, 1971, 1972, 1974*a*, 1974*b*, 1974*c*, 1979, 1980; Searight 1984; Mercer and Searight 1986). Mercer postulated a sequence of four periods of occupation from Lateglacial to late Mesolithic, based on stone tool typology and the heights of the sites relative to sea level. This sequence has yet to be confirmed by radiocarbon dating or placed in a stratigraphic context. However, a simpler two-stage sequence may be suggested for the Jura sites based on a consideration of microlith typology.

Excavations at Lussa Wood I (Mercer 1980) uncovered a structure consisting of three, contiguous, stone-lined hearths or 'cooking places'; radiocarbon determinations of 8194±350 BP (SRR-160) and 7963±200 BP (SRR-159) on samples of charcoal and carbonized hazel-nut shells appear to date the use of the hearths. A gravel deposit overlying the structure produced a very rich collection of Mesolithic artifacts with over 3000 microliths. The microliths comprise two typologically distinct series: a 'broad blade' component dominated by large partially-backed, obliquely truncated and bi-truncated (triangular and trapeze-shaped) microliths; and a 'narrow-blade' element composed of smaller, narrower microliths, including straight backed bladelets ('rods'), scalene triangles, trapezoids and rhomboids. Although there was no clear vertical separation of the 'broad blade' and 'narrow blade' microliths within the gravel, Mercer suggested that the 'broad blade' series was earlier and, in part, contemporary with the construction of the stone-lined hearths. Bonsall (1988: 32), whilst accepting the basic typological sequence proposed by Mercer, argued that the artifacts within the gravel had been reworked from pre-existing occupation surfaces and subsequently incorporated into the sediments, and were not therefore in situ. On this interpretation, the 'broad blade' series cannot be related to occupation of the Lussa Wood I site at c. 8100 BP.

The distinction between 'broad blade' and 'narrow blade' microlithic assemblages is even more evident at Glenbatrick Waterhole on the west coast of Jura (Mercer 1974). In an area of 90 m² excavated in 1970–71, two discrete concentrations of artifacts (G1 and G2) were identified. G1 produced a microlithic assemblage of 'broad blade' type, whereas the great majority of the microliths from G2 are of 'narrow blade' type. While the individual concentrations may not represent single occupation events, the clear spatial separation between 'broad blade' and 'narrow blade' microlith clusters suggests that they were deposited essentially at different stages in the Mesolithic occupation of the area (cf. Mercer 1974, 1979; see also Jacobi 1982). Radiocarbon determinations of 4225±230 BP (GX-2563) and 5045±215 BP (GX-2564) were obtained on charcoal from the Glenbatrick site, but in view of the presence of Neolithic leaf-shaped arrowheads in G2, these dates do not necessarily relate to episodes of Mesolithic occupation.

Taken together, the evidence from Glenbatrick and Lussa Wood suggests that the Mesolithic occupation of Jura can be divided into two broad phases: one characterized by a 'broad blade' microlithic industry; the other by 'narrow blade' technology. The relative and absolute dating of these two phases is not easily demonstrated on Jura, but can be established indirectly by reference to evidence for Mesolithic settlement elsewhere in Britain.

In England and Wales 'broad blade' microlithic industries are characteristic of the *early* Mesolithic, and have a probable time-range (based on *secure* radiocarbon dates from fewer than a dozen sites) of c. 9700–9000 BP. A much larger series of radiocarbon dates suggests that 'narrow blade' industries represent a *later* stage of the Mesolithic and were manufactured throughout the period c. 8800–5200 BP.

The evidence from Scotland is less precise. Radiocarbon determinations are available for a small number of Scottish sites with 'narrow blade' microlithic industries (*Table 1*). Dates of 8590±95 BP

Table 1: Radiocarbon dates for Scottish sites with 'narrow blade' microlithic assemblages. Data from published sources, with the exception of the dates from Auchareoch (Affleck, Edwards and Clarke, in press), Newton Bridge (McCullagh, in press) and Smittons (Edwards, pers. comm.)

Site	¹⁴C Age BP	Laboratory Number
Kinloch (Rhum)[b]	8590±95	GU-1873
	8560±75	GU-2040
	8515±190	GU-1874
	8310±150	GU-2150
	8080±50	GU-2146
	7975±65	GU-2039
	7880±70	GU-2147
	7850±50	GU-2145
	7570±50	GU-2149
	4725±140	GU-2043
	4080±60	GU-2148
	3890±65	GU-2042
Lussa Wood I (Jura)[a,b]	8194±350	SRR-160
	7963±200	SRR-159
Auchareoch (Arran)	8060±90	OxA-1601
	7300±90	OxA-1599
Newton Bridge (Islay)[b]	7805±90	GU-1954
	7765±225	GU-1953
North Carn 'OLS' (Jura)	7414±80	SRR-161
Castle Street (Inverness)	7275±235	GU-1376
	7080±85	GU-1377
Morton A (Fife)[a]	6450±80	Q-989
	6400±125	NZ-1193
	6300±150	Gak-2404
Morton B (Fife)	6382±120	Q-981
	6147±90	Q-988
	6115±110	Q-928
Smittons (Kirkcudbrightshire)	6260±80	OxA-1595
	5470±80	OxA-1594
Barsalloch (Wigtownshire)	6100±110	Gak-1601
Glenbatrick G2 (Jura)[b]	5045±215	GX-2564
	4225±230	GX-2563
Lussa River (Jura)[b]	4620±140	BM-556
	4200±100	BM-555

Key: a. Sites with both 'broad blade' and 'narrow blade' microliths
b. Sites with Mesolithic and later artifacts

(GU-1873), 8560±75 BP (GU-2040) and 8515±190 BP (GU-1874) (Wickham-Jones and Pollock 1987) from the site at Kinloch (Rhum) are little different from the earliest dates for 'narrow blade' sites in England, and imply that this technology had been widely adopted in Britain by the early ninth millennium BP. Taken together, the radiocarbon determinations for the Scottish sites indicate a time-range for 'narrow blade' microlithic technology at least as long as that in England. Its continuation into the fifth millennium BP cannot be assumed, however, since those sites with radiocarbon dates younger than 5200 BP have also produced evidence of post-Mesolithic occupation.

In addition to Glenbatrick and Lussa Wood I on Jura, occurrences of 'broad blade' microliths are known from a number of localities on the Scottish mainland; these include Tentsmuir (Fife), Elginhaugh (near Edinburgh), the Tweed valley (e.g. Craigsford Mains), Shewalton (Ayrshire) and Auchrocher Moss (Wigtownshire) (*Fig. 1*). It is uncertain if any of these occurrences represents a homogeneous assemblage. They are mainly surface sites in which 'narrow blade' microliths and post-Mesolithic artifacts also occur. The only major published assemblage of 'broad blade' material is that from Morton Site A (Tentsmuir, Fife), excavated by John Coles in 1969–70 (Coles 1971, 1983).[4] No secure radiocarbon dates are currently available for 'broad blade' assemblages in Scotland; but, from evidence presented above, it may be assumed that they represent an earlier phase of Mesolithic settlement than the 'narrow blade' sites, and have a time-range equivalent to that of the early Mesolithic of southern Britain (*c.* 9700–9000 BP).

The division of the Scottish material into 'broad blade' and 'narrow blade' assemblage types probably conceals a more elaborate typological sequence, but on present evidence this is difficult to demonstrate.

CONCLUDING REMARKS

From a consideration of the evidence for Mesolithic settlement, the impression is gained that sites representing single occupation events are the exception rather than the rule.

The places where 'broad blade' microliths occur together with 'narrow blade' forms are evidently 'mixed' sites created by more than one episode of Mesolithic occupation. It is not always appreciated, however, that many, apparently homogeneous, 'narrow blade' microlithic assemblages are also likely to be the result of multiple occupations of the same location, in some cases spanning a very long period of time. At Kinloch (Rhum), for example, more than one episode of occupation is implied by the spread of the radiocarbon dates (*Table 1*); while at Lussa Wood I (Jura) various lines of evidence – the

very large size of the assemblage, the wide variety of microlith types present, radiocarbon and sea-level evidence (Bonsall 1988) – suggest that occupation extended over several millennia.

Moreover, the majority of the radiocarbon dated sites were coastal at the time of their occupation. It has been shown by research elsewhere in Britain (see Bonsall *et al.*, this volume; David, this volume) that sites in coastal situations frequently reveal evidence of multiple occupation, reflecting the fact that certain locations, such as estuaries and sheltered embayments, often retained their attraction for settlement over a long period. Areas of blown sand, common around the Scottish coastline, pose particular problems. These sand dune systems were periodically unstable during the Flandrian and former land surfaces have been continually eroded by deflation, lowering artifacts from widely separated periods onto a common level (Morrison 1982). The surface collections from the sand dune areas at Shewalton on the Ayrshire coast (Lacaille 1930, 1931) and Tentsmuir in Fife (Lacaille 1954: 278–281), for example, show a mixture of Mesolithic and later artifacts; and in these situations material from different periods of Mesolithic occupation has undoubtedly become mixed together.

The fact that much of the evidence comes from surface sites has been a major obstacle to the development of a sound chronological framework for early post-glacial settlement in Scotland. Some of the interpretative problems posed by surface material may be resolved by the application of radiocarbon dating strategies of the kind advocated by Schild (this volume). Future research, however, will need to concentrate on the discovery and investigation of sites in sealed contexts – in particular, cave sites and sites associated with buried land surfaces.

Although the archaeological record for the early post-glacial period in Scotland is limited in many respects, it will be clear from the evidence presented above that a date of around 8000/8500 BP can no longer be regarded as a *terminus post quem* for the earliest settlement following deglaciation.

Notes:

1. A detailed report on the material from the 1926–27 excavations in the Creag nan Uamh caves is in preparation (Bonsall, Lawson, Murray and Rackham, forthcoming).

2. The determination of age and sex of reindeer from shed antlers is difficult. In their preliminary studies of the material from Reindeer Cave and Trou des Blaireaux, respectively, Lawson and Bonsall and Bellier and Cattelain followed procedures developed by Bouchud (1966) which rely on the size of the antler and the form of the pedicle. Spiess (1979: 97–100), however, recommends that age and sex determination should be based solely on *size* criteria. Accordingly, the interpretation of the Reindeer Cave assemblage proposed in this paper differs slightly from that put forward by Lawson and Bonsall (1986a).

3. Henderson Bishop was an amateur archaeologist who undertook fieldwork at a number of sites in the Western Isles and elsewhere in Scotland during the early part of this century.

4. For a discussion of the chronology of the Morton site – see papers by Bonsall, Myers, Wickham-Jones and Clarke, and Woodman in *Scottish Archaeological Review*, 5, 1988.

Acknowledgements: We should like to thank John Barber, Alastair Dawson, Kevin Edwards, Bill Hanson, Andrew Kitchener, Robin Livens, Euan MacKie, James Rackham, Donald Sutherland, and Gordon Thomas for their assistance in the preparation of this paper. We also thank André Gob for drawing our attention to the finds from the Trou des Blaireaux cave in Belgium. *Figures 3 & 4* are published with the permission of the Hunterian Museum.

References

AFFLECK, T.L., EDWARDS, K.J. and CLARKE, A. (in press) Archaeological and palynological studies at the Mesolithic pitchstone and flint site of Auchareoch, Isle of Arran. *Proceedings of the Society of Antiquaries of Scotland*, 118.

BANG-ANDERSEN, S. (1987) Surveying the Mesolithic of the Norwegian Highlands – a case study on test pits as a method of site discovery and delimitation. In P. Rowley-Conwy, M. Zvelebil and H.P. Blankholm (eds), *Mesolithic Northwest Europe: Recent Trends*. Sheffield, J.R. Collis: 33–45.

BELLIER, C. and CATTELAIN, P. (1983) Fouilles au 'Trou des Blaireaux' à Vaucelles (Doische – Prov. Namur): campagnes 1981–1982. *Notae Praehistoricae*, 3: 42–49.

BONSALL, C. (1988) Morton and Lussa Wood: the case for early Flandrian settlement of Scotland. *Scottish Archaeological Review*, 5: 30–33.

BOUCHUD, J. (1966) *Essai sur la Renne et la Climatologie du Paléolithique Moyen et Supérieur*. Périgueux, Imprimerie Magne.

BOWEN, D.Q., ROSE, J., McCABE, A.M. and SUTHERLAND, D.G. (1986) Correlation of Quaternary glaciations in England, Ireland, Scotland and Wales. *Quaternary Science Reviews*, 5: 299–340.

CALLANDER, J.G., CREE, J.E. and RITCHIE, J. (1927) Preliminary report on caves containing Palaeolithic relics, near Inchnadamph. *Proceedings of the Society of Antiquaries of Scotland*, 61: 169–172.

COLES, J.M. (1971) The early settlement of Scotland: excavations at Morton, Fife. *Proceedings of the Prehistoric Society*, 37(2): 284–366.

COLES, J.M. (1983) Morton revisited. In A. O'Connor and D.V. Clarke (eds), *From the Stone Age to the 'Forty-Five*. Edinburgh, John Donald: 9–18.

DAWSON, A.G. (in preparation) *Strand flat development and late Quaternary sea-level changes on Tiree and Coll, Scottish Hebrides* (paper).

JACOBI, R.M. (1982) When did man come to Scotland? *Mesolithic Miscellany*, 3(2): 8–9.

LACAILLE, A.D. (1930) Mesolithic implements from Ayrshire. *Proceedings of the Society of Antiquaries of Scotland*, 64: 34–48.

LACAILLE, A.D. (1931) Silex tardenoisiens de Shewalton. *Bulletin de la Société Préhistorique Française*, 28: 301–312.

LACAILLE, A.D. (1954) *The Stone Age in Scotland*. Oxford, University Press.

LAWSON, T.J. and BONSALL, C. (1986a) Early settlement in Scotland: the evidence from Reindeer Cave, Assynt. *Quaternary Newsletter*, 49: 1–7.

LAWSON, T.J. and BONSALL, C. (1986b) The Palaeolithic of Scotland: a reconsideration of evidence from Reindeer Cave, Assynt. In S.N. Collcutt (ed.), *The Palaeolithic of Britain and its Nearest Neighbours: Recent Trends*. Sheffield, University of Sheffield, Department of Archaeology: 85–89.

LIVENS, R.G. (1956) Three tanged flint points from Scotland. *Proceedings of the Society of Antiquaries of Scotland*, 89 (1955–56): 438–443.

LONG, D., WICKHAM-JONES, C.R. and RUCKLEY, N.A. (1986) A flint artifact from the northern North Sea. In D.A. Roe (ed.), *Studies in the Upper Palaeolithic of Britain and Northwest Europe*. Oxford, British Archaeological Reports (International Series) S296: 55–61.

LOWE, J.J. and WALKER, M.J.C. (1984) *Reconstructing Quaternary Environments*. London, Longman.

McCULLAGH, R. (in press) Excavations at Newton Bridge, Islay. *Proceedings of the Prehistoric Society*, 55.

MERCER, J. (1968) Stone tools from a washing-limit deposit of the highest Post-glacial transgression, Lealt Bay, Isle of Jura. *Proceedings of the Society of Antiquaries of Scotland*, 100 (1967–8): 1–46.

MERCER, J. (1970a) Flint tools from the present tidal zone, Lussa Bay, Isle of Jura, Argyll. *Proceedings of the Society of Antiquaries of Scotland*, 102 (1969–70): 1–30.

MERCER, J. (1970b) The microlithic succession in N Jura, Argyll, W Scotland. *Quaternaria*, 13: 177–185.

MERCER, J. (1971) A regression-time stone-workers' camp, 33 ft OD, Lussa River, Isle of Jura. *Proceedings of the Society of Antiquaries of Scotland*, 103 (1970–71): 1–32.

MERCER, J. (1972) Microlithic and Bronze Age camps, 75–26 ft OD, N Carn, Isle of Jura. *Proceedings of the Society of Antiquaries of Scotland*, 104 (1971–72): 1–22.

MERCER, J. (1974a) New C14 dates from the Isle of Jura, Argyll. *Antiquity*, 48: 189.

MERCER, J. (1974b) The Neolithic level at Lussa Wood I, N Jura, Argyll. *Glasgow Archaeological Journal*, 3: 77.

MERCER, J. (1974c) Glenbatrick Waterhole, a microlithic site on the Isle of Jura. *Proceedings of the Society of Antiquaries of Scotland*, 105 (1972–74): 9–32.

MERCER, J. (1979) The Palaeolithic and Mesolithic occupation of the Isle of Jura, Argyll, Scotland. *Almogaren*, 9–10 (1978–9): 347–367.

MERCER, J. (1980) Lussa Wood I: the Late-glacial and early Post-glacial occupation of Jura. *Proceedings of the Society of Antiquaries of Scotland*, 110 (1978–80): 1–32.

MERCER, J. and SEARIGHT, S. (1986) Glengarrisdale: confirmation of Jura's third microlithic phase. *Proceedings of the Society of Antiquaries of Scotland*, 116: 41–55.

MORRISON, A. (1982) The Mesolithic period in south-west Scotland: a review of the evidence. *Glasgow Archaeological Journal*, 9: 1–14.

MOVIUS, H.L. Jr (1942) *The Irish Stone Age*. Cambridge, University Press.

MYERS, A.M. (1988) Scotland inside and outside of the British mainland Mesolithic. *Scottish Archaeological Review*, 5: 23–29.

PRICE, R.J. (1983) *Scotland's Environment During the Last 30,000 Years*. Edinburgh, Scottish Academic Press.

ROKOENGEN, K., LOFALDII, M., RISE, L., LOKEN, T. and CARLSEN, R. (1982) Description and dating of a submerged beach in the northern North Sea. *Marine Geology*, 50: M21–M28.

SEARIGHT, S. (1984) The Mesolithic on Jura. *Current Archaeology*, 8(7): 209–214.

SPIESS, A.E. (1979) *Reindeer and Caribou Hunters. An Archaeological Study*. New York, Academic Press.

SUTHERLAND, D.G. (1984) The Quaternary deposits and landforms of Scotland and the neighbouring shelves: a review. *Quaternary Science Reviews*, 3: 157–254.

TAUTE, W. (1968) *Die Stielspitzen-Gruppen im nördlichen Mitteleuropa. Ein Beitrag zur Kenntnis der späten Altsteinzeit* (Fundamenta, A/5). Köln, Böhlau Verlag.

WICKHAM-JONES, C.R. and CLARKE, A. (1988) The ghost of Morton revisited. *Scottish Archaeological Review*, 5: 35–37.

WICKHAM-JONES, C.R. and POLLOCK, D. (1987) *Rhum – the Excavations*, 2. Edinburgh, Printed Privately.

WOODMAN, P.C. (1988) Comment on Myers: 'Scotland inside and outside of the British mainland Mesolithic'. *Scottish Archaeological Review*, 5: 34–35.

Meso–Neolithic Vegetational Impacts in Scotland and Beyond: Palynological Considerations

Kevin J. Edwards

Abstract

Palynological data (mainly pollen and charcoal analysis) can usefully provide evidence for anthropogenic impacts on past vegetation. The circumstantial nature of this evidence is most marked for pre-agricultural disturbances where proof of human impacts is uncertain. Inferences are more secure in agricultural phases, especially when cereal pollen is present. These points are discussed in the context of evidence from Scotland and elsewhere, and it is suggested that the pollen data may indicate the existence of agriculture earlier than expected, while hunter-gatherer impacts may have persisted much later than is conventionally assumed. Charcoal analysis, the Elm Decline, disturbance indicators, and the Meso–Neolithic transition are considered. It is emphasized that archaeological evidence must be fully utilized in the interpretation of the palynological record.

INTRODUCTION

While a number of archaeologists have perhaps rightly complained to the writer that Mesolithic studies in Britain and Ireland represent the poor sister, the 'Cinderella', of archaeology, this is happily not totally the case in palynology. While palynologists frequently tackle all cultural periods using the technique of pollen analysis, the Mesolithic has been blessed by the attention of some creative workers. Thus, in particular, Professors Geoffrey Dimbleby, Frank Mitchell, Ian Simmons and Alan Smith, and their associates have provided a rich harvest of material of relevance to the environmental background of Mesolithic times (see Mitchell 1976; Simmons and Tooley 1981). Pollen data are frequently open to various interpretations, and no more so than in the case of vegetational changes where proof of human impacts is frequently uncertain. This paper examines various aspects of the palynological record, using Scotland as a principal focus. It is suggested that a number of anthropogenic interpretations of the pollen record are open to alternative explanations; that agriculture may have occurred earlier than is generally indicated; that hunter-gatherer impacts may have persisted later than is generally assumed; and that archaeological evidence must also be fully utilized in the interpretation of palynological data.

ARCHAEOLOGICAL DISTRIBUTIONS AND EARLY MAN IN SCOTLAND – THE COASTAL FOCUS

The first occupation of Scotland may have been earlier than most assume (Jacobi 1982). Within deposits referred to the Allerød period (*c.* 12,500 BP) two flint points from Jura were found by Mercer (1979, 1980) (*Fig. 1*). The points were assigned to

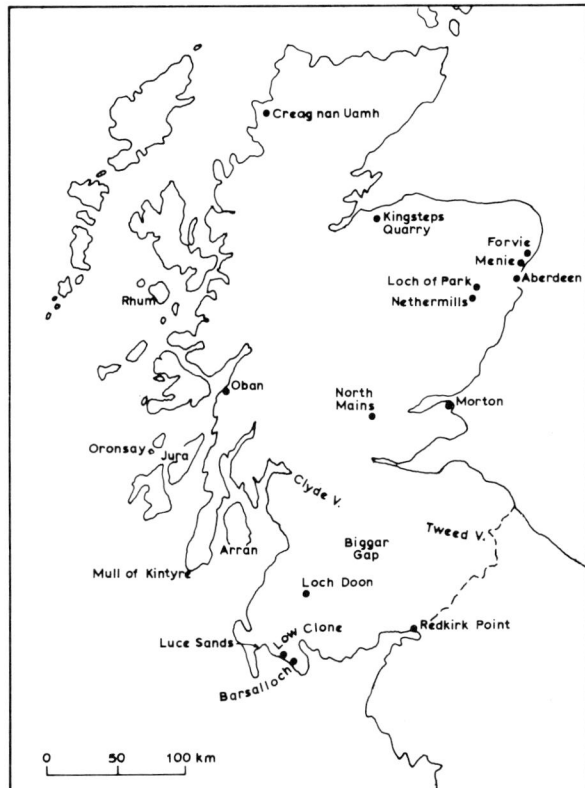

Figure 1   Scottish sites mentioned in the text.

the late Palaeolithic, but they were broken and came from secondary deposits containing many finds from later periods. Further north in the Creag nan Uamh caves near Inchnadamph, Sutherland, reindeer antlers said to be humanly cut were found in a supposedly Lateglacial context (Callander, Cree and Ritchie 1927). Although the archaeological and environmental evidence has been questioned (Lawson 1981, 1984), the most recent re-assessment suggests that the antlers were humanly collected and brought to the site in the closing stages of the Lateglacial period (Lawson and Bonsall 1986a, 1986b).

The first secure evidence for the presence of early man in Scotland during the Postglacial period is from coastal sites on both sides of the country. Carbonized hazel-nut shells associated with a bloodstone-rich lithics site at Farm Fields, Kinloch, Rhum have produced dates of 8590±95 BP (GU-1873) and 8515±190 BP (GU-1874) (Wickham-Jones, this volume). At Lussa Wood I, Jura, a triple-ringed stone feature interpreted as cooking places, contained bone fragments, a limpet shell, charred hazel-nut shells and wood (Mercer 1974). One sample of wood was dated to 8194±350 BP (SSR-160). At Redkirk Point, Dumfriesshire, a hearth site produced charcoal and twigs of birch, oak and elm (Langholme and Masters 1976) and the charcoal has been dated to 8000±65 BP (UB-2445) and 7935±110 BP (UB-2470) (Masters 1981). The site at Morton, Fife (now 4 km from the North Sea coast, but coastal during the time of high Postglacial sea levels) has produced an abundance of information upon the early Scottish prehistoric economy (Coles 1971, 1983). Lithic finds, floral and faunal remains were rich, and charcoal from the site has been dated to 8050±250 BP (NZ-1151).

Publication of Scottish archaeologically-based Mesolithic research has long had a coastal focus (e.g. Lacaille 1930, 1945, 1954; Edgar 1939; McCallien and Lacaille 1941) and this has continued into more recent times with work in the south west (Truckell 1963; Coles 1964; Cormack and Coles 1968; Cormack 1970; Jardine and Morrison 1976; Morrison 1981); the Inner Hebrides (e.g. Mercer 1968, 1970, 1974, 1979; Mellars 1979) and the east (Coles 1971, 1983). The coastal sites have been especially productive for several reasons. The sites, particularly via their lithic scatters, become noticeable in such situations as blown-sand areas, e.g. Torrs Warren in the Luce Sands (Smith 1893) and the Forvie and Menie Links sites in Aberdeenshire (Hawke-Smith 1981); on ploughed raised beach material as in Ayrshire (Lacaille 1954; Morrison 1980); at the landward end of Postglacial raised beaches, e.g. the Jura sites (Mercer 1979), the shell midden sites of Oronsay (Mellars and Payne 1971; Jardine 1977; Mellars 1981) and Aberdeenshire (Lacaille 1954); also above the raised beach as at Low Clone and Barsalloch on the Solway Firth (Cormack and Coles 1968; Cormack 1970) where the sites consisted of scooped areas or shallow pits close to where freshwater streams flow into the sea; and cave sites like those around Oban (Andersen 1895, 1898; Turner 1895; MacDougall 1907). Such sites are noticed, of course, because they were frequented by archaeologists as well as by Mesolithic peoples! This coastal concentration of finds has led to suggestions that the Mesolithic population was low; Atkinson (1962) considered a total Scottish population level of 50–70 persons, while Morrison (1980, 1982) and Price (1982, 1983) have stressed the general inhospitableness of much of inland Scotland away from the coasts and rivers. A traditional image has thus built up of the Mesolithic populace being essentially 'strand loopers' (cf. Morrison 1983). Before re-assessing this picture it is necessary to introduce the evidence provided by pollen analysis.

THE PALYNOLOGICAL RECORD AND COASTAL AREAS IN SCOTLAND

Pollen analysis suggests that after glaciation there was a spread of trees and shrubs across the relatively open landscape. This began with the pioneering taxa of birch, juniper and willow, followed by hazel and the woodland dominants of pine, oak and elm and, later, alder (*Fig. 2*; Birks 1977). The variable topography, soils and micro-climates of Scotland meant, of course, that the precise composition of the vegetation varied, but on the Scottish mainland there was woodland dominance apart from areas of basin peat. This seemed to be the rule up until the major impact of agricultural clearances during and after the period conventionally referred to as the Neolithic.

The principal broad-scale effect upon the vegetation attributed to Mesolithic man is the characteristically high representation of hazel (*Corylus avellana*) (Smith 1970, 1984; Simmons 1981). One can almost hear the note of derision in the voice of Bradley (1984: 11) when he remarked:

> ... in the literature as a whole, successful farmers have social relations with one another, while hunter-gatherers have ecological relations with hazelnuts.

The occurrence of hazel-nuts at archaeological sites of this period (e.g. Lussa Wood I, Lussa River and Glenbatrick on Jura – Mercer 1971, 1974, 1980; Morton, Fife – Coles 1971) can leave us in little doubt that they were a valuable element in the Mesolithic diet. This should not necessarily lead us to the conclusion that man encouraged the growth of hazel since it was almost certainly able to grow adequately without special tending (for the possible situation regarding offshore islands, see Boyd and Dickson 1986). Although it has been suggested that fire – perhaps in the pursuit of driving game – promoted hazel growth (Smith 1970), there is no proof that this was the case in Europe (Rackham 1980). The high Holocene (Postglacial or Flandrian stage) representation for *Corylus* pollen values may well represent a naturally progressive increase over the last few interglacials (West 1980; Edwards 1982). It is clearly dangerous to prognosticate concerning the location of early man when the archaeological

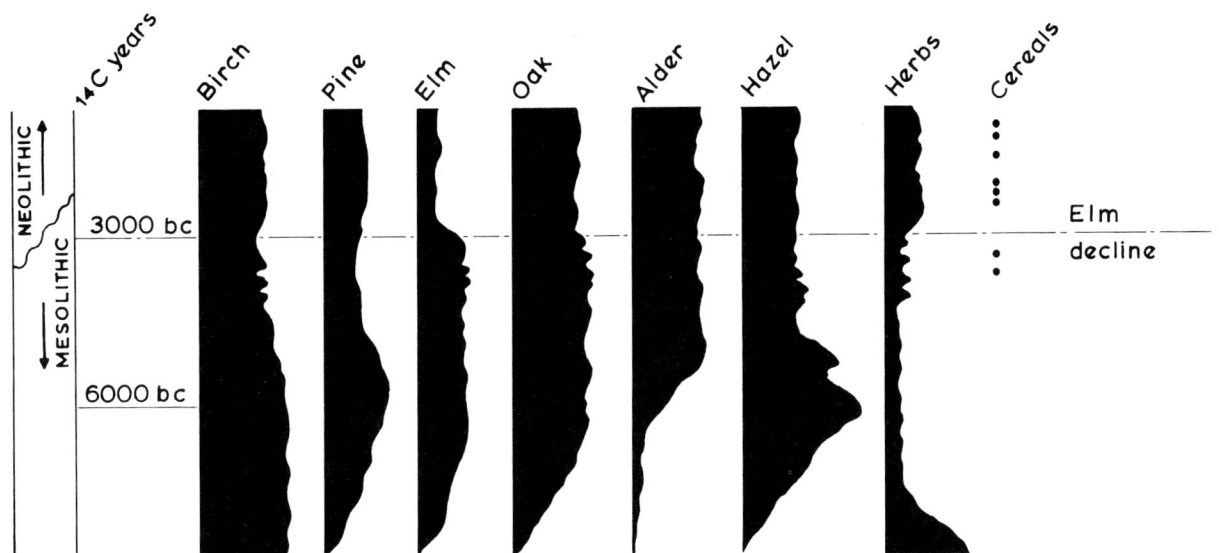

Figure 2   A schematic pollen diagram for the early and mid-Holocene period in Britain.

record at least is partial (see next section). Nevertheless, it is not difficult to find pollen sites in Scotland from areas which have not produced Mesolithic finds or are outwith the probable range of human attraction or interference, but which have produced *Corylus*-dominant pollen assemblages during the early Postglacial or even a secondary hazel peak (Edwards and Ralston 1984).

Less dramatic disturbance or interference phases (analogous to the later 'clearance' phases) are frequently found in the early Postglacial levels of pollen diagrams. They are typified by temporary reductions in tree pollen values and the rise of herbaceous taxa in spectra which occur before the conventional beginnings of Neolithic agriculture as indicated by the Elm Decline of *c.* 5100 BP (*Fig. 2*). Such perturbations in the pollen record were noted as long ago as 1954 in the little remarked paper on Kingsteps Quarry, Nairn by Knox. She analyzed a coastal peat deposit which had yielded stone artifacts (ascribed by Lacaille to the Mesolithic), lenses of charcoal, birch twigs and hazel-nuts. The pollen record indicated that the deposit was predominantly post-Boreal in age (the Boreal–Atlantic transition occurred close to the base) and featured conspicuous increases in both peat-habitat taxa (Ericaceae, Cyperaceae and Gramineae) and such non-arboreal types as *Plantago*, *Chenopodium*, Caryophyllaceae, Compositae and bracken spores. The ecological changes responsible for these patterns may be matched circumstantially with the presence of early man as indicated by the lithic finds. Alternatively, they could have been associated with such phenomena as an intermittently dry peat surface, geomorphological changes of the coastal habitat (wind-blown sand was noted in the profiles), browsing animals, or natural fires.

This difficulty in apportioning responsibility for the palynological changes applies to other sites where possible Mesolithic interference was found. These include: (i) Aros Moss on the Kintyre peninsula (Nichols 1967; but note the nearby flint finds at Machrihanish and Campbeltown – McCallien 1936; McCallien and Lacaille 1941); (ii) Loch of Park (Vasari and Vasari 1968) and Nethermills (Ewan 1981) where a possible Mesolithic hut or shelter has been reported (Kenworthy 1981), both close to the artifact-rich terraces of the River Dee lowlands of Aberdeenshire (Paterson and Lacaille 1936); and (iii) Machrie Moor in the west of Arran (Robinson 1983) where at a level dated to 8665±155 BP (GU-1427) charcoal was present, heather pollen increased to form a continuous curve and, after *c.* 7000 BP, charcoal reached high values along with those of some light demanding herbs – all at times consistent with likely Mesolithic occupation (Fairhurst 1981).

A recent discussion on pastoral episodes of clearance activity in pollen diagrams examined the role of post-occupation grazing (Buckland and Edwards 1984). It was suggested, partly from the evidence of historical and modern references to the husbandry practices and natural herbivore patterns of exploitation, that post-occupation grazing might offer a satisfactory explanation for the phenomenon of the extreme longevity of inferred pastoral phases. Given the fact that trees are continually dying, that they are subject to wind-throw, that woodland is liable to be damaged by grazing animals and that such animals existed in woodlands of the Mesolithic period, then it would not be surprising if a number of the disturbance phases in our pollen diagrams were of natural/animal origin and untouched by human hand. The presence of coeval charcoal peaks would suggest that man could be involved or, perhaps just as likely, that natural lightning fires in a dry period had opened up an area of woodland and provided stable browse for any passing roe or red deer.

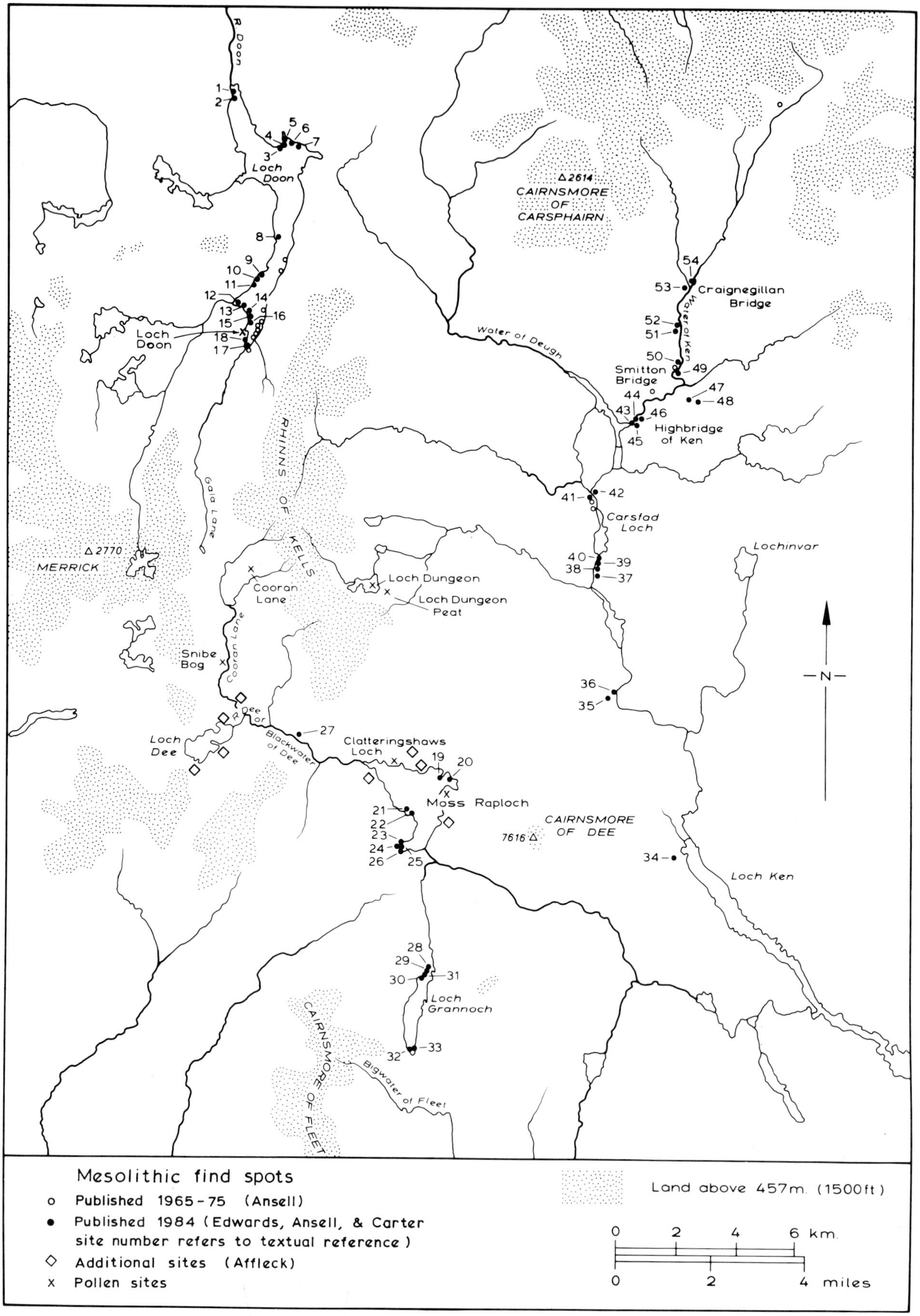

Figure 3 Mesolithic findspots and pollen sites in south-west Scotland.

INLAND PENETRATION OF ONE AREA – THE ARCHAEOLOGICAL AND PALYNOLOGICAL RECORD IN SOUTH-WEST SCOTLAND

The coastal dominance of Mesolithic finds and of palynological changes of possible anthropogenic origin in Scotland, presents a somewhat skewed pattern which would suggest that coastal resources were sufficient for most needs, with perhaps excursions along river valleys and into nearby woodland to supplement diets with animal produce or to obtain wood for fires, canoes, shelters, tools, or weapons. This pattern never looked totally convincing given the distribution of occasional inland finds, especially in south-west Scotland where the Biggar Gap flints and the more extensive spreads of the Tweed river valley (Mulholland 1970) indicated a possible Clyde–Tweed routeway. During the 1960s and 1970s Michael Ansell made a number of flint and chert finds in the Loch Doon area (Ansell 1965–1975) and these, together with more than 60 new findspots (*Fig. 3*) recorded by Ansell and workers from the Universities of Birmingham and Glasgow, portray a picture of major inland penetration within south-west Scotland (Edwards, Ansell and Carter 1984). The finds from the Loch Doon area came from various locations: (i) around the loch where they occur generally below high water level (the loch had been a hydro-electric power reservoir since 1936) and material is found below eroding peat; (ii) on castle island and another more northerly island which at times of lowered lake level is a peninsula; and (iii) beneath peat south west of the loch where upcast from forestry drainage ditches has revealed lithic finds on a small spur overlooking the Gala Lane. Other sites in mineral soils beneath peat or at the soil/peat interface (e.g. around Loch Dee) and in ploughsoil and molehills of the Ken valley present a picture of probable inland resource utilization that was perhaps every bit as concentrated as upon the coast. The existence of apparent fire settings containing carbonized materials below Starr Cottage on the south-western shore of Loch Doon (Affleck 1986), and the use of an island location within the loch, and hence possibly boats, may indicate that the Mesolithic presence was less than transient.

With the knowledge that there is considerable evidence for Mesolithic man in inland areas of south-west Scotland, what does the pollen record show? At Cooran Lane, Birks (1975) produced evidence for fire disturbance of the vegetation at *c.* 7000 BP. Tree pollen values fluctuated and Gramineae, *Melampyrum* and bracken values expanded together with the

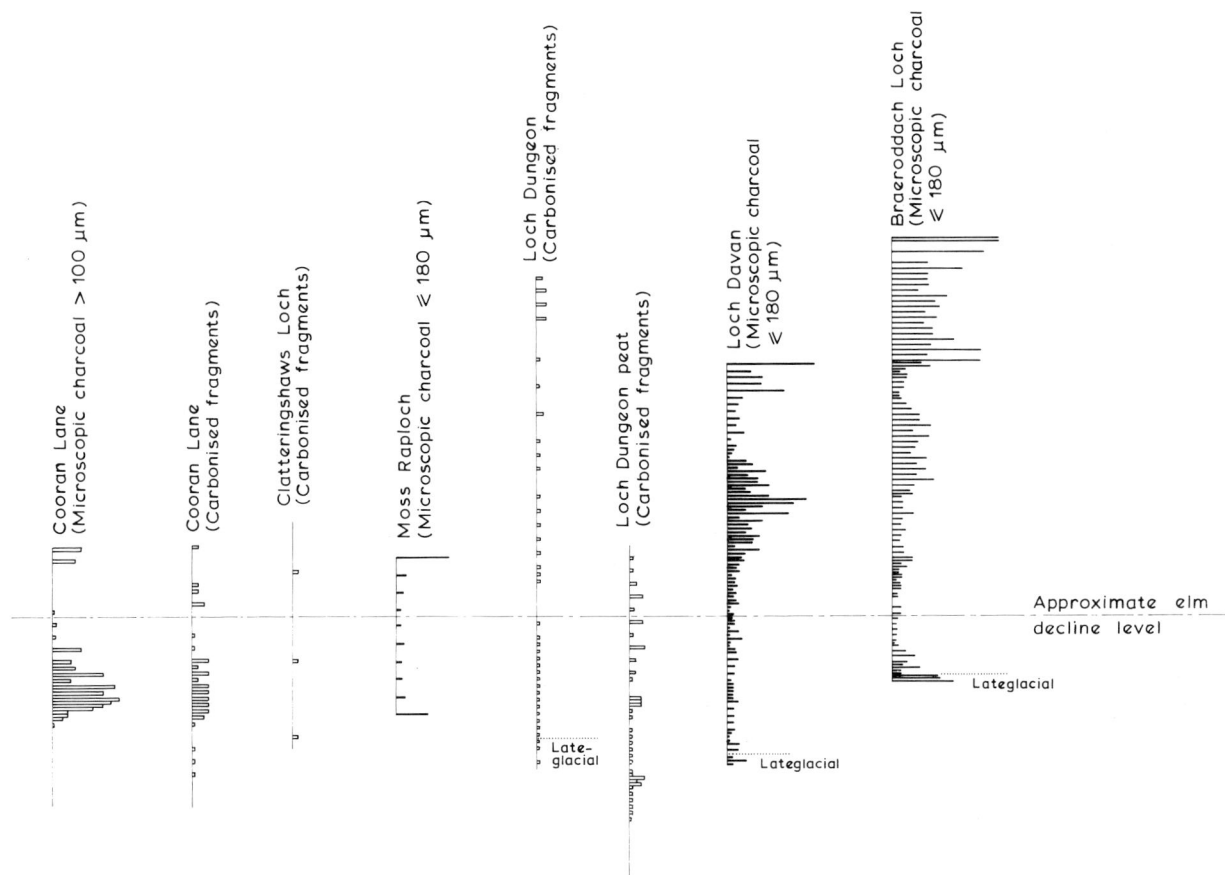

Figure 4 Charcoal profiles: Cooran Lane, Clatteringshaws Loch and Loch Dungeon peat (Birks 1975); Loch Dungeon (Birks 1972); Moss Raploch (Carter and Edwards, unpublished); Loch Davan and Braeroddach Loch (Edwards 1978).

147

appearance of large numbers of charcoal micro-fragments (*Fig. 4*). While acknowledging the clearance nature of this pattern, Birks preferred a natural interpretation (bog surface burning during a dry period) and observed that 'no evidence of occupation has been found in the hills' (1975: 206). Similarly, at Snibe Bog about 2 km to the south, Birks (1972) found pollen grains of *Plantago lanceolata*, *Fraxinus*, and *Pteridium* spores. Unaware of the archaeological evidence, she noted this:

> may reflect some human interference. If so, this was probably due to early Neolithic man, as Mesolithic remains are concentrated on the Galloway coast (1972: 206).

There were low amounts of macroscopic carbonized fragments in the pollen preparations from Clatteringshaws Loch and the Loch Dungeon lake and peat sites (Birks 1972, 1975), and there were charcoal micro-fragments in the outline profile prepared from Moss Raploch (see *Fig. 4*, where a number of charcoal curves are presented, without scales or depth data, merely to exemplify pattern for the purposes of discussion). It is obviously dangerous to talk of the implications of the data where charcoal counts, for example, are not based upon contiguous sampling, where there is little standardization in charcoal evaluation between workers (see below), and where micro-fragments are compared with carbonized macro-remains. This should not necessarily prevent speculation, however. If the Moss Raploch outline charcoal profile turns out to be a satisfactory surrogate of the final profile and if the Clatteringshaws Loch data indicate minimal local burning, it may show that these sites, or their immediate vicinities, were not used intensively by Mesolithic peoples for domestic purposes. The supposition is predicated upon the working hypothesis that domestic fires (for warmth and cooking) might produce substantial amounts of charcoal (Edwards 1979) whereas the habitual and intentional use of fire in hunting or browse-creating activities (Jacobi, Tallis and Mellars 1976; Mellars 1976; Welinder 1983) was less likely in the Scottish situation (Edwards and Ralston 1984). The lithic finds near Clatteringshaws Loch and Moss Raploch may denote hunting (but not settlement) locations, or they may show the need for pollen/charcoal sampling sites to be located much more closely to such sites of obvious human activity. The low amounts of 'occasional' or 'frequent' carbonized fragments at the Loch Dungeon lake and peat sites could indicate 'background' levels of airborne charcoal – there have, as yet, been no Mesolithic finds close to the sites. The prolonged and substantial presence of charcoal micro-fragments (>100 μm) and 'abundant' carbonized material at Cooran Lane may indicate a more permanent site or sites in that locality – these may now have disappeared or

perhaps lie hidden beneath peat and the extensive coniferous plantations. Alternatively, the data from Cooran Lane may derive from fires, however caused, on the bog surface itself (see below); Birks (1975) noted many carbonized fragments in the peat stratigraphy, and the pollen spectra are strongly indicative of local burning.

There is growing interest in applying charcoal analyses in our environmental studies (cf. Swain 1973; Cwynar 1978; Tolonen 1978; Simmons and Innes 1981; Patterson, Edwards and Maguire 1987). The presence of charcoal in pollen preparations merely tells us that combustible materials have been ignited, and not that fires have been used in any particular way by man. While much emphasis has been placed upon the role of fire in hunter-gatherer situations (Smith 1970; Simmons 1975; Mellars 1976; Robinson 1983) the associated evidence for intentional use of fire in game driving, as a mechanism to increase plant and animal biomass, or even woodland clearance, remains unproven. Obviously, changes in a suite of pollen taxa which may respond to fire (e.g. *Pinus*, *Melampyrum*, *Potentilla*, *Calluna*, and *Pteridium* spores) may encourage us to infer that vegetational burning has taken place. We know that fire existed, but it can occur naturally and there has even been a report of 23 lightning-strike fires in coniferous plantations over a two-day period in the Galloway hills (Thompson 1971). In Aberdeenshire, there are low amounts of charcoal throughout the pollen profiles from Braeroddach Loch and Loch Davan, even in the probable pre-Mesolithic levels (*Figs. 4 & 6*; Edwards 1978). The charcoal peaks across a number of fragment size classes evident from the Loch Doon peat profile (*Fig. 5*; Carter 1986) may indicate local fire occurrence above 'background' levels of airborne charcoal within the charcoal catchment area, but this does not automatically implicate man in every instance. In addition, the common occurrence of visible burnt levels within peat deposits may sometimes have human origins, but we have yet to address ourselves fully to the signal this imposes upon contemporaneous and non-contemporaneous charcoal records within the profile (see also Boyd 1982a, 1982b; Moore 1982). Lake deposits may prove to be more suitable for charcoal analysis than peat in this respect, though this might raise problems of sediment mixing and stratigraphic resolution (Green 1983).

EARLY AGRICULTURE, LATE MESOLITHIC DISTURBANCES AND THE ELM DECLINE

Since the early days of research in anthropogenic palynology, the decline in elm pollen values c. 5100 BP in north-western Europe has been seen as

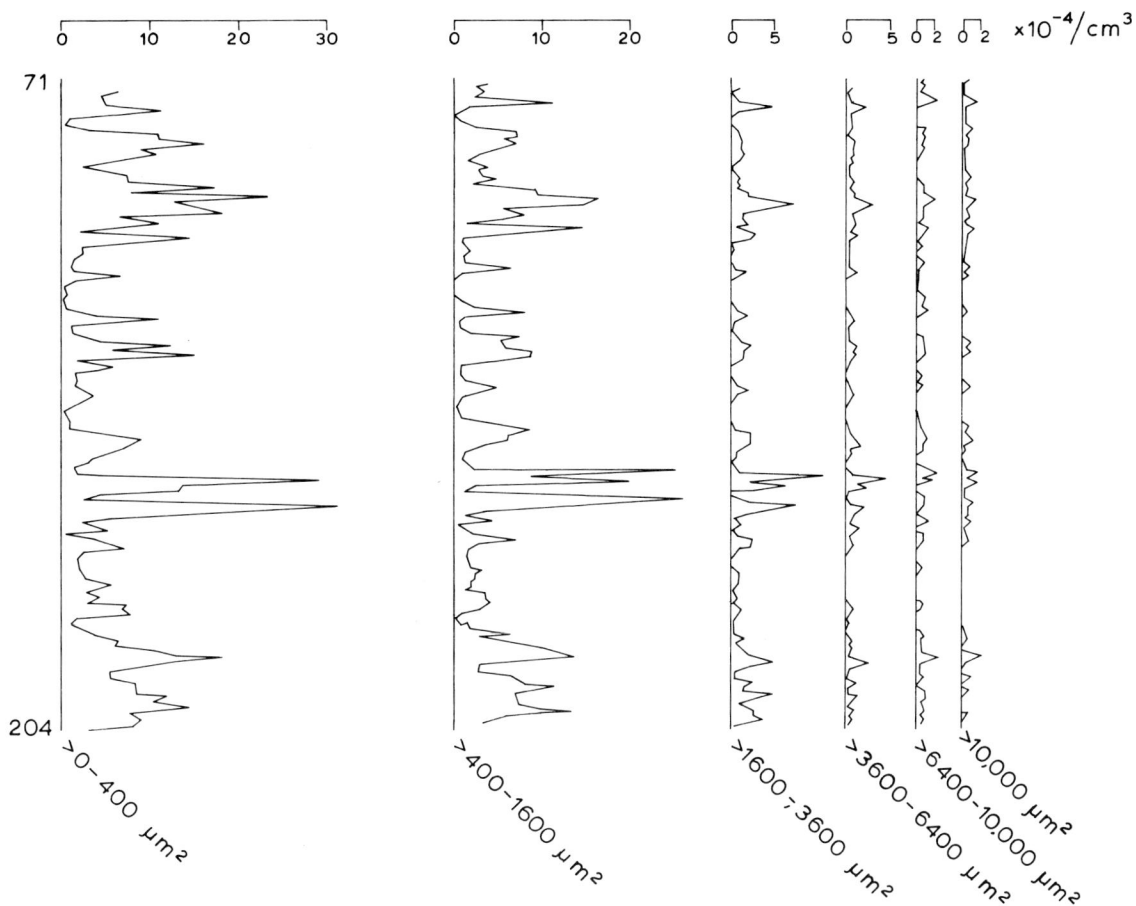

Figure 5 Charcoal size class curves for Loch Doon (after Carter 1986). A date of 4850±60 BP (GrN-13134) was obtained for core depth 186–194 cm, while the interpolated date for depth level 204 cm is 5290 BP.

marking the first horizon where incoming Neolithic communities cleared woodland for agricultural purposes (Ten Hove 1968). It has been supposed that elm trees grew particularly upon the better, more easily-worked soils, either in single stands or as part of a woodland mosaic, and that their removal by an environmentally-aware farming population was followed by cereal cultivation. It is indeed the case that the Elm Decline levels often did coincide with the appearance of cereal-type pollen and other cultural taxa (Smith, Grigson, Hillman and Tooley 1981), and an interpretation of the Elm Decline signifying the start of agriculture has held sway with a majority of both archaeologists and palynologists over alternative explanations for the *Ulmus* decline, such as climatic change or a disease hypothesis.

These views have been questioned recently in two papers which appeared independently, but cover similar areas of enquiry and came to related conclusions (Groenman-van Waateringe 1983; Edwards and Hirons 1984). Edwards and Hirons (1984) reported on eight pollen sites then known to contain cereal-type pollen and indications of vegetational disturbance immediately prior to the Elm Decline. Five of these were in Ireland, two in England, and one in Scotland (Machrie Moor, Isle of Arran – Robinson 1981). To these may now be added a further Irish example (Lough Sheeauns, Co. Galway – Molloy and O'Connell 1987), one from Hampstead Heath, London (Girling and Greig 1985) and another two from Scotland (Aros Moss, Kintyre – McIntosh 1986; Edwards, McIntosh and Robinson 1986; and North Mains, Strathallan, Perthshire – Hulme and Shirriffs 1985). There is archaeological support for such early activity. At Ballynagilly in Co. Tyrone, Northern Ireland, seven radiocarbon dates from Neolithic archaeological contexts were found to be older than the estimated date for the Elm Decline (5220 BP) and they extended back to 5745±90 BP (UB-305, Pilcher and Smith 1979). The earliest cereal-type pollen within the main Ballynagilly peat profile was found at a level dated to 5750 BP. At Carrowmore megalithic cemetery in Co. Sligo, two early radiocarbon dates have been obtained with the earliest at 5750±85 BP (Lu-1840; Burenhult 1980).

The early cereal-type pollen and archaeological dates intrude into the period which in Britain and Ireland has usually been assigned to the Mesolithic. In view of the poor distributional characteristics of most cereal pollen grains, we should be deterred from referring apparently non-arable disturbance features up to, say, 1000 radiocarbon years prior to the Elm Decline necessarily to Mesolithic activity

F

(cf. the sites mentioned above and those reviewed in Pennington 1975; Simmons, Dimbleby and Grigson 1981; Smith *et al.* 1981). If anthropogenic, they might be the result of late Mesolithic exploitation (see related discussion on the Elm Decline in Bonsall *et al.* 1986); but they might otherwise result from an early Neolithic presence, something hinted at by a number of archaeologists (e.g. Case 1969; Smith 1974; Coles 1976; Bradley 1978). There also remains the possibility that the early agricultural activities may have been effected by indigenous Mesolithic groups who had acquired the materials and techniques of cereal cultivation (Dennell 1983; Edwards and Hirons 1984). In such a connection can also be cited: (i) the finds of apparently domesticated animals in Mesolithic contexts from, for instance, Sutton (Mitchell 1956) and Dalkey Island (Liversage 1968), both in Co. Dublin and Ringneill Quay, Co. Down (Collins and Stephens 1960); (ii) domesticated sheep in southern France (Geddes 1985), together with the possible development of herding practices which span the Meso–Neolithic transition (Dimbleby and Simmons 1974; Simmons 1975); and (iii) the healed bone injury patterns on animal skeletons in Denmark which, in part, led Noe-Nygaard (1974) to hypothesize that late Mesolithic man had adopted a more settled mode of life. The interpretations surrounding cultural transitions are fraught with difficulties (Case 1969; Woodman 1976, 1977; Whittle 1977; Bradley 1984; Edwards and Ralston 1984), and the topic will be returned to below.

What of the Elm Decline which is visible in many Scottish diagrams though not always as clearly as in those from elsewhere in Britain and Ireland? Its general synchroneity (Smith and Pilcher 1973; Edwards 1985a) suggests a catastrophic event for northwest Europe. Climatic change will not explain the often specific decline of elm but not that of similarly sensitive taxa such as lime or ash. It has been suggested that agriculture may have begun before the Elm Decline, and the hitherto essential link between the Elm Decline and attendant agricultural cause must be seen as one of a number of possibilities rather than a near certainty. A pathogenic explanation, similar to the infestation of elms by the fungus *Ceratocystis ulmi* carried by the bark beetle *Scolytus scolytus*, and familiar to us as Dutch elm disease, would appear to be a good candidate. This is the conclusion reached by Groenman-van Waateringe (1983) after her consideration of the Irish evidence and would agree with suggestions made by Watts (1961; see also discussions on the second elm decline in Hirons and Edwards 1986). Rackham (1980) and Huntley and Birks (1983) – the latter after considering their European isopollen maps – both consider that an elm disease explanation, combined with the agricultural activities of early farmers who could take advantage of openings in diseased woodland, represents the best hypothesis. To this may be added the find by Girling of the bark beetle, *Scolytus scolytus*, immediately before the Elm Decline levels of West Heath Spa (Hampstead Heath, London) pollen profile analyzed by James Greig (Girling and Greig 1985) – a profile which also produced pre-Elm Decline cereal-type pollen.

THE HUNTER-GATHERER/ AGRICULTURAL TRANSITION (POST-ELM DECLINE)

While it has been shown that primary agricultural activity extended into the time period conventionally allocated to the Mesolithic, there is also the possibility that hunter-gatherer activities by indigenous Mesolithic folk continued into the period traditionally allocated to the Neolithic. Apart from the overlap in radiocarbon dates for Mesolithic and Neolithic contexts from Scotland (Morrison 1980) and Ireland (Edwards 1985b), the survival of hunter-gatherer activity and/or its local adoption in marginal areas by incoming agriculturalists, especially during those times before they had built up the resources for a settled life-style in a new and perhaps alien landscape, may surely be assumed. Indeed, if the Elm Decline is abandoned as a sure sign of clearance and agricultural activity, then the earliest post-Elm Decline disturbance phases seen in the pollen diagrams, and where cereal or arable weed pollen is absent, may be a response to hunter-gatherer impacts rather than crop and animal husbandry. Such a hypothesis has been put forward in a reconsideration of some of the data from the Howe of Cromar in Aberdeenshire (Edwards and Ralston 1984) and this is summarized below.

The Howe of Cromar is an undulating basin averaging 250 m O.D. in the foothills of the Grampians, to the north of the River Dee and some 45 km west of Aberdeen (*Fig. 6*). Mesolithic flint assemblages are known from the mouth of the River Dee (Kenworthy 1982) and the Dee terraces near Banchory especially (Paterson and Lacaille 1936; Kenworthy 1981), but microlithic finds occur as far inland as Dinnet in south Cromar and the uplands on the west (Edwards 1975). The Elm Decline at both Loch Davan and Braeroddach Loch occurs c. 5200 BP but the pollen diagrams display no definite signs of cereal cultivation, although a Neolithic-type long cairn is situated on a rise overlooking Braeroddach Loch (Edwards 1978), and both lochs at the present day have arable fields close by. Further down the Dee valley the magnificent Neolithic timber hall at Balbridie (about 50 m O.D.) produced dates for timber back to 5160±70 BP (GU-1038), while carbonized grains of emmer wheat (*Triticum dicoccum*) were dated to 4745±160 BP (GU-1421) and

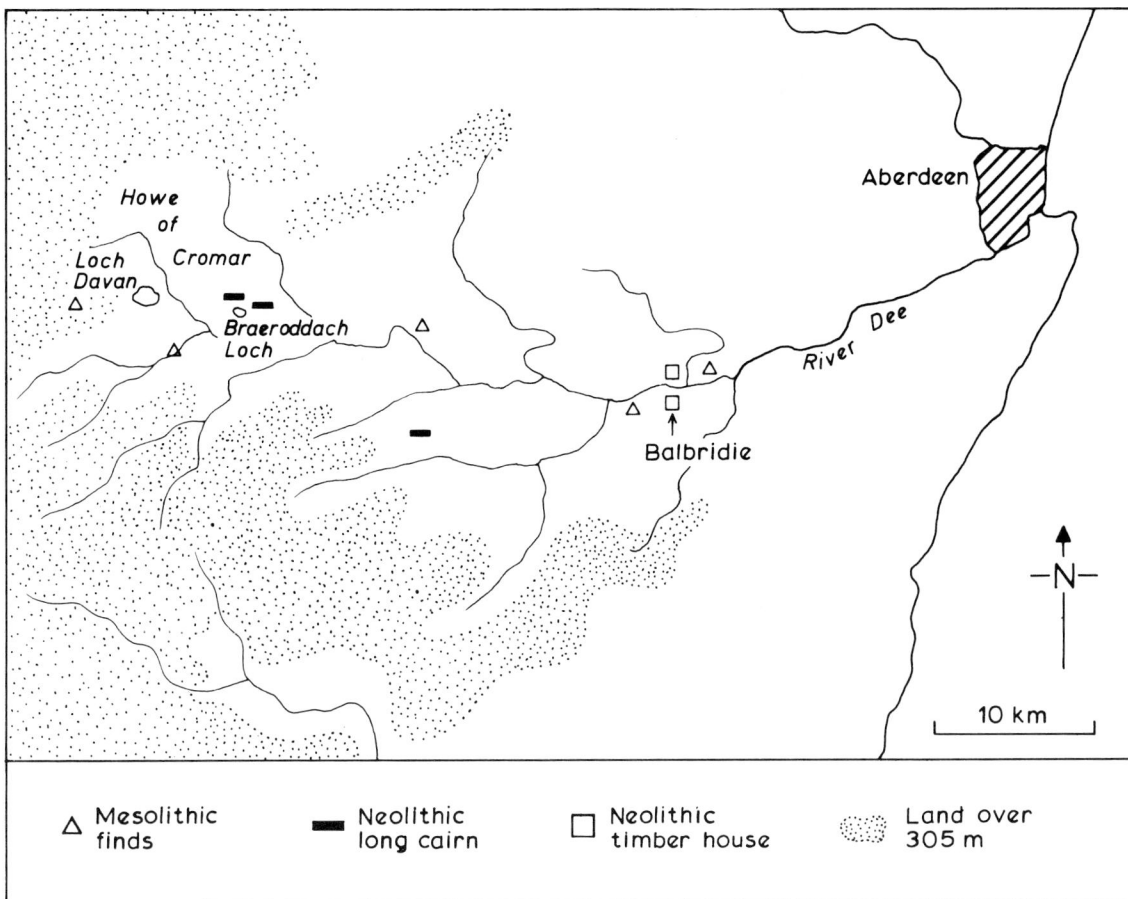

Figure 6   Mesolithic and Neolithic sites in the Dee valley, Aberdeenshire.

the youngest date from the site is 4740±135 BP (GU-1036) (Ralston 1982). The signs of immediate post-Elm Decline disturbance at the Cromar Lochs consist of a reduction in most tree pollen values and expansions for the frequencies of Gramineae, *Plantago lanceolata* and *Pteridium aquilinum*. The changes appear to represent a low level of activity at a time when cereal cultivation was probably taking place at Balbridie (there are pollen grains of Cerealia in turves associated with the structure, as well as the macro-remains of emmer). While the palynological data from the Cromar sites could represent pastoral activity, there are no clear signs from the sedimentary indicators (sediment chemistry and magnetic susceptibility measures – Edwards 1978) of any accelerated movement of soils into the loch. It is therefore conceivable that the early disturbances at and after the Elm Decline reflect the impact of hunter-gatherers taking advantage of local plant and animal resources. The longevity of the interference phases (an estimated 220 calendar years at Loch Davan and 775 calendar years at Braeroddach Loch) could represent a prolonged exploitation of the environment by hunter-gatherers, a subsequent small-scale use of the area by pastoralists or the opportunistic grazing of animals maintaining openings, however caused, within woodland (Buckland and Edwards 1984), or all such factors singly or

in combination. The long cairn perched above Braeroddach Loch may indicate late Neolithic activity within the area or may signify merely the location of a funerary monument in an area where agriculture was not being practised at this time.

CONCLUDING POINTS

A principal concern in this paper has been to examine pollen and charcoal records from Scotland and to assess them regarding the possible vegetational impacts of hunter-gatherer populations. It has been stressed throughout that the palynological evidence can be interpreted in different ways. An essential complement to the palynological record is that provided by archaeologists in terms of both material remains and ideas. It is of interest to note that enigmatic features of published pollen records from one inland area, south-west Scotland, can be resolved with some degree of satisfaction when compared with the latest archaeological evidence for inland penetration by Mesolithic peoples. Similarly, the palynological evidence for possible precocious agriculture provides a challenge for archaeologists and warns all workers against referring environmental impacts of immediate pre-Elm Decline age to Mesolithic man – that is, if we choose to regard cereal cultivation as an activity of Neolithic man by definition!

151

The suggestion that immediately post-Elm Decline disturbance phases may signify continued hunter-gatherer activities similarly raises many questions. Assuming such disturbances to be anthropogenic in origin (and not merely a response to, say, unmanaged grazing activities) then they may be due, for example, to continued activity by indigenous Mesolithic folk or by acculturated or incoming Neolithic communities. The inland, upland marginal areas may have proved attractive and safe to indigenous groups maintaining a spatially separate existence (though they may have bartered produce with farming groups while in the process of cultural amalgamation). Early farming groups in lowland areas may have valued the produce won from the upland wooded areas by those not engaged in crop husbandry.

It is unclear, as yet, whether a general reliable distinction can be made between the types of disturbances indicated in pollen diagrams such as to allow a clear differentiation of the nature of the land use other than: (i) mixed farming (with cereal pollen present – though see caveats in Edwards 1979, 1982, Edwards and Hirons 1984 – as well as the common occurrence of non-cereal grass pollen and other herbaceous taxa which could indicate pastoral activity: Behre 1981, 1986); (ii) possible cereal husbandry as part of a mixed farming system (with the pollen of weeds common to cultivated land, but without cereal pollen); and (iii) non-specific disturbances (frequently with pastoral-type indicators). This last category could indicate anything on a continuum from animal husbandry through to completely natural grazing (Buckland and Edwards 1984), or even clearings made for crop growing but which have failed to produce a sufficient supply of arable indicators at the site of pollen deposition. It is probable, however, that a closer liaison between palynologists and archaeologists could shed more light upon the data-sets available to both sets of practitioners – especially in those circumstances where researchers are both ecologically and spatially aware (e.g. Spratt and Simmons 1976).

It seems to this writer, from a palynological point of view at least, that the Mesolithic and Neolithic periods cover that section of the environmental record in which likely anthropogenic impacts will be especially discernible and potentially most easily comprehended. After this time the removal of large areas of 'palynologically-sensitive' woodland, the existence of much secondary regrowth rather than primary forest, increased soil deterioration and blanket peat growth, all combine to make the task of interpretation more difficult. While Mesolithic studies may be the 'Cinderella' of British archaeology, its subject matter holds much of interest and relevance to the palynologist as well as to the archaeologist. Let us hope they can thrive together.

Acknowledgements: I would like to thank the late Tom Affleck (Archaeology Department, Glasgow University) who allowed me to refer to his lithic finds; and Caroline Wickham-Jones (Artifact Research Unit, Royal Museum of Scotland) who provided the data on Rhum. My colleague Patrick Newell made useful comments on a draft of the paper, and Lynn Ford and Tim Grogan made great efforts to convert 'rough-outs' into a suitable typescript and artwork. Work in south-west Scotland is supported by the Science and Engineering Research Council.

References

AFFLECK, T.L. (1986) Excavation at Starr, Loch Doon 1985. *Glasgow Archaeological Society Bulletin*, 22: 10–21.

ANDERSON, J. (1875) Notice of a cave recently discovered at Oban, containing human remains and a refuse-heap of shells and bones of animals, and stone and bone implements. *Proceedings of the Society of Antiquaries of Scotland*, 29: 211–230.

ANDERSON, J. (1898) Notes on the contents of a small cave or rock-shelter at Druimvargie, Oban; and of three shell-mounds in Oronsay. *Proceedings of the Society of Antiquaries of Scotland*, 32: 298–313.

ANSELL, M. (1965–1975) Notes in *Discovery and Excavation in Scotland*.

ATKINSON, R.J.C. (1962) Fishermen and Farmers. In S. Piggott (ed.), *The Prehistoric Peoples of Scotland*. London, Routledge and Kegan Paul: 1–38.

BEHRE, K.E. (1981) The interpretation of anthropogenic indicators in pollen diagrams. *Pollen et Spores*, 23: 225–245.

BEHRE, K.E. (ed.) (1986) *Anthropogenic Indicators in Pollen Diagrams*. Rotterdam, A.A. Balkema.

BIRKS, H.H. (1972) Studies in the vegetational history of Scotland, II. Two pollen diagrams from the Galloway Hills, Kirkudbrightshire. *Journal of Ecology*, 60: 183–217.

BIRKS, H.H. (1975) Studies in the vegetational history of Scotland, IV. Pine stumps in Scottish blanket peats. *Philosophical Transactions of the Royal Society of London*, B270: 181–217.

BIRKS, H.J.B. (1977) The Flandrian forest history of Scotland: a preliminary synthesis. In F.W. Shotton (ed.), *British Quaternary Studies*. Oxford, University Press: 119–135.

BONSALL, C., SUTHERLAND, D.G., TIPPING, R.M. and CHERRY, J. (1986) The Eskmeals Project 1981–5: an interim report. *Northern Archaeology*, 7(1): 3–30.

BOYD, W.E. (1982a) Sub-surface formation of charcoal and its possible relevance to the interpretation of charcoal remains in peat. *Quaternary Newsletter*, 37: 6–8.

BOYD, W.E. (1982b) Sub-surface formation of charcoal: an unexplained event in peat. *Quaternary Newsletter*, 38: 15–16.

BOYD, W.E. and DICKSON, J.H. (1986) Patterns in the geographical distribution of the early Flandrian *Corylus* rise in southwest Scotland. *New Phytologist*, 102: 615–623.

BRADLEY, R. (1978) *The Prehistoric Settlement of Britain*. London, Routledge and Kegan Paul.

BRADLEY, R. (1984) *The Social Foundations of Prehistoric Britain*. London, Longman.

BUCKLAND, P.C. and EDWARDS, K.J. (1984) The longevity of pastoral episodes of clearance activity in pollen diagrams: the role of post-occupation grazing. *Journal of Biogeography*, 11: 243–249.

BURENHULT, G. (ed.) (1980) *The Archaeological Excavation at Carrowmore, Co. Sligo, Ireland: Excavation Seasons 1977–79* (Theses and Papers in North-European Archaeology, no. 9). Stockholm, Institute of Archaeology.

CALLANDER, J.G., CREE, J.E. and RITCHIE, J. (1927) Preliminary report on caves containing Palaeolithic relics, near Inchnadamph, Sutherland. *Proceedings of the Society of Antiquaries of Scotland*, 61: 169–172.

CARTER, B.A. (1986) *Pollen and Microscopic Charcoal Studies in South West Scotland*. Unpublished M.Phil. thesis, University of Birmingham.

CASE, H. (1969) Neolithic Explanations. *Antiquity*, 43: 176–186.

COLES, J.M. (1964) New aspects of the Mesolithic settlement of south-west Scotland. *Transactions of the Dumfriesshire and Galloway Natural History and Antiquarian Society*, 41: 67–98.

COLES, J.M. (1971) The early settlement of Scotland: excavations at Morton Fife. *Proceedings of the Prehistoric Society*, 37: 284–366.

COLES, J.M. (1976) Forest farmers: some archaeological, historical and experimental evidence. In S.J. De Laet (ed.), *Acculturation and Continuity in Atlantic Europe* (Papers presented at the 4th Atlantic Colloquium, Ghent 1975) Bruges, Acta Archaeologica Gandensis: 59–66.

COLES, J.M. (1983) Morton revisited. In A. O'Connor and D.V. Clarke (eds), *From the Stone Age to the 'Forty-Five*. Edinburgh, John Donald: 9–18.

COLLINS, A.E.P. and STEPHENS, N. (1960) The Quaternary deposits at Ringneill Quay and Ardmillan, Co. Down. *Proceedings of the Royal Irish Academy*, 61C: 41–77.

CORMACK, W.F. (1970) A Mesolithic site at Barsalloch, Wigtownshire. *Transactions of the Dumfriesshire and Galloway Natural History and Antiquarian Society*, 47: 63–80.

CORMACK, W.F. and COLES, J.M. (1968) A Mesolithic site at Low Clone, Wigtownshire. *Transactions of the Dumfriesshire and Galloway Natural History and Antiquarian Society*, 45: 44–72.

DENNELL, R. (1983) *European Economic Prehistory. A New Approach*. London, Academic Press.

EDGAR, W. (1939) A Tardenoisian site at Ballantrae, Ayrshire. *Transactions of the Glasgow Archaeological Society*, 9: 184–188.

EDWARDS, K.J. (1975) Aspects of the prehistoric archaeology of the Howe of Cromar. In A.M.D. Gemmell (ed.), *Quaternary Studies in North East Scotland*. Aberdeen, Quaternary Research Association: 82–87.

EDWARDS, K.J. (1978) *Palaeoenvironmantal and Archaeological Investigations in the Howe of Cromar, Grampian Region, Scotland*. Unpublished Ph.D. thesis, University of Aberdeen.

EDWARDS, K.J. (1979) Palynological and temporal inference in the context of prehistory, with special reference to the evidence from lake and peat deposits. *Journal of Archaeological Science*, 6: 255–270.

EDWARDS, K.J. (1982) Man, space and the woodland edge: speculations on the detection and interpretation of human impact in pollen profiles. In M. Bell and S. Limbrey (eds), *Archaeological Aspects of Woodland Ecology*. Oxford, British Archaeological Reports (International Series) S146: 5–22.

EDWARDS, K.J. (1985a) Radiocarbon dating. In K.J. Edwards and W.P. Warren (eds), *The Quaternary History of Ireland*. London, Academic Press: 280–293.

EDWARDS, K.J. (1985b) The anthropogenic factor in vegetational history. In K.J. Edwards and W.P. Warren (eds), *The Quaternary History of Ireland*. London, Academic Press: 187–220.

EDWARDS, K.J., ANSELL, M. and CARTER, B.A. (1984) New Mesolithic sites in south-west Scotland and their importance as indicators of inland penetration. *Transactions of the Dumfriesshire and Galloway Natural History and Antiquarian Society*, 58 (1983): 9–15.

EDWARDS, K.J. and HIRONS, K.R. (1984) Cereal pollen grains in pre-Elm Decline deposits: implications for the earliest agriculture in Britain and Ireland. *Journal of Archaeological Science*, 11: 71–80.

EDWARDS, K.J., McINTOSH, C.J. and ROBINSON, D.E. (1986) Optimizing the detection of cereal-type pollen grains in pre-Elm Decline deposits. *Circaea*, 4: 11–13.

EDWARDS, K.J. and RALSTON, I. (1984) Postglacial hunter-gatherers and vegetational history in Scotland. *Proceedings of the Society of Antiquaries of Scotland*, 114: 15–34.

EWAN, L. (1981) *A Palynological Investigation near Banchory: Some Local and Regional Environmental Implications*. Aberdeen, University of Aberdeen Department of Geography, O'Dell Memorial Monograph no. 11.

FAIRHURST, H.C. (1981) *Exploring Arran's Past*. Glasgow, Central Press.

GEDDES, D.S. (1985) Mesolithic domestic sheep in west Mediterranean Europe. *Journal of Archaeological Science*, 12: 25–48.

GIRLING, M.A. and GREIG, J.R.A. (1985) A first fossil record for *Scolytus scolytus* (F.) (elm bark beetle): its occurrence in Elm Decline deposits from London and the implications for Neolithic elm disease. *Journal of Archaeological Science*, 12: 347–351.

GREEN, D.G. (1983) The ecological interpretation of fine-resolution pollen records. *New Phytologist*, 94: 459–477.

GROENMAN-VAN WAATERINGE, W. (1983) The early agricultural utilization of the Irish landscape: the last word on the Elm Decline? In T. Reeves-Smyth and F. Hamond (eds), *Landscape Archaeology in Ireland*. Oxford, British Archaeological Reports (British Series) 116: 217–232.

HAWKE-SMITH, C.F. (1981) Two Mesolithic sites near Newburgh, Aberdeenshire. *Proceedings of the Society of Antiquaries of Scotland*, 110 (1978–80): 497–534.

HIRONS, K.R. and EDWARDS, K.J. (1986) Events at and around the first and second *Ulmus* declines: palaeoecological investigations in Co. Tyrone, Northern Ireland. *New Phytologist*, 104: 131–153.

HULME, P.D. and SHIRRIFS, J. (1985) Pollen analysis of a radiocarbon-dated core from North Mains, Strathallan, Perthshire. *Proceedings of the Society of Antiquaries of Scotland*, 115: 105–113.

HUNTLEY, B. and BIRKS, H.J.B. (1983) *An Atlas of Past and Present Pollen Maps for Europe: 0–13 000 Years Ago*. Cambridge, University Press.

JACOBI, R.M. (1982) When did man come to Scotland? *Mesolithic Miscellany*, 3(2): 8–9.

JACOBI, R.M., TALLIS, J.H. and MELLARS, P.A. (1976) The southern Pennine Mesolithic and the ecological record. *Journal of Archaeological Science*, 3: 307–320.

JARDINE, W.G. (1977) Location and age of Mesolithic coastal occupation sites on Oronsay, Inner Hebrides. *Nature*, 267: 138–140.

JARDINE, W.G. and MORRISON, A. (1976) The archaeological significance of Holocene coastal deposits in south-western Scotland. In D.A. Davidson and M.L. Shackley (eds), *Geoarchaeology: Earth Science and the Past*. London, Duckworth: 175–195.

KENWORTHY, J.B. (1981) *Nethermills Farm, Crathes, excavations 1978–80: interim report* (mimeo). St Andrews, Department of Archaeology.

KENWORTHY, J.B. (1982) The flint. In J.C. Murray (ed.), *Excavations in the Medieval Burgh of Aberdeen*. Edinburgh, Society of Antiquaries of Scotland Monograph Series no. 2: 200–215.

KNOX, E.M. (1954) Pollen analysis of a peat at Kingsteps Quarry, Nairn. *Transactions of the Botanical Society of Edinburgh*, 36: 224–229.

LACAILLE, A.D. (1930) Mesolithic implements from Ayrshire. *Proceedings of the Society of Antiquaries of Scotland*, 64: 34–47.

LACAILLE, A.D. (1945) The stone industries associated with the raised beach at Ballantrae. *Proceedings of the Society of Antiquaries of Scotland*, 79: 81–106.

LACAILLE, A.D. (1954) *The Stone Age in Scotland*. Oxford, University Press.

LANGHORNE, T. and MASTERS, L.J. (1976) A probable Mesolithic hearth at Redkirk Point, Gretna, Dumfriesshire. *Discovery and Excavation in Scotland*, 1976: 27–28.

LAWSON, T.J. (1981) The 1926–7 excavations of the Creag nan Uamh bone caves near Inchnadamph, Sutherland. *Proceedings of the Society of Antiquaries of Scotland*, 111: 7–20.

LAWSON, T.J. (1984) Reindeer in the Scottish Quaternary. *Quaternary Newsletter*, 42: 1–5.

LAWSON, T.J. and BONSALL, C. (1986a) Early settlement in Scotland: the evidence from Reindeer Cave, Assynt. *Quaternary Newsletter*, 49: 1–7

LAWSON, T.J. and BONSALL, C. (1986b) The Palaeolithic in Scotland: a reconsideration of evidence from Reindeer Cave, Assynt. In S.N. Collcutt (ed.), *The Palaeolithic of Britain and its Nearest Neighbours: Recent Trends*. Sheffield, University Department of Archaeology and Prehistory: 85–89.

LIVERSAGE, G.D. (1968) Excavations at Dalkey Island, Co. Dublin, 1956–59. *Proceedings of the Royal Irish Academy*, 66C: 53–233.

MACDOUGALL, A.J. (1907) Notice of the excavation of a rock-shelter at Dunollie, Oban. *Proceedings of the Society of Antiquaries of Scotland*, 38: 181–182.

153

McCallien, W.J. (1936) Late-glacial and early post-glacial Scotland. *Proceedings of the Society of Antiquaries of Scotland*, 71: 174–206.

McCallien, W.J. and Lacaille, A.D. (1941) The Campbeltown raised beach and its contained stone industry. *Proceedings of the Society of Antiquaries of Scotland*, 75: 55–92.

McIntosh, C.J. (1986) *Palaeoecological Investigations of Early Agriculture on the Isle of Arran and the Kintyre Peninsula*. Unpublished M.Sc. thesis, University of Birmingham.

Masters, L.J. (1981) A Mesolithic hearth at Redkirk Point, Gretna. *Transactions of the Dumfriesshire and Galloway Natural History and Antiquarian Society*, 56: 111–114.

Mellars, P.A. (1976) Fire ecology, animal populations and man: a study of some ecological relationships in prehistory. *Proceedings of the Prehistoric Society*, 42: 15–45.

Mellars, P.A. (1979) Excavation and economic analysis of Mesolithic shell-middens on the island of Oronsay. *Scottish Archaeological Forum*, 9: 43–61.

Mellars, P.A. (1981) Cnoc Coig, Druim Harstell and Cnoc Riach: problems of the identification and location of shell middens on Oronsay. *Proceedings of the Society of Antiquaries of Scotland*, 111: 516–518.

Mellars, P.A. and Payne, S. (1971) Excavation of two Mesolithic shell middens on the island of Oronsay. *Nature*, 231: 397–398.

Mercer, J. (1968) Stone tools from a washing-limit deposit of the highest Post-glacial transgression, Lealt Bay, Isle of Jura. *Proceedings of the Society of Antiquaries of Scotland*, 100: 1–46.

Mercer, J. (1970) The microlithic succession in N. Jura, Argyll, W. Scotland. *Quaternaria*, 13: 177–185.

Mercer, J. (1971) A regression-time stone-workers' camp 33 ft O.D., Lussa River, Isle of Jura. *Proceedings of the Society of Antiquaries of Scotland*, 103: 1–32.

Mercer, J. (1974) New C14 dates from the Isle of Jura. *Antiquity*, 48: 65–66.

Mercer, J. (1979) The Palaeolithic and Mesolithic occupation of the Isle of Jura, Argyll, Scotland. *Almogaren*, 9–10: 347–367.

Mercer, J. (1980) Lussa Wood I: the Late-glacial and early Post-glacial occupation of Jura. *Proceedings of the Society of Antiquaries of Scotland*, 110 (1978–80): 1–31.

Mitchell, G.F. (1956) An early kitchen-midden site at Sutton, Co. Dublin. *Journal of the Royal Society of Antiquaries of Ireland*, 86: 1–26.

Mitchell, G.F. (1976) *The Irish Landscape*. Glasgow, Collins.

Molloy, K and O'Connell, M. (1987) The nature of the vegetational changes at about 5000 B.P. with particular reference to the Elm Decline: fresh evidence from Connemara, western Ireland. *New Phytologist*, 106: 203–220.

Moore, P.D. (1982) Sub-surface formation of charcoal: an unlikely event in peat. *Quaternary Newsletter*, 38: 13–14.

Morrison, A. (1980) *Early Man in Britain and Ireland*. London, Croom Helm.

Morrison, A. (1981) The coastal Mesolithic in south-west Scotland. In B. Gramsch (ed.), *Mesolithikum in Europa. 2. Internationales Symposium Potsdam, 3 bis 8 April 1978 Bericht* (Veröffentlichungen des Museums für Ur- und Frühgeschichte, 14/15). Berlin, Deutscher Verlag der Wissenschaften: 441–450.

Morrison, A. (1982) The Mesolithic period in south-west Scotland: a review of the evidence. *Glasgow Archaeological Journal*, 9: 1–14.

Morrison, I.A. (1983) Prehistoric Scotland. In I. Whyte and G. Whittington (eds), *A Historical Geography of Scotland*. London, Academic Press: 1–23.

Mulholland, H. (1970) The microlithic industries of the Tweed valley. *Transactions of the Dumfriesshire and Galloway Natural History and Antiquarian Society*, 47: 81–110.

Nichols, H. (1967) Vegetational change, shoreline displacement and the human factor in the late Quaternary history of south-west Scotland. *Transactions of the Royal Society of Edinburgh*, 67: 145–187.

Noe-Nygaard, N. (1974) Mesolithic hunting in Denmark illustrated by bone injuries caused by human weapons. *Journal of Archaeological Science*, 1: 217–248.

Paterson, H.M.L. and Lacaille, A.D. (1936) Banchory microliths. *Proceedings of the Society of Antiquaries of Scotland*, 70: 419–434.

Patterson, W.A., Edwards K.J. and Maguire, D. (1987) Microscopic charcoal as a fossil indicator of fire. *Quaternary Science Reviews*, 6: 3–23.

Pennington, W. (1975) The effect of Neolithic man on the environment of north-west England: the use of absolute pollen diagrams. In J.G. Evans, S. Limbrey and H. Cleere (eds), *The Effect of Man on the Landscape: the Highland Zone*. London, C.B.A. Research Report no. 11: 74–86.

Pilcher, J.R. and Smith, A.G. (1979) Palaeoecological investigations at Ballynagilly, a Neolithic and Bronze Age settlement in County Tyrone, Northern Ireland. *Philosophical Transactions of the Royal Society of London*, B286: 343–369.

Price, R.J. (1982) The magnitude and frequency of late Quaternary environmental changes in Scotland: implications for human occupation. *Scottish Archaeological Review*, 1: 61–72.

Price, R.J. (1983) *Scotland's Environment During the Last 30,000 Years*. Edinburgh, Scottish Academic Press.

Rackham, O. (1980) *Ancient Woodland: its History, Vegetation and Uses in England*. London, Edward Arnold.

Ralston, I.B.M. (1982) A timber hall at Balbridie Farm. *Aberdeen University Review*, 168: 238–249.

Robinson, D.E. (1981) *The Vegetational and Land Use History of the West of Arran, Scotland*. Unpublished Ph.D. thesis, University of Glasgow.

Robinson, D.E. (1983) Possible Mesolithic activity in the west of Arran: evidence from peat deposits. *Glasgow Archaeological Journal*, 10: 1–6.

Simmons, I.G. (1975) Towards an ecology of Mesolithic man in the uplands of Great Britain. *Journal of Archaeological Science*, 2: 1–15.

Simmons, I.G. (1981) Culture and environment. In I.G. Simmons and M.J. Tooley (eds), *The Environment in British Prehistory*. London, Duckworth: 282–291.

Simmons, I.G., Dimbleby, G.W. and Grigson, C. (1981) The Mesolithic. In I.G. Simmons and M.J. Tooley (eds), *The Environment in British Prehistory*. London, Duckworth: 82–124.

Simmons, I.G. and Innes, J.B. (1981) Tree remains in a North York Moors peat profile. *Nature*, 294: 76–78.

Simmons, I.G. and Tooley, M.J. (eds) (1981) *The Environment in British Prehistory*. London, Duckworth.

Smith, A.G. (1970) The influence of Mesolithic and Neolithic man on British vegetation: a discussion. In D. Walker and R.G. West (eds), *Studies in the Vegetational History of the British Isles*. Cambridge, University Press: 81–96.

Smith, A.G. (1984) Newferry and the Boreal–Atlantic transition. *New Phytologist*, 98: 35–55.

Smith, A.G., Grigson, C., Hillman, G. and Tooley, M. (1981) The Neolithic. In I.G. Simmons and M.J. Tooley (eds), *The Environment in British Prehistory*. London, Duckworth: 125–209.

Smith, A.G. and Pilcher, J.R. (1973) Radiocarbon dates and vegetational history of the British Isles. *New Phytologist*, 72: 903–914.

Smith, I.F. (1974) The Neolithic. In C. Renfrew (ed.), *British Prehistory: a New Outline*. London, Duckworth: 100–136.

Smith, J. (1983) The sand-hills of Torrs Warren, Wigtownshire. *Transactions of the Geological Society of Glasgow*, 9: 293–300.

Spratt, D.A. and Simmons, I.G. (1976) Prehistoric activity and environment on the North York Moors. *Journal of Archaeological Science*, 3: 193–210.

Swain, A.M. (1973) A history of fire and vegetation in north-eastern Minnesota. *Quaternary Research*, 3: 383–396.

Ten Hove, H.A. (1968) The *Ulmus* fall at the transition Atlanticum–Subboreal in pollen diagrams. *Palaeogeography, Palaeoclimatology, Palaeoecology*, 5: 359–369

Thompson, D.A. (1971) Lightning fires in Galloway – June 1970. *Scottish Forestry*, 25: 51–52.

Truckell, A.E. (1963) The Mesolithic in Dumfries and Galloway: recent developments. *Transactions of the Dumfriesshire and Galloway Natural History and Antiquarian Society*, 40: 43–47.

TURNER, W. (1895) On human and animal remains found in caves in Oban, Argyllshire. *Proceedings of the Society of Antiquaries of Scotland*, 29: 410–438.

VASARI, Y. and VASARI, A. (1968) Late- and Post-glacial macrophytic vegetation in the lochs of Scotland. *Acta Botanici Fennici*, 45: 193–217.

WATTS, W.A. (1961) Post-Atlantic forests in Ireland. *Proceedings of the Linnaean Society of London*, 172: 33–38.

WELINDER, S. (1983) Man-made forest fires in the Mesolithic. *Mesolithic Miscellany*, 4(1): 9–10.

WEST, R.G. (1980) Pleistocene forest history in East Anglia. *New Phytologist*, 85: 571–622.

WHITTLE, A.W.R. (1977) *The Earlier Neolithic of Southern England and its Continental Background*. Oxford, British Archaeological Reports (Supplementary Series) 35.

WOODMAN, P.C. (1976) The Irish Mesolithic/Neolithic transition. In S.J. De Laet (ed.), *Acculturation and Continuity in Atlantic Europe* (Papers presented at the 4th Atlantic Colloquium, Ghent 1975). Bruges, Acta Archaeologica Gandensis: 296–307.

WOODMAN, P.C. (1977) Problems of identification of Mesolithic survivals in Ireland. *Irish Archaeological Research Forum*, 4: 17–28.

Recent Work on the Island of Rhum, Scotland

C.R. Wickham-Jones

Abstract

Until recently work on the Mesolithic of Scotland has been sporadic and concentrated in a few areas. As a result, the period is often seen as both spatially and chronologically limited. Recent work is starting to provide evidence for activity throughout Scotland during the Mesolithic period suggesting that it was both rich and chronologically extended.

Work on the island of Rhum commenced as part of a project concerned with the exploitation of lithic resources in prehistoric Scotland. In this case the occurrence and use of a chalcedonic silica, Rhum bloodstone, found both on Rhum and elsewhere along the west coast of Scotland, was of particular interest. Preliminary excavations at the site of Kinloch have revealed a rich lithic assemblage associated with undisturbed features. Microliths from the site are paralleled amongst the 'narrow blade' industries which define the later Mesolithic of the British Isles. Two radiocarbon determinations from one of the excavated pits provide some of the earliest known evidence of human activity in Scotland.

Current interpretations of the Mesolithic in Scotland are severely hampered by the uneven and sporadic interest shown in the period until recently. Concentration of work within a limited number of well-defined areas has biased many views of the period and in general the Scottish Mesolithic has been regarded as both spatially and chronologically limited. The lack of uniform coverage in archaeological fieldwork makes it unlikely that the present distribution and density of sites is representative of past settlement patterns. Woodman (1978) has shown how localized fieldwork in north-east Ireland has biased the interpretation of Mesolithic activity there. A similar bias exists, if frequently unrecognized, in most considerations of the Scottish Mesolithic. Large areas of north and west Scotland are still seen as having been uninhabited until later on in prehistory (Ritchie 1985). However, these areas have produced small amounts of Mesolithic material which is frequently associated with later artifacts, perhaps because of the type of activity that leads to its recovery. The lack of investigation into earlier prehistory in these areas has meant that the limited evidence for early settlement, together with its peripheral location, is interpreted as suggesting a late movement of population into the north and west (Lacaille 1954).

In the south, evidence for settlement is generally interpreted with emphasis upon the importance of the coastal fringe, even when sites are located well inland (Mulholland 1970). This is partly because, for a variety of reasons, early settlement is more likely to survive and be recognized on the Scottish coastlands. The lack of intensive development around the coast has led to the survival of many remains including highly visible midden deposits. Their location often coincides with that of the widespread machair systems, the formation of which can be particularly suitable for monument preservation. Sites also survive, of course, in other locations around the coast, and active coastal erosion is responsible for revealing many of these sites today. In addition, topographical conditions limit the availability of much of the Scottish mainland for settlement. Inland sites do exist, however, and lower lying inland areas would have had a rich potential throughout the Mesolithic period. Their accessibility is in many cases enhanced by the long sea lochs and glens which transect the Scottish landscape. Coastal resources were undoubtedly valuable but their general importance should not be exaggerated, particularly in view of the lack of fieldwork in many inland areas. It is salutary to note that recent work in the south west (Edwards, Ansell and Carter 1983) could increase to thirty-five the total of two inland sites previously recorded (Morrison 1982).

Few Mesolithic sites have been examined in detail in the last twenty years, with the result that little dating evidence is available. Oversimplified use of typological dating has been used to support the argument that many of the existing sites and surface collections must be late. Scotland, however, was available for settlement from early in the Postglacial period and a few sites have produced well-documented early dates (Coles 1971; Mercer 1980). It is becoming increasingly clear that human settlement in Scotland stretches back beyond what was previously accepted. On the west coast, work carried out on the island of Jura (Mercer 1980) has pushed back the earliest activity in an area already known to be rich in Mesolithic settlement. Further north, the project described here continues this process. In common with the rest of western Europe, Scotland offered a wealth of resources for exploitation throughout the Mesolithic period which was both rich and chronologically extended.

Excavations on the island of Rhum began as part of a project concerned with the exploitation of lithic

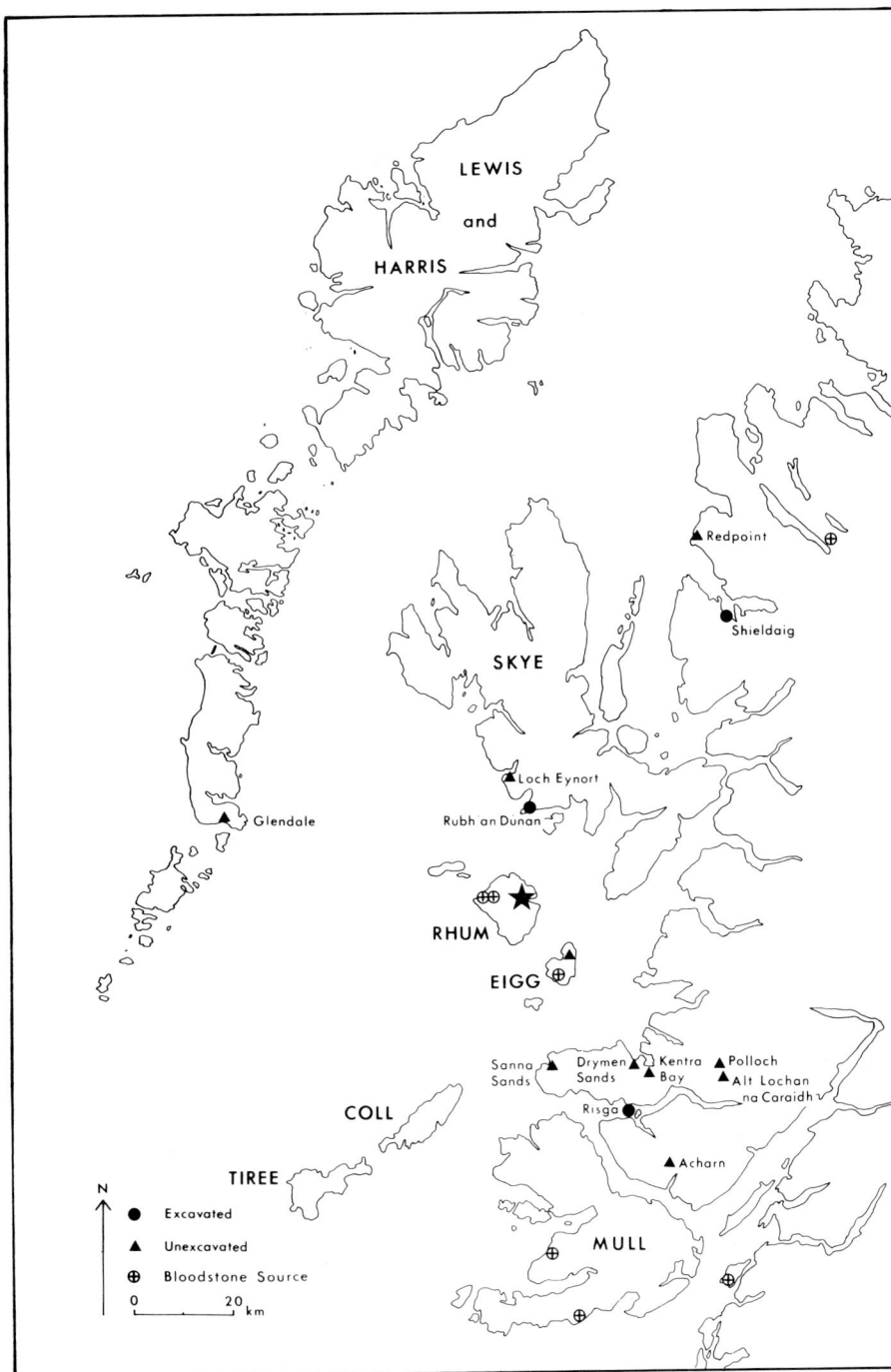

Figure 1   The geological sources of bloodstone and its archaeological occurrence on the west coast of Scotland.

resources in prehistoric Scotland. The project is at an early stage, but it is intended here to present some of the preliminary detail and discussion arising from the first year's work. Of particular interest in this case is the occurrence and use of a chalcedonic silica, Rhum bloodstone, the main source of which is found on the island. This material is formed by the crystallization of silica inside the cavities and fissures created by gas in cooling lava flows. Nodules vary greatly in size and also colour, from pale creams and greys to darker greens and purples. Geologically, a number of names apply, but for archaeological convenience these have been amalgamated here under the best known term, that of bloodstone.

Bloodstone is recorded from several sources on the west coast of Scotland, although the nature of its formation restricts these to isolated centres of Tertiary volcanic activity. Throughout prehistory it was used to supplement flint and other materials at a number of sites in the area (*Fig. 1*). Unfortunately, it is impossible to assess the archaeological importance of bloodstone at present as the paler nodules are indistinguishable from those of local flint (Wickham-Jones and Collins 1978). Both electron spin resonance (E.S.R.) spectroscopy and oxygen-isotope analysis are being considered in an attempt to differentiate between the two, as it is clearly important to recognize the true extent of the exploitation of bloodstone.

157

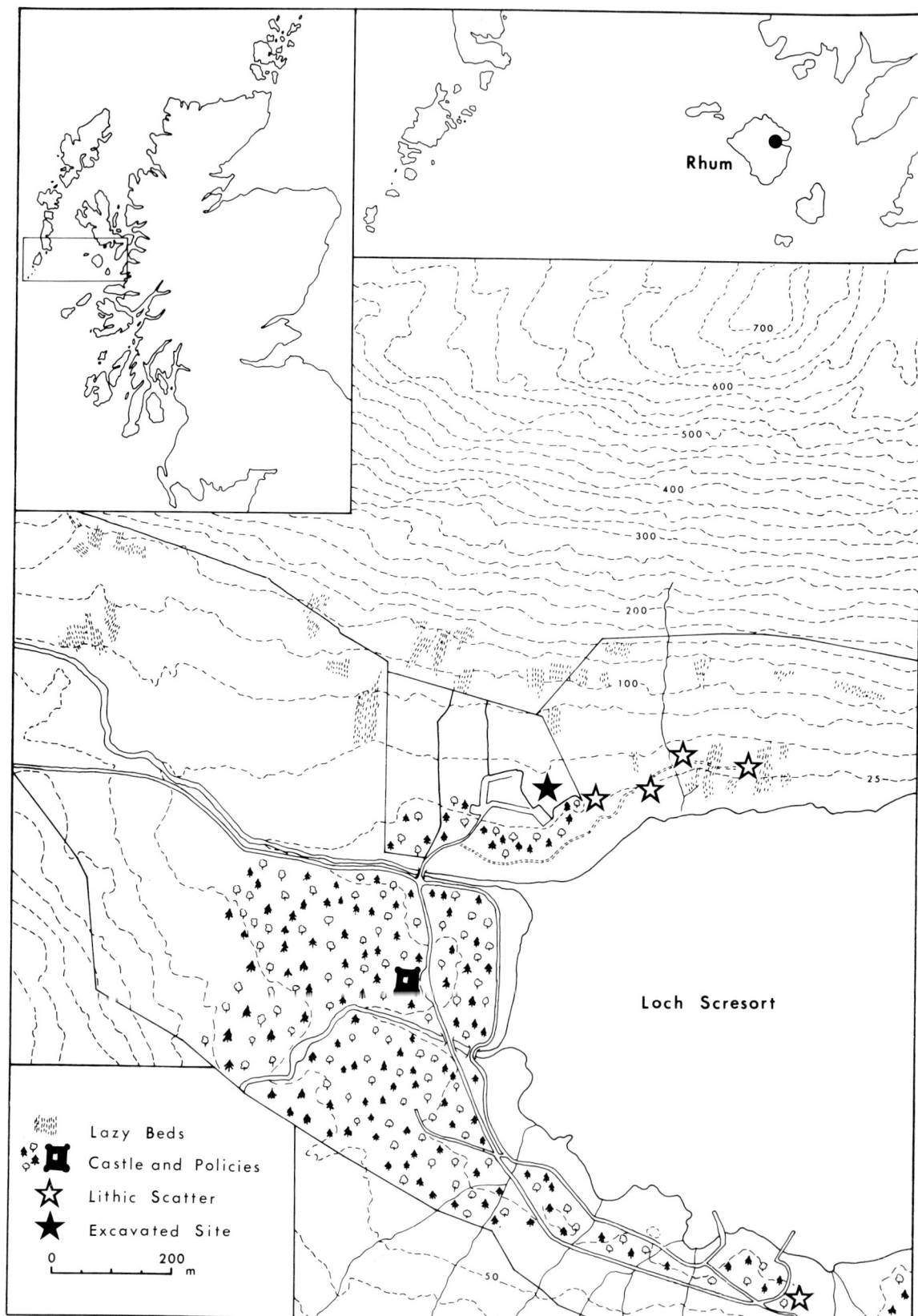

Figure 2 Farm Fields, Kinloch, Rhum: location of excavated site and nearby lithic scatters.

Prior to the excavation on Rhum, bloodstone had been recorded from other microlithic sites in the area and its use is documented over an extended period into the Early Bronze Age (Clarke, forthcoming). In spite of this, it has always been assumed that a single source, that on Rhum, was exploited through an exchange network (Ritchie 1968). A programme of E.S.R. analysis is now underway to test this theory.

Detailed work so far has concentrated on the island of Rhum, where exposure of a site by ploughing in

158

May 1983 offered the opportunity to examine a stratified assemblage at the centre of the supposed bloodstone distribution network. The island is now a National Nature Reserve. It lies off the west coast of Scotland, 25 km from the town of Mallaig. It is the largest island of the group of four known as the Small Isles. Further afield it is bounded on all sides by islands or mainland. To the north lies Skye, to the west the Outer Hebrides; the Inner Hebrides lie to the south, and there is mainland to the east and south east. Today, Rhum is mountainous and barren; the southern half of the island rises steeply to 812 m at the summit of Askival, only 2.5 km from the sea. The northern half has a gentler, though still rugged, topography. The island is transected by three broad glens, at the mouths of which lie isolated pockets of fertile land. Together with other small sheltered patches around the coast, these supported the only human settlement of the recent past.

The excavated site is situated in one of the larger of these pockets, that at Kinloch at the head of Loch Scresort on the east coast (*Fig. 2*). This is the only sheltered landfall on the island and is now the only permanently inhabited settlement. The site lies between 11–15 m O.D., occupying part of a field forming the eastern end of a band of cultivated land known as the Farm Fields. To the west, some 8 km from Kinloch lies Bloodstone Hill, the main source of bloodstone on the island (*Fig. 3*). Nodules erode in large numbers from its outcrops and are abundant today in the screes and beach gravels below. Although quarrying of the material did take place in the nineteenth century, it is likely that in prehistory there would have been sufficient material available in the scree and gravel deposits to make quarrying unnecessary. Examination of the beaches and tills elsewhere on the island suggests that little natural transportation away from the primary source has occurred.

The aims of the first season of excavation at Kinloch were to examine the distribution of material in the ploughsoil across the field, to quantify its contents and to assess the survival, if any, of stratified features. To this end a stratified random sample was constructed enabling examination of one percent of the

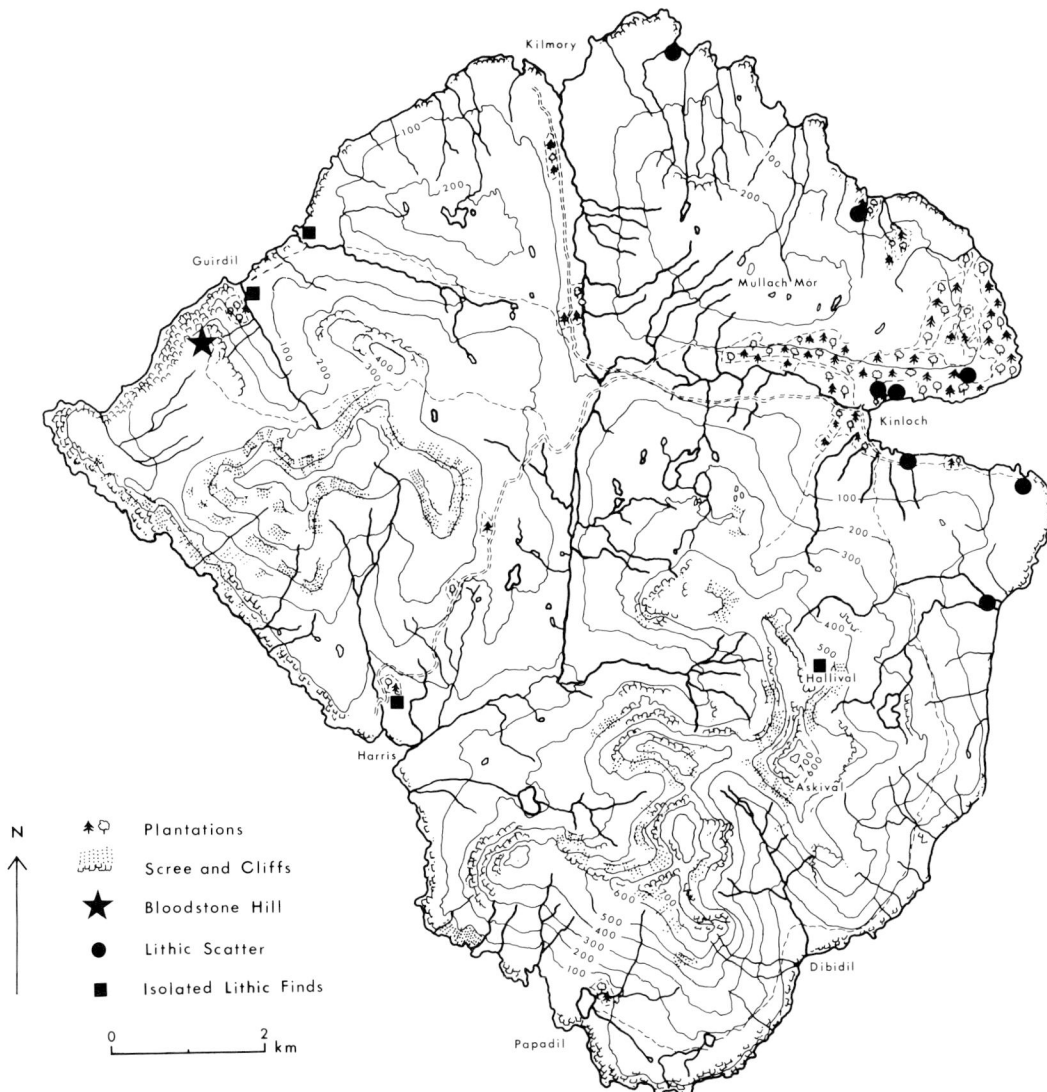

Figure 3 The island of Rhum: the location of the principal source of bloodstone (Bloodstone Hill) and lithic scatters.

159

field as a series of 38 four-metre square quadrats. All soil removed was sieved using both dry and wet techniques through meshes of minimum 3 mm dimension. Excavation of the sample revealed the detailed distribution of a microlithic scatter across the surface of the field (Wickham-Jones and Sharples 1984). The northern two-thirds of the area contained negligible quantities of lithic artifacts, but to the south the boundary of the scatter was clearly defined by an abrupt rise in the artifact density. Its northern margin lay along the upper edge of a natural hollow which opens to the south east onto Loch Scresort. Within this hollow the artifact concentration reached nearly 2000 per square metre. To the south and east the edge of the scatter was not located and surface finds outside the field indicate that it lies outwith the field boundary. A minimum area for the site would be of the order of 4500 m².

The excavation uncovered a number of features surviving across the field. Damage from ploughing proved to be remarkably shallow, owing mainly to the use of ponies for agricultural purposes until recently. Five of the sample squares within the lithic scatter contained potentially early prehistoric features and two of these were subjected to more detailed examination. An attempt was made to identify prehistoric features outside the scatter but this has so far proved unsuccessful, and it seems that the area of Mesolithic activity is largely represented by the scatter of lithic debris. Within this scatter it is clear that concentrations of material in the topsoil do not necessarily correspond with subsoil features.

Those features so far exposed comprise large hollows, small pits and isolated postholes. Present evidence suggests that they occur unevenly across the site. The two large hollows occur towards the northern edge of the scatter, on the north-west side. One was partially excavated and proved to have a complex stratigraphy containing artifact-rich, loamy fills sometimes mixed with charcoal. In the top of this lay one of the excavated small pits. Amongst other things, it contained a quantity of carbonized hazelnut shells, samples of which have produced two radiocarbon determinations of 8590±95 BP (GU–1873) and 8515±150 BP (GU–1874). The other small pit lay nearer the centre of the topsoil scatter close to an isolated stake-hole. It contained some charcoal, including burnt hazel-nut shells, together with a few lithics. As the trenches were particularly small, it is hoped that further excavation might reveal a coherent distribution of similar features.

A large assemblage of artifacts was recovered from the sample quadrats and this was examined in the field to produce a basic typological catalogue. The bulk of finds consist of flaked lithics with a few worked stones. In addition to bloodstone and the possibility of some flint, small quantities of worked agate and quartz, both locally readily available, were

Table 1: The approximate composition of the assemblage from the sample excavation, after preliminary analysis

Cores	1%
Blades	1%
Regular Flakes	7%
Non-Microlithic Retouched Pieces	1%
Microliths	2%
Débitage Flakes	69%
Chunks	19%

included. Most of this assemblage is knapping debris formed of chunks and débitage flakes with little primary waste (Table 1). The rest is composed largely of flakes, many of which are very regular, and there are a number of blades. Some conjoining flakes, blades and cores have been noted (Fig. 4, no. 10) but as this is material recovered from ploughsoil, no concerted effort has been made to locate such pieces. In addition to controlled platform work there is much evidence of bipolar knapping and both scalar and platform cores are present (Fig. 5, nos. 1–6). Retouched pieces comprise about three percent of the assemblage; of these two percent is made up of microliths. The larger retouched pieces consist mainly of scrapers and edge-retouched flakes (Fig. 6, nos. 1–8), but there are six pieces with bifacial invasive retouch (Fig. 6, nos. 9–14). The microliths consist principally of rods, backed bladelets and crescents, together with some fine points and scalene triangles, as well as microburins (Fig. 6, nos. 16–30).

The lithic assemblages from the features have yet to be studied, but preliminary analysis suggests a general similarity with that from the topsoil although there are one or two interesting differences. At the centre of the scatter, excavation of an isolated stake-hole and shallow pit produced only a few lithics including a small blade core, blades and a scalene microlith. Towards the periphery, the hollow contained a large quantity of lithics whilst the pit from which the radiocarbon sample came was filled with rounded, elongated pebbles, many of which are damaged by use (Fig. 4, nos. 1–3, 5–7). It also contained a great amount of flaked lithic material, over 1000 pieces, much of which is heavily burnt. The assemblage consists principally of débitage, but it includes a small leaf-shaped point (Fig. 6, no. 15) together with a few microliths, blades and flakes. Neither platform nor scalar cores were recovered from this pit. The hollow containing the pit produced a few platform cores but so far no scalar cores have been recognized from this complex.

As defined by the lithic scatter, the site at Kinloch is particularly large. Preliminary analysis suggests the presence of various stratified features with differing artifactual content. Recent analysis of variability in

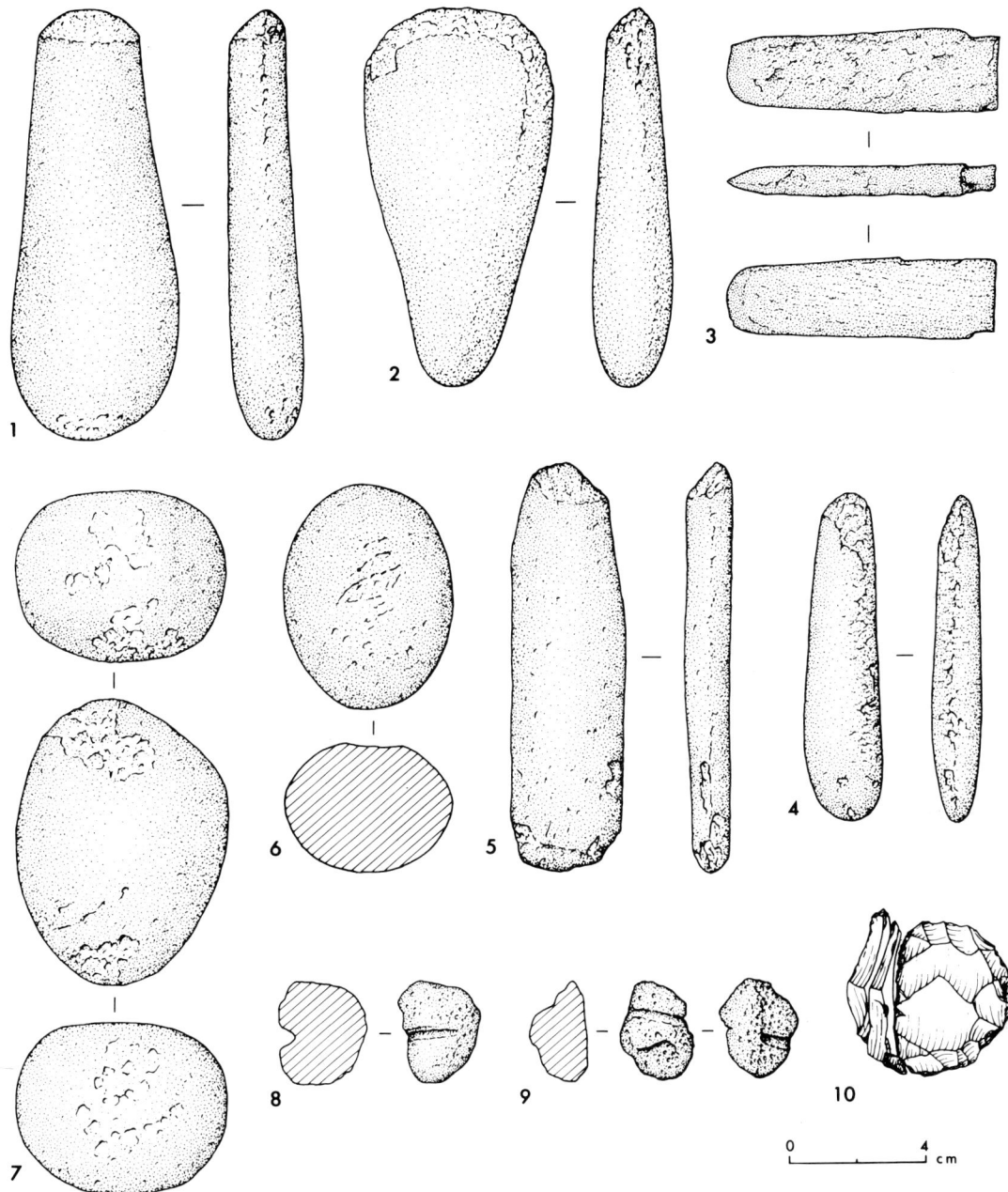

Figure 4 Farm Fields, Kinloch, Rhum: lithic artifacts – worked stone (1–7); worked pumice (8–9); conjoining blades and core (10).

site size and content during the Mesolithic has produced a number of explanations (Mellars 1976), but there is clearly much work to be done before any such interpretation could be made at Kinloch. However, the site offers great potential for an examination of both functional and chronological variation in human activity.

Additional fieldwork elsewhere on the island (*Fig. 3*) increased the number of lithic scatters previously recorded (R.C.A.H.M.S. 1983). No excavation has taken place on any of these sites, few of which have yielded any diagnostic artifacts. In most cases the number of pieces recovered is very small. In every case bloodstone was utilized, although analysis of the presence of flint must await a satisfactory method of identification. Most of these sites are concentrated

on the east coast of the island in sharp contrast to the presence of the bloodstone source in the west. The explanation for this distribution may lie in the climatic and topographical conditions of the island as this is the most sheltered area, but it is more likely that the effect of these conditions upon current human activity on the island is reflected. The majority of these sites have been recovered during agricultural or forestry work which is in general restricted to the less exposed eastern areas.

The excavations at Kinloch have produced evidence for Mesolithic activity which is at present the earliest known in Scotland. Microliths from the site are paralleled amongst the 'narrow blade' industries which define the later Mesolithic of the British Isles (Morrison 1980). The date and inception of these

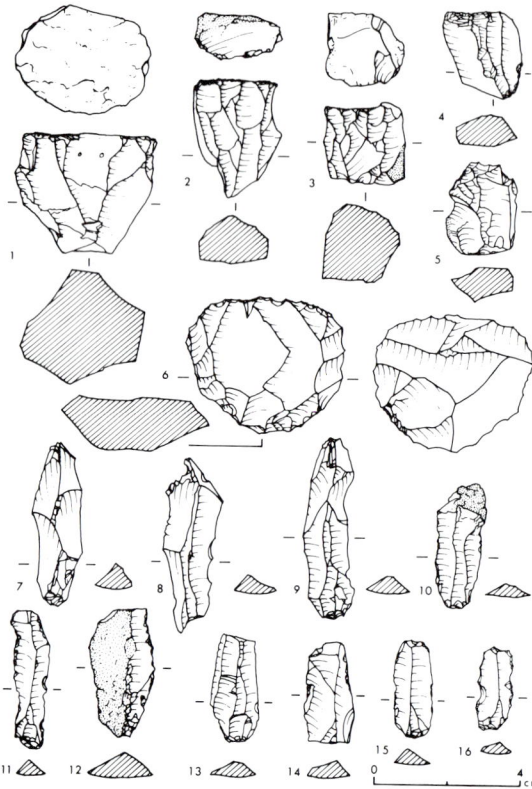

Figure 5   Farm Fields, Kinloch, Rhum: lithic artifacts – cores (1–6); blades (7–16); *n.b.* nos. 6–8 join together (cf. *Fig. 4*, no. 10).

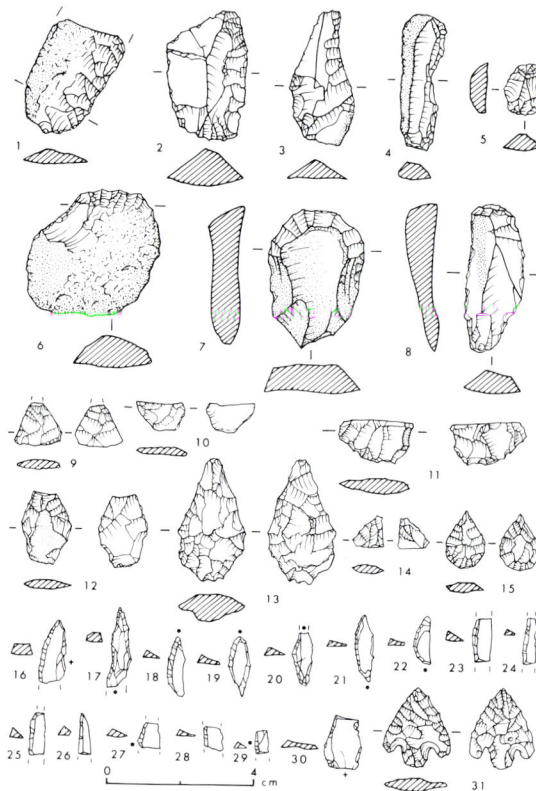

Figure 6   Farm Fields, Kinloch, Rhum: lithic artifacts – edge retouched pieces (1–4); scrapers (5–8); leaf-shaped points (9–15); microliths (16–29); microburin (30); barbed and tanged point (31); *n.b.* no. 31 was recovered from the surface of the field, to the north of the site.

industries remains open to question but several sites dating back to the ninth millennium BP are known. These sites are concentrated in the north of England but recent work in the north of Ireland at Mount Sandel (Woodman 1978) and on the island of Jura (Mercer 1980) demonstrates that the apparent lack of evidence for early sites in the north and west of the British Isles is due mainly to the lack of fieldwork. The area is large and many different environments, raw materials and site types have led to a great range of assemblage variation. By the late ninth millennium BP it is clear that local industries were established and developing with some differentiation, although a common pool of artifact types is still observable. Environmental analysis in Scotland has shown a rapid improvement in climate early on in the Postglacial period. Price (1982) discusses the rapid colonization of forests associated with a rich mammalian fauna. The islands and mainland of the west coast of Scotland offered many valuable resources including both food and raw materials, and in addition they form an inter-visible chain which would greatly facilitate movement into the area particularly by those accustomed to a peripatetic lifestyle. Changing sea levels during the early Postglacial period would only have had a minimal effect on the land mass available for settlement in the area and did little to alter the distances involved. Expansion along the west coast of Scotland would have taken place naturally and rapidly as conditions improved in the period immediately after the end of the Loch Lomond Stadial.

Acknowledgements: Many people have contributed to this work. I should like to thank the Scottish Development Department who fund the excavation and the Nature Conservancy Council, the Royal Museum of Scotland, and the Royal Commission on the Ancient and Historical Monuments of Scotland without whose assistance the project would not be taking place. Many specialists are involved; here, I should like to thank in particular Dr G. Durant and Mr P.R. Ritchie for work upon the bloodstone, and Mr D. Griffiths who is undertaking E.S.R. analysis. Acknowledgement is due to Marion O'Neil who prepared the plates, often at very short notice, and to Ian Larner and Doreen Moyes who printed them. Finally, a great debt is owed to Ann Clarke who has allowed the author to use her own research in advance of publication and who, together with Niall Sharples and Andy Barlow, has provided much stimulus in discussions of this paper. The ideas are the products of many; faults must rest with the author alone.

References

CLARKE, P.A. (forthcoming) *Bloodstone as a raw material in prehistoric Scotland* (paper).

COLES, J.M. (1971) The early settlement of Scotland: excavations at Morton, Fife. *Proceedings of the Prehistoric Society*, 37: 284–366.

EDWARDS, K.J., ANSELL, M. and CARTER, B. (1983) New Mesolithic sites in south-west Scotland and their importance as indicators of inland penetration. *Transactions of the Dumfriesshire and Galloway Natural History and Antiquarian Society*, 8: 9–15.

LACAILLE, A.D. (1954) *The Stone Age in Scotland*. Oxford, University Press.

MERCER, J. (1980) Lussa Wood I: the late-glacial and early postglacial occupation of Jura. *Proceedings of the Society of Antiquaries of Scotland*, 110 (1978–80): 1–32.

MELLARS, P.A. (1976) Settlement patterns and industrial variability in the British Mesolithic. In G. de G. Sieveking, I.H. Longworth and K.E. Wilson (eds) *Problems in Economic and Social Archaeology*. London, Duckworth: 375–399.

MORRISON, A. (1980) *Early Man in Britain and Ireland*. London, Croom Helm.

MORRISON, A. (1982) The Mesolithic period in south-west Scotland: a review of the evidence. *Glasgow Archaeological Journal*, 9: 1–14.

MULHOLLAND, H. (1970) The microlithic industries of the Tweed valley. *Transactions of the Dumfriesshire and Galloway Natural History and Antiquarian Society*, 47: 81–110.

PRICE, R.J. (1982) The magnitude and frequency of late Quaternary environmental changes in Scotland: implications for human occupation. *Scottish Archaeological Review*, 1(2): 61–72.

R.C.A.H.M.S. (1983) *Rhum, Lochaber District; Highland Region*. The Archaeological Sites and Monuments of Scotland, 20. Edinburgh, Royal Commission on the Ancient and Historical Monuments of Scotland.

RITCHIE, A. (1985) The first settlers. In C. Renfrew (ed.), *The Prehistory of Orkney*. Edinburgh, University Press: 36–53.

RITCHIE, P.R. (1968) The stone implement trade in third millennium Scotland. In J.M. Coles and D.D.A. Simpson (eds), *Studies in Ancient Europe*. Leicester, University Press: 117–136.

WICKHAM-JONES, C.R. and COLLINS, G.H. (1978) The sources of flint and chert in northern Britain. *Proceedings of the Society of Antiquaries of Scotland*, 109 (1977–78): 7–21.

WICKHAM-JONES, C.R. and SHARPLES, N. (1984) *Interim Report on the Excavations at Farm Fields, Kinloch, Rhum 1984*. Edinburgh, National Museum of Antiquities of Scotland (Artifact Research Unit).

WOODMAN, P.C. (1978) *The Mesolithic in Ireland*. Oxford, British Archaeological Reports (British Series) 58.

The Late Upper Palaeolithic and Mesolithic of the Northern Pennine Dales in the Light of Recent Fieldwork

D. Coggins, T. Laurie and R. Young

Abstract

This paper is an interim statement of the findings of three fieldworkers active in the north east of England, an area little known in British early prehistoric studies. Lithic evidence for possible late Upper Palaeolithic and early Mesolithic activity in Teesdale is presented, as is the whole range of data relating to the later Mesolithic of Weardale, Teesdale and Swaledale. The paper concludes with a brief outline of areas for future research in what is a continuing and developing project.

INTRODUCTION

In any discussion of the early prehistory of northern Britain, the northern Pennine valleys of Swaledale, Teesdale and Weardale tend to be largely neglected or mentioned only in passing. It is the aim of this paper to try to rectify this situation in a small way by bringing to a wider notice the results obtained so far from a continuing, detailed programme of field and museum research which is being carried out in the region by the authors.

R. Young has concentrated his research along the full length of the Wear valley, dealing with the whole of its prehistory (though here only sites from Weardale are discussed), while D. Coggins has worked mainly in Teesdale, with T. Laurie being active in Teesdale and Swaledale. To date, over 60 sites with Mesolithic associations have been recorded in the upland sections of these river valleys (*Fig. 1*). All of these are surface scatters with the exception of the Middle Hurth and Briar Dykes sites in Teesdale. New sites are occurring with regularity and we welcome this opportunity to present an interim statement of the results, especially as one of the sites discussed below holds out the possibility of discovering more information about late Upper Palaeolithic activity in the area.

The three dales under study lie within the Carboniferous Limestone series rocks of the Pennines, which give rise to a variety of landscape forms and valley cross-sections (Raistrick 1972), ranging from the markedly steep-sided valleys of Weardale and Swaledale to the broad undulating landscape of Teesdale which is 16 km wide at Barnard Castle on the 305 m contour. A recurrent feature in all the areas is the prominent system of stepping or terracing visible on the valley sides, produced by rock outcrops and well-formed, gravel, river terraces often used today for arable agriculture. Many of the sites recorded are located on these river terraces and the remainder come from upland locations, usually above 305 m O.D., in areas of eroding peat cover where the old land surface is exposed. Each of these areas presents its own problems in terms of recovering material and discovering new sites, and these will be mentioned again below. It is now proposed to give a brief account of previous work in the area and then move on to a discussion of some of the sites in each dale which the authors have examined in detail.

PREVIOUS WORK IN THE STUDY AREA

In terms of the late Upper Palaeolithic period no definite evidence has been recorded previously from the area. Manby (1966) has reviewed the available late Upper Palaeolithic material from the north, but the best general synthesis in terms of the distribution of finds is still that by Campbell (1977). This work shows that on the eastern side of the country the distribution of known sites stops in North Yorkshire at Flixton and Washburn Foot, while in the Pennines and on the western side of England the northernmost sites are the Kirkhead Cave in north Lancashire and the Victoria, Jubilee and Kinsey caves in West Yorkshire (Campbell 1977: maps 40 & 41). Neither Campbell nor Manby considers why this should be so and, given that in the Lateglacial and early Postglacial periods, climatic and vegetational conditions were not markedly different in the uplands (cf. Chambers 1974), this lacuna in evidence from the north is difficult to explain. It may be, as Jacobi (1976) has suggested for Lateglacial open-air sites on the Allerød soils of southern England, that Upper Palaeolithic sites do exist in the area but have been covered by solifluxion debris moving downslope and spreading out from the valley sides. In this context the site at Towler Hill in Teesdale, discussed below, may take on additional significance.

A similar gloom pervades our understanding of the earlier Mesolithic period in the study area and Jacobi's recent synthesis again serves to show the lack of early data from the northern dales. He notes

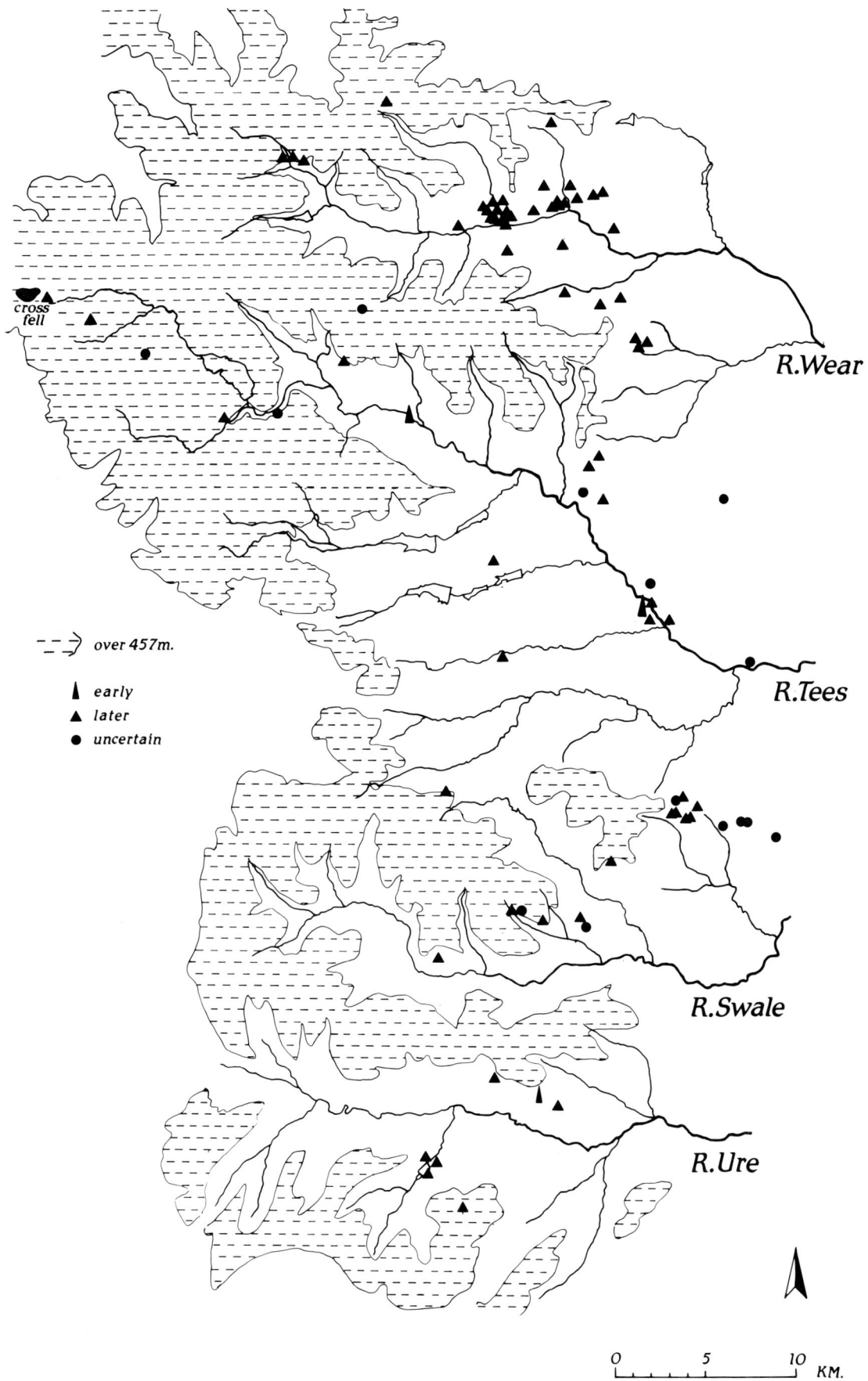

Figure 1 Mesolithic sites in the northern Pennine dales.

over 457m.

early

later

uncertain

cross fell

R.Wear

R.Tees

R.Swale

R.Ure

0   5   10
KM.

some 33 early sites on the North Yorkshire Moors and 116 sites in the Pennines, but none of the latter occur in the area under study (Jacobi 1978). It is only really with regard to sites of the later Mesolithic period that previous work in the area has made any real contribution to our knowledge. Most of the published research relates to Weardale and Teesdale.

As early as the 1870s Howchin recorded material from Wellhope and Killhope fells at the head of Weardale (Howchin 1880) and throughout the late 1880s and into the earlier part of the twentieth century lithic material was recovered by Egglestone, especially from Redburn Common in Weardale where the fumes from the smelting chimney of the Rookhope lead works had killed off the vegetation and allowed soil erosion to take place (Egglestone 1910; 1911a; 1911b).

In 1912 C.T. Trechmann, who is probably better known as a geologist/geomorphologist and for his work on the submerged forest at Hartlepool which has produced earlier Mesolithic material, turned his attention to the upland areas of Weardale and Teesdale, collecting material again from Rookhope and discovering a new site at Blackton in Teesdale. For the first time, Trechmann tried to provide a discussion of the chronology of the upland and lowland sites which he recorded, concluding that while the material may or may not be contemporary, 'there was no intercourse or exchange of materials between the two areas'. He suggested that the implements in the dales and on the fell tops had found their way there in a finished state from the south, while he thought that the coastal implements had been made *in situ* from flint nodules dug out of the boulder clay and found on the sea shore (Trechmann 1912).

It was not until the late 1920s to early 1930s and the work of Bennett-Gibbs, Cooke and Temperley that further Mesolithic material from Wager Head and Whitfield Brow in Weardale was published (Bennett-Gibbs and Temperley 1931), although throughout the 1930s and into the 1940s the site at Blackton in Teesdale was collected from by local antiquarians such as MacIntyre and Preston.

In the period 1933 to 1938 much general interest was shown in the few Mesolithic sites recorded from Weardale and Teesdale, with Raistrick's *Distribution of Mesolithic Sites in the North of England* (1933) and Raistrick and Bennett-Gibbs' *Prehistoric Invasions of Northumberland and Durham* (1934) providing the first real attempt at synthesizing the known material and setting it into a regional context. In his 1933 paper Raistrick discussed several new sites from the Yorkshire and Durham Pennines and the coastal area of Durham and Northumberland, and went on to summarize the distribution of such sites over the whole of the north of England. He followed Buckley's (1925) suggestion that the coastal material could be split into two discrete groups: (a) 'early Tardenoi-

sian with Belgian affinities'; and (b) later developed types, 'genetically connected with the earlier material and not representing a second phase of contact with the continent'. Raistrick also argued that the 'narrow blade' types of the Pennines were not distinguished on the coast, and he put forward the idea that coastal and inland sites were the direct result of connections across the North Sea between northern England and Belgium in the form of folk movement from the continent. He also noted the frequent occurrence of 'developed Tardenoisian' material with 'Neolithic' flint, first recorded by Trechmann in 1905 (Trechmann 1912), and postulated a 'telescoping' of cultural development in the north to account for this. This position, which was expanded upon by Raistrick and Bennett-Gibbs in 1934, remained seemingly unchallenged until 1970 (Harding 1970: 191)!

The most important year for the study of Mesolithic material from Weardale was 1945, as it saw the private publication of the first of Edward Hildyard's pamphlets on *The Archaeology of Weardale*. These appeared annually until 1957 and provided a regular record of new finds in the area. Hildyard was a major landowner in Weardale and turned his attention to the archaeology of the area after the Second World War finding the region, 'comparatively neglected in this as in all else' (Fell and Hildyard 1953: 99). As a result, his first concern was 'to try and examine and if possible to collect, any past finds that could still be traced to individual hands and to secure them for posterity'. This he did with some success.

He was an active fieldworker in the region, locating some 36 lithic scatters of Mesolithic, Neolithic and Bronze Age date before he left the area for Yorkshire in 1957. These were discussed in two papers by Fell and Hildyard (1953, 1956). This was the state of published knowledge about the Mesolithic of Weardale before R. Young began his research on the prehistoric archaeology of the Wear valley in 1975 (Young 1984).

In the early 1960s and 1970s research of direct relevance to the Mesolithic of Teesdale was carried out by a number of workers. 1963 saw the publication of Johnson and Dunham's survey of the geology of the Moor House Nature Reserve at the top of the dale (Johnson and Dunham 1963). During this work, at the site of Hard Hill at a height of 686 m O.D., they located Mesolithic flint artifacts in association with the fragmentary remains of two horn cores of *Bos* in cotton grass peat at a level dated palynologically towards the end of Godwin's Zone VIIa. Other *Bos* horn finds (cores and sheaths) from Teesdale and Weardale have been discussed by two of us in detail elsewhere (Coggins 1984; Young 1984, 1987). No radiocarbon date was obtained for the Hard Hill site. However, Chambers did obtain dates for a pollen sequence from Valley Bog at the head of Teesdale where, in a local pollen zone which is likely to represent the latter part of Godwin's Zone VIIa in the area, a temporary but significant increase in hazel pollen, accompanied by a relative decline in elm and oak together with an increase in bracken and several herbs, was noted. Two radiocarbon dates of 5960±60 BP (SRR–92) and 5945±50 BP (SRR–93) have been obtained for this episode, which it is thought is likely to represent Mesolithic interference with the vegetation cover (Chambers 1974). A similar sequence was also documented by Chambers at Wheelhead Moss a few miles west of Valley Bog, just below an horizon dated to 5770±110 BP; and Squires has studied two sites, Fox Earth Gill and Dufton Moss, where the picture is similar with the episodes immediately predating levels dated to *c*. 5404 BP and *c*. 5697 BP, respectively (Squires 1970).

It is against this historical background that the present field and museum work has taken place.

CURRENT RESEARCH
Weardale

In the course of R. Young's doctoral research on the prehistoric archaeology of the Wear valley, lithic material has been recorded from 196 locations throughout the area of which 83 have produced later Mesolithic forms. Of these 83 sites, 40 are in the area of the present survey, ranging in altitudinal location from 200 to 569 m O.D. covering the river terraces, lower valley slopes and upland fell areas. The greatest concentration comes from the river terraces between the villages of Stanhope and Eastgate. The distribution pattern is probably a reflection of recent and historical activities rather than the true distribution of Mesolithic activity in the area. The factors influencing the distribution have been discussed in detail elsewhere (Young 1984: 28–35), but it is worth noting that the maximum spread of sites up the dale corresponds with the maximum extent of ploughing on the terraces and lower slopes. Obviously, there may be many more sites to be found on the river terraces towards the head of the dale, but if land is not ploughed then flint and other material cannot be recovered. A similar point could be made about sites around and above 305 m O.D. In these locations considerable peat deposits cover the landscape and the highland distribution can be shown to correspond very closely to areas of peat erosion.

The commonest raw material from all the Weardale sites is grey, mottled flint which may be of Yorkshire Wolds origin (Young 1985). This regularly constitutes 60–100% of the raw material present, while chert, which could have been obtained from the local Carboniferous rock, is relatively under-used, comprising only 2–4% of the raw materials recorded. The one exception to this situation occurs at Greenhead Plantation where chert makes up some 27% of the exploited raw material. Chert does, however, show an increase on sites of probable Neolithic and Bronze Age date in the area.

Table 1: Categories of lithic material from selected Mesolithic sites in Weardale *(prepared by R. Young)*

Site Name	National Grid Reference	Altitude (metres O.D.)	Cores	Scrapers	Arrowheads	Microliths	Denticulated blades	Burins	Piercers	Notched flakes	Microburins	Unworked pebbles	Retouched flakes/blades	Hammerstones	Waste material	Retouched knives	Tanged implements
Bell's Quarry	NY 851 472	503	5	8	–	7	3	–	2	1	1	1	16	1	60	–	–
Billing Shield	NY 950 380	300	9	2	–	–	6	1	–	2	–	–	27	2	180	2	–
Cambokeels	NY 932 382	250	1	3	–	1	–	–	–	–	–	–	2	–	9	–	–
Cragside	NY 95 38	–	–	–	–	1	1	–	1	1	1	–	8	–	35	–	1
Eastfield, Eastgate	NY 962 388	330	3	1	1	1	1	1	1	1	1	1	1	1	1	–	–
Eastgate House	NY 955 387	300	3	5	–	–	–	–	–	–	–	–	3	1	32	–	–
Howel John, East Field	NY 968 388	236	2	1	–	1	–	–	–	–	1	–	–	–	27	–	–
Howel John, West Field	NY 964 388	236	31	16	2	6	3	–	2	10	1	–	37	–	420	–	–
Evenwood	NZ 155 250	160	1	3	4	1	5	–	–	3	–	–	14	–	3	3	–
Flinty Field	NY 955 385	300	1	2	1	3	1	–	1	–	–	–	16	1	10	–	–
Greenhead Plantation	NY 979 395	260	4	–	1	1	–	–	2	–	–	–	–	–	20	–	–
Police Field	NY 954 386	228	53	5	1	9	2	1	5	6	4	3	100	–	830	–	–
Rookhope, Redburn Common	NY 906 444	236	2	?	7	?	?	?	?	?	?	?	10	?	29	1	?
Whitfield Brow	NZ 006 344	335	?	3	1	?	9	?	?	?	?	?	5	?	12	?	?
Wager Head	NZ 013 337	420	6	3	–	8	–	–	–	–	–	–	180	–	?	–	–
Wellhope Fell	NY 835 416	475	–	3	–	1	4	1	1	1	–	–	21	1	114	–	–
Northgate	NY 935 401	384	1	–	–	2	–	–	–	–	–	–	9	–	12	–	–
Quarry Hill	NY 990 378	325	2	1	–	–	1	–	–	1	1	1	15	–	54	–	–

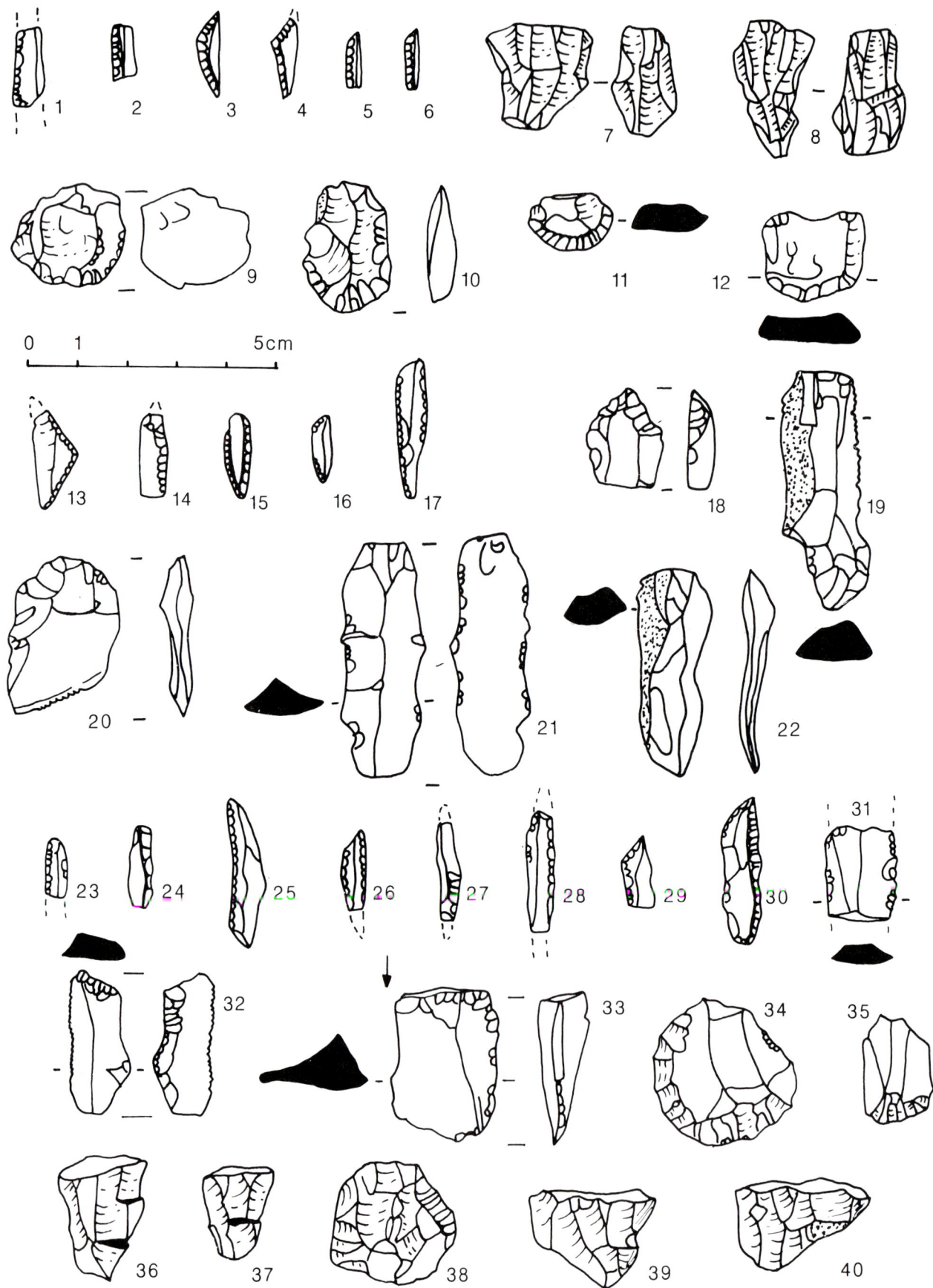

Figure 2 Lithic material from Weardale. Howel John, West Field: microliths (1–6), cores (7–8), scrapers (9–12); Bell's Quarry: microliths (13–17), piercer (18), serrated blades/flakes (19–20), utilized flakes and blades (21–22); Police Field: microliths (23–30), serrated blades/flakes (31–32), burin (33), scrapers (34–35), cores (36–40).

Table 1 gives a typological breakdown of the finds from selected sites in Weardale. As will be seen from this table, some of the sites show a mixture of Mesolithic and later forms. In all cases, these typologically later artifacts are arrowheads of leaf-shaped or barbed and tanged form, and while it could be argued that these are coincidental associations or that the assemblages represent material from more than one period, mixed by ploughing, etc., it may be that these few sites represent evidence for the latest Mesolithic activity in the area, at a time when hunters and gatherers may have been coming into contact with developing agricultural communities spreading up the dale. The sites may well be a manifestation of contact on Alexander's 'moving frontier' which he suggests may have existed between incoming colonists and indigenous groups (Alexander 1980). Here, though, is not the place to rehearse in full the arguments behind this suggestion. Statistical work on the 'mixed' and 'Mesolithic' assemblages, using discriminant function analytical techniques is underway and it is hoped that this will resolve some of the problems of interpreting these sites (Young, in preparation). In terms of artifact forms represented in *Table 1*, the commonest microlith types are edge-blunted, micro-scalene triangle and rod forms of the sort which are common in the northern and southern Pennines and the North Yorkshire Moors. Other forms present, which are common in these northern areas, are denticulated blades serrated on one or both edges, burins, usually on large flakes, piercers, and miscellaneous retouched pieces (*Fig. 2*).

The scraper and core forms are worthy of further comment. The commonest scraper types are simple end-of-flake examples making up approximately 60% of the total scraper numbers recorded so far. These are invariably on short, squat flakes ranging from 15–25 mm in length and 15–25 mm in breadth, and being usually less than 10 mm thick. Comparison with later scraper forms in the area shows a tendency for the tools to become longer, broader and thinner through time (Young 1984: 108). Differences can also be observed in other aspects of the metrical data. Angles of retouch on Mesolithic scrapers in the dale range from 20–86° ($\bar{x}$ = 64°) while angles of retouch on Neolithic and Bronze Age artifacts range from 52–92° ($\bar{x}$ = 73°). These dimensional changes may be of interest in terms of the functional interpretation of the implements. For example, Wilmsen (1970) has suggested that the edge angles can be grouped into three broad functional categories: 26–35°, having a simple cutting function; 46–55°, used for skinning, hide preparation, sinew and plant fibre shredding, heavy cutting of wood, bone or horn, and tool back blunting; 65–75°, for wood-working, bone-working, heavy shredding and skin-softening. In addition, Thomas (1971) has suggested that the very sharpest edges, those less than 20°, would have been used for whittling wood.

Viewed in this light, the angles of retouch on the Weardale Mesolithic scrapers may suggest that, while some were used as simple, sharp, cutting implements, the majority (those over 40°) were used for a wide range of domestic tasks. Comparison with the Neolithic and Bronze Age sample from the area may indicate a shift in emphasis through time away from skinning and hide-scraping to heavier tasks such as wood- and bone-working, heavy shredding of vegetable foods and skin-softening.

Turning to the core sample recovered from the Mesolithic sites in the dale, over 50% are of Clark's *Class Aii* (one platform, flakes removed part of the way round – Clark, Higgs and Longworth 1960: 216), though a wide variety of core types, with many showing multi-directional flaking, has been noted. Comparison of this sample with the Neolithic and Bronze Age cores from the area emphasizes the wide range of core types from the Mesolithic sites. In the later assemblages only four discrete core forms are visible: 47% of the sample is made up of *Class Ai* cores (one platform, flakes removed all round); 38% are of Clark's *Class C* (possessing three or more platforms); and the remainder are variants of the *Class B* (two platform) type. Further points emerge when data on core size from the area are studied. Over 50% of all Mesolithic cores from the dale are less than 25 mm in length with over 70% being less than 25 mm in breadth, indicating that cores tend to be short and squat, and arguably fully worked out when discarded. In terms of weight, only *c.* 35% of all Mesolithic cores in the dale are greater than 10 g, with the average weight being 9.9 g. Comparison with the Neolithic and Bronze Age sample shows that 54% of the cores in these assemblages are greater than 10 g when discarded, with an average weight of 11.92 g. Thus, as with the scrapers, there is a tendency for the later cores to be larger than the Mesolithic examples when discarded.

When the Mesolithic sample from the dale is compared to cores from coastal/lowland sites such as Blackhall Rocks, Filpoke Beacon and Crimdon Dene, over 90% of the latter sample are over 10 g in weight when discarded, with an average weight of 19.4 g being recorded.

The massiveness of the coastal/lowland cores from the north east may reflect the readier access that these sites might have had to sources of raw materials in the boulder clay deposits of the coast. In the dale, where flint is not locally available, we may be seeing the maximization of the use of available raw material. Flint would have had to be brought into the area and this may have been done in the course of the seasonal hunting/gathering round. The tendency for cores on Neolithic and Bronze Age sites to be larger when discarded may reflect several things, such as an in-

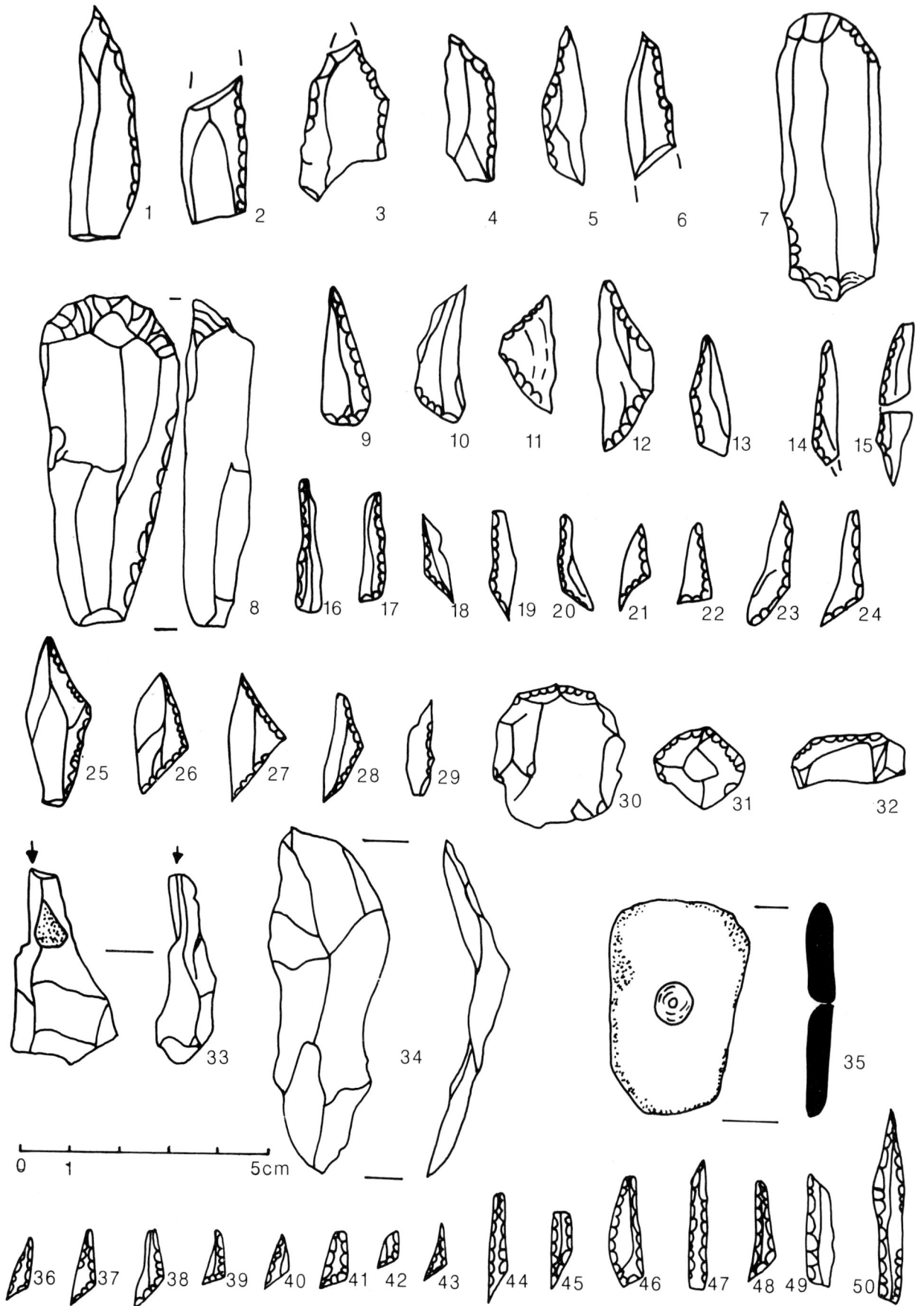

Figure 3 Lithic material from Teesdale. Towler Hill: steeply retouched points (1–6), scrapers (7–8), microliths (9–24); Staple Crag: microliths (25–29), scrapers (30–32), burin (33), blade (34), perforated shale ?bead (35); Barningham High Moor: microliths (36–50).

crease in available supplies of raw material (it is in this period that chert is used on a large scale for the first time). This would obviate the need to conserve and maximize the flint resources and it may also be indicative of a change in flint-working technology. This latter point may be supported by the restricted range of core types recorded from later sites. The wider variation in core form in the Mesolithic sample may well attest to the ingenuity of Mesolithic groups in extracting as many useful blades and flakes as possible from the available raw material, though why locally available chert was not more widely used is still a problem.

Teesdale

In Teesdale, D. Coggins has examined the sites of Blackton Smelt Mill, Briar Dykes, Middle Hurth Edge, Staple Crag, Merrygill Holm and Ravock Mire in detail, while T. Laurie has recovered material from the site at Towler Hill within the dale and and at five locations on Barningham High Moor in the interfluve area between Teesdale and Swaledale (Laurie 1984). The upper limit of arable land is 150 m O.D. in Teesdale, and the prevalence of permanent pasture is a restriction on the location of flint scatters by fieldwork.

The Towler Hill, Staple Crag and Merrygill Holm sites are located on the terraces of the Tees at 150 m, 259 m and 400 m O.D., respectively. The scatter of lithic material at Towler Hill was revealed in the course of ploughing, while the other two sites were discovered as a result of riverine erosion. The finds from Middle Hurth (457 m) and Briar Dykes (320 m) were recovered in the course of the excavation of overlying, later archaeological sites, while the remainder are located between 396 m and 457 m O.D. on erosion patches in the peat cover of the moorlands. The five sites on Barningham High Moor all occur between 420 m and 450 m O.D. The analytical work on this material is not as advanced as for the Weardale sites, but it is felt by the writers that the sites at Towler Hill and Staple Crag will prove of immense importance for an understanding of the early prehistory of the area.

Towler Hill is located on the eastern edge of a series of three river terraces on the south bank of the Tees, approximately 1.5 km north west of Barnard Castle. The terraces are in a sheltered situation and T. Laurie believes that the site is in an excellent position to exploit the fish resources of the river. The majority of the artifacts have come from the second terrace, and *Table 3* shows a breakdown of the finds recovered from the site. While it is obvious that more than one period of activity is documented at Towler Hill, two exciting points emerge.

While Campbell (1977) has indicated the difficulty of identifying late Upper Palaeolithic material in the north, we would suggest that the large backed pieces and the large end-scrapers (*Fig. 3*, nos. 1–8) may be evidence for late Upper Palaeolithic activity in the area. The pieces can be paralleled by supposed Upper Palaeolithic material from the Kirkhead, Kinsey and Victoria caves and from the possible open-air site at Sheffield's Hill in Lincolnshire and the disputed site at Brigham in Yorkshire (Campbell 1971: figs. 136–138, 141). Only further detailed collection from the terrace, which is now under pasture, will allow this suggestion to be tested, but the site holds out exciting possibilities for future work on this early period.

Similarly, among the 59 microliths recovered there is definite evidence for both earlier and later Mesolithic activity, with bi-truncated, trapeziform pieces (4 examples) and point forms (37) which can be paralleled at Star Carr, and scalene triangles (15) and rods (2) all being represented.

A further interesting point to emerge from an initial analysis of the assemblage is the preponderance of cores (171 examples), scrapers (148) and unretouched blades (138). These, along with the microliths and 22 burins make up the major part of the artifact suite. Three flat sandstone discs, chipped all round and similar to those from Deepcar and Warcock Hill South (Radley and Mellars 1964) were also recovered, in addition to six lumps of haematite, one piece of unworked jet and one struck flake of polished greenstone.

Mud-red, translucent black/brown, honey-coloured and opaque white varieties of flint, which may derive from glacial deposits on the east coast, are all present on the site, while a large proportion of black/brown banded chert, of Carboniferous origin, was also exploited for cores and flake tools. An example of the range of materials present can be seen if the cores and scrapers are considered. Just over 39% of the cores are in chert, while only just over 3% of the scrapers are in a similar material.

This large-scale utilization of local chert is also evident at Staple Crag, higher up the dale, where almost a quarter of the raw material recovered (24.6%) is chert with some 72% being made up of flint, again of various colours and probably of glacial origin. Staple Crag is another potentially early site, situated again on the south bank of the Tees on a small terrace which is subject to regular scouring by the river. All of the material seems to be from a discrete layer of cobbles below the modern ploughsoil, and the range and proportions of different tool forms recovered are shown in *Table 2* and *Fig. 3*. The main microlith forms are of isosceles triangle type and mark out the site as being of earlier Mesolithic date. Scrapers, usually small and on the ends of squat flakes, dominate the assemblage, but the presence of one perforated and one partially perforated shale object should be noted as should five flakes which on preliminary identification seem to be of Langdale rock from Cumbria.

Table 2: Categories of lithic material from selected Mesolithic sites in Teesdale *(prepared by D. Coggins)*

Site Name	National Grid Reference	Altitude (metres O.D.)	Cores	Scrapers	Arrowheads	Microliths	Denticulated blades	Burins	Piercers	Notched flakes	Microburins	Unworked pebbles	Retouched flakes/blades	Hammerstones	Waste material	Retouched knives	Tanged implements
Blackton	NY 408 258	396	4	5	2	6	–	–	–	–	–	–	21	–	120	2	–
Briar Dykes	NY 948 200	320	5	3	1	3	–	–	–	–	1	–	6	1	172	–	–
Middle Hurth	NY 867 308	457	5	5	5	12	–	1	–	1	1	–	24	1	322	1	–
Staple Crag	NY 903 278	259	5	8	–	5	–	1	–	–	–	–	28	–	173	1	–
Merrygill Holm	NY 831 284	400	1	–	1	–	–	–	–	–	–	–	4	1	8	1	–
Ravock Mire	NY 955 151	320	14	3	–	10	–	–	–	–	1	–	13	–	135	2	–

Table 3: Categories of lithic material from selected sites in Teesdale and Swaledale *(prepared by T. Laurie)*

Site Name	National Grid Reference	Altitude (metres O.D.)	Cores	Scrapers	Arrowheads	Microliths	Burins	Piercers	Mèches de Forêt	Notched flakes	Microburins	Unworked nodules	Retouched flakes	Retouched blades	Complete blades (unret.)	Hammerstones	Blade butts	Blade segments	Blade tips	Flakes and waste	Plano-convex knives
Teesdale																				
Towler Hill	NZ 0376 1772	150	171	148	7	59	22	13	3	5	19	1	83	31	138	–	95	16	67	527	1
(1) Barningham High Moor. Frankinshaw How – Arndale Springs	NZ 0578 0648	420	9	1	2	29	5	1	–	2	–	–	3	17	–	–	13	1	1	112	–
(2) Frankinshaw How, South Slope	NZ 0600 0640	427	–	1	1	1	–	–	–	–	–	–	–	5	2	–	1	1	–	2	–
(3) The Butts	NZ 0540 0675	427	20	2	5	37	2	–	–	–	2	–	5	–	14	–	9	7	3	121	–
(4) Frankinshaw Well	NZ 0642 0691	427	14	–	–	4	–	–	–	–	–	–	1	2	3	–	3	–	1	52	–
(5) Spring Heads	NX 0542 0690	435	9	–	–	29	–	–	–	–	–	–	–	17	35	–	22	3	6	158	–
Swaledale																				
Sleigill-Windegg, The Hut	NZ 0178 0404	450	8	4	2	84	2	–	–	–	–	–	6	10	40	–	17	16	6	126	–
Calvert Houses	NY 9238 9860	427	–	18	6	3	6	5	–	–	–	6	2	2	–	1	–	–	42	–	–

Further work on these two sites is in hand and if excavation occurs in the near future at the Staple Crag site, which may preserve an *in situ* occupation layer, then it will be possible to say a great deal more about the earlier Mesolithic in Teesdale.

The other sites analyzed are all later Mesolithic in character, with the assemblages dominated by rod and scalene triangle forms of microlith (*Tables 2 & 3*). One striking feature of the microliths from the Barningham High Moor area (*Fig. 3*, nos. 36–50) is their very small size. Scalene triangles on these sites go down to 2 mm in breadth and are worked on all three edges.

When these later Mesolithic assemblages are compared with the material from Weardale, two points are immediately obvious. Arrowheads of post-Mesolithic type occur on five of the Teesdale sites, but more importantly the percentages of chert in the assemblages are invariably much higher than in those from Weardale ranging from 2.7% at the Spring Heads site on Barningham High Moor to 70% at Ravock Mire. This may reflect the greater ease of obtaining chert from the Carboniferous outcrops of Teesdale. Flint type too is different in this area when compared with Weardale. On Barningham High Moor the flint is invariably multi-coloured pebble flint with brown translucent material predominating.

Swaledale

A major constraint on the recovery of sites in this area is, again, the lack of ploughing in the dale. There is no arable land in Swaledale, and the only ploughing which does occur is to allow pasture fields to be re-sown with grass. T. Laurie has examined two sites in detail (*Table 3*), both above 400 m O.D. and both from areas of peat erosion on moorland. The Sleigill site is similar to those on Barningham High Moor in terms of raw material type – 90% flint (mainly brown translucent) and 10% chert; but high quality black flint, with thick, chalky cortex has been recorded from Calvert Houses. All the microlith forms recovered so far are scalene triangles and rods, though the Calvert Houses site is of interest here as some of the scraper forms identified may be of local Neolithic type.

CONCLUSIONS AND FUTURE WORK

This paper is very much an interim statement of results from an ongoing programme of research. Fieldwork is still in progress and detailed analytical work will take place alongside it. It seems to us that the excavation of some of our surface scatter sites is now a prerequisite for setting our research onto a firmer chronological footing. Excavation may reveal sub-surface features that could produce material for radiocarbon dating and for structural and environmental analysis.

In the light of the data presented above, it would also seem important to do more work on the sources of the raw material utilized in the study area, and some attempt has been made by one of us to initiate a discussion of this problem (Young 1985). We will also be looking to move away from a basic typological approach to our material in the future, in an attempt to discuss its implications for Mesolithic settlement and subsistence patterns on a broader scale. This aspect of the research will expand on some attempts which have already been made to discuss the material in this way (Coggins 1984; Young 1984, 1987).

What we have really been concerned to do here is to demonstrate that the northern dales are not an archaeological backwater in terms of their potential for Mesolithic, and possibly earlier, research. Many parts of the area are still uncharted waters in terms of fieldwork, and we look forward to building on the results obtained in our survey and to further increasing our knowledge of earlier prehistoric activity in the region. If we have succeeded in making this point to colleagues both at home and abroad then the aims of this paper have been realized.

References

ALEXANDER, J. (1980) The frontier concept in prehistory: the end of the moving frontier. In J.V.S. Megaw (ed.), *Hunters, Gatherers and First Farmers Beyond Europe*. Leicester, University Press: 25–40.

BENNETT-GIBBS, G. and TEMPERLEY, G.W. (1931) On some flint flakes from Weardale. *Transactions of the Natural History Society of Northumberland and Durham*, New Series, 7–9: 191–192.

BUCKLEY, F. (1925) The microlith industries of Northumberland. *Archaeologia Aeliana*, Fourth Series, 1: 42–47.

CAMPBELL, J.B. (1977) *The Upper Palaeolithic of Britain. A Study of Man and Nature in the Late Ice Age* (two volumes). Oxford, Clarendon Press.

CHAMBERS, C. (1974) *The Vegetational History of Teesdale*. Unpublished Ph.D. thesis, University of Durham.

CLARK, J.G.D., HIGGS, E.S. and LONGWORTH, I.H. (1960) Excavations at the Neolithic site at Hurst Fen, Mildenhall, Suffolk, 1954, 1957 and 1958. *Proceedings of the Prehistoric Society*, 26: 202–245.

COGGINS, D. (1984) *The Archaeology of Early Settlement in Upper Teesdale*. Unpublished M.A. thesis, University of Durham.

EGGLESTONE, W.M. (1910) Neolithic flint implements in Weardale. *Proceedings of the Society of Antiquaries of Newcastle-upon-Tyne*, Third Series, 4: 205–208.

EGGLESTONE, W.M. (1911a) Neolithic flint implements, Weardale. *Proceedings of the Society of Antiquaries of Newcastle-upon-Tyne*, Third Series, 5: 106–107.

EGGLESTONE, W.M. (1911b) Neolithic flint implements in Weardale. *Proceedings of the Society of Antiquaries of Newcastle-upon-Tyne*, Third Series, 5: 115–117.

FELL, C.I. and HILDYARD, E.J.W. (1953) Prehistoric Weardale, a new survey. *Archaeologia Aeliana*, Fourth Series, 31: 98–116.

FELL, C.I. and HILDYARD, E.J.W. (1956) More flints from Weardale – a postscript. *Archaeologia Aeliana*, Fourth Series, 34: 131–137.

HARDING, D.W. (1970) The prehistoric period. In J.C. Dewdney (ed.), *Durham County and City with Teesside*. Durham, British Association for the Advancement of Science: 191–194.

HILDYARD, E.J.W. (1945) *Archaeology of Weardale: First Annual Summary of Research*. Privately published.

HOWCHIN, W. (1880) Notes on a field of prehistoric implements in Allendale, with notices of similar finds in the surrounding district. *Transactions of the Natural History Society of Northumberland and Durham*, 7: 210–222.

JACOBI, R.M. (1976) *Aspects of the Postglacial Archaeology of England and Wales*. Unpublished Ph.D. thesis, University of Cambridge.

JACOBI, R.M. (1978) Northern England in the eighth millennium bc: an essay. In P.A. Mellars (ed.), *The Early Postglacial Settlement of Northern Europe*. London, Duckworth: 295–332.

JOHNSON, G.A.L. and DUNHAM, K.C. (1963) *The Geology of Moor House*. Nature Conservancy Monograph, no. 2. London, H.M.S.O.

LAURIE, T.C. (1984) First evidence for the early Postglacial and Mesolithic occupation of the Tees valley and of the uplands between the Tees and Swale rivers. *Yorkshire Archaeological Society Prehistory Research Bulletin*, 21: 1–3, figs. 1–5.

MANBY, T.G. (1966) Creswellian site at Brigham, East Yorkshire. *Antiquaries Journal*, 46: 211–228.

RAISTRICK, A. (1933) The distribution of Mesolithic sites in the north of England. *Yorkshire Archaeological Journal*, 31: 141–156.

RAISTRICK, A. (1972) *The Pennine Dales*. London, Arrow Books.

RAISTRICK, A. and BENNETT-GIBBS, G. (1934) Prehistoric invasions of Northumberland and Durham. *Transactions of the Northern Naturalists Union*, 1(3): 187–199.

SQUIRES, R.H. (1970) *A Contribution to the Vegetational History of Upper Teesdale*. Unpublished Ph.D. thesis, University of Durham.

THOMAS, D.H. (1971) *Prehistoric Subsistence–Settlement Patterns of the Reese River Valley, Central Nevada*. Unpublished Ph.D. thesis, University of California, Davis.

TRECHMANN, C.T. (1912) Notes on Neolithic chipping sites in Northumberland and Durham. *Transactions of the Natural History Society of Northumberland and Durham*, New Series, 4: 67–85.

WILMSEN, E.N. (1970) Lithic analysis and cultural inference: a palaeo-Indian case. *University of Arizona Anthropological Papers*, 16: 70–71.

YOUNG, R. (1984) *Aspects of the Prehistoric Archaeology of the Wear Valley, Co. Durham*. Unpublished Ph.D. thesis, University of Durham.

YOUNG, R. (1985) Potential sources of flint and chert in the north east of England. *Lithics*, 5: 3–9.

YOUNG, R. (1987) *Lithics and Subsistence in North-Eastern England. Aspects of the Prehistoric Archaeology of the Wear Valley, Co. Durham, from the Mesolithic to the Bronze Age.* Oxford, British Archaeological Reports (British Series) 161.

YOUNG, R. (in preparation) *Mixed lithic scatters and the Mesolithic–Neolithic transition in the north east of England* (paper).

The Eskmeals Project: Late Mesolithic Settlement and Environment in North-West England

Clive Bonsall, Donald Sutherland, Richard Tipping and Jim Cherry

Abstract

The Eskmeals area on the coast of north-west England has been the focus of a multi-disciplinary research project since the mid-1970s. The results of fieldwork undertaken between 1981 and 1986 are described, and the evidence for Mesolithic settlement is set in its environmental context. The paper is divided into four sections. Part 1 describes the landforms and sediments which make up the Eskmeals coastal foreland, and discusses the chronology of their formation. Part 2 describes the results of excavations at a site at Williamson's Moss, where artifacts and structural remains are found in a sealed context associated with a buried land surface. Part 3 discusses the pollen record from channel deposits within the excavated area, and considers the implications of this evidence for the interpretation of the archaeological record. The final section considers three aspects of the Mesolithic settlement of the Eskmeals area: settlement location, chronology and subsistence.

INTRODUCTION

The Eskmeals Project is a study of the interaction between Mesolithic communities and their environment in a coastal setting, and centres on the area around the estuary of the River Esk, south-west Cumbria, on the edge of the English Lake District (inset, *Fig. 1*). The impetus for a major research project was provided by the important series of surface finds made here in the 1960s and 1970s by J. and P.J. Cherry (Cherry 1969; Cherry and Cherry 1986).

Fieldwork began in 1974 with a pilot excavation to test the potential of the area for further research; and was followed in 1975–77 by rescue excavations at Monk Moors Sites 1 and 2, in response to the persistent threat from ploughing (Bonsall 1981). Since 1981 a more intensive programme of fieldwork has been underway; this has been an interdisciplinary investigation in which archaeological survey and excavation are integrated with detailed palaeo-environmental studies. This research is directed at specific questions concerning the nature of late Mesolithic settlement in the Eskmeals area, the age, duration and season of occupation of the individual sites, and the environmental conditions at the time of their occupation. Two important objectives are to document the changing relationship between sea level, coastal evolution and settlement patterns during the Mesolithic period, and to assess what impact the Mesolithic population had upon the local environment. It is with these aspects of the research that this paper is principally concerned.

The authors are all actively involved in the fieldwork: *Clive Bonsall* is overall coordinator of the project and has directed the archaeological investigations; *Donald Sutherland* has supervised the geomorphological studies; *Richard Tipping* has undertaken the palynological work; while *Jim Cherry* has done much of the survey work, spending many hours in the field searching for, and locating, new sites.

It should be emphasized that this paper is in no sense a final report. The Eskmeals Project is still in progress. What follows, therefore, is an *interim* statement of some of the results already obtained.[1]

Eskmeals – the general situation

The Eskmeals coastal foreland lies to the south of the present estuary of the River Esk. The eastern margin of the foreland is defined by a sharp break of slope that can be traced from the River Esk north of Newbiggin to south of Stubb Place (*Fig. 2*). To the landward, glacial sediments underlie an undulating topography of moderate relief that rises steadily inland to over 250 m in a few kilometres. The coastal foreland itself is formed by marine, estuarine and aeolian sediments resting on an eroded surface of glacial deposits. A complex sequence of shingle ridges has been produced by the dominant northwards-directed longshore movement of littoral sediment, and in the lee of the shingle ridges estuarine sediments have accumulated. The aeolian deposits that have developed on the surface of the shingle ridges comprise a seaward area of constructional dunes eastwards of which a large, nearly flat, sand sheet has developed.

A series of channels transect the glacial deposits and apparently terminate at the edge of the coastal foreland. It is likely, however, that the lower portions of some of the channels continue below the coastal sediments. These channels, particularly along their present lower portions, have sediment infills that accumulated contemporaneously with the formation of the coastal foreland and thus preserve

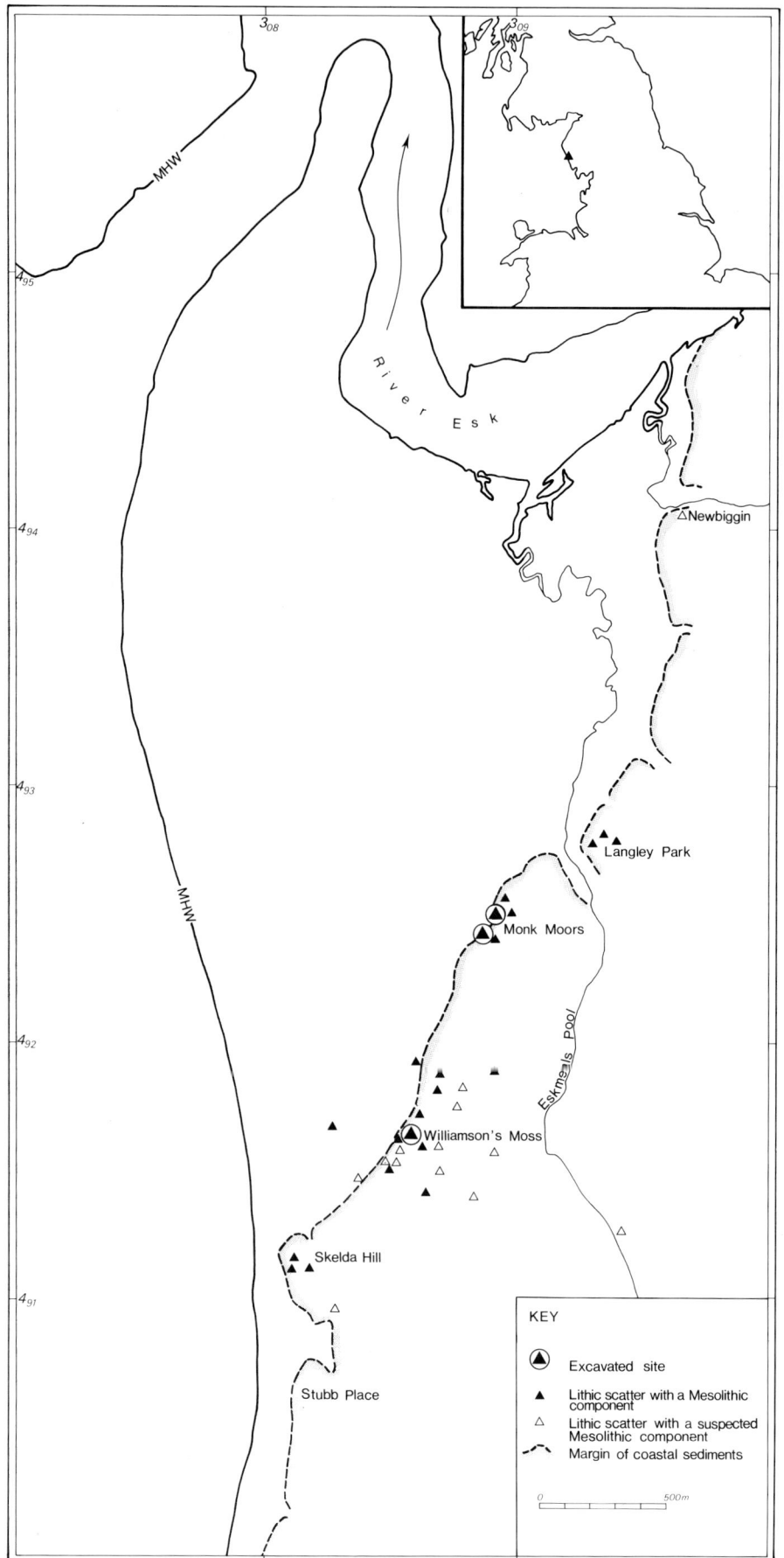

Figure 1   Distribution of Mesolithic sites in the Eskmeals area.

176

MHW

308 309

MHW

495

Reserve

River Esk

494

Newbiggin

Stockbridge

493

Monk
+ Moors

492

Williamson's
Moss

Skelda Hill

491

Stubb Place

0   500 m

Key:

1. Peat-filled basins
2. Present salt marsh
3. Estuarine sediments
4. Wind-blown sand sheet
5. Constructional sand dunes
6. Sharp break of slope
7. Moderate break of slope
8. Present streams
9. Former stream channels
10. Glacial sediments
11. Alluvial fans
12. Made ground
13. Shingle ridges

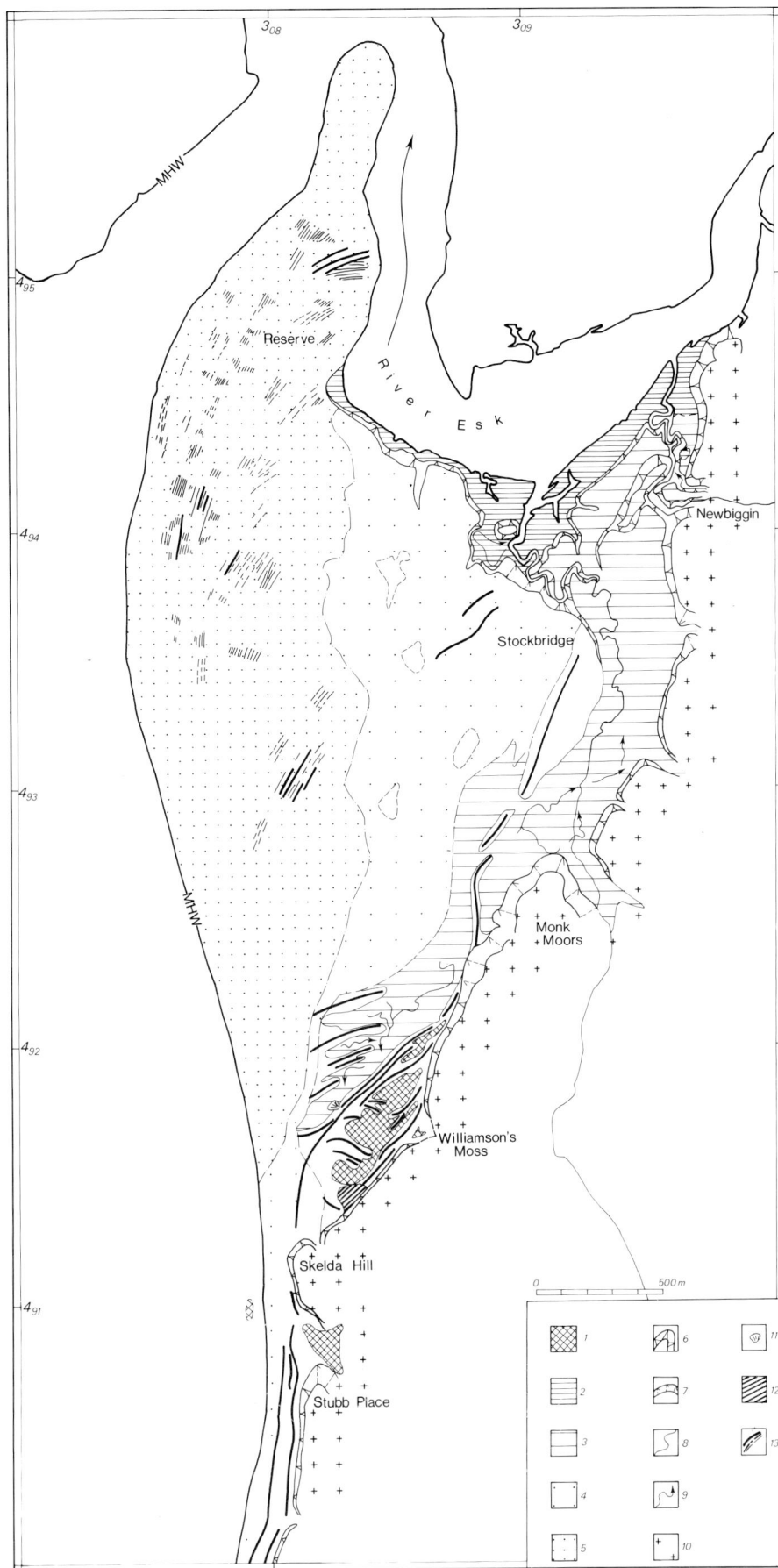

Figure 2 Geomorphological map of the Eskmeals area.

valuable evidence of mid- to late Flandrian environments.

Traces of Mesolithic occupation have been found mainly on the glacial deposits along the edge of the foreland, within a few hundred metres of the break of slope which marks the limit of the Flandrian marine transgression (*Fig. 1*). Material has also been recovered from the shingle ridges surrounding the Williamson's Moss basin which are known to have formed by 6000 BP. Of the 35 lithic scatters recorded to date, almost all were exposed where the present vegetation had been disturbed by ploughing or burrowing animals.

Archaeological distributions are frequently more a reflection of the activities of fieldworkers than of the original settlement pattern, and Eskmeals is no exception. The known sites are concentrated in areas where accessibility and modern agriculture have provided the best opportunities for fieldwalking. Some of the later shingle ridges may also preserve evidence of Mesolithic activity, and there are probably more sites to be found in the area north of Monk Moors and on the slopes above Eskmeals Pool.

DEVELOPMENT OF THE COASTAL FORELAND

Introduction

A number of previous studies have published information relating to sea-level change along the Cumbrian coast during the mid- and late Flandrian (e.g. Walker 1966; Huddart and Tooley 1972; Andrews *et al.* 1973; Tooley 1974, 1977, 1978, 1982). No synthesis of these data in the form of a sea-level curve has been published. To the south, however, in northern Lancashire, Tooley (1974, 1978) has shown that Mean High Water of Spring Tides rose rapidly from below −15 m O.D. *c.* 9000 BP to reach O.D. *c.* 6500 BP, thereafter rising to its present level of *c.* 4 m O.D.[2] To the north, in southern Scotland, Jardine (1975) has presented data that show that Mean High Water of Spring Tides rose above O.D. during the early Flandrian and reached *c.* 9 m O.D. by *c.* 6500 BP, thereafter declining to its present level of *c.* 5 m O.D. The differences in the history of sea level between the areas north and south of Cumbria are largely the result of the diminution of glacio-isostatic uplift with increasing distance from the zone of maximum ice thickness in Scotland. These differences notwithstanding, the published work suggests that the evolution of the Eskmeals foreland must be understood in the context of a rapidly rising sea level during the early Flandrian followed, after *c.* 6000–7000 BP, by a relatively stable, possibly slightly declining sea level.

Coastal development

The landforms and sediments of the Eskmeals coastal zone are shown in *Fig. 2*. The most notable features are the shingle ridges that underlie the foreland. The innermost shingle ridge can be traced from south of Stubb Place along the margin of the glacial sediments as far as Monk Moors. North west of Monk Moors the ridge is no longer in direct contact with the glacial sediments but can be traced as a clear feature as far north as Stockbridge. Instrumental levelling of this ridge indicates that it has an altitude of 8.27 m O.D. by Stubb Place, 7.52 m O.D. by Williamson's Moss and 7.63 m O.D. south of Stockbridge. The slight decline northwards suggested by these figures is in accord with observations on the modern beach. Shingle along the present beach opposite Stubb Place is moved by the sea to an altitude of 6.21 m O.D., whilst along the northern part of the foreland modern shingle is moved to an altitude of 5.36 m O.D. Comparison of the figures implies that the innermost shingle ridge was formed when sea level was 2–2.2 m higher than today.

The innermost shingle ridge was the earliest formed. Thereafter, Skelda Hill has operated as a 'hinge' northwards of which the shingle ridge complex has developed. The second group of shingle ridges to develop was that around Williamson's Moss thus isolating that basin from the sea. The main shingle ridge complex was built out subsequently with the recurving ends of the progressively-formed ridges being traceable within the area of blown sand to the north west of Stockbridge and into the Nature Reserve that occupies the northern margin of the ridge complex (*Fig. 2*). Levelling of these ridges reveals three distinct altitudes at which they were deposited. The first group includes those ridges that isolate Williamson's Moss and forms the inner group of ridges as far as the Nature Reserve. These have been levelled at three separate localities from Williamson's Moss to the Nature Reserve, giving mean altitudes at each locality of 7.29 m O.D., 7.37 m O.D. and 7.48 m O.D. The altitudes imply only a very slight fall in relative sea level between the time of deposition of the innermost shingle ridge and the formation of the greater part of the shingle ridge complex.

The second group of shingle ridges is represented by the most seaward ridge at Stubb Place and a sequence of ridges within the Reserve and immediately to the south of there. At Stubb Place the ridge occurs at 7.18 m O.D. whilst in two localities in the Reserve, where there is a clear break of slope between the first and this second group, the ridges have altitudes of 6.38 m O.D. and 6.45 m O.D. By comparison with the figures on modern shingle given earlier, these altitudes imply a sea level during deposition of these ridges of 0.9–1.1 m higher than that of the present.

The third group of ridges has only been located in

the Reserve where altitudes on three sets of these ridges have given average figures of 5.31 m O.D., 5.25 m O.D. and 5.66 m O.D. These altitudes are indistinguishable from that to which modern shingle is moved, implying no net relative sea-level change since formation of these ridges.

The development of the shingle ridges has allowed the accumulation of estuarine and lagoonal sediments on their landward sides. The first areas of such sedimentation were in the lee of the innermost shingle ridge in the area between Monk Moors and Newbiggin and in the channel mouth just north of Stubb Place. With the extension of the shingle ridge system, similar sediments began to accumulate throughout the whole area landwards of the shingle ridges between Williamson's Moss and the River Esk. Two distinct surfaces can be identified in the area of estuarine sediments. The higher occurs at 5.80–6.00 m O.D. and the lower, found only to the west of Newbiggin, at 4.64 m O.D. The inner margin of the present salt marsh along the River Esk estuary has an altitude of 3.82 m O.D., implying that the two levels identified in the estuarine sediments were formed when sea level was 2–2.2 m and 0.8 m above that of today. There is therefore good agreement between the inferences concerning altitudes of shore-line formation that have been drawn from the shingle ridges and from the estuarine sediments.

Sand dunes have formed on the surface of the intermediate and lower sets of shingle ridges. Landwards of these constructional dunes a near-flat sand sheet has been deposited on the western margin of the estuarine silts, following a brief period of peat accumulation once sea level had fallen and the higher estuarine deposits abandoned.

Chronology

Radiocarbon dating of samples associated with the construction of the shingle ridge complex has established an outline chronology of the events discussed above.

A trench was excavated across the inner margin of the earliest formed shingle ridge at Williamson's Moss (*Fig. 5*). Small wood fragments were recovered from the basal layers of the shingle ridge where it rested upon an eroded till surface. These wood fragments gave an age of 7020±80 BP (SRR-2655). In the same trench an organic sand layer with abundant rootlets, which had accumulated to the rear of the shingle ridge and was overlain by a tongue of wash-over gravels, was sampled. Because of potential contamination from rootlets, 'coarse' and 'fine' fractions were dated (SRR-2656), the former giving an age of 5060±50 BP and the latter 5640±50 BP. These results imply a degree of rootlet contamination and hence the older date is considered a minimum. Taken together, however, the dates from this trench imply that the innermost shingle

ridge was formed after 7020 BP but at some time prior to 5640 BP.

The Williamson's Moss basin was formed by growth of the shingle ridges on its seaward side, hence dates from the basal sediments in the basin provide a limiting age on the formation of these ridges. Sample SRR-2657 was divided into alkali soluble and insoluble fractions because of possible humic acid contamination (Pennington, in Harkness 1981) and these gave ages of 6140±170 BP and 5910±50 BP, indicating negligible contamination. As a further check, an alkali insoluble date was obtained from the sediment immediately overlying the above sample. This gave an age of 5760±50 BP (SRR-5657), again confirming the reliability of the lower dates. These dates may be compared with one reported by Tooley (1982) on a 'regressive overlap' from Williamson's Moss of 6230±85 BP (HV-5227). This is statistically indistinguishable from the alkali soluble fraction of SRR-2657. Taking the dates together, they imply formation of the shingle ridges seawards of Williamson's Moss by *c.* 6100 BP. Further, this also implies that the formation of the innermost shingle ridge, which is landwards of Williamson's Moss, was prior to 6100 BP and, given a period of time for construction of the shingle ridges around Williamson's Moss, may have formed prior to 6500 BP.

No *in situ* marine shells have been found in association with the uppermost group of shingle ridges. However, in deflation hollows in the sand dunes *in situ* shells are abundant on the two lower groups of shingle ridges. Two samples, each of fragments of *Arctica islandica* in a good state of preservation, were recovered from the intermediate sequence of shingle ridges. These were dated as 4830±60 BP (outer) and 4800±60 BP (inner) (SRR-2659) and 4070±60 BP (outer) and 4020±60 BP (inner) (SRR-2660). The close agreement between the inner and outer fractions of each sample indicates minimal contamination. These shell dates have been normalized for isotopic fractionation and hence, to be comparable with dates on terrestrial material, should be adjusted for the apparent age of sea water. The present best estimate for the sea around Britain is 405±40 years (Harkness 1983). Making this adjustment implies that the intermediate set of shingle ridges was being formed between 4395±70 BP and 3615±70 BP.

Two further samples were recovered from the lower sequence of shingle ridges. These were dated as 4480±70 BP (outer) and 5100±70 BP (inner) (SRR-3059) and 3270±80 BP (outer) and 3230±80 BP (inner) (SRR-3060). The inner and outer fractions of the first of these two samples are distinct at the 2s level and hence this sample is rejected. The other sample shows good agreement between the two fractions and, as with the samples from the

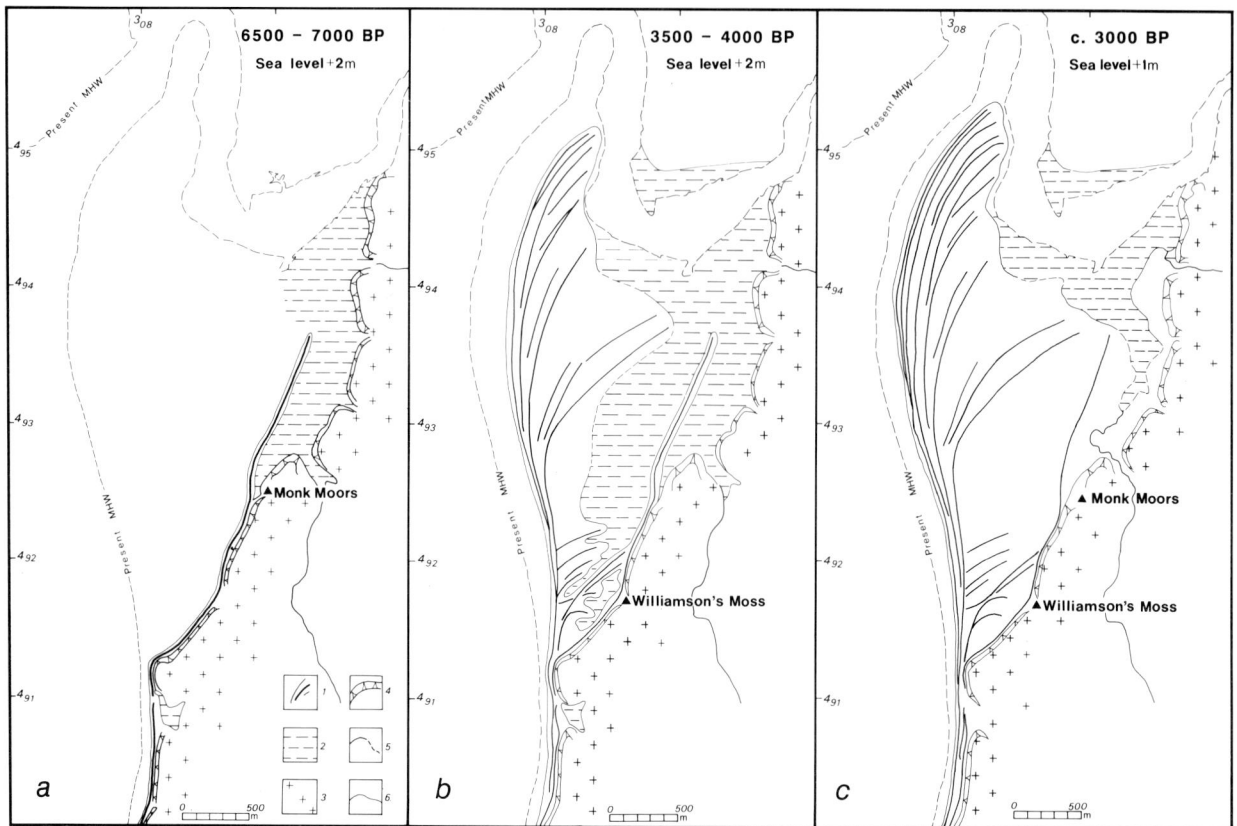

Figure 3 Evolution of the Eskmeals coastal foreland. *Key*: 1. Shingle ridges; 2. Estuarine areas; 3. Glacial sediments; 4. Marked break of slope; 5. Feature boundary; 6. Streams (on each diagram the archaeological sites known to have been occupied at the relevant period are shown).

intermediate shingle ridges, should be adjusted for the apparent age of sea water. This implies that the lower set of shingle ridges was in process of formation around 2825±90 BP.

As noted above, there was a period of peat accumulation on the estuarine flats subsequent to sea-level fall but prior to the deposition of the wind-blown sands in the lee of the developing shingle ridge and sand dune complex. A pit was dug through the sands and the peat sampled where it immediately overlay the estuarine sediments at an altitude of 5.5 m O.D., that is *c.* 0.5 m below the highest altitude to which the estuarine sediments had been deposited. Pollen analysis did not identify any marked hiatus in the sequence and a sample from the base of the peat was submitted for radiocarbon dating, giving an age of 3580±100 BP (SRR-3061). This implies retreat of the sea from this locality by approximately this date, or at approximately the time the intermediate shingle ridge sequence was being formed. This is slightly later than may have been thought probable on altitudinal comparisons alone, but given the errors inherent in radiocarbon dating and in inferring sea levels from both shingle ridges and estuarine flats, there is a broad agreement as to the chronology of development of the coastal foreland.

In the pit excavated, peat continued to accumulate till after 3310±70 BP (SRR-3062), after which the wind-blown sand was deposited. Both in the pit and in

neighbouring boreholes a thin peat horizon or disconformity separated lower, more compact sands from an upper, loose, wind-blown sand horizon. Radiocarbon dating of the thin peat layer indicated it to have accumulated between 1810±70 BP (SRR-3063) and 1460±70 BP (SRR-3064).

Conclusions

The evolution of the Eskmeals coastal zone is illustrated in *Fig. 3* and may be summarized as follows. Early Flandrian sea-level rise culminated in the contemporaneous erosion of the landward glacial deposits and formation of the innermost shingle ridge between *c.* 6500 BP and 7000 BP. Estuarine sedimentation began in the lee of this shingle ridge (*Fig. 3a*). Mean High Water of Spring Tides was then *c.* 2 m above that of today. Subsequently, and with only a slight fall in sea level, the greater part of the shingle ridge complex that underlies the Eskmeals foreland was constructed. The shingle ridges around Williamson's Moss were deposited prior to 6100 BP and a new phase of shingle ridge development, which had been preceded by a net fall in relative sea level of *c.* 1 m, was underway by 4400 BP. It seems likely, therefore, that the bulk of the Eskmeals foreland had been deposited by 5500 BP. The intermediate sequence of shingle ridges continued to form till after 3600 BP (*Fig. 3b*), their formation

180

being accompanied by progressive abandonment of the estuarine sediments landwards of the shingle ridges. The sea subsequently fell by 0.8–1.1 m and a further phase of shingle ridge development was in progress by at least 2800 BP (*Fig. 3c*). There have been at least two periods of sand dune activity on the foreland, the first between 3300 BP and 1800 BP, and the second sometime after *c.* 1500 BP. An earlier phase of sand dune activity may be suggested by a very sandy facies near the base of the estuarine sediments closest to the main shingle ridge complex. This would have occurred at sometime between 6100 BP (probably after 5500 BP) and 3500 BP.

ARCHAEOLOGY

Introduction

The excavations at Monk Moors (Bonsall 1981) were the first systematic investigation of Mesolithic sites in north-west England. Their significance derived from the fact that they produced large lithic assemblages in association with structural remains, and provided the first Mesolithic floor plans and radiocarbon dates for a part of Britain where, previously, little research had been undertaken. Nevertheless,

the evidence recovered was subject to major limitations. The sites occurred within the A-horizon of a shallow, free-draining and relatively acid soil, and had suffered extensive disturbance by ploughing. As a result, the archaeological material was unstratified and no faunal or other organic remains,[3] which would have provided an insight into economic and social aspects of the Mesolithic occupation, were preserved.

As the Eskmeals Project continued, attention shifted to the area around the basin of Williamson's Moss where fieldwalking revealed widespread evidence of Mesolithic and later habitation (*Fig. 4*). The generally low-lying, ill-drained situation and the fact that much of the land bordering the Moss had been under rough pasture for a considerable time with few signs of past cultivation, seemed to offer much better prospects of locating sites with good organic preservation, where damage from ploughing would be minimal.

The Williamson's Moss site
Location
The site chosen for excavation is situated on the glacial deposits immediately landward of the shingle

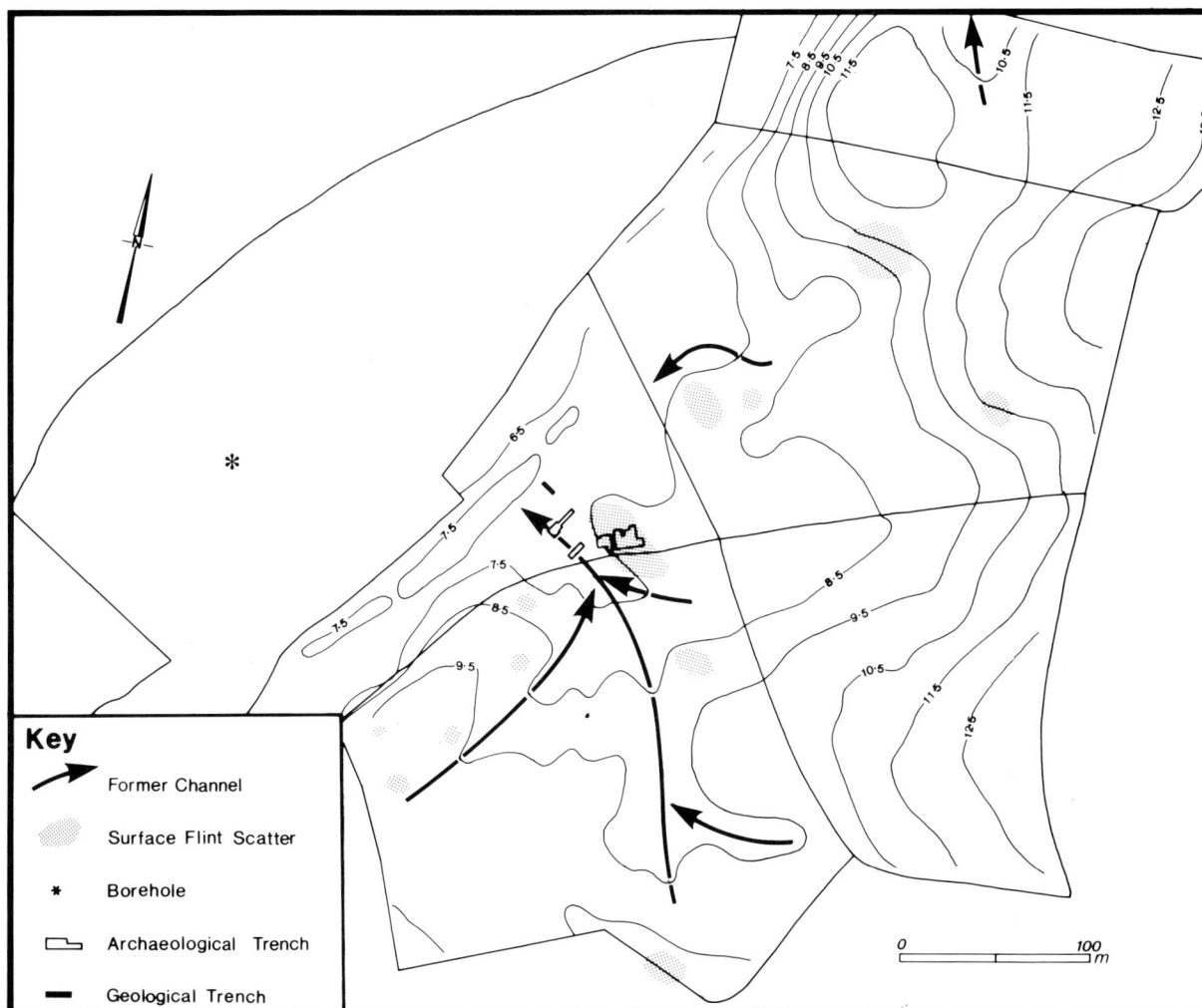

Key

→ Former Channel

▒ Surface Flint Scatter

✳ Borehole

▭ Archaeological Trench

▬ Geological Trench

Figure 4 Map of the Williamson's Moss area showing the excavated site in relation to local topography.

181

G

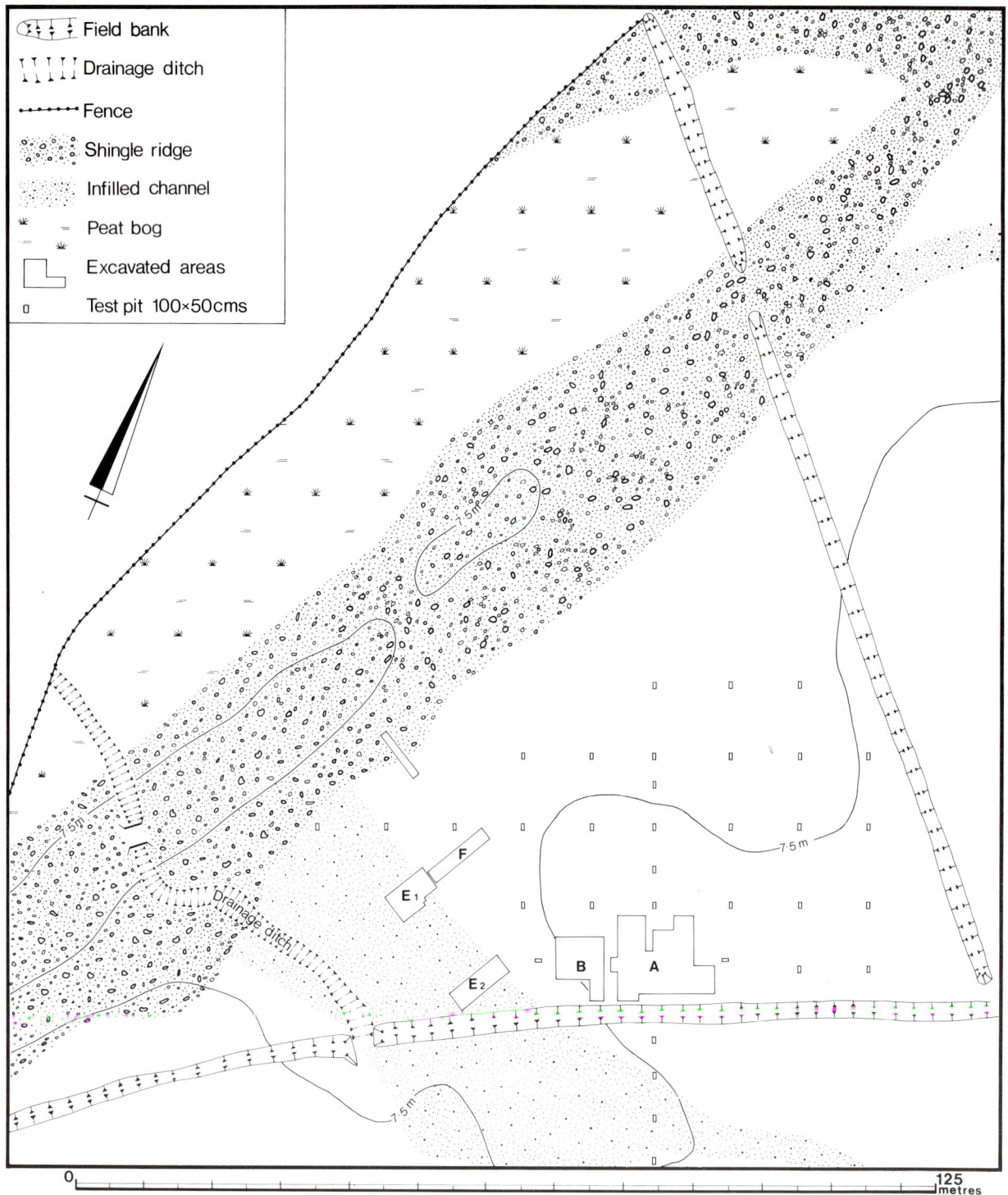

Figure 5   Map showing the Williamson's Moss excavation in relation to the shingle ridge and the infilled channel.

ridge formed by the highest Flandrian sea level, which extends along the eastern margin of Williamson's Moss (*Fig. 5*). At the time of ridge formation the edge of the glacial sediments was being eroded and a cliffline formed to the north west and south east of the Moss. Landwards of the shingle ridge the ground rises steadily for a distance of about 250 m to a height of about 15 m O.D.

The site itself occupies an area which is centred on the crest of a low ridge formed of glacial till at *c.* 8 m

O.D. Those parts of the site that lie below the 7.5 m contour have been subjected to periodic flooding which resulted in the accumulation of fine alluvial sediments. These reach their greatest depth in the southern part of the site where they infill a narrow channel cut into the till – one of a series of channels that once drained the immediately landward area. This process of alluviation was initiated by the formation of the shingle ridge which dammed up the channels and caused ponding of surface run-off from the surrounding slopes.

The *buried land surface* beneath the alluvial sediments has considerable archaeological significance, since the artifacts and structural remains associated with it are effectively in a *sealed* context. This palaeosurface appears as a thin layer of fine sand overlying the till, and can be traced over a substantial area of the site; it is preserved best where the sand infills hollows in the till surface. The origin of this sand is problematic. It may contain a wind-blown component derived from the coastal sediments. The most likely explanation, however, is that it formed *in situ* as a consequence of the removal of vegetation and the destruction/removal of the surface soil, exposing the sub-surface mineral horizon. Under these conditions, raindrop impact on the bare surface may have led to dispersal of clay and fine silt (and any remaining organic matter) which could then be removed laterally by surface wash, leading to the residual accumulation of coarser particles (coarse silt/fine sand) at the surface. This material could subsequently be redeposited in hollows by surface run-off. The fact that the palaeosurface sand frequently contains artifacts and structural features suggests that its formation coincided with a period of intensive human activity and, by extension, opens the possibility that the initial removal of trees and ground vegetation – from an area of *at least* 7500 m^2 – was the result of that activity. Whatever the origin of the sand, it is clear that it must have accumulated on an exposed land surface, and could not have formed beneath dense vegetation.

Excavation

Trial excavations were undertaken on the Williamson's Moss site in 1975–76 and again in 1979–80, with full-scale investigation beginning in 1981.

To date, an area of *c.* 275 m^2 has been exposed. This, however, represents only a very small portion of what is evidently a large and complex site. The precise limits of the site have yet to be determined, but traces of occupation have been shown to extend well beyond the area which contains the main concentration of lithic material. The excavation has been tied in to a continuous grid system. Individual one-metre and 50 cm squares have been excavated by trowel, and all the material sieved through a 3 mm mesh. Soil samples for pH, phosphate and magnetic susceptibility measurements have been taken at regular intervals across excavated areas and within stratigraphic units.

Soils, stratigraphy and archaeological preservation vary considerably over the site area. By far the best organic preservation is found in the waterlogged channel sediments, although pH values ranging from 4.2 to 5.0 have meant that very little faunal material has survived. The site is remarkably free from modern disturbance; the only major feature is an open drainage ditch which cuts through the southern part of the infilled channel (*Fig. 5*).

While the lithic assemblage gives an impression of typological homogeneity, it is clear from radiocarbon evidence and from the stratification of occupation debris in certain parts of the site that there was more than one episode of prehistoric occupation, spread over at least two millennia. The major structural remains are likely to be related to Mesolithic occupation, although there is evidence of re-use of the site during the Neolithic and Bronze Age.

For present purposes, the site may be divided into three parts: the till ridge (Area A); the lower-lying areas where the Mesolithic land surface is preserved beneath alluvial sediments; and the infilled channel which offers the best preservation and stratification of archaeological remains.

Area A

Interest focused initially on the till ridge which forms the highest ground in the site area. This affords a relatively well-drained situation and might be expected to have formed a focal point for settlement; it was anticipated, therefore, that this would be the part of the site most likely to contain the remains of dwellings. In fact, nothing was found to suggest that the till ridge had functioned primarily as a residential area.

The most notable feature was the massive concentration of artifacts – more than 34,000 pieces of worked flint, chert and volcanic tuff, including over 600 finished tools, have been recovered from an excavated area of just 125 m^2. It was established by means of test pits that the highest densities of artifacts occurred within an area about 50×30 m, coinciding with the till ridge.

A feature of prehistoric flint assemblages from the Eskmeals area generally is the almost exclusive use of small beach pebbles (the only locally available source of flint) as raw material for toolmaking. This type of material imposed severe constraints on the size and overall morphology of artifacts and on the techniques used for their manufacture. The resulting homogeneity of the assemblages – and particularly of the larger tools and débitage – makes it difficult to identify different periods of flint-working on the basis of typology and raw material characteristics. In the case of the Williamson's Moss site, the problem is compounded by the lack of radiocarbon dates for features 'associated' with the main artifact aggregation (see below) and by the absence of stratification in this part of the site.

The Williamson's Moss assemblage evidently contains an important Mesolithic component, indicated by the presence of large numbers of microliths and microburins. The microliths are all small, narrow forms similar to those from the Monk Moors sites

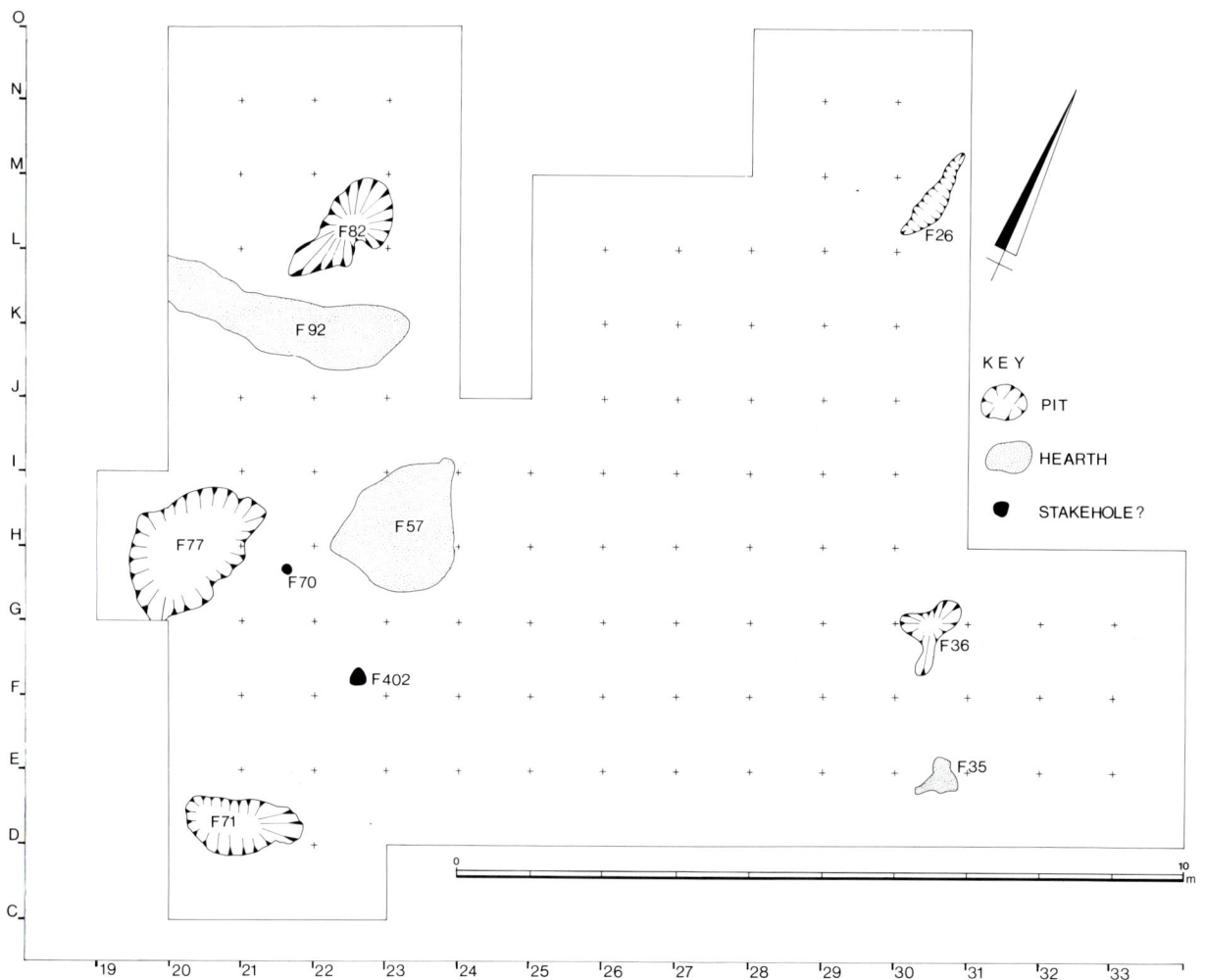

Figure 6   Area A: structural remains as revealed at the end of the 1986 season.

(cf. Bonsall 1981: fig. 6). Whilst microlithic industries of this basic type are known, from radiocarbon evidence, to have been manufactured in the north of England throughout the period *c.* 8800–5200 BP, the dating evidence discussed below suggests that the Williamson's Moss industry falls towards the end of that time-range. Other evidence suggests that the artifact concentration may also contain a Neolithic and/or Bronze Age component, although the only clearly post-Mesolithic artifact recovered so far is a single leaf-shaped arrowhead. Similarly, the possibility that more than one episode of Mesolithic activity is represented should not be discounted.

The structural remains revealed by excavation of Area A comprised hearths, small pits, and possible stake-holes (*Fig. 6*). Marked differences in the character of the hearths and of the pit infillings suggest that these features are not all of the same age, but represent a kind of 'palimpsest' resulting from successive occupations. Evidence of Neolithic and Bronze Age activity elsewhere on the site suggests that some of the features at least post-date the Mesolithic occupation. So far, the only tangible evidence to support this interpretation is the presence

of a few sherds of pottery of 'middle Neolithic' type.[4]

Another obvious product of human activity was the presence of large quantities of introduced material. Several features were infilled with loose, medium sand; while the entire area was littered with stones, many of them well-rounded cobbles. Since this material is not a normal component of the till underlying the site, it may be inferred that it has been derived from the nearby shingle ridges.

There has also been considerable vertical movement within the soil. Artifacts, imported stones and charcoal have been found dispersed through the upper 50 cm of the profile. The actions of roots, earthworms and moles, and movement down dehydration cracks in the till have all contributed to this; but the major factor was most probably *trampling* associated with successive episodes of occupation. The effects of human trampling are probably widespread on prehistoric sites in Britain, particularly those on clay soils, yet often go unrecognized. At the early Mesolithic site of Deepcar in the southern Pennines, for example, Radley (Radley and Mellars 1964: 3–4) noted that flint artifacts were dispersed through 40 cm of an unusually compact clay soil, with the largest pieces tending to occur lower down the profile. No explanation for this was offered. The same phenomenon, however, has been observed in damp clay soils in caves, where it has been attributed to trampling during human occupation (Stockton 1973). The archaeological implications of trampling are important, since re-utilization of a site can lead to severe disturbance of the remains of an earlier occupation. At the Williamson's Moss site it is therefore possible that certain kinds of structural evidence (e.g. hearths and postholes) associated with Mesolithic occupation have been destroyed by subsequent Neolithic or Bronze Age activity.

The evidence from Area A presents similar problems of interpretation to those encountered on the Monk Moors sites. There was no appreciable build up of sediment on the till ridge during the Flandrian, and hence there is no clear stratification of the archaeological remains. The only organic material to have survived is wood charcoal and a few carbonized fragments of hazel-nut shells; these samples were often too small for conventional radiocarbon dating. The most difficult problem, therefore, has been to establish the relative and absolute ages of the different features here, and to determine which, if any, were contemporary with the Mesolithic occupation. Through a detailed comparison of the archaeological sediments by means of magnetic susceptibility measurements, micromorphological examination and pollen analysis, together with the application of small counter and accelerator techniques of radiocarbon dating, it may be possible to reconstruct the sequence of events in this part of the site.

The lower-lying areas

The artifact concentration declines rapidly away from the higher ground. Material has been found over the rest of the site, but the distribution is sporadic and densities rarely exceed 5 per m². On the other hand, structural remains are widespread in these lower-lying areas.

Work so far has concentrated in a zone bordering the infilled channel (Area B and Area F), although test pits have been dug at regular intervals over the northern part of the site. Outside the channel area, the deposits overlying the till can be divided into two stratigraphic units: a thin layer of fine sand which defines the buried land surface; and, above this, a series of alluvial sediments which are up to 60 cm thick.

The alluvial sediments formed through intermittent flooding of the areas immediately behind the shingle ridge. They contain abundant evidence of human activity. Considerable quantities of well-sorted sand and fine gravel occur as narrow lenses or, where there has been mixing as a result of trampling, as irregular pockets of coarser material. This sand and gravel resembles beach material and contrasts with the surrounding sediments. It is therefore interpreted as material brought onto the site by man. Traces of fire are also widespread. High carbon and potassium values were recorded in Area B indicating the presence of large amounts of wood ash within the soil. Recognizable hearths either consist of dark lenses of charcoal powder up to 50 cm across and 10 cm thick, or appear as more extensive spreads of charcoal fragments, sometimes associated with fire-cracked stones. The absence of 'baking' of the underlying sediments suggests that the majority of these features are the remains of low temperature fires (cf. Butzer 1982: 84). Three hearths at different levels within the alluvial sediments have given dates of 3665±40 BP (UB-2568), 3756±104 BP (BM-1396), and 4925±165 BP (UB-2711), consistent with their relative stratigraphic positions (*Table 1*). The earliest of these occurred at a level just above the buried land surface.

On the basis of the evidence recovered so far, it would appear that the archaeological remains in the

Table 1: Radiocarbon dates for the Williamson's Moss Site

Lab. No.	Context	Date BP
UB-2544	Area E1. Wood (oak). Part of timber lattice of Structure 1.	6015±75
UB-2546	Area E1. Bark fragments (birch). Part of brushwood covering of Structure 1.	5650±50
UB-2545	Area E1. Bark fragments (birch). Part of decayed brushwood covering of Structure 1.	5555±40
UB-2712	Area F. Bark fragments (birch). Part of bark floor on buried land surface	5520±85
GU-1664	Area F. Bark fragments (birch). Part of bark floor on buried land surface	5500±70
UB-2713	Area E1. Bark fragments (birch). Part of bark floor on timber and earth platform (Structure 2)	5480±90
UB-2711	Area F. Charcoal from hearth in alluvial sediments overlying buried land surface	4925±165
BM-1396	Area B. Charcoal from hearth (F23) in alluvial sediments overlying buried land surface	3756±104
UB-2568	Test Pit AP36. Charcoal from hearth in alluvial sediments overlying buried land surface	3665±40
UB-2715	Area E2. Charcoal from hearth overlying Structure 5.	3480±80

Figure 7 Williamson's Moss site: areas of stone pavement – *a*. Area B (scale=20 cm divisions); *b*. Test Pit G46; *c*. Test Pit AZ26 (scales=50 cm divisions).

alluvial sediments relate mainly to Neolithic and later activity. No dwellings or other large-scale structures have been recognized. The overall impression is of frequent, but short-term, use of the site, with no indication of major or prolonged settlement.

Structural remains associated with the buried land surface are quite different in character, and comprise a number of areas of *stone pavement*. These were constructed of densely packed, well-rounded pebbles and cobbles put down as a thin layer on the contemporary ground surface. Again, these stones can only have been obtained from areas of exposed shingle along the coast. The main example uncovered so far occurs in Area B where the buried land surface slopes down towards the edge of the infilled channel (*Fig. 7a*). Similar stone concentrations have been located in test pits in the area north of the till ridge (*Fig. 7b–c*). As yet these features are undated, but their stratigraphic position below the above-dated hearths suggests that they pre-date 5000 BP, and are thus likely to relate to Mesolithic occupation of the site.

Stone pavements are known from only three other Mesolithic sites in Britain – Barsalloch in Wigtownshire (Cormack 1970), Culverwell in Dorset (Palmer 1976) and Dunford Bridge A in South Yorkshire (Radley *et al.* 1974).[5] They are found much more widely, however, on mainland European sites. Newell (1981: 245) has suggested that such features were integral parts of dwellings. This provides a plausible explanation for those examples where the paving forms a tightly confined rectangular, oval or circular area, or is related to other structural elements such as hearths and post-settings. However, interpretation of the stone pavement in Area B of the Williamson's Moss site as a 'dwelling surface' presents several difficulties, not least of which is the absence of associated structural features, and the lack of floor matting which occurs elsewhere on the site. Rather, this feature is best interpreted as a means of creating a firm, stable surface where the ground, by virtue of the damp clay subsoil, was naturally soft. The use of stones to consolidate a surface that was liable to 'puddling' as a result of constant movement of people across it does not necessarily imply a residential function.

It would be premature to suggest an interpretation of the other areas of stone pavement identified on the Williamson's Moss site. These may indeed prove to be hut floors, but a full analysis will only be possible when further excavation has been carried out.

The infilled channel

This is a small feature, less than 30 m across at its widest point. It begins a few hundred metres behind the site and is incised quite deeply into the glacial deposits, reaching a depth of 3 m where it abuts against the shingle ridge (*Fig. 5*). Once the channel

Figure 8   Area E1: structural remains as exposed at end of the 1983 field season (scale=50 cm divisions).

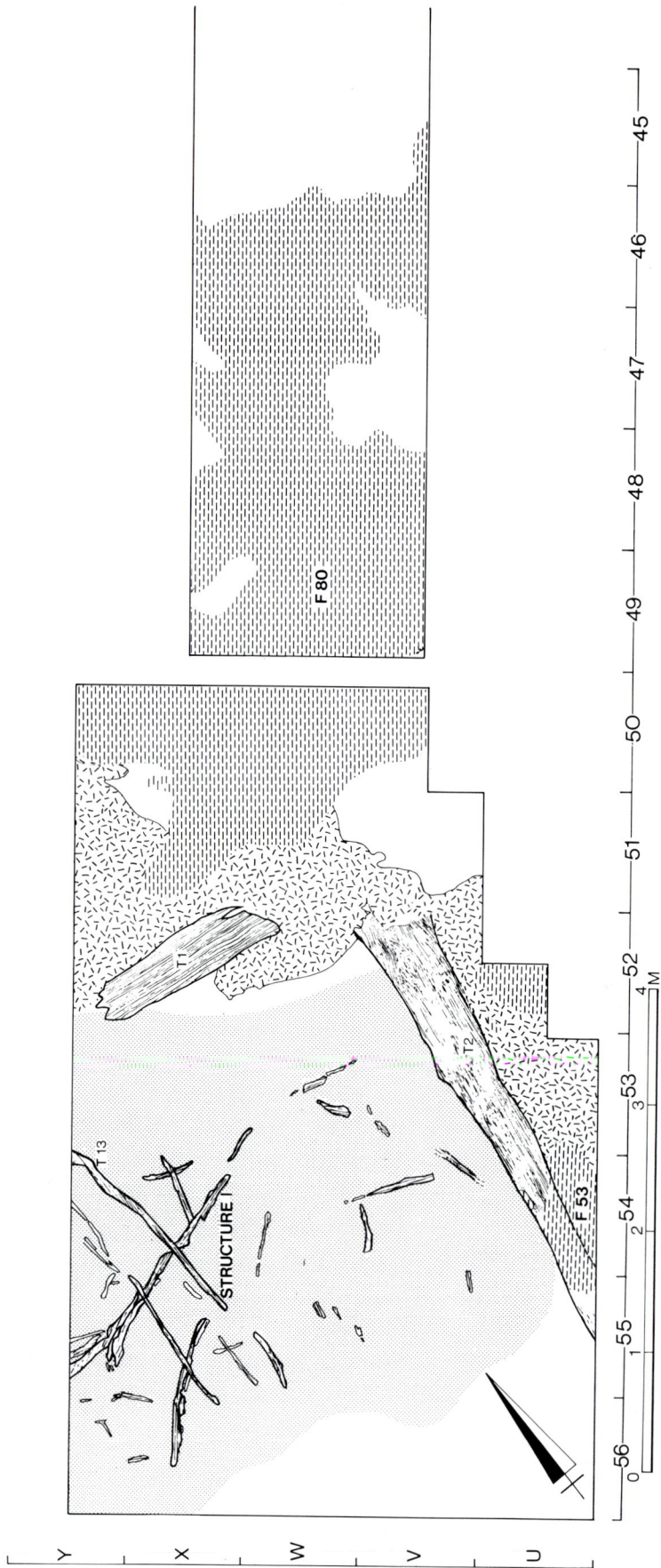

Figure 9   Area E1: plan of structural features.

Figure 10 Area E1: Structure 1 – timber lattice and decayed brushwood covering (Scale=50 cm divisions).

Figure 11 Area E1: compressed birch branch – part of decayed brushwood covering of Structure 1 (scale=5 cm divisions). Radiocarbon dating of this wood (UB-2545) gave an age of 5555±40 BP.

had been dammed up by the shingle ridge – an event that occurred between 6500–7000 BP – it filled in rapidly with sediment, predominantly silt and clay, washed down from the surrounding areas. Within less than a millennium it was converted from an active stream channel into a strip of low-lying and presumably very soft ground which, at times of high rainfall, would have been liable to flooding.

Such waterlogged ground seems an unlikely place for human occupation. Yet the channel sediments contain the clearest traces of structures found so far on the Williamson's Moss site. The construction of these features involved the use of substantial amounts of timber, made up largely of branches and sections of trunks of mature oak trees, together with quantities of brushwood and bark. These features mainly relate to a level about a metre below the present land surface.

Two trenches (Areas E1 and E2) have been opened on the north side of the channel (*Fig. 5*). These exploratory excavations are unfinished. The following discussion, therefore, is a preliminary assessment.

Area E1

Remains of two different types of structure have been uncovered in this trench (*Figs. 8 & 9*).

Structure 1. This is a raft-type foundation or platform, and is made up of two basic elements. The first is a series of oak branches laid horizontally on the channel surface. There are two sets of branches, one on top of the other, arranged in a grille or lattice pattern. The other element is a layer of black, well-humified peat up to 30 cm thick composed of twigs, thin branches and bark, which occurs between and on top of the main timbers (*Figs. 10 & 11*). This is interpreted as the decayed remains of a layer of birch brushwood placed on top of the timber lattice. This type of structure would have formed a stable foundation on which other structures could be built or which would support the weight of people. The use of this type of foundation for houses, jettys, trackways, etc., built on soft marshy ground is well documented in both ethnographic and archaeological contexts (Edwards 1934; St George Gray and Bulleid 1953; Manning 1961; Coles 1984). A timber lattice provides a rigid base that will counteract the tendency for differential settlement in response to any variation in loading. In other words, any load placed on top of such a foundation will tend to be distributed evenly across the underlying surface. Such a structure is made more stable if the timbers are fixed at the cross points. Interestingly, toolmarks have been found on one of the timbers of Structure 1 (T13) close to the point where it crosses over one of the underlying branches. These consist of fine cuts and the characteristic 'chatter-marks' left

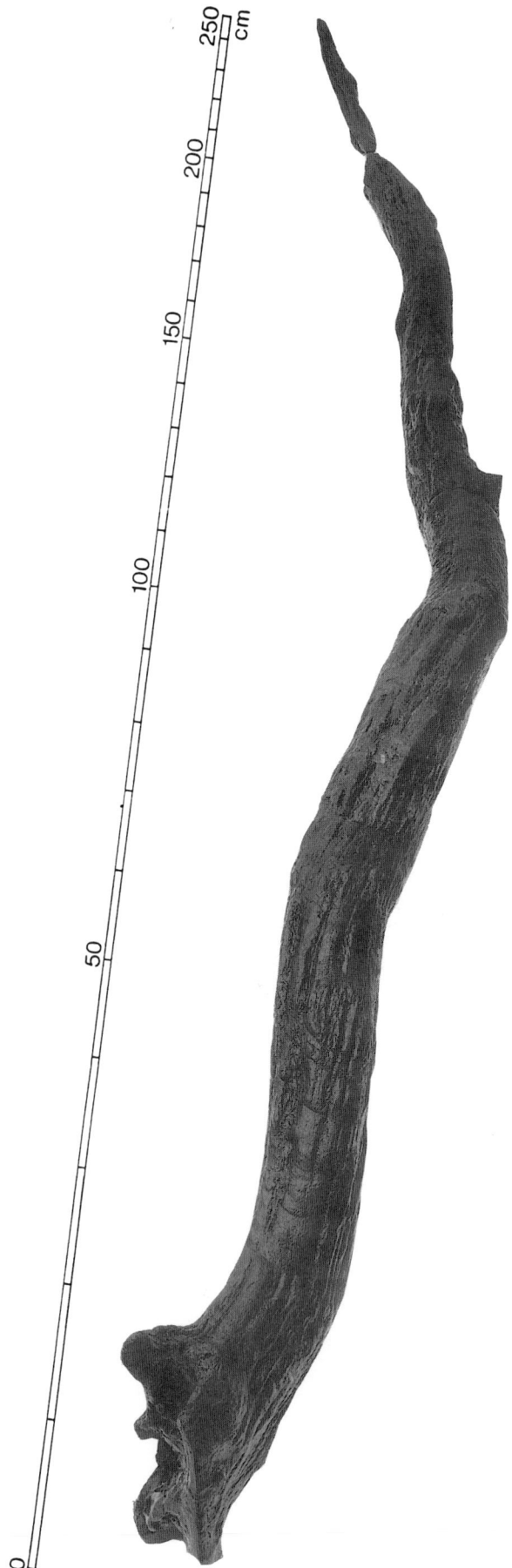

190

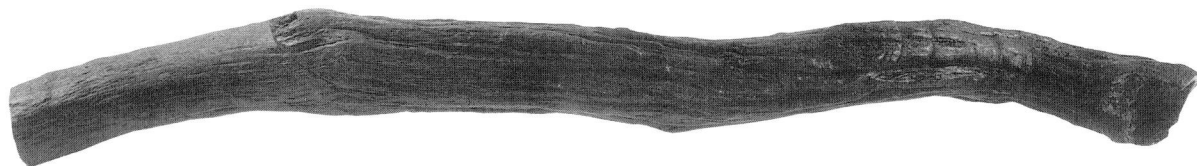

Figure 12 Opposite and above.
Area E1: oak branch (T13) with traces of working from timber lattice of Structure 1.

191

by whittling or shaving the wood with a sharp-edged implement. On another part of the branch are a series of fine grooves which may have been caused by some form of binding (*Fig. 12*). However, it is difficult to be certain if any of these traces resulted from attempts to stabilize the timber lattice. Given the low-lying, wet situation, it is suggested that this timber and brushwood structure was designed to provide a platform raised above a surface that was periodically inundated by water.

Structure 2. The two larger timbers (T1 and T2) form part of a second structural complex (*Figs. 8 & 9*). Both are sections of oak trunks, and have been placed on approximately the same alignments as the branches which form the timber lattice of Structure 1. T1 was laid on the buried land surface at the point where the channel sediments lap onto the till. T2 is a much larger piece which extends from the same point out across the channel surface. Infilling the area along the north side of T1 to a level corresponding to the upper surface of the timber, and extending in a narrow zone across the trench, is a heterogeneous mixture of clay, sand and stones with a distinctly uneven surface. This is not a naturally-formed sediment, but consists of materials from different sources that were deliberately mixed together and dumped. Similar redeposited material seems to infill the area along the east side of T2,

although this needs to be confirmed by further excavation.

This complex of features, then, represents an alternative method of constructing an artificial raised surface or platform, and of building it out across the soft ground of the infilled channel – that of using earth and stones to fill in behind a timber revetment. The ground behind these two retaining timbers was built up to a level about 40 cm above the contemporary channel surface.

Associated with this platform are the remains of extensive areas of bark flooring. In places the flooring is very well preserved and is made of superimposed layers of bark fragments laid down as a dense mat up to 10 cm thick (*Fig. 13*). Elsewhere it has decayed to form a thin layer of peat with a distinctly 'platy' structure. The largest area of bark matting (F80) can be traced for a distance of over six metres from the point where it overlies the 'made ground' into the adjoining trench (Area F), where it rests directly on the buried land surface (*Fig. 9*). Since these areas of bark matting are likely to be remnants of the *internal* floors of one or more buildings constructed on the platform and the adjacent land surface, their presence indicates a residential function for this part of the Williamson's Moss site. The use of bark as insulation for hut floors is attested at Mesolithic sites in Denmark and neighbouring areas of Northern Europe (Clark

Figure 13 Area E1: area of birch bark matting (F53) overlying Structure 2. Radiocarbon dating of this bark (UB-2713) gave an age of 5480±90 BP (scale = 10 cm divisions)

1975), birch bark often being preferred to other types because of its water-repellent properties and the ease with which it could be removed from trees.

Chronology

In order to date Structures 1 and 2, six samples were submitted for radiocarbon dating (*Table 1*, samples 1–6).

A sample of oak from the timber lattice of Structure 1 gave an age of 6015±75 BP (UB-2544). Two samples of birch bark from the base and upper part of the overlying layer of decayed brushwood respectively gave dates of 5555±40 BP (UB-2545) and 5650±50 BP (UB-2546). Three samples of birch bark from the two principal areas of bark flooring associated with Structure 2 gave ages of 5520±85 BP (UB-2712), 5500±70 BP (F80) (GU-1664), and 5480±90 BP (F53) (UB-2713).

Since dates on bark are contemporaneous with the removal of the bark from trees and its incorporation in the structures concerned, then these dates closely relate to the period of construction. The bark dates are statistically indistinguishable and indicate that Structures 1 and 2 were built *c.* 5550 BP.

No diagnostic artifacts have been found in direct association with either Structure 1 or Structure 2. Such artifacts as do occur within or immediately below the bark flooring could belong to a Mesolithic or post-Mesolithic industry. Elsewhere on the site there is a preponderance of diagnostically Mesolithic artifacts and no clearly early Neolithic artifacts (either of stone or pottery). It is therefore concluded that the structural remains in Area E1 were contemporary with occupation of the Williamson's Moss site by people who possessed a late Mesolithic technology.

The date of 6015±75 BP on a sample of oak from one of the foundation timbers of Structure 1 is *c.* 450 years earlier than the decayed brushwood covering of this feature. In common with the other oak timbers found in the channel area this sample comprised heartwood and hence would have an initial age of perhaps 100–300 years (cf. Rackham 1976; Campbell and Baxter 1979). This does not explain the whole difference. However, it is notable that there is little evidence for *in situ* decay of the timbers, implying that the bark and sapwood had already decayed prior to the use of the timber for constructional purposes (this is also implied by the well-preserved traces of working on T13). Given the limitations of Mesolithic technology[6] it may be inferred that dead timbers were utilized for the structures under discussion, and that this explains the remaining difference in age between the oak timbers and the other platform elements.

Area E2

As in Area E1, the description and interpretation of the structural remains in this trench are hampered by the incomplete state of the excavation. However, a similar pattern can be discerned (*Figs. 14 & 15*).

Structure 3. At the southern end of the trench another group of crossed timbers has been uncovered (*Fig. 15A*). This feature resembles the timber lattice of Structure 1, and is enclosed by the same type of peat deposit. It is suggested therefore that this is the remains of a second raft-type foundation of timber and brushwood. However, certain differences may be noted. The larger timbers appear to be radial sections of oak trunk with relatively flat surfaces, rather than branches as were used for Structure 1. The lowermost timbers rest on a surface at *c.* 6.25 m O.D. – some 20 cm higher than the surface underlying Structure 1. The uneven character of this surface and the presence of lumps of irregularly-mixed sand and clay, suggest that this is another example of 'made ground'. Therefore, the difference in level between Structures 1 and 3 need not necessarily imply a difference in age.

Structure 4. The timber lattice of Structure 3 abuts against a raised area of clearly redeposited material. This feature has not been fully exposed, but it appears to extend in a narrow zone along the eastern side of the trench for some 6–7 m until it abuts against the buried land surface at the northern margin of the channel sediments. It consists of the same compact mixture of clay, sand and stones that characterizes the 'made ground' associated with Structure 2 in Area E1, and has been built up to approximately the same level. The western edge, where exposed, presents an abrupt, vertical face – suggesting that the dumped material was at one time contained by a timber revetment which subsequently decayed or was removed. Unlike Structure 2 in Area E1, no traces of bark matting have been found associated with this feature. One interpretation, therefore, might be that it was a kind of earthen road or causeway linking the timber and brushwood platform to the drier, firmer ground at the edge of the infilled channel.

A mixture of sand, clay and stones provides a very suitable material for building a causeway across soft ground. If built entirely of clay, this would become deformed when put under load – it would tend to 'squeeze out' when walked on; whereas pure sand and gravel would tend to shift and fall apart, since it has little natural cohesion. On the other hand, a mixture of clay, sand and stones (in the right proportions) can be compacted to form a firm, stable surface – the clay acting as a filler giving cohesion to hold together the coarser material in a kind of natural 'concrete' (Tomlinson 1972; O'Flaherty 1974).

No radiocarbon estimates are available for either of the structures described, although in character and general configuration they resemble the struc-

Figure 14 Area E2: state of excavation at end of 1983 field season.

tural features in Area E1 which have been dated to the mid-sixth millennium BP.

Structure 5. At a higher level within the channel sediments, the remains of another structure were encountered (*Fig. 15B*). This consists of two overlapping and partially decayed timbers. The soil between and immediately above these timbers contained numerous fragments of bark – evidently the remains of a small area of floor matting. This may originally have been supported on a layer of branches and brushwood laid across the foundation timbers. On top of the bark layer was a small, but clearly defined, hearth consisting of an oval concentration of charcoal and heat-shattered stones. Traces of bark were found adhering to the undersides of some of the hearth stones.

It is evident from *Fig. 14* that the foundation timbers of this structure relate to a level well above that of the features already described, and were not in contact with either the timber and brushwood platform or the 'earthen causeway'. It is likely, therefore, that Structure 5 belongs to a later episode of occupation. A radiocarbon date of 3480±80 BP (UB-2715) on charcoal from the hearth provides a limiting date for this occupation.

Summary

In the preceding discussion, archaeological features associated with the buried land surface (the areas of stone pavement, platform structures and bark floors) and the bulk of the flint assemblage were related to Mesolithic occupation. It was further suggested that the occupation resulted in extensive removal of vegetation and soil from the site area. A question which arises from this is whether the archaeological remains are the result of a single phase of intensive occupation, or were formed during more than one episode of occupation.

A flint scatter of the size and density of that on the Williamson's Moss site is likely to have been deposited over an *aggregate* period of years, rather than months or weeks. Moreover, the intensive use by the Mesolithic population of *local* flint and other materials for toolmaking, the nature of the buried land surface and the scale and complexity of the structures associated with it (which in turn implies considerable investment of time and labour in their construction), suggest that settlement was of a permanent or semi-permanent nature.

These observations have to be considered against the suggestion made in the following section, on the basis of palynological studies, that the main artifact concentration associated with the till ridge and the platform structures within and adjacent to the infilled channel relate to *separate* episodes of occupation.

These contrasting interpretations, drawn from a consideration of the archaeological and pedological evidence on the one hand, and from pollen evidence on the other, focus attention on a fundamental problem in archaeological investigation – that of establishing whether archaeological features were formed contemporaneously or at different times, and, by extension, of distinguishing between single and multiple occupations. This is not simply a question of establishing relative chronology, but also of determining the amount of time which separated the formation of the features concerned. At present, and without more precise chronological information, these questions are incapable of being resolved for the Williamson's Moss site. Clearly, this problem will not be resolved until precise dates are obtained for individual features in different parts of the site. It is doubtful, however, if currently available dating techniques could provide the temporal resolution required.

Whilst it would be premature to attempt to draw too many conclusions from an unfinished excavation, it is worth stressing that the structural evidence from the Williamson's Moss site – in particular the use made of timber, earth and brushwood for the construction of platform foundations, and the evidence for extensive use of bark as a flooring material – is without precedent in the British Mesolithic. It remains, however, to establish the extent and precise configuration of these structures. The fre-

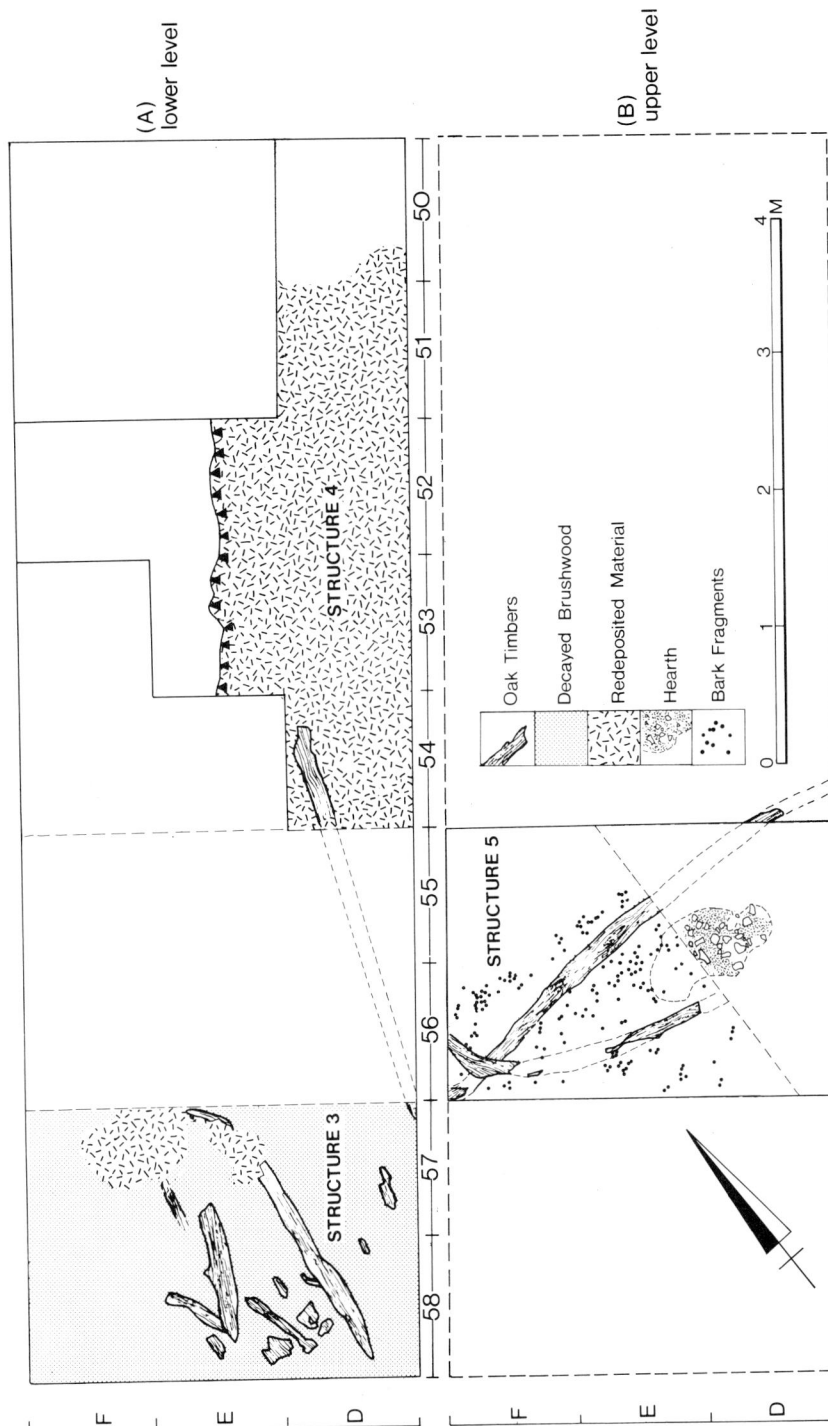

Figure 15 Area E2: structural remains – A. lower level; B. upper level (excavation unfinished, cf. *Fig. 14*).

quency with which buried timber has been encountered in systematic probing of the unexcavated areas of the infilled channel suggests that those features already uncovered form only a small sample of what is evidently a large and impressive structural complex. This view is reinforced by the discovery during the 1986 season of another infilled channel (*Fig. 5*), to the north of the till ridge, in which substantial pieces of timber were also located by probing, although the archaeological significance of this find has yet to be demonstrated by excavation.

VEGETATION HISTORY AND LAND USE CHANGES

Introduction

An earlier report on the Eskmeals Project (Bonsall, Sutherland, Tipping and Cherry 1986: 19–25) discussed the development of plant communities and land use changes near the Williamson's Moss archaeological site using palynological evidence obtained from the infilled lake basin at Williamson's Moss (*Figs 2 & 4*), from the initial deposition of lacustrine

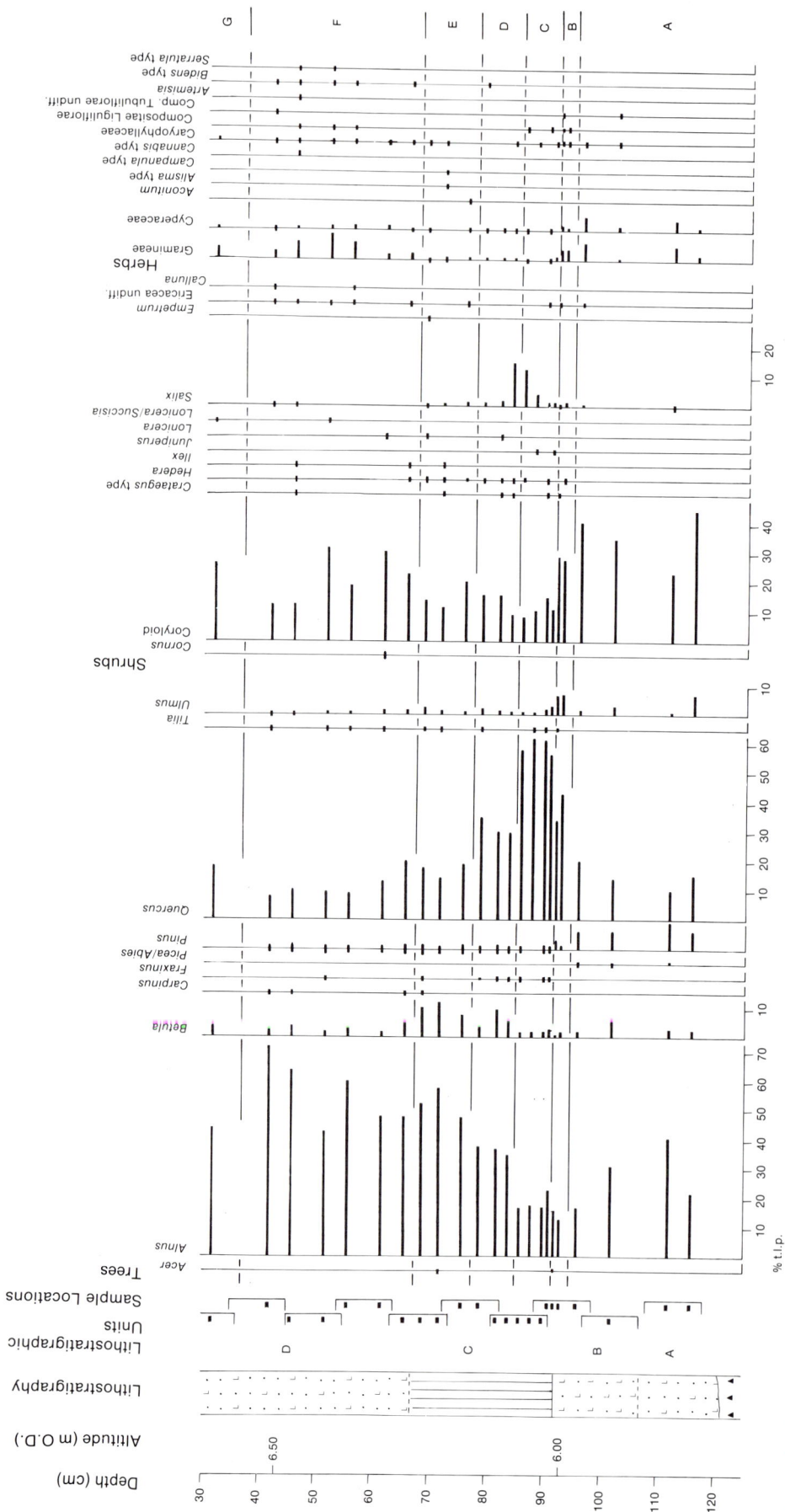

Figure 16 Relative pollen diagram from the infilled channel deposits (Area E1) of the Williamson's Moss site.

196

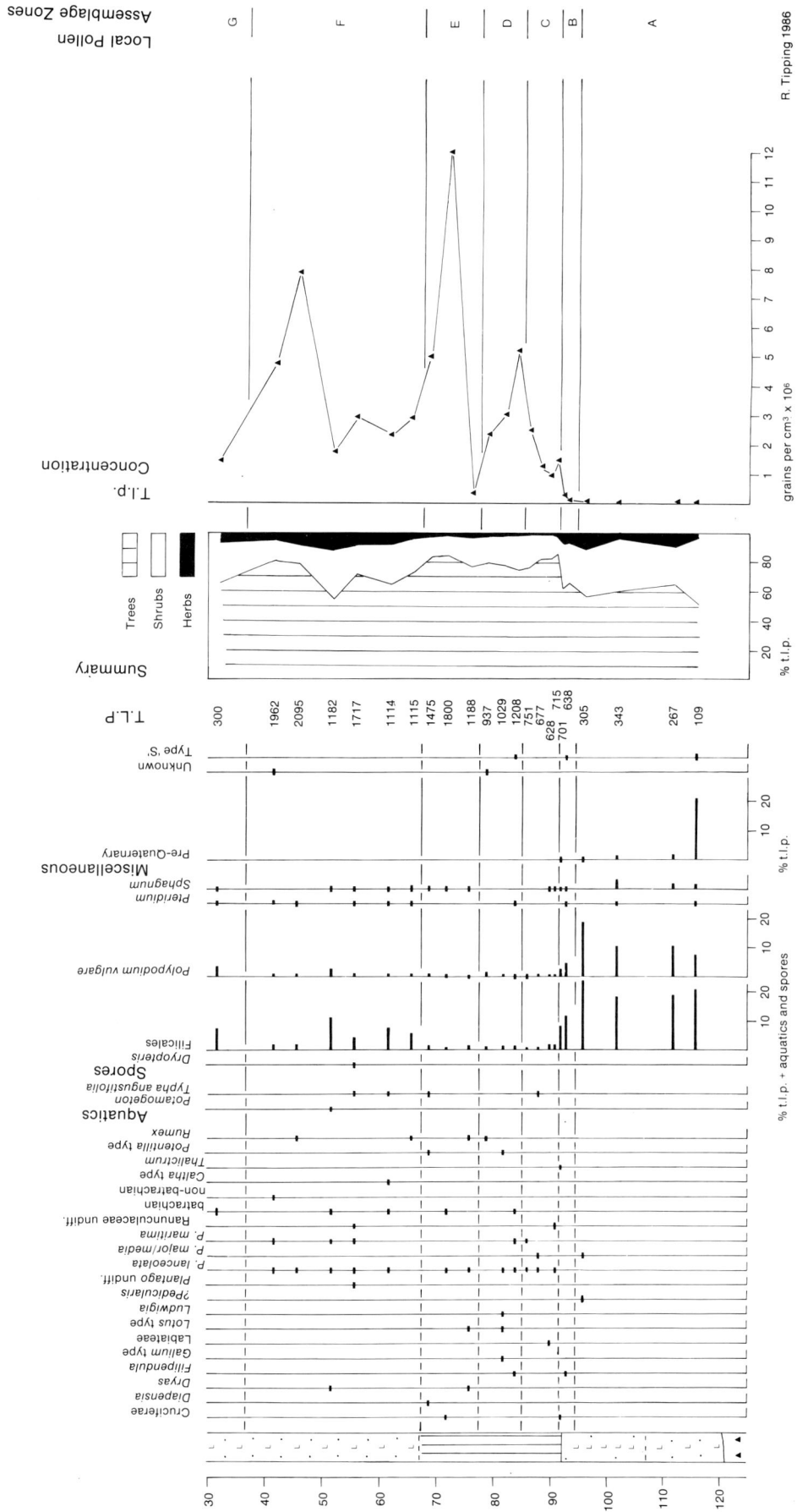

Figure 16 (cont'd) Relative pollen diagram from the infilled channel deposits (Area E1) of the Williamson's Moss site.

197

sediments in the basin at *c*. 6100 BP until, employing a tentatively developed chronology, *c*. 4800 BP. Firmer chronological control has now been provided by seven radiocarbon dates, and the palynological results from the Williamson's Moss lake basin are summarized using this refined time-scale, before a second site, from within the archaeological site considered above, is discussed.

The analyses from Williamson's Moss showed the establishment around the lake of an alder–birch carr following the isolation of the basin from marine influence at *c*. 6100 BP. The glacial deposits to the east supported a mixed-oak forest at this time, but at *c*. 5600 BP (interpolated age) small openings in the forest, characterized by the occurrence of pollen of shade-intolerant herbs and shrubs, presaged a statistically significant decline in elm pollen values at 5440±70 BP (SRR-3065: 'combined' age of two assays on (a) the humic fraction of 5520±60 BP and (b) the humin fraction of 5170±110 BP). This elm decline was associated with an increase in *Salix* (willow) percentages, thought to be due either to clearance of carr communities or a response to lowered lake levels. *Plantago lanceolata* occurred consistently from the beginning of the elm decline at values less than 1% total land pollen (t.l.p.) in counts of generally more than 800–900 land pollen grains, and persisted in the counts following partial forest regeneration at 5150±80 BP (SRR-3066: 'combined' age of (a) the humic fraction of 5260±60 BP and (b) the humin fraction of 4780±110 BP). Alder–birch carr was re-established at this time and was maintained during the second and more pronounced elm decline at 4850±80 BP (SRR-3068: 'combined' age of (a) the humic fraction of 4950±60 BP and (b) the humin fraction of 4610±100 BP), which heralded a more substantial phase of woodland clearance in the region.

The basin of Williamson's Moss is *c*. 4 hectares in extent, and the results are accordingly likely to represent a predominantly regional (*sensu* Jacobson and Bradshaw 1981) picture of the environment, a point emphasized by the absence of substantial watercourses entering the basin. The changes in vegetation and land use summarized above can only indirectly, through radiocarbon dating, be related to the prehistoric anthropogenic activities on the till slopes revealed by excavation and survey.

An attempt to overcome this problem was made by pollen analyzing the sedimentary sequence which accumulated in the infilled channel lying within the area of excavation (Areas E1, E2; *Fig. 5*) and immediately adjacent to the area of densest artifact concentration, a deposit which, because of its small size, is more likely to represent vegetation change at a local (*sensu* Jacobson and Bradshaw 1981) scale.

Methods

The sediment stratigraphy recorded in the west face of metre square J13 in Area E1 (*Fig. 9*) is shown in *Fig. 16*. Ten sample tins were used to sample the deposits, and these were sealed and stored at 4 °C in a refrigerator until analyzed. Sediment samples of 0.5 cm thickness were removed from cleaned faces and treated following standard techniques (Moore and Webb 1978) after adding *Lycopodium* tablets to determine the pollen concentrations of the samples. Residues were stained with safranine and embedded in silicon oil for counting on a Vickers M15C binocular microscope. The numbers of land pollen grains (t.l.p.) counted per spectrum are recorded in *Fig. 16*.

Results

Fig. 16 gives the complete pollen diagram for the channel deposits. The diagram has been subdivided into seven local pollen assemblage zones (l.p.a.z.), A–G. Interpretation has been based on the assumptions that the deposit represents a conformable sequence, and that vertical displacement of pollen within the decaying organic deposit has not been significant. It was indicated above that the organic remains preserved within the channel (*Fig. 16*, lithostratigraphic unit C) were probably deposited anthropogenically, and the sequence of radiocarbon dates shows the period of deposition to be less than the standard deviation on the dates, that is less than *c*. 100 years. Nevertheless, these assumptions are supported by the pollen spectra clearly showing distinct patterns (which form the basis of the zonation scheme) and no homogeneity or 'smoothing' of the spectra, which would be expected had the sediments been deposited *en masse* or had been affected by post-depositional translocation of pollen. The organic materials were probably deposited over a period of less than a century, and the anthropogenic mode of deposition has resulted in the pollen diagram showing distinctive features; the abrupt changes in major pollen taxa between l.p.a. zones C and D, and between zones D and E, suggest that accumulation was not uniform, and that the organic layer was built up in stages over this short time period. The observation that the diagram changes through time in ways which appear to be interpretable ecologically (below) also suggests that the majority of pollen grains were derived from vegetation surrounding the channel, and are not a direct consequence of the construction of the brushwood layer – for example, no major pollen taxon is so consistently highly represented in the organic unit as to suggest its introduction into the channel with the macroscopic plant remains.

L.p.a.z A shows high values of *Alnus*, *Pinus* and *Corylus*/*Myrica* (Coryloid) pollen, and very high values of Filicales (undifferentiated fern spores) and *Polypodium vulgare*. With the exception of Gramineae and Cyperaceae, herb pollen is very scarce. Pre-Quaternary palynomorphs are virtually confined to this p.a. zone, as are the broken grains of *Picea/ Abies*. At several sites on the Eskmeals foreland (Tipping, unpublished data) this distinctive suite of pollen types (Coniferales, pre-Quaternary and Polypodiaceae spores) appear to be characteristic of sediments identified as estuarine or marine from diatom analyses (J. Fulton, pers. comm.). A precise environment for the basal channel sediments cannot readily be identified in the absence of diatoms (J. Fulton, pers. comm.), but these spectra are considered to be wave-affected. The values of several pollen taxa fluctuate sharply in this p.a. zone, notably *Ulmus* and *Corylus/Myrica*, and it is probable that the pollen spectra in this zone, through being influenced by turbulence, do not give a clear indication of terrestrial plant communities surrounding the channel. The pollen concentrations in this sediment are exceedingly low, probably the result of a relatively rapid accumulation rate.

Minerogenic sedimentation continues into l.p.a.z. B and, while there is little change in sediment type and pollen concentrations, the percentages of those pollen taxa preferentially selected by wave action (*Pinus*, Filicales, *Polypodium vulgare*) decline markedly. Limited evidence from diatom analysis of a spectrum at 93 cm (J. Fulton, pers. comm.) shows these sediments to be of freshwater origin, and this p.a. zone probably reflects more closely the vegetation around the lake and on the till slopes. The change in mode of sedimentation towards the top of l.p.a.z. A is probably directly associated with the growth of the shingle ridges seaward of Williamson's Moss, and can be assigned an age of *c.* 6100 BP.

L.p.a.z. B has much lower values of *Alnus* than the basal p.a. zone, and markedly higher values of *Quercus*. These differences are thought to be due principally to the change in depositional environment noted above. *Ulmus*, erratically represented in the wave-affected sediments, rises to 7% t.l.p. Few terrestrial herbs are recorded.

The lithostratigraphic boundary between the minerogenic freshwater sediments and the overlying peat comprising the decayed remains of the brushwood cover occurs at 92 cm. Close palynological subsampling in these sediments shows the palynological boundary between l.p.a. zones B and C to lie slightly higher in the stratigraphy, so that the sedimentological boundary lies within l.p.a.z. B. It is unlikely, therefore, that the change in sediment type or depositional environment is responsible for the palynological changes occurring between these l.p.a. zones.

The l.p.a.z. boundary B/C is drawn at a pronoun-ced decline in percentages of *Ulmus*, from 7% to 1% t.l.p. The close sampling interval at this point shows the elm decline to lie entirely within the organic deposit, and so an hiatus in deposition between the minerogenic and organic deposits is not thought likely to explain this feature. The elm decline appears to be strongly associated with other indications of changing woodland structure. A reduction in values of *Corylus/Myrica* pollen is accompanied by a major expansion of *Quercus*. The direct replacement by oak trees of gaps in the woodland caused by the decline in the elm population is not thought to wholly explain the palynological changes, since there is also considerable evidence of increased openness in the canopy cover of the woodland. The pollen of *Fraxinus*, a tree which grows adventitiously in open spaces in formerly closed woodland, is recorded for the first time during the *Ulmus* decline, as are *Crataegus*-type pollen, a pollen taxon which includes hawthorn (*Crataegus*) and *Juniperus*, shrub taxa which rapidly colonize open ground. *Hedera* pollen is present from the elm decline; its representation may imply an increased population of dead host trees (cf. Garbett 1981) or, alternatively, may indicate the easier passage of pollen through the trunk space of the increasingly open woodland (cf. Tauber 1965), a mechanism which would facilitate the more effective representation of oak pollen also. Similarly, although *Tilia* is not regarded as being present at this time in the local woodland of the western Lake District (Pigott and Huntley 1980), its pollen is consistently represented during the elm decline, again implying increasing openness in the canopy cover and an increased representation of more regional pollen taxa. There are few quantitative changes in the herb taxa, but sustained counts of Compositae Liguliflorae and, importantly, *Plantago lanceolata* suggest the limited clearance of woodland in the immediate area of the channel. An alternative source for much of the herb pollen, in coastal and/or dune communities to the west of Williamson's Moss is thought unlikely given the absence of these taxa in pollen counts from the basal sediments of the channel, and from radiocarbon dating evidence that the earliest sand sheet deposits in the vicinity of the site date from *c.* 3300 BP (see above).

The elm decline at this site has a mean radiocarbon age of approximately 5550 BP. This is one of the earliest dates known to the authors for this important Flandrian biostratigraphic event in the British Isles (cf. Smith 1981) and, in addition, is very closely related to the anthropogenic deposition of the platform structures within the channel, and with the first appearance of the characteristic clearance indicator, *Plantago lanceolata*. It seems probable that the clearance of the woodland, and the elm decline itself, were through human agency. The evidence of the percentage-based pollen spectra suggests that the removal of elm was selective, but this point is difficult to establish since the pollen influx of major taxa cannot be determined given the lack of temporal separation in the radiocarbon dates. The representation of gap-phase trees, shrubs and herbs may imply some clearance of other tree species. The purpose of the clearance is uncertain due to the limited representation of diagnostic herbs (cf. Behre 1981).

The expansion of *Quercus* pollen in l.p.a.z. C has been interpreted (above) as being partly due to the ease of transfer of grains through the relatively open woodland. In l.p.a.z. D a very sharp reduction in percentages of oak occurs. There is little response seen in the proportions of open-ground taxa, however, which perhaps suggests that the reduction in *Quercus* was only partly due to continued woodland clearance. The expansion of *Salix* at the end of l.p.a.z. C, following the elm decline, is sustained into l.p.a.z. D until *Alnus*, *Betula* and *Corylus*/*Myrica* rise to replace *Quercus*. This is regarded as a successional sequence of colonizing wetland tree taxa around the infilling channel following earlier woodland clearance. The reduction in *Quercus* percentages in this zone may, therefore, represent in part the displacement of oak trees from around the channel, and in part the reduced representation of dryland taxa with the growth of carr communities around the pollen site.

The dominance of the pollen of probable wetland habitat continues in later p.a. zones. Both *Alnus* and *Betula* values peak in l.p.a.z. E. The *Quercus* curve shows a further step-wise reduction in values at the start of this p.a. zone, and this abrupt decline, together with the persistence in the pollen counts of *Plantago lanceolata* and other open-ground herbs perhaps suggests continuing dry woodland clearance. Following its initial decline *Ulmus* values are uniformly low, and it would appear that elm was almost completely removed from the vicinity of the channel.

Corylus/*Myrica* values expand in l.p.a.z. F to replace *Quercus*. It is possible that the pollen was derived from hazel (*Corylus*) expanding into gaps in the oak woodland on the till slopes away from the channel, or from sweet gale (*Myrica*) within the carr community. The boundary between the organic deposit and the overlying clay occurs at the base of l.p.a.z. F, and within l.p.a.z. F percentages of the major pollen taxa are again rather erratic, probably due to a change to an alluvial or lacustrine (cf. the increased occurrence of *Typha angustifolia* spores) depositional environment, as those taxa abundant in the wave-affected spectra of the basal p.a. zone (excepting Coniferales) are again prominent. The principal characteristic of this zone is the peak in Gramineae values. *Plantago lanceolata* is consistent-

ly represented, together with Caryophyllaceae and Compositae Liguliflorae. A phase of agricultural activity appears to be indicated at this time. In two spectra of l.p.a.z. F grass grains with long axes exceeding 40 μm (cf. Cerealia) were noted, one at 52 cm, and five at 46 cm.

Discussion

The sedimentary sequence within the channel is regarded as a conformable sequence extending from a period pre-dating the isolation of Williamson's Moss from the sea at *c.* 6100 BP to one post-dating the deposition of the brushwood at *c.* 5550 BP. Correlation between the biostratigraphy of the channel (*Fig. 16*) and that of Williamson's Moss (Bonsall *et al.* 1986: 19–25) is aided by the radiocarbon dates obtained on the sequence at Williamson's Moss and summarized above. These make it likely that the elm decline recorded in *Fig. 16* is the first of the two elm declines recorded at Williamson's Moss. The vegetational changes recorded at Williamson's Moss (also summarized above) agree well with those from the more 'local' diagram from the channel. The elm decline appears to have been of very short duration, perhaps lasting only a few years or, at most, decades, and at both pollen sites appears to have been selective.

Above the elm decline the agreement between the diagrams is less successful. A decline in *Quercus* is seen at each site. At Williamson's Moss this was interpreted (Bonsall *et al.* 1986: 23) as being the result of extended clearance of mixed deciduous woodland following the initial clearance of elm, but the interpretation presented here has been that the representation of oak pollen in the channel deposits was also reduced by the growth of dense carr around the pollen site. Either or both interpretations could be correct, as it is to be expected that pollen sites of differing pollen recruitment characteristics should reflect vegetational changes at differing scales.

At Williamson's Moss the decline in oak is ended by a short-lived regeneration phase, seen in rising *Corylus*/*Myrica* percentages, before mixed-oak forest (with *Ulmus* values approaching, but lower than, those of pre-elm decline sediments) is re-established. Nothing of this phase is seen in the pollen diagram from the channel fill (*Fig. 16*). The possibility exists of an hiatus in deposition at the top of the organic deposits. The overlying minerogenic sediments, probably alluvial in origin, are correlated with the areas of alluvial sediment adjacent to the infilled channel. The initiation of alluviation appears to pre-date 4925±165 BP (UB-2711 – see above), which is markedly later than the mean radiocarbon age of the peat deposits in the channel. However, there are no indications in the pollen record of such gaps in deposition, and this point is unclear. It is possible that the period of cereal cultivation recorded at the infilled channel in the minerogenic sediments of l.p.a.z. F (*Fig. 16*) is of the same age as the clearance episode associated with the second of the two elm declines recognized at Williamson's Moss; this correlation is made on the appearance of cereal grains with the second elm decline at Williamson's Moss in Pennington's (1975) study.

In a previous section, the platform structures (and, by implication, the elm decline, which is contemporaneous with their construction) were related to late Mesolithic occupation on the basis of the presence of a rich microlithic assemblage in the area adjacent to the channel, and the absence (to date) of early Neolithic finds. However, no chronologically diagnostic artifacts have as yet been found *directly* associated with the platform structures, and no radiocarbon dates have yet been obtained on features within the dense concentrations of late Mesolithic artifacts on the till slopes near the channel (*Fig. 4*). Thus, the contemporaneity of the platform structures and associated bark floors and brushwood covering with the Mesolithic activity around the channel remains a supposition, although a reasonable one.

There is evidence in the pollen diagram from the channel deposits (*Fig. 16*) for clearance in the vicinity of the channel at the time of the elm decline and after. However, the representation of open-ground herbs in the diagram is very restricted (percentage values of herbs are comparable with those recorded from the more 'regional' pollen spectra from the lake site of Williamson's Moss, 200 m from the excavation). Although the representation of herb pollen is known to decline very rapidly with distance from a woodland clearing (Vuorela 1973), perhaps the simplest interpretation of the pollen diagram is that during the time period covered by the organic deposit the channel was surrounded by a carr community of wetland tree and shrub taxa. The frequencies of herb pollen at the site are similar to those at the pollen site of Roudsea Wood (Birks 1982), a small woodland hollow dating from *c.* 6700–5150 BP, lying approximately 25 km to the south east of Eskmeals. Here wild grass pollen percentages are on average 5–10% of the pollen sum, and there is a restricted range of herb types. Probable cereal pollen and anthropogenic indicator herbs such as *Plantago lanceolata* occur as occasional grains from *c.* 5400 BP, but this clearance activity is envisaged by Birks to have occurred outside the wood.

The lack of evidence from the Eskmeals infilled channel pollen diagram for substantial woodland clearance adjacent to the site is problematic in view of the archaeological evidence (above) which suggests the Mesolithic occupation to have been particularly intense. There are difficulties in the interpretation of pollen records with regard to defining scale and intensity of anthropogenic activity (Edwards 1982), and the spatial distributions of plant communities around a single pollen site are not readily obtained; in addition there is only very limited empirical data on which to base an estimate of the scale of clearings in woodland for settlement prior to the Neolithic. Nevertheless, a clearing of the size suggested from the excavated areas in *Fig. 5* might be expected to have around its margins a greater proportion and variety of bare- or disturbed-ground herb taxa than is represented in the pollen diagram from the channel, only a few metres from the densest concentrations of worked flint.

The implications for late Mesolithic subsistence were the earliest elm decline at Eskmeals to be clearly related to the microlithic industry are very significant. The time-scale covered by the organic deposits within the channel can probably be measured in, at most, decades, and it may simply be that the anthropogenic activity recognized on the till surface occurred slightly earlier than the construction of the structures within the channel. At present, however, the palynological evidence cannot be taken to imply such a relationship, neither does it provide evidence to suggest that the construction of the timber structures within the channel was directly contemporary with occupation of the immediately adjoining land surface.

DISCUSSION

The preceding sections have outlined some of the results of the Eskmeals Project, and have stressed the interdisciplinary nature of the research. The following discussion will focus on three aspects of the Mesolithic settlement of the Eskmeals area: settlement location, chronology and subsistence.

Settlement location

Many factors could have influenced the location of Mesolithic sites in the Eskmeals area. Most important, perhaps, was food supply. Several authors have stressed the attractions of river estuaries in this respect (Jacobi 1973; Bonsall 1981), and it is interesting to note that nearly all the known sites at Eskmeals (*Fig. 1*) are situated on seaward-facing slopes overlooking stretches of former coastline which experienced predominantly *estuarine* conditions during the period of Mesolithic settlement. Conversely, settlement traces are lacking in areas where estuarine conditions were never established during the mid-Flandrian, for example south of Stubb Place (Cherry and Cherry 1987).

The role of other resources should not be overlooked. The only locally available source of flint would have been the shingle deposits of the coastal foreland. These deposits would also have been the most accessible sources of sand and stones for construction purposes. It is worth noting that the main site locations – at Monk Moors and Williamson's Moss – would have been ideally situated to exploit these resources.

The coast may also have been a vital source of timber for groups which lacked heavy tree-felling equipment. One reason for the apparent preference for oak heartwood as a building material exhibited by the mid-sixth millennium BP inhabitants of the Williamson's Moss site, apart from the ease with which it could be split apart along the lines of the radial rays,[7] may have been its availability as driftwood on the foreshore.

One particularly interesting feature to emerge from the current survey is the tendency for sites to occur along the margins of former channels which cut across the glacial sediments. This relationship is particularly evident to the landward of Williamson's Moss (*Fig. 4*), and also at Monk Moors where the excavated sites lie on either side of a small channel where it meets the former shoreline (*Fig. 1*). The significance of these channels for Mesolithic settlement is not certain. Certain of the channel mouths would have provided a means of access to the foreshore, particularly in the area between Monk Moors and Stubb Place where, at the maximum of the Flandrian transgression, the sea was actively eroding a cliff some 3–15 m high. It is also possible that where estuarine conditions obtained the channels had economic significance. Salmon and sea trout are known to spawn in large numbers in the mouths of small channels and feeder streams leading off the present estuary. To what extent the channels acted as sources of fresh water is, however, problematic. While they would undoubtedly have carried rainwater running off the slopes adjacent to the coastal foreland, they are unlikely during the mid-Flandrian to have been occupied by perennial streams.

Chronology

Three types of information relate to the chronology of Mesolithic settlement in the Eskmeals area: radiocarbon dating of archaeological features; the constraints imposed by the development of the coastal foreland; and the evidence for land use changes from palaeobotanical studies.

Radiocarbon dates are available from the Monk Moors and Williamson's Moss sites. Two radiocarbon dates were obtained on charcoal from a hearth at Monk Moors 1, these giving ages of 6750±155 BP (BM-1216) and 7380±370 BP (Q-1356) (Bonsall 1981). The former of these dates was from a much larger sample (hence the smaller standard deviation) and is therefore considered

more reliable. It implies occupation of Monk Moors at around 6800 BP. Post-Mesolithic occupation of the Monk Moors area is indicated by radiocarbon dates on charcoal from two hearths and a pit of *c.* 4050 BP, *c.* 3650 BP, and *c.* 2850 BP. The radiocarbon evidence from Williamson's Moss has already been discussed. The earliest evidence for occupation is around 5550 BP, and subsequent occupation during the Neolithic and earlier Bronze Age at *c.* 4900 BP and *c.* 3700 BP has also been documented.

It is apparent from the available radiocarbon evidence that both the sites investigated have been occupied on several occasions, indicating that the coastal foreland retained its attraction for settlement long after the Mesolithic period. This pattern also suggests that other site locations have witnessed repeated use over several millennia and, by extension, opens the possibility of more than one episode of Mesolithic occupation.

In the preceding section, site location was related to various environmental factors such as the nearby presence of estuarine conditions. It may therefore be presumed that the chronology of settlement at the different sites will relate to coastal evolution and the progressive establishment of suitable conditions in the Eskmeals area. For instance, as estuarine conditions were first established (between 6500–7000 BP) in the area between Monk Moors and Newbiggin, settlement may have first occurred in that area at that time. In contrast, the Williamson's Moss site faced on to the open coast till after the construction of the shingle ridges that formed the Williamson's Moss basin at *c.* 6100 BP, implying that after this date that locality would have been more attractive for settlement. It is therefore interesting that the earliest dated occupation at Monk Moors was at *c.* 6800 BP, while the earliest dated occupation at Williamson's Moss was at *c.* 5500 BP. This apparent relationship between periods of site occupation and environmental conditions suggests that as sea level fell, occupation may have continued longest in the Monk Moors–Newbiggin area where estuarine conditions lasted longest (cf. *Fig. 3*), and that Williamson's Moss retained its attraction as long as an open lake occupied the area of the present moss.

The palaeobotanical evidence from Williamson's Moss (Bonsall *et al.* 1986: 19–25, fig. 16; summarized above) indicated several phases of vegetational clearance and soil instability. The chronology established for these phases is broadly in accord with the direct dating of the archaeological evidence at the Williamson's Moss site. Both elm declines, as dated in the Williamson's Moss lake basin, coincide with dated periods of occupation on the archaeological site. The date of 5564±26 BP (pooled mean of the five determinations on bark and brushwood) for the construction of the platform structures is in close agreement with the date of 5440±70 BP (SRR-3065) for the initial elm decline and clearance recorded in the lake basin pollen diagram; and the date of 4925±165 BP (UB-2711) for a hearth is statistically indistinguishable from the date of 4850±80 BP (SRR-3068) for the second elm decline recorded in the lake basin diagram.

Subsistence

The results presented here and in Bonsall *et al.* (1986) suggest that people with a microlithic stone tool tradition occupied the Eskmeals area until the mid-sixth millennium BP; the palynological analyses from the infilled channel deposits (above) are limited in the degree to which they depict the composition of the vegetation away from the water-logged deposits, and it remains at present unresolved whether the radiocarbon dates pertaining to the platform structures and bark floors relate to the extensive occupation of the adjacent land surface.

The radiocarbon dating evidence from the channel deposits makes it clear, however, that the platforms date to a period regarded as the time of pioneer agriculture in northern England (Bradley 1978). Clearly, the results obtained from the Eskmeals Project have potentially an important bearing on the debate concerning the Mesolithic–Neolithic transition in this part of Britain.

Bonsall (1981) proposed a model of the subsistence economy of late Mesolithic groups in the Eskmeals area which emphasized the role of fishing and coastal resources, and the potential for year-round settlement. The organic sediments preserved in the infilled channel have as yet not been shown to contain faunal or other food remains, and so direct evidence to test this thesis is unavailable.

Attention instead turns to the clear palynological evidence for an early, and probably anthropogenic, elm decline within the channel deposits. The elm decline is, from provisional correlation by radiocarbon dates, contemporaneous with the first of two elm declines recognized in a pollen diagram from the lacustrine sediments in Williamson's Moss (Bonsall *et al.* 1986). The radiocarbon dates from the infilled lake basin also show the first elm decline at that site to relate to that detected by Pennington (1970, 1975) at Barfield Tarn, 4 km south east of Williamson's Moss, and dated to 5340 BP. Two elm declines at a site are not uncommon (cf. Hirons and Edwards 1986), but the Eskmeals sites are unusual in that the initial elm decline pre-dates by *c.* 300–350 years the major decline in elm commonly associated with Neolithic pastoral activities (Smith 1981); at Williamson's Moss it is the second elm decline which most readily accords in age with this period.

Oldfield (1963) recognized two elm declines at several sites in southern Cumbria, but no radiocarbon dates were obtained to test his assumption that the earliest (Oldfield's 'Primary Elm Decline') was of Neolithic date. Early elm declines dating to the early to mid-sixth millennium BP are reported from Winchester, Hampshire (Waton 1986), at 5630 BP (although here it is thought that hard-water error making the radiocarbon age older cannot be ruled out), and at Valley Bog in the northern Pennines. Here an elm decline with a radiocarbon age of 5950 BP was initially reported (Chambers, in Harkness and Wilson 1973), but on publication of the pollen diagram (Chambers 1978) this interpretation was not put forward, and a later feature, with a date of 4790 BP, was argued to be the 'Elm Decline' at this site; the significance of the earlier phase of reduced elm values is thus unclear.

The two elm declines in the Eskmeals area are considered to result from the selective removal of elm fodder for feeding to animals (above and Bonsall *et al.* 1986). The appearance at one site of two elm declines is thought to mitigate against other causes for this feature (cf. Hirons and Edwards 1986). Very early elm declines such as reported here may help to place this pastoral activity in an archaeological context. The Elm Decline no longer merits a seminal role in Neolithic agriculture (Groenman van Waateringe 1983; Edwards and Hirons 1984). In the light of this revision, it is appropriate to consider that the level of technology and understanding behind the collection of elm vegetation for fodder is little different from that invoked by Simmons and Dimbleby (1974) for Mesolithic stock control using ivy as fodder. The early date for the first elm decline in the area around Williamson's Moss may then be seen as evidence for late Mesolithic stock control. Such subsistence patterns have been postulated by Evans (1975), and interestingly Evans suggested that open maritime woodland, as would have characterized the Eskmeals area in the sixth millennium BP, would have presented very promising environments for the initial domestication of cattle.

Notes:

1. This is a substantially revised version of a paper published in the journal *Northern Archaeology*, 7(1), 1986: 3–30.

2. British Ordnance Datum (O.D.) relates to mean tide level at Newlyn, Cornwall. High Water of Spring Tides, particularly in estuaries, can therefore be several metres above O.D.

3. A small amount of carbonized plant material was recovered in the excavations at Sites 1 and 2, but its archaeological context was uncertain.

4. The pottery from the Williamson's Moss site has been identified by Dr I.H. Longworth of the British Museum.

5. Another possible example of artificial stone pavement in association with a Mesolithic flint industry was reported by Barfield (1977: 311) from Gerrard's Cross Site I in the south east of England.

6. Stone axes and other tools suitable for felling large trees are unknown from later Mesolithic contexts in northern Britain.

7. Other woods such as elm cannot be split in this way owing to the interlocked grain.

Acknowledgements: The authors wish to thank all those individuals who have assisted in the fieldwork at Eskmeals and in the preparation of this paper, especially Michael Alexander, Peter Askew, Jenny Bradbury, Peter Cherry, Gordon Cook, Roger Cornish, Clare Fell, Bill Finlayson, Joy Fulton, Alison Girdwood, Douglas Harkness, Tim Lawson, Ian Longworth, Barbara Maher, David Mann, Paul Mellars, John Nixon, Robert Payton, Gordon Pearson, Sue Pegg, Winifred Pennington, David Pheasant, Joyce Roberts, Ted Ruddock, Dave Start, David Trevarthen, and Tony Warburton. Joy Fulton also made available some of the results of her diatom analyses of the infilled channel deposits, while Robert Payton provided information on the soils of the Williamson's Moss site. A special debt of gratitude is owed to the Superintendent and staff of the Ministry of Defence Proof and Experimental Establishment, Eskmeals, for 'logistical' support, to the owner of the Williamson's Moss site, Alan Bradley, for permission to excavate, and to Edmund Strong whose ingenuity made excavation of the infilled channel a much easier task than it would otherwise have been. The illustrations were produced by Mairi Anna Birkeland, Adele Watson, Joe Rock and Gordon Thomas.

Financial support has come from many sources: the Association for Cultural Exchange, the British Academy, the Carnegie Trust for the Universities of Scotland, the Cumberland and Westmorland Antiquarian and Archaeological Society, Earthwatch, the Historic Buildings and Monuments Commission for England, the Society of Antiquaries of London, and the University of Edinburgh. Radiocarbon dates have been provided by the Scottish Universities Research Reactor Centre at East Kilbride (funded by the Natural Environment Research Council), the British Museum, and the Universities of Belfast and Glasgow. The support of all these institutions is gratefully acknowledged.

References

ANDREWS, J.T., KING, C.A.M. and STUIVER, M. (1973) Holocene sea-level changes, Cumberland coast, northwest England: eustatic and glacio-isostatic movements. *Geologie en Mijnbouw*, 52: 1–12.

BARFIELD, L.H. (1977) The excavation of a Mesolithic site at Gerrard's Cross, Bucks. *Records of Buckinghamshire*, 20(3): 308–336.

BEHRE, K-E. (1981) The interpretation of anthropogenic indicators in pollen diagrams. *Pollen et Spores*, 23: 225–245.

BIRKS, H.J.B. (1982) Mid-Flandrian forest history of Roudsea Wood National Nature Reserve, Cumbria. *New Phytologist*, 90: 339–354.

BONSALL, C. (1981) The coastal factor in the Mesolithic settlement of North-west England. In B. Gramsch (ed.), *Mesolithikum in Europa. 2. Internationales Symposium Potsdam, 3 bis 8 April 1978 Bericht* (Veröffentlichungen des Museums für Ur- und Frühgeschichte Potsdam, 14/15). Berlin, Deutscher Verlag der Wissenschaften: 451–472.

BONSALL, C., SUTHERLAND, D.G., TIPPING, R.M. and CHERRY, J. (1986) The Eskmeals Project 1981–5 : an interim report. *Northern Archaeology*, 7: 3–30.

BRADLEY, R. (1978) *The Prehistoric Settlement of Britain*. London, Routledge and Kegan Paul.

BUTZER, K.W. (1982) *Archaeology as Human Ecology*. Cambridge, University Press.

CAMPBELL, J.A. and BAXTER, M.S. (1979) Radiocarbon measurements on submerged forest floating chronologies. *Nature*, 278: 409–413.

CHAMBERS, C. (1978) A radiocarbon-dated pollen diagram from Valley Bog, on the Moor House National Nature Reserve. *New Phytologist*, 80: 273–280.

CHERRY, J. (1969) Early Neolithic sites at Eskmeals. *Transactions of the Cumberland and Westmorland Antiquarian and Archaeological Society*, 69: 40–53.

CHERRY, J. and CHERRY, P.J. (1986) Prehistoric habitation sites in west Cumbria. Part IV: the Eskmeals area. *Transactions of the Cumberland and Westmorland Antiquarian and Archaeological Society*, 86: 1–17.

CHERRY, J. and CHERRY, P.J. (1987) Prehistoric habitation sites in west Cumbria. Part V: Eskmeals to Haverigg. *Transactions of the Cumberland and Westmorland Antiquarian and Archaeological Society*, 87: 1–10.

COLES, J. (1984) *The Archaeology of Wetlands*. Edinburgh, University Press.

CORMACK, W.F. (1970) A Mesolithic site at Barsalloch, Wigtownshire. *Transactions of the Dumfriesshire and Galloway Natural History and Antiquarian Society*, 47: 63–80.

EDWARDS, K.J. (1982) Man, space and the woodland edge: speculations on the detection and interpretation of human impact in pollen profiles. In M. Bell and S. Limbrey (eds), *Archaeological Aspects of Woodland Ecology*. Oxford, British Archaeological Reports (International Series) S146: 5–22.

EDWARDS, K.J. and HIRONS, K.R. (1984) Cereal pollen grains in pre-Elm Decline deposits: implications for the earliest agriculture in Britain and Ireland. *Journal of Archaeological Science*, 11: 71–80.

EDWARDS, L.N. (1934) The evolution of early American bridges. *Transactions of the Newcomen Society*, 13 (1932–33): 95–116.

EVANS, P. (1975) The intimate relationship: an hypothesis concerning pre-Neolithic land use. In J.G. Evans, S. Limbrey and H. Cleere (eds), *The Effect of Man on the Landscape: the Highland Zone*. London, C.B.A. Research Report 11: 43–48.

GARBETT, G.G. (1981) The Elm Decline: the depletion of a resource. *New Phytologist*, 88: 573–585.

GROENMAN-VAN WAATERINGE, W. (1983) The early agricultural utilization of the Irish landscape: the last word on the Elm Decline? In T. Reeves-Smyth and F. Hamond (eds), *Landscape Archaeology in Ireland*. Oxford, British Archaeological Reports (British Series) 116: 217–232.

HARKNESS, D.D. (1981) Scottish Universities Research Reactor Centre Radiocarbon Measurements IV. *Radiocarbon*, 23(2): 252–304.

HARKNESS, D.D. (1983) The extent of natural C^{14} deficiency in the coastal environment of the United Kingdom. In W.G. Mook and H.T. Waterbolk (eds), *Proceedings of the First International Symposium ^{14}C and Archaeology* (PACT 8). Strasbourg, Council of Europe: 351–364.

HARKNESS, D.D. and WILSON, H.W. (1973) Scottish Universities Research Reactor Centre Radiocarbon Measurements I. *Radiocarbon*, 15: 554–565.

HIRONS, K.R. and EDWARDS, K.J. (1986) Events at and around the first and second *Ulmus* declines: palaeoecological investigations in Co. Tyrone, Northern Ireland. *New Phytologist*, 104: 131–153.

HUDDART, D. and TOOLEY, M.J. (1972) *The Cumberland Lowland Handbook*. London, Quaternary Research Association.

JACOBI, R.M. (1973) Aspects of the 'Mesolithic Age' in Great Britain. In S.K. Kozłowski (ed.), *The Mesolithic in Europe*. Warsaw, University Press: 237–265.

JACOBSON, G.L. Jr and BRADSHAW, R.H.W. (1981) The selection of sites for palaeovegetational studies. *Quaternary Research*, 16: 80–96.

JARDINE, W.G. (1975) Chronology of Holocene marine transgressions and regressions in south-western Scotland. *Boreas*, 4: 173–196.

MANNING, G.P. (1961) *Design and Construction of Foundations*. London, Concrete Publications.

MOORE, P.D. and WEBB, J.A. (1978) *An Illustrated Guide to Pollen Analysis*. London, Hodder and Stoughton.

NEWELL, R.R. (1981) Mesolithic dwelling structures: fact and fantasy. In B. Gramsch (ed.), *Mesolithikum in Europa. 2. Internationales Symposium Potsdam, 3 bis 8 April 1978 Bericht* (Veröffentlichungen des Museums für Ur- und Frühgeschichte Potsdam, 14/15). Berlin, Deutscher Verlag der Wissenschaften: 235–284.

O'FLAHERTY, C.A. (1974) *Highways*, vol. 2 (2nd edition). London, Edward Arnold.

OLDFIELD, F. (1963) Pollen-analysis and man's role in the ecological history of the south-east Lake District. *Geografiska Annaler*, 45: 23–40.

PALMER, S. (1976) The Mesolithic habitation site at Culver Well, Portland, Dorset: interim note. *Proceedings of the Prehistoric Society*, 42: 324–327.

PENNINGTON, W. (1970) Vegetation history in the north-west of England: a regional synthesis. In D. Walker and R.G. West (eds), *Studies in the Vegetational History of the British Isles*. Cambridge, University Press: 41–79.

PENNINGTON, W. (1975) The effect of Neolithic man on the environment in north-west England: the use of absolute pollen diagrams. In J.G. Evans, S. Limbrey and H. Cleere (eds), *The Effect of Man on the Landscape: the Highland Zone*. London, C.B.A. Research Report 11: 74–85.

PIGOTT, C.D. and HUNTLEY, J.P. (1980) Factors controlling the distribution of *Tilia cordata* at the northern limits of its geographical range. III. History in north-west England. *New Phytologist*, 84: 145–164.

RACKHAM, O. (1976) *Trees and Woodland in the English Landscape*. London, Dent.

RADLEY, J. and MELLARS, P.A. (1964) A Mesolithic structure at Deepcar, Yorkshire, England, and the affinities of its associated flint industries. *Proceedings of the Prehistoric Society*, 30: 1–24.

RADLEY, J., TALLIS, J.H. and SWITSUR, V.R. (1974) The excavation of three 'narrow blade' Mesolithic sites in the southern Pennines, England. *Proceedings of the Prehistoric Society*, 40: 1–19

SIMMONS, I.G. and DIMBLEBY, G.W. (1974) The possible role of Ivy (*Hedera helix* L.) in the Mesolithic economy of western Europe. *Journal of Archaeological Science*, 1: 291–296.

SMITH, A.G. (1981) The Neolithic. In I.G. Simmons and M.J. Tooley (eds), *The Environment in British Prehistory*. London, Duckworth: 125–209.

ST GEORGE GRAY, H. and BULLEID, A. (1953) *The Meare Lake Village*. Taunton, Printed Privately.

STOCKTON, E.D. (1973) Shaw's Creek shelter: human displacement of artefacts and its significance. *Mankind*, 9: 112–117.

TAUBER, H. (1965) Differential pollen dispersion and the interpretation of pollen diagrams. *Danmarks geologiske Undersøgelse*, Ser. II, 89: 1–89.

TOMLINSON, M.J. (1972) *Foundation Design and Construction* (2nd edition). London, Pitman.

TOOLEY, M.J. (1974) Sea-level changes during the last 9,000 years in north-west England. *Geographical Journal*, 140: 18–42.

TOOLEY, M.J. (1977) *The Isle of Man, Lancashire Coast and Lake District* (X INQUA Congess Excursion Guide A4). London, INQUA.

TOOLEY, M.J. (1978) *Sea-level Changes: North-west England during the Flandrian Stage*. Oxford, University Press.

TOOLEY, M.J. (1982) Sea-level changes in northern England. *Proceedings of the Geologists Association*, 93: 43–51.

VUORELA, I. (1973) Relative pollen rain around cultivated fields. *Acta Botanica Fennica*, 102: 1–27.

WALKER, D. (1966) The late Quaternary history of the Cumberland lowland. *Philosophical Transactions of the Royal Society London*, B251: 1–210.

WATON, P.V. (1986) Palynological evidence for early and permanent woodland on the chalk of central Hampshire. In G. de G. Sieveking and M.B. Hart (eds), *The Scientific Study of Flint and Chert*. Cambridge, University Press: 169–174.

An Application of Fine-Resolution Pollen Analysis to Later Mesolithic Peats of an English Upland

I.G. Simmons, J. Turner and J.B. Innes

Abstract

Human-induced vegetation change in the English uplands has been detected in the later Mesolithic, *c.* 7500–5500 BP. Pollen analysis of peat profiles shows a series of disturbance phases in which the forest trees recede in favour of more open and lower vegetation. These are intercalated with phases of regeneration and stability. At one site, fine-resolution pollen analysis with a vertical sampling interval of one millimetre is used to investigate a disturbance phase. It shows that these phases are composite on conventional diagrams and that ecologically intelligible information at a much finer temporal resolution can be obtained from such works. The values and limitations of the technique are also discussed briefly.

INTRODUCTION

In 7500 BP the English uplands such as Bodmin Moor, Dartmoor, the Pennines, Lake District, Cheviots and North York Moors were largely covered in high forest. Evidence from some of them can be read to indicate a few open areas at the highest altitudes, but a remote sensing satellite of the time would show them to have been mostly clad with mature oak forest in which trees such as elm, lime, alder, and the understorey shrub hazel were also of significance. If we look at such areas today then we see a vegetation dominated by low shrubs of the Ericaceae, together with grasses and sedges. Except on limestones, the soils are of highly acid types often with podsolization and gleying and, at altitudes above 300 m where the slopes are low, a thick covering (commonly 3 m, but 8 m has been found) of peat composed of the remains of ombrogenous acid-tolerant plants such as *Sphagnum* (bog-moss) and *Eriophorum* (cotton sedge).

That human agency has been a major influence in the change from one ecology to the other is now widely accepted, as is the proposition that pre-Roman cultures were amongst those contributing to the transformations (Simmons and Tooley 1981). At one stage of scholarly investigation it was thought that human-induced manipulation of the forest vegetation started with the first agricultural immigrants (i.e. the Neolithic culture) and was thereafter a consequence of the clearance of forest for his husbandry on either a shifting or a permanent basis. Following the pioneering work of G.W. Dimbleby, however, detailed investigations of both soils and organic deposits in the English uplands revealed that disturbances of the oak forest had taken place in the years prior to the decline of *Ulmus* pollen at *c.* 5500 BP, which is a chronological marker over so much of north-western Europe. Since this horizon was for long regarded as the date also of the beginning of the Neolithic in Britain, earlier Holocene disturbances of the forest, if attributed to human causes, would most likely be due to Mesolithic cultures. Now, it is customary to put back the date of early Neolithic activity in Britain by 500–700 years; and so any vegetation changes in the period 6300–5500 BP are often referred to as a 'Mesolithic–Neolithic transition', but before 6500 BP are held to be associated with the last hunter-gatherers rather than the first agriculturalists.

PALAEOECOLOGY OF THE NORTH YORK MOORS

The peats of the plateau surfaces of the North York Moors (*Fig. 1*) have for some years been recognized as interesting repositories of palaeoecological information. They occur in a region known to contain the material remains of most northern British prehistoric cultures (Spratt and Simmons 1976), and have grown at relatively uniform rates through the post-glacial chronozones Flandrian I and II during which most of the prehistoric economies impressed themselves upon the land. Further, long pollen profiles from lakes and channel mires enable the shorter sequences from the upland peats to be put into a longer chronological sequence, and the considerable density of analyzed profiles gives us a broad perspective on any change. The Moors themselves form the lowest and driest upland in England, with large plateau surfaces of 325–375 m intersected by deeply cut valleys. Glaciation has incised deep sinuous channels into the upland surface, and organic accumulation in these 'slacks' adds to the store of information in the marginal lakes and the upland 'blanket' peats. Archae-

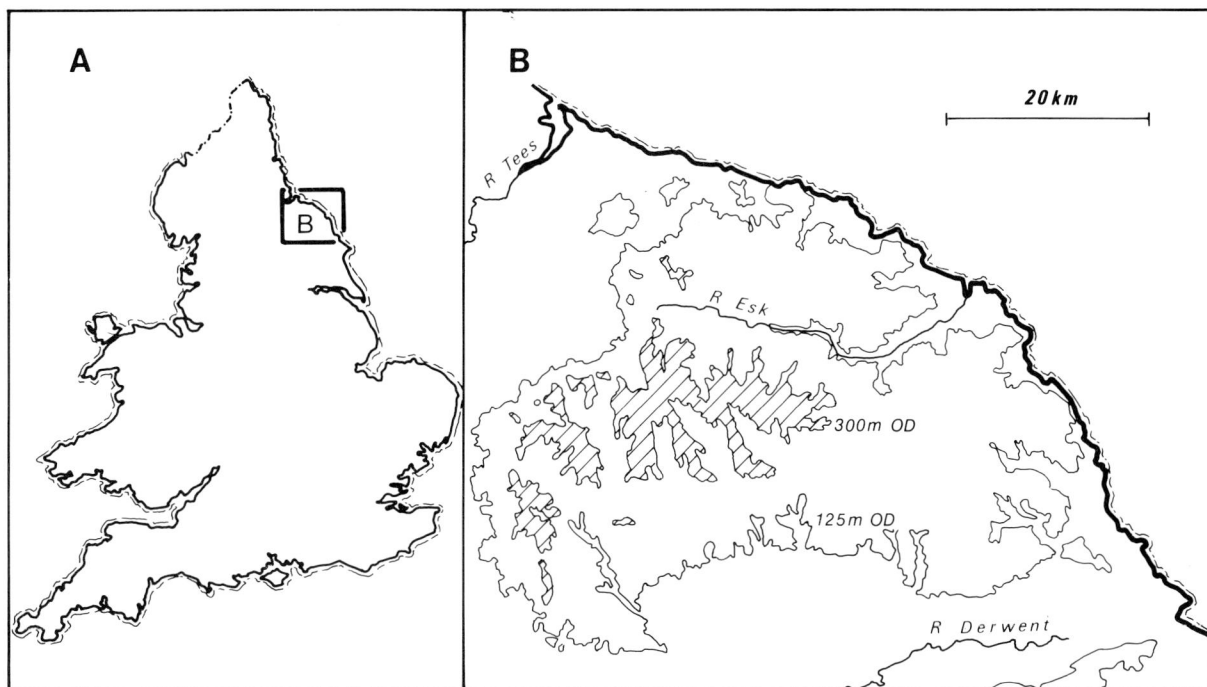

Figure 1   Location of the North York Moors.

ologists have catalogued many flint remains of Mesolithic type from the Moors (*Fig. 2*) showing the area to have been inhabited from the earliest Mesolithic period (we may recall that Star Carr is in the Vale of Pickering just south of this upland), right through to the later Mesolithic period which is of most interest here. Later Mesolithic sites consist of two main types: (i) spreads of microliths, often accompanied by charcoal, sometimes covered by peat of varying thickness, usually at high altitudes and clustering near present-day spring-heads; (ii) sites with a wider range of flint types, often marginal to the main upland ('settlement sites' in *Fig. 2*). Writers have speculated that the microlith spreads are the consequence of short-term settlements, most likely hunting camps, while the others represent a more polytechnic settlement phase with perhaps a larger gathering of people. Attempts to integrate the sparse evidence into ecological–economic models for further testing have been made (Simmons 1975, 1979).

Palaeoenvironmental work on the peats of the upland has shown that there are a number of sites where disturbance of the forest vegetation in pre-*Ulmus* decline times can be detected (*Fig. 3*). Apart from the changes in pollen frequency and pollen type which are the usual indication of such events, layers of charcoal are usually found at the appropriate horizons and it is these, occurring as they do in the damp upland climates with a current rainfall average of up to 1000 mm/yr, that give us further encouragement to think that we are dealing with human-induced processes rather than those of the natural environment. Some of these sites show a single phase of pre-*Ulmus* decline disturbance (PUDD); others have multiple

phases in the same profile. One example of a profile which not only has a number of PUDD phases but which is securely dated by ^{14}C is from Bonfield Gill Head (*Fig. 3*, site 19) whose palaeoecological data are given in a summary outline in *Fig. 4* (Simmons and Innes 1981). The top of the diagram is immediately after the *Ulmus* decline, which occurs at the zonule 7/8 transition and is marked conspicuously by a tree stump in the peat, and below it a metre or so of peat contains a number of PUDD phases interspersed by horizons which exhibit the pollen fluctuations characteristic of forest regeneration. Stratigraphic units *d* (zonule 2) and *g* (zonule 4) are PUDD phases, with ^{14}C dates of 5670±90 and 5170±90 BP respectively. These dates suggest the 'Mesolithic–Neolithic transition' zone; no cereal pollen has been detected but, as Edwards (1979) has pointed out, this is equivocal evidence. Evidence of burning is strong during the PUDD phases but ceases at the *Ulmus* decline, and the actual presence of a tree stump with roots at that level suggests woodland regeneration. This follows more or less exactly the sequence established for the Pennines by Jacobi, Tallis and Mellars (1976) who postulated that burning was a characteristic of Mesolithic land use practices but that the need for it ceased when agriculture was adopted as the most important mode of subsistence. Publication of the Bonfield Gill Head site detailed pollen analysis (Simmons and Innes 1981) revealed, however, the rather coarse resolution of the evidence for the actual nature of the PUDD phases, since in a profile analyzed even at 2 cm intervals, a PUDD phase may occupy only one or two horizons. We determined therefore to find out whether closer resolution of the pollen and charcoal frequencies of these events might

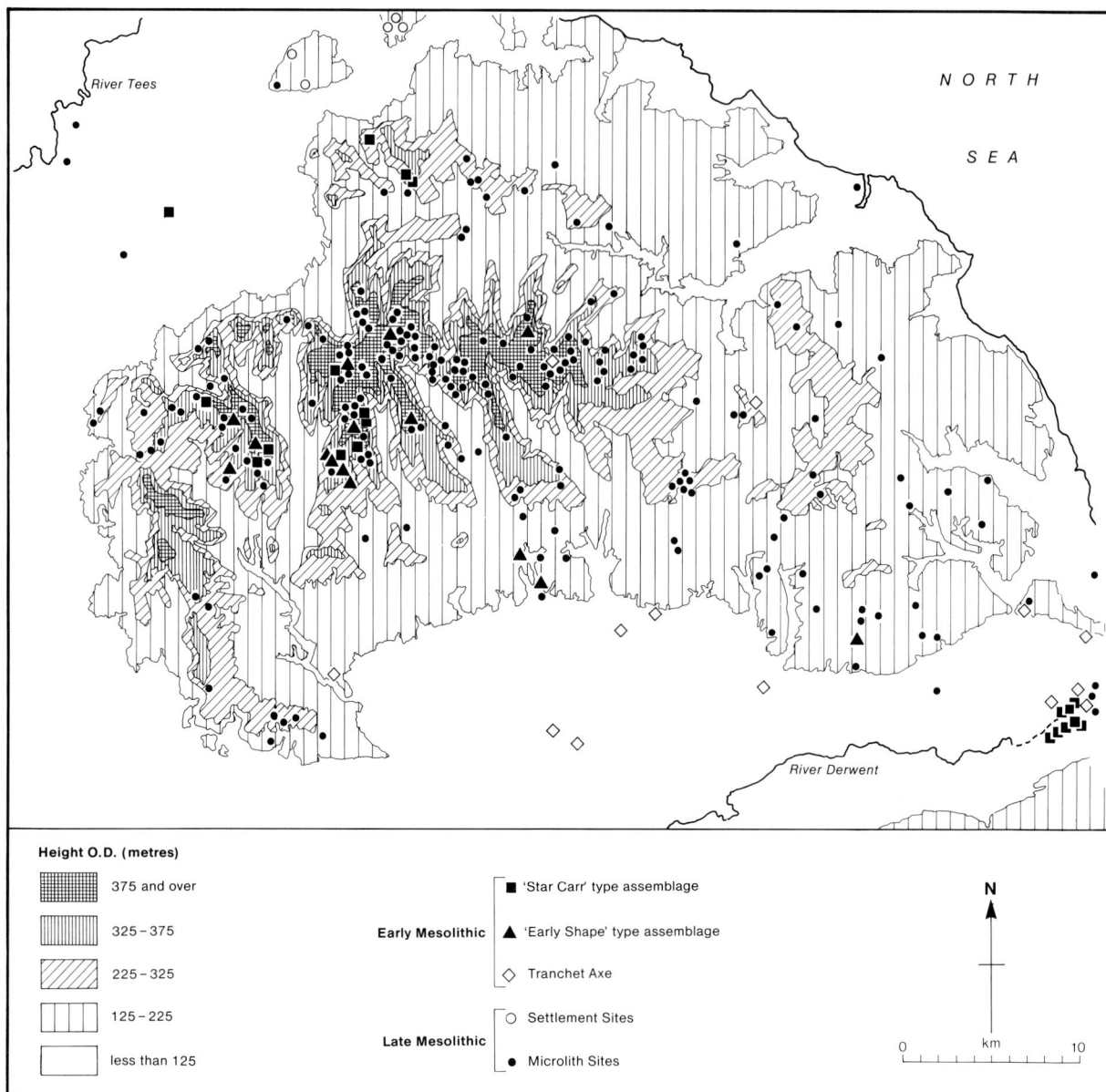

Figure 2 Distribution of early and late Mesolithic flint sites on the North York Moors.

be possible and turned to another site on the moors, North Gill (*Fig. 3*, site 21). The head of the North Gill has yielded a number of analyzed profiles (Simmons 1969a; Innes 1981) and the accumulations of peat during Flandrian II have been distinctly homogeneous. Further, certain charcoal-rich horizons have wide lateral spreads and can therefore form stratigraphic markers which enable the analyst quickly to identify segments of a profile that cover appropriate chronozones and zonules. Systematic spatial replication is therefore possible and its application limited only by available labour and time. A normal outline diagram at North Gill 5, counted at 1 cm intervals, was prepared, showing (*Fig. 5*) a number of PUDD events below the 30 cm horizon which marks the *Ulmus* decline (cf. phases *a*, *c* and *e*). Here, conditions seemed right to try and improve the resolution of the disturbance-phase information by applying fine-resolution pollen analysis.

FINE-RESOLUTION POLLEN ANALYSIS: THE TECHNIQUE

Fine-resolution pollen analysis of ombrogenous peat has been used successfully to study the detailed vegetational changes at the time of the *Ulmus* decline in both lowland (Garbett 1981) and upland (Sturludottir and Turner 1985) areas of northern England.

The technique as described by Garbett (1981) was therefore used in analyzing the North Gill 5 peat, which is highly suitable for fine sectioning. The peat was frozen for at least 72 hours at −20 °C and then transferred to a 4 °C cold room where it was cut into 2.5 cm lengths. Each length was then trimmed to fit the sample chamber of a microtome, 2.5 cm in diameter. After positioning the peat horizontally in the chamber, the microtome piston was screwed up 0.1 cm at a time and each consecutive 0.1 cm of peat sliced from the top and placed in a specimen tube.

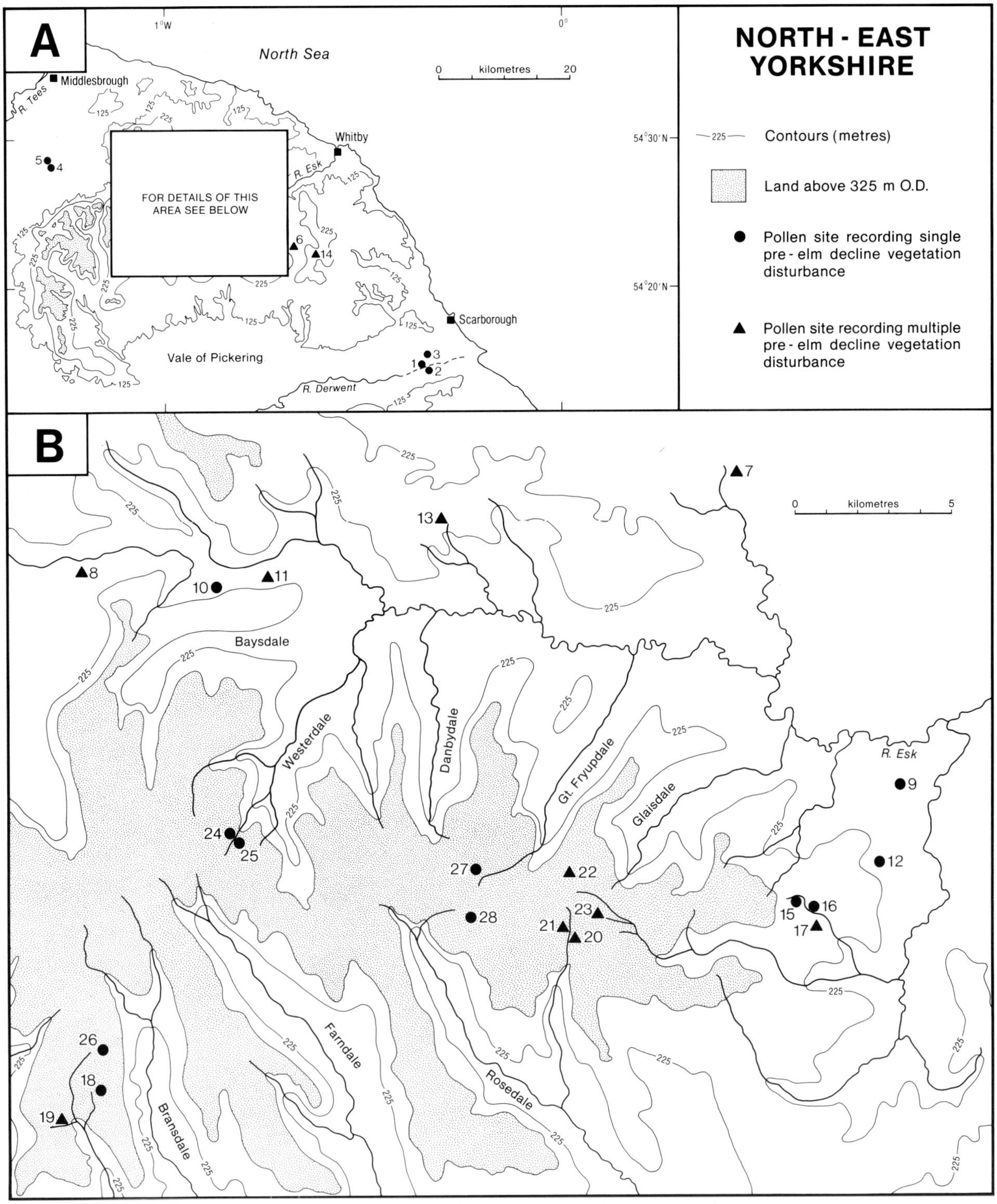

Figure 3   Distribution of sites at which evidence of pre-Elm Decline vegetation disturbance has been recorded.

Each sample therefore has a volume of approximately 0.5 cm³. Pollen was then extracted from the peat by standard methods. A few of the samples needed treatment with hydrofluoric acid to remove fine mineral material but most required only treatment with sodium hydroxide to dissolve humic materials and acetolysis to concentrate the pollen by removing cellulose (Moore and Webb 1978). Samples were mounted in silicone oil. The pollen diagram (*Fig. 6*) is a percentage diagram, but pollen concentration data were obtained by adding a *Lycopodium* tablet (Stockmarr 1972), i.e. a known number of exotic spores, at the beginning of the extraction process.

Although fine-resolution pollen analysis is essentially the same as conventional pollen analysis, the fineness of the temporal scale does call into question some of the basic assumptions of the technique.

When a peat profile is analyzed at 10 cm intervals and each sample is of the order of 1 cm thick; it is

BONFIELD GILL HEAD

CHRONOZONE

DESCRIPTION	MICROSCOPIC CHARCOAL	DEPTH (m) UNIT	PROFILE	POLLEN TYPE	ZONULE No.	AP/NAP	DIAGNOSTIC TAXA	RADIOCARBON DATING	
Cotton-grass peat		0·30	M I M I	S	9	AP	Oak - Birch - Hazel		Fl III
No charcoal		j	I M I M						
Birch stump at base		0·40		D	8	NAP	Birch - Bracken - Ruderals	4890 ±80 Har –4229	
Cotton-grass peat			I M I M	S	7	AP	Oak - Elm - Birch		
(Microscopic charcoal)		i	M I M I	D	6	NAP	Hazel - Bracken - Ruderals		
		0·50	I M I M						
Wood peat		h	V V V V	S	5	AP	Oak - Elm - Alder - Birch		
Charcoal peat		g	— ▲ — ▲	D	4	NAP	Hazel - Bracken - Ruderals	5170 ±90 Har –4226	
		0·60	M I M I						
Cotton-grass peat		f	I M I M						
			M I M I	S	3	AP	Oak - Elm - Alder - Birch		
		0·70							Fl II
Wood peat		e	I V I V						
			V I V I						
Charcoal peat		d	0·80 ▲ ▲ ▲ ▲	D	2	NAP	Hazel - Bracken - Ruderals	5670 ±90 Har –4225	
			V V V V						
Peat and wood pieces		c	V V V V						
		0·90	V V V V						
Minero-organic		b	· — · —	S	1	AP	Oak - Elm Pine - Hazel - Alder		
Sand		a 1·00	· · · ·						

0   20
% Σ Volume

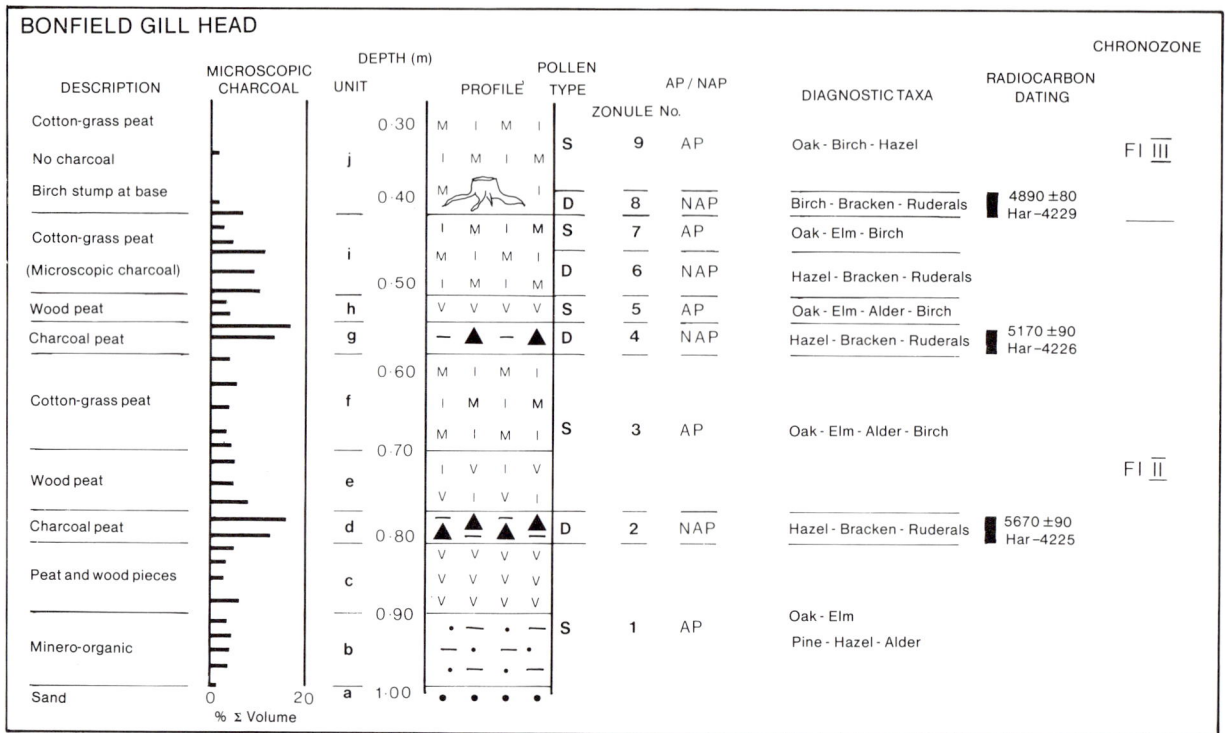

Figure 4   A summary of the pollen, stratigraphic and radiocarbon evidence at Bonfield Gill head, Bilsdale East Moor. D – disturbance, S – stability, AP – arboreal pollen, NAP – non-arboreal pollen. Stratigraphic symbols as on *Fig. 5*.

assumed that successive samples relate to different and well-separated time intervals, with a sample representing, for example, a decade of vegetation and successive samples decades with about a century between. By analogy, when consecutive 0.1 cm samples are analyzed one should be dealing with the vegetation of discrete, consecutive periods of a few years each. This will only be so, however, if each sample has chronological integrity across its 2.5 cm diameter, and the microtopography of ombrogenous mire surfaces is such that the chronological integrity of this size of sample cannot always be assumed. The 2.5 cm diameter piece of mire surface which received the pollen may not have been flat and therefore the horizontal samples may not be temporally homogeneous. Even if the samples were horizontally stratified in the mire, slight errors may have been introduced whilst sampling in the field or handling the sample in the laboratory. Any of these would mean that the pollen produced in a particular year or years might be represented in more than one sample. We cannot compensate for these possible sources of error by reducing the diameter of the sample because, in order to have the requisite number of pollen grains for a count, a sample 1 mm thick has to have this diameter. Even so at other sites some samples this size have not contained enough pollen (Sturludottir and Turner 1985), and two consecutive 0.1 cm samples have had to be amalgamated, reducing the possible resolution of that portion of the diagram to 0.2 cm.

It is now generally accepted that the pollen stratigraphy of ombrogenous mires is good and that there is less post-depositional disturbance than is the case with lake sediments. Even so, there remains the possibility that processes of bioturbation or cryoturbation may have disturbed the stratigraphy at this fine scale and set a limit to the temporal resolution that can be obtained. Even in the absence of adequate experimental data on present-day pollen incorporation into the mire surfaces, we can sometimes be reasonably confident that the pollen stratigraphy for parts of Flandrian II is good and the resolution as fine as the sample thickness. This is particularly so when the diagram shows evidence of both gradual and abrupt changes in pollen frequencies in a peat which has accumulated continuously during the period of time concerned. During such periods vegetational change will have been either sudden, as for example when plants are destroyed by natural disaster or by fire or felling or when the flowering of a species is affected by such events, or gradual, as with natural successional changes. The latter would produce smooth changes in the pollen frequency curves from sample to sample but the former would result in abrupt changes from one to the next, provided the samples have chronological integrity and that no post-depositional mixing has occurred. If these are not the case, even sudden vegetational change will be reflected in the diagram as smooth pollen frequency curves. If a diagram contains a mixture of smooth and abrupt changes in frequencies, it therefore also contains internal evidence for good resolution at the scale of the sample thickness concerned provided there is not evidence for breaks in accumulation, which is the only other factor which could have given rise to abrupt changes. The converse of this argument is not

210

necessarily true because the absence of sharp changes in pollen frequencies may simply mean that no sudden vegetational changes took place during the period being studied.

The closely-sampled diagram from North Gill (*Fig. 6*) contains a mixture of abrupt and smooth changes in pollen frequency and there is no evidence for hiatuses in peat formation, and therefore it may be considered as having fine resolution at the 0.1 cm sample interval. Another fine-resolution diagram covering the same period and taken from peat 100 m downstream, shows the same sequence of vegetational changes and thus serves to make it more probable that there were no fine-scale breaks in peat accumulation and that the samples do indeed have chronological integrity.

Placing a precise time-scale on a fine-resolution diagram is difficult because ombrogenous peat is known to form at highly irregular rates depending on the position of the water table and nature of the plants at any one time. This is difficult to quantify and any one 0.1 cm slice of peat may well have taken much longer to form than either the one above or below it. A rough estimate of mean accumulation rate is all that can be given with confidence and this has been obtained by the conventional methods of radiocarbon or pollen stratigraphic dating. Pollen stratigraphic dating at this site indicates a mean accumulation rate for the diagram in the order of 0.02 to 0.1 cm/yr, which means individual samples will have taken in the order of one to five years to form.

North Gill 5

The previous palaeoecological research carried out at the site of North Gill by Simmons (1969a, 1969b) had shown it to record particularly clear evidence of pre-Elm Decline vegetation disturbance. The thick charcoal layer which occurred at the base of the blanket peat profile was accompanied by a pollen assemblage remarkable for the variety and high percentage of ruderal herb types. Deciduous tree pollen frequencies were very low, whereas pollen values of trees and shrubs likely to be encouraged by the removal of forest canopy shade were recorded at very high levels. The presence in quantity of taxa known to be successful in post-fire habitats, such as *Melampyrum*, *Pteridium*, *Corylus* and *Pinus*, supported the charcoal evidence in suggesting that fire clearance of the local vegetation had preceded the beginning of peat growth at this site. The abundance of macrofossil remains of *Polytrichum* moss in the basal peat layers points to the pioneer recolonizing of newly burned ground (Ahlgren 1974) following this initial deforestation. The basal peat layers at North Gill have been radiocarbon dated to 6316±55 BP (BM-425) by Burleigh, Hewson and Meeks (1976), and so the forest clearance event which they record is analogous to the numerous cases of late Mesolithic age disturbance

mentioned at the beginning of this paper, and described more fully elsewhere (Simmons and Innes 1985). In addition, pollen and stratigraphic evidence of a similar nature occurred higher in the peat profile, at a point rather later in Flandrian II although still well before the Elm Decline, suggesting the recurrence of environmental disturbance.

As part of a continuing research project aimed at elucidating the cultural–environment relationships of late Mesolithic communities in Britain, it was decided to conduct a much more comprehensive analysis of the Flandrian II deposits at North Gill. One of the research techniques employed at this site for the detailed examination of the peat horizons which contain clearance evidence has been that of fine-resolution pollen analysis, as described earlier in this paper. Although still in its early stages, the initial results of this research are encouraging, and we present here in summarized form some fine-resolution pollen data from one of the later Flandrian II phases of disturbance, and assess the potential value of the technique in the study of the Mesolithic period.

A profile was selected at North Gill where the clearance horizons were stratigraphically well defined and where factors such as horizontality and humification of sediment could be shown to be favourable for application of the technique. At this site, designated North Gill 5, a silty, charcoal-rich peat rests upon coarse-grained, sandy mineral soil, and is overlain by amorphous peat which contains fragments of wood. An upper charcoal and silt horizon then occurs in the profile, incorporated within a very well humified amorphous peat composed of *Eriophorum*, *Calluna* and *Sphagnum*, and which shows varying degrees of humification. The basal 80 cm of this profile were sampled for pollen analysis at one-centimetre intervals and *Fig. 5* shows the resulting pollen frequencies for major trees and shrubs, and some selected open-habitat taxa favoured by woodland disturbance. Taxa within the tree pollen sum are shaded and about one thousand land pollen grains were counted at each level.

Seven phases in woodland history (*a–g*) are recognized from the pollen data and are used to zone the pollen diagram. The earliest phase (*a*) corresponds closely to the charcoal- and silt-rich peat which forms the basal stratigraphic unit in the profile. Although the pollen fluctuations are less well marked than in Simmons' original pollen diagram from the site, they are essentially similar, with *Quercus* and *Alnus* initially present in low frequencies while *Corylus*, *Betula*, *Melampyrum*, other ruderal herbs and *Pteridium* are recorded in high values. This phase records the regeneration of vegetation around the site through successional communities following the destructive effects of the forest fire which can be inferred from the charcoal evidence.

The succeeding phase (*b*) is one in which the effects

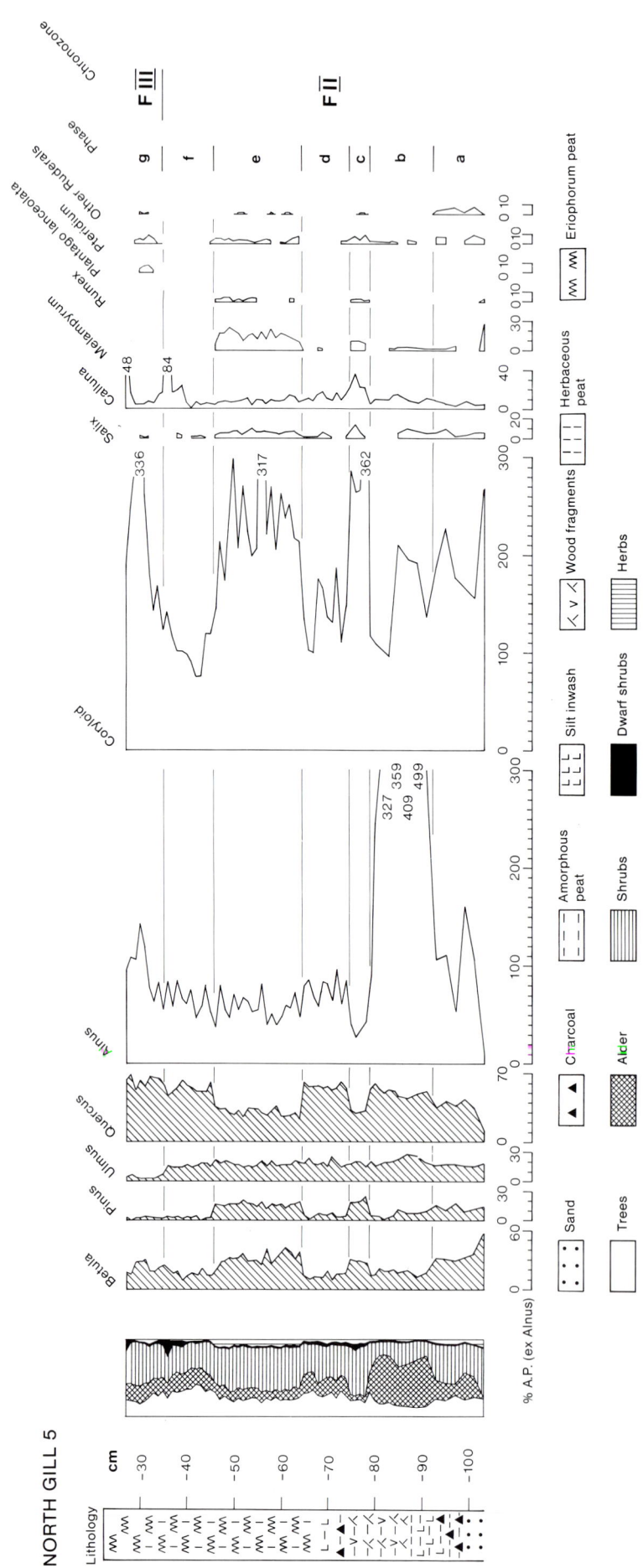

Figure 5 Conventional pollen diagram from North Gill 5, showing selected taxa as percentages of total tree pollen.

of disturbance are no longer apparent. The pollen assemblage is dominated by the deciduous woodland trees *Quercus* and *Alnus*. The latter is particularly abundant and the presence of detrital wood remains in the profile suggests an alder-dominated carr–woodland around the site itself, within a closed-canopy broadleaf forest which apparently remained largely undisturbed, although the occasional record of shade-intolerant taxa suggests that some small areas of more open vegetation may have remained in existence in the area.

Indications of fire-clearance return to the diagram during the succeeding phase (*c*) during which the pollen frequencies for *Quercus* and *Alnus* are greatly reduced, being replaced by *Betula*, *Pinus* and, particularly, *Corylus* as dominant pollen types. Other heliophyte shrubs, such as *Salix* and *Calluna*, are present in low frequencies only. Herbaceous indicators of fresh clearance are almost absent. This phase represents a period of mixed oak forest stability around the site. Phase *e* is characterized by the return of pollen fluctuations indicative of woodland clearance similar to those of phase *c*. *Quercus* is most adversely affected, little diminution being discernible in the already low *Alnus* frequencies. *Pinus*, *Betula* and *Corylus* all increase sharply in frequency, while *Salix*, *Rumex*, *Pteridium*, and especially *Melampyrum* are prominent in the assemblage. Although this phase of environmental disturbance is well marked in the pollen spectra, stratigraphic correlations are missing from the peat profile. Either bog growth had proceeded at this site beyond the point at which inwash of colluvial material into the mire was possible, or clearance took place outside the local site catchment area. Microscopic charcoal is abundant in these levels, however, presumably windblown.

A further phase (*f*) of undisturbed woodland follows, during which *Quercus* is restored to high frequencies, *Alnus* values are maintained and indicators of disturbance are either absent, like the ruderal herb group, or much reduced in importance, like *Corylus*, *Pinus* and *Betula*.

The uppermost phase (*g*) at this site is marked by a distinct decline in elm pollen frequencies which is considered to represent the boundary between the Flandrian II and Flandrian III chronozones. Throughout the previous alternating phases of disturbance and stability in woodland history, *Ulmus* frequencies remained high and virtually unchanged. The pollen evidence in phase *g* is typical of Elm Decline clearance, with *Plantago lanceolata* and *Pteridium* much in evidence and *Corylus*, *Betula*, *Alnus* and *Calluna* increasing in frequency as open areas were created in the woodland. Interestingly, *Quercus* is unaffected and *Pinus*, *Melampyrum* and *Rumex* show no response. Disturbance during this phase was apparently of a different character from that previously recorded at this site.

Fine-resolution pollen analysis at North Gill 5

Three phases of pre-Elm Decline forest disturbance (*a*, *c* and *e*) were therefore established as occurring at North Gill 5, and of these phases *c* was selected as most suitable for further study by fine-resolution pollen analysis. The well humified, amorphous nature of the sediment at this horizon facilitated its freezing and thin-sectioning in the manner described above, and contiguous sub-samples of one-millimetre thickness were obtained without difficulty. The horizontality of this deposit, as required by the method and suggested by field observation, was established by laboratory examination. Horizontally adjacent replicate samples around pollen zone boundaries at the millimetre scale showed no discernible evidence of vertical mixing of pollen assemblages. This supports the impression of chronological integrity given by the nature of the fine-resolution curves themselves, as discussed above. Pollen analysis was conducted on seventy samples of one-millimetre thickness through phase *c* and the results are shown on *Fig. 6*. Once again, only pollen curves of major trees and shrubs and selected open-habitat taxa are included. *Alnus* is not included within the tree pollen sum, and the number of land pollen grains counted at each pollen level was approximately one thousand. Ten vegetation phases have been recognized from the pollen record and these are used to subdivide the diagram.

Phase 1 may be characterized as a phase of disturbance, for pollen frequencies for *Alnus* and *Quercus* are declining, the former from high levels. This appears to correspond with the transition between phases *b* and *c* in *Fig. 5*, where similar trends may be recognized. Pollen values for *Corylus* and *Pinus*, although rising through this basal phase, remain moderate. Other open-habitat shrubs like *Calluna* and *Salix* are either present in low amounts or absent altogether. Sporadic grains of the ruderal herb types occur, but in general little evidence of the new creation of open ground conditions exists.

During phase 2 the pollen evidence is somewhat equivocal, for while *Alnus* pollen frequencies continue to fall to a low level, those of *Quercus* recover to reach their highest values for the diagram as a whole. Frequencies for *Pinus* and *Corylus* are low, which would appear to support the description of this phase as one of vegetation recovery and regeneration of woodland. *Calluna* and *Salix* values are insignificant, while ruderal herb pollen of all types and *Pteridium* spores are almost absent from the assemblage.

The evidence of phase 3 would also appear to be a record of the re-establishment of woodland communities for *Alnus* pollen frequencies rise until they are almost as high as at the base of the diagram, while the high frequencies attained by *Quercus* within the previous phase are largely maintained. No significant increases occur in *Corylus*, *Pinus*, *Calluna* or *Salix*

H

NORTH GILL 5 – PHASE C

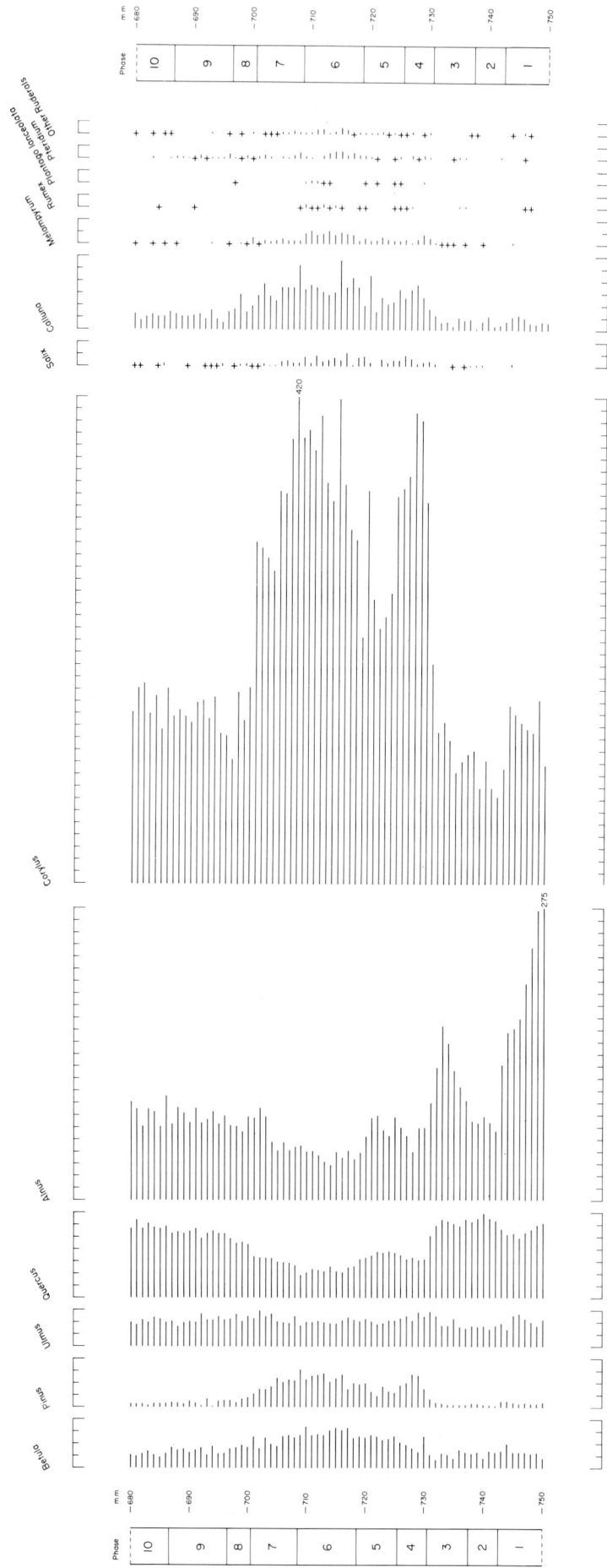

Figure 6　Fine-resolution pollen diagram from North Gill 5, showing selected taxa as percentages of total tree pollen.

214

values and there are no indications of clearance activity within the ruderal herb pollen and *Pteridium* curves. Some isolated grains of *Melampyrum* and *Rumex* occur, but in themselves cannot be considered evidence of woodland disturbance.

Phase 4 records the results of a major period of woodland disturbance, during which *Alnus* and *Quercus* are the taxa most adversely affected. *Quercus* frequencies fall to only 30% of total tree pollen, while *Alnus* values are similarly reduced. *Betula*, *Salix* and *Calluna* all rise sharply in frequency, but the most conspicuous increases are shown by *Pinus* and *Corylus*, the latter especially. Peak values of *Melampyrum* and *Pteridium* are recorded, while grains of *Rumex* and *Plantago lanceolata* also occur. These pollen fluctuations would suggest a major opening of the woodland canopy and the creation of disturbed ground conditions, followed by its recolonization by seral communities.

Phase 5 appears to record the partial regeneration of woodland near to the site, for *Corylus* frequencies fall from their peak values of the previous phase, and *Pinus*, *Salix* and *Calluna* are similarly reduced. In contrast, *Quercus* and *Alnus* frequencies rise, although they remain low in comparison to the early phases of the diagram. *Pteridium*, *Melampyrum* and *Rumex* all decline in value during this phase which seems to reflect the relaxation of disturbance pressure upon the environment.

The pollen evidence of phase 6 records the clearest evidence of forest disturbance on the entire pollen diagram. *Quercus* frequencies fall to little more than 20% of tree pollen, while *Alnus* also falls sharply, particularly in the earlier part of the phase. *Corylus* frequencies rise to very high levels indeed, while *Pinus* and *Betula* frequencies also show marked increases. High, but fluctuating frequencies of *Salix* and *Calluna* also occur. Particularly high peaks are recorded in the *Melampyrum* pollen curve, and *Rumex* and *Pteridium* are similarly prominent as are other ruderal taxa. In the second half of this phase, *Plantago lanceolata* is recorded in substantial amounts for the only time in the diagram, as part of a distinct change towards a more open type of vegetation.

During phase 7 the pollen assemblage is still dominated by taxa indicative of disturbed conditions, although their pollen frequencies are somewhat reduced and values for *Quercus* and *Alnus* begin to recover, particularly the latter. *Pinus* pollen frequencies fall gradually throughout this phase, as do those of *Corylus*, although *Betula* and *Calluna* frequencies are maintained. High *Salix* representation comes to an end during this phase. Open areas still existed apparently, for, although reduced, *Melampyrum* values remain significant and *Pteridium* spores are also still recorded in moderate frequencies. *Rumex* and *Plantago lanceolata*, however, are absent.

Phases 8, 9 and 10 contain pollen assemblages which reflect the gradual restoration of deciduous woodland at the expense of those taxa indicative of open ground and disturbed habitats. The three phases are differentiated by increasing frequencies of *Quercus* which, by the top of the diagram, regains values of up to 70% of the tree pollen. *Alnus* also increased in value, but never regains its high frequencies of the lower phases. Of those taxa which characterize the disturbance phases, *Pinus* is reduced to very low values and *Salix* is recorded only as isolated grains. *Corylus* frequencies reach minimal values during phase 8, but recover slightly in phases 9 and 10 to remain a significant contributor to the assemblage. Apart from the occasional grain, pollen of ruderal herbs of all types is no longer recorded. Although reduced in value from their maxima of the disturbance phases, *Pteridium* spores and *Calluna* and *Betula* pollen remain present in consistent amounts. *Ulmus* pollen is recorded at between 20% and 30% of tree pollen in this phase, having remained steady throughout the entire diagram at these percentages.

DISCUSSION

The results of fine-resolution pollen analysis of a pre-Elm Decline phase of disturbance at North Gill suggest that the method has potential to yield far more detailed data regarding prehistoric vegetation changes than the more conventional sampling hitherto employed in the great majority of pollen diagrams. The sensible nature of the pollen curves themselves, and the ecologically intelligible interpretations which they invite, suggest that even at this extreme level of resolution, they represent sequential and therefore reliable pollen data. They would thus seem to represent a dependable record of changes in vegetation patterns and communities, supporting the conclusions reached by Garbett (1981) and Sturludottir and Turner (1985). Indeed, their accuracy in this respect should in theory be rather greater than that of more widely spaced conventional samples, which being composed of many more years' pollen accumulation will contain a compound assemblage.

We believe, therefore, that the sequential nature of pollen data shown in *Fig. 6* demonstrates that the statistical and theoretical limits to ever-finer sampling discussed in this paper and by Moore (1980) have not been exceeded at this particular site. We do concede, however, that stratigraphic conditions suitable for the use of this technique in such an extreme form may be quite rare, and the practical limits of fine-resolution sampling may vary considerably from site to site. The potential value of high temporal resolution data, gained from pollen records with small inter-sample time intervals, is demonstrated very clearly by the North Gill 5 diagram. Perhaps of the most immediate interest is that the single disturbance event described by pollen fluctuations of phase *c* on *Fig. 5* may be recognized as actually composite in nature, comprising three discrete sub-phases of disturbance activity (*Fig. 6*, phases 1, 4 and 6). While the temporal relationships of these sub-phases are apparent, their spatial relationships are less so. Recurrent fire-disturbances of the same site may have been involved here, in which case the ecological effects of each occurrence were differential and perhaps cumulative. Most likely perhaps is that we are observing the consequences of a cluster of disturbances occurring at short intervals within the fairly limited area of the pollen catchment of our particular sampling site. Edwards (1982) has stressed the difficulties involved in relating pollen evidence of human activity to its spatial location in wooded environments. It does seem very likely, however, that these disturbances took place adjacent to the North Gill spring-head, as the stratigraphic record would suggest, and that they comprise the individual stages of an extended period of land use activity in the vicinity of the North Gill stream. As the resolution of the pollen data is too fine for the present standard error limits of the radiocarbon technique, the duration of these disturbance events cannot be known as yet, but perhaps one to two centuries for the entire period of activity may be a realistic estimate. The area around North Gill was apparently allowed time to recover between the major periods of disturbance, for woodland regeneration occurs in the intervening phases. Either a pause in disturbance occurred, or the site of activity shifted far enough away from North Gill to go unrepresented in our diagram.

The ecological evidence obtained from the selected pollen curves shown in *Fig. 6* is typical of that associated with the effects of fire-clearance in Mesolithic contexts at other sites (Simmons and Innes 1985). It may be interpreted as the creation of bare ground by fire removal of the established woodland vegetation, and the gradual recolonization of vegetation on the cleared site through successional herb, shrub and tree communities. The effects of these ecological changes would have been to produce a more productive complex of habitats in terms of food resources for wildlife, and they were thus of direct benefit to Mesolithic people in increasing the number and concentration of game animals within their hunting territory (Mellars 1976). This has led authors to postulate that Mesolithic communities were engaged in the deliberate manipulation of vegetation patterns as part of an organized land use strategy (Simmons 1975; Jacobi *et al.* 1976). If this is so, the increases in ecological detail gained by fine-resolution analysis, therefore, are likely to assist greatly our understanding of the elements of Mesolithic land use by defining the character of individual disturbances much more closely. The impact of disturbance upon the environment and consequences for ecosystem development will also be clarified. Although only selected taxa are shown on *Fig. 6*, the total number of pollen types recorded by the fine-resolution analysis is significantly increased in comparison to conventional analysis of the same phase, although the total pollen counts per level are the same magnitude. Many of the additional identifications are for ecological indicator types, again refining our interpretation of the ecological processes involved.

Green (1983) has considered problems in the interpretation of fine-resolution time series pollen data, and concludes that although the technique has special limiting factors which must be taken into account, the extraction of detailed ecological information is quite feasible and forms the major advance to be gained from it. The rapid ecological changes occurring after fire, and its effects on plant communities, are areas of research where the technique may be particularly valuable. With regard to short-lived and spatially restricted forest clearance such as we envisage took place during the Mesolithic period, fine-resolution analysis may well prove especially fruitful, and we expect its use in this context to increase. The ability of the method to identify rare indicator pollen grains may allow fine-resolution pollen analysis to be used in a culturally diagnostic way. For example, the recovery of cereal-type grains from some late pre-Elm Decline disturbance horizons (Edwards and Hirons 1984) allows their reference to an earliest Neolithic context, rather than latest Mesolithic. Fine-resolution analysis of peats of this age may thus prove most useful in the study of the Mesolithic–Neolithic transition, by defining more precisely than hitherto possible the type of land use associated with individual phases of clearance.

In conclusion, we suggest that the evidence from North Gill 5 demonstrates the potential value of fine-resolution pollen analysis as a technique for the detailed study of early prehistoric land use, perhaps particularly in relation to small scale events of Mesolithic age. The likely scarcity of suitable sediments and the high numbers of counted levels, however, mean that its application may in practice be restricted. At critical sites, however, its use may prove most rewarding, particularly in association with other sensitive techniques, such as pollen concentration and chemical analysis. We stress that our findings are preliminary, and more work is needed to further test the technique. This is under way at North Gill, and relates to a continuing research programme on the late Mesolithic levels at that site. Its relevance will be seen in relation to that body of research as a whole, the results of which will be published in due course.

Acknowledgements: J.B. Innes has been supported by a grant from the University of Durham Special Project Funds. Other support has been from the Departments of Botany and Geography in the University of Durham.

References

AHLGREN, C.E. (1974) The effects of fires on temperate forests: north central United States. In S.K. Kozlowski and C.E. Ahlgren (eds), *Fire and Ecosystems*. London, Academic Press: 195–223.

BURLEIGH, R., HEWSON, A. and MEEKS, N. (1976) British Museum natural radiocarbon measurements VIII. *Radiocarbon*, 18(1): 16–42.

EDWARDS, K.J. (1979) Palynological and temporal inference in the context of prehistory with special reference to the evidence from lake and peat deposits. *Journal of Archaeological Science*, 6: 225–270.

EDWARDS, K.J. (1982) Man, space and the woodland edge: speculations on the detection and interpretation of human impact in pollen profiles. In M. Bell and S. Limbrey (eds), *Archaeological Aspects of Woodland Ecology*. Oxford, British Archaeological Reports (International Series) S146: 5–22.

EDWARDS, K.J. and HIRONS, K. (1984) Cereal pollen grains in pre-Elm Decline deposits: implications for the earliest agriculture in Britain and Ireland. *Journal of Archaeological Science*, 11: 71–80.

GARBETT, G.G. (1981) The Elm Decline: the depletion of a resource. *New Phytolologist*, 88: 573–585.

GREEN, D.G. (1983) The ecological interpretation of fine-resolution pollen records. *New Phytologist*, 94: 459–477.

INNES, J.B. (1981) *Environmental Alteration by Mesolithic Communities in the North York Moors*. Unpublished M.Phil. thesis, University of Durham.

JACOBI, R.M., TALLIS, J.H. and MELLARS, P.A. (1976) The southern Pennine Mesolithic and the ecological record. *Journal of Archaeological Science*, 3: 307–320.

MELLARS, P.A. (1976) Fire ecology, animal populations and man: a study of some ecological relationships in prehistory. *Proceedings of the Prehistoric Society*, 42: 15–45.

MOORE, P.D. (1980) Resolution limits of pollen analysis as applied to archaeology. *MASCA Journal*, 1(4): 118–120.

MOORE, P.D. and WEBB, J.A. (1978) *An Illustrated Guide to Pollen Analysis*. London, Hodder and Stoughton.

SIMMONS, I.G. (1969a) Pollen diagrams from the North York Moors. *New Phytologist*, 63: 165–180.

SIMMONS, I.G. (1969b) Evidence for vegetational changes associated with Mesolithic man in Britain. In P.J. Ucko and G.W. Dimbleby (eds), *The Domestication and Exploitation of Plants and Animals*. London, Duckworth: 118–119.

SIMMONS, I.G. (1975) Towards an ecology of Mesolithic man in the uplands of Great Britain. *Journal of Archaeological Science*, 2: 1–15.

SIMMONS, I.G. (1979) Late Mesolithic societies and the environment of the uplands of England and Wales. *Bulletin of the Institute of Archaeology of London*, 16: 111–129.

SIMMONS, I.G. and INNES, J.B. (1981) Tree remains in a North York Moors peat profile. *Nature*, 294: 74–78.

SIMMONS, I.G. and INNES, J.B. (1985) Late Mesolithic land-use and its impacts in the English uplands. *Biogeographical Monographs*, 2: 7–17.

SIMMONS, I.G. and TOOLEY, M.J.(eds.) (1981) *The Environment in British Prehistory*. London, Duckworth.

SPRATT, D. and SIMMONS, I.G. (1976) Prehistoric activity and environment on the North York Moors. *Journal of Archaeological Science*, 3: 193–210.

STOCKMARR, J. (1972) Tablets with spores used in absolute pollen analysis. *Pollen et Spores*, 13: 615–621.

STURLUDOTTIR, S.A. and TURNER, J. (1985) The Elm Decline at Pawlaw Mire: an anthropogenic interpretation. *New Phytologist*, 99: 323–329.

The Vale of Pickering
in the Early Mesolithic in Context

R.T. Schadla-Hall

Abstract

Since the pioneering and important excavations of J.G.D. Clark at Star Carr little fieldwork has been undertaken in the Vale of Pickering. Recent excavations at Seamer Carr have shown that different types of early Mesolithic (and late Upper Palaeolithic) sites survive within the Vale, and provide a marked contrast with Clark's site. Further investigation of these sites may alter radically certain aspects of the traditional interpretation of Star Carr, and permit the development of new strategies to examine buried early Mesolithic landscapes which are widespread within the Vale.

INTRODUCTION

The Vale of Pickering in North Yorkshire is a broad flat-bottomed valley, 2–3 km wide, which runs from Malton on the edge of the Vale of York in the west, to the Yorkshire coast – a distance of some 25 km (*Fig. 1*). To the north it is bounded by the dip slope of the limestone of the North Yorkshire Moors, and to the south by the chalk scarp of the Yorkshire Wolds. This broad valley coincides with a band of Kimmeridge, Oxfordian and Speeton clays, which was modified by glacial action during the Quaternary. The eastern end of the Vale, with which this paper is primarily concerned, was last glaciated around 15,000 years ago. The basal clays are covered by a considerable depth of till, as well as superficial gravelly and sandy fluvioglacial deposits (kames and eskers) which form a highly variable and complex microtopography (Kendall and Wroot 1924; Boylan 1977; A. Franks, pers. comm.). There is good evidence for the existence of areas of open water in the Vale during the Postglacial period. The extent of these lakes and ponds at any one time is uncertain, but they seem to have decreased in area towards the end of the eighth millennium BP. Peat formation in the Vale continued into the seventh millennium BP and there is now considerable evidence to suggest that as the peat developed, occupation moved higher up the low hills of clay, sand and gravel within and around the Vale. Little evidence for late Mesolithic occupation has been found below 26 m O.D., while early Mesolithic sites have been recovered at altitudes as low as 24 m O.D. There have been few attempts to examine systematically the evidence for land use and occupation of the Vale in later prehistory (Spratt 1982), but peat cutting was certainly taking place on an extensive

scale in some areas in the later Mediaeval period when drainage work was initiated. Drainage works in the Vale were invariably localized and superficial until the end of the nineteenth century when canalization of the Hertford river and the development of the New Cut allowed certain areas to be brought into arable cultivation and reduced seasonal flooding. Since the 1940s increased drainage made possible by mechanization has begun to affect even the deeper peat deposits, and the complete drying out of shallow peat deposits over this period has led to progressive destruction of buried land surfaces as a result of more intensive ploughing.

Pioneering fieldwork by J.W. Moore in the 1940s resulted in the recognition of a number of early Mesolithic sites on the margins of the drying peat in one small area of the Vale (*Fig. 2*). Moore followed up his preliminary fieldwork with limited excavations at the early Mesolithic site of Flixton 1 in 1947–8 (Moore 1950), and the late Upper Palaeolithic site of Flixton 2 between 1948 and 1951 (Moore 1954). This work attracted the interest of the late Sir Harry Godwin and established the nature and importance of the peat stratigraphy of the Vale (Walker and Godwin 1954). Between 1949 and 1951 Professor J.G.D. Clark excavated Moore's Flixton 4 site, now better known as Star Carr, and published the now world famous site report shortly afterwards. It is a tribute to the quality of this excavation and the remarkable speed and detail with which it was published that it has been a source of constant reinterpretation ever since (Schadla-Hall 1988). It is remarkable, in view of the proven archaeological potential of this one small part of the Vale, that no further systematic excavation or fieldwork took place for the next twenty-five years, during which period the rate of drainage and agricultural activity increased markedly.

Star Carr is only one of several carr lands which comprise the eastern part of the Vale; 'carr' is the local description for an area of low-lying badly drained peaty ground which until this century meant an area prone to seasonal flooding and largely devoted to rough grazing. Star Carr is an area of over

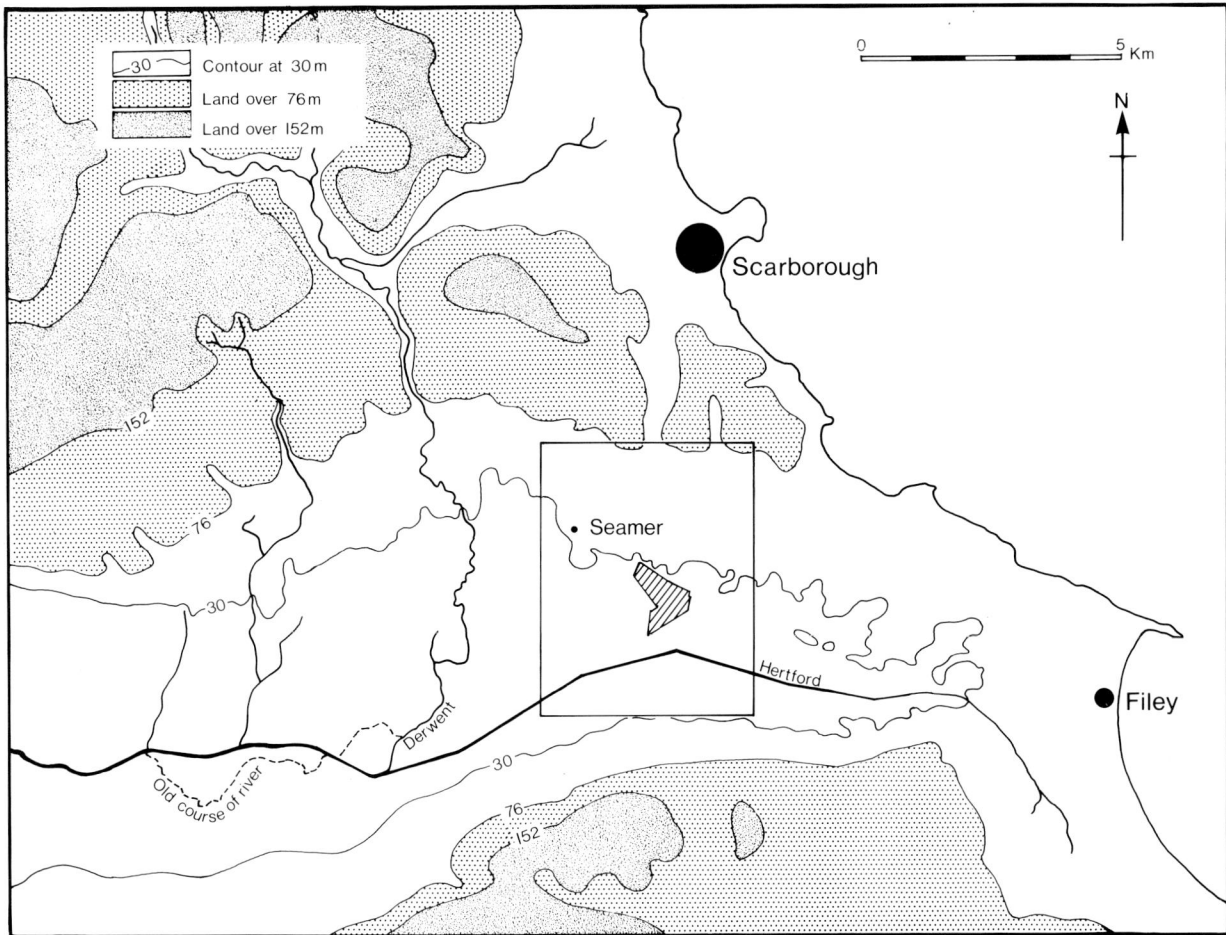

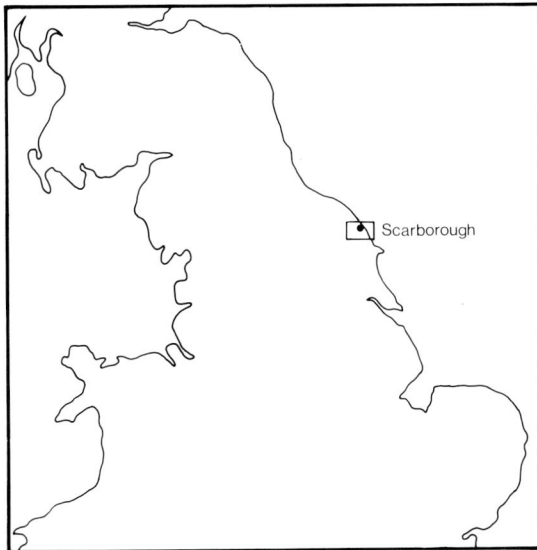

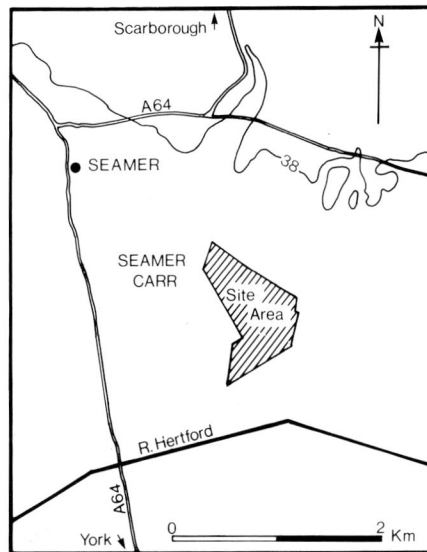

Figure 1   The eastern Vale of Pickering and the location of Seamer Carr.

200 hectares to the east of which lie Flixton Carr and Killerby Carr and to the north of which lies Seamer Carr. All these carrs are of a similar size and nature to Star Carr. In 1976 an area of some 40 hectares on the northern edge of the Vale, 0.5 km north of Star Carr, was designated as a waste disposal site (*Fig. 2*). The southern edge of this area, known as the Seamer Carr Waste Disposal Plant, took in some 15 hectares of Seamer Carr itself, including extensive peat de-

posits (*Fig. 3*). In the same year a preliminary survey of the peat stratigraphy was carried out by Dr F.M. Chambers and Dr E.W. Cloutman, under the direction of Professor A.G. Smith. This survey indicated the widespread occurrence of Zone IV–V deposits, and therefore a high probability of recovering early Mesolithic sites. Later, more detailed stratigraphic and palynological investigations indicated that the deposits spanned the late Devensian and early Fland-

219

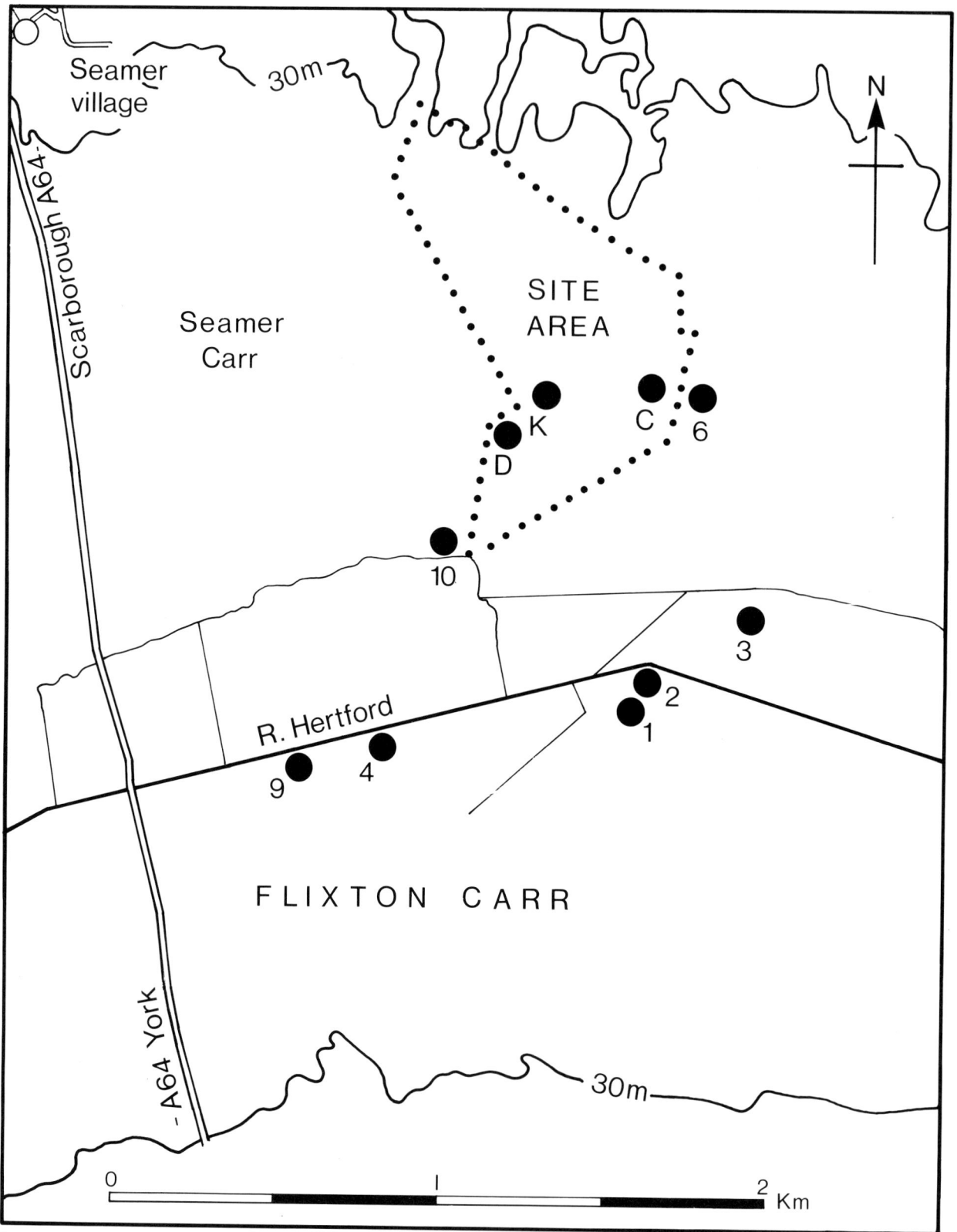

Figure 2 Postglacial sites located in the eastern Vale of Pickering (numbered sites refer to Moore (1950)).

rian and indicated an extensive reed swamp of early Mesolithic date. It also became apparent (see *Fig. 3*) that the area was unlikely on topographic grounds to contain a Star Carr-type site, as the requirements for such a site were a situation where reed swamp impinged on higher, dry ground and where the reed swamp gave way rapidly to open water (Schadla-Hall and Cloutman 1985).

In the period 1977–84 most of the 1.5 km of peat margins at Seamer Carr were investigated, much of it by using 2 × 2 m test pits (*Fig. 3*) to sample a considerable area. This strategy has almost certainly ensured

Figure 3 The southern part of the Seamer Carr site area showing the locations of test pits and major excavated areas, and the approximate extent of fen carr/reed swamp and open water in Zones IV and V.

that no extensive occupation traces on the edge of the reed swamp have been missed. However, because of high water levels and lack of resources, the deeper peat deposits could not be investigated so thoroughly, and only by means of machine-cut trenches (Schadla-Hall and Cloutman 1985).

SEAMER CARR SITE C

One area of extensive activity, Site C, was located in 1977 and was progressively excavated over a period of six years. Here, on a sandy shelf formed from a kame terrace, some 8500 pieces of worked flint were recovered and recorded. These were spread unevenly over an area of about 1000 m^2. The distribution suggests a series of activity areas (*Fig. 4*), representing a relatively short period of time. In some cases these were associated with small concentrations of burnt sand and flint which are probably the remains of hearths, and in one instance with a small stone-lined hearth. This excavation had several objectives: to excavate a large area of an early Mesolithic land surface; to delimit the main flint concentration; and to attempt to locate any extension of lithic or organic remains stratified in the peat where it would be possible to carry out more detailed environmental investigations. However, the flint scatter did not extend into the peat, and it appears that early Mesolithic activity was confined to the margins of the fen carr and reed swamp. Although preservation of bone was good and over fifty fragments were recovered, most occurred

as isolated pieces; only one small concentration was noted. Some of the bone, which included remains of red deer, aurochs, roe deer and pig (J. Clutton-Brock, pers. comm.), was clearly butchered or chopped, but the fragmentary nature and small size of the assemblage stands in clear contrast to the quantity and size of the material recovered from Star Carr, as does the overall density of flint artifacts. In terms of sources, the flint raw material may be compared with that from Star Carr, although the percentage of tools, among which scrapers predominate, is relatively small (A. David, pers. comm.). Artifacts were recorded and bagged individually, and are currently undergoing typological and functional analysis. Site C was the closest location to open water within the area under investigation, and a series of machine-cut sections were positioned in the peat on the reed swamp/open water margin (*Fig. 3*, M and U). One section produced a small quantity of bone, thought to represent a bone dump, but further investigation of this deposit proved impossible.

The sample test pits along the rest of the peat margin produced only a few worked flints, and it seems reasonable to conclude that there are no other sites comparable with Site C in the area under investigation. Site D – a low hill formed by an esker – produced a small cache of flint nodules and some 400 worked flints which may be interpreted as an isolated knapping area.

221

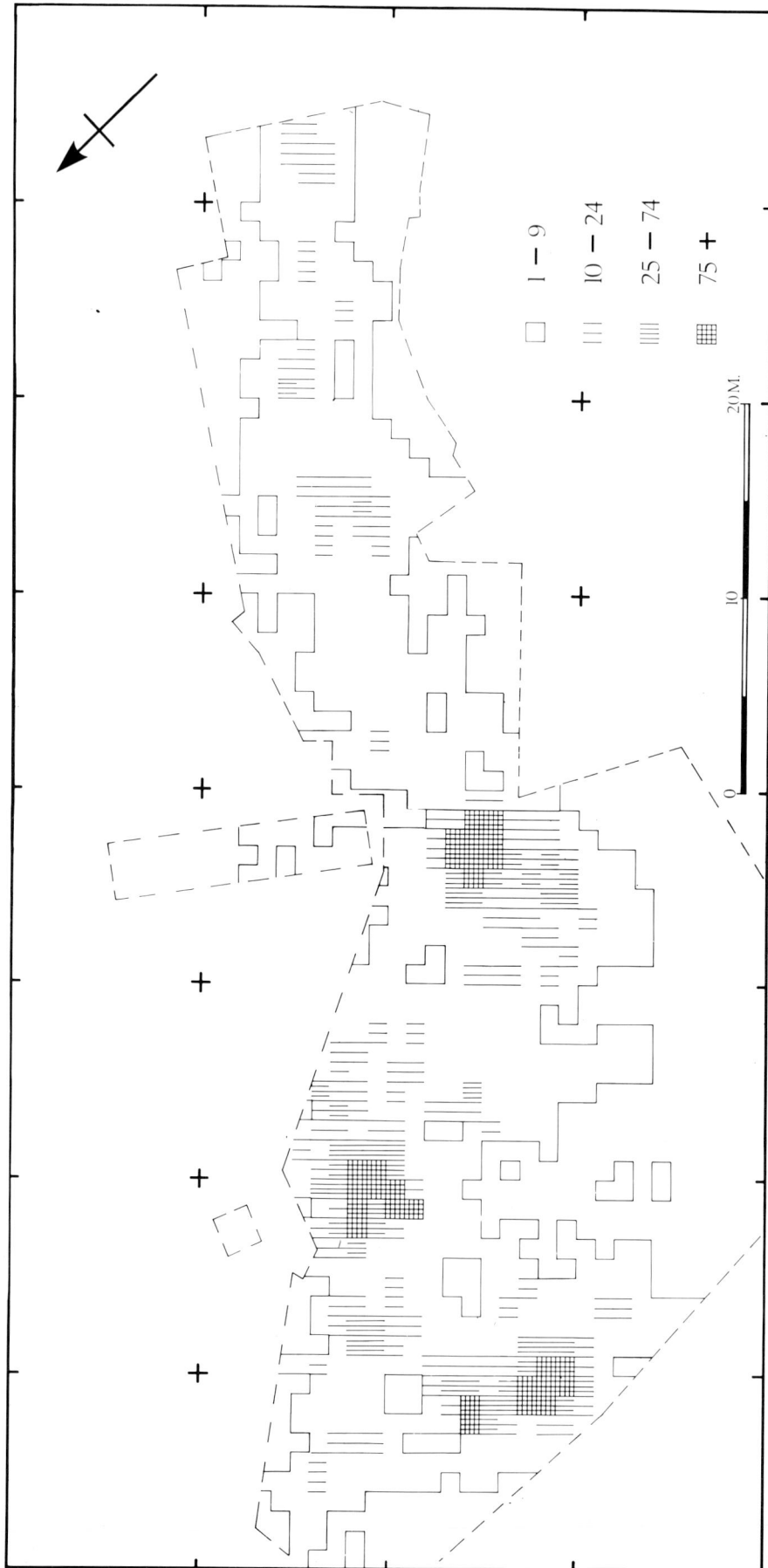

Figure 4   Seamer Carr Site C: density of worked flints per square metre.

222

SEAMER CARR SITE K

Test pits dug in 1981 and 1982 in the embayment of the western edge of the site (*Fig. 3*) indicated the presence of concentrations of worked flint. In Zones IV and V, this embayment area, which is much more extensive to the west of the site area, may have been virtually cut off from the main peat body to the south. The test pits also revealed a sandy lens 4–15 cm thick at the base of the peat, overlying an earlier peaty deposit some 3–10 cm in thickness; this stratigraphy had not been encountered elsewhere in the site area. In 1983 an area of about 150 m², Site K, was excavated and this was subsequently enlarged to over 1000 m². By the end of the 1984 season over 7000 worked flints had been recovered from this area, with variable densities similar to the pattern of Site C. In addition three stone-lined hearths and a number of shallow pits were uncovered. The similarities with Site C were marked: the main activity area was concentrated around the 24.5 m contour; like Site C the sub-soil was sandy, and attempts to recover flint in the peat deposits were unsuccessful. Again, it appears that the occupation was on and adjacent to the margins of the reed swamp. Microliths predominate among the finished tools (A. David, pers. comm.), but there are broad similarities in the raw material. Artifact densities on Site K are higher, and there seems to be a broad band of activity running from the ridge in a north-westerly direction down the slope towards the edge of what may well have been a seasonally flooded area. Although some fifty fragments of bone were recovered from this site, many with cut or chop marks and representing a similar range of fauna to Site C, the assemblage was again composed largely of isolated small fragments recovered mainly from the marginal peat deposits. One notable exception was a large red deer antler fragment which showed clear traces of the groove and splinter technique.

The aim at Site K, as at Site C, was to establish the limits of the artifact distribution, and to recover associated organic material. In 1984 two 2.5 m wide sections were excavated some 60 m to the north of Site K in an attempt to establish the extent of the distribution. These trenches, which ran east–west across the reed swamp margins on to the dry ground of the ridge, coincided with the narrowing of the shelf of land identified by Dr Cloutman's earlier work, and with the change from a sandy to a clayey palaeosurface sealed beneath the peat which had been identified in previous test pits. The southernmost trench produced well-preserved roe deer and fox bones, as well as an isolated knapping area. The more northerly section, where the palaeosurface was extremely clayey, produced no flint or other material. This tends to confirm the test pit results and underlines the impression that there was a strong preference for occupation of the less clayey areas (Schadla-Hall and Cloutman 1985). In the southernmost section the stratigraphy was similar to that recorded on Site K itself, with a lower sandy layer sealing a thin peaty layer (see above). On top of this sandy layer part of a horse jaw was recovered in a sound early Mesolithic context.

In 1984 a few tanged and backed points were recovered from the early Mesolithic occupation area. These finds, together with the recovery of flint from the peat beneath the sandy layer, suggest that this peat represents an Upper Palaeolithic (Zone II) horizon and that the thin sandy layer is a Zone III wind-blown cover sand (A. Franks, pers. comm.). Provisional radiocarbon dates suggest an age greater than 10,000 BP for the peat. Thus, in the Site K area up to 3000 m² of Zone II land surface may have been preserved. Moreover, the recovery from Site C of several sets of horse teeth stratified below the Mesolithic cultural layer, and of occasional late Upper Palaeolithic artifacts, suggests that Upper Palaeolithic remains are widespread in the Seamer Carr area, although in the case of Site C the Upper Palaeolithic and Mesolithic occupations cannot be distinguished stratigraphically. The finds from Flixton Site 2 (Moore 1954) and the recovery of some Upper Palaeolithic material from Star Carr (Clark 1954) underlines the potential for the recovery of late Upper Palaeolithic sites in the Vale.

DISCUSSION

The finds from the early Mesolithic sites at Seamer Carr are best interpreted as representing occasional activity areas. Analysis of the flint assemblages is still in progress, but it is already clear that the nature of the sites at Seamer, which have produced radiocarbon dates of *c.* 9300 BP, is in sharp contrast to Clark's site at Star Carr. The Seamer results also demonstrate the value of developing sampling strategies for examining large areas of buried land surfaces (Schadla-Hall and Cloutman 1985), as well as the need to expose large areas of such palaeosurfaces, if a coherent pattern of activity is to be established.

Within the area under consideration (*Fig. 2*) four early Mesolithic sites have now been excavated: Flixton 2 (Moore 1950), Clark's site at Star Carr (=Flixton 4: Clark 1954) and Sites C and K at Seamer. All four differ in terms of quantities, densities and frequencies of artifacts recovered. More significantly, all four sites had different local environments; Star Carr lay close to open water, whilst Seamer Sites C and K were well away from the water. There can be little doubt that all four sites belong to the period around 9300 BP, but it seems likely that each site had a different function and type of occupation. Legge and Rowley-Conwy (this volume) have now demonstrated that Star Carr was occupied during at least one summer period, and there are good reasons for doubting the seasonal occupation model traditionally applied to that site (Schadla-Hall 1988).

The recent excavations at Seamer Carr have taken place within one small area of the Vale (*Fig. 1*), and have only investigated in detail a relatively limited topographic zone concentrating around 24–25 m O.D. – an area which appears to have been dry land on the edge of, rather than in, the reed swamp of Zones IV and V. No systematic attempt has been made to locate activity on higher dry land or in the deep peat deposits, largely because of the 'rescue' nature of the project. Nevertheless, the location of two large sites and the fact that more than half of the 2 × 2 m test pits produced worked flint does suggest relatively intense activity in the early Mesolithic in this part of the Vale.

One of the most important points to emerge from the Seamer Project has been the value of detailed surveys of the buried landscape. Cloutman's initial palaeoenvironmental survey was developed by closely spaced boreholes which made it possible to reconstruct in detail the nature and topography of the Zone IV–V landscape, and to identify potential site locations which could be sampled. It has become increasingly clear that drainage now threatens the archaeological and palaeoecological integrity of the whole of the area shown in *Fig. 2*. There is a clear need to carry out further survey work in order to reconstruct accurately the Zone IV–V environment over a much larger area. A further programme of extensive fieldwork is now taking place, funded by the Science and Engineering Research Council under the direction of Professor A.G. Smith and Dr E.W. Cloutman, which should provide this clearer picture over an area of approximately 6 km² and which will in turn allow a further programme of excavation to take place (Schadla-Hall and Cloutman 1985). At the same time a programme of fieldwalking has started in an attempt to locate surface flint scatters similar to that undertaken by J.W. Moore in the 1940s (Moore 1950). Increased ploughing of the peat margins is likely to yield further results which, combined with the large scale palaeoenvironmental investigations, should provide the basis for a strategy of excavation for the foreseeable future.

In 1976 when work started at Seamer it was hoped that another 'Star Carr' would be recovered. With hindsight this was never likely, but the results have indicated the presence of other types of early Mesolithic sites within the Vale, and have demonstrated the value of large scale excavation and emphasized the levels of preservation potentially available within the Vale. The main reason for the excellent preservation on the Seamer Carr sites was the lack of drainage and cultivation in that area compared to most other areas of the peat margin in the Vale. Clark's site at Star Carr may represent only the water edge element of a larger site which extended onto the dry land to the north (Clark 1954, fig. 3). Much of that area was destroyed by the construction of the Hertford river, although there are traces of an occupation area on both sides of the river at that point. It seems likely that in the same area there are other sites similar to Flixton 4, and that within the eastern Vale as a whole other situations exist which are comparable topographically to those found at that site. It also seems probable, based on existing evidence, that the number of sites within the 6 km² which are currently being examined by Cloutman (*Fig. 2*) will be more than doubled over the next decade. Detailed palaeoenvironmental and archaeological investigations of the area are likely to provide a range of sites which will not only place Clark's site at Star Carr in a wider if still somewhat localized context, but will also change existing views on the nature of early Mesolithic exploitation of the Vale which seems likely to be far more intensive and complex than has been suggested hitherto.

Acknowledgements: I should like to thank E.W. Cloutman and A. David for information, P. Mellars for discussion, and M. Griffiths and D.W.A. Startin for support. The illustrations were drawn by R.K. Simpson. The 1976–85 investigations at Seamer Carr were funded by grants from the Historic Buildings and Monuments Commission for England and North Yorkshire County Council.

References

BOYLAN, P.J. (1977) *The Ice Age in Yorkshire and Humberside.* York, Yorkshire Museum.

CLARK, J.G.D. (1954) *Excavations at Star Carr.* Cambridge, University Press.

KENDALL, P.F. and WROOT, H.E. (1924) *The Geology of Yorkshire.* Leeds, privately published.

MOORE, J.W. (1950) Mesolithic sites in the neighbourhood of Flixton, north-east Yorkshire. *Proceedings of the Prehistoric Society*, 16: 101–108.

MOORE, J.W. (1954) Excavations at Flixton, Site 2. In J.G.D. Clark, *Excavations at Star Carr.* Cambridge, University Press: 192–194.

SCHADLA-HALL, R.T. (1988) The early Post Glacial in eastern Yorkshire. In T.G. Manby (ed.), *Archaeology in Eastern Yorkshire: Essays in Honour of T.C.M. Brewster.* Sheffield, University of Sheffield Department of Archaeology and Prehistory: 25–34.

SCHADLA-HALL, R.T. and CLOUTMAN, E.W. (1985) 'One cannot dig at random in a peat bog'. The eastern Vale of Pickering and the archaeology of a buried landscape. In C.C. Haselgrove, M. Millet and I.M. Smith (eds), *Archaeology from the Ploughsoil.* Sheffield, University of Sheffield Department of Archaeology and Prehistory: 77–86.

SPRATT, D.A. (1982) The Upper Palaeolithic and Mesolithic periods. In D.A. Spratt (ed.), *Prehistoric and Roman Archaeology of North East Yorkshire.* Oxford, British Archaeological Reports (British Series) 104: 100–111.

WALKER, D. and GODWIN, H. (1954) Lake stratigraphy, pollen analysis and vegetation history. In J.G.D. Clark, *Excavations at Star Carr.* Cambridge, University Press: 125–169.

Some Preliminary Results of a Re-examination of the Star Carr Fauna

Anthony J. Legge and Peter A. Rowley-Conwy

Abstract

Preliminary results are presented of a re-examination of the fauna from Star Carr. Two main aspects are dealt with: the numbers of aurochs, elk, red deer, wild pig and roe deer present; and the seasonality of the site.

Quantification involves some suggested re-identifications of bones. Some of the smaller 'aurochs' bones may in fact derive from elk. The anomalously small size of some of the Star Carr aurochs is thus resolved, and elk increase considerably in numbers of fragments.

Most seasonal evidence discussed suggests summer occupation of the site. This is based on tooth eruption (mainly of roe deer), neonatal bones of red deer and elk, and some other pieces of evidence. The model of seasonal migration to the uplands sometimes applied to red deer is criticized.

INTRODUCTION

Star Carr has been discussed, reviewed and reinterpreted more than any other site of its type. Many discussions of the Mesolithic of Britain have rested to a considerable degree on the information published in the site monograph (Clark 1954). Star Carr can be said to have dominated the British Mesolithic since publication, and has influenced excavation technique and interpretations throughout the world. The changes that have occurred within archaeology since the excavation of the site have been major; and the fact that many new questions can be asked of, and at least to some extent answered by, the site monograph is perhaps the greatest of the tributes that can be offered to Grahame Clark.

One aspect of the published data which has been much discussed is the fauna. Questions such as the minimum number of individuals of the major species, the seasonal evidence they provide, and the parts of the carcasses represented, have been discussed in minute detail by several authors. In spite of this, few have actually gone back to look at the bones (exceptions are Degerbøl 1961; Noe-Nygaard 1975, 1977; and Klein, Allwarden and Wolf 1983), and no complete re-examination has been attempted. Many new methods are available now which had not been developed when Fraser and King wrote their original bone report (Fraser and King 1954).

In recent years a re-analysis of the bone material has been seen as increasingly desirable (Jacobi 1978; Andresen, Byrd, Elson, McGuire, Mendoza, Staski and White 1981). The authors therefore decided to undertake a re-examination of the bones of the large mammals present at Star Carr, namely the aurochs, elk, red deer, wild pig and roe deer. Two facts must be stressed. In the first place, the study is not complete and only preliminary results are presented here. Secondly, no bone report is ever in a full sense a *final* report. Conclusions will always be subject to modification, and identifications to re-checking, as new methods and skills are developed. Many of the conclusions put forward by Fraser and King have been subject to review in the last decade. If we come to different conclusions regarding certain bone identifications, seasonal evidence, etc., we do so in the full realization that the identifications and conclusions we present will themselves be subject to modification or rejection – possibly in much less than the thirty years that have elapsed since the appearance of the original bone report.

This contribution will concentrate on two main aspects: firstly, the establishment of the number of bones and the minimum number of individuals; and secondly, the question of seasonality in so far as this can be approached via the five main food animals. Because of the preliminary nature of the report, no attempt will be made at this stage to review the large body of literature that has accumulated.

PROBLEMS OF QUANTIFICATION

This re-analysis of the bones includes those fragments in the British Museum (Natural History), the University Museum of Archaeology and Ethnology, Cambridge, and the Rotunda Museum of Archaeology and Local History, Scarborough. This represents every bone from Star Carr the whereabouts of which are known to the authors, and every piece has been examined.

Table 1 presents a basic count of fragments for the five main animals, and also the most common element within each species to give a raw minimum individual total. Several factors must be borne in mind when examining these figures. Antlers are not included. By far the most numerous category of red

Table 1: The bones of the five major animals at Star Carr (excluding antlers)

Animal	Fragments	Most common element
RED DEER, *Cervus elephas*	541	26 (left mandible)
ELK, *Alces alces*	247	12 (left astragalus)
AUROCHS, *Bos primigenius*	174	16 (13 right distal metacarpals, plus half the 6 of unknown side)
ROE DEER, *Capreolus capreolus*	103	17 (right mandible)
WILD PIG, *Sus scrofa ferus*	22	4 (left mandible)

deer remains on the site, they were interpreted as indicating the presence of the meat of a corresponding number of complete red deer (Clark 1954, 1972). Several authors have subsequently pointed out that the utility of antler as a raw material means that it may well have been collected at various times and places, stored, and moved over considerable distances. Consequently, antler (shed and unshed) could have been carried to Star Carr, and need not indicate the availability at Star Carr of the meat from as many red deer as it would take to provide the antlers (e.g. Caulfield 1978; Jacobi 1978; Pitts 1979).

The above considerations apply to red deer and elk. Roe deer antler does not seem to have been worked at Star Carr, and it may be that the specimens present do indeed derive from killed animals. If so, they could legitimately contribute towards the minimum number of individuals (cf. Pitts 1979). All determinable specimens are unshed, the total being 38 left and 39 right. If these are taken into account, the minimum number of roe deer is considerably increased.

Table 1 enumerates the bones as re-identified by the authors. One interesting development is the increase in the representation of elk. This comes about because our examination would suggest that some bones previously thought to be aurochs are in fact elk. This conclusion was also reached by Lister (1981), most (but not all) of whose re-identifications correspond with those put forward here. The re-identification of these bones as elk clears up some anomalies. The wide range of sizes of the Star Carr aurochs has been stressed (Fraser and King 1954; Jewell 1963). Re-identifying the smaller 'aurochs' as elk makes the Star Carr size range comparable to size ranges from other areas of Europe such as Denmark (Degerbøl and Fredskild 1970).

An example of this is given in *Fig. 1*. This shows the dimensions of measurable distal humeri of the five main species, and indicates the re-identifications proposed here. The width of the articulation of the smallest of 27 skeletons found in bogs in Denmark is also marked. Five Star Carr humeri falling below this were morphologically much closer to elk than to aurochs, and in terms of size also clearly fit better with elk. The two measurable aurochs distal humeri are so large that they are most probably from bulls.

Problems of recovery may contribute to the relatively small number of fragments of roe deer compared to the minimum number count (*Table 1*). The most common roe deer elements were mandibles and scapulae, most of which were relatively complete (as were the still more numerous antlers discussed above). These bones are thus considerably larger, and therefore more likely to be found, than the smaller articular ends of the long bones. The articular ends of the long bones of other species are considerably larger and will therefore be less affected by this recovery bias (Payne 1975).

Body part representation will not be discussed here, except to stress that preliminary results do appear to indicate considerable differences between the main species. This complicates any simple conversion of the raw minimum individual counts (*Table 1*) into meat weights, because differential introduction and/or removal of body parts to or from the site will bias this.

Table 2: The numbers of phalanges of the three largest animals at Star Carr

		complete	proximal	distal	MNI
RED DEER	1st phalanx	6	20	14	26
	2nd phalanx	3	12	9	
	3rd phalanx	14	–	–	
AUROCHS	1st phalanx	1	–	2	16
	2nd phalanx	7	2	–	
	3rd phalanx	–	–	–	
ELK	1st phalanx	–	37	22	12
	2nd phalanx	–	19	9	
	3rd phalanx	11	–	–	

Full discussion of body part representation will follow at a later date (Legge and Rowley-Conwy, in preparation). One small example may be quoted here. The numbers of phalanges of aurochs, elk and red deer are listed in *Table 2*. Elk, the rarest of these on the raw minimum number count, has more phalanx fragments than the other two put together. This can scarcely be due to recovery, as elk phalanges are substantially larger than those of red deer and approach aurochs in size (many of the suggested elk phalanges were indeed originally identified as aurochs). One might expect that the extremities of the aurochs would be under-represented – the larger the animal, the more likely it is that the less useful extremities would be abandoned at the kill site. One possible reason for the high representation of elk

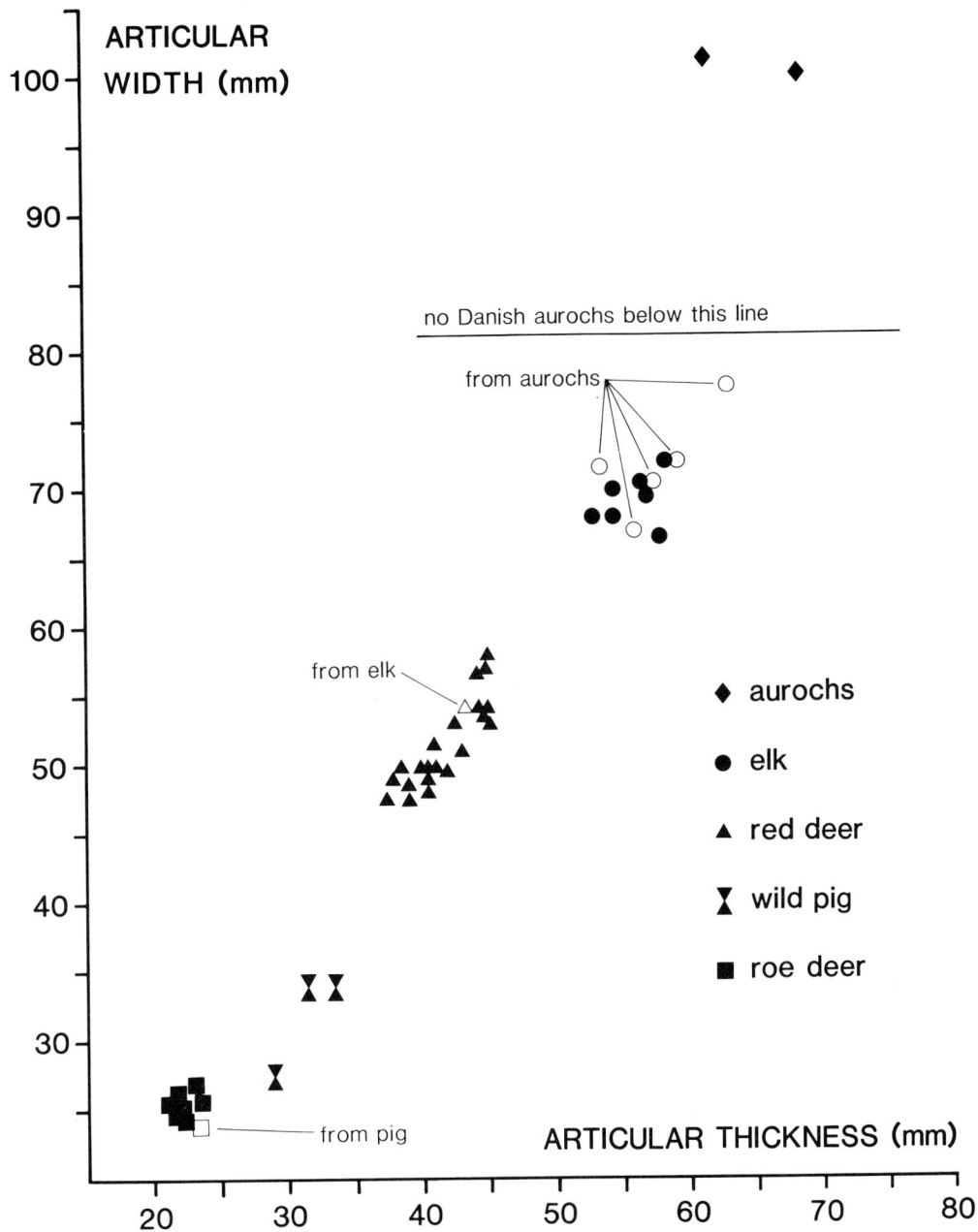

Figure 1 Dimensions of measurable distal humeri from the five main species at Star Carr, including suggested re-identifications (open symbols).

might be that this species spends much of its time in the water, particularly during summer (see below for a discussion of seasonal evidence). Red deer, on the other hand, are less well adapted to the marshes and mires (Ahlén 1965). The shallows of the lake that filled the Vale of Pickering during the Pre-Boreal would have been the most likely place for elk to be found during this season. Animals killed close to the lake edge could have been quartered and carried to Star Carr by canoe, so that the discard of peripheral parts would not be so desirable as with animals such as aurochs, killed (presumably) on dry land, often at some distance from the lake. If true, this argument would emphasize the importance of open water close offshore at Star Carr (Clark 1954: fig. 8).

SEASONALITY

The seasonality arguments presented by Fraser and King (1954) rapidly became a classic. They suggested a winter and spring occupation, an argument followed by a number of subsequent writers (e.g. Clark 1972; Mellars 1976). Some recent authorities have raised some queries, however. Jacobi (1978) suggested that occupation could have lasted at least until June on the evidence presented in the site monograph, while other recent suggestions include all-year use of the site, either briefly and sporadically (Andresen *et al.* 1981) or more continuously (Pitts 1979). A re-examination of the seasonal evidence was a major reason for the faunal re-analysis being carried out.

Much of the original argument was based on the presence of both unshed and shed red deer antlers, the former indicating an autumn/winter occupation, the latter a presence in April when the antlers are shed. A number of writers (e.g. Caulfield 1978; Pitts 1979) have pointed out that both shed and unshed antlers could have been brought onto the site from elsewhere (as discussed above). They need not therefore indicate the season of occupation of the site. The intensity of antler-working at Star Carr is a well-known feature of the site and, as with flintwork, the demand for raw material could well have exceeded the local supply. The importing of antler to the site seems to us to have a high probability. This is especially so in that measurements of limb bones of red deer show moderate sexual dimorphism, and that the results from five different bones of the body show about equal proportions of males and females, with a slight numerical bias towards the females (Legge and Rowley-Conwy, forthcoming). The mandible, scapula and metapodials all indicate 25–27 red deer at Star Carr, about half of which appear to be male. This fact makes it even less likely that the bulk of the red deer antler was obtained by hunting from the site of Star Carr.

Our preliminary work on the season of occupation is based on a number of different lines of evidence, some of which have been mentioned by other writers on the subject. These will be discussed in turn.

(a) Roe deer tooth eruption

This hitherto unexamined aspect of the fauna gives one of the clearest indications of seasonality. The roe deer jaws divide clearly into two major groups. Thir-

teen mandibles (one of them in the Scarborough Museum collection) and one maxilla either have very heavily worn deciduous teeth (with the permanent premolars in some cases visible beneath them), or have the permanent premolars in early eruption after the shedding of the deciduous teeth. When compared to modern reference material, the youngest of these jaws corresponds to animals killed in April at the earliest. The whole series of jaws suggests a restricted kill period lasting a few months at most (*Fig. 2*).

There is then a gap in the roe deer tooth eruption sequence. There are no jaws at Star Carr showing the permanent premolars and permanent M_3 in late eruption or coming into wear. Among our modern comparative specimens, amounting to over 100 of known death date, all jaws in this stage came from animals around one-and-a-half years old – i.e. those killed in their second winter. All the Star Carr jaws older than those described above have all premolars and all cusps of M_3 well in wear. This is good evidence for the seasonal killing of roe deer. All roe deer were apparently killed in late spring and summer, the younger jaws coming from one-year-old animals, the older jaws from those two years old or above.

Seasonal dating from dentition becomes more problematic once dental development is complete and all adult teeth are in wear. There is, however, some indication of a discontinuity within the fully adult group of Star Carr roe deer. Those with least tooth wear match most closely comparatives killed in their second summer, and may thus represent the two-year-old animals. The other group had more heavily worn teeth, and probably includes animals three years old and above.

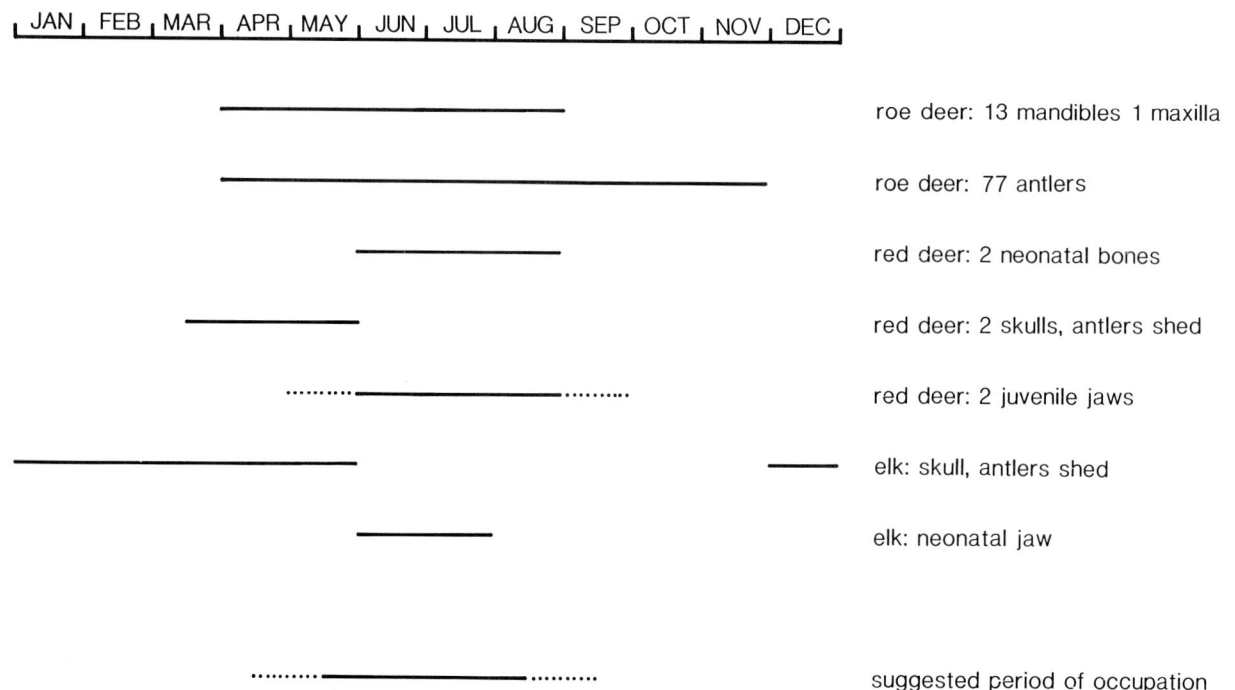

JAN | FEB | MAR | APR | MAY | JUN | JUL | AUG | SEP | OCT | NOV | DEC

roe deer: 13 mandibles 1 maxilla

roe deer: 77 antlers

red deer: 2 neonatal bones

red deer: 2 skulls, antlers shed

red deer: 2 juvenile jaws

elk: skull, antlers shed

elk: neonatal jaw

suggested period of occupation

Figure 2 Preliminary view of the seasonal evidence discussed in the text.

228

(b) Roe deer antler

As pointed out by Pitts (1979), the absence of working of the roe deer antler may indicate that they were not procured for industrial purposes, as the red deer and elk antlers demonstrably were. In this case they can legitimately be taken as seasonal indicators. The 63 unshed antlers are therefore included in *Fig. 2*, dates of cleaning and casting being taken from Prior (1968) and De Nahlik (1974).

(c) Neonatal elk and red deer

The presence of these bones was first noted by Noe-Nygaard (1975). The bones in question are a left maxilla of elk, and a left scapula and right distal humerus of red deer.

The elk maxilla contains deciduous first and second premolars, both completely unworn. These teeth start to be worn very early in life, so the Star Carr maxilla comes from an animal no more than a few weeks old at most. Most elk are born between mid-May and mid-June in Sweden today (Markgren 1969).

The red deer bones cannot be aged as precisely as the elk maxilla, but nevertheless appear to derive from neonatal animals. The distal epiphysis was fused to the shaft in a comparative specimen which we know to be aged four months at death. The Star Carr specimen was unfused and substantially smaller than the comparative. It seems most probable that both the Star Carr specimens come from animals killed in the summer.

(d) Red deer and elk skulls with antlers shed

The famous red deer frontlets are ignored as seasonal indicators, on the grounds that they might have been carried to the site if intended for some special purpose.

Two red deer and one elk skull were found not to have antlers attached. The red deer skulls indicate, as pointed out by Fraser and King (1954), that the animals were killed in spring – probably April or May. The elk skull is more problematic. This was originally taken to indicate midwinter occupation (Fraser and King 1954: fig. 31). With the benefit of more up-to-date information, it seems that wider possibilities exist. Elk shed their antlers over several months, old bulls starting as early as December, while yearlings may retain their antlers as late as April or May (Goss 1983). The Star Carr skull is thus not definite evidence of midwinter occupation, but *could* have been killed at the same time of year as the red deer not carrying antlers (*Fig. 2*).

(e) Red deer dental evidence

Most of the Star Carr red deer mandibles are in early dental maturity, with all permanent teeth in wear. A few are, however, younger than this. Two have deciduous third premolars about to be shed. In one, permanent M_4 is in the course of eruption; in the other, permanent P_4 is visible beneath the deciduous third premolar, while permanent M_4 has broken out of the jaw and cannot give any information. These jaws are very close to one another in age. According to the scheme put forward by Lowe (1967), they indicate an age of about two years, giving a kill date of late spring or summer (*Fig. 2*).

A few other jaws were not dentally mature. At present these cannot be aged as precisely as the two just described, although work now in progress may enable more exact determinations to be made. For the time being it may be said that none of these jaws comes from an animal *necessarily* killed outside the late spring/summer period.

The dentally mature animals were of little help in establishing season of kill. Study of a series of modern comparatives of known kill date in the period November to February has made it clear that, even when deer are *known* to have been killed in a restricted season, it is very difficult to demonstrate this from their jaws once all permanent teeth are in wear. Various crown height measurements were taken to supplement those of Klein *et al.* (1983), but with no greater success; we have so far been unable to develop a method to demonstrate whether animals in early dental maturity were killed seasonally or not.

Most seasonal evidence presented here suggests a late spring/summer occupation. The possibility exists that a scheduling system was in operation, and that the young adult red deer were killed in winter, so that the site could be occupied all year round. This would make sense given the model of red deer migration often employed. The animals are frequently envisaged as spending the summer in the uplands, and only coming to the lowlands in winter.

Whether this migration model would hold good for the Star Carr deer is open to question. The migration of large herds from lowland to upland on a seasonal basis is suggested by studies of animals in open, mountainous terrain such as Scotland (Darling 1937; Clutton-Brock, Guinness and Albon 1982). Studies of red deer in a woodland have revealed a very different type of behaviour, however. Little seasonal movement occurs, the deer being largely residential; and group size drops considerably. In Scottish forests, the most common group size is two animals, not the 40 or more typically found in open country (Ratcliffe and Staines 1982). In southern Sweden, average hind group size is two or three animals (i.e. one hind with one or two young at foot), while stags are overwhelmingly solitary (Ahlén 1965).

Migratory herds are thus by no means the most likely social formation for red deer in the Pre-Boreal woodlands around Star Carr. One-to-one analogies between present and prehistoric behavioural patterns may be as difficult in the zoological as in the ethnographic field. The information put forward here suggests that seasonal absence and winter yarding of red deer would not be very likely in the area around Lake Pickering. The environs of the lake would have been attractive to deer in all seasons, and there is no reason to assume a seasonal absence. This receives some support from the archaeological evidence. In at least four cases (two neonatal bones, two juvenile jaws – *Fig. 2*) we know red deer *were present in the summer*. These deer at least were not migrating to the area of the North York Moors in summer.

If it is true that the red deer were as residential as the other species are likely to have been, then seasonal scheduling is unlikely. All the preliminary evidence put forward here points to the late spring and summer, and it is most reasonable to assume that the young adult red deer were also killed at this time. Other sources of evidence may amplify this view; but at present it can be said that there is little or no evidence which necessarily indicates a winter occupation of Star Carr.

CONCLUSIONS

The above presents a preliminary view of some aspects of the Star Carr fauna. The full conclusions, including a discussion of the purpose of the site, will be presented in due course (Legge and Rowley-Conwy, in preparation).

Our initial results suggest some changes in the identifications and seasonal conclusions. If the seasonal arguments outlined above prove to be correct, then the problem arises as to where the inhabitants of Star Carr were during the rest of the year. The flint scatters on the North York Moors, which formed ideal summer sites as long as Star Carr was thought to be a winter site, seem less good candidates as winter sites. Current investigations at Seamer Carr carried out by T. Schadla-Hall are shedding much new light on the Mesolithic of the Vale of Pickering, and will do much to put Star Carr in context. Another area not to be overlooked is the sea coast. Owing to the steeply shelving sea bed, the Pre-Boreal littoral could not have been a great distance away (see Clark 1972: fig: 6).

Star Carr thus continues to yield new information thirty years after the publication of the site monograph. This article contributes to the debate, which will doubtless continue for many years to come. The fact that Star Carr can be put through such reconsiderations, and can continue to yield new information, is surely the greatest testimony to the quality of the original investigation.

Acknowledgements: We would like to thank Dr J. Clutton-Brock of the British Museum (Natural History), Dr P. Carter of the University Museum of Archaeology and Ethnology, Cambridge, and Mrs R. Palmer of the Rotunda Museum of Archaeology and Local History, Scarborough, for access to the collections in their care. We thank P. Leth Sørensen (Kalø Vildtbiologisk Station, Rønde, Denmark), P. Ratcliffe (Forestry Commission, Glenbranter, Argyll) and J. Cubby (Forestry Commission, Grizedale, Cumbria) for the provision of comparative deer jaws. Finally, we thank T. Schadla-Hall, R.M. Jacobi and M. Bracegirdle for many stimulating conversations and practical help. Any errors are our own.

References

AHLÉN, I. (1965) Studies on the red deer, *Cervus elaphus L.*, in Scandinavia. III. Ecological Investigations. *Viltrevy*, 3: 177–376.

ANDRESEN, J.M., BYRD, B.F., ELSON, M.D., McGUIRE, R.H., MENDOZA, R.G., STASKI, E. and WHITE, J.P. (1981) The deer hunters: Star Carr reconsidered. *World Archaeology*, 13: 31–46.

CAULFIELD, S. (1978) Star Carr – an alternative view. *Irish Archaeological Research Forum*, 5: 15–22.

CLARK, J.G.D. (1954) *Excavations at Star Carr*. Cambridge, University Press.

CLARK, J.G.D. (1972) *Star Carr: a Case Study in Bioarchaeology*. Addison–Wesley Module in Anthropology, no. 10. London, Cummings Publishing Company.

CLUTTON-BROCK, T.H., GUINNESS, F.E. and ALBON, S.D. (1982) *Red Deer. Behaviour and Ecology of Two Sexes*. Edinburgh, University Press.

DARLING, F.F. (1937) *A Herd of Red Deer*. Oxford, University Press.

DEGERBØL, M. (1961) On the find of a Preboreal domestic dog (*Canis familiaris* L.) from Star Carr, Yorkshire, with remarks on other Mesolithic dogs. *Proceedings of the Prehistoric Society*, 27: 35–55.

DEGERBØL, M. and FREDSKILD, B. 1970. *The Urus (Bos primigenius Bojanus) and Neolithic Domesticated Cattle (Bos taurus domesticus Linné) in Denmark*. Copenhagen, Det Kongelige Danske Videnskabernes Selskab, biologiske skrifter 17, 1.

FRASER, F.C. and KING, J.E. (1954) Faunal remains. In J.G.D. Clark, *Excavations at Star Carr*. Cambridge, University Press: 70–95.

GOSS, R.J. (1983) *Deer antlers. Regeneration, Function and Evolution*. London, Academic Press.

JACOBI, R.M. (1978) Northern England in the eighth millennium b.c.: an essay. In P. Mellars (ed.), *The Early Postglacial Settlement of Northern Europe*. London, Duckworth: 295–332.

JEWELL, P.A. (1963) Cattle from British archaeological sites. In A.E. Mourant and F.E. Zeuner (eds), *Man and Cattle*. London, Royal Anthropological Institute Occasional Paper, 18: 80–91.

KLEIN, R.G., ALLWARDEN, K. and WOLF, C. (1983) The calculation and interpretation of ungulate age profiles from dental crown heights. In G.N. Bailey (ed.), *Hunter-Gatherer Economy in Prehistory*. Cambridge, University Press: 47–57.

LISTER, A.M. (1981) *Evolutionary Studies on Pleistocene Deer*. Unpublished Ph.D. thesis, Cambridge University.

LOWE, V.P.W. (1967) Teeth as indicators of age with special reference to red deer (*Cervus elaphus* L.) on Rhum. *Journal of Zoology*, 152: 137–153.

MARKGREN, G. (1969) Reproduction of moose in Sweden. *Viltrevy*, 6: 127–299.

MELLARS, P. (1976) Settlement patterns and industrial variability in the British Mesolithic. In G. de G. Sieveking, I.H. Longworth and K.E. Wilson (eds), *Problems in Economic and Social Archaeology*. London, Duckworth: 375–399.

DE NAHLIK, N. (1974) *Deer Management. Improved Herds for Greater Profit*. London, David and Charles.

NOE-NYGAARD, N. (1975) Two shoulder blades with healed lesions from Star Carr. *Proceedings of the Prehistoric Society*, 41: 10–16.

NOE-NYGAARD, N. (1977) Butchering and marrow fracturing as a taphonomic factor in archaeological deposits. *Paleobiology*, 3: 218–237.

PAYNE, S. (1975) Partial recovery and sample bias. In A.T. Clason (ed.), *Archaeozoological Studies*. Amsterdam, North Holland Publishing Co.: 7–17.

PITTS, M. (1979) Hides and Antlers: a new look at the gatherer-hunter site at Star Carr, North Yorkshire, England. *World Archaeology*, 11: 32–42.

PRIOR, R. (1968) *The Roe Deer of Cranbourne Chase*. Oxford, University Press.

RATCLIFFE, P.R. and STAINES, B.W. (1982) Red deer in woodlands: research findings. In *Roe and Red Deer in British Forestry*. British Deer Society: 42–53.

Star Carr: the Results of a Micro-Wear Study

John V. Dumont

Abstract

This paper presents a summary of the conclusions derived from a medium magnification micro-wear analysis of 187 flints, of various types, from the British Mesolithic site of Star Carr. In addition to the interesting though trivial functional interpretations of individual artifacts, the analysis has elucidated the function of particular artifact types and has enabled an investigation of the relationship between tool morphology and function.

INTRODUCTION

Star Carr is located at the eastern end of the Vale of Pickering, 8 km south south east of Scarborough in North Yorkshire. The site is presently situated on the southern flank of a low gravel hillock, rising 1.83 m above the surrounding peat, to the north of a bend in the now defunct Little Hertford river (Clark 1954, 1972). The site belongs to the early Mesolithic 'Maglemosian technocomplex' (Jacobi 1978) and is dated to the mid-tenth millennium BP by two radiocarbon determinations – an age well in accord with the late Pre-Boreal (Zone IV) birch-dominated pollen assemblage derived from the site deposits. At that time, the low gravel hillock was a peninsula that extended into the old Glacial Lake Pickering. The site itself was located at and within the reed swamp margin of the lake when its surface stood at 22.86 m O.D.

There are four competing interpretations of the Star Carr site. Clark (1972) argues that the site was a winter or early spring base camp that was situated in the lowlands for shelter and for easy predation of the winter yards of red deer. The site being a base camp, Clark presumes that the full complement of social, economic and mystic activities were carried out at or near the excavated area. Pitts (1979), however, argues that the available evidence of seasonality indicates that the site was occupied throughout the year, though not necessarily by the same group of people or continuously. He suggests that during the winter and early spring the site would be, as Clark described, a base camp; but during the remainder of the year, the site would become the location of specialized activities and inhabited by a reduced population engaged in the processing of skins (cf. Dumont 1985). Andresen *et al.* (1981) also believe that Star Carr was not a winter base camp but rather a specialized activity area that was occupied for short periods of time throughout the year (but see Legge and Rowley-Conwy, this volume). They argue that Star Carr was a 'hunting blind' and butchering camp used for the taking and processing of red deer and other game. The prodigious quantity of lithic and organic artifacts are explained away as the detritus of 'craft manufacturing activities' produced by men in between bouts of killing and butchering as 'boredom reducers' – a rather elegant way of dismissing contrary evidence. Price (1982) is of the opinion that most of the excavated portion of Star Carr is not in fact an *in situ* living floor, but rather a spread of domestic and natural rubbish derived from a nearby occupation located on the somewhat higher and drier ground beginning at the northern border of the site.

In the light of these various interpretations, some more rational than others, I decided that a micro-wear analysis of a sample of the Star Carr lithic assemblage might help in the evaluation of the presence or absence of particular activities at the site, in addition to addressing the more basic questions of how and on what the various types of artifacts were used?

The Star Carr micro-wear analysis utilized the medium magnification, incident light method pioneered by Keeley (1977, 1980) and the technique of interferometry (Dumont 1982). The precise methodology employed in this study has been described elsewhere (Dumont 1983, 1985). The 187 artifacts examined for this study were drawn from those stored at the University Museum of Archaeology and Ethnology, Cambridge. The examined artifacts were selected from those that were apparently fresh and exhibited the least evidence of 'drawer damage'. Because the vast majority of the lithic artifacts did appear to be in a suitable condition (albeit slightly stained), it was only possible to examine a relatively small sample. The sampling procedure was governed by the aims of this research which were to determine: (i) what sorts of activities were performed with the tools found at the site; (ii) the functions of particular tool types; and (iii) the relationship between tool form and function. I came to the conclusion that sampling within each artifact type, rather than with respect to the total lithic assemblage (across types), would best serve my interests, for it would allow me to vary the sample size to take into account the variable absolute number of artifacts within each particular type. Within each of the artifact types sampled, the artifacts were selected without any conscious bias with respect to size, completeness, colour, etc., or macroscopically visible signs of wear (except for the obvious 'drawer damage').

No attempt has been made to produce a sample that would be 'random' with respect to the areal distribution of artifacts across the site. The resolution of activity areas within the site, based on micro-wear determinations, has also not been attempted. This important application of micro-wear research was not essayed because of the questions surrounding the context of the artifacts within the site (see Price 1982) and, more significantly, I felt that the lack of precise horizontal and vertical provenance, and the possibility of more than one 'occupation episode', would make a nonsense of a micro-wear-based 'spatial analysis'. Examples of the observed micro-wear traces are given in *Figs. 1–6*.

THE ARTIFACTS

Scrapers/truncated blades

Clark (1954: 96) recovered 326 pieces classified as scrapers and 48 truncated blades and flakes. Because of the general morphological similarity of the truncated blades and flakes to scrapers (end-scrapers), I have grouped the two types together during the micro-wear analysis. Fifty-six (*c.* 15%) of the 374 available scrapers/truncated blades and flakes were examined, of which 36 (64%) exhibited micro-wear traces. These traces were distributed over 49 identified utilized edges and represent at least 55 distinct use-episodes. The 55 use-episodes represent activities directed against hide (40%), bone (*c.* 22%), antler (*c.* 22%), wood (*c.* 13%) and either bone or hide (*c.* 4%). Hide-working consisted solely of scraping/planing, while all but one (*c.* 92%) of the bone-working episodes also involved this task; the manner of use of the remaining bone-working episode was not resolved. The antler-working functions were scraping/planing (*c.* 66%) and incising (*c.* 34%). Wood-working consisted primarily of whittling (*c.* 57%), while scraping/planing was responsible for the remainder of the use-episodes. Unlike the edges used against hide, bone and antler, the wood-working edges were, with a few exceptions, the unretouched lateral sides of the artifacts; the steeply retouched 'scraper edges' were generally

employed on some other material (see Dumont 1985: table 4).

The micro-wear analysis of these tools has enabled several general statements to be made with respect to tool morphology and function. After comparing the metrical attributes of the hide-, bone- and antler-working scrapers/truncated blades, the following observations were possible (Dumont 1985): (i) the antler-working tools tend to be longer than those used against bone or hide; (ii) the retouched antler-working edges are less curved than those used against bone or hide; (iii) the retouched bone-working edges are less curved than those used against hide, but more curved than those used against antler; and, of course, (iv) the retouched hide-working edges tend to be more curved than any of the others. Since these four unanticipated observations were made after the functional interpretations based on the micro-wear evidence, their derivation supports or lends credence to the ability to discriminate between at least these polish types: hide, bone and antler. I have argued elsewhere (Dumont 1983, 1985) that the differences in edge morphology reflect intentional selection or manufacture of particular types of scrapers for particular types of tasks. With respect to the manipulation of the artifacts, only three tools exhibited traces that could imply the former presence of wooden hafts.

Borers

The excavation produced 107 narrow bilaterally-backed blades whose backing converges to form a stout point, hereafter referred to as 'borers' (Clark's 'awls on narrow flakes and blades' – 1954: 96). Twenty-seven (*c.* 25%) of the 107 borers were examined, of which 14 (52%) exhibited micro-wear traces corresponding to at least 14 use-episodes. One of the borers, which in fact did not show traces of use, has been counted twice, for both of its ends are considered to have been potentially useful. In those instances where other bi-pointed borers exhibit functional traces at just one end, only that demonstrably utilized end is here considered useful. The non-utilized end is not so considered because the tool-users themselves did not view it as useful. The total examined sample of used and apparently unused borers, then, consists of 28 potentially useful tips. The 14 use-episodes indicate use against bone (*c.* 57%), wood (*c.* 7%), hide (*c.* 7%), and unidentified materials (*c.* 29%). With only a few exceptions, these tools were used in a rotary fashion to bore initial and/or to enlarge existing holes in the stated materials. It was not possible to distinguish with confidence unidirectional rotary motions (either clockwise or anti-clockwise) from reciprocal rotary actions on the basis of the observed traces.

Of the eight bone-working tools, five are confidently interpreted as having been used to bore or enlarge holes, while two others are less confidently ascribed to this activity. The manner of use of the remaining bone-working tool was not resolved. The minimum dimensions of the holes created in bone, through the rotary use of these tools, are approximated by the magnitude of the extent of traces back from the working tip and the greatest dimension (width or thickness) of the tip at the limit of the traces' extent. The holes produced, then, ranged in smallest diameter from $c.$ 1.0 or 1.6 mm to greater than 6.8 mm at a tool-penetration depth of $c.$ 1–7 mm (see Dumont 1985: table 22). It is certainly curious that although the micro-wear traces on the borers indicate that bones were being perforated, no bones have been found at the site that have perforations anywhere near the dimensions demanded by the tools' morphology. Only a single deer canine (Clark 1954: 166) was found with a perforation sufficiently small to have been produced by one of these borers. The holes in the parietals of the worked stag frontlets have diameters ranging from 1.2 to 2.5 cm (Clark 1954: 169), approximately 1.8 to 3.7 times greater than the maximum dimension of any of the borers within the distribution of the traces at the working tips. The borers, of course, could have been used to make initial perforations through the parietals which were then enlarged by other means.

With respect to wood-working and hide-working, each of these activities is represented by a single tool. Although no perforated wooden or hide artifacts were recovered from Star Carr, their former presence is easily imagined and safely assumed. The limited micro-wear evidence does suggest that the wood-working borer has made at least one perforation of at least 3 mm in diameter and up to, if not beyond, 6 mm deep, while the hide-working tool was used to make a hole of $c.$ 2 mm in diameter.

Four of the 28 stout tips were free of polish but exhibited numerous striations and edge/arête rounding. Although the type of worked material is unclear, the manner of use can be confidently interpreted as a rotary motion for all but one of the borers. Three tools have been used to produce holes of a greatest diameter of at least 2.7–5.5 mm and of a depth up to $c.$ 9 mm. The severe edge/arête rounding and numerous striations present on these three artifacts suggest that the unidentified worked material was hard and friable, as compared to the range of organic materials, and when worked produced a gritty abrasive powder. I have suggested elsewhere (Dumont 1985: 135–136) that the observed traces may have resulted from the manufacture of objects such as the Lias shale beads recovered from the site (see Clark 1954: 165–166, plate XX, A & H).

The micro-wear analysis has enabled two general observations regarding borer morphology and function (Dumont 1985): (i) the angle forming the working tips of the bone-working tools tends to be less acute than the tips of those used against other materials; and (ii) the bone-working borers tend to be thinner relative to their width than those used against other materials. The first significant difference could represent the intentional manufacture of the 'blunt' borers for bone-working, but it may be that the observed form merely reflects the effects of either severe edge damage and/or resharpening. The second difference suggests that the tool-users selected the relatively thicker blades for fashioning into the more acute working tips, perhaps in an attempt to strengthen the more delicate tips.

No traces attributable to the former presence of hafts were encountered on the examined borers.

Burins

Clark identified 336 burins from the excavation (1954: 96). Of these, 334 were fashioned on flakes and blades while two others appeared to Clark to be re-used blade cores (1954: 114). At least one other burin was not recognized as such for it had been produced on a discarded core axe resharpening flake. The minimum number of burins or burin-like cores recovered from the site, then, is 337. During this study, 20 of the 337 artifacts, representing 21 burin bits, were examined ($c.$ 6%). Burin spalls were not included in this study because of the overwhelming indications, on inspection of the burins, that the vast majority would be 'primary' removals, not resharpening spalls. Sixteen (80%) of the 20 burins exhibited micro-wear traces. The micro-wear traces on these 16 artifacts represent 11 use-episodes on nine artifacts (45% of the examined tools), of which 10 can be identified to worked material – antler ($c.$ 73% of the use-episodes) and bone ($c.$ 18%). The remaining seven artifacts exhibit either technological striations relating to the manufacture of the tools (five instances) or traces of unattributable origin (two instances). The technological striations have been described and discussed elsewhere (Dumont 1983, 1985). These broad and deep striations, caused by the truncation of the blades, were visible on a total of nine artifacts – at the truncations of four burins with functional traces, in addition to the five tools mentioned above.

With respect to the use of these tools, the eight episodes of antler-working can be subdivided into the following activities: five episodes of incising, presumably to create grooves or incised lines, one episode of either incising or planing, and two episodes of an indeterminate use, though one may actually represent 'planing'. The large number of barbed antler points and other antler objects found at the site attest to a great deal of antler-working at or near the site. These burins would have been capable of incising the grooves in the antler beams as part of the groove and splinter technique (Clark and

Thompson 1954), as well as for doing the fine reduction work (planing) on the splinters during the manufacture of the barbed points. The single bone-working episode has been confidently attributed to planing. Of the two remaining use-episodes directed against unidentified materials, the manner of use of only one has been confidently resolved – sawing with the burin facet margin. It is interesting to note that of the 11 use-episodes recognized on these tools, five or six involved the use of the bit while the remainder employed the long burin facet margins. The use of the burin facet margins, in addition to or instead of the bits, has been noted by other researchers (Keeley 1981; Moss 1983). No traces attributable to hafting were observed on these tools.

Edge-damaged/retouched blades

This group consists entirely of those artifacts described by Clark as 'utilized primary flakes' (1954: 114). The excavations produced a total of 14,743 'primary flakes' from which Clark identified 1269 'utilized' pieces, on the basis of irregular edge damage and/or the presence of macroscopically visible 'glosses' which he took to be functionally related (1954: 96, 114). During this micro-wear study, I examined 25 (c. 2%) of the 1269 'utilized primary flakes' of which 12 (48%) exhibited micro-wear traces. Of the 24 potentially usable long edges of these 12 tools, 18 were found to bear functional traces that represent at least 20 use-episodes. Six of the artifacts, then, were demonstrably utilized on both edges, while the remainder showed use of only a single edge.

The 20 use-episodes represent activities directed against wood (55%), antler (15%), antler or wood (10%), hide (15%) and meat (5%). The near absence of meat-working traces on these artifacts is surprising; the long, sharp cutting edges would seem to be ideal for cutting meat. If other artifacts of this type were used as meat knives, as the single example here was in fact used, then either I was unlucky in the composition of the artifact sample studied in this analysis and simply did not include a representative series of blades bearing this trace, or my analysis failed to resolve additional evidence of meat-cutting on the other tools. The latter possibility is probably closer to the truth because meat polish is difficult to see, especially in the early stages of its formation, and can be easily obscured by the former presence or later addition of a different polish along the same portion of the edge. With respect to the manner of use, the wood-working use-episodes were concerned primarily with whittling (10 of the 11 episodes) with the remainder being 'planing'. The antler-working episodes were of planing or whittling. The hide-working manners of use were not resolved. The two antler- or wood-working episodes concerned either whittling or planing.

This study has enabled several general observations to be made concerning artifact morphology and function. When one divides the examined sample of blades into two groups, utilized and non-utilized, on the strength of the micro-wear data, and compares their metrical attributes (Dumont 1985), it becomes clear that: (i) the utilized blades tend to have a greater thickness:width ratio than the non-utilized blades; (ii) this difference is clearly dependent upon significant differences in their thickness rather than their width; and (iii) the utilized edges tend to have greater spine angles (for the definition of 'spine angle', see Tringham et al. 1974) than non-utilized edges. The significant differences in the above metrical attributes implies that some selective criteria were applied in the choice of particular blades for use; specifically, the tool-users either selected or manufactured blades with a proportionately greater thickness for use against wood, antler, hide, and meat. The purpose of this selection may have been the desire to obtain the strongest possible blades for use. No traces attributable to hafting were observed.

Backed blades

The type name 'backed blade', as used in this study, cuts across several of Clark's types that are subsumed under his class of 'variously backed and trimmed flakes and blades' (1954: 104). This type includes, then, all of those tools known as 'convex battered back' (three examples) and 'straight battered back' (two examples), and several of the 27 'obliquely truncated' blades whose steeply retouched truncations appear more as backed lateral edges than as truncated ends (e.g. Clark 1954: fig. 38, F78). Because of my somewhat subjective selection of artifacts from Clark's 'obliquely truncated' blade type, a figure for the total number of 'backed blades' recovered from Star Carr was not ascertained (no more than 32 and probably substantially fewer, perhaps 10 examples). During this micro-wear study, seven 'backed blades' were examined of which four (c. 57%) exhibited functional traces relating to four use-episodes. Three of the four use-episodes represent wood-working – two instances of scraping/planing, and one instance of a poorly-resolved activity, either scraping/planing, sawing or whittling. The manner of use of the single antler-working episode was also poorly resolved, either planing or sawing.

The small sample of examined and even smaller number of productive backed blades makes dangerous any attempt to generalize from the observed micro-wear data. The absence of meat-, hide- and bone-working traces on the examined backed blades does not, of course, indicate that such tasks were never carried out with this type of tool. Similarly, the presence of wood polish on three utilized edges,

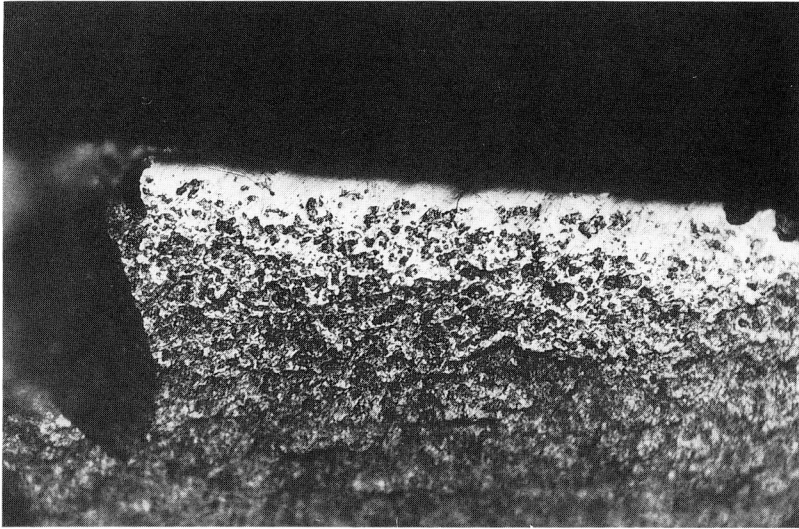

Figure 1 Wood polish and striations on an edge-damaged blade from Star Carr. Length of photograph: 0.565 mm.

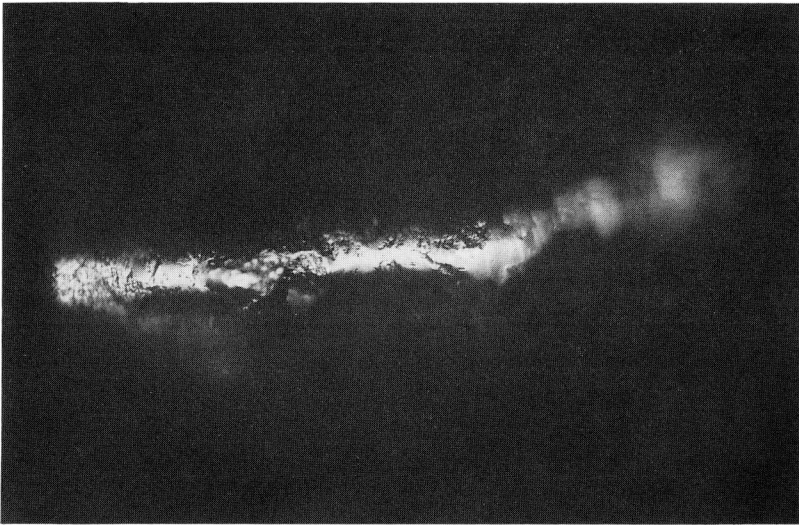

Figure 2 Bone polish on the steeply retouched edge of a scraper/truncated blade from Star Carr. Length of photograph: 0.354 mm.

Figure 3 Antler polish on the dorsal aspect of the steeply retouched truncation of a Star Carr scraper/truncated blade. Length of photograph: 0.565 mm.

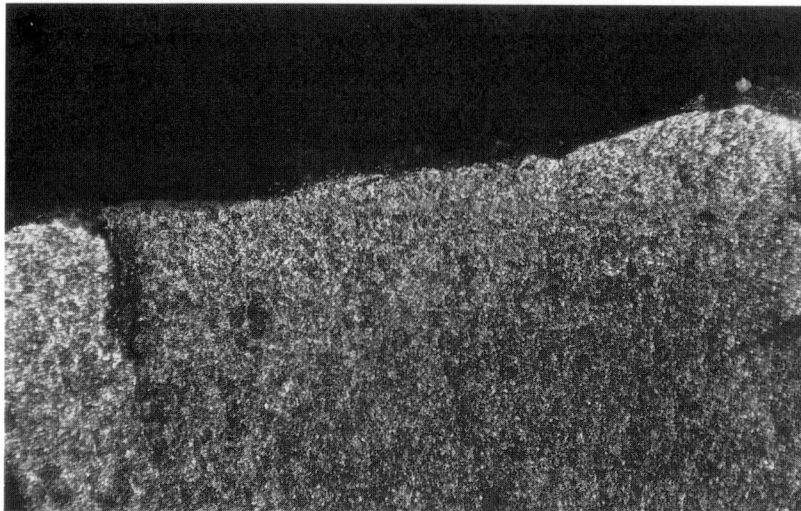

Figure 4   Hide polish on the ventral aspect of the steeply
retouched edge of a Star Carr scraper/truncated blade.
Length of photograph: 1.15 mm.

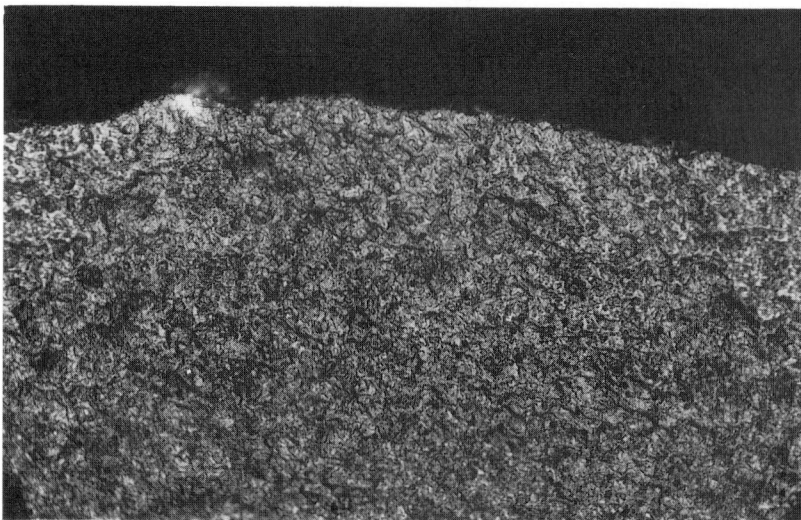

Figure 5   Meat polish on an edge-damaged blade from Star
Carr. Length of photograph: 0.354 mm.

Figure 6   'Technological striations' on the ventral aspect of the
straight truncation of a Star Carr burin. Length of
photograph: 1.15 mm.

and antler polish on one edge, cannot be taken as a strict indication of the relative importance of the activities performed with these tools. In general, the activities for which evidence was found were much what one would expect to find, given the size, shape and design of these artifacts.

Core axe resharpening flakes

The core axe resharpening flakes exhibited exceedingly few traces of use. Of the 26 resharpening (or initial sharpening) flakes recognized by Clark (1954: 96, 100), 14 (54%) were examined for micro-wear though only two exhibited functional traces – chopping wood (while attached to the core axe) and scraping/planing hide. Although the latter functional interpretation goes counter to the usually presumed function of core axes, it is not unique; hide scraping/planing was also performed by an example of this type from Mount Sandel (Dumont 1985, 1986). Another resharpening flake also exhibited functional traces, but these appear to be related to a subsequent modification of the waste flake into a burin (see above).

The micro-wear analysis of these tools has raised two related questions: why are the vast majority (c. 86%) of the examined resharpening flakes free of functional traces, and of what significance is this observation for the site of Star Carr? An answer could be that the sample studied was unrepresentative of the available population of these tools, though this would seem unlikely for the artifacts were selected on a purely random basis. One could also suggest that functional traces were not produced on the axe edges via use, though the evidence from Mount Sandel (Dumont 1985, 1986) argues strongly against such a supposition. Another response could be that the population of resharpening flakes recovered from the site was itself biased by the behaviour of the tool-makers and users; that is, perhaps the resharpening of axes generally occurred at the locality of their use rather than 'at home' provided, of course, that the two locations do not coincide. This would result in the discard of the majority of the most utilized edges, those having the greatest potential for exhibiting functional traces, away from Star Carr. If the latter possibility is to be considered, then the apparent contradiction of the presence of resharpening flakes at Star Carr must be reconciled with the proposition that 'resharpening' occurred elsewhere. This paradox can only be circumvented by suggesting that the majority of the 'resharpening flakes' found at the site were in fact detritus from the initial manufacture of the core axes and, hence, did not experience use. Although this solution is attractive, I am unable to provide any convincing arguments in its favour based on the morphology of the artifacts, because each of the 14 'resharpening flakes' appears to incorporate a working edge that to me looks potentially ready for use. Whether or not the inhabitants of the site considered these edges as potentially useful is without doubt an entirely different matter. The micro-wear analysis of the core axe resharpening flakes has clearly, then, created problems in the interpretation of tool-using and curative behaviour rather than elucidating the function of core axes.

Cores

Clark recovered at least 292 cores of various types from the excavation (1954: 98). Of these, he suggested that 120 were converted into tools, principally scrapers, on the basis of numerous small damage scars and crushing found on the striking platform. Such an argument is now generally regarded as invalid in the case of most so-called 'core-scrapers', because such traces have recently been recognized as being an effect of normal platform preparation employed in the process of blade core reduction (Tixier 1972). Nevertheless, I thought it prudent to examine a small number of these artifacts to determine whether Clark may have been correct, even if for the wrong reasons. To this end, five cores were examined of which four were in Clark's mind 'core-scrapers' and another a 'core-burin'. Each of the examined cores exhibited micro-wear traces that can be argued to have resulted from normal core platform preparation and/or from a subsequent use of the waste core as a tool. Three of the five cores exhibit a distribution of traces that lend themselves to a 'functional' interpretation and thereby provide support for Clark's belief that many of the cores were subsequently utilized. Although the micro-wear analysis has not suggested specific functional interpretations of the traces, it has at least shown that some cores were used as wedges or planes (two of the three cores), or in some other manner. This analysis demonstrates that the wholesale dismissal of the possibility that cores were liable to be re-used, after their function as sources of blades and flakes, would be unwise at any site.

Microliths

The excavations produced 248 microliths of the following types: 126 'obliquely blunted points', 45 'triangles', 45 'elongated trapezes', 12 miscellaneous, and 20 fragments (Clark 1954: 102–104). Thirty-one (c. 12%) of these microliths were examined, including examples of each type, though only three were found to exhibit micro-wear traces: evidence of hard hammer percussion, and perhaps evidence of a bone haft and a hafting adhesive. Since none of the traces observed on the artifacts can be shown to be directly related to the function of the microliths, a discussion concerning their function cannot be based on the available evidence. Although the evidence does suggest that at least two of the artifacts were hafted, whether the haft was part of a weapon or a component of some other type of tool cannot be determined. One can argue, though, that the hafting evidence (if it is such) is consistent with the traditionally assumed and occasionally documented use of microliths as projectile armatures and barbs. The absence of meat and hide polishes on their leading (cutting) edges could be explained by the extremely short duration of contact between the flint surfaces and the target animal during the projectile's penetration of the hide and flesh. The absence of bone polish could be due to careful 'aiming' to ensure maximum penetration by avoiding the skeletal frame of the animal. This sample may also be devoid of 'functional' traces because the microliths had not yet served their purpose as armatures and barbs before their incorporation within the site deposits, or because of a lack of success on the part of the hunters. None of the examined tools exhibited 'impact fractures' (Barton and Bergman 1982; Fischer, this volume).

Denticulates

Five denticulated flakes and blades were recovered from the excavations and were duly described by Clark (1954: 106) as 'saws'. Two of these denticulated pieces have been examined, though only one exhibited micro-wear traces. This tool was used against fresh hide or meat; the manner of use, however, remains unclear. It is interesting to note that the denticulation of this utilized artifact was created after or towards the end of its use; the denticulation scars are free of traces. The real function of denticulates as a type, therefore, is still unknown.

TOOL TYPES AND FUNCTION

The following section examines the relationship between particular 'functions' and the types of artifacts employed at these tasks. The discussion is organized according to six broad activity groups that are individually defined as concerning the working of hide, bone, antler, wood, meat, and unidentified materials. In order to make meaningful statements with respect to the entire lithic assemblage, it is necessary to weight the data given above for each artifact type to account for the varying sample sizes (Dumont 1985).

Hide-working

Scraping/planing would be performed primarily with scrapers/truncated blades (c. 99%) but core axes would also be used occasionally (c. 1%). Piercing/boring would only be performed by borers. If the traces on the denticulate are hide-cutting traces, then hide-cutting would be restricted to this tool type. All of the unknown hide-working functions were represented on the edge-damaged/retouched blades.

Bone-working

Although scraping/planing of bone would have been performed primarily with scrapers/truncated blades (c. 82%), a number of burin facet margins would also have been employed (c. 18%). Piercing/boring would be restricted again to borers. Sawing bone, if actually represented on the examined tools, would have been accomplished with scrapers/truncated blades. The unknown bone-working functions would be restricted to the borers.

Antler-working

The majority of the scraping/planing episodes would employ edge-damaged/retouched blades (c. 64%) with the remainder being performed by scrapers/truncated blades (c. 27%), burin facet margins (c. 9%) and perhaps the occasional backed blade. Whittling antler, if actually represented, would be restricted to the edge-damaged/retouched blades. The majority of the incising tasks would utilize the burins (c. 79%), with the remainder being performed by scrapers/truncated blades (c. 21%). Sawing antler may have been accomplished through the use of scrapers/truncated blades and/or backed blades. The unknown antler-working functions are restricted to the burins.

Wood-working

Again the majority of the scraping/planing episodes would utilize the edge-damaged/retouched blades (c. 81%), with the remainder being performed with scrapers/truncated blades (16%) and backed blades (c. 3%). Although whittling would be virtually restricted to edge-damaged/retouched blades (c. 96%), the lateral sides of some scrapers (c. 4%), and perhaps a backed blade, would also have been employed. As usual, piercing/boring would belong to the borers. Chopping would also be restricted to the core axes (as represented by the resharpening flakes). Sawing wood, if actually represented, may have been accomplished with a backed blade.

Meat-working

Cutting meat was apparently undertaken with the edge-damaged/retouched blades and, perhaps, denticulates.

The working of unidentified materials

Scraping/planing would have been performed with burins, scrapers/truncated blades and, perhaps, occasionally with cores. Piercing/boring activities would again be restricted to the borers, while sawing would be restricted to the burin facet margins. The demonstrably utilized cores that were not used for scraping/planing were evidently employed for wedging and also for unidentified activities.

Discussion

The above summary has outlined the typological composition of the activity toolkits evident at Star Carr. It is now of interest to investigate whether or not particular tool types can, in general, be correlated with particular manners of use irrespective of the nature of the worked material, or *vice versa*. As above, this discussion utilizes the weighted data to account for the differing sample sizes of the examined artifact types.

With respect to all the use-episodes likely to be found on the scrapers/truncated blades, 84.6% actually represent the eponymous use of scraping/ planing, 7.2% whittling, 6.3% incising, and 1.9% sawing. This ranking indicates that although those tools that are classified as 'scrapers/truncated blades' at Star Carr are, for the most part, concerned with scraping/planing, they were also employed at other tasks.

With respect to the burins, only 54.7% of the use-episodes would be of the presumed incising function of these tools, 25.1% would be of scraping/planing, and 10.1% each of sawing and unknown manners of use. Burins, then, may be much less specialized than had been previously thought (e.g. Clark and Thompson 1954).

With regard to the borers, 85.7% of the use-episodes would be engaged in piercing or boring activities; the remainder would represent unidentified manners of use. The Star Carr borers, then, seem to be just what they look like.

No preconceived notions surround the function of the edge-damaged/retouched blades. With reference to the total number of use-episodes likely to be present on these artifacts, 60% would be concerned with whittling, 20% with scraping/planing, 5% with cutting, and 15% would remain unidentified.

The backed blade has often been considered the 'all purpose penknife-like tool' of lithic assemblages. With respect to the activities carried out with these artifacts, 66.7% would represent scraping/planing, while sawing and whittling would each account for 16.7%. Although the absolute number of likely use-episodes is small (about six), the above presumption is not seriously challenged.

The surprising dearth of functional traces on the examined core axe resharpening flakes must surely have distorted the formal interpretation of how these tools were employed. It is, in my opinion, wholly unlikely that half of the potential use-episodes would represent hide-scraping/planing, as opposed to wood-chopping or adzing/planing, as the micro-wear data would suggest.

The use of denticulates in a presumed 'cutting' manner is not too far distant from Clark's (1954) description of these tools as saws.

Clark was correct, albeit for the wrong reasons (see above), when he suggested that some of the Star Carr cores were tools as well as the discarded residue of flake and blade production. Approximately one-third of Clark's 'utilized cores' were used in an unidentified manner, while the remainder (66.7%) were used either to wedge or to scrape/plane unidentified materials, possibly including stone in some cases. I have not yet investigated the possibility that other cores, the non-utilized cores in Clark's view, were also utilized after their role as 'cores' (*sensu strictu*) was completed.

Another way of viewing this data is to examine the types of tools utilized in a common manner, e.g. the particular tool types used for scraping/planing or piercing/boring. The following is such an examination and, as above, utilizes the weighted figures necessitated by the differing sample sizes:

1. Slightly over half (52.1%) of the scraping/ planing use-episodes would occur on the scrapers/ truncated blades. The remaining use-episodes would be found on the edge-damaged/retouched blades (33.3%), burins (9.8%), cores (0.7%), and core axe resharpening flakes (0.3%). The tool types most frequently used to scrape/plane, then, are the scrapers/truncated blades and the edge-damaged/ retouched blades which together account for 85.4% of the use-episodes.

2. Unlike the previous example, all of the piercing/ boring use-episodes would be found on borers.

3. Incising was a manner of use restricted to antler-working and would have been performed primarily by the burins (79.7%), with the remainder having been accomplished with scrapers/truncated blades.

4. Whittling would have been accomplished predominantly with edge-damaged/retouched blades (95.7%); the remaining use-episodes would have employed the scrapers/truncated blades (4.2%) and perhaps, occasionally, backed blades (0.1%).

5. The majority of the sawing episodes would seem, surprisingly, to have been performed by burins (68%) with scrapers/truncated blades and backed blades accounting for 28% and 4%, respectively.

6. The vast majority of the cutting episodes (96.2%) would have been accomplished with edge-damaged/ retouched blades, if the denticulates were indeed used in a cutting manner. If the denticulates were not so used, all of the cutting episodes would have been performed by the edge-damaged/retouched blades.

7. As one might expect, the chopping use-episodes

utilized the core axes (as represented by their resharpening flakes).

8. The wedging manner of use was exclusively associated with re-used cores.

9. The typological breakdown of the unknown manners of use is as follows: edge-damaged/retouched blades (75.6% of the use-episodes), cores (11.9%), burins (8.5%) and borers (4.0%).

FINAL COMMENTS

Since this paper is already a summary of the conclusions derived from the micro-wear analysis of 187 lithic artifacts, an additional summary at this point would be of little use. However, several general comments concerning our perception of artifacts and the original tool-users' perception of their own tools – the relationship between our imposed typology and tool function – would be appropriate. Firstly, it is clear that the retouched portions of formal tools, such as the steeply retouched 'scraper' edges of the scrapers/truncated blades, were not necessarily the only utilized portions of the tools' perimeter. Secondly, it is evident that particular tool types cannot be confidently correlated with any single type of worked material or with a particular manner of use. Similarly, there is no justification for a universal correlation between particular manners of use (e.g. scraping/planing or sawing) and specific tool types, though individual correlations are sometimes possible – for example, all of the piercing/boring episodes at Star Carr utilized the borers, and all the chopping episodes concerned the core axes (as represented by the resharpening flakes). Thirdly, this study has demonstrated that subtle morphological differences within particular tool types can occur and be associated with differing functions, such as the different working edge curvatures of the hide-, bone- and antler-working scrapers, and the acuteness and thickness of the bone-working and non-bone-working borer tips.

In addition to these conclusions regarding tool use, and the examples of tool manufacturing behaviour given above, the results of the micro-wear analysis suggest that a wide range of activities were performed at or near the site. The analysis, though, has produced no clear evidence of a specialized site function of the kind championed by Pitts (1979) or Andresen et al. (1981). As I have argued elsewhere on the basis of the weighted data (Dumont 1985) wood-working rather than hide-, bone-, antler- or meat-working, would have been responsible for the greatest number of use-episodes evident on the tools (41.8% of all the use-episodes).

References

ANDRESEN, J.M., BYRD, B.F., ELSON, M.D., McGUIRE, R.H., MENDOZA, R.G., STASKI, E. and WHITE, J.P. (1981) The deer hunters: Star Carr reconsidered. *World Archaeology*, 13(1): 31–46.

BARTON, R.N.E. and BERGMAN, C.A. (1982) Hunters at Hengistbury: some evidence from experimental archaeology. *World Archaeology*, 14(2): 237–248.

CAULFIELD, S. (1978) Star Carr – an alternative view. *Irish Archaeological Research Forum*, 5: 15–22.

CLARK, J.G.D. (1954) *Excavations at Star Carr*. Cambridge, University Press.

CLARK, J.G.D. (1972) *Star Carr: a Case Study in Bioarchaeology*. Addison–Wesley Module in Anthropology, no. 10. London, Cummings Publishing Company.

CLARK, J.G.D and THOMPSON, M.W. (1954) The groove and splinter technique of working antler in Upper Palaeolithic and Mesolithic Europe. *Proceedings of the Prehistoric Society*, 19: 148–160.

DUMONT, J.V. (1982) The quantification of microwear traces: a new use for interferometry. *World Archaeology*, 14(2): 206–217.

DUMONT, J.V. (1983) An interim report on the Star Carr microwear study. *Oxford Journal of Archaeology*, 2(2): 127–145.

DUMONT, J.V. (1985) *A Microwear Analysis of Flints from the Mesolithic Sites of Star Carr, Yorkshire, and Mount Sandel, Northern Ireland*. Unpublished D.Phil. thesis, University of Oxford.

DUMONT, J.V. (1986) A preliminary report on the Mount Sandel microwear study. In P.C. Woodman, *Excavations at Mount Sandel 1973–77* (Northern Ireland Archaeological Monographs no. 2). Belfast, Her Majesty's Stationery Office: 61–70.

JACOBI, R.M. (1978) Northern England in the eighth millennium bc: an essay. In P. Mellars (ed.), *The Early Postglacial Settlement of Northern Europe*. London, Duckworth: 295–332.

KEELEY, L.H. (1977) *An Experimental Study of Microwear Traces on Selected British Palaeolithic Implements*. Unpublished D.Phil thesis, University of Oxford.

KEELEY, L.H. (1980) *Experimental Determination of Stone Tool Uses. A Microwear Analysis*. Chicago, University Press

KEELEY, L.H. (1981) Premiers résultats de l'analyse des microtraces d'utilisation de quelques objets. In F. Audouze, D. Cahen, L.H. Keeley and B. Schmider, 'Le Site Magdalénien du Buisson Campin à Verberie (Oise)'. *Gallia Préhistoire*, 24(1): 137–141.

MOSS, E.H. (1983) *The Functional Analysis of Flint Implements. Pincevent and Pont d'Ambon: Two Case Studies from the French Final Palaeolithic*. Oxford, British Archaeological Reports (International Series) S177.

PITTS, M. (1979) Hides and antlers: a new look at the gatherer-hunter site at Star Carr, North Yorkshire, England. *World Archaeology*, 11(1): 32–42.

PRICE, T.D. (1982) Willow tales and dog smoke. *Quarterly Review of Archaeology*, 3(1): 4–7.

TIXIER, J. (1972) Obtention de lames par débitage 'sous le pied'. *Bulletin de la Société Préhistorique Française*, 69(5): 134–139.

TRINGHAM, R., COOPER, G., ODELL, G., VOYTEK, B., and WHITMAN, A. (1974) Experimentation in the formation of edge damage: a new approach to lithic analysis. *Journal of Field Archaeology*, 1: 171–196.

Some Aspects of the Human Presence in West Wales during the Mesolithic

Andrew David

Abstract

This paper describes and discusses some of the results of recent excavation and fieldwork in west Wales, and attempts to place these within the wider Postglacial scenario here and further afield. Sites within and around this peninsular extremity of the western seaboard of Britain are numerous but poorly served by dating or excavation. The proposed early and later Mesolithic presence in Wales is supported by examination of freshly excavated samples of lithic remains from two sites at Nab Head, Dyfed. These material components are compared and contrasted to those from other collections and from newly-located surface sites. Changes in emphasis amongst lithic toolkits are recognized and these, along with a consideration of more exotic items such as beads and axes, make a contribution to general speculation on the local Mesolithic economy and society.

INTRODUCTION

West Wales and its abundant flint sites have attracted the attentions of antiquarians over many decades. Compared to much of the rest of Britain, and especially the eastern part of the island, there has been little recent research or analysis relevant to the history of Welsh early post-Pleistocene occupation. The technological and environmental database has changed little since Wainwright's *Reinterpretation of the Microlithic Industries of Wales* (1963), although Jacobi has more recently discussed part of the data in the light of current Mesolithic research (Jacobi 1980*b*), and Stanton (1984) has further updated and clarified the data from Glamorgan in south Wales. However, such papers have been able to document little in the way of recent fieldwork or discovery, although the results of palaeoenvironmental and archaeological work at Waun Fignen Felen, Glamorgan, are awaited with interest.

The lack of fresh studies in Wales might be explained by an absence of contemporary environmental data from areas suggestive of maximum human exploitation. There is also a lack of humanly associated faunal collections, hence restricting the potentialities for the type of socio-economic analyses attempted elsewhere (e.g. Mellars and Wilkinson 1980). Of necessity, therefore, as for so much of Europe, it is the distribution, composition and potential function of lithic assemblages that must still dominate any discussion of Mesolithic activity in Wales.

In south and west Wales early collectors and commentators on the prolific surface flint findspots were quick to seek parallels with the copious riches of the French Upper Palaeolithic, seeing in the comparatively poor Welsh material elements of a 'Late Upper Palaeolithic' culture (Gordon-Williams 1926). Today, the evidence for the terminal Pleistocene occupation of Wales is confined to lithic items recovered from cave infillings (McBurney 1959; Savory 1973; Campbell 1977), and recent work offers no objection to regarding the totality of this material as chronologically equivalent to the Late-glacial Interstadial of *c.* 13,000–11,000 BP (Jacobi 1980*a*, pers. comm.). As yet formal linkages between artifact discard, human activity, and faunal assemblages have not been made for Wales which could allow any disentangling of human behaviour from the disturbance created by carnivores using these same locations.

So far from Wales, as for elsewhere within the British Isles, there are no artifact occurrences which convincingly link this final Pleistocene material to the lithic items which we now believe to exist within our earliest Mesolithic sequences. This picture may change, at least for the south and east of England, as a result of current research (Barton, this volume; Schadla-Hall, this volume).

Coming forward into the Mesolithic there is still as yet only poor correspondence between human and environmental information. Pollen analyses of lowland and upland areas document a succession of changing woodland environments (Godwin and Mitchell 1938; Birks *et al.* 1975; Moore 1977), and these must be seen against a background of rapidly rising sea level drastically altering the configuration of the Welsh coastline, particularly in the area of the Bristol Channel and Cardigan Bay. The mixed woodland succession with a rich hazel component, alongside an increasingly mild climate with a potentially long growing season (Webley 1976) suggests that western Wales might have experienced, as it does today, very favourable environmental conditions.

The land mammals whose exploitation might be

expected within this landscape are documented from a single faunal assemblage from King Arthur's Cave, Ross-on-Wye, which includes red deer, wild pig, aurochs, brown bear, beaver, and wild cat or marten (Taylor 1927), and by isolated bones, sometimes associated with flint débitage, from partially submerged deposits on southern and western coasts. Most dramatic amongst the latter is the find by Leach (1918) at Lydstep Haven of the skeleton of a pig with two backed bladelets within it, and having therefore apparently escaped its pursuers. Leach also records a single wild pig bone from a flint scatter sealed by peat at Freshwater West, also in Dyfed, but other such finds (Hicks 1885; Taylor 1973) of faunal material are without significant archaeological associations (see also Stanton 1984: 41–43). Data from potentially useful cave sites are either ambiguous or too poorly reported to be of direct relevance.

THE EARLY MESOLITHIC

Lithic assemblages from England dated before about 8500 years ago have a composition, especially in terms of their backed bladelet component, that distinguishes them more or less clearly from assemblages dating later in the Mesolithic. Those assemblages that appear closest to a hypothetical ancestor in the Late Devensian include backed blades consisting mostly of large convex-backed, partially-backed and, most commonly, obliquely-backed items – for instance at Thatcham II and Oakhanger V and VII. In other early assemblages, shorter obliquely-backed pieces appear combined with broad triangles, atypical trapezes and, in some areas, basally-retouched 'points'. The accompanying organic component of this latter assemblage type is well known from Star Carr (Clark 1954, 1972). In addition to backed bladelets, early Mesolithic assemblages regularly contain short end-scrapers, burins, micro-denticulates, awls and core axes/adzes. The accompanying radiocarbon record is ambiguous, but expectations derived from evolutionary trends elsewhere in Europe might lead us to expect that assemblages with many broad triangles or basally-retouched pieces may be later than those without these features.

If the latter suggestion is correct, then the first and potentially earliest assemblage type in south Wales may exist amongst the surface collections from Burry Holms, Glamorgan (Grimes 1951; Wainwright 1963), where obliquely- and partially-backed pieces are combined with short end-scrapers and micro-denticulates. This site may therefore be earlier than the three sites in north Wales from which derive our only early Mesolithic dating for the Principality. These radiocarbon dates are from Rhuddlan Site E (8739±86 BP), Rhuddlan Site M

(8548±73 BP) and Trwyn Ddu (8640±150 BP), and are notable in that they are amongst the latest dates for 'early' assemblages from the British Isles (for a fuller discussion and references, see Jacobi 1980b). Here, it might be noted that these dates are derived from bulked samples of carbonized material from soil contexts beneath major later archaeological events.

Broadly comparable to this latter group of sites, and different to Burry Holms, are the half dozen or so sites named on the map of south-west Wales in *Fig. 1*. These include surface sites at Palmerston Farm, Freshwater East, Valley Field (Caldey), Wiston and Pen Pant. Also indicated on the map are isolated finds of large backed pieces and core axes/adzes. Excavated sites are at Nab Head Site I, Waun Fignen Felen, and Daylight Rock. The last site, on the island of Caldey, was the earliest to be investigated (Lacaille and Grimes 1955), and has subsequently been referred to by Wainwright (1963) and Jacobi (1980b).

There are at least 54 backed bladelets from Daylight Rock, including 27 obliquely-backed points, 13 triangular pieces, and with no other shapes inconsistent with an early or 'broad blade' attribution. These are combined with short end-scrapers, burins, *mèches de foret*, and core axes/adzes as represented by thinning and edge-trimming flakes (*Table 1*). The most convincing analogues for this material, and for the other sites on *Fig. 1*, seem to exist amongst the published lithic assemblages from Star Carr and Flixton Site 1 in North Yorkshire (Moore 1950; Clark 1954), and also amongst the assemblages at present being recovered from the Vale of Pickering at Seamer Carr (Schadla-Hall, this volume). In each case, the dating evidence suggests a probable age between 9500 and 9000 BP.

Flora and fauna in Wales at this time might also have been generally similar to that in Yorkshire. Pollen diagrams from western Wales are few, but against a background of developing Boreal forest (Godwin and Mitchell 1938), and probably relevant to the Mesolithic diet, is the early abundance of *Corylus* noted at Tregaron and Gwarllyn and assumed to have spread from a late Pleistocene refugium on the dry land of Cardigan Bay (Moore 1977; but see Lowe 1981). As at Star Carr, exploitable land mammals would have included red and roe deer, aurochs and wild pig although, as no contemporary faunal assemblage has been sampled from Wales, it is unknown if elk was also among the potential animal resources. Horse and reindeer are unlikely to have been present so late.

Sea levels at this time would of course have been very much lower, exposing sizable areas of dry land exploitable by hunting and gathering communities. A similar situation might be envisaged to that

Table 1:   The lithic composition from selected sites in western Dyfed, Wales

	Excavated assemblages			Field assemblages			
	Daylight Rock	Nab Head I	Nab Head II	Palmerston	Cwm Bach I	Cwm Bach II	Llanunwas
Tools:							
Broad blade microliths (and fragments)	46	90	14	16	6	–	–
Narrow blade microliths (classes 5–13)	–	53	228	1	82	–	16
Unclassified microlith fragments	8	70	189	10	75	–	11
Scrapers	48	114	19	16	48	4	7
Denticulates	–	15	42	1	227	2	246
Burins	11	26	–	6	82	1	–
End-tools	–	6	5	–	73	–	20
Truncated pieces	8	–	11	2	–	–	5
Nosed pieces	1	1	6	–	8	–	1
Notched pieces	9	8	5	7	16	–	4
Awls	–	–	–	–	12	–	2
Mèches de foret and fragments	15	44	–	8	–	–	–
Axe/adze	?1	1	–	–	–	–	–
Bifacially-flaked pebbles/choppers	–	–	1	–	6	–	–
Retouched pieces	14	36	18	56	79	3	20
Utilized pieces	2	109	64	26	42	–	9
Other pieces	2	51	1	15	29	–	4
By-products:							
Microburins and related pieces	–	84	83	28	13	–	8
Burin spalls	–	21	–	0	36	–	5
Adze-sharpening/thinning flakes	10	31	–	–	–	–	–
Débitage:							
Cores, fragments and flaked nodules	–	39,103	352	72	3927	74	808
Flakes and blades	–		22,028	3401	22,000	278	4621
Scaled pieces (pièces écaillées)	–	–	–	2	133	1	15
Unmodified flint pebbles	–	–	13	–	22	–	9
TOTAL (flaked flint and stone)	175	39,863	23,079	3667	26,916	363	5811
Chert pieces	–	488	13	76	67	5	23
Other non-flint pieces (e.g. igneous)	–		61	20	47	2	27
Stone tools:							
Bevelled pebble and fragments	–	10	42	–	21	–	5
Hammerstones	–	–	1	1	13	–	1
Countersunk pebbles	–	–	–	–	2	–	–
Ground stone axes	–	–	2	–	–	–	?1
Macehead	–	–	1	–	–	–	–
Shale beads (or fragments)	–	64	–	1	–	–	–

around Trevose Head on the north Cornish coast where dry land territories have been mapped in relation to successive encroachments of the post-Pleistocene sea (Johnson and David 1982). In west Wales, a point made early on by Leach in his discussion of finds from Nanna's Cave (1916) was that, for much of its history, Caldey would have been linked to the mainland. Daylight Rock and Valley Field and those other sites now on cliff-top locations are therefore converted into inland bases with a coastline approximately at or beyond a hypothetical site territory of 10 km radius. That exploitation of the coast did take place, perhaps as part of a wider procurement strategy, is suggested by the use of beach pebble flint for tool manufacture.

Nab Head Site I

Undoubtedly one of the best known early post-Pleistocene sites in Wales is at Nab Head, a small and much eroded promontory on the southern edge of St Bride's Bay, Dyfed. The site is renowned for the publication from it of the first lithic assemblage to include a quantity of shale beads and also a small shale 'amulet' (Gordon-Williams 1925, 1926). The latter object is unique to the British Mesolithic, and has been described and illustrated by Jacobi (1980b: 159, plates 4.I–4.III), although Breuil's comments in a letter to the finder are worth quoting here:

(the amulet) interests me greatly. I have checked my impressions by showing (it) to several others. Some

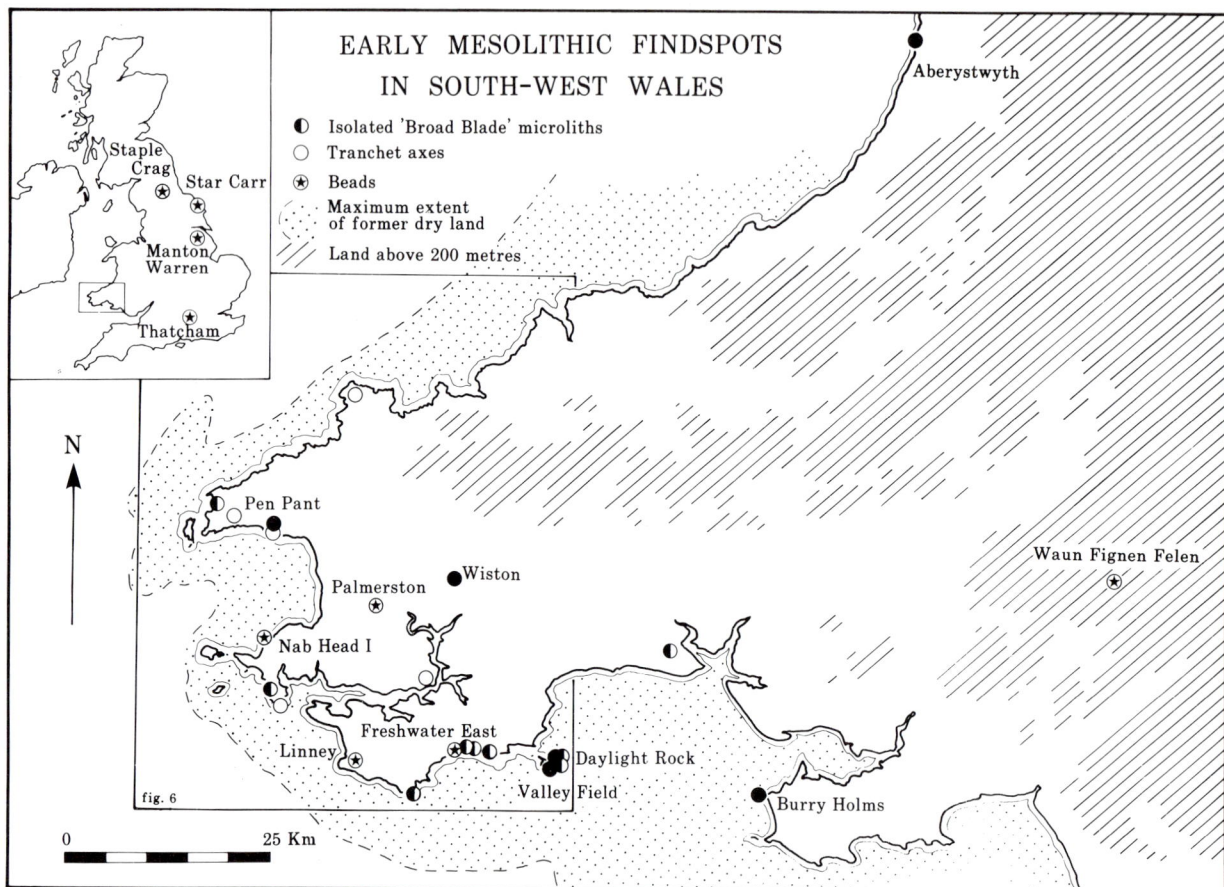

Figure 1 The distribution of early Mesolithic findspots in south-west Wales, and (inset) the distribution of probable early Mesolithic beads in England.

say a phallus with exaggerated testes; some a female steatopygic figurine. These were my own conclusions. Most likely both are right, mixed up in a sort of plastic play on words. The stem must be a human member with a very slight incision differentiating the glans; but the way in which the double spread out scrotum is treated is evidence of the will to bring to mind the hips and thighs and the lower belly of a woman.

These comments on what Breuil called 'a remarkable Palaeolithic trinket' (in the same letter) were plainly not lost on the Reverend Gordon-Williams who nevertheless felt that a full translation might be too strong a meat for his readers:

I suggest calling it 'The Duck head', in deference to ultra-refined susceptibilities; and it may as well be that as a 'Venus phallica', or what-not (1925: 80).

The flints found with these shale objects include large and simple backed bladelets, convex scrapers, burins and flaked axes/adzes, and numerous authors have subsequently figured specimens of these from the site (Wheeler 1925; Leach 1933; Grimes 1951; Wainwright 1963; Jacobi 1980*b*; Morrison 1981). With the exception of Gordon-Williams's excavations in 1925, for which documentation does not survive, the majority of collections are known to come from a denuded area of rapidly eroding sandy clay loam at the 'neck' of the Nab Head promontory. This advancing erosion, and the continuing abun-

dance of chipped flints, prompted rescue excavation at the site by the author and D.G. Benson for the Dyfed Archaeological Trust during 1979 and 1980. Altogether, some 40,000 artifacts were recovered from 186 m², and full publication of these and the subsequent excavations at Nab Head Site II (see below) is in progress.

The typology of the fresh sample of lithic material from Site I is listed in *Table 1* alongside that from Daylight Rock and a small surface collection from Palmerston Farm, some 15 km to the east of St Bride's. Nab Head Site I is in clear contrast to these other two sites in that it contains a substantial proportion of narrow backed bladelets (classes 5–13 of Jacobi 1978) whose closest parallels are with those described below under later Mesolithic assemblages. It will also be argued that the significant number of bevelled pebbles and denticulates belong with a later occupation at Nab Head. These were, however, recovered with more numerous tool types such as large triangular and obliquely-backed pieces, *mèches de foret*, a transversely-sharpened axe or adze and related thinning and sharpening flakes. These associations, as documented for Daylight Rock, Caldey, are taken to indicate early Mesolithic activity which, it has already been suggested, might be contemporary with Star Carr and Flixton Site 1.

244

Also considered to be of early date are the small perforated shale beads recovered both during excavation and from surface collection, and for which Nab Head is well known. To the author's knowledge there are now records of some 690 of these, of which 64 were recovered during the recent excavations. The majority of this latter group were found near the base of the B-horizon of the soil profile and were scattered rather generally across the breadth of the site, with the exception of a localization of 23 beads in one area of 4 m². Gordon-Williams records a concentration of nine beads associated with the shale 'amulet', and most of the 27 identical shale beads from Star Carr occurred in two clusters. Such clustering tells us little about the original context of these beads, either as adornment for the living or dead, or as items with additional prestigious or psychic (*sensu* Clark 1975) value. It is possible that graves once existed at Nab Head, but the beads were not found associated with any such features, and a detailed measurement of phosphate concentration around the main group failed to produce significant results. The acidic soil conditions at Nab Head have ensured the absence of organic material save the hardiest charred wood and hazel-nut shell fragments.

What at least seems certain is that shale beads were being manufactured at Nab Head. With the toolkit are a large number of bilaterally trimmed points or rod-like pieces interpreted as perforators or drill bits (*mèches de foret*). They are the most numerous distinct tool type after backed bladelets and scrapers (*Table 1*), and the only sites in Britain in which they occur in similar numbers are Daylight Rock and Star Carr; at the latter site they are of course also associated with shale beads. At all three sites many of these flint tools have worn and smoothed tips which also exhibit slight scaling and crushing. Similar damage has also been observed on experimental drill bits used in preparing identical beads (for a discussion of the Star Carr examples – see Dumont 1983, this volume). On-site manufacture at Nab Head is also evident from the presence of partially drilled beads and bead 'blanks' or unworked discs. Many of the fragments may also represent breakage whilst being drilled.

Identical beads can be manufactured quickly and efficiently by two people using a bow or pump drill with the flint bit embedded with resin in a small haft, so that as many as 100 beads can be processed in an hour's work. Without this mechanical aid, or by using the flint on its own, the work is considerably slower and more arduous.

Given, therefore, that beads could have been made in prodigious numbers (blanks are common on the nearest present-day beach, and there are quantities of *mèches de foret* to support this contention), it is perhaps surprising that there are so *few* beads from the site (and, incidentally, that there are *none*

recorded from Daylight Rock). Should such beads have had symbolic as well as practical status, then in this context it might be worth repeating the comments offered by Swanton (1946: 481) and recently cited by Yerkes in his discussion of shell beads in early Mississippian societies, where it is argued that these could be made instantly available as a medium of exchange while at the same time serving as 'a visible witness to the standing and credit of the wearer' (1983: 513). If not an actual currency, could not beads have served as 'a figurative expression or metaphor for social and political relationships' (Hall 1981 – quoted in Yerkes 1983: 513)?

That Nab Head might have been a production centre for such objects which were then absorbed into an exchange system is also implied by the presence of single finds of the same type of beads from other sites in south and west Wales (*Fig. 1*). Most similar, if not identical, examples come from Palmerston Farm (Joan Rees, pers. comm.), Waun Fignen Felen (Berridge 1981), and from Freshwater East (Leach 1913). The example from Linney is of an unidentified stone from a surface also with Bronze Age artifacts. English finds of beads of probable early Mesolithic date are shown on the inset map and include a shale specimen from Manton Warren, Lincolnshire, and an example, of unidentified stone material, from Thatcham. Both these finds are from unpublished records made available by R. Jacobi; that from Thatcham is from an informal collection from Site VI and is distinct from the apparently naturally 'perforated pebble' or possible bead recorded from Site V (Wymer 1962). Also included on the map, and again with apparently early Mesolithic associations, is a recent find from Staple Crag on the northern Pennines (Coggins, Laurie and Young, this volume).

With all the Welsh examples quoted above occur elements of that range of flint tools which we have argued to be of early Mesolithic age. Clark (1975) has commented on the limited chronological occurrence of *mèches de foret*; their presence also at Star Carr adds confidence to the suggestion that similar assemblages in west Wales, and the production of beads at Nab Head, must occur at some moment during the first one thousand years of the post-Pleistocene.[1]

THE LATER MESOLITHIC

Stone tool assemblages dating later than *c.* 8500 BP are identified by possession of a suite of backed bladelets usually smaller and more varied than those found amongst their early Mesolithic predecessors. With time and Britain's increasing insularity these backed bladelets have a tendency to become less similar to any mainland counterparts. In Wales, a large number of findspots have been attributed to

J

the later Mesolithic by recognition of these small backed bladelets, although few of the sites have been adequately documented. However, informative discussions of the assemblages from Prestatyn and Rhuddlan, in Clwyd, may be found in Clark (1938) and Manley and Healey (1982), respectively; while Stanton (1984) has recently provided a valuable review of the Glamorgan data.

With the recent exception of Nab Head Site II (see below), the reliable radiocarbon evidence for such apparently later Mesolithic sites is at present limited to two determinations on charcoal (7190 ± 100 BP, 7300 ± 100 BP) from a pit feature below a barrow at Brenig 53 in Clwyd. The flints from within the pit include a scalene micro-triangle, but there is no demonstrable association with the larger assemblage of later Mesolithic character from elsewhere beneath the barrow (Jacobi 1980b).

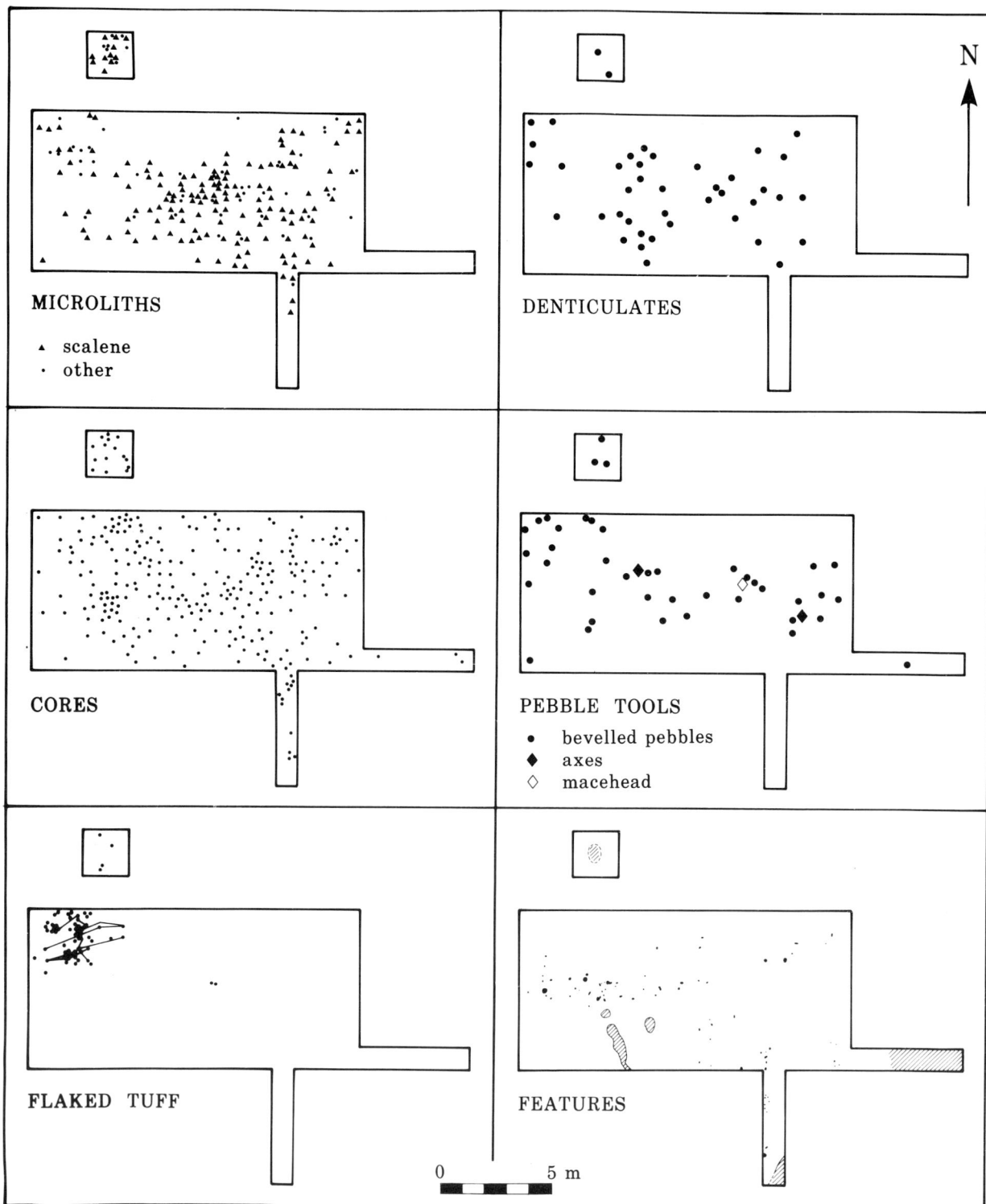

Figure 2 The distributions of selected items within the present excavated area at Nab Head Site II.

Rather less confidence can be placed in the date of 6895±80 BP (CAR-118) from a hearth, 'possibly associated with later Mesolithic flintwork elsewhere at the site', below the chambered tomb at Gwernvale (Britnell 1979). The report of a date of *c.* 7500 BP from peat apparently in association with later Mesolithic flints at Waun Fignen Felen, West Glamorgan (Berridge 1979), requires detailed confirmation.

Until recently, there were no Welsh lithic assemblages with sufficient documentation to allow for spatial analysis or any kind of social interpretation. Those so far reported are unsuitable and do not contain a sufficient backed bladelet component to

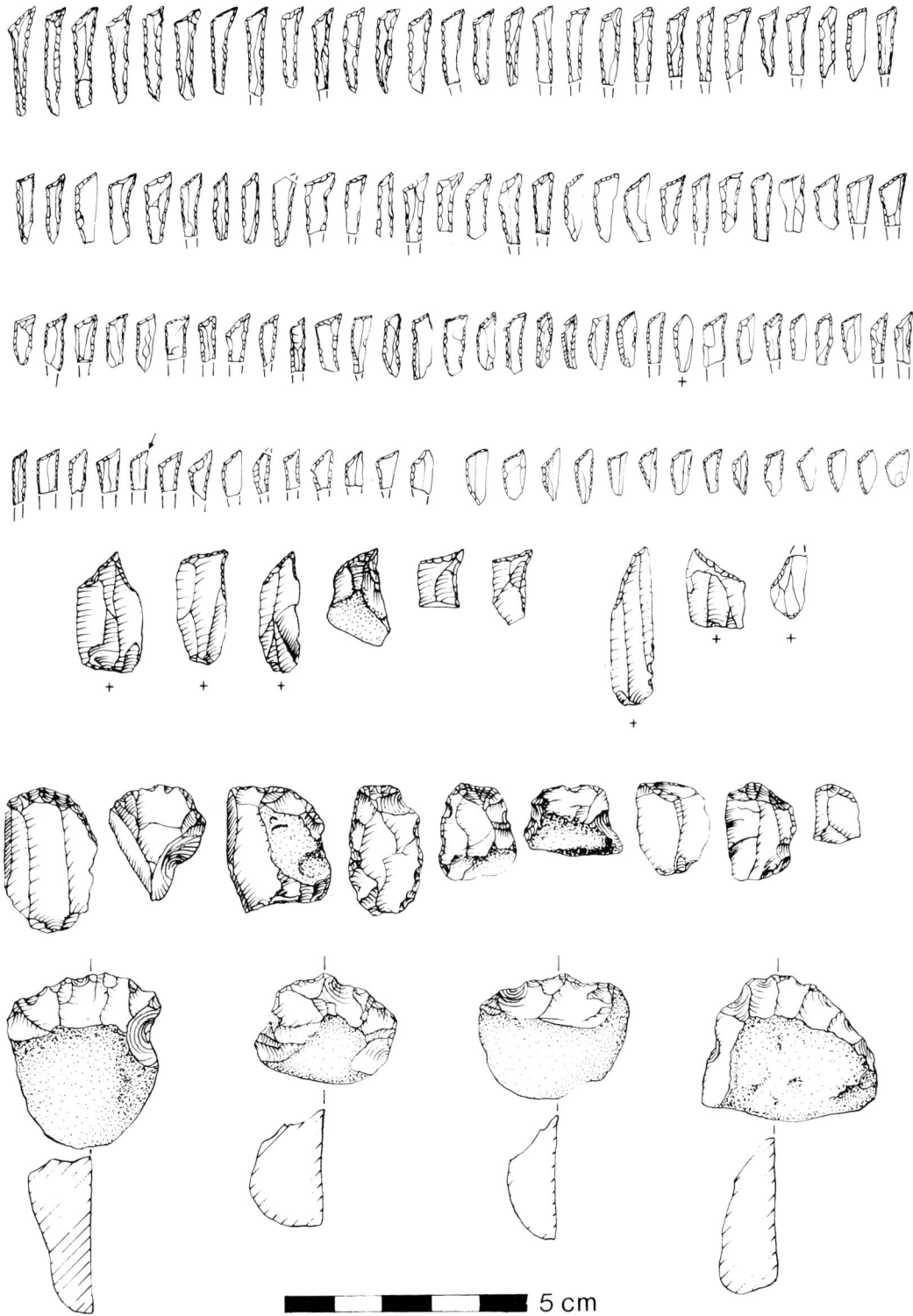

Figure 3 A selection of flint tools from Nab Head II: 'narrow blade' geometric microliths, mostly of scalene outline (top four rows); end-tools and truncated pieces (fifth row); scrapers and retouched flakes (sixth row); denticulates (bottom row).

247

suggest any meaningful conclusions on functional or other diversity. Such shortcomings hinder the search for the 'social territories' that have been tentatively identified for other parts of the British Isles (Jacobi 1979; Jacobi and Tebbut 1981; Smith 1982).

It is hoped, however, that the first steps in remedying this situation will soon be possible as a result of the exploration of a major lithic scatter at Nab Head Site II, less than a hundred metres from Site I already discussed above. Excavation in 1981 and 1982[2] was initiated by the chance find in 1980 of a flint concentration near the cliff top, but not under active erosion and beyond the range of present-day ploughing. The excavation has so far focused on a single lithic concentration, but finds of similar material over the headland area, and at Site I, suggest that Site II is just one of an aggregation of conterminous scatters. Up until 1982, 119 m[2] had been excavated through a simple shallow soil profile developed on Devonian Old Red Sandstone. Over 23,000 pieces of flaked flint and stone were retrieved, and the distribution of some of the more important lithic items is illustrated on *Fig. 2*. *Table 1* includes a breakdown of the main lithic categories (some of which are illustrated in *Fig. 3*) alongside those from a selection of other sites discussed in this paper.

The raw material is mostly flint from small beach cobbles or, more rarely, chert or fine-grained igneous rock. Many conjoining pieces emphasize the relative lack of post-depositional movement.

There are 603 recognizable tools, or their fragments, of which 71% are small backed bladelets of a predominantly scalene outline. The only remaining tools of significance are denticulates (7%), scrapers (3%), retouched pieces (3%), and end-tools and truncated pieces (3%). Denticulates and end-tools form a significant part of other site assemblages in Dyfed. The former may be described as coarsely-retouched thick primary flakes partly or wholly of denticulated outline, and frequently intermediate between cores and apparent scrapers. 'End-tools' are here defined as flakes or bladelets with distal modification to either a straight, slightly concave, or beaked outline.

Alongside items of retouched flint are modified pebbles, forming an important constituent of this and other assemblages. Apparently confined to coastal locations are elongated natural pebbles with abrasion and/or flaking at one or both ends. There are 42 of these 'bevelled pebbles' at Nab Head II, but their function, already the subject of much discussion, will remain unresolved until we are fortunate enough to find sites where the 'soft' organic component is preserved.

Still more significant, are the finds of three pecked and ground stone tools: two axes or adzes (*Fig. 4*), and a perforated stone disc bilaterally ground to an edge around its perimeter. Thin-sectioning has identified all three as of igneous material, in all probability available locally amongst beach material (Houlder, pers. comm.). The axes closely resemble each other in shape and form and are pecked and ground over most if not all of their surfaces;

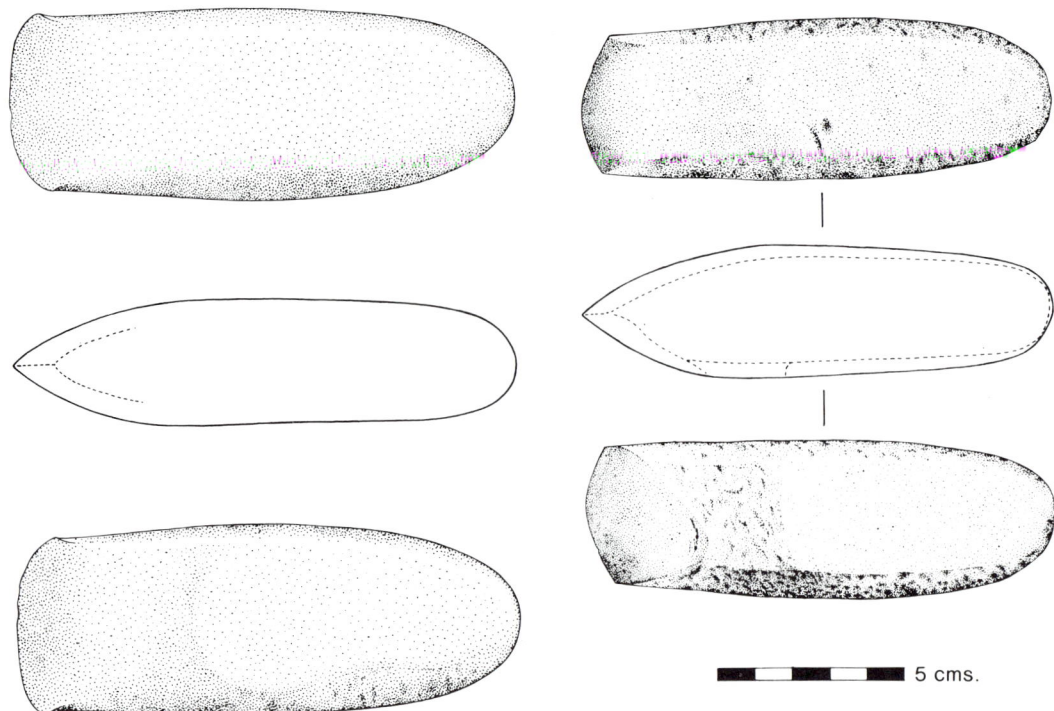

5 cms.

Figure 4 Pecked and ground stone axes or adzes from Nab Head II.

especially diagnostic is the very slight splaying at either side of the working edge, and the areas of flat polishing on either dorsal or ventral surfaces of the tools. Current research, aimed at fully studying these artifacts and their affiliations, already suggests that parallels exist (and may even be numerous) amongst other Welsh collections – e.g. from Nab Head (Jacobi 1980*b*: figs. 4.17, 4.18), the Dale area (Tenby Museum), and Cardigan (Wheeler 1921: 6). Stray finds of 'Neolithic' axes may now merit reconsideration in the light of these finds, with the 'caveat' that the Nab Head specimens cannot be proved not to be intrusive; Tower Point promontory fort is only a stone's throw away, and other later artifacts recovered from Site II include an unpatinated 'tranchet' arrowhead, a fragment of a glass bead, and a small piece of iron. It would seem more realistic, though, to include the ground stone items with the 23,000 or so other artifacts with which they were excavated, and which we confidently believe to be of pre-agricultural age. The identification of such axes from the site is the first for the British Isles in such a context and, apart from the distant Ertebølle of Denmark, offers intriguing but less exact parallels to finds from Irish Mesolithic contexts of this, or

perhaps slightly earlier date (Woodman 1978).

As already mentioned, a proportion of the flint tools excavated from Nab Head Site I are very similar to those found more exclusively here on Site II. The implication, already pointed out by Jacobi (1980*b*), is that at Site I a later Mesolithic occupation succeeded one characterized by earlier tool forms. This intuitive assessment of the two differing typologies is supported by the relative distribution within the sediment profile at Site I of the two groups. The bar chart in *Fig. 5* illustrates this differentiation where the relative representation of the two artifact groups is plotted against soil layers. The artifacts used to compile this diagram are: for the 'earlier' period – long blade cores (Johnson and David 1982), end-scrapers, large backed bladelets, axe/adze products and *mèches de foret*; for the 'later' period – narrow backed bladelets, denticulates, and small bladelet cores. It is clear from the resulting diagram that although elements of both groups are present throughout the soil profile, those subjectively attributed to some earlier use of the site increase in frequency with depth. Reciprocally, 'later' pieces are more common nearer the surface. Although post-depositional factors could have blurred this

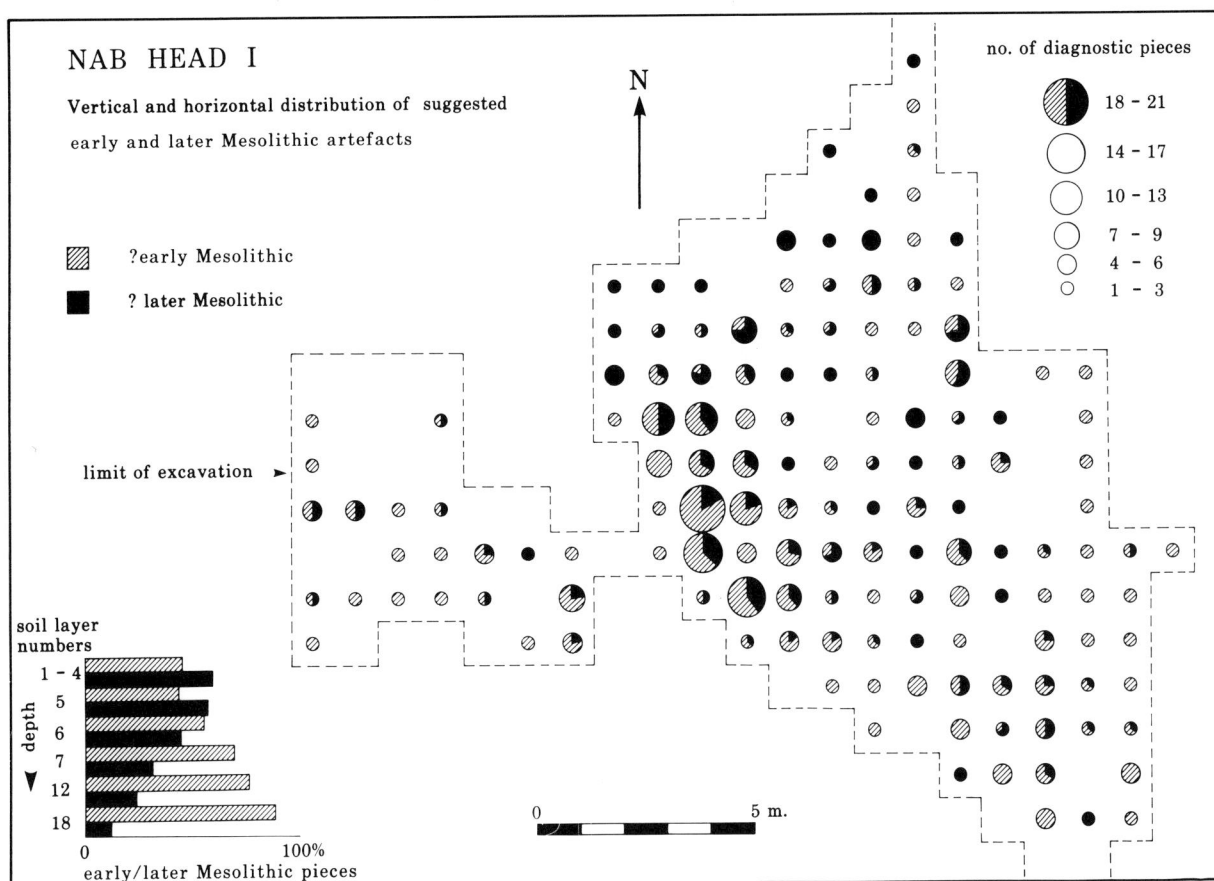

Figure 5 The vertical and horizontal distributions of suggested early and later Mesolithic artifacts at Nab Head I. The proportional circles show the number of diagnostic flint types per m², and are divided to indicate the relative contribution of those pieces assumed to be diagnostic of, respectively, early and later Mesolithic occupations. The bar chart is a schematic attempt to show, for the whole site, the relative distribution of this same subdivision vertically through the soil profile (see text for fuller explanation).

249

LATER MESOLITHIC FINDS IN WESTERN DYFED

N

○ Probable later Mesolithic sites

● Finds of bevelled pebbles

◉ Sites discussed in the text

/// Land above 200 metres

CWM BACH

LLANUNWAS

NAB HEAD II

average accumulated temp.
of 1550 day-deg. C.

0   10 Km

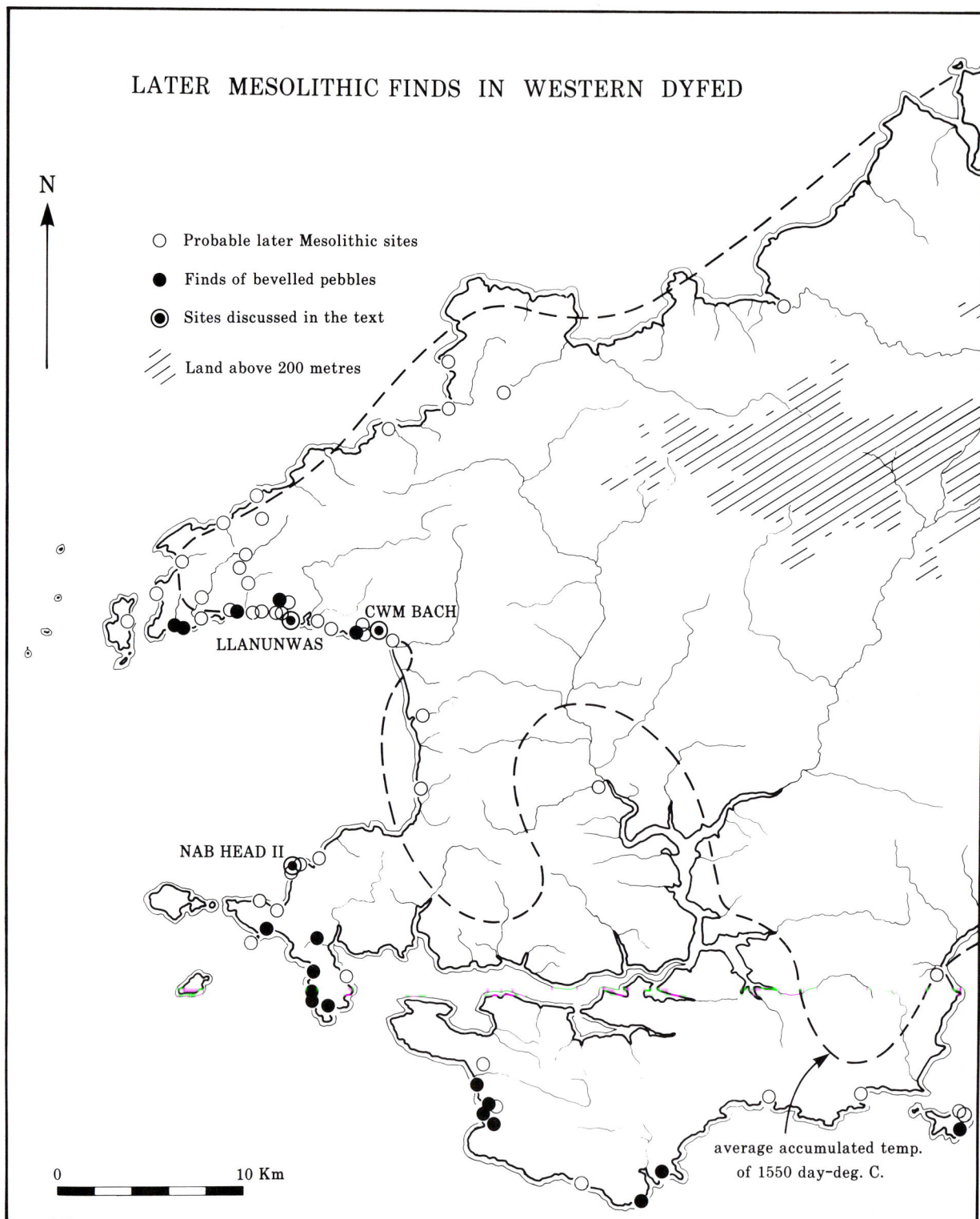

Figure 6   The distribution of later Mesolithic findspots in western Dyfed, south-west Wales. The land area to the south and west of the dashed line has a Median Accumulated Temperature above 0 °C (day-degrees) of 1550 or more for the period January to June (records for 1959 to 1978 – Rudeforth *et al*. 1984: 27, fig. 8).

vertical distribution, the evidence therefore seems to be clearly in favour of two activity phases at this site which are almost certainly widely separated in time (cf. Wawcott Site III – Froom 1976).

An approximation of the chronological setting of the later Mesolithic settlement at Nab Head II, and by implication that at Site I, is gained from two

recently obtained radiocarbon accelerator determinations (Gowlett *et al.* 1987): 7360±90 BP (OxA-860), on charcoal from a shallow pit; 6210±90 BP (OxA-861), on charcoal from a hearth area. The considerable separation in time between these two dates suggests a rather more complex site history than that originally proposed, and a fuller discussion of their significance must await the results of current submissions of additional samples from Sites I and II. It is only when such further chronological data become available, from these and other sites, that speculation on social and economic territories and systems may become more feasible, as comparable lithic assemblages are related to contemporary coastlines.

Indeed, extrapolating from the results obtained at Nab Head II, it becomes possible to recognize a series of findspots combining some or all of the artifact forms from this site. These sites, a combination of published data and fresh finds made by the author, are plotted on the map in *Fig. 6*. *Table 1* includes a typological description of the assemblages from Nab Head II and the three richest surface sites in terms of retouched forms recovered so far: Cwm Bach I and II, and Llanunwas. The purpose of *Table 1* is not only to demonstrate the apparent division between early and later sites, but in this case also to show that a distinct variability exists within the cited later assemblages.

Preliminary assessment of this typological variation suggests that it is between denticulates, scrapers, end-tools and burins. Without an exhaustive comparative description it is sufficient at this stage to indicate that marked variation occurs – e.g. burins are a very significant feature at Cwm Bach I, but are all but absent from the other three sites. Whilst admitting the error of comparing surface with excavated assemblages, the representation of denticulates and end-tools also varies. The site of Cwm Bach I, which covers some two hectares, and with a sample of some 26,000 pieces, might claim to have the most balanced assemblage, and attention is again drawn to the burins, a large number of various end-tools, 'hammerstones', and counter-sunk pebbles.

Such variability as is hinted at between these sites also has parallels to that documented by Jacobi for the Gwithian sites (1979) and is confirmed by the author in more recent studies of samples of artifacts from Westward Ho! in Devon (Balaam *et al.* 1987), and Windmill Farm, Cornwall (Smith, forthcoming). Apart from an inter-assemblage variability, which may or may not be of chronological origin, these groups of artifact forms are clearly distinct from both their earlier post-Pleistocene predecessors and the earliest succeeding Neolithic material. *Pièces écaillées*, argued to be of Bronze Age or Neolithic origin (Jacobi 1980*b*; Cherry 1982; Johnson and David 1982), are frequently present and even numerous (as at Cwm Bach) on the Welsh sites. Their post-Mesolithic age is probable in the light of the development of unpatinated *écaillée* damage on formerly patinated flakes typical of the Mesolithic material.

The number of findspots now recognized on the south-west coast of Wales appears to add confirmation to the predictions offered by Webley (1976) and ApSimon (1976) who emphasize the special climatic and environmental attractiveness of this coastal area. Thus south-west Dyfed, although presently exposed to westerly winds is one of the sunniest and mildest parts of Britain. *Fig. 6* shows the position of a line to the south and west of which average accumulated temperatures for January to June are higher than 1550 day degrees Centigrade (Rudeforth *et al.* 1984), whereby it becomes most tempting to see a correlation between a maritime fringe of exceptionally mild climate and the quite remarkable density of evidence for Mesolithic occupation within this same zone.

Exploitative territories of these sites, of whatever radius, will include tidal strips, and a substantial proportion of each catchment would extend over open sea. The indented character of western Dyfed's shore, accentuated by St Bride's Bay and Milford Haven, means that many sites are peninsular locations which at a 10 km radius would incorporate coastline well in excess of double this distance; Llanunwas and Nab Head II would, for instance, take in the entirety of the St David's peninsula and the Skomer peninsula respectively; the sites at Dale and Castlemartin to the north and south of Milford Haven would also incorporate large parts of the approaches and surroundings of this major inlet.

With the significance of the coast apparently an unavoidable conclusion, it cannot be overlooked that dry land territories, though usually of lesser extent, must also have contributed to site economics, combining with the maritime resources to provide a very wide range of subsistence alternatives indeed. The present site distribution must inevitably represent an overlay and bias of several generations of fieldwork, and it yet remains to be seen whether or not truly inland sites exist, and whether or not they might concentrate on the higher ground of the Prescelly mountains as might be predicted by economic models for the north of England (Clark 1972) or the Glamorgan uplands (Jacobi 1980*b*; Stanton 1984). Both inshore fishery, birds and seals are seasonal resources which may be taken in the warmer months. However, without further fieldwork it must remain speculative whether or not the Welsh findspots are in fact peripheral to residence or special-purpose sites better located inland for the exploitation of land mammals, fish runs, and plant foods. It is possible that the coastal sites were located with access to landward territories, and also for ease of transport, by sea, of specific maritime resources available close by. The functional variability recognizable within later Mesolithic lithic assemblages may thus reflect the processing requirements of such differing resource goals.

Bonsall (1981) has also addressed the problem of site location, within the later Mesolithic of the north west of England, and has outlined in detail the available subsistence resources surrounding the sites at Eskmeals, Cumbria. Although many of his conclusions may also hold true for our Welsh area, there are some important exceptions. Primarily, these arise from the 'hard' nature of the latter coastline in contrast to the 'soft' or estuarine conditions at Eskmeals. The west Welsh coastline of *Fig. 6* is largely the product of a hard geology much indented by the selective erosion of the weaker geology into small bays and coves interspersed amongst more forbidding cliffs and islets. These are of course ideal conditions for seals, which are absent from Eskmeals, but breed here in substantial numbers. At a 5 or 2.5 km radius (Rowley-Conwy 1983) many of the Welsh sites would have been within range of at least some sealing potential in late summer and early autumn. Are the frequently massive aggregations of chipped flint, pebble tools and lithic debris to be associated with some such resource base? Such suggestions must remain simplistic when one is reminded that important parts of the landscape, even of the latest Mesolithic age, are mostly lost to us through inundation of the contemporary shoreline and the consequent drowning of tidal zone exploitive sites that are elsewhere so fortunately preserved along shorelines of Postglacial marine regression.

Notes:

1. This dating would appear to be supported by recent AMS ^{14}C determinations on hazel-nut shell fragments from Site I, provided by the Oxford Laboratory – see Archaeometry Datelist 9 (*Archaeometry*, 31(2), forthcoming).

2. Further excavation at Site II took place in 1986, some time after the completion of this paper. The new information obtained does not substantially affect the discussion presented here, and in the meanwhile a full report on all the excavations to date is in preparation. For further recent AMS ^{14}C determinations, see Archaeometry Datelist 9 (*Archaeometry*, 31(2), forthcoming).

Acknowledgements: This paper owes an enormous debt to Roger Jacobi in the wake of whose publication on the Welsh Mesolithic in 1980 it has been difficult to follow or add to. He has cajoled me throughout and been most generous with suggestions and with his own extensive knowledge of the Welsh material. The mistakes, though, are mine. In anticipation of fuller acknowledgement of the many people who have helped me with this project, I would like to thank Don Benson, co-director at Nab Head during 1979–80, and his staff with the Dyfed Archaeological Trust whose help has been so invaluable throughout that excavation.

References

ApSimon, A. (1976) A view of the early prehistory of Wales. In G.C. Boon and J.M. Lewis (eds), *Welsh Antiquity*. Cardiff, National Museum of Wales.

Balaam, N., Bell, M.G., David, A.E.U., Girling, M.A., Levitan, B., Macphail, R.I., Robinson, M. and Scaife, R.G. (1987) Prehistoric and Romano-British sites at Westward Ho!, Devon: archaeological and palaeoenvironmental surveys 1983 and 1984. In N.D. Balaam, B. Levitan and V. Straker (eds), *Studies in Palaeoeconomy and Environment in South West England*. Oxford, British Archaeological Reports (British Series) 181.

Berridge, P. (1979) Waun Fignen Felen. *Archaeology in Wales*, 19: 11.

Berridge, P. (1981) Waun Fignen Felen. *Archaeology in Wales*, 21: 20.

Birks, H.J.B., Deacon, J. and Peglar, S. (1975) Pollen maps for the British Isles 5000 years ago. *Proceedings of the Royal Society*, B189: 87–105.

Bonsall, C. (1981) The coastal factor in the Mesolithic settlement of north-west England. In B. Gramsch (ed.), *Mesolithikum in Europa. 2. Internationales Symposium Potsdam, 3 bis 8 April 1978 Bericht*. (Veröffentlichungen des Museums für Ur- und Frühgeschichte Potsdam, 14/15). Berlin, Deutscher Verlag der Wissenschaften: 451–472.

Britnell, W. (1979) Gwernvale. *Archaeology in Wales*, 19: 10.

Campbell, J.B. (1977) *The Upper Palaeolithic of Britain: a Study of Man and Nature in the Ice Age*. Oxford, Clarendon Press.

Cherry, J. (1982) Sea cliff erosion at Drigg, Cumbria: evidence of prehistoric habitation. *Transactions of the Cumberland and Westmorland Antiquarian and Archaeological Society*, 82: 1–6.

Clark, J.G.D. (1938) Microlithic industries from tufa deposits at Prestatyn, Flintshire, and Blashenwell, Dorset. *Proceedings of the Prehistoric Society*, 4: 330–334.

Clark, J.G.D. (1954) *Excavations at Star Carr*. Cambridge, University Press.

Clark, J.G.D. (1972) *Star Carr: a Case Study in Bioarchaeology*. Addison–Wesley Module in Anthropology no. 10. London, Cummings Publishing Company.

Clark, J.G.D. (1975) *The Earlier Stone Age Settlement of Scandinavia*. Cambridge, University Press.

Dumont, J.V. (1983) An interim report on the Star Carr microwear study. *Oxford Journal of Archaeology*, 2(2): 127–145.

Froom, F.R. (1976) *Wawcott III: a Stratified Mesolithic Succession*. Oxford, British Archaeological Reports (British Series) 27.

Godwin, H. and Mitchell, G.F. (1938) Stratigraphy and development of two raised bogs near Tregaron, Cardiganshire. *New Phytologist*, 37: 5.

Gordon-Williams, J.P. (1925) Nabs Head chipping floor. *Transactions of the Carmarthenshire Antiquarian Society and Field Club*, 18: 80.

Gordon-Williams, J.P. (1926) The Nab Head chipping floor. *Archaeologia Cambrensis*, 81: 86–110.

Gowlett, J.A.J., Hedges, R.E.M., Law, I.A. and Perry, C. (1987) Radiocarbon dates from the Oxford AMS system: Archaeometry datelist 5. *Archaeometry*, 29(1): 125–155.

Grimes, W.F. (1951) *Prehistory of Wales*. Cardiff, National Museum of Wales.

Hall, R.L. (1981) *The Quartered Circle and the Symbolism of the Mississippian World*. Manuscript on file, Department of Anthropology, University of Illinois at Chicago Circle.

Hicks, H. (1885) On some recent researches in bone caves in Wales. *Proceedings of the Geologists Association*, 9: 1–20.

Jacobi, R.M. (1978) The Mesolithic of Sussex. In P.L. Drewett (ed.), *Archaeology in Sussex to AD 1500*. London, Council for British Archaeology Research Report 29: 15–22.

Jacobi, R.M. (1979) Early Flandrian hunters in the south-west. In V.A. Maxfield (ed.), *Prehistoric Dartmoor in its Context*. Torquay, Devon Archaeological Society.

Jacobi, R.M. (1980a) The Upper Palaeolithic in Britain, with special reference to Wales. In J.A. Taylor (ed.), *Culture and Environment in Prehistoric Wales*. Oxford, British Archaeological Reports (British Series) 76: 15–100.

Jacobi, R.M. (1980b) The early Holocene settlement of Wales. In J.A. Taylor (ed.), *Culture and Environment in Prehistoric Wales*. Oxford, British Archaeological Reports (British Series) 76: 131–206.

Jacobi, R.M. and Tebbutt, C.F. (1981) A late Mesolithic rock-shelter at High Hurstwood, Sussex. *Sussex Archaeological Collections*, 119: 1–36.

Johnson, N. and David, A.E.U. (1982) A Mesolithic site on Trevose Head and contemporary geography. *Cornish Archaeology*, 21: 67–103.

Lacaille, A.D. and Grimes, W.F. (1955) The prehistory of Caldey. *Archaeologia Cambrensis*, 104: 85–165.

Leach, A.L. (1913) Stone implements from soil drifts and chipping floors etc., in south Pembroke. *Archaeologia Cambrensis*, 68: 391–432.

LEACH, A.L. (1916) Nanna's Cave, Isle of Caldey. *Archaeologia Cambrensis*, 71: 155–180.

LEACH, A.L. (1918) Flint-working sites on the submerged land (submerged forest) bordering the Pembrokeshire coast. *Proceedings of the Geologists Association*, 29(2): 46–64.

LEACH, A.L. (1933) Stone implements from the Nab Head, St Bride's, Pembrokeshire. *Archaeologia Cambrensis*, 88: 229–236.

LOWE, S. (1981) Radiocarbon dating and stratigraphic resolution in Welsh Lateglacial chronology. *Nature*, 293: 210–212.

MANLEY, J. and HEALEY, E. (1982) Excavations at Hendre, Rhuddlan: the Mesolithic finds. *Archaeologia Cambrensis*, 131: 18–48.

MCBURNEY, C.B.M. (1959) Report on the first seasons's field-work on British Upper Palaeolithic cave deposits. *Proceedings of the Prehistoric Society*, 25: 260–269.

MELLARS, P.A. and WILKINSON, M.R. (1980) Fish otoliths as evidence of seasonality in prehistoric shell middens: the evidence from Oronsay (Inner Hebrides). *Proceedings of the Prehistoric Society*, 46: 101–108.

MOORE, J.W. (1950) Mesolithic sites in the neighbourhood of Flixton, north-east Yorkshire. *Proceedings of the Prehistoric Society*, 16: 101–108.

MOORE, P.D. (1977) Vegetational history. In D.Q. Bowen (ed.), Studies in the Welsh Quaternary. *Cambria*, 4: 74–83.

MORRISON, A. (1981) *Early Man in Britain and Ireland*. London, Croom Helm.

ROWLEY-CONWY, P. (1983) Sedentary hunters: the Ertebølle example. In G.N. Bailey (ed.), *Hunter-Gatherer Economy in Prehistory. A European Perspective*. Cambridge, University Press: 111–126.

RUDEFORTH, C.C., HARTNUP, R., LEA, J.W., THOMPSON, T.R.E. and WRIGHT, P.S. (1984) *Soils and their Use in Wales*. Harpenden, Soil Survey of England and Wales, Bulletin no. 11.

SAVORY, H.N. (1973) Excavations at the Hoyle, Tenby, in 1968. *Archaeologia Cambrensis*, 122: 18–34.

SMITH, G. (1982) The excavation of Mesolithic, Neolithic and Bronze Age settlements at Poldowrian, St. Keverne, 1980. *Cornish Archaeology*, 21: 23–62.

SMITH, G. (forthcoming) *Excavations at Windmill Farm, Cornwall* (paper).

STANTON, Y.C. (1984) The Mesolithic period: early Post-glacial hunter-gatherer communities in Glamorgan. In H.S. Green and Y.C. Stanton, 'The Old and Middle Stone Ages', *Glamorgan County History*, Chapter 2: 33–121.

SWANTON, J.R. (1946) *The Indians of the South-Eastern United States*. Washington, Smithsonian Institution Bureau of American Ethnology Bulletin 137.

TAYLOR, H. (1927) Second report on the excavations at King Arthur's Cave. *Proceedings of the University of Bristol Speleological Society*, 3(2): 59–83.

TAYLOR, J.A. (1973) Chronometers and chronicles: a study of palaeoenvironments in west central Wales. *Progress in Geography*, 5: 250–334.

WAINWRIGHT, G.J. (1963) A reinterpretation of the microlithic industries of Wales. *Proceedings of the Prehistoric Society*, 29: 99–132.

WEBLEY, D.P. (1976) How the West was won: prehistoric land-use in the southern Marches. In G.C. Boon and J.M. Lewis (eds), *Welsh Antiquity*. Cardiff, National Museum of Wales.

WHEELER, R.E.M. (1921) Some problems of prehistoric chronology in Wales. *Archaeologia Cambrensis*, 76: 1–18.

WHEELER, R.E.M. (1925) *Prehistoric and Roman Wales*. Oxford, Clarendon Press.

WOODMAN, P.C. (1978) *The Mesolithic in Ireland*. Oxford, British Archaeological Reports (British Series) 58.

WYMER, J.J. (1962) Excavations at the Maglemosian sites at Thatcham, Berkshire, England. *Proceedings of the Prehistoric Society*, 28: 329–361.

YERKES, R.W. (1983) Microwear, microdrills, and Mississippian craft specialization. *American Antiquity*, 48(3): 449–517.

Mesolithic Sites of Portland and their Significance

Susann Palmer

Abstract

A large number of Mesolithic sites have been discovered on the Isle of Portland in Dorset, England. This paper deals mainly with the site of Culverwell, dated to between *c.* 7370–7101 BP. Its main features are: a large shell midden with an unusual floor of limestone slabs directly overlying it, several hearths and a cooking pit, features regarded as 'ritual', and an alignment of stones which was perhaps a windbreak. The most common artifacts are pointed picks, heavy choppers and chopping tools, microliths among which scalene triangles predominate, unusual types of scrapers, knives, etc. Shell beads also occur.

THE TERRAIN

It is of some importance to appreciate the unusual environment in which a large number of Mesolithic sites occur on the Isle of Portland, Dorset. Although referred to as an 'island', it is attached to the mainland by the famous late Quaternary formation known as the Chesil Beach or Bank, which stretches from the northern end of Portland in a westerly direction to Abbotsbury where its pebbles join the mainland beach. Between the bank and the mainland's shore is a stretch of water known as the Fleet, and this area is rich in vegetation and water fowl. In prehistory it probably supported a large population of animals, including deer.

Portland reaches an elevation of 123 m at its highest point in the north and is a relatively barren, rocky prominence of Jurassic limestone. The island is full of large systems of karst caves, but it is unlikely that any of these were exposed during prehistoric times. There are, however, numerous sea caves round the southern part known as the Bill; there is adequate geological evidence to suggest that at least some of these were in existence since late Palaeolithic times, and Mesolithic people may have utilized them. These caves are also associated with a late Weichselian raised beach. Due to the durability and tectonic stability of the limestone cliffs, the present line of the cliff tops appears not to have retreated substantially from the 10 or 5 fathom lines which approximate the late Boreal and early Atlantic coastlines, respectively. This means that the coast has not changed very much since late Mesolithic times.

The topsoil on the Isle is very shallow in most areas, and immediately below this is a yellow rubbly loam with many tabular pieces of limestone. This rubble was of prime importance in the lifestyle of the Mesolithic inhabitants (see below). The limestone beds have thick veins of Portland chert, ideal for the knapping of tools which can be found in vast quantities all over the Isle.

Food was abundantly available within walking distance of the prehistoric sites, along the sea front and the Fleet. To date, there is no evidence that fishing took place.

THE SITES

All the main Mesolithic sites are in the southern part of the Isle, within quick walking distance of the present shore; access was certainly just as easy for the prehistoric food gatherers. The later, Neolithic sites are slightly further inland. Of some 30 sites, at least three contain very substantial evidence for habitation in the form of shell midden deposits and massive quantities of artifacts, many burnt.

Site 1

Site 1, immediately adjacent to the Old Lower Lighthouse, has been excavated and full reports published (Palmer 1969, 1971). A large, but shallow, shell midden was found and some stone slabs which appeared to have been artificially placed. The layout of this very large site suggested several nuclei of main living areas, perhaps four or five in number. At least one posthole was found, associated with some of the placed limestones. A semi-circular, shallow hollow, lined with small stones and associated with the remnants of a rough wall, contained much shell debris, Mesolithic artifacts and some human bones. As it also contained the crushed remains of a Bronze Age Beaker, some doubts were expressed at the time about the dating of this feature, but subsequent work on other sites on the Isle has shown that it is quite common for remains of all later periods to have become deeply trodden, or somehow incorporated, into the soft Mesolithic deposits. With hindsight, therefore, it is now believed that this burial may have been of Mesolithic date.

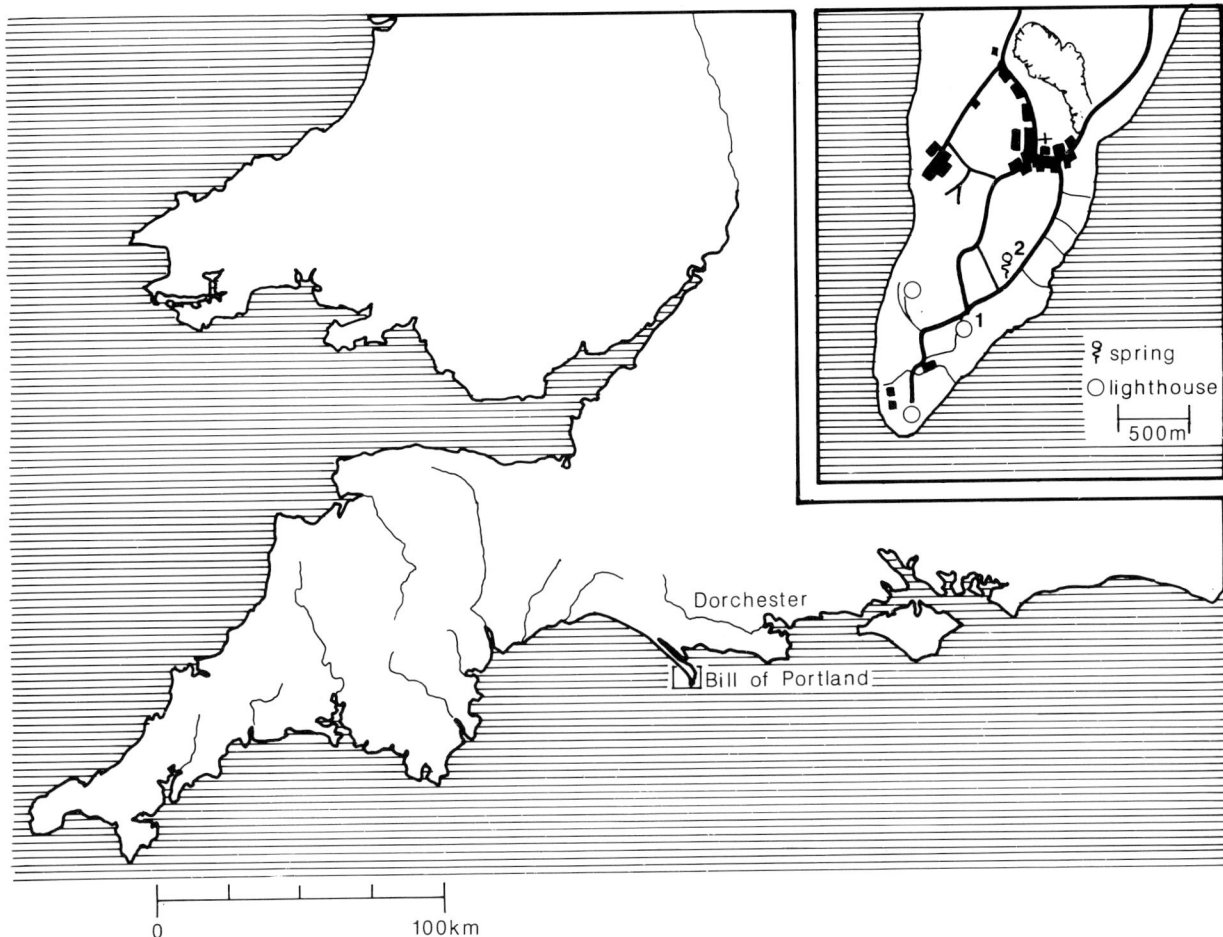

Figure 1   Map of southern England and (inset) Portland Bill with Site 1 and Culverwell (2) indicated.

Culverwell

Culverwell is the name of a stream near which several of the main sites are situated. It is also the name by which a major site, of at least 300 m², has become known. This site, which is situated on the south slope of a hill at the Bill, is still being excavated and may prove most interesting and prolific in finds (Palmer 1970, 1976, 1977). Charcoal from a hearth has given radiocarbon dates of 7150±135 BP (BM-473) and 7101±97 BP (BM-960); the weighted average of three samples of burnt limestone from the same area has given a thermoluminescence date of 7370±640 BP (OxTL-501 b, m), thus providing a reasonably acceptable timescale. An amino-acid date of a shell sample is in broad agreement with this.

A very important feature of the site is a large floor of limestone slabs with roughly parallel sides and measuring approximately 12 × 3.6 m; the original length is uncertain as it disappears under the road at the southern end. This floor lies directly on top of a thick shell midden, contained in a large (possibly natural) hollow; in places, it is also covered by midden material, so that the dating of this feature is also secure. The midden contains mostly *Littorina* sp., *Patella* sp. and *Monodonta lineata* (da Costa)

with the occasional *Nucella lapillus*. It is thought likely that several small huts of a mixture of stone, wood and skin were erected in a row on the floor, which would have provided excellent drainage into the midden below.

Several hearths have been found, all east of the floor, and winds coming from a westerly or southwesterly direction (as today) would have blown the smoke away from the huts. One large hearth, which provided the charcoal for dating, was in a scooped-out hollow in the clayey soil immediately below the midden. Round the edge of it were found a large number of pounders, a cupped pebble, picks, microliths and some hazel-nuts, as well as a few fragmented bits of bone of wild pig and sea bird.

At the northern end of the site – but also on the eastern edge of the floor – a hearth of more than a metre in diameter was found under a deposit of midden nearly a metre thick. In tracing the structural development of the floor, it was concluded that the earliest settlement of the site was in this area, directly on the loamy clay above the raised beach, and that subsequently the settlement gradually expanded downhill after the midden had accumulated sufficiently to fill the hollow. The floor was then laid down on the relatively level surface so provided.

255

Round the eastern perimeter of this hearth, a small area was paved with limestone slabs in order to provide seating and working space adjacent to the hearth. Here a *cache* of 12 picks in all stages of completion was found, exactly as they had been abandoned during the actual process of manufacture.

About 4.5 m east of the floor there is a very impressive cooking pit, excavated into the hard rubbly loam; it is a metre deep and about the same in diameter. This is an unusual feature for this period and would have required hard work with only simple stone tools. At the bottom were several large slabs of limestone, showing ample signs of burning. Food placed on these stones could have been covered with earth or turves and would have cooked slowly, protected against the fierce coastal winds.

During work on the site, it was realized that the generally parallel-sided stone floor was slightly out of alignment at a number of points. It was argued that these points probably coincided with development phases of the floor as it was extended southward. Each one of these points was also found to be marked by a larger-than-average slab of limestone, often sub-triangular in shape. On excavation, one of these slabs was found to have a large beautifully rounded beach pebble immediately adjacent to it, and there appeared to be a hollow underneath the slab. The slab was lifted and the midden debris cleared away to reveal a small hollow about 20 cm in diameter, and in it an axe, a pierced scallop shell and a round, very smooth pebble. This feature is regarded as a sort of 'foundation offering'. The other similarly shaped and placed slabs on the site have since also been lifted and, although they had holes underneath them, no objects were found. These may have contained organic offerings originally.

At the southern end of the site a substantial alignment of irregularly-shaped limestones had been placed at an approximately 90° angle to the eastern edge of the main floor, thus forming an L-shaped structure. Recent work in this area has shown that this minor alignment is also closely associated with the floor and midden and with vast quantities of Mesolithic artifacts, but its precise nature and chronological relationship to other features on the site requires further investigation. It could have been a windbreak on the southern perimeter of the 'backyard' where knapping and other activities took place. At one point it appears to be associated with a hollowed-out area of approximately circular or sub-circular shape, marked out by stones around the circumference, and perhaps two or more metres diameter. It can be suggested tentatively that this is the remains of a hut immediately adjacent to the main floor.

ARTIFACTS

Portland has become known for the exceptionally large numbers of 'picks' found on all the Mesolithic sites in the Bill area; between 4000 and 5000 have so far been collected from ploughsoil and from the excavated sites. At Culverwell several hundred picks have so far been found all over the living site and in the midden, as well as clearly associated with the floor. They are mostly made from tabular pieces of limestone from the Isle's rubble beds. Many are extremely crude and, often, only a few flakes have been removed from the piece of stone in order to produce a sharp pointed tool; at other times these tools have been neatly flaked all round. They vary in size from 7 to 27 cm, but a few larger ones have been found. Axes and adzes, made in the same manner, also occur but are far less common than the picks; a few axes are sharpened by a *tranchet* blow.

Pebble 'mace-heads' with hour-glass perforations, countersunk or 'cupped' pebbles, pounders and choppers are some of the other types of core tools which are fairly common on the site, often associated with the hearths.

Microliths are prolific on all the excavated sites. There is a very noticeable difference between the microliths from Site 1 and those from the habitation site of Culverwell. On Site 1 only 66 were found and they tend to be relatively crude; obliquely blunted forms predominate, although 'rods' blunted along one or two sides are also common. At Culverwell, microliths are very common and are invariably beautifully made; an estimated one-third of these are scalene triangles with the rods second in numbers. Other geometric forms also occur. As there is no absolute date for Site 1, it is not possible to argue over the question of time differences between the two sites, particularly as the rest of the tools are identical.

SIGNIFICANCE OF PORTLAND SITES

Until recently it was a generally held belief that Mesolithic people were invariably nomadic and wandered about in loosely-formed groups, particularly along the coasts. The sites on Portland are all grouped in one part of the Isle and there is an element of cohesion about their spatial arrangements. The elaborate structures at Culverwell indicate clearly that social groups were stable and relatively well settled, almost in 'village' style. The archaeological evidence suggests that they did not migrate seasonally; sea-food supplies would have been more than adequate all the year round, and the stone structures appear to indicate that they were intended to protect against inclement weather.

The use of the natural products of the environment indicates good economic sense and ingenuity. The unusual and extensive use of limestone slabs for building the floor must be seen as an excellent prehistoric example of how the availability of natural commodities can actually dictate the lifestyle of a community. This means that, in tracing the origins of a particular type of structure, we must always look first in an area where there is an abundant supply of the building material. This availability of tabular pieces of limestone on Portland also explains why the Mesolithic folk on the Isle produced so many thousands of picks, while on other sites in England and throughout Europe these tools can usually be counted in tens or even less – in other words, Portland is a 'natural' place for the type of tools and unusual structures which occur at this early date on its living sites.

The picks are further evidence of a persistent and stable interest in either, or both, of two types of activities – digging up edible plants, or prizing fresh chert from seams in the limestone beds. Portland chert artifacts are widely distributed over southern England, suggestive of barter. Portland, however, must not be regarded as just a 'factory' site or workfloor; it is primarily a large habitation area, and the production of tools was part of the living activities.

The deposit of pierced scallop shell, axe and round pebble under a carefully chosen and placed stone within the living area at Culverwell is strongly suggestive of a well-established ritual belief system amongst Mesolithic people, and also of a thorough appreciation of symbolism. This is also indicated by the placing of big, round, beach pebbles in relatively strategic positions all over the site; round pebbles are of symbolic importance in virtually every culture of the past and in many even today.

It is on sites like those on Portland that we must look for the origins of later, Neolithic culture traits.

References

PALMER, S. (1969) A Mesolithic site at Portland Bill. *Proceedings of the Dorset Natural History and Archaeological Society*, 90: 183–206.

PALMER, S. (1970) The Stone Age industries of the Isle of Portland, Dorset, and the utilization of Portland chert as artifact material in southern England. *Proceedings of the Prehistoric Society*, 36: 82–115.

PALMER, S. (1971) Second report on excavations at Portland Site 1, 1967 to 1968. *Proceedings of the Dorset Natural History and Archaeological Society*, 92: 168–180.

PALMER, S. (1976) The Mesolithic habitation site at Culverwell, Portland, Dorset. Interim Report. *Proceedings of the Prehistoric Society*, 42: 324–327.

PALMER, S. (1977) *Mesolithic Cultures of Britain*. Poole (Dorset), Dolphin Press.

A Mesolithic Flint Assemblage from Hazleton, Gloucestershire, England, and its Implications

Alan Saville

Abstract

This paper describes the discovery of a mixed late Mesolithic and early Neolithic flint assemblage in the buried soil beneath a laterally-chambered Cotswold–Severn tomb. The diagnostic typology of the assemblage is described and its spatial distribution, reflecting basically separate foci of late Mesolithic and early Neolithic activity, is depicted. Discussion centres on the problem of isolating late Mesolithic flintwork from that of the early Neolithic, and on the implications of the recurrent discovery of mixed lithic assemblages beneath laterally-chambered Neolithic long cairns.

Between 1979 and 1982 the Neolithic chambered tomb known as Hazleton North, situated some 13 km (8 miles) east of Cheltenham in the county of Gloucestershire, was totally excavated. Details of the excavation of this example of a laterally-chambered Cotswold–Severn tomb have been published in interim form (Saville 1984*a*) and need not be repeated here. It can be noted, however, that one radiocarbon date of 4450±90 BP (OxA-383) has recently become available for human bone from what is thought to be a late stage of the burial activity, implying that the construction and use of the monument is likely to fall well within the fifth millennium BP.

Subsequent to the investigation of the funerary monument the whole of the pre-cairn surface preserved beneath it was excavated. Within the total excavation area of 1606 m² stripped to subsoil/bedrock level, some 770 m² were directly sealed by the monument, and a further 86 m² were sealed by the peripheral collapse of cairn stonework. 4843 pieces of struck flint were recovered from the pre-cairn surface. When plotted in terms of density per square metre, two clear centres of concentration emerged (*Fig. 1*).

The concentration located immediately to the west of the two burial chambers matched the position of a 'midden' deposit containing Neolithic pottery, quernstone fragments, animal bones and carbonized cereal grains, and the position of an adjacent 'structure' suggested by the presence of a hearth and post- and stake-holes (*Fig. 2*). The other concentration (located beneath the west terminal of the monument)

partly correlated with the area usually termed the *forecourt* which is situated between the two protruding horns of the cairn, and also ran underneath the cairn, particularly under the southern horn.

Analysis of this flint assemblage is in progress, a task which is both complicated and enlivened by the existence of a clear typological subdivision within the material. The two elements involved can be defined as formally Mesolithic and formally Neolithic. The Mesolithic element is exemplified by 71 microliths and five microburins. About half of the microliths are complete enough for classification, comprising a mixture of geometric and edge-blunted forms (*Fig. 3*). The geometrics include crescents (*Fig. 3*, nos. 1–2), a micro-tranchet (*Fig. 3*, no. 3), and scalene microtriangles (*Fig. 3*, nos. 4–10). The edge-blunted microliths include several examples of narrow needle-point types (*Fig. 3*, nos. 11–16). These microlith types are characteristic of the Mesolithic occupation of the Cotswold area (Saville 1984*b*), where the few assemblages recovered to date are exclusively of later Mesolithic character. No absolute dates are available for these assemblages, although the range of microlith shapes, especially the presence of the micro-tranchet, points to a period after 7000 BP (Jacobi 1980). The only potential contrast within the Hazleton microlith component is provided by two obliquely blunted points (*Fig. 3*, nos. 17–18), of which one (no. 18) is an extremely broad-bladed form quite out of character with the rest of the assemblage. This raises the question of non-homogeneity, perhaps reflecting more than one phase of Mesolithic activity at the site. Corroborating evidence from other typological indicators or from distinctive spatial patterning has not been recognized, however, and the presence of a few such 'errant' forms should probably be given no more weight than that of the occasional transverse or barbed-and-tanged arrowhead from later contexts at Hazleton.

The Neolithic element from the buried soil is exemplified by the presence of three leaf-shaped

258

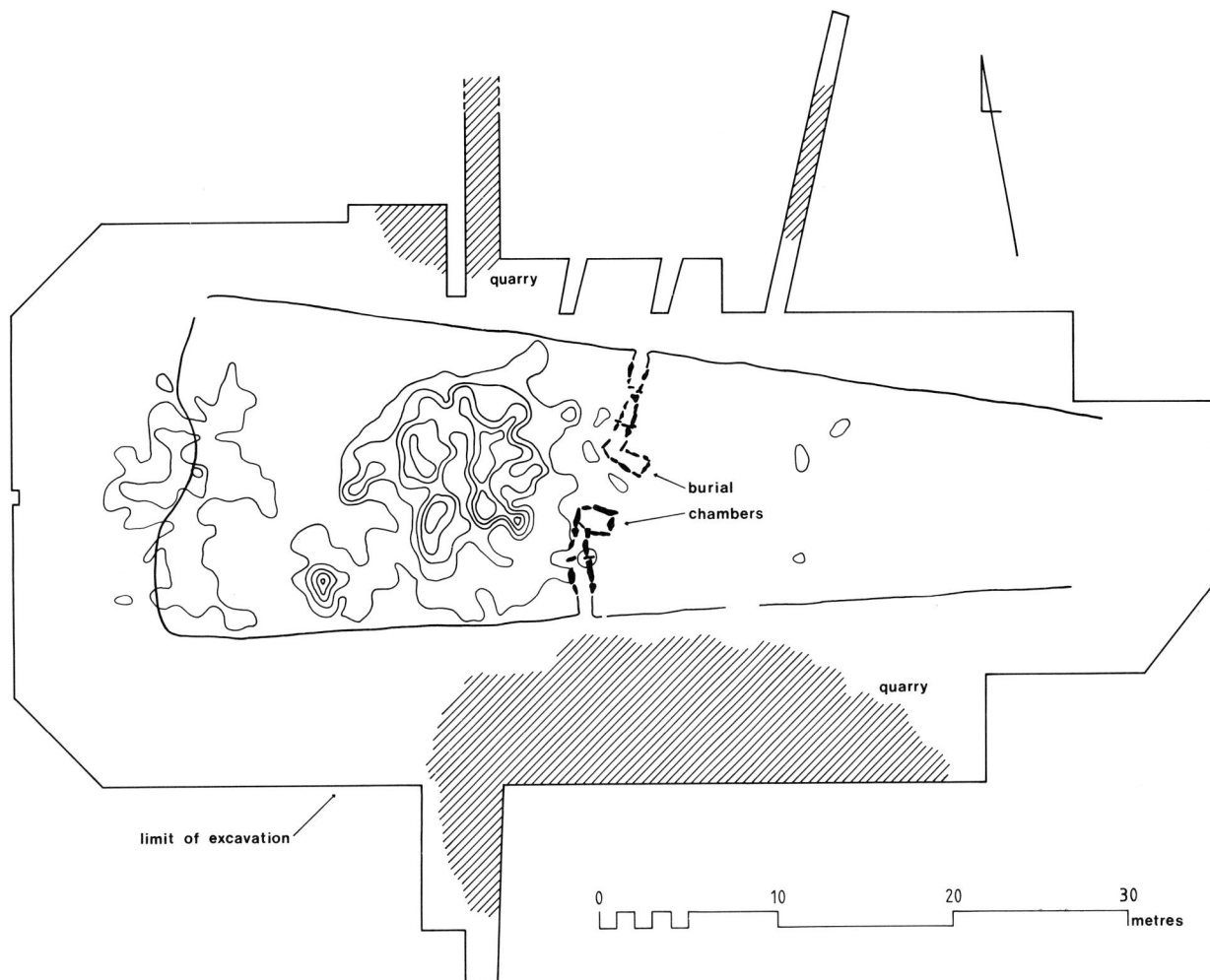

Figure 1 Hazleton North: distribution of pieces of struck flint in the pre-cairn soil shown by contours of density, drawn at intervals of 5, 15, 30, 45 & 60 flints per square metre (the outline of the overlying long cairn and the positions of the burial chambers are superimposed for convenience). *Drawn by J. Hoyle*

arrowheads, one so-called laurel-leaf and some 15 fragments and flakes from polished flint implements, presumably axe-heads. These implement types are characteristic of the English early to middle Neolithic flint industries, best known from causewayed enclosure sites such as Windmill Hill, Wiltshire (Smith 1965). At Hazleton the Neolithic flints are found in association with undecorated pottery of Grimston–Lyles Hill type. No radiocarbon dates are available yet for the Hazleton pre-cairn assemblage, but it is envisaged that the Neolithic activity was immediately pre-cairn, at a date of *c.* 5000/4900 BP by analogy with the dates from other sites (cf. Darvill 1982: 26–27).

The buried soil beneath the Hazleton North tomb provided no internal vertical stratigraphy by which to separate finds or features of different chronological phases. Horizontal 'stratigraphy' did, however, suggest a validity to the typological subdivision of the assemblage. The Mesolithic microliths and microburins had a distribution which was heavily weighted towards the west end of the excavation area (*Fig. 4*), and which correlated strongly with the separate concentrations of flints already noted beneath the south horn area (*Fig. 1*). In contrast, the Neolithic material, though not abundant, had a distribution (*Fig. 5*) which avoided the westernmost concentration and correlated strongly with the flint concentration im-

mediately to the west of the chambered area (*Fig. 1*). It therefore correlated with both the midden area and the postulated structure (*Fig. 2*). The most economical explanation for this spatial diversity is that it reflects chronologically (and presumably culturally) separate foci of activity.

Microliths are by far the most common diagnostically Mesolithic implement type at Hazleton, and there are few other artifacts which can be directly linked to them, except the microburins and perhaps the single burin present. The Mesolithic and Neolithic distributions are not mutually exclusive, as is clear from the occurrence of microliths in the Neolithic midden. Hence the ascription of the remaining flint assemblage to one or other grouping is difficult. The implements, which so far include only three scrapers, four piercers, two worn-edged pieces and an *outil écaillé*, are not easily characterized as either Mesolithic or Neolithic on typological grounds, and are too few for any reliable conclusions to be drawn from their spatial distribution. For what it is worth, however, the burin and three of the piercers fall within the 'Mesolithic concentration' in the forecourt area, the others within the 'Neolithic concentration'. The only other implement category of any numerical significance from the buried soil is the edge-trimmed flake, of which there are some 27 so far. This is not a typologically diagnostic implement,

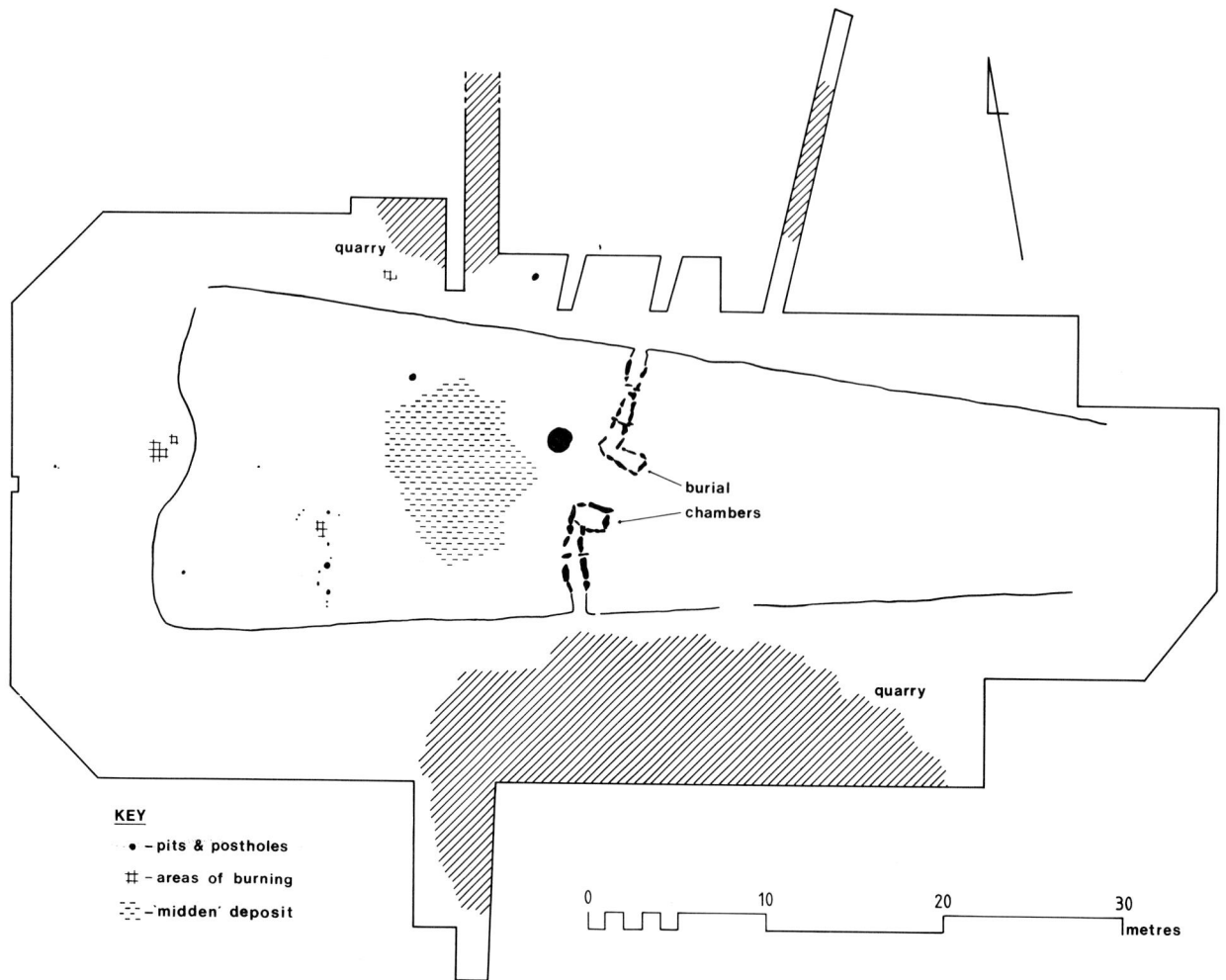

Figure 2 Hazleton North: distribution of archaeological features in the pre-cairn soil (with the outline of the cairn and the positions of the burial chambers superimposed). *Drawn by J. Hoyle*

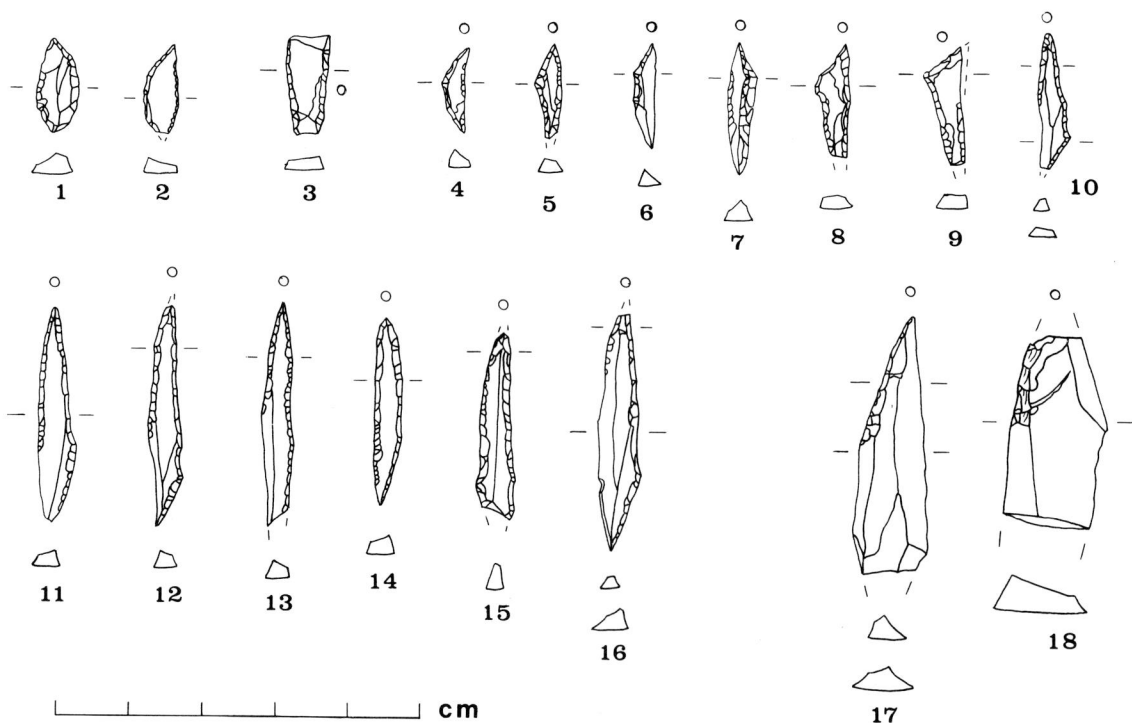

Figure 3 Hazleton North: flint microliths. *Drawn by A. Saville*

occurring elsewhere in both Mesolithic and Neolithic flint assemblages; at Hazleton it is distributed equally between the two concentrations.

The bulk of the buried soil assemblage inevitably comprises débitage, principally tiny chips, spalls and broken segments of flakes, giving little scope for typological or metrical analysis. In subjective, qualitative terms the main product of core reduction at Hazleton

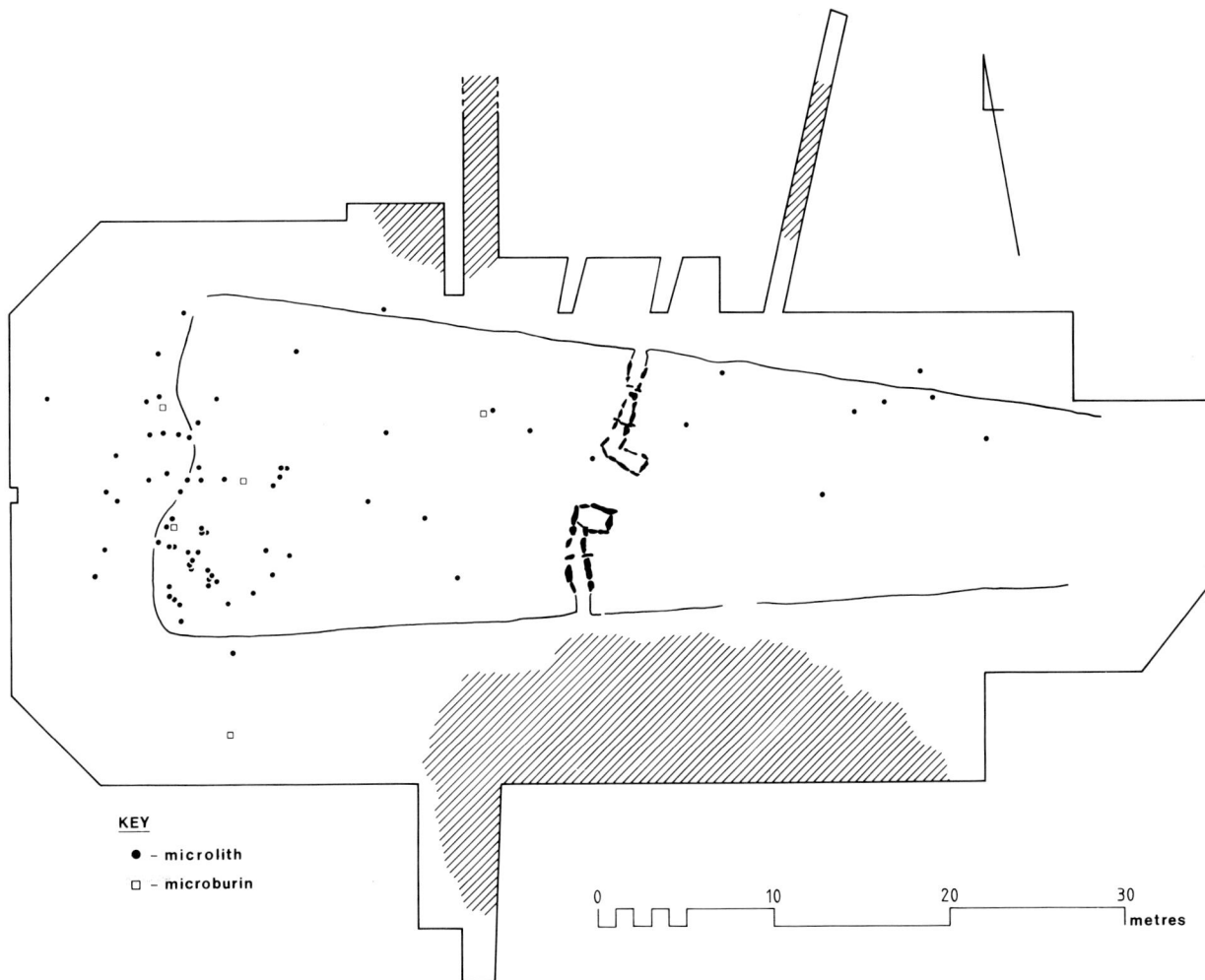

Figure 4   Hazleton North: distribution of diagnostic Mesolithic flints in the pre-cairn soil (with the outline of the cairn and the positions of the burial chambers superimposed). *Drawn by J. Hoyle*

seems to have been blades and bladelets. These might equally be seen as indicating late Mesolithic or earlier Neolithic knapping, since the discrimination found possible between material of these two phases from sites in southern and eastern England (Pitts and Jacobi 1979) has yet to be demonstrated in other parts of the country.

Further analysis of the flint assemblage from Hazleton will seek to isolate the Mesolithic and Neolithic elements more precisely. The very existence of these two elements is of considerable interest, however, in view of the fact that similarly subdivisible assemblages have also been recovered from the buried soils beneath the only two other Cotswold–Severn tombs which have seen extensive excavation in recent years – namely Ascott-under-Wychwood, Oxfordshire (Selkirk 1971) and Gwernvale, Powys (Britnell 1984). This recurrent association of Mesolithic and Neolithic elements seems unlikely to be coincidental and demands an archaeological explanation.

It is not possible at any of the three sites to tie the Neolithic pre-cairn occupation incontrovertibly to the phase of cairn construction. At Ascott-under-Wychwood the pre-cairn Neolithic activity is interpreted as representing a settlement, or a series of settlements, which was abandoned and made over to open grassland for a considerable period before the tomb was built (Evans 1971; Selkirk 1971). At

Gwernvale the evidence was taken to suggest both small-scale settlement and the presence of ceremonial structures, the latter immediately pre-dating the tomb (Britnell 1984). At Hazleton both the structure and the midden could have been in use while the monument was being constructed, although this cannot be demonstrated conclusively. However, in view of the spatial relationship between the midden and the cairn there is likely to have been at most only a short interval between the activity producing the midden and the construction of the monument. This is because the central position of the midden beneath the cairn is difficult to accept as a fortuitous occurrence; it seems much more likely that its presence was visible in some way to the tomb-builders.

In each case, therefore, it seems likely that areas already cleared for settlement in the earliest Neolithic were used as convenient, and perhaps ritually appropriate, locations for tomb construction by members of the same population or their descendants. If correct, this provides a readily acceptable explanation for the recurrent Neolithic settlement evidence beneath the Cotswold–Severn tombs.

The presence of Mesolithic material in the buried soil at all three of the above sites has been seen in each case as representing activity which certainly pre-dates, perhaps considerably, the following Neolithic pre-cairn activity. In no case is there any absolute dating evidence for the time-gap involved, although

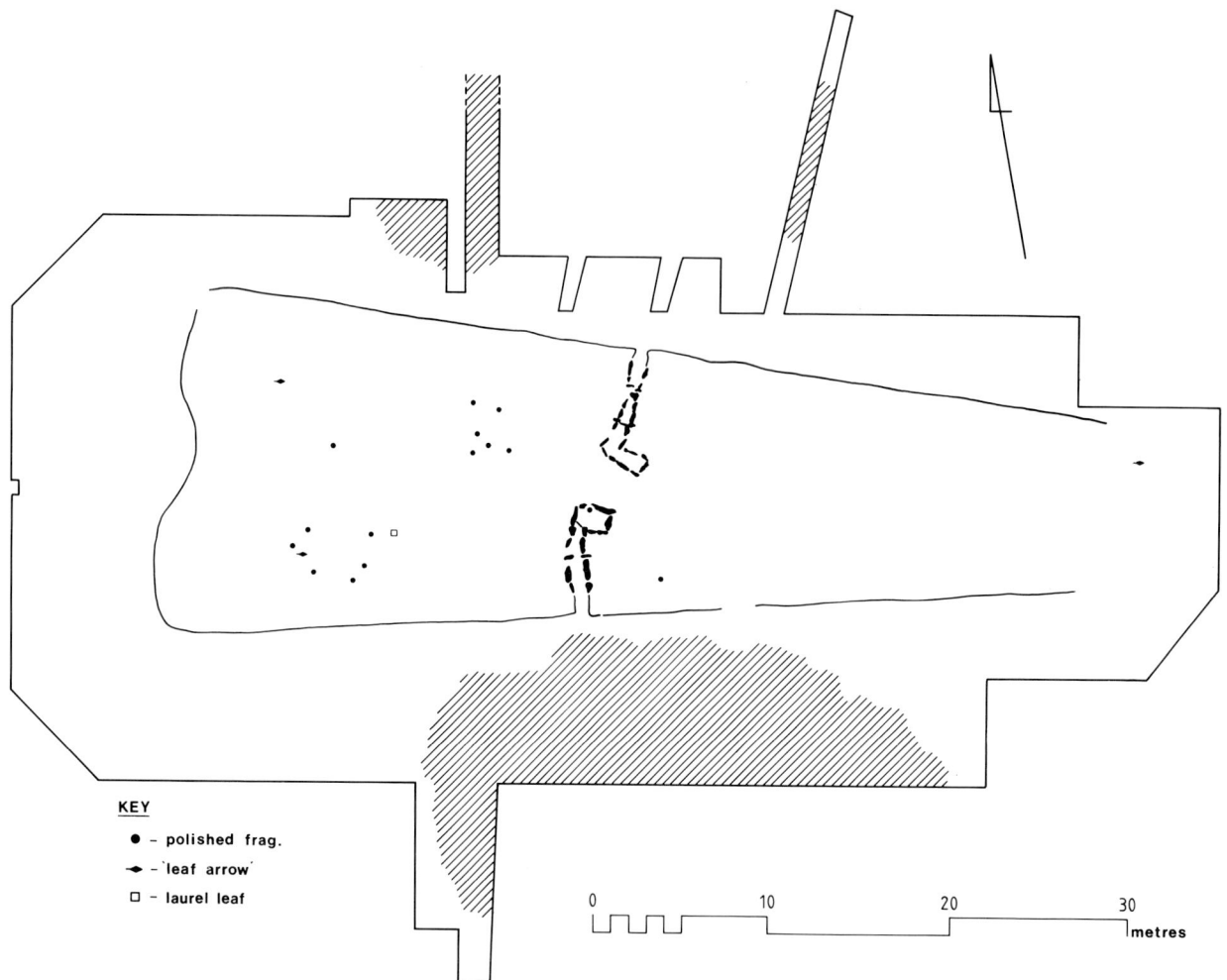

Figure 5   Hazleton North: distribution of diagnostic Neolithic flints in the pre-cairn soil (with the outline of the cairn and the positions of the burial chambers superimposed). *Drawn by J. Hoyle*

it has been suggested that the unassociated radio-carbon date of 6895±80 BP (CAR-118) from Gwernvale (Britnell 1984: 136) could be linked with the late Mesolithic industry. At Ascott-under-Wychwood the environmental evidence suggested a phase of dense woodland and new soil formation intervening between the late Mesolithic and early Neolithic activity (Evans 1971). At Gwernvale, Healey and Green (1984) have interpreted the typology of the flintwork as indicative not only of later Mesolithic activity, but also of early Mesolithic and late Upper Palaeolithic activity.

Such postulated continuous re-use of the same location over millennia seems extraordinary when the Gwernvale site does not appear to offer any particular advantage of location. The same could be said of the sites of Ascott-under-Wychwood and Hazleton. None of these locations is topographically distinct in terms of prominence or slope; the locations are not situated at changes in soil type or geology (except Gwernvale which lies at the edge of a terrace – Britnell 1984); they are not adjacent to permanent water supplies; nor do they offer lithic resources other than for cairn building. The only kinds of resources they may have offered, such as concentrations of edible vegetable foodstuffs, are likely to remain archaeologically invisible. It is perhaps more likely that the advantage offered by the location in each case was simply that it had been used previously for settlement

activity. In other words, these locations had already been cleared of vegetation and obstacles, becoming marked by the act of clearance and by the deposition of cultural debris, particularly flint débitage (a re-usable resource!). Such a location might continue to remain visible through a predominance of vegetation types associated with human habitation, and by its proximity to tracks and paths remaining in constant use by both animals and humans.

However, this kind of visibility can surely only apply if the gap between successive occupations of each site is not excessively long, since the regenerating Postglacial vegetation cover in the Cotswold region can be expected to have been both dense and obscuring. It is difficult to obtain data which would enable the placing of any realistic time-brackets on such a process, but a gap in the region of 700 or more radiocarbon years between late Mesolithic and earlier Neolithic settlement, as indicated by the evidence currently available (Bradley 1984), would seem to be far too large. If this gap in the radiocarbon data becomes reduced, it will then be difficult in the case of mixed assemblages to determine whether the dates relate to Mesolithic or Neolithic activity; and it is a current theoretical problem as to whether late sixth millennium BP Mesolithic activity, or early sixth millennium BP Neolithic activity is the more likely (Bradley 1984).

This conundrum would best be resolved by the

location and accurate dating of culturally discrete assemblages of late Mesolithic and early Neolithic assemblages in areas like the Cotswolds. For the Neolithic this is more hopeful, since the lithic assemblages from the recently excavated causewayed enclosures at Crickley Hill and The Peak (Darvill 1984) may provide suitable models for the earliest Neolithic flintwork in the region. Uncontaminated late Mesolithic sites with dating potential are only likely to be found by chance, however, and may take a long time to be discovered. For the present it will be necessary to place some interpretation upon the evidence available from sites like Hazleton where both Mesolithic and Neolithic industries are represented. The 'best guess' to fit this evidence is perhaps that late Mesolithic activity did continue well down into the sixth millennium BP, probably overlapping with initial Neolithic activity, but certainly occurring close enough in time for the existence of Mesolithic settlement areas to be readily visible to Neolithic settlers.

Further speculation on this point might centre on the nature of these sites, which have been assumed to represent unspecified domestic settlements in both the late Mesolithic (a temporary camp for ungulate exploitation at Gwernvale – Healey and Green 1984) and the pre-cairn early Neolithic. In the absence of information about Mesolithic funerary practices in Midland England it is just conceivable as an alternative to suggest that a burial *and/or* ritual aspect could have attached to continuous use of the same locations, and that this factor, through regularized veneration, accounted for the continuing visibility or awareness of the same sites. Following this scenario it may be relevant that each of the tombs discussed, at Hazleton, Ascott-under-Wychwood, and Gwernvale, is of the laterally-chambered type, which is now thought to be potentially the earliest within the Cotswold–Severn group (Darvill 1982), and that Mesolithic assemblages have not been recorded from beneath terminally-chambered Cotswold tombs.

From here it is perhaps but a short step to the concept of a Mesolithic ancestry for the earliest Cotswold tomb-builders.

References

BRADLEY, R. (1984) Regional systems in Neolithic Britain. In R. Bradley and J. Gardiner (eds), *Neolithic studies: a Review of some Current Research*. Oxford, British Archaeological Reports (British Series) 133: 5–14.

BRITNELL, W.J. (1984) The Gwernvale long cairn, Crickhowell, Brecknock. In W.J. Britnell and H.N. Savory, *Gwernvale and Penywyrlod: Two Neolithic Long Cairns in the Black Mountains of Brecknock*. Cardiff, The Cambrian Archaeological Association: 41–154.

DARVILL, T.C. (1982) *The Megalithic Chambered Tombs of the Cotswold–Severn Region*. Highworth (Wiltshire), Vorda Archaeological and Historical Publications.

DARVILL, T.C. (1984) Neolithic Gloucestershire. In A. Saville (ed.), *Archaeology in Gloucestershire: from the Earliest Hunters to the Industrial Age*. Cheltenham, Cheltenham Art Gallery & Museums and the Bristol & Gloucestershire Archaeological Society: 80–112.

EVANS, J.G. (1971) Habitat change on the calcareous soils of Britain: the impact of Neolithic man. In D.D.A. Simpson (ed.), *Economy and Settlement in Neolithic and Early Bronze Age Britain and Europe*. Leicester, Leicester University Press: 27–73.

HEALEY, E. and GREEN, H.S. (1984) The lithic industries. In W.J. Britnell and H.N. Savory, *Gwernvale and Penywyrlod: Two Neolithic Long Cairns in the Black Mountains of Brecknock*. Cardiff, The Cambrian Archaeological Association: 113–132.

JACOBI, R.M. (1980) The early Holocene settlement of Wales. In J.A. Taylor (ed.), *Culture and Environment in Prehistoric Wales*. Oxford, British Archaeological Reports (British Series) 76: 131–206.

PITTS, M.W. and JACOBI, R.M. (1979) Some aspects of change in flaked stone industries of the Mesolithic and Neolithic in southern Britain. *Journal of Archaeological Science*, 6: 163–177.

SAVILLE, A. (1984*a*) Preliminary report on the excavation of a Cotswold–Severn tomb at Hazleton, Gloucestershire. *Antiquaries Journal*, 64: 10–24.

SAVILLE, A. (1984*b*) Palaeolithic and Mesolithic evidence from Gloucestershire. In A. Saville (ed.), *Archaeology in Gloucestershire: from the Earliest Hunters to the Industrial Age*. Cheltenham, Cheltenham Art Gallery & Museums and the Bristol & Gloucestershire Archaeological Society: 59–79.

SELKIRK, A. (1971) Ascott-under-Wychwood. *Current Archaeology*, 3(1): 7–10.

SMITH, I.F. (1965) *Windmill Hill and Avebury: Excavations by Alexander Keiller, 1925–1939*. Oxford, The Clarendon Press.

Long Blade Technology in Southern Britain

R.N.E. Barton

Abstract

This paper deals with a group of flint assemblages characterized by long blades (>12 cm) which have recently been recognized in southern Britain. Although the size of the débitage is undoubtedly linked to the abundance of high quality raw material, the long blade toolkit is sufficiently distinct from local Upper Palaeolithic and early Mesolithic facies to be classified separately. Amongst the recurring elements are heavily bruised blades (*lames mâchurées*) which appear to be connected with bone- and antlerworking activities. Chronological arguments are advanced to suggest that the British assemblages fit within the terminal Pleistocene/earliest Holocene time-range.

INTRODUCTION

In this paper attention is drawn to a particular group of flint assemblages which have received little attention in the archaeological literature. They bear strong resemblances to the later Upper Palaeolithic but appear to date to the latter part of Dryas III and the first part of the succeeding Pre-Boreal chronozone. By implication, they could overlap chronologically with the earliest Mesolithic material in Britain, although allowance may have to be made for an apparent 370-year compression in the radiocarbon record which occurs around 9600 BP, according to recent tree-ring evidence (Becker and Kromer 1986).

This advanced Palaeolithic industry combines heavily edge-damaged or 'bruised' blades (*lames mâchurées* – cf. Bordes 1971; Barton 1986a) with small backed blades, sometimes including microliths (cf. Clark 1934: 55). The assemblages are characterized by long blades (>12 cm in length) and are quite unlike the late 'Federmesser-type' Upper Palaeolithic industries already described for Britain (Campbell 1977; Jacobi 1980), or the local early Mesolithic as seen at Thatcham (Wymer 1962) or Star Carr (Clark 1954). The 'long blade' assemblages (as it is suggested they be called, cf. Wymer 1976) are also sufficiently distinct both typologically and technologically to remove any suggestion that they are simply functional variants of one or other of the major complexes. Finally, distinct parallels can be observed with long blade assemblages on the European mainland which have been dated on or near the Pleistocene/Holocene boundary (Rust 1943; Rozoy 1978; Fagnart 1984).

LOCATION OF BRITISH LONG BLADE SITES

So far, only a few sites of this type have been excavated. These include Avington VI (Froom 1970; Barton and Froom 1986), Sproughton (Wymer 1976), and Springhead (Burchell 1938). To this list can be added several rich surface collections, most notably from Wawcott XII (Froom, pers. comm.), Swaffham Prior (David, pers. comm.) and Riverdale (Barton 1986b), where characteristic 'bruised' blades have been found amongst other long blade material (*Fig. 1*). If account is taken of numerous isolated findspots, the total number of British sites of this kind may be well over sixty (Barton 1986b).

Figure 1   Location of selected long blade assemblages in southern Britain. Key: A – Avington VI; R – Riverdale; S – Sproughton; SH – Springhead; SW – Swaffham Prior; W – Wawcott XII.

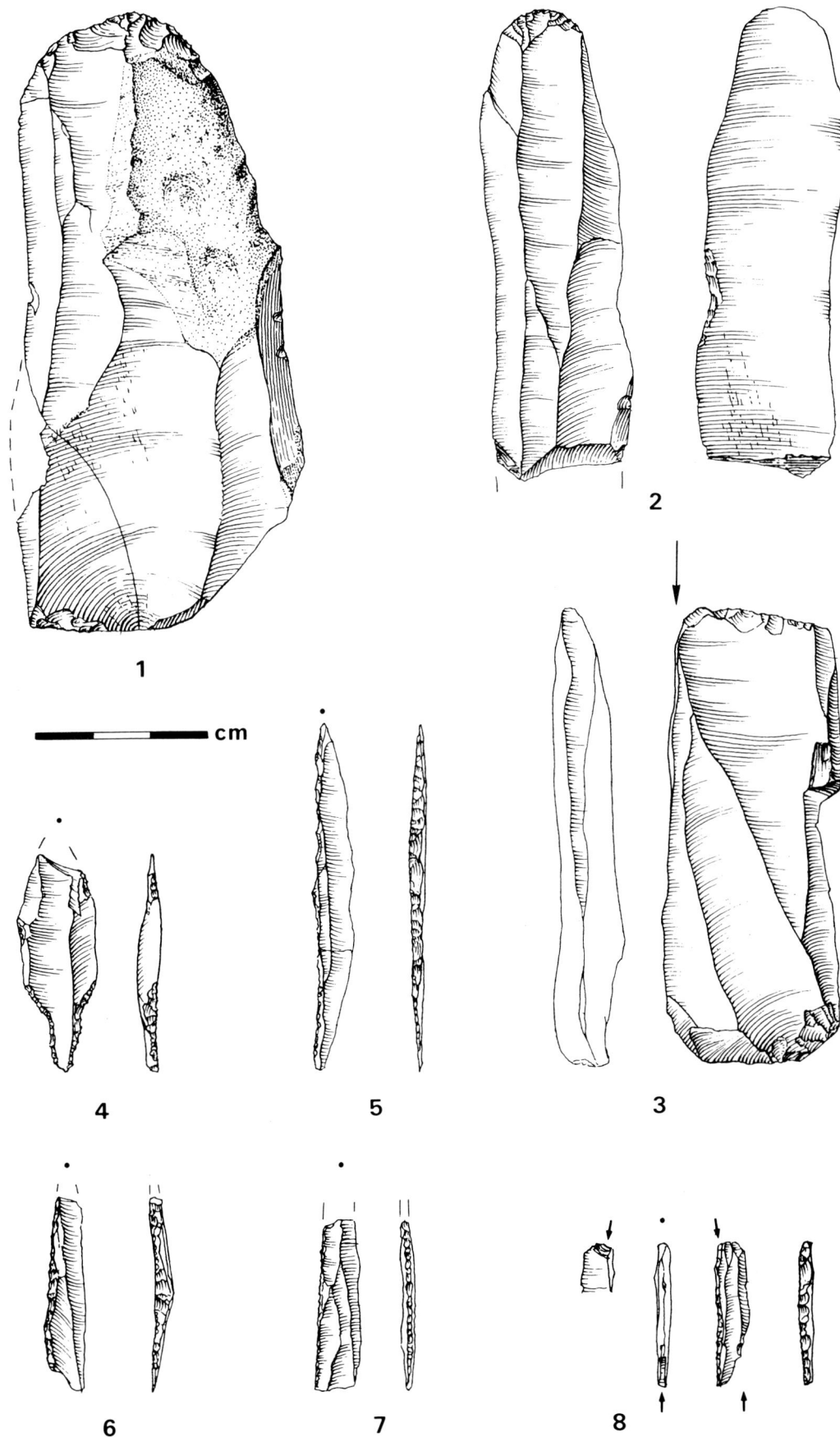

Figure 2 Avington VI: retouched tools – end-scrapers (1–2); burin on truncation (3); tanged point (4); backed bladelets (5–8).

265

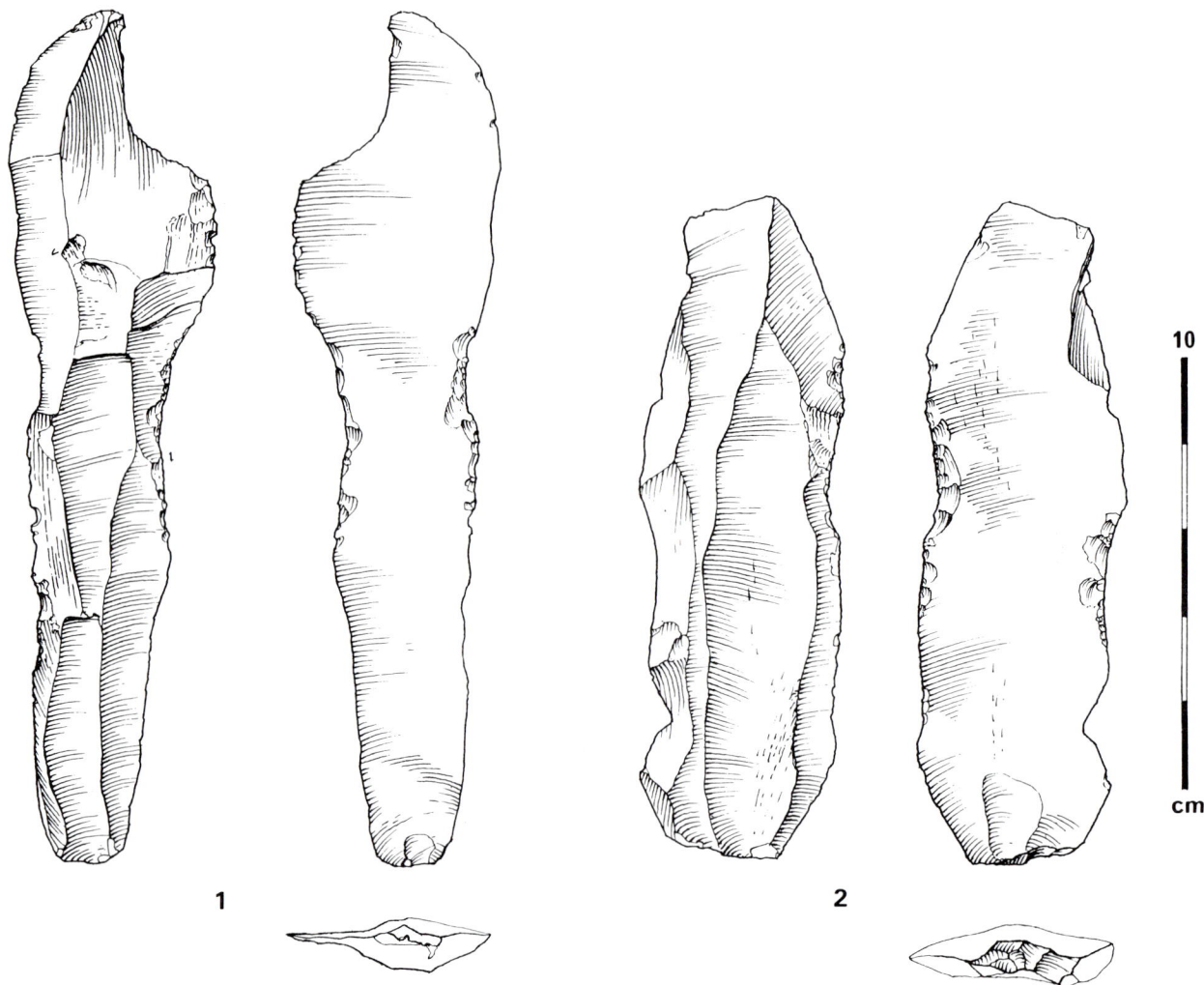

Figure 3   Avington VI – 'bruised' blades.

All of the above material comes from southern Britain from open-air sites in areas which correspond closely to the known distribution of the rich flint-bearing Upper Cretaceous chalk deposits. Noticeable, too, is the apparent preference shown for low-lying floodplain situations, which may reflect special functional requirements (e.g. riverside butchery activities) or accessibility of raw materials (e.g. flint sources exposed on denuded valley slopes), or both. It should be noted also that a very high proportion of the finds from these sites consist of flaking waste.

TYPOLOGICAL AND TECHNOLOGICAL CHARACTERISTICS

Although one of the most striking features of the long blade group is the large size of the artifacts, there are important typological and technological characteristics which link it with other Upper Palaeolithic flintwork from southern Britain. In the first place, the technique of core preparation is essentially that of the Upper Palaeolithic. The initial stages normally consisted of the production of one, and sometimes two, crests (frontal and posterior) and

the preparation of two opposed striking platforms. During the reduction process (i.e. the detaching of blades), minor adjustments were regularly made to the platforms by the removal of tiny flakes, resulting in a characteristically 'faceted' blade butt (*Fig. 3*, no. 2). The occurrence of such faceting seldom falls below 20% in the long blade assemblages examined by the author (Barton 1986*b*).

By contrast, the method of core preparation in British early Mesolithic assemblages rarely involved more than a single anterior crest. Furthermore, the main series of removals were commonly detached from one platform only and rejuvenation of the striking platform was achieved by removing sizable tablets from the top of the core. Although core tablets certainly occur in the long blade assemblages, the author has never seen any trace of faceting on Mesolithic cores from southern Britain.

Retouched tools are on the whole poorly represented in the long blade assemblages – they form, for example, less than 2% of the total excavated collection from Sproughton (Barton 1986*a*). Scrapers occur predominantly on the ends of large flake or blade supports (*Figs. 2 & 4*). Amongst the burins,

266

Sites	RETOUCHED TOOLS					DEBITAGE	
	Scrapers	*Scraper/ Burins*	*Burins*	*Backed Bladelets*	*Microliths*	*Bruised Flakes/Blades*	*Microburins*
Avington VI[*]	4	–	2	9	6	6	–
Springhead (lower floor)	5	–	7	–	1	4	–
Riverdale (Canterbury)	–	–	–	–	–	16	–
Sproughton (Devil's Wood Pit)	6	1	9	3	2	6	2
Swaffham Prior[*]	113	4	26	2	1	18	2

([*] estimated or incomplete counts)

dihedral forms are more common than truncation burins (*Figs. 4 & 5*) – a feature that has also been noted at some British Upper Palaeolithic sites (Barton 1986*b*; Bergman and Barton 1986; Jacobi, pers. comm.). On the other hand, a more 'Mesolithic' characteristic of the long blade assemblages is the occasional occurrence of geometric and non-geometric microlith forms (*Table 1*; *Figs. 4 & 5*). Rarely present, however, are the typical by-products of microlith manufacture (microburins) which feature so prominently in most of the Mesolithic assemblages. It may also be noted that some of the smaller backed pieces found with the long blades retain part or all of their butt ends (*Fig. 5*), again indicating much greater similarity to Upper Palaeolithic counterparts. A single example of a tanged point, identical to an Ahrensburgian point, has been recovered from Avington VI (*Fig. 2*, no. 3). The presence of many heavily 'bruised' blades seems to be something that is restricted to assemblages of long blade type (*Fig. 3*).

DATING EVIDENCE FOR THE BRITISH ASSEMBLAGES

In spite of the fact that direct dating evidence for late Pleistocene/early Holocene contexts in Britain remains scanty, recent coleopteran studies suggest that the major warming episode which marks the end of the Pleistocene began in this country close to 10,500 years ago, slightly earlier than is traditionally accepted (Atkinson *et al.* 1987). Evidence of the early warming is also provided in some British pollen records (Lowe and Walker 1977; Lowe 1981). It is, therefore, highly significant that several examples of worked bone and antler have recently been shown to belong to this same period, when much of Britain was thought to have been unoccupied. One such find, so far unique in Britain, is a Lyngby axe of reindeer antler from Earl's Barton in Northamptonshire which has been dated to 10,320±150 BP (OxA-803: Gowlett *et al.* 1986). Another comprises an

incised and decorated horse mandible (Sieveking 1971). Neither object was associated with flint artifacts, but the mandible was found with other possible burial items at Kendrick's Cave in Gwynedd, north Wales and gave a date of 10,000±200 BP (OxA-111: Gillespie *et al.* 1985). Both finds offer direct evidence for a human presence in Britain at this time. Close parallels for the Northamptonshire antler axe exist over a wide area of the European mainland from southern Scandinavia to Poland. In north Germany they are found in contexts dating to Dryas III (Clark 1975).

Some indication that the long blade technology also fits within this same period is available from three of the excavated sites. At Avington VI in Berkshire the long blade horizon is stratified well above a dark organic layer which appears, on palynological grounds, to be of Allerød age; while pollen from the long blade layer itself is not inconsistent with a Dryas III dating (Holyoak 1980). In Kent, at the long blade site of Springhead, mollusca of probable Dryas III type (Kerney's Mollusc Zone A) indicate the likely age of the archaeological horizon (Jacobi 1982). At Sproughton, Suffolk, the long blade horizon lies at the top of a sequence of river channel deposits which gave a latest radiocarbon date of 9880±120 BP – corresponding approximately to the Dryas III/Pre-Boreal boundary. Although none of these data constitute hard evidence in themselves, collectively they may be regarded as tending to support the proposed framework.

EUROPEAN AFFINITIES WITH THE BRITISH MATERIAL

Several important points of similarity can be recognized between the British long blade occurrences and certain assemblages on the European mainland. In particular, technological and typological comparisons may be made with the north German final Palaeolithic groups and with sites in the Somme

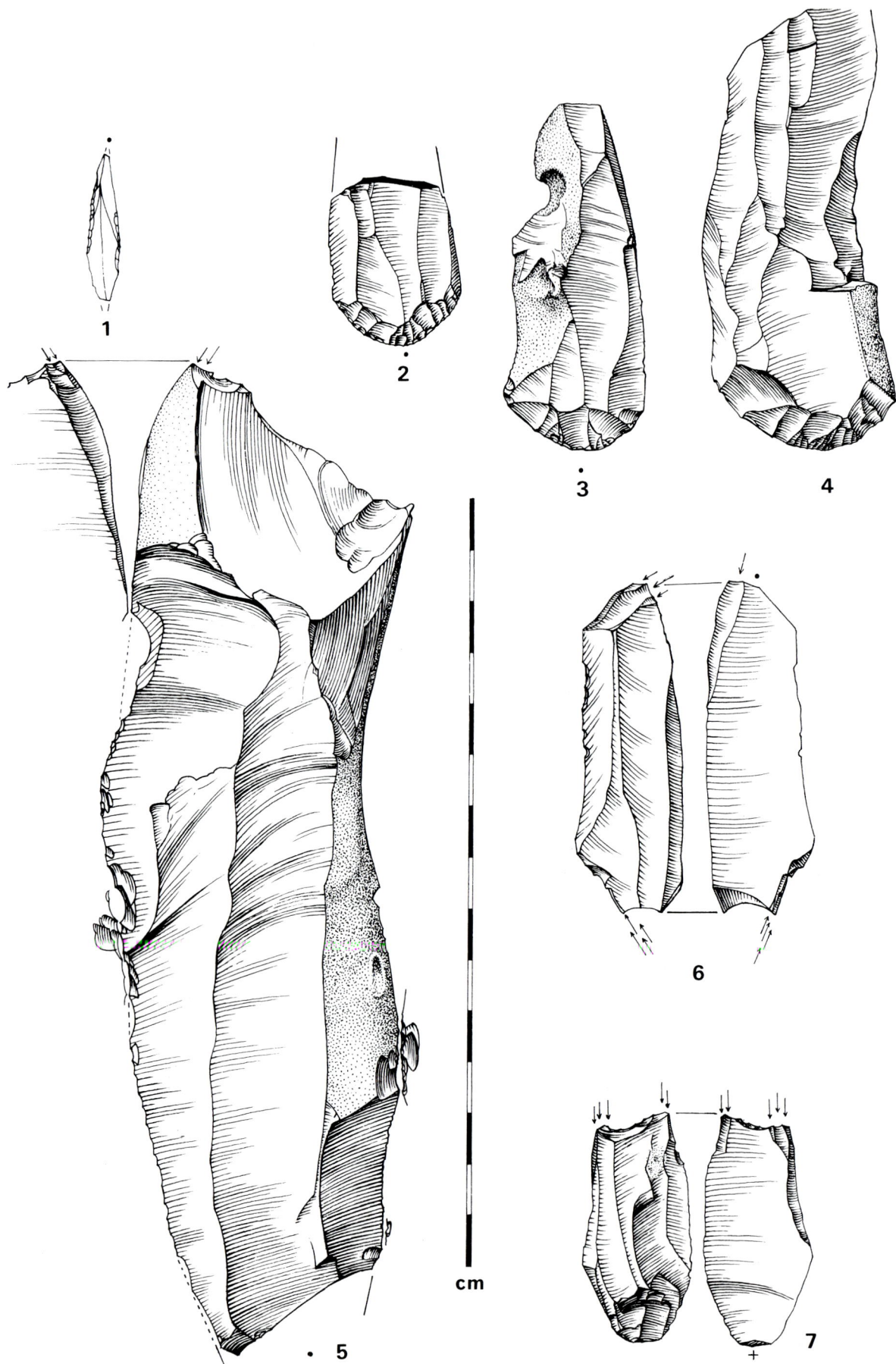

Figure 4 Springhead, lower floor: microlith (1); end-scrapers (2–4); atypical truncation burin (5); multiple mixed dihedral burin (6); multiple burin on a concave truncation (7). (*Source*: Jacobi 1982)

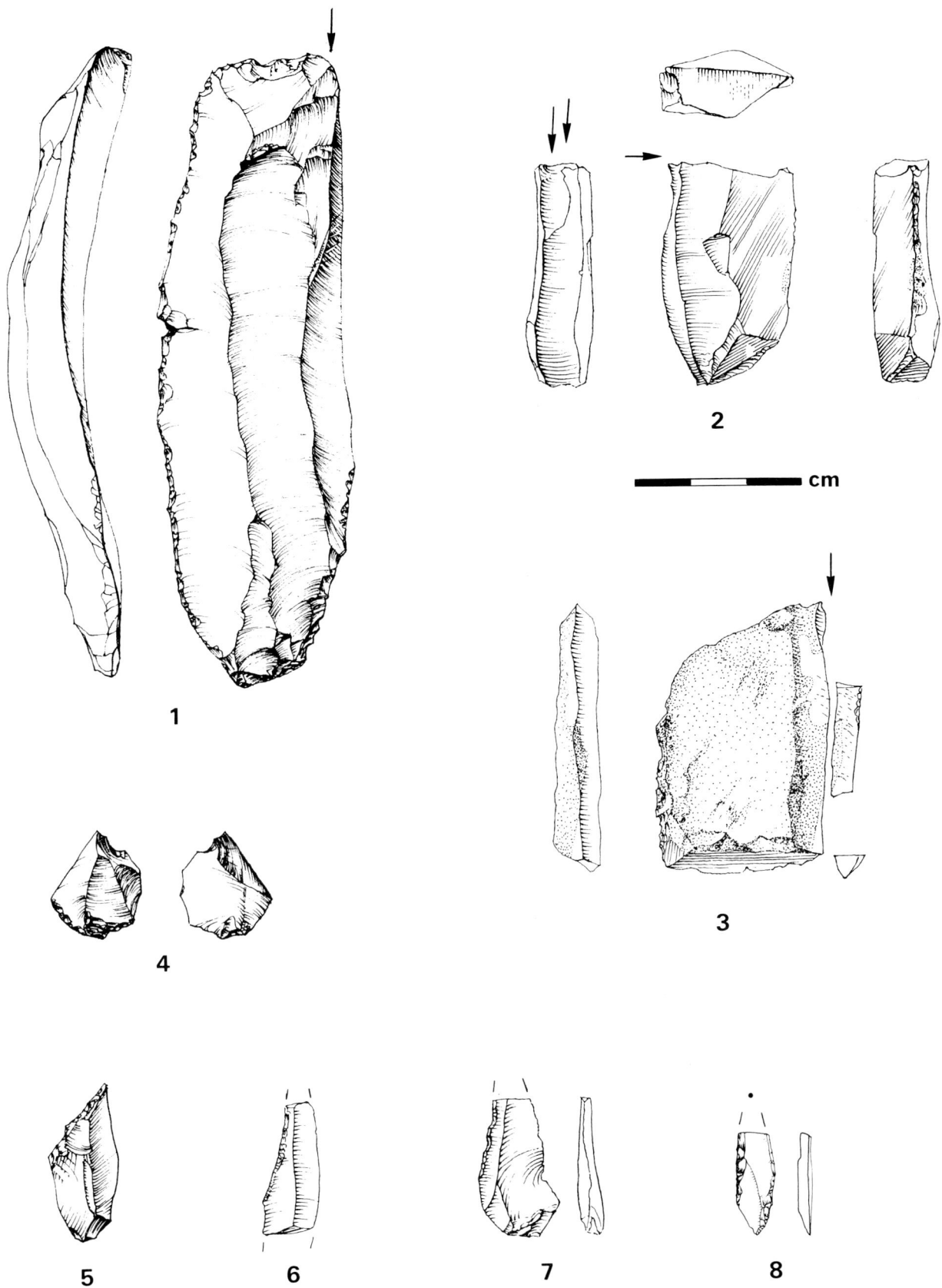

Figure 5   Sproughton: burin on a straight truncation (1); angle burin (2); burin on a natural surface (3); proximal microburin (4); retouched bladelets (5–7); microlith (8).

valley in northern France, which in each area can be dated to late Dryas III.

Typologically, the southern British toolkits bear closest resemblance to the north French assemblages of Belloy-type. These are best known from Belloy-sur-Somme, Flixecourt, and Villers-Tournelle in the Somme valley and its tributaries (Fagnart 1984, pers. comm.). The finds are characterized by end-scrapers and burins on large supports, whilst backed components are sometimes made on bladelets. Among the informal tools are long 'bruised' blades. At Belloy itself faunal remains consist mainly of horse (*Equus przewalski*). From a technological point of view, it is noteworthy that similar core preparation techniques to the British ones are used and that an important proportion of the blades have faceted butts. Structurally, these flint assemblages are very similar indeed to the southern British long blade assemblages.

Parallels may also be drawn with the Ahrensburgian sites with long blades on the North German Plain. Here, the tools on smaller supports include diminutive tanged 'Ahrensburgian' points, obliquely truncated 'Zonhoven' points and various geometric microliths, e.g. broad triangles and lanceolate forms. At the sites of Eggstedt, Teltwisch 2 and the type site of Stellmoor, typical examples of 'bruised' blades also occur (cf. Rust 1943: fig. 47; Taute 1968: figs. 80, 81). At the latter site the artifacts are associated with a sizeable reindeer kill (Rust 1943).

Overall, the most common stone projectile types at many of the long blade Ahrensburgian sites in Germany and the Low Countries are the obliquely-blunted 'Zonhoven' points (Taute 1968). It is also worth mentioning that although small tanged points do occasionally occur in France (Hinout 1985), none has so far been found in a long blade assemblage (Fagnart, pers. comm.). If the appearance of particular point types is not time-transgressive, it may be that the French–British–German long blade sites represent a continuum – an extensive Ahrensburgian social territory with some regional variation in flint projectile equipment. Such localized preferences might account for the occurrence of fewer tanged points in the western regions.

The most accurately dated continental assemblages with long blades, so far, are those of Stellmoor and Belloy-sur-Somme. The Ahrensburgian (upper) level at Stellmoor has been dated to 10,320±250 BP (Y-152.2: Lanting and Mook 1977); a recent unpublished date on reindeer antler from the same level (Bokelmann, pers. comm.) confirms the published date. From Belloy there is now a series of four AMS radiocarbon dates on horse teeth from the long blade horizon (Gowlett *et al.* 1986) which range from 9720±130 BP (OxA-462) to 10,260±160 BP (OxA-724). All of these dates fall close to the Pleistocene/Holocene boundary and provide additional circumstantial evidence for the time-range of the British long blade technology.

DISCUSSION

Recent palynological work in Europe has suggested a rather complex sequence of events during the closing stages of the Pleistocene and the beginning of the Holocene, marked by a series of short-lived climatic fluctuations (Behre 1978). An early warming phase within Dryas III (c. 10,200 BP) is indicated by various pollen profiles from the European mainland (Van der Hammen 1951; Casparie and Van Zeist 1960; Behre 1967, 1978). The term 'Friesland Oscillation' is now generally applied to this warmer episode (Van der Hammen 1971). In the Netherlands this is succeeded by a much cooler period, the 'Rammelbeek' phase, lasting no more than a few hundred years (Van der Hammen 1971).

Some evidence for an early climatic amelioration during Dryas III is also present in Britain according to palynological and beetle studies (Lowe and Walker 1977; Walker and Lowe 1980; Lowe 1981; Atkinson *et al.* 1987). However, no direct evidence yet exists for succeeding cooler conditions equivalent to the 'Rammelbeek' phase, although mega-faunal dates suggest a late persistence of horse (9770±80 BP: BM-1619) and reindeer (9760±70 BP: BM-1674) in south-eastern Britain (Clutton-Brock and Burleigh 1983).[1] If these dates are taken at face value, they would appear substantially to match that of a worked beam of red deer antler from Thatcham IV, also in the southern part of the country. This object is tentatively associated with Mesolithic activity in the Kennet valley and has an age of 9760±120 BP (OxA-732: Gowlett *et al.* 1987). Similar dates have been obtained on birch wood and charcoal from adjacent locations. These are likewise said to reflect early Mesolithic site activities in this area (Wymer 1962).

In conclusion, the radiocarbon dates from southern Britain hint at a much more complicated mosaic of habitats during the Lateglacial/early Postglacial than previously supposed. If the long blade technologies are linked to the killing and processing of large game, as they would appear to be on the north European mainland, and if conditions were such as to permit the presence of reindeer and horse as late as the early Pre-Boreal, the apparent survival of Upper Palaeolithic-like industries in Britain up to this time need not be surprising.

Note:
1. The reader's attention is drawn to the statement issued by the British Museum radiocarbon laboratory – *Antiquity*, 61 (1987): 168. BM-1674 was measured during the critical period (S. Bowman, pers. comm.) and may be subject to the error discussed in that statement. (Ed.)

Acknowledgements: I should like to thank Mrs C. Wilson and Mr G. Wallis for the line drawings, and Dr R.M. Jacobi for his permission to reproduce *Fig. 4*, originally by Mrs H. Martingell.

References

ATKINSON, T.C., BRIFFA, K.R. and COOPE, G.R. (1987) Seasonal temperatures in Britain during the past 20,000 years, reconstructed using beetle remains. *Nature*, 325: 587–592.

BARTON, R.N.E. (1986a) Experiments with long blades from Sproughton, near Ipswich, Suffolk. In D.A. Roe (ed.), *Studies in the Upper Palaeolithic of Britain and Northwest Europe*. Oxford, British Archaeological Reports (International Series) S296: 129–141.

BARTON, R.N.E. (1986b) *A Study of Selected British and European Flint Assemblages of Late Devensian and Early Flandrian Age*. Unpublished D.Phil. thesis, University of Oxford.

BARTON, R.N.E. and FROOM, F.R. (1986) The long blade assemblage from Avington VI, Berkshire. In S.N. Collcutt (ed.), *The Palaeolithic of Britain and its Nearest Neighbours: Recent Advances*. Sheffield, Department of Archaeology and Prehistory, University of Sheffield: 80–84.

BECKER, B. and KROMER, B. (1986) Extension of the Holocene dendrochronology by the Preboreal pine series, 8,800 to 10,100 BP. *Radiocarbon*, 28(2b): 961–967.

BEHRE, K.E. (1967) The Late Glacial and early Postglacial history of vegetation and climate in northwestern Germany. *Review of Palaeobotany and Palynology*, 4: 149–161.

BEHRE, K.E. (1978) Die Klimasschwankungen im europäischen Präboreal. *Festschrift in Honour of Professor H. Kliewe's 60th Birthday* (Petermann's Geographische Mitteilungen, 2). Gotha/Leipzig, VEB Hermann Haack: 97–102.

BERGMAN, C.A. and BARTON, R.N.E. (1986) The Upper Palaeolithic site of Hengistbury Head, Dorset, England. In S.N. Collcutt (ed.), *The Palaeolithic of Britain and its Nearest Neighbours: Recent Advances*. Sheffield, Department of Archaeology and Prehistory, University of Sheffield: 69–72.

BORDES, F. (1971) Essai de préhistoire expérimentale: fabrication d'un épieu de bois. *Mélanges de Préhistoire, d'Archéocivilisation et d'Ethnologie Offerts à André Varagnac*. Ecole Pratique des Hautes Etudes, VIᵉ Section, Centre de Recherches Historiques. Paris, SEVPEN: 69–73.

BURCHELL, J.P.T. (1938) Two Mesolithic 'floors' in the Ebbsfleet valley of the lower Thames. *The Antiquaries Journal*, 18: 397–401.

CAMPBELL, J.B. (1977) *The Upper Palaeolithic of Britain. A Study of Man and Nature in the Late Ice Age* (two volumes). Oxford, Clarendon Press.

CASPARIE, W.A. and VAN ZEIST, W. (1960) A Late Glacial lake deposit near Waskemeer (Prov. of Friesland). *Acta Botanica Neerlandica*, 9: 191–196.

CLARK, J.G.D. (1934) The classification of a microlithic culture: the Tardenoisian of Horsham. *Archaeological Journal*, 90: 52–77.

CLARK, J.G.D. (1954) *Excavations at Star Carr*. Cambridge, University Press.

CLARK, J.G.D. (1975) *The Earlier Stone Age Settlement of Scandinavia*. Cambridge, University Press.

CLUTTON-BROCK, J. and BURLEIGH, R. (1983) Some archaeological applications of the dating of animal bone by radiocarbon with particular reference to post-Pleistocene extinctions. In W.G. Mook and H.T. Waterbolk (eds), *1st International Symposium on ¹⁴C and Archaeology* (PACT 8). Strasbourg, Council of Europe: 409–419.

FAGNART, J-P. (1984) Le Paléolithique supérieur dans le nord de la France: un état de la question. *Bulletin de la Société Préhistorique Française*, 81: 291–301.

FROOM, F.R. (1970) The Mesolithic around Hungerford. *Transactions of the Newbury District Field Club*, 12: 58–67.

GILLESPIE, R., GOWLETT, J.A.J., HALL, E.T., HEDGES, R.E.M. and PERRY, C. (1985) Radiocarbon dates from the Oxford AMS system: Archaeometry datelist 2. *Archaeometry*, 27(2): 237–246.

GOWLETT, J.A.J., HEDGES, R.E.M., LAW, I.A. and PERRY, C. (1986) Radiocarbon dates from the Oxford AMS system: Archaeometry datelist 4. *Archaeometry*, 28(2): 206–221.

GOWLETT, J.A.J., HEDGES, R.E.M., LAW, I.A. and PERRY, C. (1987) Radiocarbon dates from the Oxford AMS system: Archaeometry datelist 5. *Archaeometry*, 29(1): 125–155.

HINOUT, J. (1985) Le gisement épipaléolithique de La Muette 1, commune de Vieux–Moulin (Oise). *Bulletin de la Société Préhistorique Française*, 82: 377–388.

HOLYOAK, D.T. (1980) *Late Pleistocene Sediments and Biostratigraphy of the Kennet Valley, England*. Unpublished Ph.D. thesis, University of Reading.

JACOBI, R.M. (1980) The Upper Palaeolithic of Britain with special reference to Wales. In J.A. Taylor (ed.), *Culture and Environment in Prehistoric Wales: Selected Essays*. Oxford, British Archaeological Reports (British Series) 76: 15–99.

JACOBI, R.M. (1982) Later hunters in Kent: Tasmania and the earliest Neolithic. In P.E. Leach (ed.), *Archaeology in Kent to AD 1500*. London, C.B.A. Research Report 48: 12–24.

LANTING, J.N. and MOOK, W.G. (1977) *The Pre– and Protohistory of the Netherlands in Terms of Radiocarbon Dates*. Groningen, University Press.

LOWE, J.J. and WALKER, M.J.C. (1977) The reconstruction of the Lateglacial environment in the southern and eastern Grampian Highlands. In J.M. Gray and J.J. Lowe (eds), *Studies in the Scottish Lateglacial Environment*. Oxford, Pergamon Press: 101–118.

LOWE, S. (1981) Radiocarbon dating and stratigraphic resolution in Welsh Lateglacial chronology. *Nature*, 293: 210–212.

ROZOY, J-G. (1978) *Les Derniers Chasseurs. L'Epipaléolithique en France et en Belgique*. Bulletin de la Société archéologique champenoise, numéro spécial. Charleville, J-G. Rozoy.

RUST, A. (1943) *Die alt– und mittelsteinzeitlichen Funde von Stellmoor*. Neumünster, Karl Wachholz.

SIEVEKING, G. DE G. (1971) The Kendrick's Cave mandible. *The British Museum Quarterly*, 35: 230–250.

TAUTE, W. (1968) *Die Stielspitzen–Gruppen im nördlichen Mitteleuropa*. Köln, Böhlau Verlag.

VAN DER HAMMEN, T. (1951) Late–glacial flora and periglacial phenomena in the Netherlands. *Leidse Geologische Mededelingen*, 17: 71–184.

VAN DER HAMMEN, T. (1971) The upper Quaternary stratigraphy of the Dinkel Valley. In T. Van der Hammen and T.A. Wijmstra (eds), *Upper Quaternary of the Dinkel Valley*. *Mededelingen Rijks Geologische Dienst*, Neuwe Serie 22: 59–72.

WALKER, M.J.C. and LOWE, J.J. (1980) Pollen analysis, radiocarbon dates and the deglaciation of Rannoch Moor, Scotland, following the Loch Lomond Advance. In R.A. Cullingford, D.A. Davidson and J. Lewin (eds), *Timescales in Geomorphology*. London, J. Wiley and Sons: 247–259.

WYMER, J.J. (1962) Excavations at the Maglemosian sites at Thatcham, Berkshire, England. *Proceedings of the Prehistoric Society*, 28: 329–361.

WYMER, J.J. (1976) A long blade industry from Sproughton, Suffolk. *East Anglian Archaeology*, 3: 1–10.

British Antler Mattocks

Christopher Smith

Abstract

Red deer antler mattocks can be divided into four types; antler-base mattocks (*Type A*), laterally perforated antler-base mattocks (*Type B*), antler-beam mattocks (*Type C*) and unbalanced, or laterally perforated antler-beam mattocks (*Type D*).

Implements of this kind are well known from the lands around the North Sea where they seem to be of predominantly Mesolithic and early Neolithic date. In Britain Types A and B were probably contemporary and were in use from the ninth to the sixth millennium BP, when they appear to have been replaced by Types C and D. Type C is rare in Britain, whereas Types A and D are difficult to parallel elsewhere. Two-thirds of the British finds come from the Thames valley. Macroscopic examination of wear and damage suggests that these implements were heavy-duty digging tools and the term antler mattock is used in preference to antler axe, adze, perforated antler pick or hoe.

INTRODUCTION

Antler was one of the most versatile raw materials available to Stone Age man and its infrequent survival in the archaeological record gives only a limited view of the extent of its use. Antler, being both robust and durable but also easy to work, is in many respects similar to wood and the French term *bois de cerf* seems particularly appropriate. Like wood, antler is a readily renewable resource and a regular supply could be maintained by the collection of naturally shed antlers, while animals slaughtered in the hunt would have provided additional supplies.

Four species of cervid indigenous to Britain during the early Flandrian experienced an annual cycle of antler growth and casting – reindeer (*Rangifer tarandus*), elk (*Alces alces*), red deer (*Cervus elaphus*) and roe deer (*Capreolus capreolus*). Both male and female reindeer produce antlers, but with the others only the males are thus adorned and the growth of antlers is closely associated with the hormonal cycle leading up to the autumnal rut. Antler from all the British cervids was to some extent utilized by late Upper Palaeolithic and Mesolithic man but it is only the antlers of the elk and red deer that were selected for the heavy-duty implements known variously as antler axes, adzes, perforated picks, hoes and mattocks.

While this varied terminology reflects the variety of functional interpretations proposed in respect of these implements, it has also led to some imprecision

as to their nature and, as a consequence, to uncertainty in respect of their chronological range (Jacobi 1978). This uncertainty can to some extent be reduced by the adoption of a more precise definition. For the purpose of this study I have defined antler mattocks – the term that I prefer for reasons to be given below – on the basis of the following two criteria: (i) the presence of a round, oval or subrectangular perforation suitable for hafting; and (ii) the presence of a working edge of antler made by an oblique transverse truncation of the beam forming a facet within about 50° of the main axis.

Both these features must be present for the implement to be classed as an antler mattock. On the basis of these criteria, it is possible to exclude the antler axes of Lyngby type and the antler picks characteristic of Neolithic sites which do not have perforations, and the numerous perforated antler sleeves, sockets, hammers, and maces which do not have working edges made by transverse truncation.

So far I have been able to identify, either by inspection in museum collections or from published sources, 71 implements of red deer antler that may be described as mattocks within the terms of the above definition. The main published sources referred to have been the *Gazetteer of Mesolithic Sites in England and Wales* published by the Council for British Archaeology (Wymer 1977), two papers on the Thames valley by Lacaille (1961, 1966) and one by Lawrence (1929), Lacaille's *The Stone Age in Scotland* (1954), and Clark's account of Obanian bone- and antler-working (Clark 1955). To these 71 red deer antler mattocks may be added the six well-known elk antler implements from Star Carr (Clark 1954: 157–159). These 77 implements are listed in *Table 1* with details of their location and type according to the classification proposed below. In addition, I have found references to a further 22 implements, but in the absence of illustrations these cannot be classified prior to inspection and indeed all may not be mattocks within the definition proposed. These unauthenticated examples are listed in *Table 2*. The approximate locations of 94 authenticated and unauthenticated antler mattocks are shown in *Fig. 1*,

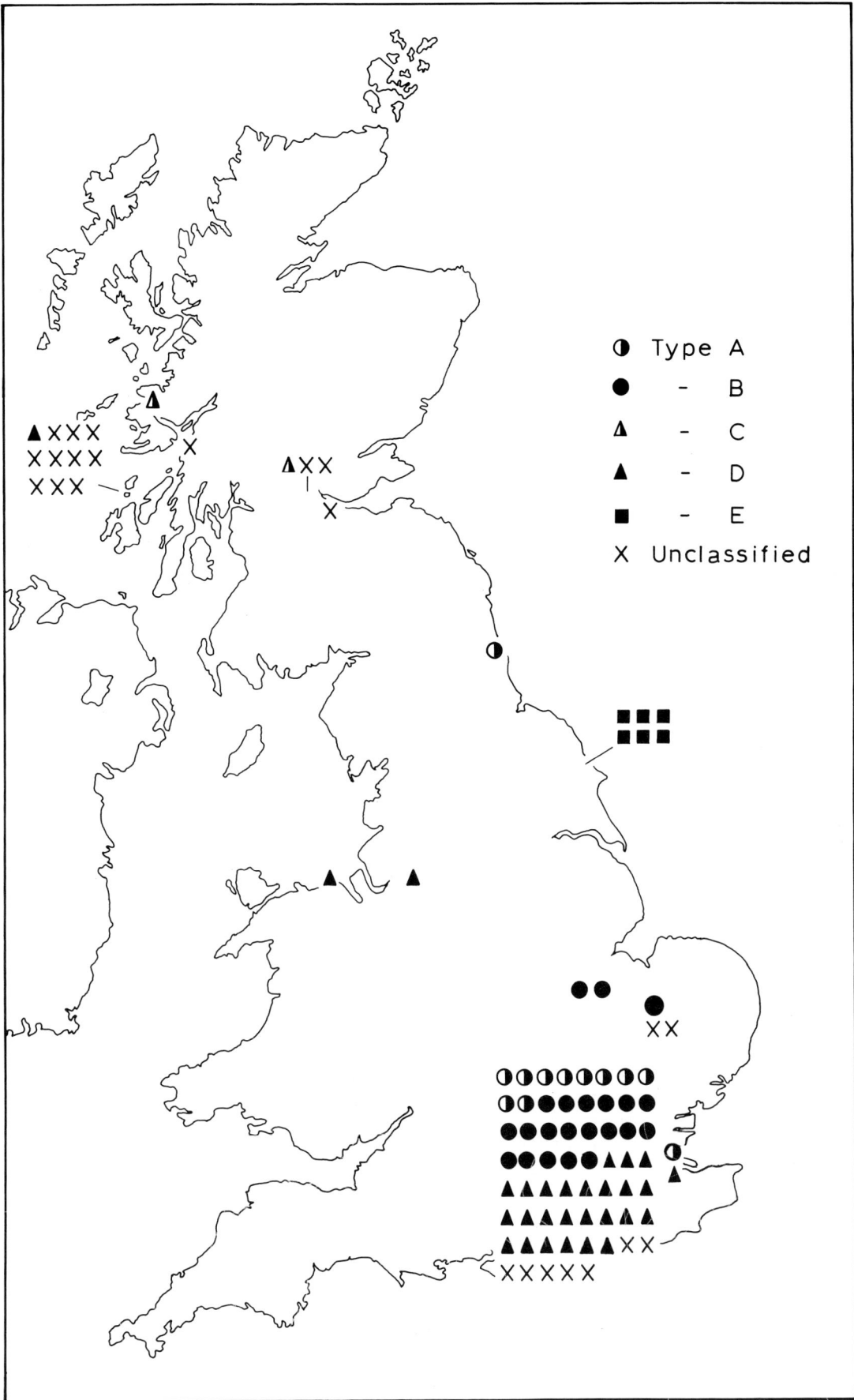

Figure 1   The approximate findspots of 94 antler mattocks shown according to type.

273

Table 1:   British antler mattocks (authenticated examples)

	Site	National Grid Reference	Type	Location	Registration Number	Reference
1.	Bankside Power Station	TQ32008050	A	Museum of London	38.187	Lacaille 1966: 19, fig. 3.10
2.	Barn Elms	TQ233 765	D	Museum of London	A18231	Wymer 1977: 193
3.	Battersea Reach	TQ270 775	D	Museum of London	A7350	Wymer 1977: 199
4.	Boveney Lock	SU94507780	D	Museum of London	ML898	Wymer 1977: 20
5.	Brentford	TQ179 769	B	Museum of London	0.1157a	Wymer 1977: 190
6.	Brentford Eyot (or Ait)	TQ183 778	A	Museum of London	A28142	Wymer 1977: 190
7.	Unknown		A	British Museum		
8.	Unknown		A	B.M.N.H.		
9.	Chelsea Reach	TQ280 777	D	Museum of London	60.176.299	
10.	Cliff Creek 1	TQ710 770	A	Sunderland Museum	G12298	Wymer 1977: 147
11.	Cliff Creek 2	TQ710 770	D	Sunderland Museum	G12297	
12.	Cnoc Sligeach	NR37208900	D	Hunterian Museum	B1914.516	Clark 1955: 93–98
13.	County Hall Extension 1	TQ30707980	A	Museum of London	A27513	Lacaille 1966: 14, fig. 3.7
14.	County Hall Extension 2	TQ30707980	A	Museum of London	A26935	Lacaille 1966: 14, fig. 3.8
15.	County Hall Extension 3	TQ30707980	A	Museum of London	27514	Lacaille 1966: 14, fig. 3.8
16.	Eel Pie Island	TQ165 731	D	Museum of London	49.107.902	Lacaille 1961: 133, fig. 7.2
17.	Feltwell	TL710 905	B	King's Lynn Museum	KL20.962	Wymer 1977: 206
18.	Finsbury Circus	TQ32808140	A	Museum of London	10.561	Lacaille 1961: 134–136, fig. 7
19.	Grangemouth	NS935 825				Lacaille 1954: 172–173, fig. 66
20.	Hammersmith 1	TQ225 783	B	Museum of London	C708	Wymer 1977: 188
21.	Hammersmith 2	TQ225 783	B	British Museum	121	
22.	Hammersmith 3	TQ225 783	B	British Museum	B 108	
23.	Hammersmith 4	TQ225 783	D	British Museum	WG 113	
24.	Hammersmith 5	TQ225 783	D	British Museum	WG 1223	
25.	Hammersmith 6	TQ225 783	B	Museum of London	A14691	Wymer 1977: 188
26.	Hammersmith 7	TQ225 783	D	Museum of London	A13728	Wymer 1977: 188
27.	Hammersmith 8	TQ225 783	D	Museum of London	A22556	Wymer 1977: 188
28.	Hammersmith 9	TQ225 783	D	Museum of London	A13648	Wymer 1977: 188
29.	Hammersmith 10	TQ225 783	D	Museum of London	71	Wymer 1977: 188
30.	Hammersmith 11	TQ225 783	B	Lost		Lawrence 1929: 86, pl. VIIIb
31.	Kew 1	TQ190 778	B	Museum of London	A13478	Wymer 1977: 194–195
32.	Kew 2	TQ190 778	B	Museum of London	A13684	Wymer 1977: 194–195
33.	Kew 3	TQ190 778	D	Museum of London	A13685	Wymer 1977: 194–195
34.	Kew 4	TQ190 778	D	Museum of London	A13647	Wymer 1977: 194–195
35.	Kew Bridge	TQ19007780	B	Museum of London	49.107.897	Lacaille 1961: 133, fig. 7.1
36.	Unprovenanced		A	Museum of London	49.107.901	
37.	Unprovenanced		A	Museum of London		
38.	Manchester Ship Canal	SJ88 67	D	Unknown		Newstead 1889: 152–155
39.	Meiklewood	NS726 956	C	Royal Museum of Scotland		Clark 1955: 93–98
40.	Moorfields	TQ327 817	B	Museum of London	70	Guildhall Museum 1908: pl. III
41.	Mortlake 1	TQ203 762	B	Museum of London	L139	Wymer 1977: 195
42.	Mortlake 2	TQ203 762	D	Museum of London	A13641	Wymer 1977: 195
43.	Mortlake 3	TQ203 762	D	Museum of London	C714	Wymer 1977: 195
44.	Mortlake 4	TQ203 762	D	Private Collection		Lacaille 1966: 14, fig. 3.5
45.	New Scotland Yard	TQ30407980	A	Museum of London	49.85	Lacaille 1961: 134, fig. 7.3
46.	Old England 1	TQ190 778	A	Museum of London	0.1159a	
47.	Old England 2	TQ190 778	B	Museum of London	0.1159f	
48.	Peterborough 1	TF10	B	B.M.N.H.		
49.	Peterborough 2	TF10	B	B.M.N.H.		
50.	Priory Midden	NR34508890	x	Paul Mellars		
51.	Putney 1	TQ240 759	B	Museum of London	A13497	
52.	Putney 2	TQ240 759	B	Museum of London	81.167.3	
53.	Richmond	TQ178 744	D	Museum of London	0.1157d	Wymer 1977: 196
54.	Risga	NM610 602	C	Kelvingrove Museum		Clark 1955: 93–98
55.	Splash Point	SJ020 825	D	National Museum of Wales	47.101.4	
56.	Staines	TQ030 715	D	Museum of London	49.107.900	Wymer 1977: 285
57.	Star Carr EM1	TA02708100	E	British Museum	1958.2-8.5	Clark 1954: 157–159, fig. 69
58.	Star Carr EM2	TA02708100	E	B.M.N.H.	1958.9.17.212	Clark 1954: 157–159, fig. 69
59.	Star Carr EM3	TA02708100	E	C.U.M.A.E.	1963.68	Clark 1954: 158
60.	Star Carr EM4	TA02708100	E	C.U.M.A.E.	1963.68	Clark 1954: 157–159, fig. 69
61.	Star Carr EM5	TA02708100	E	C.U.M.A.E.	1963.68	Clark 1954: 157–159, fig. 69
62.	Star Carr EM6	TA02708100	E	C.U.M.A.E.	1963.68	Clark 1954: 157–159, fig. 69
63.	Sunbury Lock	TQ110 685	B	Kingston-on-Thames Museum	650	Wymer 1977: 285
64.	Syon Reach	TQ175 765	D	Museum of London	33.153.5	Wymer 1977: 190
65.	Teddington	TQ165 716	B	British Museum	WG 120	Wymer 1977: 196
66.	Twickenham 1	TQ 165 731	D	Museum of London	49.107.899	
67.	Twickenham 2	TQ 165 731	D	Museum of London	49.107.906	

Table 1 (cont'd): British antler mattocks (authenticated examples)

	Site	National Grid Reference	Type	Location	Registration Number	Reference
68.	Twickenham 3	TQ 165 731	D	Museum of London	Lloyd 9 oz	Lacaille 1961: 136, fig. 7.2
69.	Wandsworth	TQ 255 754	D	British Museum	B 108	Wymer 1977: 200
70.	Willington Quay	NZ 324 662	A	Museum of Antiquities, Newcastle	1934.7	Smith and Bonsall 1985
71.	Windmill Lane, Brentford 1	TQ 168 783	B	Museum of London	0.1158e	Wymer 1977: 190
72.	Windmill Lane, Brentford 2	TQ 168 783	B	Museum of London	0.1158h	Wymer 1977: 190
73.	Windmill Lane, Brentford 3	TQ 168 783	A	Museum of London	0.1158g	Wymer 1977: 190
74.	Windmill Lane, Brentford 4	TQ 168 783	A	Museum of London	0.1158f	Wymer 1977: 190
75.	Windmill Lane, Brentford 5	TQ 168 783	D	Museum of London	0.1158a	Wymer 1977: 190
76.	Windsor 1	SU 75 77	B	Museum of London	81.167.2	
77.	Wormingford Bridge	TL 9320 3290	D	Unknown		Smith 1898: 310–312

Key:	B.M.N.H.	British Museum (Natural History)
	C.U.M.A.E.	University Museum of Archaeology and Ethnology, Cambridge

Table 2: British antler mattocks (unauthenticated examples)

	Site	National Grid Reference	Type	Reference
78.	Airthrey Castle	NS 817 965	x	Lacaille 1954: 171
79.	Blair Drummond Moss	NS 721 985	x	Lacaille 1954: 171
80.	Caisteal-nan-Gillean 1	NR 357 880	x	Lacaille 1954: 214
81.	Caisteal-nan-Gillean 2	NR 357 880	x	Lacaille 1954: 214
82.	Caisteal-nan-Gillean 3	NR 357 880	x	Lacaille 1954: 214
83.	Caisteal-nan-Gillean 4	NR 357 880	x	Lacaille 1954: 214
84.	Caisteal-nan-Gillean 5	NR 357 880	x	Lacaille 1954: 214
85.	Caisteal-nan-Gillean 6	NR 357 880	x	Lacaille 1954: 214
86.	Caisteal-nan-Gillean 7	NR 357 880	x	Lacaille 1954: 214
87.	Caisteal-nan-Gillean 8	NR 357 880	x	Lacaille 1954: 214
88.	Cnoc Coig	NR 3620 8870	x	Paul Mellars, pers. comm.
89.	Druimvargie Rockshelter	NM 86 30	x	Clark 1955: 93
90.	Grays	TQ 610 770	x	Wymer 1977: 94
91.	London area		x	Wymer 1977: 411
92.	Richmond Lock and Weir	TQ 1700 7500	x	Wymer 1977: 195
93.	St John's Square, Clerkenwell	TQ 3170 8280	x	Wymer 1977: 199
94.	Strand on the Green	TQ 194 777	x	Wymer 1977: 191
95.	Walthamstow	TQ 350 880	x	Wymer 1977: 198
96.	West Row 1	TL 652 775	x	Wymer 1977: 262
97.	West Row 2	TL 652 775	x	Wymer 1977: 262
98.	Windsor 2	SU 950 770	x	Wymer 1977: 11
99.	Windsor 3	SU 950 770	x	Wymer 1977: 11

the large number from the London area being shown *en bloc*. The remaining five are without known findspots.

The antler mattocks from the British Isles may be subdivided on the basis of their raw material. It has already been noted that both elk and red deer antler were used for the manufacture of mattocks but the only elk antler mattocks known from Britain are those from Star Carr. All the other implements of this type are made from red deer antler, and it is these which form the basis of the present study. At the time of writing, this study is still underway and only a brief summary of the main points to emerge so far can be offered here. I hope on another occasion to offer a more complete consideration of the points raised and also to publish the morphological and biometric data that have been collected.

TYPOLOGY

Red deer antler mattocks may be divided into four types on morphological grounds. The fact that these are mutually exclusive, and that there is usually never any doubt as to which type any individual implement belongs, suggests that this is a valid way of subdividing the material. The four types are illustrated in *Fig. 2* and are defined as follows:

A   Antler-base mattocks

These implements are made from the basal portion of antlers truncated between the bez and trez tines. The perforation, which is in the same plane as the tines, may be through the stump of the bez tine or between it and the brow tine. Type A includes one atypical example (*Table 1*, no. 8), an unprovenanced find in

275

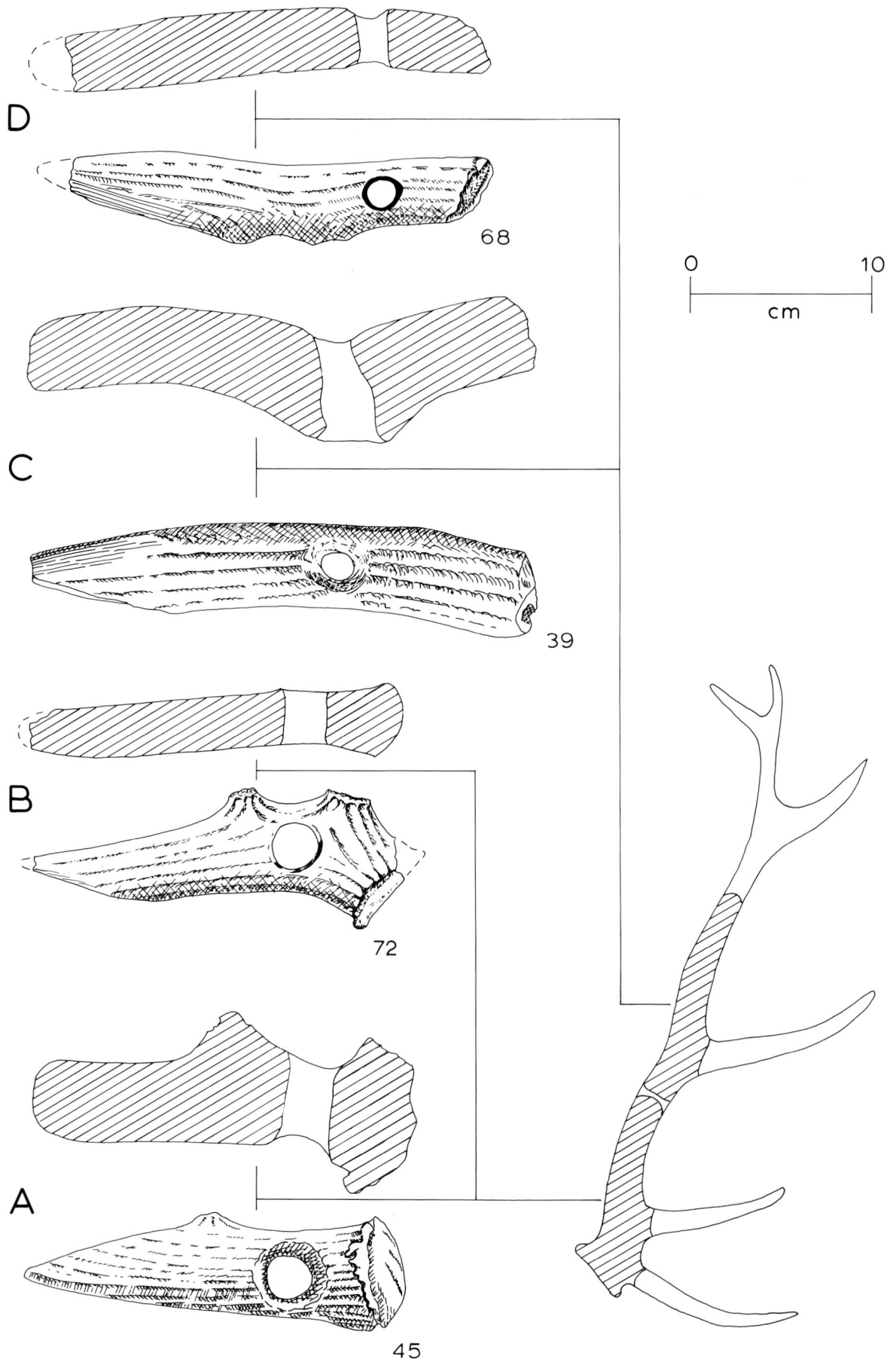

Figure 2   Types of red deer antler mattock found in Britain (numbers refer to *Table 1*).

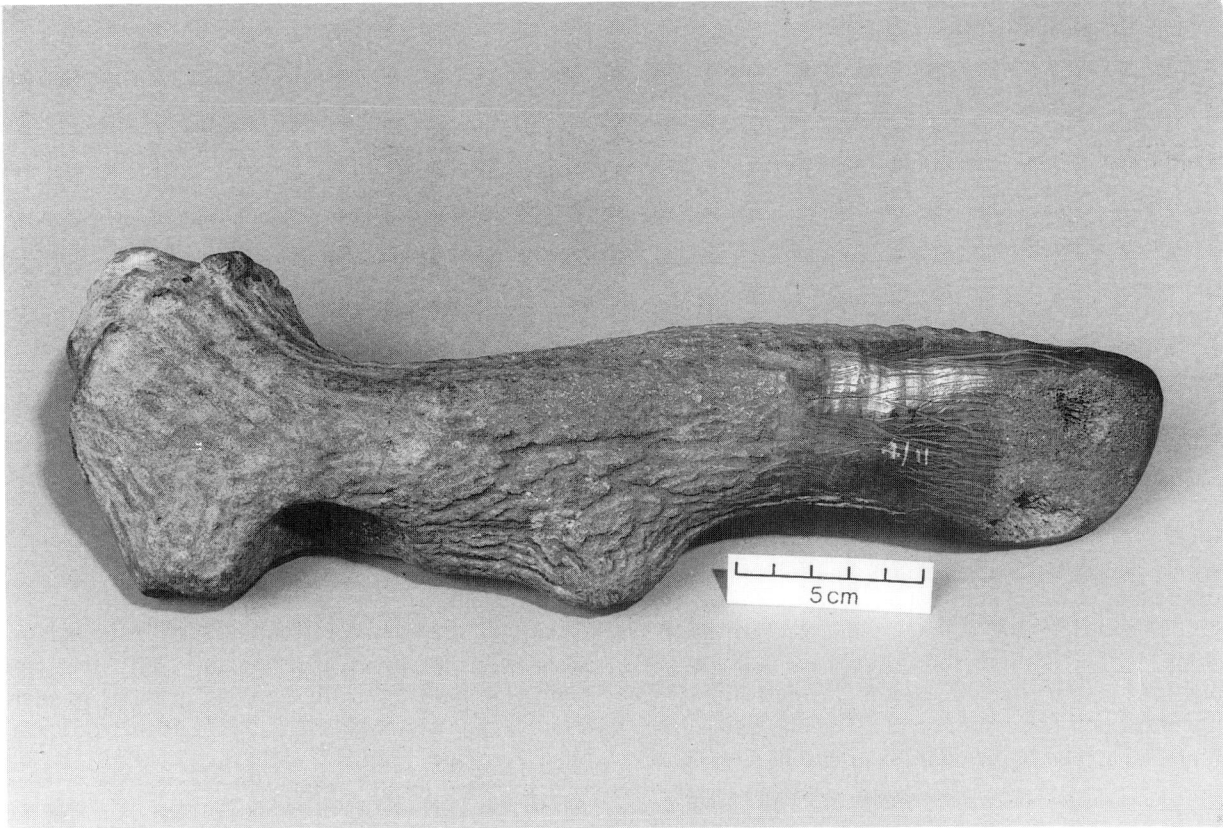

Figure 3a Antler-base mattock (Type A) from Willington Quay (*Table 1*, no. 70). Photo: University of Newcastle upon Tyne.

Figure 3b Detail of the Willington Quay mattock showing chatter marks and wear striations. Photo: University of Newcastle upon Tyne.

K

the British Museum (Natural History) which, although made from the basal portion of an antler, has its working edge formed out of the brow tine, the rest of the beam having been removed. The example illustrated in *Fig. 2A* is from New Scotland Yard, London, while *Fig. 3* shows two views of the Type A mattock from Willington Quay, Wallsend.

B Laterally perforated antler-base mattocks

These implements are similar to Type A but the perforation, which is made through the side of the beam, is at right angles to the plane of the tines. The example illustrated in *Fig. 2B* is from Windmill Lane, Brentford, while a further example, from Kew Bridge, is shown in *Fig. 4a*.

C Antler-beam mattocks

These implements are made from the beams of antlers, the basal portions of which have been removed from a point approximately midway between the bez and trez tines. They usually incorporate the stump of the trez tine and an approximately equal length of beam to either side. The perforation is made through the stump of the trez tine and in the same plane. The implement illustrated in *Figs. 2C &*

4b is from Meiklewood in the Carse of Stirling, Scotland.

D Unbalanced, or laterally perforated, antler-beam mattocks

These implements are made from much the same portion of the antler as Type C but the perforation is made close to the butt-end making a noticeably unbalanced implement. The perforation is not made through a tine stump and is usually at right angles to the plane of the tines. These implements can be of considerable length. I have handled specimens over 400 mm long but the mean size of complete examples is approximately 260 mm. Type D includes a small group of unbalanced implements made from tines as opposed to sections of beam. They are, however, so similar to the unbalanced beam implements that a separate category does not seem to be called for. The example illustrated in *Fig. 2D* is from Twickenham, while *Fig. 5a* shows a particularly long specimen from Hammersmith; *Fig. 5b* is an example of more usual length from Staines, and *Fig. 5c* is the Type D specimen from Splash Point, Rhyl.

Figure 4a Laterally perforated antler-base mattock (Type B) from Kew Bridge (*Table 1*, no.33). Photo: Museum of London.

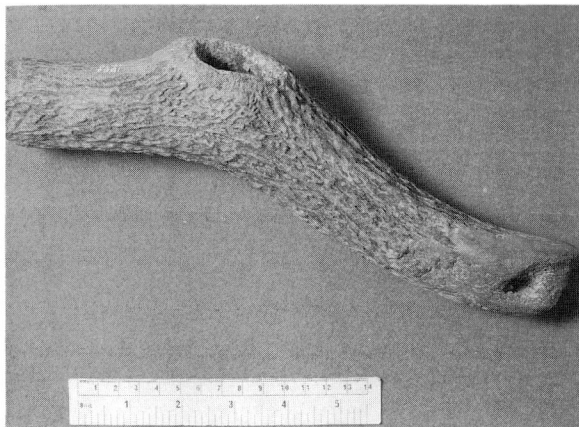

Figure 5a Unbalanced, or laterally perforated, antler-beam mattock (Type D) from the River Thames at Hammersmith (*Table 1*, no. 27). Photo: Museum of London.

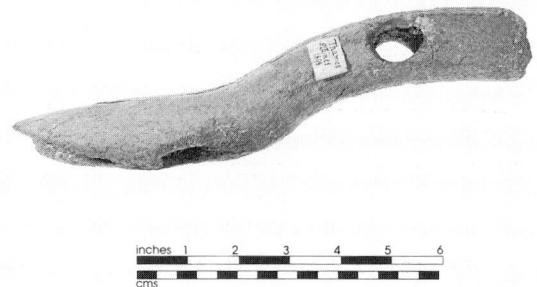

Figure 4b Antler-beam mattock (Type C) from Meiklewood (*Table 1*, no. 39). Photo: Royal Museum of Scotland.

Figure 5b Unbalanced, or laterally perforated, antler-beam mattock (Type D) from Staines (*Table 1*, no. 56). Photo: Museum of London.

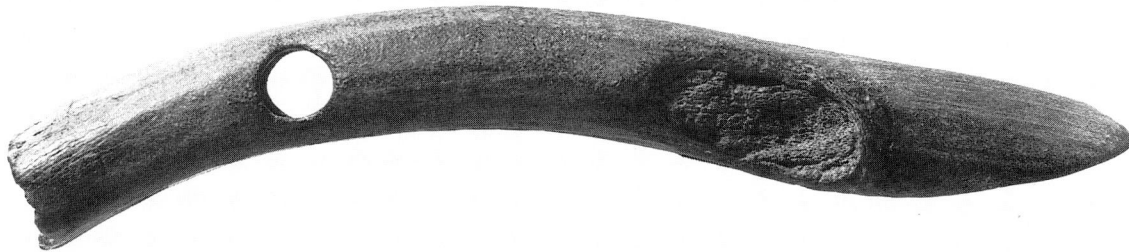

Figure 5c Unbalanced, or laterally perforated, antler-beam mattock (Type D) from Splash Point, Rhyl (*Table 1*, no. 55). Photo: National Museum of Wales.

The six elk antler mattocks from Star Carr constitute Type E. They have been included in *Table 1* and *Fig. 1* for the sake of completeness.

AFFINITIES AND DATING

Antler mattocks are a relatively common find from areas bordering the North Sea and are particularly well known from southern Scandinavia, and there seems little doubt that they are predominantly a Mesolithic type. Mattocks made from the basal portions of red deer antlers appear to have come into use around the beginning of the ninth millennium BP, superseding forms made of elk antler. Antler-base mattocks were replaced by the antler-beam variety around the middle of the sixth millennium BP, at the beginning of the Younger Ertebølle phase. This typological change, which is documented stratigraphically at sites such as Ringkloster (Andersen 1974) and Tybrind Vig (Andersen 1984), is quite abrupt and suggests that the two types fulfilled essentially the same function. On the North European Plain antler-beam mattocks appear rather earlier in the sixth millennium BP, and are known from Ertebølle (Schwabedissen 1980) and Neolithic sites (Clark 1975).

Up to the time of writing, I have found no indication among the published continental examples that the division of antler-base mattocks into two types as proposed here has any chronological significance. However, it is also true to say that all illustrations I have seen show the implements in question to be laterally perforated, that is of Type B, and that Type A appears at present to be an exclusively British variant. Most antler-beam mattocks from continental sites are of Type C and the chronological position of this type in the later Mesolithic and early Neolithic periods seems well established. Apart from two not

entirely typical examples from Hagestad in Scania (Salomonsson 1961: 18–20, fig. 10) and Pechor in southern Podolia (Semenov 1964: 181, fig. 96), the unbalanced antler-beam implements of Type D have proved difficult to parallel outside Britain. Although the Hagestad implement is unprovenanced it is decorated with what Salomonsson regards as typical Maglemose ornamentation, thus suggesting a date in the earlier part of the Mesolithic period, whereas according to Semenov the Pechor mattock was found on an Early Bronze Age settlement.

As yet no British antler mattocks have been directly dated[1] and there are only a few useful archaeological associations, such as the radiocarbon dates from Star Carr which suggest a mid-tenth millennium BP date for the elk antler mattocks from that site. Similarly, several red deer antler mattocks have been found in middens in south-west Scotland associated with assemblages of late Mesolithic 'Obanian' type at present dated, at least on the island of Oronsay, to the middle centuries of the sixth millennium BP (Mellars 1978). The implements in question appear to be of both Type C (Risga) and Type D (Cnoc Sligeach), although the latter, as an antler-tine mattock, is rather atypical.

A much less precise date may be suggested for the fine Type C mattock from Meiklewood in the Carse of Stirling (*Fig. 4b*). The carse clay of the Forth valley was deposited during the Main Postglacial Transgression and subsequent regression, deposition having commenced around 8500 BP. The surface of the carse is diachronous, the age depending on the period of abandonment of the relevant shorelines. At Meiklewood carse deposition may be estimated to have ceased prior to 4120 ± 105 BP (Sissons and Brooks 1971, site 7). However, since the Meiklewood mattock is reported as having been found within the carse

(Turner 1890) its age can only be bracketed between 8500 and 4120 BP (Smith and Bonsall 1985).

A similarly imprecise absolute date may be quoted in respect of the Type D mattock from off Splash Point, Rhyl (*Fig. 5c*). According to its label this implement was found in 'Estuarine Blue Clay'. Clays of this description have long been known off the Rhyl foreshore and are assumed to be derived from a marine inundation of a land surface. In such circumstances the implement can be assumed to have been found in a derived position. The clays in question are intercalated with two peat beds and the base of the lower of these has a radiocarbon date of 4725 ± 65 BP (J. Manley, pers. comm.). As it is not known which layer of blue clay the implement came from this date could be either a *terminus ante quem* or a *terminus post quem*; but in either case it would not be inconsistent with a dating on typological grounds to the late Mesolithic or early Neolithic.

An attempt has been made to suggest a date on palynological grounds for a Type B antler-base mattock found in the River Thames at Kew Bridge (*Fig. 4a*). According to Lacaille (1961) pollen collected from mud adhering to this implement indicated a late Boreal (Zone VI) date for its deposition. However, this must be treated as very tenuous, particularly as the implement had presumably sunk into the mud and was in a derived context. For what it is worth, such a date in the seventh millennium or the first half of the eighth millennium BP would place this implement somewhat earlier than the dated examples of Types C and D.

The size of red deer, and their antlers, is known to have declined during the course of the Flandrian and contemporary representatives of this species give a poor idea of the stature of the animals familiar to Mesolithic man. The publication of a large group of dated antler picks from the Neolithic sites of Grimes Graves and Durrington Walls (Clutton-Brock 1984) offers some possibility that other antler implements may be tentatively dated on the basis of biometric data. Neolithic antler picks were made from substantially complete antlers and Clutton-Brock was able to record measurements in respect of up to 15 characteristics (Clutton-Brock 1984: 11, fig. 3). Antler mattocks are made from parts of antlers and it was found that measurements could be collected for only three of Clutton-Brock's characteristics: numbers 2 and 15 in the case of antler-base implements, and number 10 in the case of beam implements. Even so, measurement was not possible in every case owing to the incomplete state of preservation of some implements. In the event, it proved possible to record measurements for characteristic 2, the anterior–posterior diameter of the burr and for characteristic 15, the distance from the base of the brow tine to post bez tine, in 21 cases each; and for characteristic 10, the diameter of the beam at the point where the trez tine starts, in 18 cases.

The mean measurement for characteristic 2 in respect of 11 Type A mattocks was 69.2 mm, which is very close to the mean of 68.3 mm recorded by Clutton-Brock from 276 picks from Grimes Graves (Clutton-Brock 1984). The same measurement in respect of 10 Type B mattocks was calculated as 64.3 mm and might be tentatively taken to suggest that rather smaller animals supplied the antlers used for Type B implements. Clutton-Brock does not quote a mean value in respect of characteristic 15 but the mean values for both Type A and Type B mattocks of 106 mm and 91 mm respectively lie well within the range illustrated in her diagram (Clutton-Brock 1984: fig. 9), and again it may be significant that Type B mattocks seem to be somewhat smaller than Type A in this dimension. Type C and D mattocks can be assessed only in respect of characteristic 10, their values being 45 mm and 37.7 mm respectively. Both of these values are smaller than the mean of 50 mm calculated from 228 Neolithic picks from Grimes Graves (Clutton-Brock 1984: fig. 17). This is more likely to be a reflection of the selection of robust antlers by the Grimes Graves miners than an indication that Type C and D mattocks are later in date.

However, it must be admitted that the population of mattocks from which these measurements were taken is too diverse and the number of measurements too small for these data to provide a satisfactory basis for statistical analysis. But they can be used as a basis for comparing individual antler mattocks with the dated Neolithic antler picks. For example, the Willington Quay Type A mattock (*Fig. 3a*), with a burr diameter of 90 mm and a span of 150 mm from the base of the brow tine to the distal base of the bez tine, was made from an antler considerably larger than most of the Neolithic picks. This can be taken, very tentatively, to lend support to the argument for a date earlier than Grimes Graves or Durrington Walls (Rackham, in Smith and Bonsall 1985).

From these admittedly tenuous strands of evidence it is possible to view the British antler mattocks within the following chronological framework. The earliest in the series appear to be the elk antler mattocks which were in use in the lands around the North Sea Basin during the Pre-Boreal and Boreal periods (Zones IV–VI) (Clark 1975). Star Carr is the only British site where implements of this type have been found, and the mid-tenth millennium BP radiocarbon dates are in accordance with their established chronological range. A decline in the elk population during the Boreal period meant that their antlers ceased to be available in sufficient numbers and led to the adoption of red deer antlers for the production of heavy-duty implements. The Type A and B antler-base mattocks are very similar to the longer specimens from Star Carr (i.e. EM1, EM2, and EM4;

Clark 1954: 157–9) and it may be assumed that they served a similar function. Types A and B cannot be separated chronologically at present though there is just a hint in the biometric data that Type A, which used rather larger antlers than Type B, could be earlier. Antler-base mattocks continue to be used on the European mainland down to about the mid-sixth millennium BP when they are replaced by beam implements. A similar chronological range may be accepted for the British examples, and Type C antler-beam mattocks have been dated in the north of Britain to the middle and later sixth millennium BP. The only date available for a Type D implement in Britain is the early fifth millennium BP radiocarbon date tenuously associated with the mattock from Splash Point, Rhyl. If such a date can be applied to this group as a whole, Type D mattocks would appear to lie at the end of the British series. When antler mattocks ceased to be used in Britain cannot at present be established. The fact that none, to my knowledge, have been found in Britain in contexts dated later than the Mesolithic, in spite of the excellent opportunities for preservation offered by many Neolithic and later sites, suggests that antler mattocks are a specifically Mesolithic type and that later populations had little use for them.

It is a notable feature of the distribution of the British antler mattocks (*Fig. 1*) that whereas Type C appears to be confined to the north, Types A and B have not been found outside the south east. The Type A mattock from Willington Quay on the Tyne (*Fig. 3a*) might be thought to provide an exception, but there is a good chance that this implement originated in the Thames and was brought north in a load of ballast early this century (Smith and Bonsall 1985). Type D is rather more widespread although by far the majority of implements of this kind also come from the south east where it appears to be the regional equivalent of Type C. The confinement of antler-base mattocks to the south east should not necessarily be interpreted as a cultural phenomenon. The fact is we know of virtually no pre-sixth millennium BP sites in the north where soil conditions are such that antler implements could be preserved. The polarity of the distribution pattern could be more apparent than real.

MANUFACTURE AND USE

In the absence of any systematic study by microscopy there are few observations in respect of the manufacture and use of these implements that are unlikely to need qualification or revision at some time in the future. In the meantime a few points can be made, arising mainly from my inspection of 59 antler mattocks in various museums.

The manufacture of an antler mattock involved a number of distinct operations. First, a blank had to be produced by the division of a complete antler into a number of small segments, usually a basal segment and one or more segments of beam. This process is illustrated by Clark who also illustrates a blank from Caisteal-nan-Gillean (Clark 1955: figs. 4 & 5a). Traces of this stage in the process do not usually survive on antler-base mattocks as they are removed by subsequent wear, but they can often be clearly seen at the butt-end of beam implements. To break an antler into segments it is first necessary to penetrate the hard outer layer. This is done either by the 'nibbling' technique with a flint burin as described by Clark (1954, 1956) or by sawing with a flint knife. Both techniques leave characteristic scars. Secondly, it was necessary to remove extraneous material such as tines and this was generally acomplished by the 'nibbling' method. The third stage in the process entailed the provision of the working edge and facet. This took the greatest wear in use and manufacturing traces are usually hard to detect. However, the initial formation of the facet was probably achieved by chopping away surplus antler with a stone axe. After this the surface had to be pared down to produce a fairly smooth face. This was done with a flint blade and traces of this part of the process do occasionally survive in the form of 'chatter marks' at right angles to the long axis of the implement. These can clearly be seen in the accompanying detailed photograph of the Willington Quay mattock (*Fig. 3b*) and appear in Clark's illustration of the broken Type C mattock from Risga (Clark 1955: fig. 1). The final stage in the manufacturing process involved the perforation of the implement for hafting. This again entailed cutting through the hard outer layer and was accomplished by a variety of means. Often 'nibbling' was employed but in some cases nearly rectangular segments were cut out by a variation of the grooving technique otherwise known to have been used in the production of blanks for barbed points. Grooves parallel to the main axis of the beam were scored in the surface about 20 mm apart and then others cut across these at right angles. The resulting perforation tends to be sub-rectangular or oval. A third technique employed, mainly in the formation of nearly round perforations, was drilling probably with a bow drill and flint bit. This process can be recognized from the presence of nearly circular grooves around the opening and spiral scoring within the shaft hole.

Determining the function of antler mattocks is both one of the most controversial and difficult aspects of their study, and firm conclusions will remain an impossibility until a series of these implements has been the subject of a micro-wear study. Nonetheless, some basic observations can be made which may at least reduce the area of uncertainty.

The names that have been given to these implements – axes, adzes, perforated picks, hoes, and mattocks – all have in common the implication that the implements were hafted, but not even this may be regarded as a certainty. In publishing the Type D mattock from Wormingford Bridge, Worthington Smith suggested that the perforation was not for hafting but for suspension, a view apparently shared by Charles Read of the British Museum (Smith 1898). Smith and Read based their suggestion upon the size of the perforation which at 20 mm they thought to be rather too small for a haft. Perforations of this size or smaller are not uncommon, especially amongst the Type D implements, and at one time I also entertained doubts that they were all hafted. There is, however, a good deal of evidence that the majority of the implements considered here were indeed hafted. In the first place, the careful perforation of the beam was quite unnecessary if a means of suspension was all that was required. A thong tied around the beam and with a loop attached would have been quite sufficient. Secondly, a number of the implements studied have actually broken around the perforation (*Fig. 5a*) suggesting that this was a point of particular weakness that was subject to considerable stress. The presence of a haft and the use of the implement for digging or chopping would produce just this kind of stress. Thirdly, and most importantly, several implements have been found with parts of their hafts intact. Lawrence (1929: plate VIIIb) has illustrated a fine Type B mattock from Hammersmith which was found with about 50 cm of its haft, and Turner (1890) reported that both the Blair Drummond and Meiklewood implements had small sections of their hafts *in situ* when found. The recently found Peterborough 1 mattock also retains a small section of its haft. I now have little doubt that most of the implements studied were hafted and this clearly has a bearing on any considerations of the manner in which they were used. Any implements that were not hafted cannot be described as mattocks.

Three broad categories of use have in the past been proposed for these implements: wood-working, flenching and digging. The wood-working view has given rise to the terms antler axe and antler adze to describe implements with working edges parallel with or at right angles to the haft. In the course of collecting data for this study consideration was given to this distinction and to the angle of the working edge in relation to the vertical axis of the perforation. Apart from three elk antler mattocks (Star Carr EM4, EM5, and EM6) only three other implements were found to have adze-like working edges at 90° to the haft and one of these, the implement from Grangemouth, may not be of antler. Of the 59 implements examined, 29 had working edges within 10° of the haft and in this respect could be described as axes, while 27 had edges at varying angles between 10 and 45° with a mean value of 26°. Whether these should be called axes or adzes is uncertain. No correlation has been detected between implement type and angle of cutting edge,

and it may be assumed that the latter was mainly fortuitous. When newly made these implements would have had quite sharp cutting edges and may have been suitable for some wood-working tasks including chopping, lopping and perhaps debarking as suggested by Read (Smith 1898) and Lovett (1898). However, the shape of most of these implements is quite unsuitable for use as an axe being far longer than necessary, poorly balanced and awkward to use for chopping purposes. It is also difficult to see how wood-working could produce the patterns of wear observed on many of the better preserved implements and described below.

The suggestion that these implements may have been used as flenching axes arises from the fact that three examples recorded from the Firth of Forth – Airthrey, Blair Drummond, and Meiklewood – were found with the skeletons of stranded whales (Turner 1890; Clark 1947; Lacaille 1966). The stranding of whales must have been a comparatively rare and adventitious event and is unlikely to have generated a specific type of tool. Moreover, it is difficult to imagine how the removal of blubber and soft tissue from whale carcasses could account for the wear on the facets of some of the mattocks.

This wear has been noted in three forms: a fine lustrous polish, striations which are deep and angular in profile, and flaking around the tip. Polishes have been noted on the surfaces of many of the better-preserved implements but only those on the facet or around the tip may be attributed to use. Other areas of polish may be assumed to be due to natural abrasion after deposition or to rubbing of the original antler by the deer before it was shed. The details of the wear polishes noted on the facet and at the tip of various implements are too fine to be studied except with the aid of a powerful microscope, and assessment of wear has been based on consideration of the striations which are clearly visible to the naked eye and may be seen in the detailed photograph of the Willington Quay mattock (*Fig. 3b*). These striations usually occur in roughly parallel groups of varying depth but angular profile. They are often slightly convex and this may be used to give an indication of which way up the implement was used, the convexity being towards the upper surface. These striations correspond closely to those described by Semenov (1964) on mattock-type implements of bone, walrus ivory and antler, and attributed by him to wear caused by digging in gritty soil. The polish could also have resulted from digging, but in rather finer material with a high organic content. The flaking noted at the tip of a number of implements is likely to have been caused when a large stone was struck, and it was probably the shock of such impacts which caused some mattocks to fracture around the perforation (*Fig. 5a*).

I feel the arguments for regarding these as digging

implements are strong, and it is for this reason that the term mattock has been used throughout this study. They should not be called picks for this would imply some association with quarrying or mining and lead to confusion with Neolithic antler picks of the Grimes Graves type, and the term hoe has an implication of cultivation which is probably unjustified. However, it would be a mistake to try and attribute a single function to such a wide range of implements, and it is unlikely that the long slender Type D mattocks were used for precisely the same function as the robust elk antler mattocks from Star Carr. All the British antler mattocks appear to come from coastal or riverine situations and their use may have been specifically related to activities on the river bank or foreshore such as digging for roots, aquatic plants, small animals, mollusca or bait, setting snares or fish traps, and occasionally the butchering of stranded marine mammals. But this is all conjectural and we must await the results of micro-wear studies before a more subtle interpretation of the function of British antler mattocks can be proposed.

Note:
1. A programme of AMS ^{14}C dating of antler mattocks is being undertaken jointly by the author and Clive Bonsall of the University of Edinburgh. Samples from six of the mattocks listed in *Table 1* and illustrated in *Figs. 3–5* – Hammersmith 8, Kew Bridge, Meiklewood, Splash Point, Staines, and Willington Quay – have been submitted for dating to the Oxford Radiocarbon Accelerator Laboratory. The results of this dating programme will form part of a separate publication.

Acknowledgments: I should like to thank the following individuals for help in the prosecution of this research and in the preparation of this paper: Miranda Armour-Chelu, Clive Bonsall, Andrew Foxon, Kevin Greene, Stephen Green, Maria Hinton, Elizabeth James, Avril Lansdell, Jean MacDonald, John Manley, Roger Miket, Elizabeth Owles, and Penny Robinson.

Postscript

At the Symposium Alison Roberts kindly drew my attention to an article by Noel Broadbent published in *Tor*, 17 (1975–7): 63–106. In this article, which is entitled 'Perforated stones, antlers and stone picks – evidence for the use of the digging stick in Scandinavia and Finland', Broadbent makes the interesting suggestion that the well-known antler axes and mattocks from southern Scandinavia may have been digging stick handles. Whilst some of the more balanced implements could have been suitable for use in this way, it is difficult to account for the signs of wear and tear evident on their facets, or indeed why they should have facets at all, if they were only used as handles. Broadbent appears to place less importance than I on these traces of use.

References

ANDERSEN, S.H. (1974) Ringkloster: en jysk inlandsboplads med Ertebøllekultur. *Kuml*, 1973–4: 11–108.

ANDERSEN, S.H. (1984) Tybrind Vig. *Current Archaeology*, 93: 314–317.

CLARK, J.G.D. (1954) *Excavations at Star Carr*. Cambridge, University Press.

CLARK, J.G.D. (1955) Notes on the Obanian with special reference to antler and bone work. *Proceedings of the Society of Antiquaries of Scotland*, 89: 91–106.

CLARK, J.G.D. (1975) *The Earlier Stone Age Settlement of Scandinavia*. Cambridge, University Press.

CLUTTON-BROCK, J. (1984) *Neolithic Antler Picks from Grimes Graves, Norfolk, and Durrington Walls, Wiltshire: a Biometric Analysis*. London, British Museum Publications.

GUILDHALL MUSEUM (1908) *Catalogue of the Collection of Antiquities in the Guildhall* (2nd edition). London, Guildhall Museum.

JACOBI, R.M. (1978) Northern England in the eighth millennium bc: an essay. In P. Mellars (ed.), *The Early Postglacial Settlement of Northern Europe*. London, Duckworth: 295–332.

LACAILLE, A.D. (1954) *The Stone Age in Scotland*. Oxford, University Press.

LACAILLE, A.D. (1961) Mesolithic facies in Middlesex and London. *Transactions of the London and Middlesex Archaeological Society*, 20(3): 100–150.

LACAILLE, A.D. (1966) Mesolithic facies in the transpontine fringes. *Surrey Archaeological Collections*, 66: 1–43.

LAWRENCE, G.F. (1929) Antiquities from the middle Thames. *The Archaeological Journal*, 86: 69–98.

LOVETT, E. (1898) Observations on the implement made from a deer's antler in the Museum of the Essex Field Club. *Essex Naturalist*, 10: 351–353.

NEWSTEAD, R. (1889) On the discovery of the two prehistoric horn implements at Lymm, Cheshire. *Chester Archaeological Society's Journal*, 6(2): 152–155.

SALOMONSSON, B. (1961) Some early Mesolithic artefacts from Scania, Sweden. *Meddelanden från Lunds universitets historiska museum*, 1960–61: 5–26.

SCHWABEDISSEN, H. (1981) Ertebølle/Ellerbeck – Mesolithikum oder Neolithikum in Europa? In B. Gramsch (ed.), *Mesolithikum in Europa. 2. Internationales Symposium Potsdam, 3 bis 8 April 1978 Bericht* (Veröffentlichungen des Museums für Ur- und Frühgeschichte Potsdam, 14/15). Berlin, Deutscher Verlag der Wissenschaften: 129–142.

SEMENOV, S.A. (1964) *Prehistoric Technology*. Bath, Adams and Dart.

SISSONS, J.B. and BROOKS, C.L. (1971) Dating of early Postglacial land and sea level changes in the western Forth valley. *Nature Physical Science*, 234: 124–127.

SMITH, W.G. (1898) An implement made from a stag's antler, from Wormingford, Essex. *Essex Naturalist*, 10: 310–312.

SMITH, C.A. and BONSALL, C. (1985) A red deer antler mattock from Willington Quay, Wallsend. *Archaeologia Aeliana*, 13: 203–211.

TURNER, W. (1890) On some implements of stag's horn associated with whales' skeletons found in the Carse of Stirling. *Report of the British Association for the Advancement of Science, 1889*: 789–791.

WYMER, J.J. (ed.) (1977) *Gazetteer of Mesolithic Sites in England and Wales*. London, Council for British Archaeology Research Report no. 20.

Ten Years' Research on the Mesolithic of the Belgian Lowland: Results and Prospects

P.M. Vermeersch

Abstract

Research on the Mesolithic of the Belgian lowland is hampered by a biased geographical site distribution resulting from modern exploitation systems – sod manuring, alluviation, and soil erosion. Information on palaeobotany and archaeozoology is scanty. Although some thirty radiocarbon dates are available, many problems related to dating and stylistic relationship remain to be solved. It is argued that the pedoturbatory history of the soil at each site should be looked at carefully before internal site structure can be understood. New, well-preserved sites will have to be located in order to enhance the quality of the archaeological information.

INTRODUCTION

Evaluation of the present data on the Mesolithic of the Belgian lowland has led the author to the conclusion that most of the sites, which for many years had been cited in the international literature on the Mesolithic of Belgium and of western Europe, should be discarded as of little scientific value (Vermeersch 1984). This is mainly due to the fact that most of the existing assemblages originated as surface collections over large areas. However, survey and excavation during the last decade have resulted in the discovery of many new Mesolithic sites.

Thus, in a recent search for sites of some value (Vermeersch 1984), 32 of the 38 sites mentioned by Kozłowski (1980) were rejected. There are about 40 sites (*Fig. 1*) which can be considered as of sufficient quality to be utilized in a search for understanding the Mesolithic occupation of the region in question. Well-preserved sites are even less numerous, and only a few of these – e.g. Brecht-Moordenaarsven 2, Opgrimbie-Onder de Berg 1, Opgrimbie-De Zijp 1 and 2 and Weelde-Paardsdrank 5 – are relatively undisturbed and were carefully excavated. All other sites were either severely damaged or collected from unsystematically, or else the excavation results are inaccessible. North of the Belgian lowland, in the Netherlands south of the Meuse valley, the situation is even worse. Indeed, since Bohmers' excavations which have remained unpublished, no new research has been extensively reported.

THE GEOGRAPHICAL DISTRIBUTION OF THE SITES

The Belgian lowland can roughly be divided into three main landscapes (*Fig. 1*): the northern sandy zone of the Kempen and the adjacent southern Netherlands, the transitional area with loamy sand soils, and the southern loam area.

The sandy heathlands

In the sandy area, sites are located on the highest ground in the interfluve areas. Very often these sites

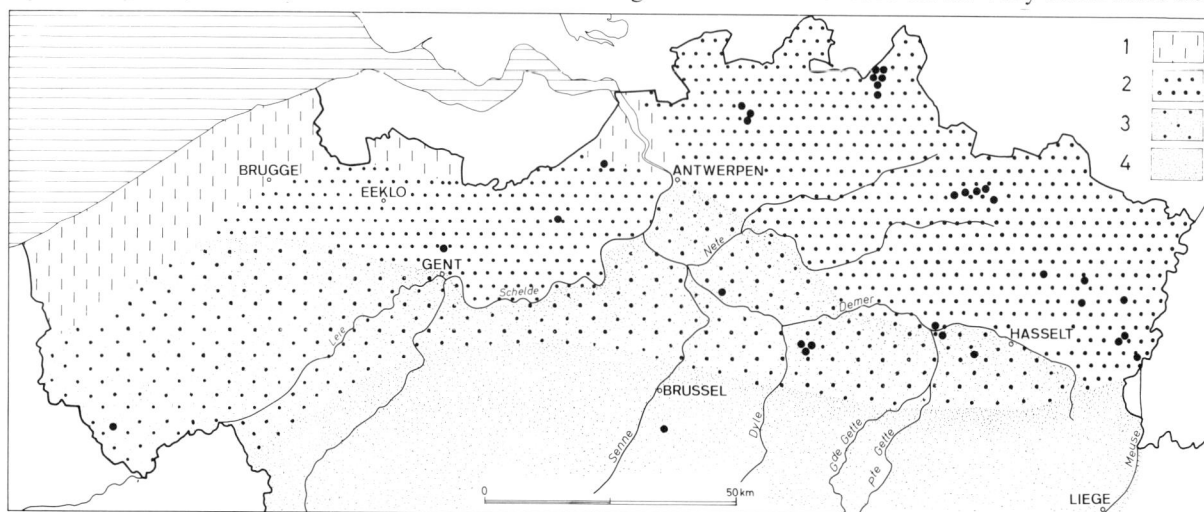

Figure 1   Mesolithic sites on the Belgian lowland. *Key*: 1 – marine clay; 2 – sand; 3 – loamy sand; 4 – loam.

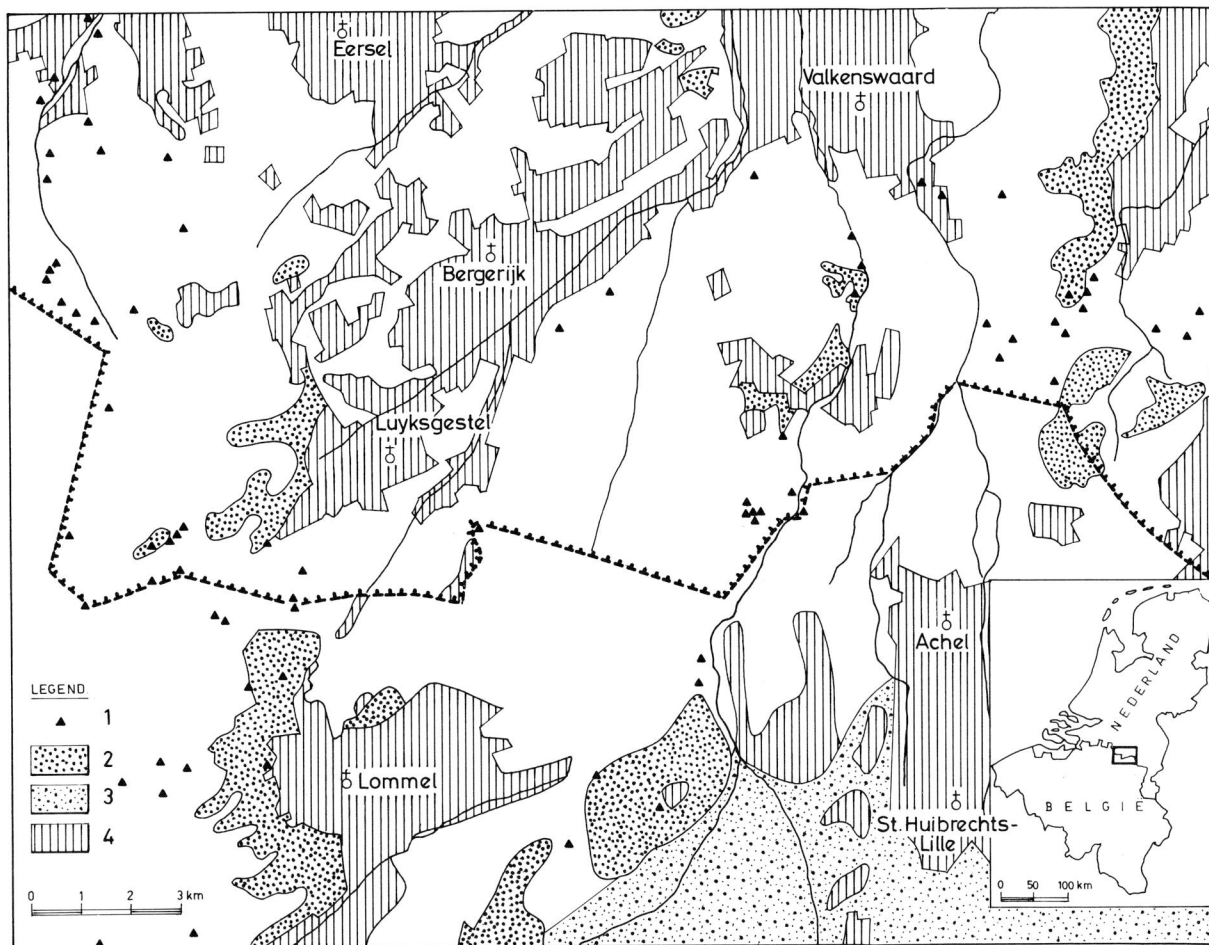

Figure 2   Mesolithic site distribution in a restricted area. *Key*: 1 – site; 2 – eroded aeolian sands; 3 – loamy sand soils; 4 – 'eerdgronden'.

are situated on Lateglacial dunes near a fen ('ven'), and usually occur in clusters. Their geomorphological position does not appear to be significantly different from that of the earlier Epi-Palaeolithic sites.

It is becoming evident that the present distribution of the sites does not necessarily reflect their original distribution. The present distribution (*Fig. 2*) is an artifact of differences in survey intensity from region to region and of the fact that large areas are forested. In addition, factors related to historical geography must be considered. Indeed, most of the sites are located on soils which have long been covered by a heath vegetation and have only recently been exploited for agriculture.

In order to understand the present site distribution it has to be taken into account that large areas of the region are covered by humic sand accumulations owing to the practice of sod manuring – known as 'esgronden' in Belgium and 'eerdgronden' in the Netherlands. These soils can be up to 50 cm or more in thickness. They extend around the present villages and are the traditional cultivated fields. As a result, it would be difficult to recover Mesolithic sites by surface survey in these areas since any sites would now be covered by thick sod-manuring

deposits. It is only recently that the utilization of deep ploughing has begun to reverse this situation. Other parts of the landscape lack the thick A2 horizon of the typical humic-iron podzol, even on dry ground. This is probably due to the same sod-cutting practice which resulted in soil truncation outside the cultivated areas. Unfortunately, the extent of these phenomena has not been adequately mapped, so that it remains incompletely understood. Taking into account the large extent of the sod-manured fields around the present villages, the distribution of the truncated soil is certainly extensive. As most of the Mesolithic sites occur within the A2 horizon of the podzols (Vermeersch 1976), it is likely that the sites on these soils were destroyed before archaeological survey was undertaken.

Therefore, the areas where Mesolithic sites have a chance of being preserved or easily discovered correspond to those which are farthest from the villages. They include the driest and poorest soils of the sandy region.

We therefore have to contend with a serious sampling bias, which renders it difficult to generalize about Mesolithic utilization of the landscape. Further survey and research will be continually hampered by this biased geographical site distribution.

The region with loamy sand soils

In the region with loamy sand soils, south of the sandy heathlands, most sites are situated in small river valleys such as those of the Winge, the Herk and the Demer. Here the agricultural situation is different. Sites on the valley margins have generally been destroyed by ploughing, as was the case with the Winge sites (Vermeersch 1972). Sometimes, however, as at Schulen 1, the sites have been covered by recent alluvial deposits, owing to sub-recent to recent soil erosion in the higher basin area. Moreover, large areas of the river valley soils are covered by grassland, thus rendering an intensive survey difficult. Taking into account all the limitations on site visibility and recovery, Mesolithic people seem to have favoured a valley edge situation for settlement location. Indeed, sites outside the valleys are rare. It is not clear if this is the result of deliberate choice by Mesolithic man, or of the impact of soil erosion processes on site preservation. Recent soil erosion surveys in the same region (H.J. De Ploey, pers. comm.) have revealed that in certain situations major soil erosion has resulted in the extensive accumulation of colluvial deposits on lower valley slopes. On the other hand, the inter-valley areas have yielded some Neolithic sites, suggesting that prehistoric sites can nevertheless survive this erosion.

The loam region

To the south of the area with loamy sand soils, Mesolithic sites are virtually unknown. I suspect that sites were located in the valley floors and are now covered by many metres of thick alluvial cover. It seems reasonable to assume that, if sites were also located on the loam slopes, they have now disappeared as a result of soil erosion. Such an hypothesis is suggested by the fact that even on very gentle slopes, Danubian sites, such as Wange (Lodewijckx 1984), show evidence of major soil erosion, resulting in the removal of nearly one metre of soil material. As it is generally accepted that loess accumulation came to an end before the beginning of the Holocene, it seems likely that Mesolithic sites, if they were present, were surface sites. Their survival up to the present time is therefore unlikely.

All these considerations have made me sceptical about the possibilities of studying the way in which the Mesolithic population utilized its geographical space. The impact of modern agriculture has been much too severe.

PALAEOBOTANY AND ARCHAEOZOOLOGY OF THE MESOLITHIC SITES

Anthracological analyses are rare. When they have been produced, the charcoal has been found to consist mainly or exclusively of pine. Some sites have proved rich in hazel-nut shells.

Palynology is informative about the vegetation of the valley floors but, for the time being, very little information is available on the vegetational history of the dry interfluvial areas during the period concerned. Palynological analyses of the artifact-bearing layers of sandy soils have always produced Sub-Boreal or Sub-Atlantic spectra, evidently too young.

In some spectra at Weelde (Munaut 1982), *Hedera* scored relatively high percentages. If we accept contemporaneity between these spectra and the late Mesolithic occupation – which has yet to be proven – the presence of *Hedera* can be attributed to disturbance of the Postglacial forest by the Mesolithic population. A similar phenomenon has been observed on some Mesolithic sites in Britain (Dimbleby 1967) and France (Planchais 1976). Troels-Smith (1960) has suggested that *Hedera* served as winter fodder. Such an interpretation implies that some kind of animal keeping was practised by the Mesolithic groups. Unfortunately, since animal bones have not been preserved in the acid soils of northern Belgium, this hypothesis cannot be evaluated.

DATING THE MESOLITHIC

Although some thirty radiocarbon dates are available for northern Belgium (*Fig. 3*) – a reasonable number compared to some other regions of similar extent in Europe – it remains difficult to discern the time limits of the Mesolithic occupation. As in other European regions, it begins sometime between 10,000 and 9000 BP. The main problem with the radiocarbon dates is that about 40% of them can be considered too young and outside the expected age range. This is probably to be attributed to the fact that the association of the Mesolithic remains with the charcoal samples is sometimes questionable. However, there are no criteria which could help us evaluate the reliability of these dates.

Some authors have favoured the idea of the survival of late Mesolithic groups after the introduction of agriculture (Newell 1973; Rozoy 1978). Radiocarbon dates and the presence of Danubian points in late Mesolithic and early Neolithic contexts were considered to provide support for this interpretation. However, the present author is still not in favour of a late dating of sites such as Weelde-Paardsdrank 1 and 5, in which trapezes represent 14–18% of the total tool count and which contain some Danubian (-like) points (Huyge and Vermeersch 1982). New accelerator dates are available for Weelde-Paardsdrank 1 on a hazel-nut fragment from the base of the vertical artifact distribution – 8160±150 BP (OxA-141), 7090±150 BP (OxA-142)

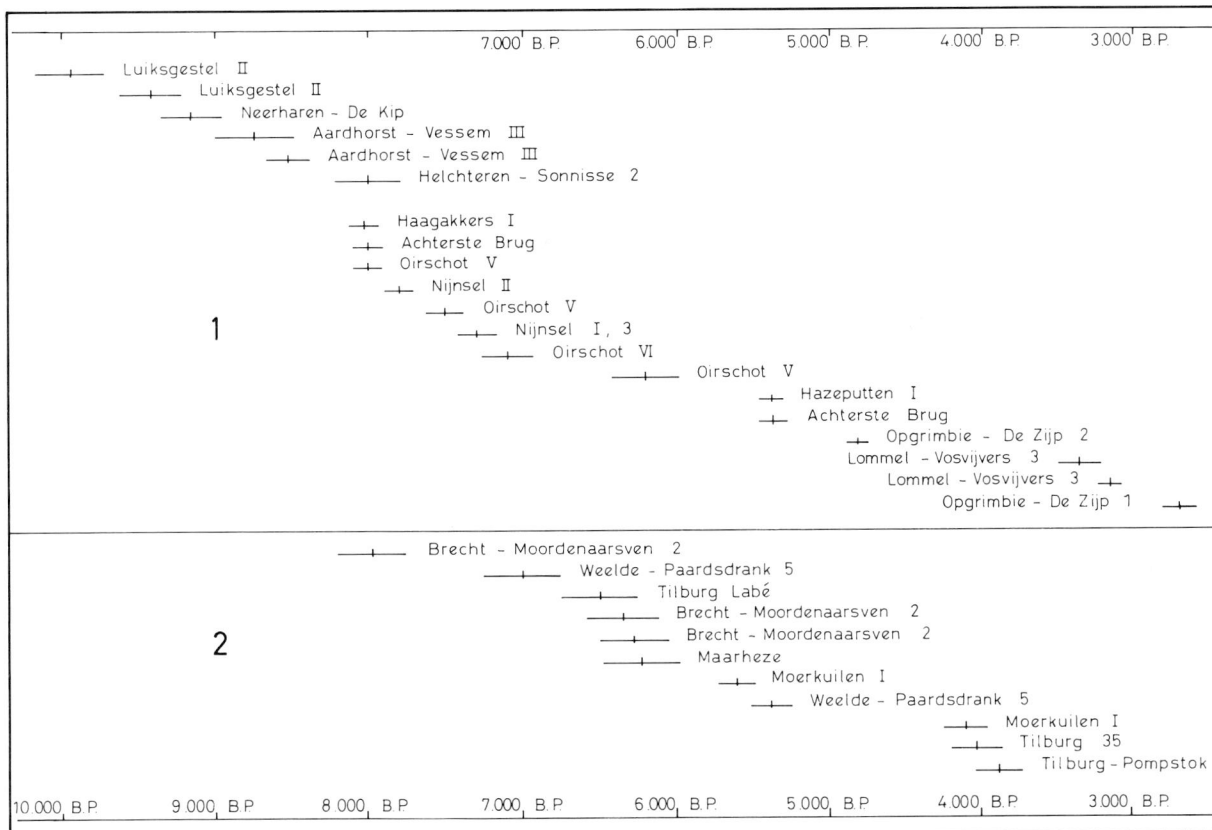

Figure 3   Radiocarbon dates for Belgian Mesolithic sites (±2s). *Key*: 1 – sites without trapezes; 2 – sites with trapezes.

and 3330±130 BP (OxA-143) – the first being the most secure date for the hazel-nut (Gillespie *et al.* 1985). If one accepts the association between the hazel-nut and the lithic material, it proves that such late Mesolithic sites predate the introduction of the Danubian. Moreover, it is important to stress the significant differences in flaking techniques that exist between the Mesolithic and the Danubian (Vermeersch 1982).

There is certainly some evidence for a late Mesolithic occupation of the region. It is conspicuous indeed that in some middle Neolithic sites a microlithic component is always present. This could be observed at Michelsberg sites such as Le Gué du Plantin (De Heinzelin, Haesaerts and De Laet 1977) and Thieusies-Ferme de l'Hosté (Vermeersch and Walter 1980), where typical bladelets of clearly Mesolithic affinities were produced on the site (Vermeersch, in press). The increased utilization of thumbnail scrapers on late Neolithic sites such as Geistingen-Huizerhof (Heymans and Vermeersch 1983) or Koningsbosch (Van Haaren and Modderman 1973) could be interpreted as an influence or an acculturation of a local Mesolithic population, whereas the Danubian was fully intrusive. Even if the range of late Mesolithic hunter-gatherers was confined to the poorer (for agriculture) sandy soils, it would be difficult to justify using the radiocarbon dates from that region (e.g. Lommel-Vosvijvers) to suggest the existence of Mesolithic groups during the

Bronze Age. It is always possible that the two concordant dates of *c.* 3300 BP are from two intrusive hearths relating to a Bronze Age occupation, even if in the broader surroundings of the site no Bronze Age remains have been discovered to date.

Hopefully, with increasing numbers of radiocarbon dates, this dating problem will have a solution; although a secure correlation between charcoal and Mesolithic occupation will perhaps always remain problematical.

SITE STRUCTURES

Wood and Johnson (1978) have stated that:

> a reasonably accurate assessment of the pedoturbatory history of the soils and sediments at every archaeological site is absolutely prerequisite to valid archaeological interpretations (1978: 370).

Everybody who has been excavating in the sandy soils of northern Belgium will agree with this statement. Indeed, in such soils the artifacts are dispersed through the different horizons of the Holocene soil profile, normally a humic-iron podzol. Pedoturbation must be held responsible for this vertical distribution. It is generally accepted that the processes responsible for the formation of the present soil are of much younger age than the Mesolithic occupation.

Occasionally, during the excavations, one gains

Square H1; West section

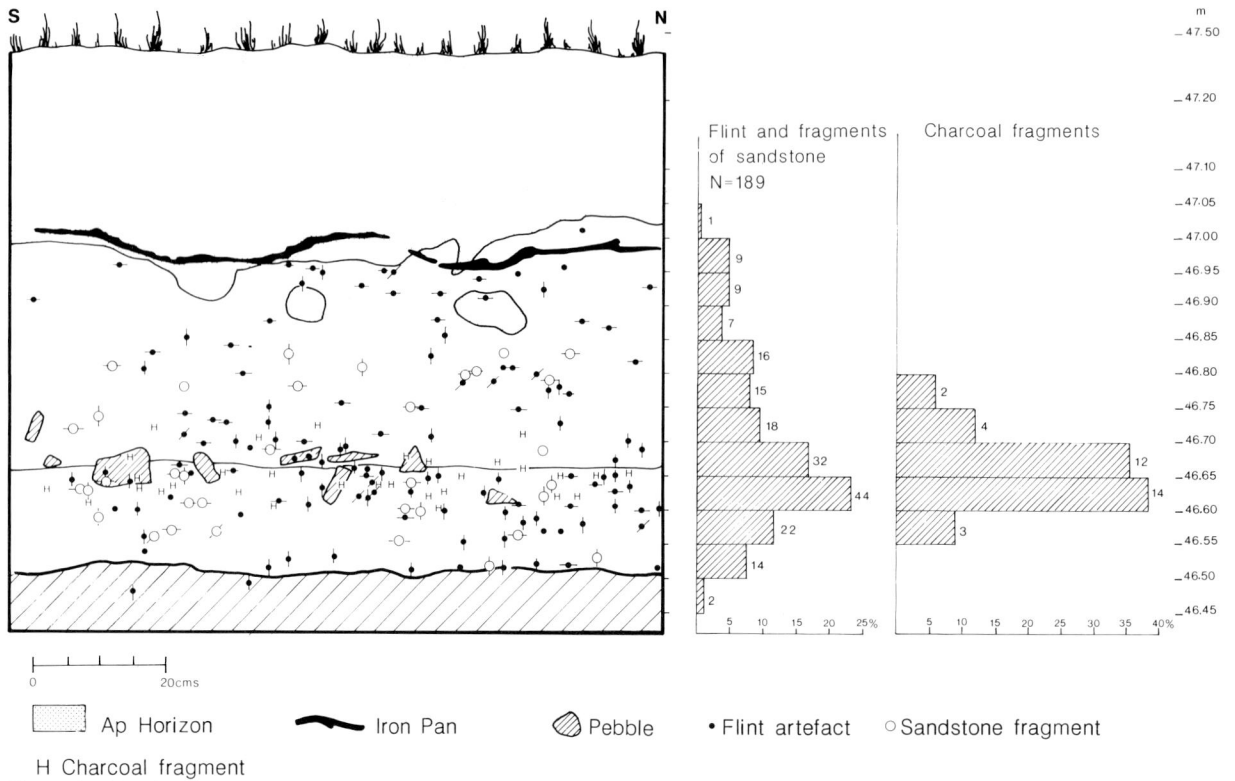

Figure 4   Neerharen-De Kip: section of square H1 showing vertical distribution of artifacts. Their inclination is indicated by a bar (after Lauwers and Vermeersch 1982).

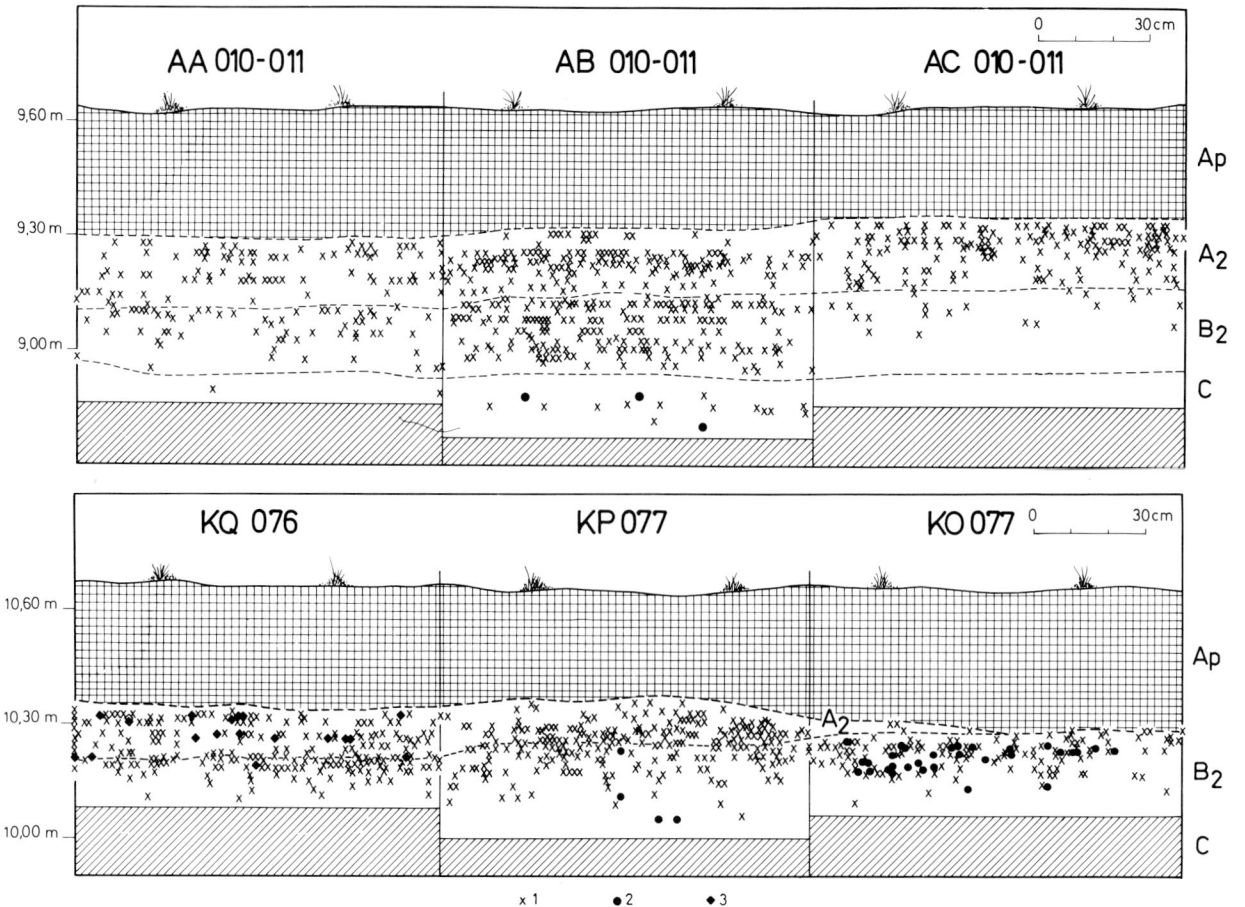

Figure 5   Weelde-Paardsdrank: sections from squares in Sector 1 (upper) and Sector 5 (lower), with superimposed: 1 – stone artifacts; 2 – hazel-nut shells; 3 – charcoal (after Huyge and Vermeersch 1982).

288

the impression that the original occupation surface can be traced by the position of large manuports such as hearth stones, which generally coincides with the level of maximum artifact concentration. This was the situation at the site of Neerharen-De Kip (*Fig. 4*). There, it was clear that the Mesolithic occupation level was covered by aeolian sand. On other sites, however, such as Weelde-Paardsdrank 5 (*Fig. 5*), it is not possible to draw such a conclusion and the original occupation horizon cannot be traced. This is the case on the majority of sites.

In general, pedoturbation seems to have resulted in downward movement of the artifacts within the soil profile, but occasionally movement seems to have been in the opposite direction.

In situations where there was reoccupation of the same site (as was probably often the case), pedoturbation has resulted in mixing together of the archaeological remains of the different occupations. Therefore, great care is needed in interpreting the intra-site horizontal patterning of the archaeological material unless it can be established that one is analyzing the remains of a single occupation. But how can one be sure? A very small occupation scatter can be an indication that the site was occupied for only a very restricted period. In these situations, only a limited aspect of the total material culture may be present, thus limiting the scope for inter-site typological and technological comparisons. Such small occupation sites may also be the result of specialized activity. It seems to me, therefore, that it will always be difficult to make judgements about the homogeneity of the excavated material of larger sites.

Except for some hearth features, such as those at Opglabbeek-Ruiterskuil (Vermeersch 1982), attempts to collect new data about Mesolithic structures have so far proved unsuccessful.

THE ARCHAEOLOGICAL MATERIALS

Studies on technology and tool type frequencies of the regional Mesolithic have led to different classificatory schemes such as those by Bohmers (Bohmers and Wouters 1956), Narr (1968), Newell (1973), Arora (1976), Rozoy (1978), J. and S. Kozłowski (1979), Gob (1981), and Gendel (1982). It is difficult to adopt and work with any of these schemes because the definitions of the different taxonomic groupings are too vague and cannot be used for reconstructing the history of the Mesolithic occupation of the Belgian lowland.

It is clear that the north Belgian materials fit quite well in the west and central European Mesolithic. But some distinctive features can also be found, such as the use of flat bifacial retouch on the leaf-shaped points ('feuilles de gui').

Gendel (1984) has shown that differences in assemblage composition between the various 'cultures' are of little diagnostic value. If we add to his mostly stylistic considerations the difficulties of isolating homogeneous entities and of dating the different occupations, my hesitation towards a taxonomic approach can be understood. It is, of course, always possible to define taxonomic groups based on the typological differences between the sites. But what is the meaning of such groups? Are they cultural, chronological, or functional? Perhaps a first step toward solving this problem is to understand the empirical distribution of typological and stylistic elements (e.g. Gendel 1984), rather than to force ill-defined data-sets within preconceived notions of cultural taxonomy.

CONCLUSIONS

Excavations of many new sites in northern Belgium have provided a considerable amount of new data. Unfortunately, these excavations have not provided answers to the many questions we have to face. It seems to me that some of the problems, especially those related to geographical site distribution and internal site structure, will remain unsolved. Others, especially those related to dating and stylistic relationships, are, if we are lucky in locating good new sites, capable of solution.

Acknowledgement: I should like to thank Peter Gendel and Clive Bonsall for correcting the English of my original text.

References

ARORA, S. (1976) Die mittlere Steinzeit im westlichen Deutschland und in den Nachbargebieten. In *Beiträge zur Urgeschichte des Rheinlandes*, 2. Köln, Rheinische Ausgrabungen 17: 1–65.

BOHMERS, A. and WOUTERS, A. (1956) Statistics and graphs in the study of flint assemblages. III. A preliminary report on the statistical analysis of the Mesolithic in north-western Europe. *Palaeohistoria*, 5: 27–38.

DE HEINZELIN, J., HAESAERTS, P. and DE LAET, S.J. (1977) *Le Gué du Plantin, Site Néolithique et Romain*. Bruges, Dissertationes Archaeologicae Gandenses 17.

DIMBLEBY, G.W. (1967) *Plants and Archaeology*. London, John Baker.

GENDEL, P. (1982) An analysis of stylistic variation in some late Mesolithic assemblages from northwestern Europe. *Bulletin de la Société royale belge d'Anthropologie et de Préhistoire*, 93: 51–62.

GENDEL, P. (1984) *Mesolithic Social Territories in Northwestern Europe*. Oxford, British Archaeological Reports (International Series) S218.

GILLESPIE, R., GOWLETT, J.A.J., HALL, E.T., HEDGES, R.E.M. and PERRY, C. (1985) Radiocarbon dates from the Oxford AMS system: Archaeometry datelist 2. *Archaeometry*, 27: 237–246.

GOB, A. (1981) *Le Mésolithique dans le Bassin de l'Ourthe* (Mémoire de la Société wallonne de Palethnologie, 3). Liège, Presses Universitaires.

HEYMANS, H. and VERMEERSCH, P.M. (1983) Siedlungsspuren aus Mittel- und Spätneolithikum, Bronzezeit und Eisenzeit in Geistingen, Huizerhof. *Archaeologia Belgica*, 255: 15–64.

HUYGE, D. and VERMEERSCH, P.M. (1982) Late Mesolithic settlement at Weelde-Paardsdrank. In P.M. Vermeersch (ed.), *Contributions to the Study of the Mesolithic of the Belgian Lowland* (Studia Praehistorica Belgica, 1). Tervuren, Koninklijk Museum voor Midden-Afrika: 115–209.

KOZŁOWSKI, J. and KOZŁOWSKI, S.K. (1979) *Upper Palaeolithic and Mesolithic in Europe. Taxonomy and Palaeohistory* (Prace Komisji Archeologicznej 18). Wrocław, Polska Akademia Nauk.

KOZŁOWSKI, S.K. (1980) *Atlas of the Mesolithic in Europe (First Generation Maps)*. Warsaw, University Press.

LAUWERS, R. and VERMEERSCH, P.M. (1982) Un site du Mésolithique ancien à Neerharen-De Kip. In P.M. Vermeersch (ed.), *Contributions to the Study of the Mesolithic of the Belgian Lowland* (Studia Praehistorica Belgica, 1). Tervuren, Koninklijk Museum voor Midden-Afrika: 15–52.

LODEWIJCKX, M. (1981) De Bandkeramische Nederzetting te Wange. *Notae Praehistoricae*, 1: 26–27.

MUNAUT, A.V. (1982) Analyses palynologiques. In P.M. Vermeersch (ed.), *Contributions to the Study of the Mesolithic of the Belgian Lowland* (Studia Praehistorica Belgica, 1). Tervuren, Koninklijk Museum voor Midden-Afrika: 139–143.

NARR, K. (1968) *Studien zur älteren und mittleren Steinzeit der Niederen Lande*. Bonn, Habelt.

NEWELL, R. (1973) The Post-glacial adaptions of the indigenous population of the Northwest European Plain. In S.K. Kozłowski (ed.), *The Mesolithic in Europe*. Warsaw, University Press: 399–440.

PLANCHAIS, N. (1976) La végétation au Pleistocène supérieur et au début de l'Holocène dans le Bassin de Paris et les plaines de la Loire moyenne. In H. de Lumley (ed.), *La Préhistoire Française*, tome 1. Paris, Centre National de la Recherche Scientifique: 534–538.

ROZOY, J-G. (1978) *Les Derniers Chasseurs. L'Epipaléolithique en France et en Belgique*. Bulletin de la Société archéologique champenoise, numéro spécial. Charleville, J-G. Rozoy.

TROELS-SMITH, J. (1960) Ivy, mistletoe and elm. Climate indicators – fodder plants. A contribution to the interpretation of the pollen zone border VII–VIII. *Danmarks geologiske Undersøgelse*, Series IV, 4: 4–32.

VAN HAAREN, H.M.E. and MODDERMAN, P.J.R. (1973) Ein mittelneolithischer Fundort unter Koningsbosch. *Analecta Praehistorica Leidensia*, 6: 7–49.

VERMEERSCH, P.M. (1972) *Twee Mesolithische sites te Holsbeek*. Brussels, Archaeologia Belgica 138.

VERMEERSCH, P.M. (1976) La position lithostratigraphique et chronostratigraphique des industries épipaléolithiques et mésolithiques en Basse Belgique. *Congrès Préhistorique de France, 20ᵉ session. Provence, 1974*: 616–621.

VERMEERSCH, P.M. (ed.) (1982) *Contributions to the Study of the Mesolithic of the Belgian Lowland* (Studia Praehistorica Belgica, 1). Tervuren, Koninklijk Museum voor Midden-Afrika.

VERMEERSCH, P.M. (1984) Du Paléolithique au Mésolithique dans le nord de la Belgique. In D. Cahen and P. Haesaerts (eds), *Peuples Chasseurs de la Belgique Préhistorique dans leur Cadre Naturel*. Brussels, Institut royal des Sciences naturelles de Belgique: 181–193.

VERMEERSCH, P.M. (in press) Le Néolithique moyen en Belgique. In D. Cahen, A. Cahen-Delhaye and R. Langohr (eds), *Peuples Agriculteurs de la Belgique Préhistorique dans leur Cadre Naturel*. Brussels, Institut royal des Sciences naturelles de Belgique.

VERMEERSCH, P.M. and WALTER, R. (1980) *Thieusies, ferme de l'Hosté, site Michelsberg*. Brussels, Archaeologia Belgica 230.

WOOD, R. and JOHNSON, D.L. (1978) A survey of disturbance processes in archaeological site formation. In M.B. Schiffer, W.R. Wood and D.L. Johnson (eds), *Advances in Archaeological Method and Theory*, 1: 315–381.

Archaeology, Environment and the Social Evolution of Later Band Societies in a Lowland Area

Nico Arts

Abstract

Using geological, radiocarbon and typological evidence, six evolutionary stages are distinguished for the final Palaeolithic and Mesolithic of the southern Netherlands (*c.* 12,400–6000 BP). In order to indicate long-term variation in the available environmental and archaeological record, the relevant evidence is summarized thematically. This data-set provides tangible evidence for social evolution. Six evolutionary components are identified and expressed as indices: temperature, primary productivity of the environment, population density, exchange, settlement variation and territorial intensification; several of them appear to be statistically interrelated. Comparing the indices for successive stages, decreasing values are true for three stages, suggesting that several collapses of the social system occurred, evidenced by: (a) a marked reduction in population density during two stages (the early Mesolithic and, probably, the early Neolithic) and a decrease in the volume of exchange; and (b) an increase in the proportion of smaller settlements during these same stages, from which a decrease in the size of individual residence groups may be inferred, which probably indicates a fragmentation of social organization. During two stages these decreases contrast with the increasing values of the environmental components that indicate more 'favourable' conditions.

A tentative explanatory hypothesis is formulated in order to explain the observed collapses. Most collapses may have been caused by social stress, due to persistent stressors. Three possible persistent stressors are discussed: a natural disaster, overspecialization, and an immigration.

INTRODUCTION AND PROBLEM FORMULATION

This paper is an attempt to explore the topic of social evolution. It is concerned with lithic assemblages left by later band societies, with special reference to a specific study area. For the purpose of this exploration, social evolution is defined as the cumulative effect of dynamic change, with the probability that social systems will become increasingly complex. Complexity refers to variables (or components) which should intensify as social evolution proceeds. These components are measured by indices which incorporate the expected degree and direction of intensification. The model of social evolution may be thought of as an indefinable set of components which interact together to form change. The term *band societies* used in the title of this paper refers to final Palaeolithic and Mesolithic hunter-gatherers; the adjective *later* is used to distinguish them from earlier (e.g. Middle Palaeolithic) band societies.

Following Newell (1984) on Mesolithic social evolution, this paper has two objectives. The primary objective is to identify those evolutionary components which leave tangible and quantifiable environmental and archaeological remains. This will be presented in such a way that the more important differences can be assessed, so that statements can be made about the comparative complexity of archaeological stages. The second objective is to generate a tentative explanatory hypothesis for the more conspicuous patterns which emerge from this presentation.

The study area is a portion of the Northwest European Plain, encompassing most of the southern Netherlands. This area was occupied throughout much of prehistory, but it will be demonstrated that the Lateglacial and early Holocene are to be considered as one chronologically well-defined sequence of archaeological stages. The existing body of information will demonstrate a series of differing components, which justify a consideration of prehistoric social evolution in more precise terms than has generally been attempted.

The rate and level of social evolution depends on the interrelationship of components, and one obvious path towards the understanding of social evolution is through its simplified components. From a close study of their working and interactions, the behaviour of rates and levels may be analyzed (Naroll 1956; Carneiro 1970; Tatje and Naroll 1970; Berreman 1981). Such is the perspective of systems theory (cf. Wenke 1981), and such a strategy has been suggested for archaeology by a number of authors (Clarke 1978; Jochim 1979; Ellen 1982). For band societies, including later prehistoric ones, a number of specific evolutionary components, some of which are considered as causal, have been discussed, implicitly or explicitly, in relation to social evolution. These include subsistence activities and environmental factors (Mikkelsen 1978; Hayden 1981; Bahn 1983; Bailey 1983), demographic patterns (Harris 1977; Clark and Straus 1983; Constandse-Westermann, Newell and Meiklejohn 1984; Newell and Constandse-Westermann 1986), ornaments and arts (Conkey 1980; Gamble 1983; Jochim 1983), technology (Gouldner and Peterson 1962; Oswalt 1973; Boserup 1981), exchange (Conkey 1978; Moore 1981; Van der Leeuw 1981; Gamble 1983; Root 1983), settlement variation (David 1973; Newell 1973; Mellars 1976; Conkey 1980), and burial analysis (Alekshin 1983; O'Shea and Zvelebil 1984).

In the present study, six components will be discussed: two environmental components, population density, exchange, settlement variation and territorial intensification, while there is also some evidence for changes in land use. The archaeological record from the study area also provides data on technological change and on ornaments and arts, but, as will become apparent, technological change is minimal and difficult to quantify, and data on ornaments and arts are too scarce.

As this paper deals with prehistoric remains, this in itself imposes severe limitations on any work of a more general nature that, beyond description, attempts to approach archaeological remains as a residue of social behaviour. Therefore, this paper should be considered as a provocative attempt at understanding change in past life-ways.

THE STUDY AREA: GEOLOGICAL AND ENVIRONMENTAL EVIDENCE

The area considered in the present study corresponds to the southern part of the lower catchment of the River Meuse; it includes the southern Dutch provinces of North Brabant and Limburg, and has a surface area of 7400 km^2 (Figs. 1 & 2). This area has been selected for study because it contains a high number, as well as a high diversity, of relevant prehistoric sites. For practical reasons, such as access to archaeological data, the borders of this region are the current political borders of the above-mentioned provinces. In the south the limit corresponds roughly with the watershed of the rivers Meuse and Schelde; the entire northern limit is formed by the course of the Meuse.

The area is predominantly flat and tilts down towards the north; a similar, but less pronounced decline, occurs to the west (Fig. 3). The entire region is well watered with rivers, streams and fens, the major river drainages flowing north and east to the River Meuse. A striking feature is the contrast between the loess-covered hills and plateaus in the south, which cover an area of c. 600 km^2, and the

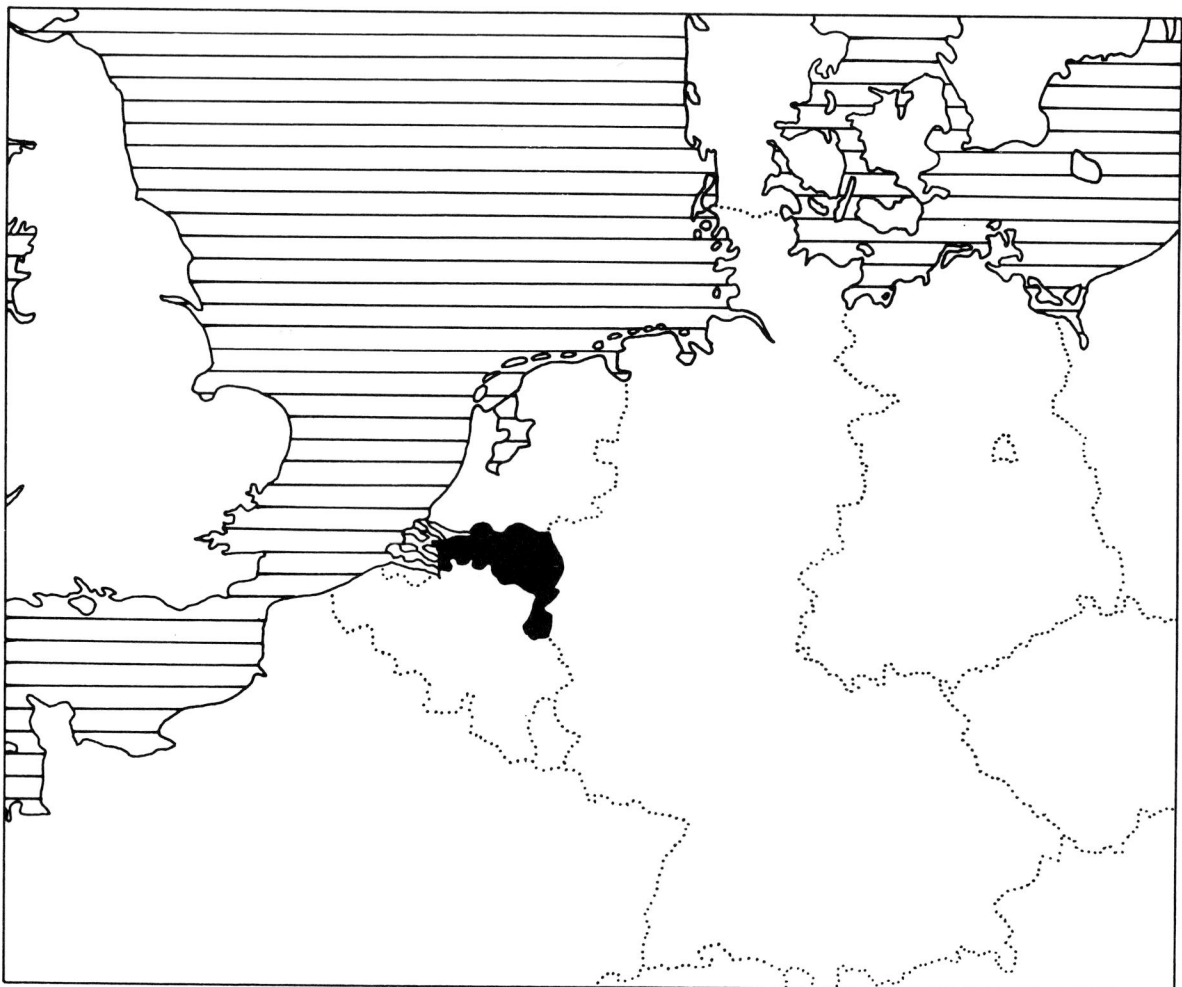

Figure 1   Location of the study area.

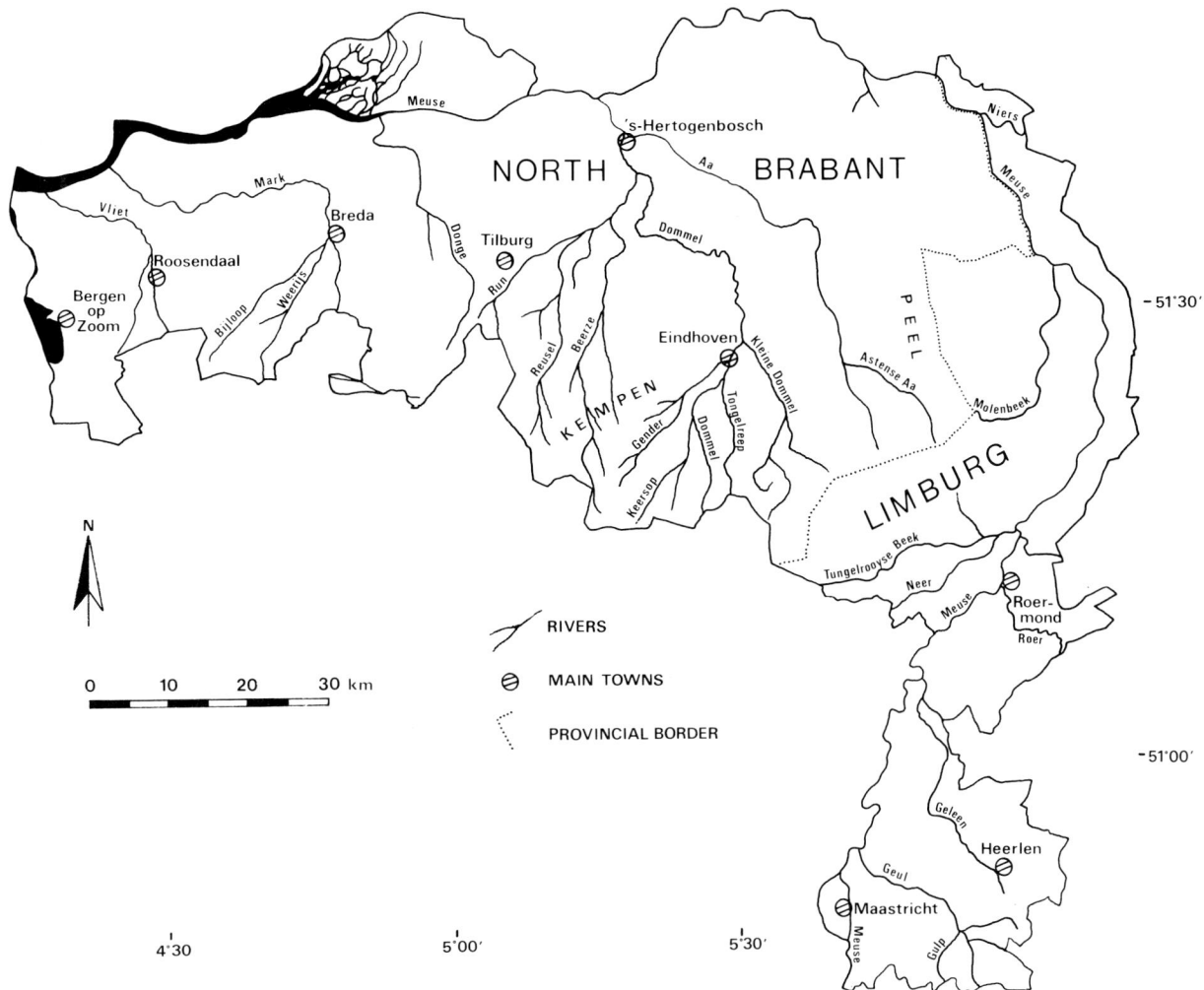

Figure 2 Major river systems and modern towns in the study area.

sandy lowland plain in the north with a surface area of *c.* 6100 km^2. As will be demonstrated, this division is also reflected in vegetation successions and in the archaeological record.

Geologically, the area is very young (*Fig. 4*). The greater part of the modern landscape is dominated by aeolian deposits up to four metres thick (Van den Toorn 1967), in which podzolic soils have developed. In the north west these aeolian deposits are covered by mainly post-Atlantic marine clay deposits; hence this region, with an area of *c.* 700 km^2, is excluded from the present study. In the south there are occasional outcrops of Cretaceous and Tertiary deposits, generally containing flint (Kuyl 1980). In the extreme north east there is a Middle Pleistocene ice-pushed ridge that is not covered by younger deposits. Middle Pleistocene coarse-grained sandy deposits occur at, or close to, the surface especially in river valleys. These deposits contain gravel, including flint.

The greater part of the area is a coversand landscape. Coversands were deposited during different periods, and the ideal coversand stratigraphy is as follows:

1. The lowermost stratum is generally a Pleni-glacial loamy or gravel deposit (Bisschops 1973).

2. Most older coversand I was deposited during the Upper Pleniglacial and is characterized by solifluction and frost wedges (Bisschops 1973). In a number of places, elongate coversand ridges were deposited (*Fig. 4*), some of them diagonally across river valleys, leading to diversions of river channels. These ridges were accentuated by later coversand deposition.

3. The Beuningen layer is characterized by a thin layer of rounded gravel. It originates from Upper Pleniglacial sand drifts, when fine-grained material was blown away and coarse-grained material was left behind on the surface. It is a type of arctic desert pavement, and indicates a dry, high-arctic environment (Van der Hammen *et al.* 1967).

4. The older coversand II was deposited during the final Upper Pleniglacial. It is characterized by thin, horizontally-layered loamy beds (Van den Toorn 1967), which may be deposited by alternating wet and dry surfaces during sedimentation (Van der Hammen 1952).

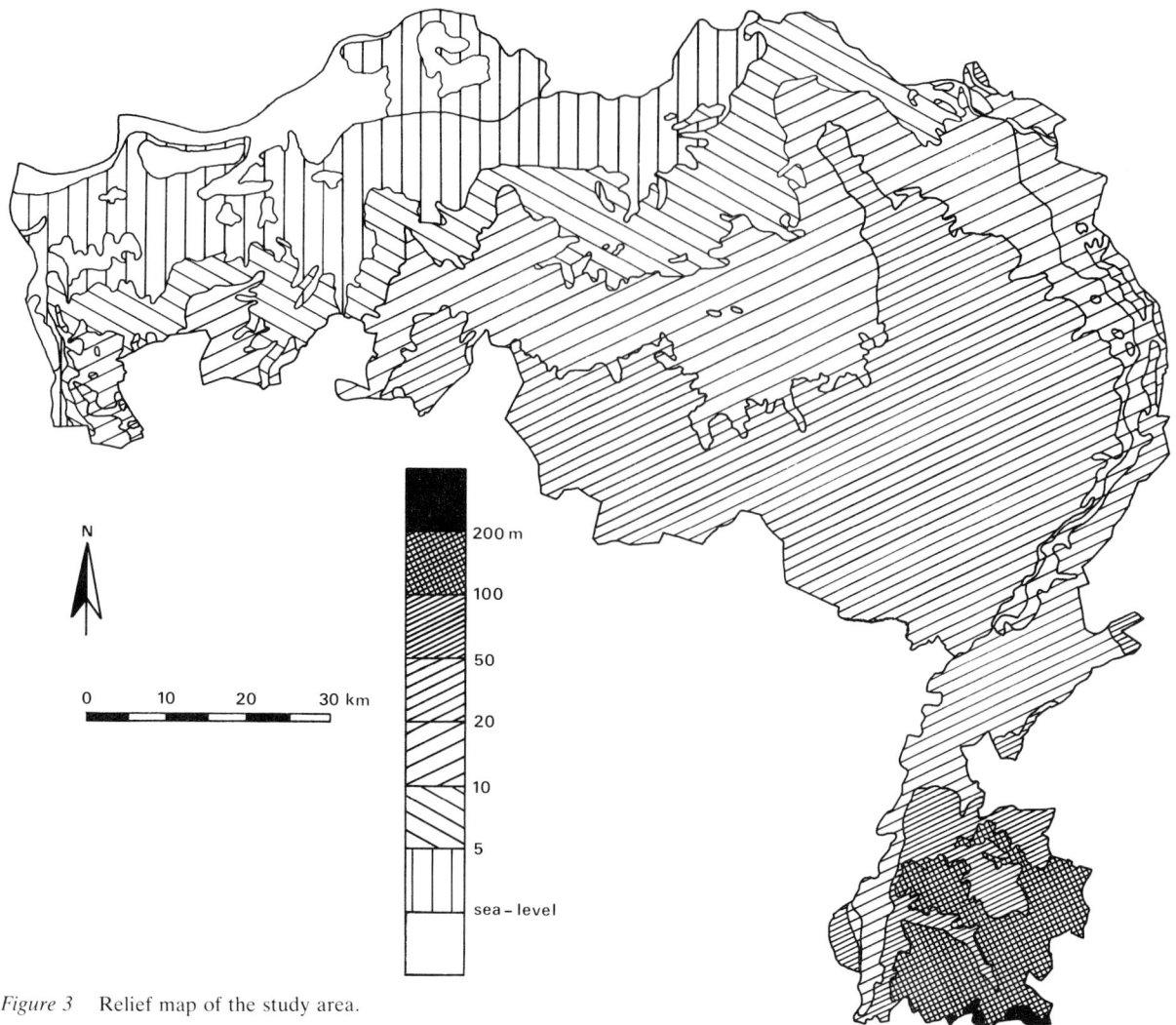

Figure 3 Relief map of the study area.

5. A loamy coversand layer marks the transition between older coversand and younger coversand, and presumably represents a soil formed during the Bølling Interstadial.

6. Younger coversand I was deposited during the Older Dryas, carried by prevailing west-north-west winds (Maarleveld 1960); generally it contains frost wedges (Bisschops 1973).

7. The Usselo layer, a bleached 10–20 cm thick soil with small lumps of fir charcoal in it (Van den Toorn 1967), represents a soil from the Allerød Interstadial. It is believed that the charcoals in it are remains of extended forest fires sparked by intense volcanic eruptions of the Laacher See in the German Eifel *c.* 11,030 BP (Bosinski 1983). In the study area carbonized twigs or trunks are never present; this suggests deposition of the charcoal by wind (Van den Toorn 1967).

8. Younger coversand II was deposited during the Younger Dryas and is often characterized by finger-shaped structures. According to Brussaard and Runia (1984) these structures represent fossil tunnels dug by dung-beetles. Younger coversand II was

deposited by prevailing west-south-west winds (Maarleveld 1960).

Coversands were also deposited during the early Holocene but, owing to the increased vegetational mat over much of the land surface, their source was primarily restricted to periodically dry river beds. Archaeological evidence indicates that coversand deposition continued at least into the Atlantic (Bisschops 1973). During the Sub-Boreal and Sub-Atlantic sand-drift areas began to develop, due to clearance of vegetation. Therefore, coversands may be covered by a layer of blown sand up to a metre thick. Such wind-blown sands frequently contain thin horizontal organic layers, which are the remnants of buried soils.

This description of coversand stratigraphy is idealized and, so far, the only complete sequence known to the author is from Tilburg (Arts, in press *a*). In most areas several layers are missing, owing to Lateglacial and Holocene erosion or to modern human activities. In the southern hilly region loess deposits do not record such detailed Lateglacial/Holocene stratigraphy.

Before reclamation, the coversand landscape was

294

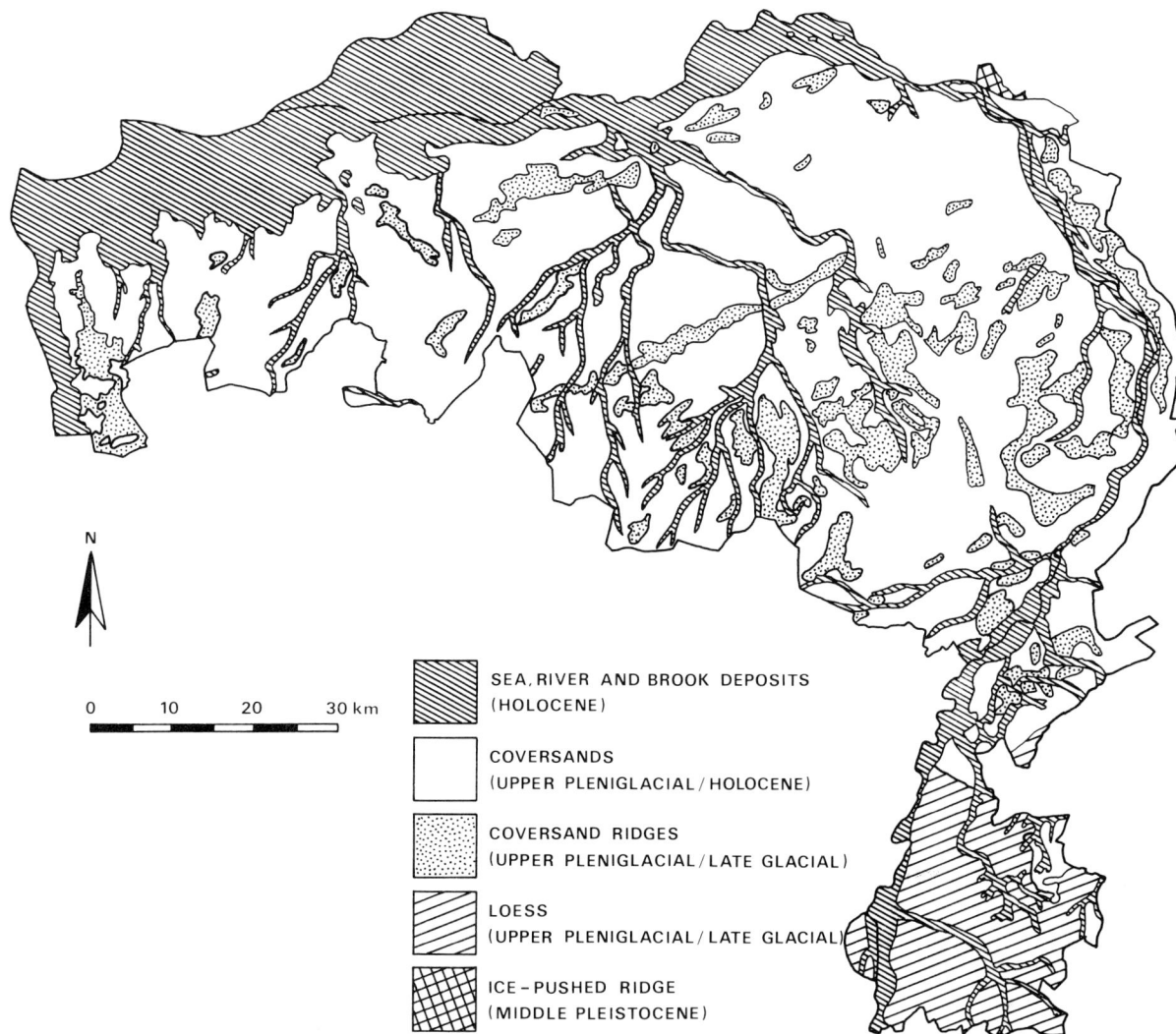

Figure 4 Simplified geological map of the study area.

Legend:
- SEA, RIVER AND BROOK DEPOSITS (HOLOCENE)
- COVERSANDS (UPPER PLENIGLACIAL / HOLOCENE)
- COVERSAND RIDGES (UPPER PLENIGLACIAL / LATE GLACIAL)
- LOESS (UPPER PLENIGLACIAL / LATE GLACIAL)
- ICE-PUSHED RIDGE (MIDDLE PLEISTOCENE)

characterized by numerous fens, which were developed in Lateglacial fossil pingos, abandoned river beds and deflation hollows (Van den Toorn 1967; Broertjes 1977).

Beginning in the final Upper Pleniglacial peat began to develop, especially in river valleys and fens. In the region which corresponds roughly to the provincial borders of North Brabant and Limburg, bad drainage conditions resulted in the development of an extensive peat-bog – the Peel. Archaeological evidence suggests that its growth made human occupation difficult from Neolithic times onward; in historical times the Peel bog attained a surface area of *c.* 400 km².

Based on palynological studies, seven vegetational periods are described for the Lateglacial and early Holocene of the study area (Van der Hammen 1952; Janssen 1960; De Ploey 1963; Munaut 1967; Buurman 1970; Zagwijn 1975; Kalis 1980; Van Leeuwaarden 1982). These are: the Bølling Interstadial (*c.* 12,400–12,000 BP), the Older Dryas Stadial (*c.* 12,000–11,800 BP), the Allerød Interstadial (*c.* 11,800–11,000 BP), the Younger Dryas Stadial

(*c.* 11,000–10,000 BP), the Pre-Boreal (*c.* 10,000–8700 BP), the Boreal (*c.* 8700–7500 BP), and the Atlantic (*c.* 7500–5000 BP). Vegetational evidence suggests a partition of the Atlantic into the early Atlantic (*c.* 7500–6700 BP), when vegetation was not yet stable, and the late Atlantic (*c.* 6700–5000 BP) with a climax forest.

Quantified data on environmental components, such as sunlight, wind and fauna, are not available. Mean July temperatures have been estimated for various time periods (Van der Hammen *et al.* 1967; Zagwijn 1975), but the work of Coope *et al.* (1971) on beetle remains suggests that these estimates may need correction in future.

A common measure of vegetational mass is gross primary productivity, which is defined by Odum (1983: 99) as the total rate of photosynthesis, including the organic matter required for respiration during a measurement period. Productivity of an environment refers to its fertility or richness (Odum 1983: 100), and it represents a dynamic component which summarizes a number of biotic sub-systems. In this paper it is considered as a key environment

Table 1: Geological evidence, vegetational periods and environmental components (*a* from Zagwijn 1975; *b* estimated from Odum 1983)

Geology	Vegetational period	Years BP	Mean July temperature (°C)[a]	Gross primary productivity (kcal/m²/yr)[b]
	EARLY HOLOCENE			
	Late Atlantic	6700–5000	18	8000
Coversand	Early Atlantic	7500–6700	17	7000
	Boreal	8700–7500	16	3000
	Pre-Boreal	10,000–8700	13	2750
	LATE GLACIAL			
Younger Coversand II	Younger Dryas	11,000–10,000	9	2000
Usselo layer	Allerød	11,800–11,000	14	2500
Younger Coversand I	Older Dryas	12,000–11,800	8	800
Loamy layer	Bølling	12,400–12,000	12	1000
Older Coversand II	UPPER PLENIGLACIAL	31,000–12,400	<5	200
Beuningen layer				
Older Coversand I				

variable; estimates for the study area are presented in *Table 1*, and have been derived from vegetational evidence as presented in *Fig. 5* (this diagram presents the average of the palynological works listed above). The reconstruction of forest successions suggests that the environment in the hilly loess region was more productive than in the sandy lowland plain, but such differences are difficult to quantify.

The present-day landscape has been altered significantly by agricultural activities, large-scale reclamation projects and re-allotments of farm property. During the last one hundred years large tracts of heath have been reclaimed and forested,

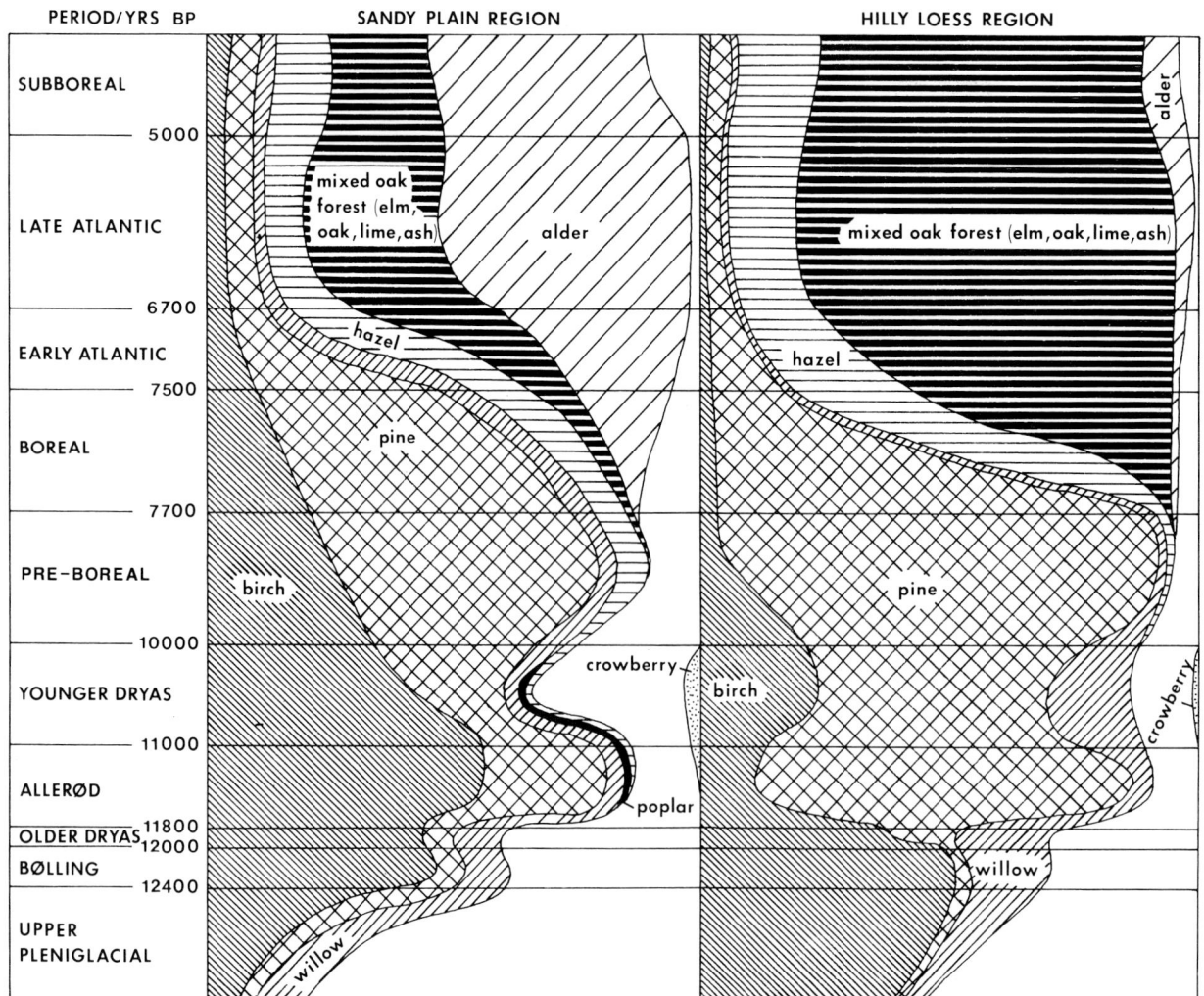

Figure 5 Generalized reconstruction of forest successions in the study area.

most of the Peel peat has been removed, the landscape has been levelled to accommodate farm machinery, and villages and towns have been greatly extended. These disturbances to the former landscape, together with sand drifts and road construction, have greatly increased archaeological visibility in the field, making possible surveys which have resulted in a fairly detailed knowledge of prehistoric occupation.

THE ARCHAEOLOGICAL RECORD OF THE STUDY AREA

Compared to the surrounding areas, Belgium and West Germany, research on the final Palaeolithic and Mesolithic in the study area started late. It was only during the 1920s that the first artifacts dating to these periods became known. At the end of the 1940s fewer than ten sites were mentioned in the published record (Arts, in press b). Most pioneering work must be attributed to A. Bohmers and A. Wouters. The latter recorded a number of important sites and published the first synoptic articles on the periods under study here (Wouters 1953, 1954).

From that time onward the number of known surface sites began to increase dramatically. Twenty-four sites were excavated under the direction of A. Bohmers of the Biologisch–Archaeologisch Instituut, University of Groningen, between 1948 and 1962. Other professional institutions and amateur investigators have further enlarged the number of excavated sites. To date, 46 sites have been excavated to an acceptable standard (*Fig. 6*), but only eleven of them have been analyzed (Bohmers and Wouters 1964; Heesters 1967, 1969, 1971; Heesters and Wouters 1968, 1970; Arts and Deeben 1976, 1978, 1981; Leysen 1984; Deeben 1985). Archaeological data from excavated sites and a number of surface sites have been used in the synthetic works of Bohmers and Wouters (Bohmers 1958, 1960, 1963; Bohmers and Wouters 1958; Wouters 1981a, 1981b, 1982), but their work was mainly directed toward the solution of chronological and typological problems. Although they generally recorded artifact distributions, these did not get any attention in most of their published work. Only one plan was published, but it was not analyzed (Bohmers and Wouters

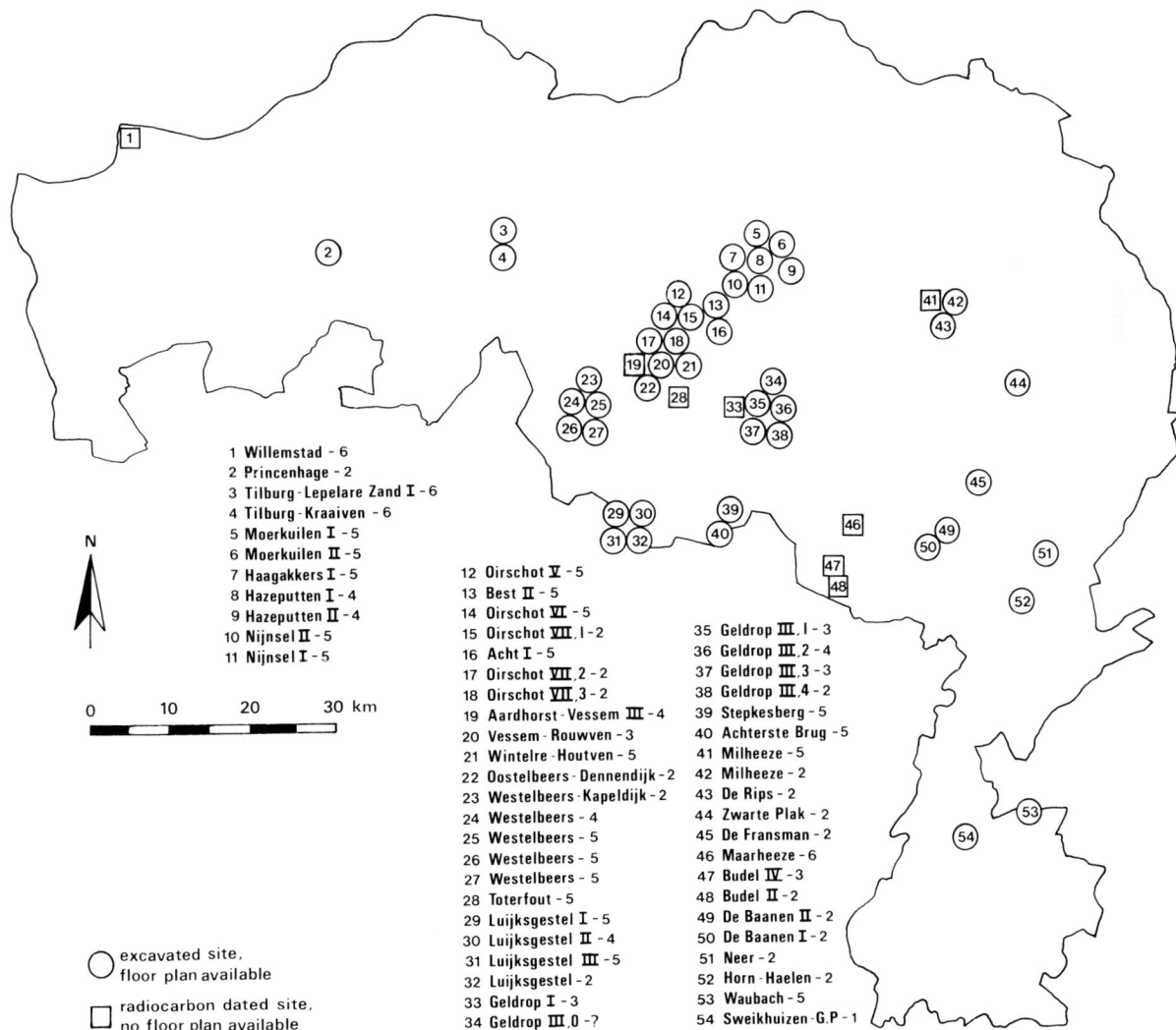

1 Willemstad - 6
2 Princenhage - 2
3 Tilburg - Lepelare Zand I - 6
4 Tilburg - Kraaiven - 6
5 Moerkuilen I - 5
6 Moerkuilen II - 5
7 Haagakkers I - 5
8 Hazeputten I - 4
9 Hazeputten II - 4
10 Nijnsel II - 5
11 Nijnsel I - 5

12 Oirschot V - 5
13 Best II - 5
14 Oirschot VI - 5
15 Oirschot VII.1 - 2
16 Acht I - 5
17 Oirschot VII.2 - 2
18 Oirschot VII.3 - 2
19 Aardhorst - Vessem III - 4
20 Vessem - Rouwven - 3
21 Wintelre - Houtven - 5
22 Oostelbeers - Dennendijk - 2
23 Westelbeers - Kapeldijk - 2
24 Westelbeers - 4
25 Westelbeers - 5
26 Westelbeers - 5
27 Westelbeers - 5
28 Toterfout - 5
29 Luijksgestel I - 5
30 Luijksgestel II - 4
31 Luijksgestel III - 5
32 Luijksgestel - 2
33 Geldrop I - 3
34 Geldrop III,0 -?

35 Geldrop III.1 - 3
36 Geldrop III.2 - 4
37 Geldrop III.3 - 3
38 Geldrop III.4 - 2
39 Stepkesberg - 5
40 Achterste Brug - 5
41 Milheeze - 5
42 Milheeze - 2
43 De Rips - 2
44 Zwarte Plak - 2
45 De Fransman - 2
46 Maarheeze - 6
47 Budel IV - 3
48 Budel II - 2
49 De Baanen II - 2
50 De Baanen I - 2
51 Neer - 2
52 Horn - Haelen - 2
53 Waubach - 5
54 Sweikhuizen - G.P - 1

N

0   10   20   30 km

○ excavated site, floor plan available

□ radiocarbon dated site, no floor plan available

Figure 6   Excavated sites in the study area. Numbers after site names refer to archaeological stages.

1962). Further chronological and typological studies, which include data from the study area, are contained in a number of other works (Newell 1970a, 1970b, 1972; Paddayya 1971; Stapert 1975; Rozoy 1978; Arts, in press a, b).

During the 1970s research was reformulated by Newell (1973, 1975), who analyzed artifact distributions as a residue of human activities (see below); an identical approach was attempted by Price (1975, 1978). As most descriptive excavation reports are still lacking, however, we are still unable to evaluate these studies properly. Other, more behavioural approaches to archaeological data from the study area include those by Arts and Deeben (1981) on migratory movements during the Younger Dryas, and those by Gendel (1982a, 1982b, 1983, 1984) on social territories and raw material exploitation during the Mesolithic.

The great majority of recorded sites are surface scatters. Although a number of publications have reported individual surface assemblages, little analysis has been done. Thanks to the work of more than one hundred amateur workers, a total of 1182 final

Palaeolithic and Mesolithic sites have been registered. Since 1949 much of the amateur work has been recorded by G. Beex, formerly provincial archaeologist of North Brabant, and by the Dutch State Service for Archaeological Investigations at Amersfoort. Their records contain mainly data on topographic locations of sites and on the circumstances of finds; in general no data are available on typological dating, individual site sizes, or their contents. In order to gain some insight into the character and contents of each individual site and into the overall picture of their distribution, during the 1970s a project, initially suggested by R.R. Newell, was started in North Brabant to record such data in detail, and in 1981 the province of Limburg was also included. This project, entitled the *Later Band Project*, is currently conducted from the Institute of Pre- and Protohistory, University of Amsterdam, in collaboration with the Dutch State Service for Archaeological Investigations. The aims include the systematic registration and documentation of final Palaeolithic and Mesolithic surface sites, analysis of unpublished excavated sites, and the problem-

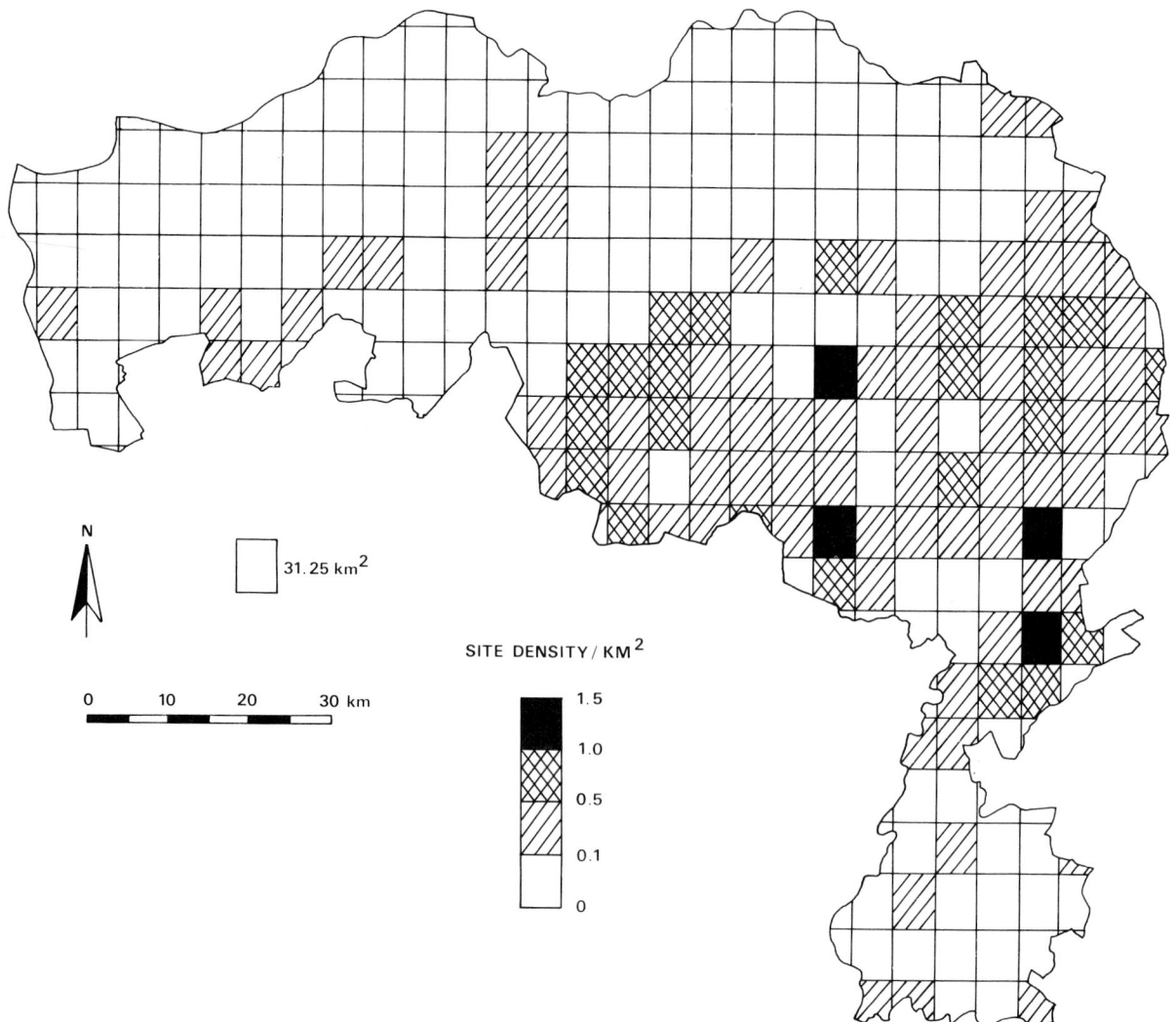

Figure 7 Overall distribution and density of recorded final Palaeolithic and Mesolithic sites in the study area.

orientated excavation of new sites. This paper includes some of the results of this ongoing project.

On the basis of work conducted so far, a number of archaeological characteristics for the study area that are relevant for the present paper will be discussed.

The overall distribution of recorded sites is presented in *Fig. 7*. It is partly biased by regionally bound field surveys of amateur workers. Other surveys in 'empty' regions and in regions with fewer sites (e.g. Slofstra *et al.* 1982; Verhagen 1984), however, suggest that the map is a more or less accurate representation of site distribution and concentration. Areas with denser site concentrations are generally located in regions between 20 and 50 m a.s.l., in particular on coversand ridges (cf. *Figs. 3 & 4*). The large amount of material dredged up from modern river beds, including those in 'empty' regions (Bosscha Erdbrink *et al.* 1975, 1983; Bosscha Erdbrink 1982; Arts, in press *a*), however, suggests that present river valleys were also commonly occupied. Thus, due to river erosion and sedimentation, an unknown proportion of sites is almost entirely lacking. The same is true for the clay-covered coastal area in the west.

Final Palaeolithic and Mesolithic sites are known mainly from flint artifacts. The number of artifacts per site varies between one and 80,000; so far, an estimated one million artifacts have been collected. In many assemblages there is considerable variation in tool types, which allows relative chronologies to be constructed. Typological sequences for the study area (*Figs. 8 & 9*) have been developed by using the principle of frequent association among artifacts (partly summarized in former studies – see above) and by comparison with material from areas bordering the study area (Arora 1976; Gob 1981; Vermeersch 1984). In particular, the presence or absence of certain lithic point types (*Fig. 8*) has been used as diagnostic for relative dating. Chronologies are further aided by coversand stratigraphy and radiocarbon dating. The theoretical and practical difficulties in interpreting radiocarbon dates (e.g. Newell 1979) have led to difficulties in establishing a generally accepted chronology for the study area. The 24 sites that have been dated by radiocarbon have provided 41 dates (*Fig. 10*), most summarized by Lanting and Mook (1977). One-third of these dates do not agree with typological dating; moreover, there is a tendency to emphasize those dates that fit preconceived ideas and to minimize other dates, without explaining rejected dates properly. For the study area, an important problem in interpreting radiocarbon dates is the lack of information concerning the stratigraphic context of most of the radiocarbon samples within sites. Furthermore, most samples were taken from highly bioturbatic podzolic soils and, owing to the reoccupation of a

number of sites, some samples are obviously mixed with younger or older materials. In addition, pits in excavated sites from which radiocarbon samples were taken are not necessarily fire-places used by the prehistoric inhabitants, as is often suggested by their excavators, but may be the remnants of natural fires (Newell and Dekin 1978; cf. Newell 1981).

The lack of archaeological materials from the Upper Pleniglacial suggests that the study area, and also other parts of the North European Plain, were not occupied by human societies during most of this period (cf. Clark 1975; Vermeersch 1984). The dry high-arctic environment was probably not conducive to human occupation for some twenty millennia. The area was reoccupied during the Lateglacial by final Palaeolithic band societies. Generally, three stages are accepted for the final Palaeolithic (Paddayya 1971; Stapert 1975; Arts, in press *a*): the Magdalenian (stage 1), Federmesser (stage 2), and Ahrensburgian (stage 3). Despite this uniformity in chronological ordering, there is no complete agreement on the absolute dating of each stage. In the study area there is only one site with dating evidence for the Magdalenian. Wouters (1983) described a Magdalenian site found in a soil (probably a Bølling soil) stratigraphically below the Allerød soil. Typological similarities with sites in adjacent Belgium and West Germany, which have been dated stratigraphically or by radiocarbon, suggest that Magdalenian occupation continued into the Older Dryas (cf. Arts and Deeben 1987). Geological evidence shows that the Federmesser is dated to the Allerød; when not in eroded soils, Federmesser sites are always located in the Allerød soil, and there is no geological evidence for an earlier or later date. Radiocarbon dates from Dutch and Belgian Federmesser sites range from the twelfth to the seventh millennium BP (Lanting and Mook 1977; Vermeersch 1982), while the Allerød soil is radiocarbon dated to 11,800–11,000 BP (Lanting and Mook 1977). The discrepancy between radiocarbon dates from archaeological sites and those from strictly geological sites, and the need for a working chronology forced us to adapt (at least temporarily) dating of the Federmesser. The Federmesser stage in this study is restricted to the Allerød, a date supported by most of the radiocarbon dates from the study area (*Fig. 10*). Geological (e.g. Wouters 1957) and radiocarbon evidence (Lanting and Mook 1977) indicate a dating of the Ahrensburgian to the Younger Dryas.

The chronology of the Mesolithic relies on radiocarbon dates (*Fig. 10*) and typology; geological evidence is lacking, although there are several instances in coversand ridges where a Federmesser layer lies stratigraphically below a Mesolithic layer. One well-excavated site, not yet published, at Westelbeers provided micro-stratigraphic evidence

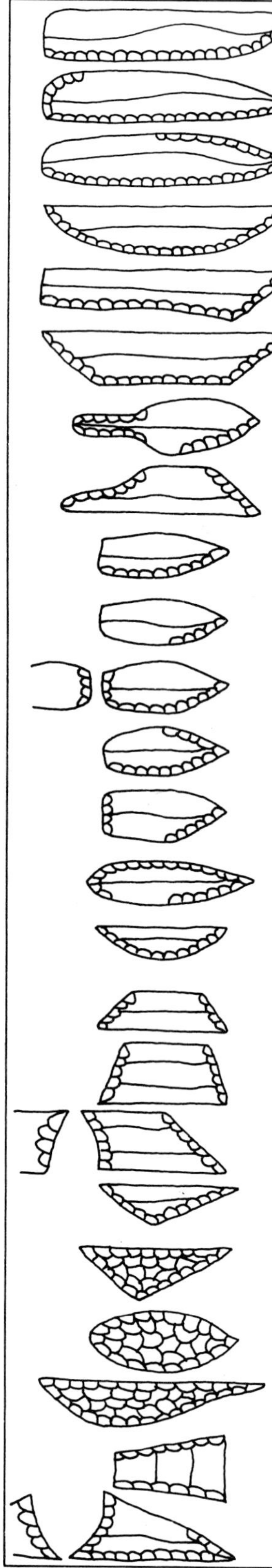

Figure 8 table:

TYPE	1	2	3	4	5	6
Tjonger point		high	high			
Gravette point		high	low			
Kremser point		low				
Azilian point		low	low			
Creswell point		low	low			
Cheddar point		low				
tanged point		low	high			
shouldered point		low	low			
a-point				high	low	low
b-point		low	high	high	high	high
c-point					high	high
d-point					low	high
Zonhoven point			low	low		
lancette point					low	low
crescent					low	low
narrow trapeze					low	high
broad trapeze			low		low	high
rhombic trapeze						high
triangle			low	high	high	high
surface retouched triangle					low	high
leaf-shaped point					high	high
feuille de gui					high	high
transverse point						low
Danubian point						low

Figure 8 Typological classification, sequence and relative frequencies of lithic points (frequency of individual types is indicated by the size of dots: 'high' (large dots), 'moderate' (medium-sized dots), 'low' (small dots).

300

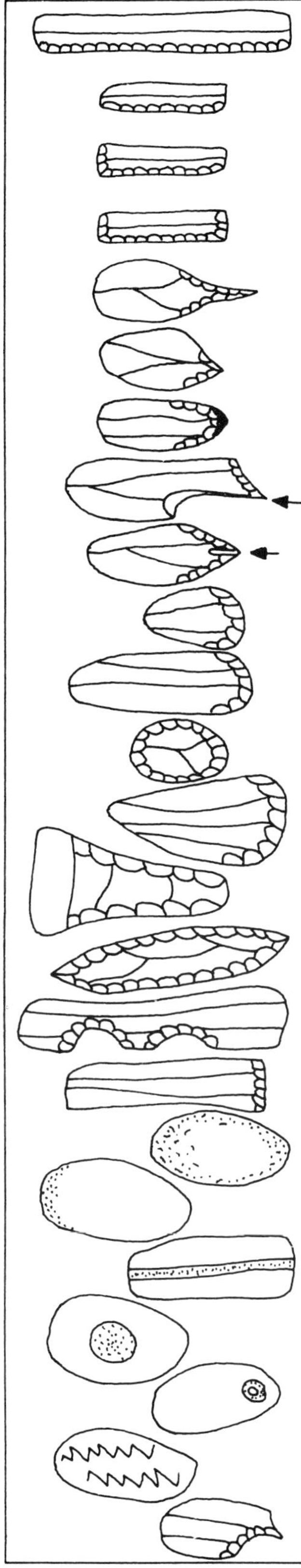

TYPE	STAGE / FREQUENCY					
	1	2	3	4	5	6
large backed blade	●	●				
small backed blade	●		●	●	●	●
triangular backed blade				·	·	●
rectangular backed blade					·	·
needle-pointed borer	●	·				
borer (other types)	·	·	·	·	·	·
reamer		·				
burin	●	●	●	●	·	·
beaked burin	·	·	·			
short end scraper	·	●	●	●	●	●
long end scraper	●	·	·	·	·	·
circular scraper			·		·	·
large end scraper						●
axe						·
pic						·
notched blade	·	·	·	·	●	●
truncated blade	·	·	●	·	·	·
retouchoir		●	·			
hammer stone	●	●	·	·	●	●
needle/shaft sharpener		·	·	·		·
mace-head					·	·
pendant			·			
decorated stone		·	·			
micro-burin			·	●	●	●

Figure 9   Typological classification, sequence and relative frequencies of other artifact types (frequency of individual types is indicated by the size of dots: 'high' (large dots), 'moderate' (medium-sized dots), 'low' (small dots).

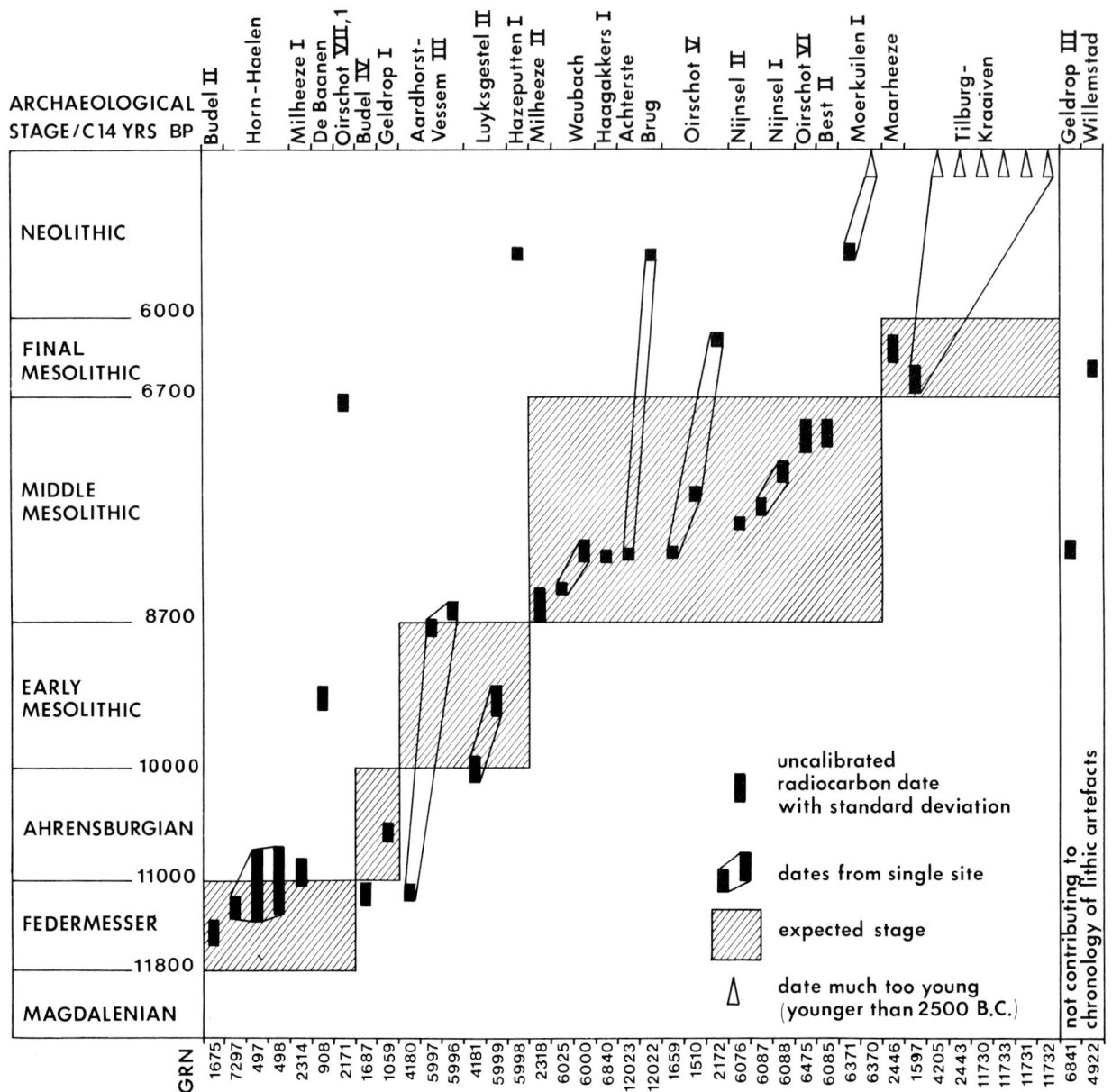

Figure 10 Radiocarbon dates for archaeological stages.

for two Mesolithic layers – typologically, an early and a middle Mesolithic layer.

Newell (1975) defined five Mesolithic stages for the Netherlands: the *Basal Mesolithic* (c. 10,250–8850 BP), the *Early Mesolithic* (c. 8850–8350 BP), the *Boreal Mesolithic* (c. 8350–7700 BP), the *Late Mesolithic* (c. 7700–7350 BP), and the *Late Mesolithic Survival* (c. 7350–6150 BP). A critical re-examination of Newell's (1975: 41) typological scheme, practical difficulties in ordering Mesolithic sites from the study area into his stages, and new evidence from lowland Belgium (Vermeersch (ed.) 1982; Vermeersch 1982, 1984) permit a revision and simplification of Newell's scheme for the southern Netherlands. Three Mesolithic stages will be distinguished: the early Mesolithic (stage 4, c. 10,000–8700 BP), the middle Mesolithic (stage 5, c. 8700–6700 BP), and the final Mesolithic (stage 6, c. 6700–6000 BP). The typological regularity of these stages in the study area suggests that this three-fold division is basically correct. New radiocarbon evidence, however, might revise its absolute chronology.

Based on the typological schemes presented above (*Figs. 8 & 9*), a total of 670 (56.7%) of the 1182 recorded sites provided sufficient data to be attributed to one of the six stages: stage 1, $n = 5$; stage 2, $n = 128$; stage 3, $n = 32$; stage 4, $n = 13$; stage 5, $n = 343$; stage 6, $n = 149$. Within these totals, the frequency of sites found in the hilly loess region is very low: stage 1, $n = 3$; stage 2, $n = 3$; stage 3, $n = 4$; stages 4 and 5, $n = 0$; stage 6, $n = 4$. All other sites are in the sandy lowland plain.

The transition from the Mesolithic to the Neolithic in the study area is poorly understood. Around 6400 BP Bandkeramik (Danubian) agriculturalists immigrated into the hilly loess region. The distribution of Bandkeramik sites is strongly correlated with the hilly loess region (De Grooth and Verwers 1984). During the Bandkeramik occupation there is some evidence of contact with contemporaneous Mesolithic people in the sandy lowland plain, illustrated by the presence of Danubian flint points in 24 final Mesolithic sites; these are considered as the archaeological remains of exchange between Mesolithic hunter-gatherers and Neolithic agriculturalists (Newell 1970a, 1972, 1975). In the study area there is no typological or radiocarbon evidence for a continuation of the Mesolithic *after* the Bandkeramik occupation, which lasted only four centuries. There are two hypotheses concerning the adoption of agriculture in the study area. The first hypothesis states that the Bandkeramik flint industry is developed from the Younger Oldesloe (Newell 1970a, 1970b, 1972) which has axes and picks and is located to the north of the Bandkeramik area, and which then migrated south during the final Mesolithic (cf. Newell 1970c, 1975; Wouters 1981b). The other hypothesis states that the early Neolithic Limburg pottery (Modderman 1981) reflects the material manifestation of a Mesolithic population undergoing acculturation (Modderman 1982). Both hypotheses refer to events which took place in the Meuse valley and do not explain what then happened outside the Meuse valley. Further, if Mesolithic groups were acculturated during the Bandkeramik in the Meuse valley, their influence on the Bandkeramik flint industry is much less conspicuous than Newell (1970a, 1970b, 1972) suggests (Louwe Kooijmans 1976; Howell 1983; De Grooth and Verwers 1984). Lack of continuity in flint assemblages might indicate either rather rapid acculturation, or simply that acculturation is not the correct model (Howell 1983). The early Neolithic successor of the Bandkeramik, the Rössen stage, does not shed any light on the problem of the Mesolithic–Neolithic transition, because Rössen artifacts are extremely scarce in the study area (Van der Waals 1972; Louwe Kooijmans 1976). Only from the middle Neolithic (c. 5100 BP and later) does the number of sites increase, but an overview of the middle Neolithic in the study area is not available. The above discussion suggests that the study area was probably largely uninhabited during the sixth millennium BP.

Most raw materials recovered from final Palaeolithic and Mesolithic sites are of local origin, and were probably collected from local gravel deposits. Only one quarry site has been found, which was exploited during stages 2 and 5 (Arts 1984). Local raw materials vary in quality from stage to stage. During stages 5 and 6 inferior, eroded, coarse-grained flint nodules with frequent internal cracks were often used. During stages 1–4 local raw materials were generally of better quality. Besides flint, most sites also contain quartz, quartzite and sandstone in small quantities, with an average frequency of c. 5%. One stage 1 site, however, produced large numbers of stones other than flint, arranged in a circular pattern, which have been interpreted as a tent-ring (Arts, in press a). A striking aspect of the material remains of the largest sites of stage 6 (see below) is the presence of large numbers of fire-cracked rocks, which might be interpreted as cooking stones. At least six types of exotic raw materials have been found in the study area: fine-grained dark flint, chalcedonic flint, Wommersom quartzite, black chert, micaceous sandstone, and ochre. Most of them are unique to one or a few archaeological stages, and there is variation in their average absolute frequencies among the total of artifacts per stage (*Table 2*). Petrological analyses of exotic materials are generally lacking and, thus, the locations mentioned below are the most probable sources.

The fine-grained dark flint only occurs in Federmesser sites, and it probably originates from Obourg in Hainault, Belgium (F. Van Noten, pers. comm.; cf. Hubert 1980). This exotic raw material may include several petrological variants, one or more of them possibly originating in the North Sea basin (Wouters 1984). Because inventories conducted so far have not recognized such variations, in this paper the Obourg outcrop is considered the source, even though this interpretation might need revision in future. Chalcedonic flint probably originates from the German Rhineland, where a source is known from Bad Godesberg (Arora and Bosinski 1978).

Table 2: Absolute frequencies of exotic materials. Frequencies shown as .01 should be read as ≤ .01; *distance* and *direction* refer to the absolute distance between, and the direction to the source and the centre of the study area

Exotic material	Distance (km)	Direction	Stage 1	Stage 2	Stage 3	Stage 4	Stage 5	Stage 6
Fine-grained dark flint	180	S	–	.05	–	–	–	–
Chalcedonic flint	120	SE	–	–	.02	–	–	–
Wommersom quartzite	95	S	–	–	–	–	.07	.13
Black chert	130	S	–	–	–	–	.01	.01
Micaceous sandstone	95	S	–	–	–	–	.01	.01
Ochre	120	S	.01	.01	.01	.01	.01	.01
Danubian points	60	SE	–	–	–	–	–	.01

Distinctive of stages 5 and 6 is Wommersom quartzite, a siliceous sandstone from Wommersom, near Tienen in Belgium (Gendel 1982a). It is frequently used for producing surface retouched points (surface retouched triangles, leaf-shaped points and 'feuilles de gui' – e.g. Ophoven et al. 1948; Newell 1973, 1975), and notched blades. In the study area frequencies of Wommersom quartzite decline sharply east of the River Meuse. Black chert (phtanite) originates from Ottignies/Céroux-Mousty in Belgium (Caspar 1984). Micaceous sandstones (grès lustré) might originate from sources near Wommersom (Huyge and Vermeersch 1982). Ochre most probably originates from the Meuse region in Belgium (Coninx 1984).

During the periods under study technological change is minimal, but there is a gradual reduction in the size of cores through time, with a corresponding reduction in the dimensions of blades, flakes and tools. During the periods under study there were two innovations in flint-working: the microburin technique (Bordaz 1970) during stage 3 (the Ahrensburgian), and surface retouch during stage 5 (the middle Mesolithic) (Newell 1973, 1975).

Objects of art and ornaments are scarce. Some decorated stone artifacts are known from stages 2 and 3. Stone and ochre pendants are known from stage 3 (Arts, in press a). Some rock engravings in the loess region (Span 1983) have been attributed to stage 3 but, since they are not associated with other archaeological material, this date is not convincing. In the extreme north west of the study area a unique wooden statuette was dredged up from a coversand at a depth of 8 m below modern sea level which, according to radiocarbon dating, is of final Mesolithic origin (Van Es and Casparie 1968). Some ornamented antlers of *Rangifer tarandus* and *Cervus elaphus* have been dredged up from river beds and are presumably of final Palaeolithic origin (Arts, in press a). Finally, material remains of a large final Mesolithic site at Tilburg include a thin, 15 cm long, polished piece of stone with a pierced hole at one end and scratches marked on both sides (Arts, in press b).

Most soils have been decalcified and, in general, little organic material, such as bone refuse, has been preserved. Pits from excavated sites, however, frequently contain charcoal and sometimes also carbonized hazel-nut remains and small fragments of calcined bone. Large amounts of bone material, including worked bone, have been dredged from river beds, but never in association with inorganic artifacts (Arts, in press a). Some human bones, dredged up from the River Meuse, have been attributed to the Mesolithic (Bosscha Erdbrink et al. 1975), but there are doubts about their ages and affinities (Newell et al. 1979). However, nitrogen/fluorine analysis (Bosscha Erdbrink et al. 1983) suggests a Pleistocene to early Holocene, or an early Holocene to middle Holocene date for a recently found skull from the River Meuse.

Site-size data are available for 21 excavated sites (for Mesolithic sites – see Newell 1973, 1975; Price 1975, 1978) and for 220 surface sites in the study area. Since these data are based on artifact distributions, it is difficult to demonstrate that the entire area of distribution represents a single occupation (Mellars 1976; Lewarch and O'Brien 1981). However, association between areas sharply defined by artifact densities and typologically homogeneous assemblages, suggests a single episode of occupation. It is possible, however, that the larger sites do not represent large settlements, but repeated visits during the same stage to the same locality. Therefore, the types mentioned below must be approached with some degree of caution.

Four settlement types are distinguished here (*Table 3*), more or less in conformity with the types defined by Newell (1973, 1975), who used a larger sample of excavated sites for the Mesolithic. Absolute

Table 3: Absolute frequencies of settlement types (underlined) and total surface areas of settlements (median values, m²). Numbers in parentheses signify sites in the hilly loess region

Settlement type	Surface area (km²)	Stage 1	Stage 2	Stage 3	Stage 4	Stage 5	Stage 6	N
I	52	–	36 / 1872	10 / 520	4 / 208	101 / 5252	28 / 1456	179 / 9208
II	450	2(2) / 900	–	1 / 450	1 / 450	31 / 13,950	6 / 2700	41(2) / 18,450
III	2250	–	12 / 27,000	–	–	–	–	12 / 27,000
IV	3500	–	–	–	–	–	9(1) / 31,500	9(1) / 31,500
n⁺		2(2) / 900	48 / 28,872	11 / 970	5 / 658	132 / 19,202	43(1) / 35,656	241(3) / 86,258
Total dated sites		5(3)	128(3)	32(4)	13(0)	343(0)	149(4)	670(14)
Frequency n⁺		.20(.67)	.38(0)	.34(0)	.39	.39	.29(.25)	.36(.21)

data on tool density, waste material and so forth, are not given here because they are incomplete for surface sites. Furthermore, the excavation techniques employed in most excavated sites were not ideal for recovering an unbiased sample of the assemblages; hence, these data are also incomplete.

Type I settlements are more or less circular small areas, ranging between 4 m² and c. 100 m², with comparatively few artifacts. They occur in all stages except stage 1, and are comparable to Newell's (1973) types 2 and 3. Type II settlements are usually oval or circular in plan with a surface area ranging between c. 200 m² and c. 700 m². They are comparable to Newell's (1973) type 1, and occur in all stages except stage 2. Type III and IV settlements are much larger. Usually they are oval-shaped artifact scatters which contain several concentrations; they are comparable to Newell's (1973) type 4. Type III, with a surface area ranging between c. 2000 m² and c. 2500 m², only occurs during stage 2; and type IV, with a surface area ranging between c. 3000 m² and c. 4000 m², only during stage 6.

AN ANALYSIS OF EVOLUTIONARY COMPONENTS

In the preceding discussion of the environmental and archaeological record of the study area, several changes were noted. In this section the six evolutionary components – temperature, primary productivity of the environment, population densities, exchange, settlement variation and territorial intensification – will be examined separately, followed by a comparison of these components through time.

Environment

As discussed above, there have been major environmental changes during the stages under study. Quantification of these changes, an estimate of the mean July temperature and an estimate of the primary productivity, all show the same pattern – an increase in the estimates from stage 1 to stage 2, followed by a decrease in stage 3, and successive increases for the remaining stages (*Table 4*).

Population densities and land use

Following Plog (1974) and Welinder (1979), among others, site counts have been used to infer relative population densities, which has proved to be a reasonable way to estimate prehistoric hunter-gatherer population densities (Constandse-Westermann, Newell and Meiklejohn 1984). This rests upon the supposition that there is a relationship between the area that a population occupies in a given stage, the number of settlements in that area, and the number of individuals in that population (cf. Plog 1974: 87). In this paper, relative population densities (*PD*) are measured by the formula:

$$PD = \frac{NS.10^4}{SF.TS}$$

where *NS* is the number of sites during a given stage, *SF* the surface area in km² (cf. *Table 5*), and *TS* (time-span) the number of years of that stage (*Table 4*). The factor 10^4 is added in order to avoid very small numbers. Calculated this way, there is evidence for population increases and decreases throughout the periods under study (*Table 5*). Moreover, visual comparison of *Figs. 3, 4* and *7*, and a comparison of population densities between the sandy lowland plain and the hilly loess region (*Table 5*), suggest changing patterns in land use.

As mentioned above, during the period prior to stage 1 there were no inhabitants in the study area; thus the population density starts at zero. During stage 1 a population immigrated into the study area and, in contrast to most other stages, seems to have favoured the loess region. In the lowland plain population density increased significantly during stage 2, and then decreased from stage 2 through

Table 4: Summary of raw scores of environmental and archaeological components

Evolutionary component	Stage 1	Stage 2	Stage 3	Stage 4	Stage 5	Stage 6
Time-span (years)	600	800	1000	1300	2000	700
Mean July temperature (°C)	10.7	14	9	13	16.4	18
Gross primary productivity (kcal/m²/year)	933	2500	2000	2750	4600	8000
Number of sites (lowland)	2	125	28	13	343	145
Number of sites (hills)	3	3	4	0	0	4
Number of sites (study area)	5	128	32	13	343	149

Table 5: Relative population densities

Zone	Surface area (km²)	Stage 1	Stage 2	Stage 3	Stage 4	Stage 5	Stage 6
Sandy lowland	6100	.05	2.56	.46	.16	2.81	3.40
Hilly loess region	600	.83	.62	.67	0	0	.95
Entire study area	6700	.12	2.39	.48	.15	2.56	3.18

stage 4. During stages 4 and 5 the loess region seems to have been uninhabited, and was reoccupied again during stage 6. During stage 5 in the sandy lowland plain a significant population increase seems to have occurred. This increase has also been noted by Newell (1973) for a larger geographical area and, according to him, was due to the Holocene rise of sea level, causing portions of the population in the bordering North Sea basin to move into the study area. It is interesting to note that the hilly loess region was sparsely occupied during the final Mesolithic, when Bandkeramik agriculturalists immigrated into this region. In contrast, the sandy lowland plain had the largest population during this stage compared to all other stages.

Exchange

Exchange has been measured by the amount of exotic materials found in the archaeological record. Exotic materials are defined as source-specific materials where both distance from the source and frequent occurrence in sites suggest acquisition through a regional exchange system. In this paper it is suggested that the more regularly an exotic material occurs in archaeological sites, the more likely it is that it reflects exchange through 'trade' partners within a social system, rather than frequent movements of individual groups to the source. The index of exchange is influenced by the distance to and the direction of the source, since it is possible that different exotic materials from the same direction were exchanged on one occasion, and the number and the density of sites participating in the exchange network. The index of exchange (EX), then, is measured by the formula:

$$EX = \frac{D(S).F(S)}{\sqrt{N(S)}} + \frac{D(SE).F(SE)}{\sqrt{N(SE)}}$$

where S and SE represent the two directions from which exotic materials were exchanged (Table 2), D is the distance, F is the frequency, and N the number of exotic materials. From the raw data in Table 2 we get the following indices of exchange: stage 1, 1.2; stage 2, 7.2; stage 3, 3.6; stage 4, 1.2; stage 5, 5.1; stage 6, 8.5. These indices are averages for the entire study area; data from the loess region are too few to calculate separate indices for both environmental regions.

Settlement variation

In a previous section four settlement types were discussed. Ethnographic evidence (e.g. VanStone 1974; Campbell 1968; Mauss and Beuchat 1979) suggests that smaller settlements were limited-activity areas, occupied by a small number of individuals; while larger settlements were multifunctional areas,

occupied by a larger number of individuals (cf. David 1973; Newell 1973; Mellars 1976). Larger settlements, probably at best to be interpreted as aggregation settlements, or large more permanent settlements, suggest greater social interaction. In order to compare such interaction per stage, an index of aggregation (AG) will be measured by the formula:

$$AG = \frac{SF(LS)^2}{SF(n).SF(N)}$$

where $SF(LS)$ is the sum of the areas of the largest settlement type per stage, $SF(n)$ the sum of the areas of all settlements per stage, and $SF(N)$ the sum of the areas of all settlements of all stages. Calculated from the data in Table 3, the following indices of aggregation for the entire study area are obtained: stage 1, 0.010; stage 2, 0.293; stage 3, 0.002; stage 4, 0.004; stage 5, 0.118; stage 6, 0.323. Data on frequencies of settlement types from the hilly loess region (Table 3) are insufficient to enable separate indices to be calculated for both environmental regions.

Territorial intensification

Visual inspections of archaeological culture maps (e.g. Kozłowski and Kozłowski 1977; Kozłowski 1980) indicate that areas of cultural territories decreased from the final Palaeolithic to the end of the Mesolithic (cf. Price 1983; Newell 1984). An archaeological culture is defined by Clarke (1978: 247) as a polythetic set of specific and comprehensive artifact types which consistently recur together in assemblages within a limited geographical area; it may be considered as the material manifestation of an area of maximized group intercommunication (Clarke 1978: 270). We may expect that the smaller the cultural territory, the greater the chance of frequent social interaction. Territorial areas, estimated from Clark (1975), Kozłowski and Kozłowski (1977), Rozoy (1978) and Kozłowski (1980) were calculated using $x.10^{-5}$ km^2 where 10^{-5} is the constant and x is the estimated territorial extent based on the site distribution. This produces the following territorial sizes: stage 1, ≥ 5.0; stage 2, 3.0; stage 3, 1.2; stages 5 and 6, 0.8. It is noticeable that the territorial size decreases through time. No data were available for stage 4, and for this stage the average of stages 3 and 5 (1.0) was used. The index of territorial intensification, then, is the mathematical inverse of these areas, producing the following indices: stage 1, ≤ 0.20; stage 2, 0.33; stage 3, 0.83; stage 4, 1.00; stage 5, 1.25; stage 6, 1.25.

So far the analysis has been a static one, with fixed scores for each evolutionary component. In order to observe variation in the overall picture of social

Table 6: Indices of evolutionary components, relative to their sum, with growth (+) or decline (−) comparative to previous stage

Evolutionary component	Stage 1	Stage 2	Stage 3	Stage 4	Stage 5	Stage 6
1. Rank stage	.05	.10(+.05)	.14(+.04)	.19(+.05)	.24(+.05)	.29(+.05)
2. Time-span	.09	.13(+.04)	.16(+.03)	.20(+.04)	.31(+.11)	.11(−.20)
3. Temperature	.13	.17(+.04)	.11(−.06)	.16(+.05)	.20(+.04)	.22(+.02)
4. Primary productivity	.04	.12(+.08)	.10(−.02)	.13(+.03)	.22(+.09)	.38(+.16)
5. Index of exchange	.04	.27(+.23)	.13(−.14)	.04(−.09)	.19(+.15)	.31(+.12)
6. Index of aggregation	.01	.39(+.38)	.01(−.38)	.01(0)	.16(+.15)	.43(+.27)
7. Index of territorial intensification	.04	.07(+.03)	.17(+.10)	.21(+.04)	.26(+.05)	.26(0)
8. Population density – lowland	.01	.27(+.26)	.05(−.22)	.02(−.03)	.30(+.28)	.36(+.06)
9. Population density – hills	.27	.20(−.07)	.22(+.02)	0(−.22)	0(0)	.31(+.31)
10. Population density – study area	.01	.27(+.26)	.05(−.22)	.02(−.03)	.29(+.27)	.36(+.07)

Sum of (+) and (−) – environmental components 3 and 4, only		(+.12)	(−.08)	(+.08)	(+.13)	(+.18)

Sum of (+) and (−) – social components 5, 6, 7 and 10, only		(+.90)	(−.58)	(−.08)	(+.62)	(+.46)

evolution, each component is expressed as a proportion of its respective raw total (*Table 6*; *Fig. 11*). The direction of change for each of the components differs significantly from the rank stage, i.e. the expected direction of increasing values under the supposition that evolution is a continuous process of growth. There are also significant differences among most components. An interesting negative correlation is found when the sum of the environmental components is compared to the sum of the more social components (*Table 6*). This seems to indicate that social evolution is not always stimulated by environmental change, as is suggested by Service

(1962), although there is generally a relationship between vegetational periods and archaeological stages (*Table 1*; *Fig. 10*). The change that occurs during stage 4, where the environmental sums increase and the social sums decrease, is particularly striking.

Components might be interrelated and, in order to measure such possible relations, Spearman r_s measures (Siegel 1956) were calculated (*Table 7*). It is noticeable that there are several statistically significant correlations: between population density (lowland plain and entire study area) and index values for exchange; between index values for

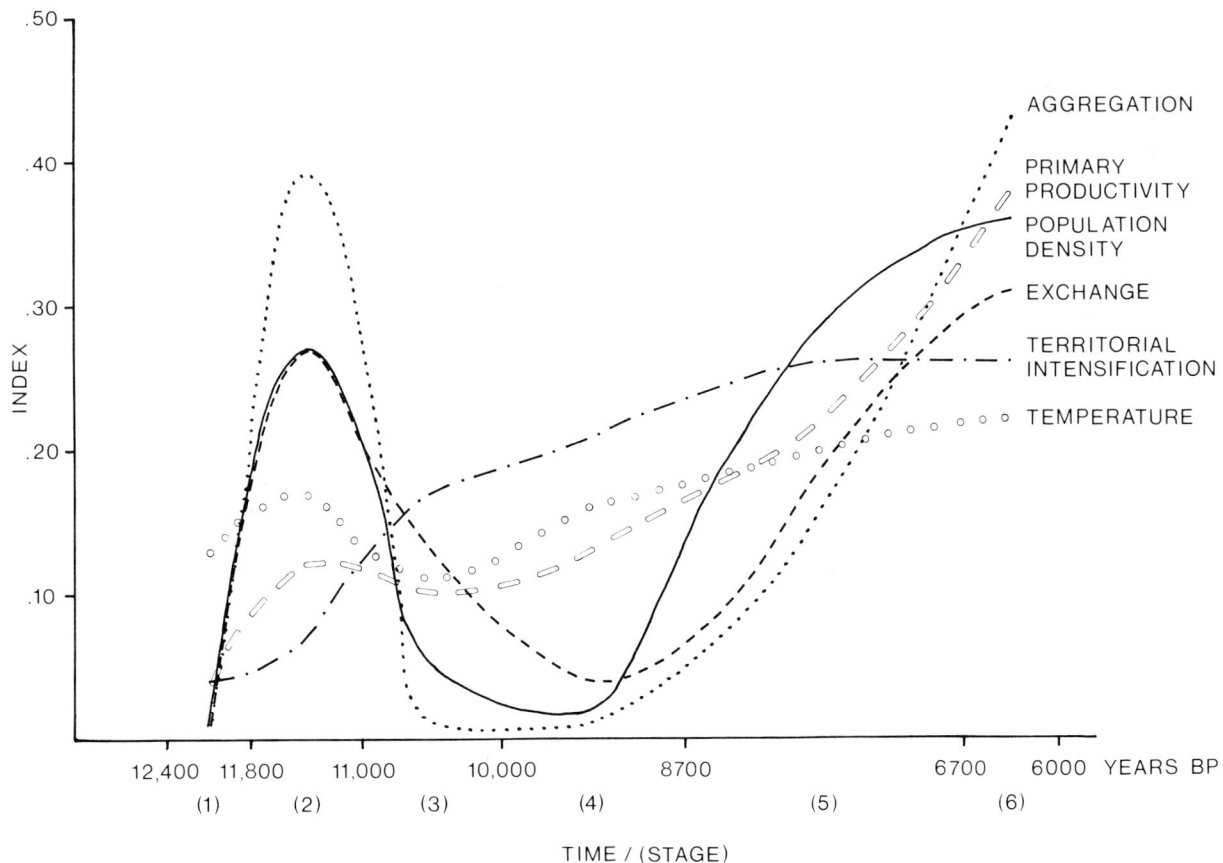

Figure 11 Indices for evolutionary components expressed as graphs (source: *Table 6*).

Table 7: *Spearman r_s measures of correlation (N=6). Significant correlations at .01 level are underlined; significant correlations at .05 level are underlined and in parentheses*

Evolutionary component	10	9	8	7	6	5	4	3	2	1
1. Rank stage	.771	.043	.771	<u>.986</u>	.371	.529	<u>.943</u>	.714	.771	–
2. Time-span	.200	−.871	.200	.433	−.314	−.071	.714	.086		
3. Temperature	.829	.029	.829	.700	(<u>.886</u>)	.757	(<u>.886</u>)			
4. Primary productivity	.829	−.100	.829	(<u>.929</u>)	.600	.643				
5. Index of exchange	(<u>.929</u>)	.329	(<u>.929</u>)	.486	.814					
6. Index of aggregation	.714	.329	.714	.329						
7. Index of territorial intensification	.757	−.157	.757							
8. Population density – lowland	<u>1</u>	.129								
9. Population density – hills	.129									
10. Population density – study area	–									

territorial intensification and both rank stage values and primary productivity values; between values for the index of aggregation and mean July temperature; and between values for primary productivity and both the rank stage values and mean July temperature values. The correlation between primary productivity and temperature is what is expected logically (see above). The values for the indices of territorial intensification and those for primary productivity are positively correlated with the expected unidirectional change in social evolution (the rank stage), as are the correlations between territorial intensification and primary productivity, and between aggregation and temperature. Whether or not these correlations are spurious is difficult to ascertain. Interesting is the positive correlation between population density and rate of exchange, which suggests that in this case population density selects for exchange activity, or vice-versa, or that both are related to another significant component.

SUMMARY, INTERPRETATION AND EVALUATION

In this paper several components related to social evolution were discussed in the context of the final Palaeolithic and Mesolithic of the southern Netherlands. If the major points of this study are valid, there are several implications concerning social evolution in the study area, and probably also for bordering areas. The overwhelming impression is one of discontinuity; it can be concluded that changes in social components have not been continuous or unidirectional, when evaluated against the theoretical expectation in the definition presented at the beginning of this paper, which has implications for evolutionary studies (Steward 1955; White 1959; Sahlins and Service (eds) 1960). Comparison among stages shows that the Federmesser stage, the middle Mesolithic and the final Mesolithic (stages 2, 5 and 6) were periods of increasing complexity as measured by the indices. Decreasing complexity occurred during the Ahrensburgian stage and the early Mesolithic (stages 3 and 4), and also during the final Mesolithic (stage 6) when compared with the succeeding early Neolithic. Such evidence suggests several collapses of the social system, which may be summarized as follows:

1. A marked reduction in population density occurred during stages 3 and 4 which led to a virtual abandonment of the study area during stage 4, and probably also during the early Neolithic, with a related decrease in the volume of exchange.

2. An increase in the proportion of smaller settlements occurred during stages 3 and 4, from which a decrease in the size of individual residence groups may be inferred. Despite the increase in territorial intensification, this trend and the reduction in population density probably indicate a fragmentation of social organization.

3. During stages 4 and 6 these decreases contrast with the increasing rates of environmental components, which suggests that social evolution is not always stimulated by environmental change.

In an attempt to understand the order and logic of such social collapses, the concept of social stress furnishes perhaps the best available theory. Stress theory is applicable to situations where forces produce sudden effects, which may be termed catastrophes on account of their discontinuous nature (Selye 1976). Social stress may be defined as the group of effects that are in excess of the normal or known effects of a situation; stressors are characterized as new, intense, rapidly changing, sudden, fatigue producing, and/or boring (Edwards 1972: 88). Selye (1976) developed the concept of systemic stress, which is described as following a time-course called the general adaptation syndrome; it is characterized by four successive phases: (i) an alarm reaction (or the shock phase); (ii) a countershock phase, when defence mechanisms are resurgenced; (iii) a phase of resistance, which is marked by maximum adaptation; and finally (iv) when a persistent stressor exhausts the defensive reactions, a phase of exhaustion is entered in which adaptation mechanisms do not function.

If stress theory is applicable to the archaeological case studied in this paper, the observed collapses of the social system must be the result of phases of exhaustion, and must be caused by some persistent stressors. In the case of the study area, three successive events might have produced the necessary stress to result in 'catastrophe' situations: a natural disaster, overspecialization, and a migration.

The natural disaster, the intense volcanic eruption of the Laacher See in the German Eifel, at a distance of only 160 km from the centre of the study area, is recorded at the end of stage 2 (Bosinski 1983). According to Bosinski, this eruption lasted for only a few days, producing ash falls, atmospherics and solar eclipses over a wide area surrounding the Laacher See. Growth disturbances to trees in northern Switzerland, 250 km south of the Laacher See, seem to be related to the eruption (K.F. Kaiser, cited by Bosinski 1983: 52) and suggest that the eruption was followed by several years of climatic deterioration, a common phenomenon after volcanic activity (Lamb 1977) in a large part of north-west Europe. Charcoal in soils from this period possibly indicates extensive forest fires, ignited by falls of hot volcanic ash. This was followed by the climatic deterioration of the Younger Dryas. If this event can be considered as a stressor which contributed to the observed social collapse during stage 3, it fulfils a number of characteristics mentioned by Edwards (1972): it was new, it was intense, it caused a rapidly changing environment, and it was sudden.

Archaeological evidence suggests a highly specialized adaptation during stage 3, when reindeer formed the overwhelming bulk of man's food supply (Rust 1943; Burch 1972; Clark 1975; Sturdy 1975). Butzer (1971) has argued that:

> the disappearance or emigration of ... the reindeer herds ... during the Preboreal removed the cornerstone of the European meat supply. Such changes would have introduced a major food crisis for specialized hunters (1971: 537).

Such a crisis would seem to be due to overspecialization (cf. Clarke 1978: 98), and its social consequences would conform to the Law of Evolutionary Potential which states that the more adapted a form is to a given stage, the smaller is its potential for passing to the next stage (Sahlins and Service (eds) 1960: 97). Whether this stressor caused the observed collapse during stage 4 is difficult to ascertain; although it was new, it is unknown how rapid, sudden or intense it was.

Ample evidence, both typological and technological, of population continuity through all stages suggests that migrations were not the cause of the observed changes in the social components. Only the Bandkeramik agricultural settlement during the final Mesolithic is seen as direct colonization by intrusive migrant groups. Bandkeramik settlement was short-lived and, during its final stage, fortified sites (e.g. Lüning 1982, 1983) suggest some crisis (De Grooth

and Verwers 1984). It was followed by a rapid disintegration, probably indicating that agricultural innovation in the study area and bordering areas was not very successful (cf. Newell 1984). The as yet unknown effects of agricultural innovation on neighbouring band societies, which might include social and demographic pressures, may have caused the social collapse at the end of stage 6, resulting in a depopulation of the study area. In terms of characteristics of stressors, Bandkeramik immigration was new and rapid; to what extent it was sudden, fatigue producing and/or boring is difficult to substantiate. Nevertheless, it is interesting to note that this social collapse was simultaneous with the Bandkeramik crisis. Finally, archaeological evidence from the western and central Netherlands suggests that both Mesolithic and Neolithic adaptations were more successful in the Dutch coastal areas during the sixth millennium BP (e.g. Louwe Kooijmans 1976), than in the study area.

Many of the interpretations and propositions in this paper are based on evidence that is less than satisfactory. The archaeological record in the study area is poor in some aspects, particularly in faunal remains, and most of the data are derived from surface material, which has its own interpretative problems (cf. Lewarch and O'Brien 1981). Furthermore, some of the statements in this study are frankly speculative and open to question on a number of grounds. As always in studies like this, the need for more tangible evidence, including more well-excavated sites and more absolute dates, is underscored. It is interesting, nevertheless, that the relationships among individual components are not random, but change in a systematic way throughout the periods under study. The correlation obtained suggests that this case study will provide a reasonably solid base for further research. It would be interesting to compare the results of this study with data from a comparable time period in the North-west European Plain.

Acknowledgements: This work has been supported by the University of Amsterdam, the Dutch State Service for Archaeological Investigations at Amersfoort, and the Archeologische Sectie, Noordbrabants Genootschap at 's-Hertogenbosch. This paper has profited greatly from critical reviews of an earlier draft provided by Jos Deeben, Susan Loving, Ray Newell, Louise van Wijngaarden, and Willem Willems. Ray Newell also kindly made available some of his unpublished data; Susan Loving also edited the English text. It will be evident that this paper could not have been attempted without the collaboration of numerous amateur workers in the study area, who showed me their collections, talked them over, and offered me their hospitality over the past few years. Finally, my greatest personal indebtedness is to Marion; she knows why.

References

ALEKSHIN, V.A. (1983) Burial customs as an archaeological resource. *Current Anthropology*, 24: 137–149.

ARORA, S.K. (1976) Die mittlere Steinzeit in westlichen Deutschland und den Nachbargebieten. *Rheinische Ausgrabungen*, 17: 1–65.

L

ARORA, S.K. and BOSINSKI, G. (1978) Naturräume und Rohstoffe für die Steinwerkzeugherstellung. In S. Veil (ed.), *Alt- und mittelsteinzeitliche Fundplätze des Rheinlandes*. Bonn, Rheinisches Landesmuseum: 22–23.

ARTS, N. (1984) Waubach: a late Upper Palaeolithic/Mesolithic lithic raw material procurement site in Limburg, the Netherlands. *Helinium*, 24: 209–220.

ARTS, N. (in press *a*) A survey of final Palaeolithic archaeology in the southern Netherlands. In M. Otte (ed.), *Les Civilisations du Paléolithique Final de la Loire à l'Oder*. Oxford, British Archaeological Reports (International Series).

ARTS, N. (in press *b*) Mesolithische jagers, vissers en voedselverzamelaars in noordoost België en zuidoost Nederland. *Het Oude Land van Loon*.

ARTS, N. and DEEBEN, J. (1976) *Een Federmesser Nederzetting Langs de Kapeldijk te Westelbeers, Provincie Noord-Brabant*. Eindhoven, Stichting Brabants Heem.

ARTS, N. and DEEBEN, J. (1978) Een Federmesser nederzetting te Oostelbeers: een rapport betreffende de noodopgravingen in 1976. *Brabants Heem*, 30: 60–75.

ARTS, N. and DEEBEN, J. (1981) *Prehistorische Jagers en Verzamelaars te Vessem: een Model*. Eindhoven, Stichting Brabants Heem.

ARTS, N. and DEEBEN, J. (1987) On the northwestern border of late Magdalenian territory: ecology and archaeology of early Late Glacial band societies in northwestern Europe. In J.M. Burdukiewicz and M. Kobusiewicz (eds), *Late Glacial in Central Europe. Culture and Environment*. Wrocław, Zakład Narodowy imienia Ossolińskich.

BAHN, P.G. (1983) Late Pleistocene economies of the French Pyrenees. In G. Bailey (ed.), *Hunter-Gatherer Economy in Prehistory. A European Perspective*. Cambridge, University Press: 168–186.

BAILEY, G. (1983) Economic change in late Pleistocene Cantabria. In G. Bailey (ed.), *Hunter-Gatherer Economy in Prehistory. A European Perspective*. Cambridge, University Press: 149–165.

BERREMAN, G.D. (1981) Social inequality: a cross-cultural analysis. In G.D. Berreman and K.M. Zaretsky (eds), *Social Inequality. Comparative and Developmental Approaches*. New York, Academic Press: 3–40.

BISSCHOPS, J.H. (1973) *Toelichtingen bij de Geologische Kaart van Nederland 1:50.000. Blad Eindhoven Oost (51 O)*. Haarlem, Rijks Geologische Dienst.

BOHMERS, A. (1958) Statistics and graphs in the study of flint assemblages. II. A preliminary report on the statistical analysis of the Younger Palaeolithic in northwestern Europe. *Palaeohistoria*, 5: 8–25.

BOHMERS, A. (1960) Statistiques et graphiques dans l'étude des industries préhistoriques. V. Considérations générales au sujet du Hambourgien, du Tjongerian, du Magdalénien et de l'Azilien. *Palaeohistoria*, 8: 15–37.

BOHMERS, A. (1963) A statistical analysis of flint artefacts. In D.R. Brothwell and E.S. Higgs (eds), *Science in Archaeology*. London, Thames and Hudson: 469–481.

BOHMERS, A. and WOUTERS, A. (1958) Statistics and graphs in the study of flint assemblages. III. A preliminary report on the statistical analysis of the Mesolithic in northwestern Europe. *Palaeohistoria*, 5: 27–38.

BOHMERS, A. and WOUTERS, A. (1962) Belangrijke vondsten van de Ahrensburgcultuur in de gemeente Geldrop. *Brabants Heem*, 14: 3–20.

BORDAZ, J. (1970) *Tools of the Old and New Stone Age*. Newton Abbott, David and Charles.

BOSERUP, E. (1981) *Population and Technological Change. A Study of Long-Term Trends*. Chicago, University Press.

BOSINSKI, G. (1983) *Eiszeitjäger im Neuwieder Becken. Archäologie des Eiszeitalters am Mittelrhein*. Koblenz, Landesamt für Denkmalpflege Rheinland-Pfalz.

BOSSCHA ERDBRINK, D.P. (1982) Red deer keratic artefacts in Dutch collections. *Berichten van de Rijksdienst voor het Oudheidkundig Bodemonderzoek*, 32: 103–137.

BOSSCHA ERDBRINK, D.P., MEIKLEJOHN, C. and TACOMA, J. (1975) River Valley People: fossil human remains from the Limburg province, the Netherlands. *Proceedings of the Koninklijke Nederlandse Akademie van Wetenschappen*, C78: 226–264.

BOSSCHA ERDBRINK, D.P., MEIKLEJOHN, C. and TACOMA, J. (1983) River Valley People: cranial and postcranial material from the lower Meuse between Maasbommel and Hedel in the Netherlands. *Proceedings of the Koninklijke Nederlandse Akademie van Wetenschappen*, B86: 343–377.

BROERTJES, J.P. (1977) Het onstaan van de Brabantse vennen. In N. Roymans, J. Biemans, J. Slofstra and W.J.H. Verwers (eds), *Brabantse Oudheden*. Eindhoven, Stichting Brabants Heem: 19–25.

BRUSSAARD, L. and RUNIA, L. (1984) Recent and ancient traces of scarab beetle activity in sandy soils of the Netherlands. *Geoderma*, 34: 229–250.

BURCH, E.S. (1972) The caribou/wild reindeer as a human resource. *American Antiquity*, 37: 339–368.

BUTZER, K.W. (1971) *Environment and Archaeology. An Ecological Approach to Prehistory* (2nd edition). Chicago, Aldine.

BUURMAN, P. (1970) Pollen analysis of the Helvoirt river valley. *Geologie en Mijnbouw*, 49: 381–390.

CAMPBELL, J.M. (1968) Territoriality among ancient hunters: interpretations from ethnography and nature. In B.J. Meggers (ed.), *Anthroplogical Archaeology in the Americas*. Washington D.C., Anthropological Society of Washington: 1–21

CARNEIRO, R.L. (1970) Scale analysis, evolutionary sequences, and the rating of cultures. In R. Naroll and R. Cohen (eds), *A Handbook of Method and Theory in Cultural Anthropology*. New York, Natural History Press: 834–871.

CASPAR, J-P. 1084) Matériaux lithiques de la préhistoire. In D. Cahen and P. Haesaerts (eds), *Peuples Chasseurs de la Belgique Préhistorique dans leur Cadre Naturel*. Brussels, Institut royal des Sciences naturelles de Belgique: 107–114.

CLARK, G.A. and STRAUS, L.G. (1983) Late Pleistocene hunter-gatherer adptations in Cantabrian Spain. In G. Bailey (ed.), *Hunter-Gatherer Economy in Prehistory. A European Perspective*. Cambridge, University Press: 131–148.

CLARK, J.G.D. (1975) *The Earlier Stone Age Settlement of Scandinavia*. Cambridge, University Press.

CLARKE, D.L. (1978) *Analytical Archaeology* (2nd edition). London, Methuen.

CONINX, Y. (1984) Oker en zijn relatie tot de mens van de steentijd. *Archaeologische Berichten*, 15: 131–144.

CONKEY, M.W. (1978) Style and information in cultural evolution: toward a predictive model for the Palaeolithic. In C.L. Redman, M.J. Berman, E.V. Curtin, W.Y. Langhorne, N.M. Versaggi and J.C. Wanser (eds), *Social Archaeology: Beyond Subsistence and Dating*. New York, Academic Press: 61–85.

CONKEY, M.W. (1980) The identification of prehistoric hunter-gatherer aggregation sites: the case of Altamira. *Current Anthropology*, 21: 609–630.

CONSTANDSE-WESTERMANN, T.S., NEWELL, R.R. and MEIKLEJOHN, C. (1984) Human biological background of population dynamics in the western European Mesolithic. *Proceedings of the Koninklijke Nederlandse Akademie van Wetenschappen*, B87: 139–223.

COOPE, G.R., MORGAN, A. and OSBORNE, P.J. (1971) Fossil coleoptera as indicators of climatic fluctuations during the Last Glaciation in Britain. *Palaeogeography, Palaeoclimatology, Palaeoecology*, 10: 87–101.

DAVID, N. (1973) On Upper Palaeolithic society, ecology, and technological change: the Noaillian case. In C. Renfrew (ed.), *The Explanation of Culture Change. Models in Prehistory*. London, Duckworth: 277–303.

DEEBEN, J. (1985) *Een Federmesser Nederzetting te Geldrop. De Aktiviteiten Rond Twee Vuren*. Unpublished Masters thesis, Institute of Pre- and Protohistory, University of Amsterdam.

DE GROOTH, M.E.T. and VERWERS, G.J. (1984) *Op Goede Gronden. De Eerste Boeren in Noordwest Europa*. Leiden, Rijksmuseum van Oudheden.

DE PLOEY, J. (1963) Palynological investigations of Upper Pleistocene and Holocene deposits in the lower Kempenland (Belgium). *Grana Palynologica*, 4: 428–438.

EDWARDS, D.C. (1972) *General Psychology* (2nd edition). New York, Macmillan.

ELLEN, R. (1982) *Environment, Subsistence and System. The Ecology of Small-scale Social Formations.* Cambridge, University Press.

GAMBLE, C. (1983) Culture and society in the Upper Palaeolithic of Europe. In G. Bailey (ed.), *Hunter-Gatherer Economy in Prehistory. A European Perspective.* Cambridge, University Press: 201–211.

GENDEL, P.A. (1982*a*) The distribution and utilisation of Wommersom quartzite during the Mesolithic. In A. Gob and F. Spier (eds), *Le Mésolithique entre Rhin et Meuse.* Luxembourg, Société Préhistorique Luxembourgeoise: 21–50.

GENDEL, P.A. (1982*b*) An analysis of stylistic variation in some late Mesolithic assemblages from northwestern Europe. *Bulletin de la Société royale belge d'Anthropologie et de Préhistoire*, 93: 51–62.

GENDEL, P.A. (1983) *Mesolithic Social Territories in Northwestern Europe.* Unpublished Ph.D. thesis, University of Wisconsin–Madison.

GENDEL, P.A. (1984) *Mesolithic Social Territories in Northwestern Europe.* Oxford, British Archaeological Reports (International Series) S218.

GOB, A. (1981) *Le Mésolithique dans le Bassin de l'Ourthe* (Mémoire de la Société wallone de Palethnologie, 3). Liège, Presses Universitaires.

GOULDNER, A.W. and PETERSON, R.A. (1962) *Notes on Technology and the Moral Order.* Indianapolis, Bobbs–Merill.

HARRIS, D. (1977) Settling down: an evolutionary model for the transformation of mobile bands into sedentary communities. In J. Friedman and M.J. Rowlands (eds), *The Evolution of Social Systems.* London, Duckworth: 401–417.

HAYDEN, B. (1981) Research and development in the Stone Age: technological transitions among hunter-gatherers. *Current Anthropology*, 22: 519–548.

HEESTERS, W. (1967) Mesolithicum te Nijnsel. *Brabants Heem*, 19: 168–178.

HEESTERS, W. (1969) Mesolithische variaties. *Brabants Heem*, 21: 14–20

HEESTERS, W. (1971) Een Mesolithische nederzettenis te Sint-Oedenrode. *Brabants Heem*, 23: 94–115.

HEESTERS, W. and WOUTERS, A. (1968) Een Vroeg-Mesolithische kultuur te Nijnsel. *Brabants Heem*, 20: 98–108.

HEESTERS, W. and WOUTERS, A. (1970) De Tjongerkultuur in de Rips (gem. Bakel). *Brabants Heem*, 22: 2–20.

HOWELL, J.M. (1983) *Settlement and Economy in Neolithic Northern France.* Oxford, British Archaeological Reports (International Series) S157.

HUBERT, F. (1980) Obourg, Gem. und Kr. Mons, Prov. Hainaut. In G. Weisgerber (ed.), *5000 Jahre Feuersteinbergbau.* Bochum, Deutschen Bergbau-Museum: 422–423.

HUYGE, D. and VERMEERSCH, P.M. (1982) Late Mesolithic settlement at Weelde-Paardsdrank. In P.M. Vermeersch (ed.), *Contributions to the Study of the Mesolithic of the Belgian Lowland* (Studia Praehistorica Belgica, 1). Tervuren, Koninklijk Museum voor Midden-Afrika: 115–203.

JANSSEN, C.R. (1960) On the Late-glacial and Post-glacial vegetation of south Limburg (Netherlands). *Wentia*, 4: 1–112.

JOCHIM, M.A. (1979) Breaking down the system: recent ecological approaches in archaeology. In M.B. Schiffer (ed.), *Advances in Archaeological Method and Theory*, 2. New York, Academic Press: 77–117.

JOCHIM, M.A. (1983) Palaeolithic cave art in ecological perspective. In G. Bailey (ed.), *Hunter-Gatherer Economy in Prehistory. A European Perspective.* Cambridge, University Press: 212–219.

KALIS, A.J. (1980) *Palynologisch onderzoek van de vegetatiegeschiedenis in verband met de bewoningsgeschiedenis van het Duits-Nederlandse loesslandschap.* Paper presented to the 10th Congress of Dutch Archaeologists, Maastricht, 13–14 November 1980.

KOZŁOWSKI, J.K. and KOZŁOWSKI, S.K. (1977) *Epoka Kamienia na Ziemiach Polskich.* Warsaw, Państwowe Wydawnictwo Naukowe.

KOZŁOWSKI, S.K. (1980) *Atlas of the Mesolithic in Europe (First Generation Maps).* Warsaw, University Press.

KUYL, O.S. (1980) *Toelichtingen bij de Geologische Kaart van Nederland 1:50,000. Blad Heerlen (62 W oostelijke helft, 62 O westelijke helft).* Haarlem, Rijks Geologische Dienst.

LAMB, H.H. (1977) *Climate. Present, Past and Future. 2. Climatic History and the Future.* London, Methuen.

LANTING, J.N. and MOOK, W.G. (1977) *The Pre- and Protohistory of the Netherlands in Terms of Radiocarbon Dates.* Groningen, Radiocarbon Laboratory.

LEWARCH, D.E. and O'BRIEN, M.J. (1981) The expanding role of surface assemblages in archaeological research. In M.B. Schiffer (ed.), *Advances in Archaeological Method and Theory*, 4. New York, Academic Press: 297–342.

LEYSEN, V. (1984) *Materiaalstudie van het Site Achterste Brug (Valkenswaard).* Unpublished Masters thesis, Instituut voor Aardwetenschappen, University of Leuven.

LOUWE KOOIJMANS, L.P. (1976) Local developments in a borderland. A survey of the Neolithic in the Lower Rhine. *Oudheidkundige Mededelingen van het Rijksmuseum van Oudheden te Leiden*, 57: 227–297.

LÜNING, J. (1982) Siedlung und Siedlungslandschaft in Bandkeramischer und Rössener Zeit. *Offa*, 39: 9–33.

LÜNING, J. (1983) Stand und Aufgaben der siedlungsarchäologischen Erforschung des Neolithikums im Rheinischen Braunkohlenrevier. *Rheinische Ausgrabungen*, 24: 33–46.

MAARLEVELD, G.C. (1960) Wind directions and coversands in the Netherlands. *Biuletyn Peryglacjalny*, 8: 49–58.

MAUSS, M. and BEUCHAT, M.H. (1979) *Seasonal Variations of the Eskimo. A Study in Social Morphology.* London, Routledge and Kegan Paul.

MELLARS, P. (1976) Settlement patterns and industrial variability in the British Mesolithic. In G. de G. Sieveking, I.H. Longworth and K.E. Wilson (eds), *Problems in Economic and Social Archaeology.* London, Duckworth: 375–399.

MIKKELSEN, E. (1978) Seasonality and Mesolithic adaptation in Norway. In K. Kristiansen and C. Paludan-Müller (eds), *New Directions in Scandinavian Archaeology.* Copenhagen, National Museum of Denmark: 79–119.

MODDERMAN, P.J.R. (1981) Céramique du Limbourg: Rhénanie-Westphalie, Pays-Bas, Hesbaye. *Helinium*, 21: 140–160.

MODDERMAN, P.J.R. (1982) Eléments non-rubanes du Néolithique ancien entre les vallées du Rhin inférieur et de la Seine. *Helinium*, 22: 272–273.

MOORE, J.A. (1981) The effects of information networks in hunter-gatherer societies. In B. Winterhalder and E.A. Smith (eds), *Hunter-Gatherer Foraging Strategies. Ethnographic and Archaeological Analyses.* Chicago, University Press: 194–217.

MUNAUT, A.V. (1967) *Recherches Paleo-écologiques en Basse et Moyenne Belgique.* Louvain, Institut de Geographie.

NAROLL, R. (1956) A preliminary index of social development. *American Anthropologist*, 58: 687–716.

NEWELL, R.R. (1970*a*) *The Mesolithic Affinities and Typological Relations of the Dutch Bandkeramik Flint Industry.* Unpublished PhD thesis, University of London.

NEWELL, R.R. (1970*b*) The flint industry of the Dutch Linearbandkeramik. In P.J.R. Modderman, *Linearbandkeramik aus Elsloo und Stein.* 's-Gravenhage, Staatsuitgeverij: 144–183.

NEWELL, R.R. (1970*c*) Een afslagbijl uit Anderen, gem. Anloo en zijn relatie tot het Atlantisch Mesolithicum. *Nieuwe Drentse Volksalmanak*, 1970: 177–184.

NEWELL, R.R. (1972) The Mesolithic affinities and typological relations of the Dutch Bandkeramik flint industry. In J. Fitz and J. Makkay (eds), *Die aktuellen Fragen der Bandkeramik.* Székesfehérvár, Musei Stephani Regis: 9–38.

NEWELL, R.R. (1973) The Post-glacial adaptations of the indigenous population of the Northwest European Plain. In S.K. Kozłowski (ed.), *The Mesolithic in Europe.* Warsaw, University Press: 399–440.

NEWELL, R.R. (1975) Mesolithicum. In G.J. Verwers (ed.), *Noord-Brabant in Pre- en Protohistorie.* Oosterhout, Anthropological Publications: 39–54.

NEWELL, R.R. (1979) Comment on: D. Cahen, L.H. Keeley and F. Van Noten, 'Stone tools, toolkits, and human behavior in prehistory'. *Current Anthropology*, 20: 675–676.

NEWELL, R.R. (1981) Mesolithic dwelling structures: fact and fantasy. In B. Gramsch (ed.), *Mesolithikum in Europa. 2. Internationales Symposium Potsdam, 3 bis 8 April 1978 Bericht* (Veröffentlichungen des Museums für Ur- und

Frühgeschichte, 14/15). Berlin, Deutscher Verlag der Wissenschaften: 235–284.

NEWELL, R.R. (1984) On the Mesolithic contribution to the social evolution of western European society. In J. Bintliff (ed.), *European Social Evolution: Archaeological Perspectives*. Bradford, University of Bradford: 69–82..

NEWELL, R.R. and CONSTANDSE-WESTERMANN, T.S. (1986) Population growth, density and technology in the western European Mesolithic: lessons from analogous historical contexts. *Palaeohistoria*, 26: 1–18.

NEWELL, R.R., CONSTANDSE-WESTERMANN, T.S. and MEIKLEJOHN, C. (1979) The skeletal remains of Mesolithic man in western Europe: an evaluative catalogue. *Journal of Human Evolution*, 8: 1–228.

NEWELL, R.R. and DEKIN, A.A. (1978) An integrative strategy for the definition of behaviourally meaningful archaeological units. *Palaeohistoria*, 20: 7–38.

ODUM, E.P. (1983) *Basic Ecology*. Philadelphia, Saunders.

OPHOVEN, M., SACCASYN DELLA SANTA, E. and HAMAL-NANDRIN, J. (1948) *Utilisation à l'Age de la Pierre (Mésolithique) du Grès-quartzite de Wommerson*.

O'SHEA, J. and ZVELEBIL, M. (1984) Oleneostrovski mogilnik: reconstructing the social and economic organization of prehistoric foragers in northern Russia. *Journal of Anthropological Archaeology*, 3: 1–40.

OSWALT, W.H. (1973) *Habitat and Technology. The Evolution of Hunting*. New York, Holt, Rinehart and Winston.

PADDAYYA, K. (1971) The late Palaeolithic of the Netherlands – a review. *Helinium*, 11: 257–270.

PLOG, F.T. (1974) *The Study of Prehistoric Change*. New York, Academic Press.

PRICE, T.D. (1975) *Mesolithic Settlement Systems in the Netherlands*. Unpublished PhD thesis, University of Michigan.

PRICE, T.D. (1978) Mesolithic settlements in the Netherlands. In P.A. Mellars (ed.), *The Early Postglacial Settlement of Northern Europe*. London, Duckworth: 81–113.

PRICE, T.D. (1983) The European Mesolithic. *American Antiquity*, 48: 761–778.

ROOT, D. (1983) Information exchange and the spatial configurations of egalitarian societies. In J.A. Moore and A.S. Keene (eds), *Archaeological Hammers and Theories*. New York, Academic press: 139–219.

ROZOY, J-G. (1978) *Les Derniers Chasseurs. L'Epipaléolithique en France et en Belgique* (Bulletin de la Société archéologique champenoise, numéro spécial). Charleville, J-G. Rozoy.

RUST, A. (1943) *Die mittel- und altsteinzeitlichen Funde von Stellmoor*. Neumünster, Karl Wachholtz.

SAHLINS, M. and SERVICE, E.R. (eds) (1960) *Evolution and Culture*. Ann Arbor, University of Michigan Press.

SELYE, H. (1976) *The Stress of life* (2nd edition). New York, McGraw Hill.

SERVICE, E.R. (1962) *Primitive Social Organization. An Evolutionary Perspective*. New York, Random House.

SIEGEL, S. (1956) *Nonparametric Statistics for the Behavioral Sciences*. Tokyo, McGraw Hill–Kogakusha.

SLOFSTRA, J., VAN REGTEREN ALTENA, H.H., ROYMANS, N. and THEUWS, F. (1982) *Het Kempenproject. Een Regionaal-Archeologisch Onderzoeksprogramma*. Waalre, Stichting Brabants Heem.

SPAN, A. (1983) Prehistorische grotwand–kunst ook in Nederland? *Archaeologische Berichten*, 14: 138–145.

STAPERT, D. (1975) Paleolithicum. In G.J. Verwers (ed.), *Noord-Brabant in Pre- en Protohistorie*. Oosterhout, Anthropological Publications: 19–38.

STEWARD, J.H. (1955) *Theory of Culture Change*. Urbana, University of Illinois Press.

STURDY, D.A. (1975) Some reindeer economies in prehistoric Europe. In E.S. Higgs (ed.), *Palaeoeconomy*. Cambridge, University Press: 55–95.

TATJE, T.A. and NAROLL, R. (1970) Two measures of societal complexity: an empirical cross-cultural comparison. In R. Naroll and R. Cohen (eds), *A Handbook of Method in Cultural Anthropology*. New York, Natural History Press: 766–833.

VAN DEN TOORN, J.C. (1967) *Toelichting bij de Geologische Kaart van Nederland 1:50.000. Blad Venlo West (52 W)*. Haarlem, Rijks Geologische Dienst.

VAN DER HAMMEN, T. (1952) Late-glacial and periglacial phenomena in the Netherlands. *Leidse Geologische Mededelingen*, 17: 71–185.

VAN DER HAMMEN, T., MAARLEVELD, G.C., VOGEL, J.C. and ZAGWIJN, W.H. (1967) Stratigraphy, climatic succession and radiocarbon dating of the Last Glacial in the Netherlands. *Geologie en Mijnbouw*, 46: 79–95.

VAN DER LEEUW, S.E. (1981) Information flows, flow structures and the explanation of change in human institutions. In S.E. van der Leeuw (ed.), *Archaeological Approaches to the Study of Complexity*. Amsterdam, University of Amsterdam: 229–329.

VAN DER WAALS, J.D. (1972) Die durchlochten Rössener Keile und das frühe Neolithikum in Belgien und in den Niederlanden. In H. Schwabedissen (ed.), *Die Anfänge des Neolithikums vom Orient bis Nordeuropa. Va. Westliches Mitteleuropa*. Köln, Bohlau Verlag: 153–184.

VAN ES, W.A. and CASPARIE, W.A. (1968) Mesolithic wooden statuette from the Volkerak, near Willemstad, North Brabant. *Berichten van de Rijksdienst van het Oudheidkundig Bodemonderzoek*, 18: 111–116.

VAN LEEUWAARDEN, W. (1982) *Palynological and Macropalaeobotanical Studies in the Development of the Vegetation Mosaic in Eastern Noord-Brabant (the Netherlands) during Lateglacial and Early Holocene Times*. Unpublished Ph.D. thesis, University of Utrecht.

VANSTONE, J.W. (1974) *Athapaskan Adaptations. Hunters and Fishermen in the Subarctic Forests*. Arlington Heights, AHM Publishing Corporation.

VERHAGEN, J.H. (1984) *Prehistorie en Vroeggste Geschiedenis van West-Brabant*. Waalre, Stichting Brabants Heem.

VERMEERSCH, P.M. (ed.) (1982) *Contributions to the Study of the Mesolithic of the Belgian Lowland* (Studia Praehistorica Belgica, 1). Tervuren, Koninklijk Museum voor Midden-Africa.

VERMEERSCH, P.M. (1982) Quinze années de recherches sur le Mésolithique en basse Belgique. Etat de question. In A. Gob and F. Spier (eds), *Le Mésolithique entre Rhin et Meuse*. Luxembourg, Société Préhistorique Luxembourgeoise: 343–351.

VERMEERSCH, P.M. (1984) Du Paléolithique final au Mésolithique dans le nord de la Belgique. In D. Cahen and P. Haesaerts (eds), *Peuples Chasseurs de la Belgique Préhistorique dans leur Cadre Naturel*. Brussels, Institut royal des Sciences naturelles de Belgique: 181–193.

WELINDER, S. (1979) *Prehistoric Demography*. Lund, Gleerup.

WENKE, R.J. (1981) Explaining the evolution of cultural complexity: a review. In M.B. Schiffer (ed.), *Advances in Archaeological Method and Theory*, 4. New York, Academic Press: 79–127.

WHITE, L.A. (1959) *The Evolution of Culture*. New York, McGraw Hill.

WOUTERS, A. (1953) Het Palaeolithicum en Mesolithicum in Limburg. *Publications de la Société Historique et Archéologique dans le Limburg*, 88/89 (1952–1953): 1–18.

WOUTERS, A. (1954) Voorneolithische culturen in Brabant. *Brabants Heem*, 6: 122–148.

WOUTERS, A. (1957) Een nieuwe vindplaats van de Ahrensburg-cultuur onder de gemeente Geldrop. *Brabants Heem*, 9: 2–12.

WOUTERS, A. (1981a) Laat-Oldesloe uit Kesseleik (Midden-Limburg) en de typologie van deze 'Maglemose'-component (de Leien–Wartena-Complex). *Archaeologische Berichten*, 9: 128–130.

WOUTERS, A. (1981b) Wat is het 'De Leien–Wartena-Complex'....? *Archaeologische Berichten*, 9: 127, 140.

WOUTERS, A. (1982) Het Jong-Palaeolithicum. *Archaeologische Berichten*, 11/12: 5–27.

WOUTERS, A. (1983) Magdalenien uit het Peelgebied. *Archaeologische Berichten*, 14: 99–108.

ZAGWIJN, W.H. (1975) Indeling van het Kwartair op grond van veranderingen in vegetatie en klimaat. In W.H. Zagwijn and C.J. van Staalduinen (eds), *Toelichting op de Geologische Overzichtskaarten van Nederland*. Haarlem, Rijks Geologische Dienst: 109–114.

Excavations near Friesack: an Early Mesolithic Marshland Site in the Northern Plain of Central Europe

Bernhard Gramsch and Klaus Kloss

Abstract

Excavations have been conducted since 1977 at an early Mesolithic marshland site near Friesack, Potsdam District (G.D.R.). The site lies in the Warsaw–Berlin *Urstromtal* which is now filled with fluvioglacial sands and has extensive peat cover. At the time of occupation, the sands formed a topography of low hills with lakes and ponds in process of peat formation. The former habitation site is a low sand hill which had a small lake on its eastern and southern side.

The excavated part of the 'refuse area' in the shore zone of the lake consisted of a sequence of humic sands, peats and sands. Certain layers are directly associated with episodes of human activity, when sands were carried from the hill by wind and surface run-off. This resulted in a multi-stratified sequence of sediments. The results of sedimentological analysis, palynology and radiocarbon dating have suggested the following periods of occupation: (1) middle to late Pre-Boreal, 9700–9450 BP; (2) Pre-Boreal/Boreal transition, 9350–9150 BP; (3) early Boreal, 9050–8800 BP; (4) late Boreal/early Atlantic, 8150–7000 BP.

The finds comprise artifacts of flint, stone, bone, antler, teeth and wood. The stratigraphy allowed a detailed chronological subdivision of the finds. Of particular note are the numerous surviving artifacts of organic materials, including hafted bone points, antler mattocks and sleeves with wooden shafts, a perforated stone club with wooden handle, objects of wood and bast, fragments of arrows and spears, winding-boards, a wooden trough-like vessel, a carrying-handle of twisted rods or withes, and fragments of nets. Most of these objects came from the layers belonging to the second and third settlement phases. Among the many remains of hunted animals, red deer, roe deer and wild pig are the most numerous; but remains of beaver and tortoise are also important.

The sediments also indicate the frequency of occupation during the different settlement phases – altogether about 40 occupations can be distinguished. From the Pre-Boreal to early Boreal (according to the antler evidence) the season of occupation was spring, whereas in late Boreal/early Atlantic times the site was visited in the autumn. In the second and third settlement phases the social units occupying the site seem to have been larger than in the earlier and later periods. Until the early Boreal, hunting was the main subsistence activity; in the later periods the collecting of hazel-nuts was also important. Human influence on the natural environment can be seen in the palynological evidence for clearance of trees and the distribution of nitrogen-loving plants.

INTRODUCTION

Until now the earlier Mesolithic of the lowland region between the Rhine and the Oder has not been nearly so well researched as might be supposed from general reviews. Our knowledge relies for the most part on surface finds of flint artifacts from almost completely destroyed settlement sites, or on single finds of bone and antler artifacts from rivers, lakes and marshes. This situation contrasts with the state of research in northern countries, particularly Denmark, although similar geographical conditions should have ensured equally good preservation of early Mesolithic sites.

Apart from a few excavations of limited significance, only the excavations at Duvensee Moor (Schwantes 1925, 1939; Schwabedissen 1946, 1951; Bokelmann 1971, 1981) and Hohen Viecheln (Schuldt 1961) have given a significant insight into the range of material culture, settlement forms, economy, and ecology of early Mesolithic hunter-gatherer-fisher populations of the Rhine–Oder region. The findings from just two sites can, however, hardly be regarded as representative of a region of some 200,000 km². Any new site with well-preserved stratigraphy and archaeological remains must therefore receive particular attention. Friesack, about 60 km north west of Berlin in the Potsdam district, would appear to be such a site (*Fig. 1a*).

THE SITE OF FRIESACK AND ITS INVESTIGATION

The early Mesolithic site of Friesack lies within the Warsaw–Berlin *Urstromtal* (ice-marginal valley), about 30 km from the Elbe. The landforms and basic sediments date from the Weichsel Glaciation. The *Urstromtal* is filled with fluvioglacial sands (*Talsande*), which for the most part are covered with Holocene peats. Reclamation since the eighteenth century has lowered the surface by at least one metre and numerous sandy hills project above this level. The differing geomorphological conditions of the area, including the moraines to the south and north of the valley, have produced a wide variety of soils and vegetation.

In the early Holocene (Pre-Boreal and Boreal) the topography of the *Urstromtal* differed from that of today. There were flat, sandy plains with water-filled hollows, mostly small lakes and ponds of no great depth, and (probably) meandering streams. Some 30 sites within a 20 km length of the *Urstromtal* indicate that Mesolithic man seemed to prefer this watery landscape.

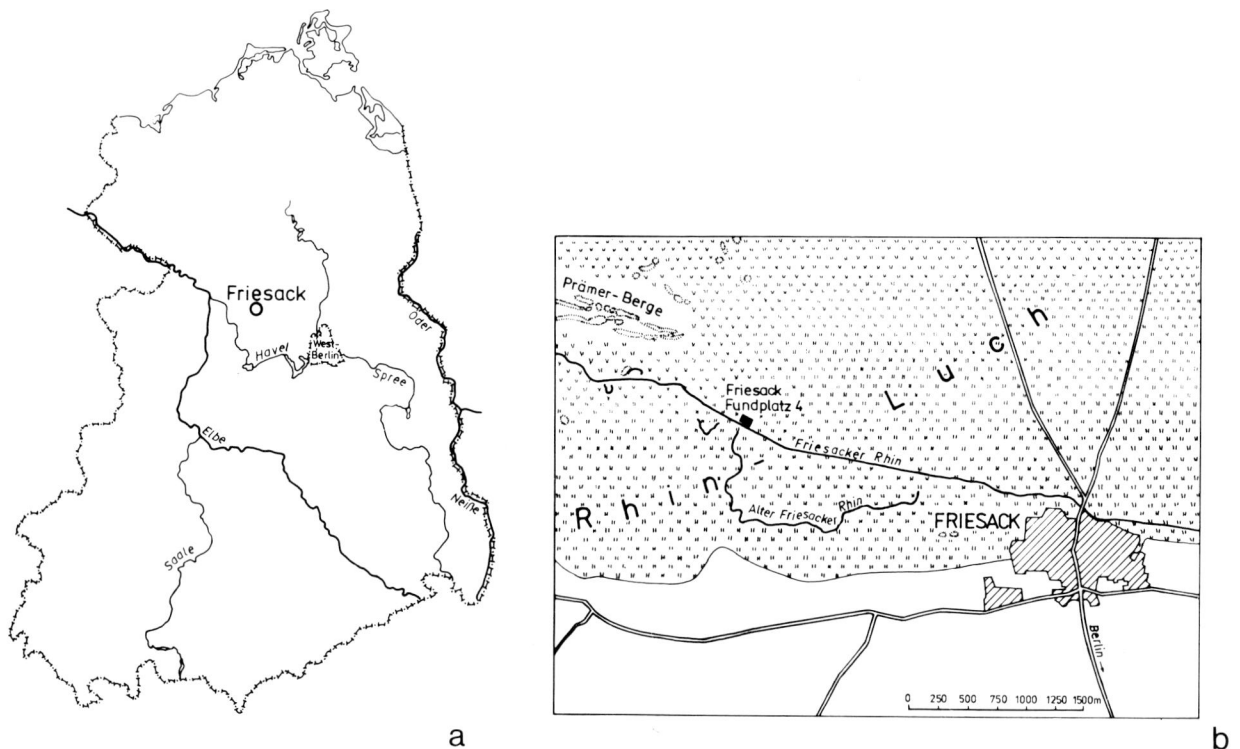

Figure 1   Friesack: *a*. location of the site in the German Democratic Republic; *b*. topographic situation.

The Friesack site is a low sandy hill which rises to a maximum height of 1.5 m above the surrounding area (*Fig. 1b*). Borings revealed a small channel to the east and a large depression to the south which in the early Holocene were filled with water. The site was discovered in 1910 and first excavated between 1916 and 1925 (Schneider 1932); a further, unpublished, excavation was carried out by Reinerth in 1940, some documentation of which is in the Potsdam Museum. These early investigations revealed an undisturbed deposit with Mesolithic and Neolithic flint, bone and antler artifacts on the eastern margin of the sandy hill – the former water-covered 'refuse area' of the habitation site. The habitation site itself has been largely destroyed by sand removal since the eighteenth century.

The present excavations have been in progress since 1977 because of a new reclamation project which will lower the water table by a further 0.5 m, thus endangering any prehistoric organic materials.

In the formerly water-covered margins of the habitation site a total area of 256 m² has been examined since 1977 (Gramsch 1979, 1981, 1985, 1987). In the early stages, the 2–3.5 m deep trenches were kept dry by pumping, but more recently by artificial lowering of the water table. All materials foreign to the sediments, with the exception of unworked roots of former and existing vegetation, were recorded separately according to layer and grid square. General sieving of the sediments was abandoned because of negligible results, but numerous samples were taken for sediment analysis and plant

macrofossil analysis, and column samples taken for pollen analysis.

STRATIGRAPHY

The investigation yielded surprising results on sediment formation and stratigraphy in the former underwater 'refuse area' of the habitation site. Below the present surface, with its middle to late Holocene peats containing two Neolithic artifact horizons, and overlying the late Weichselian sands, were layered sands containing undecayed plant remains, humic sands and sandy organic muds, as well as peats (*Fig. 2*). The peats and sandy organic muds form the basal layer, and the majority of the sedimentary layers between the late Pleistocene sands and later peats contain Mesolithic artifacts: flint and pebble artifacts as well as objects of bone, antler, wood, and bark. According to the geological investigations of Königsson (Uppsala) and Jäger (Halle), the formation of the sandy sediments was closely linked to human activity. During periods of settlement the vegetation on the hill and slope was destroyed and the sandy subsoil exposed, so that wind and surface water could transport the sand material to the lake or pool that once existed on the margin of the habitation site. In this area layered sediments incorporating archaeological remains formed during periods of settlement. The intervening layers contained sand with quantities of plant remains and, in deeper water, sandy organic muds with charcoal particles carried by the wind from the hearth areas of the former settlements. This multi-

314

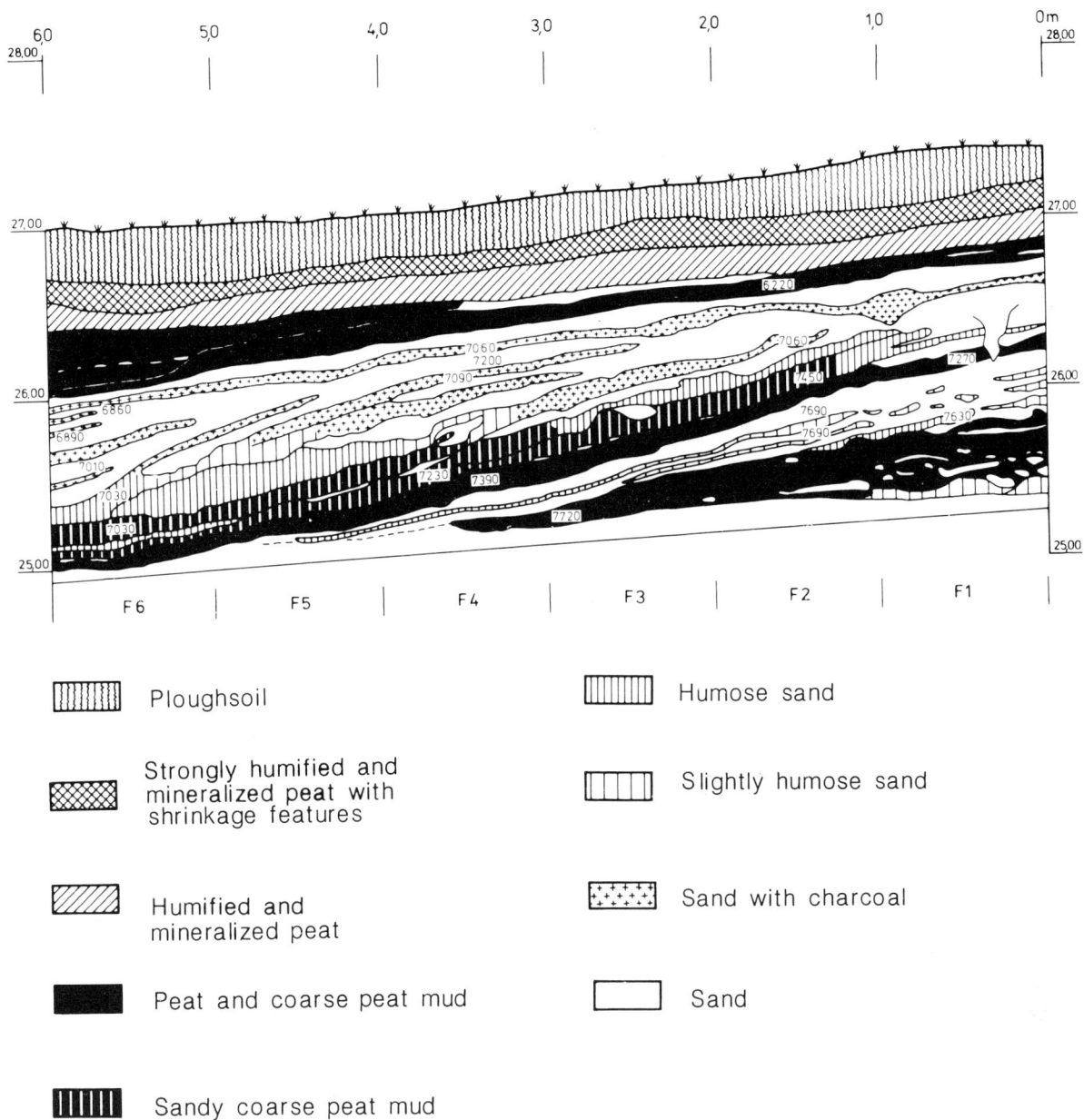

Figure 2 Friesack: Section Z (WNW–ESW). Radiocarbon dates in years BC. *Scale*, 1:40

Legend:
- Ploughsoil
- Strongly humified and mineralized peat with shrinkage features
- Humified and mineralized peat
- Peat and coarse peat mud
- Sandy coarse peat mud
- Humose sand
- Slightly humose sand
- Sand with charcoal
- Sand

layered stratigraphy appears to have formed in a zone that was sheltered from the prevailing wind by the hill.

So far, three such layered-sand complexes have been discovered, two of which have been studied in detail. They are similar in size – the maximum width at right angles to the shoreline is about 12 m, while the maximum depth or thickness is 0.7–0.8 metres. The volume of a one-metre wide average segment is 6–7 m^3. The lower, older complex was built up closer to the former shoreline than the upper, later complex (*Fig. 2*). According to the radiocarbon dates, both complexes appear to have been formed over quite short and approximately similar periods of time – the lower complex between 9700 and 9450 BP, the upper complex between 9050 and 8800 BP. The deposition of such a large body of sediments in a short period of time suggests some indirect human

influence in the process of wind and water transportation of material from the hill to the lake or pond edge. The third, only partially investigated, complex is further away from the former shore and the excavated section. It is stratigraphically later than the other two and has been partly removed by erosion.

The layers of the sand complexes overlie one another obliquely at an angle of 15–20°; the mud layers farthest from the shore cannot be separated with any certainty.

The middle peat formed after the deposition of the lower, older sand complex. Archaeological material is found only in the upper few centimetres of this complex and on top of it, indicating that the formation of the peat took place when man was absent. The interruption of peat development and the resumption of the deposition of the later sand

315

complex could again be associated with human activity and interference.

Occupation of the hill by hunter-fisher-gatherer groups began towards the end of the period of formation of the oldest Holocene peat – the beginning of the *Verlandung*[1] process of the bodies of water on the eastern and southern margins of the hill. The archaeological finds occurred in the upper strata of the peat. The surface of the peat showed three elongated hollows, at right angles to the former shore, each about 2–3 m wide and filled with alternating layers of sand and humic sand with charcoal. Radiocarbon dating indicates that these sand layers with their contents were being deposited at the same time as the archaeological material in the upper layers of the peat. This, coupled with underwater disturbance of the sediments, suggests regular use of the long hollows as 'pathways' into the shallow water. This suggestion is supported by the disturbance of the alignment of wood fragments and branches in the peat directly alongside the hollows, in contrast to the alignment of such objects parallel to the shoreline in areas away from the hollows. Similar features – the formation of elongated hollows and disturbance of sediments – can be observed at present-day bathing places with restricted access to the water.

Above the Pre-Boreal to early Atlantic sediments, the late Atlantic and Sub-Boreal peats have two dry horizons with indications of Neolithic settlement. The finds in the older horizon were few but characteristic; remains of pottery and T-shaped antler mattocks indicated a settlement of the earliest TRB culture, before 5000 BP. The later dry horizon had more numerous remains of the Havelland culture, a regional form of the middle Neolithic TRB, contemporary with and related to the Bernburg culture.

CHRONOLOGY

The chronology of Mesolithic settlement at the habitation site of Friesack has been secured by palynological and radiometric dating. All the sedimentary layers contained pollen, although the quantities were somewhat uneven. Pollen analyses have revealed that the layers containing artifacts accumulated between the middle Pre-Boreal and earlier Atlantic periods. The radiocarbon dates agree well with the palynological evidence. Fifty-four dates are at present available, all from the laboratory of the Academy of Sciences of the German Democratic Republic in Berlin. Almost all sediment layers were dated at least once, so that the concordance between the same layers in different cuttings could be checked. The radiocarbon determinations for samples from Section Z are shown in *Fig. 2*. Standard deviations range from ±60 to ±100 years.

The material for dating was, with one exception, charcoal, probably originating from hearths. In one case fir cones were dated because the level from which they came – the lowest peat layer, lacking archaeological finds – contained no charcoal.

The earliest date, 9940±100 BP (Bln-2754), relates to the lowest level of the basal peat, which produced no archaeological finds. The period from the uppermost level of the basal peat, which contained artifacts, to the end of the deposition of the lower layered-sand complex was covered by nine dates between 9680±70 BP (Bln-3036) and 9450±65 BP (Bln-1914). The peat layer above this and its overlay of sandy organic muds and humic sands have eight dates between 9340±70 BP (Bln-3025) and 9180±70 BP (Bln-3024). There is an anomalous date of 9400±70 BP (Bln-3018), probably from 'old' charcoal. Above this is the upper layered-sand complex with eighteen dates between 9040±70 BP (Bln-3008) and 8810±70 BP (Bln-3010); two further dates of *c.* 9150 BP are, according to the stratigraphic position of the samples, obviously too old. There then follows a gap, also indicated by the palynological evidence. The latest complex of sands containing artifacts, humic sands and organic muds is spread over a wider chronological range, having nine dates between 8170±60 BP (Bln-2999) and 6990±70 BP (Bln-3029).

Four settlement phases can thus be distinguished:

Phase 1: 9700–9450 BP (average 9590 BP)
Phase 2: 9350–9150 BP (average 9240 BP)
Phase 3: 9050–8800 BP (average 8960 BP)
Phase 4: 8150–7000 BP

Between these periods of settlement (and this is confirmed by the nature of the intervening sedimentation), the site appears not to have been visited. The same may be assumed for the periods immediately before 9700 BP and after 7000 BP.

A reliable chronological framework for the stratigraphic sequence of 75 sediment layers from the Pre-Boreal to the earlier Atlantic has thus been provided by pollen analysis and radiocarbon dating. This means that the archaeological remains from these layers have been dated with a relatively high degree of precision.

THE FINDS

The concentration of finds in the sediment layers of the former underwater 'refuse area' is extraordinarily high. The average for flint artifacts is 600 per m^2, and the maximum 4000 per m^2. The sand complex of the early Boreal is the most prolific part of the sequence, while the middle to late Pre-Boreal layer complex has significantly fewer flint artifacts (10–15% of the total from the early Boreal complex). Animal remains and artifacts of bone, antler and animal teeth have also survived in relatively large quantities (50–200 pieces per m²) with the early Boreal levels again having the largest numbers. Fragments of naturally-occurring and worked wood, including wooden artifacts, are found in all levels, but particularly in the peats and organic muds.

Lithic artifacts

Since the site consists of stone-free fluvioglacial sands, all the lithic material must have been brought to the site by human agency.

Analysis of the lithic finds has only just started,

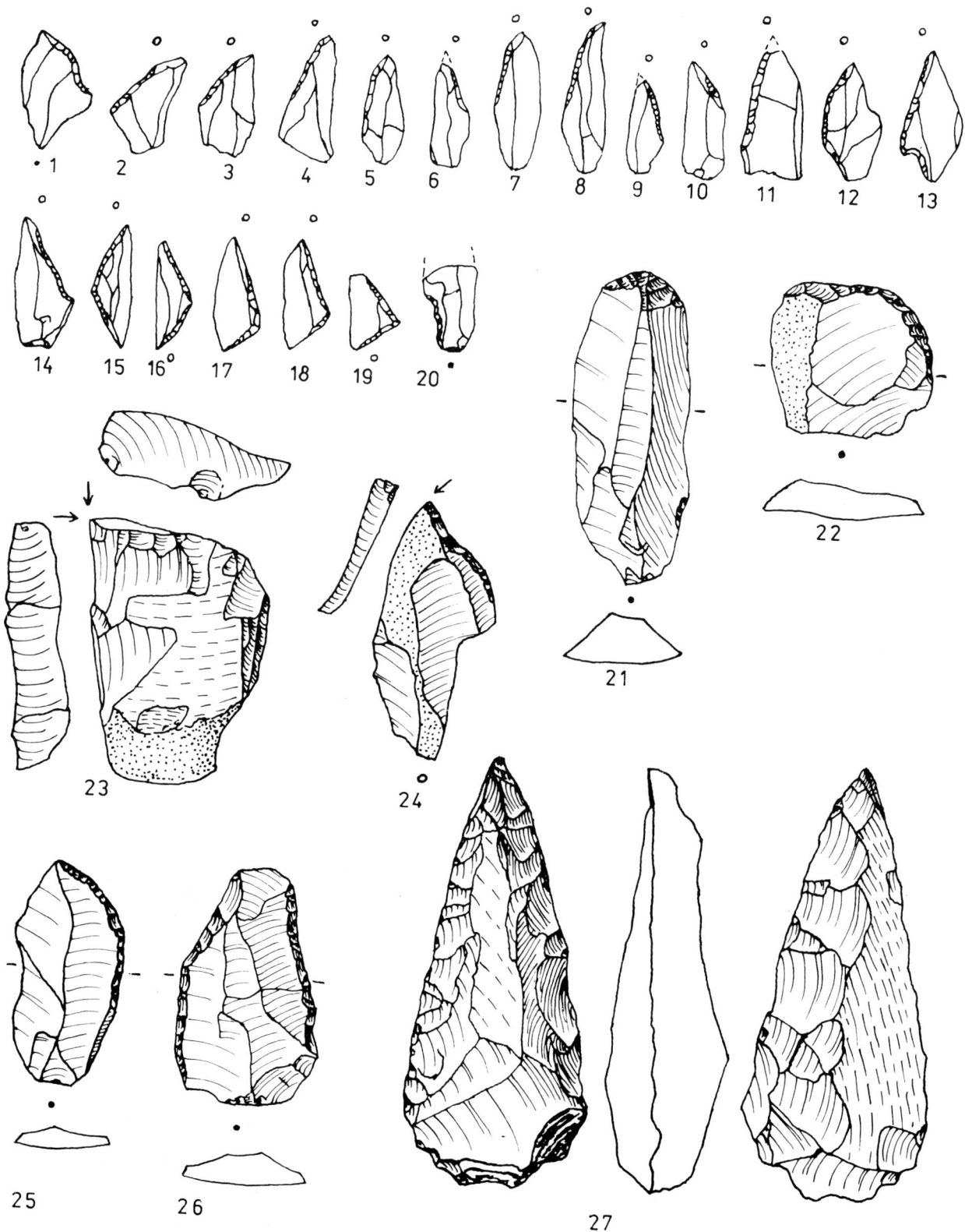

Figure 3 Friesack: flint tools from the Pre-Boreal layers. *Scale*, 1:1

but something can be said about the quantities. Among the 120,000 flint artifacts (all of northern flint) flakes, flake fragments, splinters and debris are by far the most numerous; blades and blade fragments constitute 10%; and cores (3–4%) are relatively numerous. Retouched artifacts, or 'tools', amount to about 2% of the total.

In the Mesolithic sediments microliths (c. 2000) form the largest tool group with, moreover, numerous microburins. Most (c. 60%) of the microliths come from the early Boreal complex; they are rarer (c. 30%) in the late Boreal/early Atlantic complex, and least frequent (c. 10%) in the middle to late Pre-Boreal horizons.

A preliminary view of the microliths from the Pre-Boreal period shows that the majority are points (c. 70% of all microliths), with triangular microliths (c. 25%) and edge- and end-retouched forms (c. 5%). The relatively broad points with oblique retouch (*Fig. 3*, nos. 1–3) and the points with partial retouch on one edge (*Fig. 3*, nos. 4–10) together form more than two-thirds of all points. Noteworthy is the occurrence of a few points retouched on both edges ('awls') and basal-retouched points. The percentage of triangular forms is astonishingly high for such an early period. There is a preponderance of scalene triangles with a length ratio of the two retouched edges of less than 2:1 (*Fig. 3*, nos. 17–19) over isosceles triangles (*Fig. 3*, nos. 15–16).

In the early Boreal levels the frequency of points drops to about 60%. Points with oblique retouch and points with partial retouch of one edge are the most numerous forms although they amount to only 45% of all points, while the percentage of points with total retouch of one edge increases. Points with basal retouch amount to 10% of all points. Triangles form 35% of all microliths and are generally narrower than in the Pre-Boreal period. Isosceles triangles, which constitute 30% of all triangles, are more numerous than in the Pre-Boreal period. Among the scalene triangles, forms with a length ratio of the retouched sides of greater than 2:1 appear for the first time (c. 20% of all triangles). The remaining triangles are scalene with a length ratio of the retouched sides of less than 2:1.

In the late Boreal–early Atlantic layers, points make up only 45% of all microliths. Points with partial retouch of one edge and points with oblique retouch together form rather less than 40%. Points with total retouch of one edge occur in about the same quantity. Points with basal retouch form 10% of all points. The triangles are all relatively narrow, isosceles forms making up 25% of all triangles. Narrow scalene triangles with a retouched side ratio of less than 2:1 are most numerous (c. 45% of all triangles). The triangles with a length ratio of the retouched edges of 3:1 or greater form 30% of all triangles, including a relatively large number of long narrow forms. Trapezes appear for the first time in this level (early Atlantic layers), although they represent only about 1% of all microliths.

The 700 implements on blades, flakes and waste pieces are treated only summarily here (*Fig. 3*, nos. 21–26). True scrapers are, in the Pre-Boreal as well as in later layers, extremely rare, but flakes, blades and waste pieces with edge retouch are numerous. Burins are also few.

Axes and 'picks' of flint are represented by 60 examples of relatively small size (*Fig. 3*, no. 27), and they show just as little careful working as the core tools of the Brandenburg Mesolithic as a whole (cf. Gramsch 1973: 23). That these were axe blades is shown by the discovery of a red deer antler sleeve with a small, and only crudely flaked, core axe still socketed in it (*Fig. 5*, no. 1). In the Pre-Boreal and early Boreal layers only core axes and 'picks' have so far been found; there are no flake axes. Individual tools resembling flake axes first appear in the later Boreal and early Atlantic periods.

Remarkable are nine implements of stone. From the early Boreal layers came two complete and two fragmentary pebble-axes (*Fig. 6*, no. 1), as well as three fragments of clubs (*Fig. 6*, nos. 2–3), and a fragment of a sandstone arrow-smoother. Particularly interesting is a complete stone club, with drilled shaft-hole in which the wooden shaft has survived, from the early Atlantic level. This has parallels with a find from Segebro, Scania (Larsson 1982: 57). In one of the Pre-Boreal levels, a piece of pyrites smoothed on all sides was discovered – this was probably used for working bone artifacts.

Bone, antler and tooth artifacts

So far, almost 500 objects of bone, antler and animal teeth have been recovered from all levels, as well as partly-worked and waste pieces. More than 100 artifacts were also removed by mechanical diggers from the channel on the southern side of the habitation site.

The excavated objects include 284 bone points and fragments. These are, with only a few exceptions, manufactured from cervid limb bones. Only five points with small barbs, found close together, are of red deer antler. Simple bone points (*Fig. 4*, nos. 1–4) occur from the middle Pre-Boreal to the early Atlantic. Points with notches (*Fig. 4*, nos. 5–7) occur mainly in the Pre-Boreal and early Boreal, although a few single finds came from late Boreal and early Atlantic levels. Points with small barbs near the tip (*Fig. 4*, nos. 8–12) appear at the Pre-Boreal/Boreal transition, but also occur in later layers.

Particular mention must be made of three simple bone points still attached to their broken wooden shafts by means of bast binding and pitch. *Fig. 6*, no. 11 shows the best preserved example. The bast binding under the pitch is easily recognizable by X-

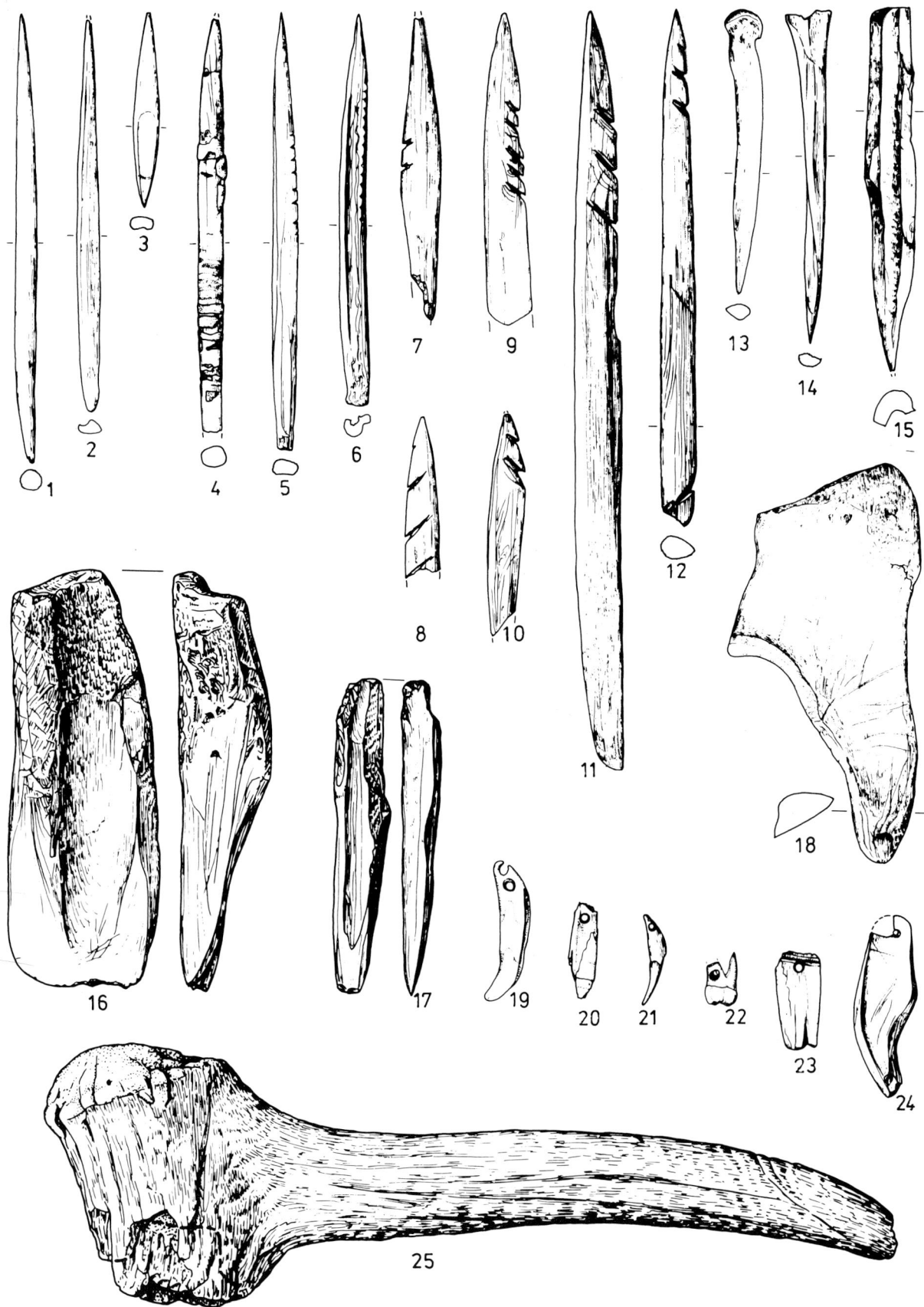

Figure 4   Friesack: bone and antler tools (1–18, 25); animal teeth and bone ornaments (19–24). *Scale*, 1:2

ray photography. Other points with traces of pitch must also have been hafted in similar fashion. The three hafted examples and some points with traces of pitch appear to have been bound to the haft along two-thirds of their length, and some points with notches had some of their notches in the area of binding with the haft. Comparable examples of hafted points from the early Mesolithic are so far unknown.

Other points had been hafted by binding with narrow strips of bast, but without pitch (*Fig. 6, no. 12*). On one point a small fragment of wooden shaft survived. Comparable is a barbed point fastened to a hazel shaft with bast cord, from Ulkestrup Lyng (Andersen, Jørgensen and Richter 1982: 45, fig. 68). This method of hafting was probably restricted to points with barbs; several points of this type have recognizable narrow corrosion strips running obliquely to, and across, the long axes.

Other bone or antler artifacts include 38 awls (*Fig. 4, nos. 13–15*), 12 chisel-like tools or insets for sockets (*Fig. 4, nos. 16–17*), 20 'axe-blades' of deer and elk antler (*Fig. 5, no. 4*), 34 perforated deer antler mattocks or sockets (*Fig. 5, no. 3*), three with surviving wooden shafts, and two unperforated tool mounts (*Fig. 4, no. 25*). There are also an unperforated deer antler implement with a cutting edge, deer antler points with blunt or obliquely cut ends, a bone 'needle' perforated at one end, perhaps for making nets, two dorsal vertebrae with knife-like sharpened projections, an aurochs ulna with sharpened edge (*Fig. 4, no. 18*), a fragment of perforated bone mattock made from an aurochs ulna, a bird's mandible with sharpened ramus, a small bird-bone splinter with pointed end and one barb, two carefully worked bone splinters with edge 'retouch', and a small perforated bone plate (*Fig. 4, no. 23*).

Only wild boar teeth had been made into tools for scraping or smoothing; otherwise teeth were perforated and used as ornaments (20 examples),

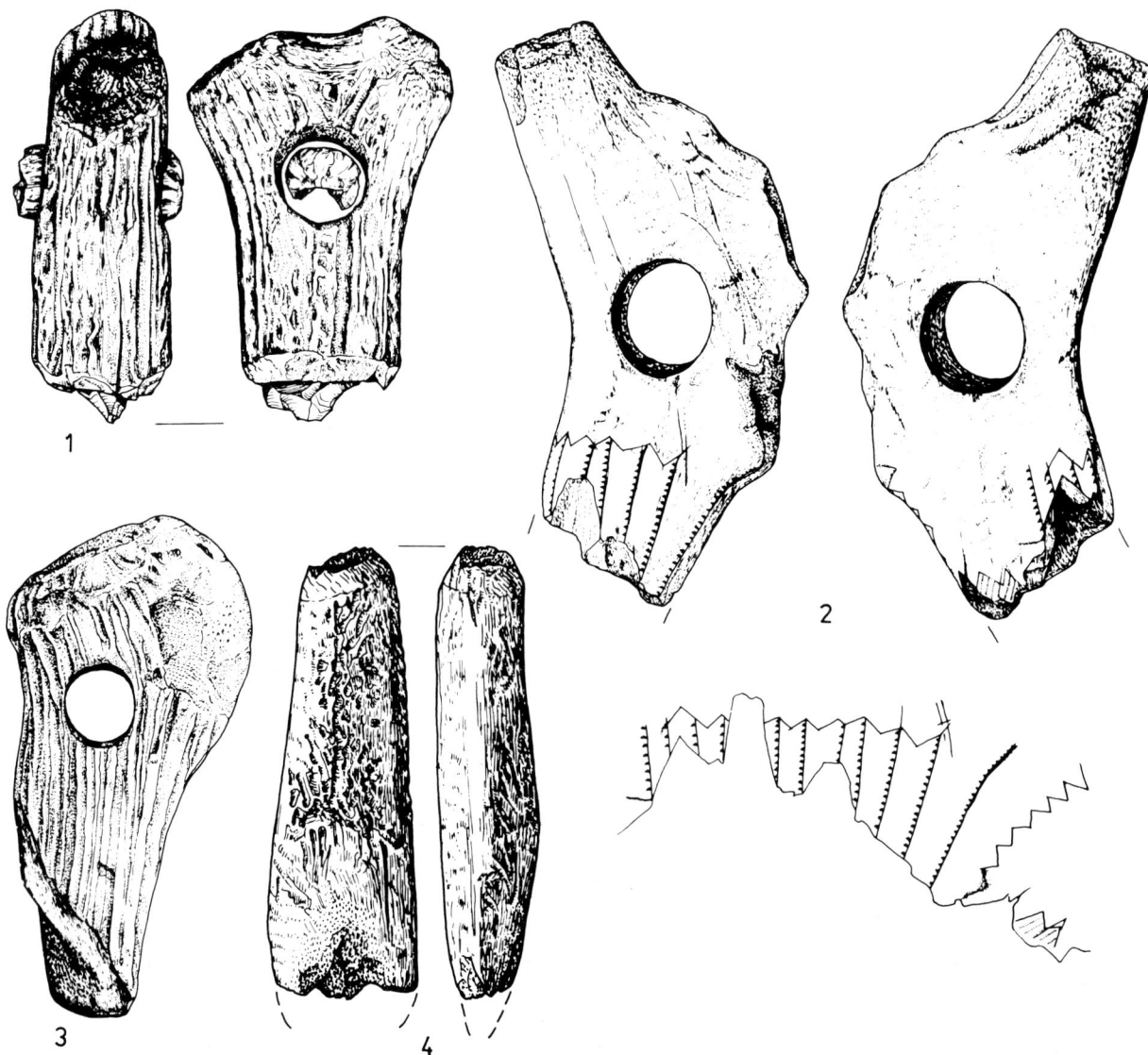

Figure 5   Friesack: red deer antler artifacts. *Scale,* 1:2

320

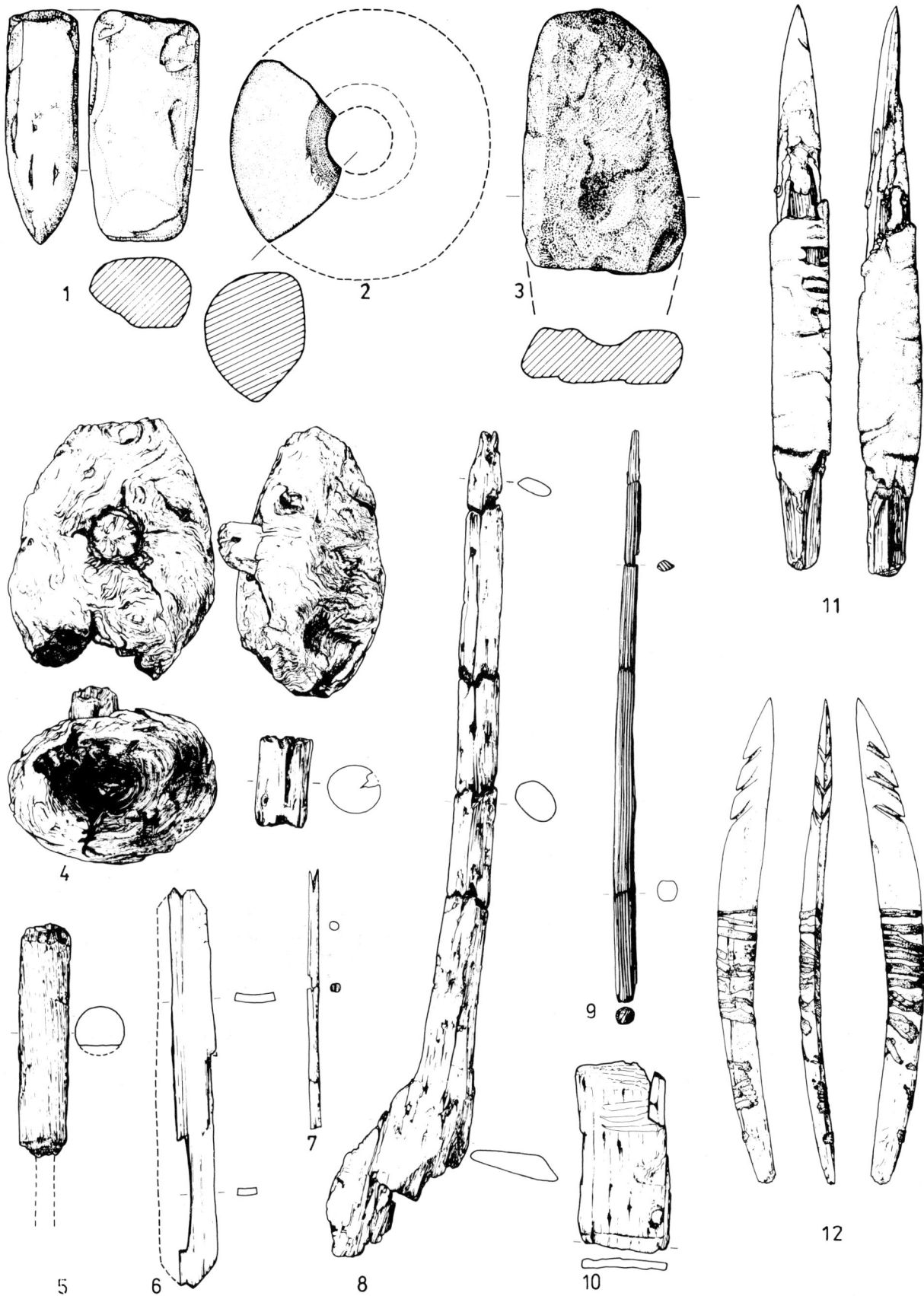

Figure 6 Friesack: stone tools (1–3: *scale*, 1:2); artifacts of wood and bark (4–10: *scale*, 1:3); bone point with wooden shaft and pitch (11: *scale*, 2:3); bone point with bast binding (12: *scale*, 1:2).

including teeth of cervids, wild pig, (*Fig. 4*, no. 20), aurochs, wolf (*Fig. 4*, no. 19), fox (*Fig. 4*, no. 21), and one human canine and one human molar (*Fig. 4*, no. 22) – an occurrence so far unique in the early Mesolithic of central and northern Europe.

Only four decorated bone or antler pieces have so far been recovered: from the Pre-Boreal, a burnt bone fragment with a few carefully engraved double zig-zag lines; from the early Boreal, a phalanx with three parallel short grooves; from the late Boreal, an antler axe-sleeve made from a broken 'bâton de commandement' (with the remains of an incised motif of grooves and zig-zag lines – *Fig. 5*, no. 2), and an awl with two rows of parallel grooves. In the material removed from the channel by mechanical diggers were found fragments of three decorated 'bâtons de commandement' of deer antler, a fragment of a decorated antler point, and part of a decorated shell of a European pond tortoise dating (based on pollen analysis of the attached peat) to the late Boreal/early Atlantic period.

The bone–antler–tooth industry from Friesack includes almost all the characteristic forms of the west Baltic Maglemose complex; but the range of forms of Maglemose type emerges only at the transition from Pre-Boreal to Boreal, whilst the Pre-Boreal Mesolithic of Friesack has in addition to 103 simple and notched bone points, *inter alia*, only six bone awls, two bone chisels or scrapers, including a large example of the type found at Star Carr (Clark 1954: fig. 73), three 'axe-blades' of deer and elk antler, an unperforated sleeve or socket of deer antler, four perforated animal teeth, and a perforated human tooth.

Artifacts of wood and bark

Since 1981 more than 100 wooden artifacts have been recovered, but the condition of many does not allow much to be said about function. They include fragments of spears (*Fig. 6*, no. 9), arrows (*Fig. 6*, no. 7), blunted arrows for bird hunting or the recovery of undamaged pelts (*Fig. 6*, no. 5), a bow, two small boards with opposed notches (perhaps for winding bast cord? – *Fig. 6*, no. 6), a possible digging-stick with fire-hardened semi-circular end, fragments of two paddles (*Fig. 6*, no. 8), and an apparently worked knot[2] of pine wood. Other wooden objects had been mechanically excavated from the channel, including three axe sockets (*Fig. 6*, no. 4). The high level of wood-working in the early Mesolithic is emphasized by the discovery of fragments of a carefully worked, pointed-ended trough, like the Australian aboriginal 'koolamon'. Unique for the Mesolithic is a handle, made of twisted rods, for a basket or carrying net. The wood is mostly pine (*Pinus sylvestris*) – particularly the spear and arrow remains, the bow, the majority of board and plank-like pieces, and the winding board. The digging-stick

is ash (*Fraxinus excelsior*), while the paddles are probably of *Sorbus*. Alder (*Alnus*), hazel (*Corylus*) and poplar (*Populus*) are also represented.

As at other Mesolithic marshland sites in Europe, numerous rolls of birch bark were found, at least some of which must have been used to produce pitch or resin for hafting implements, as indicated by one roll with pitch adhering to it. Lumps and flat pieces of resin occur in the Pre-Boreal and early Boreal levels, teeth marks suggesting that some of these had been chewed. Other pieces of tree bark may have formed part of a vessel (*Fig. 6*, no. 10).

The use of plant fibres, or bast, has been shown by the bone point hafting in the early Boreal and by the fragments of nets from the same period. The technique of net manufacture (*Fig. 7*) has so far only been seen in the Neolithic of Switzerland and Denmark and, more recently, at the early Ertebølle site of Tybrind Vig on the Danish island of Funen (Andersen and Bender Jørgensen 1985). Whether the Friesack nets were for fishing or carrying purposes is not clear. The oldest fragments of bast at Friesack belong to the period around 9600 BP.

ECOLOGY, SETTLEMENT AND ECONOMY

The list of fauna so far includes: otter (*Lutra lutra*), wolf (*Canis lupus*), brown bear (*Ursus arctos*), lynx (*Lynx lynx*), wild cat (*Felis silvestris*), wild pig (*Sus scrofa*), red deer (*Cervus elaphus*), roe deer (*Capreolus capreolus*), elk (*Alces alces*), aurochs (*Bos primigenius*), beaver (*Castor fiber*), hare (*Lepus europaeus*), pike (*Esox lucius*), catfish (*Siluris glanis*), European pond tortoise (*Emys orbicularis*), and large species of birds – mostly water birds. Human remains are so far represented only by a small skull fragment and the perforated teeth already mentioned.

The main animals hunted were red deer, roe deer and wild pig, but there are also significant quantities of beaver and tortoise remains. There are a few elk remains in the Pre-Boreal, and fish are not numerous.

The environment around the site in the early Postglacial period has been reconstructed from evidence of pollen and sediment borings (Kloss 1987a, 1987b). Around the inhabited sand hill were small, reed-fringed lakes, sandy areas, marshes, and birch woods. The sandy areas had pine woods of varying density.

It was vital for human occupation that the small, shallow lakes were more and more organically productive as the climate became warmer, contributing to a rich flora and fauna, and above all providing food for fish and birds, and eventually man. These small, shallow lakes were thus more important to the contemporary economy and settlement than larger, deeper, and thus colder, bodies of water.

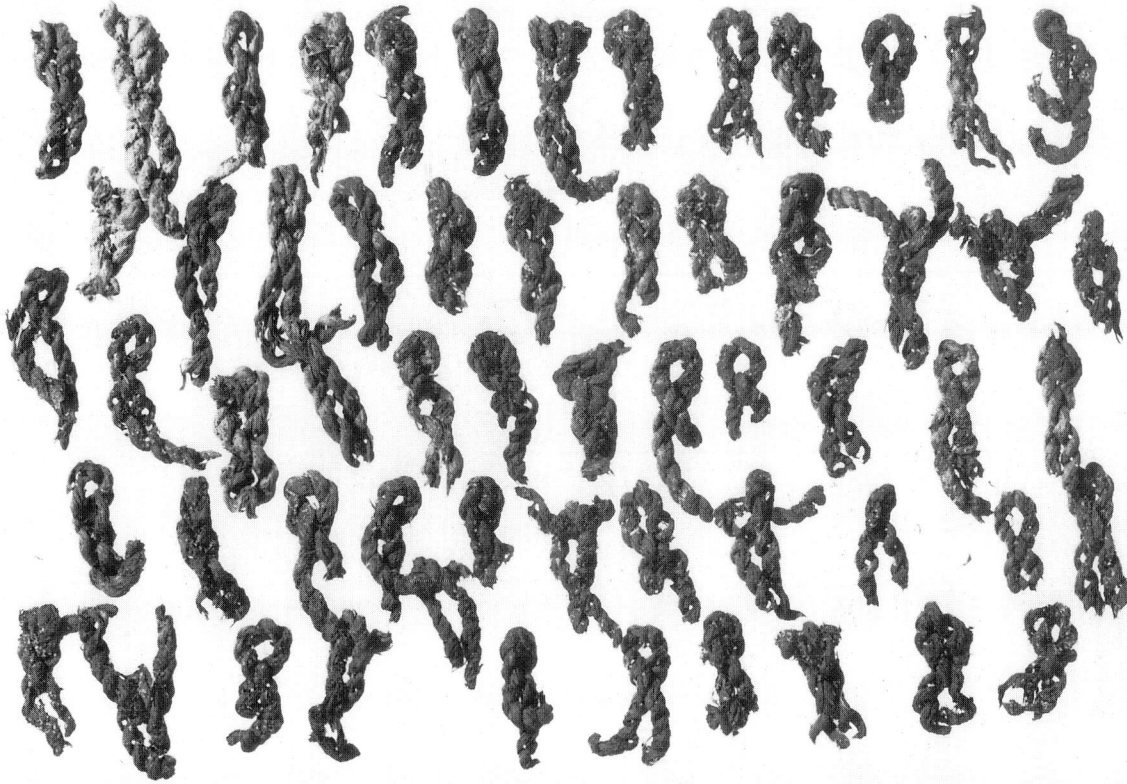

Figure 7   Friesack: fragments of a net made of plant fibres. *Scale*, 4:3

In the Boreal period, the vegetation of woods and marshes were of equal importance. Reeds were the main vegetation type in treeless areas, but there were also areas free of trees on the sand hills in the wet, low-lying areas.

In the late Boreal and early Atlantic, mixed-oak forest became more significant. There was a marked reduction in pine, birch and hazel, and ash appeared. Water bodies diminished due to the progressive *Verlandung* of the area, with the development of eutrophic vegetation, particularly broad-leaved reeds (*Typha latifolia*).

The sediments near the margins of the water to the east and south of the hill suggest discontinuous occupation of the site. Anthropogenic sediments intercalated with undisturbed 'natural' layers indicate times when people were absent. The following settlement phases are indicated: middle to late Pre-Boreal (9700–9450 BP) – approximately 15 settlement episodes; Pre-Boreal/Boreal transition (9350–9150 BP) – approximately five settlements; early Boreal (9050–8800 BP) – approximately 15 settlements; late Boreal to early Atlantic (8150–7000 BP) – approximately five settlements, separated by long intervals.

On the basis of the sedimentary sequence, it may be suggested that the site was occupied on a seasonal, non-permanent basis, not every year but at intervals of 5–25 years. The sediment layers associat-ed with settlement appear to have formed more quickly than the layers formed when man was absent.

The frequency and quantity of finds suggest longer occupation by larger groups in the Pre-Boreal/Boreal transition and early Boreal periods, than in the Pre-Boreal and late Boreal/Atlantic periods.

Antler evidence suggests spring occupation of the site in Pre-Boreal to early Boreal times, and occupation around September/October in the late Boreal to early Atlantic period. Further zoological and botanical research (studies of bird and fish remains, age-structure of young animals, plant macro-remains) is being applied to the problem of season and duration of occupation.

In the Pre-Boreal and early Boreal periods, the preponderance of mammal bones suggests that hunting was the most important source of food. Fishing was less important. Since these periods were of mainly spring occupation, there may have been a scarcity of plant foods.

All Mesolithic activities are represented at Friesack: working of flint and other stone, bone- and antler-working, the manufacture of all kinds of utensils and implements, collecting and working of wood, collecting and working of plant fibres, making fires (evidenced by masses of charcoal including charred branches and larger wood splinters), extracting resin, probably working of skins, prepar-

323

ation of food, and other activities. Some type of building activity (probably a dwelling structure) seems to be indicated by the occurrence of cut logs and tree trunks.

The finds indicate considerable material possessions. Some intact artifacts may have been left lying deliberately – for example, two groups each of six bone points – to be picked up at some later time, if the possibility of deposition in shallow water for cult or religious purposes is ruled out. They might also have been laid in the shallow water to protect them against gnawing by animals (cf. Larsson 1978, 1983).

Apart from seasonal use by medium to large Mesolithic social units for their food resources, Friesack might have been a meeting-place at which, from time to time, the whole group came together, as among some Australian aborigines (Spencer 1928).

The pollen analyses and numerous finds of wooden artifacts and fragments show that man had influenced the natural environment from his first appearance, with the clearance of trees, particularly pine in the Pre-Boreal and Boreal, and the destruction of ground vegetation leading to changes in the relief of the area through erosion and downhill movement of masses of sand. A careful estimate indicates that at least 1000 m^3 of sand were carried down from the hill to the shore areas of the adjacent lake in the early Holocene.

FINAL REMARKS

This report is only a general review of the results of the Friesack excavations, and no comparisons have been made here with other north-central European or south Scandinavian sites.

Friesack is an unusual site in terms of finds and stratigraphy. Such sites may well be confined to the lower-lying areas of Pleistocene *Urstromtäler* between the Elbe and Oder. Similarities can be seen with sites such as 'Fiener Bruch' (Bicker 1934) and Hohen Viecheln (Schuldt 1961).

The Friesack excavations will continue for some years alongside a more detailed evaluation of the archaeological, geological, sedimentological, botanical, and zoological evidence.

Notes:

1. Literally, 'becoming land' – as a result of peat formation. (Ed.)

2. The part of a branch which forms inside the trunk of the tree. (Ed.)

Acknowledgements: Thanks are due to the following for improving methods of investigation and for critical advice on the interpretation of results during visits to Friesack: Søren H. Andersen (Århus), Amilcare Bietti (Rome), Klaus Bokelmann (Schleswig), Erik Brinch Petersen (Copenhagen), Noel Broadbent (Umeå), Jan Burdukiewicz (Wrocław), Volkmar Geupel (Dresden), Witold Guminski (Warsaw), Michał Kobusiewicz (Poznań), Stefan K. Kozłowski (Warsaw), Raymond Newell (Groningen) and Thomar Weber (Halle), as well as the following representatives of the natural sciences, Pavel Doluchanov (Leningrad), Klaus-Dieter Jäger (Halle), Lars-König Königsson (Uppsala), Dietrich Kopp (Eberswalde), Gerhart Mundel (Paulinenaue), Michael Succow (Eberswalde) and Roland Weisse (Potsdam). Finally, I am indebted to Alex and Sigrid Morrison (Glasgow) who have produced the English translation of this paper.

References

ANDERSEN, K., JØRGENSEN, S. and RICHTER, J. (1982) *Maglemose hytterne ved Ulkestrup Lyng*. Copenhagen, Det Kongelige Nordiske Oldskriftselskab.

ANDERSEN, S.H. and BENDER JØRGENSEN, L. (1985) Gamle klude. *Skalk*, 1985(1): 8–10.

BICKER, F.K. (1934) *Dünenmesolithikum aus dem Fiener Bruch*. Halle, Niemeyer Verlag.

BOKELMANN, K. (1971) Duvensee, ein Wohnplatz des Mesolithikums in Schleswig-Holstein und die Duvenseegruppe. *Offa*, 28: 5–26.

BOKELMANN, K. (1981) Duvensee, Wohnplatz 8. *Offa*, 38: 21–31.

CLARK, J.G.D. (1954) *Excavations at Star Carr*. Cambridge, University Press.

GRAMSCH, B. (1973) *Das Mesolithikum im Flachland zwischen Elbe und Oder*. Berlin, Deutscher Verlag der Wissenschaften.

GRAMSCH, B. (1979) Neue Ausgrabungen auf dem mesolithisch-neolithischen Fundplatz Friesack, Kr. Nauen. *Ausgrabungen und Funde*, 24: 56–61.

GRAMSCH, B. (1981) Der mesolithisch–neolithische Moorfundplatz bei Friesack, Kr. Nauen, 2. Vorbericht. *Ausgrabungen und Funde*, 26: 65–72.

GRAMSCH, B. (1985) Der mesolithisch–neolithische Moorfundplatz bei Friesack, Kr. Nauen, 3. Vorbericht. *Ausgrabungen und Funde*, 30: 57–67.

GRAMSCH, B. (1987) Ausgrabungen auf dem mesolithischen Moorfundplatz bei Friesack, Bezirk Potsdam. *Veröffentlichungen des Museums für Ur- und Frühgeschichte Potsdam*, 21: 75–100.

KLOSS, K. (1987*a*) Pollenanalysen zur Vegetationsgeschichte, Moorentwicklung und mesolithisch-neolithischen Besiedlung im Unteren Rhinluch bei Friesack, Bezirk Potsdam. *Veröffentlichungen des Museums für Ur- und Frühgeschichte Potsdam*, 21: 101–120.

KLOSS, K. (1987*b*) Zur Umwelt mesolithischer Jäger und Sammler im Unteren Rhinluch bei Friesack. *Veröffentlichungen des Museums für Ur- und Frühgeschichte Potsdam*, 21: 121–130.

LARSSON, L. (1978) *Ageröd I:B – Ageröd I:D. A Study of Early Atlantic Settlement in Scania* (Acta Archaeologica Lundensia, Series in 4°, no. 12). Lund, CWK Gleerup.

LARSSON, L. (1982) *Segebro, en tidigatlantisk boplats vid Sege ås mynning*. Malmö, Malmö Museum.

LARSSON, L. (1983) *Ageröd V, an Atlantic Bog Site in Central Scania*. Lund, Institute of Archaeology.

SCHNEIDER, M. (1932) *Die Urkeramiker*. Leipzig, Curt Kabitzsch.

SCHULDT, E. (1961) *Hohen Viecheln, ein mittelsteinzeitlicher Wohnplatz in Mecklenburg*. Berlin, Akademie-Verlag.

SCHWABEDISSEN, H. (1946) Die Bedeutung der Moorarchäologie für die Urgeschichtsforschung. *Offa*, 8: 46–74.

SCHWABEDISSEN, H. (1951) Grabungen auf dem Moorwohnplatz von Duvensee. *Germania*, 29: 208.

SCHWANTES, G. (1925) Der frühneolithische Wohnplatz von Duvensee. *Praehistorische Zeitschrift*, 16: 173–177.

SCHWANTES, G. (1939) *Die Vorgeschichte Schleswig-Holsteins (Stein- und Bronzezeit)*. Neumünster, Karl Wachholtz.

SPENCER, W.B. (1928) *Wanderings in Wild Australia*. London, Macmillan.

Vænget Nord: Excavation, Documentation and Interpretation of a Mesolithic Site at Vedbæk, Denmark

Erik Brinch Petersen

Abstract

Within the overall context of the results of the Vedbæk Project – the discovery of a substantial number of sites, a subsistence economy based on faunal diversity but with a marine dominance, evidence of a transgressive coastline, and a long Mesolithic chronology – the excavation of the site of Vænget Nord (*c.* 7000 BP) is described with an emphasis on gaining information using methods such as horizontal *décapage*, photographic recording, and wet-sieving. An anthropogenic zonation of the settlement is proposed based on evidence from use-wear analysis of the lithics, refitting, the distribution of charcoal and fire-cracked stones, and the overall arrangement of structural features on the site.

INTRODUCTION

The Vedbæk Project has been in operation since 1975 with the aim of describing and explaining the changes observable in the behaviour of a Mesolithic population around a Zealand fjord during the Atlantic and early Sub-Boreal periods, *c.* 7500–4500 BP.

The fossil Vedbækfjord (*Fig. 1*) was chosen for a number of reasons. First and foremost, it was considered important to concentrate on one particular area in order to avoid regional differences when comparing sites. Secondly, a number of sites were known from the area, and of these the National Museum had earlier investigated two, Henriksholm-Bøgebakken (1924) and Vedbæk-Boldbaner (1944–45); both excavations are, however, still largely unpublished (Mathiassen 1946). Some interesting stray finds had also been unearthed by peat cutting, and among these the so-called reindeer antler hammer is the most spectacular (Mathiassen 1941; Troels-Smith 1941) – this piece is in fact made from elk (*Alces alces*) and not reindeer antler (Vang Petersen 1982). Furthermore, information compiled by a local amateur indicated that many more Mesolithic sites could still be located and investigat-

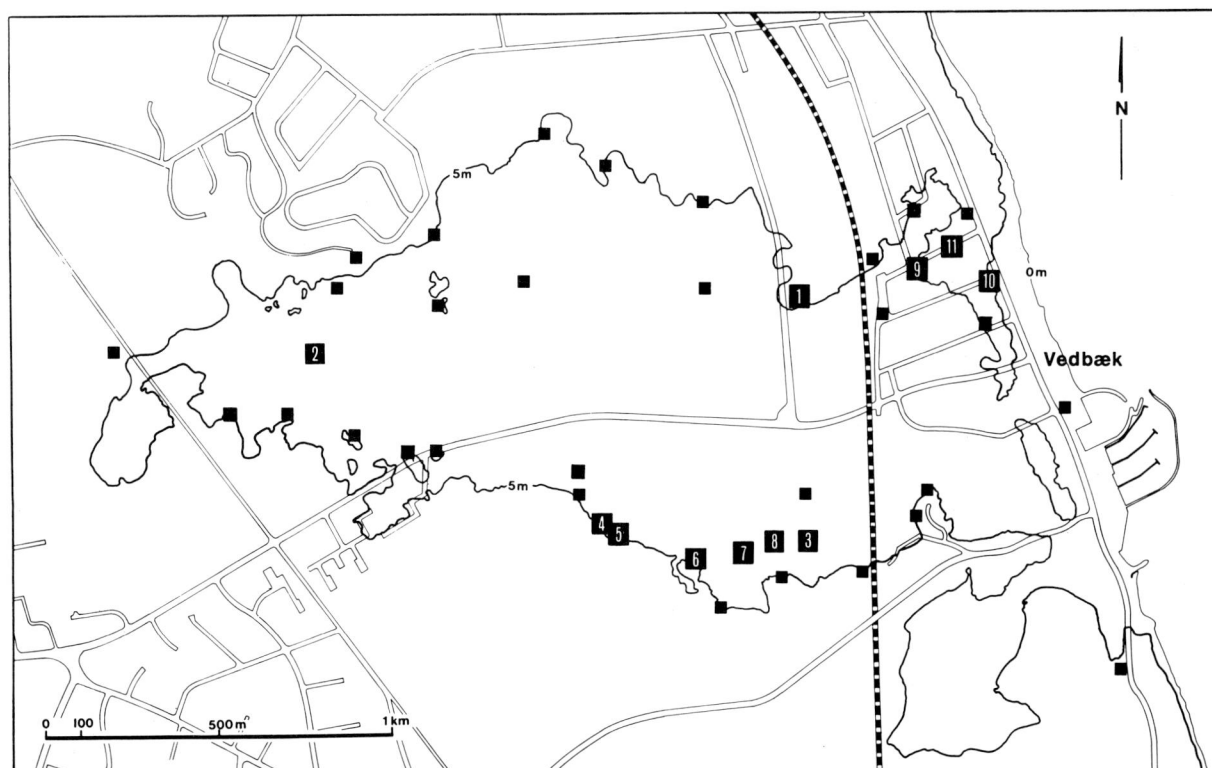

Figure 1 The fossil Vedbækfjord as indicated by the 5 m contour. Vænget Nord is site no 7. *Drawn by S.A. Knudsen*

ed. Finally, owing to its strategic position with regard to eustatic and isostatic movements, Vedbæk provides a longer time-scale than most other coastal areas.

FAUNAL EXPLOITATION

Identification of the bone material recovered from the excavated sites at Vedbæk shows quite a diversity with some 60 species of fish, reptiles, birds, and mammals (Aaris-Sørensen 1980a, 1980b, 1982). The sylvan fauna is dominated by red deer, roe deer and wild boar, in spite of the fact that the absolute number of these animals is severely affected by taphonomic loss (Aaris-Sørensen 1983). However, it is the marine component of the fauna that dominates, with fish as the staple part of the Mesolithic diet (Aaris-Sørensen 1980b; Enghoff 1983). This is corroborated by $\delta^{13}C$ measurements of the human skeletons from Henriksholm-Bøgebakken which show a pronounced marine $\delta^{13}C$ value (Tauber 1981).

SEA-LEVEL CHANGES

The most dramatic change in the environment was the change in sea level. For Vedbæk, during the period in question, a shore displacement curve can now be drawn, extending from below zero at c. 7500 BP and reaching a transgression maximum of nearly 5 m a.s.l. c. 5500 BP. Furthermore, this curve has been tied in with the Mesolithic chronology of the area (Christensen 1981).

MESOLITHIC CHRONOLOGY

In a recent study, a chronology for the Kongemose and Ertebølle stages of the middle and late Mesolithic of Zealand has been put forward. The foundation of this chronology is provided by the Vedbæk sites, but other sites from the region of Øresund have been included as well. This chronology stresses the value of the microlithic points as time markers, with rhomboids as the earliest type, and the slender transverse arrowheads as the latest type of the Mesolithic sequence (Vang Petersen 1984).

SITE EXCAVATION

To date, more than forty sites have been located (Fig. 1) but excavations have taken place at only 11 of these, including the extensive rescue excavation at Henriksholm-Bøgebakken that led to the discovery of beautifully preserved burials (Albrethsen and Brinch Petersen 1975, 1976; Albrethsen et al. 1976). Normally, however, sites at Vedbæk have been affected by cultivation, peat cutting, drainage, and by the building of houses, roads and parking places, by a railway, a sewer, a sporting ground, and by our predecessors, professional as well as illicit diggers.

Likewise, it must be kept in mind that only a small part of each site has been investigated, and that these excavations have been placed more or less at random on the original site, thus complicating any comparison.

Vænget Nord

When at Vænget Nord a virgin site was discovered in 1976 and subsequently tested in 1977, it became tempting to undertake a total excavation of that site. As a result of the testing, it was evident that the site was situated on a small island and, based on the lithic industry plus a few radiocarbon dates, the age of the habitation could be placed at c. 7000 BP, thus making it one of the oldest sites discovered so far in the Vedbæk area. Furthermore, as this island attains a maximum height of only 2.75 m a.s.l., the transgression c. 6800 BP put an end to the habitation, and the ongoing transgression sealed off the site completely. That, at least, was the theory.

In all, 506 m² have been investigated (Fig. 2) and, of the these, 226 m² were exposed during a horizontal décapage of the central part of the island. This horizontal exposure was undertaken in two stages. During the first exposure all lithics, manuports and fire-cracked stones were left in situ, and could thus be recorded against the soil discolorations (Fig. 3). The next step was to remove all the artifacts leaving behind only the features. This situation was again recorded. Meanwhile, all the backdirt was wet-sieved and sorted out per 25 cm square.

The photographic recording has certainly added another dimension to the standard backplotting, and the site zonation proposed at the end of this paper would perhaps never have been so evident were it not for the visual inspection that can still be performed (Price and Brinch Petersen 1987).

The wet-sieving has, of course, augmented the lithic material quite substantially. Not only are there fragments of rhomboid points, but unbroken points, microburins, and microburins of Krukowski type are also frequently encountered among the sieved material; even small axe-sharpening flakes are often missed by trowelling. Charcoal and hazel-nuts (charred or uncharred) are also successfully recovered by wet-sieving. Faunal remains were, unfortunately, not preserved on the top of the island; only in front of the site to the north was it possible to recover fish remains and mammalian bones.

Another effect of the horizontal exposure was the identification of a number of anthropogenic features, an often neglected aspect of a Mesolithic site. However, interpretation of the function of many of these features, as well as their exact definition, has proved difficult.

So far, various types of features have been discerned. Hearths consist of simple pits with charcoal and, often, patches of charcoal can be found

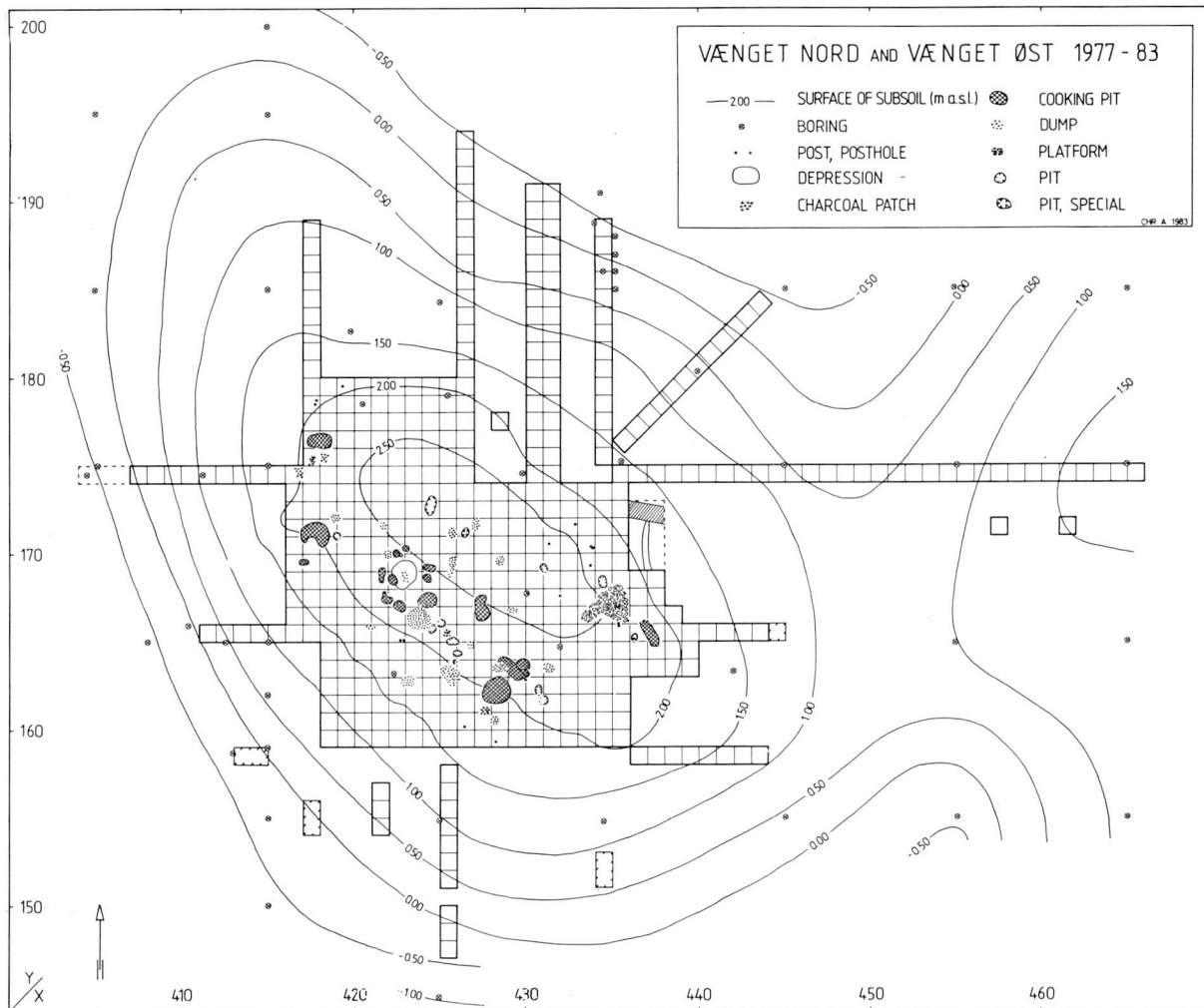

Figure 2　Vænget Nord: excavation plan. *Drawn by C. Adamsen*

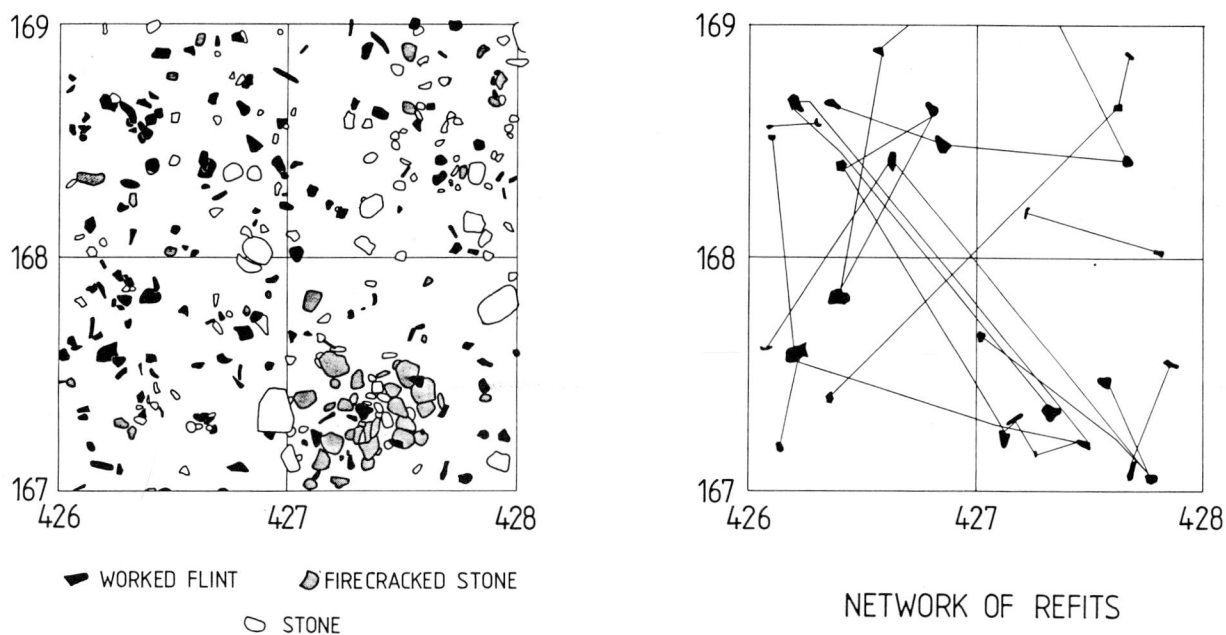

Figure 3　Vænget Nord: *décapage* and refits in four central metre squares. *Drawn by C. Adamsen*

around them. Cooking pits tend to be larger than hearths, and in them can be found charcoal as well as fire-cracked stones. Such fire-cracked stones may subsequently be dumped together on the ground after use, or they may be spread all over the site. When found on other sites, such dumps have often been mistaken for hearths.

In the central part of the site there was a depression, perhaps not a deliberately made feature, but one that was caused by trampling. That at least was the impression gained. A number of small pits did not give any clue as to their function, except one in which was found a small flint core with some thirty flakes that could be refitted back onto the core. Even the smallest flint chips from the core reduction were present. This was evidently some sort of cache.

One man-size pit has been interpreted as a burial, in spite of the fact that no skeleton or red ochre were to be seen. However, a heavy flint blade and two core axes neatly placed in the pit do support this suggestion. Moreover, the location of this burial (*Fig. 2*) is identical to that of the burial recovered at Vedbæk-Boldbaner (Mathiassen 1946).

Finally, some 15 wooden posts were still preserved on the site, but they tend to appear, not on the top of the island, but on the slope just outside the main concentration of the other features. In the centre of the site more than 200 stake-holes were discovered during the last field season, and it is quite possible that an even greater number were missed during the earlier seasons. However, neither the posts nor the stake-holes can be said to form discernible structures.

Zonation

In a recent wear analysis of parts of the lithics from Vænget Nord (Juel Jensen and Brinch Petersen 1985) it has been suggested that a bipartition of the central part of the site can be worked out. One area is characterized by burins for working bone or antler, whereas hide-working tools such as end-scrapers, truncated pieces and unretouched blades dominate the other. The burin area coincides with that part of the site where features are abundant, and where the depression mentioned above occurs. Although rhomboid points and microburins tend to be distributed all over the site, their maximum concentration occurs within the burin area. It is therefore tempting to relate this zone, called a primary occupation zone, to the area where the huts must have been placed.

The adjacent zone, termed the hide-working zone, covers an area to the east of the primary occupation zone. In accordance with the suggested function of this area, there are only a few features here, and these occur mainly along the periphery of the zone.

Surrounding and sometimes merging with the hide-working zone, there is a zone of intensive flint-working. Most of the refits so far worked out for the site fall within this zone. Six different networks can for the moment be defined here, and *Fig. 3* shows one of these networks, where the three zones mentioned so far merge into one another. Perhaps that is why this particular area is so rich in flint tools and débitage. However, there is a *caveat*. The refitting analysis of the site is still in progress, and the present author and investigator may find it easier to conjoin flakes from axe production rather than from core reductions.

Behind and to the south of these three zones comes the garbage zone. This is a zone, dark in colour and rich in charcoal and fire-cracked stones, with only a few dispersed flakes. It is practically devoid of features, but the refuse must have been deposited on dry land. The 'midden' has its maximum thickness immediately adjacent to the primary occupation zone.

On the very highest part of the island and just to the north of the primary occupation zone lies the single burial which, based on the grave goods and comparison with other Mesolithic burials, might have contained the corpse of an adult male.

On the eastern side of the island, around the 2 m contour, is a well-developed erosion terrace corresponding to the highest shoreline of the occupation. Beyond this is a zone with a high density of worked flint, some originally deposited here, some swept together and thrown out from the primary occupation zone and from the flint-working zone, and some finally redeposited following the erosion. The outermost and lowest-lying zone is a rather small area, where bones survive and where shells of hazelnuts attain their maximum concentration. This, of course, is a matter of preservation.

Finally, in a few cases, it has been possible to isolate individual flint dumps, represented by a large number of refits lying close together within a limited area. In one case, this was the material left over from the making of an axe, with débitage of all the stages of the axe production present – only the axe itself was missing; but this is not the knapping place proper, as the smallest chips are missing and, furthermore, deposition took place in a saturated part to the north of the site.

The picture (*Fig. 4*) proposed for the site of Vænget Nord is of course a gross simplification of a very complicated situation. It can also be argued that several of the differences observed are due to secondary phenomena, such as differential preservation conditions. Furthermore, as the island must have seen a number of occupations over several hundred years, such a clear-cut pattern as the one proposed here may not be true or, at best, be valid only for the youngest occupation.

Similarly, it has not yet been possible to suggest a

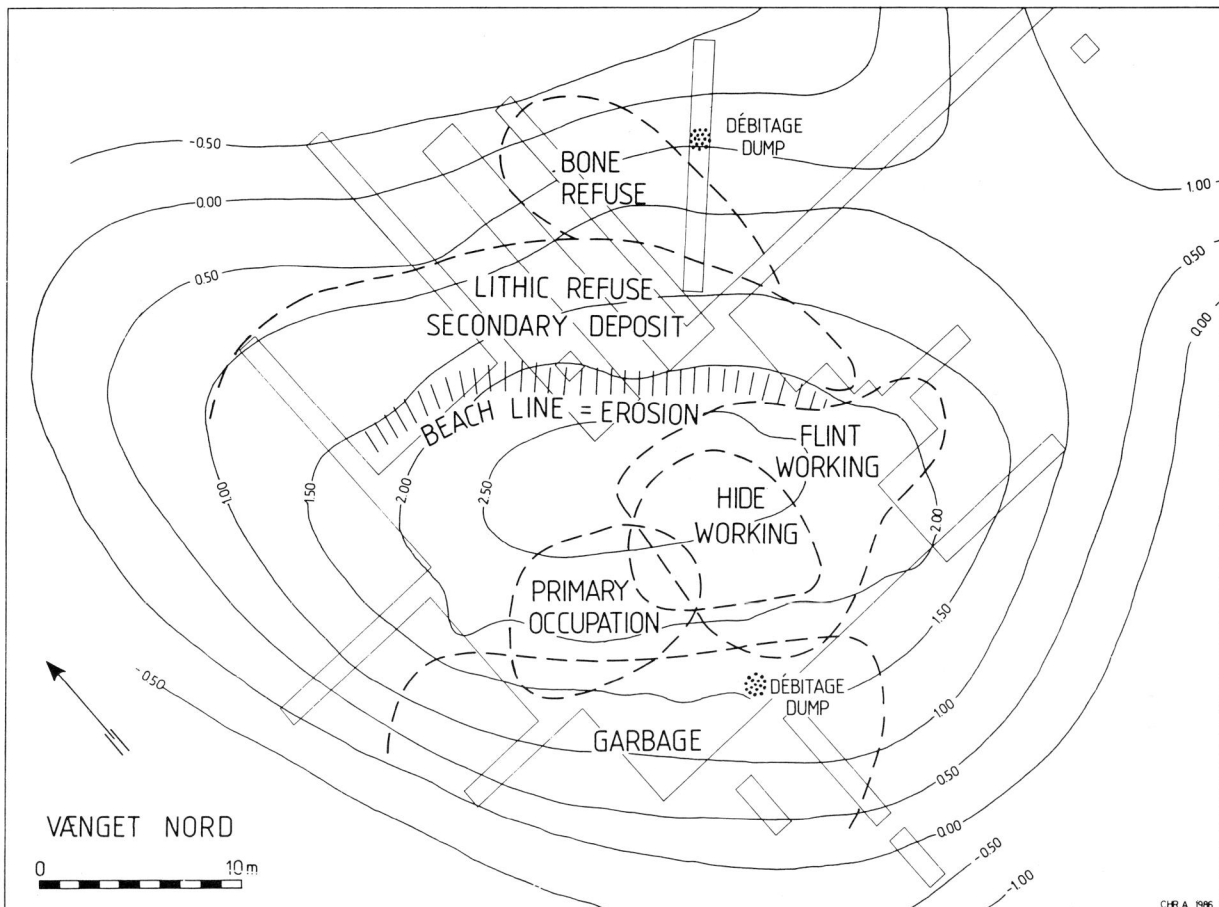

Figure 4   Vænget Nord: zonation of the island and its habitation. *Drawn by C. Adamsen*

zonation for the western flank of the island, and the white space here should really be seen as a big question mark. There are at least two possibilities – either the primary occupation zone extended into this area, or it was occupied by another specialized activity area.

However, the site is not simply a palimpsest of a number of occupations, but does show some zonation. For the ongoing analysis, this is a most comforting thought. Finally, it must not be forgotten that, although the island was totally submerged after 6500 BP, it still attracted people, as witnessed by, *inter alia*, a dug-out canoe moored there underwater some time after 5700 BP. In short, a site is a site is a site.

Acknowledgements: The excavation at Vænget Nord was undertaken as a joint venture between the University of Copenhagen (Institute of Prehistoric Archaeology and the Zoological Museum), the National Museum of Denmark, and the University of Wisconsin, Madison, U.S.A. The fieldwork has been made possible by generous grants from the Danish Research Council for the Humanities, Dronning Margrethe II's arkæologiske Fond, Sparekassen for Lyngby og Omegns Fond, Søllerød Museum, and the National Science Foundation, U.S.A. Numerous students from the universities of Copenhagen and Wisconsin (Madison) shared the experience and provided their enthusiasm. Christian Adamsen of the Institute of Prehistoric Archaeology managed, as always, to convert the author's vague ideas into persuasive illustrations. Finally, Sigrid and Alex Morrison (Glasgow) not only helped the author in sorting out his post-symposium reflections, but also scrutinized his English prose.

References

AARIS-SØRENSEN, K. (1980a) Depauperation of the mammalian fauna of the island of Zealand during the Atlantic period. *Videnskabelige Meddelelser fra dansk naturhistorisk Forening*, 142: 131–138.

AARIS-SØRENSEN, K. (1980b) Atlantic fish, reptile and bird remains from the Mesolithic settlement at Vedbæk, north Zealand. *Videnskabelige Meddelelser fra dansk naturhistorisk Forening*, 142: 139–149.

AARIS-SØRENSEN, K. (1982) A classification code and computerized data-analysis for faunal materials from archaeological sites. *Ossa*, 8: 3–29.

AARIS-SØRENSEN, K. (1983) An example of taphonomic loss in a Mesolithic faunal assemblage. In J. Clutton-Brock and C. Grigson (eds), *Animals and Archaeology. I. Hunters and their Prey*. Oxford, British Archaeological Reports (International Series) S163: 243–247.

ALBRETHSEN, S.E. and BRINCH PETERSEN, E. (1975) Gravene på Bøgebakken, Vedbæk. *Søllerødbogen*: 9–60.

ALBRETHSEN, S.E. and BRINCH PETERSEN, E. (1976) Excavation of a Mesolithic cemetery at Vedbæk, Denmark. *Acta Archaeologica*, 47: 1–28.

ALBRETHSEN, S.E., BRINCH PETERSEN, E., BALSLEV JØRGENSEN, J. and ALEXANDERSEN, V. (1976) De levede og døde ... for 7000 år siden. *Nationalmuseets Arbejdsmark*: 5–23.

CHRISTENSEN, C. (1981) Havniveauændringer 5500–2500 f.Kr. i Vedbækområdet, NØ Sjælland. *Dansk Geologisk Forenings Årsskrift*: 91–107.

ENGHOFF, I. B. (1983) Size distribution of cod (*Gadus morhua* L.) and whiting (*Merlangus merlangus* (L.)) (Pisces, Gadidae) from a Mesolithic settlement at Vedbæk, north Zealand, Denmark. *Videnskabelige Meddelelser fra dansk naturhistorisk Forening*, 144: 83–97.

JUEL JENSEN, H. and BRINCH PETERSEN, E. (1985) A functional study of lithics from Vænget Nord, a Mesolithic site at Vedbæk, N.E. Sjælland. *Journal of Danish Archaeology*, 4: 40–51.

MATHIASSEN, T. (1941) Two new Danish implements of reindeer antler. *Acta Archaeologica*, 12: 125–134.

MATHIASSEN, T. (1946) En boplads fra ældre stenalder ved Vedbæk Boldbaner. *Søllerødbogen*: 19–35.

PRICE, T.D. and BRINCH PETERSEN, E. (1987) Prehistoric settlement in Mesolithic Denmark. *Scientific American*, 256(3): 90–99.

TAUBER, H. (1981) ^{13}C evidence for dietary habits of prehistoric man in Denmark. *Nature*, 292: 332–333.

TROELS-SMITH, J. (1941) Geological dating of a reindeer antler hammer from Vedbæk. *Acta Archaeologica*, 12: 135–144.

VANG PETERSEN, P. (1982) Jægerfolket på Vedbækbopladserne. *Nationalmuseets Arbejdsmark*: 179–189.

VANG PETERSEN, P. (1984) Chronological and regional variation in the late Mesolithic of eastern Denmark. *Journal of Danish Archaeology*, 3: 7–18.

Mesolithic House Sites in Arctic Norway

Ericka Engelstad

Abstract

A brief description of Mesolithic/Early Stone Age sites, particularly Komsa sites in Finnmark, is presented. Dating is based primarily on lithic typology and shoreline displacement. Possible early sites in Finnmark and Troms are described. The transition between the Early Stone Age and the Late Stone Age is now believed to be gradual in most areas of arctic Norway, with some new technological additions to essentially Mesolithic assemblages. Recent surveys have increased the number of Mesolithic localities, particularly in the area south of the previous Komsa distribution. Both coastal and interior Mesolithic sites are now known. The chronological problems relating to the Mesolithic/Early Stone Age in this area are discussed. The known habitation sites with tent or house structures, which have been tested or excavated, are described and discussed. These include several sites in the Varanger fjord area, particularly Karlebotn and Mortensnes at the base of the fjord. Also discussed are sites at Tverrvikraet, Simavik, and Træna. Newly discovered and excavated Mesolithic pit houses at Karlebotn (the Starehnjunni site) are described and discussed. The habitation sites are set in relation to previous interpretations of Mesolithic settlement and socio-economic patterns. It is postulated that the settlement pattern shows greater residential stability and the use of short-range transhumance. The continuity between the Early Stone Age (Mesolithic) and the Late Stone Age in terms of lithic assemblages, settlement patterns, and economy is emphasized.

INTRODUCTION

The present paper describes some of the newly found habitation sites with remains of pit houses and tent rings which can be dated to the Mesolithic in arctic Norway. Since very few are familiar with the Mesolithic (or Early Stone Age as it is called) in this area, I will first give a brief summary of our present knowledge of these lithic assemblages and the problems of their chronological placement. The newly found house remains in Finnmark and Troms will then be described and related to interpretations of settlement patterns and socio-cultural inferences.

DATING THE MESOLITHIC IN ARCTIC NORWAY

The primary method of dating the Mesolithic/Early Stone Age in this area is by shoreline displacement chronology. Most sites lack organic material and, therefore, radiocarbon dating is not extensive. In fact, there are only a handful of radiocarbon dates from this time period. The beginning of the Early Stone Age is assumed to be close to the beginning of

the deglaciation of this area and is dated by means of shoreline displacement. On the outer coast of Troms this can be as early as 14,000 BP and in Finnmark c. 12,000 BP. It should be remembered that this is a geological dating of terraces which could have been occupied at that time, but there are as yet few archaeological finds which can be related to these high-lying terraces.

In Troms, on the outer coast, the highest-lying, known sites have a clearly Mesolithic assemblage and can be shoreline dated to c. 10,000 BP. There is, in addition, one early radiocarbon date of 9200±200 BP from the Simavik site (Sandmo 1986). In Finnmark the oldest sites are located near Karlebotn at a height of 85 m above sea level (E. Helskog 1982). This terrace is associated with the marine limit and can have a maximum age of 12,000 BP. The structural remains of two possible tents were found. Unfortunately, the associated assemblages, which consisted solely of unretouched quartz flakes and retouched flake scrapers of quartz, is equivocal. These types of artifacts are found throughout the Stone Age (both Early and Late) in arctic Norway and, thus, could be dated to either period. However, the geographical/topographical context of the Karlebotn sites points toward an early dating; and the use of coarse-grained quartz and quartzite points toward an affiliation with Komsa. At present, these two sites (Simavik and Karlebotn) are the only sure indication of an early Holocene habitation of the arctic Norwegian coast. Sites which could be equally as early are reported from some coastal surveys, but none have been investigated further.

The end of the Mesolithic is more difficult to date by means of shoreline displacement. Only one of the latest Mesolithic sites is dated by radiocarbon. The end of the Mesolithic is very simply dated in relation to the beginning of the Late Stone Age. The chronological sequence for the Late Stone Age in Finnmark (particularly Varanger fjord, Ivers fjord and Sørøya) is relatively well dated by radiocarbon (Engelstad 1985). Of course, this has the effect of making the transition between the Mesolithic and the Late Stone Age seem rather abrupt, and many

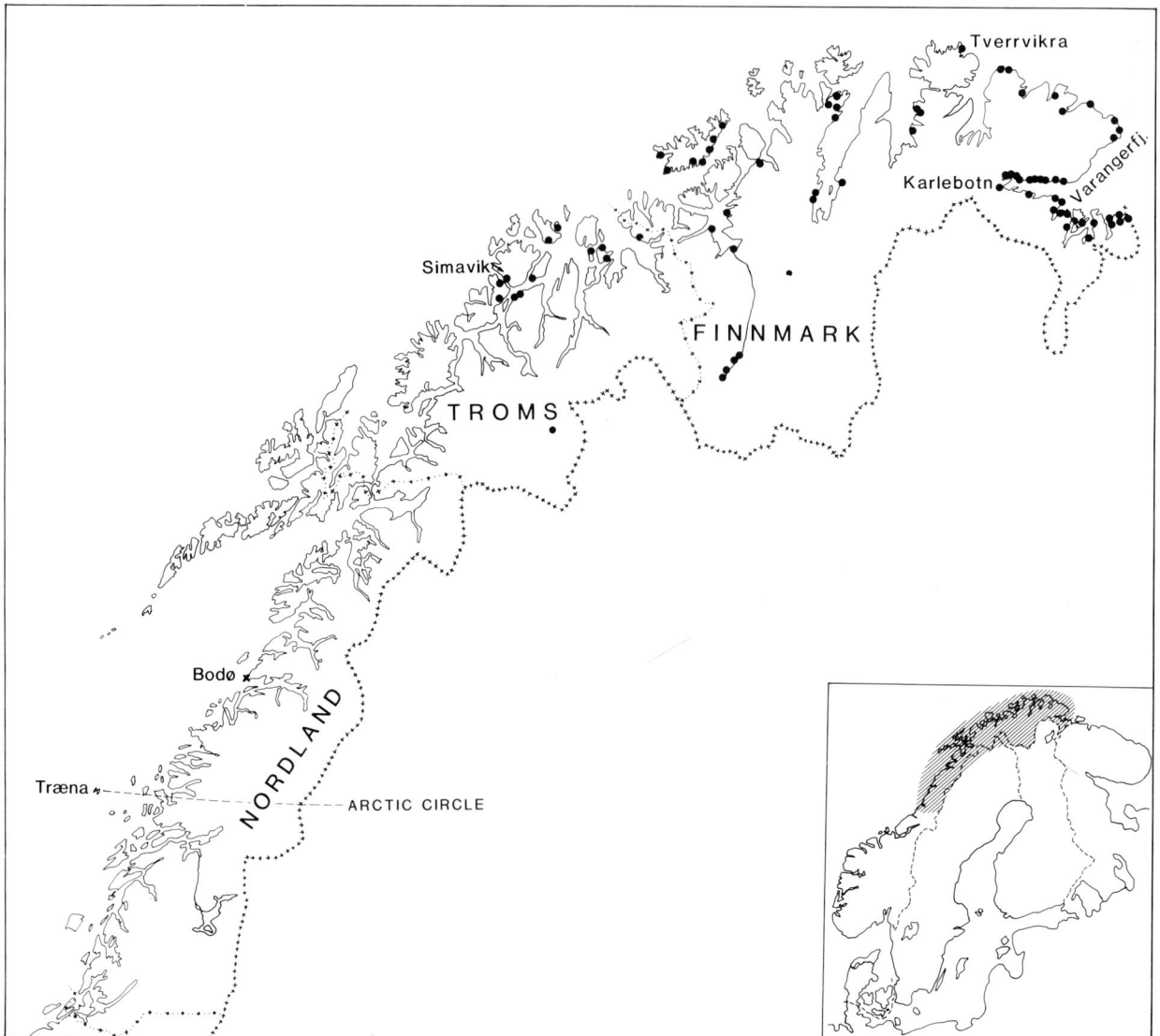

Figure 1   Map of arctic Norway, showing the location of Early Stone Age/Mesolithic sites in Troms and Finnmark. The majority of sites in Finnmark are classified as Komsa.

early Late Stone Age sites are actually Mesolithic in character. A good example of this is the site of Sæleneshøgda in Karlebotn. Sæleneshøgda is the type site for Period I (the Sæleneshøgda phase) of the Late Stone Age. Although the assemblage is Mesolithic (microlithic technology, transverse points, etc.) it is traditionally placed at the beginning of the Late Stone Age because of the presence of four ground axes (Simonsen 1961; K. Helskog 1978a, 1978b; Engelstad 1985). The ground axes are a minimal part of the entire assemblage. However, the presence of ground or polished tools should not be considered as an absolute defining characteristic of the beginning of the Late Stone Age in this area. Polished slate points are found on Finnish Mesolithic sites, in particular the Suomusjärvi sites (Luho 1967; Siiriäinen 1970, 1973, 1981; Matiskainen, this volume). It is interesting to note that as the Late Stone Age is now being more extensively dated by radiocarbon, it is revealed to be as much as 1000 years earlier than the previous relative dating of the

same assemblages would allow. This not only pushes back the transition between the Late Stone Age and the Mesolithic to between 6500–6200 BP, but also has affected our understanding of the possible dating of the beginnings of the Mesolithic/Early Stone Age.

MESOLITHIC SITES IN ARCTIC NORWAY

Until recently the Mesolithic in arctic Norway (*Fig. 1*) was synonymous with the Komsa culture (Bøe and Nummedal 1936; Clark 1936, 1975; Helskog 1974). Komsa consists of a series of lithic assemblages from open-air sites along the coast of Finnmark, the northernmost part of arctic Norway. In Norway the geographically closest group of Mesolithic sites were the so-called flint sites from the coastal area around the Arctic Circle in the province of Nordland. Typologically, these last assemblages were characterized as being between Komsa and the Fosna culture, the southern Norwegian coastal Mesolithic assemblages (Clark 1936, 1975; Gjessing 1937).

332

The coastal area between these two groups of assemblages was devoid of similar finds. In the outer coastal area (for example, the Lofoten islands) the relevant land areas which could have been inhabited are now either submerged or under sediments deposited during the Tapes transgression, c. 7000–6000 BP. In the inner coastal and fjordal areas sites were also lacking. For this latter area the situation changed in the late 1970s and early 1980s when intensive surveying resulted in the discovery of several open-air sites in the Bodø area and some 10 sites in the northern part of the province of Troms. The analysis of these new assemblages is now in progress and they can be presented only cursorily in the present paper.

The Komsa sites are purely coastal in their distribution. There are, however, two interior areas which have sites which can be dated to the late Mesolithic. One of these areas is the interior of Finnmark (Finnmarksvidda) where there are now five sites with stray finds of quartzite transverse points which are dated to c. 6000 BP (E. Helskog 1978). Unfortunately, four of these sites are in wind-blown sand and the Mesolithic finds are often mixed with artifacts which are clearly from later time periods. Only one of these five sites has been excavated. The other interior area is in inner Troms at the site of Devdis I. This site was excavated in 1970 (K. Helskog 1980b) and had an assemblage characterized by transverse points, single-edged points, oblique points, retouched flakes, and platform cores of chert and quartzite. Devdis I is a single component site and is dated between 7000 and 6000 BP on the basis of typology and one radiocarbon date of 6575±150 BP (T-1343). The majority of previously mentioned assemblages come from open-air sites without any evidence of habitation structures.

HABITATION STRUCTURES

Some of the earliest evidence of habitation structures is of tent remains – circles or rectangles of stones supposedly marking the periphery of a skin tent. Less than ten of these are now known from both the Varanger fjord and the islands in Troms. Here, I will include only those which have been investigated either by excavation or testing. However, numerous structures which, because of their height above sea level could be Mesolithic, have been reported along the outer coast of Finnmark. Since these are only summarily reported in surveys and none have been investigated further, and because both their cultural and chronological placement is unsure, I will only name them here. However, they do represent an enormously large research potential that can greatly increase our knowledge of the Early Stone Age.

To date, the oldest structures are of two stone formations marking the border of rectangularly shaped tents. These features are located at a height of 85 m above sea level in Karlebotn. As stated earlier, this terrace is associated with the marine limit in the area and can have a maximum date of 12,000 BP. There are no radiocarbon dates from either of these structures. Dating by height above sea level is of course only an approximation, and these two structures are probably somewhat later than the maximum of 12,000 BP. The associated assemblages give no help in getting a better dating since they are of a character which is generally defined simply as Mesolithic/Early Stone Age.

Also in the Varanger fjord area four sites with structural remains possibly dating to the Mesolithic/Early Stone Age were excavated in the early 1960s (Odner 1966). These sites are Småstraumen I, Bugøynes III, Nesseby IB, and Trifandalen. All four sites are dated to the Mesolithic/Early Stone Age on the basis of lithic typology and height above sea level. Småstraumen I and Bugøynes III are on raised cobble beaches where rectangular floor areas have been cleared by the removal of large cobbles. These cleared areas, which are believed to be the remains of rectangular tents, are 2×4 m to 2.5×3.5 m in size. None contained evidence of a hearth. Three of five tent foundations at Småstraumen I were test excavated and contained numerous lithics – primarily flakes, but also scrapers, burins, cores, and tanged points of quartz and quartzite (Odner 1966: 17–20). Bugøynes III contained a single rectangular area with flakes, blades, scrapers, burins and one chisel, all of quartz and quartzite (Odner 1966: 51–55).

The two other Varanger sites, Nesseby IB and Trifandalen, had evidence of shallow, round (c. 2.5 m in diameter) floor depressions in sand and gravel terraces. Again, none contained evidence of a hearth. Nesseby IB contained four depressions, all of which were excavated. However, only one of these was with some certainty interpreted as the foundation of a sod house. The lithic assemblage associated with this house foundation included blades, transverse points, single-edged points, scrapers, and flakes of quartz and quartzite (Odner 1966: 75–77). A depression with possible peat wall was excavated at Trifandalen. The interpretation of this depression as a tent structure is highly tentative. The site as a whole was rather rich in lithics. The possible tent structure contained flakes, blades, scrapers, and tanged points of quartz and quartzite (Odner 1966: 28–42). However, it should be remembered that two radiocarbon samples resulted in exceptionally late (Iron Age) dates (E. Helskog 1974: 264), and it is possible that the 'structure' is actually of Iron Age date.

At Mortensnes, on the north side of the Varanger

fjord, a new survey in 1984 found a total of 34 Mesolithic house or tent structures (Schanche 1985). These were divided into five clusters associated with four different prehistoric shorelines dated between 9000 BP and 6000 BP. The structures are shallow (5–20 cm in depth), small and often circular, with a diameter of 3–5 metres. Excavations of several of the structures were carried out in 1985 and 1986, and material is still under analysis. However, it is possible to state that the few radiocarbon dates from this site appear to support the shoreline dating.

A more substantial type of structure and, therefore, probably the remains of a house, was excavated at Tverrvikraet in Gamvik, on the outer coast of Finnmark (K. Helskog 1975). This site is located 15 m above sea level on the top of a ridge which at 6000–5000 BP would have been on a point exposed to the sea on three sides. The structural remains consisted of a stone wall about 10 cm high and varying between 60 and 100 cm wide. The stone wall formed a rectangle approximately 3.5 × 4.0 metres. Although the interior contained no signs of a hearth, it did contain large quantities of quartz and quartzite flakes. Numerous flakes were also found exterior to the house walls. This is in many ways a typical Komsa assemblage, which most often consists of only quartz and quartzite flakes and few (or sometimes no) finished tools. The location – an exposed area on the outer coast – is also typical of Komsa locations. This is one of the few house structures which can with certainty be associated with Komsa. This house foundation is similar to a house foundation excavated by Gjessing (1943) on the island of Sanna, Træna, which is dated by him to the Mesolithic. This house ('Langhågen') was 4.5 × 6 m with stone wall foundations, postholes along the interior of the walls, and a single, centrally placed hearth. The assemblage consisted primarily of blades, scrapers, burins, and cores of flint and quartz. In addition, Gjessing interpreted certain linear stone concentrations adjacent to the house as a pathway from the house to a landing place for boats ('båtstø') by the contemporary shore. The house is dated partially by typology and partially by the geological dating of this terrace to the Atlantic period (c. 8000–6000 BP). This house is a unique phenomenon in the Mesolithic of the area and should be considered as evidence for the complexity of the Early Stone Age/Mesolithic adaptation to the arctic maritime environment.

The newly discovered site of Starehnjunni lies on the north side of Karlebotn, one of the most central and best studied locations in Stone Age research in the Varanger fjord (Engelstad 1985). This site lies 42.5 m above sea level on a terrace which is dated by shoreline displacement to c. 9000 BP (Møller 1987). The site lies c. 500 m west of the Sæleneshøgda site with three pit houses which, as stated earlier, despite a traditional placement at the beginning of the Late Stone Age, is best considered Mesolithic (K. Helskog 1980a; Engelstad 1985).

The Starehnjunni site consists of the remains of four pit houses in a line on the upper part of the terrace. All four pit houses were test excavated in 1983 (Engelstad 1984). Because of their height above sea level and topographical relationship between the Sæleneshøgda site and the Late Stone Age Nordli site with early Comb Ceramics of the Säräis-niemi I type, it was believed before excavation that the site was possibly transitional between the Mesolithic and the Late Stone Age. In addition, the pit house remains were morphologically similar to early Late Stone Age houses of the 'Karlebotn' type (Simonsen 1976; Engelstad, in press). Previously, pit houses were associated primarily with the Late Stone Age. However, the test excavations revealed assemblages which were clearly Mesolithic in character.

The houses range from 12 to 15 m^2 in area, from 10 to 30 cm deep, and are rectangular in form. Only one of these houses had signs of an entrance passage and this was orientated towards the sea. None of the houses had an interior stone-lined hearth. Flakes, blades, and lithic tools were found spread throughout the floor area. Several metres in front of one of the houses (A) was an activity area with lithic remains. Only one square metre of this area was excavated but it contained a lithic assemblage similar to those found in the houses.

Charcoal of birch from the activity area outside of house A was radiocarbon dated to 7710±480 BP (T-5428). Unfortunately, no organic material which could be radiocarbon dated was found in any of the other house excavations. But, on the basis of similarities in assemblages, they can be dated with some likelihood to the same time-range. Thus, this is one of the earliest radiocarbon dated archaeological sites in Finnmark. This date supports the results of the recent radiocarbon dating of Late Stone Age sites in the area (K. Helskog 1978a, 1978b, 1980a) and places this site and related assemblages well within the Mesolithic.

The assemblages are characterized by blades and microblades and the use of various types of local chert, quartzite, quartz, and rhyolite. The source of much of this lithic material is probably nearby outcrops of Eocambrian tillite, both the Bigganjar'ga tillite and the Mortensnes tillite, which contain small nodules of diverse cherts. These nodules are seldom larger than fist size and the lithic technology bears witness to the intensive use of small cores.

The only other house structures from the Mesolithic or Early Stone Age are found at Simavik in Troms. Here, on a high-lying terrace (27–28 m a.s.l.), there is a row of four pit houses with the remains of thick sod walls, two of which had a possible tunnel-like, covered entrance passage which was probably also covered with sod (Sandmo 1983). Only two of the houses have been partially excavated. The lithic assemblage at this site is also clearly Mesolithic, but appears to be most similar to Fosna assemblages and not at all related to Komsa (Sandmo 1986). At present, Simavik, dated to *c.* 9200 BP, is the oldest known Mesolithic site in Troms.

SETTLEMENT PATTERNS AND CULTURAL INFERENCES

Surveying during the last 10 to 15 years has increased the number of possible Early Stone Age sites. Although only a very few of these have been the subject of further investigations (all of them rather limited) it is now clear that site type variation is greater than previously known. The overwhelming dominance of open-air transitory sites located on beach terraces led to the view of Early Stone Age society consisting of extensively transhumant fishing and sea mammal hunting groups (Odner 1964). Komsa groups are often referred to as being 'bound to the coast' ('kystbundet') although their movements along the coastline are considered to be wide ranging. For example, Odner (1964) postulated seasonal transhumance between the inner fjord and the outer coast for Komsa groups in the Varanger fjord area. This hypothesis was based on ethnographically known Sami patterns in this same area and on a comparison of the absolute size (total number of artifacts) of 63 Komsa assemblages. Since most of these assemblages consisted of scattered surface finds variously collected, and since their size was calculated based on the assumption of a standard ratio of 10 flakes to every finished tool (no matter what type of stone was used or what kind of flaking qualities it had), his conclusions should be considered tentative. Odner's and others' (Simonsen 1974; Gjessing 1975) models of Early Stone Age mobility patterns were based primarily on open-air surface sites, and it is not surprising that Komsa seemed rather overly mobile as a result. The new habitation site finds change this picture. Pit houses and houses with stone foundations and peat walls indicate more permanent habitation. They also indicate greater continuity in settlement pattern with the Late Stone Age.

Although the evidence is as yet sparse, pit houses, house foundations and tent remains are found both in the inner fjord area and on the outer coast in arctic Norway. These structures appear to indicate a greater stability of settlement than the open-air sites. Although open-air sites were previously considered typical for Komsa and the Early Stone Age in general, they can now be regarded as only one aspect of the settlement pattern. It is possible to consider these habitation remains in a hierarchical

classification of sites, with: (i) more settled sites (similar to, but not the same as, what are often called 'base camps') represented by pit houses and house foundations; (ii) temporary sites, satellite sites or seasonal camps represented by open-air sites with tent rings or rectangles; and (iii) special activity areas represented by open-air scatters of flakes and a few tools. In Varanger all of these habitation site types exist in one localized area at the base of the fjord. It is possible that this smaller area represents the transhumant range of Mesolithic groups.

An analysis of the lithic assemblages from the Varanger fjord area also seems to indicate the possibility of two localized transhumant ranges. Using a correspondence analysis of 43 Early Stone Age lithic assemblages in Varanger, K. Helskog (in Bolviken *et al.* 1982: 48–51) found that the assemblage clusters were equivalent to two geographical areas within the fjord: (1) the base of Varanger fjord and the adjacent coastline; and (2) the small sheltered fjord–island area on the south-east part of the Varanger fjord. Interestingly enough, this last area is the same as that used by the Øst Sami who were transhumant hunter-fishers until the middle of the last century (Vorren 1979; Olsen 1984). Thus, the Stone Age transhumant pattern has most likely been short range with longer habitation of various localities, rather than long range with one primary settlement and distant, small, transitory hunting or fishing camps.

In the Varanger fjord both long-range and short-range mobility are known to have occurred ethnographically/historically among the Sami population (Kolsrud 1961). However, it is particularly the long-range pattern which has been used by archaeologists when interpreting both Early and Late Stone Age settlement patterns. This is, I believe, a mistake and makes Stone Age hunter-fisher transhumance appear to be much more extensive than it in reality was. The pattern of long-range mobility which existed among the Sami on the north side of the Varanger fjord was based on a mixed economy where domestic animals, particularly sheep, played an important role. Thus, the long-range movements of this group were based as much, if not more, on the need to save grass for winter hay and move the animals to summer pasture (in Norway this is a well-known pattern called 'sætring'). Summer pasturing was combined with the more traditional (perhaps going as far back as the Stone Age) utilization of spring/early summer resources on the outer coast – egg and dun gathering, and so forth; but where as before only small task groups undertook this activity, the requirements of domestic animals (sheep) now necessitated that the entire family moved to summer pastures. Thus, this long-range pattern is related most closely to an economy dependent on the use of domestic animals (in this case sheep, and not reindeer) rather than on methods of utilizing local resources.

In an area of rich maritime resources where fishing and sea mammal hunting mean a certain regularity and predictability of food supply, local resource utilization can be, and is, most effctive with the use of short-range transhumance, and this was probably the case during the Early Stone Age. The archaeological data also appear to support this hypothesis. Both assemblage variation and habitation site variation exist within small local areas. It is here suggested that the Early Stone Age in Finnmark and probably the whole of arctic Norway consisted of several groups of transhumant hunter-fishers who utilized localized resources via restricted residential mobility.

Previously, the Early Stone Age in Finnmark was placed in a socio-economic category equivalent to an early, highly mobile hunting stage of human evolution. From what we today know of hunter-gatherer/hunter-fisher societies ethnographically, this 'type' seems obviously an overemphasis of the 'primitive'. That it has managed to overlive such a long time is a reflection of the lack of new research in the Early Stone Age in arctic Norway.

Previously, the contrast between the Early Stone Age extensive mobility and the Late Stone Age more settled, residential mobility was quite clear. However, now we are finding more house remains associated with Early Stone Age lithic assemblages, and this reduces the differences between Early and Late Stone Age in terms of settlement patterns. Combined with the apparently strong continuity between Early and Late Stone Age lithic assemblages – there are, for example, numerous transverse points found associated with Säräisniemi I ceramics at the Nordli site in Varanger dated to c. 6500–5700 BP (K. Helskog 1980a) – it can be seen that there is little difference between the Early and Late Stone Age in arctic Norway. In fact, I would suggest that this two-fold chronological division has little relevance in terms of socio-cultural patterns, and one should instead simply refer to the Stone Age. A detailed chronology for the earlier part of the Stone Age awaits future research.

References

BØE, J. and NUMMEDAL, A. (1936) *Le Finnmarkien. Les Origines de la Civilisation dans l'Extrême-nord de l'Europe.* Oslo, Institutt for Sammenlignende Kulturforskning, Serie B, Skrifter 32.

BØLVIKEN, E., HELSKOG, E., HELSKOG, K., HOLM-OLSEN, I.M., SOLHEIM, L. and BERTELSEN, R. (1982) Correspondence analysis: an alternative to principle components. *World Archaeology*, 14(1): 41–60.

CLARK, J.G.D. (1936) *The Mesolithic Settlement of Northern Europe.* Cambridge, University Press.

CLARK, J.G.D. (1975) *The Earlier Stone Age Settlement of Scandinavia.* Cambridge, University Press.

ENGELSTAD, E. (1984) *Rapport om arkeologiske utgravninger ved Karlebotn, sommeren 1983.* Unpublished report, Tromsø Museum, University of Tromsø.

ENGELSTAD, E. (1985) The Late Stone Age of arctic Norway. A review. *Arctic Anthropology*, 22(1): 79–96.

ENGELSTAD, E. (in press) Pit houses from the Stone Age of arctic Norway: classification and meaning. *Proceedings of the Symposium on Multivariable data analyse i nordisk arkeologi, University of Aarhus, 25–29 November 1984.*

GJESSING, G. (1937) Mellom Komsa og Fosna. Noen eldre steinaldersfunn fra Nordland. In *Från stenålder till rokoko: Studier tillagnade Otto Rydbeck.* Lund, Gleerup: 1–16.

GJESSING, G. (1943) *Træn-funnene.* Oslo, Instituttet for Sammenlignende Kulturforskning, Serie B, Skrifter 41.

GJESSING, G. (1975) Maritime adaptations in northern Norway's prehistory. In W. Fitzhugh (ed.), *Prehistoric Maritime Adaptations of the Circumpolar Zone.* The Hague, Mouton: 87–100.

HELSKOG, E. (1974) The Komsa culture: past and present. *Arctic Anthropology*, 11 (supplement): 261–265.

HELSKOG, E. (1978) Finnmarksviddas forhistorie. In *Finnmarksvidda: natur – kultur* (Norges Offentlige Utredninger, 18A). Oslo, Universitetsforlaget: 135–144.

HELSKOG, E.(1982) *Undersøkelse av steinalderstufter ved Karlebotn, Nesseby k., Finnmark.* Unpublished report, Tromsø Museum, University of Tromsø.

HELSKOG, K. (1974) Two tests of the prehistoric cultural chronology of Varanger, north Norway. *Norwegian Archaeological Review*, 7(2): 98–103.

HELSKOG, K. (1975) Nord-Norges eldste hustuft? *Ottar*, 83: 5–7.

HELSKOG, K. (1978a) Late Holocene sea-level changes seen from prehistoric settlements. *Norsk geografisk Tidskrift*, 32: 111–119.

HELSKOG, K. (1978b) *Varangers forhistorie i lys av ^{14}C dateringer.* Paper read at the Symposium in Honour of the 25th Anniversary of the Radiocarbon Laboratory in Trondheim, 8–10 May, 1978.

HELSKOG, K. (1980a) The chronology of the Younger Stone Age in Varanger, north Norway. Revisited. *Norwegian Archaeological Review*, 13(1): 47–60.

HELSKOG, K. (1980b) *Subsistence-Economic Adaptations to the Alpine Region of Interior North Norway.* Unpublished Ph.D thesis, University of Wisconsin, Madison. University Microfilms, Ann Arbor, Michigan.

KOLSRUD, K. (1961) Sommersete: til problemet om halvnomadisme og seterflytting blant norske sjøsamer. *Samiske Samlinger*, 5(1). Norsk Folkemuseum and Universitetsforlaget.

LUHO, V. (1967) Die Suomusjärvi kultur. Die mittel- und spätmesolithische Zeit in Finnland. *Finska Fornminneforeningens Tidsskrift* (Suomen muinaismuistoyhdistyksen aikakauskirja), 66: 1–124.

MØLLER, J. (1987) Shoreline relation and prehistoric settlement in northern Norway. *Norsk geografisk Tidskrift*, 41: 45–60.

ODNER, K. (1964) Erhverv og bosetning i Komsakulturen. *Viking*, 27: 117–128.

ODNER, K. (1966) *Komsakulturen i Nesseby og Sør-Varanger.* Tromsø, Tromsø Museums Skrifter 12.

OLSEN, B. (1984) *Stabilitet og Endring. Produksjon og Samfunn i Varanger 8000 f.Kr.–1700 e.Kr.* Magistergradsavhandling i arkeologi, University of Tromsø.

SANDMO, A-K. (1983) På spor av den eldste bosetningen i Nord-Norge – nye funn fra Troms. *Ottar*, 141: 10–19.

SANDMO, A-K. (1986) *Råstoff og redskap – mer enn teknisk hjelpemiddel. Om symbolfunksjonen som et aspekt ved materiell kultur.* Magistergradsavhandling i arkeologi, University of Tromsø.

SCHANCHE, K. (1985) Registrering og kartlegging av fornminner på Mortensnes, sommeren 1984. In E. Engelstad and I.M. Holm-Olsen (eds), *Arkeologisk feltarbeid i Nord-Norge 1984.* Tromsø, Universitetet i Tromsø, Tromura, Kulturhistorie 5: 147–150.

SIIRIÄINEN, A. (1970) Archaeological background of the ancient Lake Päijänne and the geological dating of the Mesolithic–Neolithic boundary in Finland. *Bulletin of the Geological Society of Finland*, 42: 119–127.

SIIRIÄINEN, A. (1973) Shore displacement and Stone Age chronology of Finland. *Finskt Museum*, 80: 5–22.

SIIRIÄINEN, A. (1981) Problems of the east Fennoscandian Mesolithic. *Finskt Museum*, 84 (1977): 5–31

SIMONSEN, P. (1961) *Varanger-Funnene II. Fund og udgravninger på fjordens sydkyst.* Tromsø, Tromsø Museums Skrifter 7(2).

SIMONSEN, P. (1974) *Veidemenn på Norkalotten, hefte 1: Innledning – Eldre Steinalder.* Tromsø, Universitetet i Tromsø, Institutt for Samfunnsvitenskap, Stensilserie B – historie, nr. 1.

SIMONSEN, P. (1979) Steinalderens hustyper i Nord-Norge. *ISKOS*, 1: 23–25.

VORREN, O. (1979) Den samiske bosetning i Sør-Varanger. In Å. Lunde (ed.), *Sør-Varangers historie.* Kirkenes, Sør-Varanger kommune: 51–96

Mesolithic Adaptations
in the Southern Norwegian Highlands

Sveinung Bang-Andersen

Abstract

Archaeological investigations were undertaken from 1974 to 1978 in the Ryfylke and Setesdal mountains in the southernmost part of the Norwegian highlands, as part of an interdisciplinary research project – the *Ulla-Førre undersøkelsene.*

The indications are that this marginal highland area was first settled *c.* 7000 BP, that is between 1300 and 1800 years later than the Hardangervidda plateau and the Oppdal mountains in the central and northern parts of the highlands. This delay seems to be due to environmental factors, viz. a longer Postglacial regeneration phase before a stable plant cover and fauna were established.

The archaeological material consists of a limited number of lithic artifacts from 11 open-air Mesolithic sites located near the most critical point on the present main migration route of reindeer. Specialized reindeer hunting, performed during short seasonal expeditions in the early autumn by small task groups moving in from more permanent residence areas in the outer westerly fjord areas, stands out as the most plausible interpretation of the highland sites.

Mesolithic exploitation of the reindeer resources in the Setesdal mountains concentrated around two periods, *c.* 7000–6700 BP and *c.* 6100–5700 BP, possibly as a result of economic stress in the adjacent lowland. The hiatus between 6700 and 6100 BP, which is considered to represent a real settlement lacuna, is tentatively interpreted as the result of a decline in the reindeer population due to climatic change.

Further information, in particular data from palynological studies and from archaeological investigations of Mesolithic sites in the western fjord districts, is needed before more definite cultural–historical conclusions can be drawn.

INTRODUCTION

In this survey I will first give an account of the present state of research concerning Mesolithic settlement in the southern Norwegian highlands. I will then draw attention to some major archaeological problems within the Ryfylke–Setesdal mountains in the southernmost part of the highlands: when was this marginal highland area first settled; who settled it; what were the main resources sought after, and how did Mesolithic man utilize these resources? Particular consideration will be given to the question of stability or discontinuity in the Mesolithic exploitation of the Ryfylke–Setesdal mountains. Finally, some preliminary conclusions will be drawn and outlines for further research suggested.

THE SOUTHERN NORWEGIAN HIGHLANDS AND THEIR ARCHAEOLOGICAL BACKGROUND

The southern Norwegian highlands are formed by a continuous but heterogeneous range of mountains from the Rørosvidda plateau in the north east to the Ryfylke–Setesdal mountains in the south west. Geographically they cover 55,000 km^2, about one-third of the total area of southern Norway. Geologically the highlands belong to the Caledonian mountain range, the main areas lying between 900 and 1300 m above sea level. The highlands exhibit a diverse and dissected terrain with large areas of moderate slopes and plateaux, broken abruptly by high summits (up to 2500 m), valleys, gorges, and extensive drainage systems. Some areas, especially in the central and western highlands, are covered by glaciers up to 500 km^2 in extent. Snow generally covers the ground for about eight months of the year. These highlands effectively divide the southern peninsula of Norway into an eastern and a western zone, with marked differences in climate, vegetation and topography. Towards the west the mountains and high plateaux end abruptly at the sea, with deep valleys and fjords penetrating far into the uplands from the coast. In consequence, the western coastal zone is very steep and dissected. To the east and south east the highlands exhibit a more gradual gradient, with long parallel valleys that slope gently from the highland plateaux towards the coast. The main faunal resources above the 900 m contour line are wild reindeer (*Rangifer tarandus*), comprising some 50,000 individuals according to recent summer counts (Krafft 1981). Trout (*Salmo trutta*) is the most common species of fish both in the lakes and rivers, and ptarmigan (*Lagopus mutus*) the most important edible bird.

Archaeological investigation of the southern Norwegian highlands began less than fifty years ago. Several reasons could account for this, not least the remoteness and relative inaccessibility of the mountains, combined with the extreme climatic conditions which prevail here, even in summer. As a result, until

338

1940 it was widely believed that the Mesolithic population of southern Norway was predominantly coast-oriented, and only to a moderate degree made expeditions into the lower inland. The highland resources, it seemed, were first exploited in the Migration Period, c. AD 400. When in 1942 the Bergen archaeologist, Johannes Bøe, published the results of his excavations at Sumtangen, at an altitude of 1200 m in the northern part of the Hardangervidda plateau, the foundations for a radical new understanding of highland prehistory were laid. The excavations had uncovered one of the most extensive open-air Stone Age dwelling sites known at that time in Norway. The artifact assemblage, which consisted mainly of flint, was found to correspond in every respect with the material from Stone Age hunter-gatherer sites previously known from the west coast. Less extensive archaeological investigations in the central region of the Hardangervidda confirmed the findings from Sumtangen. Stone Age groups from the lowland must have undertaken regular seasonal hunting expeditions far into the interior of southern Norway (Bøe 1942).

After Bøe's pioneer work came a period of stagnation with virtually no archaeological investigations carried out in the highlands.

In contrast, during the next two decades from 1958 to the end of the 1970s, a continuous series of extensive archaeological investigations covering almost every major part of the southern Norwegian highlands were undertaken. These brought to light well over a thousand Stone Age sites, a considerable number of them Mesolithic (Martens and Hagen 1961; Hagen 1963; Indrelid 1973, 1975; Johansen 1978). Plans for development of hydro-electric power were responsible for practically all of this activity. As time limits were often short, many of the Stone Age investigations performed during this period were more like rescue excavations than well-founded research projects. However, the last three or four highland projects to be carried out have shown a more positive trend, as the archaeological investigations have been performed within the framework of interdisciplinary projects with problem-orientated research strategies. Although many projects are of merit, particular attention should be drawn to the achievements of the Hardangervidda Project (HTK) which was organized by Bergen University from 1969 to 1975 (Johansen 1973; Indrelid 1973, 1975; Kjos-Hanssen and Moe 1978; Indrelid and Moe 1983).

GENERAL STATUS OF MESOLITHIC RESEARCH IN THE SOUTHERN HIGHLANDS

First colonization

The oldest radiocarbon dated settlements have been found in the Oppdal mountains south of the city of

Trondheim, and along the Lærdal watercourse near the main divide in the high mountains east of Sognefjord, Norway's longest fjord. Here a small number of sites have been dated to c. 8800–8500 BP (*Fig. 1*). These results establish that man resided in the northern and central parts of the southern Norwegian highlands soon, perhaps only 200–300 years, after deglaciation. It is assumed that the areas in question became ice-free c. 9000 BP. The oldest site on the Hardangervidda, which is just a stone's throw away from Bøe's classic locality at Sumtangen, has been dated to c. 8300 BP (Indrelid, pers. comm.).

In the southern part of the highlands, to the east and north east of the city of Stavanger, the earliest sites are radiocarbon dated to c. 7200–6900 BP. However, the oldest date, from the Indre Agder area, should be accepted with some reservation as the context of the charcoal sample is not entirely convincing. The oldest reliable evidence of Mesolithic activity in the southernmost highlands comes from the Årdal mountains, where a site with microliths and microburins has been dated to 7130±140 BP (T-452: Bang-Andersen, in preparation).

Considerable effort has been made during the last decade to find older sites in the southern highlands, but with no success. As the excavation methods and criteria for the choice of sites have been virtually identical in all areas, the differences in the dates of the earliest occupation may be accepted as real. There is thus a gap of 1300–1800 years between the first use of the northern and central highlands by man and his appearance in the southernmost parts of the highlands.

Regional variants

Typologically, there appear to be good reasons for dividing the Mesolithic dwelling sites into two contemporary geographical groups: a northern group located primarily on the north side of the Jotunheimen mountains, and a southern group widely represented within the Hardangervidda. While the assemblages from the northern sites closely resemble those from dwelling places of the so-called 'Fosna culture' on the north-west coast, the central and southern sites demonstrate clear affinity with the artifact assemblage of the 'Nøstvet culture' (Indrelid 1975). However, the full extent of these regional variations is not known.

Another important trend to be noted is the lack of Mesolithic sites in the highlands between the major fjords of central-western Norway. In spite of a number of surveys, very few sites of clearly Mesolithic age have been found. The difference between these areas and the more inland parts of the highlands is so distinct that one may speak of a 'western frontier' for Mesolithic highland sites (Indrelid 1975; Gustafson 1981).

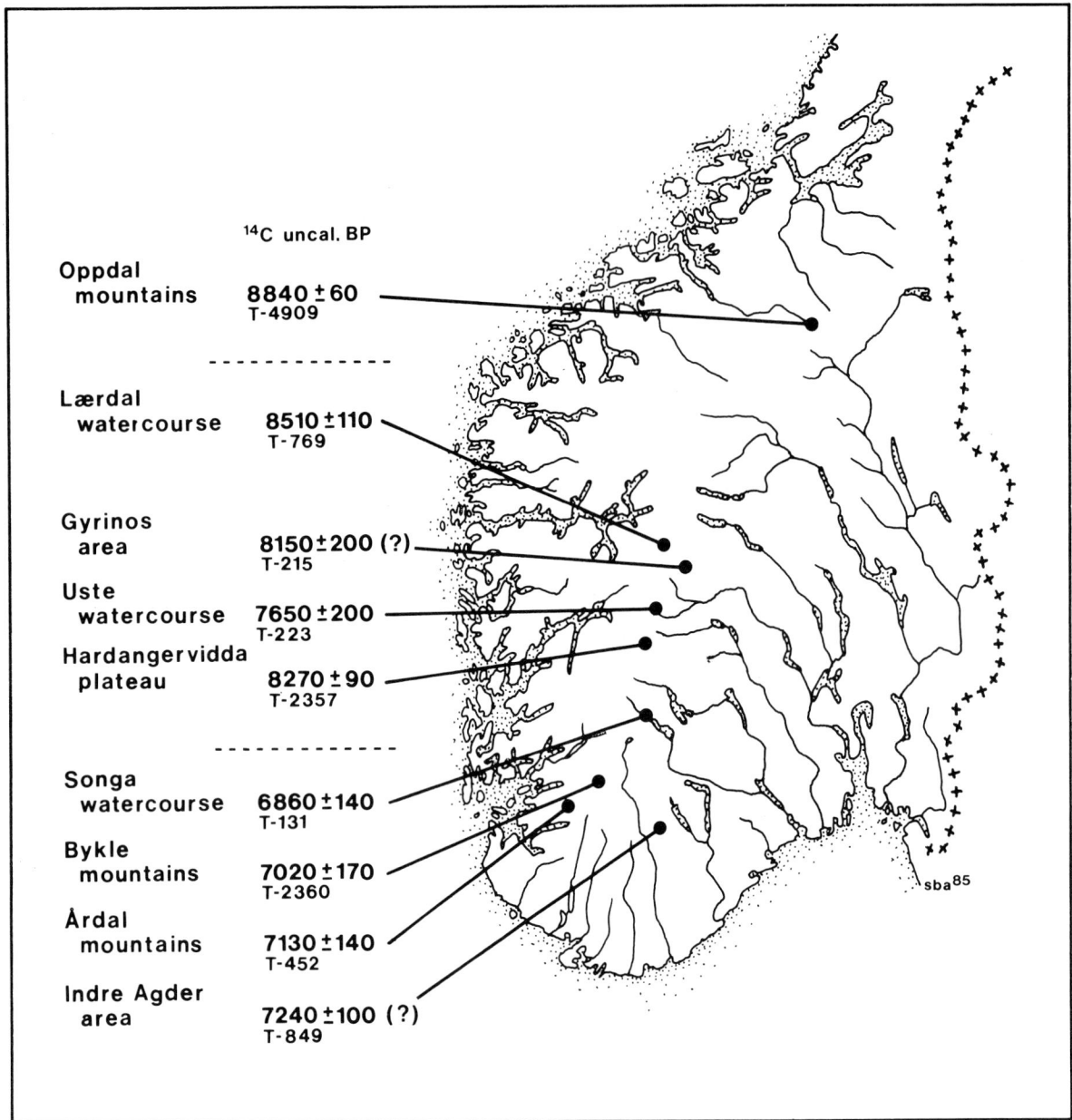

Figure 1   Earliest radiocarbon dates for Mesolithic sites in the southern Norwegian highlands. Question marks indicate dubious results.

Site types and settlement pattern

A clear majority, perhaps as many as 99%, of the Mesolithic highland sites were located along lakes and watercourses. However, as waterside areas have been far more thoroughly surveyed than off-water areas, this disparity may partly reflect the mode of archaeological registration. Regardless, it seems obvious that watersides would have been preferred dwelling places. Another significant tendency is that the further a site lies from the waterside, the smaller is the artifact scatter and the lower the number of distinct artifact types. This may be interpreted as a result of different activities.

The highland sites appear to consist of dwelling sites of differing size and character, butchering spots, and other localities reflecting highly specialized activities, such as quarries for extraction of quartzite.

Alternatively, no graves or votive sites, nor any rock carvings or paintings have been found. With relatively few exceptions the sites are of the unsheltered or 'open-air' type, where the finds are restricted to lithic artifacts. The settlement layers are usually thin, heavily leached and unstratified. Based primarily on archaeological evidence from the Hardangervidda, Indrelid (1973) has grouped the highland sites into four main categories, which for the sake of clarity are presented here in the slightly simplified form of a frequency diagram (*Table 1*). Type 2 emerges as the most common, while Type 4 occurs only rarely. This grouping will be further commented upon later.

Owing to the lack of faunal material, our assumptions about Mesolithic resource exploitation in the highlands will be purely theoretical. They are based partly on the artifact inventory from the settlement

340

Site elements \ Locality types	1	2	3	4
Waste material	÷	+	+	+
Tool inventory	÷	÷	+	+
Charcoal/hearths/cooking stones	o	÷	+	+
Site size	÷	÷	+	?
Dwelling constructions	o	o	o	+

Key symbols: + many/large ÷ few/small o lacking

sites, and partly on the topographic location of the sites, combined with deductions from the behaviour of game living in the area today. Briefly, it may be suggested that the early presence of man everywhere in the southern Norwegian highlands was related to reindeer hunting.

Practically all Mesolithic highland sites are devoid of traces of permanent dwelling structures. They contain highly specialized toolkits which usually include artifacts of flint, a material which in Norway only occurs naturally in coastal beach deposits. This indicates that the exploitation of reindeer may be attributed to Mesolithic groups that remained in the western or eastern lowlands for most of the year (Indrelid 1975; Johansen 1978; Mikkelsen 1978; Bang-Andersen and Kjos-Hanssen 1979).

Neolithic impacts

The introduction of agriculture in southern Norway is manifested osteologically by the occurrence of bones of domestic animals (sheep/goat) in a small number of cave dwellings on the western coast, and palynologically by the occurrence of pollen from plants favoured by grazing activity, primarily ribwort plantain (*Plantago lanceolata*). Archaeologically, this coincides roughly with the cessation of the 3000-year-long microblade tradition, and the introduction of slate and rhyolite artifacts. This major technological change has been radiocarbon dated to *c.* 5200 BP (Indrelid 1976).

The effects of this process in the lowlands seem, however, to have varied considerably within the different regions of the southern Norwegian highlands. At Hardangervidda Neolithic elements, such as cord-decorated pottery and flakes derived from polished flint axes of southern Scandinavian types, have frequently been found on the settlement sites. This, together with palynological data, indicates regular stock-keeping on the plateau itself from *c.* 5000 BP onwards (Indrelid and Moe 1983). In other areas, as for example along the Lærdal watercourse which is only 75 km further north, any indication of agricultural activity appears to be lacking according to Johansen (1978).

So, while significant economic changes took place

within some of the traditional Mesolithic reindeer hunting territories, economic and cultural stability may have persisted in other areas, provided that these highlands *were* still in use in the Neolithic period – a premiss which is not necessarily secure.

CASE STUDY OF A MARGINAL SOUTHERN HIGHLAND AREA

The investigation area

The investigation area is in the southernmost part of the Norwegian highlands, half-way between the heads of the long, narrow, east–west orientated Ryfylke fjords and the upper part of the Setesdal, a 150 km long glacial valley which penetrates the highlands in a north–south direction (*Fig. 2*). The area lies between 900 and 1300 m above sea level.

There are clear differences between the western part of the area, usually called the *Ryfylke mountains*, and the eastern part, the *Setesdal mountains*. While most of the the area to the west of the main watershed consists of bare rock surfaces with little or no soil cover or vegetation, the eastern mountains exhibit more till and drift deposits. This, in combination with more moderate snowfall and shorter winter seasons, provides the Setesdal mountains east of the divide with the best grazing land for reindeer, the only big game of importance in the area. According to airplane counts the reindeer population in the Ryfylke–Setesdal mountains, the southernmost reindeer population in Norway, consists of approximately 3500 animals (Kjos-Hanssen and Gunnerød 1977). Climatically there is also a marked east–west divide within the investigation area, as the western highlands are dominated by Atlantic wet and cloudy weather and the Setesdal mountains by a drier, more continental climate.

The central part of the Ryfylke–Setesdal mountains is characterized by a multitude of lakes. Five main watercourses drain the area – one to the east, one to the south, and three to the west. Extensive plans for hydro-electric development formed the basis of an interdisciplinary research project, the Ulla-Førre Investigation (*Ulla-Førre undersøkelsene*), managed by the Arkeologisk museum i Stavanger from 1974 to 1980. The main objective of this project was cultural–historical – to investigate the human exploitation of the Ryfylke–Setesdal mountains and the surrounding country from the end of glaciation to the present day (Vinsrygg 1973; Johansen 1975).

The archaeological evidence

A coherent highland area of about 450 km^2 on both sides of the watershed has been more or less thoroughly investigated in order to locate Stone Age sites. Most of the surveying was completed between

M

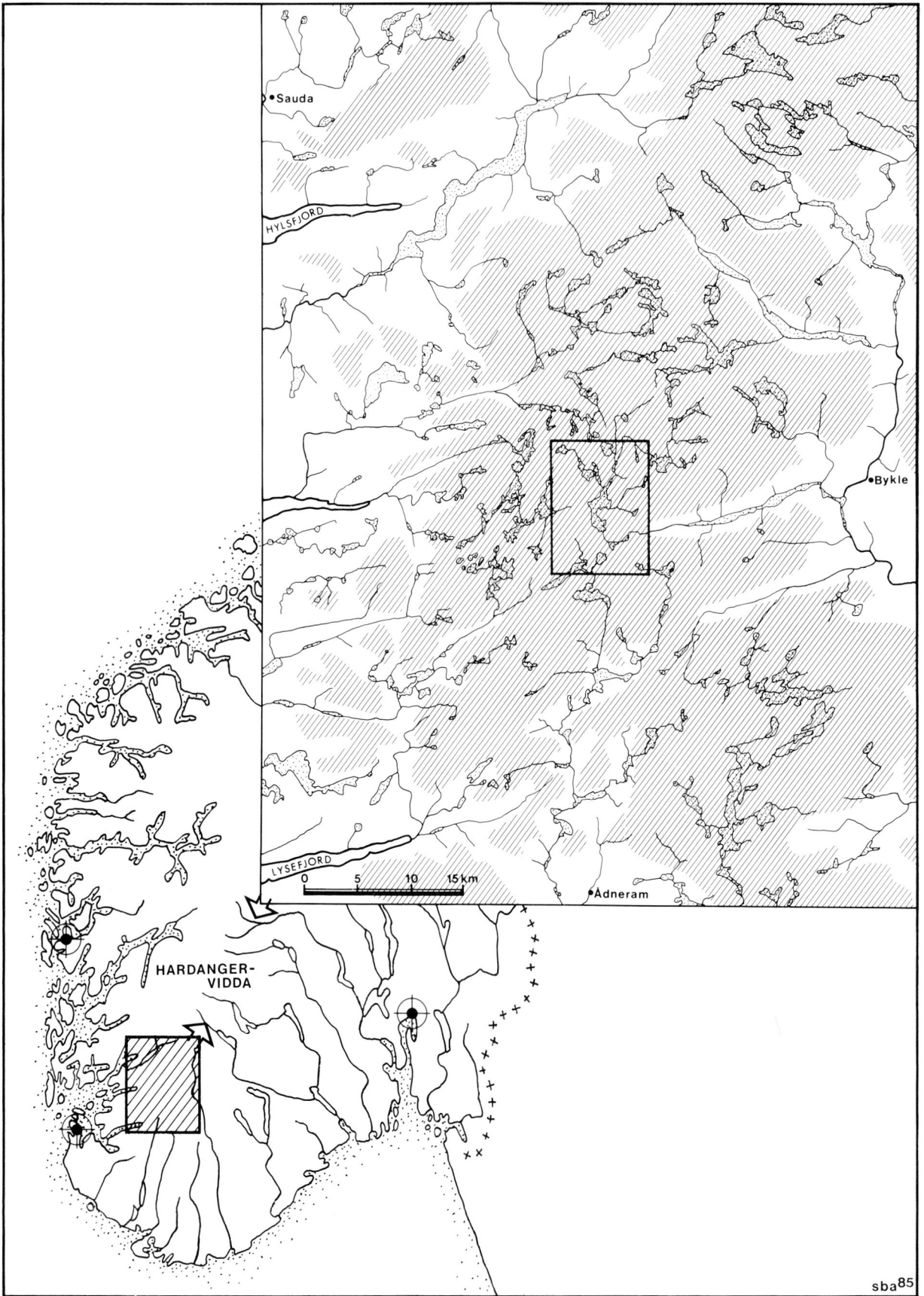

Figure 2 Location of the Ryfylke–Setesdal mountains: land above 900 m is shaded; inner square indicates the extent of *Fig. 3*.

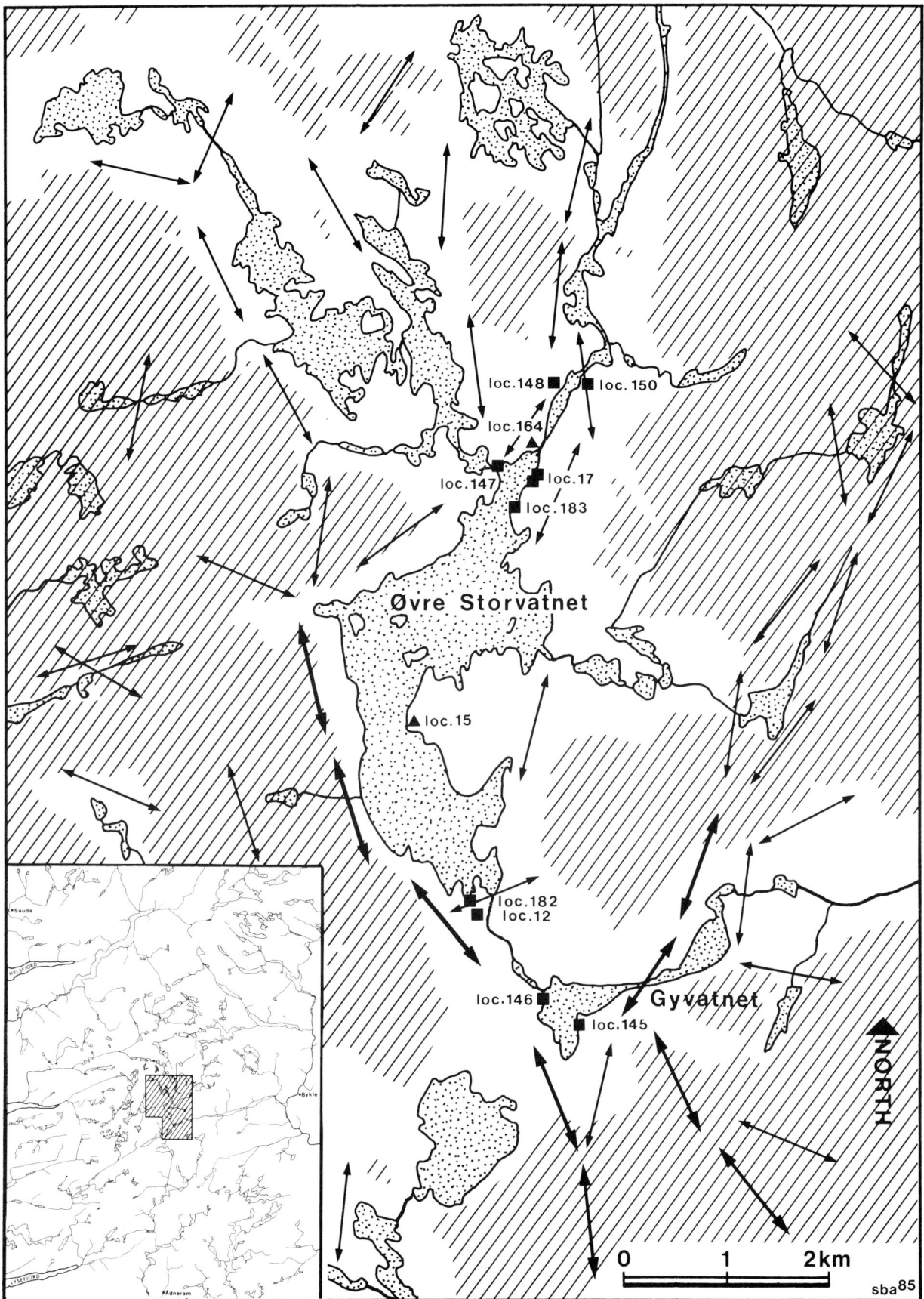

Figure 3 The area around the lakes of Øvre Storvatnet and Gyvatnet with Mesolithic sites indicated by black squares, and the main reindeer migration routes indicated by arrows (land above 1050 m is hatched).

1973 and 1976, and archaeological excavations were undertaken from 1974 to 1978. Subsequently, only minor control work has been performed, mainly water sieving of soil dumps from previous excavations (Bang-Andersen 1985).

With two exceptions, all localities of Mesolithic date (older than 5200 BP) are located within a limited area, near the lakes of Øvre Storvatnet and Vestre Gyvatnet in the Setesdal mountains, just to the east of the main divide (Bang-Andersen 1976a; Bang-Andersen and Kjos-Hanssen 1979; *Fig. 3*). The exceptions are an open-air dwelling site, radiocarbon dated to *c.* 6240 BP, at Store Urevatn approximately 20 km to the north east (Løken 1977), and a rock-shelter dwelling, radiocarbon dated to *c.* 7130 BP, at Storhillervatn 25 km further south west (Bang-Andersen, in preparation).

A striking feature is that a highland territory embracing at least 300 km² around the watershed and westward of it, is completely devoid of Stone Age sites. That is, there are no traces of settlement where they would generally be expected – along the watercourses and near the most important reindeer trek routes. After years of intensive searching, and 4000 empty test pits, it seems likely that the absence of sites in the Ryfylke high mountains is a reality.

Of 11 Mesolithic sites located in the Storvatnet–Gyvatnet area, nine have been excavated. As shown in *Fig. 3*, all sites are clearly waterfront oriented, situated either close to the water's edge (Localities 17 and 183), or at most 100 m away (Localities 12 and 150). With the exception of three localities near river mouths, in low-lying and damp terrain, the Mesolithic sites are situated on the tops of dry, well-drained gravel ridges. These are exposed to wind, but compensate by offering a very good view of the surrounding terrain. All sites are open-air (unsheltered) localities. Several usable rock-shelters have been located in the vicinity, but these contain no indication of use during the Stone Age.

The artifact material consists mainly of flint of variable quality. In addition, smaller amounts of rock-crystal and quartz normally occur. Scrapers form the only identifiable tool group, although there is also a relatively strong element of retouched chippings and microblades, which to a large extent seem to have functioned as tools. The microblades were obtained mainly from handle cores. It should also be mentioned that traces of red ochre have been found at two localities (Bang-Andersen 1982).

Remains of dwelling structures such as postholes or distinct cut and stone-lined fireplaces have not been observed. Cultural layers are, with a few exceptions, thin, unstratified and strongly leached in such a way that organic material other than charcoal is not preserved.

As soil phosphate surveys have failed to yield meaningful results, the site areas have to be defined by the horizontal distribution of the lithic material. The excavated find-bearing area varies considerably from 1 to 56 m². As can be seen from *Table 2*, six out of nine excavated sites have floor areas of between 25 and 40 m². It is, however, the extreme cases which attract the greatest interest, and which will be commented upon further.

Table 2: Comparison of the total lithic artifact assemblages and the horizontal extent of Mesolithic sites excavated in the Setesdal mountains

Locality no.	Find material			Locality size		
	Total	Distinct tools	Microblades & fragments	Excavation area in m²	Find-bearing area in m²	Estimated overall area in m²
12	276	1	22	28	21	35-40
17	1078	30	181	62	56	80-100
145	411	7	68	4	3	30-35
146	361	2	0	5	5	25-30
147	130	3	22	20	14	25-30
148	7	0	1	9	1	1-5
150	144	5	7	30	24	30-35
182	394	12	33	25	21	40-45
183	48	3	3	12	11	15-20

Locality 148 is situated on a slight slope, 15 m away from the water's edge. A reindeer path lies only 3–4 m away. During the archaeological excavation only seven flint artifacts – six chippings from the same nodule, and one microblade fragment (*Fig. 4*) – were

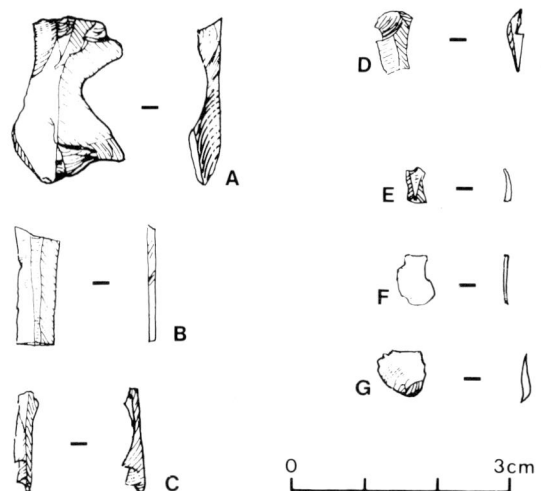

Figure 4 The total artifact assemblage from Locality 148 in the Setesdal mountains. All pieces, except B, are from the same flint nodule.

found. The artifacts, which have a total weight of 1.3 g, came from an area of less than 1 m² around a small charcoal patch which has been radiocarbon dated to c. 5870 BP. With such a small number of finds from this limited area, it is impossible to call this locality a dwelling place in the real sense of the word. It is more likely to represent a solitary situation, for example, a short halt in connection with the skinning of game.

This 'clean' locality type, which reflects specialized activities, has until now rarely been found in the southern Norwegian highlands. The reason is obvious; they are almost impossible to trace through test pits. A similar locality was previously reported from Grjotflott on the Hardangervidda, where the finds consisted of eight flint artifacts (Indrelid 1973).

If we omit Locality 148, it is difficult, but not impossible, to determine how many occupations each site represents. For example, this can be demonstrated at Locality 17, which is the largest both in area and quantity of finds. The site is situated on the top of a dry gravel ridge, 10–15 m from the water's edge and 4–5 m higher. An area of 62 m² was excavated. The total extent of the site was originally somewhat larger, about 90 m². The archaeological finds indicate that the site experienced at least three distinct settlement phases. This impression is partially supported

by the stratigraphy. The first occupation, radiocarbon dated to c. 6870 BP, is reflected in the use of quartz as artifact material. A later Mesolithic phase, dated to c. 6000 BP, is distinguished by the production of microblades (*Fig. 5*) and the extensive use of flint scrapers. The most recent use of the locality, which took place c. 4040 BP, is represented by slate arrowheads and certain other Neolithic elements. The distribution of artifact material from the oldest and youngest settlement phases wa restricted, and may be the result of single visits. The finds from the middle phase were, however, widely dispersed and demonstrate a far more intensive occupation. Find distribution analysis and conjoining experiments, which have not yet been completed, indicate that this phase includes at least two, and possibly as many as four or five separate occupations (Bang-Andersen, in preparation). To conclude, the site was occupied a number of times, perhaps as many as seven. Archaeologically, it is clearly mixed, but mixed in a distinctive manner.

Altogether, 16 radiocarbon dates are available from the sites. As can be seen from *Table 3*, as many as 13 of these fall into the period 7000–5700 BP, two are c. 4000 BP and one c. 2500 BP. All the dates seem to be consistent with the archaeological evidence. The distribution of the Mesolithic dates is striking, as they cluster around two limited periods, c. 7000–6700

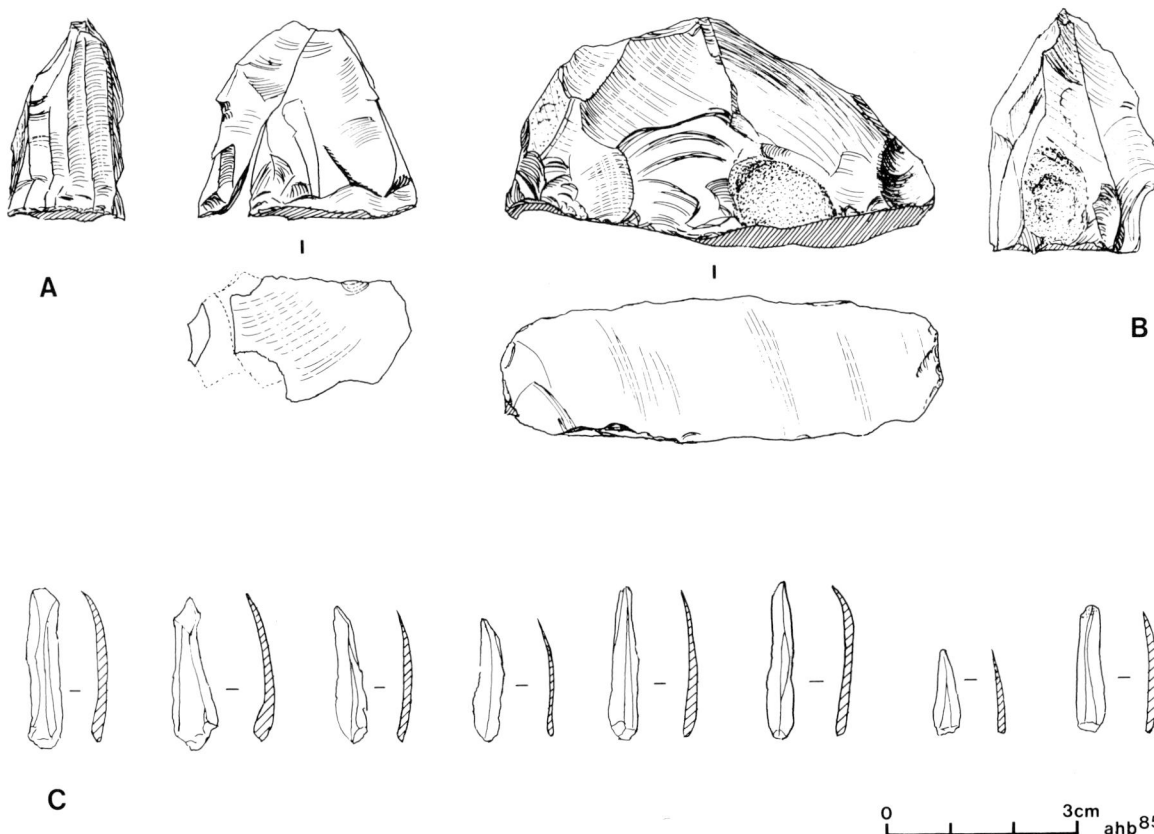

Figure 5 Representative series of flint artifacts from the microblade industry at Locality 17 in the Setesdal mountains: A – conjoined handle core with an obvious blade-flaking front; B – handle core with no blade scars; C – microblades, all produced from the same core.

345

	Mesolithic Stone Age	5200 Neolithic Stone Age	3500 "Bronze Age" 2500
T-2360 (LOC.147)			
T-2651 (LOC.182)			
T-2652 (LOC.183)			
T-2650 (LOC.17s)			
T-2074 (LOC. 12)			
T-3542 (LOC. 12)			
T-2359 (LOC.146)			
T-2073 (LOC.17s)			
T-3076 (LOC.147)			
T-2072 (LOC.17N)			
T-3072 (LOC.148)			
T-3073 (LOC.150)			
T-3074 (LOC.145)			
T-3075 (LOC.17M)			
T-3077 (LOC. 13)			
T-3078 (LOC.146)			

| 7000 | 6000 | 5000 | 4000 | 3000 | 2000 |

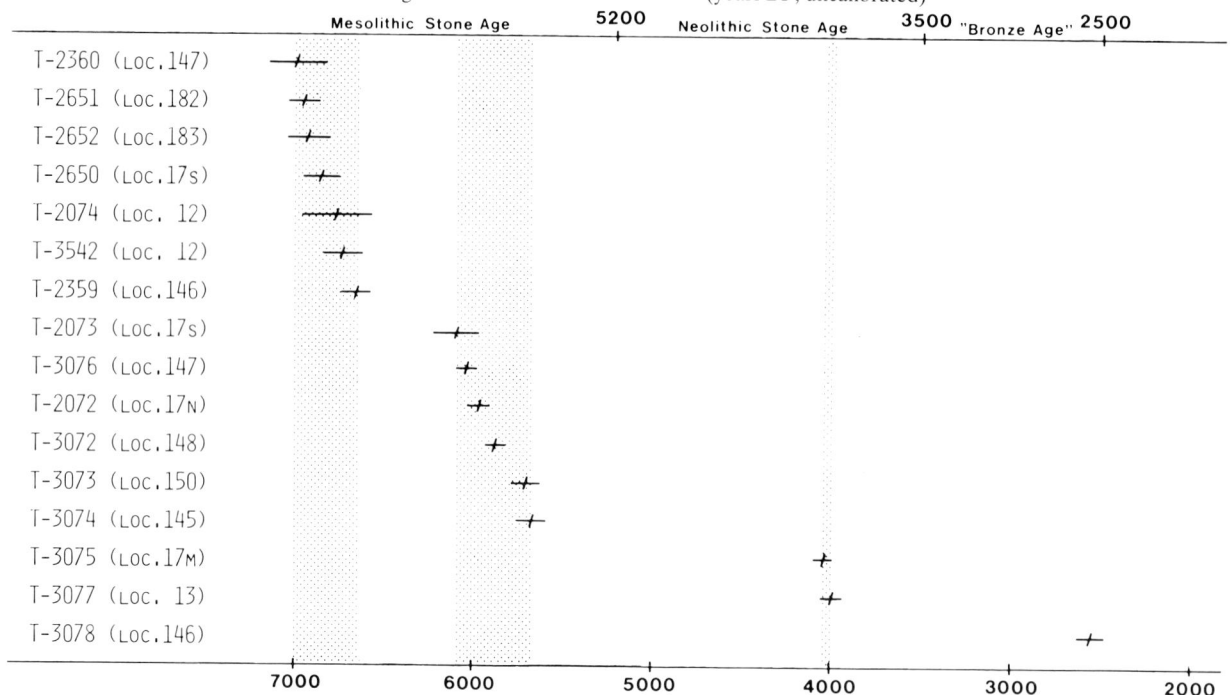

BP and *c.* 6100–5700 BP. The intervening period of 350–800 radiocarbon years is not covered.

There could be several explanations for this lacuna, including the possibility of inaccurate radiocarbon determinations. However, the possibility that extensive use of fossil firewood has created a false older phase may be ruled out, as wood anatomy analysis shows that the charcoal in practically all samples was from branch and twig fragments.

One element of uncertainty is that future dendro-calibrations may lead to the adjustment of conventional radiocarbon dates, so that the gap will be narrowed or even disappear. For the moment, however, the oldest group of dates lie beyond the range of the MASCA-curve. A third source of error, which is possible though unlikely, is that the highland area *was* used in the period concerned, without this being identified archaeologically.

A gap of about 600 years in the middle of a 1300–1400 year long cultural tradition within a restricted area, represents a great challenge. It implies that Mesolithic hunting groups for approximately twenty generations, for reasons unknown, found this part of the highland of limited interest, until they again made use of it.

A partly contemporaneous lacuna from *c.* 6800 to *c.* 6400 BP in the Hardangervidda has been tentatively interpreted as the result of a decline in the reindeer population, due to a marked increase in precipitation and snow cover (Moe, Indrelid and Kjos-Hanssen 1978). This also provides a plausible explanation for the hiatus in the Setesdal mountains.

The ecological setting

The Setesdal mountains were deglaciated by *c.* 8800

BP (P. Blystad, pers. comm.). Assuming that the earliest occupation is represented in the excavated archaeological material, this indicates that the highland area remained unexploited for perhaps 1500–2000 years, before Mesolithic man found it attractive.

Further north in the southern Norwegian highlands there was, as previously noted, a gap of only a few hundred years between deglaciation and the first appearance of man. In spite of this, the lacuna in the Setesdal mountains is felt to be real, given the thinner soil cover and the length of time it must have taken here – compared, for example, with the Hardangervidda – to establish a plant cover which could provide sufficient extensive, stable grazing land for reindeer.

Little is known about the climate and vegetation in this area in the period from 7000 to 5500 BP, as the results of palynological fieldwork performed as part of the Ulla-Førre Project are still awaited. However, preliminary estimates based on radiocarbon dating of fossil pine stumps and trunks, and on meteorological inferences, indicate that the highlands remained unforested, in spite of a generally higher tree line. The mean summer temperature in the Atlantic period may have been 1–2 °C higher, and the climate more marked by high-pressure zones, than today (Selsing 1978; Selsing and Wishman 1983).

Wood anatomy analysis carried out on a collection of some 350 pieces of charcoal from Mesolithic contexts from the excavated sites, shows a clear dominance of birch (65%), with smaller amounts of juniper (18%), rowan (9%), pine (5%) and willow (3%). If the choice of firewood was random – it seems unlikely, in an area where trees were not common, that Mesolithic hunters would have selected particular woods for their higher output of energy – then the results of the wood anatomy analyses probably give a representative picture of the vegetation in the immediate vicinity of the sites. The composition of this sparse arctic–alpine vegetation must have been virtually identical to that of the present.

What kinds of food resources were available at that time? As osteological material is lacking, we are obliged to use indirect evidence. Trout or other fish species were definitely not the prime factor which first attracted Mesolithic groups to the area, as high waterfalls both to the east and west effectively prevent natural occurrences of fish. Other resources such as small game (hare, ptarmigan) and berries (bilberry, crowberry) may have been exploited to some extent. In this respect, however, the lowland areas must have been far more alluring.

It is difficult to imagine resources other than *reindeer* that may have attracted Mesolithic groups to the Setesdal mountains. As indicated in *Fig. 3*, the early spring and late summer migrations pass in a north–south direction through points on both sides of Lake Gyvatnet and along the western shore of Øvre Storvatnet. Only a few kilometres further north and north east the reindeer find the best summer pastures, as they probably did 7000 and 6000 years ago. Here mother-and-calf herds consisting of up to 300 animals roam until the rut begins in October, while the bucks live in the rocky areas west of the watershed.

Economic interpretation

These inferences regarding the ecological setting, combined with a knowledge of the archaeological material, provide the basis for a more detailed economic interpretation of the Mesolithic sites in the Setesdal mountains.

The almost overwhelming dominance of flint as artifact material indicates a close connection with the coast, and therefore two possible areas of origin: the southern coast of Norway (*Sørlandet*) and the fjord area of south-west Norway (*Ryfylke*). Of these, the latter area is the more likely, as it involves a very much shorter migration route than the southern coast alternative. By *c.* 7000 BP, the reindeer population in the Setesdal mountains had become numerous and sufficiently stable to represent a viable subsistence base for hunter-gatherer groups inhabiting the densely wooded western fjord districts.

The reindeer hunt took place around a 'bottleneck' area a few kilometres east of the watershed, where topographical features funnelled the main treks and created seasonal aggregations of prey. The hunt seems to have focused on mother-and-calf bands, as no Mesolithic sites have been found in the more sparsely populated buck areas to the west of the divide.

What archaeological evidence do we have then for the Mesolithic exploitation of this area? Debris from the manufacture and maintenance of flint tools, the general occurrence of scrapers and microblades, together with clear evidence of camp fires, justifies the interpretation of the majority of sites as dwelling locations. When this material is compared with Indrelid's grouping of the Hardangervidda sites (*Table 1*), it is seen that only sites of Types 1 and 2 occur in the Setesdal mountains. Type 2, or most probably an intermediate state between Types 1 and 2, is the one most commonly found.

The neighbouring reindeer territories were searched from these dwelling places. The procurement activities are partly recognizable through special purpose sites (hunting stands, butchering spots) of Type 1, which are evidently strongly underrepresented. The small quantities of artifacts, the very limited number of distinct tool types, the absence of dwelling structures, and restricted floor areas clearly indicate that these were not permanent settlements or encampments that were occupied for the greater part of the year. Individual occupations are likely to have lasted days or at most weeks, rather than months.

The artifact assemblages from the sites give no direct indication of the hunting techniques employed, as not a single projectile point of undoubted Mesolithic age has been found. However, hunting with bows and arrows is implied by the presence of large numbers of microblades which may be interpreted as flint edges that were inserted into slotted arrowpoints (Mikkelsen 1975; Bang-Andersen 1979).

The tendency for sites to be located in elevated positions near water provides further indirect evidence, since the reindeer tend to follow watercourses during migrations (*Fig. 3*). The majority of the dwelling sites are located near obvious river crossing points (Locality 150), river outlets (Localities 146 and 147), or at places where hunters could rapidly manoeuvre to the opposite beach of a lake by boat (Localities 17 and 183).

In addition to bow hunting, it would have been easy to carry out game drives, with the water bodies as reception and killing areas. Reindeer killed in water will float almost indefinitely, thus enabling hunters to continue the kill and not worry about immediate retrieval. This form of reindeer driving is known from ethnographic sources in southern Norway, and is also well documented from circumpolar areas, especially among Eskimos and Indians (e.g. Birket-Smith 1929; Burch 1972; Spiess 1979). The reindeer hunt most probably took place in the early autumn, when the meat and hides were in prime condition.

Two further questions merit consideration: who were the Mesolithic reindeer hunters foraging in this highland area, and where did they come from?

All the site characteristics seem to indicate that the hunting groups were small, each possibly comprising between 5 and 10 persons (most of them likely to

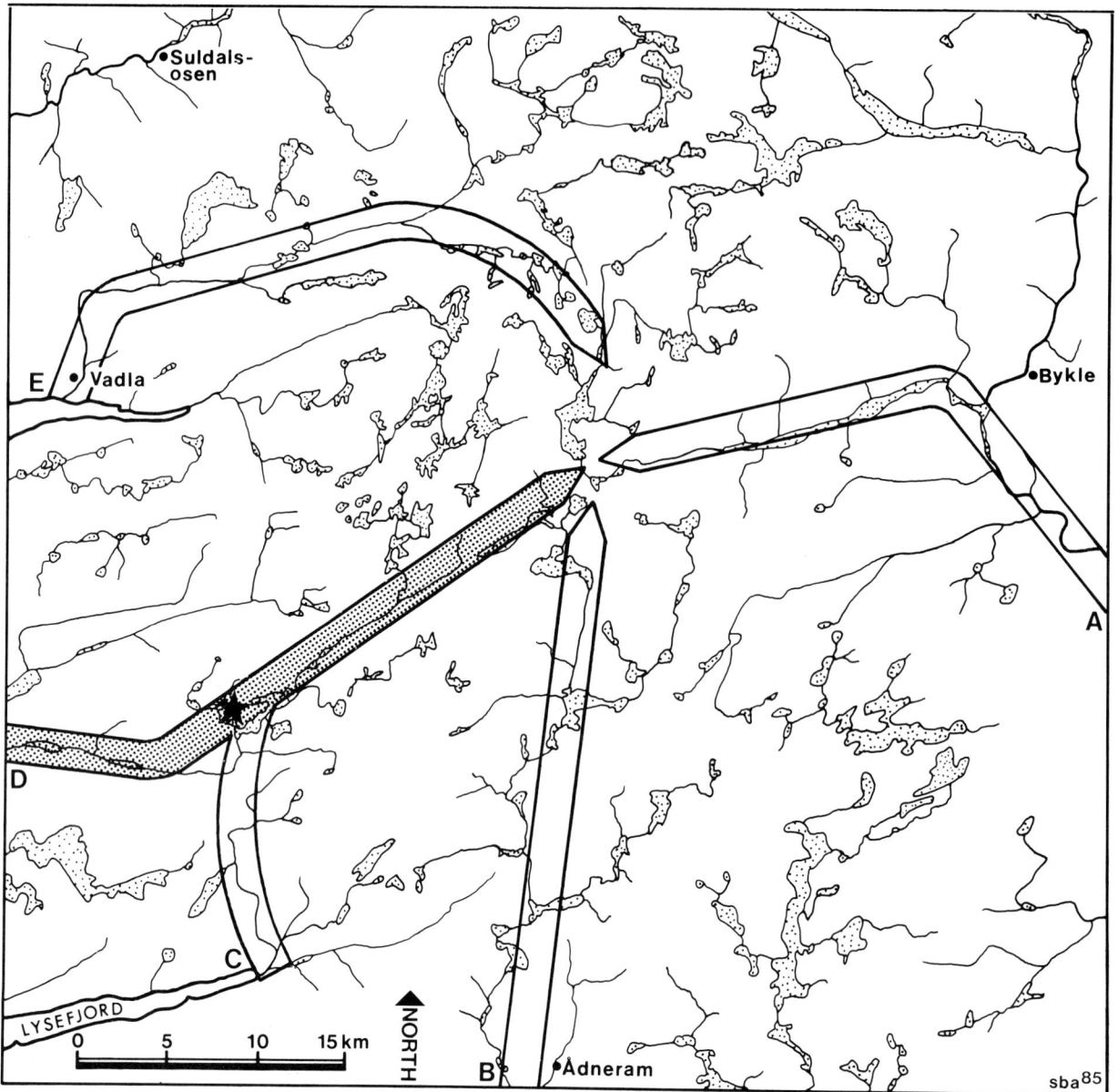

Figure 7 Possible seasonal movement routes following the main watercourses of the Storvatnet–Gyvatnet area. D stands out as the most likely route. A possible transit site, Storhiller, is indicated by a star.

have been adult males). However, as a small lump of resin with distinct human milk tooth imprints (*Fig. 6*) found at Locality 17 demonstrates, children also participated to some extent. It is tempting to take this as an indication of apprenticeship training (Bang-Andersen 1976*b*).

Figure 6 Lump of charred resin with series of tooth imprints (probably made by a child aged 6–12 years), found at Locality 17 in the Setesdal mountains.

Eight alternatives for explaining the background to Mesolithic exploitation of the Setesdal mountains

are summarized in *Table 4*. Of these Pattern A, which implies year-round occupation in the highlands, may be rejected on the basis of what has been stated above.

Table 4: Schematic representation of alternative mobility patterns underlying the Mesolithic settlement of the Setesdal mountains

Ecological zones / Mobility patterns	A	B	C	D	E	F	G	H
Highland	●	●	●	●	⊙	⊙	⊙	⊙
Valleys & fiord heads		⊙	⊙		●	●		⊙
Fiord mouths & outer coast			⊙	⊙		⊙	●	●

Key symbols: ● base camps   ⊙ hunting stations   ←——→ moves

348

The other models imply that the mountains were used within established mobility patterns, which to a large extent must have been linear along easily recognizable natural routeways. Patterns B, C and D, which postulate base camps in the highlands combined with some seasonal exploitation of the surrounding western valleys and fjord areas, may also be taken out of consideration. Of the remaining alternatives, Patterns G and H may be emphasized. These imply home bases most probably near fjord mouths, or on the outer coast of south-west Norway. In particular, the sounds in the middle of the Ryfylke fjord system appear to be well suited as base areas for settlement; and a number of Mesolithic sites have been discovered here during the last decade.

From Årdalsfjord, which is one of the likely alternatives, it is not more than 50–60 km as the crow flies – a two-day walk – through a continuous corridor of river valleys to the reindeer hunting spots in the Setesdal mountains (*Fig. 7*). Storhiller, a rock-shelter with its oldest occupation layer radiocarbon dated to *c.* 7130 BP, may have been a transit camp half-way on this migration route (Bang-Andersen, in preparation).

The cultural–historical interpretation which at present seems most probable, is that Mesolithic groups with base territories in the outer western fjord areas, exploited the reindeer population in the marginal southern Norwegian highlands primarily during periods of subsistence stress in the lowlands (Pattern H). Small task groups would have left their base camps in the early autumn, and followed the main watercourses up to their hunting grounds in the Setesdal mountains where they stayed for a few weeks.

Some time after 5700 BP this tradition appears to end. When the reindeer resources in the highlands were again exploited, *c.* 4000 BP, the hunters were probably Neolithic groups making sporadic short-term expeditions from summer-pasture camps in the surrounding valleys and low-lying lake basins.

PRELIMINARY CONCLUSIONS

The Setesdal mountains, and in all probability the other areas of the southernmost highlands, were first settled 1300–1800 years later than the central and northern parts of the southern Norwegian highlands.

Specialized reindeer hunting, performed during short seasonal expeditions in the early autumn from more permanent residence areas in the western fjord districts, supplies the most plausible interpretation of the highland sites.

Mesolithic exploitation of the reindeer resources in the Setesdal mountains was concentrated in two periods, *c.* 7000–6700 and *c.* 6100–5700 BP. The intervening hiatus in settlement may be linked to environmental changes.

Finally, further information, in particular data from palynological studies and from archaeological investigations of the Mesolithic sites in the western fjord districts, is needed before more definite cultural–historical conclusions can be drawn.

Acknowledgements: All radiocarbon dates mentioned in this article have been carried out by the Trondheim Radiological Dating Laboratory. The wood anatomy determinations were performed by laboratory technician Aud Simonsen, Arkeologisk museum i Stavanger, and the tooth imprints in a lump of resin have been investigated by dentist Ole Andreas Tomasgaard, Stavanger. The fieldwork was financed by the Norwegian Watercourse and Electricity Board (NVE); and travel grants from Arkeologisk museum i Stavanger and the Norwegian Research Council for Sciences and Humanities (NAVF) enabled the author to present the preliminary results at the III International Mesolithic Symposium, in Edinburgh. To these individuals and institutions I offer my sincere thanks.

References

BANG-ANDERSEN, S. (1976*a*) Steinalderboplasser i Bykleheiene 1000 meter over havet. *Frå haug ok heidni*, 6: 92–101.

BANG-ANDERSEN, S. (1976*b*) Mystiske tanninntrykk i harpiks. *Frå haug ok heidni*, 6: 130–131.

BANG-ANDERSEN, S. (1979) Fra barnets munn til arkeologens hånd. *AmS-Småtrykk* (Stavanger), 5: 25–27.

BANG-ANDERSEN, S. (1982) Om okerbruk blant forhistoriske jeger-samler grupper i Sør-Norge. In A. Lillehammer (ed.), *Faggrenser brytes*. Stavanger, AmS-Skrifter 9: 57–73.

BANG-ANDERSEN, S. (1985) Utgravd-tapt-gjenfunnet. En analyse av steinartefakttapet ved utgravning av boplasser. In J.R. Naess (ed.), *Artikkelsamling I*. Stavanger, AmS-Skrifter 11: 5–23.

BANG-ANDERSEN, S. and KJOS-HANSSEN, O. (1979) På spor etter de første mennesker i høyfjellet. *AmS-Småtrykk* (Stavanger), 3: 31–45.

BURCH, E.S. Jr (1972) The caribou/wild reindeer as a human resource. *American Antiquity*, 37: 339–368.

BØE, J. (1942) Til høgfjellets forhistorie. Boplassen på Sumtangen ved Finsevatn på Hardangervidda. *Bergens Museums Skrifter*, 21: 81–82.

GUSTAFSON, L. (1981) Om 'vestgrensa' i høyfjellet. *Arkeo*, 1980: 6–10.

HAGEN, A. (1963) Mesolitiske jegergrupper i norske høyfjell. *Universitetets Oldsaksamlings Årbok* 1960/1961: 109–142.

INDRELID, S. (1973) Mesolitiske tilpasningsformer i høyfjellet. *Stavanger Museums Årbok* 1972: 5–27.

INDRELID, S. (1975) Problems relating to the early Mesolithic settlement of southern Norway. *Norwegian Archaeological Review*, 8(1): 1–18.

INDRELID, S. (1976) *Das Spätmesolithikum und die Anfänge des Neolithikums im westlichen Norwegen*. Unpublished manuscript.

INDRELID, S., KJOS-HANSSEN, O. and MOE, D. (1978) A Study of environment and early man in the southern Norwegian highlands. *Norwegian Archaeological Review*, 11(2): 73–83.

INDRELID, S. and MOE, D. (1983) Februk på Hardangervidda i yngre steinalder. *Viking*, 46: 36–71.

JOHANSEN, A.B. (1973) The Hardangervidda Project for Interdisciplinary Cultural Research: a presentation. *Norwegian Archaeological Review*, 6(2): 60–66.

JOHANSEN, A.B. (1975) Ulla/Førre-undersøkingane sidan sist. *Frå haug ok heidni*, 5: 286–291.

JOHANSEN, A.B. (1978) *Høyfjellsfunn ved Lærdalsvassdraget* (Bind II). Oslo, Universitetsforlaget.

KJOS-HANSSEN, O. and GUNNERØD, T.B. (1977) *Villreinundersøkelser i Setesdalsheiene i 1975 og 1976*. Trondheim, Direktoratet for vilt og ferskvannsfisk, Rapport 2–1977.

KRAFFT, A. (1981) Utbredelse og bestandsstørrelse av villrein i Norge. *Viltrapport*, 18: 23.

LOKEN, T. (1977) Langs elv og vatn i Bykle Vesthei. *Frå haug ok heidni*, 6: 160–163.

MARTENS, I. and HAGEN, A. (1961) Arkeologiske undersøkelser langs elv og vann. *Norske Oldfunn*, 10: 1–96.

MIKKELSEN, E. (1975) *Frebergsvik. Et Mesolitisk Boplassområde ved Oslofjorden.* Oslo, Universitetets Oldsaksamlings Skrifter, ny rekke nr. 1.

MIKKELSEN, E. (1978) Seasonality and Mesolithic adaption in Norway. In K. Kristiansen and C. Paludan-Müller (eds), *New Directions in Scandinavian Archaeology.* Copenhagen, National Museum of Denmark: 79–119.

SELSING, L. (1978) Gamle furustubber i fjellet. *AmS-Småtrykk* (Stavanger) 3: 71–85.

SELSING, L. and WISHMAN, E.H. (1982) Klimaet og furuskoggrensen. *Frá haug ok heidni*, 9: 103–111.

SPIESS, A.E. (1979) *Reindeer and Caribou Hunters. An Archaeological Study.* New York, Academic Press.

VINSRYGG, S. (1973) Ulla/Førre-undersøkingane. *Frá haug ok heidni*, 5: 56–60.

A Case Study of Rørmyr II: a Norwegian Early Mesolithic Site

Birgitte Skar and Sheila Coulson

Abstract

The Pre-Boreal site of Rørmyr II, one of the three well-known Høgnipen sites of southern Norway, excavated in the 1960s, is re-examined. By use of the method of conjoining, it is shown that Rørmyr II consists of the remains of a single short-term occupation. Three activity areas are shown to have co-functioned and various contemporary activities are suggested for the areas.

INTRODUCTION

The site of Rørmyr II, or Høgnipen as it is more commonly known, is a cornerstone in the chronological framework of the Norwegian Mesolithic and is considered to be one of the earliest Postglacial sites in Scandinavia (Mikkelsen 1975, 1978; Fischer 1978; Lindblom 1984). Although it was excavated in the early 1960s, only a brief article has been published on the finds (Johansen 1964). Bearing in mind the importance of the site in Scandinavian prehistory and the difficulties encountered in attempting to use the published material for comparative purposes, the present authors decided to re-examine the lithic remains. To answer questions regarding the possible mixing of the site, in addition to commenting upon on-site activities and the length of occupation, the method of conjoining was used. This method has been applied to a limited extent in Scandinavia, although in other countries conjoining has been employed with impressive results (Leroi-Gourhan and Brézillon 1960, 1962; Bosinski 1975; Cahen, Keeley and Van Noten 1979). The following paper discusses the results of this study and the related technological and chronological implications.

ENVIRONMENT

At the time of occupation, the site of Rørmyr II was situated on the beach of a small rocky island, or skerry, in the outer archipelago of the eastern Oslofjord (*Fig. 1*). No absolute dates are available for the site, but it is possible to estimate from the shoreline displacement curve that Rørmyr II, at 155 m above sea level, could not have been occupied until *c.* 9600 BP (during the Pre-Boreal chronozone), as the Postglacial marine limit in this area is 185 m above sea level (Hafsten 1983). The climate at that time would have been subarctic; although the glacier was reced-

ing rapidly by 9600 BP, it must be remembered that the icefields were still only 70–80 km north of the Rørmyr II site (Sørensen 1978).

Vegetation was sparse on the skerry which contained the site. The environment would have closely resembled that of the islands off the modern coast of western Sweden, with sand-filled rock fissures providing the only growing places for herbs, shrubs, and occasional birch and pine trees. Edible resources would have included sea mammals, sea birds, fish, shellfish and eggs, in addition to crowberries, sea buckthorn and juniper.

It is because of its geographic position that Rørmyr II figures prominently in theories on the early occupation of Norway (Hagen 1963; Indrelid 1975; Welinder 1981). The most recent theory is that the deglaciated coast of southern Norway and western Sweden was originally part of the exploitation territory of groups based on the continent. During the estimated time of occupation of Rørmyr II these areas are presumed to have become more permanently occupied (Welinder 1983).

METHOD

Excavation

Rørmyr II is one of three sites at Høgnipen excavated in the early 1960s by Statsstipendiat Dr Erling Johansen. Excavation notes have not been made available, but the museum catalogue indicates that 140 m² were excavated. It also states that 613 lithic artifacts were located in a gravel layer which was found beneath 30–40 cm of turf and topsoil. No organic remains were recovered and no fireplaces or structural remains were reported.

On a recent visit to the site it was observed that large sections of the eastern area of Rørmyr II were excavated. Therefore, the discrepancy that was noted between the number of squares excavated and those with replotted finds is most probably explained by excavated squares that did not contain lithic material (*Fig. 6*). During the visit it was also observed that an area to the north of the site was undisturbed. It thus appears that Rørmyr II was not fully excavated, in

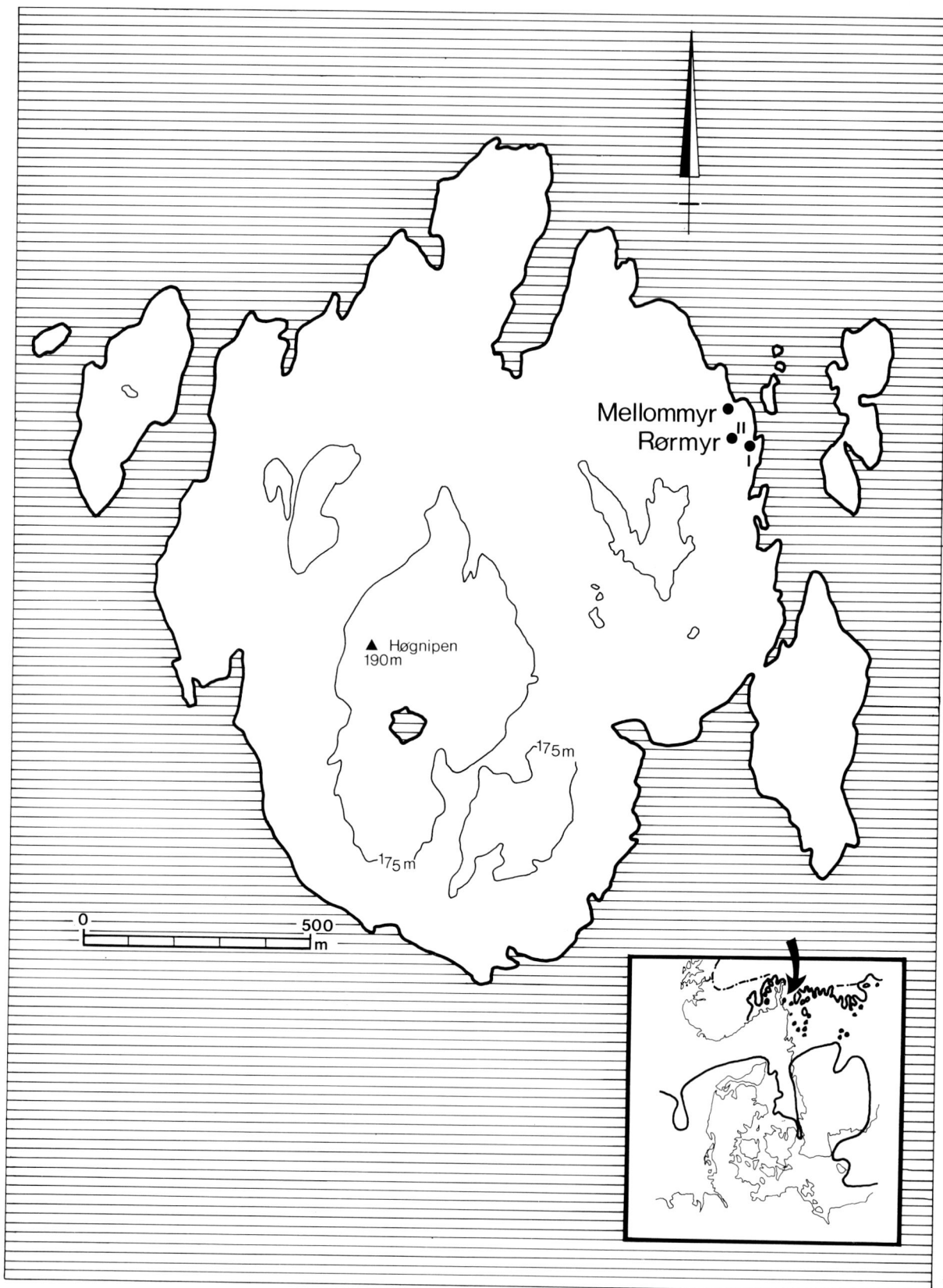

Figure 1 The location of the Rørmyr II settlement (insert, after Indrelid 1975).

contrast to the two other Høgnipen sites – Rørmyr I and Mellommyr (Johansen 1964).

Analysis

An initial examination of the material indicated that most of the artifacts were made from a limited number of nodules. In addition, replotting of the individual artifacts suggested that there was a possibility of tracing activity areas. The latter impression was further supported by the results of the repositioning of the burnt flints which showed two definite

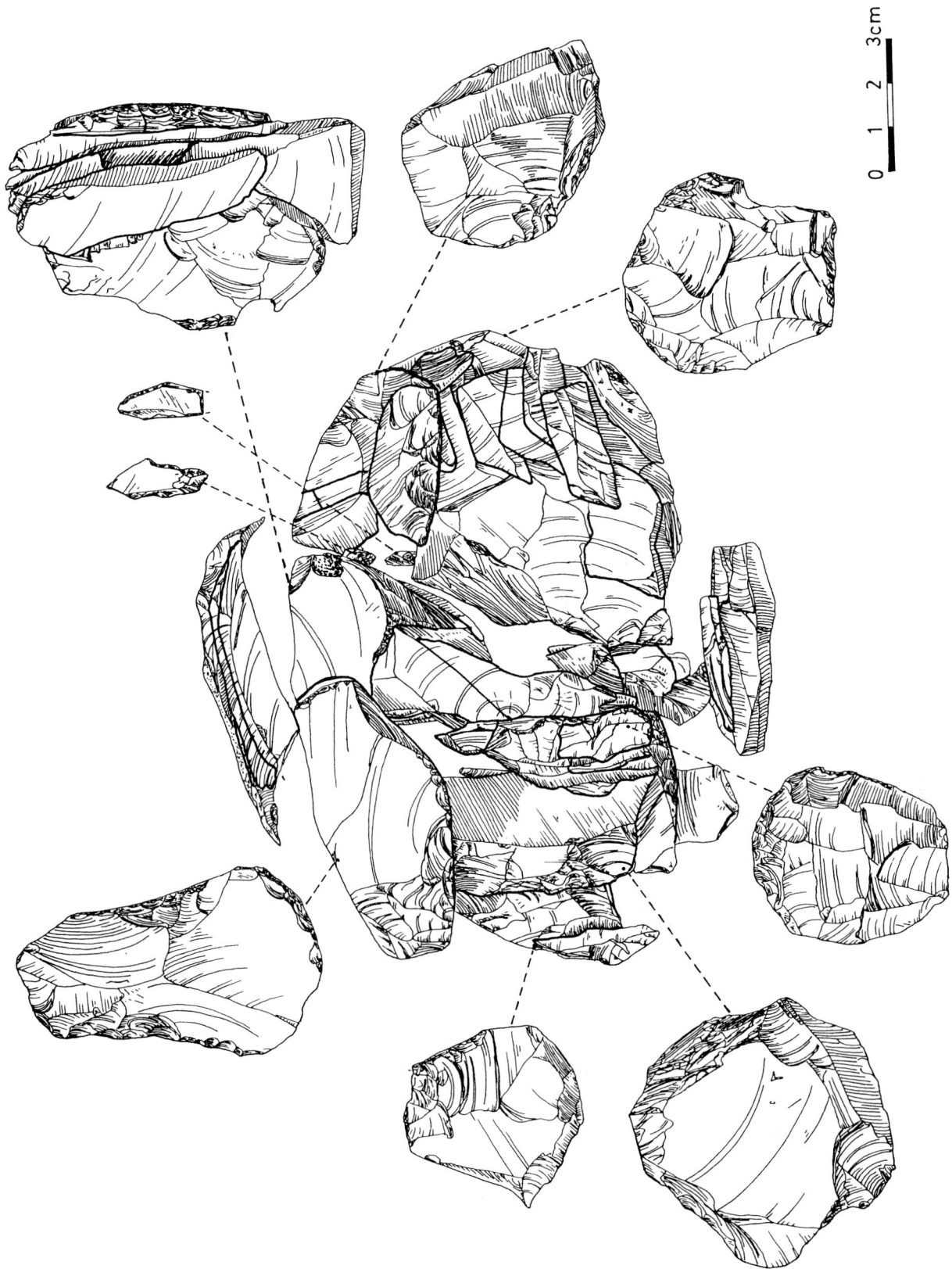

Figure 2   Block A7: explosion showing the different tools that were refitted. The five discs are illustrated in their final state (for the various stages of reworking and resharpening, see *Fig. 3*).

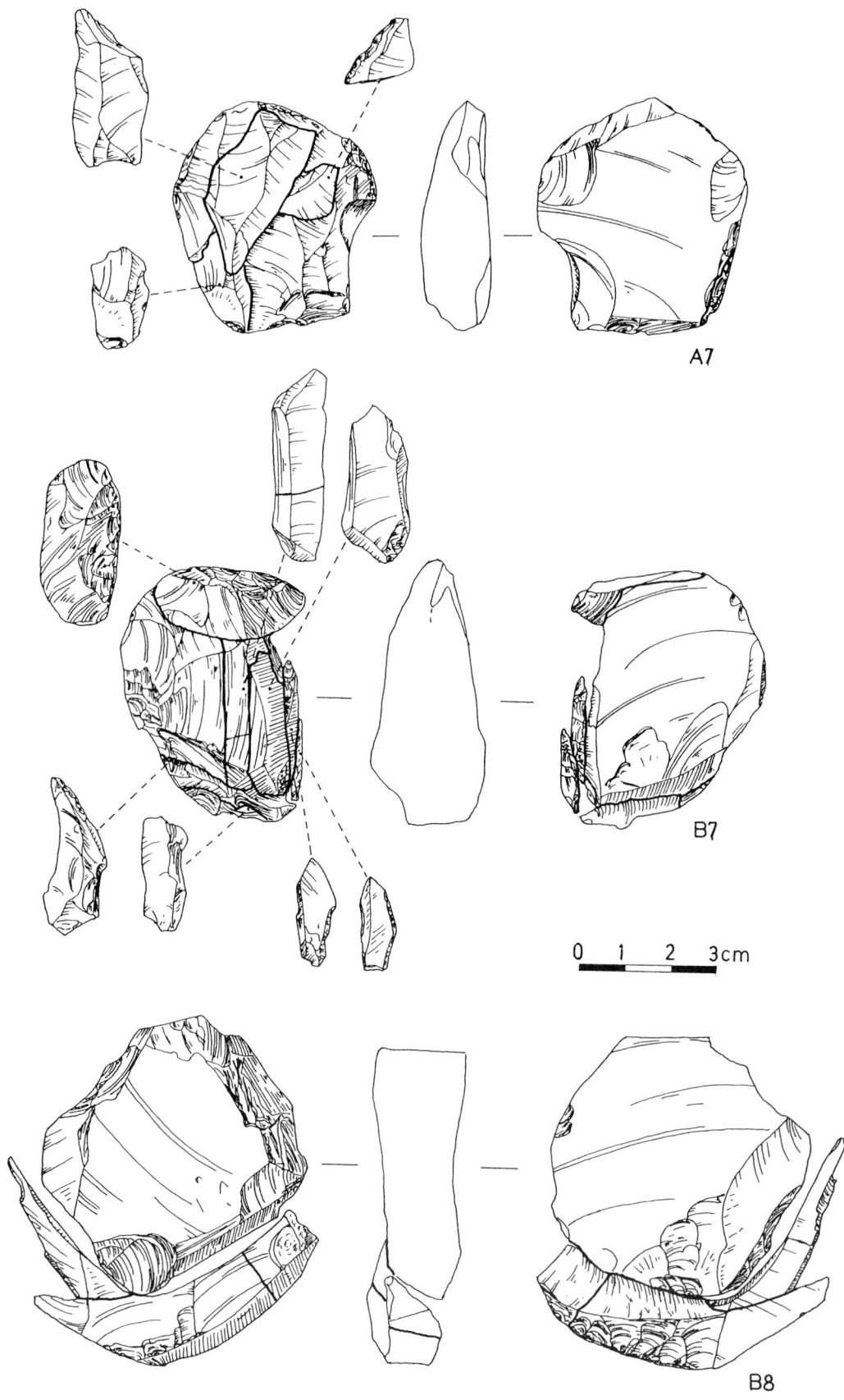

Figure 3 Discs A7, B7 and B8: dorsal side and exploded view, profile, and ventral face. Exploded view shows resharpening flakes, points, and points abandoned in manufacture.

354

concentrations of burning, hereafter referred to as Areas I and II (*Fig. 6*, Area I – squares 5–12, A–H; Area II – squares 1–4, A–H). A third area (III) could also be identified as a distinct cluster of unburnt flints approximately 8–10 m to the east of the other two (*Fig. 6*, Area III – squares I–Q). In an attempt to investigate the nature of these three areas further the method of refitting or conjoining was employed.

RESULTS OF THE CONJOINING

167 (27%) of the 613 artifacts recovered from the site were conjoined, of which the vast majority fit into one large nodule, called the A7 block, a flake core and a blade core (the blue-line core). The remainder, or non-conjoined artifacts, comprise pieces from the three conjoined cores which have not yet been re-fitted, a core of dark flint, the various tools and débit-age produced from it, and some virtually exhausted cores which had only a few removals taken from them before they were abandoned.

All the artifacts are in good condition with only minimal edge damage, most of which is recent. Only 26 (4%) of the pieces are patinated to any substantial degree, while 103 artifacts (17%) are burnt or fire-cracked. The technique of manufacture used throughout is uniform, with tools made on both flakes and blades. The simplest means of describing the technological traits, however, is by following the re-duction process of the three conjoined nodules. In this way, the inter-relationship of the individual activity areas will also become apparent.

Block A7

This nodule contains 65 artifacts of which 10 are finished tools or tools abandoned in production (*Fig. 2*). The cortex layer had been cleaned from the nodule off-site, although small patches of remaining cortex give an indication of the boundaries for three of the sides. The nodule is rounded in shape (16 × 13 × 10 cm) and weighs slightly less than one kilogram.

The reduction of this nodule can be traced through the following stages. The first removals were four irregular blades which have retained some cortex. These artifacts, plus the flake axe which was removed next, were found in Area I. The concave sides of the axe were formed by large removals, with secondary retouch used to shape the edges. The front edge, or what is normally considered to be the cutting edge, was only cut back 3–4 mm (*Fig. 2*, no. 1).

The first disc to be removed from this nodule had been resharpened in Area III, used as a core to pro-duce at least one blank in Area I, then used as a scraper, and finally resharpened and used again be-fore being abandoned (*Fig. 2*, no. 2). Between this disc and the next is a single removal that was found in Area II. Although this flake appears to be one of the few true 'waste' flakes from the nodule, the location it was found in indicates that it was perhaps moved from the main manufacturing area to serve as a blank.

The next disc to be removed differs from the others in that the refitted formation flakes show extensive bifacial trimming (*Fig. 2*, no. 3; *Fig. 3*, B8). The intent behind these removals is unknown. This disc, which served as a scraper, was, in common with all the discs, abandoned in Area I.

A core made on a flake was then removed from the nodule (*Fig. 2*, no. 4). Flakes were taken from both faces of this piece in Areas I and II before the core was discarded in Area I. These removals were fol-lowed by the detachment of another waste flake (also left in Area II) and another disc (*Fig. 2*, no. 5). Again the 'history' of the tool follows the common pattern for the site: the disc acted as a core for blanks (in Area I), then as a scraper (resharpened in Area II), and was finally discarded as an exhausted scraper (back in Area I).

The next stage in the reduction of the A7 block was the removal of a large flake which was used to produce a blade core (*Fig. 2*, no. 6). The piece was crested and seven blades were removed before the core split in two. An attempt to continue working the remaining sections resulted in four more blades and flakes being produced before the piece was left. All the 'waste' blades and flakes and the sections of split core were found within one square of Area I, except for the large blade (*Fig. 2*, no. 6a), which was found six metres away in Area II.

Following the detachment of preparatory flakes another disc was removed. This disc, B7, has the most informative history of all the tools on the site (*Fig. 2*, no. 7; *Fig. 3*, B7). Of the seven refitted pieces, two are tools and one is a tool abandoned in production. The disc first served as a core from which a point was produced (*Fig. 3*, B7, no. 1). This was found with a broken tang-end in Area III. Next, the disc was used as a scraper, since a resharpening flake from it was recovered from the far north end of Area I (*Fig. 3*, B7, no. 2). The piece was then either carried to Area II or produced blanks which were taken there (*Fig. 3*, B7, nos. 3–4). One of these blanks was worked at the distal end in an attempt to form a point before it was discarded (*Fig. 3*, B7, no. 4). Returned to Area I, the disc was again used to produce three blanks (*Fig. 3*, B7, nos. 5–7), of which one was used to make a single-edged point that was found in un-damaged condition (*Fig. 3*, B7, no. 5). Before the disc was finally abandoned it again served as a scraper.

The last disc to be taken from block A7 (*Fig. 2*, no. 8) was also used as a core (*Fig. 3*, A7, no. 1), produc-ing a point abandoned in production within Area II (*Fig. 3*, A7, no. 2), before it was resharpened and used as a scraper in Area I (*Fig. 3*, A7, no. 3). The final removals from the A7 block were a series of seven blades, all but one of which was found in Area

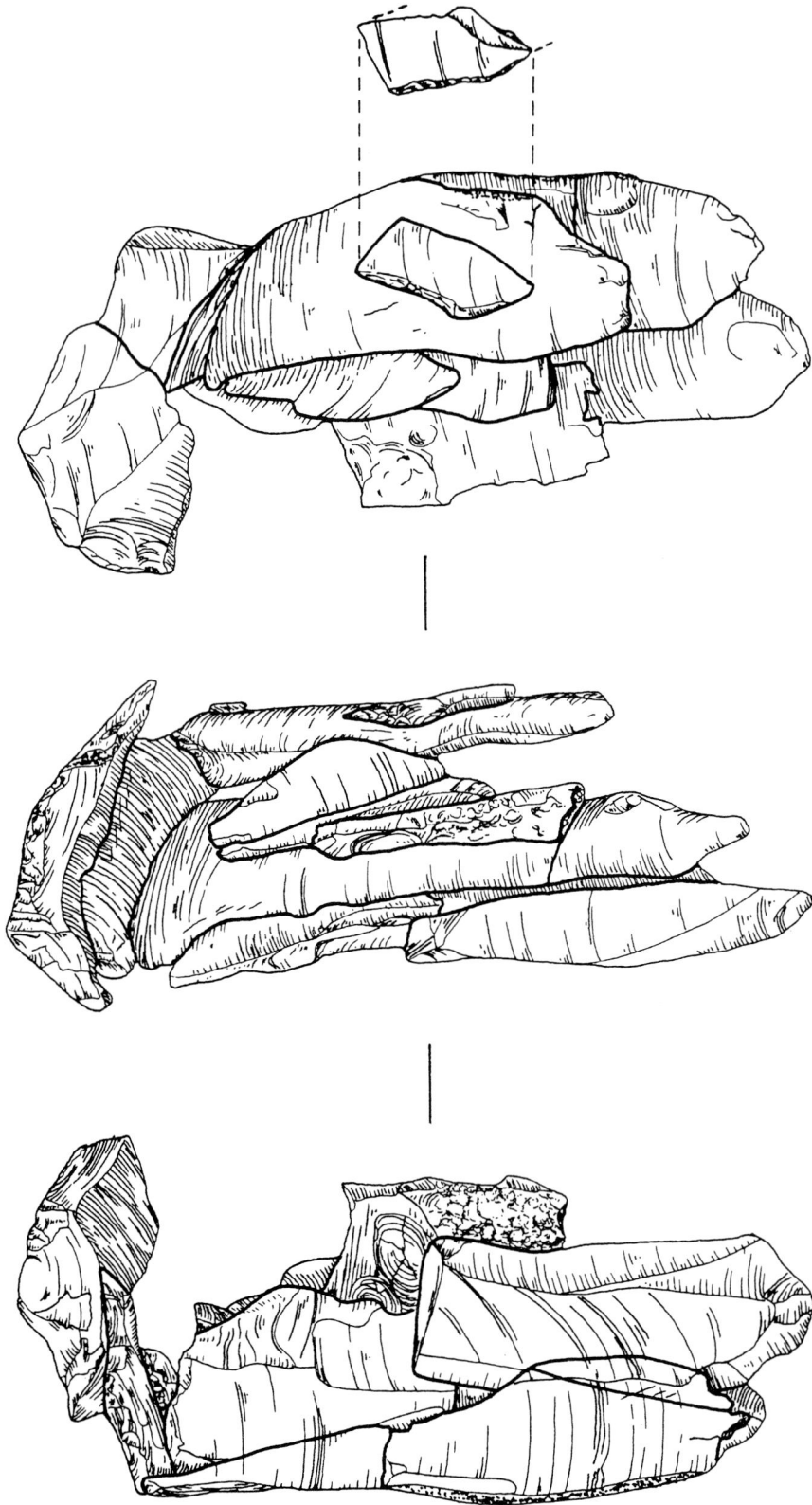

Figure 4   Flake core: dorsal, profile and ventral faces – showing impact-fractured, simple lanceolate point.

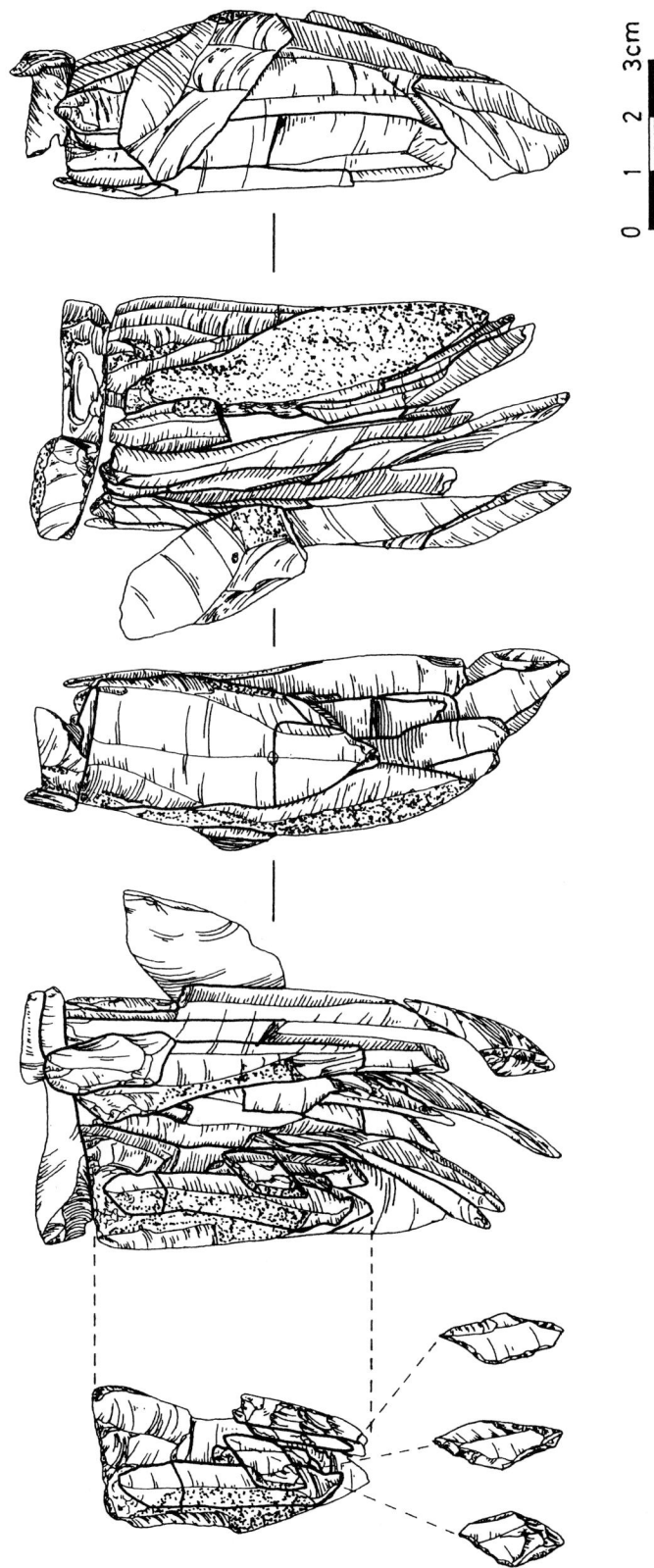

Figure 5 Blue-line blade core: on the left the conical core and the three refitted single-edge points.

I, and another series of flakes and a platform rejuvenation flake (recovered in Area II). The remaining irregular cherty core, from square A7, was left in Area I.

Flake core

The flake core is represented by 13 artifacts of which three are tools (*Fig. 4*). The residual core and nearly all of the initial cortex-removal flakes were not found. The conjoined flakes and tools form a piece which is approximately 12 × 5 × 4 cm.

One of the two platform rejuvenation flakes was removed before the first elongated flake was detached. This flake was made into a burin on an oblique truncation. The core was turned again and the second platform rejuvenation flake removed. The entire series of flakes which would have followed the platform reworking are missing. On the opposite platform three more flakes were detached, the second of which was made into a burin on a straight truncation. Again the core was inverted and another series of flakes were removed, none of which were modified. Finally, the core was turned and the last conjoined flakes are seen terminating in a blank that was used to make a simple lanceolate microlith, which subsequently suffered massive impact damage (Fischer 1985; *Fig. 4*; *Fig. 7*, no. 6).

Blue-line blade core

The blue-line blade core was made from a nodule with a naturally 'keeled' face, a form ideal for such a purpose (*Fig. 5*). The striking platform is flat and unmodified, and was partially formed by the removals seen in *Fig. 5*. Neither end of this nodule was recovered. The refitted core consists of 28 artifacts, of which four are tools, and measures approximately 10 × 7 × 4 cm. With the exception of one flake, all initial preparation stages are missing. The removals between this flake and the remainder of the core were not recovered. A small patch of cresting is the only indication of the preparatory phases that took place before the removal of 14 blades. Two proximal and two distal ends are missing; otherwise the blades are complete. Although the core was struck from the opposite platform halfway through this series, the final blades are still noticeably curved.

The core, which is now in the form seen on the extreme left in *Fig. 5*, was again crested. This was executed in the same one-sided manner seen on the blade core removed from the A7 block (*Fig. 2*, no. 6). Two blades were then taken from the core and used as blanks for the production of single-edged points (*Fig. 5*, nos. 1–2). These were followed by another blade which is unmodified and was recovered with a burnt proximal end. The final removal in this series has also been made into a single-edged point (*Fig. 5*, no.3). The exhausted core, which is fire-cracked, was abandoned in the same square where the A7 block

blade core was worked (square D8). With the exception of one flake (found in Area II), all the artifacts from this core were also confined to Area I.

ACTIVITY AREAS

The palaeotopographical study of the site of Rørmyr II reveals from the distribution of conjoined materials, three inter-related areas of activity. These can be defined as Area I (*Fig. 6*, squares 5–12, A–H), the main activity area where most manufacturing and tool use was undertaken, Area II (squares 1–4, A–H), characterized by retooling and blank modification, and Area III (squares H–Q), a concentration separated from the others and identified as a possible butchering location.

The remaining 73% of the lithic material that was not conjoined includes the artifacts from the A7 block and two cores that have not yet been refitted, in addition to various small groups which normally contained an exhausted core and a few flakes. The replotting of these pieces to their original excavation squares not only confirms the existence of the three areas, but adds considerable strength to the interpretation of the activities within these concentrations.

Area I

This is the main activity area for the site where 76% of all the artifacts were found. The distribution of burnt pieces showed a clear concentration between squares C7 and D8, which was interpreted as a fireplace. It is directly around this area that most of the flint knapping was undertaken (*Fig. 6*: the redistribution of conjoined artifacts from the A7 block).

Nearly all the cores, core fragments and crested blades were abandoned in this area. As mentioned previously, there are indications that cores and discs could have been carried to Area II, in that flakes, blades and platform rejuvenation flakes are found here. In any case, whether the cores were moved or whether only potential blanks were selected and taken to this area, the cores were finally worked out and abandoned back in Area I.

All discs were also found concentrated around the fireplace within Area I. Although most disc-resharpening flakes are confined to this area, their appearance (from conjoined discs) in both of the other areas shows that these tools were used and reworked before being taken back to Area I. When discs served as cores, as noted for tools A7 and B7 from the A7 block, the knapping was carried out in Area I, but potential blanks were frequently taken to Area II.

All of the 13 burins from this collection, one of the two flake axes and three of the six truncated pieces are restricted to Area I, with the remainder of the truncations being found in Area II. Finally, of the 62 points found on the site, 39 were recovered within Area I. Only four points in this group have suffered impact fractures (*Fig. 7*, nos. 1 & 6), eight have

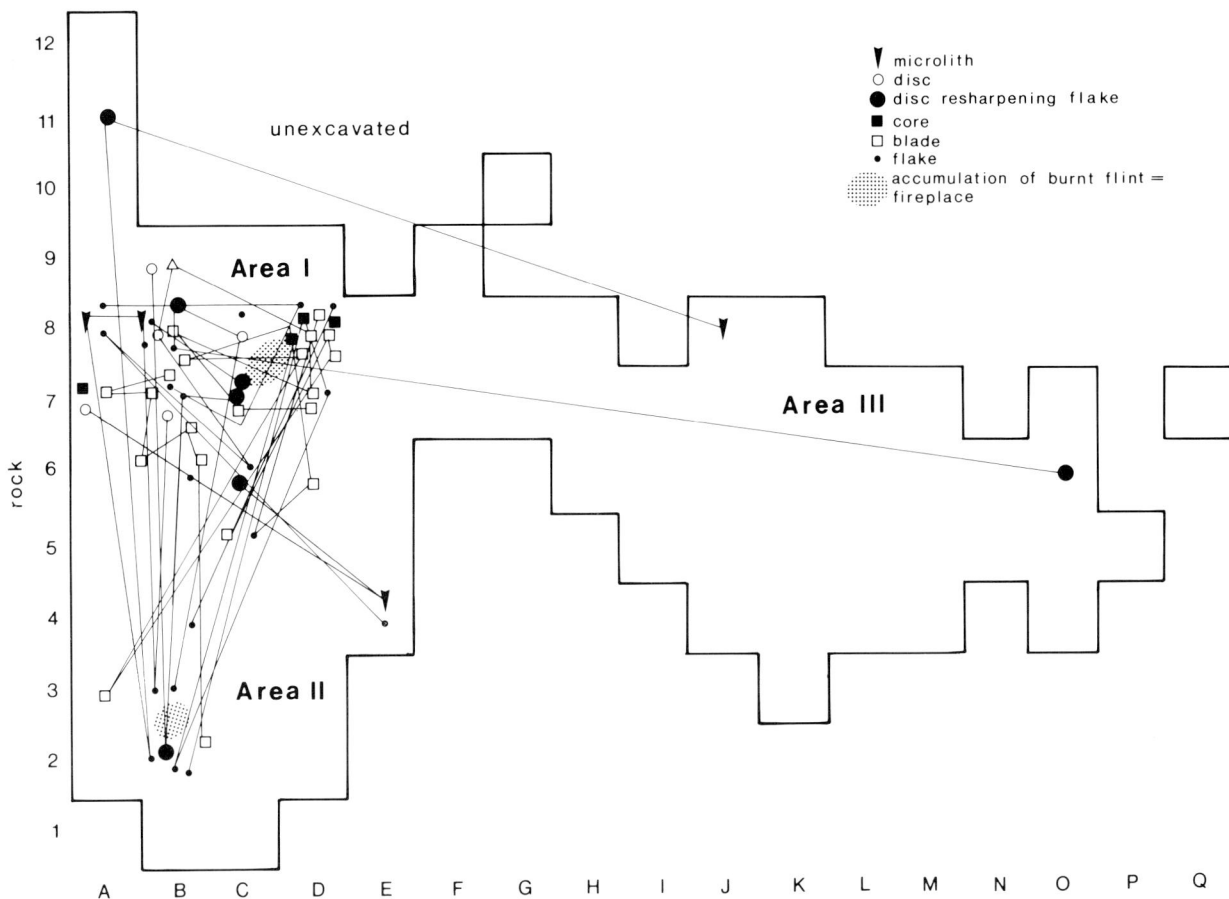

Figure 6 Distribution of refitted artifacts from the A7 block.

snapped (*Fig. 7*, no. 5), four were abandoned in production and 23 appear undamaged. Most pieces from this latter group are skewed, twisted or exhibit a fault which appeared in the final stages of production. As point manufacture was undertaken in Area I, it would seem likely that the large number of apparently unused points were found unsuitable for retooling and therefore discarded.

Area II

This area is considered to represent retooling activities, which were centred around a second fireplace at the junction of squares B2 and B3 (*Fig. 6*). As mentioned above, potential blanks were moved from Area I to Area II; this can be seen in the redistribution diagram for block A7 (*Fig. 6*). The plots for both conjoined and non-conjoined artifacts show a close connection between Areas I and II, but there are only minor indications of initial manufacturing being undertaken in Area II (for example, this area accounts for only five of the 57 cores and core fragments recovered). The impression that Area II represents retooling activities is best illustrated by examining the points.

All but two of the 12 points from Area II were damaged: four have impact fractures (*Fig. 7*, nos. 2–4); and four were snapped, possibly during the manufacturing or retooling process (*Fig. 7*, nos. 5 & 7). The exceptions are points abandoned in manufacture (e.g. *Fig. 3*, A7).

Further support for retooling activities is obtained from two sections of a point that were recovered in square B2 (*Fig. 7*, no. 2). This point has an impact fracture on the tip and is snapped at the base, which was subsequently burnt. It was probably produced at Rørmyr II, as other artifacts of the same material were found on-site. It is conceivable that this point was shot into game that was brought back to the site. The damaged tip remained in the meat while the snapped tang was lodged in the shaft. The shaft was retooled by the fireplace and the snapped tang ended up in the fire. The tip was discarded when removed from the meat, in the same square, but far enough from the fire for it to be unaffected by the heat.

Tools that have been considered to represent processing, such as scrapers and burins, are not found in this area (although the recovery of a disc-resharpening flake, mentioned above, would indicate that a disc had been used here at some point). However, there are as many truncated flakes and blades in Area II as were found in Area I. It is possible to interpret this occurrence by seeing these tools as having served a multi-purpose function that was undertaken in both areas where work was performed close to a fire.

Area III

Area III is the smallest of the concentrations on Rørmyr II, containing only 9% of the total artifacts. A few of the pieces are burnt but there is no indication

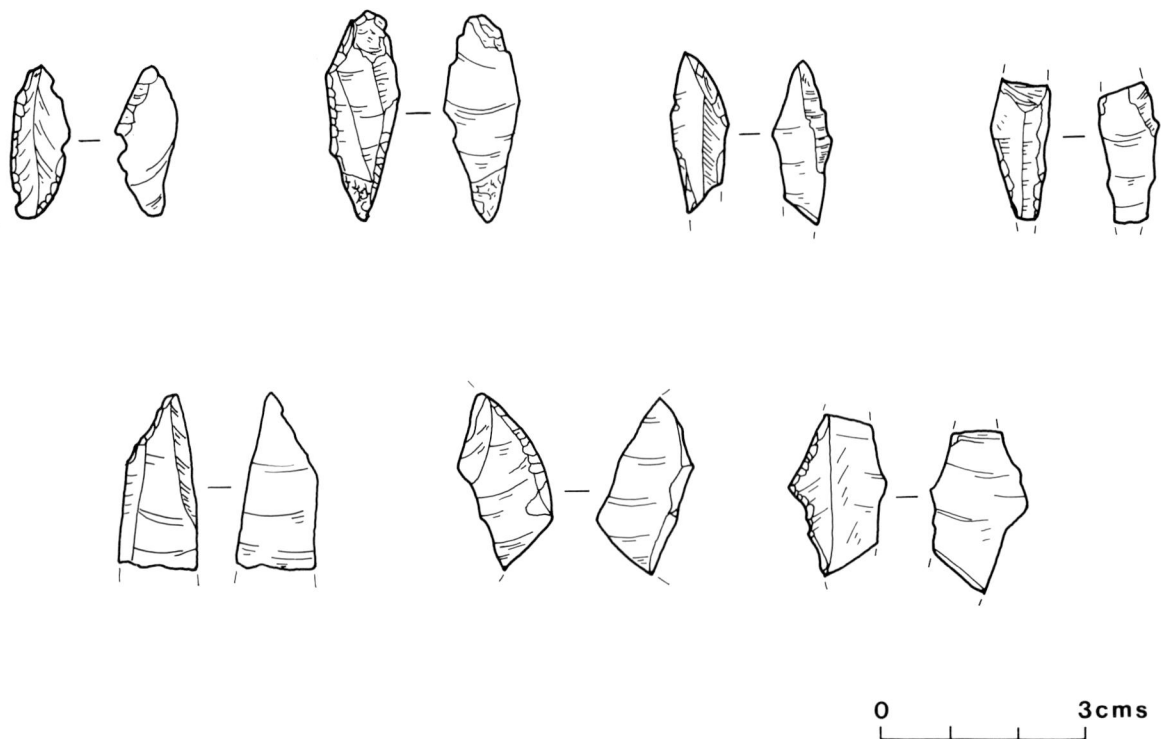

Figure 7   Examples of impact-fractured and snapped microliths. No. 2 has, in addition to the impact fracture, a refitted burnt tang.

of any meaningful clustering. It is connected to Areas I and II both by the refitted block and by pieces made from material found in both areas (*Fig. 6*).

This area is characterized by single examples of a number of tool types, such as a flake axe, a borer that resembles a Lateglacial 'zinken', a blade with two notches, an exhausted core, assorted blades and flakes, and 11 points, nine of which are impact fractured. The exceptionally high number of damaged points in combination with an assortment of tools leads to the conclusion that this area could represent butchering activity.

CONCLUSIONS

By combining the method of conjoining with a re-examination and replotting of the artifacts from Rørmyr II, it has been demonstrated that there were three main areas of activity on this site. A large concentration of manufacturing debris was found around a fireplace in the northern part of the site. This area was also the location of virtually all the work which required heavy scrapers and burins. Six metres south of this, a second smaller fire was identified where it appears points were made and retooled, and occasionally some lighter scraping activity took place. Eight to ten metres to the east was found the final activity area, characterized by an abnormally large number of impact-fractured points and various tools that could be considered consistent with the butchering of game.

A traditional re-analysis of the lithic material would have indicated that these activities took place at Rørmyr II, but the fact that these three zones are directly related, and were the result of a single period of occupation, was demonstrated through the use of conjoining. It can now also be stated that the artifacts on Rørmyr II were brought to the site in the form of partially prepared nodules, which were knapped, made into tools, used, reworked and abandoned on-site. The 'history' of many of the tools can be traced from when and where they were made, through their various 'lives', to the point where they were finally abandoned. Some of these pieces, for example the discs, were previously unidentified, as their various forms and functions could only be seen when they were refitted to their original flakes. In addition, many personal knapping characteristics of the inhabitants of the site can be seen.

The importance of the position of the site of Rørmyr II within the chronological framework of the Scandinavian Mesolithic is indisputable. Evidence from an examination of the shoreline displacement curve indicates that Rørmyr II could not have been occupied before 9600 BP. The fact that the area in front of the site drops away sharply and that sea level at that time was falling at the rate of 6.5 m a century, indicate that the site would not have been suitable as a coastal occupation site for very long.

Acknowledgements: We wish to express our thanks to the following people for their help and support: to Professor Stig Welinder for originally turning our attention to the site, to Statestipend Dr Erling Johansen who gave us permission to publish, and to our colleagues at the Institute of Archaeology and the University Museum, Oslo, for their encouragement and advice.

360

References

BOSINSKI, G. (1975) Die Rekonstruktion des Gönnersdorfer Hauses: Kommentar zum Model. *Ausgrabungen in Deutschland*. Mainz, Monographien des Romisch-Germanischen Zentralmuseums 1, vol. 3: 255–257.

BRINCH PETERSEN, E. (1966) Klosterlund – Sønder Hadsund – Bollund. *Acta Archaeologica*, 37: 77–186.

CAHEN, D. (1976) Nouvelles fouilles à la pointe de la Gombe (expointe de Kalina), Kinshasa, Zaire. *L'Anthropologie*, 80: 573–602.

CAHEN, D., KEELEY, L.H., and VAN NOTEN, F.L. (1979) Stone tools, tool-kits, and human behavior in prehistory. *Current Anthropology*, 20(4): 661–683.

FISCHER, A. (1978) På sporet af overgangen mellem palæoliticum og mesoliticum i Sydskandinavien. *Hikuin*, 4: 27–50, 150–153.

FISCHER, A., VEMMING-HANSEN, P., and RASMUSSEN, P. (1985) Macro and micro wear traces on lithic projectile points. Experimental results and prehistoric examples. *Journal of Danish Archaeology*, 3: 13–46.

HAGEN, A. (1963) Mesolitiske jegergrupper i det norske høyfjell. *Universitetets Oldsaksamling Årbok*, 1960/61: 109–143.

HAFSTEN, U. (1983) Shorelevel changes in south Norway during the last 13,000 years. *Norsk Geografisk Tidsskrift*, 37(2): 63–79.

INDRELID, S. (1975) Problems relating to the early Mesolithic settlement of southern Norway. *Norwegian Archaeological Review*, 8: 1–18.

JOHANSEN, E. (1962) Nyt lys over den eldste innvandring til Norge. Forste epistel fra Høykneppe. *Østfoldarv. Årbok for museer og historielag i østfold*, 6.

JOHANSEN, E. (1964) Høgnipen funnene. Et nyt blad av Norges eldste innvandringshistorie. *Viking*, 27: 177–181.

LEROI-GOURHAN, A. and BRÉZILLON, M. (1966) L'habitation magdalénienne no. 1 de Pincevent près Montereau (Seine-et-Marne). *Gallia Préhistoire*, 9: 263–371.

LEROI-GOURHAN, A. and BRÉZILLON, M. (1972) *Fouilles de Pincevent: Essai d'analyse ethnographique d'un habitat magdalénien* (VIIe Supplément à Gallia Préhistoire). Paris, Centre National de la Recherche Scientifique.

LINDBLOM, I. (1984) Former for økologisk tilpasning i mesolitikum, østfold. *Universitetets Oldsaksamling Årbok*, 1982/83: 43–86.

MIKKELSEN, E. (1975) Mesolithic in south-eastern Norway. *Norwegian Archaeological Review*, 8: 19–36.

MIKKELSEN, E. (1978) Seasonality and Mesolithic adaption in Norway. In K. Kristiansen and C. Palludan-Müller (eds.), *New Directions in Scandinavian Archaeology*. Copenhagen, National Museum of Denmark: 79–120.

SØRENSEN, R. (1979) Late Weichselian deglaciation in the Oslo fjord area, south Norway. *Boreas*, 8: 241–247.

WELINDER, S. (1981) Den kontinentaleuropeiska bakgrunden till Norges äldsta stenalder. *Universitetets Oldsaksamling Årbok*, 1980/81: 21–34.

Mesolithic Forest Clearance in Scandinavia

Stig Welinder

Abstract

Six sites in Norway, Sweden and Finland with pollen data and/or charcoal layers interpreted as indicating intentional forest clearance during the period 9000–5000 BP are presented. The sites are regarded as the best evidence available today. If the evidence is accepted, then hypotheses of when and where to find forest clearance during the Mesolithic can be put forward.

INTRODUCTION

It is a fascinating idea that forest was intentionally cleared during the pre-farming period in order to improve grazing for wild ungulates, thus improving hunting grounds. The idea is sound palaeoecologically and there is ethnographic evidence in its favour.

In this article the idea will be looked at from a Scandinavian point of view. Six sites in Norway, Sweden and Finland with pollen data and/or charcoal layers indicating forest fires during the period 9000–5000 BP will be discussed. The question is: are they evidence of intentional forest clearance by hunter-gatherers, or natural forest succession where fire plays an essential part in vegetational structure.

The sites represent the best evidence available in Scandinavia at present. Furthermore, they represent a typical and representative selection of sites. If the evidence is accepted, then hypotheses of when and where to find forest clearances during the Mesolithic can be put forward.

From each of the sites (*Fig. 1*) a simplified pollen diagram (*Figs. 2–7*) and a diagram of the occurrence of charcoal is presented (no charcoal graph is available for *Fig. 6* and no pollen diagram for *Fig. 7*). The intention is to present the types of evidence that have been used in order to demonstrate the occurrence of forest fires and their possible causation by man. The suggested one or more forest fires are denoted by black bars in the diagrams. In the following site descriptions, the original publication of the full pollen record for each site is referred to (no pollen diagram is available in connection with *Fig. 7*).

The pollen percentages quoted for broadleafed tree species refer to recalculated pollen diagrams (e.g. *Tilia* × 8, *Ulmus* × 2, etc. – cf. Andersen 1970).

DESCRIPTION AND DISCUSSION OF SITES

Aspö (Blekinge, Sweden)

Aspö is an island, 6.5 km² in area, in the archipelago of south-easternmost Sweden. The pollen diagram from a bog (Berglund 1966: 126–127, fig. 54, pollen diagram V) can be regarded as representative of this island and no more.

The rational *Tilia* limit of the area is dated to *c*. 8000 BP, and at *c*. 6000 BP the broadleafed tree species constituted more than 50% of the arboreal pollen sum. The fairly rocky island itself continued to be dominated by pine woods after 8000 BP.

The only possible Mesolithic artifact from the island is a single find of a pecked axe.

The pollen diagram (*Fig. 2*) spans the period 8000–6500 BP. A forest fire at *c*. 8000 BP is indicated by minima in the *Pinus* and *Corylus* curves. A charcoal

Figure 1   Pollen sites discussed in the text. The dashed line denotes the northern limit of more than 25% broadleafed tree species in the forest at *c*. 6000 BP.

362

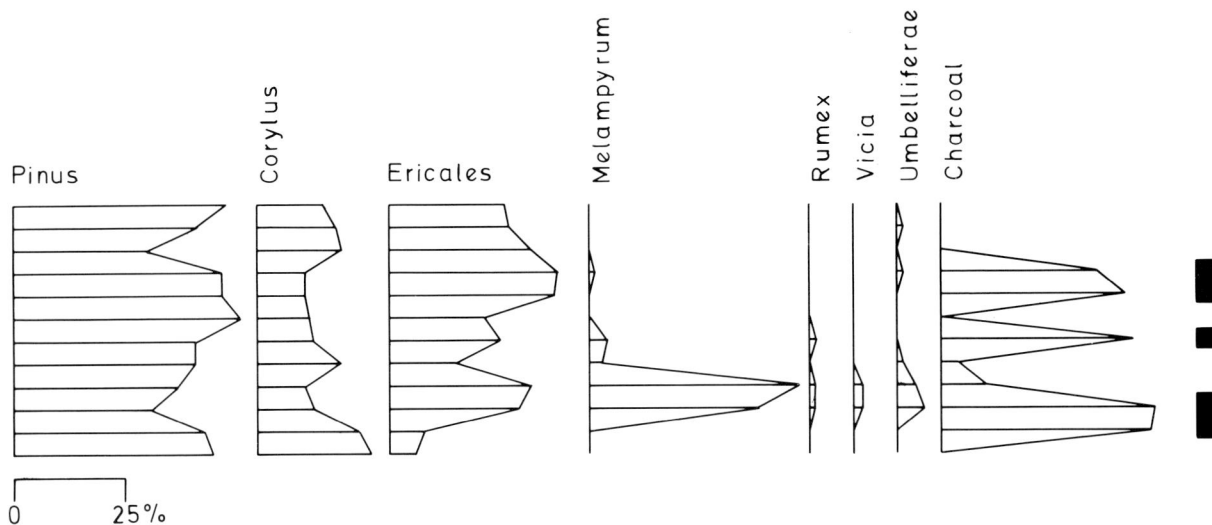

Figure 2   Aspö (after Berglund 1966: pollen diagram V).

layer and maxima for a number of herb species, especially *Melampyrum*, makes the interpretation almost unequivocal. Two further forest fires may have taken place during the succeeding millennium.

The Aspö pollen diagram displays the most unambiguous case of a forest fire during Mesolithic times. There is no close relation to Mesolithic sites, nor other evidence to suggest that the forest of the island was intentionally cleared by man. Consecutive forest fires may have kept the vegetation of the island open with patches of heathland during the late Mesolithic.

Sturup (Scania, south Sweden)

The pollen site is situated in an undulating landscape of low clayey morainic hills and intervening marshland.

The rational *Tilia* limit of the area is dated to *c.* 8000 BP. Broadleafed tree species account for well over 50% of the arboreal pollen sum at *c.* 6000 BP. The supposed forest fire occurred in pine–hazel woodland, mixed with brushwood in low-lying areas.

Less than 200 m away there are two Mesolithic sites, which have yielded flint artifacts datable to the period 9000–8000 BP. No ecofacts have been recorded at the sites.

When the pollen diagram (*Fig. 3*) was published for the first time (Welinder 1971: 193–195; see also Welinder 1983: 40–42), the charcoal maximum at *c.* 9000 BP, accompanied by a continuous *Urtica* curve, was interpreted as indicating the actual settlement area, where nettles may have thrived on the garbage heaps. An alternative interpretation is that the above features, together with the *Pinus* minimum and the generally increasing *Corylus* curve, indicate a series of forest fires. At the end of the period of fires, *c.* 8500 BP, the burned area would have been invaded by bracken.

If the latter interpretation is correct, then the close proximity to contemporary Mesolithic sites strongly suggests that the forest was intentionally set on fire by Mesolithic hunters.

It remains to be noted that at this site, in contrast to Aspö, there is no macroscopic charcoal layer.

Mabo mosse (Östergötland, south Sweden)

Mabo mosse is a raised bog in an area where evidence of farming has been recognized in pollen diagrams at a surprisingly early date (Göransson 1977: 109–110). The site was investigated in order to study this phenomenon recorded in a peat deposit well suited to radiocarbon dating, which had perhaps not been the case with the lake deposits previously investigated.

The rational *Tilia* limit of the area is dated to *c.* 7000 BP. The broadleafed tree species make up 5–25% of the arboreal pollen sum at *c.* 6000 BP. The charcoal maximum in the top part of the diagram (*Fig. 4*) is radiocarbon dated to *c.* 5100 BP. It is connected with an elm decline and the first occurrence of a Cerealia pollen grain in a way that is reminiscent of the classic Danish landnam horizons.

Further down in the pollen diagram there are a series of *Betula* maxima, a *Pteridium* maximum, and a lot of charcoal dust. The scattered pollen grains of *Rumex* and *Vicia* are to be noted, too. The relation of

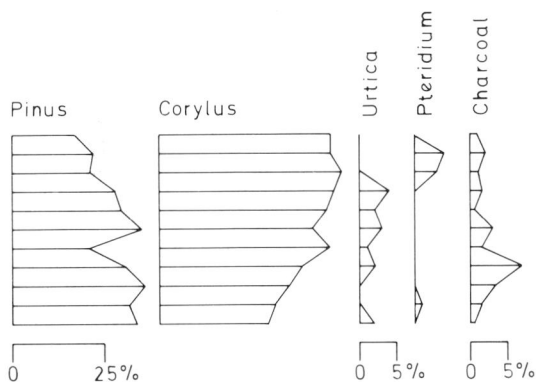

Figure 3   Sturup (after Welinder 1983: fig. 8.2).

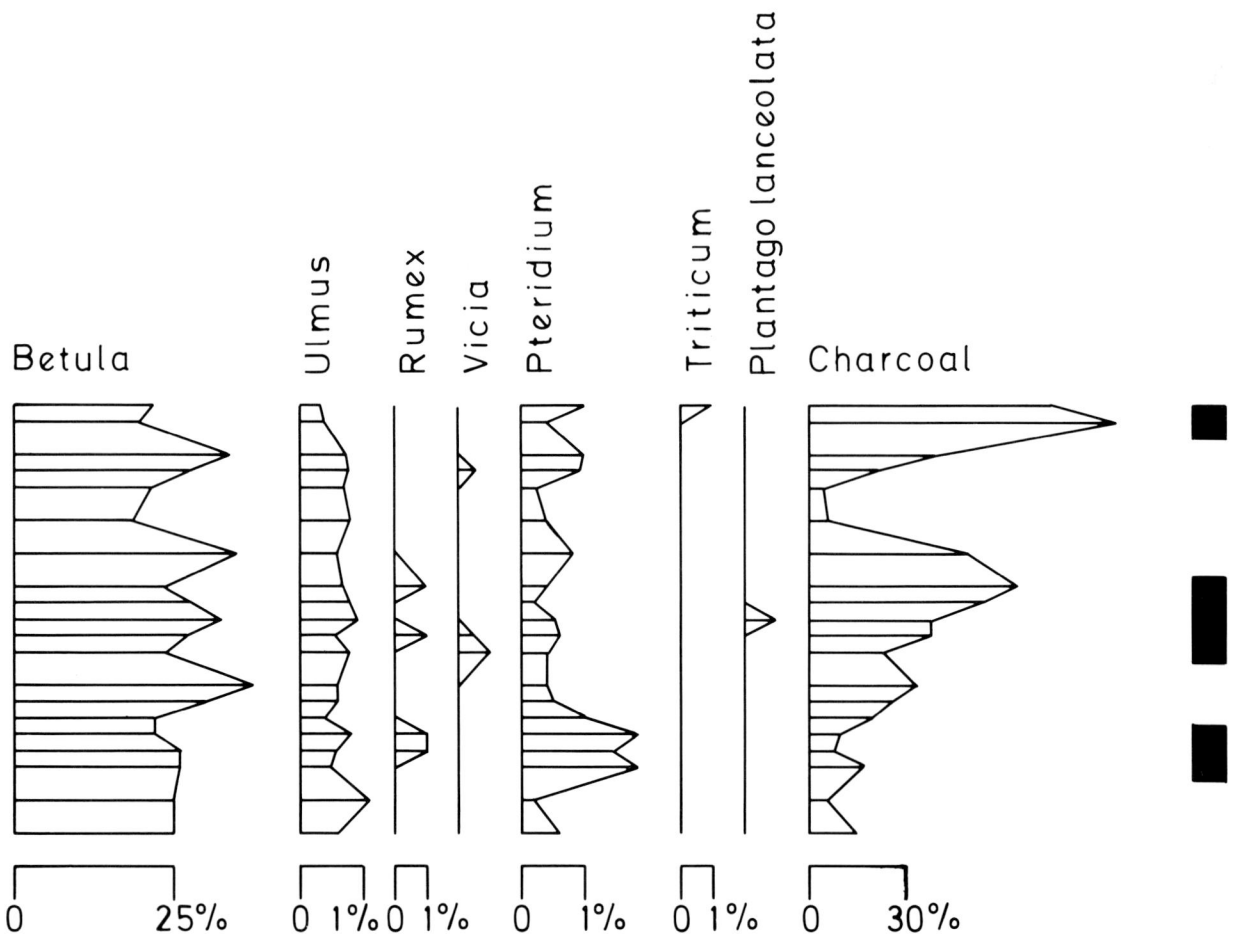

Figure 4   Mabo mosse (after Göransson 1977: Mabo mosse 1975).

these features to a number of macroscopic charcoal layers, three to five in different parts of the bog, is not clear.

The above indications of forest fires belong to the period 6500–5500 BP. The number and character of possible forest fires is not clear, but a single pollen grain of *Plantago lanceolata* is recorded at the beginning of the maximum occurrence of charcoal particles.

Sites and isolated finds of Mesolithic and Neolithic age are rare in the area, but have not been looked for systematically.

Dalkarlstorp (Västmanland, middle Sweden)

Dalkarlstorp is an extensive Mesolithic site on a sandy terrace at the foot of an esker. During the earliest period of occupation, radiocarbon dated to 6500–6000 BP, a layer of clayey, brackish water mud was deposited in a Litorina Sea bay, at the present time the basal sediments of a raised bog which forms the other edge of this site.

Pollen diagrams from sections and cores taken 25, 75, and 300 m away from the site are available (Welinder 1983: 38–40). The rational *Tilia* limit is dated to c. 6500 BP, and c. 500 years later broadleafed trees accounted for more than 25% of the arboreal pollen sum.

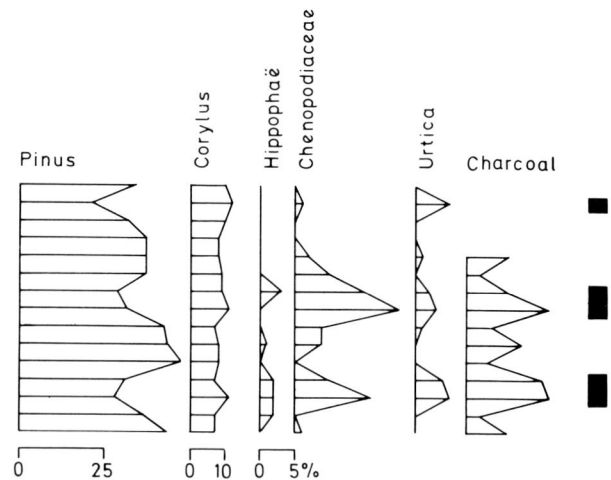

Figure 5   Dalkarlstorp (after Welinder 1983: fig. 8.1).

The three diagrams from the brackish water layer have been summarized in a single diagram (*Fig. 5*), which spans the period 6500–6000 BP. Three consecutive *Pinus* minima are each accompanied by maxima of *Corylus*, Chenopodiaceae, and *Urtica*. The earliest two *Pinus* minima are also accompanied by *Hippophaë* and charcoal maxima. The suggestion is that the pine forest of the sandy deposit along the esker burned three times in a period of no more than 500 years. Each time, the landscape remained open for some time before the forest regenerated.

364

An alternative interpretation is that the charcoal dust was blown away from the actual settlement site area during periods of occupation, during which the light- and nourishment-demanding goosefoots and nettles were growing in the garbage of the site. In any event, the close relation in time and space between the pollen sites and the Mesolithic site is striking.

Kaakotinlampi (Sysmä, south Finland)

Lake Kaakotinlampi is a mire pool enclosed by forest (Vuorela 1981: 55–56, figs. 3–6). It is situated in an area which is generally rich in Stone Age sites, although the nearest sites to the lake are some 7–9 km away. At least some of these sites belong to the late Mesolithic, 7000–4500 BP.

The date of the rational *Tilia* limit is *c.* 6500 BP. Broadleafed tree species never account for more than 20% of the arboreal pollen sum in the area.

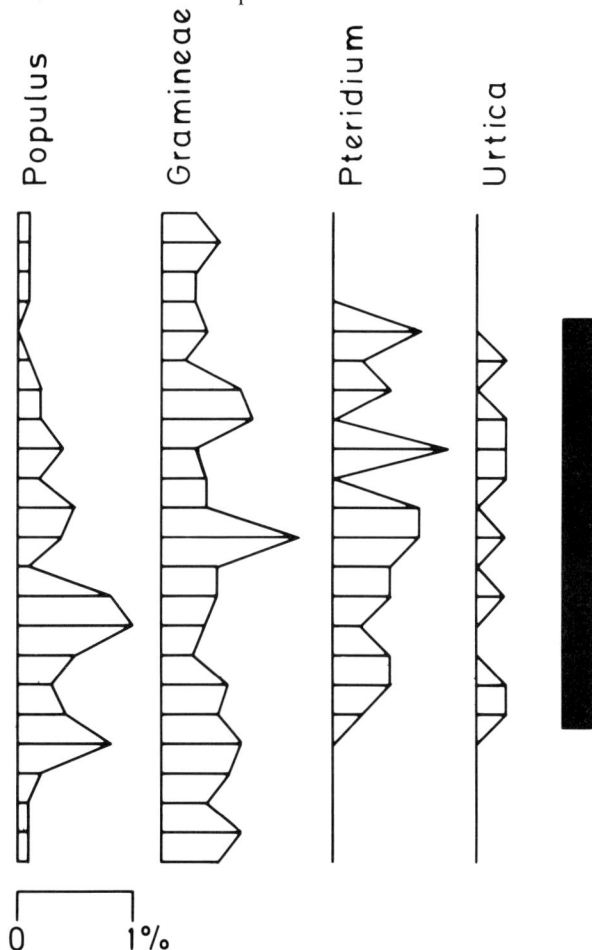

Figure 6   Kaakotinlampi (after Vuorela 1981: figs. 3–6).

The pollen diagram (*Fig. 6*) spans the period 8000–5000 BP. In that part of the sequence corresponding to 7500–5500 BP, there are a number of *Populus* and Gramineae maxima and continuous curves for *Pteridium* and *Urtica*. These features are interpreted as indicating forest clearance by means of burning.

Telemark (south Norway)

Charcoal horizons have been found at eight out of a total of eighteen pollen sites reported by Mikkelsen

et al. (1979: 40–45, fig. 4) from Telemark. Three of these horizons belong to the pre-farming period.

Notable is a charcoal layer, dated to *c.* 6000 BP, in a bog a few hundred metres from the late Mesolithic and Neolithic site at Rognlien (*Fig. 7*). There is no pollen diagram available for this site.

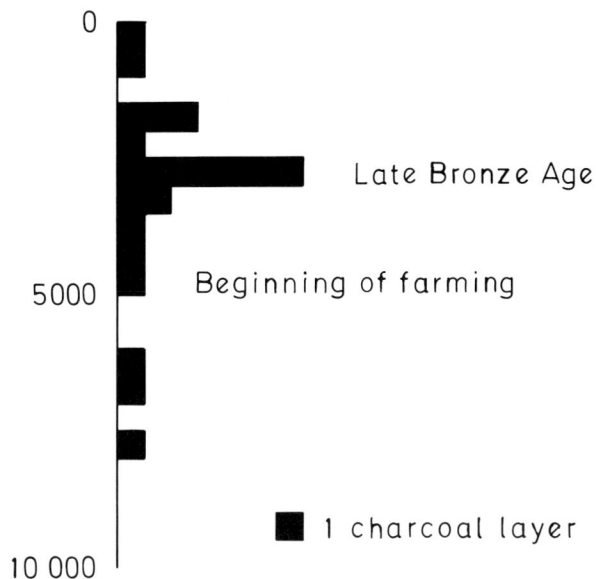

Figure 7   Telemark (after Mikkelsen *et al.* 1979: fig. 4). Time-scale in ^{14}C yrs BP.

The rational *Tilia* limit in the area is dated to *c.* 6500 BP. Broadleafed tree species account for less than 20% of the arboreal pollen sum at *c.* 6000 BP.

CONCLUSIONS

Four lines of evidence serve as indicators of pre-farming forest fires at the sites described:

1)   the presence of macroscopic charcoal layers or horizons of charcoal dust;
2)   dynamic changes in the forest species composition indicating opening and regeneration, e.g. maxima of *Populus*, *Betula* and *Corylus*;
3)   maxima of *Melampyrum* and *Pteridium*, both of which spread rapidly in burned forest areas;
4)   maxima for light-demanding herbs, i.e. Gramineae, *Rumex*, *Urtica* and *Vicia*, generally indicating open ground.

At some of the sites the occurrence of forest fires seems well documented – for example, at Aspö, where there is a charcoal layer and a pollen diagram which records episodes of reduced tree cover, and at Mabo mosse and Rognlien where at least the bog surfaces themselves have burned, as demonstrated by charcoal layers.

The evidence from the other three sites seems less clear-cut, consisting of maxima of *Pteridium* and various herbs, and the presence of charcoal dust. Sturup and Dalkarlstorp are the two sites most closely associated with Mesolithic settlement sites.

Thus, there is no site with both strong evidence of

forest fires during Mesolithic times and a close relation to Mesolithic settlement sites. The evidence, however, is interesting enough to make it worth considering seriously the possibility of intentional burning of woodland in order to improve hunting-grounds during the Mesolithic.

If all six sites are accepted as demonstrating intentional forest fires, then a pattern may be suggested. In the southern part of the Scandinavian peninsula, where the broadleafed tree species were early immigrants and soon formed the dominant forest type, forest fires are found either early or in marginal areas. The Sturup site is an example of the former. The Aspö and Mabo mosse sites are examples of the latter (*Fig. 1*).

Further to the north, and in south Finland, the sites occur in a mixed forest environment. The three sites described, Rognlien, Dalkarlstorp, and Kaakotinlampi, are more or less contemporary and belong to the late Mesolithic, *c.* 7000–5500 BP.

Even further to the north, in the coniferous forest environment, forest fires, whether spontaneous or intentional, are not known. Without doubt forest fires must have been an integral part of the regeneration of the forest ecosystem, but data are lacking. In the northern area extensive use of trapping pits is documented both above the tree limit, for reindeer, and below it, for elk. Thus, it is possible that intentional forest fires were not used in this area.

References

ANDERSEN, S.T. (1970) *The Relative Pollen Productivity and Pollen Representation of North European Trees and Correction Factors for Tree Pollen Spectra*. Copenhagen, *Danmarks geologiske Undersøgelse*, Series II, 96.

BERGLUND, B.E. (1966) *Late Quaternary Vegetation in Eastern Blekinge, South-eastern Sweden. A Pollen-analytical Study. II. Post-glacial Time*. University of Lund, Publications from the Institutes of Mineralogy, Palaeontology and Quaternary Geology, no. 135.

GÖRANSSON, H. (1977) *The Flandrian Vegetational History of Southern Östergötland*. University of Lund, Department of Quaternary Geology, thesis 3.

MIKKELSEN, E. and HOEG, I.H. (1979) A reconstruction of Neolithic agriculture in eastern Norway. *Norwegian Archaeological Review*, 12(1): 33–47.

VUORELA, I. (1981) The vegetational and settlement history in Sysmä, central south Finland, interpreted on the basis of two pollen diagrams. *Bulletin of the Geological Society of Finland*, 53(1): 47–61.

WELINDER, S. (1971) *Tidigpostglacialt mesoliticum i Skåne*. Lund, Acta Archaeologica Lundensia, series in 8° minore, no. 1.

WELINDER, S. (1983) *The Ecology of Long-term Change*. Lund, Acta Archaeologica Lundensia, series in 8° minore, no. 9.

Late Mesolithic Settlements and Cemeteries at Skateholm, Southern Sweden

Lars Larsson

Abstract

A trial excavation of a site at Skateholm, south Scania, Sweden, was initiated in the spring of 1980. It was soon established that the site contained a combination of settlement area and cemetery, both of late Mesolithic age. Investigations have been conducted during five seasons of excavation (1980–84) at the first site to be discovered, designated Skateholm I, and three years of excavation (1982–84) have been undertaken at a more recently discovered site nearby, designated Skateholm II. Altogether, 65 graves and some 200 other features have been examined at Skateholm I, together with *c.* 100 m² of occupation layer. Twenty-two graves have been examined at Skateholm II, as well as a small section of the occupation layer. Studies of sea-level changes during the late Atlantic period show that the sites were then located on small islands in an ancient lagoon, the extent of which varied considerably in the course of sea-level movements, owing to the flatness of the terrain. The well-preserved bone material in the occupation layers testifies to the great variety of species within the various environments in and around the lagoon. Much of the material consists of fish bones. The sites were, evidently, strategically located to exploit the habitats of several species of fish.

The burials display considerable variation in terms of positioning of the body, with the supine, hocker and sitting positions all being represented. Indications exist, however, to show that the choice of position and also the choice of grave goods and their number was dependent upon sex and/or age. By virtue of the chronological difference between the Mesolithic occupations at Skateholm I and Skateholm II, it is possible to analyze burial customs in terms of a time perspective. The results of the Skateholm investigations suggest that the combination of inter-related settlement area/graveyard was not an unusual occurrence in late Mesolithic society. This suggestion is supported by the discovery of another late Mesolithic site, Skateholm III, which promises to produce similar evidence.

BACKGROUND

Finds made in Denmark in 1975 resulted in a dramatic reappraisal of aspects of late Mesolithic settlement patterns. This concerned the accidental discovery of a Mesolithic cemetery at Bøgebakken (Albrethsen and Brinch Petersen 1976). At the foot of a slope and directly associated with an ancient shoreline – a classic location – were found the remains of a late Mesolithic settlement. The cemetery area was located higher up the slope. The results of the Bøgebakken excavation served to place the study of the infra-structure of the late Mesolithic settlement in a completely new perspective. The question immediately arose – was this combination of settlement and cemetery complex unique, or did the Bøgebakken phenomenon merely reflect the paucity of our knowledge regarding the infra-structure of Mesolithic settlements. An opportunity to test this question arose in connection with the investigation of the early Atlantic coastal site of Segebro on the Swedish side of the Øresund coast, where an extensive area at a higher level than the shore-associated occupation layer became the object of investigation in 1976 (Larsson 1982*b*). This area proved to contain a considerable number of subsoil disturbances. Three adjacent features were distinguished from the rest on the basis of their oblong shape and mixture of humus and sand infilling. Flint blades were found in these features and traces of red ochre were noted in one of them. Owing to the unsuitability of the soil for the preservation of bone, it was not possible to establish beyond doubt that these features were, in fact, graves. The Segebro investigation, nevertheless, provided a hint that interment in conjunction with settlement might not be unique to Bøgebakken.

In spite of the fact that interment could not be proved, the Segebro excavation provided other valuable results, in the form of numerous features which were definitely not graves. In themselves, these might constitute an important factor in the study of a Mesolithic settlement's infra-structure. The value of such peripheral features has generally not been recognized, owing to the fact that past research has been biased towards a more stratigraphy-orientated analysis of the occupation and refuse areas.

THE EXCAVATIONS

The archaeological investigation at Skateholm in southernmost Scania, Sweden, started in 1980 (*Fig. 1*). The area, a former lagoon, contains a number of late Mesolithic sites. Skateholm I, the first site to be discovered, consists of a cultivated sand and gravel knoll which rises gently above the surrounding pastureland. The intention, initially, was to make a preliminary study of the knoll's southern slope prior to spring sowing. A small number of trial trenches were opened in an attempt to document the extent

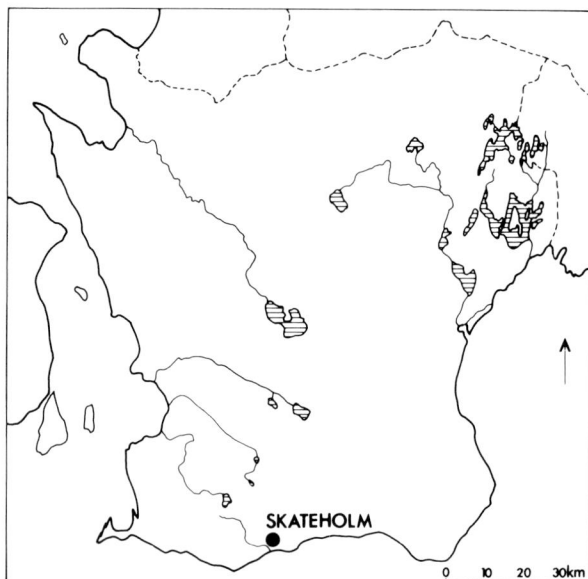

Figure 1 The location of the research area in southernmost Scania.

of the settlement and to establish whether or not any traces of the occupation layer remained. The presence of an intact occupation layer was recorded over a wide area, with an abundance of bone material indicating good preservation conditions. The knowledge gained from the excavations at Bøgebakken and Segebro (see above), regarding the relationship between occupation layer and features such as graves, was a major factor in the decision to allocate a part of the preliminary investigation at Skateholm to a higher section of the slope. A small trial trench was assigned to the upper reaches of the slope, where the occupation layer proved to be only a few centimetres thick. Barely a few centimetres below it a human skull was uncovered. Removal of the topsoil reinforced the assumption that the skull was part of a grave and, furthermore, revealed that several other subsoil disturbances were in fact

graves. A larger area was expropriated for the purpose of further examination. This area was expanded in stages to 3000 m², within which a total of 65 graves have been discovered and fully excavated (Bjelm and Larsson 1984; Larsson 1980a, 1980b, 1981a, 1981b, 1982a, 1982b, 1982c, 1982d, 1983a, 1983b, 1984a, 1984b, 1984c, 1984d, 1985b, 1986, 1987, 1988b).

THE RELATIONSHIP BETWEEN SETTLEMENT AND CEMETERY

The major question concerns the relationship between settlement and cemetery – were they in use at the same time, or at different times?

In this respect stratigraphic observations, combined with radiocarbon dating, have been of importance. Twelve radiocarbon determinations are available – seven on samples from graves and five on samples from the occupation layer or from pits. Those for the graves range from 6290±95 BP to 5930±125 BP, whereas those for the occupation layer or pits range from 6020±70 BP to 5640±60 BP (Table 1). This suggests that some graves are older than the occupation layer. It must be stated that all but one of the samples from the occupation layer, apart from being few in number, were taken from a relatively small area, before the full extent of the site had been realized. Four dates from graves below the occupation layer ranged from 6290±95 BP to 5930±125 BP.

No fewer than eleven graves were found to lie below an undisturbed occupation layer, indicating that these are older than the overlying settlement remains. In others, where no trace of the occupation layer survives today, the composition of the filling suggests that one had once existed. These observations are, of course, not proof that the site was actually occupied at that precise juncture. Several

Table 1: The radiocarbon dates from Skateholm

Site	Lab. No.	Material	Context	¹⁴C Age BP
Skateholm II	Lu-2114	charcoal	pit below occupation layer	6910±70
Skateholm II	Lu-2113	charcoal	occupation layer	6590±70
Skateholm II	Lu-2115	charcoal	occupation layer	6380±70
Skateholm II	Lu-2478	charcoal	occupation layer	6300±100
Skateholm II	Lu-1957	charcoal	occupation layer	6050±100
Skateholm II	Lu-1956	charcoal	occupation layer	5470±105
Skateholm I	Lu-1835	charcoal	grave below occupation layer	6290±95
Skateholm I	Lu-2109	bone	grave	6270±70
Skateholm I	Lu-1834	bone	grave below occupation layer	6240±85
Skateholm I	Lu-1888	charcoal	grave below occupation layer	6220±100
Skateholm I	Lu-2347	charcoal	grave	6180±70
Skateholm I	Lu-2116	charcoal	grave	5990±70
Skateholm I	Lu-1886	charcoal	grave below occupation layer	5930±125
Skateholm I	Lu-1853	hazel-nut shells	pit below occupation layer	6020±70
Skateholm I	Lu-1849	charcoal	occupation layer	5800±70
Skateholm I	Lu-1848	charcoal	occupation layer	5790±70
Skateholm I	Lu-2229	charcoal	pit	5640±60
Skateholm III	Lu-2156	bone	grave	5850±90

indications exist which suggest that the occupation layer originally covered a much greater area than it is possible to establish today. The highest limit of the latter agrees well with the assumed optimum of the transgressional high-water mark. Parts of the occupation layer probably lay unprotected during this period, with the result that substantial amounts of occupational evidence were washed away.

In this context, the typology of the transverse arrowheads provides certain clues to the chronology of settlement at Skateholm I. This suggests that occupation first took place here when the shoreline was at c. 3 m a.s.l., but that the settlers were forced to move higher up the slope and to assign their various activities to new areas. In this way, the older graves would come to be covered by a younger occupation layer.

An insight into settlement patterns in other parts of the ancient lagoon has proved to be of great significance for further studies. Late Mesolithic settlement has been documented at several other locations within the confines of the lagoon. One of these, Skateholm II, yielded promising results which have significance for the project as a whole. This site is located barely 150 m south east of Skateholm I on what was, during Mesolithic times, a small island, 300 m long and 100 m wide, separated from the Skateholm I promontory by a mere 50 m of shallow water. A trial excavation in 1981 indicated the presence of late Mesolithic settlement. In the course of a reconnaissance of the site in 1982, fragments of human bones were found to be present in molehills. This discovery led to a systematic excavation which revealed evidence of burials on the crown of the knoll. At the same time, the presence of an intact occupation layer, with an abundance of flint and bone material, was recorded along the southern slope of the knoll. By the end of the excavation in 1984 a total of 22 graves had been discovered.

None of the graves was associated with the occupation layer. Finds in the grave infillings, however, as well as the nature and typology of certain grave goods, provided evidence that the two phenomena were related. Both graves and occupation layers at Skateholm II have produced arrowheads of the same type – a transverse arrowhead displaying one long straight side and a shorter, concave side, with the cutting-edge running diagonally between the two.

The dominant arrowhead form at Skateholm I, in both occupation layer and graves, is a type consisting of two concave or straight sides. It has, however, been established that the oblique-edge type occurred in the lowest-lying occupation layers at Skateholm I. The highest level of the occupation layer at Skateholm II was at c. 3 m a.s.l., which agrees well with the lowest level of the occupation layer at Skateholm I. This observation supports the hypothesis that both the settlement and burials at Skateholm II are older than, or partly contemporaneous with, the oldest settlement at Skateholm I.

Radiocarbon dates from the settlement at Skateholm II confirm the difference in age. Charcoal from a pit below the occupation layer gave the value 6910±70 BP, while the four dates from the occupation layer range from 6590±70 BP to 5470±195 BP (*Table 1*).

Thus, research at Skateholm has established a connection between settlement and graveyard at two separate sites no more than 150 m apart. A third cemetery complex may have existed barely 250 m west of Skateholm I. This section of the lagoon once constituted a cape and comprises an area in which late Mesolithic settlement had already been established. It is reliably reported that, during gravel extraction in the 1930s, a number of skeletons were encountered. One surviving skeleton was found in the archives of the Historiska museet in Stockholm. A radiocarbon determination on bones from this skeleton (a female, supine burial) gave an age of 5850±90 BP, which clearly shows that the grave is of late Mesolithic age, and therefore provides a strong indication that this third site – Skateholm III – also contained an inter-related graveyard and settlement area.

Even though no direct evidence exists to support the hypothesis that the three sites were not contemporaneous – either in terms of their use as settlements or burial areas, or both – several indications suggest that they were not. Skateholm II is the oldest site, belonging to a late phase of the Kongemose culture and the oldest phase of the Ertebølle culture. Skateholm I is somewhat younger, and belongs to a middle phase of the Ertebølle culture. Finds from the vicinity of Skateholm III indicate that this site belongs to an even later phase of the Ertebølle culture.

THE TOPOGRAPHY AND ENVIRONMENT IN THE SKATEHOLM AREA

The question as to why the ancient lagoon at Skateholm should comprise several late Mesolithic settlement sites cannot be answered without first considering the variables that govern the ultimate choice of site location in the context of a hunter–gatherer society at the close of the Atlantic period (Gaillard and Lemdahl 1988; Gaillard *et al.* 1988; Göransson 1988; Håkansson 1988; Lemdahl 1988; Lemdahl and Göransson 1988).

The relationship between water and land altered radically as a result of rising sea levels during the late Mesolithic. Just how important it is to obtain a knowledge of these relative sea-level movements can be seen in the fact that the Skateholm area comprises a lowland terrain with occasional, gently rising

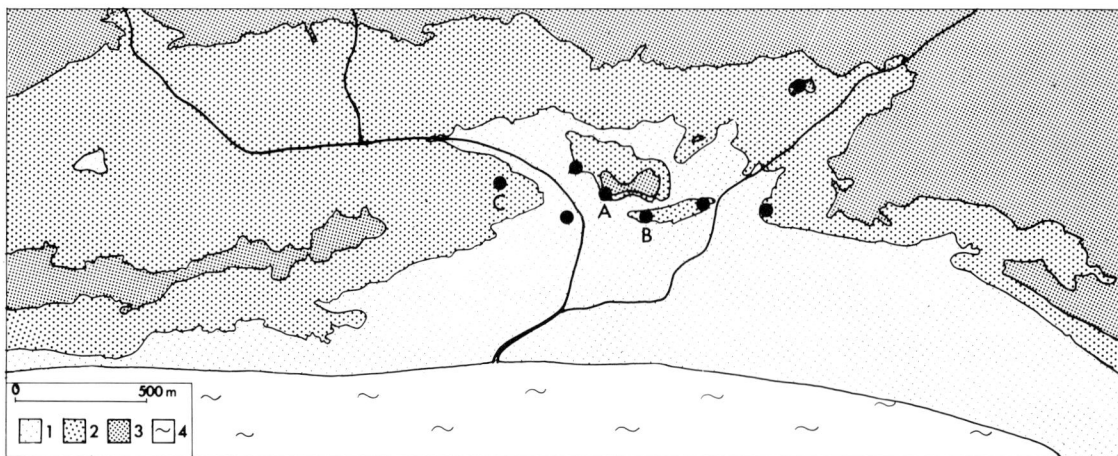

Figure 2   The research area at Skateholm. Black dots mark sites with Mesolithic settlement. *Key*: A – Skateholm I; B – Skateholm II; C – Skateholm III; 1 – area lower then 3 metres a.s.l.; 2 – area between 3 and 5 metres a.s.l.; 3 – area higher than 5 metres a.s.l.; 4 – present sea level.

knolls and hills. *Fig. 2* clearly shows that even a small increase in sea level would have significantly affected the relationships between water and land. It is precisely these relationships between sea levels and land areas that are basic to the study of Skateholm. Sea levels during the late Mesolithic period varied between 1 m and 4 m above present sea level. Skateholm I would have been habitable for the major part of the period. The island on which the site was located decreased in area as sea level rose to a point where, at the Mesolithic–Neolithic transition, it would only have constituted a skerry. At the same time, the lagoon increased in size. Low-lying islands, such as the one on which Skateholm II was located, and capes, like that on which Skateholm III is situated, disappeared, only to be replaced by others in the form of partially submerged promontories. The Litorina bank running parallel to the present shoreline, but now a good 200 m inland, probably had a precursor in the form of sand bars and spits which at times may have afforded protection against storm waves in the sheltered lagoon.

Several small freshwater streams flowed into the lagoon with the result that it became brackish. The shallowness of the lagoon and its long, narrow shores would have facilitated a broad zonation of plant life. The composition of the afforested hinterland meant that habitats for a wide variety of animal species existed within an extremely limited area around Skateholm, a fact which is reflected in the very large number of species identified in the faunal material. Apart from humans and dogs, 85 different species of mammals, fowl and fish have been identified, together with a few species of amphibians and reptiles (Jonsson 1988). This variety provides not only a clue to the diversity of food resources, but also an indication of the nature of the surrounding environment. Wild boar, red deer and roe deer appear to have been the most hunted big game, but considerable quantities of grey seal bones show that

this area of activity was also pursued. The relatively high frequency of bones of fur-bearing animals, such as otter, marten, wild cat and beaver, suggests that the demand for pelts was high. The number of bird bones is relatively small; even so a wide variety of species are represented.

Considerable quantities of fish bones have been recovered. The use of fine sieving has revealed the presence of large numbers of bones of the smaller species, such as roach and herring, and small specimens of pike, eel and perch. Their presence in such large numbers indicates the extensive employment of fixed equipment in the form of wicker-work fish traps. Topographically, the conditions within the site locality were highly conducive to the use of such trapping methods. A comparative study of the bone material from Skateholm I and Skateholm II proved to be highly informative, particularly in the light of evidence for changes in the local environment during the late Mesolithic period. Certain differences in the proportions of the various species between the two sites can be observed. Some of these can be explained as being due to ecological changes, in that the proportions of saltwater fish and seal are greater at Skateholm I, where the effects of the higher sea level on the catchment resources are clearer. Other differences, such as the larger percentage of roe deer at Skateholm II and, conversely, the larger percentage of wild boar at Skateholm I may be explicable in terms of changes in the environment.

THE GRAVES AT SKATEHOLM I

By the close of excavations, the number of graves examined at Skateholm I was sixty-five (*Fig. 3*). Of these, 57 were human burials (including five double graves), comprising 62 individuals; the remaining eight graves contained dogs. In all probability, these represent *all* the graves preserved within the confines of this cemetery. The graves themselves exhibit a considerable degree of variation in burial customs,

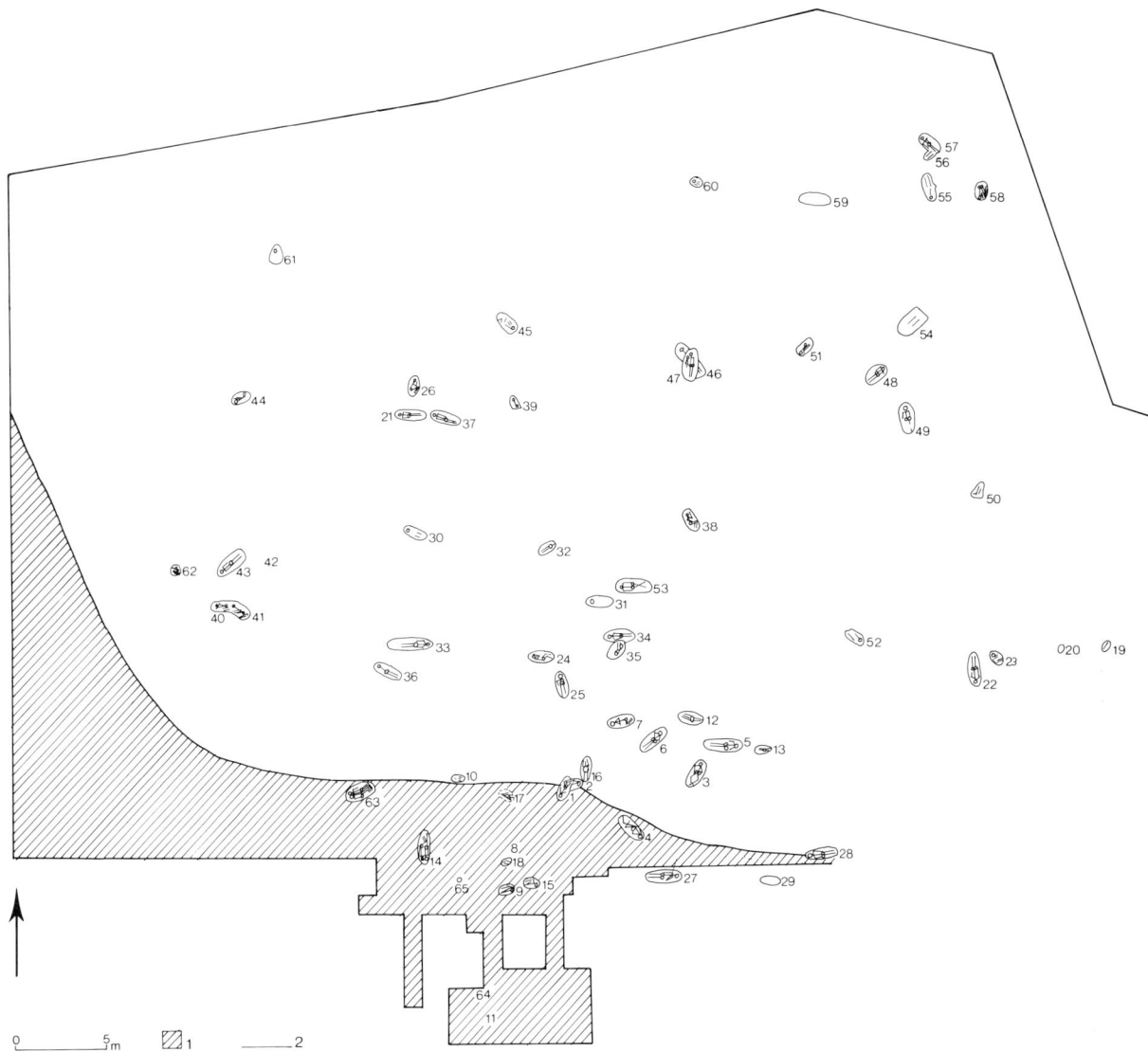

Figure 3 Plan of the research area at Skateholm I. *Key*: 1 – occupation layer; 2 – limit of topsoil removal. Arabic numerals denote graves.

encompassing every conceivable method of burial including both inhumation and cremation. These range from the sitting position to the hocker position to the outstretched, supine attitude. Variations even occur within these groupings: seated burials comprise upright sitting as well as reclined, half-sitting postures, while the hocker position ranges from individuals with slightly bent extremities in relaxed attitudes to others in extremely contorted, drawn-up positions. A radical deviation within the extended burial group is represented by a grave where a man was placed on his stomach.

The age distribution is markedly skewed; remarkably, there are only six instances of child burials, normally associated with adults, including two graves where only the teeth remained and one in which a prematurely born child was placed on the left hip of an adult female (Persson and Persson 1984, 1988; Alexandersen 1988).

The burials display varying degrees of preservation, from relatively good to extremely bad. This is due to a variety of factors. The sediments are seldom uniform, with very stony strata alternating with strata consisting of coarse, medium and fine gravel, as well as very light sand. The composition of the strata will have facilitated drainage in some areas but hindered it in others, thus providing one explanation why the degree of preservation varies so much at Skateholm I. The majority of graves located close to the modern surface tend to display more or less advanced stages of dissolution. The fragile condition of the majority of individuals necessitated on-the-spot osteological examination of the remains. As regards the stratigraphic location of the individual graves, only in very few cases was it possible to establish with any degree of certainty that these had retained their original depth in relation to the ancient ground level. Modern cultivation has inevitably led to a depletion of the topsoil covering.

It will always remain an unanswerable question as to how many graves have been totally destroyed. Fragments of human bones have been found in the

occupation layer, suggesting that graves were obliterated even in prehistoric times. This is supported by the fact that perforated tooth beads have been found in considerable numbers and were not confined to any particular area of the site.

It is not possible, in this article, to give an account of each individual grave. However, some of the more interesting examples will be cited.

Grave 6 contained two individuals: a female aged 35–40 years, in an upright-sitting position, and a prematurely born child placed on her hip. Both were copiously covered with red ochre. A decoration consisting of some 30 perforated teeth of wild boar partly underlay the child's skeleton. The unperforated tooth of an elk was also found, an animal which at that time would have been a rare sight in southern Scania.

Grave 11 comprised a 10 m^2 area below the occupation layer, in which the burnt bones of an adult male lay spread about in shallow discolorations in the sand, as well as in small, but deep, soil marks interpreted as postholes. The distribution of these features indicates the presence of a wooden structure which presumably had some connection with the burial act.

Grave 13 consisted of a metre-long pit in which the skeletal parts of a grown man were found jumbled up. Only the hand and foot bones lay in their correct anatomical position. No remains of the right hand or left foot could be identified. A transverse arrowhead, found embedded in a section of the pelvis, indicated that death was caused by a projectile which pierced the abdomen.

Grave 14 contained a fifty-year-old man in a supine attitude, beside whom a girl aged between 17 and 19 years had been placed in a hocker position in such a way that her legs overlay those of the man. A large portion of a marten cranium, together with fragments of jaws from red deer, roe deer and wild boar, was found in the grave filling immediately above the skeletons.

Grave 26 held a female. That part of the feature containing the burial merely constituted the central depression of a large pit. Surrounding the pit were four postholes marking the position of a trapeze-shaped, timber structure that had been built over the grave. Abundant charcoal on a level immediately above the skeleton proved to come from logs of ash which had been placed across the grave. The indications are that some kind of wooden structure above the grave had been burned down in the course of the burial ritual.

Grave 41 was a double grave in the westernmost section of the research area. It contained an adult and a child (*Fig. 4*). The adult, probably male, was

Figure 4   Skateholm I. Grave 41 with an old man in the hocker position and a child placed in front of him (above). Two perforated eye-teeth of bear lay on the child's chest (below). Beneath these can be seen lumps of amber, which also turned out to be pendants.

placed in the hocker position. The child lay turned towards the adult. Grave goods in the form of two perforated eye-teeth of bear were found on the child's chest, and under these were four pieces of amber, all with perforations. A short bone point and a flint knife lay adjacent to the child's thigh. Red ochre was strewn over the child.

Grave 53 contained a young female in the supine position, but with crossed extremities. Grave goods consisted of perforated teeth of elk, red deer and wild boar. Some 30 teeth, some from elk, were found distributed around the woman's lower arms and under her hips.

A feature of particular interest at Skateholm I is the burial of dogs. Two well-preserved examples – *grave 9* and *grave 23* – show that these were similar in size to German Shepherds. They had all been placed in hocker positions. Although these graves are the first direct evidence, there are several indications that the burial of dogs was practised at other late Mesolithic sites, in the form of well-preserved, intact bones and crania (Dahr 1937; Aaris-Sørensen 1977; Lepiksaar 1982). Moreover, ritual dog burial in pre-agrarian societies has been documented in other parts of the world – for example, the American Middle West and Kamchatka (Cantwell 1982; Dikov 1983).

Studies have shown that the positioning of the body itself, as well as the *post mortem* arrangement of the extremities, is in some cases relatable to sex and/or age. For example, of the number of individuals placed in the hocker position, only one-third are men, the other two-thirds women. Moreover, almost all males were laid with their feet close together, whereas the hands of the elderly women were positioned in front of the face.

The distribution of red ochre may variously take the form of concentrations about the head, thorax and pelvic regions, either singularly or in combination. Considerable variations also exist in the amounts applied. In certain cases the red ochre occurs beneath the skeletal parts, indicating that it was not strewn over the corpse after burial, but was already adhering to the skin or clothing prior to burial.

An interesting phenomenon, observed in several graves, is the occurrence of concentrations of fish bones at varying points within the graves. In a few cases these are associated with distinct, dark soil stains (Jonsson 1986). These soil marks have been interpreted as the remains of containers made of an organic material, holding fish, which were deposited in the form of grave goods.

The distribution of grave goods in relation to the age of buried individuals shows a distinct pattern. It is the younger females and older males who have been furnished with the great majority of grave goods recorded.

In several cases the question arises as to what may or may not be validly described as a grave offering. This applies to those graves where flint artifacts and animal bones occurred in the filling immediately above the body and which seem to be inconsistent with the composition of the main mass of the filling. The position of several of these objects suggests that some connection exists between them and the burial.

The actual size of the Skateholm I graveyard has been established; the excavated graves are located in an area 50×40 metres. There also appears to be a tendency for graves to occur in groups. A few cases of overlapping occur, but in only one instance has any great damage been caused to the older grave.

THE GRAVES AT SKATEHOLM II

Altogether, 22 graves have been investigated at Skateholm II within an area 30×15 m (*Fig. 5*). It was not the intention to conduct a total and definitive investigation of the cemetery. The section examined might represent part of a larger area containing graves. Several of the graves at Skateholm II display interesting features which complement the complex picture regarding Mesolithic burial customs.

A long and narrow band of dark-coloured soil, oblong–oval in form, was observed at a level immediately above the body in *grave IV*, and more or less matched the outline of the grave. This band is the remains of a structure of wood. The deceased, a male, was placed in the supine position. A bone harpoon and a pecked stone axe were tucked in below the left upper arm. A collection of grave goods had also been placed in a small area of dense red ochre behind the head. This included a pecked stone axe, two grinding plates, four blades, a round stone and a long, narrow, bone needle. A slotted bone knife, found in a mole run close to the grave, was probably associated with the burial.

Grave VIII contained a woman in the sitting position, as well as a dog which had been placed across the woman's shins. It had apparently been decapitated prior to burial. The body of the woman had been ornamented with a row of some 100 tooth beads from red deer which encircled the rear of her hips.

Grave XI, with a young adult male in a supine position, featured a veritable network of red deer antlers placed transversely across the man's shins. Two antlers were still attached to a cranial fragment.

Grave XII held two children, 2 and 4 years old respectively, placed close together. One child had received two flint blades, while the other was given a long bone point as a grave offering. Both crania were strewn with red ochre.

Grave XV was encountered in the central section of the research area, where there was a high concentration of graves. It contained a young male,

N

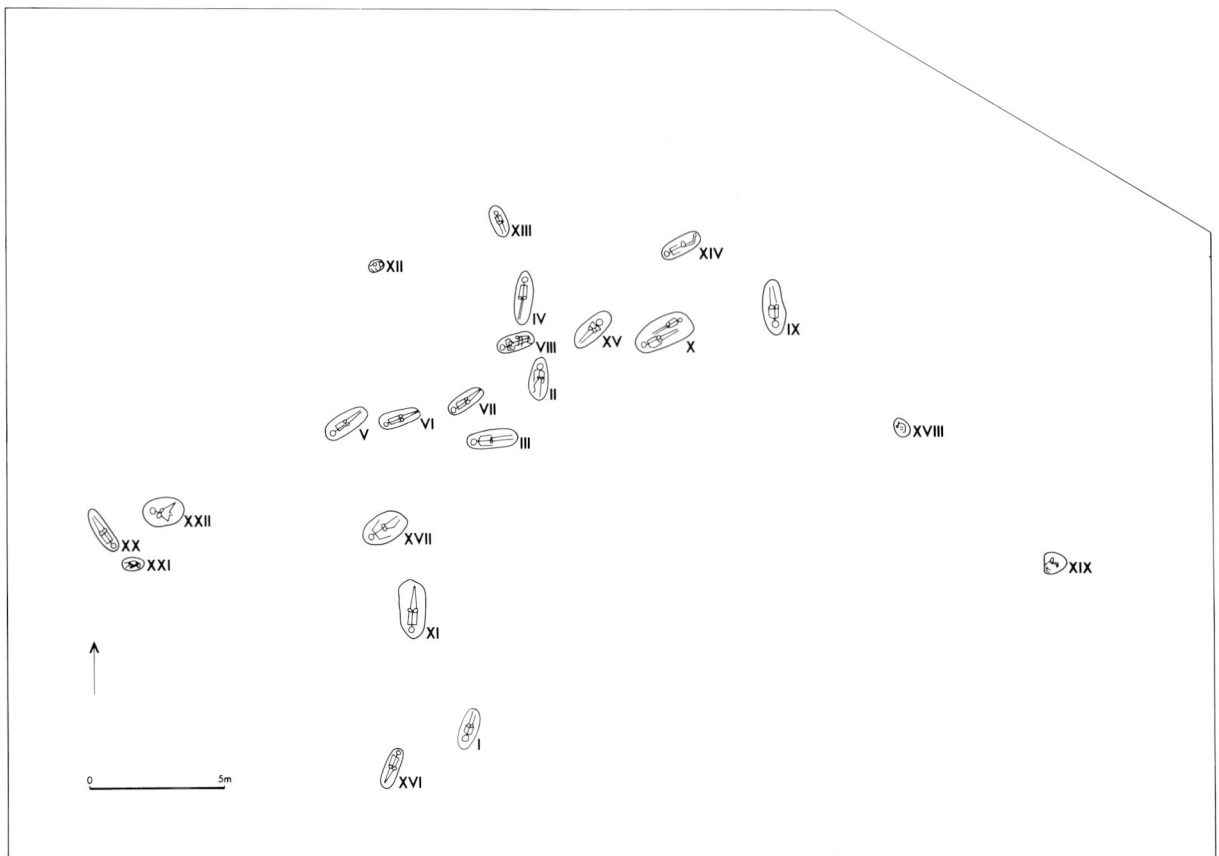

Figure 5　Plan of the cemetery at Skateholm II. Roman numerals denote the graves.

placed in a sitting position (*Fig. 6*). Two antlers of red deer lay by the man's head, while a large antler lay by his feet. A row of perforated teeth of red deer ran across the top of the cranium – evidently the remains of a more elaborate head-dress. Two flint blades lay by the hip and a core axe at the left of the thigh. Several teeth of wild boar lay below the right underarm.

Grave XX contained a young female in a supine attitude. A row of perforated tooth beads extended around the waist, including teeth from aurochs. The latter are evidence of long distance contact, since the aurochs was by that time extinct in southern Scania. Tooth beads also occurred behind the head. A dog was found in a pit behind grave XX, a red deer antler lying along its back (*Fig. 7*). In addition, three flint knives and an ornamented hammer of red deer antler were found on the dog's stomach. It is not impossible that a connection exists between grave XX and the pit containing the dog, but this could not be established; the latter is therefore assumed to be a separate burial – *grave XXI*.

THE RELATIONSHIP BETWEEN SKATEHOLM I AND SKATEHOLM II

The occurrence of graves at both Skateholm I and II provides a unique opportunity for studying the relationship between a hunter-gatherer society and

its deceased members over a period spanning several generations and within an extremely limited area. Certain elements can be noted. Much of what has been said about the Skateholm I graves also applies to those at Skateholm II; but differences exist which may be significant for the study of late Mesolithic burial customs in terms of a time perspective. One difference is that the hocker position does not occur in any grave at Skateholm II, whereas it is the most frequently occurring feature at Skateholm I. Another difference concerns the burial of dogs. At Skateholm I they appear to have been accorded the same burial rites as humans, while their presence in three graves at Skateholm II is of a secondary nature and they are not shown the same degree of respect evident in the Skateholm I canine burials.

Another difference between the sites concerns the number and variety of grave goods accorded to the deceased. While Skateholm II, like Skateholm I, features graves in which non-perishable grave goods occur, the frequency of graves with many and varied grave goods is greater at the former site than at the latter. Whereas the majority of graves at Skateholm I contain one artifact, the majority of those at Skateholm II feature at least two and, in most cases, three or more.

In contrast to the seemingly random distribution of graves at Skateholm I, a concentration is more readily discernible at Skateholm II. At the latter site

374

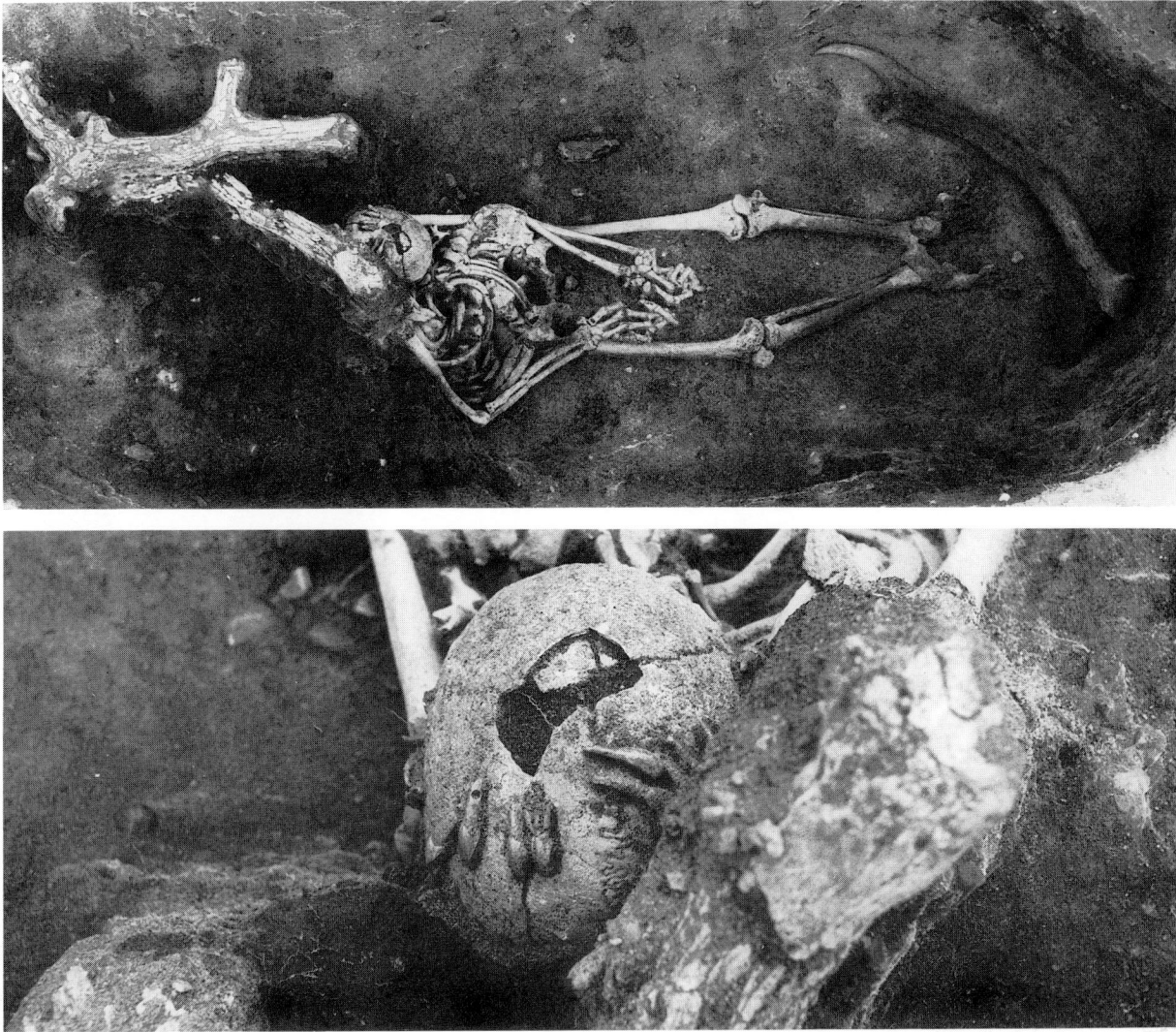

Figure 6 Skateholm II. Grave XV with a young man placed in sitting position (above). Antlers were placed behind the interred's head and in front of his feet. A core axe was found close to the left thigh. A row of perforated teeth of red deer ran across the top of the cranium (below).

the graves are, with two exceptions, all situated within a narrow belt along the crest of the slope and above the settlement area.

OTHER ARCHAEOLOGICAL FEATURES

The fact that the upper section of the settlement areas at Skateholm I and Skateholm II has been subjected to detailed examination has meant that features other than graves have been recorded. As is the case with other archaeological investigations, regardless of period, the precise function of the majority of these cannot be explained. A few exhibit, both in terms of form and composition of the filling, close similarities to the documented graves. That the cenotaph phenomenon, which is well known from other late Mesolithic cemeteries, may be represented at Skateholm by these features cannot be discounted (Péquart *et al.* 1937; Péquart and Péquart 1954; Albrethsen and Brinch Petersen 1976). A pit, similar in form to the surrounding graves, was investigated at Skateholm II. While no

trace of a skeleton was recorded, three large deer antler beams were found in the pit. This feature has, with some reservation, been interpreted as a cenotaph. Another form of construction is that of the house found at both Skateholm I and Skateholm II. At Skateholm I a shallow pit, 11 m long by 6 m wide, was encountered directly adjacent to the cemetery (Larsson 1985a). This pit had been counter-sunk into the side of the hill in order to obtain a level surface. The distinctive marks of postholes were also documented beneath the relatively level surface of the pit floor. These had held sturdy posts up to 25 cm in diameter, as well as poles of lesser dimensions.

A peculiar feature was located in the middle of the graveyard at Skateholm II. It consisted of an almost rectangular area, *c.* 4 m long, bounded by a narrow band of intensive red ochre (Larsson 1988a). The area was covered by a thin layer of red ochre, and the presence of postholes showed that some kind of structure had been raised, the filling of which consisted of a mixture of soot and sand. The

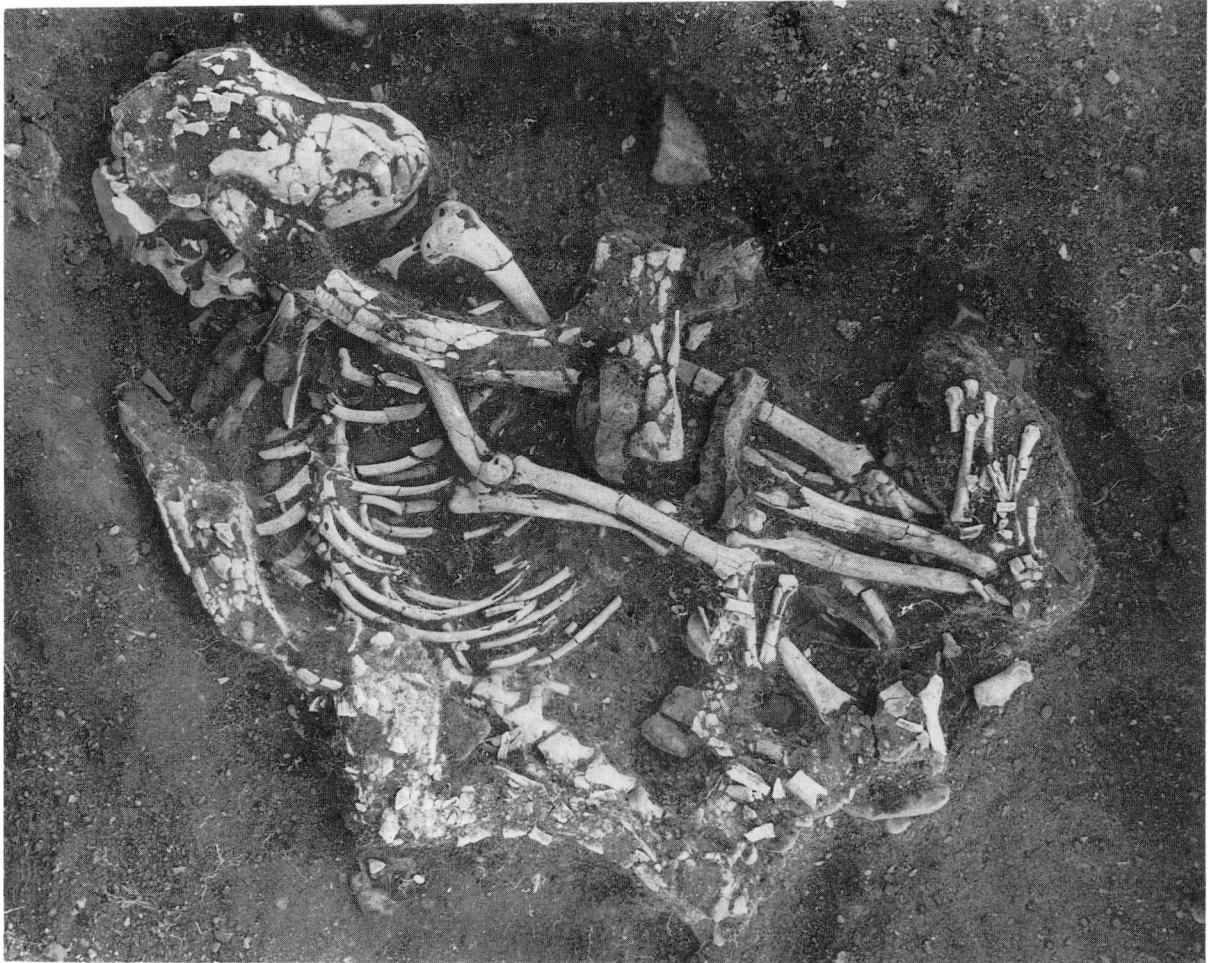

Figure 7   Skateholm II. Grave XXI with a buried dog. A red deer antler lay along the back of the dog and three flint knives were found on its stomach (above). A decorated hammer of red deer antler was placed on the chest of the dog (below).

conjoining bones from the skeletal parts of various animals were found in the band of red ochre. This feature is interpreted as a cult–ceremonial area.

SKATEHOLM AND THE OUTSIDE WORLD
Another important aspect of the project concerns the relationship between the sites already investigated

376

and those subsequently documented within the Skateholm area in general and the ancient lagoon in particular. Coincidental observations had established the existence of other sites. A more definitive reconnaissance led to the recognition of more than twenty Stone Age sites. Surface finds at some of these suggested late Mesolithic occupation. One of these sites, Skateholm IX, in the eastern part of the former lagoon, has a topographical situation which is strongly reminiscent of the position of Skateholm I–III.

The investigations at Skateholm show that late Mesolithic settlement was concentrated in and around the ancient lagoon. As regards the nearest settlement concentrations, a complex of sites from the same period is known along the former beach ridges adjoining Öja-Herread's bog, situated c. 25 km east of Skateholm (M. Larsson 1986). Late Mesolithic sites have also been found on low islands in the former lagoon. As for settlement on the coast west of Skateholm, the remains of a very large late Mesolithic site exist on the shore of a prehistoric bay at Kämpinge, c. 30 km away. Here, the inhabitants were able to move higher up the slope as sea level rose, in contrast to Skateholm where marine transgressions forced an evacuation to other, higher-lying islands.

Acknowledgements: I would like to thank the following individuals who contributed information for this article: Dr Hans Göransson, Dr Hannelore Håkansson, Mrs Marie-José Gaillard Lemdahl, and Mr Geoffrey Lemdahl (Quaternary geology), Dr Sören Håkansson (radiocarbon dates), Mr Leif Jonsson, Dr Ove Persson and Mrs Evy Persson (osteology and anthropology), and Dr Verner Alexandersen (odontology). Mr William Troy has been of great help in the English revision of the article.

References

AARIS-SØRENSEN, K. (1977) Vedbæk-jægeren og hans hunde. In E. Brinch Petersen, J.H. Jønsson, P. Vang Petersen and K. Aaris-Sørensen, Vedbækprojektet. I marken og i museerne. *Søllerodbøgen*, 1977: 170–176.

ALBRETHSEN, S.E. and BRINCH PETERSEN, E. (1976) Excavation of a Mesolithic cemetery at Vedbæk, Denmark. *Acta Archaeologica*, 47: 1–28.

ALEXANDERSEN, V. (1988) Description of the human dentition from the late Mesolithic grave-fields at Skateholm. In L. Larsson (ed.), *The Skateholm Project. I. Man and Environment* (Acta Regiae Societatis Humaniorum Litterarum Lundensis, LXXIX). Lund, Royal Society of Letters: 106–163.

BJELM, L. and LARSSON, L. (1984) Application of georadar in archaeological research. Results from a test at Skateholm, southern Sweden. *Meddelanden från Lunds universitets historiska museum*, 1983–1984: 39–46.

CANTWELL, A-M. (1982) Middle Woodland dog ceremonialism in Illinois. *The Wisconsin Archeologist*, 61(4): 480–496.

DAHR, E. (1937) *Studien über Hunde aus primitiven Steinzeit-kulturen in Nordeuropa* (Lunds Universitets Arsskrift, Neue Folge Avd. 2, Bd 32, Nr 4). Lund, University of Lund.

DIKOV, N.N. (1983) The stages and routes of human occupation of the Beringian land bridge based upon archaeological data. In P.M. Masters and N.C. Fleming (eds), *Quaternary Coastlines and Marine Archaeology*: 347–364.

GAILLARD, M-J. and LEMDAHL, G. (1988) Plant-macrofossil analysis (seeds and fruits) at Skateholm–Järavallen, southern Sweden. A lagoonal landscape during Atlantic and early Subboreal time. In L. Larsson (ed.), *The Skateholm Project. I. Man and Environment* (Acta Regiae Societatis Humaniorum Litterarum Lundensis, LXXIX). Lund, Royal Society of Letters: 34–38.

GAILLARD, M-J., GÖRANSSON, H., HÅKANSSON, H. and LEMDAHL, G. (1988) The palaeoenvironment at Skateholm–Järavallen (southern Sweden) during Atlantic and early Subboreal time on the basis of pollen-, macrofossil-, diatom- and insect-analysis. In L. Larsson (ed.), *The Skateholm Project. I. Man and Environment* (Acta Regiae Societatis Humaniorum Litterarum Lundensis, LXXIX). Lund, Royal Society of Letters: 52–55.

GÖRANSSON, H. (1988) Pollen analytical investigations at Skateholm, southern Sweden. In L. Larsson (ed.), *The Skateholm Project. I. Man and Environment* (Acta Regiae Societatis Humaniorum Litterarum Lundensis, LXXIX). Lund, Royal Society of Letters: 27–33.

HÅKANSSON, H. (1988) Diatom analysis at Skateholm–Järavallen, southern Sweden. In L. Larsson (ed.), *The Skateholm Project. I. Man and Environment* (Acta Regiae Societatis Humaniorum Litterarum Lundensis, LXXIX). Lund, Royal Society of Letters: 39–45.

JONSSON, L. (1986) Fish bones in late Mesolithic human graves at Skateholm, Scania, south Sweden. In D.C. Brinkhuizen and A.T. Clason (eds), *Fish and Archaeology. Studies in Osteometry, Taphonomy, Seasonality and Fishing Methods*. Oxford, British Archaeological Reports (International Series) S294: 62–79.

JONSSON, L. (1988) The vertebrate faunal remains from the late Atlantic settlement Skateholm in Scania, south Sweden. In L. Larsson (ed.), *The Skateholm Project. I. Man and Environment* (Acta Regiae Societatis Humaniorum Litterarum Lundensis, LXXIX). Lund, Royal Society of Letters: 56–88.

LARSSON, L. (1980a) Gravar från jägarstenåldern. *Ale*, 1980(3): 32–36.

LARSSON, L. (1980b) Stenåldersjägarnas boplats och graver vid Skateholm. *Limhamniana*, 1980: 13–39.

LARSSON, L. (1981a) En 7000-årig sydkustboplats. Nytt om gammalt från Skateholm. *Limhamniana*, 1981: 17–36.

LARSSON, L. (1981b) The Mesolithic settlement and graveyard from Skateholm, southern Sweden. *Mesolithic Miscellany*, 2(1): 4–5.

LARSSON, L. (1982a) A 7000 years old site at the southern coast. New things about old things from Skateholm. *Mesolithic Miscellany*, 3(1): 3–5.

LARSSON, L. (1982b) Segebro. En tidigatlantisk boplats vid Sege as mynning. *Malmöfynd*, 4: 1–140.

LARSSON, L. (1982c) *Skateholmsprojektet. En utställning om ett fångstsamhälle för 7000 år sedan*. Lund, Institute of Archaeology, Report Series no. 13.

LARSSON, L. (1982d) Skateholmsprojektet. Nya gravar och ett nytt gravfält. *Limhamniana*, 1982: 11–41.

LARSSON, L. (1983a) Skateholmsprojektet. Jägare–fiskare–bönder. *Limhamniana*, 1983: 7–40.

LARSSON, L. (1983b) The Skateholm Project. More graves and a newly discovered cemetery. *Mesolithic Miscellany*, 4(1): 4–6.

LARSSON, L. (1984a) Gräberfelder und Siedlungen des Spätmesolithikums bei Skateholm, Südschonen, Schweden. *Archäologisches Korrespondenzblatt*, 14(2): 123–130.

LARSSON, L. (1984b) The Skateholm Project. A late Mesolithic settlement and cemetery complex at a southern Swedish bay. *Meddelanden från Lunds universitets historiska museum*, 1983–1984: 5–38.

LARSSON, L. (1984c) The Skateholm Project. Hunters–fishers–farmers. *Mesolithic Miscellany*, 5(1): 5–9.

LARSSON, L. (1984d) Skateholmsprojektet. På spåren efter gravsedsförändringar, ceremoniplatser och tama rävar. *Limhamniana*, 1984: 49–84.

LARSSON, L. (1985a) Of house and hearth. The excavation, interpretation and reconstruction of a late Mesolithic house. *Archaeological Environment*, 4: 197–209.

LARSSON, L. (1985b) The Skateholm Project. On the trail of changes in burial custom, ritual areas and tame foxes. *Mesolithic Miscellany*, 6(1): 1–5.

LARSSON, L. (1986) Skateholm. *Skalk*, 1986(4): 21–30.

LARSSON, L. (1987) Ett rikt liv på stenåldern. *Forskning och Framsteg*, 1987(2): 32–38.

LARSSON, L. (1988*a*) A construction for ceremonial activities from the late Mesolithic. *Meddelanden från Lunds universitets historiska museum*, 1987–1988: 5–18.

LARSSON, L. (1988*b*) The Skateholm Project. Late Mesolithic settlement at a south Swedish lagoon. In L. Larsson (ed.), *The Skateholm Project. I. Man and Environment* (Acta Regiae Societatis Humaniorum Litterarum Lundensis, LXXIX). Lund, Royal Society of Letters: 9–19.

LARSSON, M. (1986) Bredasten – an early Ertebølle site with a dwelling structure in south Scania. *Meddelanden från Lunds universitets historiska museum*, 1985–1986: 5–49.

LEMDAHL, G. (1988) A Postglacial insect fauna from Skateholm–Järavallen, southern Sweden. In L. Larsson (ed.), *The Skateholm Project. I. Man and Environment* (Acta Regiae Societatis Humaniorum Litterarum Lundensis, LXXIX). Lund, Royal Society of Letters: 46–51.

LEMDAHL, G. and GÖRANSSON, H. (1988) Geological investigations at Skateholm, southern Sweden. In L. Larsson (ed.), *The Skateholm Project. I. Man and Environment* (Acta Regiae Societatis Humaniorum Litterarum Lundensis, LXXIX).

Lund, Royal Society of Letters: 20–26.

LEPIKSAAR, J. (1982) Djurrester från den tidigmesolitiska boplatsen vid Segebro nära Malmö i Skåne (Sydsverige). In L. Larsson, Segebro. En tidigatlantisk boplats vid Sege ås mynning. *Malmöfynd*, 4: 105–128.

PÉQUART, M., PÉQUART, ST-J., BOULE, M. and VALLOIS, H. (1937) *Téviec. Station-Nécropole Mésolithique du Morbihan.* (Archives de l'Institut de Paleontologie Humaine, Mémoire 18). Paris, Masson.

PÉQUART, M. and PÉQUART, ST-J. (1954) *Hoëdic. Deuxième Station-Nécropole du Mésolithique Côtier Armoricain.* Anvers, de Sikkel.

PERSSON, O. and PERSSON, E. (1984) *Anthropological Report on the Mesolithic Graves from Skateholm, Southern Sweden. I. Excavation Seasons 1980–1982.* Lund, Institute of Archaeology, Report Series no. 21.

PERSSON, O. and PERSSON, E. (1988) Anthropological report concerning the interred Mesolithic populations from Skateholm, southern Sweden. Excavation seasons 1983–1984. In L. Larsson (ed.), *The Skateholm Project. I. Man and Environment* (Acta Regiae Societatis Humaniorum Litterarum Lundensis, LXXIX). Lund, Royal Society of Letters: 89–105.

The Chronology of the Finnish Mesolithic

Heikki Matiskainen

Abstract

The study presents a chronology by artifact type of the Finnish Mesolithic with the aid of shore displacement chronology as based on the history of the Baltic. The method is the so-called stratigraphic method as used in present-day Quaternary geology, whereby the elevations of radiocarbon-dated isolation thresholds of lakes and bogs are used to date Mesolithic sites by comparing information on their elevations with shorelines formed at various stages.

METHOD

The main grounds for the dating of the Stone Age of Finland have been provided by shore displacement chronology based on Holocene land upheaval and the history of the Baltic. Apart from Finland the method has also been used elsewhere in the land upheaval areas of Fennoscandia – in Norway, Sweden and Soviet Karelia. This means of dating can be regarded as an original Finnish method, whereby archaeological dates have been made possible by an active Quaternary geological study of Postglacial shore displacements (Siiriäinen 1969, 1973; Matiskainen 1978; Nunez 1978a, 1978b; Hyvärinen and Eronen 1979).

The methods used in the study of shore displacement can be summarized as follows: (i) field observations and levelling of ancient Baltic shorelines, providing relative and distance diagrams and gradient datings of them; (ii) stratigraphic methods, viz. microfossil-determined isolation horizons of the various phases of the Baltic in lake and bog sediments; and (iii) dating of isolation thresholds from the isolation horizons with the aid of pollen zones or radiocarbon dates.

During the past decade research has concentrated less on the synchronization of ancient shorelines, traditionally a central feature of Quaternary geological studies of shoreline displacement in Finland. Relative and distance diagrams based on shoreline observations have been the object of less interest, because of the uncertainties of interpretation of shoreline data. The presently used method can be described as stratigraphic. Limnic layer series from bogs and lakes isolated from the Baltic through land upheaval are selected for study. From these, the isolation horizon is determined through observed changes in diatom flora. In the process of isolation marine or large lacustrine species of diatoms are replaced by smaller lacustrine forms, and in the same connection changes in layer formation can be observed through loss-on-ignition. In this sense, pollen analysis has taken the role of a routine method solely for providing a basis for chronology when attempting to date the contact horizons by radiocarbon.

The stratigraphic method is at its most useful in limited and uniform areas of land upheaval, where isostatic tilting does not skew the dating of the shoreline displacement curve. A type area of this kind can be defined from isobases of present land uplift as in this study; alternatively, elevation isobases of the Litorina Sea can be used.

The archaeological shoreline displacement chronology is based on two main conditions. The first requirement is that a prehistoric site must be located at or near the shoreline of its time. The second requirement is a Quaternary dating of that shoreline. In defining the lower limit of the site a fixed point of elevation is chosen for the shoreline displacement curve, the precision of which, in turn, depends on the Quaternary geological methods used. Both indices contain numerous sources of error. The location of a hunter-gatherer dwelling site on the shore of the ancient Baltic is hard to demonstrate without precise excavation with soil phosphate analyses. In the main, dwelling sites of the Finnish Stone Age were linked to the shoreline, but there are also numerous examples to the contrary. Factors affecting the precision of the shoreline displacement curve based on the stratigraphic method include sources of error in radiocarbon determinations, contamination skewing dating of limnic sediments, and misinterpretations of diatom ecology. It is also difficult to demonstrate minor fluctuations in the water level.

ARCHAEOLOGICAL DATA

The chronological model is based on some 200 Mesolithic dwelling sites in southern and central

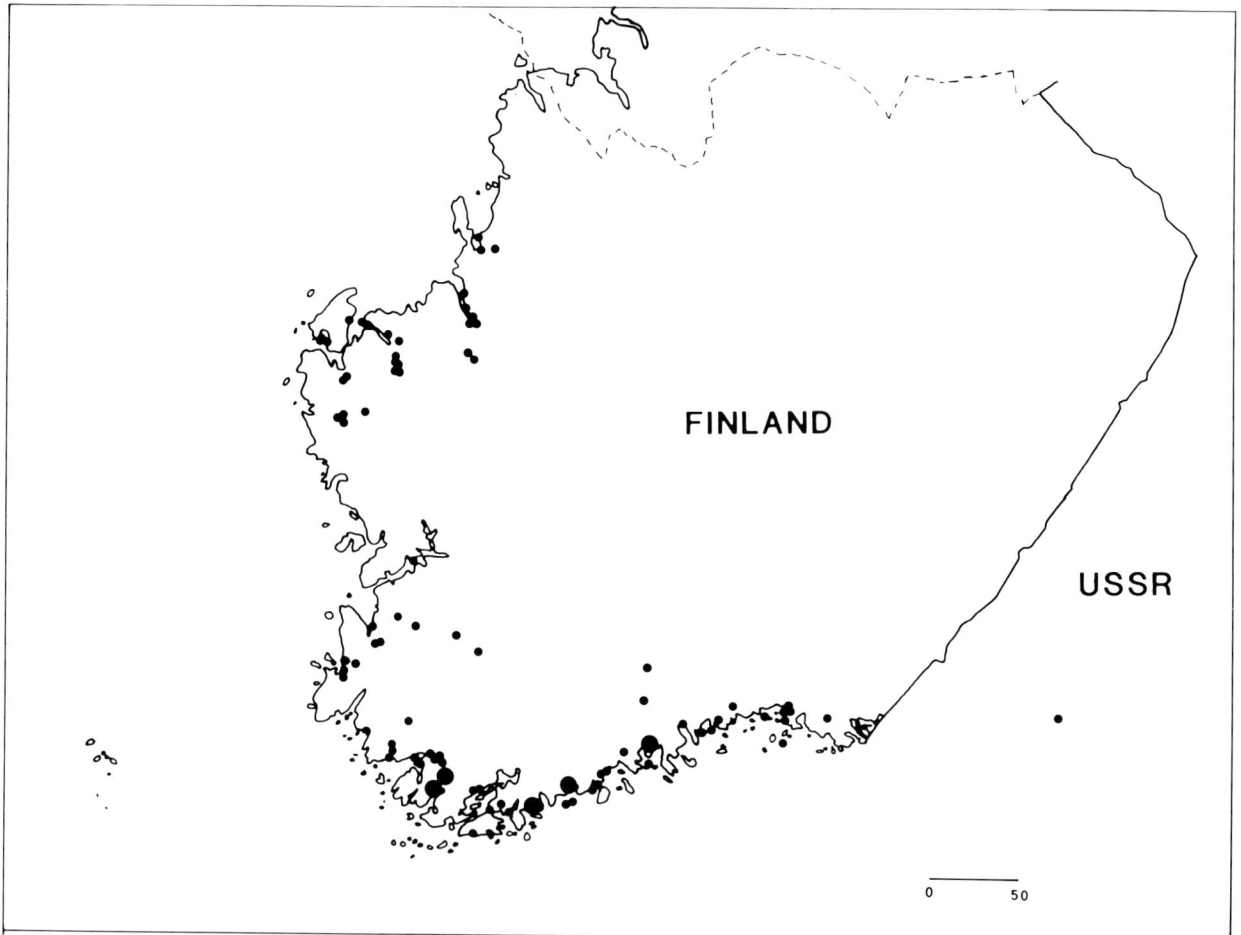

Figure 1   Distribution of Mesolithic sites dated in the study – shown in relation to the shoreline at the highest phase of the Litorina Sea, *c.* 7500 BP.

Finland, of which 60 have been excavated. It is assumed that these sites were 'shoreline' sites, i.e. located at or near the ancient shore of the Baltic (*Fig. 1*). The chronology is constructed so that the finds from these sites include one or more type artifacts suitable for dating. The artifact types are stone artifacts dated to the Mesolithic by Äyräpää (1950): the primitive axe, the coniform-holed globular stone mace-head, the leaf-shaped slate point, the curved-backed grooved adze, the South-Finnish even-bladed adze, and the oblique-bladed quartz points. The relative chronological ordering of the artifacts was partly known. The leaf-shaped slate point has been regarded as an early form, whereas the South-Finnish even-bladed adze and the oblique-bladed quartz point have been dated to the final stages of the Finnish Mesolithic (Äyräpää 1950; Luho 1967; Siiriäinen 1981).

To form the Mesolithic chronology, the study presents eight shoreline displacement curves based on the stratigraphic method from different zones of land uplift from the Karelian isthmus to southern Ostrobothnia. The curves have been prepared according to the dates of isolation horizons of bodies of water separated from the Baltic. A key shoreline displacement curve is that from the Askola area,

which is described in more detail in order to illustrate the method (see Appendix).

EARLY HOLOCENE SHORELINE DISPLACEMENT IN ASKOLA

The most important find area in the Finnish Mesolithic is located in Askola, south Finland (Luho 1956).

Isolations and facies changes from six bodies of water have been studied at Askola. The material is based on research by Matti Eronen and this author (Eronen, Haila and Matiskainen 1982). The main aim has been to define the culmination of the Ancylus transgression and to date it, as well as determining the rate of the Ancylus regression and defining the development of the Litorina Sea on stratigraphic grounds.

Developments relating to the Ancylus Lake can be clearly observed in two of the bodies of water studied, Huiskaissuo and Kopinkallio bogs. In both of these the layer sequence was similar. At the base was clay overlain by a deposit of detritus mud. The organic layer is covered by a layer of gyttja indicating that the body was affected by a transgression. After this the sea regressed and bogs gradually developed.

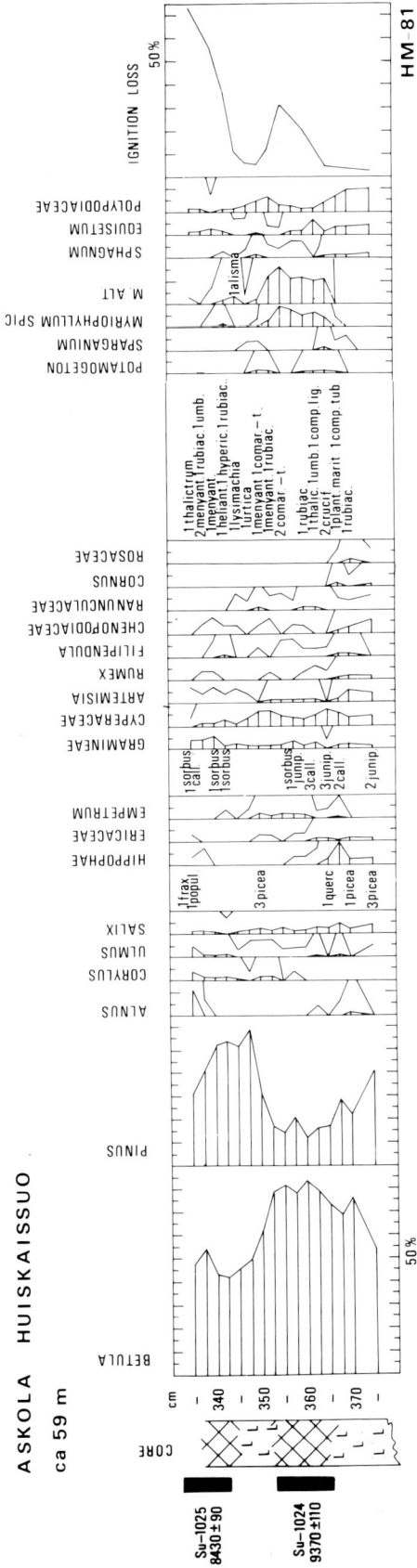

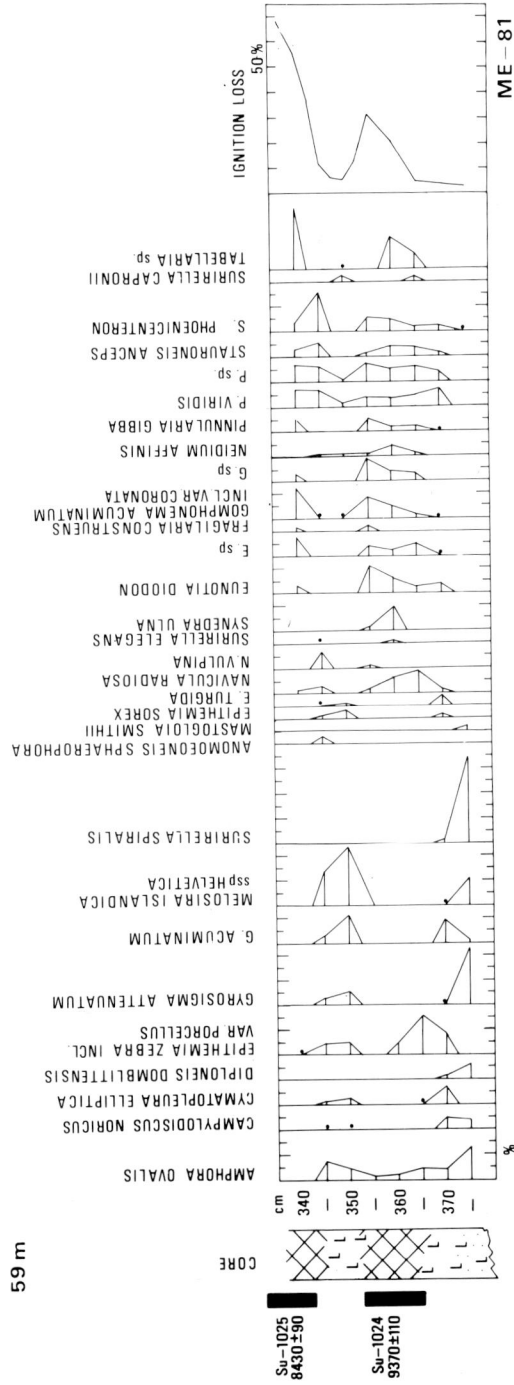

Figure 2 Diatom and pollen diagrams from Askola Huiskaissuo bog.

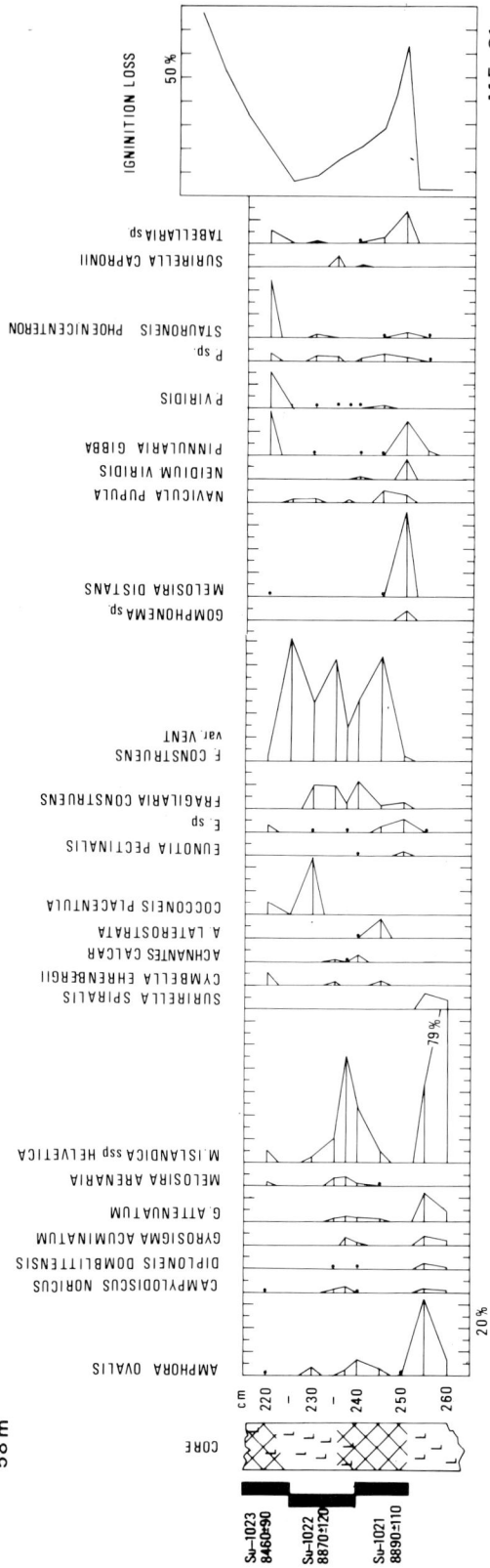

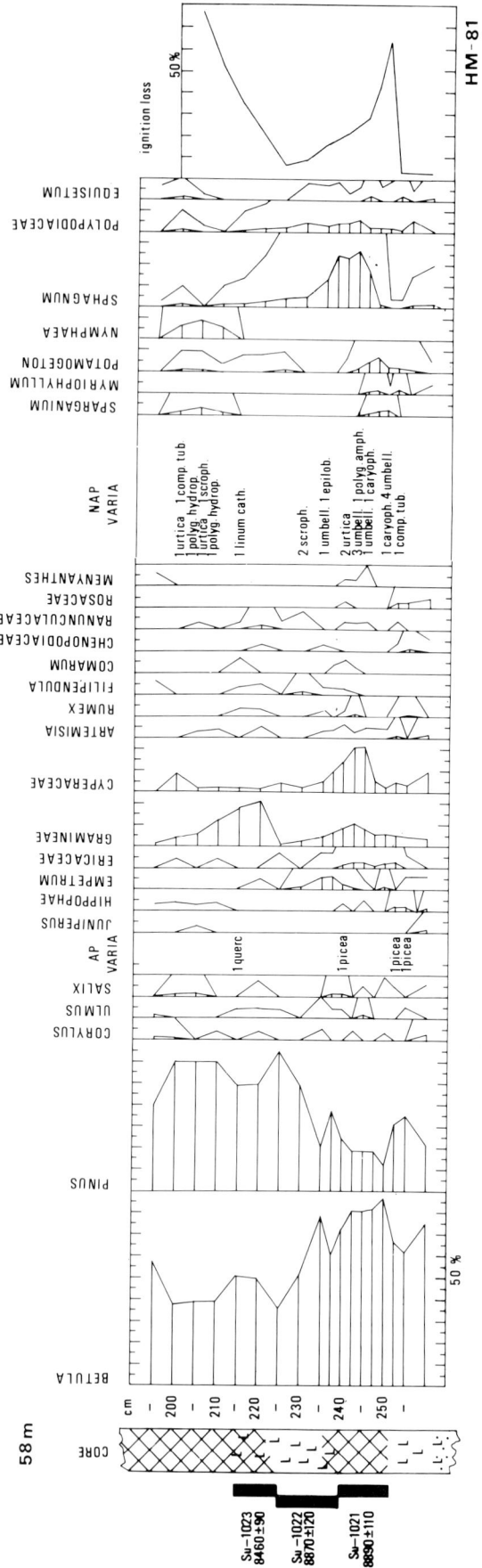

Figure 3 Diatom and pollen diagrams from Askola Kopinkallio bog.

ca 39 m

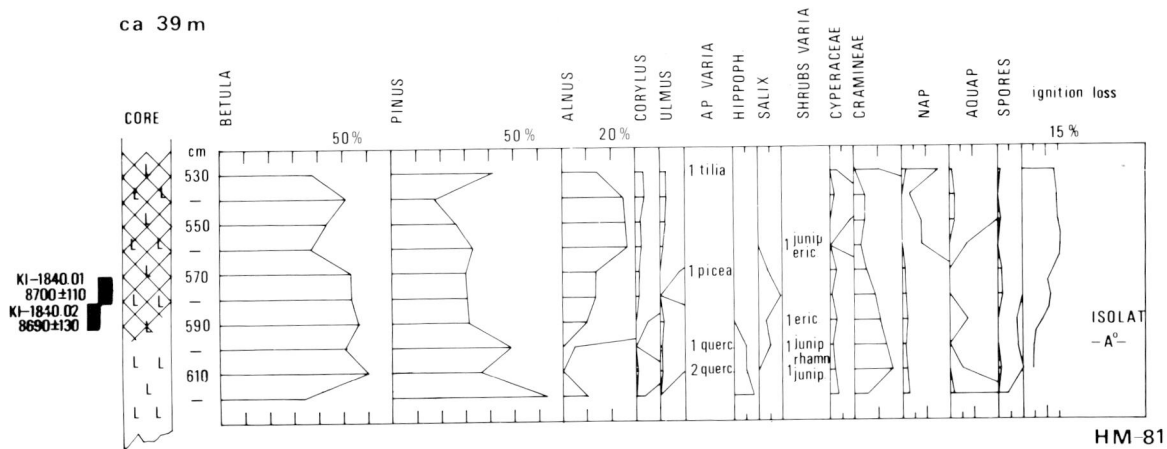

Figure 4   Pollen diagram from Askola Aborreträsk basin.

ASKOLA   LAMMINSUO

ca 32 m

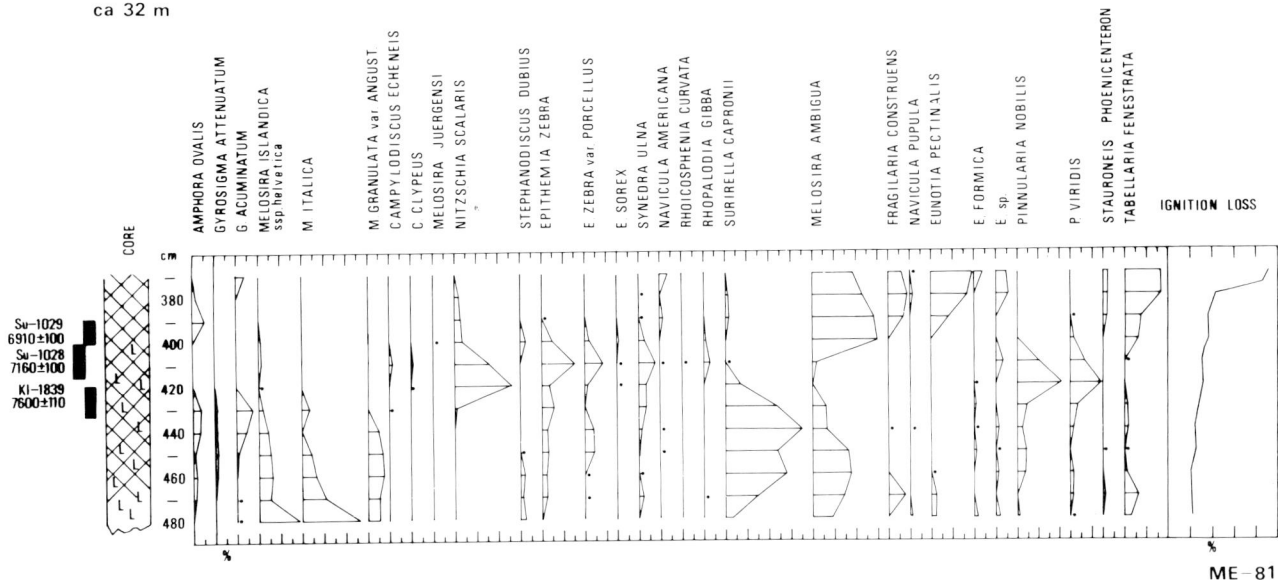

Figure 5   Diatom diagram from Askola Lamminsuo bog.

On the basis of diatom analytical interpretation the large lacustrine diatoms change into small lake forms in the organic layer, after which large lacustrine forms increase strongly in the clay mud layer as an indication of transgression, changing back finally to small lacustrine forms. The threshold elevations are 58 and 59 m a.s.l, indicating that the altitude attained by the Ancylus transgression exceeded that of both bodies of water. These events are radiocarbon dated (*Figs. 2 & 3*).

According to pollen analysis the first isolation occurred in the birch-dominated Pre-Boreal period. Contact with the Baltic was renewed at the boundary of the Pre-Boreal and Boreal periods, and the final isolation occurred in the early part of the Boreal period.

In order to determine the rate of regression, the isolation of a pond called Aborreträsk was studied. This pond is located at an elevation of 39 m a.s.l. and is in a zone between the Ancylus and Litorina levels.

The isolation limit occurs at the very beginning of the Atlantic period above the rational increase of *Alnus* (*Fig. 4*).

The Litorina limit is dated from two bodies of water, Lamminsuo bog and Lake Käärmejärvi. The diatom stratigraphy of Lamminsuo bog shows a small lake stage following isolation from the Ancylus Lake and a weak indication of the effect of the saline Litorina Sea on the body of water. The marine indications are however so weak that the Litorina Sea could not have risen much above 32 m a.s.l., the threshhold elevation of the bog. A layer sequence from Lake Käärmejärvi from below the Litorina limit indicates isolation and hence regression of the Litorina Sea later than the rational rise of *Tilia*, at which stage there had been a regression in the development of the Litorina Sea (*Figs. 5 & 6*).

The sixth body studied was Stormossen bog in Porvoo, located at an elevation of *c.* 27.5 m a.s.l. The isolation of this bog is problematic, as halophilic

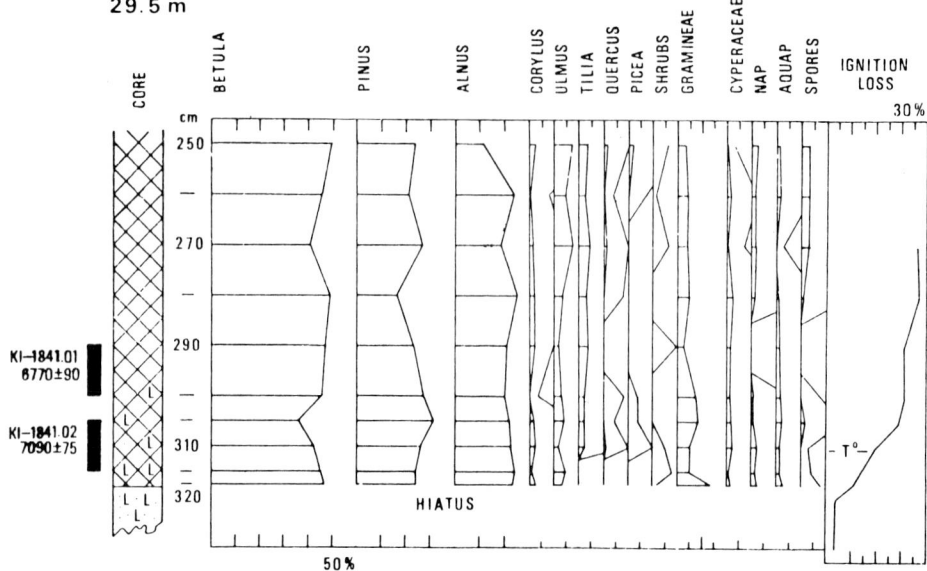

Figure 6   Pollen diagram from Porvoo Käärmejärvi basin.

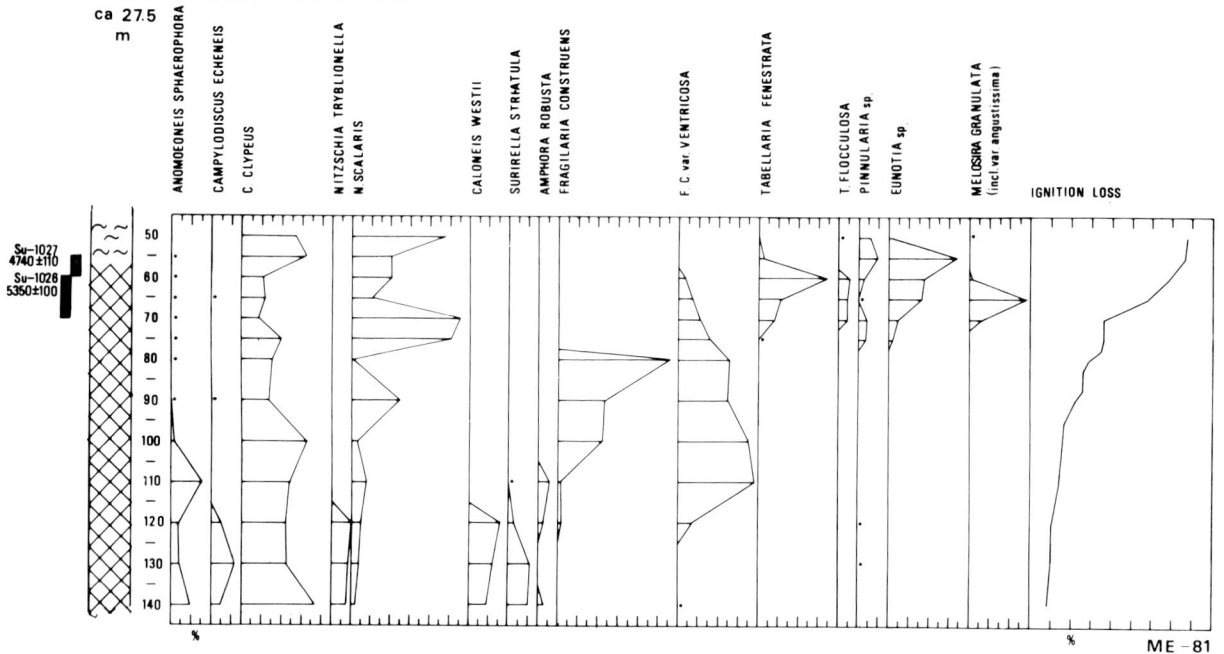

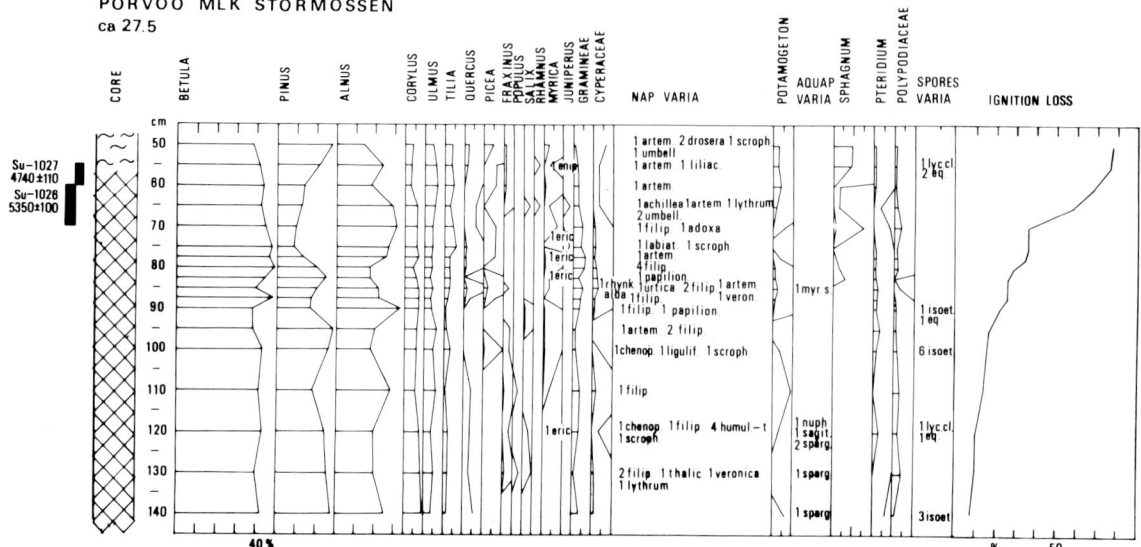

Figure 7   Diatom and pollen diagrams from Porvoo Stormossen bog.

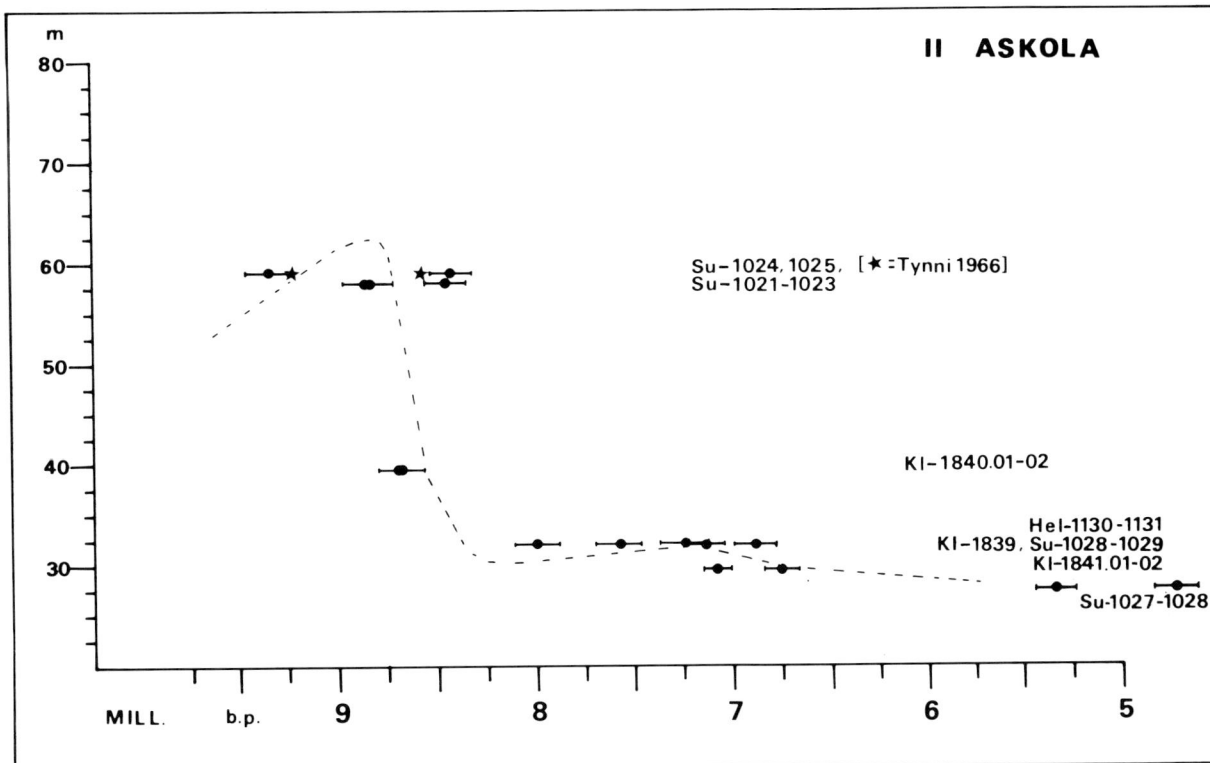

Figure 8 Shoreline displacement curve for the Askola area in the vicinity of the present 3 mm/yr uplift isobase.

diatom species seem to occur even after isolation (*Fig. 7*).

These datings provide the basis for the shoreline displacement curve of the Postglacial period in the Askola area. The shoreline displacement is characterized by an Ancylus transgression at *c.* 61 m a.s.l. *c.* 8800 BP and a rapid regression *c.* 8600 BP. Following these developments a eustatic rise partly exceeding land uplift can be observed in the transgression phase of the Litorina Sea at an elevation of 31–32 m *c.* 8000–7000 BP, followed by a gradual fall of the water level. In the Askola area the rapid developments of the Ancylus phase were followed by a period in which the shorelines remained fairly stable for *c.* 2000 years. In other words, eustatic rising of the water level has been nearly as great as the Askola land uplift (*Fig. 8*).

EARLY HOLOCENE SHORELINE DISPLACEMENT OF THE BALTIC IN FINLAND

To the east of Askola, in the Karelian isthmus area where land uplift is weaker, the Litorina transgression can be clearly observed. It can also be observed that the transgression has destroyed at least some of the Mesolithic sites in the area (*Fig. 9*, Curve I).

To the west of Askola, in the Helsinki area, the Litorina transgression cannot be observed and the curve is regressive from the Ancylus transgression onwards. The shoreline remained at the same

elevation for 2500 years, from *c.* 8500 to *c.* 6000 BP (*Fig. 9*, Curve III).

Further to the west the following shoreline displacement curve has been produced for the Kisko area with the westernmost observations of the Ancylus transgression. The 'old' dates may have been caused by the small amount of available organic material and contamination by redeposited carbon (*Fig. 9*, Curve IV). In the area of Salo, southwest Finland, the Ancylus regression is distinct and the Litorina phase can be seen as a slowing of shoreline displacement (*Fig. 9*, Curve V). There are two isolation observations from the Turku area (*Fig. 9*, Curve VI).

Two curves have been prepared from the area of rapid uplift, from Laitila and Lauhanvuori. The variability in elevation is great and is thus best suited to providing an archaeological shoreline displacement curve. The rapid land uplift in the Lauhanvuori area indicates extremely rapid negative changes in shoreline displacement during the Ancylus phase. The eustatic Litorina phase does not seem to have had much effect on the rate of shoreline displacement (*Fig. 9*, Curves VII & VIII).

In summary the presented curves form the following picture of developments in the Baltic during the Mesolithic:

1) The Yoldia regression is followed by the regressive development of the beginning of the Ancylus period which became transgressive *c.* 9000 BP. The almost catastrophic Ancylus regression occurred *c.* 8800–8500 BP.

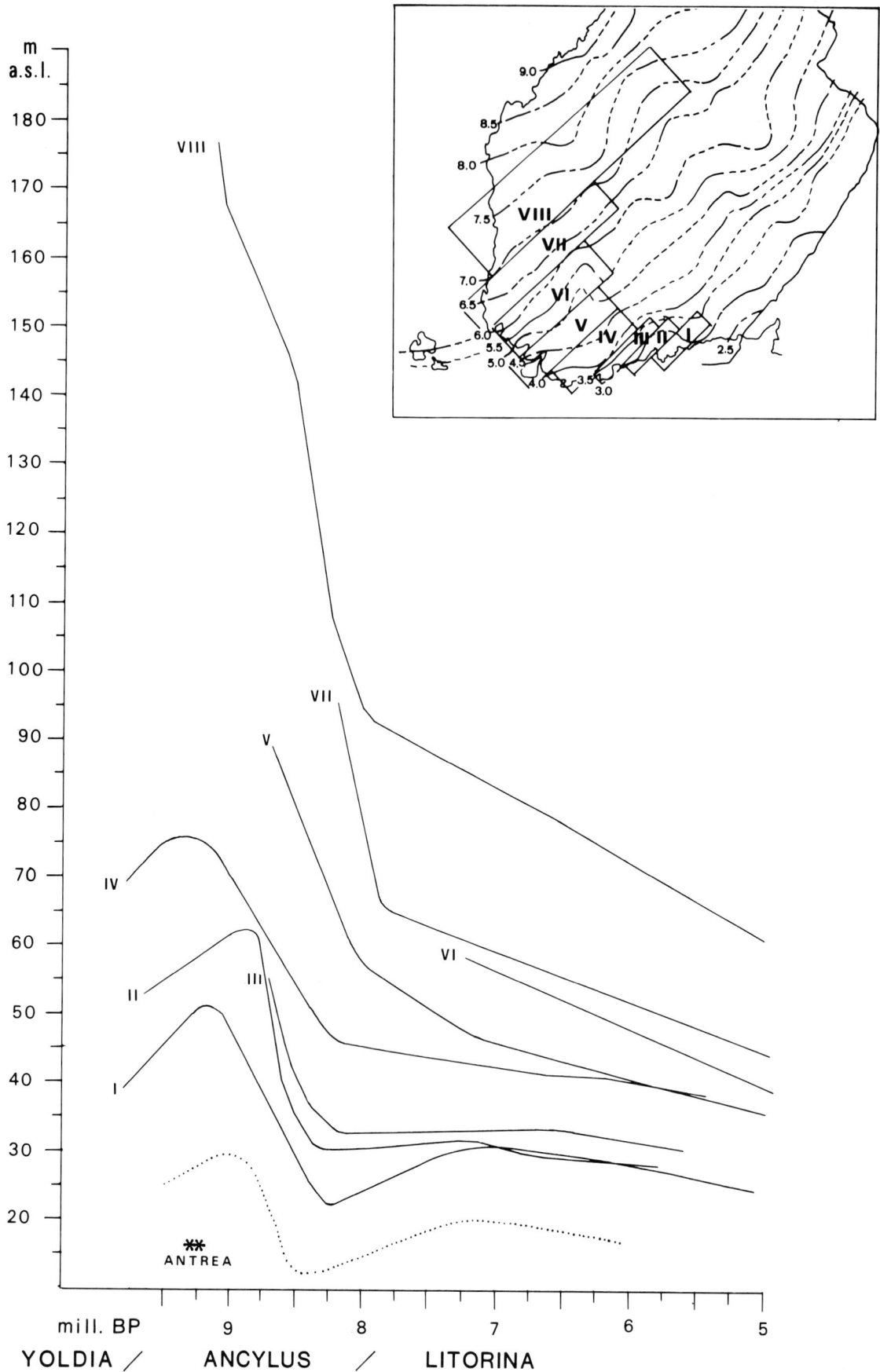

Figure 9 Postglacial shoreline displacement in south and central Finland based on radiocarbon evidence. The curves relate to different uplift zones: I – 2.5 to 3 mm/yr; II – 3 mm/yr; III – 3.5 mm/yr; IV – 4 mm/yr; V – 4.5 mm/yr; VI – 5.5 mm/yr; VII – 6.5 mm/yr; VIII – 7.5 mm/yr (zones according to present rates of uplift: Kiviniemi 1981). The dotted line curve is based on shore observations from the Karelian isthmus with the dates projected from curve I. The Antrea net find is located on the curve.

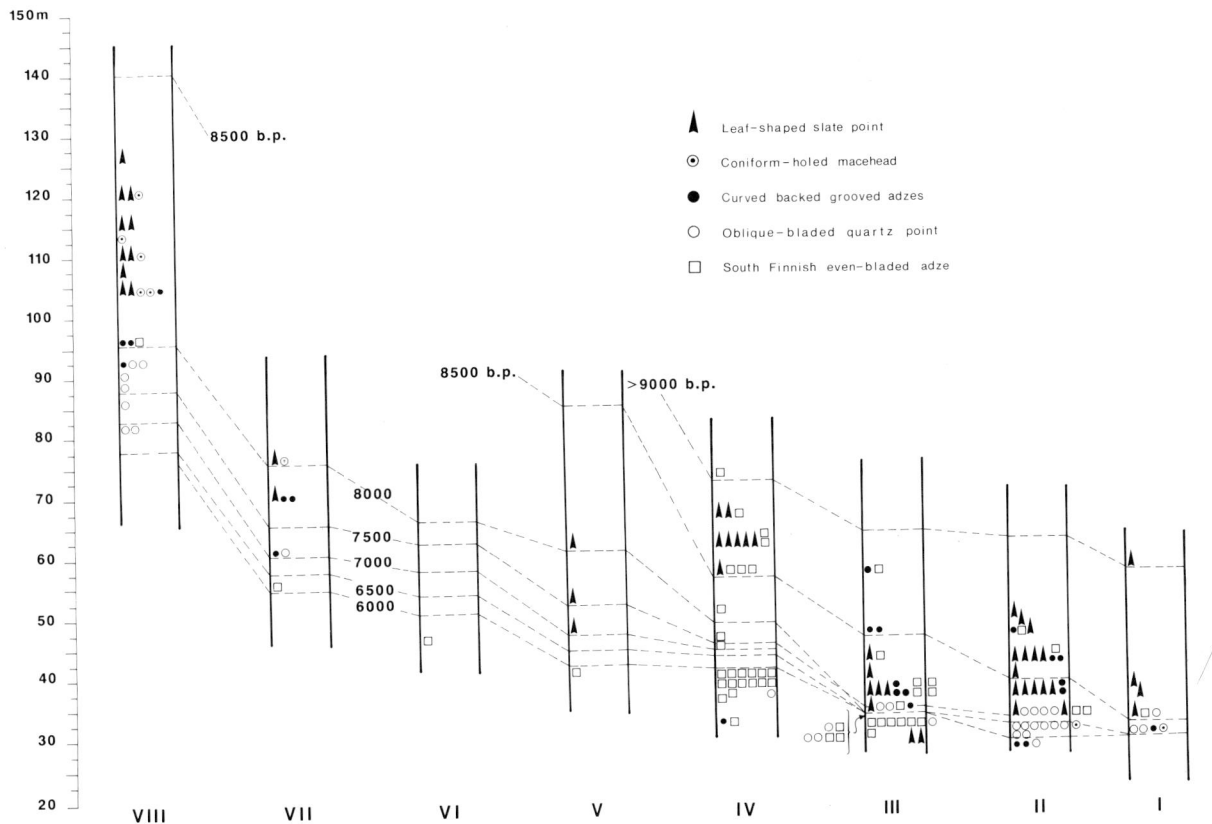

Figure 10 Sites from zones in *Fig. 9* combined on shoreline displacement curves I–VIII. Chronological limits have been established by comparing elevations of limits between 9000 and 6000 BP at 500 year intervals (^{14}C error limits of ±150 years on a ±0.5 m elevation zone). Sites marked with symbols indicate type artifacts found in the assemblages.

2) The first saline *Mastogloia* indication can be distinguished in layer sequences at *c.* 8000 BP.

3) The Litorina transgression occurs to the east of the 3 mm/yr land uplift isobase and is at its maximum *c.* 7600–7500 BP.

CHRONOLOGY OF THE MESOLITHIC

The Mesolithic chronology was developed by placing the sites located on the shore of the ancient Baltic on the shoreline displacement curves in accordance with their location in a particular uplift zone. The dating of a site is based on the presence of a Mesolithic type artifact and the use of quartz as a raw material. Sites with only quartz artifacts and flakes, except where they include oblique-bladed points, have not been included in the dating even though they could be dated to the Mesolithic on the basis of their elevation. The Mesolithic quartz material does not provide possibilities for typological dating, with the exception of the oblique points.

The Mesolithic artifact forms of Finland are dated as follows (*Fig. 10*):

Leaf-shaped slate points. The leaf-shaped slate points (*Fig. 11*) form the earliest artifact group of the Mesolithic, although some specimens seem to date to the later stages of the period. The main chrono-

Figure 11 Leaf-shaped slate points (NM 1811 – Utajärvi; NM 3678.8 – Haapajärvi; NM 8927.1 – Punkalaidun; NM 4119.3 – Kuortane). Scale=1:2

logical emphasis is on the Ancylus period (cf. Luho 1967; Siiriäinen 1981).

Coniform-holed globular mace-heads. This singularly Finnish artifact form (*Fig. 12*), the distribution of which is centred on southern Ostrobothnia and central Finland, is also dated to the early Mesolithic, i.e. the Ancylus period. The chronological model confirms Luho's (1967) relative dating of this artifact group to the early Mesolithic.

387

Figure 12 Coniform-holed globular mace-heads (NM2386.75 – Alajärvi; NM 10620.5 – Liljendal). Scale=1:2

Curved-backed grooved adzes. The distribution of this artifact (*Fig. 13*) is centred mainly on south Finland, although specimens have been found

Figure 13 Curved-backed grooved adze (NM 2040.47 – Kylmäkoski). Scale=1:2

throughout the country. Many of these artifacts are of so-called Onega green slate, the sources of which are on the western shores of Lake Onega, north of Petrozavodsk. The dating obtained for these is very broad, from the final stages of the Ancylus regression to the end of the Mesolithic, although the chronological emphasis is on the late Ancylus period and early Litorina period.

Figure 14 Oblique-bladed quartz points (MN 1171.3, 7, & 8 – Alajärvi). Scale=1:1

Oblique-bladed quartz points. Oblique-bladed quartz points (*Fig. 14*) have traditionally been dated to the late Mesolithic. The earliest specimens have been found in early Litorina contexts and the artifact form remains in use to the end of the Mesolithic (Luho 1967; Siiriäinen 1981).

Figure 15 South-Finnish even-bladed adzes (NM 3875.1 – Kisko; NM 7347 – Lohja). Scale=1:2

South-Finnish even-bladed adzes. As indicated by its name this artifact group (*Fig. 15*) has a southern Finnish distribution. Mostly the adzes are of diabase, which is found associated with intrusive minerals in west Uusimaa. Traditionally the group has been dated to the end of the Mesolithic. Some South-Finnish even-bladed adzes have been found on Mesolithic sites in the Suomusjärvi region associated with slate points and at elevations corresponding to the Ancylus level. This could be taken to indicate that the chronological distribution is a broad one, but it is, however, more likely that they are from sites which were not in direct contact with the shoreline of the period. The majority of sites with

388

these artifacts are dated to the end of the Mesolithic.

Figure 16 Primitive axes (NM 3712.4, NM 4576.1 – Suomusjärvi). Scale=1:2

Primitive axes. The so-called primitive axes (*Fig. 16*) were in use throughout the Mesolithic. The earliest find is that associated with the well-dated Antrea net (9300–9200 BP) and axes have also been found on later sites. The primitive axe characterizes the Finnish Mesolithic; its more exact dating requires a more detailed typological classification, wherein the subdivisions may also have chronologicalal significance.

In the presented chronology the most critical problem is presented by the question of whether all of the sites were located on the shore of the ancient Baltic. Some of the sites chosen for *Fig. 1* are clustered near river outlets flowing from ancient inland lakes to the sea, as for example the sites at Askola. In these cases it may be presumed that settlement by river estuaries was at higher elevations than the sea.

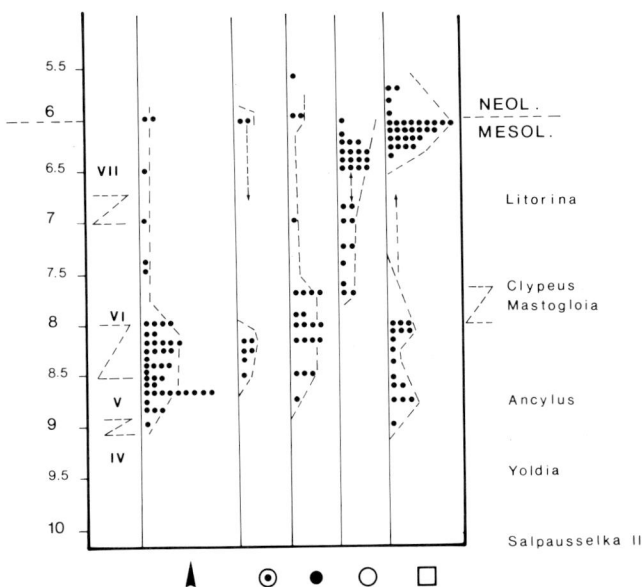

Figure 17 Chronological distribution of Mesolithic artifact forms in relation to the major phases in the development of the Baltic (see *Fig. 10* for key).

Fig. 17 presents artifact finds from sites in accordance with the radiocarbon-dated shoreline displacement chronology. Certain anomalies have been shifted in the direction of the main chronological groups. These came about mainly as a result of interpreting the stable shoreline displacement zones of the east Uusimaa region. *Fig. 17* shows the degree of precision available in sketching the chronology. The main chronological phases of the artifact forms are as follows: leaf-shaped slate points, *c.* 8800–8000 BP; coniform-holed globular mace-heads, *c.* 8500–8000 BP; curved-backed grooved adzes, *c.* 8500–7500 BP; oblique-bladed quartz points, *c.* 7700–6000 BP; South-Finnish even-bladed adzes, *c.* 6500–6000 BP.

The Finnish Mesolithic can thus be divided into two chronological phases, corresponding to the two major phases in the development of the Baltic. Also the artifact typology supports the biostratigraphic division. The chronological divisions are as follows:

Ancylus Mesolithic, 9300–8000 BP – characterized by leaf-shaped slate points and coniform-holed globular mace-heads.

Litorina Mesolithic, 8000–6000 BP – characterized by oblique-bladed quartz points and South-Finnish even-bladed adzes.

In addition to the Baltic, it is also possible to date the Mesolithic sites in the lake region of the Finnish interior. However, the above stratigraphic method cannot be applied and dating must be based on relative and distance diagrams of shoreline formations. The early Holocene development of the large lakes of the Finnish interior was one of transgression, which meant that sites were destroyed. It was only in the northern part of this area that rapid land uplift saved sites from destruction.

Note:

This paper is a summary of the author's unpublished Lic. phil. thesis (Matiskainen 1983).

APPENDIX: *Radiocarbon dates (years BP) relating to shoreline displacement curves I–VIII*

Curve I

Sippola Hangassuo, 47 m a.s.l. (Eronen 1976): (Hel-663) 9519±200; (Hel-662) 9530±200; (Hel-661) 9280±190; (Hel-660) 8870±170; (Hel-664) 8780±160; (Hel-665) 8360±190.
Porvoo Bastuberg, 28 m a.s.l. (Eronen 1974): (Hel-394) 8480±190; (Hel-393) 7960±180; (Hel-392) 7250±240; (Hel-391) 6230±220; (Hel-390) 5970±200.

Curve II

Askola Kopinkallionsuo, 58 m a.s.l. (Eronen and Haila 1982): (Su-1021) 8890±110; (Su-1022) 8870±120; (Su-1023) 8460±90.
Askola Huiskaissuo, 59 m a.s.l. (Eronen and Haila 1982): (Su-1024) 9370±110; (Su-1025) 8430±90.
Askola Aborreträsk, 39 m a.s.l. (Eronen and Haila 1982): (Ki-1840.01) 8690±130; (Ki-1840.02) 8700±110.
Askola Lamminjärvensuo, 32 m a.s.l. (Eronen and Haila 1982): (Ki-1839) 7600±110; (Su-1028) 7160±100; (Su-1029) 6910±100.
Porvoo Käärmejärvi, 29.5 m a.s.l. (Eronen and Haila 1982): (Ki-1841.01) 6770±90; (Ki-1841.02) 7090±75.

Porvoo Stormossen, 27.5 m a.s.l. (Eronen and Haila 1982): (Su-1026) 5300±100; (Su-1027) 4740±110.

Sipoo Bakunkärrträsk, 33 m a.s.l. (Hyvärinen 1979): (Hel-1131) 7250±120; (Hel-1130) 8010±120.

Curve III

Vantaa Marsupolku, 44 m a.s.l. (Eronen and Haila 1982): (Hel-1240) 8570±190; (Hel-1239) 8490±120.

Espoo Odinlampi, 34.9 m a.s.l. (Hyvärinen 1980): (Hel-1266) 8010±120; (Hel-1267) 7370±100; (Hel-1268) 6390±110.

Vantaa Lammaslampi, 31.8 m a.s.l. (Alhonen *et al.* 1978): (Hel-996) 7740±170; (Hel-997) 7470±160; (Hel-998) 7310±160; (Hel-999) 6550±170; (Hel-1000) 6160±160.

Kauniainen Gallträsk, 31 m a.s.l. (Alhonen 1972; Eronen 1974): (Hel-351) 7410±250; (Hel-350) 6180±230.

Curve IV

Karjalohja Lehmälampi, 71.2 m a.s.l. (Glückert and Ristaniemi 1980): (Su-885) 9710±150; (Su-886) 9060±160.

Kisko Leilänlampi, 42 m a.s.l. (Eronen 1974): (Hel-287) 6620±170; (Hel-395) 7780±230.

Tenhola Träskmossen, 41 m a.s.l. (Eronen 1974): (Hel-669) 6260±200.

Curve V

Halikko Hiitteenmäensuo, 88.9 m a.s.l. (Glückert 1976): (Hel-767) 8620±190.

Paimio Meltolansuo, 67 m a.s.l. (Glückert 1976): (Hel-730) 8110±170.

Salo Santamäensuo, 57.5 m a.s.l.: (Hel-1455) 7960±130.

Dragsfjaärd, Sandbrinksmossen, 47 m a.s.l. (Glückert 1976): (Hel-726) 7150±170.

Kemiö Slätmossen, 38 m a.s.l. (Glückert 1976): (Hel-658) 5490±180.

Curve VI

Vahto, Neittesuo, 58 m a.s.l. (Glückert 1976): (Hel-727) 7100±140.

Turku Isosuo, 40 m a.s.l. (Glückert 1976): (Hel-564) 4950±140.

Curve VII

Yläne, Iso-Vuohensuo, 58 m a.s.l. (Glückert 1976): (Hel-652) 8050±250.

Yläne Muurassuo, 67 m a.s.l. (Glückert 1976): (Hel-729) 7450±230.

Eura Vähäjärvi, 61.5 m a.s.l. (Eronen 1974): (Hel-385) 8070±250; (Hel-384) 7360±170; (Hel-383) 6960±170.

Laitila, Sammalsuo, 47 m a.s.l. (Glückert 1976): (Hel-647) 5030±200.

Eura Pyhäjärvi, 47 m a.s.l. (Eronen, Heikkinen and Tikkanen 1982): (Hel-1391) 7420±120; (Hel-1392) 5630±120; (Hel-1393) 5580±120.

Curve VIII

Kauhajoki Juurakkojärvi, 167 m a.s.l. (Salomaa 1982): (Hel-1293) 8920±180; (Hel-1294) 9070±190.

Kauhajoki Kauhajärvi, 143.9 m a.s.l. (Salomaa 1982): (Hel-1291) 7960±170; (Hel-1294) 9070±190.

Isojoki Haukilampi, 107 m a.s.l. (Salomaa 1982): (Hel-1171) 8230±160.

Isojoki Kodesjärvi, 94.1 m a.s.l. (Salomaa 1982): (Hel-1175) 8010±160.

Siikainen Haapajärvi, 80.6 m a.s.l. (Salomaa 1982: (Hel-1366) 6410±150; (Hel-1367) 6760±150.

Kuortane Porraslampi, 90 m a.s.l. (Eronen 1974): (Hel-450) 7750±260.

References

ALHONEN, P. (1972) Gallträsket: the geological development and paleolimnology of a small polluted lake in southern Finland. *Commentationes Biologicae Societas Scientiarum Fennica*, 57: 1–34.

ALHONEN, P., ERONEN, M., NUNEZ, M., SALOMAA, R. and UUUSINOKA, R. (1978) A contribution to Holocene shore displacement and environmental development in Vantaa, south Finland: the stratigraphy of Lake Lammaslampi. *Bulletin of the Geological Society of Finland*, 50: 69–79.

ÄYRÄPÄÄ, A. (1950) Die ältesten steinzeitlichen Funde aus Finnland. *Acta Archaeologica*, 21: 1–43.

ERONEN, M. (1974) The history of the Litorina Sea and the associated Holocene events. *Commentationes Physico-Mathematicae Societas Scientiarum Fennica*, 44: 79–195.

ERONEN, M. (1976) A radiocarbon-dated Ancylus transgression site in south eastern Finland. *Boreas*, 5: 65–76

ERONEN, M., HAILA, H. and MATISKAINEN, H. (1982) Holocene shoreline displacement in southern Finland. *Abstracts, XI INQUA Congress, Moscow 1982*.

ERONEN, M. and HAILA, H. (1982) Shoreline displacement near Helsinki, southern Finland during the Ancylus Lake stage. *Annales Academiae Scientiarum Fennicae* AIII, 134: 111–129.

ERONEN, M., HEIKKINEN, O. and TIKKANEN, M. (1982) Holocene development and present hydrology of Lake Pyhäjärvi in Satakunta, southwestern Finland. *Fennia*, 160(2): 195–223.

GLÜCKERT, G. (1976) Postglacial shore level displacement of the Baltic in S.W. Finland. *Annales Academiae Scientiarum Fennicae* A III, 118: 1–92

GLÜCKERT, G. and RISTANIEMI, O. (1980) Ancylustransgressio Karjalohjalla toisella Salpausselällä. *Publications of the Department of Quaternary Geology University of Turku*, 41: 1–22.

HYVÄRINEN, H. (1979) Helsingin seudun rannansiirtyminen Litorina-aikana Sipoossa tutkitun näytesarjan valossa. *Terra*, 91(1): 15–20.

HYVÄRINEN, H. (1980) Relative sea-level changes near Helsinki, southern Finland during early Litorina times. *Bulletin of the Geological Society of Finland*, 52(2): 207–219.

HYVÄRINEN, H. and ERONEN, M. (1979) The Quaternary history of the Baltic. Northern part. In V. Gudelis and L-K. Königsson (eds) *The Quaternary History of the Baltic*. Uppsala, Acta Universitatis Uppsalaensis Symposium Universitas Uppsala Annum Quinguentesimum Celebrantis, 1: 7–27.

KIVINIEMI, A. (1980) Some results concerning crustal movements in Finland. *Tectonophysics*, 71: 67–71.

LUHO, V. (1956) Die Askola-Kultur. Die frühmesolitische Steinzeit in Finnland. *Suomen muinaismuistoyhdistyksen aikakauskirja*, 57: 1–227.

LUHO, V. (1956) Die Askola-Kultur. Die frühmesolithische Steinzeit in Finnland. *Suomen muinaismuistoyhdistyksen aikakauskirja*, 57: 1–227.

MATISKAINEN, H. (1979) Paijanteen arkeologinen rannansiirtymiskronologia. Lahden Museo- ja Taidelautakunta. *Tutkimuksia*, 16: 1–33.

MATISKAINEN, H. (1983) *Suomen mesoliittisen kivikauden sisäinen kronologia ^{14}C – ajoitukseen tukeutuvan Itämeren kehityshistorian perusteella*. Unpublished Lic. phil. thesis, University of Helsinki, Department of Archaeology.

NUNEZ, M. (1978a) A model to date Stone Age sites within an area of abnormal uplift in southern Finland. *ISKOS*, 2: 25–51.

NUNEZ, M. (1978b) On the date of the early Mesolithic settlement of Finland. *Suomen Museo*, 1977: 5–13.

SALOMAA, R. (1982) Post-glacial shoreline displacement in the Lauhanvuori area, western Finland. *Annales Academiae Scientiarum Fennicae* A III, 134: 81–97.

SIIRIÄINEN, A. (1969) Uber die Chronologie der steinzeitlichen Kustenwohnplätze Finnlands im Lichte der Uferverschiebung. *Suomen Museo*, 1969: 40–75.

SIIRIÄINEN, A. (1973) Studies relating to shore displacement and Stone Age chronology in Finland. *Finskt Museum*, 1973: 5–22.

SIIRIÄINEN, A. (1981) Problems of the east Fennoscandian Mesolithic. *Finskt Museum*, 1977: 5–31.

Some Mesolithic Wooden Artifacts from the Site of Vis I in the European North East of the U.S.S.R.

Grigoriy M. Burov

Abstract

The author has devised a method of locating ancient wooden objects and structures in peat bogs formed by the infilled ox-bow lakes of meandering rivers. Archaeological sites of different periods have been discovered with the help of this method, the Mesolithic settlement of Vis I (8300–7000 BP) among them. Notable among the wooden artifacts recovered from this site were two types of skis and a series of small bows used for boring or for making fire. Examples of Mesolithic art (sculpture, relief and engraved ornaments) are found on these skis and bows.

INTRODUCTION

The comparatively small number of ancient wooden objects known throughout the world were found either in conditions of constant dryness (Carter and Mace 1927), in natural (Raushenbakh 1969) or tumulus (Rudenko 1953) permafrost, or in salt-affected soils (Ebert 1924). Mainly, however, they occur in regions of excessive dampness, usually in settlements situated in hollows, often in peat bogs. Such settlements rarely leave surface traces and are often discovered not by archaeologists but by peat workers. This was the case with the peat-bog sites of Shigir (Dmitriev 1951) and Gorbunovo (Eding 1929, 1940a, 1940b) in the Transurals, Sarnate in Latvia (Vankina 1970), and a site in the floodplain of the River Kuznechikha (Smirnov 1941) in the European north east of the U.S.S.R. Many ancient sledge runners and skis have also been found accidentally in bogs and lake deposits in Finland, Sweden and Norway (Itkonen 1930, 1931–1932, 1934, 1936, 1938, 1941, 1946, 1949; Burov 1981b).

It is only on rare occasions that waterlogged archaeological sites are discovered in the course of deliberate prospecting, usually when the site is disturbed as a result of natural erosion by the water of a lake, sea, river, or stream. Thus, falling water levels have revealed pile dwellings in lakes in Switzerland (Mongayt 1973) and on the Modlona river in the Onega region (Bryusov 1951; Oshibkina 1978), and settlements on the north-west coast of North America (Croes 1976). In cases when artifacts are not entirely buried in bottom deposits (as in Lake Constance), they may be discovered during underwater prospecting (Reinerth 1960). A slight rise at the peat-bog site of Nizhneye Veretye in the region of Lake Onega (Foss 1952) led A.Ya. Bryusov (1963) to the conclusion that similar features might indicate peat-bog settlements where wooden artifacts could be found. However, this hypothesis has not yet been confirmed by fieldwork. Of some interest are sites on slightly higher ground with cultural layers extending down into waterlogged hollows. In such conditions wooden and other perishable artifacts are often preserved (Croes 1976), but sites of this kind are very rare. In burials, as a rule, wooden artifacts are poorly preserved.

Prospecting for wooden artifacts yields good results in areas where there are many easily accessible settlements on isolated hillocks and terraces (Burov 1964, 1969, 1974a, 1974b). Such settlements usually include those associated with infilled ox-bow lakes which have become, or are in process of becoming, peat bogs. It is well known that ancient man preferred to settle along rivers. Thus, when abandoned meanders ('cut-offs') gradually became infilled and converted into bogs, organic objects inevitably found their way into these back-swamps where they remained intact owing to the preservative properties of water and peat.

The location of ox-bow peat bogs is not difficult in most cases owing to the fact that they usually occur in river floodplains. Outcrops of ox-bow deposits rising at least partially above the water level can often be observed in river cliffs. In the absence of such outcrops, prospecting along small and medium-sized rivers with ox-bow meanders is simpler than on large ones with ox-bow lakes of another genetic type, known as 'channels' (Baranovskaya 1937). A bow-shaped terrace edge can point to the presence of an ox-bow peat bog (Shchukin 1960). Hence, such peat bogs can be discovered and delimited by digging or augering along the bow-shaped edge.

When wooden objects find their way to the bottom of an ox-bow, they are preserved in the sapropel and, subsequently, by the peat of the bow-shaped bog that eventually forms. Some objects may sink before a meander is cut off, but occasionally they are not carried away by the current. It goes without saying that many of the piles and posts of fish weirs driven into the bottom will remain there. The accumulation of wooden objects is interrupted by mineral overburden which, with the passage of time, covers the peat bog.

From what has been said above, it follows that the 'archaeological stage' in the history of the ox-bow hollow, during which the cultural layer is formed, is limited. If people settled on the terrace after the peat bog was covered by mineral overburden, or if a settlement had ceased to exist before the river migrated into its vicinity, there will be no cultural layers in the ox-bow deposits. Success is more likely if a settlement is explored which existed intermittently over a long period. The duration of occupation is also of great importance; people who left only a few flints and sherds of pottery would hardly have left enough wooden objects to be found in the course of exploratory excavations.

Peat bogs with potentially a lot of manufactured wooden objects which are situated near lake outflows are, from a practical point of view, most suitable for archaeological prospecting – flooding is not a major problem, there is practically no alluvium, and there is no overburden to hamper access to the ancient ox-bow deposits.

THE VIS SITES

An ideal place for archaeological excavations is the region of Lake Sindor in the Vychegda basin. Exploratory excavations were started in 1960 and continued in 1962 (Burov 1967). They revealed two horseshoe-shaped, ox-bow peat bogs relating to the Simva and Vis rivers (the latter is an outlet of Lake Sindor), in which many wooden artifacts have been found. These peat bogs are located at the bow-shaped edges of the higher ground on which two multi-period settlements, Vis I and II, existed for a long time (*Fig. 1*, sites 15, 16). The peat bogs are 16–20 m wide; the length of the first is 150 m and of the second 250 m; the maximum depths are 1.6 m and more than 3.3 m, respectively.

In the peat bog adjacent to the site of Vis I, 168 organic (wooden, bark, sedge) objects and 39 pieces of wood with traces of working were found in 1960–67. These finds date back to the period 8300–7000 BP. Five radiocarbon dates for the bog were obtained: 8080±90 BP (LE-776), 7820±80 BP (RUL-616), 7150±60 BP (LE-684), 7090±80 BP (LE-685) and 7090±70 BP (LE-713) (Burov *et al.* 1972). The dates were obtained on wooden artifacts and pieces of

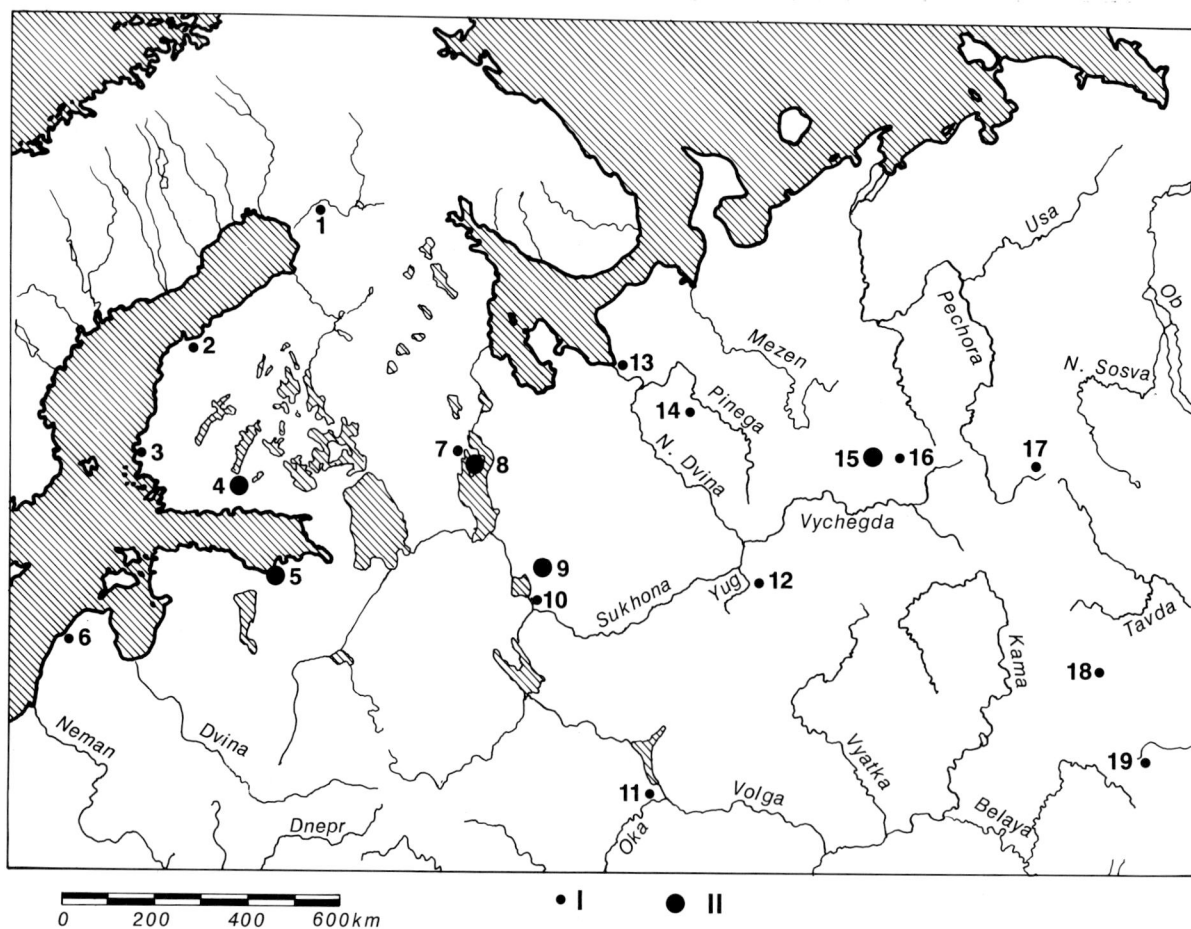

Figure 1 Map showing sites mentioned in the text. *Key*: I – sites of the Neolithic, Bronze and Iron Ages; II – Mesolithic sites; 1 – Rovaniemi; 2 – Alahärmä; 3 – Noormarkku; 4 – Heinola; 5 – Tõrvala; 6 – Sarnate; 7 – Padozero; 8 – Oleniy Ostrov; 9 – Nizhneye Veretye; 10 – Modlona; 11 – Seyma; 12 – Marmugino; 13 – Kuznechikha; 14 – Yavron'ga; 15, 16 – Vis I, II; 17 – Kanin cave; 18 – Gorbunovo peat bog; 19 – Shigir peat bog.

wood with traces of working – in one case (RUL-616) the dated sample was a log found at a level below a sledge runner, but above a bow.

In the middle layers of peat bog II (Vis II) weirs made of stakes and horizontal rods were discovered in 1962–66, together with a large quantity of ceramics of the Vanvizdino culture (AD 400–600), hundreds of wooden and birch bark objects, and bone and glass artifacts.

In 1968, along the bow-shaped edge of the hillock on which the site of Yavron'ga I (in the Pinega basin) is situated, the present author found an ox-bow peat bog containing remains of fish weirs and a fragment of a simple bow dating from the Iron Age (Burov 1974a). In 1966 an infilled ox-bow lake at the village of Marmugino on the Yug river (a tributary of the Northern Dvina) revealed Neolithic fish traps made of wooden laths. Radiocarbon determinations indicated a date of c. 5000–4500 BP (Burov 1969; Burov et al. 1972).

WOODEN ARTIFACTS FROM VIS I

Since organic artifacts are extremely rare in sites dating back to the period 9000–7000 BP anywhere in the world, the extensive collection from Vis I assumes considerable significance. It includes, among other objects, a variety of sledge runners and skis, bows for hunting and other purposes, arrows and spears, throwing-sticks, hoops of landing-nets or fish traps, a wooden disc from an implement for frightening fish (botalo), an oar, an arched scraper, and a series of stakes. Also found were a fragment of a fishing basket or mat, a net made of sedge fibre, a pine bark float and a birch bark vessel (Burov 1964, 1966a, 1966b, 1967, 1968, 1973a, 1973b, 1981a, 1981c).

This paper will consider just two of the categories of wooden objects from Vis I – the skis and the small bows.

Skis

One group of artifacts made of hardwood is represented by a series of end fragments (Fig. 2, no. 1; Fig. 3). When whole, these appear to have tapered gradually, with a projection resembling the prow of a ship at one end. The end was noticeably turned up, a result of its having been cut out of a massive log divided into two. The flat lower surface, corresponding to the flat face of the split log, became convex as it tapered. There was a slight projecting rim, or flange, along both edges on the upper surface; while the upturned projection at the front end was triangular in section. There were no holes in these artifacts. The largest fragment (which measures 45 cm in length) comes from an object more than 15 cm wide, and the end is turned up more than 14 cm (Fig. 2, no. 1). Three of the fragments are ornamented;

the edges and underside of the upturned end are covered with notches, while the upper surface is engraved with zig-zags.

It is evident that these are fragments of winter means of transportation. The absence of holes in the fore-part, the symmetry of the artifacts, and the flat lower surface allow them to be interpreted as skis, rather than as sledge runners. The sharply upturned end of the Vis I objects is reminiscent of east Siberian Yakut skis, known from a seventeenth century print reproduced in a book by N. Witsen (Antropova 1953: fig. 1), which some authors have considered to be unbelievable. The Vis I artifacts have no archaeological analogues. In some respects, however, they resemble the Heinola-type hardwood sledge runners (examples of which have been found at Heinola, Finland, and at Vis I) which are arched in profile, with a sharply curved fore-part, a projecting rim along one edge, and holes through the ends for fastening them together in pairs using straps (Burov 1981c: fig. 4).

There is also an unusually finely-made object in the collection (Fig. 2, no. 2; Fig. 2a) which differs greatly from the Vis-type skis described above, but possesses some features in common with runners of the Vis type which resemble those of toboggans used by Canadian indians (Burov 1981c: fig. 5). In both cases softwood was used; the lower surface is flat; the fore-part is not sharpened, but is turned up and has a pair of small holes (0.2–0.3 cm in diameter) bored from both surfaces. On the lower surface there is also a carved projection bevelled backwards. Almost the whole of the lower surface is covered with marks left by a shaving instrument (arched scraper or 'spokeshave') fitted with worn microliths[1] – this has been proved experimentally.

There are a number of differences between this object and skis of the Vis type: the absence of a rim along the edges; the presence of a ridge in the form of a wave pattern 0.6 cm high along the middle of the upper surface, which adds to the strength of the object; and the presence of a projection in the form of an elk's head. The crown and ears of this sculpture are placed in a specially-made hollow in the front end, while the neck is represented by a protruberance, extending from which is the wavy ridge. The absence of lateral flanges, the width (which is not less than 12.5 cm), and the wavy ridge testify to the fact that this object served as a ski and not as a sledge runner. Moreover, indisputable runners of the same style (Vis-type runners) were also found in the peat bog.

The pair of holes was probably used for attaching a belt when going downhill. As an Arabian traveller, Abu-Hamid, wrote in the twelfth century about the skis of the northern Urals and the region beyond the Ural mountains:

Both small planks, which are put on the feet, are bound together with a long belt looking like a horse's bridle which is held in the left hand (Mongayt 1965: 35–36).

The carved elk's head projection, which was bevelled backwards, also had a practical use. Being lower than the gliding surface of the ski, it would have prevented the reverse movement of the ski over packed snow. It would also have served as a stabilizer preventing the lateral displacement of the ski end. In recent times (nineteenth and twentieth centuries AD), Siberian and certain other peoples covered the lower ski surface with fur and edged their skis with flat strips of wood (*nashchep*) for the same purpose (Antropova 1953). The effectiveness of these devices has been proved by experiments.

At the same time, the sculpture of the elk's head probably symbolized rapid movement. In this res-

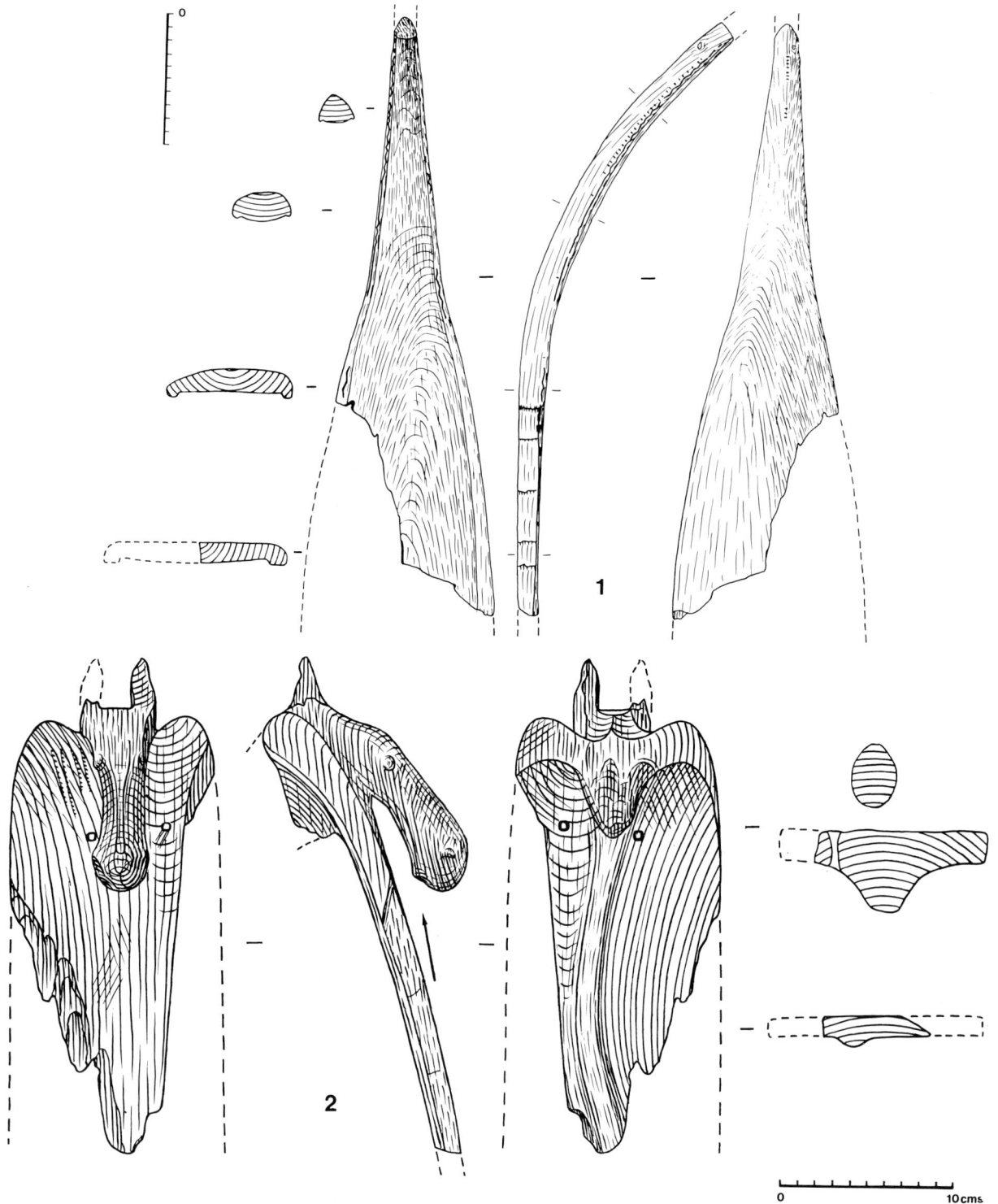

Figure 2 Vis I: Vis- (no. 168) and Veretye-type (no. 17) skis.

Figure 2a Veretye-type ski (no. 17) from Vis I.

pect, the Vis find may be compared with the late Neolithic runner from Noormarkku in Finland which is crowned by a sculpture of an elk's head (Salo 1967), and to ancient ships with prows in the form of a bird's head. It may be supposed that the people believed that these sculptures made skiing easier.

The brake in the form of an elk's head on this second type of Vis ski is a masterpiece of Mesolithic applied wooden sculpture. The ears and muzzle are reproduced very realistically, with bulges corresponding to the eyes and the lower lip. The surface of the head has been smoothed with an indented shaving instrument. The lower surface of the ski is covered with marks of longitudinal shaving, and the upper surface has wavy shave marks along the central ridge. Antler sculptures of the elk from the Mesolithic burial site of Oleniy Ostrov (Gurina

1956: figs. 113, 114, 118, 131) are similar to the Vis I sculpture. There are also parallels among the plastic art of later times, mainly of the Neolithic and Bronze Age. Four wooden artifacts from sites in the area beyond the Ural mountains and from Finland are of particular interest – namely, the sculpture of the she-elk from the Gorbunovo peat bog (Raushenbakh 1956: fig. 3; Moshinskaya 1976: fig. 14), a carved bucket with a handle in the form of an elk's head from the Shigir peat bog (Moshinskaya 1976: plate 13), the runner with an elk's head sculpture on the front end from Noormarkku (similar to that from Vis I), and the sculpture of an elk's head from Rovaniemi (Erä-Esko 1958; Hyypää 1958). The Shigir bucket is undated, but the other objects are dated to the Neolithic. In addition, an antler sculpture of an elk from the Shigir peat bog (Moshinskaya 1976: fig. 10) which has parallels in Finland (Ailio and Hackman 1911: 118, fig. 21), a stone head from the Modlona site (Oshibkina 1978: plate 51), a shaft-hole axe with the butt in the shape of an elk's head from Padozero in Karelia (Aspelin 1877: no. 72), and a bronze dagger with a pommel shaped like an elk's head from the Seyma burial ground in the Volga–Oka region (Bader 1970: fig. 50) are all analogous to the Vis I sculpture.

Almost all of the sculptures mentioned above are similar to the Vis I sculpture in the form of the muzzle. Exceptions are the carved butt of the Padozero axe and the head from burial no. 153 at Oleniy Ostrov, although the latter is similar to the Vis I sculpture in the form of the ears. Sculptures which have eyes without hollows to represent pupils are particularly close to the Vis I sculpture – specifically, the carved protruberance of the Noormarkku runner, the shaft of the Shigir bucket, and the pommel of the Seyma dagger.

The Seyma dagger provides a clue to the significance of the wavy ridge decorating the upper surface of the Vis I ski. In the Mesolithic antler and bone plastic art of north-eastern Europe (Oleniy Ostrov, Tõrvala) only the images of man, elk and snake occur (Gurina 1956, 1961). This fact allows us to regard the wavy ridge as a relief image of a reptile. The cult of the snake was preserved throughout the Neolithic – finds at sites in the eastern Baltic region (Loze 1973; Vankina *et al.* 1973) and in the Gorbunovo peat bog (Raushenbakh 1956) testify to this. Daggers of the Seyma type (Bader 1970: fig. 50; Chernykh 1970: 164, fig. 59), dated to 1500–1200 BC, bear images of the snake; moreover, on the hilt of the Seyma site dagger, as well as on the ski from Vis I, the snake stretches from the head of an elk. Thus, these subjects are probably linked with a cult involving the elk and reptiles which lasted for thousands of years. A special variant of this may have been preserved up to the second millennium

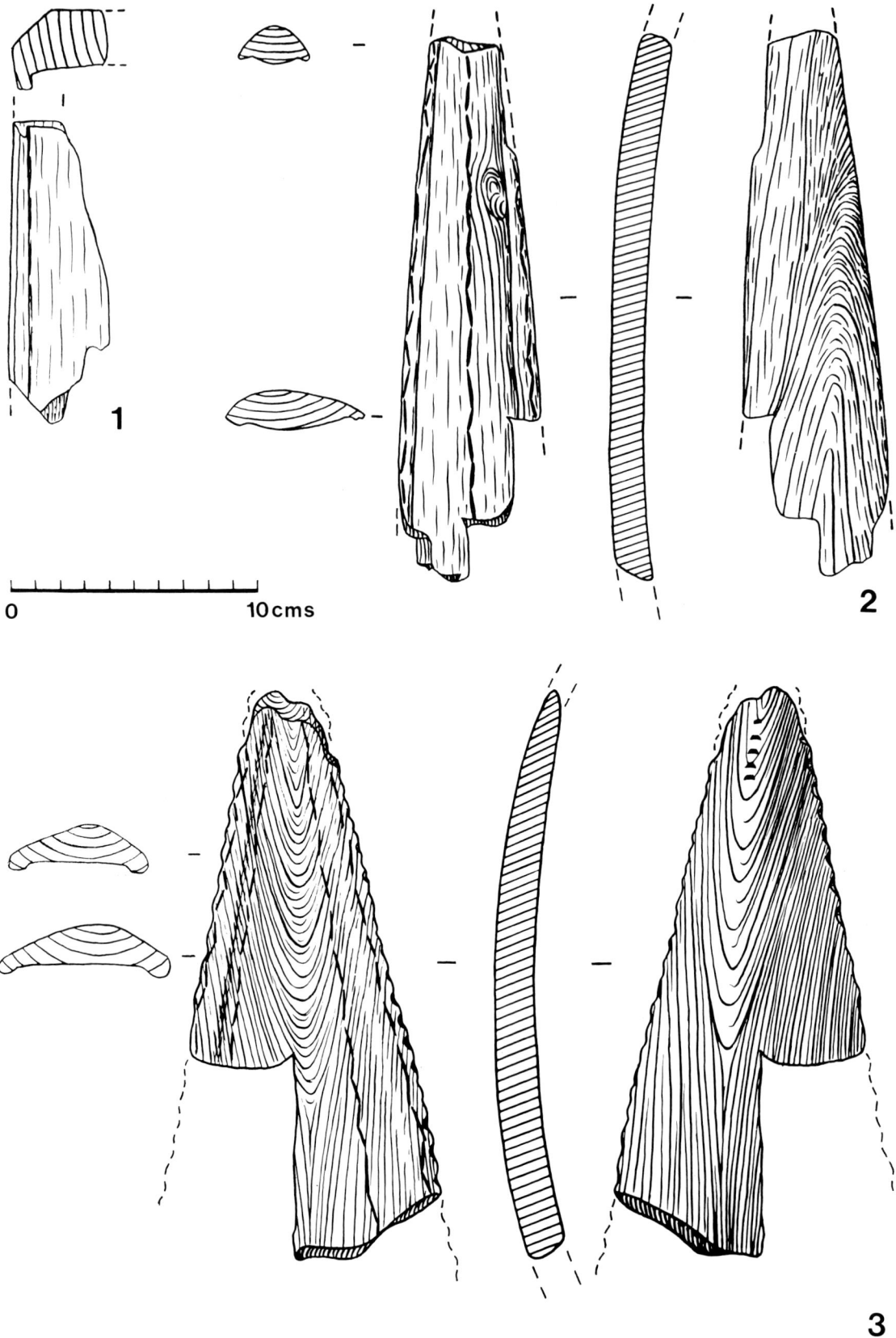

Figure 3   Vis I: Vis-type skis: 1 – no. 51; 2 – no. 116; 3 – no. 52 (nos. 51 & 52, on the basis of their relative stratigraphic positions, could belong to the same object).

BP on bronze cult plaques picturing a man–elk on a pangolin (Spitsyn 1906).

The evolution of elk-head images from the Mesolithic (Oleniy Ostrov) to the Middle Ages was noted by B.A. Rybakov (1976: 63). On the plaques of the Perm 'animal' style (Urals region, AD 570–800) they form part of compositions or serve as an addition to the heads of anthropomorphic figures, while in the Kanin cave on the upper reaches of the River Pechora in the European north east a bronze plaque with an elk head (of Iron Age date) was found, its eyes shown as engraved protruberances (Kanivets 1964: fig. 31).

The second type of Vis I ski has an indisputable analogue at the Mesolithic site of Nizhneye Veretye (*Fig. 4*; State Historical Museum registration no. 76792). This artifact was recovered in excavations in 1933 but, being a small fragment, was not recognized for what it was by the excavator, M.E. Foss, and was never described. It is only the comparison provided by the Vis I ski which allows us to determine the function of this rare object and to reconstruct it to a certain degree. Both the Veretye ski and the Vis I ski were made of softwood and had a raised-up forepart with a pair of bored holes and a carved brake. The brake, apparently, had the shape of an animal's head but, judging by the outlines of the muzzle, it was the sculpture of a bear rather than an elk. In this connection, it is worth mentioning the Neolithic runner from Alahärmä in Finland, the fore-part of which is finished with a carved bear head (Kopisto 1964: fig. 1; Carpelan 1974: 66–68). The other differences are that the carved projection is not bevelled backwards, but has a steep rear part, and there is no wavy ridge on the upper surface, which is smoothly convex.

Stratigraphic observations indicate that, given the similarity in style, the skis of the first (Vis) type and the runner of the first (Heinola) type are more ancient than skis of the second (Veretye) type and runners of the second (Vis) type.

Small bows

A special category of tools from Vis I is formed by objects of more or less curved profile with almond-shaped terminals on both ends. These terminals are directed inwards at an obtuse angle, as is the case with the hunting bow of the Vis type (Burov 1981a), in contrast to an arched scraper haft where they are directed outwards (Burov 1973b: fig. 5).

The outer surface corresponds to the bark-less surface of a wooden trunk or branch. The object widens and thickens gradually towards the middle. The section is pointed-oval, triangular or segment-shaped (*Table 1*). In all cases softwood was used, and in at least half of the cases (*Fig. 5*, no. 2; *Fig. 5a*; *Fig. 6*, nos. 1, 2) this is white spruce.

These artifacts can be divided into two groups according to their size. The first group includes two

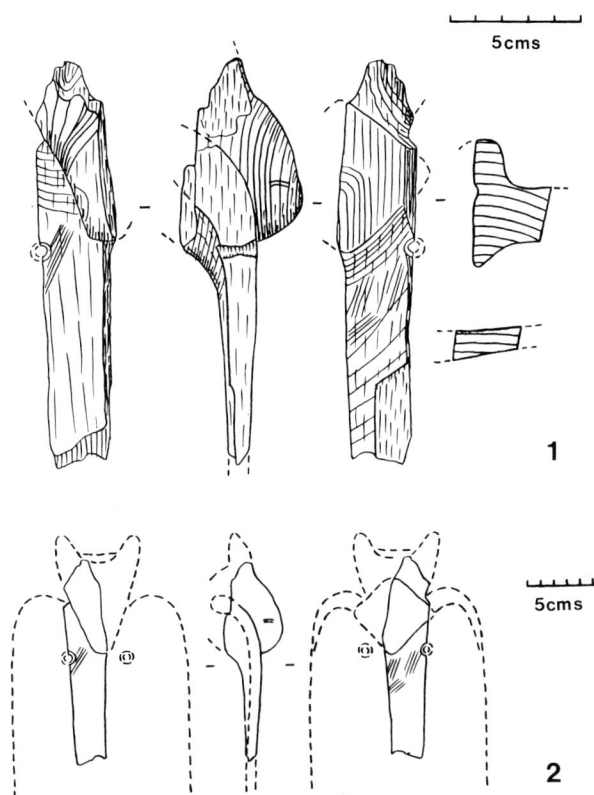

5cms

Figure 4   Ski of Veretye type from Nizhneye Veretye: 1 – fragment of fore-part; 2 – its reconstruction.

Table 1:   Characteristics of the small bows from Vis I – width (W) and thickness (Th) measurements in centimetres

No.	Fig.	Length (cm)	Middle part		Ends before carved terminals		Section	Presence of Ornament
			W	Th	W	Th		
74	5.1	c. 56	4.6–5.2	2.0–2.1	5.0	2.2	pointed-oval	–
95	5.2	54.2	4.2	1.1	2.3	1.4	triangular	–
128	6.1	c. 26	2.1	1.4	1.7	1.1	pointed-oval	+
189	5.3	–	>1.9	>1.2	1.5	1.0	triangular	?
92a	6.2	c. 27	1.9	1.8	1.4	1.1	pointed-oval	+
184	6.3	c. 27	1.8	0.5	0.6	0.4	segment-shaped	+

Note: 74 – crudely made, but has an arc-shaped profile indicating its use; 95 – complete; all the others are broken

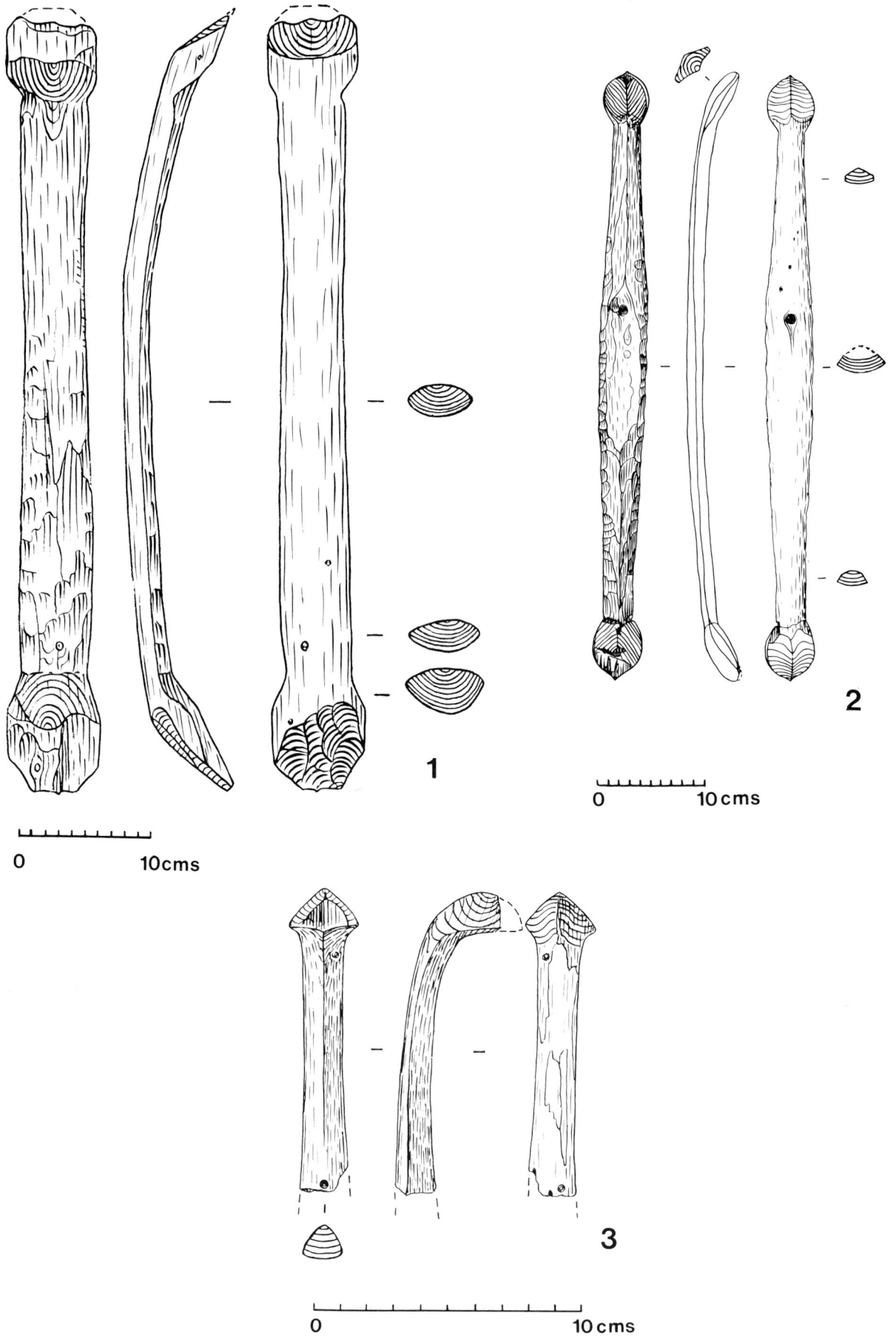

Figure 5   Small bows from Vis I: 1 – no. 74; 2 – no. 95; 3 – no. 189.

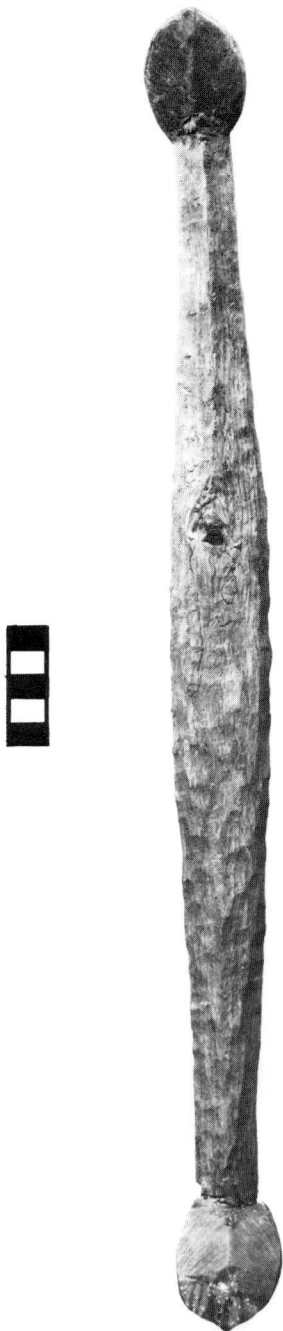

Figure 5a Small bow (no. 95) from Vis I

especially to those which have no holes for the string, should be taken into consideration. The similarity lies in the location of the carved terminals, in the arc-shaped profile, in the use of the external part of coniferous trees, and in the character of the section intended for bowing. The differences are in the symmetry of these artifacts (almond-shaped terminals on both ends), their shortened proportions, their small size, and the absence of hollows for engaging arrows.

These artifacts with two carved terminals can be compared, therefore, with small bows from archaeological sites of a number of regions and periods. Primitive small bows were discovered at the site of Modlona (Bryusov 1951: 39) and in the Gorbunovo peat bog (Eding 1929: 9). Small, rather elaborate copies of bows (23–43.5 cm in length) were found in Switzerland at Fenil near Bern (Adler 1915: 182, fig. 5) and on Saint Lawrence Island in Alaska (Collins 1937: plate 59).

Small bows could have had a number of uses. Some authors (Bryusov 1951; Okladnikov and Beregovaya 1971) have interpreted them as equipment for boring or as tools for making fire, while others (Eding 1929; Collins 1937) have considered them to be children's toys. Adler (1915) believes that small bows were toys, handles of vessels, or arcs of traps. The small bows from Vis I, which differ greatly from true bows, cannot be considered as models for them. The suggestion that they were children's toys seems unacceptable because their shortened proportions and the broadening of the middle part (*Fig. 5*, no. 2; *Fig. 5a*) make them unsuitable for shooting. This feature links the small bows to one of the types of large bows (type III) from Vis I, which is distinguished by its very large size and the fact that it is made of hardwood (Burov 1981a: fig. 6, no. 1); yet this object could hardly have served for hunting purposes. The form of its ends remains unknown. The elaborate finishing makes it unlikely that the small bows were parts of traps. The possibility that they were handles of birch bark boxes must not be excluded, however, although the birch bark box from the site has no trace of a handle.

Thus, the conclusion has to be drawn that the tools with two carved terminals were used in the same manner as ancient Egyptian small bows – for boring (Childe 1958) or for making fire (Harrison 1958). In order to test this hypothesis, an experimental copy of the Vis small bow was made of pine wood. It proved to be quite suitable for boring, even if it was slightly bowed (since this action requires the string to be well drawn). It is not difficult to fasten the string to the bow. As the cross-section thickens rather abruptly towards the middle part, it is sufficient to wind the string two or three times round the neck of the bow to fix it firmly. In the course of

specimens about 55 cm long, their maximum width being 5 cm (*Fig. 5*, no. 1). The second group (*Fig. 5*, no. 3; *Fig. 6*) consists of four tools, which are half the length of the artifacts in the first group (three objects are *c.* 26–27 cm in length) and much narrower (1.8–2.1 cm in width). The artifacts of the first group have facets on the inner face made by a cutting or hacking instrument. All the smaller artifacts have a carefully finished surface, and on top of that, in at least three cases, there is an engraved decoration.

With regard to the function of these objects, their similarity to the hunting bows of Vis type, and

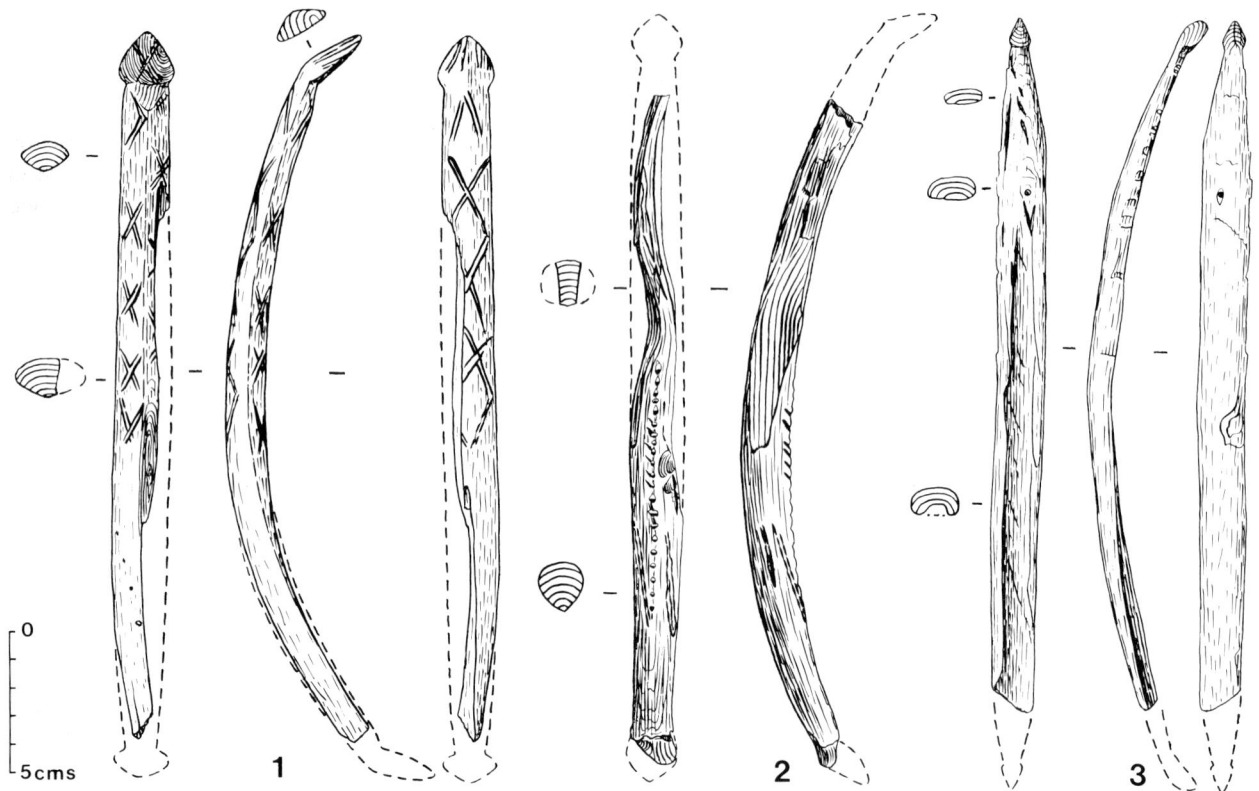

Figure 6 Small bows from Vis I: 1 – no. 128; 2 – no. 92a; 3 – no. 184.

use the bow probably acquired residual strain and the string had to be tightened from time to time. When a wooden pivot is put in the loop for rotation, the string may be pulled up excessively and the bow can be broken. Naturally, irregular width and thickness and careless surface preparation make this more likely. Furthermore, it has been proved experimentally that almond-shaped terminals not only fix the string firmly, but also make it easier to use the bow. For this reason, arched scraper hafts also possess such terminals.

It is quite possible that the Vis bow-borers were used for work on antler and bone. An antler pick and a bone device for straightening spear shafts from the site of Nizhneye Veretye have large holes bored through them (Foss 1952: figs. 20, 26). Moreover, bows for making fire were, apparently, used in the Mesolithic. It may be supposed, therefore, that larger bows were used for boring, while smaller ones were used for making fire. Fungi of the Polyporaceae family (bracket fungus) found in the Vis I peat bog recall similar finds at the Mesolithic site of Hohen Viecheln in Mecklenberg; in the opinions of Schuldt (1961) and Gramsch (1973), this form of tinder was used for keeping, rather than striking, fire which could be made with the help of small bows.

Two other finds from Vis I deserve mention. An arched *Juniperus* switch (25 cm in length) with a cut at the thicker end is believed to be a small bow. A pine artifact in the form of a 'shovel' with traces of shaving on one side and made, apparently, from a

Vis-type runner (Burov 1973*b*: fig. 5) is similar in form to the bows. This object was evidently unfinished. The fragment found by archaeologists is more than 70 cm long, and the 'blade' is 5.7 cm wide and 1.1–1.2 cm thick. The small size of the 'blade' and the gradual widening of the 'handle' away from the 'blade' make it possible to think of this object as an unfinished and broken hunting or boring bow with one or two almond-shaped terminals.

Note:

1. Bladelets with a jagged (indented) edge resulting from use.

References

ADLER, B. (1915) Die Bogen der Schweizer Pfahlbauten. *Anzeiger für schweizerische Altertumskunde*, 17(3): 177–191.

AILIO, J. and HACKMAN, A. (1911) Trouvailles préhistorique. *Suomen muinaismuistoyhdistyksen aikakauskirja*, 25: 1–97.

ANTROPOVA, V.V. (1953) Lyzhi narodov Sibiri. *Sbornik Muzeya antropologii i etnografii*, 14: 5–36.

ASPELIN, J.R. (1877) *Antiquités du Nord Finno-Ougrien*, vol. 1. Helsingfors, Edlund – St Petersburg, Eggers.

BADER, O.N. (1970) *Basseyn Oki v epokhu bronzy*. Moscow, Nauka.

BARANOVSKAYA, Z.N. (1937) O geneticheskikh tipakh rechnykh starits. *Zemlevedenie*, 39(2): 116–121.

BRYUSOV, A.YA. (1951) Svaynoe poselenie na r. Modlone i drugie stoyanki v Charozerskom rayone Vologodskoy oblasti. *Materialy i issledovaniya po arkheologii SSSR*, 20: 7–76.

BRYUSOV, A.YA. (1963) *Metody raskopok torfyanikovykh stoyanok*. Moscow, Izdatel'stvo Akademii nauk SSSR.

BUROV, G.M. (1964) Torfyaniki rechnykh starits kak mesta arkheologicheskikh nakhodok. *Izvestiya Komi filiala Vsesoyuznogo geograficheskogo obshchestva*, 9: 99–103.

BUROV, G.M. (1966*a*) Arkeologicheskie nakhodki v starichnykh torfyanikakh basseyna Vychegdy. *Sovetskaya arkheologiya*, 1: 155–173.

BUROV, G.M. (1966b) Naydeno v vychegodskikh torfyanikakh. *Priroda*, 9: 74–79.

BUROV, G.M. (1967) *Drevniy Sindor*. Moscow, Nauka.

BUROV, G.M. (1968) Rezul'taty raskopok Visskikh tortyanikov v 1963–1963 gg. *Uchenye zapiski Permskogo gosudarstvennogo universiteta*, 191: 194–209.

BUROV, G.M. (1969) O poiskakh drevnikh derevyannykh veshchey i rybolovnykh sooruzheniy v starichnykh torfyanikakh ravninnykh rek. *Kratkie soobshcheniya Instituta arkheologii AN SSSR*, 117: 130–134.

BUROV, G.M. (1973a) Plemena Vychegodskogo kraya v epokhu neolita i ranney bronzy. *Materialy i issledovaniya po arkheologii SSSR*, 172: 83–94.

BUROV, G.M. (1973b) Die mesolithischen Kulturen im äussersten europäischen Nordosten. In S.K. Kozłowski (ed.), *The Mesolithic in Europe*. Warsaw, University Press: 129–149.

BUROV, G.M. (1974a) *Arkheologicheskie kul'tury Severa evropeyskoy chasti SSSR (Severodvinskiy kray)*. Ul'yanovsk, Pedagogicheskiy institut.

BUROV, G.M. (1974b) Prochnaya osedlost' i zakol'noe rybolovstvo u neoliticheskikh plemen Severo-Vostochnoy Evropy. In I.P. Gerasimov *et al.* (eds), *Pervobytnyy chelovek, ego material'naya kul'tura i prirodnaya sreda v pleystotsene i golotsene*. Moscow, Institut geografii: 283–287.

BUROV, G.M. (1981a) Der Bogen bei den mesolithischen Stämmen Nordosteuropas. In B. Gramsch (ed.), *Mesolithikum in Europa. 2. Internationales Symposium Potsdam, 3 bis 8 April 1978 Bericht* (Veröffentlichungen des Museums für Ur- und Frühgeschichte Potsdam, 14/15). Berlin, Deutscher Verlag der Wissenschaften: 373–388.

BUROV, G.M. (1981b) Drevnie sani Severnoy Evropy. *Skandinavskiy sbornik*, 26: 151–171.

BUROV, G.M. (1981c) Fragmenty saney s poseleniy Vis I (mezolit) i Vis II (I tysyacheletie n.e.). *Sovetskaya arkheologiya*, 2: 117–131.

BUROV, G.M., ROMANOVA, E.N. and SEMENTSOV, A.A. (1972) Khronologiya derevyannykh sooruzheniy i veshchey, naydennykh v Severodvinskom basseyne. In B.A. Kolchin (ed.), *Problemy absolyutnogo datirovaniya v arkheologii*. Moscow, Nauka: 76–79.

CARPELAN, C. (1974) Hirven- ja karhunpääesineita Skandinaviasta Uralille. *Suomen museo*: 29–88.

CARTER, H. and MACE, A.C. (1927) *The Tomb of Tut-ankh-Amen Discovered by the Late Earl of Carnarvon and H. Carter*, vol. 1. London, Cassell.

CHERNYKH, E.N. (1970) *Drevneyshaya metallurgiya Urala i Povolzh'ya*. Moscow, Nauka.

CHILDE, V.G. (1958) Rotary motion. In C. Singer, E.J. Holmyard and A.R. Hall (eds), *A History of Technology*, vol. 1. Oxford, Clarendon Press: 187–215.

COLLINS, H.B. (1937) *Archaeology of St Lawrence Island, Alaska*. Washington D.C., Smithsonian Institution.

CROES, D.R. (1976) The definition, distribution, and time depth of water-saturated archaeological sites ('wet sites') on the Northwest Coast of North America. In D.R. Croes (ed.), *The Excavation of Water-saturated Archaeological Sites (Wet Sites) on the Northwest Coast of North America*. Ottawa, National Museum of Canada: 1–12.

DMITRIEV, P.A. (1951) Shigirskaya kul'tura na vostochnom sklone Urala. *Materialy i issledovaniya po arkheologii SSSR*, 21: 28–93.

EBERT, M. (1924) *Reallexikon der Vorgeschichte*, vol. 1. Berlin, De Cruyter.

EDING, D.N. (1929) *Gorbunovskiy torfyanik*. Tagil.

EDING, D.N. (1940a) Novye nakhodki na Gorbunovskom torfyanike. *Materialy i issledovaniya po arkheologii SSSR*, 1: 41–57.

EDING, D.N. (1940b) *Reznaya skul'ptura Urala*. Moscow, Gosudarstvennyy istoricheskiy muzey.

ERÄ-ESKO, A. (1958) Die Elchkopfskulptur von Lehtojärvi in Rovaniemi. *Suomen museo*: 8–18.

FOSS, M.E. (1952) *Drevneyshaya istoriya Severa evropeyskoy chasti SSSR*. Moscow, Izdatel'stvo Akademii nauk SSSR.

GRAMSCH, B. (1973) *Das Mesolithikum im Flachland zwischen Elbe und Oder*. Berlin, Deutscher Verlag der Wissenschaften.

GURINA, N.N. (1956) *Oleneostrovskiy mogil'nik*. Moscow, Izdatel'stvo Akademii nauk SSSR.

GURINA, N.N. (1961) *Drevnyaya istoriya Severo-Zapada evropeyskoy chasti SSSR*. Moscow, Izadatel'stvo Akademii nauk SSSR.

HARRISON, H.S. (1958) Fire-making, fuel, and lighting. In C. Singer, E.J. Holmyard and A.R. Hall (eds), *A History of Technology*, vol. 1. Oxford, Clarendon Press: 216–237.

HYYPÄÄ, E. (1958) Geologische Datierung der Elchkopfskulptur vom Lehtojärvi bei Rovaniemi. *Suomen museo*: 19–25.

IIKONEN, T.I. (1930, 1931–1932, 1934, 1936, 1938, 1941, 1946, 1949) Muinaissuksia ja -jalaksia. *Suomen museo*.

KANIVETS, V.I. (1964) *Kaninskaya peshchera*. Moscow, Nauka.

KOPISTO, A. (1964) Uusia jalaslöytöjä. *Suomen museo*: 17–25.

LOZE, I.A. (1973) Reznaya skul'ptura kamennogo veka Vostochnoy Pribaltiki v sootnoshenii s ural'skoy skul'pturoy. In A.P. Smirnov (ed.), *Problemy arkheologii Urala i Sibiri*. Moscow, Nauka: 174–182.

MONGAYT, A.L. (1965) XII vek. Puteshestvie v Rossiyu. *Nauka i zhizn'*, 1: 34–38.

MONGAYT, A.L. (1973) *Arkheologiya Zapadnoy Evropy. Kamennyy vek*. Moscow, Nauka.

MOSHINSKAYA, V.I. (1976) *Drevnyaya skul'ptura Urala i Zapadnoy Sibiri*. Moscow, Nauka.

OKLADNIKOV, A.P. and BEREGOVAYA, N.A. (1971) *Drevnie poseleniya Baranova mysa*. Novosibirsk, Nauka.

OSHIBKINA, S.V. (1978) *Neolit Vostochnogo Prionezh'ya*. Moscow, Nauka.

RAUSHENBAKH, V.M. (1956) *Srednee Zaural'e v epokhu neolita i bronzy*. Moscow, Goskul'tprosvetizdat.

RAUSHENBAKH, V.M. (1969) *Novye nakhodki na Chetyrekhstolbovom ostrove*. Moscow, Sovetskaya Rossiya.

REINERTH, H. (1960) Unterwasserfotografie in Vor- und Frühgeschichte. In H.U. Richter, *Unterwasserfotografie und -fernsehen*. Halle (Saale): 288–296.

RUDENKO, S.I. (1953) *Kul'tura naseleniya Gornogo Altaya v skifskoe vremya*. Moscow, Izdatel'stvo Akademii nauk SSSR.

RYBAKOV, B.A. (1976) Novye dannye o kul'te nebesnogo olenya. In L.V. Kol'tsov *et al.* (eds), *Vostochnaya Evropa v epokhu kamnya i bronzy*. Moscow, Nauka: 57–63.

SALO, U. (1967) Die Elchkopfkufe von Noormarkku. *Suomen museo*: 42–45.

SCHULDT, E. (1961) *Hohen Viecheln. Ein mittelsteinzeitlicher Wohnplatz in Mecklenburg*. Berlin, Reimer (Vohsen).

SHCHUKIN, M.S. (1960) *Obshchaya geomorfologiya*, vol. 1. Moscow, Izdatel'stvo Moskovskogo universiteta.

SMIRNOV, V.I. (1941) Stoyanka na r. Kuznechikha v g. Arkhangel'ske. *Kratkie soobshcheniya Instituta istorii material'noy kul'tury*, 9: 90–98.

SPITSYN, A.A. (1906) Shamanskie izobrazheniya. *Zapiski otdeleniya russkoy i slavyanskoy arkheologii Russkogo arkheologicheskogo obshchestva*, 8(1): 29–145.

VANKINA, L.V. (1970) *Torfyanikovaya stoyanka Sarnate*. Riga, Zinatne.

VANKINA, L.V., ZAGORSKIS, F.A. and LOZE, I.A. (1973) Neoliticheskie plemena Latvii. *Materialy i issledovaniya po arkheologii SSSR*, 172: 210–217.

The Material Culture of the Veretye-type Sites in the Region to the East of Lake Onega

S.V. Oshibkina

Abstract

The Veretye-type sites are found in the central region of the north of eastern Europe. They are grouped around large glacial lakes to the east of Lake Onega, and are quite distinctive when compared to other Mesolithic cultures of the forest belt and the north of eastern Europe. The 17 known findspots include several camp sites, a burial ground, and places where random finds have been made. Nizhneye Veretye I and the Popovo burial ground are the best studied sites. A wide variety of objects were recovered from Nizhneye Veretye I where the cultural layer was sealed by peat. Among them are weapons, tools, objects of everyday use and ornaments, as well as remains of dwellings, stone-working shops, and hearths. There are also some unique items, including ornamented objects and wooden sculptures.

Investigation of the Popovo burial ground revealed its affiliation to the Veretye culture, as well as details of the burial rite. To obtain a clearer picture, ethnographic evidence has been widely drawn upon. These findings are important for understanding the historical and cultural development of the population concerned.

The Veretye sites are dated mainly to the ninth millennium BP. They belong to the Kunda–Maglemose complex of cultures and were peopled by a Europoid population which settled along the southern shores of Lake Antsilovoe in the Boreal period.

INTRODUCTION

A number of Mesolithic sites have been discovered recently in the central regions of the Russian north. Some of them have been excavated, while others have produced random finds. These investigations have identified two groups of sites belonging to two archaeological cultures. One is called the Sukhona culture, since its sites are found mainly in the middle reaches of the Sukhona river; the other is termed 'sites of the Veretye type', from the name of the first site of this type to be described, and comprises peat-bog sites in the region to the east of Lake Onega. The present article offers a concise description of the latter group.

A number of large glacial lakes are situated to the east of Lake Onega. This area was deglaciated by 14,500–13,500 BP. The present-day relief and hydrology of the region took a long time to form. The present outline of the southern part of Lake Onega was formed as late as the Allerød Interstadial (11,800–10,200 BP – Kvasov 1976: 231). Evidently the Vozhe, Lacha and Beloye lake systems had formed by that time, although the lakes themselves were for a long time somewhat larger than today. Pine and birch forests replaced the tundra as the levels of large bodies of water gradually stabilized and ecological zones shifted northwards. Environmental conditions favourable to settlement were established in the Pre-Boreal period. To date, no Pre-Boreal sites have been found in the region. People of the Veretye culture appeared there in the Boreal, and their sites are considered to represent the earliest settlement of the region (*Fig. 1*).

There are now 17 sites which have produced material of Veretye-type. These include camp sites, findspots of isolated artifacts or small groups of material, and a burial ground. The sites are mainly associated with peat bogs which originated in the Boreal. The cultural layers of the main sites (Nizhneye Veretye I, Nizhneye Veretye, Pogostishche I) are found beneath peat, which facilitates their dating and accounts for their description as peat-bog sites.

The Nizhneye Veretye I site is especially clearly stratified. The sequence from the modern surface downwards is: a turf layer (25–30 cm), black peat (30–40 cm), brown peat (25–40 cm), sand and gravel (10–15 cm), and sandy bedrock. The Mesolithic horizon coincides with the sand-and-gravel layer. Pollen analyses have shown that the sequence spans the greater part of the Holocene, beginning in the Pre-Boreal. The sand-and-gravel layer, containing the cultural remains, and the lower part of the brown peat layer are dated to the Boreal between 9000 and 8000 BP (established by N.A. Khotinsky). They are characterized by the predominance of pine and birch pollen, the absence of pollen of broad-leaved trees, and an insignificant quantity of wormwood and goosefoot pollen. Thus, the cultural layer is found in Boreal deposits and directly overlies Pre-Boreal strata. Radiocarbon dates for Nizhneye Veretye I fall around the middle of the Boreal period – 9050±80 BP (GIN-4031); 8790±100 BP (GIN-4869.Mg-P); 8750±70 BP (LE-1472); 8560±120 BP (GIN-2452.U); 8520±80 BP (GIN-4030); 8520±130 BP (GIN-2452.D).[1]

Since the Mesolithic horizons at the Nizhneye Veretye and Pogostishche I sites occur in a similar stratigraphic context, they can also be referred to the

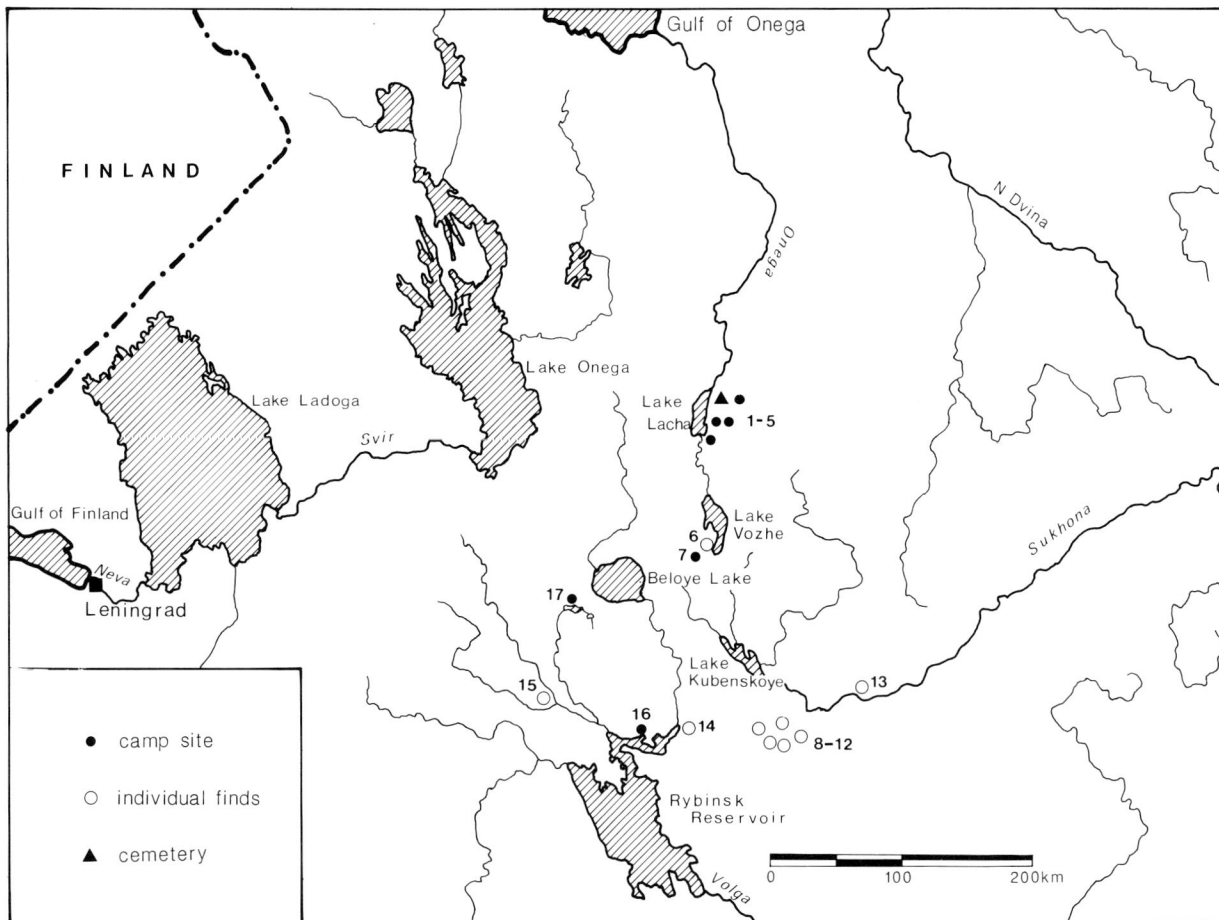

Figure 1 The Veretye-type sites. a – camps; b – individual finds; c – burial ground. 1 – Nizhneye Veretye I; 2 – Nizhneye Veretye; 3 – Popovo; 4 – the Popovo burial ground; 5 – Sukhoe; 6 – the Vyazovyy Cape; 7 – Pogostishche I; 8 – Kanifolnyy; 9 – Kanifolnyy I; 10 – Liminskaya; 11 – Vologda; 12 – Priluki; 13 – Shuyskoe; 14 – Sheksna; 15 – Chagodoshcha; 16 – Yagorba; 17 – the Andozero-M site.

mid-Boreal. Dating of other sites and of the burial ground near Popovo has traditionally been based on typological comparisons with the above-mentioned sites, although it has been established that the Andozero-M and Yagorba sites belong to the late Mesolithic. A series of radiocarbon dates on human bone (*Table 1*) that have recently become available for the Popovo cemetery indicate that three burials (I, III, IX) are as old as the tenth millennium BP, and that two (burials VI, VIII) can be dated to the eighth millennium BP. Research at this site is still in progress and is directed at identifying the reasons for the great difference in the ages of the burials. Most of the Veretye-type sites can thus be referred to the ninth and tenth millennia BP, although some date to a later period.

NIZHNEYE VERETYE I

The Nizhneye Veretye I site is the best studied archaeologically. Some 1316 m^2 have been excavated, and extensive drainage work has been effected to counteract flooding. The site is situated on the left bank of the Kinema river, a kilometre from where it flows into Lake Lacha (Arkhangelsk region). Since the lake was much larger in the Boreal, the site

Table 1: Radiocarbon dates on human bone for the cemeteries of Popovo and Oleniy Ostrov produced by the Laboratory of Geochemical Isotopes and Geochronology at the Geological Institute of the Academy of Sciences (GIN), U.S.S.R. (L.D. Sylerzhitskiy)

Site	Context	Lab. No.	Date BP
POPOVO:	Burial IX	GIN-4856	9730±110
	Burial III	GIN-4442	9520±130
	Burial I	GIN-4447	9430±150
	Burial VI	GIN-3887	7510±150
	Burial VIII	GIN-4857	7150±160
OLENIY OSTROV:	Burial 100	GIN-4836	9910±80
	Burial 70	GIN-4450	7470±240
	Burial 142	GIN-4451	7220±110
	Burial 84–85	GIN-4839	7210±50
	Burial 152–153	GIN-4452	7140±140
	Burial 71	GIN-4449	7130±140
	Burial 158	GIN-4454	7130±170
	Burial 118	GIN-4840	7080±80
	Burial 108–109	GIN-4838	7070±100
	Burial 151	GIN-4453	6980±200
	Burial 73	GIN-4841	6960±100
	Burial 10	GIN-4456	6950±90
	Burial 19	GIN-4457	6870±200
	Burial 3–3a	GIN-4459	6830±100
	Burial 16	GIN-4458	6790±80

would then have been at the mouth of the river. It overlooked the river and extended along its banks. The drainage made it possible to strip away the peat and to locate *in situ* the remains of dwellings, hearths and fire spots, and stone-working areas, as well as animal and fish bones. The dwellings were ground-based and had a framework of wooden stakes (8–12 cm in diameter) driven vertically into the sandy ground; the walls and roof would have been covered with soft materials. The results of the excavations have thus provided the means for studying the site's infra-structure, for identifying residential and economic zones within the site area, for investigating the lay-out of individual dwellings, and for determining the equipment and methods used for fishing and hunting. The present article, however, is an attempt to give a concise description of the material culture of the Veretye-type sites and to provide general information about the excavations conducted between 1979 and 1984.

The peat bog of the Nizhneye Veretye I settlement has preserved a wide range of organic materials – artifacts made of bone and antler, and objects of wood and bark. The exceptionally good preservation has made it possible to reconstruct the shapes of many objects, to establish the purpose of others, and to determine how some of them were used. In all, 8256 artifacts were found, in addition to large numbers of flakes and other flint débitage. Bone and antler tools account for 20–25% of all the artifacts, wooden objects for about 10%, and stone tools for about 70%. However, since bone and wooden objects have not been preserved on the higher parts of the site, which dried out periodically, the actual percentage of organic materials used by the local population was higher. Owing to the large number of finds, this paper will concentrate on the most interesting and distinctive objects, providing ample information about the material culture and economic activities and, to some extent, about the spiritual life of the inhabitants.

The stone industry

Stone implements (*Fig. 2*) are represented by axes, adzes, chisels, wedges, hoes, arrowheads, points on blades, end-scrapers, racloirs, burins on blades and flakes, awls, drills, knives, daggers, retouched and unretouched regular blades, stones with holes and hollows, instruments for chipping and retouching stone, grinding stones and slabs, and flint 'spheres'.[2] The ratio of flakes to blades is almost 4:1.

Axes, or to be more exact axe-heads, were made of flint or shale, the ratio being 1:1. Primary working of the surface of both types was basically similar. The blades of the axe-heads, however, were treated differently; while shale blades were ground, flint blades were simply trimmed by chipping. In some cases, axes were made of hard granite-like stone,

with pecking of the surface and with ground blades. Four basic axe types can be identified on the basis of their shape: I – axe-heads with pointed butts (*Fig. 2*, nos. 12, 14); II – short axe-heads with broad butts and an oval cross-section (*Fig. 2*, no. 13); III – axe-heads that are rectangular in plan and rectangular in cross-section; IV – axe-heads that are oval in plan and in section. The first type was an especially stable form, found on almost all Veretye-type sites. It had a tapering butt, with transverse chipping or grinding on the end. A number of wooden handles were recovered, and indicate the way in which some stone and antler axe-heads were hafted. On one occasion, a stone axe-head was found still mounted in its wooden haft (Oshibkina 1982a: fig. 4).

Adzes and chisels are not numerous; they comprise no more than 1.5% of the total finds. Adzes were invariably made of shale with ground surfaces. They were rectangular in form, oval in section, narrowing towards the butt.

Flint wedges, round or square in section, were crudely sharpened. The more massive wedges were probably used to split wood or bones.

Five 'hoes' are of particular interest. All of them are similarly trimmed and worked. They have broad working edges with rounded sides and short handles, carefully worked and finished with transverse chipping. The surface of the implement was largely unworked; the broad working edge was trimmed along the sides. Most of them range from 10 to 12 cm in length. Only one was significantly larger – 22 cm long, 16 cm wide at the blade and 3.5 cm wide at the butt (*Fig. 2*, no. 15). The function of these implements is not clear. In a number of Neolithic cultures in the Caucasus and the Near East, similar artifacts are regarded as land-tilling implements. It is probable, however, that 'hoes' like those from Nizhneye Veretye I had a different origin and purpose among the Mesolithic population of the north of eastern Europe. It seems likely that they were intended to imitate implements made from elk antlers which retained much of the natural form of the antler, the beam serving as a handle. The broad central part of the antler was shortened and sharpened along the sides. A similar hoe was found at Nizhneye Veretye.

Twelve stone arrowheads were found. Judging by their scarcity on the site, they were replaced by bone and wooden arrowheads. There were two types of flint arrowheads: (i) broad and comparatively massive blades were used to make tanged arrowheads trimmed both at the tip and at the end (*Fig. 2*, nos. 2, 5), the stem designed to be fitted into an arrowshaft; (ii) thin, small blades were used to make willow-leaf arrowheads trimmed at the tip (*Fig. 2*, no. 4).

At Nizhneye Veretye I several small, obliquely-retouched blades were also found. It has been

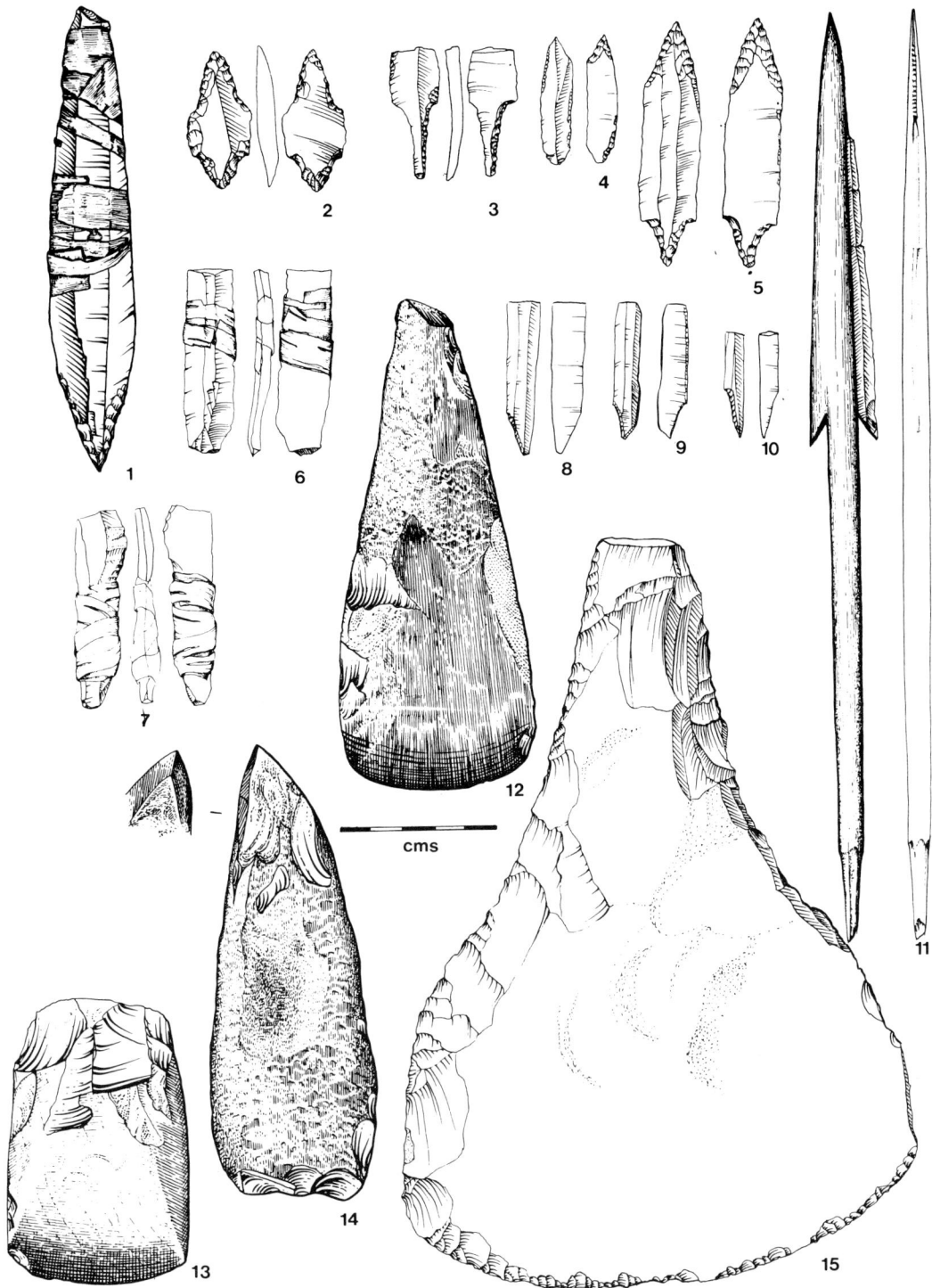

Figure 2 Stone artifacts from Nizhneye Veretye I: dagger (1); arrowheads (2–5); knives (6–7); backed blades (8–10); backed blade fixed in a bone arrowhead (11); axes (12–14); flint hoe (15).

established that these points were the lower barbs inserted into slotted bone arrow-shafts along with other regular bladelets. Such a flint barb corresponded to a barb cut into the other side of the bone shaft (*Fig. 2*, nos. 8–11). Some intact bone arrowheads were found inset with similarly retouched blades.

Stone implements used for domestic tasks, such as scrapers, awls, burins and knives, were made mainly on flint flakes. End-scrapers and large racloirs

(which were rare) had retouched working edges and cortex on their upper surfaces. Burins are second in numerical importance in the stone industry of Nizhneye Veretye I, comprising 18–20% of the stone implements. This suggests that they were widely used for working bone, antler and wood. Flakes, split cores, and lumps of stone were used for their manufacture. On the basis of their morphological attributes, various types of burins can be

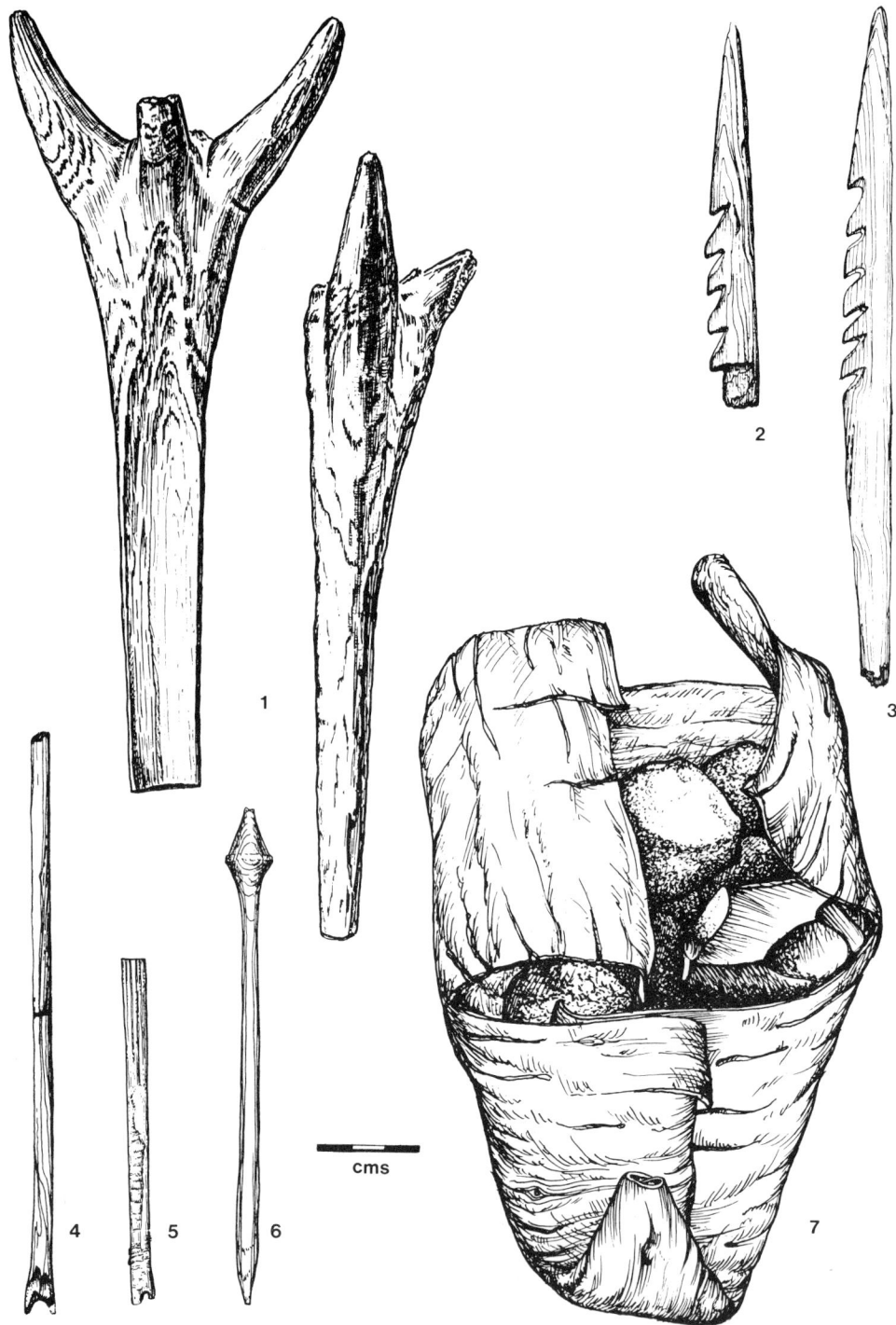

Figure 3 Objects made from wood and bark from Nizhneye Veretye I: anthropomorphic figure (1); barbed points (2–3); basal portions of arrows (4–5); arrowhead (6); birch bark container with semi-prepared flint artifacts (7).

distinguished (cf. Sonneville-Bordes and Perrot 1956): (i) dihedral straight burins (10% of the burins); (ii) offset dihedral burins; (iii) angle burins on a broken blade; (iv) multiple dihedral burins. The first type is also known from the later Palaeolithic of Lithuania, and such assemblages are considered to belong to the Baltic–Magdalenian facies (Rimantiene 1971: fig. 16, no. 6). Blades were rarely used to make burins, but some larger blades were used without previous working. This is supported by finds of burins made on large blades, one end of which was

protected by birch bark to serve as a handle, while the other end bore traces of intensive use.

Large, regular blades with sharp edges were used without additional working. Special stone knives were also made to cut out hides; they had distinctive rounded blades and were shaped to fit the hand. Broad blades or shale plates were used for their manufacture. In the first case, the working edge was trimmed; in the second it was ground. The Nizhneye Veretye I population also used daggers made from large, regular blades. One such dagger was found

406

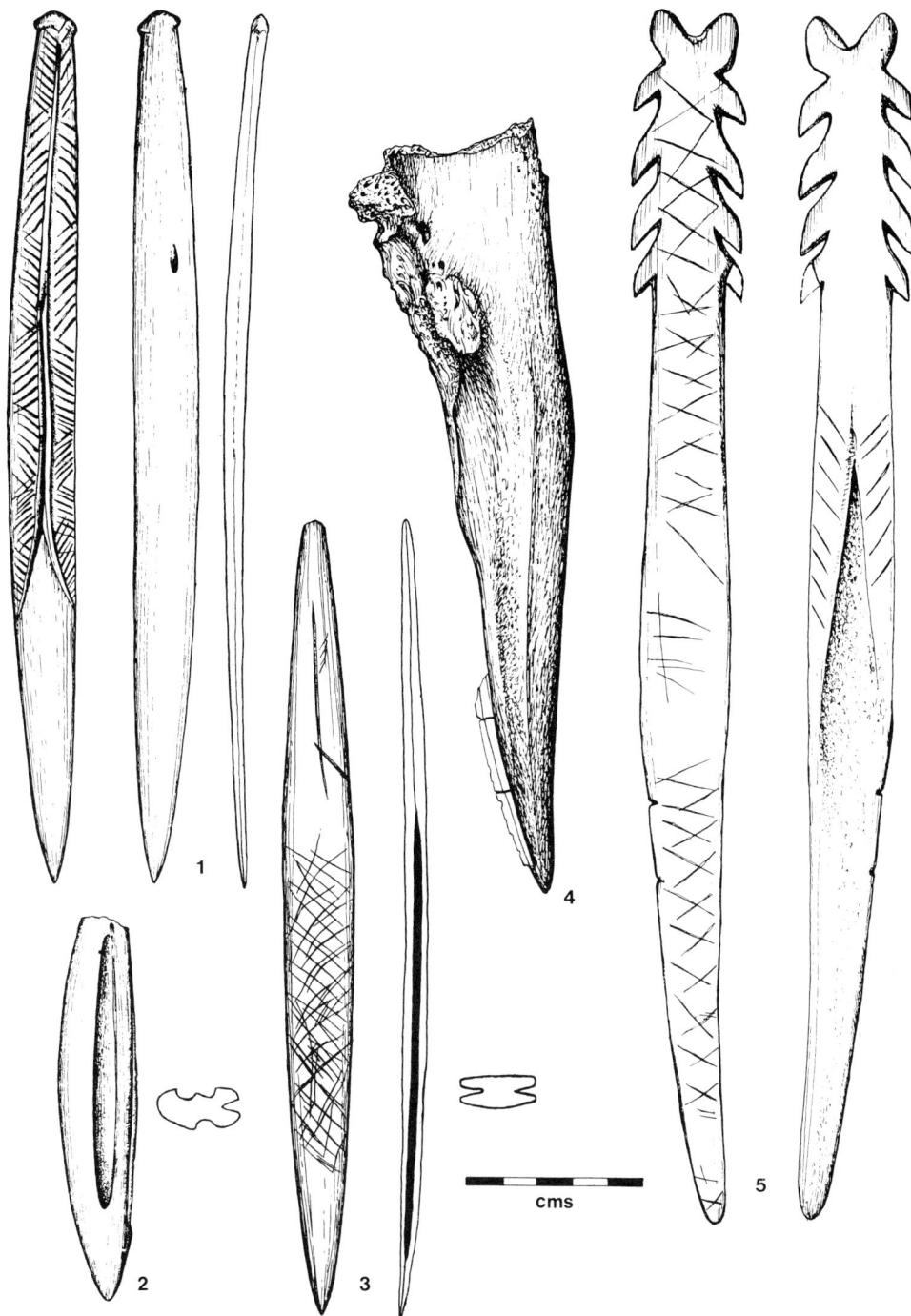

Figure 4 Bone knives from Nizhneye Veretye I.

intact with its handle protected by birch bark. Beneath the bark wrapping the end is crudely trimmed, and the tip of the dagger is sharpened (*Fig. 2*, no. 1).

Stone-working and toolmaking took place on the site itself, but in places specially assigned to that task. The general lay-out of the Nizhneye Veretye I site clearly indicates that these activities were localized outside the dwelling zone. One such place, located nearer to the forest, was evidently a workshop with stores of raw materials and blanks, and production waste. An anvil made of a dark-green

diorite boulder stood in the centre. Its surface was considerably damaged. A birch bark container, resembling a box, was found nearby (*Fig. 3*, no. 7). It was cut out of a single strip of birch bark, its ends serving as a lid. The sides of the strip are bent over to form the walls. Inside were found 29 objects – five cores of grey-blue high grade flint, 13 other cores, nine flakes, one unfinished scraper on a retouched blade, and one implement for flint-flaking. An analogous find was made in another part of the site, also outside the dwelling zone. This consisted of a birch bark container strengthened in the corners

407

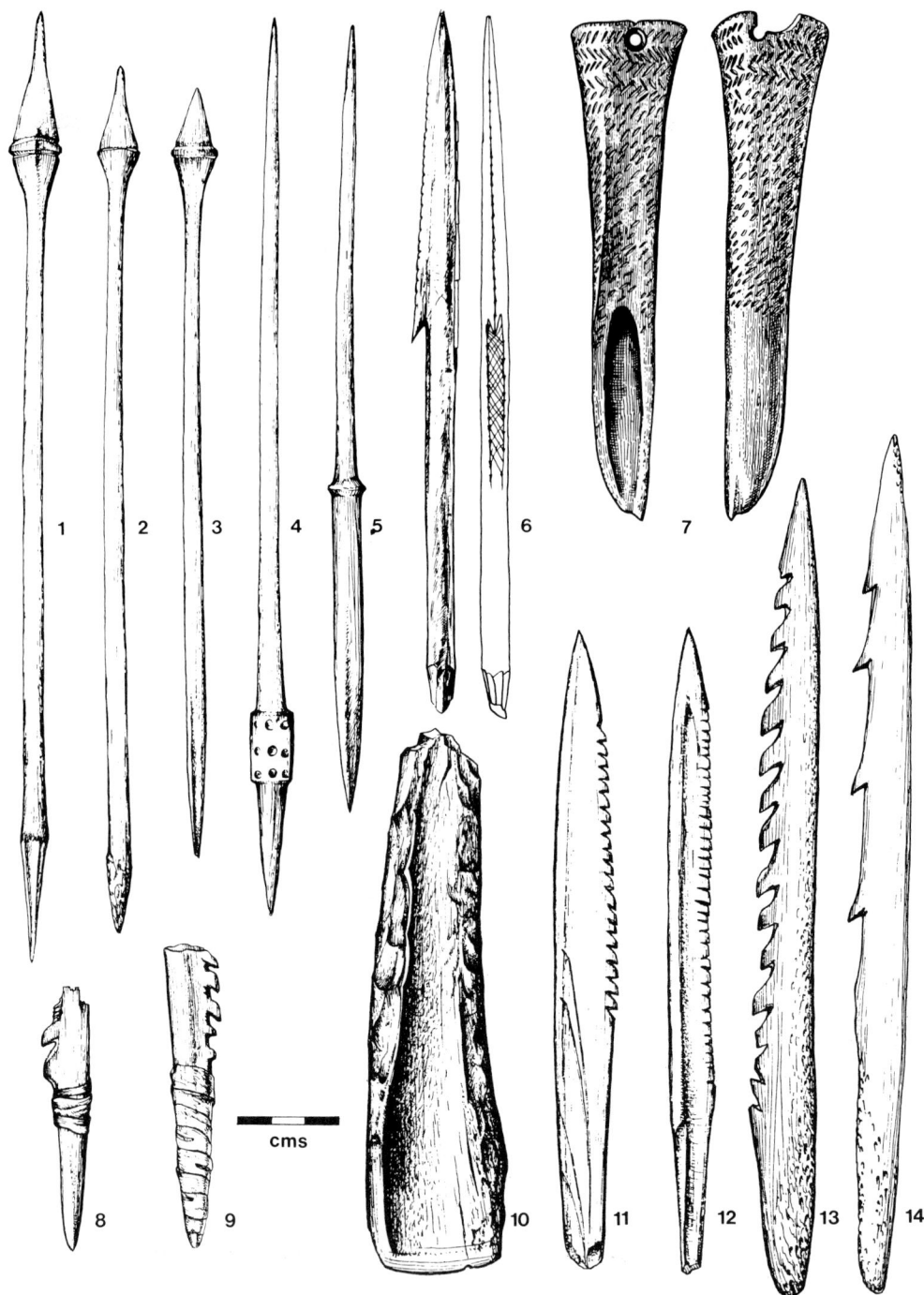

Figure 5 Other bone implements from Nizhneye Veretye I: arrowheads (1–6); decorated implement (7); basal fragments of a barbed spear-head (8–9); scraper (10); barbed points (11–14).

with wooden pegs, containing flint raw materials and flakes. Evidently, the inhabitants stored high grade raw material in places where it was worked.

Small grinding plates were used for working shale and bone objects. Occasionally, massive grinding plates are found, both sides of which bear traces of grinding in the form of three to five oval depressions.

On the whole, the Nizhneye Veretye I stone industry is distinguished by a high level of technical accomplishment, the diversity of tools produced, and evidence for rational organization of labour on the site.

Objects of bone, antler and wood

Bone and antler objects are numerous and varied. A prominent place is taken by hunting implements – arrowheads, barbed points or harpoons, large knives or daggers, various kinds of points made of sharpened bones, ribs and metapodials. Wooden bows, fragments of arrows and bark binding on knives add to our knowledge of hunting implements at Nizhneye Veretye I.

In all, 184 arrowheads and their fragments have been found so far (*Fig. 5*). They are divided into 10 main types: I – biconical forms (nos. 1–3); II –

narrow, pointed forms with an expanded ring or a narrow block above the stem (no. 5); III – narrow, pointed forms with cylindrical widening above the stem (no. 4); IV – plain, narrow, pointed arrowheads; V – narrow, pointed forms with slots for a series of stone or flint inserts (no. 6); VI – symmetrical arrowheads with a single flint insert; VII – arrowheads with biconical widening above the stem; VIII – oar-shaped arrowheads; IX – blunted arrowheads; X – asymmetrical forms. There are also a number of arrowheads that are unique in form, and these are treated separately. The latest excavations will probably produce one or two additional groups. The proposed typology is based on the shape of the arrowheads and the method of hafting, since many of the stems retained resin traces.

All arrowheads can be subdivided into two large groups according to their functions – blunted arrowheads intended for hunting fowl and fur-bearing animals (types I, IX and X), and arrowheads with long, sharpened, heavy tips, intended for hunting big game, but which could be used in encounters with hostile tribes. In the case of the second group, the stem of the arrowhead and the shaft above it were usually carefully worked and often bore ornamental incised notches and circles. These may represent a sign system and can be investigated as such. The purpose of these signs does not seem to have been purely a decorative one; they were a means of identifying arrows, which was of importance when the catch was apportioned. It is likely that this factor was taken into account when arrowheads were manufactured and that each hunter had his own, distinctively marked arrows. As a rule, however, the arrowheads of the first group were more or less uniform and had no signs on them. This may be because they were used at closer ranges and both arrows and prey were rarely lost. Thus, wooden arrowheads belong exclusively to the first group. There were approximately equal numbers of arrowheads of the first and second groups (47.6% and 52.4%, respectively).

A total of 182 barbed points or harpoons were found (*Fig. 5*). They can be divided into five main types: I – uniserial points with small hooked barbs (no. 11); II – uniserial points with straight, widely-spaced barbs (no. 14); III – uniserial points with small notched barbs (no. 12); IV – short uniserial points with two or three barbs; V – points with barbs along one side and an inset flint blade along the other. Several other points were also found: a point made from a small metapodial with two barbs at the end, and a short, wide implement with three barbs. Barbed points of type I were the most common.

The barbed points fall into three size-groupings: 6–10 cm, 15–16 cm, and 22–25 cm. All types were designed to be inserted into a wooden shaft. Some of them retained fragments of birch bark strips glued on with an organic resin-like substance (*Fig. 5*, nos. 8, 9). Fragments of wooden shafts were also recovered, including the upper part of a shaft with slots along its sides into which the stems of barbed points were fitted. In this case the projectile was originally fitted with two points and could have been a fishing spear.

It is probable that ancient hunters used throwing spears equipped with barbed points. According to Alfred Rust (1937) the inhabitants of Meiendorf used similar spears when hunting reindeer, although not everybody subscribes to this view. Many researchers believe that such lances were used in spearing fish, mainly pike, and term them 'fishing spears' (Zagorska 1974). The barbed points from Nizhneye Veretye I bear no ornament or other signs. Ornamented points are extremely rare on other sites of the Nizhneye Veretye type.

Daggers and large knives (*Fig. 4*) had sharpened tips with grooves into which flint blades were fitted. They may be divided into several types: those inset with one or two blades, and those without any. They can be further classified according to the material the weapon was made of: those made from elk bones, and those made from the ribs of some other animal. Being personal weapons, the knives and daggers were carefully worked; many of them had polished surfaces and long, sharpened tips. Some are decorated with fine incised designs, or with carved notches along the sides and around the hilt (no. 5). Some have net-like incised ornament (nos. 1, 3); others are marked with small slanting crosses (Oshibkina 1983: fig. 29). The knives and daggers are a graphic illustration of the ancient hunters' ingenuity and imagination which prompted them to create new, more sophisticated weapons based, as they were, on traditional forms. Thus, simple daggers made of elk bones were quite common in the Mesolithic cultures. The Nizhneye Veretye I people not only sharpened them, but made grooves and inserted blades in them (*Fig. 4*, no. 4). Several daggers made from straightened and sharpened elk ribs, perhaps intended as combat weapons, were found. Also among the finds is a knife the hilt of which is crowned with a carved zoomorphic figure. Its entire surface on both sides is covered with an incised ornament of crossed lines. Evidently this weapon was not of utilitarian value; it was probably intended for use in hunting rituals, since its hilt can be regarded as a stylized elk's head.

Many bone and antler objects of everyday use found at Nizhneye Veretye I merit closer study and ethnographic comparison. This paper will concentrate on those which have analogues in other Mesolithic cultures and which therefore permit more precise dating and establishment of the cultural affinities of the Veretye-type sites. Among these objects are needle cases with needles, and bone scrapers.

Scrapers made from split long bones (also referred

to as implements with hollow working edges) were used in the Mesolithic for processing hides. The earliest implements of this type were found at Star Carr, Great Britain. They were made from aurochs long bones (Clark 1954: 161–164). In the eastern Baltic region scrapers manufactured from elk bones are found on sites of the Kunda culture dated to the Boreal. There are two types of scrapers – with plain and with barbed working edges, the latter probably being used for processing fish (Indreko 1948: 333, fig. 47; Jaanits and Jaanits 1975: 67). Both types were found on the Veretye-type sites, especially Nizhneye Veretye I.

There were nine needle cases made from hollow swan bones and one from a specially treated dog joint. Bones with epiphyses sawn off were usually employed for this purpose. They were polished and ornamented with notches or an incised net-like motif. A narrow groove provided the means of suspending the needle case. In one needle case two needles, a needle blank, and three cutting tools on irregular flint bladelets were found (Oshibkina 1983: fig. 39, nos. 1–3). Analogous objects have been found on Palaeolithic sites. Similar needle cases made of swan bones were discovered in the Hamburgian level at Meiendorf; these were interpreted as containers for some kind of paint or abrasive powder (Rust 1937: 108, fig. 49). Artifacts of bird bones, including swan bones, were also found at Avdeyevo, an Upper Palaeolithic site on the Don. They are lavishly ornamented and a little bit larger than those from Nizhneye Veretye I (Gvozdover 1953: 208, fig. 14).

It is probable that swan bones were preferred for the manufacture of needle cases because they were larger than those of other birds, were light, and looked nice. It can also be surmised that such objects were the product of an ancient tradition.

In the cultural layer of Nizhneye Veretye I bone and antler artifacts tended to be better preserved than wooden ones. Nevertheless, the latter comprise 6–10% of the organic materials depending on the degree to which the deposits had been waterlogged. There were many wooden fragments of dwellings – various kinds of pegs, stakes, blocks and beams. Objects of everyday use were found in large numbers. These include implements for dressing hides, an oblong knife-board, a flat round board with a handle and a hole in it, a small flat shovel with a long handle, and many other items. In some cases the function of the artifacts remains unclear since they were associated with the economic and everyday life of an ancient population. Ethnographic parallels may be of help here, although direct comparisons are possible only with peoples living in a similar natural environment and at a similar stage of historical and cultural development.

Most of the wooden objects recovered are connected with hunting. Bows are represented only by fragments. One fragment was 102 cm in length, with only its ends missing. It has been established that the inhabitants of the Nizhneye Veretye I site used bows 120–150 cm long, the surfaces of which were covered with cut notches. There is a cut-out grip in the centre of the bow, protected by strips of birch bark. Nocks were cut near the ends to retain the bowstring. The bows were round or oval in section at the centre and oval towards the ends, and were made of both pine and spruce.

A comparatively small number of bows have been found on Stone Age sites across Europe and in the Urals. Most are dated to the Neolithic, although bows dated to the Mesolithic have been found at the peat bog site of Vis I, in the Vychegda basin (Burov 1967, 1981). In spite of the fact that Nizhneye Veretye I belongs to the same ecological zone as Vis I and is dated to the same period, the bows found on these sites, like many of the other artifacts, are quite different from one another. The Nizhneye Veretye I bows are more like the bows found at Holmegaard IV, Denmark (Brøndsted 1960: 73). A comparison of Mesolithic bows reveals that, despite wide variations in shape and size and in the way in which the strings were attached, they were rather primitive. The design of the bow progressed in the Neolithic and, especially, in the Bronze Age as testified by archaeological finds in England, Switzerland, the German Democratic Republic and Latvia (Clark 1963; Vankina 1970; Wetzel 1970).

At the same time the Nizhneye Veretye I finds show that arrows had different forms and were more advanced technologically. They had either bone or wooden heads and nocks to engage the bowstring. Some of them bore traces of fletching. Arrows made of a single piece of wood were also found. From these it could be established that the total length was 60–65 cm. A large number of wooden arrowheads were found. They closely resembled bone arrowheads of type I with a biconical tip (e.g. *Fig. 3*, no. 6), and had a sharpened stem for fitting into the arrow-shaft. Some examples bore traces of pitch. Both arrowheads and arrows were mostly made of pine wood. Being blunted arrows, they were presumably used to hunt fur-bearing animals.

Among other wooden objects from Nizhneye Veretye I were two primitive sculptures. One of them represents a bird's head on an outstretched neck. The shape of the beak suggests a swan. The sculpture was not finished because the craftsman could not remove a knot on one side. It is clear, nevertheless, that the object was intended for a wide pedestal. Its total length is 26 cm, the pedestal being 12 cm wide. The second sculpture represents an idol with raised hands. It is 22.5 cm long and its lower part is shaped so as to fit in a vertical position. Both objects can be termed 'sculptures' with certain reservations.

OTHER SITES

Although other sites of the Veretye type have not yielded collections as representative and varied as that from Nizhneye Veretye I, the objects recovered from them clearly betray their cultural affiliation. This is true both of camp sites and of individual finds.

Nizhneye Veretye

Nizhneye Veretye, second in size after Nizhneye Veretye I, is situated some 60–70 m away, and was discovered in 1929 by M.E. Foss. Only 154 m² were excavated, yielding 314 bone, antler and wooden objects, and 156 stone artifacts (Foss 1941: 33). In general, the cultural layer proved to be rather poor, and was contaminated by Neolithic and Bronze Age material.

The Nizhneye Veretye flint industry consists of large scrapers on flakes with retouch along the lateral edges, retouched blades, fragments of knives on blades, a burin, and two arrowheads on blades. A shale axe with an oblong butt and polished blade was also found. In terms of its shape, surface and blade treatment, it resembles type I implements from Nizhneye Veretye I. Fragments of axes and wedges were also found. The recovery of 16 grinding slabs illustrates the extent and development of stone grinding on this site. There were also stones with hollows, chipping implements and cores. The entire assemblage comprises 37 objects.

The following antler and bone objects were found: 36 arrowheads, 50 barbed points, an axe, a pickaxe, three hoes, a small antler shovel, 14 chisel-like implements and points, two grooved knives, 23 awls, 14 points on metapodials, two bone rings, and an antler implement for straightening arrows.

Among the wooden objects found at Nizhneye Veretye were two bow fragments, four arrowheads, a fragment of an arrow, spear shafts, and fragments of arrow-shafts.

A number of art objects thought to be associated with magic rituals, including sculptures of birds and fish and bone plates with carved ornamentation (Foss 1941: fig. 7), were also recovered from the site. In some cases bone plates were decorated with drawings rather than abstract designs. The style of the drawings and of the incised and deeply carved lines has much in common with the way that the numerous bone artifacts from Nizhneye Veretye I were decorated.

A comparison between the stone and bone industries of the two sites reveals their considerable similarity. This is especially evident in the case of certain artifact categories. All the types of arrowheads identified at Nizhneye Veretye I, except types VI and X and certain special forms, are also represented at Nizhneye Veretye; and there are a few grooved objects, including arrowheads. Barbed points are found mainly as fragments, the intact examples belonging to types I, II and V. Absent are points of type III (equivalent to Clark's type 2 – Clark 1936: 117, fig. 41), and short points with two or three barbs (type IV); the latter are replaced by long single-barbed points. The absence of the above-mentioned types could be due to the small size of the sample, but it is more likely that the differences are chronological. The two sites may be regarded as of broadly the same age, but there are grounds for placing Nizhneye Veretye slightly later in time.

Andozero-M

The Andozero-M site is considered to be the latest of the Veretye-type sites. It is situated to the west of the main group of sites, on the shore of the lake of the same name. This is a multi-period site with Neolithic and Mesolithic horizons, separated by a sterile clay layer 20 cm thick. No bone artifacts were preserved, but the composition of the stone industry and its most important types link Andozero-M to the sites of the Veretye type.

Tiny arrowheads on blades were found on the site. Eight of them are willow-leaved, and one has a definite stem. In addition, thick rounded scrapers, retouched along both lateral edges and with cortex on the upper surface were also found, together with awls, shale axes with sharp blades (type I), short axes (type II), and drilled shale objects. Palynologically, the site is dated to the sixth millennium BP (Oshibkina 1979). The composition and character of the stone implements link the Andozero-M site to the Veretye-type sites, on the one hand, and to the sites of the Suomusjärvi culture in Finland, on the other (Luho 1967). There are some sites near the eastern shore of Lake Onega which are similar to Andozero-M and can be regarded as remnants of a population related to that of the Veretye-type sites which expanded westwards towards the end of the Mesolithic.

Popovo

At Popovo, on the right bank of the Kinema river 1.5 km upstream from Nizhneye Veretye I, there is a cemetery. Ten burials, four of them completely destroyed, were found in the 440 m² that were excavated. The cemetery was situated on the top of a sand-and-gravel glacial hill. The bodies were placed in two rows along the river bank. In five instances the head was orientated to the east, and in one instance to the west. The graves were 0.35–0.7 m deep. The dead were placed in extended position

411

with the hands along their sides. All the graves contained traces of red ochre with which the bodies had been covered, together with small lumps of coal, fish bones and vertebrae. Two burials (I, VI) were associated with complete fish skeletons. In burial VI the fish was placed next to the buried man's left hand; in burial I, next to the right hand. The date and cultural affinities of the cemetery are indicated by artifacts discovered in five of the graves and in ritual pits associated with them. These pits produced faunal remains and fragments of distinctive stone and bone artifacts (Oshibkina 1982b).

In addition to the burials and accompanying ritual pits, the hilltop contained a cultural layer darkened by organic residues which yielded a series of Mesolithic artifacts. The stratigraphy and planigraphy of the site, and comparisons between the finds from the burials, the ritual pits and the cultural layer, have made it possible to pose the question of the relationship between the cemetery and the camp site. The fact that the cultural layer is thin, discontinuous and exceedingly poor in artifacts suggests that it was formed in the period when the cemetery was being established there and that it contained randomly discarded objects. There was thus no camp in the proper sense of the word. The burials were not made in the camp site itself, but on a vacant, specially chosen plot of land. However, the problem of the relationship between settlement and cemetery remained and demanded further investigation. In the course of this work the cultural layer of another site was discovered 120 m upstream. Excavations there are at an early stage; a new Mesolithic site has been discovered, but the question of its relationship to the cemetery awaits solution.

The bulk of the finds from the Popovo cemetery consist of stone and bone implements. They include shale axes with oblong butts and ground blades, flint chisel-like tools, arrowheads made from long blades, scrapers on flakes and blades, and dihedral burins on massive flakes. Bone implements include barbed points, knives made from elk shoulder-blades and bones, fragments of a slotted knife with an inset flint blade, a fragment of a needle-shaped arrowhead, scrapers with hollow edges, and a fish hook. Stone axes, bone knives, barbed points, and pendants made of animal teeth also deserve mention. Thus, burial III contained 11 pendants made of the canine teeth of beaver and marten, together with an axe. All the objects of everyday use were found in ritual pits and were associated with the burial rite.

All the ritual pits contained animal bones, consistently from particular parts of an animal. Usually they were fragments of elk jaws, joints and phalanges, and jaws and teeth of beavers and dogs; fragments of scapulae and ulnae were also discovered in the pits. They were probably cooked and eaten elsewhere, and only bone fragments symbolizing the animal were placed in the pits. Much importance was attached to the dog which probably had an important role to play in the economic life of the population. Apart from the bones and teeth found in the pits, and the above-mentioned necklace of canine teeth in burial III, skeletons of two dogs were found in a pit associated with the burial of a 7 to 9-year-old child. This is an example of a burial rite connected with the guarding role of the dog.

When compared, materials from the Popovo cemetery and the Nizhneye Veretye I and Nizhneye Veretye sites exhibit striking similarities. This can be seen in the form, techniques and other characteristics of stone and bone implements. Evidently, they belonged to a related population. The cemetery was probably associated either with one of the sites mentioned above or with a similar site not yet discovered.

Five skulls from the Popovo cemetery were clearly identifiable. All of them belonged to individuals with distinctive Europoid features (I.I. Gokhman and A.A. Zubov, pers. comm.).[3]

A number of radiocarbon dates have recently been obtained on human bone from the Popovo cemetery and are given in *Table 1*.

CONCLUDING REMARKS

Several Mesolithic cultures are known today in the European north and the forest belt of eastern Europe. They include the sites of Vis I type along the Vychegda river, the Mesolithic sites in Karelia, and the Butovo culture sites in the Volga–Oka basin – all dating to the Boreal period. A comparison of stone tools from these sites and the Veretye-type sites reveals significant differences. The same can be said of the well-known cemetery of Oleniy Ostrov; the artifacts from this site bear a slight resemblance to those from the Veretye-type sites. Against a broader historical background the closest parallels for the stone and bone industries (and certain economic traits) of the Veretye population are to be found on the sites of the Kunda culture in the eastern Baltic region and the Maglemose culture in the southern Baltic region. There is some justification, therefore, for considering the Veretye-type sites as part of the Kunda–Maglemose complex.

Notes:
1. Suffixes to Geological Institute of the Academy of Sciences (GIN) radiocarbon laboratory numbers indicate the nature of the samples dated: D – wood (Russian: *drevesina*); Mg-P – small particles of peat (Russian: *melkie fraktsii torfa*); U – charcoal (Russian: *drevesina ugol'*).
2. Rounded nodules of flint, 5–8 cm in diameter and retaining the cortex, are found in large numbers on sites of the Veretye culture. Some show traces of use or working in the form of heavily worn areas and depressions. They resemble objects of 'bola' type known from ethnography.
3. In Soviet anthropology the term 'Northern Europoids' is used to refer to the descendants of the 'Cromagnon' race. The southern populations of eastern Europe are referred to the 'Mediterranean' racial type.

References

BRØNDSTED, J.K. (1960) *Nordische Vorzeit I. Steinzeit.* Neumünster, Karl Wachholtz.

BUROV, G.M. (1967) *Drevniy Sindor.* Moscow, Nauka.

BUROV, G.M. (1981) Der Bogen bei den mesolithischen Stämmen Nordosteuropas. In B. Gramsch (ed.), *Mesolithikum in Europa. 2. Internationales Symposium Potsdam, 3 bis 8 April 1978 Bericht* (Veröffentlichungen des Museums für Ur- und Frühgeschichte Potsdam, 14/15). Berlin, Deutscher Verlag der Wissenschaften: 373–388.

CLARK, J.G.D. (1936) *The Mesolithic Settlement of Northern Europe.* Cambridge, University Press.

CLARK, J.G.D. (1954) *Excavations at Star Carr.* Cambridge, University Press.

CLARK, J.G.D. (1963) Neolithic bows from Somerset, England, and the prehistory of archery in north-west Europe. *Proceedings of the Prehistoric Society*, 29: 50–98.

FOSS, M.E. (1941) Stoyanka Veret'e. *Trudy Gosudarstvennogo Istoricheskogo Muzeya*, 12: 21–70.

GVOZDOVER, M.D. (1953) Obrabotka kosti i kostyanye izdeliya Avdeevskoy stoyanki. *Materialy i issledovaniya po arkheologii SSSR*, 39: 192–226.

INDREKO, R. (1948) *Die mittlere Steinzeit in Estland.* Stockholm, Kungl. Vitterhets Historie och Antikvitets Akademiens Hadlingar, 66.

JAANITS, L. and JAANITS, K. (1975) Frühmesolithische Siedlung in Pulli. *Izvestiya AN ESSR*, obshchestvennye nauki 24/1: 64–70.

KVASOV, D.D. (1976) *Pozdnechetvertichnaya istoriya krupnykh ozer i vnutrennikh morey Vostochoy Evropy.* Leningrad, Nauka.

LUHO, V. (1967) Die Suomusjärvi-Kultur. Die mittel- und spätmesolithische Zeit in Finnland. *Suomen muinaismuistoyhdistyksen aikakauskirja*, 66: 1–124.

OSHIBKINA, S.V. (1979) Mezoliticheskaya stoyanka Andozero-M. *Kratkie soobshcheniya Instituta arkheologii AN SSSR*, 157: 21–27.

OSHIBKINA, S.V. (1982a) Derevyannye izdeliya stoyanki Nizhnee Veret'e. *Archeologicke rozhledy*, 34: 414–429.

OSHIBKINA, S.V. (1982b) Mogil'nik v mestnosti Popovo. *Sovetskaya archeologiya*, 3: 122–138.

OSHIBKINA, S.V. (1983) *Mezolit basseyna Sukhony i Vostochnogo Prionezh'ya.* Moscow, Nauka.

RIMANTIENE, R.K. (1971) *Paleolit i mezolit Litvy.* Vilnyus, Izdatel'stvo Mintis.

RUST, A. (1937) *Das altsteinzeitliche Renntierjägerlager Meiendorf.* Neumünster, Karl Wachholtz.

SONNEVILLE-BORDES, D. DE and PERROT, J. (1956) Lexique typologique du Paléolithique supérieur. Outillage lithique – IV Burins. *Bulletin de la Société Préhistorique Française*, 53: 408–412.

VANKINA, L.V. (1970) *Torfyanikovaya stoyanka Sarnate.* Riga, Zinatne.

WETZEL, G. (1966) Ein Eibenholzbogen von Barleben, Kr. Wolmirstedt. *Ausgrabungen und Funde*, 11, hft 1: 9–10.

ZAGORSKA, I. (1974) Videja akmens laikmeta zivju skepi Latvija. *Arheologija un etnografija* (Riga), 11: 25–38.

The Bone and Antler Inventory from Zvejnieki II, Latvian SSR

Ilga Zagorska and Francis Zagorskis

Abstract

The Stone Age of the Latvian SSR is characterized by a rich inventory of antler and bone artifacts. These have been obtained as stray finds and also, during the past two decades, from excavated sites. The middle level of the settlement of Zvejnieki II belongs to the middle Mesolithic, *c.* 9000–8000 BP. Together with a rich flint inventory, this site has yielded numerous artifacts of bone and antler – tools, hunting and fishing equipment, and decorative objects. These artifacts show close similarities, both in typology and in the relative proportions of the different types, to those found at Kunda-Lammasmägi in northern Estonia. Taking into account the distribution of sites and stray finds, the heartland of the Kunda culture appears to correspond to the territories of Estonia and northern and south-eastern Latvia, although its influence can be observed over a much wider area.

INTRODUCTION

Archaeologists in Soviet Latvia have paid particular attention to research on the Mesolithic period over the last two decades. The Mesolithic cultures of the east Baltic area, represented particularly by finds in the Kunda marsh, the Pernava valley and the Kunda-Lammasmägi site in Estonia (Indreko 1948; L. Jaanits 1966), have been noted for their rich bone and antler industry since the last century. The evidence from Latvia has consisted mainly of stray finds from the area around Lake Lubana, the first of which came to light in the 1930s (Šturms 1939, 1970; Loze 1964, 1966). The settlement of Zvejnieki II in northern Latvia was discovered in the 1970s and investigated by F. Zagorskis of the Institute of History, Academy of Sciences of the Latvian SSR. Amongst other finds, the site has produced a rich and varied collection of bone and antler artifacts. Several middle Mesolithic sites with bone artifacts have also recently been exposed in central Estonia – Moksi, Siimusaare, Umbusi – and on the banks of Lake Lubana in Latvia, at Zvidze (K. Jaanits 1981; Loze 1981).

THE SITE AND ITS CONTEXT

The site of Zvejnieki II is situated on the northern shore of Lake Burtnieki, on the northern slope of a long gravel ridge formed by a drumlin. The excavations exposed an area of 665 m² and yielded nearly 1500 flint and 1000 bone artifacts. On the upper part of the slope, overlying the primary yellowish sand, there was a layer of light-coloured gravel and marl. This layer yielded early Mesolithic artifacts (Zagorska 1981). All over the slope, partly covering the early Mesolithic horizon, there was a 0.4–0.7 m thick layer of gravel varying from dark- to light-grey in colour, in which middle Mesolithic artifacts were found. The bone and antler inventory from this layer is similar to the Kunda-Lammasmägi finds and belongs to the main stage of the Kunda culture, between 9000 and 8000 BP.

This report will consider the bone and antler assemblage found in the middle Mesolithic layer of Zvejnieki II. During the middle Mesolithic, which coincides with the Boreal, the animal life of Latvia was that of a forest zone. The faunal assemblage from Zvejnieki II is dominated by elk (77%), then beaver (12%), wild boar (5.4%), aurochs (0.26%), horse (0.4%), red deer and roe deer. Predators are represented by brown bear, marten, and wolf. Some bones of otter and European pond tortoise were found, as well as those of dog (1.8%) – the only domesticated animal represented on the site.

THE BONE AND ANTLER INVENTORY

For the manufacture of tools use was made mainly of elk bone and antler, while bones of other animals – such as roe deer, horse, beaver and bear – were used comparatively rarely (V. Danilchenko, Moscow).

Of the finds from Zvejnieki II, *c.* 900 bone and antler objects are considered to belong to the middle Mesolithic occupation. They comprise: (i) raw bone and antler, bearing traces of working; (ii) finished artifacts of bone and antler – tools, fishing and hunting equipment, decorative items, and miscellaneous pieces.

Tools

For the manufacture of tools a large long bone was divided into strips by first making parallel longitudinal incisions, and then removing splinters 1.2–2.5 cm broad and 4–6 mm thick. The articular end was removed at some stage by cutting a deep

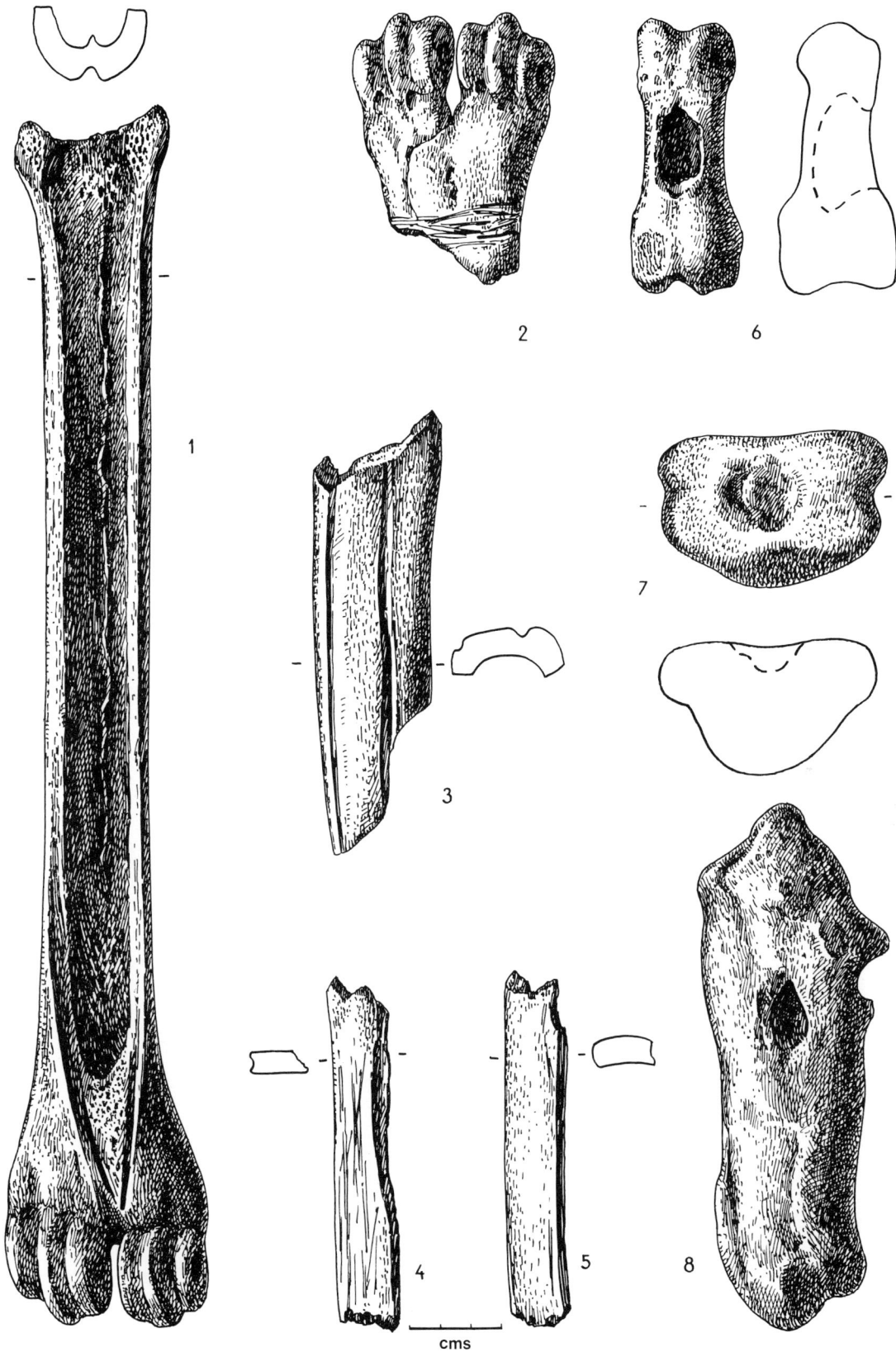

Figure 1 Raw bone and antler specimens with traces of working from Zvejnieki II. Registration numbers (Collection No. 158, Institute of History, Academy of Sciences, LSSR): 1 – 1857; 2 – 452; 3 – 991; 4 – 354; 5 – 341; 6 – 662; 7 – 472; 8 – 1158.

415

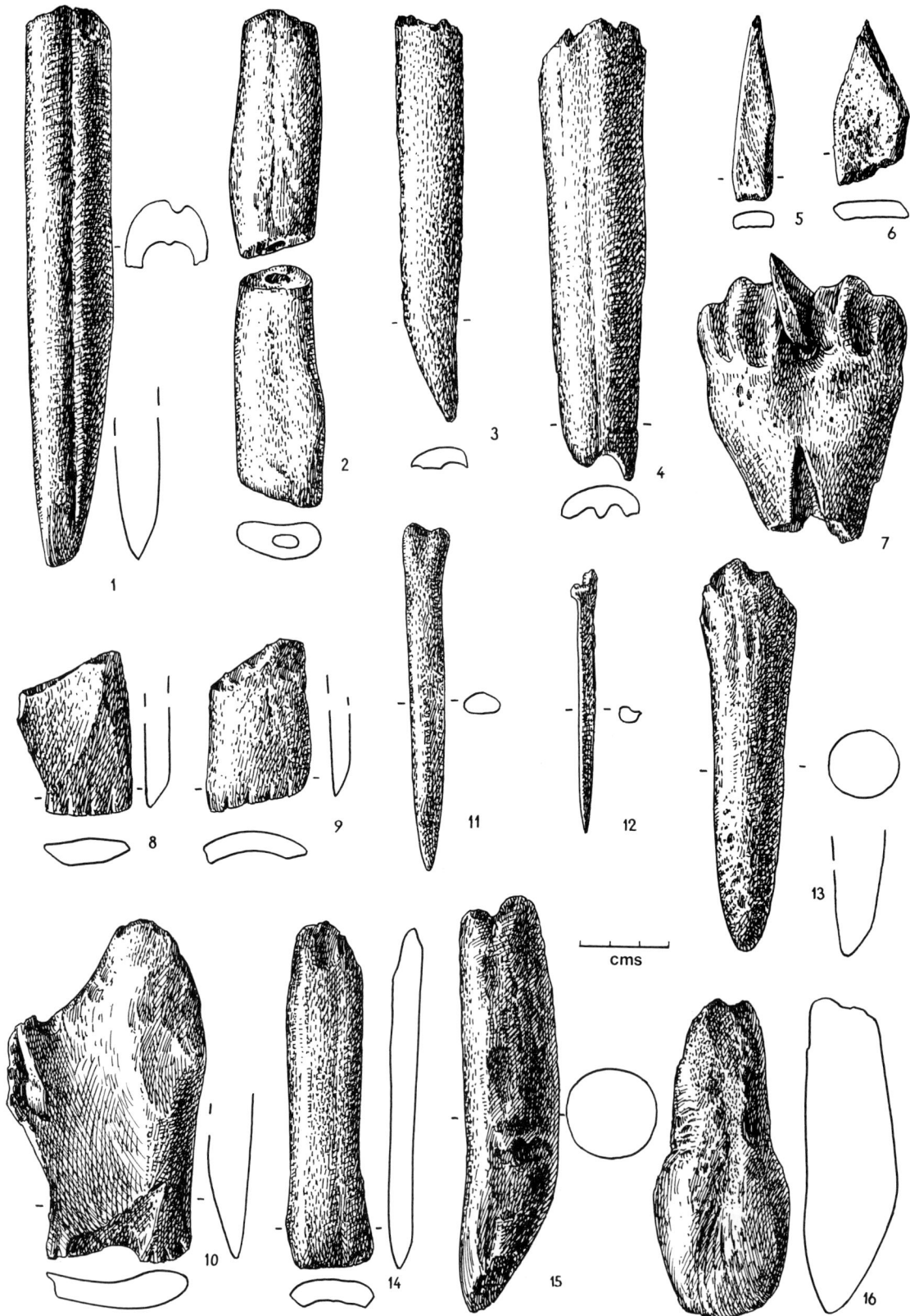

Figure 2   Bone and antler tools from Zvejnieki II. Registration numbers: 1 – 154; 2 – 1843; 3 – 221; 4 – 763; 5 – 2683; 6 – 1544; 7 – 2302; 8 – 303; 9 – 177; 10 – 203; 11 – 1948; 12 – 362; 13 – 47; 14 – 1168; 15 – 1848; 16 – 2753.

416

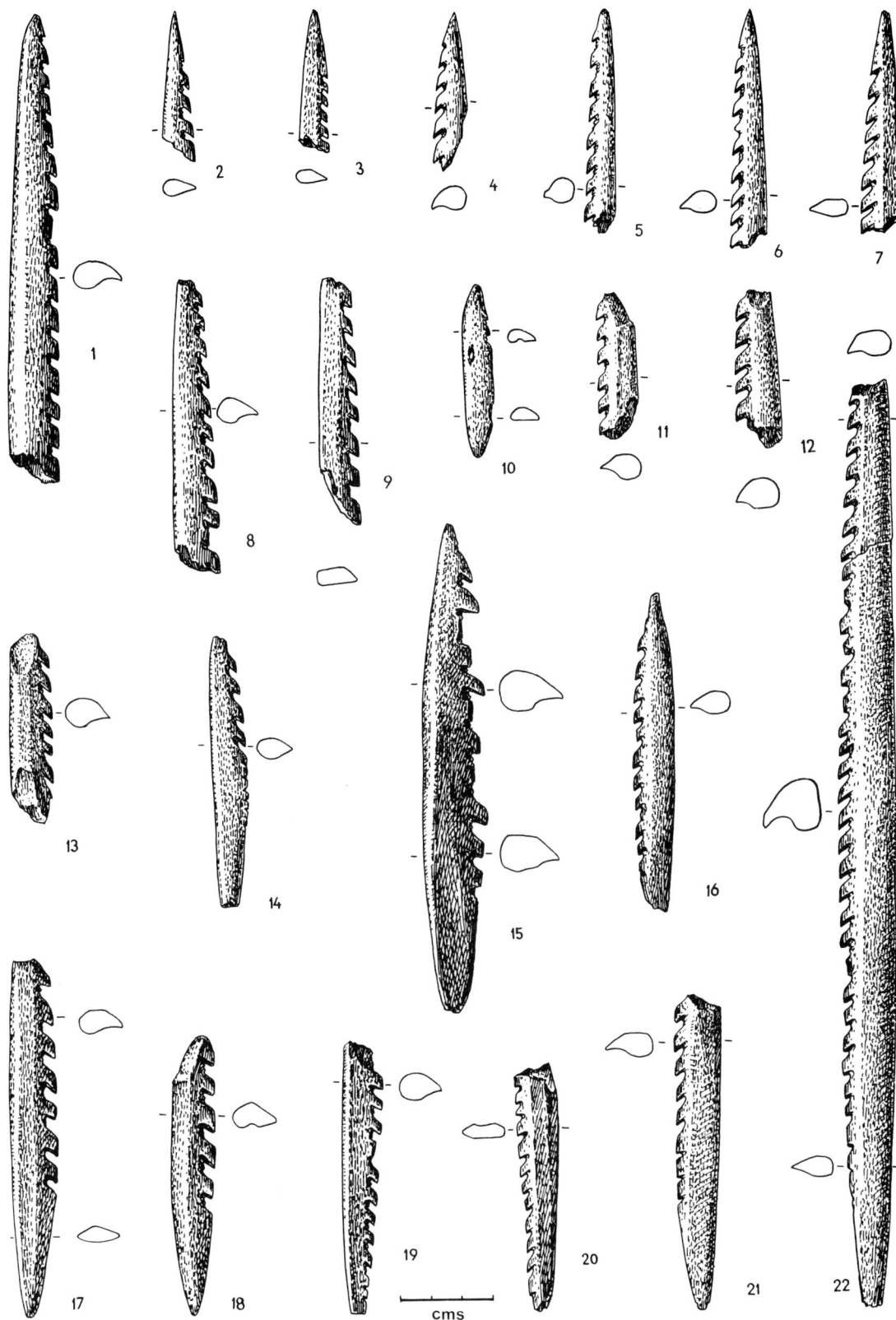

Figure 3 Fish spears of Kunda type from Zvejnieki II. Registration numbers: 1 – 774; 2 – 925; 3 – 1407; 4 – 731; 5 – 883; 6 – 912; 7 – 908; 8 – 889; 9 – 1283; 10 – 80; 11 – 176; 12 – 180; 13 – 113; 14 – 921; 15 – 1929; 16 – 1197; 17 – 779; 18 – 719; 19 – 250; 20 – 1795; 21 – 1886; 22 – 277.

transverse notch or circular groove, after which it could be knocked off (*Fig. 1*, nos. 1–5). Tools were also made from other bones, such as ribs, shoulder blades and antler tines. The excavations have produced a large number of first and second phalanges and other limb bones of elk, some of which have circular or oval perforations (*Fig. 1*, nos. 6–8). Numerous pieces of antler bearing traces of heavy cutting were also found. In the middle Mesolithic, techniques of working antler and bone were very uniform across the forest belt of northern Europe extending from the eastern shores of Lake Onega in the east (Oshibkina 1983) to the site of Star Carr in England in the west (Clark 1954).

Of the 212 tools recovered from the middle Mesolithic horizon, most are well-known types, although there are some which may be regarded as novel.

Antler tine implements

The antler tools include a rich collection of chisels made from elk antler tines. These have a facet at one end formed by oblique cutting, with the other end occasionally slightly modified for insertion into a haft. They vary in length from 8 to 14 cm (*Fig. 2*, nos. 15, 16). A similar find at the site of Zvidze on the shore of Lake Lubana in eastern Latvia clearly shows the manner in which the implement was attached to a wooden haft (Loze 1981: fig. 2, no. 6). Specimens of particularly slender tines with the tips often bevelled on one face or preserved intact, and varying from 7 to 15 cm in length, were also found (*Fig. 2*, no. 13). Similar objects made of red deer antler are known from Star Carr, where they were interpreted as implements used for working leather or skins (Clark 1954: figs. 65, 66).

Antler adzes

Fragmentary pieces of antler adzes with perforations for a haft – a well-known type across northern Europe – were also preserved.

Handles

A distinctive group is formed by a series of comparatively small objects (7–8 cm in length) of antler or bone with a surface, edges and ends smoothed, and with natural or artificial sockets (*Fig. 2*, no. 2). These were presumably used as handles for an inset of flint or bone in order to perform stabbing, cutting or perforating actions (Semenov 1957: 209). Such hafts have been known since the Upper Palaeolithic and have been found at sites in the basins of the rivers Dnestr, Dnepr, Don (Molodova I, Molodova V, Mezin, Eliseevitchi), as well as in Czechoslovakia (Pekarna, Pavlov) and further west (Feustel 1973; Chernysh 1982: fig. 36).

Tools with a hollow working edge

A large number of tools with a hollow working edge were found. They were made of longitudinally split tubular bones, smoothed on both surfaces, with a convex working edge bevelled on the inner face. Some of these tools have rough traces of flaking on the outer face at the working edge; they vary in length from 6 to 16 cm. There are three kinds of these tools: (i) with a blade in the form of a beak (*Fig. 2*, no. 4); (ii) with a notched blade (*Fig. 2*, nos. 8–10); and (iii) with a smooth blade (*Fig. 2*, no. 14). Clark has emphasized the close similarity of these objects to tools used by various groups of the Central Eskimo for working caribou skins (Clark 1954: 161–162, fig. 73).

Narrow-bladed chisels

Other specimens made from tubular bones have their working edge narrowed and bevelled on both faces. They may be classed as narrow-bladed chisels (*Fig. 2*, no. 1).

Ice-picks

Fragments of tools manufactured from long tubular bones, smoothed, and normally with the tip broken off were also among the finds from Zvejnieki II. Similar, but complete and undamaged, specimens are known amongst the stray finds on the banks of Lake Lubana; they have been classified as ice-picks (Šturms 1970: 36, fig. 18, no. 5).

Wedge-shaped tools

The most numerous group of tools is formed by wedge-shaped splinters of bone, of varied size and form (length: 4–17 cm), and with the edges split off on both sides (*Fig. 2*, nos. 5, 6). Exceptionally, some specimens are split off on one side only (*Fig. 2*, no. 3). The largest examples were evidently gripped in the hand for use, while the smallest pieces were set in some form of haft, such as the articular end of a large long bone (*Fig. 2*, no. 7). Wedge-shaped tools were known already in the Upper Palaeolithic and are thought to have been used for removing spongy tissue from the core of antlers (Semenov 1957: 190, fig. 80, no. 2). The wedged-shaped tools from Zvejnieki II were probably used for working antler and bone, de-barking wood, flaking flint, and for other purposes. The large number of wedge-shaped tools found on the site suggests that they must have seen extensive use.

Knives

These were made from animal ribs and shoulder blades and the tusks of wild boars, and have either one or both edges worked.

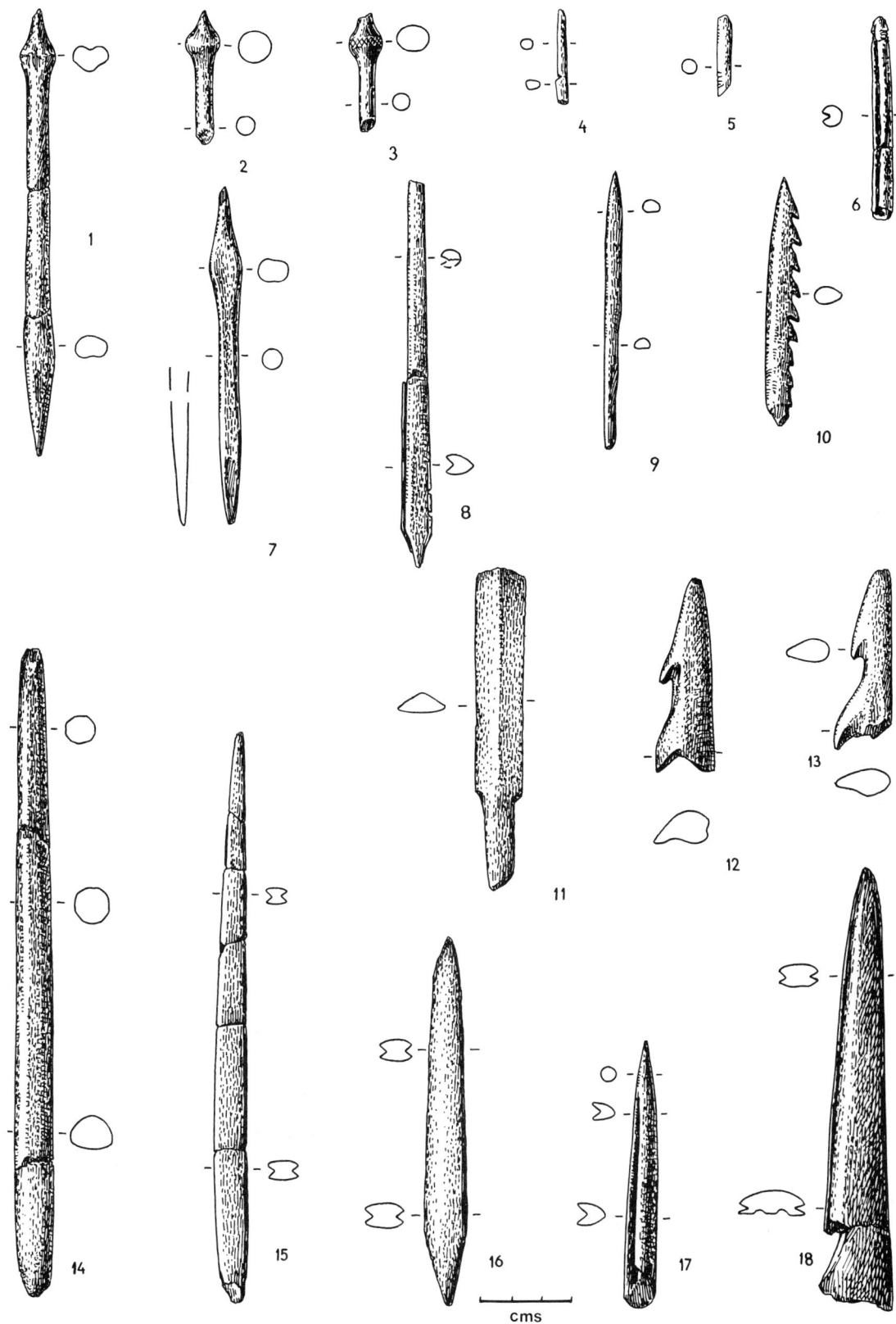

Figure 4 Fishing and hunting equipment from Zvejnieki II. Registration numbers: 1 – 528; 2 – 1100; 3 – 1204; 4 – 1194; 5 – 625; 6 – 624; 7 – 1800; 8 – 306; 9 – 1110; 10 – 170; 11 – 923; 12 – 1518; 13 – 983; 14 – 11; 15 – 997; 16 – 986; 17 – 929; 18 – 1198.

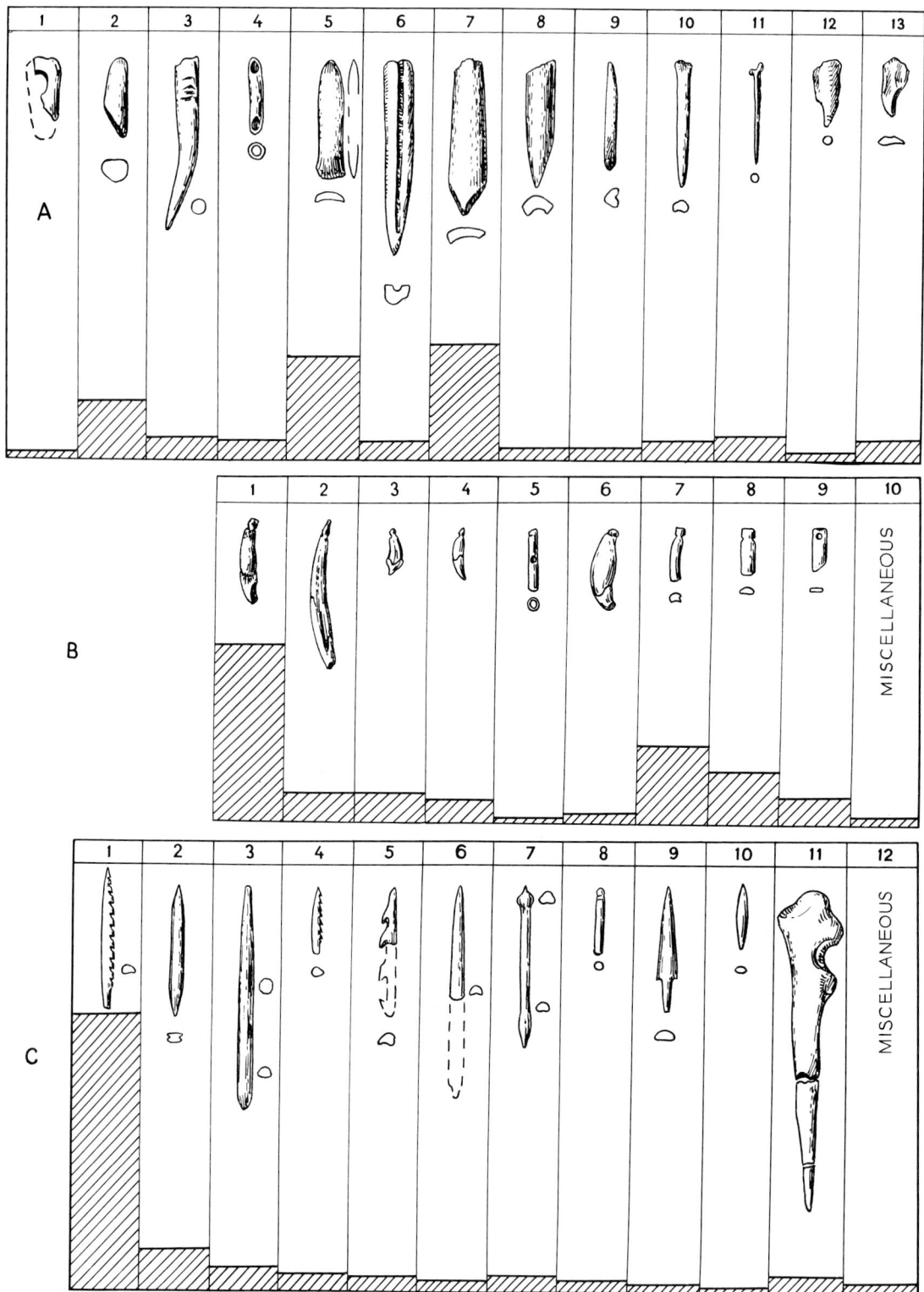

Figure 5   The different categories of bone and antler artifacts from Zvejnieki II.

A. *Tools*: 1 – adzes (0.9% of the total of 212 objects); 2 – chisels (13.2%); 3 – antler tine implements (5.2%); 4 – handles (4.3%); 5 – tools with a hollow working edge (25%); 6 – narrow-bladed chisels (3.8%); 7 – wedged-shaped tools (26.9%); 8 – ice-picks (2.8%); 9 – skin smoothers (2.8%); 10 – blunt-ended awls (4.3%); 11 – awls (5.6%); 12 – drills (0.9%); 13 – knives (4.3%).

B. *Decorative articles*: 1–4, 6 – tooth pendants; 5 – bird bone tube; 7 – beaver canine pendants; 8, 9 – bone tablets; 10 – miscellaneous items. (1=41.2% of the total of 136 items; 2=6.6%; 3=6.6%; 4=5.1%; 5=0.7%; 6=1.5%; 7=19.1%; 8=11.8%; 9=5.9%; 10=1.5%).

C. *Fishing and hunting equipment*: 1 – fish spears of Kunda type (63.8% of the total of 324 objects); 2 – slotted points (9.3%); 3 – needle-shaped points (4.9%); 4 – harpoons with slanting barbs (3.7%); 5 – harpoons with beak-shaped barbs (3.1%) 6 – fish spears of Lubana type (1.9%); 7 – arrowheads with a conical tip (3.4%); 8 – stems of compound fish-hooks (1.9%); 9 – spear-heads with symmetrical barbs (1.2%); 10 – arrowheads, leaf-shaped (0.6%); 11 – daggers (4.3%); 12 – miscellaneous items (1.9%).

420

Miscellaneous tools

A variety of smaller, thinner ribs and bone splinters with the end rounded and thoroughly polished were presumably used for smoothing seams of skin or leather. Bird bones and elk metacarpals were converted into bodkins, pins, awls and drills.

The overall classification of the bone and antler tools from the middle Mesolithic horizon of Zvejnieki II is summarized in *Fig. 5A*. Many of these objects – slender antler tines, handles, rib and shoulder-blade knives, skin smoothers, bodkins, etc. – are types that were already in use in the Upper Palaeolithic of middle and north-west Europe. The early Mesolithic in the east Baltic region, as attested by the finds from the lower layer of Zvejnieki II and the site of Pulli in Estonia (Jaanits and Jaanits 1978), is characterized by almost all of the artifact types mentioned above. Yet the middle Mesolithic toolkit shows certain differences in the variety of artifact forms, their quantity, and frequency of occurrence. This toolkit consists of thirteen different types. Most numerous are the wedge-shaped artifacts, tools with a hollow working edge, and antler chisels (*Fig. 5A*, types 7, 5, 2). Less frequent are worked tines, handles, awls, and bodkins (*Fig. 5A*, types 3, 4, 10, 11). Other forms are represented only by a few examples (*Fig. 5A*, types 1, 6, 9, 12, 13).

Some of these tools, such as the antler chisels and the tools with a hollow working edge, were widespread over the North European Plain during the Mesolithic (e.g. Nizhneye Veretye, Hohen Viecheln, Star Carr). Bone and antler handles are found more rarely, for example at Maglemosian sites in Denmark (Mathiassen 1948: figs. 191–193). Wedge-shaped tools, which are particularly prominent among the finds from Zvejnieki II, are an artifact type that is rarely mentioned in the archaeological literature. The closest analogue for the toolkit from Zvejnieki II is the assemblage from Kunda-Lammasmägi (Indreko 1948).

Decorative articles

The category of decorative articles, comprising 136 items, is represented by pendants cut from bone, pendants made from beaver canines, tooth-beads, and bird bone tubes (*Fig. 5B*). The bone pendants are either rectangular tablets that are smoothly polished with incised grooves and drilled holes, or simply irregular fragments of bone with a transverse groove at one end (*Fig. 5B*, types 8, 9). The beaver tooth pendants were made of the middle sections of split canines and were similarly grooved at one or both ends (*Fig. 5B*, type 7). The tooth-beads were likewise grooved at the root end (*Fig. 5B*, types 1–4). The tooth-beads found at Zvejnieki II are representative of the animal life of the east Baltic

during the Boreal period; elk incisors dominate, being twice as numerous as beaver canines, while the teeth of small carnivores are less common still, and there are only a few examples of teeth of wild boar and bear and of bird bones.

Hunting and fishing equipment

The hunting and fishing equipment found at the site consists of 324 items (*Fig. 5C*).

The largest category is formed by fish spears with a single row of small, beak-shaped barbs and a pear-shaped cross-section. They taper towards both ends, the tangs being smooth or marked with fine incisions. Their lengths range from 6 to 30 cm (*Fig. 3*). The fish spears belong to the so-called Kunda type – Clark's type 6 (Clark 1936: 116–117).

Also well represented are slotted bone points with grooves along one or both sides for insertion of flint blades – Clark's types 21A and 21B (*Fig. 4*, nos. 8, 15–18), smoothed needle-shaped points with a cross-section that is circular, sometimes oval or irregular – Clark's type 1 (*Fig. 4*, nos. 9, 14), harpoons with obliquely-cut or slanting barbs – Clark's type 10 (*Fig. 4*, no. 10), harpoons with large, widely-spaced, beak-shaped barbs – Clark's type 12A (*Fig. 4*, nos. 12, 13), and arrowheads with a conical tip – Clark's type 16 (*Fig. 4*, nos. 1, 2, 3, 7,).

Also present, but few in number, were the stems of compound fish-hooks (*Fig. 4*, nos. 4–6), spear-heads with a long blade and two symmetrical barbs at its lower end – a variety of Clark's type 17 (*Fig. 4*, no. 11), and examples of spear-heads with a tri-angular cross-section – the Lubana type or Clark's type 13. There are also some arrowheads of leaf-shaped form, and a large number of daggers made from long tubular bones or humeri.

The most important component of the hunting and fishing equipment at Zvejnieki II (*Fig. 5C*) are the spear-heads of Kunda type (*Fig. 5A*, type 1) which, together with the spear-heads of Lubana type (*Fig. 5A*, type 6), were the main artifacts for fish spearing. Fish-hooks were also used (*Fig. 5A*, type 8). In the Boreal period the main species of fish caught at Zvejnieki II were pike, bream, tench and perch, which were probably taken during the summer months (determined by J. Sloka, Riga).

The most important hunting weapons were probably the spear-heads with flint inserts (*Fig. 5C*, type 2), the arrows with a conical tip (*Fig. 5C*, type 7), the harpoons with slanted or beak-shaped barbs (*Fig. 5C*, types 4, 5), and daggers (*Fig. 5C*, type 11). The smoothed needle-shaped points (*Fig. 5C*, type 3) were probably used as arrowheads for bird hunting.

Several of the middle Mesolithic hunting and fishing weapon types apparently originated in European Upper Paleolithic cultures. The needle-shaped points and the spear-heads with flint inserts appear

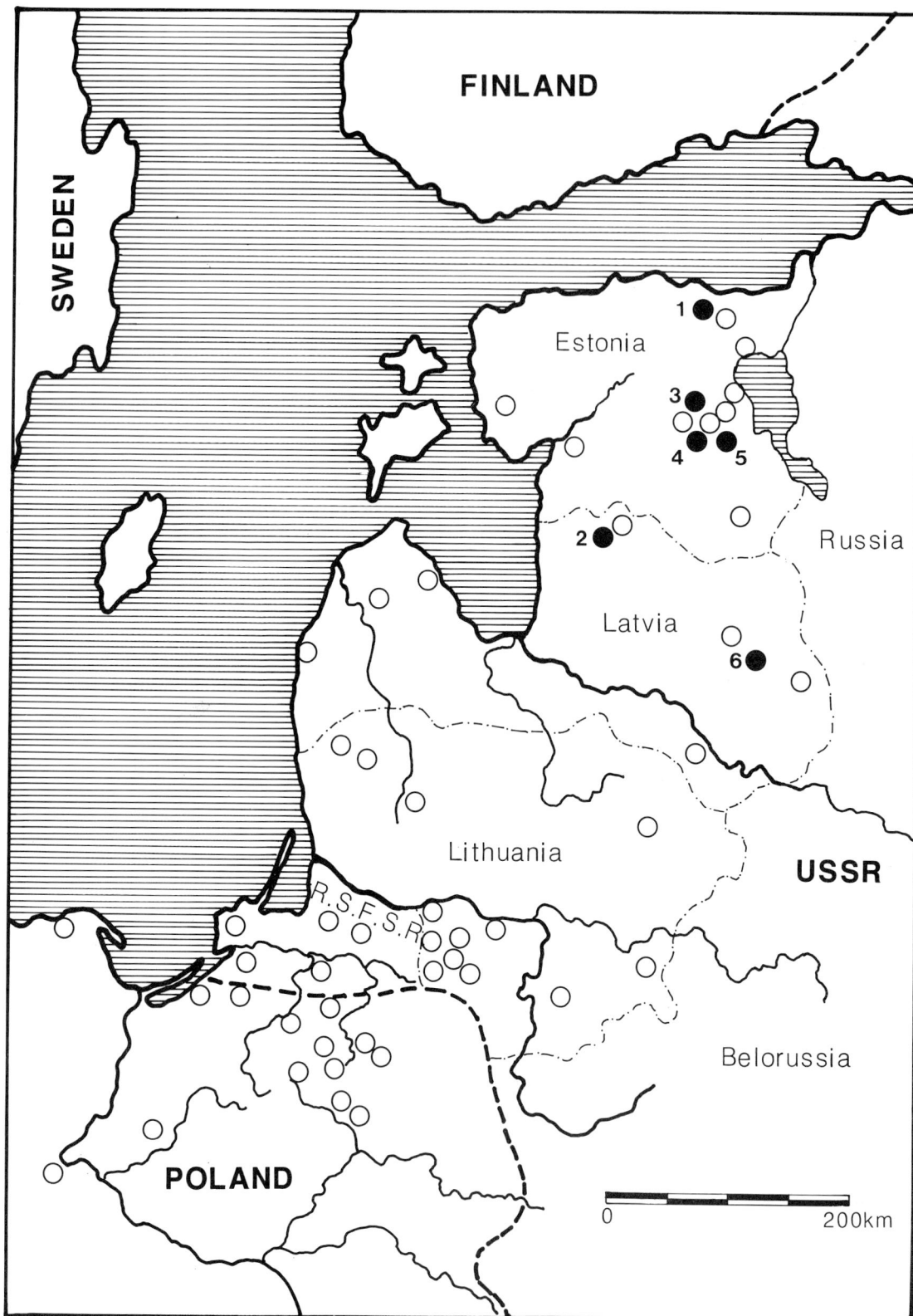

●   sites with antler/bone assemblage

○   stray finds of antler/bone hunting and fishing equipment

Figure 6   The distribution of Kunda culture Boreal period sites with a bone and antler inventory in the east Baltic region: 1 – Kunda-Lammasmägi; 2 – Zvejnieki II; 3 – Umbusi; 4 – Moksi; 5 – Siimusaare; 6 – Zvidze.

in the middle European Upper Palaeolithic – at sites of the Molodova group throughout the basin of the River Dnestr (Chernysh 1973: fig. 21). Harpoons with beak-shaped barbs turn up as Clark's type 12A in the tanged point cultures on the southern and south-western shores of the Baltic Sea (Kozłowski 1981: 84). Spears of Lubana type and arrowheads with a conical tip are first encountered in the early Mesolithic of the east Baltic area – in the lower layer of Zvejnieki II and at Pulli in Estonia (Jaanits and Jaanits 1978). In the middle Mesolithic the fish spear of Kunda type becomes the main fishing implement. The Kunda spear-head probably emerged in the east Baltic region from the broad, barbed harpoons of the early Mesolithic (Zagorska 1981: fig. 2, no. 10; fig. 5, no. 6). The middle Mesolithic stratum at Zvejnieki II has produced some specimens with symmetrical barbs (*Fig. 5C*, type 9), which become more widely used in the following phase – i.e. at the end of the Mesolithic (Zagorskis 1973: 656, fig. 2, nos. 3, 4, 7, 8, 11).

The assemblage of hunting and fishing equipment from Zvejnieki II shows close similarities in both typology and the proportions of the different types to that found at Kunda-Lammasmägi (Indreko 1948; L. Jaanits 1966). Kunda type spear-heads and points with flint inserts were also found at the sites of Siimusaare, Moksi and Umbusi in Estonia (K. Jaanits 1981). Sporadic finds of hunting and fishing equipment like those from the middle Mesolithic level at Zvejnieki II are known from all over Estonia, throughout Latvia (though here mainly in the south-eastern part, especially around Lake Lubana), from Lithuania and the district of Kaliningrad, and from north-eastern Poland (Rimantiene 1971; Kozłowski 1972; Zagorska and Zagorskis 1977; L. Jaanits et al. 1982). Judging by the distribution of settlements and the density of bone and antler stray finds, the centre of the Kunda culture lies in Estonia and the northern and south-eastern parts of Latvia (*Fig. 6*). The extension of similar stray finds even further to the south west testifies to mutual influence and relationships between the Kunda and Neman cultures.

References

CHERNYSH, A. (1973) *Paleolit i mezolit Pridnestrovya*. Moscow, Nauka.

CHERNYSH, A. (1982) Mnogosloynaya paleoliticheskaya stoyanka Molodova I. In G.I. Gorecki and I.K. Ivanova (eds), *Unikal'noe must'erskoe poselenie na Srednem Dnestre*. Moscow, Nauka: 6–102.

CLARK, J.G.D. (1936) *The Mesolithic Settlement of Northern Europe*. Cambridge, University Press.

CLARK, J.G.D. (1954) *Excavations at Star Carr*. Cambridge, University Press.

FEUSTEL, R. (1973) *Technik der Steinzeit*. Weimar, Herman Böhlaus Nachfolger.

INDREKO, R. (1948) *Die mittlere Steinzeit in Estland*. Stockholm, Kungl. Vitterhets Historie och Antikvitets Akademiens Handlingar, 66.

JAANITS, K. (1981) Die mesolithischen Siedlungsplätze mit Feuersteininventar in Estland. In B. Gramsch (ed.), *Mesolithikum in Europa. 2. Internationales Symposium Potsdam, 3 bis 8 April 1978 Bericht* (Veröffentlichungen des Museums für Ur- und Frühgeschichte Potsdam, 14/15). Berlin, Deutscher Verlag der Wissenschaften: 389–399.

JAANITS, L. (1966) Novye dannye po mezolitu Estonii. *Materialy i issledovaniya po arkheologii SSSR*, 126: 114–124.

JAANITS, L. and JAANITS, K. (1978) Ausgrabungen der Frühmesolithischen Siedlung von Pulli. *Eesti NSV Teaduste Akademiya Toimetised*, 27(1): 56–63.

JAANITS, L., LAUL, S., LOUGAS, V. and TONISSON, E. (1982) *Eesti esiajalagu*. Tallinn, 'Eesti Raamat'.

KOZŁOWSKI, S.K. (1972) *Pradzieje ziem polskich od IX do V tysiaclecia p.n.e.* Warsaw, Państwowe Wydawnictwo Naukowe.

KOZŁOWSKI, S.K. (1981) Single-barbed Havel type harpoons in the European Lowland. *Archaeologia Interregionalis*, 1: 77–88.

LOZE, I. (1964) Mezoliticheskie nakhodki Lubanskoy nizmennosti. *Izvestiya Akademii Nauk Latv. SSR*, 3: 7–20.

LOZE, I. (1966) Nekotorye mezoliticheskie nakhodki na territorii Latvii. *Materialy i issledovaniya po arkheologii SSSR*, 126: 108–113.

LOZE, I. (1981) Spätmesolithikum und Frühneolithikum in Lettland. In B. Gramsch (ed.), *Mesolithikum in Europa. 2. Internationales Symposium Potsdam, 3 bis 8 April 1978 Bericht* (Veröffentlichungen des Museums für Ur- und Frühgeschichte Potsdam, 14/15). Berlin, Deutscher Verlag der Wissenschaften: 183–190.

MATHIASSEN, T. (1948) *Danske Oldsager. I. Ældre Stenalder*. Copenhagen, Nordisk Forlag.

OSHIBKINA, S. (1983) *Mezolit basseyna Sukhony i Vostochnogo Prionezh'ya*. Moscow, Nauka.

RIMANTIENE, R.K. (1971) *Paleolit i mezolit Litvy*. Vilnyus, Izdatel'stvo Mintis.

SEMENOV, S. (1957) *Pervobytnaya technika* (Materialy i issledovaniya po Arkheologii SSSR, 54). Moscow–Leningrad, Izdatel'stvo Akademii Nauk SSSR.

ŠTURMS, E. (1939) Mezolīta atradumi Latvijā. *Senatne un māksla* (Riga), 1: 31–44.

ŠTURMS, E. (1970) *Die steinzeitlichen Kulturen des Baltikums*. Bonn, Rudolf Habelt Verlag GMBH.

ZAGORSKA, I. (1981) Das Frühmesolithikum in Lettland. In B. Gramsch (ed.), *Mesolithikum in Europa. 2. Internationales Symposium Potsdam, 3 bis 8 April 1978 Bericht* (Veröffentlichungen des Museums für Ur- und Frühgeschichte Potsdam, 14/15). Berlin, Deutscher Verlag der Wissenschaften: 73–82.

ZAGORSKA, I. and ZAGORSKIS, F. (1977) Mezolit Latvii. *Kratkie soobshcheniya Instituta arkheologii* (Moscow), 149: 69–75.

ZAGORSKIS, F. (1973) Das Spätmesolithikum in Lettland. In S.K. Kozłowski (ed.), *The Mesolithic in Europe*. Warsaw, University Press: 651–669.

A Survey of Early Holocene Cultures of the Western Part of the Russian Plain

Stefan Karol Kozłowski

Abstract

This article presents a survey of the early and middle Holocene hunter-gatherer cultures of the western part of the east European plain (the Estonian, Latvian, Lithuanian, Byelorussian, Moldavian, and the western part of the Ukrainian Soviet Socialist Republics). The ecological/latitudinal subdivision of this territory is presented (zones A–C) and the characteristics of the landscape, river network, soils, flora, fauna, and flint raw material sources described. This is followed by remarks on the chronology of the Mesolithic cultures and a concise description of the main taxonomic units (zone A – Kunda, Post-Swiderian and Neman cultures; zone B – Post-Swiderian, Kudlaevka and Janisławice cultures; zone C – Shan-Koba, Belolesye, Murzak-Koba, Kukrek and Grebeniki cultures). Separate sections deal with the Mesolithic art of the region and the burial evidence. Finally, the Mesolithic settlement network is discussed.

INTRODUCTION

The present article is a tentative synthesis of early Holocene hunter-gatherer cultures from the area adjacent to the eastern borders of Poland, Czechoslovakia, Hungary and Romania. A presentation of this kind has never been attempted by Soviet archaeologists, but it is an indispensable part of the present author's research into the European, and especially the central European, Mesolithic.

This research is based primarily on the available literature, but also incorporates numerous previously unpublished finds studied by the author in Soviet and Polish museums.

The study area is a natural eastward extension of central Europe; hence some of the cultural phenomena apparent there are also known from Poland. Thus, not only is the Russian material complementary to that from Poland, the evidence from Poland contributes towards a better understanding of the phenomena from the western part of the Russian Plain.

This report first brings together basic information about the archaeology and chronology, and about the most important elements of the natural environment, and then describes the characteristics of the principal taxonomic units against their environmental background.

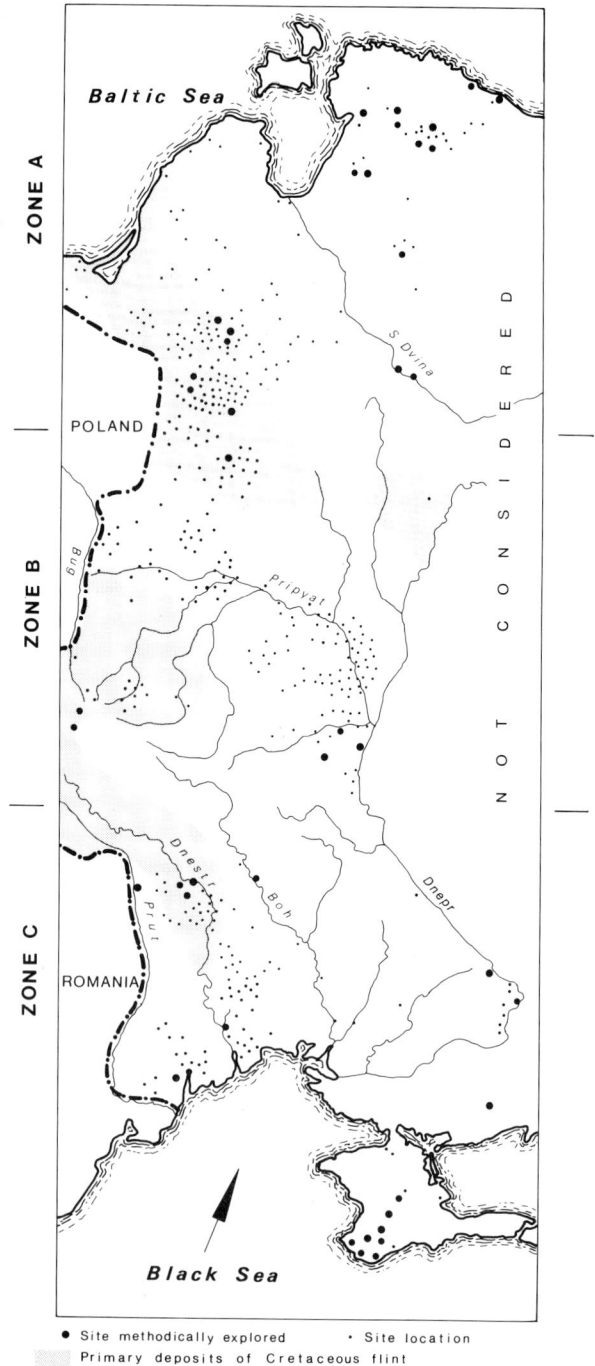

● Site methodically explored   · Site location
Primary deposits of Cretaceous flint

Figure 1   Map of early and middle Holocene sites in the western part of the Soviet Union showing primary deposits of Cretaceous flint (stipple). Large dots denote methodically explored sites (see *Table 1*). Based on information from Jaanits (1981), Zagorskis (1974), Rimantiene (1971, 1984), Zalizniak (1984), Telegin (1982), Kraskovski (1978), and S.K. Kozłowski (1972, 1975, 1980).

Table 1:   Methodically explored sites shown in *Fig. 1*

Republic	Site	Culture
Estonian S.S.R	Pulli	Kunda
	Narva	Kunda
	Kunda-Lammasmägi	Kunda
	Jälevere	Kunda
	Lepakose	Kunda
	Moksi	Kunda
	Siimusaare	Kunda
	Umbusi	Kunda
Latvian S.S.R.	Osa	Kunda
	Zvejnieki I	Kunda
	Zvejnieki II	Kunda
Lithuanian S.S.R.	Lampédžiai	Neman
	Niatesiai 1	Swiderian & Neman
	Žemiai-Kaniukai	Neman
	Paštuva	Neman
	Maksimonys 4	Janisławice
	Dubičiai 2	Neman
Byelorussian S.S.R.	Semenov Khutor	Neman
	Krumplevo	Neman
	Nesilovichi I	Janisławice
Ukrainian S.S.R.	Borodianka 3V	Janisławice
	Rudoi Ostrov	Janisławice
	Vishgorod DVS	Janisławice
	Igren 8	Kukrek
	Žankovtsi II	Grebeniki
	Vorotsiv II	Grebeniki
	Kamyanitsa 1	Grebeniki
	Mirnoe	Kukrek
	Girjevo	Grebeniki
	Belolesye	Belolesye
	Kamennaya Mogila	Kukrek
	Vasilevka III	Murzak-Koba
	Kukrek	Kukrek & Murzak-Koba
	Laspi 7	Murzak-Koba
	Shan-Koba	Shan-Koba, Imeretinska, Murzak-koba & Grebeniki
	Fat'ma-Koba	Shan-Koba, Imeretinska, Murzak-Koba & Grebeniki
	Zamil-Koba	Shan-Koba & Murzak-Koba
	Siuren II	Shan-Koba
	Murzak-Koba	Murzak-Koba
	Kara-Koba	Murzak-Koba
Moldavian S.S.R.	Soroki I	Grebeniki
	Soroki II	Grebeniki
	Butesty	Belolesye
	Frumusika	Grebeniki

Territorial range

Since the objective of this study is the presentation of a direct comparative background for Polish Mesolithic finds, the territory to be considered is not a discrete geographical region, but a stretch of land directly adjacent to the Polish border. Accordingly, the western limits of the area coincide with the political boundaries of Poland, Czechoslovakia, Hungary and Romania. The eastern boundary extends from the Gulf of Finland to the upper Dnepr valley and then along this river to the base of the Crimean peninsula (the Kerch peninsula is excluded). The author will therefore be looking at the following Soviet Republics: the Estonian, Latvian, Lithuanian and Moldavian Republics, at the greater part of the Byelorussian and the western part of the Ukranian Republics, and also at the Kaliningrad district of the Federal Russian Republic (*Fig. 1*) – an area of about 680,000 km².

Inevitably this area is very diversified ecologically, and cultural development in the final stages of the existence of hunter-gatherer communities was multi-channel and complex.

Chronological range

The chronological scope of the present study is arbitrary. The lower limit is set at the conventional boundary between the Pleistocene and the Holocene, *c.* 10,300/10,000 BP. I am fully aware of the discretionary nature of this delimitation, the more so since the area in question appears to provide evidence that divisions into climatic periods did not coincide with cultural or economic phases. The nature of the evidence (viz. few homogeneous assemblages and few dates) does not make things any easier; for this reason, the proposed interpretations of the initial stages of cultural development of some (western) parts of the territory must be treated with caution.

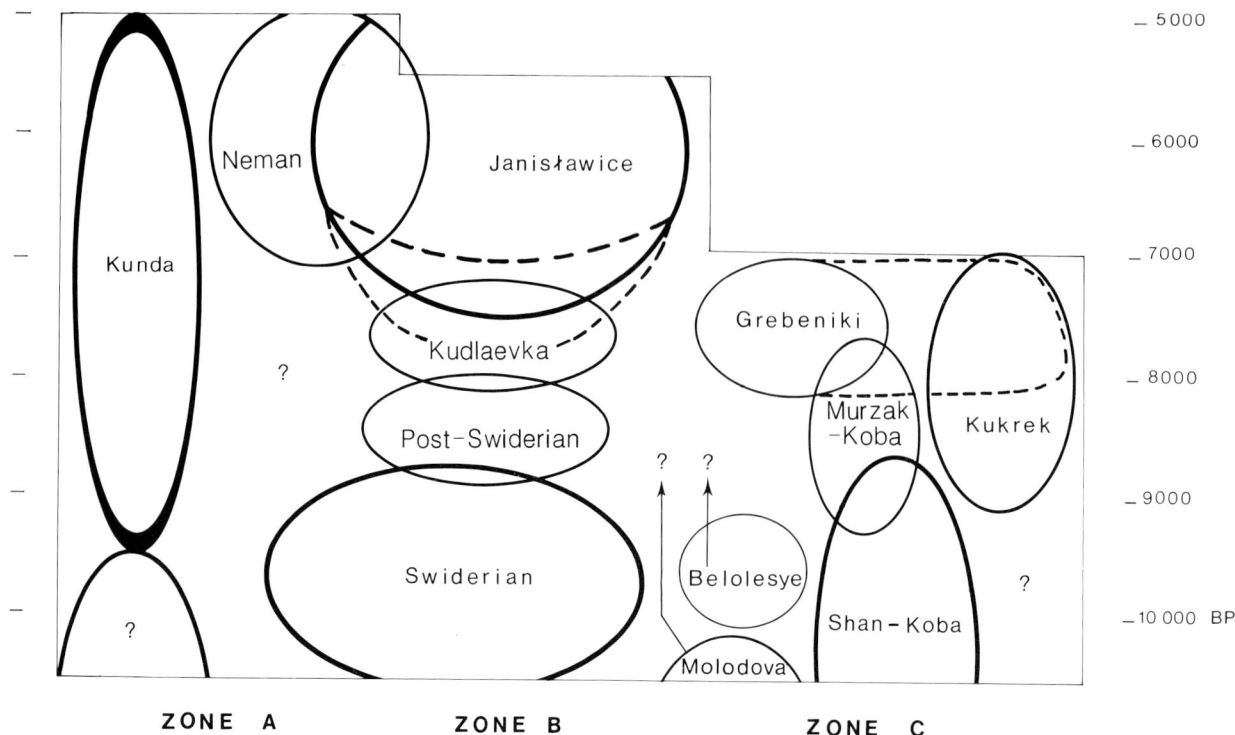

Figure 2   Chronology of the early and middle Holocene cultures of the western part of the Soviet Union (radiocarbon dates BP, uncalibrated).

The upper limit of the chronology is set by the appearance of ceramics. This, of course, occurred at different times, depending on the ecological zone; in the south it was generally earlier than in the north. The chronology of the appearance of the first ceramics in the area under consideration has yet to be fully determined, but we know that the first pottery appeared in the southern zone in the middle of the eighth millennium BP, while in the central and northern zones it was probably in the sixth millennium BP. The appearance of ceramics in a hunter-gatherer community does not always indicate neolithization in economic terms, but apparently signifies important changes in these communities. Consequently, the appearance of ceramics seems to be a good indicator of the decline of the old way of life, a decline which nevertheless could have gone on for quite some time.

NATURAL ENVIRONMENT

It is obvious that such a vast area as the one under consideration, and one stretching for about 1800 km from north to south, must have been highly diversified ecologically. This is indeed the case today, and may be inferred for the past.

The differentiation is of zonal character and the different zones are arranged latitudinally, this being conditioned on the one hand by climate, and on the other by terrain, geological structure, soils and hydrology.

The combined effect of all these factors led to the appearance of three main floral–faunal and landscape zones in the western part of the USSR in the early and middle Holocene (*Fig. 1*):

A. the lowland zone of young lakelands in the north;

B. the lowland zone of great river valleys in the central part; and

C. the upland–lowland steppe zone in the south.

Each of these zones – still discernible today – significantly influenced the character of early and middle Holocene settlement, creating barriers to its future development.

Zone A

The zone of young lakelands covers the areas of the Soviet Baltic republics and is bounded in the south by the moraine of the maximum of the Valdai (Würm) Glaciation. The hills of the frontal moraine (rising to over 200 m above sea level) form the watershed between the Baltic and Black Sea catchment areas. This glacial landscape declines in both relief and altitude towards the Baltic Sea.

Almost all of zone A is covered by boulder clays, which are sometimes sandy. This type of cover does not favour the discovery of Mesolithic sites. In the frontal moraine zone, as well as in several other regions, there are patches of outwash sands. The geological substratum was of course one of the fundamental factors conditioning the dominant soil types of this zone. These are podzol–grassland soils with two islands (Estonia and the borderland be-

426

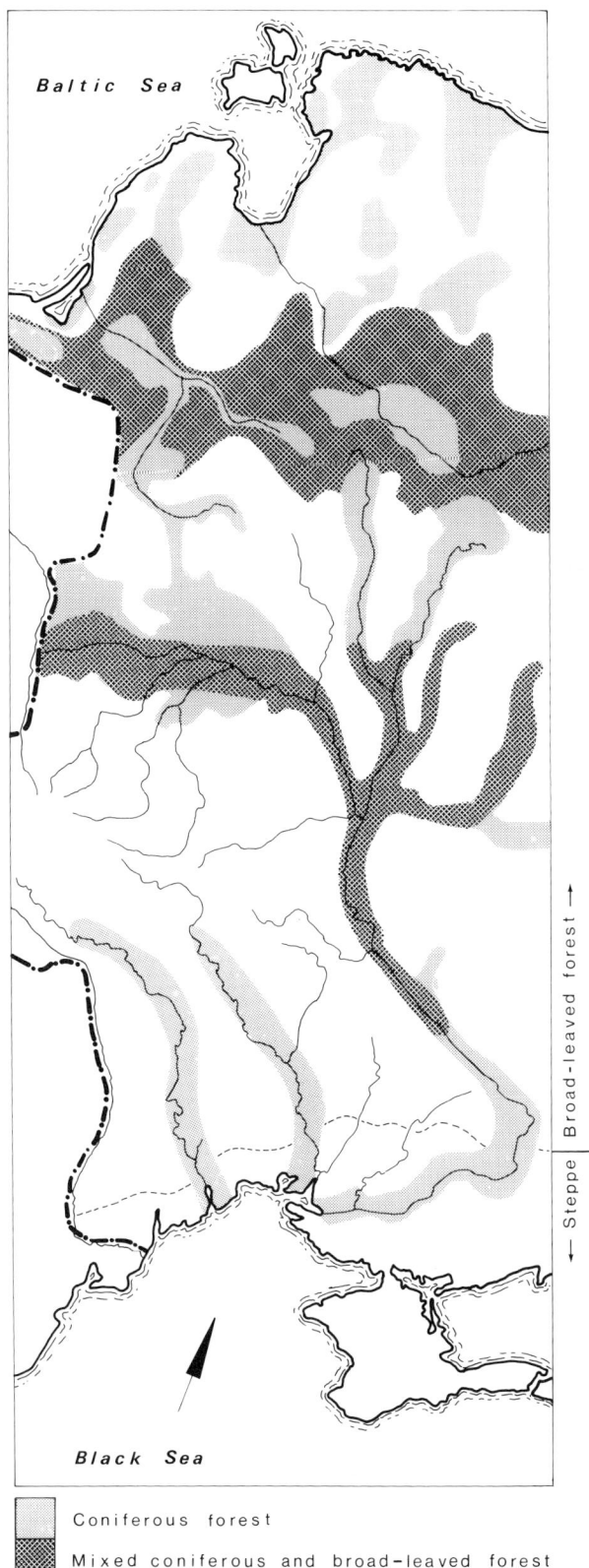

Figure 3 Vegetation map of the western part of the Soviet Union for the period from c. 8000 to 6000 BP. After Dolukhanov (1979).

tween Lithuania and Latvia) of brown earth and limestone soils.

Zone A is completely within the Baltic Sea catchment area. The drainage system is particularly

well developed, consisting, on the one hand, of medium-sized rivers flowing directly into the Baltic (Dvina, Neman) and, on the other, of numerous small rivers flowing either into the sea or into one of the mentioned rivers, together with many post-glacial lakes which are frequently connected by the dense river network.

This type of drainage system provides very favourable conditions for hunter-gatherer-fishing settlement (*Fig. 1*). In zone A, settlement is confined either to sandy river terraces (Lithuanian sites) or to lake terraces and islands (Latvia, Estonia).

The present-day climate of zone A is transitional between oceanic and continental. Mean July temperature ranges from 15 to 20 °C, the figure for January ranging from 0 to −10 °C; in this respect zone A does not differ from zone B. Annual precipitation is 600–1000 mm. There are many indications (mainly from pollen analyses) that zone A was also relatively distinct in the early and middle Holocene.

Zone A belongs mainly to the vast province of taiga-type European lowland forests (*Fig. 3*). The composition of the forest is of course conditioned by the climate and by soil type. Around 10,000 BP Estonia was covered by birch forests, and Lithuania and Latvia by birch–pine forests. Around 9000 BP the birch–pine forests expanded northwards, partly eliminating the birch forests from Estonia. Latvia and Lithuania were overgrown by northern mixed conifer–deciduous forest (*Pinus* variant), while the remaining area was already overgrown by mixed deciduous forest. One may of course look more closely at the local composition of these forests, for example at the peculiar features of vegetation complexes in large river valleys, but for present purposes this is not necessary.

The large mammal fauna (*Fig. 4*) is known in zone A from Mesolithic sites in Estonia and Latvia, and also from the Mesolithic grave at Gizycko-Pierkunowo in north-eastern Poland. Throughout the period the elk dominates among large mammals. On sites belonging to the tenth and ninth millennia BP elk bones comprise over 95% of large mammal bones, and in later periods the figure remains over 50%. Early sites contain small numbers of bones of red deer, roe deer, wild boar, *Bos*, and wild horses. On later sites the numbers of these bones increase, with boar and *Bos* bones being particularly numerous.

Gross (1940) suggested that in this area (strictly speaking, in what was formerly East Prussia) reindeer and elk were present not only in the late Pleistocene but also in the early Holocene (especially the Pre-Boreal period). This theory about the local survival of the reindeer till a relatively late period is acceptable given that it correlates well with data concerning the survival of the Swiderian culture

ZONE A (NE)

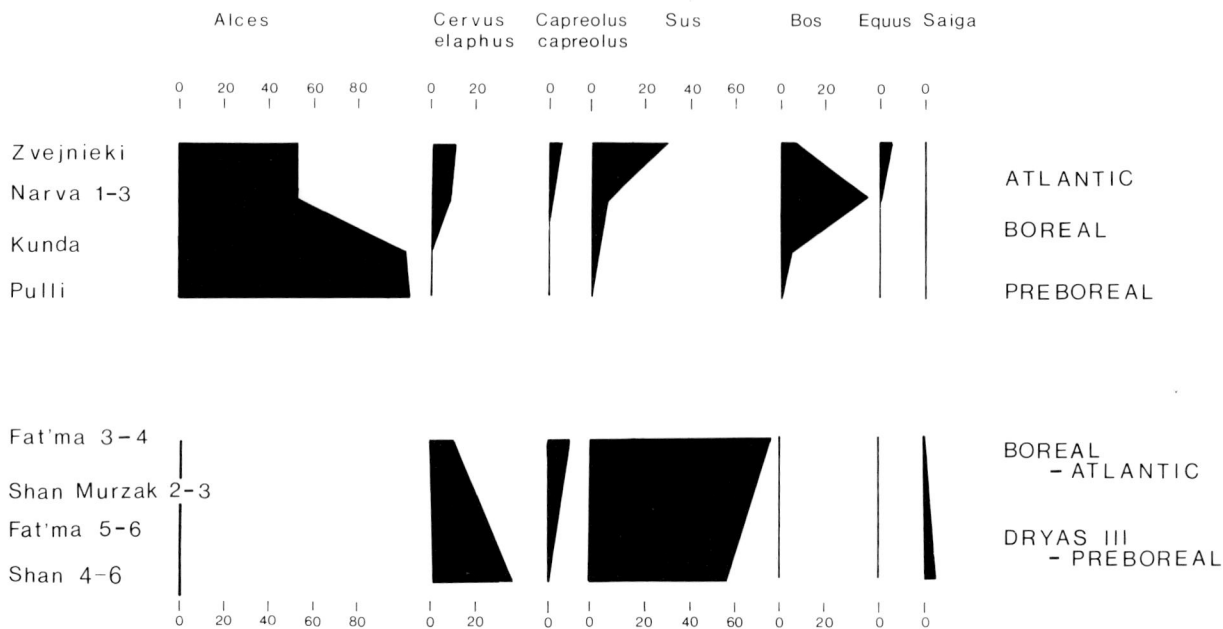

Figure 4 Evolution of large mammal faunas in Estonia/Latvia (zone A) and the Crimean peninsula (zone C).

in Lithuania and northern Byelorussia well into the tenth millennium BP. It must be added that Gross substantiated his theory with results of pollen analysis. Evidence from well-dated sites appears to show that the reindeer survived well into the Holocene only in the south-western part of zone A, vanishing in the north-eastern part by the beginning of the tenth millennium BP.

Finally, mention should also be made of the lithic raw materials which had an obvious bearing on local settlement and material culture. The availability of raw materials in zone A varies considerably (*Fig. 1*). In Lithuania there are abundant deposits of good Cretaceous flint, while Latvia and Estonia are almost totally devoid of flint; this led, on the one hand, to partial substitution of flint by other materials (quartz and schist in Estonia) and, on the other, to a much greater use of bone and antler as tool materials. There even appeared in the literature a theory, now obsolete, about the existence of unique 'bone cultures' in this area. The raw material situation not only affected the form of the material culture but also had a direct bearing on the settlement network, with sites visibly concentrated around raw material outcrops.

As will be evident from the above description, zone A is distinct in certain respects, but similar to zone B in other respects; in some periods both zones were characterized by similar features of material culture.

Zone B

The zone of large east–west orientated river valleys coincides mainly with Byelorussia and some of the northern extremeties of the Ukraine. It is a natural extension of a similar zone in Poland and Germany. In the north it is bounded by the frontal moraines of the Last Glaciation and in the south by the loess uplands of Volhynia and Podolia. In all, it is a distinctly lowland area, called Polesie, made up of depositional landforms of the Riss (Dnepr) Glaciation and the Warta (Moscow) Stadial. These include sandy forms of ground and frontal moraine, outwash, and elevated loess patches (rising to over 200 m above sea level) of north-western Byelorussia. The soils of zone B developed on sandy substrata are mostly of the grassland–podzol variety, as in zone A, whereas on heavier substrata (e.g. loess) brown earth soils dominate. The entire area is drained by a dense network of small and medium-sized rivers flowing into the major river of this zone, the Pripet, which flows latitudinally to join the Dnepr (Black Sea catchment area). The Pripet valley is, of course, a marginal valley of one of the Pleistocene glaciations (Moscow) and has all the attributes of such a feature (extensive marshlands, lakes, etc.).

The dense drainage network of zone B, and especially its medium-sized rivers (Styr, Horyn, Uborch, Uzh, Ptych, Shchara, upper Neman, and Pripet) with their sandy terraces, formed an excellent framework for early and middle Holocene settlement which, it seems, developed along different lines from

428

that in zone A (at least in its north-eastern part). The settlement map (*Fig. 1*) shows 'chains' of sites localized in valleys of at least the medium-sized rivers; the valleys of small water courses, the uplands, and even the relatively low-lying areas of ground moraine were avoided (the latter are poorly watered in the sense of having a low density of surface drainage). The river valleys were not only the most attractive settlement niche, but appear to have been the *only* environment exploited by the hunters and gatherers of those times. The same might apply to a part of zone A (southern Lithuania). The climate of the large valley zone is continental, with less annual precipitation than in zone A (500–600 mm) but with similar temperatures (15 to 20 °C in July and 0 to −10 °C in January).

Zone B is, of course, a forest zone of lowland taiga type (*Fig. 3*), differentiated territorially according to differences in soil substratum. By *c.* 10,000 BP the area was already overgrown by mixed forests which, about a thousand years later, were replaced in south-western Byelorussia by northern mixed conifer–deciduous forest (*Pinus* variant). The river valleys thus provided a particularly rich environment.

The forests were inhabited by large forest mammals. The only direct evidence of this fauna comes from the ceramic site of Zatsenye on the River Tsna in central Byelorussia, dated to the sixth millennium BP. The dominant species was the elk (comprising over 50% of large mammal bones); also fairly plentiful are boar (*c.* 30%) and red deer (*c.* 20%). This composition of fauna more or less corresponds to that of the zone of large valleys on the Polish lowland.

Finally, a few words about the stone raw materials from zone B. Readily accessible flint raw materials, mainly of Cretaceous age, dominate. These were obtained from various sources, both from primary chalk deposits and from Cretaceous rafts transported by the Rissian ice sheet. Primary chalk deposits crop out all over northern Byelorussia (upper Neman and upper Dnepr river basins) and also in Volhynia. These deposits were cut by the larger rivers (Neman, Dnepr, Desna, Styr, Horyn). The other source of flint raw material is the so-called Cretaceous rafts with flint nodules, scattered almost throughout Byelorussia as a result of ice sheet transport; these rafts are especially plentiful in Polesie. The flint raw material from both these sources is usually of good quality. An inferior raw material (occurring as small nodules, often with cracks) is Cretaceous erratic flint which is scattered through glacial deposits over practically all of Polesie. It also seems that nodules of good Cretaceous flint from the primary deposits of Volhynia were transported towards the Pripet valley by its southern tributaries, and were extracted by man from river alluvia. The more important outcrops of better-quality raw materials naturally attracted Mesolithic settlement. This is evidenced by the particularly numerous Neman sites, the sites on the Desna river, and probably also some of the Pripet sites.

Zone C

This is the vast area between the line of Volhynian loess uplands and the coast of the Black Sea. It is principally an upland area (the Moldavian upland in Romania, the Bessarabian, Podolian and Dnepr uplands in the USSR) bounded in the south by the Black Sea lowland and the Crimean mountains. It is of plate structure (the Black Sea plate) bounded in the west by the eastern Carpathians, and is built of loess and loess-like deposits on which have evolved chernozem-type soils (locally differentiated).

Zone C belongs, of course, to the Black Sea catchment area and is cut by large (Dnepr, Dnestr, Boh) and medium-sized rivers, often flowing in deep gorges. The river network is much less dense than in zones A and B. There are few small water courses, and so the zones of Mesolithic settlement, concentrated in valleys (terraces and upland peripheries), are split up and separated by poorly watered stretches of loess uplands, usually devoid of traces of human activity. It seems that owing to its specific hydrological features, zone C had a smaller settlement capacity than zones A and B. This situation appears to be due to the local climate which today is characterized by relatively high mean January temperatures (0 to −5 °C), high mean July temperatures (20 to 25 °C), and modest annual precipitation (400–500 mm). This type of continental climate must also have obtained in the lower and middle Holocene when zone C was overgrown by steppe-like vegetation mixed with some forest elements (*Fig. 3*). In the tenth and ninth millennia BP Volhynia and Podolia were overgrown by mixed deciduous forests of continental type; further south there was forest–steppe and steppe proper. In the eighth and seventh millennia BP most of zone C became dominated by continental-type deciduous forest, bounded in the south by a narrow belt of steppe. Throughout the early Holocene the valleys of large rivers were overgrown by rich gallery forests.

The zone C fauna (*Fig. 4*) is marked by local differentiation and is known primarily from eighth and seventh millennia BP sites. On the Black Sea coast, at the site of Mirnoe near the Danube mouth the dominant large mammal is *Bos* (over 80% of large mammal bones) with the horse (14%) in second place. There are infrequent bones of red deer, boar and ass. Elsewhere, in the middle Dnestr river basin, the dominant animal on Mesolithic and early Neolithic sites is red deer which is accompanied locally by numerous roe deer (over 30%) and in other cases by numerous *Bos* or boar. This indicates that the generally similar fauna of the southern zone is locally differentiated into open landscape and forest faunas. The former occurs mainly on the Black Sea lowland; the latter in forest-covered uplands and in large river valleys. The composition of the upland fauna is similar to the local late Pleistocene fauna from layer 1a at the site of Molodova V although, of course, the proportions of the species in Holocene layers are different from those in the Pleistocene layers.

A full sequence of large mammals is known from the Crimea. The fauna is composed of three thermophilous species (red deer, roe deer and boar) which until the late Pleistocene were probably still accompanied by the Saiga antelope.

In the Shan-Koba development phase (final Pleistocene and probably early Holocene) the dominant species in the Crimea was the boar (60%); red deer accounts for over 30% of the fauna, but roe deer and saiga were scarce. Subsequent periods saw an increase in the importance of boar (up to 80%) and roe deer (up to 10%), the gradual disappearance of red deer, and the complete disappearance of saiga. The palaeozoological evidence does not permit a distinction to be made between Boreal and Atlantic faunas, since they tend to be lumped together in publications dealing with bone assemblages of the Murzak-Koba and Grebeniki phases. It is reasonable to suppose, however, that the role of red deer was greater in the ninth millennium BP than in the eighth and seventh millennia.

Zone C also abounds in good quality flint raw materials which, however, are not evenly distributed throughout its territory. Richest in this respect is the western part with *in situ* Cretaceous flint close to the ground surface known from Volhynia, Podolia, the eastern Carpathians (Prut, Ibaneşti), and the upper and middle course of the Dnestr. The Cretaceous rocks in these areas are cut by river valleys, and the rivers transport raw material nodules which can therefore be found in the alluvia of these rivers. In the Crimean mountains there are also Cretaceous flints that can be transported by the local rivers. The eastern part of zone C has fewer sources of lithic raw materials, but there are siliceous rocks along the middle course of the Boh river and erratic flint along the middle Dnepr (Nadporozhye). In this zone too the settlement network is in part influenced by the distribution of raw material deposits, and Mesolithic settlement in the eastern part of zone C is less intense not only, it seems, because of the less thorough exploration of this area.

ARCHAEOLOGICAL EVIDENCE

The early and middle Holocene evidence from the western part of the Russian Plain differs considerably as regards its cognitive value and is unevenly distributed. This is due to several factors which include, on the one hand, the geological structure of the various regions (resulting in differences in raw material availability) and, on the other, the different activities of archaeologists, not all of whom are specialists in collecting evidence of the social activities of hunter-gatherer communities. For example, the sandy regions of Lithuania and Byelorussia have produced numerous collections but, since these are largely the products of surface exploration, there are very few homogeneous assemblages. This is because Stone Age settlement in this region was generally confined to dry sandy elevations in river valleys on which sedimentation had already ceased by the eleventh millennium BP. Thus, repeated settlement in the same locations led to the appearance of mixed sites which should be explored very methodically indeed if homogeneous assemblages are to be obtained.

The situation is different in Estonia and Latvia where sites are frequently located on clayey lake and river terraces. In many cases the sites were covered by layers of organic sediments. The result is that in these republics sites are few but have often been excavated methodically, yielding homogeneous assemblages and numerous radiocarbon or pollen dates (*Fig. 5*).

In the southern regions (Ukrainian and Moldavian Republics) the situation is different again. The sites are admittedly few, but they often contain homogeneous assemblages. This appears to be due to the less intensive settlement of the area and to the undoubtedly greater potential for choosing sites, compared to the sandy zone of Byelorussia and Lithuania. In effect, the loess-covered southern zone provides a fair number of homogeneous assemblages and, as in Estonia and Latvia, data about fauna and chronology.

Separate mention should be made of the multilayered sites of the Crimean peninsula which provide a basis for the relative chronology of this part of the Ukraine (*Table 2*).

As will be appreciated from this brief review, the state of research into early and middle Holocene materials from the western republics of the USSR varies, hence many of the conclusions proposed in this paper continue to have the value of working hypotheses. It is fortunate, however, that there are several valuable assemblages from outside the region, and these add to the evidence at our disposal.

To conclude these remarks about the archaeological evidence, some consideration must be given to the reconstruction of early and middle Holocene settlement in the western regions of the USSR. Although this task is very difficult in view of the previously mentioned disparities in the exploration of the region, the following points may be made:

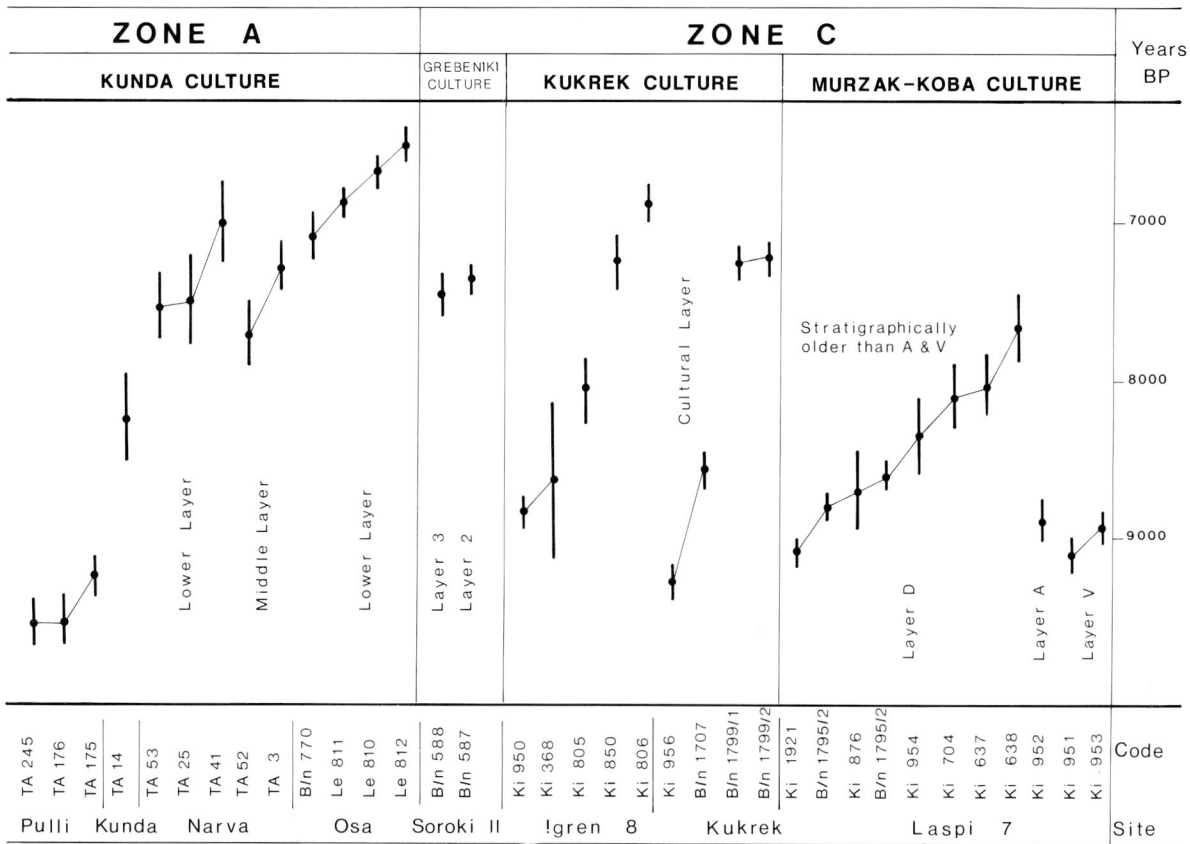

ZONE A			ZONE C		Years
KUNDA CULTURE		GREBENIKI CULTURE	KUKREK CULTURE	MURZAK–KOBA CULTURE	BP

Lower Layer · Middle Layer · Lower Layer · Layer 3 · Layer 2 · Cultural Layer · Stratigraphically older than A & V · Layer D · Layer A · Layer V

— 7000
— 8000
— 9000

																																	Code
TA 245	TA 176	TA 175	TA 14	TA 53	TA 25	TA 41	TA 52	TA 3	B/n 770	Le 811	Le 810	Le 812	B/n 588	B/n 587	Ki 950	Ki 368	Ki 805	Ki 850	Ki 806	Ki 956	B/n 1707	B/n 1799/1	B/n 1799/2	Ki 1921	B/n 1795/2	Ki 876	B/n 1795/2	Ki 954	Ki 704	Ki 637	Ki 638	Ki 952	Ki 951	Ki 953
Pulli		Kunda		Narva						Osa			Soroki II					Igren 8						Kukrek							Laspi 7			Site

Figure 5 Radiocarbon dates for early and middle Holocene sites in the western part of the Soviet Union.

a)   In the young lakelands (Estonia, Latvia, northern Lithuania) the probably sparse settlement was concentrated around post-glacial lakes, and also spread onto terraces of medium-sized rivers.

b)   In the sandy regions of southern Lithuania (zone A), Byelorussia and north-western Ukraine (zone B), settlement was confined to terraces of medium-sized rivers (Neman, Pripet).

c)   The upland regions of Würm and Rissian moraines of northern Byelorussia and Lithuania were not settled at all; the same is true of the loesses of Byelorussia.

d)   The loess uplands of the western Ukraine were also probably sparsely settled or not at all; the same applies to the eastern Carpathians bend.

e)   The Black Sea lowland and the lower part of the lower Dnepr river basin featured settlement mainly along the few medium-sized rivers (Dnestr, Boh) and possibly around the shallow lakes of the Black Sea coast.

f)   The Crimea is characterized primarily by cave sites in the mountain zone.

The settlement network was thus based on the entire system of medium-sized rivers characterized by an exceptionally rich environment, and on the lake system in the north. It clearly avoided the poorly watered areas of loess and of frontal ground moraines.

The drainage network in the western part of the USSR is, of course, highly differentiated along the north–south axis – from the lakeland belt in the north, through the belt of great river valleys, through the upland belt where rivers are rare, to the poorly watered zone of the Black Sea lowland in the south. The exceptional density of settlement in the northern-most zones is therefore understandable.

Variations in biomass (nearly always lower in the forest zone) do not seem to have had an important bearing on settlement structure. In all parts of the region the biomass was so abundant that even if it was greater in the steppe zone, this is unlikely to have affected settlement.

However, the settlement network was certainly influenced by the distribution of stone raw material outcrops. This is particularly evident in the middle Neman and Pripet river basins and also along the Dnestr. It appears that the exceptional concentration of sites there may be due to the outcrops of good quality lithic raw materials found on river terraces.

CHRONOLOGICAL FOUNDATIONS

One of the main difficulties in the study of the Mesolithic of the western part of the USSR stems from the fact that very few sites are dated (*Fig. 5*). The situation is so serious that several large taxonomic units are not dated at all. In spite of this, a basic chronology may be derived relying in part on

Table 2:   Stratigraphy and relative chronology of the major sites in zone C

NORTH CAUCASUS SLOPES		CRIMEA				CULTURE
Gubski Naves	*Sosruko*	*Shan-Koba*	*Fat'ma-Koba*	*Zamil-Koba*	*Kukrek*	
–	–	layer 2	layer 3/4a	–	–	GREBENIKI
upper layer	–	layer 3	layer 4b	upper layer	upper layer	MURZAK-KOBA
–	layer 1	–	–	–	lower layer	KUKREK
–	–	layer 4	layer 5	–	–	IMERETINSKA
lower layer	layer 3	layers 5/6	layer 6	lower layer	–	SHAN-KOBA

dates based on typological analysis and site stratigraphy. It is also possible to make use of existing dates for sites in neighbouring regions – Poland, Hungary, Romania, or the upper Volga area.

It must be stressed, of course, that some of the proposed datings are no more than hypotheses.

Zone C

The Crimean peninsula provides data for relative dating of Mesolithic assemblages based on stratified cave and rock-shelter sites. Unfortunately, most of the assemblages from this area do not have absolute dates since they were obtained before the Second World War.

Table 2 contains the most important data concerning the stratigraphy of the Crimean and Caucasian sites. Generally speaking, the first assemblages to appear in this area were those with arched-backed pieces (Shan-Koba culture), which were succeeded by quasi-Gravettian assemblages (Imeretinska culture of the Caucasian tradition); the latter, however, appears to have been a brief episode connected with a short-lived north-westward penetration of Caucasian peoples. Nevertheless, it seems that the tradition of arched-backed pieces (Shan-Koba) survived in this area (e.g. the uppermost layer of the site of Siuren II). The tradition of arched-backed pieces probably originated in the final phase of the Pleistocene (evidenced by the presence of the antelope, *Saiga tatarica*, indicating a continental climate, and elements of the Swiderian culture in some assemblages); it probably survived until the appearance of cultures with trapezes – this is indicated, among other things, by infrequent arched-backed pieces of the Murzak-Koba culture. Such a dating for arched-backed point assemblages is in agreement with the dating of similar elements in the Balkans, the Carpathian basin, and also in the Near East (e.g. Zarzi).

The assemblages with arched-backed pieces are succeeded by assemblages with trapezes. This is indicated not only by the stratigraphy of sites in this area, but also by observations from the Near East and the Balkans. These assemblages (which are mainly those of the Murzak-Koba culture) are characterized by an entirely new technology of a carefully prepared core flaked by the pressure technique, by regular blades, denticulated blades, and finally by the presence of trapezes. Problems arise, however, when it comes to dating the appearance of these elements in the Crimea, and hence in the whole of zone C. On the one hand, we know that similar technological and typological elements appeared in central, southern and western Europe only *c.* 8000 BP; on the other, there are radiocarbon determinations from the sites of Laspi 7 and Igren 8 (*Fig. 5*) which suggest an earlier date (ninth millennium BP) for such elements. Since there are no grounds for questioning the above datings, and because there are similar dates for trapezes from Franchthi in Greece and for late Capsian sites in North Africa, it may be assumed tentatively that the intercultural trend which introduced the trapezes was generally earlier than 8000 BP in the Black Sea zone and in the south-eastern part of the Mediterranean. It follows that this trend may have had two developmental phases and that it spread to zone C in the first phase (ninth millennium BP).

The Murzak-Koba culture is followed in Crimean sites by assemblages of Grebeniki and Kukrek types (the latter may be earlier). The time of their emergence is uncertain, with the (suspect) radiocarbon dates from Igren 8 on the Dnepr (Kukrek culture) indicating a date perhaps as early as the ninth millennium BP.

The proposed scheme for zone C is shown in *Fig. 2*.

Zone A

Relatively good chronological data are provided by zone A. There is a full sequence of dates from Estonia and Latvia (*Fig. 5*) for the Kunda culture, as well as pollen dates for single bone and antler artifacts from the late Palaeolithic and the Mesolithic. To these can be added radiocarbon dates from the nearby Poland and upper Volga regions.

The cultural sequence of zone A begins in the Dryas III period and the early Pre-Boreal when the Swiderian culture is documented in north-eastern Poland (youngest dates=c. 9700 BP), and also in Lithuania and the Kaliningrad district (pollen dates for Lyngby-type axes, Havel-type single-barbed harpoons, and processed reindeer antlers). It is difficult to date the moment of disintegration of the Swiderian culture, i.e. when the classic structure of the reindeer hunters' culture breaks down, giving way to the ephemeral, forest-based post-Swiderian cultures. If it is true that the reindeer survived in what was formerly East Prussia till the Pre-Boreal period, then this point in time might be hypothetically assumed to be the moment of transition to the rare post-Swiderian assemblages, which cannot be dated directly.

The latter should be younger than the Swiderian assemblages (having evolved from them) and older than the Neman culture assemblages which occur on lower river terraces and contain chronologically diagnostic elements such as trapezes or Janisławice elements (points), and which are thus probably of late Atlantic age. The finds of *Trapa natans* shells at the site of Lampédžiai, together with its geomorphological position, confirm the proposed dating of the Neman culture to a period after the post-Swiderian culture. Also significant are the data supplied by the analysis of well dated (tenth to seventh millennium BP) Kunda sites from Estonia and Latvia (*Fig. 5*) containing typological elements (e.g. micro-retouched bladelets) known from post-Swiderian (e.g. Ełk I in Poland) and Neman sites. This, of course, suggests the parallel development of these cultures and the Kunda culture.

A separate problem is presented by sites of the so-called Janisławice culture, which occur mainly in southern Lithuania. The dates for this culture from Poland suggest that it was already in existence in the seventh millennium BP, and this is in accord with its technological and typological characteristics (regular cores and blades, trapezes, retouched blades). The problem to be solved is its position with respect to the Neman culture which dominates in Lithuania. Relying more on intuition than on facts, the present author is inclined to believe that the two cultures, which shared only part of their territorial ranges, developed in parallel, with the Janisławice culture dominating earlier. The chronological scheme for zone A is shown in *Fig. 2*.

Zone B

The chronology of Mesolithic sites from zone B is the most difficult and least reliable, since there are no direct datings from this area. One must thus make use of information from zones A and C and also from the Polish equivalent of zone B.

The final phase of the Pleistocene (Dryas III) is characterized in Poland by the presence of the Swiderian culture; the same is true of the very beginning of the Pre-Boreal period (cf. remarks about zone A). It may thus be assumed that the Swiderian assemblages in Byelorussia, identical to the Polish ones, date to the same period. These are probably succeeded by post-Swiderian assemblages corresponding to those from Lithuania. However, the post-Swiderian assemblages in Byelorussia are poorly defined.

The next developmental stage in the Mesolithic of zone B is represented by assemblages of the Kudlaevka type, characterized by the presence of backed pieces with a straight back and (but not always) of tanged points. Judging by their morphology, the tanged points are of post-Swiderian origin and they are accompanied by, among other things, small double-platform cores, also associated with the Swiderian tradition. The backed pieces, on the other hand, are related either to some relatively unknown late Gravettian tradition or to the 'Maglemosian' Komornica culture from Poland. There are also trapezes and regular retouched blades which might suggest an early Atlantic age for the cultural units concerned.

After the Kudlaevka-type assemblages comes the Janisławice culture, the appearance of which is dated in Poland to the seventh millennium BP. It features trapezes and regular blades, and therefore appears to be generally of Atlantic age (the second phase of the proliferation of the trend with trapezes – cf. remarks about zone C). Neman culture assemblages, analogous to the Lithuanian ones, may have existed alongside the Janisławice assemblages in central Byelorussia (cf. remarks about zone A).

Fig. 2 shows the chronological scheme for zone B. This scheme, however, will need to be improved and perhaps corrected in the future.

Overview

The chronological evidence may be summarized as follows:

1. The western areas of the USSR are characterized by a latitudinal zonal structure which had considerable influence on the development of local early and middle Holocene cultures.

2. Zones A and B were at first dominated by the Swiderian and related cultures (in general, these were traditions associated with tanged points) and by traditions arising from them. Zone C was dominated by arched-backed piece traditions of Near East and Mediterranean origin.

3. In the Boreal period there (apparently) occurs in zone C a technological and stylistic change – which, among other things, sees the introduction of trapezes and a new blade technology – associated

with the Murzak-Koba and perhaps also the Kukrek cultures.

4. In the Atlantic period a new technology with trapezes appears in zone B, signifying a complete cultural change (Kudlaevka and Janisławice cultures) which undoubtedly originated in the south. The change, barely perceptible in the Kudlaevka culture, becomes complete in the Janisławice culture. The trend also spreads to zone A where, however, it introduces only slight modifications in the local cultural environment based on the tanged point tradition. Nevertheless, the Janisławice culture also appears there locally. During that time further morphological changes occur in the flint industries of zone C – Kukrek (earlier?) and Grebeniki – which are doubtless the foundation of local neolithization.

5. All the evidence presented above indicates a process of constant northward 'pulsation' of the southern environment during the period from the final phase of the Pleistocene to the middle Holocene.

TAXONOMIC DIVISIONS

In what follows an attempt is made to present the basic elements of the stylistic and technological differentiation of flint materials, together with information about their place in time and space and about their environmental conditioning. The characterizations are based on material from the western republics of the Soviet Union, as well as on data from neighbouring regions which contained similar material.

As far as possible the descriptions are set out according to the scheme of taxonomic units of the late Palaeolithic and Mesolithic previously proposed by the author (Kozłowski 1975).

Tanged point technocomplex

The technocomplex with tanged points is represented in the south-western part of zone A and probably in all of zone B by the Swiderian culture and by the post-Swiderian assemblages that evolved from it

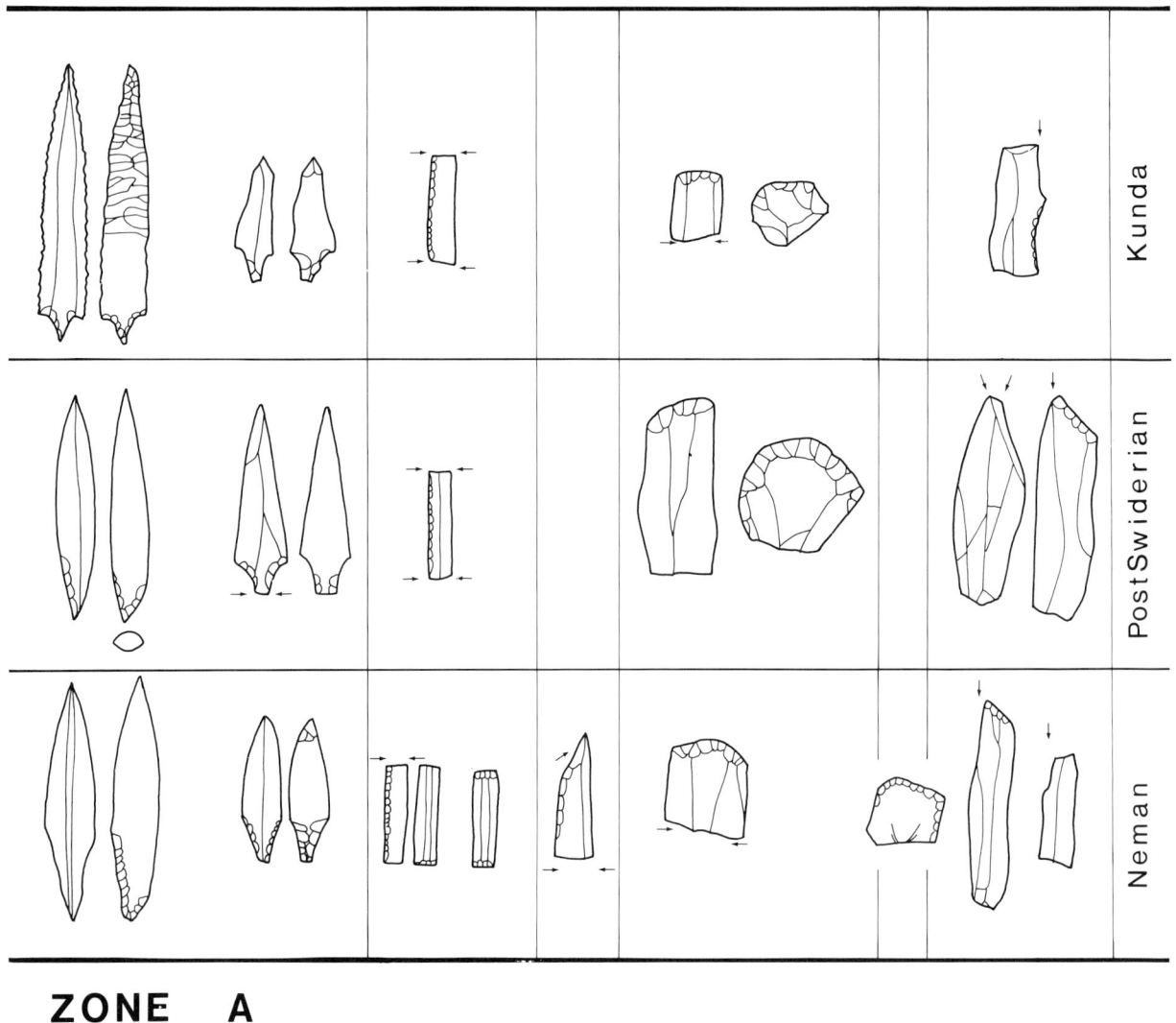

ZONE A

Figure 6   Flint industries of zone A.

434

(*Fig. 2*). The Swiderian culture also extended over almost the whole of Poland, but the post-Swiderian assemblages are found only in the north-eastern part of the country.

The Swiderian in Poland is dated to the Dryas III period and to the beginning of the Pre-Boreal period. It seems that it may be similarly dated in zones A and B, despite the lack of age estimates from these regions. Zones A and B, as well as north-eastern Poland, could have been inhabited by the Swiderian people throughout the Pre-Boreal period; this is suggested by pollen dates for reindeer antlers from that period.

The direct continuation of the Swiderian culture in the area of the closing stages of its development is represented by the post-Swiderian assemblages which still retain some of its stylistic and technological features. Moreover, the post-Swiderian assemblages differ considerably from one another. The few data from north-eastern Poland place them generally in the Pre-Boreal–Boreal period.

Technologically, the two taxonomic units are similar; the double-platform core technique dominates in both, the difference being that in the post-Swiderian assemblages the cores are often small. This is due to the abandonment of mined flint in favour of erratic flint, which is one of the features of the disintegration of the forest-tundra Swiderian and its adaptation to a forest environment.

The dominant stylistic elements in both units are non-pedunculate and pedunculate tanged points, slim and short scrapers, and burins. Post-Swiderian assemblages often, but not always, include other forms of tanged points, e.g. forms with semi-abrupt (*vs* flat) retouch on the ventral face, or forms with an intentionally truncated peduncle. Also found in these assemblages are finely retouched bladelets, undoubtedly of east European origin.

North-eastern technocomplex

The cultural environment described above is no doubt partly responsible for the emergence of the western section of the Mesolithic north-eastern technocomplex (Kozłowski 1975), which in the area under consideration is represented by three taxonomic units: in zone A there is the Kunda culture developing at least from the middle of the tenth millennium BP, and the considerably younger Neman culture; while in zone B there is the Kudlaevka culture (also quite late), accompanied in some regions by Neman sites. The latter two cultures are also known from north-eastern Poland, while the Kudlaevka culture is additionally present east of the Dnepr. The relatively late chronological position (Atlantic period) of the Kudlaevka and Neman cultures is documented only typologically.

The three taxonomic units differ technologically.

The Kudlaevka culture still retains, in very degenerate form, elements of the post-Swiderian technology, but both the units from zone A are based on the technique of single-platform cores for blades and bladelets, probably originating to the east of Europe and perhaps even in Siberia. The broken blade technique is present in all three units, and in the zone A units such blades were used to produce numerous end-scrapers and burins, retouched blades and finely retouched bladelets.

The link between all three units and the forest environment is beyond doubt. The main hunted animal was the elk; the people lived in small temporary camps, chiefly on lake shores in the north-eastern part of zone A, and on river banks in the other areas.

Stylistically, all three units are characterized by the presence of non-pedunculate and pedunculate tanged points with local variations. Some of these may have a post-Swiderian origin; others (e.g. some of the Kunda points) may derive from a different tradition (i.e. an unknown culture of reindeer hunters from the area between Estonia and the upper Volga river basin). The tanged points are accompanied by finely retouched bladelets, very characteristic of the entire Mesolithic between zones A and B and the Ural mountains, slim and short end-scrapers (the former often on broken blades), and burins (often on broken blades), as well as retouched blades. The remaining elements are specific to the separate units. In the Neman culture there are infrequent Janisławice-type points and scrapers together with unpolished axes and trapezes. The Kudlaevka culture is marked by the presence of backed pieces and backed bladelets, segments, as well as short scrapers and trapezes. The Kunda culture assemblages also occasionally contain partially polished axes. It seems that the eastern branch of the Kudlaevka culture lacks tanged points.

Janisławice culture

A separate taxonomic position is occupied by the Janisławice culture which occurs mainly in zone B but also in the south-western part of zone A. This culture is also known from the Vistula river basin in Poland and from areas to the east of the Dnepr. The radiocarbon dates from Poland and the presence of trapezes in the assemblages place this unit in the Atlantic period; it is logical to assume that it is later than the Kudlaevka culture, continuing the earlier local traditions.

Technologically, the Janisławice culture is distinct from the units with tanged points described above. The dominant technique is that of regular single-platform cores which, however, differ from those of, for example, the Kunda culture. The blades from such cores are regular and fairly large, and this

ZONE B

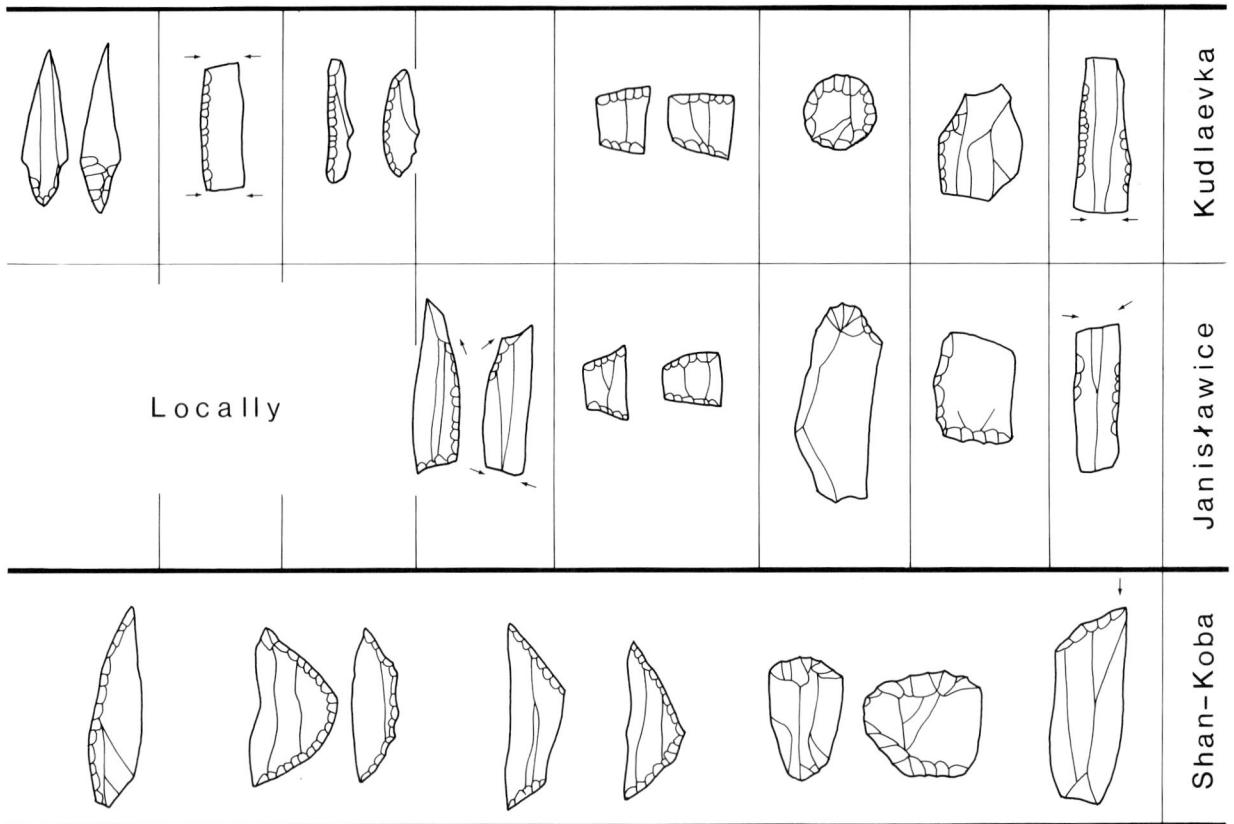

Locally

ZONE C

Figure 7   Flint industries of zones B and C.

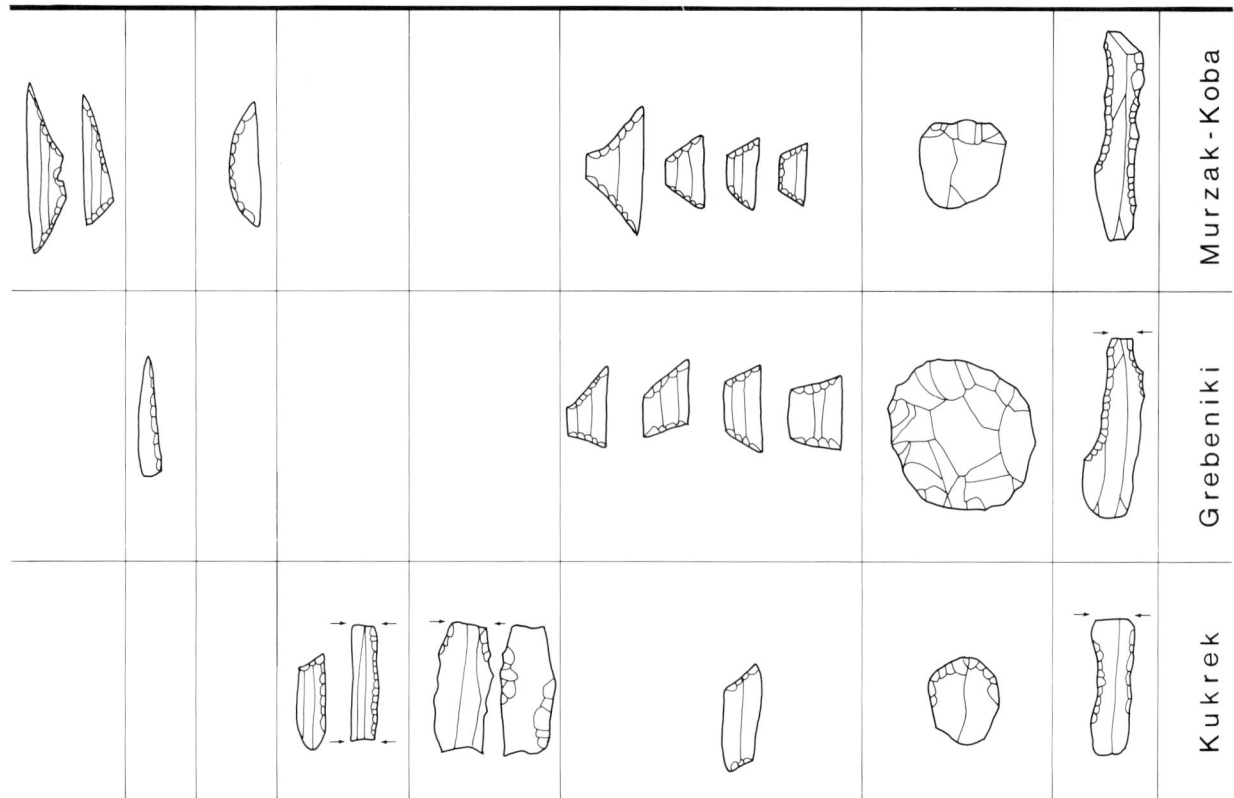

ZONE C

Figure 8   Flint industries of zone C

436

forced the Janisławice people to seek better quality raw materials, often of the mined variety. These blades were used in the production of Janisławice points and trapezes, rarely of end-scrapers; the implements were also retouched on the lateral edges. The flakes were used to make irregular scrapers. The Janisławice unit must be genetically related to the southern environment (zone C) from which the technological and typological innovations (e.g. trapezes) spread, probably at the beginning of the eighth millennium BP, to become superimposed on the local substratum. In conclusion, it is worth mentioning that various other types of tools characterize the Janisławice assemblages depending on the local substratum: in Poland – triangles and narrow trapezes; in central Byelorussia and Lithuania – broad trapezes; further to the east – tanged points (remains of the Kudlaevka tradition); and in Lithuania – Janisławice points with truncated base. Janisławice camps usually occur on river terraces, and the people of this culture hunted elk and red deer.

Zones A and B are marked by broad similarities in cultural taxonomy, undermined only in the late period by the successive waves of southern influences (regular blade technology, trapezes and, perhaps, backed pieces); but zone C is markedly distinct typologically.

Shan-Koba and Belolesye-type assemblages

The transition from the Pleistocene to the Holocene is poorly researched in zone C, but it is known that at that time there were two related cultural units: the Shan-Koba culture and assemblages of the Belolesye type. Both of these, as well as the typologically similar Balkan, east Ukrainian and Caucasian units, appear towards the end of the Pleistocene. There are many indications that they survived until the beginning of the Boreal period. In the western extremities of zone C the units may even have survived until the end of the Boreal. Genetically, they are probably related to the Near East (e.g. industries of Zarzi and Shanidar type), and the maximum range of industries of this type originally covered at least the southern belt of the whole of zone C. Still awaiting explanation is their position with respect to the Tardigravettian industries of the Carpathian basin which are contemporaneous with the Shan-Koba culture and the Belolesye-type assemblages, and similar to them as regards artifact morphology. The technology of the Shan-Koba culture and of Belolesye-type assemblages is based on fairly wide, not very regular and short blades, and often also on flakes. Dominant in the assemblages are large segments and equilateral triangles, as well as short end-scrapers on flakes. The Shan-Koba culture is further distinguished by double retouched truncations.

The third, very poorly explored element in zone C comprises the youngest Eastern Gravettian assemblages known from the Dnestr river basin (Ataki, Oselivka) and elsewhere. In addition to obvious features of the Molodavian culture, they contain segments, double retouched truncations and short end-scrapers; in these respects the assemblages are similar to the Shan-Koba and Belolesye assemblage types.

The early Holocene environment inhabited by the hunters of zone C was mainly steppe cut by valleys of large rivers which were overgrown by gallery forests; the fauna of these forests included red deer, *Bos*, boar, and horse.

Local cultures of zone C

We now proceed to cultures which developed after the phase described in the previous section – the Murzak-Koba, Kukrek and Grebeniki cultures. The first and the last of these appear to be genetic successors of the local early Holocene cultures, suggested by the diversified backed pieces and segments present in their inventories. The Kukrek culture appears to be unrelated. Elements shared by all three cultures are: slim, conical, single-platform cores for regular blades and bladelets with around-perimeter flaking surface, blades with denticulated retouch, and short end-scrapers. All these elements, together with the trapezes known from the Murzak-Koba and Grebeniki cultures, and possibly the Kukrek rhombs, are probably of Near Eastern origin and are thus exotic elements in zone C. The features which distinguish these cultures one from another are the special triangles of the Murzak-Koba culture and the finely retouched bladelets and ventrally retouched inserts of the Kukrek culture, and the Gravettian backed pieces of the Grebeniki culture.

The range of the Murzak-Koba culture is marginal to the area under consideration (in the east it spreads all the way to the Caucasus), but the other two units occupy the whole of zone C (the Grebeniki culture in the west, and the Kukrek culture in the east as far as the Caucasus). They are thus steppe and deciduous forest cultures based on red deer and *Bos*.

A separate problem is presented by the dating of the Kukrek and Murzak-Koba cultures which apparently appear in zone C as early as the ninth millennium BP (see the section on chronology).

As regards settlement, the network is not as dense as in zones A and B. The settlement sites include flood terraces of large and medium-sized rivers, the edges of loess uplands, and caves and rock-shelters. Large open sites are known which are either remains of large settlements or traces of repeated visits of settlers to the same spot.

Q

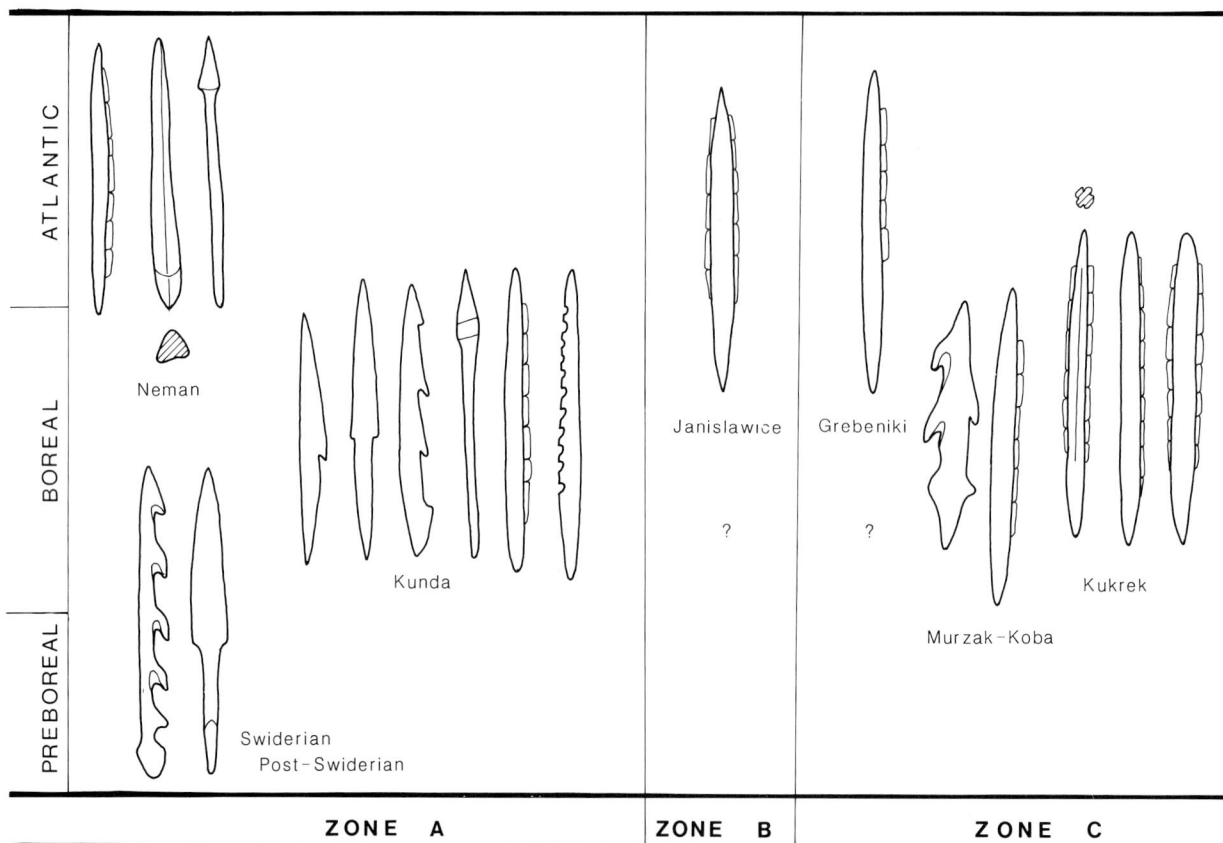

Figure 9 Bone points and harpoons of early and middle Holocene cultures of the western part of the Soviet Union.

BONE INDUSTRIES

The distribution of bone and antler artifacts in the western part of the Russian Plain is very uneven. Vast regions are devoid of them, probably due to the character of certain Holocene sediments which do not favour their survival. It must also be borne in mind that such artifacts are very often accidental finds without stratigraphic or cultural contexts. For this reason, emphasis will be placed on classes of artifacts with diagnostic features that make it possible to reconstruct their original cultural context with a high degree of probability, especially as single specimens of these artifacts are known from systematically excavated and explored sites – specifically, harpoons, points and ornamented hoes. It is worth noting that the study of bone and antler artifacts is particularly important in zone A (especially in its north-eastern part) where good stone raw materials were not always available and where organic materials had to take their place.

The bone points and harpoons known from the western areas of the USSR are very varied morphologically (*Fig. 9*); their territorial ranges differ, as does their popularity. Some classes appear to be inter-regional; others are confined to one zone, or even to a fragment thereof.

The most widespread type are spindle-shaped points with a single groove and unretouched blades as inserts (type 21 in Clark's classification: Clark

1936). These occur in zone C and are connected with the local cultures there (Murzak-Koba, Kukrek, Grebeniki) – i.e. with cultures of the ninth–seventh millennia BP; eastwards they spread as far as the Caucasus (Sosruko). One specimen of this type is known from zone B, while in zone A the points with a single groove are fairly numerous and are characteristic of the middle (and late?) Kunda culture, probably of the Atlantic period (on the basis of a pollen date from Zinten, near Kaliningrad), and of the Neman culture in Lithuania and north-eastern Poland. It may be that this extensive distribution is due to a specific factor – an intercultural trend spreading from the south in the ninth millennium BP.

Another intercultural type are pin-shaped points (Clark's type 16) known from vast areas of the forest zone in the USSR, reaching as far west as north-eastern Poland, and in the east spreading beyond the Ural mountains. In our area they occur mainly in zone A but also (rarely) in zone B. From the very beginning of the Holocene they are characteristic of the Kunda culture, and later, in Lithuania, of the Neman culture; they continue to be present in the 'Neolithic' of the USSR forest zone. In all, they appear to be among the key elements characterizing the so-called north-eastern Mesolithic culture complex of the Taiga.

All the other types are of local character only. In all of zone A there occur since the beginning of the

438

Holocene single-barbed harpoons with large barbs, probably derived from the late Palaeolithic (Swiderian, etc.) Havel-type specimens (Clark's type 12A); somewhat later (ninth millennium BP) points with small barbs (Clark's type 6) appear. In Latvia and Estonia the first type belongs to the Kunda tradition, while in Lithuania it is post-Swiderian or, perhaps, Neman. The second type is attributable to the Kunda and Neman traditions.

Also from zone A, we should mention points of Clark's types 17 and 18, linked with the Kunda culture since the ninth millennium BP, and the Neman points with triangular cross-section (Clark's type 13) which are undated but probably belong to the Neman culture. These points are also known from north-eastern Poland. The cultural affinities of the various types of points are confirmed by their occurrence on Kunda culture sites, several pollen dates for single finds, and by their geographic position.

The last type characteristic of zone A, or rather mainly of its north-western part, is the spindle-shaped point with two grooves equipped with broken bladelets (Clark's type 21B). However, its territorial range in the west is markedly different from that of the Neman culture types 13, 16, and 21A. This suggests a link with the Janisławice culture, which accords with the context of a similar specimen discovered in Byelorussia.

Finally, in zone C, in addition to the points with a single groove described at the beginning of this section, there appear – probably by the ninth millennium BP (Murzak-Koba culture) – the characteristic flat double-barbed harpoons with widened base. Similar specimens (but single-barbed), unfortunately undated, are known from the Mesolithic of the Caucasus (Kvachara), the middle Volga, and the southern Ural mountains (Davlekanovo). This type apparently originates much further south (in the Pleistocene it is known from the Natufian) and marks a stage of stronger influences from the south. The subsequent elements of this phenomenon are the Mesolithic flat harpoons from the Balkans (e.g. Vlasac, Odmut) and the Alps (e.g. Birsmatten-Basisgrotte, Liesbergmühli, etc.) dated to the eighth millennium BP.

BURIALS

The western republics of the Soviet Union have yielded a number of Mesolithic skeleton burials, both single graves and inhumations grouped in cemeteries.

In zone C single graves are known from rock-shelters in the Crimea (Murzak-Koba, Fat'ma-Koba) containing skeletons lying full-length, and there is also a small cemetery at Vasilevka III (three graves) with crouched skeletons. Vasilevka yielded several flint artifacts of Murzak-Koba type and a decorated bone point with two grooves and equipped with unretouched blades. These artifacts allow the cemetery to be dated to the ninth millennium BP, assuming that the chronology of the Murzak-Koba culture proposed here is correct. The graves from Murzak-Koba and Fat'ma-Koba contained no artifacts, but their stratigraphic position suggests a similar dating.

The presence of single inhumations on settlement sites corresponds well with the contemporary situation in other parts of Europe. It will suffice to mention the isolated Mesolithic graves at Vatte di Zambana (Italy), Cuzoul de Gramat (France) and Birsmatten-Basisgrotte (Switzerland). However, the date (admittedly only typological) for the Vasilevka cemetery is older than all the known dates for Mesolithic cemeteries in Europe, which are generally of Atlantic age (Moita do Sebastião, Cabeço da Arruda, Cabeço da Amoreira, Hoëdic, Téviec, Vedbæk-Boldbaner, Skateholm, Zvejnieki, Oleniy Ostrov, Vlasac). There can only be two explanations for this – either the dating of Vasilevka (and of the entire Murzak-Koba culture) is wrong, or the phenomenon of Mesolithic cemeteries in the Black Sea region, or perhaps even in the entire eastern part of the Mediterranean, is pre-Atlantic. It is worth pointing out here that in the Ukraine the tradition of cemeteries was already in existence at the end of the Pleistocene.

Zone B lacks Mesolithic burials, leaving aside the single inhumation from Janisławice in central Poland which is connected with the Janisławice culture (also characteristic of the western part of the Russian Plain). The Janisławice grave contained an individual of lappoidal type in a sitting position, together with a rich inventory of flint (microliths, cores, blades, hammerstone) and bone artifacts (necklace of animal teeth, daggers, needles). Ochre was also present.

Zone A, on the other hand, has produced two burial sites belonging to the Janisławice culture: at Gizycko-Perkunowo in north-eastern Poland a single and a double inhumation of lappoidal type were found with ochre, a few flint artifacts and necklaces of animal teeth; and at Zvejnieki (Latvian SSR) there is a large cemetery consisting of upwards of 100 graves belonging to the Kunda culture. The Zvejnieki cemetery is characterized by supine skeletons, ochre, abundant bone and antler artifacts (especially points), and animal teeth necklaces. It is dated typologically to the Atlantic period and was also used during the local 'Neolithic'. It resembles the large (over 100 graves) late Mesolithic cemetery from Oleniy Ostrov in Karelia, both as regards inhumation type and grave offerings.

The present evidence does not provide a sound

basis for drawing conclusions. All that can be said with certainty is:

1. There is zonal and, probably, cultural differentiation of inhumations, reflected in differences in skeleton position, number of inhumations in a grave, and grave offerings.

2. It is possible to differentiate the burials chronologically, but only in zones north of the steppes, into the generally earlier single burials, and the later cemeteries.

3. It would seem that cemeteries are a relatively late phenomenon in Mesolithic Europe, appearing (except perhaps in the south-eastern zone) only in the eighth millennium BP. They are apparently an expression of increased settlement stability or perhaps greater population density than existed earlier; this is possibly confirmed by the increased area and artifact content of settlements.

ART

Zones B and C have yielded no examples of Mesolithic art. Such artifacts are known only from zone A and most of them are single finds uncovered during drainage work, although their Mesolithic date is quite certain; a few come from methodically excavated sites (Zvejnieki, Kunda-Lammasmägi, Narva). The art objects may be divided into two groups: figurative art objects, and ornamented tools and weapons.

The first group includes the amber 'horse' head from Juodkrante (Lithuanian SSR) which resembles the zoomorphic figurines known from Jutland and Poland, and is therefore related to the Maglemosian tradition in its broadest sense, and the heavily stylized antler elk head from the Zvejnieki cemetery (Latvia). This carved figure, together with the 'bâton' which it crowns, is very similar to the more realistic representations and analogous 'bâtons' from the Oleniy Ostrov cemetery and the Veretye settlement on the bank of the River Sukhona. All these sites belong to the Kunda culture.

The second group comprises tools and weapons made largely of bone and antler, rarely of stone, and decorated with various incised ornaments. These are mostly bone points of Clark's types 16 and 12A.

The following conclusions may be drawn:

1. Two different traditions of Mesolithic art are represented in the lakeland zone: the Maglemosian tradition in the south west, and the Kunda tradition in the north east.

2. In both traditions there are figurative representations of animals, and geometric ornaments on artifacts, usually made of bone (e.g. the 'Maglemosian' hoes from north-eastern Poland).

3. The remaining two zones (great valleys and steppe) are virtually devoid of these kinds of relics, leaving aside the single Maglemosian hoe from eastern Poland (Woźniki).

CONCLUSIONS

The evidence concerning the early and middle Holocene cultures of the western part of the Soviet Union may be summarized as follows:

1. The narrow strip of land between the western border of the USSR and the line of the Dnepr was highly diversified ecologically in the early and middle Holocene; this diversification was latitudinal.

2. Three ecological zones (A, B and C) may be distinguished in this area. Zones A and B are formerly glaciated landscapes, and differ primarily in hydrology, geomorphology, soils and abundance of flint raw materials. Zone A may be further subdivided into the south-western (sandy) part and the north-eastern (clayey) part; the former is related to zone B as regards landscape characteristics. Zone C is distinguished by its upland landscape, less developed river network, markedly warmer climate, soils, and the presence of steppe elements.

3. In the earliest Holocene the differences between zones A and B are not very pronounced, and increase only later. For this reason the cultural development of both zones is at first similar (the Swiderian culture, post-Swiderian assemblages, and the separately developing Kunda culture). With time the differences between zones A and B increase; new cultural units appear which are related to the earlier units with tanged points but differ considerably from one another. Their territories correspond more or less to those of the two zones. At that time the Janisławice culture, characteristic of zone B, emerges. Zone C develops along different lines from the very beginning, the similarity of industries from zones C and B in the Atlantic period being due to the cultural influence of zone C on zone B.

4. In zone C the settlement network is less dense, which suggests that the settlement was sparser in this area. In all three zones settlers preferred valleys of medium-sized rivers, and the large valleys were either avoided or the sites there are buried by alluvia. It is not possible, however, to offer a definitive explanation of the groups of sites evident in the map (*Fig. 1*). These may be remains of small local groups, i.e. actual social groupings that existed in the past; but it is also evident that these groups of sites are related to the presence of rich flint sources nearby. The two observations may of course be in mutual agreement, and local groups could have formed around raw material deposits. There are evidently regions that were not settled, usually elevated clayey and loess areas with few rivers and lakes.

5. Environmental data leave no doubt as to the hunter-gatherer-fishing character of the economy. The zonal arrangement of the vegetation cover and of the large mammal fauna is evident, and it is reasonable to suppose that fishing was well developed, especially in the north-eastern part of zone A. Unfortunately, all these observations are only of a general nature. The temporal evolution of the environment involved the Atlantic northward expansion of thermophilous elements which were followed by the southern cultural elements.

6. Data about camp sites and their lay-out are too scarce to permit reconstructions. The same goes for the alleged seasonality of Mesolithic communities.

7. Further studies, including consideration of the basic issues, need to be continued in the future.

APPENDIX: *Mesolithic of the U.S.S.R. – Select Bibliography*

1. Environment

DĄBROWSKI, M.J. (1959) Późnoglacjalna i holoceńska historia lasów Puszczy Białowieskiej (Lateglacial and Holocene history of the Białowieża primary forest). *Acta Societatis Botanicorum Poloniae*, 28: 197–248.

DOLUKHANOV, P.M. (1979) *Ecology and Economy in Neolithic Eastern Europe*. London, Duckworth.

FIRBAS, F. (1949) *Waldgeschichte Mitteleuropas*. Jena, Gustav Fischer.

FRENZEL, B. (1960) *Die Vegetations-Landschaftszonen Nord-Eurasiens während der letzen Eiszeit und während der postglazialen Warmezeit*. Mainz, Abhl. Akad. Wiss. Lit.

HUNTLEY, B. and BIRKS, H.J.B. (1983) *An Atlas of Past and Present Pollen Maps for Europe: 0–13000 years ago*. Cambridge, University Press.

NEISHTAT, M.I. (1957) *Istoriya lesov i paleogeografiya SSSR v golotsene* (History of forests and palaeogeography of the USSR in the Holocene). Moscow, Nauka.

2. General works on the central and east European Mesolithic.

BADER, O.N. (1970) Mezolit (Mesolithic). In A.A. Formozov (ed.). *Kamennyy vek na territorii SSSR. Materialy i issledovaniya po arkheologii SSSR*, 166: 90–104.

CLARK, J.G.D. (1936) *The Mesolithic Settlement of Northern Europe*. Cambridge, University Press.

GURINA, N.N. (ed.) (1966) *U istokov drevnikh kultur* (The origins of the old cultures) (Materialy i isseldovaniya po arkheologii SSSR, 126). Moscow, Nauka.

GURINA, N.N. (ed.) (1977) *Pamyatki epokhi mezolita* (The Mesolithic monuments) (Kratkie soobshcheniya Instituta arkheologii AN SSSR, 149). Moscow, Nauka.

KOLTSOV, L.V. (1977) *Finalnyy paleolit i mezolit yuzhnoy i vostochnoy Pribaltiki* (Late Palaeolithic and Mesolithic of the southern and eastern regions of the Baltic Sea). Moscow, Nauka.

KOLTSOV, L.V. (1983) The main types of Mesolithic flint arrowheads and microliths in the north-west USSR. *Archaeologia Interregionalis*, 2: 271–276.

KOZŁOWSKI, J.K. and KOZŁOWSKI, S.K. (1975) *Pradzieje Europy od XL do IV tysiąclecia p.n.e.* (Prehistory of Europe from 40th to 4th millennium B.C.). Warsaw, Państwowe Wydawnictwo Naukowe.

KOZŁOWSKI, J.K. and KOZŁOWSKI, S.K. (1977) *Epoka kamienia na ziemiach polskich* (The Stone Age in Poland). Warsaw, Państwowe Wydawnictwo Naukowe.

KOZŁOWSKI, J.K. and KOZŁOWSKI, S.K. (1979) *Upper Palaeolithic and Mesolithic in Europe. Taxonomy and Palaeohistory* (Prace Komisji Archeologicznej, 18). Wrocław–Warsaw–Kraków–Gdańsk, Ossolineum.

KOZŁOWSKI, S.K. (1972) *Pradzieje ziem polskich od IX do V tysiaclecia p.n.e.* (Prehistory of the Polish territories from ninth to fifth millennium B.C.). Warsaw, Państwowe Wy-

dawnictwo Naukowe.

KOZŁOWSKI, S.K. (1975) *Cultural Differentiation of Europe from 10th to 5th Millennium B.C.* Warsaw, University Press.

KOZŁOWSKI, S.K. (1980) *Atlas of the Mesolithic in Europe.* Warsaw, University Press.

3. Regional works

a. *Lithuanian, Latvian and Estonian SSR and Kaliningrad region*

GROSS, H. (1940) Die Renntierjäger-Kulteren Ostpreussens. *Praehistorische Zeitschrift*, 30/31: 39–67.

INDREKO, R. (1948) *Die mittlere Steinzeit in Estland* (Kungl. Vitterhets Historie och Antiqvitets Akademiens Handlingar, 66). Stockholm, Almquist and Wiksell.

JAANITS, K. (1981) Die mesolithischen Siedlungsplätze mit Feuersteininventar in Estland. In B. Gramsch (ed.), *Mesolithikum in Europa. 2. Internationales Symposium Potsdam, 3 bis 8 April 1978 Bericht* (Veröffentlichungen des Museums für Ur- und Frühgeschichte Potsdam, 14/15). Berlin, Deutscher Verlag der Wissenschaften: 389–399.

LOZE, I. (1973) Mesolithic art of eastern Baltic region. In S.K. Kozłowski (ed.), *The Mesolithic in Europe*. Warsaw, University Press: 391–398.

LOZE, I. (1981) Spätmesolithikum und Frühneolithikum in Lettland. In B. Gramsch (ed.), *Mesolithikum in Europa. 2. Internationales Symposium Potsdam, 3 bis 8 April 1978 Bericht* (Veröffentlichungen des Museums für Ur- und Frühgeschichte Potsdam, 14/15). Berlin, Deutscher Verlag der Wissenschaften: 183–190.

RIMANTIENE, R.K. (1971) *Paleolit i mezolit Litvy* (Palaeolithic and Mesolithic of Lithuania). Vilnyus, Izdatel'stvo Mintis.

RIMANTIENE, R.K. (1984) *Akmens amžius Lietuvoje* (Stone Age in Lithuania). Vilnyus, Mokslas.

ZAGORSKA, I. (1981) Das Frühmesolithikum in Lettland. In B. Gramsch (ed.), *Mesolithikum in Europa. 2. Internationales Symposium Potsdam, 3 bis 8 April 1978 Bericht* (Veröffentlichungen des Museums für Ur- und Frühgeschichte Potsdam, 14/15). Berlin, Deutscher Verlag der Wissenschaften: 73–82.

ZAGORSKIS, F. (1974) Mezolits (Mesolithic). *Latvijas PSR Archeologia* Riga, Zinatne: 23–29.

b. *Byelorussian and the northern part of the Ukrainian SSR*

ISAENKO, V.F. (ed.) (1970) *Ocherki po arkheologii Belorussii* (Works on the archaeology of Byelorussia). Minsk, Nauka i Tekhnika.

ZALIZNIAK, L.L. (1984) *Mezolit Yugo-vostochnogo Polesia* (Mesolithic of south-eastern Polesie). Kiev, Naukova Dumka.

c. *Southern part of the Ukrainian SSR and the Moldavian SSR*

BADER, O.N. (1961) O sootnoshenii kultury verkhnego paleolita i mezolita Kryma i Kavkaza (Interrelations of the Upper Palaeolithic and Mesolithic cultures of the Crimea and the Caucasus). *Sovetskaya Arkheologiya*: 9–25.

CHERNYSH, A.P. (1975) *Starodavnie naselenniya Podnistrovia v dobu mezolitu* (The prehistoric settlement of the Dnestr river basin during the Mesolithic period). Kiev, Naukova Dumka.

DANILENKO, V.N. (1969) *Neolit Ukrainy* (The Neolithic of the Ukraine). Kiev, Naukova Dumka.

GATSOV, I. (1982) The archaeological cultures of the late Pleistocene and early Holocene in the western Black Sea region, and their significance for the formation of the Neolithic flint industries. In J.K. Kozłowski (ed.), *Origin of the Chipped Stone Industries of the Early Farming Cultures in Balkans*. Warsaw–Kraków, Państwowe Wydawnictwo Naukowe: 111–130.

KRASKOVSKI, V.I. (1978) *Karta Paleolita i Mezolita severozapadnogo Prichernomoria* (Palaeolithic and Mesolithic sites of the north-eastern part of Prichernomorie). Kiev, Naukova Dumka.

MARKEVICH, V.I. (1974) *Bugo-dnestrovskaya kultura na territorii Moldavii* (The Bug–Dnestr culture in Moldavia). Kishinev, Shtintsa.

STANKO, V.N. (1972) Tipy pamyatnikov i lokalnye kultury v mezolite severnogo Prichernomoria (Types of monuments and local cultures in the northern regions of the Black Sea). *Materialy i issledovaniya po arkheologii SSSR*, 185: 252–261.

TELEGIN, D.Y. (1982) *Mezolitichnye pamyatki Ukrainy* (Mesolithic monuments of the Ukraine). Kiev, Naukova Dumka.

Procurement of Flint in the Mesolithic of the Polish Plain

Michał Kobusiewicz

Abstract

The area of northern Poland covered by thick glacial sediments is devoid of primary sources of flint. However, erratic nodules of Cretaceous flint of Baltic origin occur in glacial sands and clays. Collecting this raw material from the surface did not satisfy the needs of local Mesolithic communities who compensated by importing *chocolate flint* from the south, though only on a small scale. In their quest for raw material, the Mesolithic population of this part of Europe discovered specific localities that were particularly rich in erratic pebbles of Cretaceous flint. These concentrations of flint resulted from unusual geomorphological processes which operated here at the end of the Pleistocene. Knowledge of at least some of these natural concentrations enabled the Mesolithic people to exploit them and to provide themselves with the necessary supply of flint.

INTRODUCTION

The Polish Plain is part of the large belt of plains in northern Europe. It covers all of central and northern Poland and was largely overridden by ice during the Last (Vistulian) Glaciation and completely covered by ice during earlier glacials. The Quaternary sediments which cover the Polish Plain reach an average depth of 40 metres. Hence, all the primary sources of flint lie well below the present surface. However, pieces of flint of various sizes do occur in sands and clays which were brought from the north by glacier ice. This type of raw material is referred to in geological literature as erratic Cretaceous Baltic flint. It was used extensively on the Plain during the Mesolithic. It was probably obtained simply by collecting it from the surface wherever it was found. This, however, did not satisfy the needs of the Mesolithic population who attempted to compensate by importing raw material from the south, though only on a small scale. This imported material is represented by finds of *chocolate flint* which originated in the late Oxfordian or early Kimmeridgian limestones and the karstic clays, the natural outcrops of which are on the northern slopes of the Swietokrzyskie (Holy Cross) mountains on the southern edge of the Plain.

In the late Palaeolithic and Mesolithic chocolate flint was imported over a considerable distance to the north, particularly along the basins of the Vistula and Warta rivers which provided natural communication routes (Schild, Marczak and Królik 1975;

Więckowska 1975; Schild 1976a, 1976b, 1984). Such imports are frequently encountered over 100 km from their source, less frequently at 200 km, and occasionally reach even further. However, apart from those regions which were relatively close to the natural sources of flint in the south, the remaining areas of the Polish Plain were beyond the reach of southern imports and the inhabitants there had effectively to depend on deposits of erratic Cretaceous Baltic flint.

EXPLOITATION OF ERRATIC FLINT

Searching for erratic pebbles of flint in the late Pleistocene tundra or in the early Holocene forests with their thick undergrowth, could not have been easy and was certainly strenuous. Moreover, erratic flint found on the surface is the least suitable material for toolmaking, usually being brittle and cracked by heat and frost. In spite of this, no tendency to use this material sparingly can be observed in the Mesolithic archaeological materials collected from the Plain. Research on late Pleistocene and early Holocene communities in the north west of Poland has, however, led to the discovery of specific sources of erratic flint and suggests that these communities were aware of these sources and of their significance.

Such natural secondary concentrations of erratic flint are known from a number of regions of the Plain. The following is an account of two well-documented examples.

Poznań–Starołęka

The first lies in the central part of the valley of the River Warta just beyond Poznań, where the river cuts across the Poznań Stadial moraines of the Vistulian Glaciation in a north–south direction. Research by Pawłowski and Bartkowski (1961) has shown that the River Warta cut through the Poznań Stadial moraines forming terrace VII which, at 20 m above the present level of the river, is the highest terrace. The river removed the finer material, leaving behind the coarser fraction such as gravel

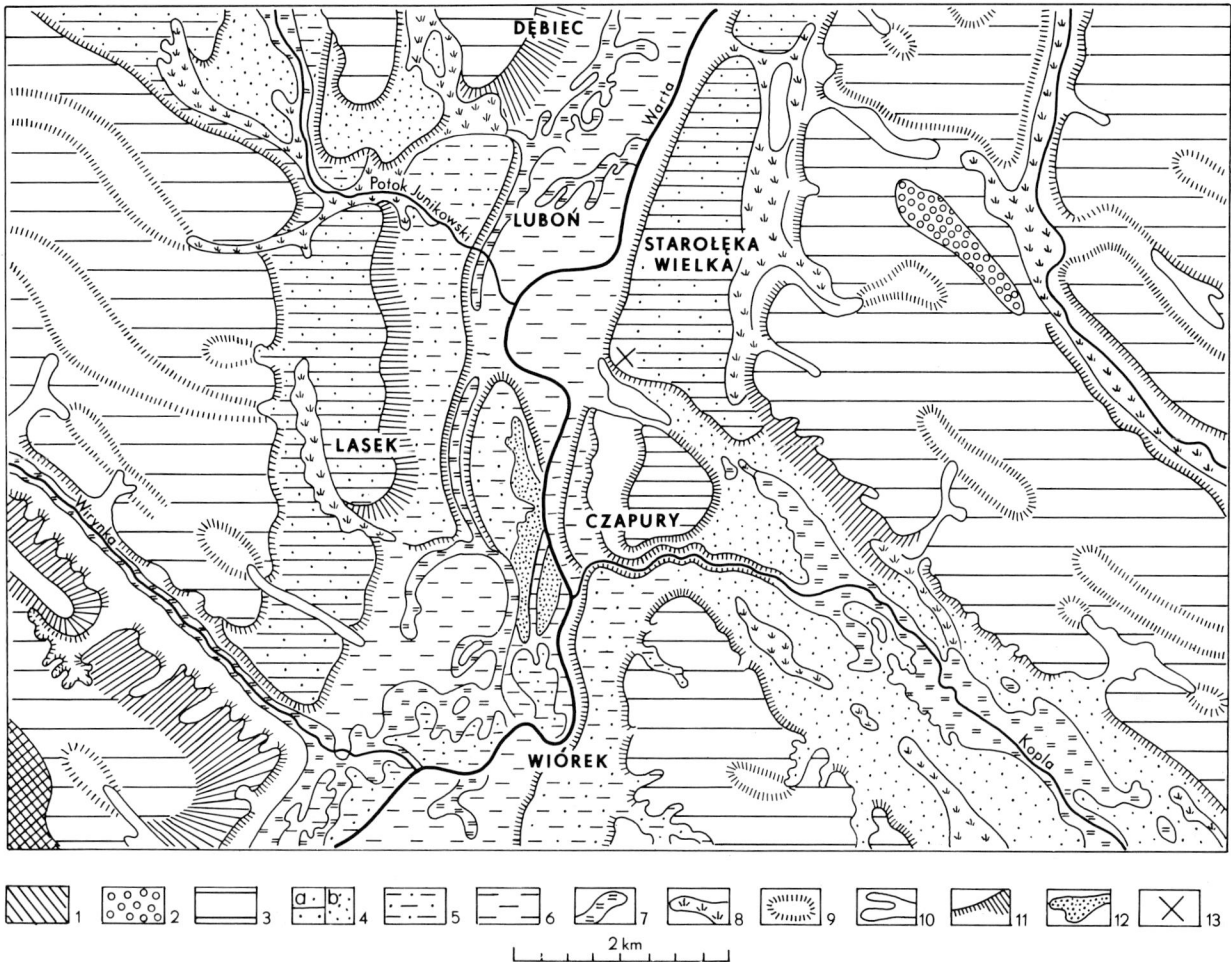

Figure 1 Geomorphology of the area with secondary concentration of erratic flint near Poznań–Starołęka, north-west Poland (after T. Bartkowski 1961). *Key*: 1 – frontal moraine; 2 – esker; 3 – morainic plateau; 4a – terrace VII; 4b – terrace VI; 5 – terrace II; 6 – terrace I; 7 – marshes; 8 – flat wet valley bottoms; 9 – sub-glacial valleys dissecting the plateau; 10 – small sub-aerial valleys; 11 – scarps; 12 – dunes; 13 – Swiderian and Mesolithic archaeological site.

and small erratic pebbles of which there is a high concentration covering the surface of terrace VII. Among these are numerous nodules of Cretaceous flint. Exceptionally rich concentrations of the residue from this dissected moraine can be found in the Warta river valley extending for several kilometres to the south of Poznań in the localities of Starołęka, Czapury, Luboń, and Lasek (*Fig. 1*). This phenomenon can be accounted for by the fact that here the River Warta formed a sharp curve eroding and sorting the material across a relatively large area of moraines.

Flint nodules are as numerous on the surface of terrace VII as they are at a relatively shallow depth beneath it, and sometimes exceed 20 cm in diameter. Because of their size and the small number of internal fractures, they constitute very good raw material for toolmaking. The formation of these flint-rich deposits must have begun during the Pomeranian Stadial of the Vistulian Glaciation and must have come to an end by the Younger Dryas, since a Swiderian culture site of that age at Poznań–Starołęka is situated on the surface of terrace VII.

The identification of the geomorphological processes involved explains the occurrence of such a rich deposit of erratic flint nodules in this relatively small area south of Poznań, and the numerous Stone Age sites associated with it. In a 7 km stretch of the valley 47 sites were found, most of which were Mesolithic though some were late Palaeolithic and Neolithic. They are all exceptionally rich in flint materials. Among them are two flint-processing workshops from Poznań–Starołęka (Kobusiewicz 1961) which have been thoroughly excavated. They possess characteristics which are typical of workshops associated with flint quarries in the regions where there are natural flint outcrops – for example, on the northern slopes of the Swietokrzyskie mountains or other places where flint was mined. These characteristics are: (i) an abundance of forms such as pre-cores and cores from the first stages of processing; (ii) numerous large primary and secondary flakes; (iii) the presence of macrolithic tools like those known from the true mining areas; and (iv) the preponderance of pre-cores, cores (5%) and débitage (93.3%) over retouched tools (1.7%).

443

The Mesolithic sites combined the functions of sites associated with flint quarries – that is, places in which raw material underwent preliminary processing – with that of workshops producing blades.

The characteristics of the sites associated with mines or workshops are also found at other sites in the region of Starołęka. Since these sites are known only from surface finds, a detailed analysis is not possible. The flint assemblages are distinguished by the presence of erratic nodules of flint with barely noticeable marks showing that work was begun on them, pre-cores, numerous cores (frequently including large specimens in the initial stages of reduction), and a vast quantity of various types of débitage also often of large size. Examples of such sites are: Lasek 16, 3 and 13, Luboń 16, and Wiórek 2.

The entire group of sites from the Poznań–Starołęka region recalls similar, though larger and richer, complexes of sites which accompany flint quarries in areas where flint occurs naturally. The following is a list of all the similarities: (i) a marked concentration of sites; (ii) products and proportions of products characteristic of flint workshops; and (iii) an abundant use of flint material. The fourth essential element of the flint 'basin' is the presence

of raw material deposited in a secondary location as a result of the unique geomorphological conditions in this region.

Międzychód

The second example of a flint 'basin' on the Plain is the region of Międzychód approximately 70 km west north west of Poznań. Here, too, secondary deposits of flint were the result of exceptional geomorphological processes. During the Poznań Stadial subglacial rivers cut across the former river valley which was covered by glacial deposits of this and earlier glacial episodes. The tunnel valleys of the present lakes following these river channels run perpendicular to the Warta river valley below Międzychód. The pressure of the sub-glacial river waters was considerable. In order to escape from under the glacier the meltwaters had to rise 30 m in a few kilometres. It is not surprising, therefore, that they cut deeply into the moraine washing away finer materials and leaving behind gravels and variously sized stones which included large quantities of erratic Cretaceous Baltic flint, frequently up to 20 cm across.

The size of the region around Międzychód which

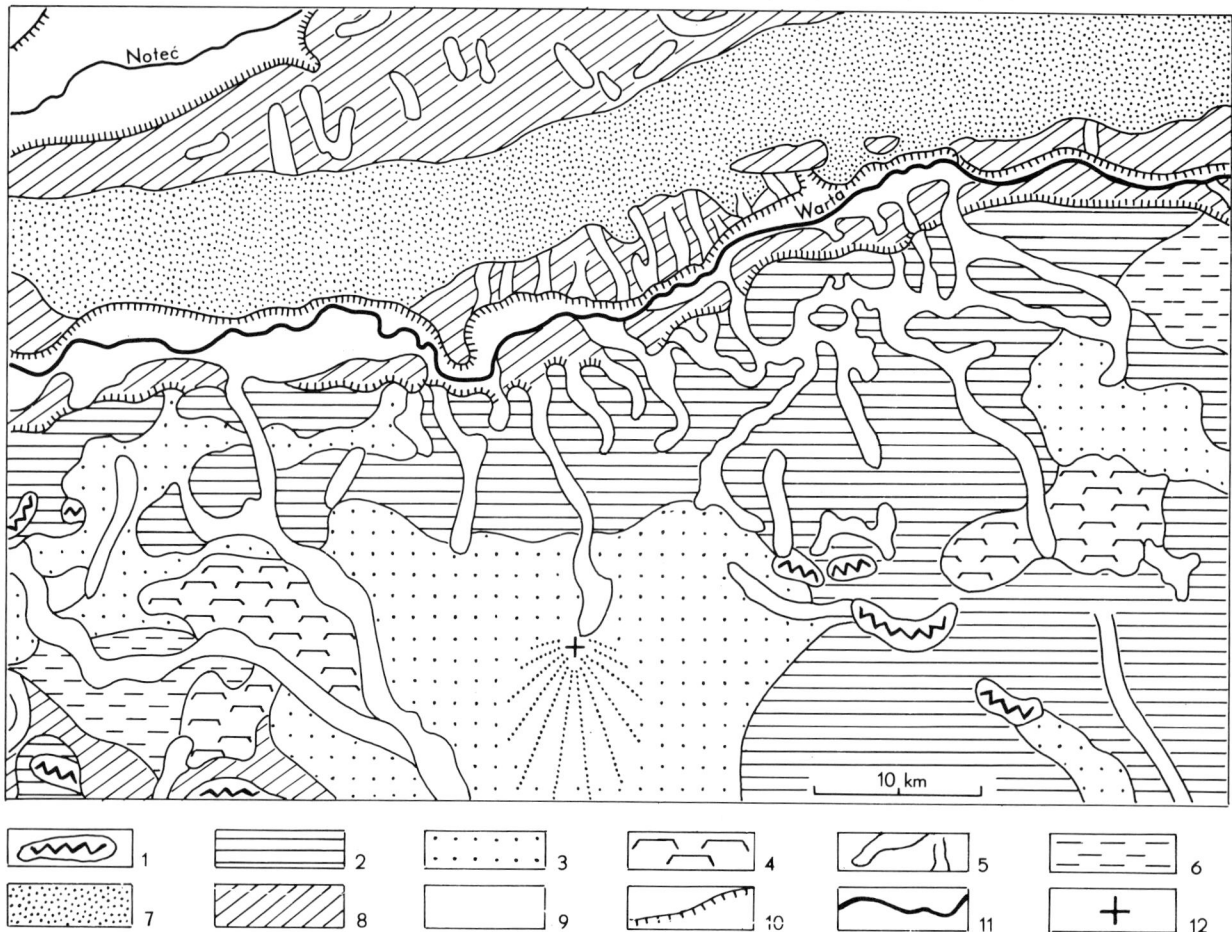

Figure 2 Geomorphology of the area with secondary concentration of erratic flint near Międzychód, north-west Poland (after L. Starkel (ed.), *Przeglądowa Mapa Geomorfologiczna Polski* 1983). *Key*: 1 – frontal moraine; 2 – morainic plateau; 3 – sander plains and fans; 4 – kames; 5 – sub-glacial channels; 6 – sedimentary plains; 7 – aeolian forms; 8 – high terraces; 9 – floodplain terraces; 10 – scarps; 11 – rivers; 12 – site at Lewice.

444

is rich in flint derived from the moraine by the action of the glacial waters is difficult to estimate. It certainly includes all of the area crossed by the north–south trending outlets of the present lakes – namely, a section of the Warta river valley approximately 25 km long and 8–15 km wide (*Fig. 2*). In this area there are numerous sites with flint assemblages. These assemblages, known only from surface finds, include principally cores which are usually large or very large, as well as forms characteristic of initial and advanced phases of processing. These include large and very large primary flakes, lames à crête, and rejuvenating flakes. The majority of sites in this area are characterized by the abundant use of flint. At the same time, the assemblages have few retouched tools which means that a precise assessment of their age is difficult to make. In general terms, the Międzychód 'basin' was already known

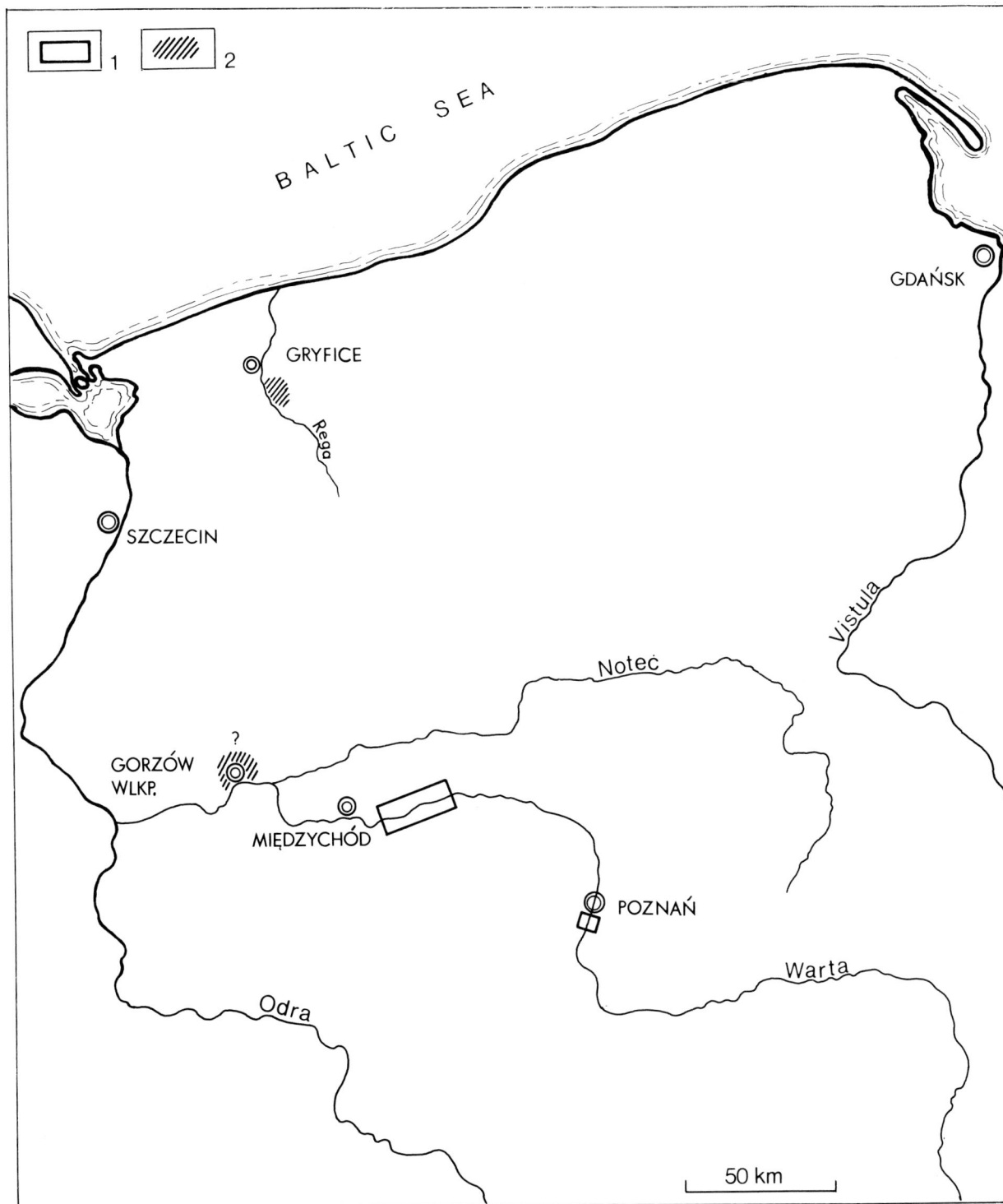

Figure 3   The 'flint basins' in the north-western Polish Plain. *Key*: 1 – well-documented 'flint basins'; 2 – possible 'flint basins'.

445

by the end of the Palaeolithic, but was exploited mainly during the Mesolithic period. Traces of Neolithic settlement in this region are rather sparse.

CONCLUDING REMARKS

It would be interesting to be able to trace how far the materials from the areas discussed above actually reached. This, however, is not possible since the erratic flint from the regions of Poznań–Starołęka and Międzychód does not differ significantly from erratic flint found in small amounts across all of the formerly glaciated areas of the Polish Plain.

Other areas are known on the Plain of north-west Poland in which there are sites with workshops exhibiting an abundant use of flint. They include a group of late Palaeolithic sites in Kocierz near Gryfice, west Pomerania (Czarnecki 1973) and the region of Gorzów Wielkopolski (*Fig. 3*). However, insufficient archaeological research has been carried out in these areas to enable further comment. Nevertheless, these occurrences serve to indicate that there were probably more of these 'flint basins' and that they provided the main sources of flint raw material for the early Holocene inhabitants of the Polish Plain.

References

BARTKOWSKI, T. (1961) Wiek teras w przełomowej dolinie Warty pod Poznaniem a stanowisko archeologiczne w Poznaniu Starołęce (L'âge des terrasses dans la vallée de brèche de la Warta près de Poznań et la station archéologique à Poznań–Starołęka). *Fontes Archaeologici Posnanienses*, 12: 24–33.

CZARNECKI, M. (1973) Wstępne badania wykopaliskowe paleolitycznego stanowiska w Kocierzu, pow. Gryfice (Die ersten Ergebnisse über Forschungsausgrabungen in der paläolithischen Fundstelle in Kocierz, Kreis Gryfice). *Materiały Zachodniopomorskie*, 17: 7–16.

KOBUSIEWICZ, M. (1961) Stanowisko z końca paleolitu i początków mezolitu z Poznania-Starołęki (Une station de la fin de l'ère paléolithique et des débuts de l'ère mésolithique à Poznań–Starołęka). *Fontes Archaeologici Posnanienses*, 12: 1–22.

SCHILD, R. (1976a) The final Palaeolithic settlements of the European Plain. *Scientific American*, 234: 88–99.

SCHILD, R. (1976b) Flint mining and trade in Polish prehistory as seen from perspective of the chocolate flint of central Poland. A second approach. *Acta Archaeologica Carpatica*, 16: 147–170.

SCHILD, R. (1984) Terminal Palaeolithic of the North European Plain: a review of lost chances, potential and hopes. In F. Wendorf and A.E. Close (eds), *Advances in World Archaeology*, 3. Orlando, Academic Press: 193–274.

SCHILD, R., MARCZAK, M. and KRÓLIK, H. (1975) *Późny Mezolit* (The Late Mesolithic). Wrocław, Ossolineum.

WIĘCKOWSKA, H. (1975) Społeczności łowiecko-rybackie wczesnego holocenu. In W. Hensel (ed.), *Prahistoria Ziem Polskich. I. Paleolit i Mezolit*. Wrocław, Ossolineum.

Elements of a Food-Producing Economy in the Late Mesolithic of the Polish Lowland

Lucyna Domańska

Abstract

This paper considers some of the problems of the Mesolithic–Neolithic transition on the Polish Plain. Of particular relevance are the results of recent investigations at the eighth millennium BP site of Dęby 29. The lithic assemblage from this site belongs to the 'Janisławice' culture and includes high percentages of microliths, burins, and blades. This is associated with the remains of fireplaces and a hut. No pottery has been found on the site but, significantly, some of the flint blades show micro-wear traces similar to those found on Neolithic flint sickles. The faunal assemblage is dominated by the bones of small ruminants (roe deer or sheep/goats), with a smaller proportion of pig bones. Thin-section analysis will show whether these are from wild or domesticated animals. The evidence from Dęby 29 raises questions concerning the subsistence economy of the inhabitants, and the relationship between this 'Janisławice' group and the local Neolithic. Several possible interpretations are considered.

INTRODUCTION

This paper discusses some of the problems of the Mesolithic–Neolithic transition on the Polish Plain between the Oder and Vistula rivers. This part of the Polish Plain, particularly the belt of the Great Valleys, has been chosen for an analysis of the problem because, here, evidence of contacts between Mesolithic and Neolithic communities offers the possibility of explaining the origin of the local Neolithic (Domańska and Kośko 1974, 1983). Intensive field and laboratory studies of late Mesolithic sites conducted in this region over the last few years (*Fig. 1*), and in particular the finds made at the site of Dęby 29, have enabled us to investigate the nature of the transition.

THE MESOLITHIC BACKGROUND

During the Atlantic period this part of the Polish Plain was dominated by sites belonging to the so-called 'Northern Technocomplex' (Kozłowski and Kozłowski 1977); although recent investigations have identified another important element in the settlement of the Great Valleys during this period, attributable to the 'Janisławice' population (see below).

Results of recent investigations by the present author (Domańska 1986, in press) indicate the presence within this region of two late Mesolithic groups which have their origins in the north Euro-

Figure 1   Location map of the more important sites referred to in the text.

pean Mesolithic: the Chojnice group, in the maritime lowlands and the Pomeranian uplands; and the Kolankowo group, in the belt of the Great Valleys.

The Chojnice group

The characteristics of the Chojnice group are best represented by the site of Jastrzębia Góra 4 (*Fig. 1*), radiocarbon dated to 6705±80 BP (Bln-1926). The most important features of the Chojnice group are: (i) a predominance of conical and subconical single-platform cores which were used to produce blades that are very long, thin and regular (*Fig. 2*); (ii) microliths which comprise numerous points with a retouched base and various categories of triangles, such as wide-angled, elongated triangles ('Pieńki triangles' – Kozłowski 1972), triangles retouched on all edges, and narrow rectangular scalene triangles; trapezes and the so-called 'Nowy Młyn' points were also discovered (*Fig. 3*). Flint assemblages identical to those found at Jastrzębia Góra 4 have been found

447

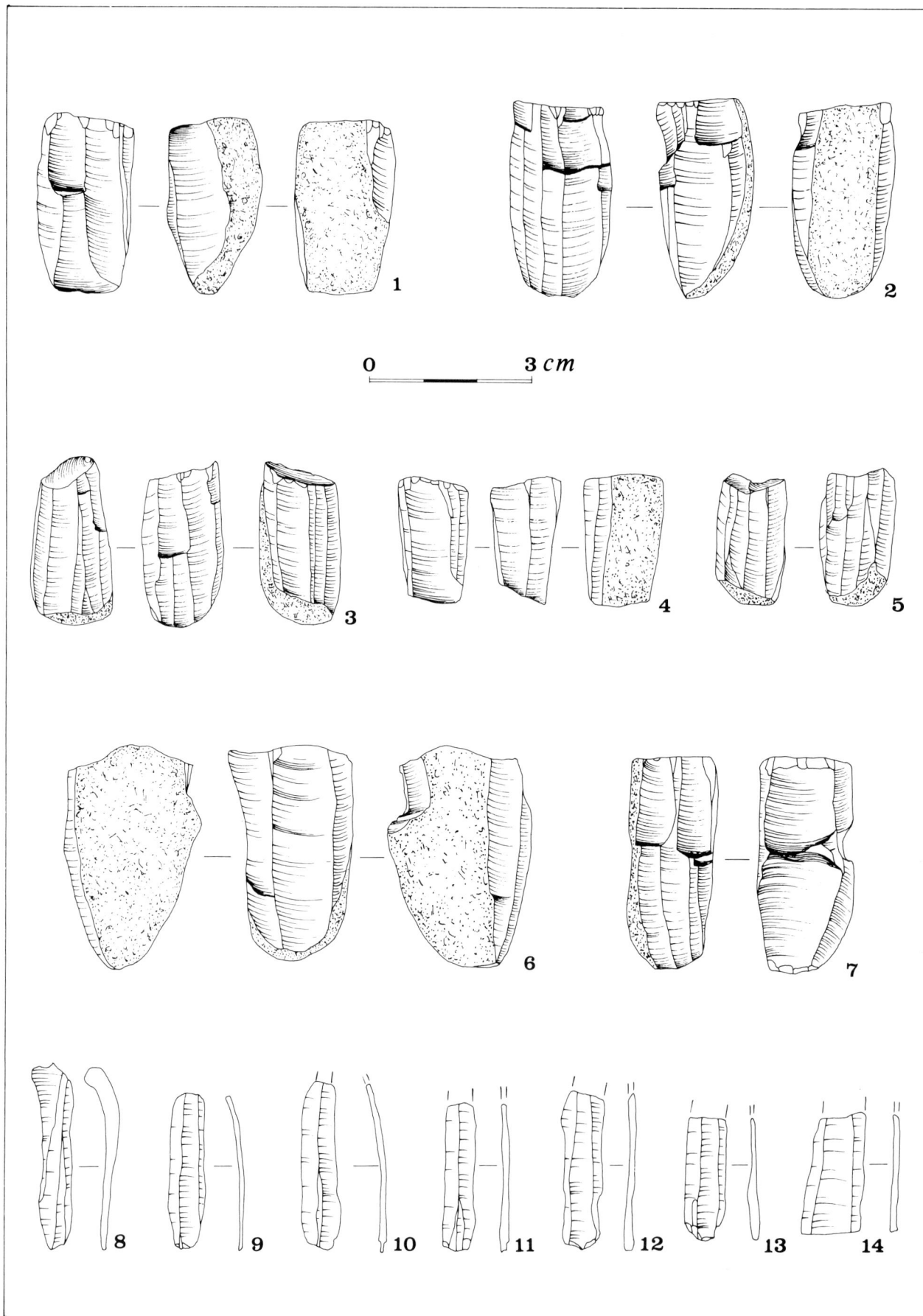

Figure 2 Jastrzębia Góra Site 4: cores and blades.

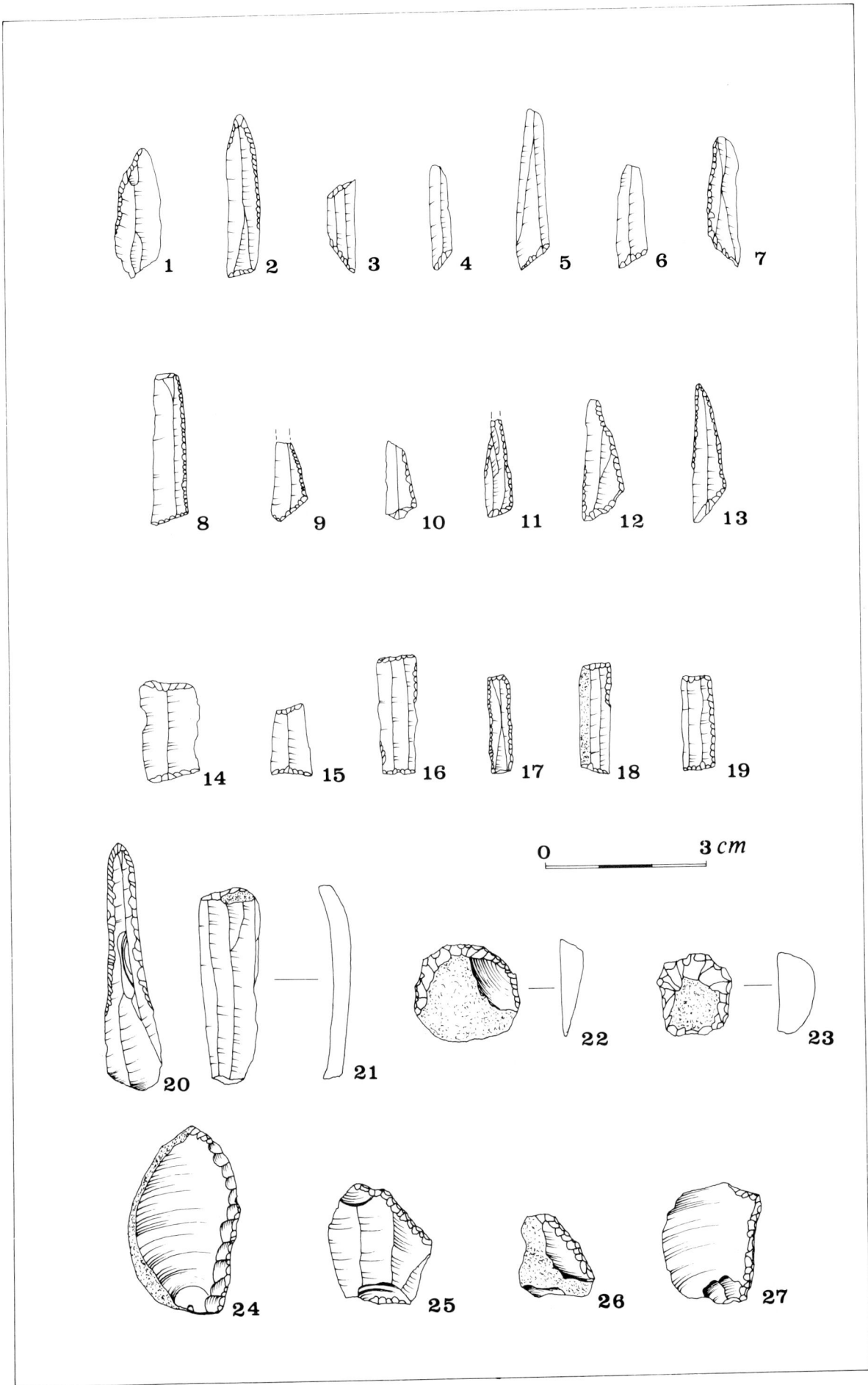

Figure 3 Jastrzębia Góra Site 4: retouched tools.

449

in various parts of the maritime lowlands and the Pomeranian uplands (Domańska 1976, in press).

There appear to be close typological links between the flint assemblages of the Chojnice group and those of the Maglemose culture (Brinch Petersen 1971; Andersen, Jørgensen and Richter 1982), and this is reinforced by the similarity in the method of blade production. The number of points with a retouched base, scalene triangles retouched on all edges, and narrow rectangular triangles in Chojnice assemblages suggest that this group is most closely related to the Zealand sites.

Further support for a link with the Maglemose sites is provided by a comparison of the horizontal distribution of various tool types on Danish Maglemose sites with those of the Chojnice group conducted by Ole Grøn (1983; Domańska, in press). The sites of Jastrzębia Góra 4 in northern Poland and Ulkestrup I on Zealand both showed two concentrations of microliths, indicating a considerable similarity of settlement structure.

The Kolankowo group

The Kolankowo group is found in the Great Valleys zone (*Fig. 1*). The assemblages (*Fig. 4*) are characterized by: (i) a predominance of single-platform cores for blades and flakes, although cores with changed orientation and cores with two platforms also occur; (ii) a predominance among the microliths of forms such as trapezes, broad scalene triangles, isosceles triangles, segments, obliquely-blunted points, and backed bladélets.

A direct comparison of the assemblages of Kolankowo type with late Mesolithic cultures from northern Poland is not possible at present. Future studies may show that these assemblages are merely the youngest phase of the Komornica culture. The few radiocarbon dates available show only that this group developed in the second half of the seventh and in the sixth millennium BP.

EVIDENCE OF CONTACT BETWEEN LATE MESOLITHIC AND EARLY NEOLITHIC GROUPS

This 'Mesolithic' population occupied the area which was also settled by the earliest Neolithic food producers, and evidence exists which indicates contact between these groups. Two important stages of contact have been recognized: Stage I, which covers the final phase of the Linear Pottery (LBK) culture; and Stage II, associated with the earliest phase of the Funnel Beaker (TRB) culture.

Stage I coincides with the process of rapid demographic expansion among Danubian communities, which populated the region of the so-called 'black earth' soils. This population increase forced the LBK groups to migrate into the areas of podzolic soils already occupied by the 'Mesolithic' population. Evidence for this process is found at sites like Podgaj 32, where pottery of the LBK culture was found associated with a flint inventory similar to that of the Mesolithic Kolankowo group (*Fig. 5*).

These observations may be interpreted in two ways (Czerniak, in press): either assemblages of the Podgaj type are the result of Danubian groups adopting Mesolithic methods of flint knapping and their use of local raw materials; or, some Mesolithic groups were assimilated by the Danubians.

Another question to be considered is the extent to which the 'Mesolithic' population participated in the origin of the local early farming culture, the TRB culture. Assemblages belonging to the earliest phase of the TRB culture show close links with the flint industry of the Danubian communities (Lech and Młynarczyk 1981). This can be seen in: (i) the size characteristics of the blanks; (ii) the extensive use of chocolate-coloured flint; (iii) the use of similar techniques for producing blanks, e.g. the use of the splinter technique; and (iv) the predominance of end-scrapers and side-scrapers among the tools.

It may be concluded from the above observations that the TRB culture assemblages from the belt of the Great Valleys had closer links with the flint industries of the Danubian communities than with those of the 'Mesolithic' peoples.

However, proof of the extent to which the 'Mesolithic' population participated in the origin of local early farming culture was found at the site of Łącko 6 (Domańska and Kośko 1974, 1983) which has been dated on the basis of the pottery to the earliest phase of the TRB culture. The flint inventory from this site contains a number of Mesolithic elements of the Kolankowo group. It was concluded that the presence of these Mesolithic elements in the assemblage was the result of the neolithization of some of the 'Mesolithic' groups.

Dęby 29

It now seems certain that contacts occurred between the 'late Mesolithic' population and the earliest Neolithic food producers in this part of the Polish lowland. However, we still know very little about the changes that must have taken place among the 'Mesolithic' population – in particular, those changes which occurred during the middle and late Atlantic period.

Investigations at the site of Dęby 29 have made a significant contribution towards solving this problem. This site was excavated for only one month in 1984, but has already produced evidence which permits new hypotheses to be formulated. These interpretations must be regarded as tentative, since analysis of the finds is incomplete.

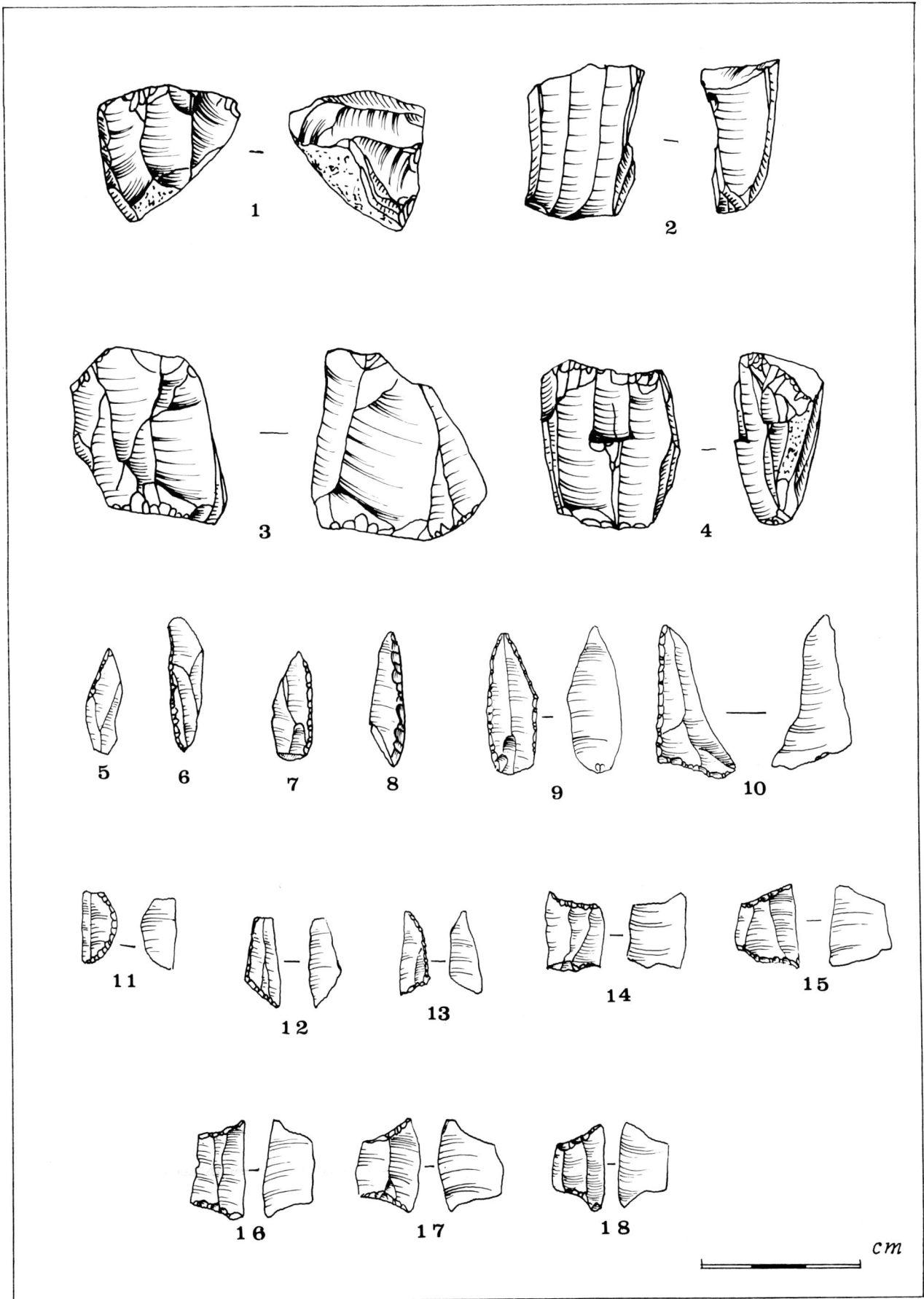

Figure 4 Kolankowo Site 1: cores (1–4); microliths (5–18).

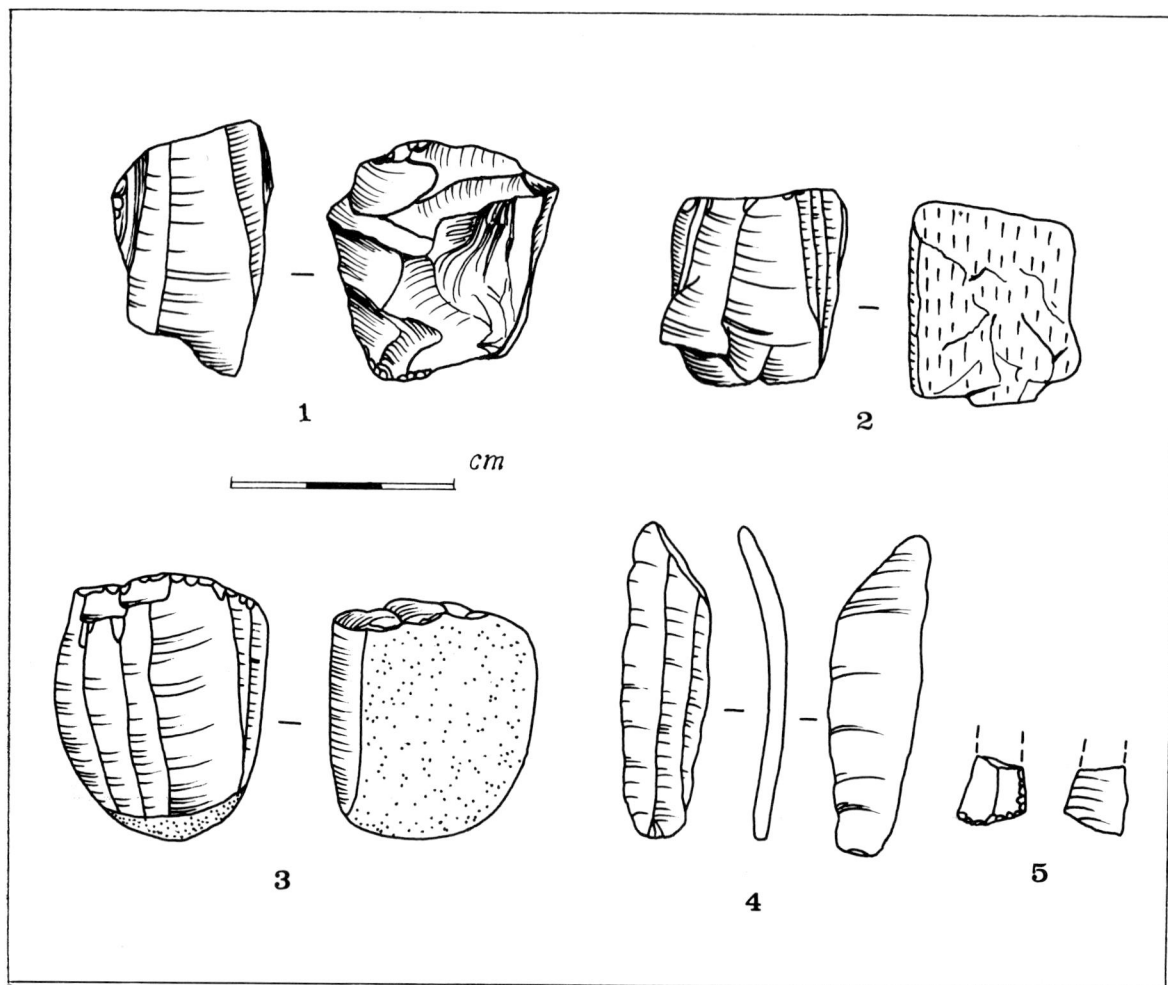

Figure 5 Podgaj Site 32: flint artifacts.

Of prime importance to the interpretation of the site is the undisturbed nature of its stratigraphy. Sections through the site show two different soil horizons separated by a layer of sand. The lower horizon is podzolized and contains the Mesolithic assemblage. This was covered by the sand layer on which the recent soil has developed. All the post-Mesolithic material occurred in this upper soil.

The Mesolithic assemblage (*Figs. 6 & 7*), radio-carbon dated to 7250±100 BP (Gd-2278), belongs to the 'Janisławice' culture. The artifacts occurred in two concentrations, and there were also remains of fireplaces and a hut. No pottery was found on the site. The raw material utilized was exclusively chocolate-coloured flint which comes from deposits on the north-east fringes of the Holy Cross mountains, some 200 km from the site. The main characteristics of the flint assemblage are: (i) extensive use of the blade technique; and (ii) a significant microlithic component – microburins comprise 5% of the artifacts, while 72% of the tools are microliths which include narrow rectangular triangles, short rectangular triangles of the Janisławice type, Janisławice points, and trapezes. Of

particular note was the discovery of blades which, on microscopic examination, showed use-wear similar to that found on Neolithic flint sickles.

Also of interest was the discovery of faunal material, among which bones of apparently domesticated animals predominate. Thin-section analysis of the bones, which would indicate whether or not they are from domesticated animals, has not yet been undertaken. At present, therefore, it is only possible to suggest that about 80% of the bones are from small ruminants such as roe deer or sheep/goats; although the porous structure of some of the long bones suggests that the majority are from sheep or goats. However, the presence of pig has been positively identified by teeth and ankle bones. The remaining part of the faunal material is composed of the bones of wild large mammals.

As the analysis of the faunal material is incomplete, a number of interpretations are still possible. This 'Janisławice' group may have specialized in roe deer hunting, and may already have had domesticated pig. On the other hand, thin-section analysis may show that the majority of the faunal remains are from domesticated animals. If

452

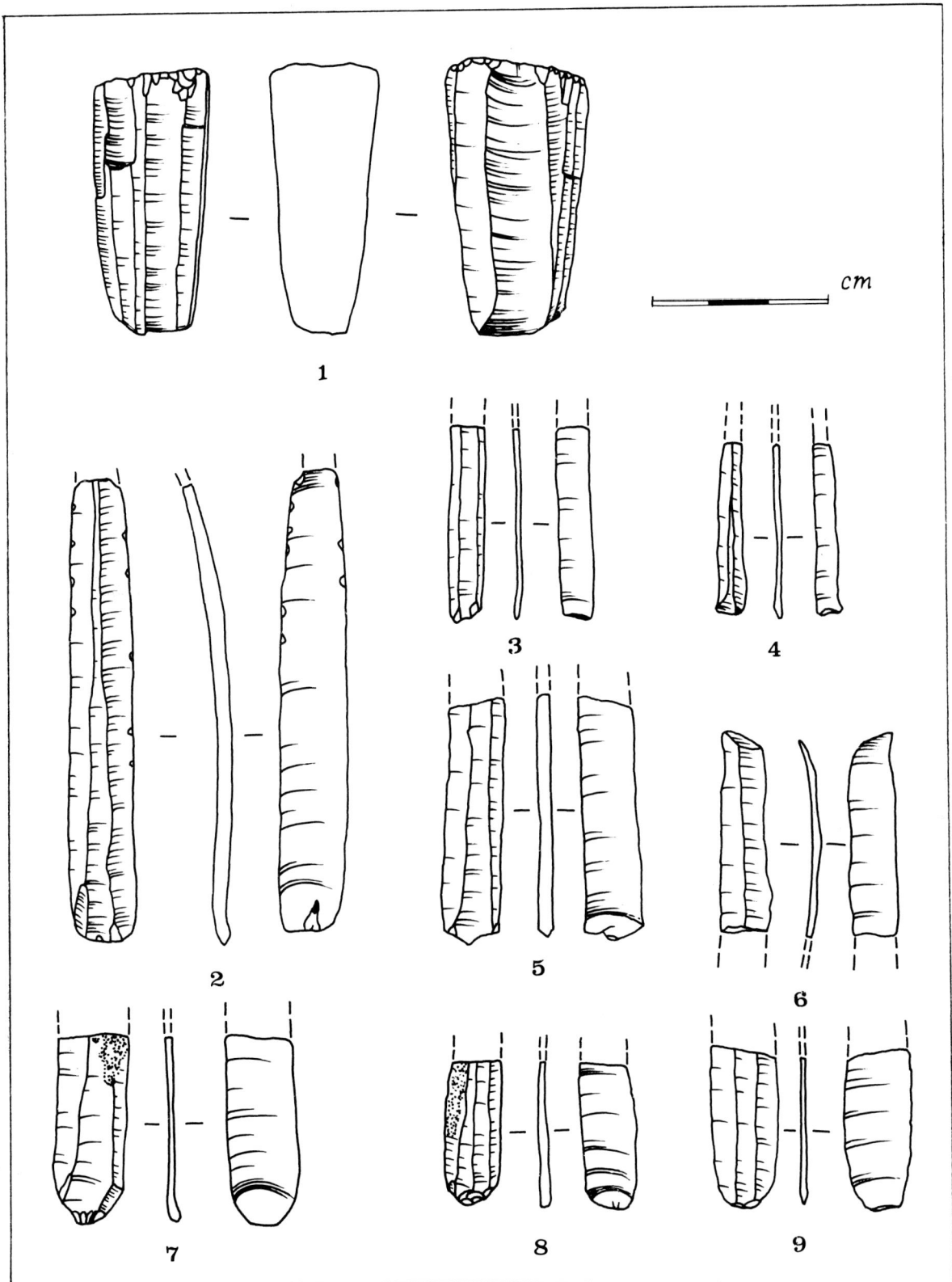

Figure 6 Dęby Site 29: core (1); blades (2–9).

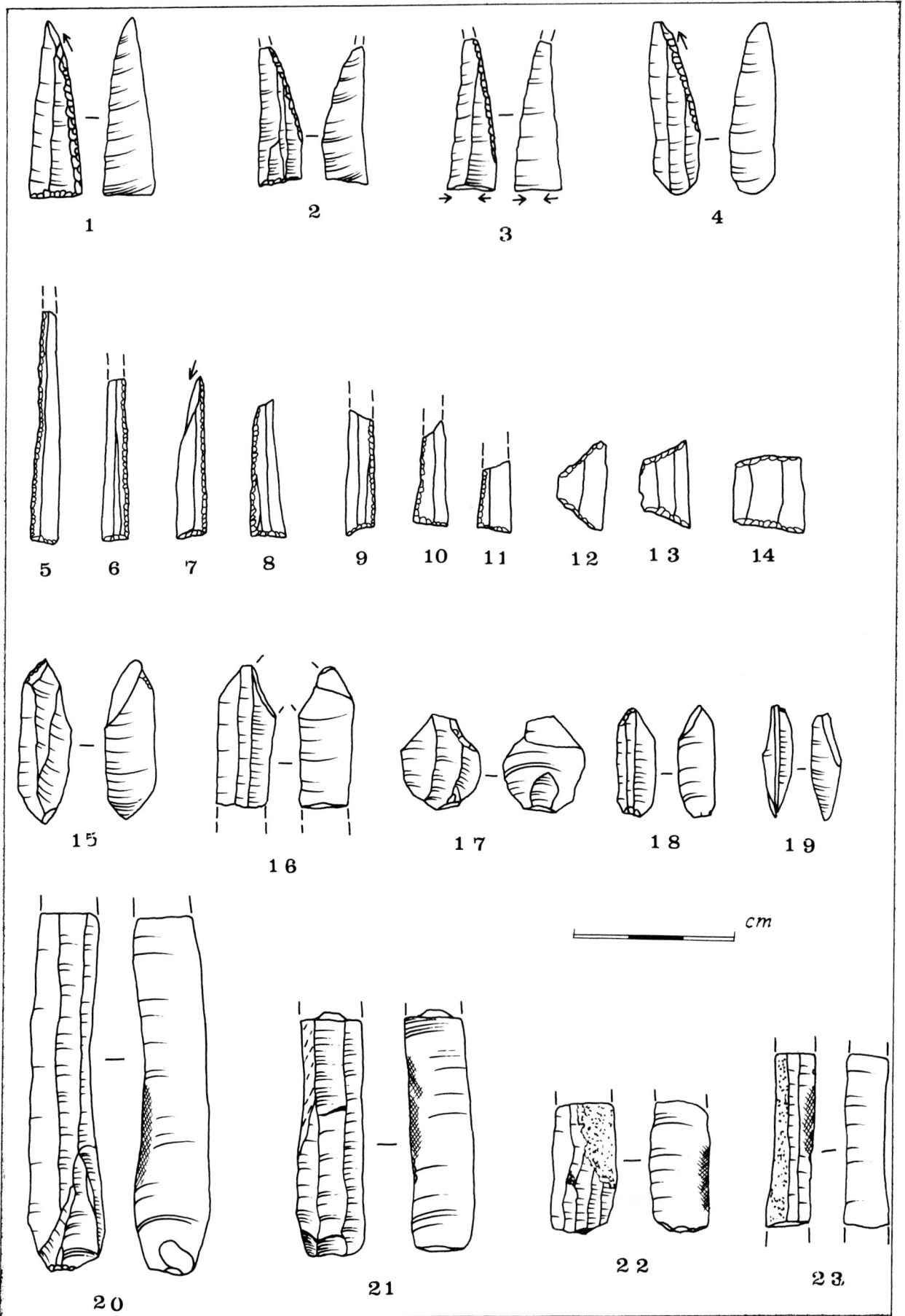

Figure 7 Dęby Site 29: microliths (1–14); microburins (15–19); blades with micro-wear polish (20–23).

this proves to be the case, it may be suggested that Dęby 29 represents the pre-pottery stage of the Neolithic on the Polish Plain.

It is hoped that further investigation of this unique site will provide the information necessary to support one of the hypotheses presented.

References

ANDERSEN, K., JØRGENSEN, S. and RICHTER, J. (1982) *Maglemose hytterne ved Ulkestrup Lyng*. Copenhagen, Det Kongelige Nordiske Oldskriftselskab.

BRINCH PETERSEN, E. (1971) Sværdborg II. A Maglemose hut from Sværdborg bog, Zealand, Denmark. *Acta Archaeologica*, 42: 43–47.

CZERNIAK, L. (in press) Czynniki zewnętrzne w rozwoju kulturowym społeczeństw Kujaw w okresie wczesnego i środkowego neolitu. In A. Cofta-Broniewska (ed.), *Kontakty społeczeństw pradziejowych Kujaw z innymi ludami Europy*. Poznań.

DOMAŃSKA, L. (1976) Knochenhacke der Maglemose-Kultur aus Trudna, Kr. Zlotow, Polen. *Bonner Hefte*, 11: 55–59.

DOMAŃSKA, L. (1986) Selected problems of coastal zone flint industry in the Stone Age. In T. Malinowski (ed.), *Problems of the Stone Age in Pomerania* (Archaeologia Interregionalis). Warsaw–Kraków–Słupsk, Wydawnictwa Uniwersytetu Warszawskiego: 233–245.

DOMAŃSKA, L. (in press) Rozwój kulturowy społeczeństw Kujaw w okresie późnego mezolitu. In A. Cofta-Broniewska (ed.), *Kontakty społeczeństw pradziejowych Kujaw z innymi ludami Europy*. Poznań.

DOMAŃSKA, L. and KOŚKO, A. (1974) Z badań nad charakterem więzi kulturowej stref pojezierno-nadmorskiej i wielkodolinnej Niżu w międzyrzeczu Odry i Wisły w dobie początków neolityzacji. In F. Lachowicz (ed.), *Studia Archaeologica Pomeranica*. Koszalin, Muzeum Archeologiczno–Historyczne w Koszalinie: 23–52.

DOMAŃSKA, L. and KOŚKO, A. (1983) Łącko, woj. Bydgoszcz stanowisko 6 – obozowisko z fazy I ('AB') kultury pucharów lejkowatych. Z badań nad genezą rozwoju i systematyką chronologiczną kultury pucharów lejkowatych na Kujawach. *Acta Universitatis Lodziensis. Folia Archaeologica*, 4: 3–55.

GRØN, O. (1983) Social behaviour and settlement structure. Preliminary results of a distribution analysis on sites of the Maglemose culture. *Journal of Danish Archaeology*, 2: 32–42.

LECH, J. and MŁYNARCZYK, H. (1981) Uwagi o krzemieniarstwie społeczeństw wstęgowych i wspólnot kultury pucharów lejkowatych. Próba konfrontacji. In T. Wiślański (ed.), *Kultura pucharów lejkowatych w Polsce*. Poznań, Polska Akademia Nauk–Oddział w Poznaniu: 11–36.

KOZŁOWSKI, J.K. and KOZŁOWSKI, S.K. (1977) *Epoka kamienia na ziemiach polskich*. Warsaw, Państwowe Wydawnictwo Naukowe.

KOZŁOWSKI, S.K. (1972) *Pradzieje ziem polskich od IX do V tysiąclecia p.n.e.* Warsaw, Państwowe Wydawnictwo Naukowe.

Hunting of Brown Bears in the Mesolithic: Evidence from the Medvedia Cave near Ružín in Slovakia

Juraj Bárta

Abstract

In a cave, near the village of Ružín in east Slovakia, speleologists found a bear skull protruding from a sinter deposit, and during subsequent amateur excavations recovered an obsidian blade and the tip of a slotted bone point. Another obsidian flake and a similar bone point with microlithic blades fixed in by cement were found by the author when excavating a second skeleton of *Ursus arctos*. The typology of the bone points suggests that the sinter layer containing the bear skeletons and the archaeological remains was formed during the Atlantic period. The Medvedia cave represents the most southerly findspot of this type of late Mesolithic bone point, and the first evidence for hunting of *Ursus arctos* in a cave situation.

INTRODUCTION

The area around the now flooded village of Ružín, district of Košice, in the eastern part of the Slovak Ore mountains has several caves with evidence of prehistoric habitation (*Fig. 1*). They are situated above the karst valley of the Little Ružínok river, and one of them, the Medvedia cave, has only recently become significant archaeologically. It is

the highest of the caves, is generally difficult of access, and was originally buried under debris (*Fig. 2*). It was discovered accidentally by speleologists several years ago.

Compared to other caves in the vicinity of Ružín, the Medvedia cave has few natural advantages for settlement. The entrance passage, which is 32 m long and aligned north west, is very narrow and barely passable. Its largest space is a 7 m long, roughly oval chamber, known as the 'Chapel' (*Fig. 3*), which drops steeply to a depth of 5 m below the level of the entrance passage. Two-thirds of the floor of the passage are covered by debris and muddy humus, which are a remnant of the original filling; the rest is bedrock, with sinter lakelets further from the entrance. The floor of the Chapel consists of a horizontal layer of grey-yellow, granular sinter, 40 cm thick, in which several phases of sedimentation can be distinguished on the basis of slight colour variations (*Fig. 4*).[1]

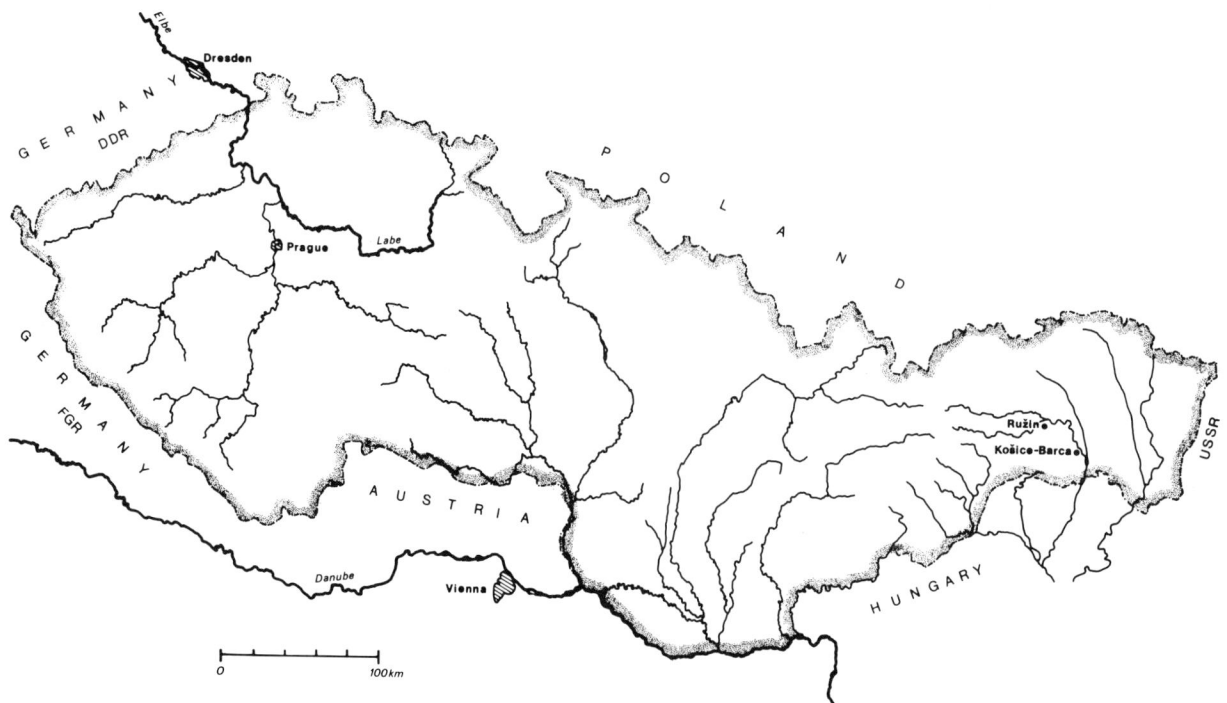

Figure 1 Geographical location of the Ružín area.

Figure 2   Medvedia cave: the entrance.

Figure 3   Medvedia cave (the 'Chapel'): archaeological trench.

Figure 4   Medvedia cave (the 'Chapel'): section through the sinter layer with remains of *Ursus arctos*.

HISTORY OF INVESTIGATION OF THE CAVE

Soon after the discovery of the Medvedia cave, the frontal portion of a bear skull was found protruding from the sinter in the south-west part of the Chapel. This was dug out amateurishly by the speleologists and handed over to the East Slovak Museum in Košice. In 1978 members of the Slovak Speleological Society attempted to recover the rest of the skeleton of the bear which they thought was a juvenile cave bear (*Ursus spelaeus*). They carried out an amateur archaeological excavation during which they found an obsidian blade and later, among the bones of the skeleton, a bone point with grooves on opposite sides, which they considered to be an awl. Unfortunately, they failed to record the precise stratigraphic context of these finds. Subsequently, the bone point was brought to the author's attention; it was immediately evident that this was not an awl, but the tip of a 'composite' artifact that originally had been inset with microliths.

Systematic archaeological investigation of the cave began in July 1980. It was fairly exhaustive, but lasted only a short time because of a lack of labour. The complicated access to the cave also posed problems, making it difficult to transport excavated material to the mouth of the cave for processing. In spite of these difficulties, and under weak lighting from acetylene lamps, the professional speleo-archaeological method brought unexpected success. Remains of another bear were found near the base of the sinter layer in the western part of a small trench aligned along the long axis of the Chapel, that was dug to extend the amateur excavation (*Fig. 4*). They were later identified by C. Ambros as belonging to brown bear (*Ursus arctos arctos*). An obsidian flake and a longer bone point with two opposed grooves and broken at the base – type 21B in the classifications of Clark (1936) and Kozłowski (1969) – were found among the bones. The point still had seven extremely small blades of limnoquartzite[2] fixed in by cement (*Fig. 5*).

This find also helped to establish the function of the similar bone point that had been found by the speleologists who, because of insufficient archaeological experience and poor lighting, probably failed to notice the stone microblades that had originally been inserted into the grooves. Thus, for the first time, composite artifacts have been discovered in Czechoslovakia. These particular finds represent arrowheads which Mesolithic hunters used to kill forest predators from a distance. In the European context, this is an important discovery that explains the function of a class of microlithic artifacts found mainly in open-air Mesolithic settlements.

The investigation continued in 1984 under better technical conditions. The trench was extended to the

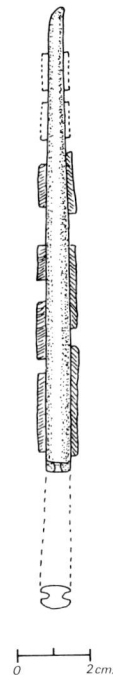

Figure 5   Medvedia cave: bone point with microlithic inserts of flint.

west, into a steeply sloping passage which forms a continuation of the Chapel. This excavation yielded results that were primarily of palaeontological interest. It was demonstrated that, in all, remains of three bear skeletons had been recovered from the cave, all belonging to the species *Ursus arctos arctos* (brown bear), and that these had been scattered by repeated floods during the humid Atlantic period of the Holocene. Beneath the sinter crust was a dark-brown sticky clay of Pleistocene age which contained a few remains of chamois (*Rupicapra rupicapra*) and charcoals of conifers. The latter, according to an analysis done by E. Hajnalová, came from white fir (*Abies alba*), pine (*Pinus* sp.) and *Pinus–Picea*. During this second phase of investigation, a fragment of a Palaeolithic blade was found. This was made from a different kind of obsidian than the two obsidian artifacts found during the previous excavations.

INTERPRETATION OF THE EVIDENCE

The bear remains

With the onset of warmer conditions in the Holocene, brown bear (*Ursus arctos arctos*) gradually replaced the cave bear (*Ursus spelaeus*) (Kahlke 1955). In the palaeontological collection from the Medvedia cave the bones of two of the bears have the same colour as the sinter crust, while some of the bones of the third bear skeleton from the base of the sinter, at the contact with the Pleistocene sub-layer, have a different, grey-brown colour – suggesting that they are somewhat older. None of the bones shows any trace of fire or other marks which would point to their presence near a fireplace. If a hearth had existed in the relatively small space of the Chapel, it should have left some trace in spite of the repeated flooding. Charcoals of unidentifiable conifers from the middle of the sinter crust near the archaeological finds, and those (*Pinopsida*) which were scattered in the Pleistocene sub-layer, have no growth rings. This suggests that they came from burning branches, probably used as torches.

The presence of Holocene and Pleistocene charcoals suggests that prehistoric hunters made at least two visits to the cave. The clearest evidence is for occupation during the humid Atlantic period, when granular sinter deposits formed in a number of Czechoslovak caves (Ložek and Bárta 1952). This deposit was the main stratigraphic horizon in the Medvedia cave, and confirms the Mesolithic age attributed to the sparse archaeological remains on the basis of artifact typology.

The composite arrowheads indicate the killing of at least one bear. It is possible, however, that two bears were killed by arrows (the third bear skeleton comes from an older layer). If the latter is the case, then both bears may have been killed or fatally wounded in a single hunting action, each by one composite arrowhead.

Although it is possible that the Medvedia cave served as a den for brown bears, and that the bears were killed inside the cave where the entrance passage leads into the gulf-like Chapel, the general geomorphological situation and the particular morphology of the interior of the cave suggest another interpretation. None of the bear bones shows any traces which would indicate that the animals were hit by the weapons that were found close to one of them; but it is possible that the animals were hit 'softly' (in hunters' terminology) in the abdominal cavity while outside the cave, and that, fatally wounded with arrows in the body, they resorted to the cave where at the end of the passage they fell into the bottom of the Chapel. From the depth of the Chapel with its steep and slippery access, there was no escape. Here, the Mesolithic hunters probably killed them and butchered them with their obsidian knives, which they left behind. The cave may have acted as a kind of cold store from which the meat could have been consumed gradually.

Interpretation of the evidence from the Medvedia cave is complicated by the fact that none of the bear skeletons is complete, since bones found during the first excavations were removed by amateurs. It is just possible, however, that the bones recovered from the middle of the sinter layer represent a bear family. These are of the same colour as the sinter, but there is no unequivocal evidence that they are contemporary.

The bone points

The most significant archaeological finds from the Medvedia cave dating to the Mesolithic, are the two thin, slotted bone points which originally were inset with limnoquartzite microblades fixed in by organic cement. Most archaeologists interpret implements of this type as spearheads (Kozłowski 1969) and, in the case of shorter and narrower specimens, as arrows, more rarely as harpoons (Wyss 1966; Rimantiene 1971).

Composite artifacts of this type, which are known mainly from numerous Mesolithic cultures in north-western and north-eastern Europe, the Russian Plain and the Crimea, may have either one or two grooves for the insertion of microliths. An analysis of the Mesolithic sites in these territories has shown, however, that there is no obvious chronological link between the single-rowed points (type 21A) and the two-rowed points (Clark's types 21B–25). These slotted points have their origin in the final Palaeolithic, but their general development falls within the Mesolithic in which they are the leading type of bone industry in some cultures. The two-rowed forms, however, occur mainly at the end of the middle Mesolithic and in the late Mesolithic (Kozłowski 1975: fig. 27). Thus, it is reasonable to suppose that the specimens from the Medvedia cave belong to the late Mesolithic; and this is confirmed by their stratigraphic context, viz. their occurrence in a sinter layer formed during the Atlantic period.

Of the two 'composite' bone points from the Medvedia cave, one was inset with unretouched microblades and contained remnants of cement which held these stone inserts in place. Chemical analyses of stabilizing cements for the fixation of microliths are rare, partly because preservation of the cement is exceptional, and partly because the technique of analysis is complicated. Analysis of the specimen from the Medvedia cave, the first of its kind to be undertaken in central Europe, was carried out by Dr M. Strnad who identified the cement in this case as the resin of a conifer.

DISCUSSION

Archaeological research in east Slovakia has so far revealed only one Mesolithic site, Košice-Barca I, dating to the Atlantic period (Prošek 1959). Since on this site obsidian was used for the production of chipped stone artifacts, it may be included in the so-called Tisza Mesolithic group on the basis of Romanian analogues (Bárta 1972, 1981). The newly-discovered artifacts from the Medvedia cave are also made from obsidian; hence, the possibility of a link with Košice-Barca I, the nearest site geographically, cannot be excluded.

The two-rowed composite bone points from Ružín represent the most southerly findspot of this implement type in Europe. In spite of the fact that these points are concentrated predominantly in north-east Europe, it seems, given the use of obsidian in the production of the other blades from the Ružín sites, that we should seek the origins of this developed Mesolithic industry in the south-east region – viz. in the Tisza basin, east of the Carpathians, where primary outcrops of obsidian are known. The flint inserts of the Ružín composite arrowheads are very narrow and refined. They are made from narrow conical cores, which are characteristic of the late Mesolithic and early Neolithic of the Black Sea steppe region (Telegin 1973, 1982). Although it is not possible to draw detailed conclusions concerning the origin of the Mesolithic collection from the Medvedia cave, as Mesolithic sites are rare in east Slovakia, analogues might be sought in the direction of the Black Sea.

The evidence from the Medvedia cave indicates 'soft' hits by two composite arrows in the breast of one or two brown bears. It is the first find of its kind, and the first instance in which hunting of brown bear in a Mesolithic cave situation has been convincingly demonstrated.

The significance of the Mesolithic site in Ružín is further underlined by the discovery of a human femur in the Hadia cave, which lies some 50 m below the Medvedia cave. This was found at the base of Holocene sediments, without any associated archaeological or palaeontological material, by the same speleologists who explored the Medvedia cave. Chemical analysis was undertaken by J. Čejka of three bones of *Ursus arctos arctos* and one of the composite bone artifacts from the Medvedia cave, and of the isolated human femur from the Hadia cave. One of the bear bones, the bone point and the human femur showed the same degree of fossil-ization, which points to their contemporaneity.

According to Dr E. Vlček the femur may be the first anthropological find from Slovakia belonging to the period of hunters who used composite arrowheads. The isolation of the human femur can be loosely explained as the result of a bear killing a man whose thigh the animal then took into its den in the Hadia cave.

Notes:

1. The term *sinter* refers to a deposit formed by the evaporation of spring or lake water.
2. *Limnoquartzite* is a type of 'flint' of volcanic origin found in central Europe.

References

Bárta, J. (1972) Die mittlere Steinzeit in der Slowakei. *Acta Praehistorica et Archaeologica*, 3: 57–76.

Bárta, J. (1981) Das Mesolithikum in nordwestlichen Teil des Karpatenbeckens. In B. Gramsch (ed.), *Mesolithikum in Europa. 2. Internationales Symposium Potsdam, 3 bis 8 April 1978 Bericht* (Veröffentlichungen des Museums für Ur- und Frühgeschichte Potsdam, 14/15). Potsdam, Deutscher Verlag der Wissenschaften: 295–300.

Clark, J.G.D. (1936) *The Mesolithic Settlement of Northern Europe*. Cambridge, University Press.

Kahlke, H.D. (1955) *Großsäugetiere im Eiszeitalter*. Leipzig, Urania-Verlag.

Kozłowski, S.K. (1969) Z problematyki polskiego mezolitu (Cz 10), Kościane harpuny i ostrza mezolityczne. *Światowit*, 30: 135–152.

Kozłowski, S.K. (1975) *Cultural Differentiation of Europe from 10th to 5th Millennium B.C.* Warsaw, University Press.

Ložek, V. and Bárta, J. (1952) K otázce stáří holocenních travertínových poloh v našich jeskyních. *Československy kras* (Brno), 5: 137–139.

Prošek, F. (1959) Mesolitická obsidiánová industrie ze stanice Barca I, *Archeologické rozhledy*, 11: 145–148.

Rimantiene, R.K. (1971) *Paleolit i mezolit Litvy*. Vilnyus, Izdatel'stvo Mintis.

Telegin, D.Y. (1973) Pozdniy mezolit Ukrainy. In S.K. Kozłowski (ed.), *The Mesolithic in Europe*. Warsaw, University Press: 531–549.

Telegin, D.Y. (1982) *Mezolitichni pamyatki Ukrainy*. Kiev, Izdatel'stvo Naukova dumka: 206–208.

Wyss, R. (1966) Mesolithische Harpunen in Mitteleuropa. In R. Wyss (ed.), *Festschrift Emil Vogt, Schweizerisches Landesmuseum*. Zürich, Separatum: 9–20.

The Mesolithic Site of Smolín, South Moravia

Karel Valoch

Abstract

In 1959–1960 the Anthropos Institute of the Moravian Museum in Brno undertook the investigation of a Mesolithic (final Palaeolithic) settlement near Smolín, 35 km south of Brno.

Two semi-subterranean dwellings and an extensive area covered with flint were found in the 520 m² excavated. The industry contains typical geometric microliths, while short end-scrapers dominate among the larger tools. Cobbles of various rocks were used as retouchers, choppers, pounding stones, millstones, and grindstones.

The faunal remains indicate that the inhabitants hunted a range of animals, including large herbivores. Charcoal analyses indicate that the surrounding forests were mostly coniferous, with an admixture of deciduous trees. Radiocarbon dates place the settlement in the Boreal period.

INTRODUCTION

The site of Smolín holds an important position in the Mesolithic of Czechoslovakia. It is the richest Mesolithic settlement, and the only one of this period to be dated by the radiocarbon method.

Although several Mesolithic findspots are known from Bohemia, these consist mainly of small clusters of artifacts or isolated finds. Geographically, it is possible to distinguish three areas of occurrence of Mesolithic settlement: (i) sandy areas in the lake country of southern Bohemia; (ii) sandy deposits along the River Elbe in central Bohemia; and (iii) the Ohře river valley in north-west Bohemia. In addition to these areas, several isolated locations occur in the Bohemian karst in the vicinity of Beroun. A distinctively microlithic industry was also collected from the site of Ládví in Prague-Kobylisy. In the Ohře valley systematic excavation has been carried out at only one site, Tašovice 1, near Carlsbad, where Prošek identified a residential structure containing two hearths (see Sklenář 1976: fig. 32).

Apart from Smolín and the neighbouring site of Přibice, only five other Mesolithic sites have been found in Moravia. These are located on sandy banks along the Dyje and Morava rivers. Two further lithic assemblages were collected at Opava and Luhačovice, but these are characterized by tanged and rhombic points and are therefore different typologically from the industries mentioned above.

In Slovakia only two sites have been investigated:

Sereď-Mačanské Vršky, on the lower Váh, and Barca, near Košice in eastern Slovakia. The former site contained an extensive microlithic industry, the latter an obsidian assemblage. In addition to these two major finds, three smaller assemblages were collected along the lower reaches of the River Váh and along the Donau. Cultural classification of the industries from Smolín, Přibice, Sereď and Barca has been carried out by S.K. Kozłowski (1975).

SMOLÍN

Settlement of Moravia during the Mesolithic (final Palaeolithic) was very sparse. The archaeological record consists of only small collections of stone tools found on sandy soils close to rivers in the southern part of Moravia. Only two large settlements have been found – Přibice and Smolín, about 5 km apart and some 35 km south of Brno on the terraces above the River Jihlava. Large stone industries have been collected from both sites but, so far, research has only been carried out at Smolín.

The settlement of Smolín is at the foot of a south-facing slope, at *c.* 200 m above sea level (*Fig. 1*). In the west and in the south the slope ends with an abrupt drop, representing the Pleistocene banks of the River Jihlava, whose present-day floodplain is

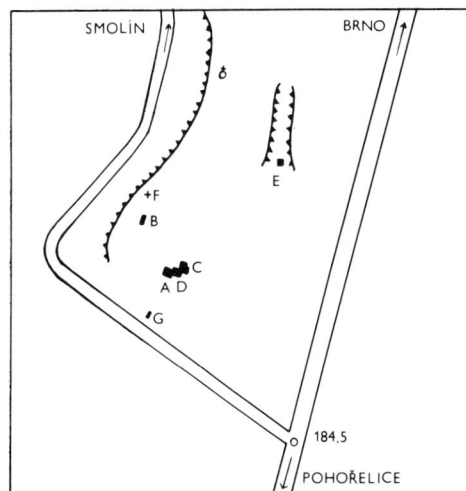

Figure 1   Smolín: plan of the site showing the location of the excavated sectors.

some 180 m above sea level; the present river channel is several hundred metres away from the Mesolithic settlement.

The geology of the site area has been studied by digging vertical shafts. At the base of the sequence are river terrace gravels of Middle Pleistocene age, overlain by a fossil soil developed in loess. The overlying layers are up to 250 cm thick and consist of wind-blown sands formed during the Lateglacial. The sands contain an Usselo-type soil of Allerød age and are sealed by a Holocene soil. At the base of the Holocene soil there is a sub-fossil 'marbled horizon'[1] containing the Mesolithic industry.

A radiocarbon date of 8315±55 BP (GrN-7622R) was obtained on burnt bones from sector C, indicating that the site dates to the Boreal period.

Charcoal from the site has been identified by E. Opravil (in litt., 2 February 1979). Of five fragments collected from pit B, two were of fir (Abies sp.) and one each of lime (Tilia sp.) and maple (Acer sp.). Seven fragments recovered from sector D are all spruce/larch (Picea/Larix).

The animal remains consist mostly of loose teeth, with only a few identifiable bone fragments (Table 1). The majority belong to large herbivores (Musil, in Valoch 1978).

A single snail shell found in sector A has been identified by J. Kovanda as Lymnae cf. palustris (Mühl).

A total of 520 m² of the site were examined, divided between four trenches (sectors A–D). Most of this area contained Mesolithic artifacts. According to their location we can distinguish between two major complexes of finds. In sectors A and B well-defined living pits were found, while sectors C and D were characterized by an extensive horizontal spread of flint artifacts, the eastern limit of which was not reached in the excavations.

Sector A was excavated in an area rich in surface finds of flint artifacts and on a relatively exposed part of the slope. It can be presumed that most of the dwelling pit had been destroyed by ploughing or by removal of the soil through rainwash. Only the the truncated base of the pit was found, about 50 cm below the surface. It appeared as an oval depression infilled with dark soil within light-yellow sand, and

measured 9×12 metres. Flints and animal bones were confined to the infilling of this feature.

The situation was better in sector B. The Holocene soil had not been preserved and the dark cultural deposit, oval in shape, was clearly discernible in the light sand, with thinly scattered flints visible on the surface. The dark deposit containing an abundance of flints was dug out to reveal an oval pit (pit B), almost 100 cm deep and measuring 10×5 metres. On the north-east side of the pit, at a distance of about 150 cm, another small patch of dark soil, 100 cm in diameter, was visible on the surface. This infilled a 20 cm deep conical, almost circular pit, on the bottom of which were several pieces of charcoal (Fig. 2). In three places within pit B fire-cracked

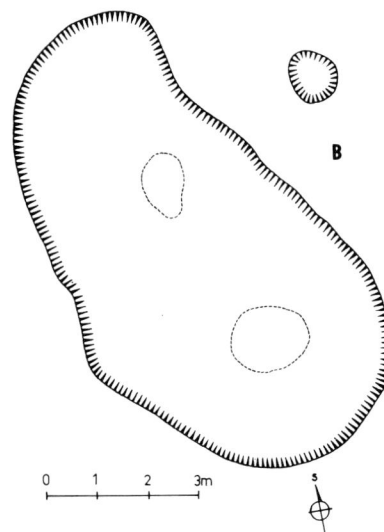

Figure 2   Smolín: plan of pit B.

cobbles of various rocks were found. These occurred at a depth of 60 cm in metre squares 58, 59 (28 pieces) and at a depth of 100 cm (i.e. the bottom of the pit) in metre square 67 (7 pieces), and in metre square 85 (8 pieces). The cobbles can be regarded as paving under the fireplace, although no charcoal was found in these places.

The cultural layer in sectors C and D formed in a completely different way. Here, there was a layer of sub-fossil, 'marbled' soil. It was c. 15 cm thick over the whole surface and contained flints, the density of

Table 1:   Mammalian remains from Smolín

Species	MNI	Body part representation
HORSE (Equus sp.)	6–9	30 teeth, 1 metacarpus, 1 fragment of astragalus
BOVIDAE (Bos/Bison)	5	13 teeth, 1 phalange, 1 calcaneus, 1 fragment of tibia
BEAVER (Castor fiber)	3	9 teeth, 1 mandible fragment
PIG (Sus scrofa)	2	
FOX (Vulpes vulpes)	1	
RED DEER (Cervus elaphus)	1	

Table 2: Flaked lithic assemblages from Smolín

	Sector A		Sector B		Sectors C–D	
	n	%	n	%	n	%
Tools	202	4.08	170	3.43	589	2.40
Partially retouched pieces	24	0.48	21	0.42	72	0.29
Cores	171	3.45	136	2.79	478	1.94
Blades <3 cm	104		26		154	
Blades 3–5 cm	132		80		468	
Blades >5 cm	15		8		62	
Flakes	186		56		288	
Core-edges and Burin spalls	57		39		204	
Waste	4062		4424		22,263	
Total	4953		4960		24,578	

TOOLS:	%	%	%
Microliths	30.69	50.59	21.61
End-scrapers (*Fig. 3*, nos. 40–45)	37.62	21.18	44.24
Burins (*Fig. 3*, nos. 46, 47)	14.85	8.24	15.09
others (*Fig. 3*, nos. 48–50)	16.84	19.99	19.06
Total	100.00	100.00	100.00

MICROLITHS:	%	%	%
Triangles (*Fig. 3*, nos. 26–30)	11.29	5.81	5.83
Trapezes (*Fig. 3*, nos. 31–39)	1.61	3.49	5.56
Tardenois points (*Fig. 3*, nos. 21–25)	3.23	11.63	10.27
Backed points (*Fig. 3*, nos. 12–14, 17)	17.74	17.44	15.83
Oblique points (*Fig. 3*, nos. 1–11)	30.65	36.05	42.72
Microburins	12.90	10.47	10.83
others (*Fig. 3*, nos. 15, 16, 18–20)	22.58	15.11	8.96
	100.00	100.00	100.00

which increased towards a centre situated seemingly at the south-eastern corner of sector C. There the number of flints per m² exceeded 500 pieces. In this area, in metre square 140, there was another paved fireplace; the paving consisted of about eighty fragments of burnt and cracked pebbles, and there were burnt fragments of animal bones. These were used for radiocarbon dating. The whole area was covered with flints, the total extent of which (including as yet unexcavated areas) was estimated at 400 m².

The flaked stone industry was abundant in all sectors and its typological composition was basically the same everywhere. There were no significant differences between living pits A and B on the one hand, and between sectors C and D on the other, which would suggest differences between the activities of the people living there (*Table 2*). In general the Smolín industry is very close to the central European Beuronian (Taute 1974); it contains, however, a large number of short end-scrapers on flakes and shortened blades, reflecting the traditions of the local late Palaeolithic (*Fig. 3*).

The pebble tools fall into several morphologically and functionally different types, and warrant special attention (Valoch 1977). They comprise:

1. Six pebbles of quartz and igneous rock from various sectors, which have been pounded to the form of choppers.

2. Five quartz and hornstone pebbles from sector C with scars caused by blows on one or both ends; these may be interpreted as hammerstones.

3. Four small flat slate pebbles with concentrations of scars at their ends, which served as retouchers; these were found in sectors A, B and C (*Fig. 4*, nos. 3–5).

4. Two grindstones found in sector D; these are of sandstone, are semi-circular in cross-section, and have a longitudinal groove on the flat side (*Fig. 4*, nos. 1–2).

5. Eight greywacke pebbles from sectors C and D; these are mostly fragments of oval or spherical shape, and are covered by scars on their rounded surfaces which have obviously resulted from pounding. Since the material is not very hard, they could not have been used for shattering bones or stones. It

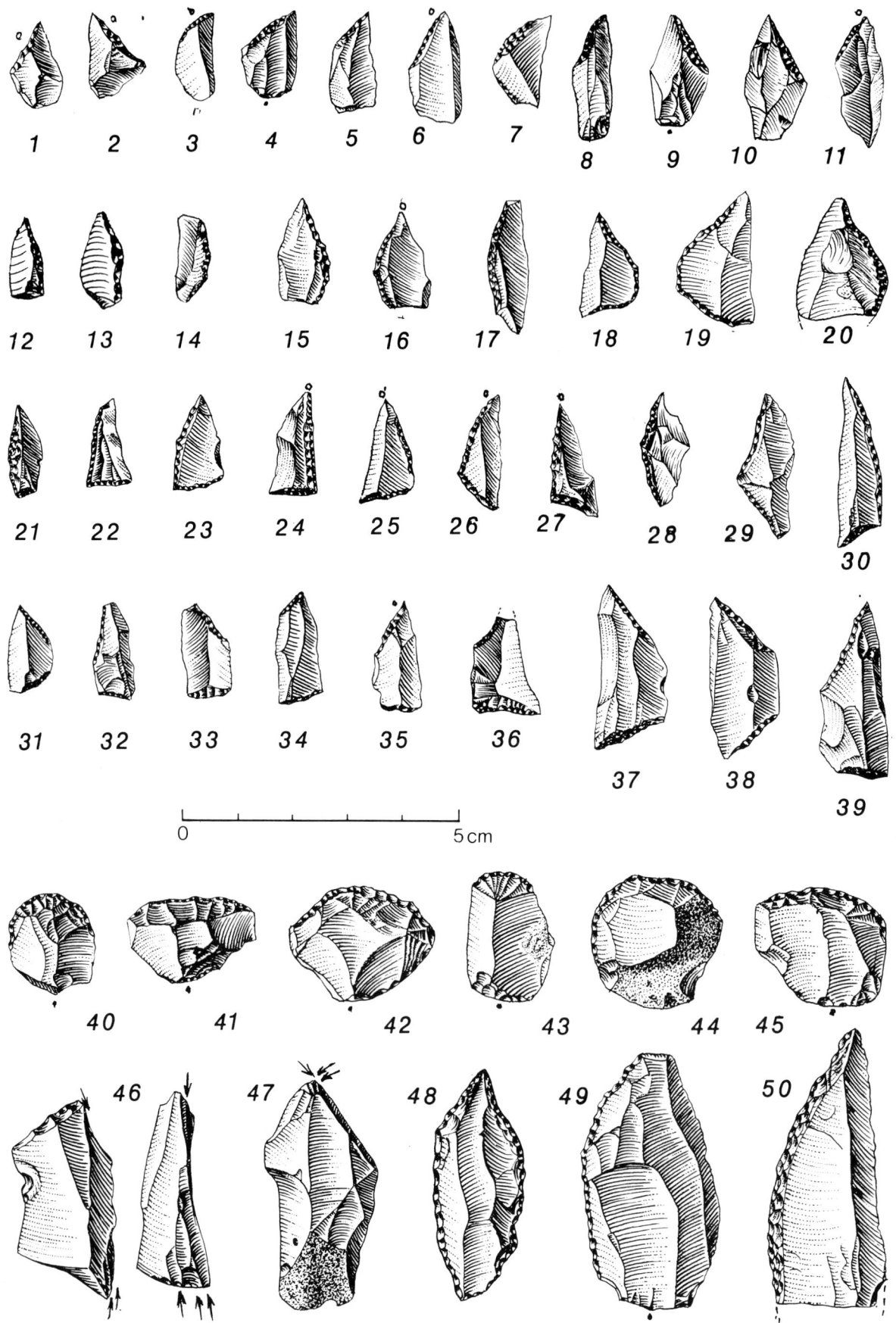

Figure 3 Smolín: the Mesolithic flaked stone industry from sectors C and D.

464

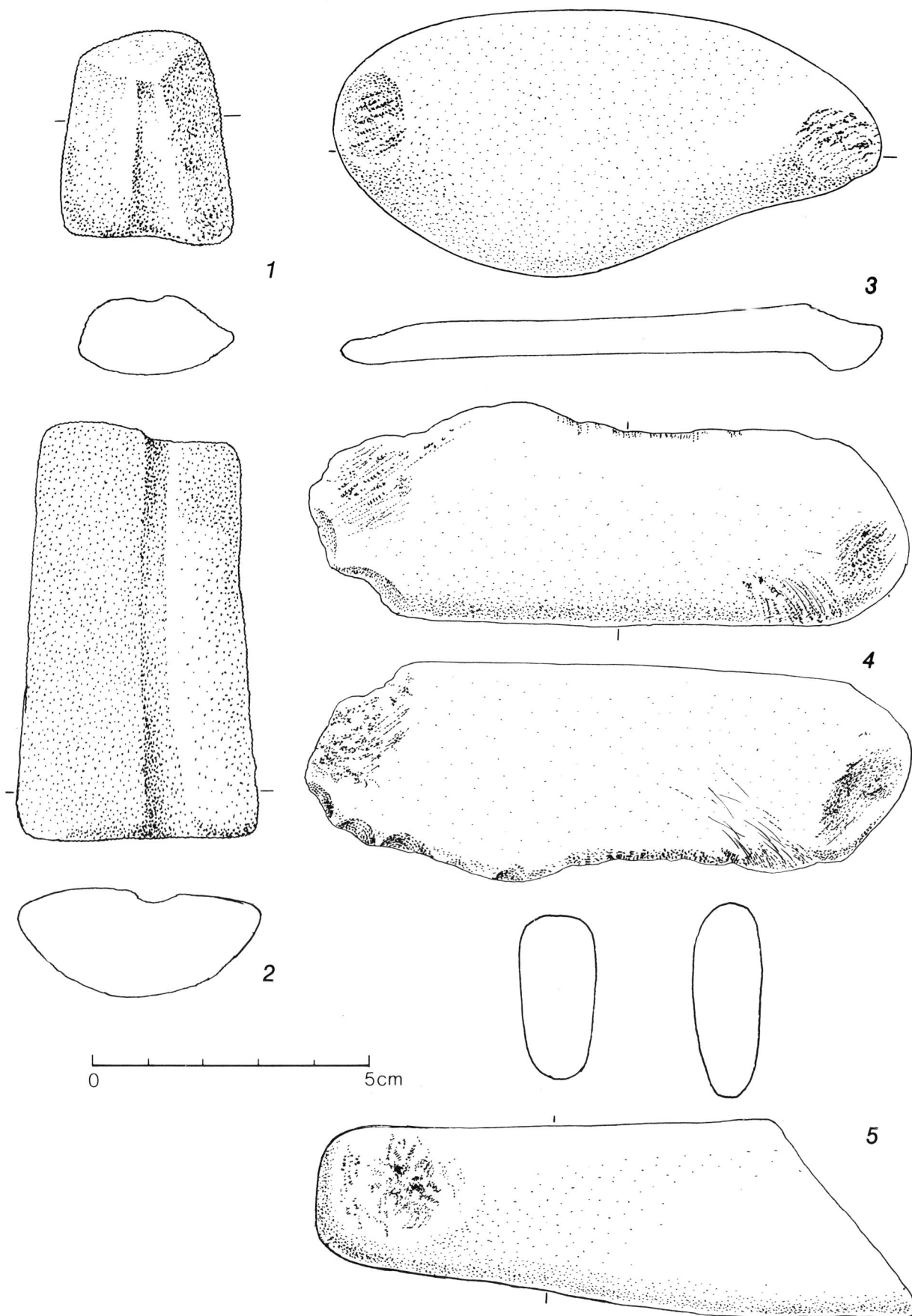

Figure 4 Pebble tools: sandstone grindstones from sector D (1–2); slate retouchers from sectors C, A and B (3–5).

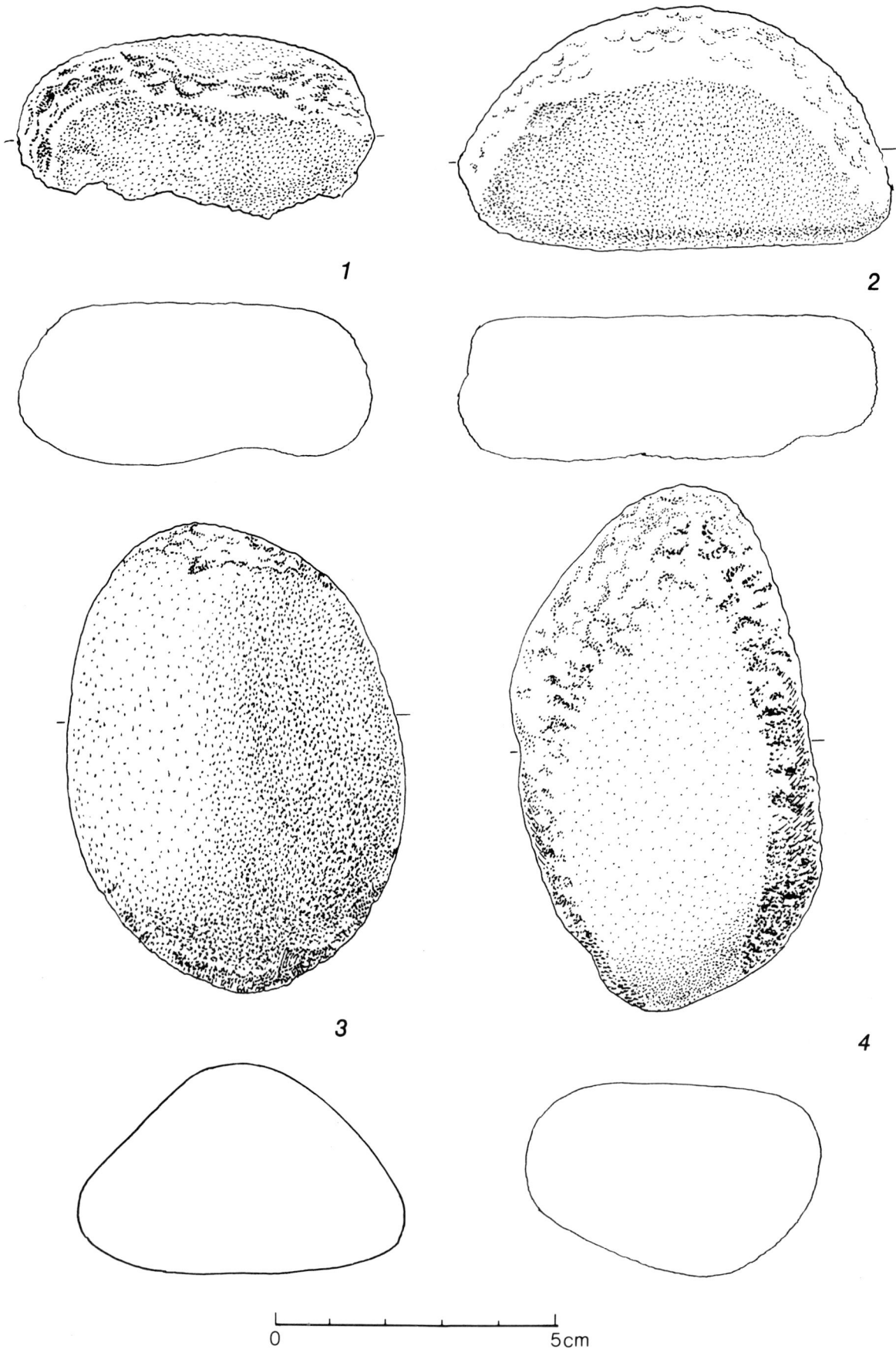

Figure 5 Pounding stones (greywacke) from sectors D (3) and C (1, 2, 4).

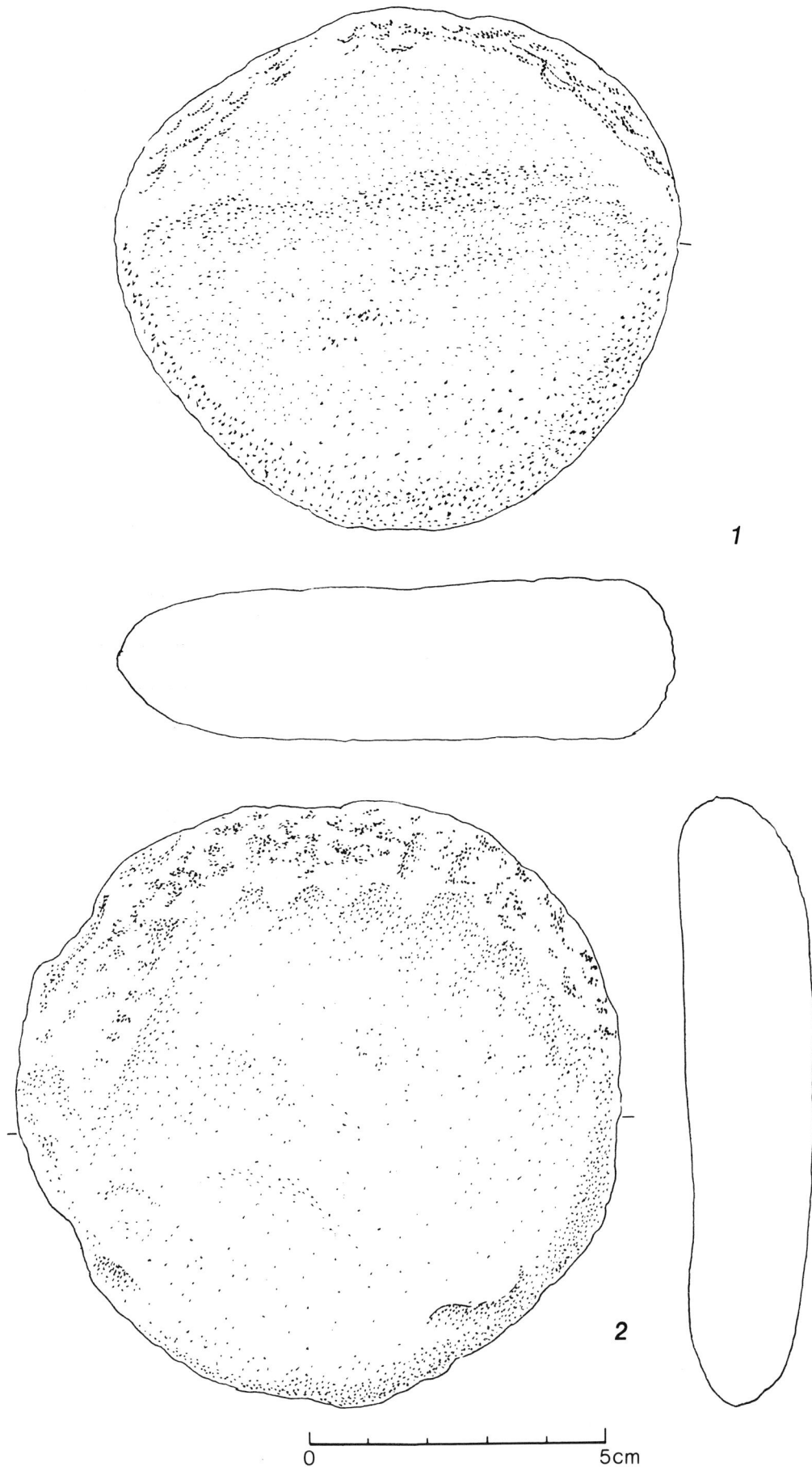

Figure 6   Pounding stones (greywacke) from sector C.

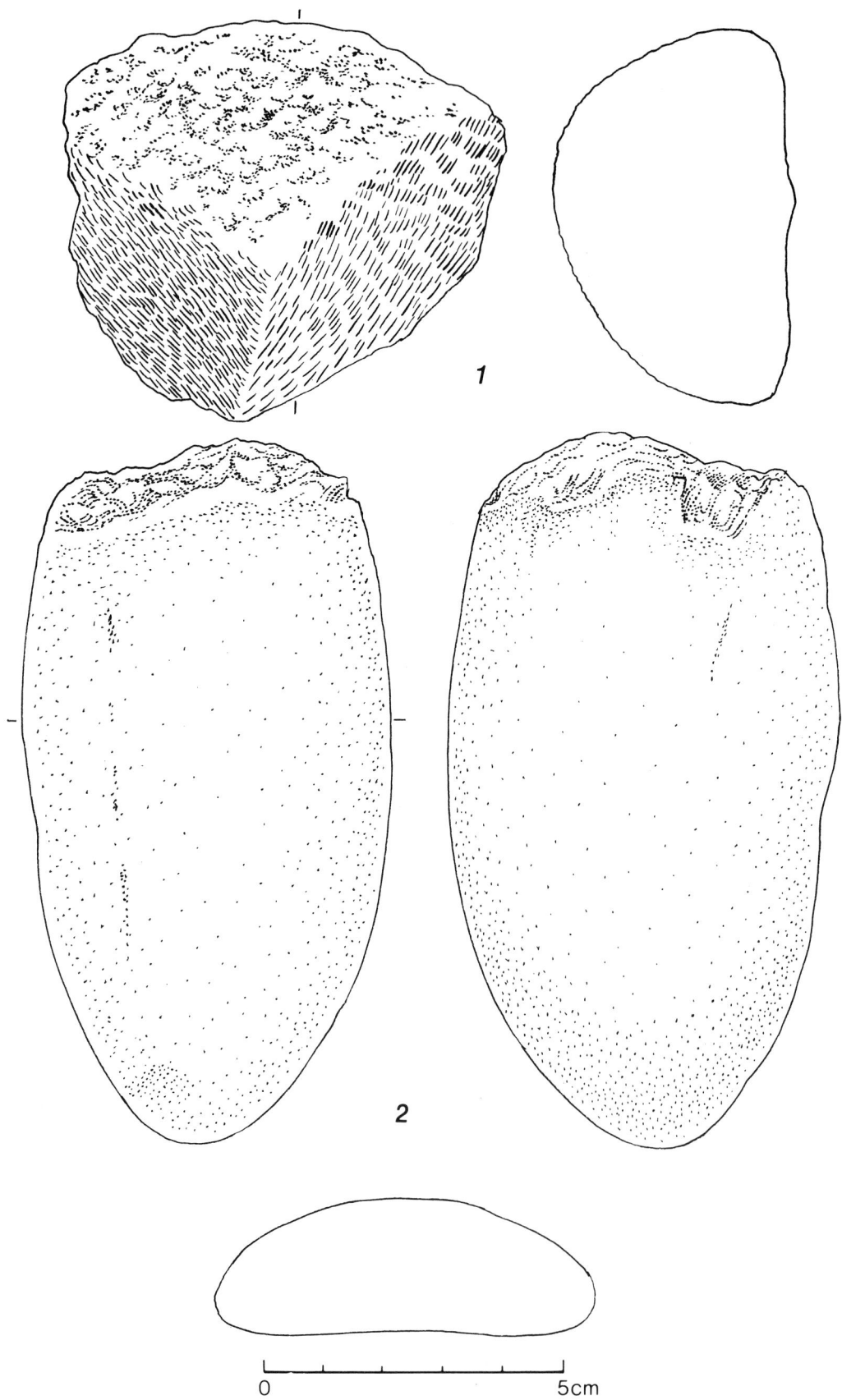

Figure 7   Pebble tools (amphibolite): millstone (1) from sector A; ?axe (2) from sector D.

468

seems more likely that they were used for inflicting light blows (e.g. for cracking hazel-nuts or for crushing the seeds of various Gramineae). They can thus be regarded as pounding stones (*Figs. 5 & 6*).

6. In pit A was found a natural, three-sided amphibolite fragment whose convex dorsal surface had been rounded by numerous scars, resembling a Neolithic millstone (*Fig. 7, no. 1*); while a small, semi-circular pebble whose rounded surface has been polished by numerous scars was found in sector C. Both may have been used for crushing seeds with a rocking movement of the stone, although mineral pigments can also be crushed in this way.

7. Pit A also produced a fragment of a flat pebble of an unidentified rock. One side of the pebble is more lustrous than the other; it has evidently been polished and is covered by fine cross-wise striations. The polishing and the striations are the result of some intensive activity.

8. An interesting artifact was found in sector D. It is an oblong amphibolite pebble of plano-convex cross-section with one of its ends transversely flaked away (*Fig. 7, no. 2*). The traces of wear suggest that the function of the tool was very similar to that of an axe. Its morphology and the raw material used also resemble those of Neolithic axes.

INTERPRETATION

Ecology

The settlement of Smolín dates to the Boreal period. It was situated some 20 m above the floodplain of the River Jihlava, on wind-blown sand deposited over Pleistocene gravel. The floodplain was covered with closed forest, mostly of coniferous trees with an admixture of deciduous trees. On the plateau above the settlement, open woodland alternated with grassland dotted with shrubs and groups of trees, supporting herds of grazing herbivores.

Economy

It seems that the river in the vicinity of the settlement was rich in fish, but fishing is not documented archaeologically. The main source of food was game, mainly large herbivores. The comparatively large number of stones with traces of wear among the finds (pounding stones, millstones), however, indicates preparation of food of vegetable origin (grains, nuts, roots, tubers, etc.); vegetal food probably formed a very important component of the diet.

Certain aspects of the economy can be deduced from raw materials used for the manufacture of stone tools. They delineate the territory within which people moved and also reveal that they had contacts with distant regions. In the case of Smolín

these aspects are somewhat limited; most raw materials come from the immediate vicinity of the settlement, both from Miocene sediments containing various hornstones mostly of Jurassic origin, and also from the pebbles of the river terraces. The river transported rocks to these terraces from the vast area of the Bohemian–Moravian uplands and from the igneous rock massif in the Brno area. The porcellanite is obviously not of local origin; it comes from eastern Moravia, from a distance of some 75 km. Also of foreign origin are the flint, presumably from the deposits in southern Polonia (a minimum distance of 270 km), and the obsidian from east Slovakia (some 370 km away).

The flint from southern Poland is without doubt a high quality raw material. It can be substituted, however, by local hornstones with fracture properties as good as those of flint. Hornstones were used for the manufacture of all kinds of tools in the Palaeolithic. Porcellanite is both fragile and soft, and tools made of this material had no special properties. Nevertheless, there are several tools and blades made of this material. Only two flakes made of obsidian were found – in sectors A and C. Flakes of rock crystal (found in all sectors) and smoky quartz (sector B), which could have been derived from local gravels, were also found.

The occasional use of pieces of exotic rocks, often of low quality, goes back to the Middle Palaeolithic. It was never caused by special needs or by special technological properties of the raw materials. As regards the raw materials brought from regions hundreds of kilometres away, they were certainly not picked up accidentally on a hunting trip. Palaeolithic hunters as a rule did not undertake hunting trips to such distant regions. These materials may have been obtained through exchange or as gifts from other groups, and their use probably had no functional significance. They were presumably connected with traditional, perhaps ritualized, customs within the spiritual sphere of the contemporary society (cf. Oliva 1982).

Settlement

Pit A and the adjoining sectors C and D with their abundance of flint artifacts and fireplaces can be regarded as a single settlement complex. It is quite possible that the isolated pit B forms part of another, as yet unexplored, complex. Test pit F, situated to the north of sector B, revealed a further concentration of flints. It seems unlikely that such an extensive area was settled contemporaneously, and it may be suggested that it was a repeated (seasonal?) settlement. It is possible that the shelters erected over the living pits were renewed several times; this is perhaps suggested by the fireplaces in different positions in pit B (*Fig. 2*).

469

R

The interpretation of the flint concentration in sectors C and D is less straightforward. Its extent precludes the possibility that it was a single roofed shelter. The area with the largest concentration of flints and with the fireplace, covering roughly 8×6 m, could conceivably be regarded as a shelter without a pit, but this hypothesis seems doubtful. The large number of burnt animal bones associated with a fireplace in sector C indicates that it was not simply a workshop for the manufacture of flaked stone tools. This area also produced nearly all the pounding stones and millstones, indicating that it was used for processing food of vegetable origin. A combination of activities arising from the daily life of hunters and gatherers probably took place within this area.

Note:

1. This is a term used in Czechoslovakia for an horizon formed by thin iron-rich bands, often found in early Holocene aeolian sands.

Acknowledgement: I should like to thank Marek Zvelebil for his help in improving the English of the original manuscript.

References

KOZŁOWSKI, S.K. (1975) *Cultural Differentiation of Europe from 10th to 5th Millennium B.C.* Warsaw, University Press.

OLIVA, M. (1982) La variabilité des industries paléolithiques et le comportement humaine (human behaviour). *Archeologické rozhledy*, 34(6): 622–647.

SKLENÁŘ, K. (1976) Palaeolithic and Mesolithic dwellings: an essay in classification. *Památky Archeologické*, 67: 249–340.

TAUTE, W. (1974) Neue Forschungen zur Chronologie von Spätpaläolithikum und Mesolithikum in Süddeutschland. *Archäologische Informationen*, 2/3 (1973–1974): 59–66.

VALOCH, K. (1977) Felssteinartefakte aus dem Endpaläolithikum von Smolín. *Anthropologie*, 15(2–3): 107–110.

VALOCH, K. (1978) Die endpaläolithische Siedlung in Smolín. *Studie Archeologického ústavu ČSAV v Brně*, 6(3): 1–116.

Early Holocene Flint Assemblages from the Bulgarian Black Sea Coast

Ivan Gatsov

Abstract

From Bulgaria, the only flint artifacts relating to the Pleistocene/Holocene transition are those found in the region of 'Pobiti Kamani', near Varna. The collection consists of *c*. 1300 cores and tools, including 428 microliths, as well as *c*. 900 blades, bladelets and their fragments, and *c*. 9000 flakes. The Bulgarian Black Sea coast represents the eastern limit of the Epi-Tardigravettian tradition. The characteristics, development and external relations of this tradition are discussed.

INTRODUCTION

In recent years intensive exploration of archaeological sites in Europe dating to the end of the Pleistocene and the early Holocene has been carried out. In spite of this, the problems connected with settlement around the Pleistocene/Holocene transition are poorly reflected in Bulgarian archaeological literature. The reasons lie in inadequate investigation of sites belonging to the period from the eleventh to the ninth millennium BP (Schild 1973).

The only materials from Bulgaria dating to this period are those collected by the Varna archaeologist, Ara Margos. In all, Margos collected *c*. 11,000 artifacts from surface sites in the 'Pobiti Kamani' region, an area of about 50 km^2 to the west of Varna. To the south this region borders on the Varna lake and to the north it stretches to the Varna plateau. The terrain is covered by fine-grained sands and dunes whose formation pre-dates the Allerød interstadial. Specialists differ as to the origins of the 'column-shaped' limestone formations of the region.

The first description of this area was made by a British Army Captain, T. Spratt, during the Crimean War. The region has attracted a number of researchers, especially during the past fifty years. Yet, the most important archaeological finds are still the flint artifacts collected by Margos, although they are unstratified and are strongly patinated. They were gathered from the surface of 11 sites – defined as the places where their concentration was greatest.

TECHNOLOGICAL AND TYPOLOGICAL CHARACTERISTICS

In technical–typological terms, the collection is characterized by the following features:

Cores

Based on the number of platforms, and the number and location of the flaking surfaces, the cores (*Fig. 1*) comprise: single-platform cores, double-platform cores, cores with changed orientation, discoidal cores, flakes and nodules bearing traces of core processing, and fragments of undefined cores. According to the types of blanks obtained, they are respectively for blades, for blades and flakes, and for flakes. Other attributes taken into consideration are: the type of blank used for the core (pebble, flint nodule, flake), the presence and type of core preparation, the platform type, the phase of processing, colour of patina, state of preservation of the inter-scar areas ('nervures'), the eventual secondary use of the cores, and the dimensions (Gatsov 1984).

Half of the single-platform and double-platform cores bear traces of preparation, consisting of the striking off of a one-sided or two-sided trimming blade, and the preparation of one or two sides and a platform. Usually, the flaking face was deliberately narrowed before or during processing by striking off one or two massive side-flakes. Similarly, the flaking face was made on the narrowest side, and these cores resemble dihedral burins in form. Similar 'plate cores' are known from the flint assemblage from Vlasac, in the Iron Gates region of Yugoslavia (Kozłowski and Kozłowski 1982). Both the narrowing of the flaking face and the choice of the narrowest side for a processing surface facilitated the production of blades and bladelets.

The double-platform cores and the cores with two perpendicular flaking faces can be viewed as intermediate stages in the transformation of the single-platform cores into different types of double-platform cores, and then into cores with changed orientation which have three or more flaking faces. Another characteristic feature of the technique of core processing is the tendency toward maximum use of the cores. This is confirmed by evidence of use of the splintering technique in those cases where hand-processing was impossible. It is no accident, therefore, that most of the cores have a length range of only 20–50 mm and widths ranging from 10 to 40

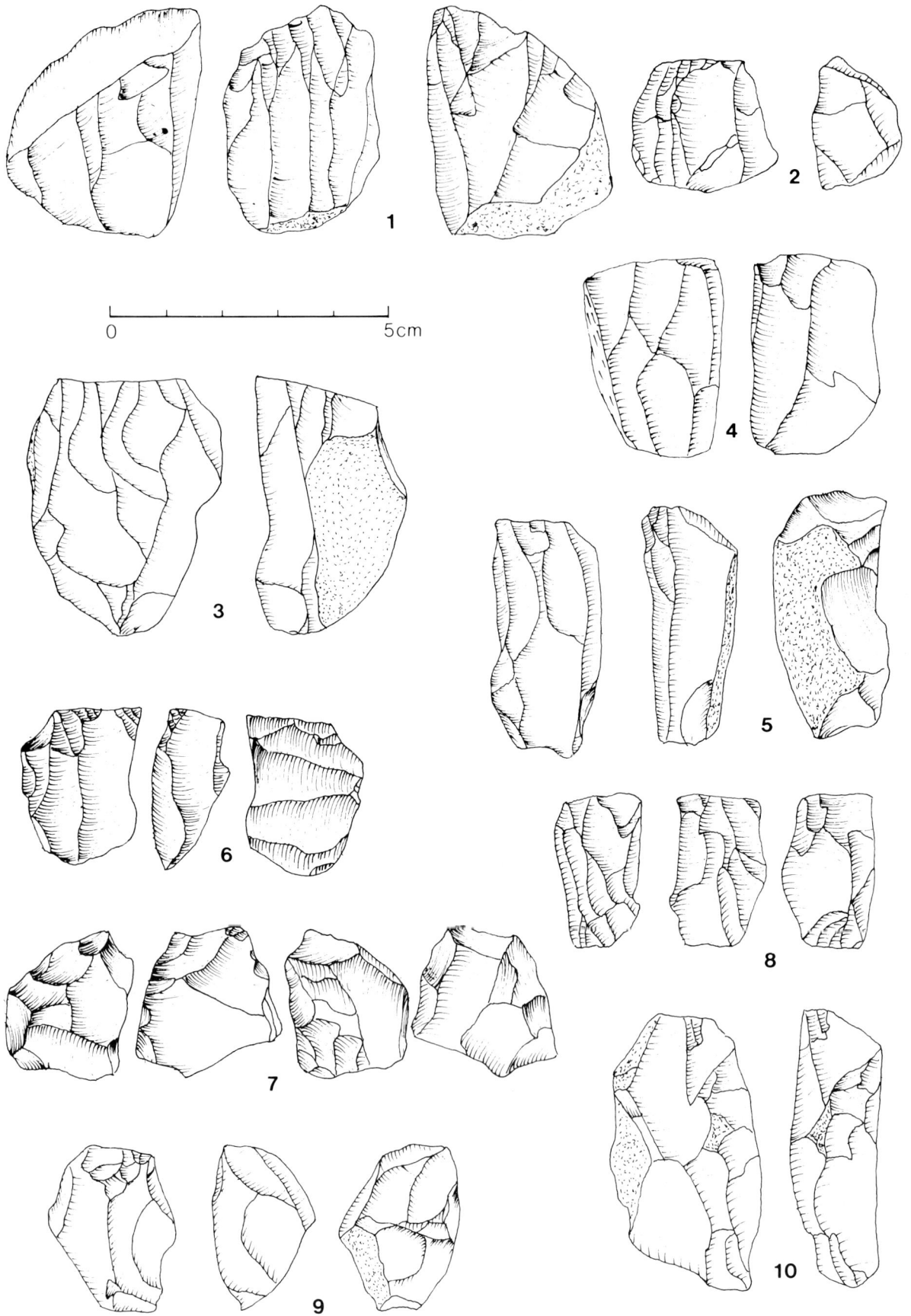

Figure 1 Pobiti Kamani: cores.

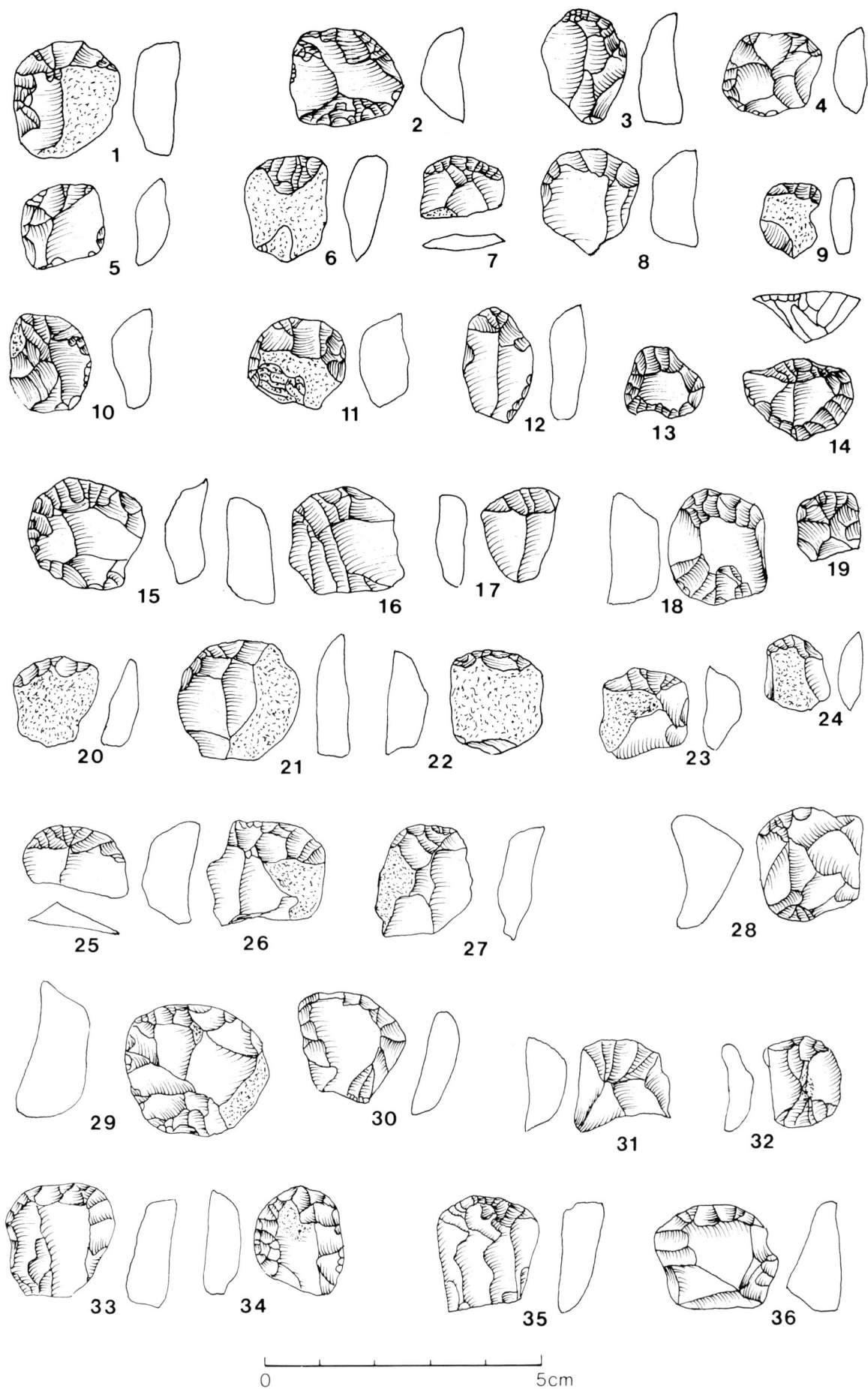

Figure 2 Pobiti Kamani: end-scrapers.

mm. Larger examples can be found among the discoidal cores and in certain specimens with two flaking faces.

In the case of the discoidal cores, the circumference served as a platform and blanks were detached from one or both surfaces. Most of these cores are made on massive flakes.

Flakes and blades

Like most of the artifacts, the flakes and blades are very strongly patinated, which makes it virtually impossible to distinguish the type of core from which they were struck. Nearly one-third of them are wholly or partially corticated on the dorsal face, which shows that processing was done on the spot.

Complete blades and flakes are rare. The most common fragments are the mid-sections, while proximal and distal fragments occur in about the same proportions. The dorsal scar patterns show that nearly all of the blades were struck from single-platform cores or from double-platform cores where the processing was done by alternation of the flaking faces. Most of the flakes are from cores with changed orientation.

Tools

Among the tools, end-scrapers are the most important category (*Fig. 2*). They are made on short, massive flakes or their fragments. The scraper front is characteristically shaped on the more massive end of the blade and is set at an angle close to 90°. There is no retouch along the lateral edges. Among these tools, there are a significant number of micro-end-scrapers, up to 20 mm in diameter, which are usually circular or subcircular in form.

The tools also include burins, combination tools (end-scraper/burin), perforators, alternate perforators, other types of scrapers, raclettes, and retouched flakes. The individual types are found either as single examples or in very significant quantities.

Microliths

The collection contains 424 microliths. These consist of arch-backed points, straight-backed points, crescents, triangles, trapezes, truncated bladelets, transversely-and-laterally-backed bladelets, obliquely-and-laterally-backed bladelets, backed bladelets, bladelets with alternate retouch, and unilateral micro-retouched bladelets.

Half of the microliths are fragmentary backed bladelets, which rarely occur unbroken. Next in order of frequency are the different types of truncated bladelets (14.15%), trapezes (12.5%) and crescents (5.9%). The remaining types are found in smaller series or as single examples. Among the trapezes, asymmetric forms predominate, several with concave retouched edges.

GENERAL OBSERVATIONS

The technology of the cores and typology of the tools are the reason for their being considered together. Parallels in technique and typology can be found at sites such as Vlasac and Cuina Turcului in Yugoslavia (Păunescu 1970). The northern Black Sea coast of Bulgaria represents the eastern limit of the Epi-Tardigravettian tradition. The assemblages from the Black Sea steppes, which belong to the Grebeniki culture, are characterized by a completely different technique of core processing – the 'nucleus de crayon' technique (Stanko 1980).

Within Bulgaria, two cultural facies can be identified in the development of the Tardigravettian tradition – one in south Bulgaria (the mid-Rhodopes), represented by the high-mountain, late Palaeolithic site of Orpheus I (Ivanova and Gatsov 1985); the other in the locality of 'Pobiti Kamani'. The latter assemblages belong to a later period; typologically they can be referred to the beginning of the Holocene, and are characterized by the presence of local elements – namely, an absence of burins, large numbers of end-scrapers, the use of the splintering technique, and the scarcity of blades and bladelets (Kozłowski and Kozłowski 1983). These elements can also be found in Neolithic assemblages in north-eastern and central Bulgaria – e.g. at the sites of Usoe and Kachitza.

As regards the terminology of the early Holocene finds from Bulgaria, the terms Epi-Palaeolithic and Epi-Tardigravettian are both used by researchers, in some cases to refer to the same materials.

For the Bulgarian finds, it is probably more appropriate to use the term Epi-Palaeolithic, because the Epi-Palaeolithic tradition continued here up to the Neolithic. This Epi-Palaeolithic tradition resulted from the mixing of local Palaeolithic elements (see above) with Tardigravettian influences found mainly along the lower Danube valley.

References

GATSOV, I. (1984) Technology and typology of cores from the collection 'Pobiti Kamani'. In J.K. Kozłowski and S.K. Kozłowski (eds), *Advances in Palaeolithic and Mesolithic Archaeology*. Warsaw, Wydawnictwa Uniwersytetu Warszawskiego: 135–151.

IVANOVA, S. and GATSOV, I. (1985) A late Palaeolithic find from the end of the Pleistocene in the surroundings of the 'Orphey' hut in the middle Rhodopes. *Bulletin des musées de la Bulgarie du sud*, 11: 65–76.

KOZŁOWSKI, J.K. and KOZŁOWSKI, S.K. (1982) Lithic industries from the multi-layer Mesolithic site Vlasac in Yugoslavia. In J.K. Kozłowski (ed.), *Origin of the Chipped Stone Industries of the Early Farming Cultures in Balkans*. Warsaw, Państwowe Wydawnictwo Naukowe: 11–109.

KOZŁOWSKI, J.K. and KOZŁOWSKI, S.K. (1983) Chipped stone industries from Lepenski Vir, Yugoslavia. In, *Il Popolamento delle Alpi in Età Mesolitica, VIII–V Millennio a.C.* (Preistoria Alpina, 19). Trento, Museo Tridentino di Scienze Naturali: 259–294.

PĂUNESCU, A. (1970) *Evoluția uneltelor şi armelor de piatră cioplită descoperite pe teritoriul României*. Bucharest, Editura Academiei Republicii Socialiste România.

SCHILD, R. (1973) Paleogeografia Niżu Europejskiego w późnym glacjale. *Przegląd Archeologiczny*, 21: 9–63.

STANKO, B. (1982) *Mirnoe*. Kiev, Naukova Dumka.

Thoughts on the Chronological Relations Between the Epi-Palaeolithic and the Neolithic of the Low Danube

Vasile Boroneanţ

Abstract

Excavations undertaken in 1964 in the Iron Gates gorge, where the Porţile de Fier I and II power stations were built, brought to light remains of two cultures – the Clisurean culture (thirteenth to tenth millennium BP) and the Schela Cladovei–Lepenski Vir culture (ninth to eighth millennium BP). They reflect local evolution keeping abreast of the dynamics of invention of that period. Through their control over cervid populations, selective slaughter of suids, the invention of soil tilling tools made of red deer antler, bone or stone (sometimes ground and polished), ornamental designs, increasing sedentism and burial systems, these cultures bear witness to radical economic, social, ideological and behavioural changes that were to become more widespread in the Neolithic.

INTRODUCTION

In 1964 a series of archaeological excavations were undertaken in the Porţile de Fier straits (Iron Gates gorge), where the Porţile de Fier I hydro-electric station was built. A second station, Porţile de Fier II, is now under construction about 100 km downstream, and it is here that excavations dealing with the Epi-Palaeolithic have been undertaken (*Fig. 1*).

The Porţile de Fier straits consist of Cretaceous and Jurassic limestone and are rich in karst phenomena, of which the most important archaeologically are a series of caves and rock-shelters which were inhabited by human communities in prehistoric times. The straits are winding with numerous basins, narrow passages and sheltered micro-zones. Before the flooding which resulted from dam construction and the creation of an artificial lake, the river was characterized by a series of shallows, with stretches of deeper water up to 40 m deep. The climate is sub-mediterranean with relict fauna and flora. During glacial episodes, the climate was less severe than in the Carpathians or in central Europe. In the Palaeolithic and Epi-Palaeolithic movement of people and materials along the river was difficult, if not impossible in some places, particularly in winter, owing to the cliffs that rise more or less directly from the river's edge. Settlement, therefore, shifted to the higher plateaus which were more accessible. The economic potential of the area was high and there were natural resources such as flint, quartz, quartzite, and other raw materials.

The Porţile de Fier II hydro-electric station is being built downstream of the straits, where the river enters the Romanian plain. The topography changes into an open valley which takes the form of a plain on the Romanian shore and 100–300 m high hills, descending gradually to the Danube, on the Yugoslav border. Once out of the straits, the Danube meanders and contains islets, some of which are very large – for example, Ostrovul Mare which is 17.5 km long and 7 km wide. On the Romanian shore, the beaches are wide and covered either with fine alluvium or with gravels and sands. There are no sheltered areas and, therefore, no micro-climates. The vegetation is typical meadow and gallery grove. The fauna is fairly uniform, although the distribution of the species varies. The climate is more severe than in the straits, with hotter and drier summers and colder winters, while the winds blow harder and longer from the west.

The archaeological record is richer for the straits and includes evidence for habitation in the Middle Palaeolithic, Upper Palaeolithic and Epi-Palaeolithic; whereas in the downstream area data are available only for the late Epi-Palaeolithic, since fieldwork has concentrated on the area that would be directly affected by the construction of the hydro-electric station or the lake created by it.

EVOLUTION OF THE EPI-PALAEOLITHIC

In general terms, the evolution of Epi-Palaeolithic society in the area concerned can be divided into three cultures – the Epi-Gravettian (Proto-Clisurean culture), the Clisurean, and the Schela Cladovei–Lepenski Vir cultures. In the Porţile de Fier II area, only sites belonging to the Schela Cladovei–Lepenski Vir culture have been identified. Thus, whereas in the straits the cultural evolution can be traced back to the period between the sixteenth and the eighth millennium BP (Boroneanţ 1970*b*, 1979), in the downstream area only the period between the ninth and the eighth millennium BP is represented (Boroneanţ 1980, 1982).

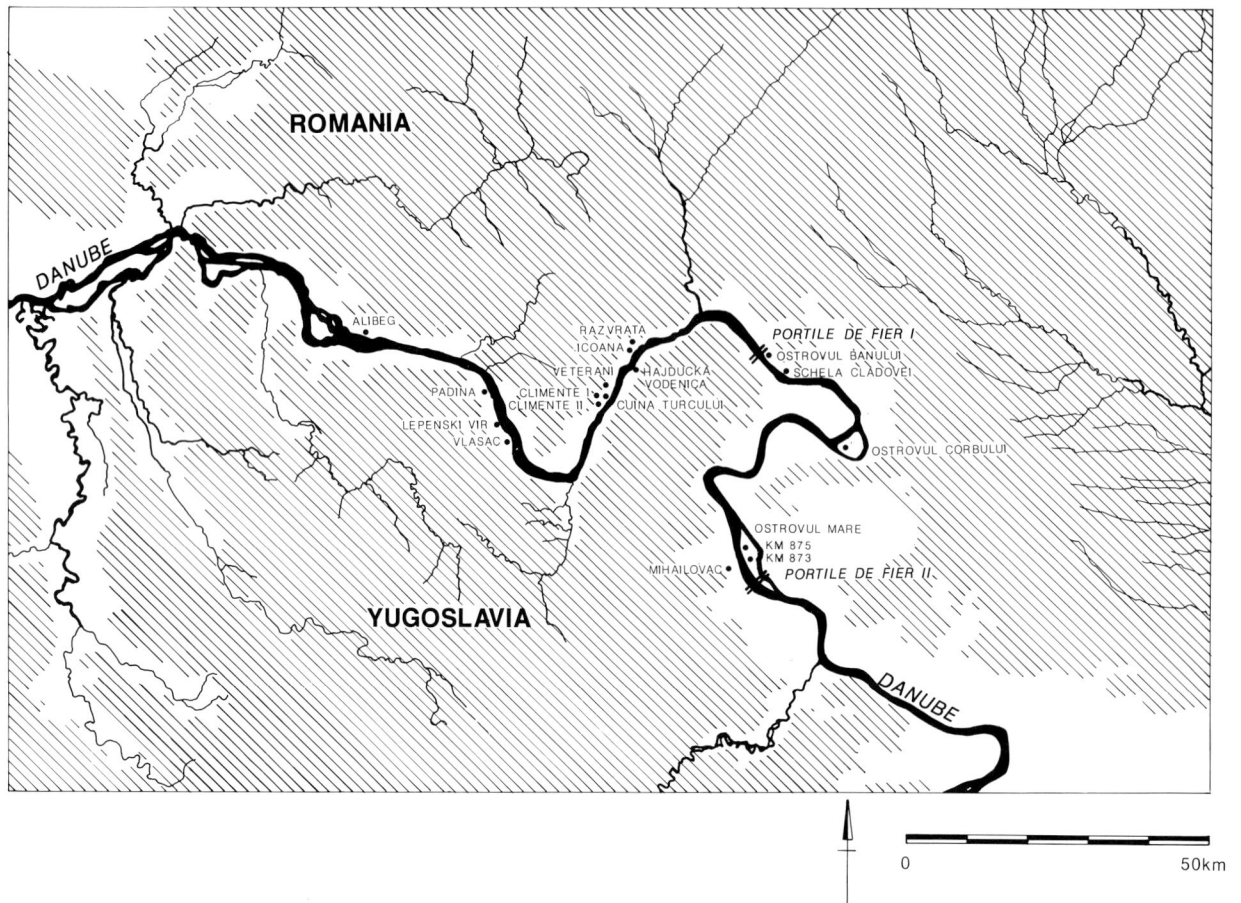

Figure 1   Map of the Iron Gates gorge showing the location of the Porţile de Fier sites and other important sites mentioned in the text.

Proto-Clisurean culture

The Proto-Clisurean culture was identified and investigated in the Climente I cave at Dubova in 1965–1969. The flint industry is dominated by microliths (up to 53% of the toolkit). The tools include backed bladelets, bladelets with fine retouch (some of Dufour type), tanged points and some geometric pieces (e.g. segments of circles, triangles or trapezes), and notched or shouldered bladelets. This proves that the communities were in a process of microlithization against the background of a lithic technology based on blades (Boroneanţ 1979).

Clisurean culture

The microlithization process continued in the Clisurean culture cycle and was accompanied by a reduction in blade débitage. The flint industry of this phase is very rich – over 39,400 pieces were found at Cuina Turcului and over 2700 in the Climente II cave – and is generally characterized by bipolar ('scalar') débitage. The most frequent tools are scrapers in the form of circles, parts of circles and of thumb-nail form, tanged points, 'pièces esquillées', and retouched splinters. The apparent changes in the general flint inventory can be attributed to the process of 'segregation' (Palma di Cesnola 1976), or what the French term 'regionalization' (Escalon de Fonton 1976), but are also linked to a reduction in the size of the territory within which the communities moved and gathered their supplies of food and raw materials.

Radiocarbon dating at Cuina Turcului indicates Clisurean occupations between 12,600±120 BP (Bln-803) and 10,125±200 BP (Bln-802) (Păunescu 1970: 29), associated with considerable economic stability.

Schela Cladovei–Lepenski Vir culture

The segregation or regionalization process becomes more evident during the Schela Cladovei–Lepenski Vir cultural cycle, reflecting a further confinement of economic activities against the background of a warmer climate. Human groups left the caves and rock-shelters to settle on the banks of the Danube and explore the economic resources of much more restricted areas. This is demonstrated by the larger number of settlements with economic characteristics resembling the sedentary settlements of the Neolithic.

Another development which accompanied this process was the integration into exchange networks of raw materials that only occasionally attracted the attention of earlier communities, such as quartz and other rocks, horns, teeth, tusks, bones resulting from the consumption of game, and all kinds of rocks and boulders available on the beach. It was no

Table 1: Schela Cladovei culture sites – weights (g) and percentages of the three major categories of raw materials

Material	Veterani Terasă		Ostrovul Banului		Icoana		Răzvrata		Schela Cladovei		Alibeg	
	wgt	%	wgt	%	wgt	%	wgt	%	wgt	%	wgt	%
Flint	2,241	37.77	946	13.69	1,586	1.48	88	0.57	1,083	4.18	1,625	5.15
Quartzitic rocks	2,921	49.07	2,953	42.75	34,775	32.51	3,858	25.00	6,663	25.72	3,389	10.74
Quartz	781	13.16	3,009	43.56	70,598	66.01	11,484	74.43	18,161	70.10	26,538	84.11
TOTAL	5,933	100.00	6,908	100.00	106,959	100.00	15,430	100.00	25,907	100.00	31,552	100.00

Table 2: Schela Cladovei culture sites – weights (g) and percentages of quartz and quartzitic rocks *vs* flint

Material	Veterani Terasă		Ostrovul Banului		Icoana		Răzvrata		Schela Cladovei		Alibeg	
	wgt	%	wgt	%	wgt	%	wgt	%	wgt	%	wgt	%
Flint	2,241	37.77	946	13.69	1,586	1.48	88	0.57	1,083	4.18	1,625	5.15
Quartzite & Quartz	3,692	62.23	5,962	86.31	105,373	98.52	15,342	99.43	24,824	95.82	29,927	94.85
TOTAL	5,933		6,908		106,959		15,430		25,907		31,552	

longer necessary for people to travel long distances to procure such materials. This, then, was an ergonomical process.

Weighing of all the lithic materials found in the Schela Cladovei settlements (*Tables 1 & 2*) has shown that in the initial stages (Veterani Terasă) flint still constitutes a high percentage (37.77% of the assemblage), while in the main stage of development (Icoana) it averages only 1.48%, with other rocks accounting for 98.52% of the material used. Towards the final stage of the culture (Alibeg) flint starts to gain ground again, reaching 5.15% of the total.

For activities such as the cutting of meat, gutting of fish, peeling of roots or skinning, where previously flint tools were used, people now used boars' tusks or the shafts of long bones. Ingenuity and adaptation are the hallmarks of this stage; an attempt was made to integrate all the local raw material resources into the economic system to the limit of available technology. From this period on, there was no other major technological innovation until the discovery of metallurgy and, particularly, iron processing. Clay baking was an Epi-Palaeolithic invention, and the introduction of pottery into the economic system was just a deviation from the straight road of progress of Epi-Palaeolithic society. This does not mean, however, that the introduction of pottery was not a significant event.

INNOVATION AND CULTURE CHANGE IN THE LATE EPI-PALAEOLITHIC

In the light of the sequence of inventions made, the Epi-Palaeolithic appears to have been a period in which experiments were made in restricted areas rather than across whole regions – experiments that were to be consolidated and extended in the Neo-lithic. A culture so rich in inventions and so dynamic could only be matched by the introduction of iron metallurgy, which was eventually to lead to the disappearance of traditional stone tools. The introduction of iron-working was, in fact, a crucial change in the history of the means of production and in the traditional behaviour of individuals and of society, equivalent to that which occurred towards the end of the Epi-Palaeolithic.

The segregation and regionalization phenomena resulted, therefore, in these historic consequences over vast areas but not always simultaneously (Rozoy 1978: 1–3), since they followed the evolution of the climate.

The latest excavations to be undertaken at Porţile de Fier II have yielded further evidence of this process. The finds from the two excavated localities at Ostrovul Mare, kilometres 873 and 875, include several bone objects with a similar morphology and an active end that appears worn on one side only. Their technical–functional characteristics have been analyzed and compared with the so-called ground stone 'axes', which also have a worn working end, and with the red deer antler ard tips of 'Aratrum type' (Boroneanţ and Boroneanţ 1983). The results suggest that they all represent a single functional type. Consequently, both bone and stone examples of these implements were mounted for use as tips of ards of Aratrum type. They could not have been axes, otherwise they would have had two equal active surfaces forming a wedge-shaped working end (Boroneanţ 1983). Examples of these implements made of bone were recovered from the upper levels at Ostrovul Mare, together with those made of ground stone. At Ostrovul Mare km 875, quartzite tools of the same type were identified. Similar implements, made of the same range of raw materials,

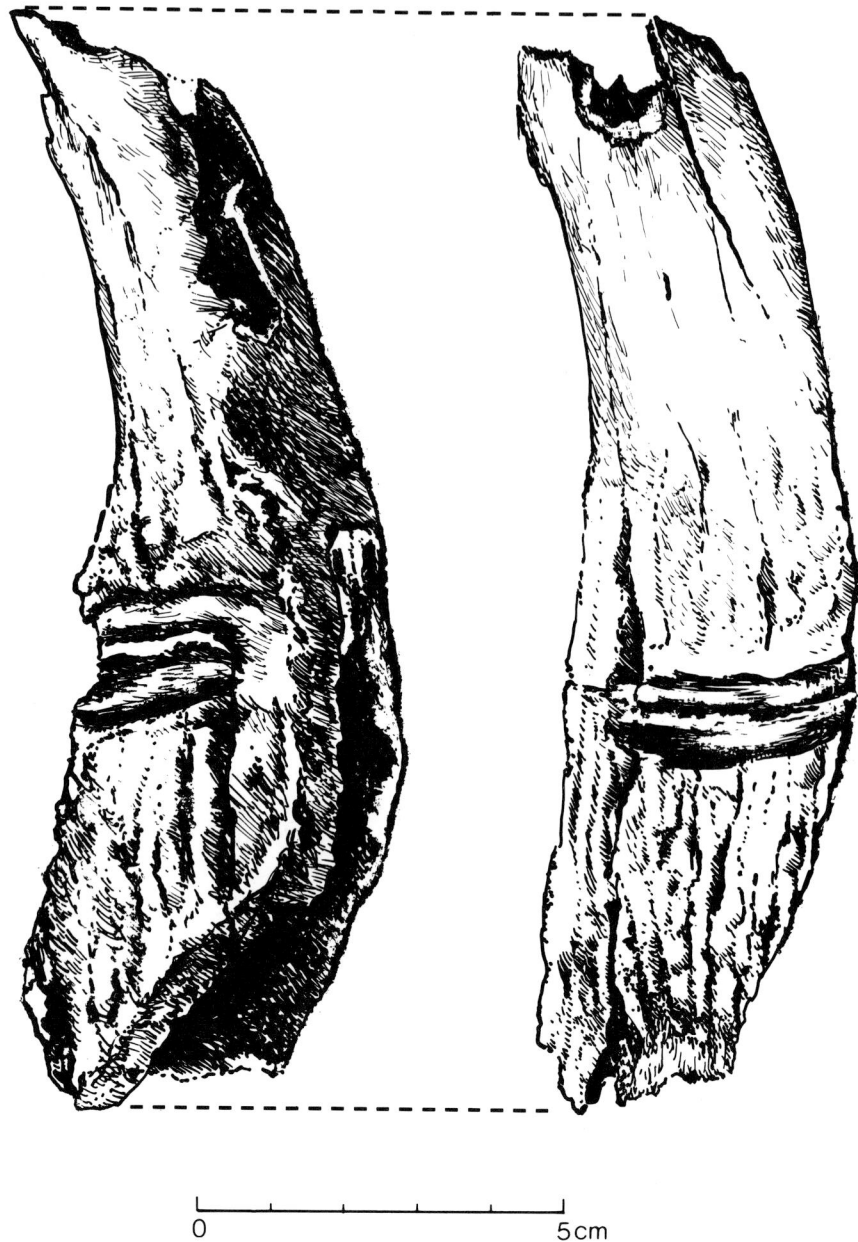

Figure 2 Ostrovul Mare km 873: ard tip made from a red deer antler.

were found during the recent excavations at Schela Cladovei.

A new kind of ard tip was found at Ostrovul Mare km 873 (*Fig. 2*). It is made from a red deer antler and the passive end has been thinned so that it could be inserted into a wooden handle, and has a polish resulting from prolonged use. Towards the active end is a lateral groove where a cord or thong was attached to fasten the tip to the ard. This find adds to the inventory of tools known from this period and affords a clearer insight into the ingenuity of the late Epi-Palaeolithic communities.

Another very important find for our understanding of the development of these communities came from Ostrovul Mare km 875. This was a small sunken hut, inside which was a fireplace with sides made of burnt clay. It marks the transition to the Neolithic oven.

At Mihailovac, on the Yugoslav border, remains of a trapeze-shaped dwelling were found within which there was burnt clay, possibly from the walls. Pieces of burnt clay within dwellings were also found at Alibeg.

In the light of this data, the road taken by the human communities of the Low Danube is absolutely clear.

THE EPI-PALAEOLITHIC–NEOLITHIC TRANSITION

A site of utmost importance for the chronology of the Epi-Palaeolithic–Neolithic transition is that of Schela Cladovei. The 1982 excavations there revealed a Proto-Sesklo dwelling, whose construction had disturbed the latest Schela Cladovei–Lepenski Vir deposit. The cultural remains suggest that the disturbed layer must have been contemporary with the final habitations at Lepenski Vir (Srejović 1969), Padina (Jovanović 1969) and Alibeg (Boroneanţ 1973). It follows that the earliest Balkan Neolithic overlaps in time with the final stages of the Schela Cladovei culture.

How did this transition from one culture to another and from one stage to another occur? If the Neolithic was introduced from outside, where did it come from? The present author believes that it did not come from outside. The achievements of the previous stage during the Schela Cladovei culture cannot be overlooked (Boroneanţ 1973). If one looks objectively at the Proto-Sesklo culture in this area and, indeed, over its entire geographical range, it is evident that much of the ornamentation on bone, horn and stone tools is dominated by the motifs of the Schela Cladovei culture. The prevailing designs are the network, rhombs, squares, small circles, zigzags, wavy lines, and so forth. Moreover, the syntax or the way in which these elements are interrelated is the same, which indicates that very little time had passed since the bone, horn or wood elements of this culture were transferred to pottery. There are obviously progressive elements too, which represent an advance over the late Epi-Palaeolithic, but these elements are naturally and generally linked to the more flexible medium of ceramics, where the individual's artistic talent and imagination were freer to develop.

The idea of manufacturing ceramics may not have originated in the region of the Low Danube, but then pottery was not of overriding importance – it was merely part of the general process of cultural development. A new culture does not have to come from elsewhere, since that would deny the law of progress; the best example of this is the Schela Cladovei culture. A culture is born out of the general background of the age and has its own unique character. It reflects the ecosystemic cultural character of its zone or area. The Schela Cladovei culture also incorporated traditions that were characteristic of the intra-Balkan and intra-Carpathians territories and quite different from those of the peri-Mediterranean coast of the time. It would never have evolved towards the monumental; it was inward-looking, with its own mythology, and presented a different face to the outside world.

Consequently, it cannot be said that the evolution of the Schela Cladovei–Lepenski Vir culture was halted by the development of Neolithic society within this zone. Nor can it be determined whether the achievements of this time were part of a general evolution of society which marked the very transition

from one culture to another and from one stage to another.

Let us turn to the unparalleled, unique and unmistakable in the development of human society in the Low Danube – the carved boulders ornamented with abstract and naturalistic motifs from Lepenski Vir (Srejović 1969), Padina (Jovanović 1969), Hajdučka-Vodenica (Jovanović 1966), Vlasac (Srejović and Letica 1978), Cuina Turcului (Boroneanţ 1974), Schela Cladovei and elsewhere, that were connected with religious and functional (production) magic – in order to highlight the effects of an invention on certain categories of raw materials that had become traditional at a certain stage of prehistoric human development. The present author believes that the discovery of clay baking and processing towards the end of the Epi-Palaeolithic in this particular zone led to the abandonment of the processing of river boulders in artistic forms in favour of the processing of clay into pottery and idols. A parallel trend was the decline of the flint arrowheads characteristic of the Clisurean culture and the concomitant spread of bone arrowheads during the Schela Cladovei culture.

Obviously, many other things could be said about the finds from Porţile de Fier II on both banks of the Danube, but space does not permit such a lengthy treatment.

CONCLUDING REMARKS

In conclusion, it is worth underlining the fact that the emergence of the Neolithic in the Low Danube was not a sudden or radical change; the human communities there were embarked on an evolutionary course that would inevitably lead in that direction. Local experience led to the emergence of new activities which were undertaken by means of new specialized equipment. The new activities and the new equipment were interdependent. The soil could not be tilled without appropriate tools; animals could not be tamed if the communities did not become sedentary; pottery could not exist without the improvement of fireplaces and the construction of ovens. Even the human type of this area underwent morpho-structural adjustments in the face of ecological change (Nicolăescu-Plopşor 1976).

The discovery at Schela Cladovei of a Proto-Sesklo cultural horizon typical of the Balkan early Neolithic fills the gap that seemed to exist between the Schela Cladovei–Lepenski Vir culture and the early Neolithic, formerly represented in the Low Danube by the Criş–Starčevo culture. Previously, there had been speculation on the part of some researchers that the Schela Cladovei culture was a late development of the Epi-Palaeolithic (Mesolithic) parallel to the Proto-Sesklo early Neolithic, unlike the situation in the rest of the Balkan peninsula and in the Near East. This interpretation deliberately overlooked the radiocarbon evidence. Together with the previous finds at Cuina Turcului (Boroneanţ 1970a), the recent discoveries at Schela Cladovei demonstrate that cultural evolution in the Porţile de Fier area was normal. The Schela Cladovei culture of the Epi-Palaeolithic was succeeded by the Proto-Sesklo culture which, in its turn, gave way to the Criş–Starčevo culture. This evolution was an integral part of the evolution of Balkan society over the time-range concerned. The lack of Proto-Sesklo discoveries in the western part of Romania, apart from the finds from Gura Baciului (Vlassa 1972) and Cîrcea (Nica 1977), does not mean these are isolated occurrences resulting from the movement of people from the south west. They merely mark a gap in the study of the period which is just beginning to be filled – a point reinforced by the recent discovery at Ocniţa near Ocna Sibiului in Transylvania (Paul, in press).

References

BORONEANŢ, V. (1970a) La civilisation Criş de Cuina Turcului. *Actes du VIIe Congrès International des Sciences Préhistoriques et Protohistoriques, Prague 1966*: 407–410.

BORONEANŢ, V. (1970b) La période épipaléolithique sur la rive roumaine des Portes de Fer du Danube. *Praehistorische Zeitschrift*, 45(1): 1–25.

BORONEANŢ, V. (1973) Recherches archéologiques sur la culture Schela Cladovei de la zone des 'Portes de Fer'. *Dacia*, 17: 5–39.

BORONEANŢ, V. (1974) Noi date despre cele mai vechi manifestări de artă plastică pe teritoriul României. *Studii şi Cercetări de Istoria Artei*, 18(1): 114.

BORONEANŢ, V. (1979) Descoperiri arheologice în unele peşteri din defileul Dunării. In T. Orghidan and S. Hegrea (eds),

Speologia–Porţile de Fier (Academia Republicii Socialiste Romania – Grupul de cercetări complexe Porţile de Fier, seria monografică). Bucharest, Editura Academiei: 140–185.

BORONEANŢ, V. (1980) Probleme ale culturii Schela Cladovei–Lepenski Vir în lumina noilor cercetări. *Drobeta*, 4: 27–42.

BORONEANŢ, V. (1982) General survey of Epipalaeolithic (Mesolithic) research in Romania (1978–1981). *Mesolithic Miscellany*, 3(1): 11–12.

BORONEANŢ, V. and BORONEANŢ, C. (1983) Consideraţii asupra parametrilor tehnico funcţionali ai uneltelor preistorice de lucrat pămîntul. *Ialomiţa*, 1: 115–122.

ESCALON DE FONTON, M. (1976) Les civilisations de l'Epipaléolithique et du Mésolithique en Provence littorale. In H. de Lumley (ed.), *La Préhistoire Française*, tome 1. Paris, Centre National de la Recherche Scientifique: 1367–1378.

JOVANOVIĆ, B. (1966) Sculptures de la nécropole de l'âge du fer ancien à Hajdučka Vodenica. *Archaeologia Iugoslavica*, 7: 31–34.

JOVANOVIĆ, B. (1969) Chronological frames of the Iron Gates group of the early Neolithic period. *Archaeologia Iugoslavica*, 10: 23–38.

NICA, M. (1977) Nouvelles données sur le Néolithique ancien d'Oltenie. *Dacia*, 21: 13–54.

NICOLĂESCU-PLOPŞOR, D. (1976) Deux cas de mort violente dans l'Epipaléolithique final de Schela Cladovei. *Annuaire Roumain d'Anthropologie*, 13: 3–5.

PALMA DI CESNOLA, A. (1967) Il Paleolitico della Puglia. *Memorie del Museo Civico di Storia Naturale di Verona*, 15: 76–75.

PAUL, I. (in press) Unele probleme ale neoliticului timpuriu în zona carpato-dunăreana. *Studii şi Cercetări de Istorie Veche şi Arheologie*, 40(1).

PĂUNESCU, A. (1970) Epipaleoliticul de la Cuina Turcului–Dubova. *Studii şi Cercetări de Istorie Veche*, 21(1): 3–47.

ROZOY, J-G. (1978) *Les Derniers Chasseurs. L'Epipaléolithique en France et en Belgique* (Bulletin de la Société archéologique champenoise, numéro spécial). Charleville, J-G. Rozoy.

SREJOVIĆ, D. (1969) *Lepenski Vir. Nova praisorijska Kultura u Podunavlju*. Belgrade, Srpska književna zadruga.

SREJOVIĆ, D. and LETICA, Z. (1978) *Vlasac. Mezolitsko naselje u Djerdapu*. Belgrade, Srpska Akademija Nauka i Umetnosti.

VLASSA, N. (1972) Eine frühneolithische Kultur mit bemalter Keramik der Vor-Starčevo-Körösszeit in Gura Baciului, Siebenbürgen. *Praehistorische Zeitschrift*, 47(2): 174–197.

The Mesolithic of Serbia and Montenegro

Dragoslav Srejović

Abstract

This paper argues, on the basis of an analysis of the main features of the relevant finds from the Iron Gates region and from Montenegro, that the Mesolithic cultures of Serbia and Montenegro represent a direct continuation of the local final Palaeolithic cultures, which are themselves merely regional variants of the Epi-Tardigravettian. During the Pre-Boreal the existing traditions exerted a very strong influence on the local cultures, and their evolution was therefore uniform. At the beginning of the Boreal a differentiation took place; the culture in the Iron Gates region became progressive and achieved in time almost all the basic elements of the so-called 'Neolithic Revolution'. The culture in the inland and coastal parts of Montenegro, however, remained unaltered for a long time and acquired Neolithic features only under external cultural influences.

INTRODUCTION

The territory of Serbia and Montenegro is not large. It comprises the central part of the Balkan peninsula and its axis extends from the north east to the south west, so that it links the Pannonian plain with the shores of the Adriatic Sea. It is a territory, therefore, which cuts across several climatic and vegetation zones, and comprises three natural regions: (i) the Morava valley and part of the Danubian region; (ii) the central area comprising the watershed of the Adriatic, Aegean and Black Sea river systems; and (iii) the maritime region. Each of these regions has specific ecological features, and therefore one should not expect a uniform development of Mesolithic cultures in Serbia and Montenegro.

As recently as the 1950s it was held that the territories of Serbia and Montenegro were either uninhabited during the Mesolithic period or lay outside the region of the major population movements and cultural developments. Because of this misconception the origin of the Neolithic was explained in a very facile way – as a result of the migrations of people and ideas from the southern parts of the Balkan peninsula or from distant Anatolia (Milojčić 1949; Childe 1957).

It was only in the 1960s, when some areas threatened by flooding as a result of the construction of hydro-electric power plants were investigated in detail, that a considerable number of Mesolithic sites were discovered in Serbia and Montenegro. Only a few of these sites have been adequately explored so far (*Fig. 1*). They include those in the area of the Iron Gates (eastern Serbia), in the gorges of the rivers Piva and Ćehotina (northern Montenegro), and in the Trebišnica valley (south-west Montenegro). Although of limited scope, these investigations have established a new and important fact; during the Mesolithic gaps in habitation and cultural development in Serbia and Montenegro were far fewer than in Anatolia or the Aegean – the regions from which until recently it was believed that people, economic innovations and culture had spread to the inland parts of the Balkan peninsula.

The Mesolithic flint industry was discovered first in the Crvena Stijena rock-shelter in the south-western part of Montenegro (Benac 1957; Basler 1975). It was, however, the investigation of the Lepenski Vir terrace in the Iron Gates that first promoted intense interest in the study of the Mesolithic culture in the central parts of the Balkan peninsula. Remains of seven successive settlements of fishers, hunters and food gatherers were discovered beneath an early Neolithic layer (Lepenski Vir III) in this small and inaccessible retreat (Proto-Lepenski Vir, Lepenski Vir Ia–e, Lepenski Vir II). Each of these levels consisted of a number of dwellings of uniform plan. Graves and stone, bone and antler tools were discovered in all the settlements, while the Lepenski Vir I and II settlements also yielded sanctuaries with sculptures made of large boulders (Srejović 1969, 1972a). Lepenski Vir then took its place on the archaeological map of Europe as an exceptionally important, but isolated, centre of culture. The archaeological material found in it, however, gave grounds for hope that we might expect similar archaeological discoveries in the future, which would make the developments on this small Danubian terrace more intelligible.

In subsequent years these expectations were fulfilled. Fourteen more settlements dating from the same period have been discovered on the banks of the Danube and in the Iron Gates region so far, the most important of them being Vlasac and Schela Cladovei (Boroneanţ 1970, 1973; Srejović and Letica 1978). The stratigraphy of these sites and the

481

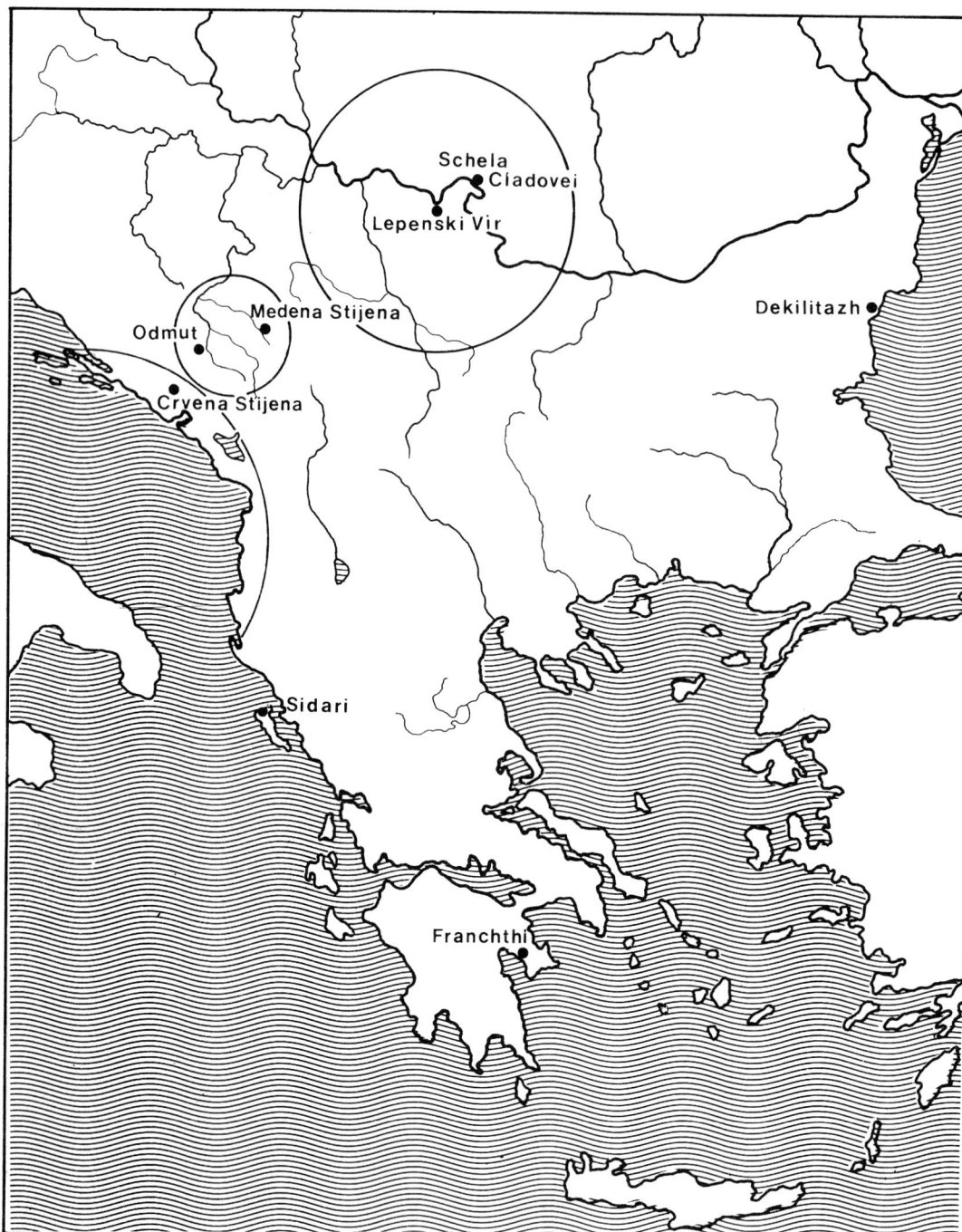

Figure 1   Map of the Balkan peninsula showing sites referred to in the text.

material discovered in them show that Lepenski Vir should be considered the centre of a distinctive and long-lived Danubian culture, known as the Lepenski Vir culture (Srejović 1969) or the Schela Cladovei–Lepenski Vir culture (Boroneanţ 1980).

THE IRON GATES SITES: THE LEPENSKI VIR CULTURE

The Iron Gates region was the cradle of the Lepenski Vir culture, but it was not its sole territory, as Jovanović (1969), Nandris (1972), and Tringham (1971) supposed. Sites belonging to the Lepenski Vir culture have recently been discovered in the open

country far from the Iron Gates (Mogoşanu 1978; Boroneanţ 1980, 1981; Srejović and Babović 1981, 1983). This shows that David Clarke was right when he observed:

> In this light, we should perhaps see the Danube gorge sites of the Lepenski Vir complex as not so much a unique local adaptation but a restricted sample of the once extensive lower Danube riverine Mesolithic, preserved for us by its unusual location, where the deeply-channelled and constrained Danube cuts high ground (1976: 468).

Today, we know not only the distribution of the Lepenski Vir culture, but also the tradition on which it was founded. We also have other data necessary for a thorough study of this culture – evidence concerning the location and structure of its settlements (Srejović 1969, 1972a; Jovanović 1969, 1984a, 1984b; Boroneanţ 1973; Srejović and Letica 1978), the forms of burial (Letica 1975), the lithic industry (Radovanović 1981; Kozłowski and Kozłowski 1982), art (Srejović and Babović 1983), anthropological remains (Nemeskéri 1972; Živanović 1975; Nicolăescu-Plopşor 1976; Nemeskéri and Szathmáry 1978), fauna (Bökönyi 1972, 1978; Bolomey 1973; Clason 1980) and flora (Cărciumaru 1973). Moreover, the stratigraphy of the settlements of the Lepenski Vir culture and the radiocarbon dates (Srejović and Letica 1978; Boroneanţ 1980; Srejović and Babović 1981; Prinz 1982) make it possible for us to distinguish two basic stages in the development of the Lepenski Vir culture, and the phases which link it with the local final Palaeolithic and early Neolithic cultures.

Chronology and development

Table 1 outlines the chronology of prehistoric settlement in the Iron Gates region. In this continuous cultural development, the period between 10,000 and 9000 BP represented a long interval during which some of the local forms of the final Palaeolithic (the Cuina Turcului culture) disappeared, and some were transformed into the forms of the Lepenski Vir culture. The final transformation of the traditional culture – the constitution of the distinctive Lepenski Vir culture – took place, however, only at the beginning of the Boreal; its apogee was

c. 8000 BP, and its disintegration occurred in the middle of the eighth millennium BP.

Three factors exercised a decisive influence over the emergence and evolution of the Lepenski Vir culture – climatic change, population increase, and isolation. The rising temperature in the Boreal enriched the vegetation of the Iron Gates region and made it possible for the local populations to live in the open, but the factor of isolation made their existence a very complex one. The earliest settlements of the Lepenski Vir culture (Proto-Lepenski Vir, Vlasac Ia, Padina A, Icoana I) were built on low terraces which are always small and isolated, because they are cut out by the Danube longitudinally and enclosed by the steep slopes of the surrounding hills. The communities which inhabited these terraces were compelled to engage in a number of new activities, primarily to build dwellings and to establish a combined settled–mobile economy – that is, to make seasonal camps in addition to their permanent settlements.

Architecture

The Mesolithic architecture of the Iron Gates region lacks orthogonal plans and vertical walls. Tent-like dwellings with the ground plan derived from a circle or a triangle were the only forms constructed in all the phases. Dwellings with sunken floors, almost triangular in plan and with circular or ellipsoid hearths surrounded with pebbles or broken stones, were discovered in the earliest settlements (Vlasac Ia, Proto-Lepenski Vir, Padina A, Schela Cladovei I, Ostrovul Banului IIIa). Later dwellings were constructed with the ground plan in the form of the truncated sector of a circle, and with rectangular hearths made of large stone blocks. In some dwellings the hearth was surrounded with stone slabs, altars and sculptures made of large boulders, so that a separate sacred area (a kind of sanctuary) was formed at their centre (Srejović 1972a: 64–72).

Art, sculpture and burial

Unlike architecture, which was a new development, not based on traditional forms, sculptures were made of the 'sacred stone', the boulder, which for centuries had played an important role in the traditional culture of the Iron Gates region, both in every-day activities (as the basic material for the making of stone implements) and in religious practice (boulders coloured with ochre). The intricate arabesques shown on a number of sculptures are also associated with the traditional artistic forms of expression, with the engravings found at Cuina Turcului and with the similar ornaments found on the objects belonging to the Magdalenian, Epi-Gravettian and Romanellian cultures (Boroneanţ 1970; Păunescu 1970; Srejović and Babović 1983).

Table 1: The chronology of the Iron Gates region

Stages	Sites	^{14}C dates BP
Early Neolithic	Lepenski Vir IIIa Cuina Turcului III Padina B–3	
Transitional Mesolithic/Neolithic	Kula; Padina B–2 (?) Alibeg; Ostrovul Mare	7195±100
Late Mesolithic	Lepenski Vir I and II Vlasac II and III Padina B–1 Icoana II Hajdučka Vodenica Schela Cladovei II Ostrovul Banului IIIb	7930–7440
Early Mesolithic	Proto-Lepenski Vir Vlasac I Padina A Schela Cladovei I Ostrovul Banului IIIa Icoana I	8565–7950
Transitional Palaeolithic/Mesolithic	Cuina Turcului II Ostrovul Banului I–II	8565±100
Final Palaeolithic	Cuina Turcului I	12,600±100

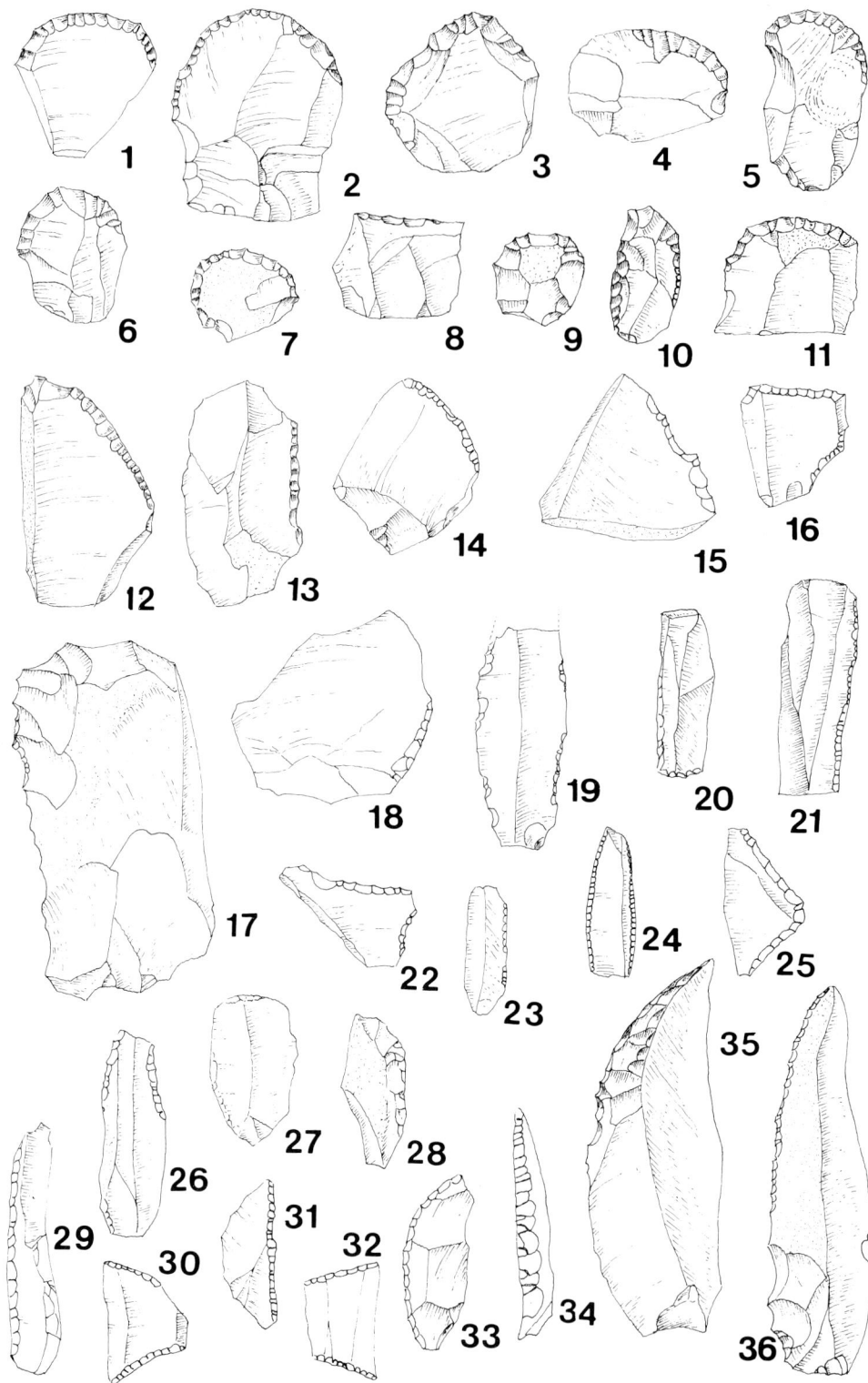

Figure 2 Vlasac (Serbia), layers I–II: flint industry of the Lepenski Vir culture.

The sinuous furrows on the sculptures and the broken lines on the traditional engravings probably represent signs denoting water, torrents and the river, or allusions to the inexhaustible sources of life and to constant propagation. Since the river is the basic subject of artistic expression, it may be assumed that the figural sculptures represent river demons or the first creatures born out of water, the forefathers of mankind and of everything else in this world (Srejović and Babović 1983). They may also have been representations of ancestors, for human skulls, jaw bones and, in a few cases, entire skeletons were discovered near the sculptures in some dwellings. New-born infants and some adults were buried under the floor of the sanctuaries. Some male burials, perhaps belonging to shamans and sorcerers, were interred in a seated position in special stone structures, the plans of which resemble those of the dwellings (Letica 1975).

The sanctuaries with sculptures and special forms of burial were found only in permanent settlements (Lepenski Vir I and II, Hajdučka Vodenica), which were undoubtedly also religious centres where all the communities inhabiting the Iron Gates region held periodic gatherings. The contemporaneous seasonal settlements and camps (Vlasac II and III, Icoana II, Schela Cladovei II) yielded, on the other hand, a large number of very varied implements and weapons, and only occasionally a ritual instrument made of stone or antler. This separation of the sacral and secular activities, i.e. the employment of human faculties for the achievement of different goals, resulted in the rapid development of the Lepenski Vir culture, which was reflected in a number of innovations. The remains of fauna and pollen in the coprolites from Vlasac and Icoana provide evidence of the cultivation of cereals *in loco* and the domestication or selection of animals (Bökönyi 1972, 1978; Bolomey 1973; Cărciumaru 1973). On the other hand, all the settlements and camps from the late phase of the Lepenski Vir culture yielded stone mortars and pestles, heavy axes made of polished boulders, and antler tools which were used for farming (Boroneanţ 1973; Srejović and Letica 1978).

The lithic industry

These innovations were accompanied by archaizing elements, which are particularly noticeable in the lithic industry. The flint industry of the Lepenski Vir culture – characterized by short end-scrapers (*Fig. 2*, nos. 1–7), lanceolate points (*Fig. 2*, no. 28), crescents (*Fig. 2*, no. 33), rectangles (*Fig. 2*, no. 20), isosceles triangles (*Fig. 2*, no. 25), and backed blades (*Fig. 2*, no. 36) – represents a direct continuation of the local traditions, i.e. of the flint industry of Cuina Turcului, which is very close to the Epi-Tardigravettian (Păunescu 1970). Some regional Balkan, intercultural elements, such as splintered pieces, irregular scrapers, micro-retouched bladelets and trapezes (*Fig. 2*, nos. 12–15, 23, 24, 30, 32) were also found; they seem to be evidence of the existence of some links between the Iron Gates region and the sites in the southern and eastern parts of the Balkan peninsula, such as Odmut, Sidari and, particularly, Dekilitazh (Srejović 1972b, 1974; Radovanović 1981; Gatsov 1982; Kozłowski and Kozłowski 1982). The flint industry of the Lepenski Vir culture remained virtually unaltered, but it was gradually replaced by implements made of polished stone, and especially by a surprising growth of quartz and quartzite industry. The settlements belonging to the phase of the disintegration of the Lepenski Vir culture (Kula II, Ostrovul Mare, Ostrovul Corbului) yielded only quartz and quartzite implements and tools made of polished stone (Mogoşanu 1978; Boroneanţ 1980).

Thus, the end of the Lepenski Vir culture was marked both by extremely archaizing elements (the quartz and quartzite industry) and by elements anticipating the subsequent Neolithic epoch (implements made of polished stone, farming tools made of antler).

THE MONTENEGRO SITES

The Mesolithic culture of Montenegro has many links with the Mesolithic of the Iron Gates region, but its evolution followed a different course. It is also based on the traditions of the local final Palaeolithic culture, which is in many respects similar to the Cuina Turcului culture and to the Mediterranean Epi-Tardigravettian. This is clearly illustrated by the flint industry discovered in the Medena Stijena rock-shelter in the gorge of the Ćehotina river. A culture layer, 1.40 m thick, has been investigated there in the last two years. Although investigations have not been completed yet and not all the necessary analyses have been carried out, we may nevertheless give a preliminary account of the stratigraphy of Medena Stijena and describe the most important archaeological finds from it.

Medena Stijena

Eight culture layers can be clearly distinguished in the Medena Stijena deposit. The first two (I, II) lie directly beneath the surface, and hearths and pottery of the Copper and Early Bronze Ages have been found in them. Layers III–VIII yielded only flint implements and a small quantity of animal bones (*Figs. 3–5*). Layers III and IV were separated from layers V–VIII by a sterile layer 0.25 m thick. Layer III, soft and grey in colour, was certainly formed in the early Holocene; layer IV may also date from that period, although it is closer to layers V–VIII as regards its structure, colour and archaeological material. These layers are reddish in colour and differ only in the quantity of stones, ash and charcoal they contain. All the retouched implements found in layers VIII–IV have almost identical technical and morphological features (*Figs. 3–5*). The most common are end-scrapers, backed blades, backed pieces, isosceles triangles and truncations. It is noticeable, however, that the size of the retouched implements gradually decreases in the later layers; only comparatively large tools were found in layer VIII, while layer IV yielded mainly micro-points and small scrapers. The flint industry from layers VIII–IV may be defined as a whole as Tardigravettian or Epi-Tardigravettian, and it shows close analogies with the flint industry from layers IX–VII of Crvena Stijena (Basler 1975: figs. 9–11). It also has certain similarities with the flint industry from Cuina Turcului I (Păunescu 1970: figs. 3–6). The flint imple-

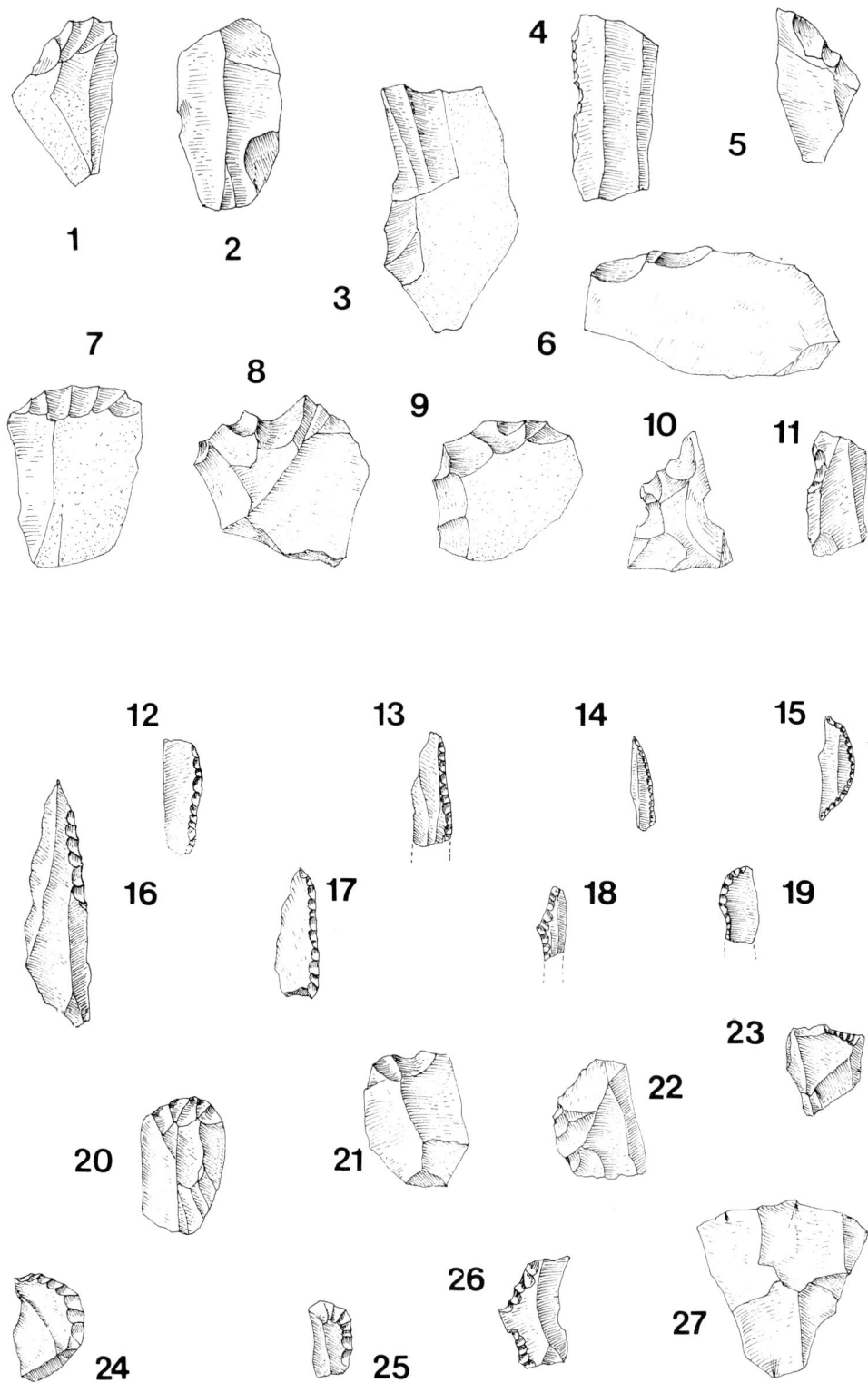

Figure 3 Medena Stijena (Montenegro) rock-shelter: flint industry – layer III (1–11); layer IV (12–27).

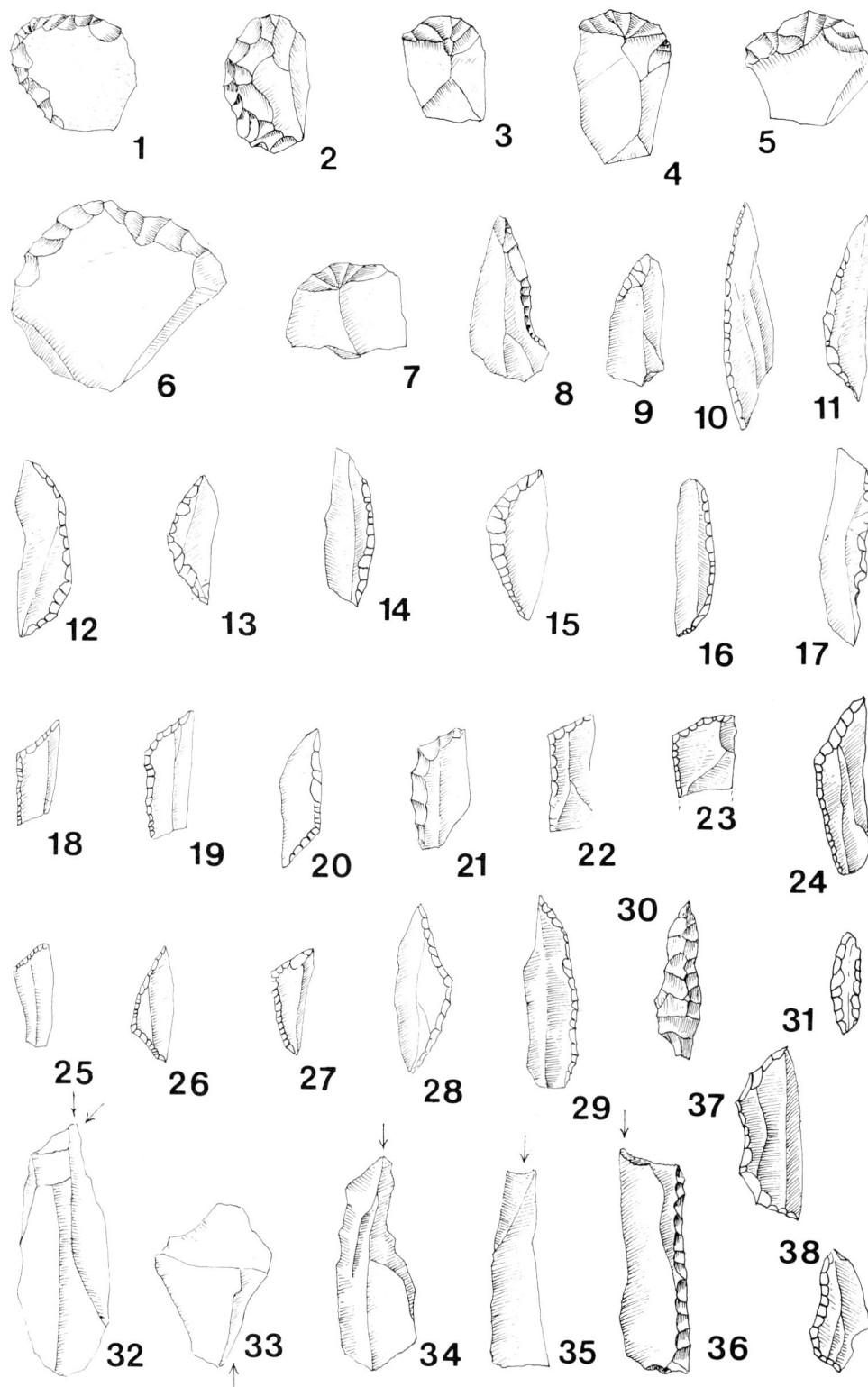

Figure 4 Medena Stijena rock-shelter, layers V and VI: flint industry.

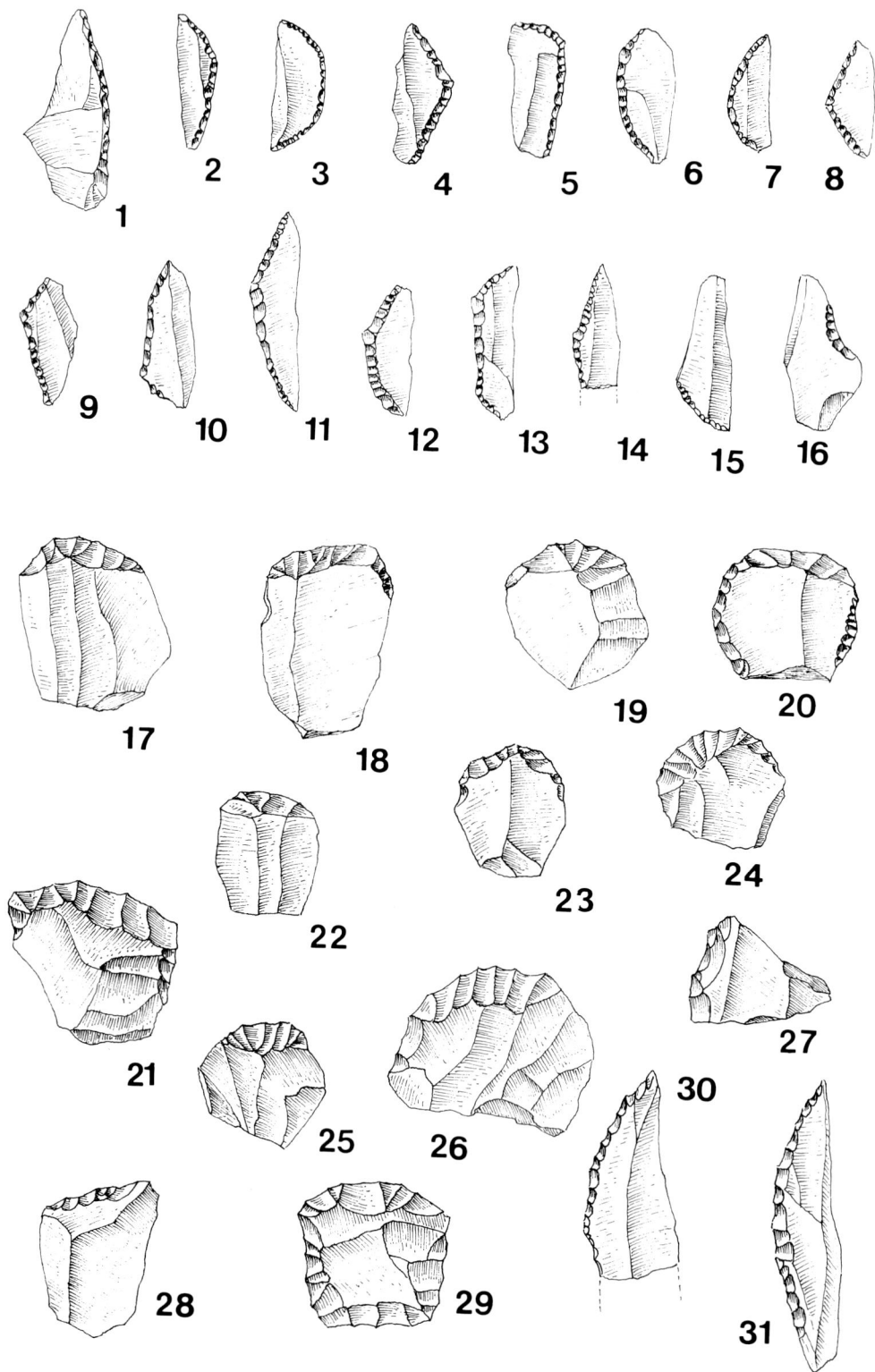

Figure 5 Medena Stijena rock-shelter: flint industry – layer VII (1–16); layer VIII (17–31).

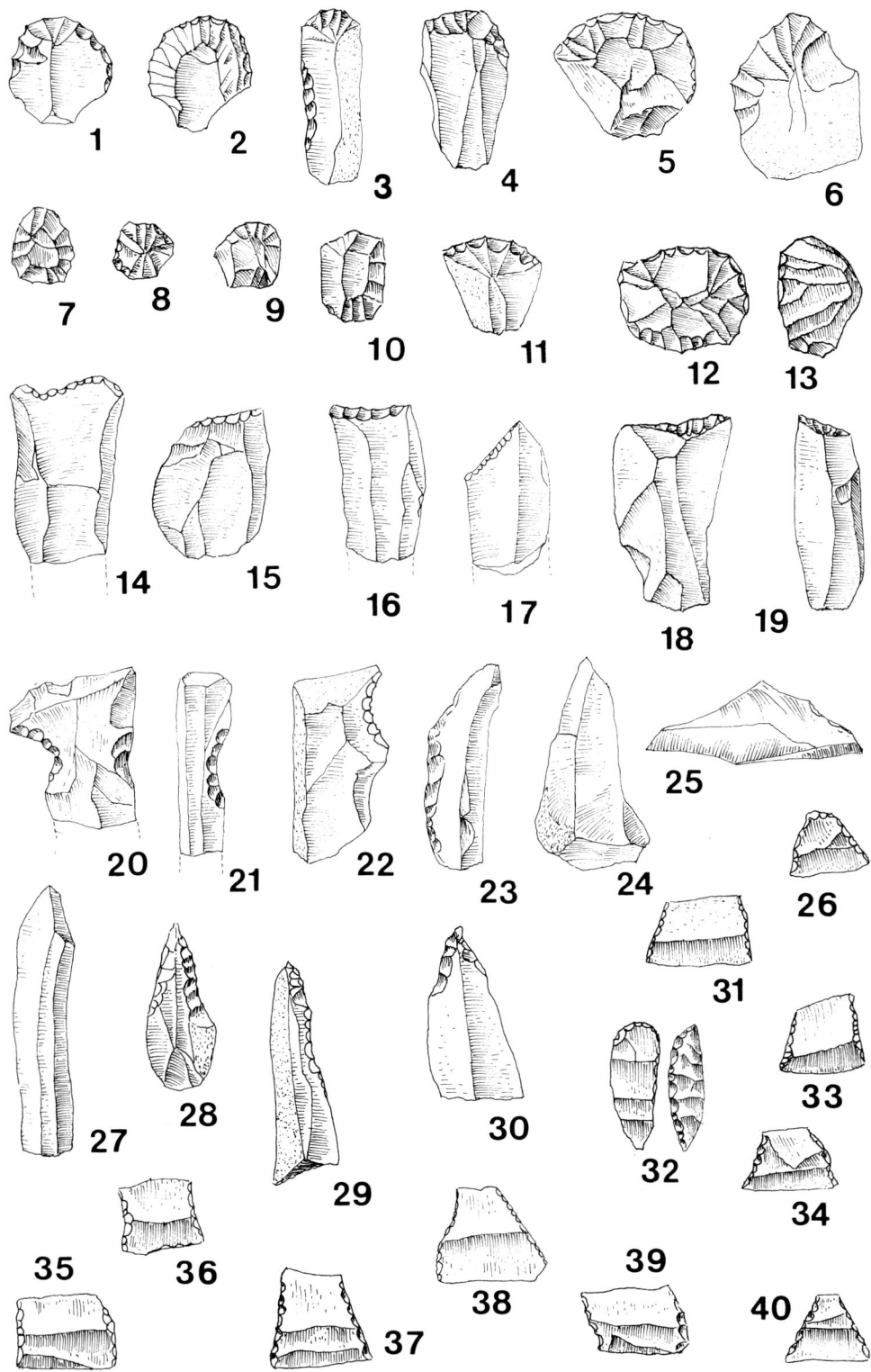

Figure 6 Odmut cave (Montenegro), layer I: flint industry.

ments from layer III are undoubtedly Mesolithic (*Fig. 3*, nos. 1–11). They are based on the local traditions, but show such technological and morphological impoverishment in comparison with the tools from layer IV that they must be separated by a rather wide chronological gap.

Odmut cave

It was precisely during that gap that the Mesolithic deposit in the Odmut cave seems to have been formed.

The Odmut cave is situated in the gorge of the Piva river, at an altitude of 558 m above sea level (*Fig. 1*). A deposit 4 m thick was investigated there and was found to consist of seven culture layers. The earliest of these (Odmut I) contained flint implements, a number of bone harpoons, bone tools and a very large quantity of fish and animal bones, especially those of the ibex (*c.* 65%). The radiocarbon dates show that this layer was formed in the early Holocene, between 10,000 and 7200 BP (Srejović 1974). The next layer (Odmut II) yielded a large number of flint artifacts, but it also contained sherds of early Neolithic ware. This means that the finds from layer I of the Odmut cave represent the Mesolithic of the inland regions of Montenegro.

The largest part of the flint industry of Odmut I consisted of unretouched flakes and unretouched microblades. The most common among the retouched tools were short end-scrapers and burins (*Fig. 6*, nos. 1–13, 24, 25, 27), truncations, notches and geometric microliths (*Fig. 6*, nos. 14–19, 20–22, 26, 31–40), while backed blanks, piercers and points were very rare (*Fig. 6*, nos. 28–30). The flint industry from layers VII–V of Crvena Stijena is very similar (Basler 1975: figs. 6–9) and some of its technical features associate it with the Mesolithic layer D at Sidari (Sordinas 1970: 10–11). A strong Romanellian component is noticeable even in the flint industry from the layers containing early Neolithic ware (Odmut II, Crvena Stijena III).

CONCLUSION

In conclusion, we may say that the Mesolithic cultures of Serbia and Montenegro represent a direct continuation of the local final Palaeolithic cultures (Cuina Turcului I, Medena Stijena VIII–V, Crvena Stijena IX–VIII), which are themselves merely regional variants of the Epi-Tardigravettian. During the Pre-Boreal the existing traditions exercised a very strong influence on the local cultures, and their evolution was uniform. At the beginning of the Boreal a differentiation took place; the culture in the Iron Gates region became progressive and achieved in time almost all the basic innovations of the so-called 'Neolithic Revolution'. The culture in the inland and coastal parts of Montenegro remained, however, unaltered for a long time, and acquired Neolithic features only as a result of external cultural influences.

References

BASLER, D. (1975) Stariji litički periodi u Crvenoj Stijeni. In D. Basler (ed.), *Crvena Stijena*. Nikšić, Zajednica kulturnih ustanova: 11–103.

BENAC, A. (1957) Crvena Stijena. *Glasnik Zemaljskog muzeja u Sarajevu*, 12: 19–50.

BÖKÖNYI, S. (1972) The vertebrate fauna. In D. Srejović, *Europe's First Monumental Sculpture: New Discoveries at Lepenski Vir*. London, Thames and Hudson: 186–189.

BÖKÖNYI, S. (1978) Vlasac und die Fragen der mesolithischen Domestikation. *Mitteilungen des Archäologischen Institut der Ungarischen Akademie der Wissenschaften*, 7: 85–92.

BOLOMEY, A. (1973) An outline of the late Epipalaeolithic economy at the 'Iron Gates': the evidence on bones. *Dacia*, 17: 41–52.

BORONEANȚ, V. (1970) La période épipaléolithique sur la rive roumaine des Portes de Fer du Danube. *Praehistorische Zeitschrift*, 45(1): 1–25.

BORONEANȚ, V. (1973) Recherches archéologiques sur la culture Schela Cladovei de la zone des 'Portes de Fer'. *Dacia*, 17: 5–39.

BORONEANȚ, V. (1980) Probleme ale culturii Schela Cladovei–Lepenski Vir in lumina noilor cercetări. *Drobeta*, 4: 27–42.

BORONEANȚ, V. (1981) Betrachtungen über das Epipaläolithikum (Mesolithikum) in Rumänien. In B. Gramsch (ed.), *Mesolithikum in Europa. 2. Internationales Symposium Potsdam, 3 bis 8 April 1978 Bericht* (Veröffentlichungen des Museums für Ur- und Frühgeschichte Potsdam, 14/15). Berlin, Deutscher Verlag der Wissenschaften: 289–294.

CÂRCIUMARU, M. (1973) Analyse pollinique des coprolithes livrés par quelques stations archéologiques des deux bords du Danube dans la zone des 'Portes de Fer'. *Dacia*, 17: 53–60.

CHILDE, V.G. (1957) *The Dawn of European Civilisation* (6th edition). London, Routledge and Kegan Paul.

CLARKE, D.L. (1976) Mesolithic Europe: the economic basis. In G. de G. Sieveking, I.H. Longworth and K.E. Wilson (eds), *Problems in Economic and Social Archaeology*. London, Duckworth: 449–481.

CLASON, A.T. (1980) Padina and Starčevo: game, fish and cattle. *Palaeohistoria*, 22: 141–173.

GATSOV, I. (1982) The archaeological cultures of the late Pleistocene and early Holocene in the western Black Sea region, and their significance for the formation of the Neolithic flint industries. In J.K. Kozłowski (ed.), *Origin of the Chipped Stone Industries of the Early Farming Cultures in Balkans*. Warsaw–Kraków, Państwowe Wydawnictwo Naukowe: 111–130.

JOVANOVIĆ, B. (1969) Chronological frames of the Iron Gates group of the early Neolithic period. *Archaeologia Iugoslavica*, 10: 23–38.

JOVANOVIĆ, B. (1984a) Padina, naselje mezolita i starijeg neolita. *Starinar*, 33/34: 159–166.

JOVANOVIĆ, B. (1984b) Hajdučka Vodenica, praistorijska nekropola. *Starinar*, 33/34: 305–312.

KOZŁOWSKI, J.K. and KOZŁOWSKI, S.K. (1982) Lithic industries from the multi-layer Mesolithic site Vlasac in Yugoslavia. In J.K. Kozłowski (ed.), *Origin of the Chipped Stone Industries of the Early Farming Cultures in Balkans*. Warsaw–Kraków, Państwowe Wydawnictwo Naukowe: 11–109.

LETICA, Z. (1975) Ensevelissement et les rites funéraires dans la culture de Lepenski Vir. In *Valcamonica Symposium 72 – Les Religions de la Préhistoire*. Capo di Ponte, Edizioni del Centro Camuno di Studi Preistorici: 95–104.

MILOJČIĆ, V. (1949) *Chronologie der jüngeren Steinzeit Mittel- und Südosteuropas*. Berlin, Archäologisches Institut.

MOGOȘANU, F. (1978) Mezoliticul de la Ostrovul Corbului, o noua asezare de tip Schela Cladovei. *Studii și Cercetări de Istorie Veche și Arheologie*, 29(3): 335–351.

NANDRIS, J. (1972) Review of D. Srejović, 'Europe's First Monumental Sculpture: New Discoveries at Lepenski Vir'. *Proceedings of the Prehistoric Society*, 38: 426–429.

NEMESKÉRI, J. (1972) The inhabitants of Lepenski Vir. In D. Srejović, *Europe's First Monumental Sculpture: New Discoveries at Lepenski Vir*. London, Thames and Hudson: 190–204.

NEMESKÉRI, J. and SZATHMÁRY, L. (1978) Taxonomical structure of the Vlasac Mesolithic subpopulation. In D. Srejović and Z. Letica (eds), *Vlasac. Mezolitisko naselje u Djerdapu*, vol. 2. Belgrade, Srpska Akademija Nauka i Umetnosti: 177–184.

NICOLĂESCU-PLOPŞOR, D. (1976) Deux cas de mort violente dans l'Epipaléolithique final de Schela Cladovei. *Annuaire Roumain d'Anthropologie*, 13: 3–5.

PĂUNESCU, A. (1970) Epipaleoliticul de la Cuina Turcului–Dubova. *Studii şi Cercetări de Istorie Veche*, 21(1): 3–47.

PRINZ, B. (1982) *Stone Tools, Cultural Continuity, and Mesolithic Adaptations on the Lower Danube* (Ph.D. thesis, University of Pittsburgh). Ann Arbor, University Microfilms.

RADOVANOVIĆ, I. (1981) *Ranoholocenska kremena industrija sa lokaliteta Padina u Djerdapu*. Belgrade, Arheološki Institut.

SORDINAS, A. (1970) *Stone Implements from Northwestern Corfu, Greece*. Memphis, Memphis State University Anthropological Research Center Occasional Papers 4.

SREJOVIĆ, D. (1969) *Lepenski Vir. Nova praistorijska Kultura u Podunavlju*. Belgrade, Srpska književna zadruga.

SREJOVIĆ, D. (1972a) *Europe's First Monumental Sculpture: New Discoveries at Lepenski Vir*. London, Thames and Hudson.

SREJOVIĆ, D. (1972b) Kulturen des frühen Postglazials im südlichen Donauraum. *Balcanica*, 3: 11–44.

SREJOVIĆ, D. (1974) The Odmut Cave – a new facet of the Mesolithic culture of the Balkan peninsula. *Archaeologia Iugoslavica*, 15: 3–6.

SREJOVIĆ, D. and BABOVIĆ, L. (1981) *Lepenski Vir, Menschenbilder einer frühen europäischen Kultur*. Mainz am Rhein, von Zabern.

SREJOVIĆ, D. and BABOVIĆ, L. (1983) *Umetnost Lepenskog Vira*. Belgrade, Jugoslavija.

SREJOVIĆ, D. and LETICA, Z. (1978) *Vlasac. Mezolitsko naselje u Djerdapu*. Belgrade, Srpska Akademija Nauka i Umetnosti.

TRINGHAM, R. (1971) *Hunters, Fishers and Farmers of Eastern Europe 6000–3000 BC*. London, Hutchinson University Library.

ŽIVANOVIĆ, S. (1975) Mesolithic population in Djerdap. *Balcanica*, 6: 1–10.

Rethinking the Mesolithic: the Case of South-East Europe

Barbara A. Voytek and Ruth Tringham

Abstract

This paper questions a number of preconceptions which have been entertained about Mesolithic hunting-gathering populations, with a specific focus on south-east Europe. It attempts to model the interaction that may have characterized the Iron Gates gorges (the Djerdap) *c.* 7000 BP, when the earliest evidence for food production is known from the area. Two arguments are discussed as possible explanations for the major changes within the Mesolithic society represented by archaeological sites in this region such as Vlasac, Lepenski Vir, Schela Cladovei, and others. The first of the arguments is that the changes were due to the introduction of a food-producing technology by an intrusive population known as the Starčevo-Criş archaeological culture. An alternative argument is made that a complex of factors, including sedentism, food storage and exchange practices, signalled the social transformation of the Mesolithic society. The paper also examines critically the nature of so-called egalitarianism in hunting-gathering populations, including possible bases for social differentiation. In recognizing and accepting organizational variation in hunter-gatherer societies, the aim of the paper is to provide a dynamic view of a population traditionally studied as a static entity.

INTRODUCTION

This paper questions a number of preconceptions which have been entertained about Mesolithic hunting-gathering populations, with a specific focus on south-east Europe. The term 'Mesolithic' is being used here to denote the Postglacial period, during which time the human population of Europe was engaged in hunting-gathering or foraging subsistence practices. We shall be considering the nature of socio-economic changes which characterize Mesolithic society just prior to the evidence for food production in south-east Europe and how these changes may have contributed to the acceptance and spread of food-producing techniques and practices, especially animal domestication.

Traditionally, it was believed that there had been little contact between the indigenous hunter-gatherers in south-east Europe and the intrusive food producers who brought with them knowledge of ceramic manufacture, domesticated sheep and goat, and domesticated wheat and barley (Tringham 1971). Also part of the traditional view was the belief that the indigenous population had eventually been assimilated by the food producers or, in some cases, forcibly eradicated (Jovanović 1969; Mogoşanu 1978;

Boroneanţ 1980). In spite of the fact that data to disprove these theories are still preliminary, there is growing scepticism that the intrusive food producers had entered an empty landscape with no contacts with the indigenous population (Nandris 1971; Dennell 1983; Tringham, forthcoming). One of the major problems with the older view is that it assumes that the indigenous populations were both passive and static, almost incapable of socio-economic or cultural change until effected by an intrusive group with a different economic base.

The traditional view of what is commonly called the 'neolithization' of hunting-gathering societies in south-east Europe is thus now being questioned. This paper is an attempt to model the interaction that may have characterized one region of south-east Europe *c.* 7000 BP, when the earliest evidence for food production is known from the area. The model is also applicable and testable in other hypothetical contact situations between hunter-gatherers and food producers in Europe. The paper discusses two alternative arguments for the major changes within the society represented by archaeological sites in the Iron Gates gorges (the Djerdap). The first argument is that the introduction of a food-producing technology was responsible. An alternative claim is that a complex of factors, including increased sedentism, food storage and exchange practices, signalled the social transformation of the Mesolithic society. The paper also critically examines the nature of so-called egalitarianism in hunting-gathering populations, including the question of differential access to resources. The aim of the paper is to provide a dynamic view of a population traditionally studied as a static entity.

ARCHAEOLOGICAL BACKGROUND

Before elaborating on the model of neolithization to be presented here, we might consider the geographic area in question. V. Gordon Childe in the most recent edition of *The Dawn of European Civilisation* suggested that in the Balkan peninsula and along the lower Danube, a Mesolithic population 'might be postulated to explain peculiarities in the local Neo-lithic culture' (Childe 1957: 84). However, although Childe had been aware of the importance of the interaction of Mesolithic and Neolithic populations in prehistoric Europe, he wrote relatively little on the subject. In *The Danube in Prehistory* he noted the probability of persistent groups of hunters after the glacial period in some areas, who would have accepted food production when they contacted Neolithic peoples and would 'multiply rapidly and exercise a decisive influence on the subsequent development of civilization' (Childe 1929: 20–21). Specific to the Danube region, Childe noted the survival of 'epipalaeolithic elements' which had given the Danubian culture an 'individuality of its own' (Childe 1929: 414). Subsequent to Childe's work, there were arguments against interaction between the indigenous hunter-gatherers and the food producers, mainly due to a lack of substantive data with which to prove co-existence (Tringham 1968, 1973).

In the 1960s the Yugoslav and Romanian govern-ments began construction of a dam in the area of the Iron Gates gorge (the Djerdap) which was completed in 1971. A number of settlements based on hunting, gathering and fishing were uncovered and excavated on both sides of the Danube (*Fig. 1*). The Djerdap itself represents a number of micro-zones whose climatic conditions vary according to altitude and location within the gorges. Post-Pleistocene environ-mental changes had not been radical and the climate had been relatively stable. Vegetational diversity in a relatively small area can be noted, including mixed-oak forest, beech, walnut and hackberry, and abundant river resources (Srejović 1969, 1972; Prinz 1982).

The Mesolithic occupation

Structural remains, stone tools and facilities, and faunal data from the sites in the Djerdap suggest at least semi-sedentary or possibly year-round perm-anent settlement based on hunting, fishing and gathering. The quantity of cultural debris from Vlasac II, for example, suggests to some researchers that this site represents a permanent settlement (Srejović 1969, 1972; Prinz 1982). In levels II and III there are a variety of stone structures – some are possible dwellings while others may represent the remains of storage, perhaps for smoked fish. Similar claims have been made for Lepenski Vir (Tringham 1971). Large stone hearths found in Padina A follow the same rectangular pattern of construction (Jovan-ović 1969). The Romanian sites present a similar pattern in terms of hearth types and the heavy use of stone to suggest permanent settlement (Păunescu 1970, 1978; Mogoşanu 1978; Boroneanţ 1980).

Stone rings which have been interpreted as tent rings have been found at Vlasac (Prinz 1982). Lack of dwelling debris or evidence for fires within the rings may suggest that they represent remains of shelters for food-processing activities such as wild seed removal. A number of pounders and mortars found at Lepenski Vir and Padina have been interpreted as clubs and altars (Srejović 1969, 1972).

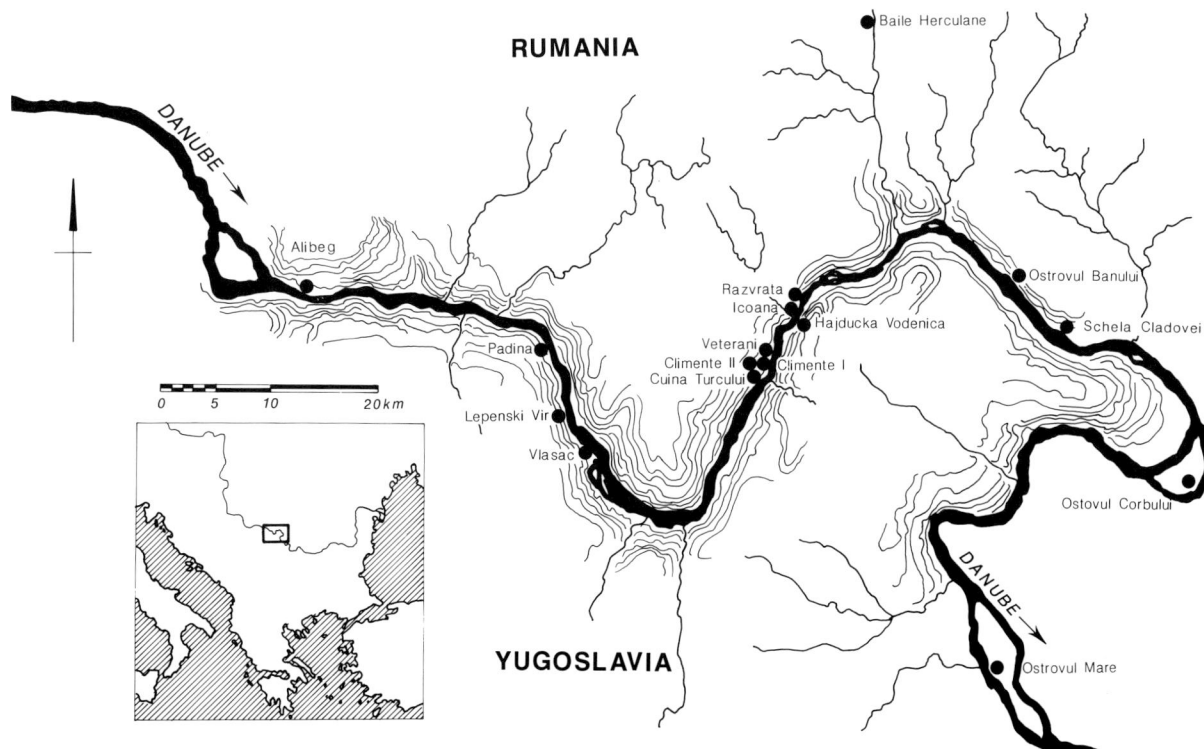

Figure 1   Map of the Djerdap (Iron Gates gorge).

493

At least some of these artifacts may have been used for grinding and/or pounding of foodstuffs such as seeds and nuts, which is suggested by the wear patterns on the stone implements. The exploitation of plant foods has been suggested by a number of other sources – for example, in terms of the antler tools found at Vlasac which appear to have been used in working the soil (Letica 1969). In addition, pollen analysis of coprolites from Vlasac and Icoana shows Gramineae of cereal type (Cărciumaru 1973). Finally, dental studies indicate that plant foods played an important part in the diet of the Mesolithic occupants at some of the sites (y'Edynak 1978; Boroneanţ 1980; y'Edynak and Fleisch 1983).

Faunal data such as those from Icoana support the theory of year-round occupation. Fishing had been the base of subsistence at most of the sites, but there is also evidence for pig and deer, wild ox and other animals, including wild cat, badger, and lynx. There is some evidence for early domestication of dog at Vlasac and at Lepenski Vir, and possibly of pig at Icoana (Letica 1969; Srejović 1969, 1972; Bolomey 1973). In brief, although the subsistence data from the Djerdap sites are not sufficient to *prove* year-round occupation of the sites, the studies do suggest that the wide range of locally available resources could have supported the settlements on at least a semi-permanent basis. Furthermore, as mentioned, there is some evidence for possible storage facilities which could have helped to accommodate and encourage a sedentary lifestyle.

The use of rock resources reflects a permanence of residence and an intensive use of local resources (Voytek 1985). Obsidian *had* been used by the earlier Epi-Palaeolithic populations at sites such as Ostrovul Banului I, Cuina Turcului I and Băile Herculane. However, its usage declined in the later occupation levels. In addition, the Epi-Palaeolithic sites and occupation horizons have few, if any, tools made from local quartz and/or quartzite (Boroneanţ 1981). However, chronologically later sites and levels (which date after *c.* 8000 BP) have rich quartz and/or quartzite industries (Radovanović 1981; Prinz 1982). These include the sites of Vlasac III, Icoana II, Răzvrata, Ostrovul Banului III, Schela Cladovei II, Alibeg, Lepenski Vir, and Ostrovul Mare (*Table 1*).

There are at least two possible explanations for the change in the use of rock resources: (a) there was no longer a reliance on pooling within a larger population which could have brought in the distant stone and/or other materials and resources to supplement local subsistence strategies (Wiessner 1982); or (b) long-range foraging practices had ceased and only local materials were being exploited (Boroneanţ 1981; Ambrose, n.d.).

These possible explanations are not mutually

Table 1: General chronology of the Djerdap (after Bolomey 1973; Prinz 1982; Tringham, forthcoming)

Stage	Sites	^{14}C dates BP
EARLY NEOLITHIC	Vlasac IV Lepenski Vir IIIb Cuina Turcului III Schela Cladovei III Icoana III Ostrovul Banului IV	
7000 BP		
TRANSITIONAL EARLY NEOLITHIC/ LATE MESOLITHIC	Alibeg Ostrovul Mare III Lepenski Vir IIIa Padina B	7195±100
7500 BP		
LATER MESOLITHIC	Vlasac II & III Lepenski Vir I & II Padina A Ostrovul Corbului III Răzvatra II Schela Cladovei II Ostrovul Banului IIIb Icoana II	7475±100 7565±100
8000 BP		
EARLIER MESOLITHIC	Vlasac I Ostrovul Banului IIIa Veterani Terasă Răzvrata I Icoana I Schela Cladovei I Pestera Veterani	8040±160 8265±100
8500 BP		
POST-PLEISTOCENE	Cuina Turcului II Băile Herculane II Ostrovul Banului II	10,125±200
TERMINAL PLEISTOCENE	Climente II Ostrovul Banului I Cuina Turcului I Băile Herculane I	 12,600±120

exclusive. The former deals with the indirect procurement of resources through some form of exchange, while the latter explanation deals with resources that are acquired directly. All that can really be said at this time is that there was a progressive decline in the exploitation of long-distance rock resources and an increase in local resource exploitation (either directly or through exchange with neighbouring peoples) during the Mesolithic in the Iron Gates.

Early Neolithic occupation

During a period dating roughly between 7500 and 6500 BP, there is evidence for changes in the material culture and, to some extent, in the subsistence base of sites in the Djerdap as well as other parts of the Danube basin (e.g. sites in the outlying zones of the Iron Gates such as those of Pojejena-Moldova, Gornea-Liubcova, Orsova, Gura Baciului, Cîrcea, Donja Branjevina, Kozluk, and others – Lazarovici 1979: 28). For example, no domestic animal remains (aside from dog) are found at Lepenski Vir until level III. Then an increase occurs in the proportion of both wild and domestic cattle, although wild fauna in general continues to dominate (Srejović 1972: 187).

In level III at Lepenski Vir, attempts at domestication had received new impetus at the time of other changes in resource use. All the stone at Lepenski Vir had been local until III. In the later building phase of IIIa, there is an influx of non-local stone including beads of azurite and malachite, as well as shoe-last axes of andesite. These new materials are not exclusive – local stone continues to be used, including sandstone and quartz.

During IIIb at Lepenski Vir, there is a firm association of pottery and domestic animal remains. A new axe form – a small trapeze of a classic early Neolithic type – is found made in serpentinite. This type of rock had not been found in the earlier levels. The axes were found within a ceramic vessel, suggesting perhaps a cache or storage. Also uncovered within two separate pots were pieces of chert. A number of large blades and flakes of a waxy, yellow chert with white inclusions were found in one pot, and in the other, cores of the same chert (Srejović 1969, 1972). Again, this type of raw material is not known from the earlier occupations. It was also found in Neolithic levels at the sites of Padina B and Cuina Turcului III as well as other early Neolithic sites in Romania, such as Cîrcea (Radovanović 1981; Voytek 1985). In addition, obsidian appears for the first time in level III of Lepenski Vir (Srejović 1972: 145). Other evidence for possible exchange in distant goods includes pottery forms and shells (Srejović 1972: 147–148).

At the site of Padina, the early Neolithic occupation (Padina B) has some similarities with the earlier levels of Padina A, namely, the architecture and the bone tool industry (Jovanović 1969). As mentioned, in Padina B a new type of chert had been introduced. The differences between the Mesolithic and Neolithic occupations at the Romanian sites are not very clear. The early Neolithic horizons appear to be well-developed, later stages of the early Neolithic archaeological culture, Starčevo-Criş. At Cuina Turcului, there is a sterile layer separating the latest Mesolithic layer and the Neolithic Starčevo layer, suggesting that some time had passed between occupations (Păunescu 1978). At other sites, evidence of possible violence has been noted in the burial remains and has been interpreted as violent confrontations between the indigenous and intrusive populations (Mogoşanu 1978; Boroneanţ 1980). It is clear from the literature that the stone industry does change, although it is not clear whether the changes are due largely to new raw materials. For example, obsidian use increases proportionately with the appearance of the food producers, as was the case at Lepenski Vir (Păunescu 1978).

The nature of the early Neolithic settlement reflected by sites such as Lepenski Vir III, Padina B, Alibeg, Cuina Turcului II, Schela Cladovei III, Climente Pestera, Ostrovul Golu I/II is still open to question (Lazarovici 1979). The early Neolithic archaeological culture assigned to the appearance of food-producing techniques and a particular material culture, including ceramics, in this region is the Starčevo-Criş culture. Because of the complexity of the Mesolithic society in the Djerdap (suggested by the structural remains, attempts at animal domestication, etc.), the relationship between this society and the bearers of the Starčevo-Criş culture has been difficult to explain. Labels such as 'Proto-Starčevo' have been considered for the situation in the Djerdap in which the evidence suggests more than a simple replacement by a new cultural group. It is in such situations that we would offer the model outlined below in which the presence of new materials, such as ceramics and some lithic materials, is examined in a framework different from that of cultural replacement. The model suggests that the indigenous population did interact with an intrusive group of people who practised a different economy and that there was a period of co-existence. Furthermore, during this period, some exchange of goods and services occurred which helped to maintain the co-existence but, at the same time, helped to bring about changes in both societies.

MODELLING MESOLITHIC TRANSFORMATION

The model to be discussed in reference to the Mesolithic and the inherent changes of Mesolithic society in south-east Europe has three principal components – sedentism, food storage, and exchange.

Sedentism

David Harris (1977a, 1977b) has argued for population increase following on sedentism and leading to social differentiation. The process which he and others have discussed is not necessarily one of linear evolution. To understand the process, we have to ask the question: why does sedentism occur, and how does one study it? Some work on this question has been done in ethnographic situations (e.g. Hitchcock 1982). The results suggest that in contemporary situations sedentism is usually *not* voluntary – encompassing forced sedentism or involving circumscribed territories (Hitchcock 1982; Price and Brown 1985: 10–12).

Archaeologists have also addressed the problem of studying sedentism. It is becoming more and more apparent that the consequences of 'settling down' are among the most important and, in many cases, least reversible in the growth and development of a society (Kaiser and Voytek 1983; Brown 1985; Tringham, forthcoming). It is also becoming increasingly apparent that a single causal factor for reduced mobility cannot be cited for all instances where this process appears to be in evidence (Brown 1985: 205). Understanding the process of reduced residential mobility or increased sedentism is perhaps one of the greatest challenges at present for archaeologists. In an archaeological perspective, such a process would have been gradual, slow, and uneven. One can theoretically envision the process as involving a decrease of residential mobility for combined reasons of demography, economics and social relations – culminating, in some instances, in permanent settlement. Such a process, extending over hundreds of years, is an elusive topic. One must adopt an historical approach in which to consider the effects of reduced mobility on the interactions between individuals, socio-cultural practices, resource use and availability, environment, and so forth. A recent attempt by Brown is an example of a similar approach – at least insofar as it is contrasted with 'general systems' approaches – done within the framework of optimal foraging strategy (Brown 1985: 206).

The physical remains which are available for the study of sedentism in prehistory include permanent structures, evidence for population growth and/or environmental conditions and change, differentiation of settlements, features, and so forth. Because of the provisioning risks involved in subsistence strategies based on reduced mobility, food storage, to reduce the risks, is also considered possible evidence for permanent or semi-permanent settlement.

Food storage/food processing

Among the material remains which are considered workable data for studying sedentism are those which reflect food storage and permanent facilities for food processing (Brown 1985; Bender 1985a). Food storage and food processing can be considered technological innovations which facilitate a sedentary lifestyle. However, as with other technological systems, they occur within a social context and their development can have important social repercussions. In our model, food storage and food processing are regarded as means by which the returns from production are delayed, as opposed to immediate returns (Woodburn 1982).

Recently, arguments have been advanced, mainly by Testart (1982), that food storage, which can accompany and in fact encourage sedentism, provides a base for the development of social differentiation and inequality. It can also be argued, however, that food storage mainly strengthens a tendency toward inequality which is latent within every society, no matter what its subsistence base (Beteille 1981).

In a 1982 article, Woodburn considers the fact that there are many hunting-gathering societies with social systems in which there is a marked inequality and that groups such as the Hadza and the !Kung distinguish themselves by their efforts to restrict or eliminate inequality or, at least, tendencies toward inequality. The subsistence system of these groups may be described as being one of 'immediate returns' and includes such practices as food sharing, restricted hoarding, and so forth.

Other groups follow a system of 'delayed returns' (Woodburn 1982). Within delayed-return systems, rights can be held over valued assets of some sort which present a delayed yield or return for labour applied over time. Alternatively, if not actually a matter of rights, then assets are held and managed in a way which resembles and has similar social implications to delayed yields on labour. Food storage fits within the system of delayed returns. Some of the assets in question include technical facilities, processed/stored foods or materials usually in fixed dwellings, wild products which have been improved or increased by human labour, and assets in the form of rights held by men over female kin (Meillassoux 1982; Bender 1985a).

Along these lines, domestication as well as food storage, as a means of ensuring a renewable source of animal products, would have entailed a change in social structure to allow some households or units the keeping of, and access to, domestic stock and products, and to accommodate the fact that the knowledge of domestication would not have been distributed evenly among the population (Meadows 1983). These practices, in effect, signal a break in the pattern of apparent egalitarianism and a change in the social relations which structure productive forces. Unequal access to knowledge combines with unequal access to goods. Temporary leadership positions are then strengthened and extended to other areas within the society, including exchange (Bender 1985b).

Exchange

Having discussed the elements of sedentism and storage and their consequences on the Mesolithic society, we should now consider the last element of our model, namely, exchange. The type of exchange discussed here is specifically that which can occur between hunter-gatherers and food producers. It is realized that exchange and alliance networks had probably characterized the Mesolithic society of south-east Europe before the arrival of an intrusive population and/or a new economy. However, we would argue that the inter-societal exchange with the new peoples would have had a different dimension and would have provided yet another arena for social differentiation and socio-economic change (Gardner 1972). One example of hunter-gatherer/

agriculturalist exchange was presented by Jean Peterson in her work in the Philippines. Her study dealt with exchange between the Palanan, a food-producing group, and the Agta, hunter-gatherers (Peterson 1978). Items exchanged include non-domestic protein for domestic carbohydrates and natural products (such as honey and rope) for trade goods. In addition, the Palanan achieve access to cleared land (cleared by the Agta) and access to labour for future clearing, harvesting and/or planting.

The food exchange between the Agta and Palanan is economically rational. The hunter-gatherers receive a dependable carbohydrate source with little direct labour, while the food producers receive non-domestic protein. One important point is that the resource exploitation system in which these two groups participate could be upset if, for example, the Agta intensify their land use in an attempt to derive more returns from their own production. At present, they cultivate small swidden plots, abandoning them after two or three years. The Palanan, on the other hand, clear plots for intended permanent cultivation.

If the Agta were to change their subsistence strategy and engage in permanent cultivation, two outcomes may be postulated. First, such cultivation would interfere with their hunting practices. Secondly, it would put them into direct competition with the Palanan for land. The Palanan, in turn, require access to this land. In effect, by maintaining their demand for the wild meat and fish protein which they obtain from the Agta, the Palanan help ensure that access to the land and provide a constant 'market' for the Agta hunting. In sum, the exchange of domestic and non-domestic subsistence resources represents more than just dietary satisfaction or a means of redistributing diverse resources. It maintains the social reproduction of each society and is part of the reason co-existence occurs.

Another factor that helps maintain the exchange between these peoples is the institution known as the 'ibay'. The 'ibay' mediates exchange between the Agta and Palanan. 'Ibay' relationships exist between individuals in each of the two groups. In fact, the 'ibay' is an alliance that serves as a basic institution for exchange. Even when the demand for these goods and services is not immediate, the 'ibay' contract for future exchanges on almost a credit basis. If all exchange transactions were to become concentrated within the 'ibay', which is currently not the case, the social position of the individuals in the 'ibay' may change. That is, a change would occur in the social relations of production, with the 'ibay' fulfilling an important function within the society.

Admittedly, such future development can be only speculation at this point. However, there are other hunter-gatherer and farmer exchange systems through which individuals have acquired certain positions of leadership. The Birhors of central India, for example, are involved in inter-tribal trade with food producers (Sinha 1972). Within the minimal socio-economic unit of this group (the 'tanda'), positions of leadership are found. Such positions are considered to be rare in hunting-gathering groups. The role of these leaders in the trading systems is not explained in the literature, but is compared with that of the Mistassini Cree. Among the Cree, strong leadership patterns developed in well-defined hunting territories and allied with trading camps as fur trade became a major part of their subsistence strategy. Thus, changes within the Cree social structure have been linked to contact with Europeans who had provided the impetus for the trade (Rogers 1972).

Although these few examples do not obviously create a cause-and-effect relationship between exchange systems and the development of a social institution to organize that system, they do suggest that the two may be related in some way. At least, they suggest the possibility of change within the social structure, given exchange or trade practices with groups that are external to the society (Gardner 1972; Morris 1982).

Other ethnographic accounts of inter-societal exchange indicate that exchange in certain commodities can lead to situations in which the commodities or materials become less accessible to all members of the community because of differences in labour input, capacity and control. By definition, the community thus becomes less egalitarian (Fried 1960). The commodities in question are produced by a limited number of families or individuals and the returns are used exclusively by the production unit without sharing with the larger social unit (the band or tribe). One example of such 'private' production among a group of hunter-gatherers is the fur trade in eastern Canada. Another example is found in southern Africa where the Okiek produce honey on an individual household basis. The households do not share the returns from the production of this commodity, although they do share in other activities. Exchange such as this not only threatens egalitarianism in resource access, but also tends to weaken collective arrangements among foragers. The result can lead to individualization of the economic unit, breakdown of the band organization, and a change in the social structure of the foragers (Peterson 1978; Leacock and Lee 1982).

CONCLUSION

In brief, the model which is being suggested for the Djerdap combines the three factors of sedentism, food storage and exchange, as discussed above. The archaeological evidence does suggest that the indigenous hunter-gatherers in the Djerdap had become less mobile and that this process was accompanied by an intensified use of local resources for tools and food, as well as the development of storage techniques and facilities. Domestication of the dog and possibly pig also occurred during this period of *c.* 8000 BP. The permanent facilities for acquiring resources and storing them, as well as the techniques of animal-keeping could have become foci of control by individuals – perhaps the heads of households – and the bases for social differentiation. Thus, we would argue that the social structure of the indigenous hunter-gatherers of the Djerdap had already been in a state of changing, transforming in a way that would accommodate and encourage co-existence and exchange between the indigenous population and the intrusive food producers known as the Starčevo-Criş archaeological culture. During the period *c.* 7500–6500 BP, the food producers accelerated the processes of change which had already begun and helped to bring about the resolution of internal contradictions within the Mesolithic society itself.

The exchange which we have postulated between the hunter-gatherers and the agriculturalists would have played a major role in the socio-economic transformation witnessed in the Djerdap. New stone products and materials were involved as well as new subsistence goods. It is possible that the ceramic vessels in which the stone had been found were part of the exchange transactions. Other ceramics may also represent exchange activities rather than on-site manufacture, a theory which could be tested with more detailed analyses of the ceramics and ceramic technology. Moreover, the food producers would have benefited from the exchange, receiving non-domestic protein from the hunter-gatherers as well as services, especially labour. As mentioned earlier, the nature of the intrusive food producers and their organization is still to be understood. At least from some sites in the Djerdap, we know that their diet was not completely different from that of the indigenous population (Necrasov 1961; Clason 1980; y'Edynak and Fleisch 1983). As we have suggested, the exchange would have afforded new roles in both societies, strengthening and confirming emergent social differentiation. The acts of controlling the exchange, maintaining it, and leading negotiations with the other group would sustain and confirm status positions. In addition, the exchange activities working together with the elements of food storage would help strengthen the productive individuality of the household unit under a particular head.

While the evidence for exchange can be examined with the archaeological record, the changes in the two societies in question must be studied mainly in terms of the subsequent developments in the region. Among these is abandonment during the Neolithic period of the Djerdap which, although to some extent suitable for early Neolithic agriculture with tillable land and river communication, was also a circumscribed region. The limited land area could not accommodate intensification of economic production and population growth which accompanied the increasingly sedentary indigenous population and the interaction of that population with the intrusive food producers (Tringham, forthcoming). It is feasible that even without the contact with the Starčevo-Criş archaeological culture, however, there would have been an end to the way of life of the hunter-gatherers along the Danube, as represented by sites such as Vlasac and Lepenski Vir I–II.

Developments elsewhere along the Danube suggest that the interaction of the hunter-gatherers and the agriculturalists had lasting effects and played a major role in the distribution and spread of food production in south-east and central Europe. This base must be considered part of the historical trajectory of subsequent Neolithic archaeological cultures known as the Linear Pottery and the Vinča cultures.

To conclude, we would argue that the nature of the Mesolithic structure in the Djerdap was such that the introduction of food production did not in itself effect major changes. The greater changes in the mode of production had occurred prior to that time. The power of the apparently egalitarian collective had already begun to disperse among the individual households and heads, perhaps with some having obtained the level of status represented in the ritual remains seen at Lepenski Vir. The social relations of production which were dynamically transforming in the Djerdap helped the spread of food production in the Danube basin by providing a structure in which this economy could operate. The situation was thus not one of violent replacement but of internal structural change.

References

AMBROSE, S. (n.d.) Optimal foraging strategies in different climates in the Middle Stone Age of Southern Africa. *Unpublished manuscript.*

BENDER, B. (1985a) Emergent tribal formations in the American Midcontinent. *American Antiquity*, 50: 52–62.

BENDER, B. (1985b) Prehistoric developments in the American Midcontinent and in Brittany, northwest France. In T.D. Price and J.A. Brown (eds), *Prehistoric Hunter-Gatherers: the Emergence of Cultural Complexity*. New York, Academic Press: 21–57.

BETEILLE, A. (1981) The idea of natural inequality. In G. Berreman (ed.), *Social Inequality*. New York, Academic Press: 59–80.

BOLOMEY, A. (1973) An outline of the late Epipalaeolithic economy at the 'Iron Gates': the evidence on bones. *Dacia*, 17: 41–52.

BORONEANŢ, V. (1980) Probleme ale culturii Schela Cladovei–Lepenski Vir în lumina noilor cercetări. *Drobeta*, 4: 27–42.

BORONEANŢ, V. (1981) Betrachtungen über das Epipaläolithikum (Mesolithikum) in Rumänien. In B. Gramsch (ed.), *Mesolithikum in Europa. 2. Internationales Symposium, Potsdam 3 bis 8 April 1978* (Veröffentlichungen des Museum für Ur- and Frühgeschichte Potsdam, 14/15). Berlin, Deutscher Verlag der Wissenschaften: 289–294.

BROWN, J.A. (1985) Long-term trends to sedentism and the emergence of complexity in the American Midwest. In T.D.

Price and J.A. Brown (eds), *Prehistoric Hunter-Gatherers: the Emergence of Cultural Complexity*. New York, Academic Press: 201–234.

CĂRCIUMARU, M. (1973) Analyse pollinique des coprolithes livrés par quelques stations archéologiques des deux bords du Danube dans la zone des 'Portes de Fer'. *Dacia*, 17: 53–60.

CHILDE, V.G. (1929) *The Danube in Prehistory*. Oxford, Clarendon Press.

CHILDE, V.G. (1957) *The Dawn of European Civilisation* (6th edition). London, Routledge and Kegan Paul.

CLASON, A.T. (1980) Padina and Starčevo: game, fish and cattle. *Palaeohistoria*, 22: 141–173.

DENNELL, R. (1983) *European Economic Prehistory: a New Approach*. New York, Academic Press.

Y'EDYNAK, G.J. (1978) Culture, diet and dental reduction in Mesolithic forager-fishers of Yugoslavia. *Current Anthropology*, 19(3): 616–618.

Y'EDYNAK, G.J. and FLEISCH, S. (1983) Microevolution and biological adaptability in the transition from food-collecting to food-producing in the Iron Gates of Yugoslavia. *Journal of Human Evolution*, 12: 279–296.

FRIED, M. (1960) On the evolution of social stratification and the state. In S. Diamond (ed.), *Culture in History*. New York, Columbia University Press: 713–731.

GARDNER, P.M. (1972) The Paliyans. In M.G. Bicchieri (ed.), *Hunters and Gatherers Today*. New York, Holt, Rinehart and Winston: 404–450.

HARRIS, D. (1977a) Alternative pathways towards agriculture. In C.A. Reed (ed.), *Origins of Agriculture*. The Hague, Mouton: 179–243.

HARRIS, D. (1977b) Settling down: an evolutionary model of the transformation of mobile bands into sedentary communities. In J. Friedman and M. Rowlands (eds), *The Evolution of Social Systems*. London, Duckworth: 401–417.

HITCHCOCK, R. (1982) Patterns of sedentism among the Basarwa of eastern Botswana. In E. Leacock and R. Lee (eds), *Politics and History in Band Societies*. Cambridge, University Press: 223–267.

JOVANOVIĆ, B. (1969) Chronological frames of the Iron Gates group of the early Neolithic period. *Archaeologia Iugoslavica*, 10: 23–38.

KAISER, T. and VOYTEK, B. (1983) Sedentism and economic change in the Balkan Neolithic. *Journal of Anthropological Archaeology*, 2: 323–353.

LAZAROVICI, G. (1979) Die Starčevo-Criş-Kultur (Allgemeine Fragen). *Studii şi Comunicari de Istorie* (Caransebes): 27–31.

LEACOCK, E. and LEE, R. (eds) (1982) *Politics and History in Band Societies*. Cambridge, University Press.

LETICA, Z. (1969) Vlasac – nouvel habitat de la culture de Lepenski Vir. *Archaeologia Iugoslavia*, 10: 7–11.

MEADOWS, R. (1983) Animal domestication in the Middle East: a view from the eastern margin. *Paper presented at the 4th International Conference on Archaeozoology, Oxford*.

MEILLASSOUX, C. (1982) *Femmes, Greniers et Capitaux*. Paris, François Maspero.

MOGOŞANU, F. (1978) Mezoliticul de la Ostrovul Corbului, o noua asezare de tip Schela Cladovei. *Studii şi Cercetări de Istorie Veche şi Arheologie*, 29(3): 335–351.

MORRIS, B. (1982) *Forest Traders: a Socio-Economic Study of the Hill Pandaram*. New Jersey, Humanities Press.

NANDRIS, J. (1971) Relations between the Mesolithic, the First Temperate Neolithic, and the Bandkeramik: the nature of the problem. *Akten der Pannonien Konferenzen I, 1970* (Alba Regia, 12). Székesfehérvár, István Király Muzeúm Évkönyve: 61–69.

NECRASOV, O. (1961) Study of wild and domestic fauna of the early Neolithic Criş culture. *Analele Stiintifice* (Iaşi), 7: 265–274.

PĂUNESCU, A. (1970) Epipaleoliticul de la Cuina Turcului-Dubova. *Studii şi Cercetări de Istorie Veche*, 21(1): 3–47.

PĂUNESCU, A. (1978) Cercetările arheologice de la Cuina Turcului-Dubova (jud. Mehedinti). *Tibiscus Istorie* (Timisoara), 7: 11–56.

PETERSON, J.T. (1978) Hunter-gatherer/farmer exchange. *American Anthropologist*, 80: 335–349.

PRICE, T.D. and BROWN, J.A. (eds) (1985) *Prehistoric Hunter-Gatherers: the Emergence of Cultural Complexity*. New York, Academic Press.

PRINZ, B. (1982) *Stone Tools, Cultural Continuity, and Mesolithic Adaptations on the Lower Danube* (Ph.D. thesis, University of Pittsburgh). Ann Arbor, University Microfilms.

RADOVANOVIĆ, I. (1981) *Ranoholocenska kremena industrija sa lokaliteta Padina u Djerdapu*. Belgrade, Arheološki Institut.

ROGERS, E.S. (1972) The Misatassini Cree. In M.G. Bicchieri (ed.), *Hunters and Gatherers Today*. New York, Holt, Rinehart and Winston: 90–137.

SINHA, D.P. (1972) The Birhors. In M.G. Bicchieri (ed.), *Hunters and Gatherers Today*. New York, Holt, Rinehart and Winston: 371–403.

SREJOVIĆ, D. (1969) *Lepenski Vir. Nova praistorijska Kultura u Podunavlju*. Belgrade, Srpska književna zadruga.

SREJOVIĆ, D. (1972) *Europe's First Monumental Sculpture: New Discoveries at Lepenski Vir*. London, Thames and Hudson.

TESTART, A. (1982) *Les Chasseurs-Cueilleurs ou l'Origine des Inéqalités*. Paris, Société d'Ethnographie.

TRINGHAM, R.E. (1968) A preliminary study of the early Neolithic and latest Mesolithic blade industries in south-east and central Europe. In J.M. Coles and D.D.A. Simpson (eds), *Studies in Ancient Europe*. Leicester, University Press: 45–70.

TRINGHAM, R.E. (1971) *Hunters, Fishers and Farmers of Eastern Europe 6000–3000 BC*. London, Hutchinson University Library.

TRINGHAM, R.E. (1973) The Mesolithic of southeastern Europe. In S.K. Kozłowski (ed.), *The Mesolithic in Europe*. Warsaw, University Press: 551–572.

TRINGHAM, R.E. (forthcoming) *Domesticating the humans: the role of sedentism in the 'neolithisation' of south-east Europe* (Paper).

VOYTEK, B.A. (1985) *The Exploitation of the Lithic Resources in Neolithic Southeast Europe*. Unpublished Ph.D. thesis, University of California, Berkeley.

WIESSNER, P. (1982) Beyond willow smoke and dogs' tails: a comment on Binford's analysis of hunting-gathering settlement systems. *American Antiquity*, 47: 171–178.

WOODBURN, J. (1982) Egalitarian societies. *Man*, 17: 431–451.

Demographic Trends in Neothermal South-East Europe

John Chapman

Abstract

The perspective of network analysis is used as a framework for the explanation of forager–farmer interactions. The Wobstian notion of mating networks is combined with a re-appraisal of forager exchange to produce testable propositions about social structures of early Holocene populations. The model is tested against datasets from south-east Europe – in particular, those of the Iron Gates Mesolithic and early Neolithic. An attempt is thereby made to explain the appearance and collapse of 'central places' such as Lepenski Vir.

INTRODUCTION

The question of population growth is inextricably linked to models designed to explain the origins of food production. By far the most influential accounts rely on demographic factors as the proximate, if not the long-term, cause of the adoption of agriculture (Binford 1968; Flannery 1973; Cohen 1977; Harris 1977; Hassan 1977). A similar assumption concerning the potential for population growth generated by the adoption of farming lies at the heart of a cluster of models explaining the spread of these behavioural innovations into secondary areas such as Europe (Ammerman and Cavalli-Sforza 1973, 1979; Green 1980; Hamond 1980; Starling 1985). All the models in this second group share a common failing, namely an inability or an unwillingness to take into account the population densities of indigenous hunters, gatherers or fishers. This striking omission is reminiscent of the 'hiatus' theory of the Mesolithic so clearly rejected by Clark (1980). To her credit, Ruth Tringham (1968, 1971) introduced Mesolithic populations into the debate, although her original hypothesis of the separate development of local hunter-gatherers and pioneer farmers has been the subject of a devastating auto-critique (Tringham 1983; see also Voytek and Tringham, this volume). Yet despite the discovery of the Iron Gates Mesolithic sequence, with Lepenski Vir as the super-nova of the European Mesolithic (Jovanović 1969; Srejović 1969; Boroneanț 1970; Srejović and Letica 1978), no single model has done full justice to the contribution of Balkan Mesolithic populations *over the whole peninsula*. In this paper, a model of demographic development is presented for the central Balkan area, covering the period 10,000–6000 BP. My aims are threefold: (i) to define the demographic profiles of pioneer farming communities and indigenous societies; (ii) to discuss their interactions, both biological and cultural; and (iii) to explain the growth of 'central places' such as Lepenski Vir.

THEORY

The three central trends affecting Pleistocene human populations have been defined by Denham (1974) as: (a) local episodes of relatively rapid growth; (b) episodes of decline and stasis; and (c) episodes of local group extinction. It is Denham's contention that the absence of long-term cumulative population growth in the Palaeolithic period can be explained by the overall balance between these trends, a cyclic pattern of greater and lesser success in the maintenance of viable breeding populations. By contrast, one of the defining traits of the Neothermal period (*c.* 13,000 BP to present) is the rapid increase in global population, the archaeological relevance of which can best be appreciated at the regional population level.

In view of the anthropological evidence for overall continuity in the human populations of Europe from the late Pleistocene into Neothermal times (Barrière 1956; Ferembach 1974; Vallois and de Félice 1977; Živanović 1982), one key question is the method by which the European population maintained and increased its size through a series of relatively rapid environmental fluctuations. One way of approaching this question is through the examination of models of hunter-gatherer mating networks.

Two contrasting approaches to human mating networks have been formulated within the last decade – the simulation studies of Martin Wobst (1974, 1975, 1976) and the bio-archaeological approach of a team of researchers in Holland, led by Raymond Newell and Trinette Constandse-Westermann (Newell, Constandse-Westermann and Meiklejohn 1979; Constandse-Westermann and Newell 1984, this volume; Newell 1984; Newell *et al.*, in press).

Martin Wobst (1974) approximated the minimal size of mating networks in a series of computer simulations designed to answer the question, 'how large does an exogamous mating network have to be to ensure that any member, upon reaching maturity, will find a suitable mate?' (1976: 50). The answer ranged from 175 to 475 members, with the majority of cases in the upper part of this range (1974: 161–170). On this basis, Wobst took 475 people to be the practical lower limit for a mating network. Given the range of modern hunter-gatherer population densities, defined as 0.5 to 0.005 persons/km², Wobst calculated the areal extent of the minimum mating networks (e.g. 950 km² at a density of 0.5 persons/km², 9500 km² at 0.05 persons/km², etc.). Such networks would comprise *c*. 18 minimum bands, the local groups who engage in face-to-face interactions, with a size range of 15–75 and mean size of 25. Wobst revised his earlier (1974) opinion of band exogamy and tribal endogamy in the Palaeolithic period to argue that overlapping mating systems with no sharp social boundaries characterized much of the Palaeolithic period, whilst in the late Upper Palaeolithic and Mesolithic closed networks evolved under conditions of increased population density, selection for communal tasks such as group-hunting, and increased locational constraints. The component parts of Wobst's model are summarized below (*Fig. 1*).

The Constandse-Westermann and Newell (C-WN) model of mating networks is fully presented elsewhere in this volume. In summary, the C-WN model defines three hierarchical levels in the social structure – the band, the dialectic tribe, and the language family – which can be classified in two levels of social complexity, band level societies and tribal level societies. Basing their demographic data on early post-contact studies of a sample of 263 North American societies, Constandse-Westermann and Newell (this volume) define a range of population sizes, densities and territorial extent for these units. Their conclusion is that overlapping band networks characterized bands and dialectic tribes at the band level, whilst endogamy would have been practicable in dialectic tribes at the tribal level. The essential difference here concerns population density at the tribal level, which is high enough to support breeding networks in a smaller territorial area than was possible at the band level. At the highest hierarchical level (language families) a system of overlapping breeding networks is proposed.

Although both of these models succeed admirably in focusing on the key issue of population (genes)–society (communication) interactions, each maintains a questionable view of mating network size and composition. Wobst's model specifically excludes those specialized marine, lacustrine and riverine hunter-gatherer-fisher populations likely to be of greatest interest to prehistoric archaeology, thereby artificially depressing the mean size of his sample population (Wobst 1976: 51). Hence the areal extent of the mating networks of these specialized groups is, by definition, likely to be far smaller than the smallest area (950 km²) postulated by Wobst. A

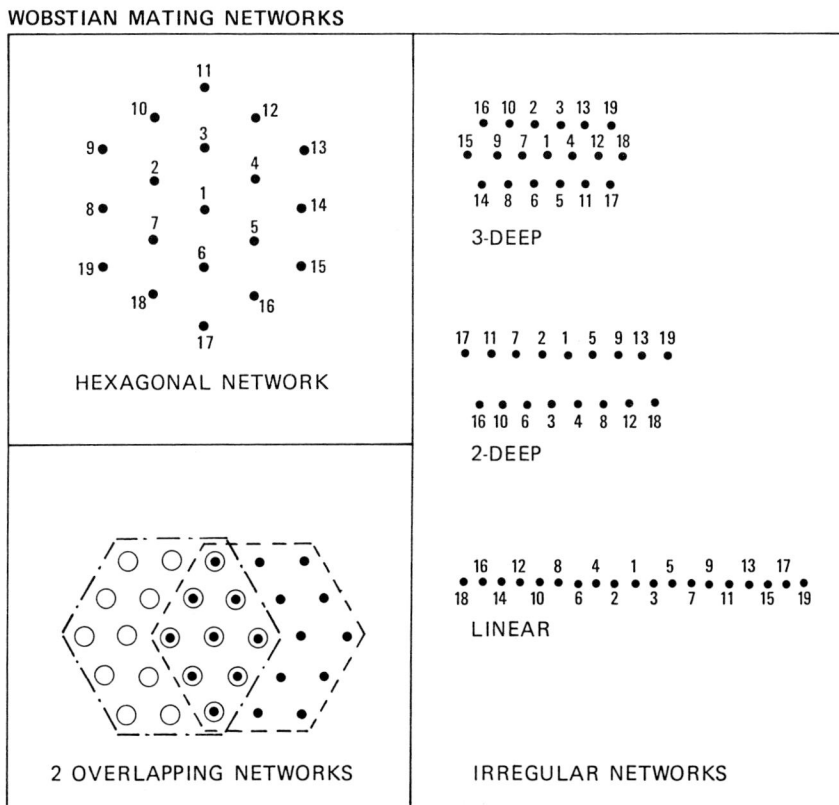

WOBSTIAN MATING NETWORKS

HEXAGONAL NETWORK

2 OVERLAPPING NETWORKS

3-DEEP

2-DEEP

LINEAR

IRREGULAR NETWORKS

Figure 1 Wobstian mating networks (after Wobst 1974).

second problem is that the behavioural adjustments by which mating networks of fewer than 475 members have long-term viability are not clearly distinguished (Wobst 1975).

One of the difficulties with the C-WN model is the wide range of societies included within the ethnographic sample on which band and tribal level population statistics are calculated. Inclusion of societies whose social development is far more complex than that exhibited in the European Palaeolithic and Mesolithic not only excessively extends the range of population estimates, but raises group means and standard deviations to an unacceptably high level. Secondly, in Adams and Kasakoff's (1975) study of endogamous breeding populations, there are many groups practising 80%-endogamy whose size rarely exceeds 1400 and, of these, the smallest groups are invariably hunter-gatherers (e.g. Adams and Kasakoff 1975: fig. 1b).

Furthermore, and of especial relevance to the relationship between open and closed breeding networks, Spuhler (1967) has identified many contemporary primitive populations of Europe, South America and North Africa which operate closed networks of 1500–4000 individuals. Adams and Kasakoff stress that the actual endogamous group size is always much smaller than the maximum possible size of 10,000 people.

These objections lead to a re-formulation of the parameters on which a hunter-gatherer model of breeding systems can be based. It is proposed to define the most likely breeding network size as greater than 500 (Wobst's effective minimum) and less than 1000 – the point at which hunter-gatherer populations became rare in Adams and Kasakoff's (1975) survey. The population density range of Mesolithic hunter-gatherers, many of whom are demonstrably exploiting coastal, lacustrine and riverine environments, may be assumed to fall nearer the upper end of Wobst's density range of 0.5–0.005 people/km^2.

Such a re-definition alters the theoretical pathways from open to closed breeding networks. For the Wobst formulation, higher population densities themselves increase the likelihood of a transition, as does the probable facilitation of communal task-sharing but, as a countervaling tendency, locational constraints would be diminished. For the C-WN model, there is a far greater likelihood that ethnic groups will equal or exceed the size of endogamous breeding networks, with the possibility that the transition to closed breeding networks occurred in pre-farming contexts.

The important spatial component of Wobst's (1974) model concerns the extra transport costs attached to any deviation from the ideal hexagonal distribution of an open mating network (*Fig. 1*).

Increasing centre–periphery costs can be acute with network closure, whilst a linear pattern of settlement (e.g. coastal, riverine) is likely to lead to locational inequalities which would be exacerbated still further in a closed linear system. In each case, the predicted response would be an increase in ritual to favour within-group cohesion and/or territorial symbolism designed to define group boundaries more clearly. It may be objected that, in the real world, such locational constrasts are so abundant as to provoke responses from an early date of settlement. However, in a low-density breeding network of wide areal extent, linear settlement patterns on a small scale can be absorbed into a wider pattern with minimal extra transport costs. Conversely, in a higher-density network covering a smaller area, locational contrasts would be more likely to stand out as an important density-dependent factor with the potential for triggering social inequality and requiring measures for increased social cohesion.

The contrast between linear (coastal) and non-linear (interior) environments has been more rigorously defined through the simulation studies of James Moore (1981). He concludes that it is easier to increase settlement and subsistence efficiency in coastal than in interior environments, with the higher potential for closer site packing and higher population densities. Social costs of such developments may well be intensification of alliance formation and exchange, often with higher levels of ritual activity.

The second major element in a theoretical discussion of Neothermal demography is the spread of a population of pioneer farmers into regions previously settled by indigenous hunter-gatherer-fisher populations. The demographic characteristics of such an agricultural colonization have been modelled by Stanton Green in an approach which is applicable to both incoming pioneer farmers and indigenous groups developing their own farming strategies (Green 1980; cf. Dennell 1984).

Green's model stresses the ecological conditions which favour colonizers and their demographic correlates. In a frontier context populations require high mobility, the ability to use a wide range of resources, and a high reproductive potential. Hence successful colonizing populations are likely to be relatively fast-growing, with a predominantly young age-structure and male-biased sex ratio, and organized in incomplete family groups. Assuming that frontiers are low-density areas some distance from more densely populated areas, Green argues that the frontier problem is a balance between relatively low subsistence costs, with land easy to acquire, and the higher social, demographic and exchange costs of pioneer living. Great stress is laid on regular exchange and co-operation between pioneer groups,

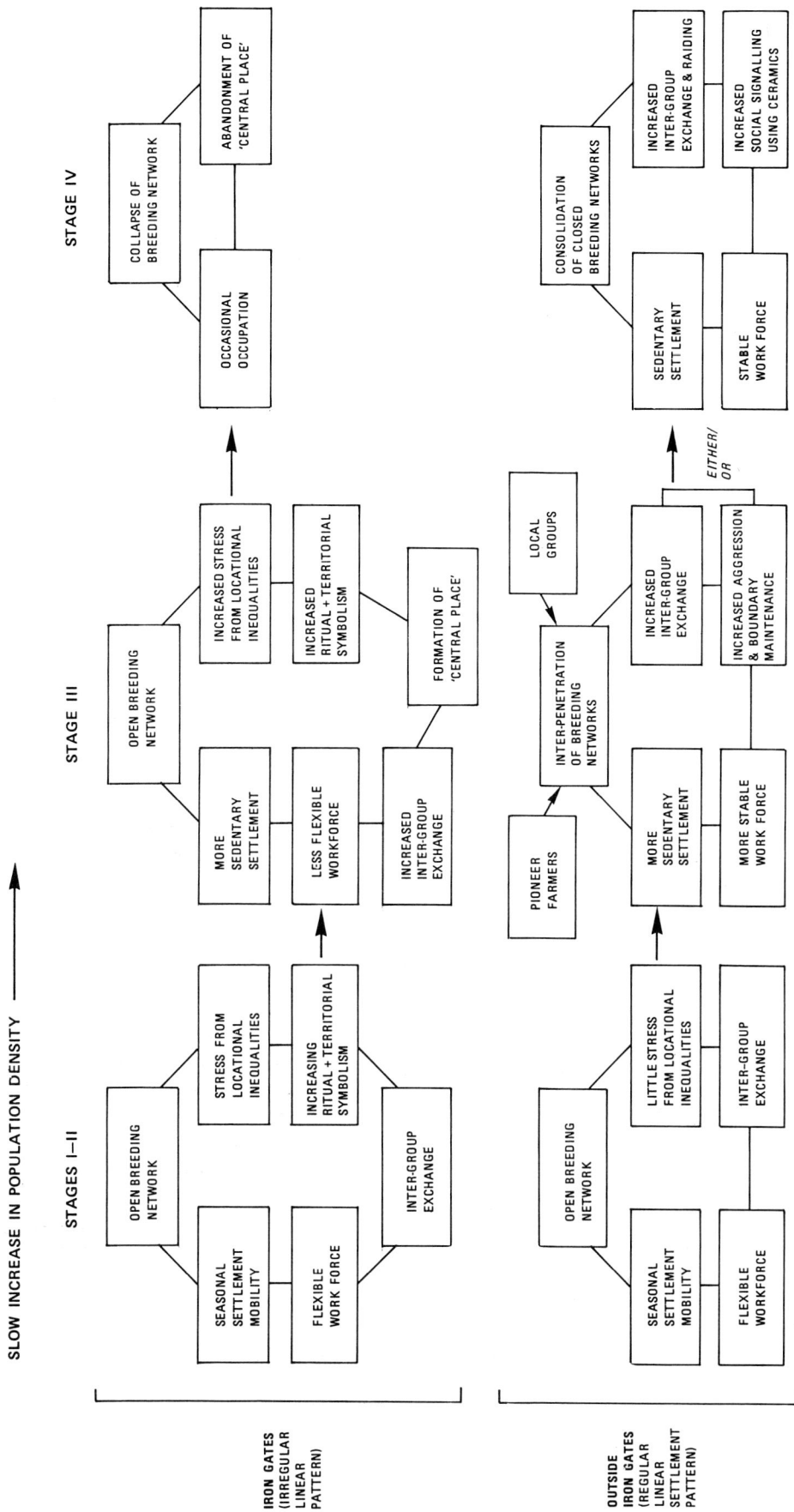

Figure 2   A model for the demographic interaction of foragers and farmers in the central Balkans.

SLOW INCREASE IN POPULATION DENSITY ⟶

STAGES I–II

STAGE III

STAGE IV

IRON GATES
(IRREGULAR
LINEAR PATTERN)

OPEN BREEDING NETWORK

SEASONAL SETTLEMENT MOBILITY

FLEXIBLE WORK FORCE

INTER-GROUP EXCHANGE

STRESS FROM LOCATIONAL INEQUALITIES

INCREASING RITUAL + TERRITORIAL SYMBOLISM

OPEN BREEDING NETWORK

MORE SEDENTARY SETTLEMENT

LESS FLEXIBLE WORKFORCE

INCREASED INTER-GROUP EXCHANGE

INCREASED STRESS FROM LOCATIONAL INEQUALITIES

INCREASED RITUAL + TERRITORIAL SYMBOLISM

FORMATION OF 'CENTRAL PLACE'

COLLAPSE OF BREEDING NETWORK

OCCASIONAL OCCUPATION

ABANDONMENT OF 'CENTRAL PLACE'

OUTSIDE
IRON GATES
(REGULAR
LINEAR SETTLEMENT PATTERN)

OPEN BREEDING NETWORK

SEASONAL SETTLEMENT MOBILITY

FLEXIBLE WORKFORCE

LITTLE STRESS FROM LOCATIONAL INEQUALITIES

INTER-GROUP EXCHANGE

PIONEER FARMERS

LOCAL GROUPS

INTER-PENETRATION OF BREEDING NETWORKS

MORE SEDENTARY SETTLEMENT

MORE STABLE WORK FORCE

INCREASED INTER-GROUP EXCHANGE

INCREASED AGGRESSION & BOUNDARY MAINTENANCE

EITHER/OR

CONSOLIDATION OF CLOSED BREEDING NETWORKS

SEDENTARY SETTLEMENT

STABLE WORK FORCE

INCREASED INTER-GROUP EXCHANGE & RAIDING

INCREASED SOCIAL SIGNALLING USING CERAMICS

503

who benefit from population increase as a way of increasing the labour force.

Apart from the dubious assumption that colonizing farmers would adopt an extensive agricultural strategy, perhaps the most significant omission from Green's model – and his case study of the Scandinavian Neolithic (Green 1980: 231–236) – is the role played by local populations, whose densities in some areas are likely to have important implications for the pioneer farmers (but cf. Green et al., in press). Negative implications include the kind of inter-group aggression caused by resource competition and a threat to traditional territories. On the positive side, the exchange of agricultural produce and stock, decorated pottery and other novel artifacts for local wild foods and information about techniques of exploiting local flora and fauna, raw material sources, etc., would begin the integration of two culturally diverse populations. Given the probability of a high male sex ratio, strategies of mate selection from local populations would bring obvious benefits to the incoming farmers, in terms of increased reproductive potential, an expanded gene pool but, most importantly, a quantum increase in the number of local links of kinship and alliance.

The time-scale of this genetic and social interaction is clearly crucial to the argument. Dennell (1984) has argued that recruitment of sub-adult foragers by expanding agriculturalists would lead to a loss of foraging breeding potential within two to three generations, thus leaving the latter with the 'choice' of extinction or assimilation into farming villages. It is hard to see how or why hunter-gatherer leaders would condone their own genetic suicide by acceding to such rapid changes in alliance structure. Rather, the impact of the expanding farmers would have occurred over a longer period of time, with local forager intensification of land use (perhaps via horticulture – Green et al., in press) as common as the adoption of profitable hunting strategies by farmers in rich environments. A social and economic mosaic of farmers and foragers in a rich but diverse environment requires a concomitant increase in information-processing strategies, whether territorial, stylistic, or ritual (cf. Moore 1983).

These theoretical arguments can be summarized in a model which attempts to relate important variables in the total system: type of breeding network, degree of settlement mobility, level of long-distance exchange, level of ritual and/or territorial symbolism, degree of social inequality, and type of work-force (Fig. 2).

It should be noted that the factor of increased population density is a necessary but insufficient cause of the change from open to closed mating networks. Important related factors include the arrival of an initially distinct population of pioneer

farmers and the importance of stable work-forces for communal agrarian tasks.

The demographic model will be tested using the available data from the early Neothermal period in the central Balkans. Before this operation, it is necessary to comment on the relative frequency of hunter-gatherer-fisher and early farming sites in this area in order to clarify specific survey and taphonomic bias in the existing record.

GEOMORPHOLOGY AND RECOVERY BIAS

At first sight, the Balkans would seem to be the perfect candidate for the 'hiatus' model of the disappearing European Mesolithic (cf. Waterbolk 1968). Whilst intensive and extensive surveys have been geared to the discovery of lowland farming sites in areas of relative geomorphological stability (Ecsedy et al. 1981; Sherratt 1983; Vasiljević and Trbuhović 1972, 1973; Chapman, in press), there is a preservational and recovery bias against hunting and fishing sites in unstable floodplain environments, against open hunter-gatherer flint scatters in the hill-country, and a strong bias in favour of hunter-gatherer occupation of cave or gorge sites, whether upland or lowland. The lengthy sequence of Mesolithic and later sites in the Iron Gates gorge of the Danube (Trifunović 1969; Boroneanţ 1970) and the concentration of cave sites in the limestone karst of the north Adriatic zone (Mirosavljević 1959; Cannarella and Cremonesi 1967) exemplify the last-named contexts. Rare examples of the preservation of floodplain Mesolithic sites such as the Soroki group on the Dnestr and the site of Pechera on the southern Bug can be explained by the fall of glacial lake levels which led to a lowering of river levels in the Anathermal period in the south Russian Plain (Dolukhanov 1979).

The principal geomorphological factors masking most sites are the deposition of deluvium, alluvium, or wind-blown sand on Altithermal-age occupation surfaces.[1] On rare occasions, hunter-gatherer-fisher sites are uncovered on the floodplains of the major rivers, and the same is true for a few early Neolithic floodplain sites.[2] The evidence of known low-lying sites and the clear-cut, well-dated, geomorphological data point to a sizable yet largely undiscovered population of Mesolithic and Neolithic sites exploiting the rich seasonal resources of the lower terraces and floodplains of all the major rivers.

The range of wild resources exploited at Soroki and Pechera exemplify the broad spectrum economies which were available in all the major river valleys of south-east Europe from the tenth millennium BP onwards – viz. anadromous and local fish, molluscs, and a wide range of herbivores (Markyevich 1968). Unless the 'hiatus' theory is deemed valid for the Balkan Mesolithic, ecological reasoning makes it

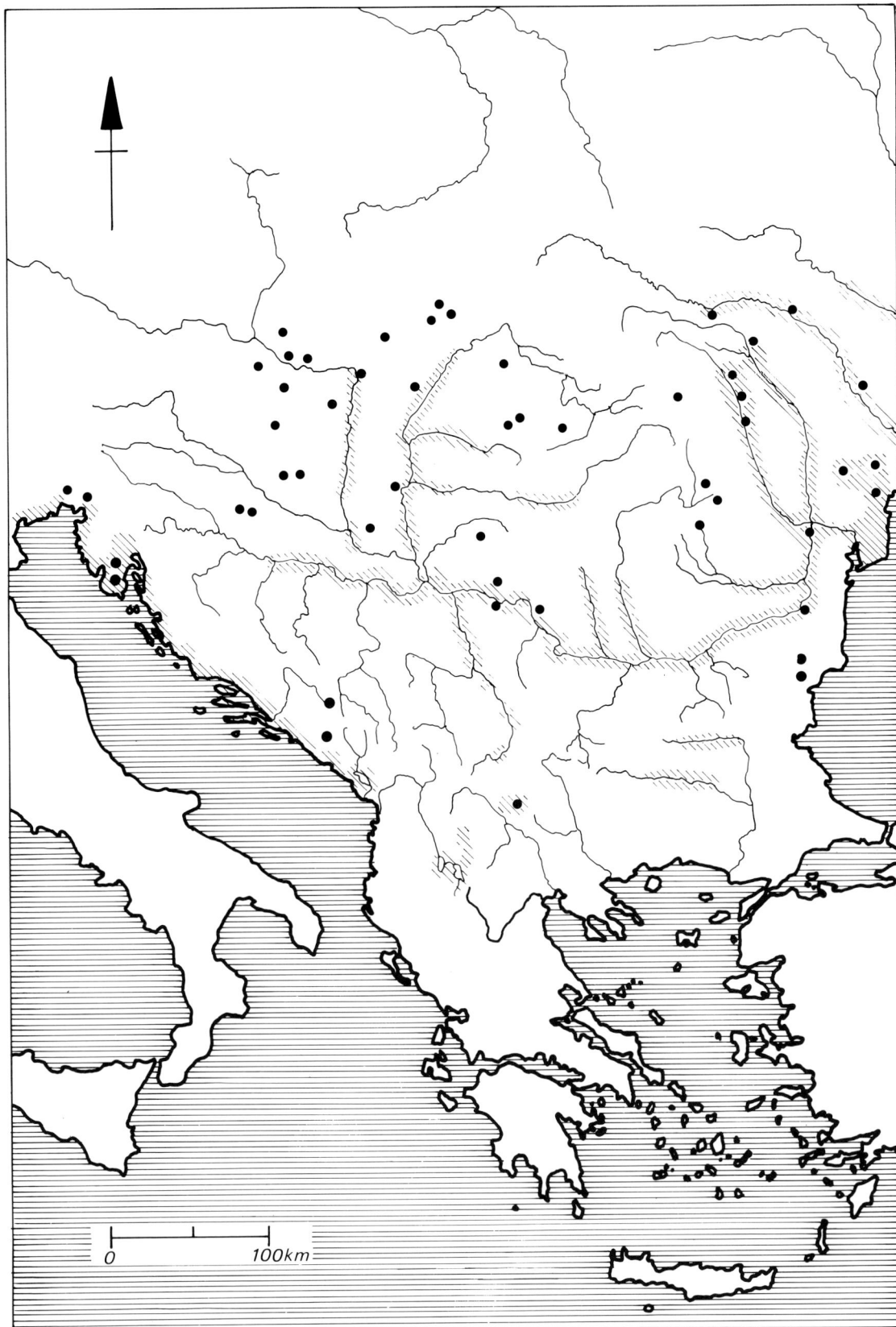

●   Known Mesolithic site

▨   Ecological zone with high potential for Mesolithic settlement

Figure 3   Recovery bias and ecological potential in the Balkan Mesolithic.

clear that the main lowland valleys would have provided the richest resource base of all available environmental niches (*Fig. 3*).

It should be stressed that the shortage of water and reduced ecological diversity of interfluvial zones renders intensive use of these areas unlikely in the Mesolithic period. The demographic implications of such seasonal or semi-permanent sites await investigation.

THE DATA

In order to test the implications of the model, a period of 4000 radiocarbon years (10,000–6000 BP) is abstracted from the Neothermal sequence, as the time-span encapsulating the clearest evidence for long-term processes of demographic and cultural change. In particular, three changes are highlighted: (i) the development of the Iron Gates later Mesolithic (Lepenski Vir/Schela culture) from the late ninth millennium BP; (ii) the first indications of domesticated plants and animals in the central Balkans, shortly after 7500 BP; and (iii) the almost total abandonment of settlements within the Iron Gates gorge as bases for fishing, gathering and hunting, after 6500 BP. A persistent theme of the model is the different potentialities opened up by Neothermal environmental changes within the Iron Gates gorge as contrasted with areas outside the gorge, despite the common cultural (i.e. cognitive and technological) heritage of all populations in the central Balkan area prior to 10,000 BP.

The Anathermal period, 10,000–8300 BP

At the beginning of this period, the difference between the vegetation inside and outside the Iron Gates reflected the fact that the Djerdap had remained a refuge area for thermophilous trees and wild grasses including Cerealia through most of the Last Glaciation (Cărciumaru 1971), whilst forest–steppe or steppe associations with high non-tree pollen (NAP) values but few Cerealia characterized Balkan lowland areas such as the lower Danube valley (Leroi-Gourhan *et al.* 1967) and the Morava valley (Gigov 1964). With the Anathermal rise in temperature and precipitation, re-colonization of steppe areas began from refuge areas such as the Iron Gates; but high NAP values are found in pollen diagrams dated *c.* 10,000 BP in western Hungary (Zólyomi 1953), south Hungary (Miháltz-Farago and Mucsi 1971), and Oltenia (Leroi-Gourhan *et al.* 1967). However, by this time, more rapid re-colonization of deciduous trees was occurring in Serbia (Gigov 1964). Through the tenth and ninth millennia BP, a gradual spread of mixed-oak forests in the Balkan lowlands narrowed the vegetational contrast between the plains and the Iron Gates micro-region, a divergence that had virtually dis-

appeared by the start of the Altithermal period (Pop 1929, 1932; Marković-Marjanović and Gigov 1971).

The increasing precipitation and rising sea level of the Anathermal period provided favourable conditions for the build-up of stocks of both non-migratory and migratory fish in the Danube catchment. It is difficult to assess the significance of non-migratory fish populations in the middle Danube valley and its tributaries. The movement of anadromous fish was probably limited to the lower Danube valley because of the deep nick-point at the eastern end of the Iron Gates gorge, which acted as a barrier to upward fish movement. Hence the lower Danube valley may well have been more favourable for fishing in this period than the Iron Gates gorge itself.

The archaeological evidence for clearly dated tenth to ninth millennium BP sites outside the Iron Gates gorge is so far minimal, but on ecological grounds we can predict a low density of mobile fishers, hunters and gatherers in the major river valleys, with home bases on the river terraces, and field camps for temporary operations in the flood-plain and in the hill country. Logistical strategies (*pace* Binford 1980) would have been increasingly necessary as fish resources became more important, since their peak densities coincided with summer movement of deer into the uplands.

In the Djerdap, a similar pattern of home base in the gorge (e.g. Cuina Turcului) and seasonal field camp in the uplands (e.g. Băile Herculane, with its Danube fish bones: Nicolăescu-Plopşor *et al.* 1957) can be identified from the tenth millennium BP onwards. Within a broad-spectrum economy, red deer and pigs were staple foods, with relatively few fish bones and little evidence for digging implements (hoes, mattocks). Cave sites were more frequent than open sites, and there is no evidence for facilities at these sites.

It is assumed that population densities in the Iron Gates gorge are lower in this period than in the eighth millennium BP. Nemeskéri's estimate of the entire Djerdap Epi-Palaeolithic population at the time of the Vlasac site was 60–115 people (Nemeskéri 1978). Here the lower figure of 60 people is taken as a first approximation. Taking the area of the Djerdap as *c.* 1200 km^2, a mean population density of 0.05 persons/km^2 is reached. Given the minimum size of viable mating networks as 500–1000 people, the areal extent of the network is in the range of 10,000–20,000 km^2. A possible configuration of mating networks is presented below (*Fig. 4*), based on these calculations and assuming lower population densities outside the Iron Gates gorge than inside.

Three comments arise from this heuristic. First, Nemeskéri's claim that the Djerdap Epi-Palaeolithic breeding population is relatively closed seems im-

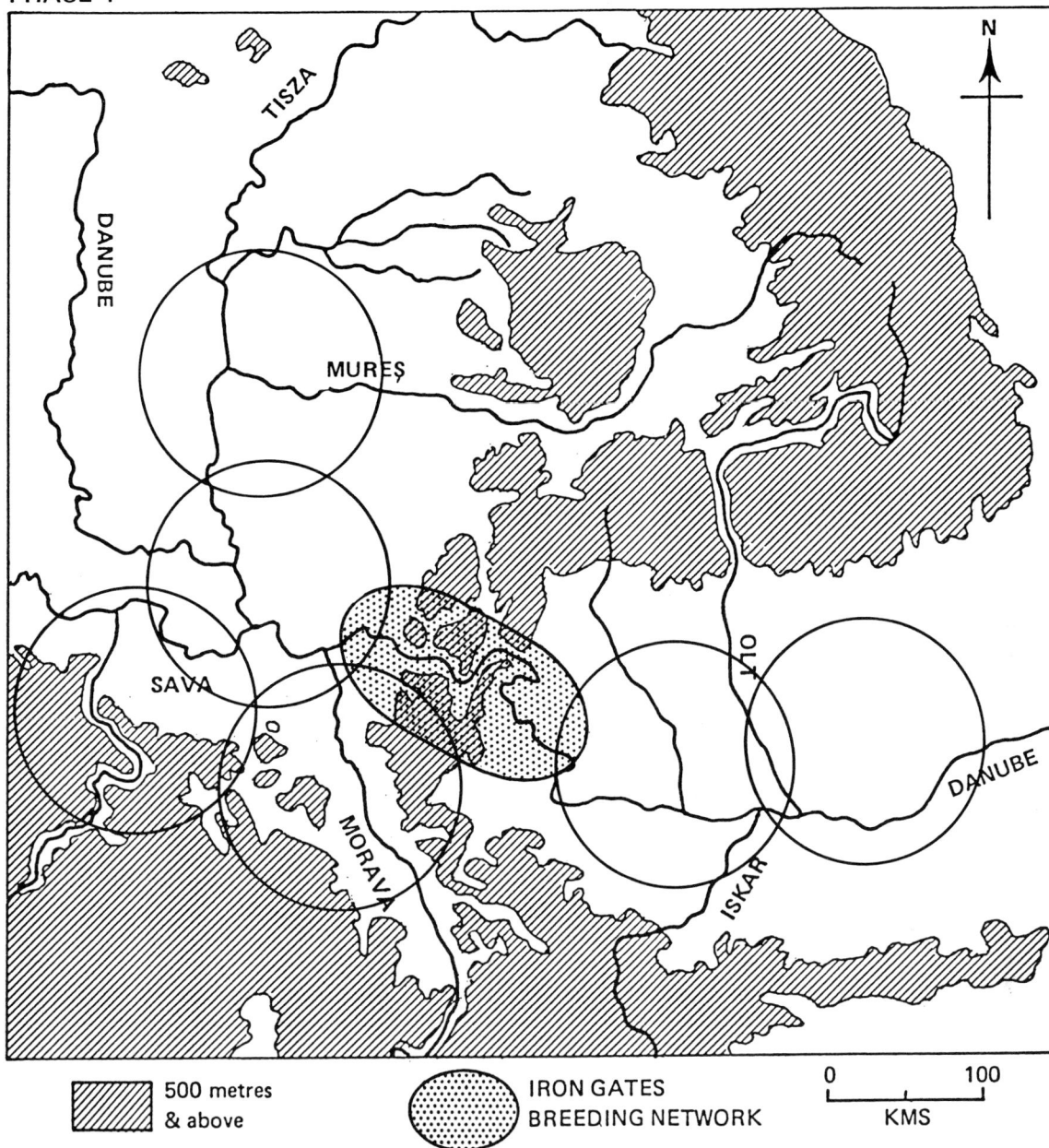

Figure 4   Breeding networks in the central Balkans: Phase I.

probable, since the Djerdap covers less than a quarter of the area of the network. Secondly, given such low population densities, open, overlapping mating networks would be advantageous to minimize transport costs over already large distances (cf. Wobst 1974). Thirdly, the fluidity of the open breeding networks allows the exchange of goods and information, both stylistic and cognitive, across large areas of land, thereby explaining the far-flung typological parallels cited for the Iron Gates sites (Boroneanţ 1970; Păunescu 1970a; Radovanović 1981), as well as the similarities in artistic motifs in sites as distant as Denmark and Italy (Marshack, in press). The appearance of Hungarian obsidian in the Iron Gates sites of Cuina Turcului I–II, Ostrovul Banului I–II, and Băile Herculane (Păunescu 1970b),

as well as the Mediterranean gastropods at Cuina Turcului (Grossu 1970) corroborates these long-distance exchanges.

The early Altithermal period, 8300–7500 BP

By the early part of the Holocene climatic optimum, or Altithermal period, the vegetational contrasts between the thermophilous forests of the Iron Gates and other less heavily-wooded areas had diminished. Over most of the Serbian lowlands below 1000 m a.s.l., oak, beech, walnut, hazel and hornbeam forests were flourishing (Gigov 1964), whilst in western Hungary non-tree pollen values fell to below 30%, with closed mixed-oak forest over most loess surfaces and gallery groves of willow and alder (Zólyomi 1953). Only on the drier parts of the middle Danube basin were there more open oak-woods (Miháltz-Farago and Mucsi 1971; Marković-Marjanović and Gigov 1971), whilst in Oltenia there is some evidence for a slightly denser tree cover (Leroi-Gourhan *et al.* 1967). These developments brought a decline in browse and graze for most herbivores, a drop in biomass hardly compensated for by increasing yields of acorns, hazel-nuts and berries (cf. Waterbolk 1968; for a critique of Clarke's (1976) discussion of forest resources, see Jarman, Bailey and Jarman 1983). The higher water temperatures of the Altithermal led to greater densities of fodder for both anadromous and non-migratory fish and the creation of greater opportunities for the growth of freshwater molluscs. New riverine areas became available for colonization by both fish and shellfish populations, following the marine transgression indicated in the Black Sea area (Ostrovsky 1967; Banu 1971).

The economic evidence from the Iron Gates sites indicates that the greater opportunities for fishing and, indeed, shell collecting were rapidly exploited in addition to the established culling of suids (Icoana) and cervids (Vlasac, Padina). Limp and Reidhead (1979) have stressed the higher labour inputs and more elaborate technology required for successful fishing in major river channels as compared with backwater lakes, oxbows and dead meanders. Local dog domestication has been demonstrated at Vlasac (Bökönyi 1978); close man–pig relationships are defined at Icoana (Bolomey 1973*a*, 1973*b*); whilst domesticated sheep, cattle, pigs and dogs are claimed in small numbers from early eighth millennium BP levels at Padina (Clason 1980). The large number of antler hoes and mattocks has been interpreted as evidence of planting, if not yet domesticating, wild cereals (Boroneanţ 1970), an activity reminiscent of Bronson's (1977) distinction between cultivation (including selective exploitation, intervention, accidental planting, near-cultivation and quasi-domestication) and farming (the creation of artificial habitats for domesticated plants). Prinz (1982) has ingeniously extended the interpretation of Cărciumaru's study of the coprolite pollen from Vlasac (Cărciumaru 1978) to suggest a wide range of plant use at Vlasac, culminating in a probable specialization on seeds (Chenopodiaceae, Gramineae, Cerealia) in Vlasac III (Prinz 1982: 152–155). This economic intensification of a wide range of species led to the investment of more effort on facilities and structures on open sites in the gorge. At these home bases, there is the first evidence for trapezoidal houses (Padina: Jovanović 1969) and square paved areas with hearths (Schela Cladovei: Boroneanţ 1970), in each case associated with the first signs of formal burial. In addition, larger numbers of more elaborate decorated objects in stone, bone and antler reveal increased intensity in social signalling

(Marshack, in press).

The settlement pattern in this period indicates an increase in population, attested by a larger number of sites in the gorge, increase in site size and the founding of new sites on the Danube outside the gorge (e.g. the seven Schela sites on Ostrovul Mare: Boroneanţ 1982, this volume). This increased population density is accompanied by signs of nutritional problems, episodes of acute food shortages and dental problems[3] – all signs that, despite the supposed high level of Mesolithic culture, the food quest was not wholly satisfactory.

The increase in population density inside the gorge may well differentiate the Djerdap from other areas of the central Balkans in the early eighth millennium BP. It is suggested that the areal extent of the Djerdap mating network decreases as a result of a higher estimated density of 0.1 person/km^2, whilst there is a minimal change in other areas (*Fig. 5*).

Whilst the Djerdap mating network continues as an open system, the diminution in size leads to constraints on mobility in the gorge which represents a highly irregular terrain linked by a linear route, namely the Danube. The locational advantages of centrality in the gorge led to differential transport requirements for finding a suitable mate (Wobst 1976). One of the principal strategies for overcoming these differences is in-group ceremonial and territorial symbolism – precisely the attributes found in the elaborate art and burial ritual of the Schela sites.

The discovery of exotic materials used in display or burial ritual – Hungarian obsidian at Vlasac I, Padina A1 and Ostrovul Banului (Kozłowski and Kozłowski 1982; Radovanović 1981), and Bulgarian graphite at Vlasac (Srejović and Letica 1978) – complements the discovery of small quantities of exotic raw materials for chipped stone tools. For example, at Vlasac, Kozłowski and Kozłowski (1982) have identified two types of brown flint (A3, A4), one igneous rock (C1), and the yellow flint from the pre-Balkan platform (A1) – all but the latter derived from areas north or west of the gorge. All these finds indicate the continuation of exchange networks at both local and inter-regional scale, across widespread open mating networks.

The middle Altithermal, 7500–6500 BP

The major changes in south-east Europe in this millennium are not so much environmental, for the trends noted in the early Altithermal continue, but rather cultural – namely, the spread of food production from areas of Mediterranean Greece and Anatolia northwards across the Balkan peninsula, reaching the southern rim of the Carpathians by 7000 BP (Bökönyi 1974; Renfrew 1979). In view of the absence of temperate Balkan prototypes for domesticated plants such as emmer, the hexaploid

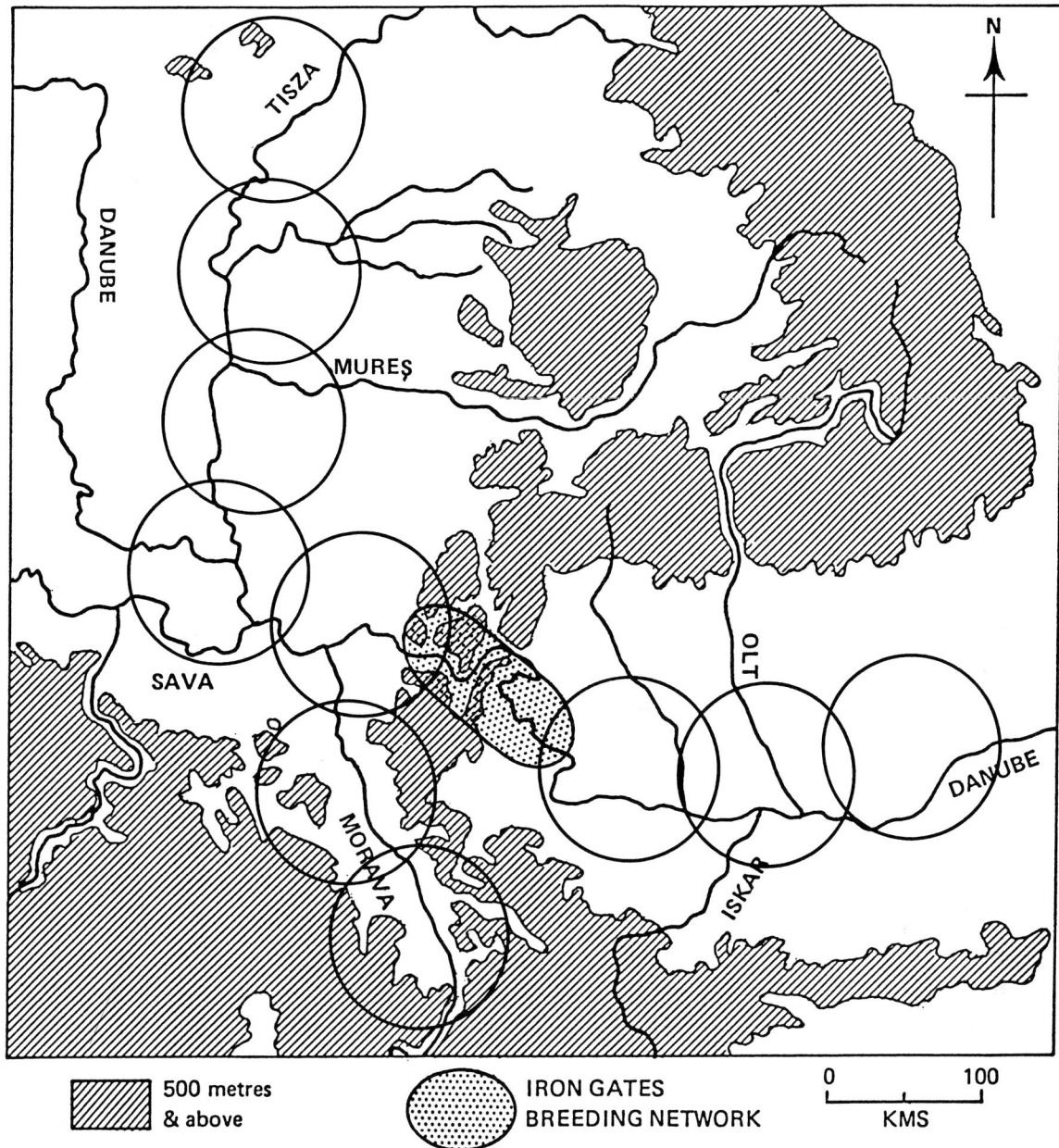

Figure 5   Breeding networks in the central Balkans: Phase II.

wheats and barleys and certain pulses, and animals such as sheep and goat, it is assumed that many of the important novel resources which later formed the basis for established farming in the Balkans were introduced and then widely diffused by small groups of pioneer agriculturalists. The small number of known First Temperate Neolithic (FTN) sites dated by radiocarbon or ceramic typology to before 7000 BP would suggest that the population incursion was on a relatively small scale (*Fig. 6*). The pattern of radiocarbon dates is best interpreted as the development of a more or less static frontier between agriculturalists and hunter-gatherers in the Macedo-Bulgarian transition zone (for definition of term, see Nandris 1970) for a period of up to 400 radiocarbon years, *c.* 7800–7400 BP, followed by a rapid spread

of food production as far north as Hungary within 200 radiocarbon years (for date list, see Renfrew 1979).

Contemporary with the dissemination of mixed farming into the central Balkans, the further intensification of broad-spectrum strategies in the Iron Gates gorge is set in the context of startling innovations in hunter-gatherer-fisher art and architecture – the Lepenski Vir complex (Nandris 1968, 1972; Srejović 1969). The economic basis of levels I and II at Lepenski Vir, as well as contemporary Criş sites such as Cuina Turcului, Icoana, Schela Cladovei and Padina, is intensive fishing and the selective culling of red deer or pigs with the aid of the domestic dog (Bökönyi 1969, 1978; Bolomey 1973a, 1973b; Clason 1980). There is some evidence for

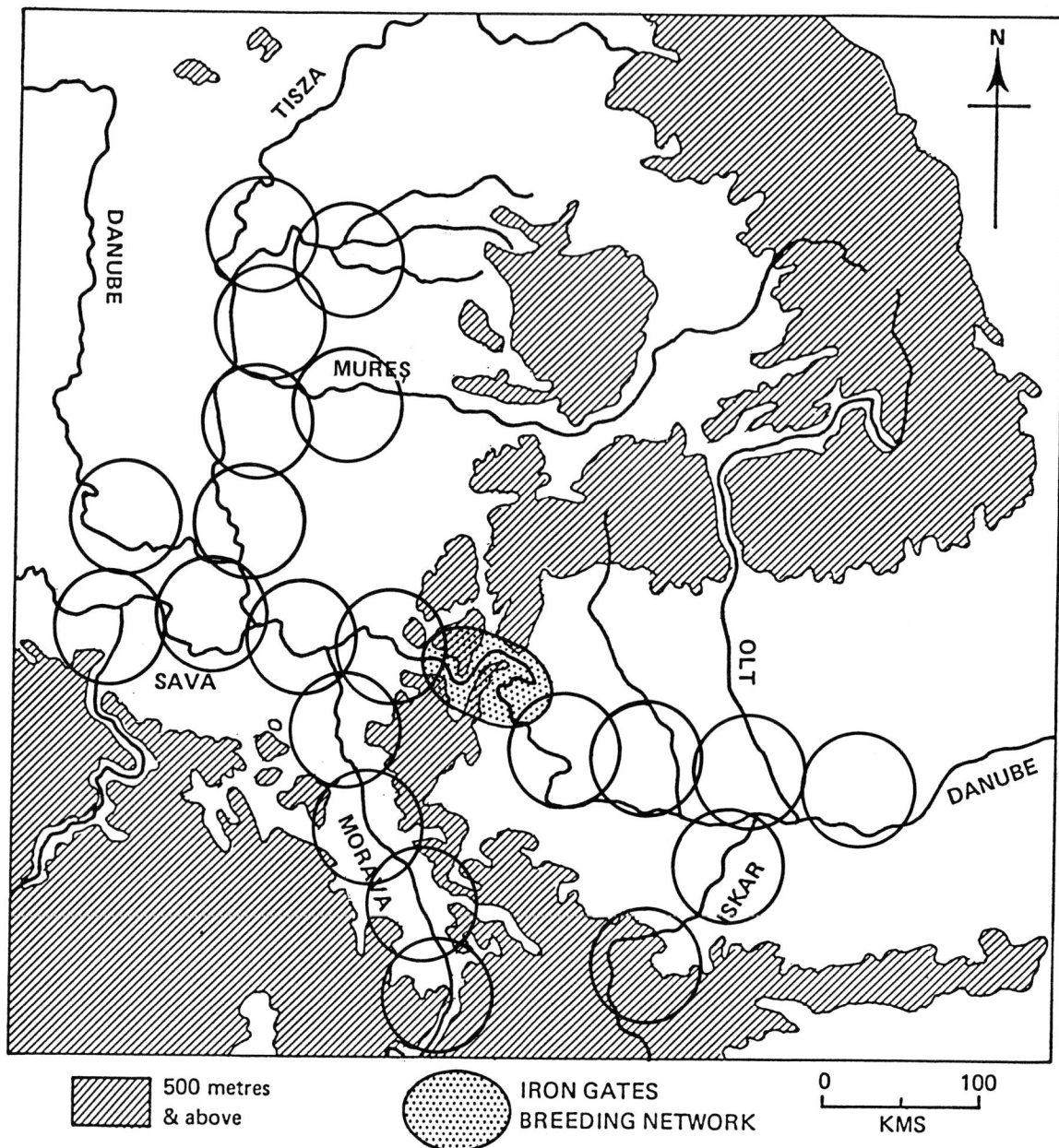

Figure 6 Breeding networks in the central Balkans: Phase III.

exchange of information and resources between the pioneer farmers and local inhabitants: (i) the cultivation of domestic einkorn wheat at Cuina Turcului and Icoana supported by the discovery of a fungus parasitic on a type of stem-rust that specifically attacks wheat (Cărciumaru 1973); (ii) the occurrence of low frequencies of domestic animals at Padina (Clason 1980) and the Romanian sites (Bolomey 1973b); (iii) the existence at Lepenski Vir II of a type of domestic dog whose morphology resembles those of domestic dogs from other Neolithic sites rather than that of the Vlasac dog population (Prinz 1982: 389); (iv) the import, and then widespread use, of FTN pottery in gorge sites; (v) the yellow flint (A1) from the pre-Balkan platform of north

Bulgaria found in large quantities at Padina B, Vlasac IV, Lepenski Vir III and the Romanian Criş sites (Kozłowski and Kozłowski 1983; Radovanović 1981); and (vi) the import into Lepenski Vir III of A3 and A4 brown flint, C3 and C4 igneous rock, and C5 basalt from north and west of the gorge (Kozłowski and Kozłowski 1983). The increased range and volume of products indicates intensification of exchange over and above hunter-gatherer levels in period II, with an important exchange route of pre-Balkan flint along the lower Danube corridor.

The sophistication of the trapezoidal houses of Padina and Lepenski Vir I and II should not conceal the strong probability that these sites would have been uninhabitable for parts of each spring due to flooding. The settlement pattern continuity in home bases located in the gorge and seasonal camps in the uplands is striking, despite the high density of large artifacts, facilities and structures. The pattern of semi-permanent, repeated occupation of the Lepenski Vir I–II village stands in contrast to the shorter-term but all-year-round use of river terrace locations which typified many pioneer farming sites north of the Macedo-Bulgarian zone (Chapman 1977, 1981).

The evidence of the large villages at Lepenski Vir and Padina, as well as an increased number of open sites on the Romanian bank, indicates a continued rise in population density in the gorge. An estimate of 300–400 people at this period implies a mean density of 0.25–0.33 person/km^2 within the Djerdap. Outside the gorge the relatively wide spacing of localized areas of high population density (the pioneer farming sites), as well as a scatter of lower-density seasonal hunter-fisher sites, would suggest a higher population size than was ever supported before in the Neothermal period; for heuristic reasons, let us assume a population density of 0.5 person/km^2 by the late seventh millennium BP.

Although the development of higher population densities outside the gorge would have made mating network closure possible, such an option would not have benefited the pioneer farming groups with their inbuilt need to develop kinship alliances with local populations. The formation of such alliances would have led to the interchange of information on comparative subsistence strategies, as an important mechanism for the diffusion of early farming (e.g. the Schela sites with hunter-fisher levels stratified beneath pottery-using food-producing levels: Boroneanţ 1970, 1982).

The further fall in the areal extent of a closed Djerdap breeding network meant that locational inequalities were unavoidable. Hence, two kinds of social signalling were important – an integrative set of ceremonial symbols to offset extra economic costs of peripheral groups, and a territorial-based symbolism to differentiate breeding populations. There can be no doubt that social and locational inequality in the central Balkans Mesolithic is exemplified by the village of Lepenski Vir I–II which operated as a low-level central place for the sites of the gorge. The evidence for communal feasting, mortuary ritual and the increasing body of geometric art symbols is convincingly interpreted as a range of integrative strategies, whilst the unique monumental art embodies in the water deities of the Danube a set of territorial and economic signals differentiating the Djerdap from other closed breeding networks outside the gorge. On this interpretation, the cultural achievements of the Lepenski Vir craftsmen can be regarded, at least partially, as signs of intra-group stress arising out of the problems associated with irregular linear settlement patterns.

The late Altithermal, 6500–6000 BP

The environmental evidence for the late seventh millennium BP indicates that the vegetational cover and the availability of fish were substantially the same as in the preceding millennium (Pop 1929, 1932; Zólyomi 1953; Gigov 1964; Miháltz-Farago and Mucsi 1971). It is therefore to the cultural that we turn for an explanation of a dramatic change in settlement pattern – the almost total abandonment of the Iron Gates gorge by hunter-gatherer-fisher populations.

The major residential site in the gorge in this period was the occupation of Lepenski Vir III. This reoccupation of the village site after abandonment by the inhabitants of level II[4] marks a cultural but not an economic break with the past, defined negatively by the absence of trapezoidal houses, boulder and geometric art and formal burial, and positively by the widespread use of Starčevo pottery and a wide range of exotic raw materials (Srejović 1969). The three-phase settlement represents a longer occupation than most FTN sites in Serbia and Romania (Chapman 1976) and was based largely on fishing, hunting of red deer, pig and aurochs, and cattle herding (Bökönyi 1969). The site was finally abandoned some time in the late seventh millennium BP, contemporary with the last occupations of Oltenian Criş sites such as Cîrcea-la Viaduct (Nica 1976). Lepenski Vir III apart, the only evidence of residence in the gorge in this period is short-term use of the cave of Cuina Turcului (Nicolăescu-Plopşor et al. 1965).

This sequence of changes raises many questions, of which the following are perhaps most pertinent: (i) what caused the abandonment of most period III sites in the Djerdap gorge; (ii) why was Lepenski Vir reoccupied when other contemporary sites were abandoned; and (iii) why did the occupants of Lepenski Vir III adopt such a different set of social symbols from those used in periods I–II?

To the first question, three hypotheses can be proposed. Srejović and Letica (1978) have argued that the development of food production was fatal to the cognitive system of the Djerdap fishers, and that the loss of the worldview underpinning the ceremonial centre at Lepenski Vir provoked irreversible damage to their culture. In an extension of Nandris's (1968, 1972) evolutionary argument that hunting and fishing survived so long in the gorge because it was as adaptively successful as pioneer farming, I suggested (1977, 1981) that the consolidation of FTN agriculture into a well-adapted, more productive mixed farming economy by the late seventh millennium BP made this a more viable strategy than the Iron Gates hunter-gatherer-fisher economy. Neither of these hypotheses explains the apparent anomaly of Lepenski Vir III. A third hypothesis, not necessarily irreconcilable with the first two, proposes that the high social and energy costs of maintaining a viable mating network in a highly dissected, mountainous terrain with the degree of inequality implicit in the use of a 'central place', such as Lepenski Vir, introduced insoluble conflicts into the social fabric, and the finely-balanced system collapsed. A ready alternative to a closed Djerdap network existed in the form of breeding networks outside the gorge – the clusters of latest FTN sites in the Liubcova basin (Comşa 1969; Lazarovici 1977; Chapman 1981) and the Kladovo–Korbovo area (Chapman 1981). In fact, the economic evidence from Liubcova and Gornea shows that as wide a range of Danube fish, forest and mountain game were captured by 'Neolithic' farmers as by the Djerdap hunter-fishers (Comşa 1969). Hence the Iron Gates breeding network was replaced by two networks centred, respectively, on the arable land at either end of the gorge – networks whose social symbolism was at least partly based on decorated ceramics.

The selection of Lepenski Vir III for reoccupation in the late seventh millennium BP reflects a combination of symbolic and functional considerations. The symbolic advantages in reoccupying a previously venerated site, whether temple, megalith or enclosed camp, reside in the overt links which current social leaders can claim with their past ancestors (Evans 1985); in short, re-using the 'central place' of a past social network has considerable ideological power for new settlers. The other advantages of Lepenski Vir were those recognized by the earlier occupants – viz. its centrality in the gorge and its excellent location for fishing. Centrality for Lepenski Vir III consisted not so much of a 'central place', but rather a link between two overlapping breeding networks. The exotic items found in Lepenski Vir III reflect as wide a range of exchange networks as ever existed for the Djerdap – Hungarian obsidian, azurite and malachite, *Spondylus* shells from the Aegean, marble, and a necklace of paligorskite whose nearest source is either the Urals or Anatolia (Srejović 1969).

Finally, the abandonment of monumental rivergods in elaborate shrines in Lepenski Vir III indicates the acceptance of a social order at once less complex and less intensive. One of the principal material components of the new social order – decorated ceramics – was adopted for reasons as much symbolic as practical, not least of which concerns the preparation and consumption of fish and meat (cf. Arnold 1985). Once ceramics became integral to social life in the breeding networks on the periphery of the gorge, it was inevitable that their use should spread to the sole surviving major occupation site in the Djerdap gorge. These new, flexible symbols rapidly became one of the principal vehicles for social signalling amidst the increasingly localized mating networks of mature agrarian populations.

CONCLUSION

A series of currently untestable assumptions have been made concerning the demographic structure of a population of which little is known – the Altithermal hunters, fishers and gatherers of the central Balkans. It does not need to be stressed that the attempts at portraying the effects of postulated population growth on hypothetical breeding network size should be regarded as a heuristic device, to aid comprehension rather than to represent reality. Yet, at present, modelling is the only way of introducing population dynamics into an otherwise static and over-simplified picture of the hunter/ farmer interface. Does this approach yield any new insights into this critical interface?

On a theoretical level, mating network theory is a type of middle-range theory by which general demographic concepts can be related to basic data. Mating network concepts allow the integration of settlement pattern data, economy, and the various classes of artifacts carrying symbolic information.

Secondly, mating network theory provides an opportunity to explain, rather than merely celebrate, artifactual and architectural complexity in the hunterfisher record. The inequalities which characterize closed networks in irregular terrain can clearly stimulate internal social tensions of the type thus far recognized to result from inter-group stress (Hodder 1979).

Thirdly, mating network theory provides a spatially broad perspective on the production, distribution and consumption patterns of communities living in small sites. Whilst much information can be yielded from a study of household archaeology (Wilk and Rathje 1982; Tringham 1983), processes of social and physical reproduction are necessarily grounded in a wider network of people and behaviour.

On an empirical level, the use of mating network theory has encouraged the study of the Iron Gates Mesolithic as part of a broader set of issues and within the context of regional hunter-gatherer settlement systems. In this way, a more refined idea of hunter/farmer interactions is possible, based on the inter-dependence of pioneer farmers and indigenous groups.

A further aspect of the mating network model is its ability to predict the occurrence of 'central places' even at relatively low population densities and in allegedly egalitarian hunter-fisher contexts. Instead of the attempt to identify social ranking through the distribution of ornaments in hunter-gatherer graves (cf. critique by Fiedel 1983), it is surely more profitable to analyze the constraints on mobility in mating networks covering different kinds of terrain in order to assess the likelihood of locational inequalities whose existence may well be *suppressed* by the distribution of personal ornaments.

Finally, what of the Iron Gates Mesolithic? Its achievements in art, artifacts and architecture are unparalleled in the European Mesolithic, yet their context reveals tension as much as originality, child malnutrition as much as sculptural precocity, and the struggle for cognitive survival as much as religious innovation. In its juxtaposition of whirlpools and mountains, plants and animals, woods and river, the Iron Gates environment is unique in south-east Europe, as indeed are the sculptures and shrines of Lepenski Vir; but the social constraints of forager mating networks, especially in linear environments, are common to many areas and populations, prompting convergent strategies of symbolic order and economic adaptation. The conjuncture of an area of high environmental potential with a successful social structure using well-adapted technology produced the Iron Gates Mesolithic. It was only after a millennium of farming that this conjuncture lost its adaptive significance and the Iron Gates gorge lost its inhabitants.

Notes:

1. Examples of the process of post-Altithermal deposition masking early sites include: (i) Sub-Atlantic alluviation in the middle Tisza and middle Danube valleys (Bukurov 1961); (ii) Sub-Atlantic alluviation in the Körös depression, Ko. Békés (Molnár *et al*. 1971); (iii) wind-blown sand deposited in the Sub-Boreal period in the Tiszazug (Nagy 1954); (iv) Sub-Atlantic alluviation in the middle Morava valley which, near Niš, buried a Roman anchor to a depth of 2 m (I.F. Partyonov, pers. comm.); (v) colluvial deposits masking light valley soils and floodplain in the Azmak valley, central Bulgaria (Dennell and Webley 1975).

2. Apart from the examples of Soroki and Pechera, the Aceramic Neolithic site of Kamennya Mogila near the Sea of Azov was found buried 2 m in flood loams of the River Molochnaya (Dolukhanov 1979). Similarly, the Mesolithic site of Mirnoye was found beneath the sandy clay of the New Black Sea Transgression (Dolukhanov 1979). Flint scatters of Mesolithic date are also known from the middle Danube near Budapest (Dobosi 1971) and the floodplains between the Danube delta and the lower Dnestr (Boriskovski and Kraskovski 1961). Similar examples of floodplain Criş sites are known from Basarabi, buried 2 m (Jarman 1983), and Ostrovul Mare (Boroneanţ 1982, this volume).

3. The evidence from Vlasac that 40% of the children suffered from rickets has been interpreted as indicating Vitamin D deficiency (Nemeskéri and Lengyel 1978). However, Prinz has claimed that Vitamin D deficiency is unlikely in a population so reliant on fishing, and has proposed the alternative of chronic, seasonal calcium deficiency (Prinz 1982: 162–164). At Padina, enamel hypoplasia indicating episodes of acute food shortage are more common in the late Mesolithic than in the early Neolithic (y'Edynak 1978), whilst severe periodontal disease, dental attrition, relative high frequency of arthritis and a low level of rickets characterized the late Mesolithic population (Živanović 1976, 1979, 1982).

4. The evidence for a break in occupation of a century of more is the weathering of a fine sandy layer deposited on top of the Lepenski Vir II occupation to form a buried soil (Brunnacker 1971: figs. 5 & 6b). Additionally, the sands which form the matrix for levels II and III are of different colour and geological origin (1971: 30). It should be stressed that Professor Srejović's (1969) alternative view of the chronology of the Iron Gates sequence

does not affect the main postulates of the model. A date for Lepenski Vir I–II in the late ninth to early eighth millennium BP, rather than *c*. 7400–6600 BP, would mean that the need for a 'central place' in the Iron Gates developed rather earlier but for the same reasons as suggested above. The main difference for the demographic model is that the collapse of the Iron Gates hunter-fisher system is even more dramatic, viz. the ceramic-based symbolic system of the pioneer farmers was adopted by the local populations in the Iron Gates (Lepenski Vir III) and was abandoned almost completely in the gorge after 6500 BP. One example of the adoption of decorative elements of the hunter-fisher cognitive system in the ceramic repertoire is the occurrence of a fishing-net motif in white-on-red painted ware of the Starčevo style (Nandris 1968; for others, see Gimbutas 1974).

Acknowledgements: I am grateful to my colleagues at the Mesolithic Symposium for discussing the first draft of this paper, and especially to Stefan Kozłowski, Stan Green, Jim Moore and Chris Smith. Stan Green, Jim Moore and Marek Zvelebil kindly sent a pre-publication draft of their paper to the Cork conference. Hans-Peter Uerpmann was kind enough to discuss with me the recent evidence for Mesolithic fishing in Germany. I thank Wendy Dennis for converting an incomprehensible manuscript into a legible text, and Clive Bonsall for his many editorial felicities.

References

ADAMS, J.W. and KASAKOFF, A.B. (1975) Factors underlying endogamous group size. In M. Nag (ed.), *Population and Social Organization*. The Hague, Mouton: 147–174.

AMMERMAN, A.J. and CAVALLI-SFORZA, L.L. (1973) A population model for the diffusion of early farming in Europe. In C. Renfrew (ed.), *The Explanation of Culture Change*. London, Duckworth: 343–357.

AMMERMAN, A.J. and CAVALLI-SFORZA, L.L. (1979) The wave of advance model for the spread of agriculture. In C. Renfrew and K. Cooke (eds), *Transformations. Mathematical Approaches to Culture Change*. London, Academic Press: 275–293.

ARNOLD, D.E. (1985) *Ceramic Theory and Cultural Process*. Cambridge, University Press.

BANU, A. (1971) *Delta Dunării*. Unpublished Ph.D. thesis, University of Bucharest.

BARRIÈRE, C. (1956) *Les Civilisations Tardenoisiennes en Europe Occidentale*. Paris, Bière.

BINFORD, L.R. (1968) Post-Pleistocene adaptations. In L.R. Binford and S.R. Binford (eds), *New Perspectives in Archaeology*. Chicago, Aldine: 313–341.

BINFORD, L.R. (1980) Willow smoke and dogs' tails: hunter-gatherer settlement systems and archaeological site formation. *American Antiquity*, 45: 4–20.

BÖKÖNYI, S. (1969) Kičmenjači (Prethodni Izveštaj). In D. Srejović, *Lepenski Vir. Nova praistorijska Kultura u Podunavlju*. Belgrade, Srpska književna zadruga: 224–228.

BÖKÖNYI, S. (1974) *History of Domestic Mammals in Central and Eastern Europe*. Budapest, Akadémiai Kiadó.

BÖKÖNYI, S. (1978) The vertebrate fauna of Vlasac. In D. Srejović and Z. Letica (eds), *Vlasac. Mesolitsko Naselje u Djerdapu*, vol. 2. Belgrade, Srpska Akademija Nauka i Umetnosti: 35–68.

BOLOMEY, A. (1973a) An outline of the late Epipalaeolithic economy at the 'Iron Gates': the evidence on bones. *Dacia*, 17: 41–52.

BOLOMEY, A. (1973b) The present stage of knowledge of mammal exploitation during the Epipalaeolithic and earliest Neolithic on the territory of Romania. In J. Matolcsi (ed.), *Domestikationsforschung und Geschichte der Haustiere*. Budapest, Akadémiai Kiadó: 197–203.

BORISKOVSKI, P.I. and KRASKOVSKI, V. (1961) *Pamyatniki drevneishei chelovyecheskoi kulturi severo-zapadnovo Prichernomorye*. Odessa.

BORONEANŢ, V. (1970) La période épipaléolithique sur la rive roumaine des Portes de Fer du Danube. *Praehistorische Zeitschrift*, 45(1): 1–25.

BORONEANŢ, V. (1982) General survey of Epipalaeolithic (Mesolithic) research in Romania (1978–1981). *Mesolithic Miscellany*, 3(1): 11–12.

BRONSON, B. (1977) The earliest farming: demography as cause and consequence. In C.A. Reed (ed.), *Origins of Agriculture*. The Hague, Mouton: 23–48.

BRUNNACKER, K. (1971) Geologisch-pedologische Untersuchungen in Lepenski Vir am Eiserner Tor. In D. Srejović, 'Die Lepenski Vir-Kultur und der Beginn der Jungsteinzeit an den Mittleren Donau'. *Fundamenta*, A/3: 20–32.

BUKUROV, B. (1961) Geomorfološke prilike Severnog Banata. *Glasnik Srpskog Geografskog Društva*, 41(1): 15–23.

CANNARELLA, O. and CREMONESI G. (1967) Gli scavi nella Grotta Azzurra di Samatorza nel Carso triestino. *Rivista di Scienze Preistoriche*, 22(2): 281–330.

CĂRCIUMARU, M. (1971) Analiza polinică a unor sedimente Würmiene dîn Peştera Hoţilor de la Băile Herculane. *Studii şi Cercetări de Istorie Veche*, 22(1): 15–19.

CĂRCIUMARU, M. (1973) Analiza polinică a coprolitelor dîn staţiunea arheologică de la Icoana (Defileul Dunăru). *Studii şi Cercetări de Istorie Veche*, 24(1): 5–14.

CĂRCIUMARU, M. (1978) L'analyse pollinique des coprolithes de la station archéologique de Vlasac. In D. Srejović and Z. Letica (eds), *Vlasac. Mesolitsko naselje u Djerdapu*, vol. 2. Belgrade, Srpska Akademija Nauka i Umetnosti: 31–34.

CHAPMAN, J.C. (1976) Biosocial aspects of the Balkan Neolithic. *IXᵉ Congres UISPP Résumés des Communications*. Nice, UISPP: 295.

CHAPMAN, J.C. (1977) *The Balkans in the Fifth and Fourth Millennia bc*. Unpublished Ph.D thesis, University of London.

CHAPMAN, J.C. (1981) *The Vinča Culture of South East Europe. Studies in Chronology, Economy and Society*. Oxford, British Archaeological Reports (International Series) S117.

CHAPMAN, J.C. (in press) The Neolithic period in the Moravo-Danubian confluence area: a regional assessment of settlement pattern. In R. Tringham and D. Krstić (eds), *Selevac: a Neolithic Village in Yugoslavia*. Los Angeles, UCLA Institute of Archaeology Press.

CLARK, J.G.D. (1980) *Mesolithic Prelude*. Edinburgh, University Press.

CLARKE, D.L. (1976) Mesolithic Europe: the economic basis. In G. de G. Sieveking, I.H. Longworth and K.E. Wilson (eds), *Problems in Economic and Social Archaeology*. London, Duckworth: 449–481.

CLASON, A. (1980) Padina and Starčevo: game, fish and cattle. *Palaeohistoria*, 22: 141–173.

COHEN, M.N. (1977) *The Food Crisis in Prehistory*. New Haven, Yale University Press.

COMŞA, E. (1969) Données concernant la civilisation de Vinča en sud-ouest de la Roumaine. *Dacia*, 13: 11–44.

CONSTANDSE-WESTERMANN, T.S. and NEWELL, R.R. (1984) Human biological background of population dynamics in the western European Mesolithic. *Proceedings of the Koninklijke Nederlandse Akademie van Wetenschappen*, B87: 139–223.

DENHAM, W.W. (1974) Population structure, infant transport and infanticide among Pleistocene and modern hunter-gatherers. *Journal of Anthropological Research*, 30: 191–198.

DENNELL, R.W. (1984) The expansion of exogenous-based economies across Europe: the Balkans and central Europe. In S.P. de Atley and F.J. Findlow (eds), *Exploring the Limits. Frontiers and Boundaries in Prehistory*. Oxford, British Archaeological Reports (International Series) S223: 93–115.

DENNELL, R.W. and WEBLEY, D. (1975) Prehistoric settlement and land use in southern Bulgaria. In E.S. Higgs (ed.), *Palaeoeconomy*. Cambridge, University Press: 97–109.

DOBOSI, V. (1971) Mesolithische Fundorte in Ungarn. *Alba Regia*, 12: 39–60.

DOLUKHANOV, P. (1979) *Ecology and Economy in Neolithic Eastern Europe*. London, Academic Press.

ECSEDY, I., KOVACS, T., MARÁZ, B. and TORMA, I. (1981) *Békés Megye Régészeti Topográfiája a Szeghalmi Járás*. Budapest, Akadémiai Kiadó.

Y'EDYNAK, G.J. (1978) Culture, diet and dental reduction in Mesolithic forager-fishers of Yugoslavia. *Current Anthropology*, 19(3): 616–618.

EVANS, C. (1985) Tradition and the cultural landscape: an archaeology of place. *Archaeological Review from Cambridge*, 4(1): 80–94.

FEREMBACH, D. (1974) Les hommes de l'Epipaléolithique et du Mésolithique de la France et du nord-ouest du bassin Méditerranéen. *Bulletin et Mémoires de la Société d'Anthropologie de Paris*, 1: 201–236.

FIEDEL, S.J. (1983) Ornaments in hunter-gatherer burials: do they imply ranking? *Paper read at the 48th Annual Meeting of the Society for American Archaeology, Pittsburgh*.

FLANNERY, K.V. (1973) The origins of agriculture. *Annual Review of Anthropology*, 2: 271–310.

GIGOV, A. (1964) Typen der Pollen-Diagramme am Gebiet Jugoslawien im Laufe der Nacheiszeit. *Advancing Frontiers of Plant Sciences*, 9: 9–14.

GIMBUTAS, M. (1974) *The Gods and Goddesses of Old World Europe. Myths and Cult Images*. London, Thames and Hudson.

GREEN, S.W. (1980) Broadening least-cost models for expanding agricultural systems. In T. Earle and A. Christenson (eds), *Modelling Change in Prehistoric Subsistence Economies*. London, Academic Press: 209–241.

GREEN, S.W., MOORE, J.A. and ZVELEBIL, M. (in press) Conceptual approaches to Ireland's Mesolithic and Neolithic. *Paper presented at the Symposium on the Irish Mesolithic, Cork 1985*.

GROSSU, A. (1970) Unele observaţii asupra gasteropodelor descoperite în straturile Romanello-Aziliene de la Cuina Turcului. *Studii şi Cercetări de Istorie Veche*, 21: 45–47.

HAMOND, F. (1980) The colonisation of Europe: the analysis of settlement process. In I. Hodder, N. Hammond and G.L. Isaac (eds), *Patterns of the Past*. Cambridge, University Press: 211–248.

HARRIS, D. (1977) Alternative pathways towards agriculture. In C.A. Reed (ed.), *Origins of Agriculture*. The Hague, Mouton: 179–243.

HARRISON, G.A. and BOYCE, A.J. (eds) (1972) *The Structure of Human Populations*. Oxford, Clarendon Press.

HASSAN, F. (1977) The dynamics of agricultural origins in Palestine: a theoretical model. In C.A. Reed (ed.), *Origins of Agriculture*. The Hague, Mouton: 589–609.

HODDER, I. (1979) Economic and social stress and material culture patterning. *American Antiquity*, 44: 446–454.

JARMAN, M.R., BAILEY, G. and JARMAN, H.N. (1983) *Early European Agriculture*. Cambridge, University Press.

JOVANOVIĆ, B. (1969) Chronological frames of the Iron Gates group of the early Neolithic period. *Archaeologia Iugoslavica*, 10: 23–38.

KOZŁOWSKI, J.K. and KOZŁOWSKI, S.K. (1982) Lithic industries from the multi-layer Mesolithic site Vlasac in Yugoslavia. In J.K. Kozłowski (ed.), *Origin of the Chipped Stone Industries of the Early Farming Cultures in Balkans*. Warsaw–Kraków, Państwowe Wydawnictwo Naukowe: 11–109.

KOZŁOWSKI, J.K. and KOZŁOWSKI, S.K. (1983) Chipped stone industries from Lepenski Vir, Yugoslavia. In *Il Popolamento delle Alpi in Età Mesolitica: VIII–V Millennio a.C. (Preistoria Alpina, 19)*. Trento, Museo Tridentino di Scienze Naturali: 259–294.

LAZAROVICI, G. (1977) *Gornea – prehistorie*. Reşiţa, Muzeul de Istorie al Judeţului Caraş-Severin.

LEROI-GOURHAN, A., MATEESCO, C.N. and PROTOPOPESCU-PAKE, E.M. (1967) Contribution à l'étude du climat à la station de Vădastră du Paléolithique à la fin du Néolithique. *Bulletin de l'Association Française pour l'Etude du Quaternaire*, 1967(4): 271–279.

LIMP, W.F. and REIDHEAD, V.A. (1979) An economic evaluation of the potential of fish utilization in riverine environments. *American Antiquity*, 44(1): 70–78.

MARKOVIĆ-MARJANOVIĆ, J. and GIGOV, A. (1971) Geološki sastav i istorija vegetacije tresetišta kereš na subotičkoj peščari. *Glasnik Prirodnačkog Muzeja Beograd*, Series A, 26: 129–148.

MARKYEVICH, V.I. (1968) *Neolit Moldavii*. Thesis for Kandidat Istoricheskikh Nauka, University of Moscow.

MARSHACK, A. (in press) Epipaleolithic, early Neolithic Iconography: a cognitive, comparative analysis of the Lepenski Vir/Vlasac iconography and symbolism, its roots and later influence. *Paper presented to the Lepenski Vir Conference, Köln, March 1981*.

MIHÁLTZ-FARAGO, M. and MUCSI, M. (1971) Geologische Entwicklungsgeschichte von Natronteichen auf Grund der Palynologische Untersuchungen, *Acta Geografica* (Szeged), 11(1–7): 93–101.

MIROSAVLJEVIĆ, I. (1959) Jamina Sredi – prilog prethistorijskoj kulturi na otoku Cresu. *Arheološki Radovi i Razprave*, 1: 131–169.

MOLNÁR, B., MUCSI, M. and MAGYAR, L. (1971) Latest Quaternary history of the southern stretch of the Tisza valley. *A Móra Ferenc Múzeum Évkönyve*, 1971(1): 5–14.

MOORE, J.A. (1981) The effects of information networks in hunter-gatherer societies. In B. Winterhalder and E. Smith (eds), *Hunter-Gatherer Foraging Strategies: Ethnographic and Archaeological Analyses*. Chicago, University Press: 194–217.

MOORE, J.A. (1983) The trouble with know-it-alls: information as an ecological social resource. In J.A. Moore and A.S. Keene (eds), *Archaeological Hammers and Theories*. New York, Academic Press: 173–191.

NAGY, M.A. (1954) Taljfoldrajzi Megfigyelések a Tiszazugban, *Földrajzi Értesitö*, 3(3): 507–543.

NANDRIS, J.G. (1968) Lepenski Vir. *Science Journal*, 1: 64–70.

NANDRIS, J.G. (1970) The development and relationships of the earlier Greek Neolithic. *Man*, 5: 192–213.

NANDRIS, J.G. (1972) Review of D. Srejović, 'Europe's First Monumental Sculpture: New Discoveries at Lepenski Vir'. *Proceedings of the Prehistoric Society*, 38: 426–429.

NEMESKÉRI, J. (1978) Demographic structure of the Vlasac Epipaleolithic population. In D. Srejović and Z. Letica (eds), *Vlasac. Mesolitsko naselje u Djerdapu*, vol. 2. Belgrade, Srpska Akademija Nauka i Umetnosti: 97–133.

NEMESKÉRI, J. and LENGYEL, I. (1978) The results of paleopathological examinations. In D. Srejović and Z. Letica (eds), *Vlasac. Mesolitsko naselje u Djerdapu*, vol. 2. Belgrade, Srpska Akademija Nauka i Umetnosti: 231–260.

NEWELL, R.R. (1984) On the Mesolithic contribution to the social evolution of western European society. In J. Bintliff (ed.), *European Social Evolution: Archaeological Perspectives*. Bradford, University of Bradford: 69–82.

NEWELL, R.R., CONSTANDSE-WESTERMANN, T.S. and MEIKLEJOHN, C. (1979) The skeletal remains of Mesolithic man in western Europe: an evaluative catalogue. *Journal of Human Evolution*, 8: 1–228.

NEWELL, R.R., KIELMAN, D., CONSTANDSE-WESTERMANN, T.S., VAN GIJN, A. and VAN DER SANDEN, W.A.B. (in press) *An Inquiry into the Ethnic Resolution of Mesolithic Regional Groups: a Study of their Decorative Ornaments in Time and Space*. Leiden, E.J. Brill.

NICA, M. (1971) O Aşezare de tip Starčevo-Criş lînga Basarabi (Jud. Dolj). *Studii şi Cercetări de Istorie Veche*, 22(4): 547–556.

NICA, M. (1976) Cîrcea. Cea mai veche asezare neolitică de la sud de Carpaţi. *Studii şi Cercetări de Istorie Veche şi Arheologie*, 27(4): 435–463.

NICOLĂESCU-PLOPŞOR, C., COMŞA, E. and PĂUNESCU, A. (1957) Şantierul arheologic Băile Herculane (reg. Timişoara, r. Almas). *Materiale*, 3: 51–58.

NICOLĂESCU-PLOPŞOR, C., DAVIDESCU, M., ROMAN, P.L. and BORONEANŢ, V. (1965) Cercetările arheologice de la Cazane. *Studii şi Cercetări de Istorie Veche*, 16: 407–411.

OSTROVSKY, A.B. (1967) Regressivnyye urovni Chernogo morya i ikh svyaz's pyeruglublyenyim ryecnykh dolin kavkazsogo pobyeryezhya (Izvyestiya AN SSSR, Seriya Geografichyeskaya, 1). Moscow.

PĂUNESCU, A. (1970a) Epipaleoliticul de la Cuina Turcului-Dubova. *Studii şi Cercetări de Istorie Veche*, 21(1): 3–47.

PĂUNESCU, A. (1970b) Evoluţia uneltor şi armelor de piatră cioplită descoperite pe teritoriul Romaniei. Bucharest, Academia di Ştiinţe Sociale şi Politice (Institutul de Arheologie).

POP, E. (1929) Analize de polen în turba Carpaţilor Orientali (Dorna Lucina). *Buletinul Grădinii Botanice* (Cluj), 9(3–4): 81–120.

POP, E. (1932) Contribuţii la istoria vegetăţiei cuaternare din Transilvania. *Buletinul Grădinii Botanice* (Cluj), 12(1–2): 29–102.

POP, E., BOŞCAIU, N. and LUPŞA, V. (1970) Anexa Nr. 1, Analiza sporopolinică sedimentelor de la Cuina Turcului-Dubova. In A. Păunescu 'Epipaleoliticul de la Cuina Turcului-Dubova'. *Studii şi Cercetări de Istorie Veche*, 21(1): 31–34.

PRINZ, B. (1982) *Stone tools, Cultural Continuity, and Mesolithic Adaptations on the Lower Danube* (Ph.D. thesis, University of Pittsburgh). Ann Arbor, University Microfilms.

RADOVANOVIĆ, I. (1981) *Ranoholocenska kremena industrija sa lokaliteta Padina u Djerdapu*. Belgrade, Arheološki Institut.

RENFREW, J. (1979) The first farmers in south-east Europe. *Archaeophysika*, 8: 243–265.

SHERRATT, A.G. (1983) Early agrarian settlement in the Körös region of the Great Hungarian Plain. *Acta Archaeologica Hungarica*, 35(1–2): 155–169.

SPUHLER, J.N. (1967) Behaviour and mating patterns in human populations. In J.N. Spuhler (ed.), *Genetic Diversity and Human Behaviour*. Chicago, Aldine.

SREJOVIĆ, D. (1969) *Lepenski Vir. Nova praistorijska Kultura u Podunavlju*. Belgrade, Srpska književna zadruga.

SREJOVIĆ, D. and LETICA, Z. (1978) *Vlasac. Mesolitsko naselje u Djerdapu*. Belgrade, Srpska Akademija Nauka i Umetnosti.

STARLING, N. (1985) Colonization and succession: the earlier Neolithic of central Europe. *Proceedings of the Prehistoric Society*, 51: 41–57.

TRIFUNOVIĆ, L. (1969) *Anciennes Cultures du Djerdap*. Belgrade, Narodni Muzej Beograd.

TRINGHAM, R. (1968) A preliminary study of the early Neolithic and latest Mesolithic blade industries in south-east and central Europe. In J.M. Coles and D.D.A. Simpson (eds), *Studies in Ancient Europe*. Leicester, University Press: 45–70.

TRINGHAM, R. (1971) *Hunters, Fishers and Farmers of Eastern Europe 6000–3000 BC*. London, Hutchinson University Library.

TRINGHAM, R. (1983) The development of the household as the primary unit of production in Neolithic and Eneolithic south-east Europe. *Paper read at the 48th Annual Meeting of the Society for American Archaeology, Pittsburgh*.

VALLOIS, H. and DE FELICE, S. (1977) *Les Mésolithiques de France*. Paris, Masson.

VASILJEVIĆ, M. and TRBUHOVIĆ, V. (1972) Rekognosciranje u Podrinju i sondažna ispitivanja. *Arheološki Pregled*, 14: 164–189.

VASILJEVIĆ, M. and TRBUHOVIĆ, V. (1973) Rekognosciranje u Podrinju i sondažna ispitivanja, *Arheološki Preglad*, 15: 133–161.

WATERBOLK, H.T. (1968) Food production in prehistoric Europe. *Science*, 162: 1093–1102.

WILK, R.R. and RATHJE, W.L. (1982) Household archaeology. *American Behavioural Scientist*, 25(6): 617–639.

WOBST, H.M. (1974) Boundary conditions for Palaeolithic social systems: a simulation approach. *American Antiquity*, 39: 147–178.

WOBST, H.M. (1975) The demography of finite populations and the origins of the incest taboo. In A.C. Swedlund (ed.), *Population Studies in Archaeology and Biological Anthropology*. Washington, Memoirs of the Society for American Archaeology 30: 75–81.

WOBST, H.M. (1976) Locational relationships in Palaeolithic society. *Journal of Human Evolution*, 5: 49–58.

ŽIVANOVIĆ, S. (1976) The masticatory apparatus of the Mesolithic Padina population. *Zbornik Radova: Antropološko Društvo Jugoslavije*, 3: 79–96.

ŽIVANOVIĆ, S. (1979) Further evidence on Cro-Magnon Man in the Iron Gates gorge of the Danube. *Current Anthropology*, 20(4): 805.

ŽIVANOVIĆ, S. (1982) *Ancient Diseases. The Elements of Palaeopathology*. London, Methuen.

ZÓLYOMI, B. (1953) Die Entwicklungsgeschichte der Vegetations Ungarn seit dem letzten Interglazial. *Acta Biologica Academiae Scientiarum Hungaricae*, 4(3–4): 364–430.

Riparo Salvini: a New Dryas II Site in Southern Lazio.
Thoughts on the Late Epi-Gravettian of Middle and Southern Tyrrhenian Italy

E. Avellino, A. Bietti, L. Giacopini, A. Lo Pinto and M. Vicari

Abstract

This paper describes the finds from the rock-shelter site of Riparo Salvini in southern Italy and discusses their significance for our understanding of the cultural processes which marked the Pleistocene–Holocene transition. The paper is divided into four sections: the introductory section outlines the background to the project; section two describes the site and its stratigraphy, and discusses the archaeological problems caused by modern disturbance; section three deals with the faunal remains and the lithic industries, emphasizing the evidence for intra-site variability in the distribution of the archaeological remains; in the final section an attempt is made to draw some preliminary conclusions about the nature of the site and to establish comparisons with other relevant sites in the middle and southern Tyrrhenian zone of Italy.

INTRODUCTION

The problems which arise from the analysis of the cultural processes at the Pleistocene–Holocene transition in Europe – and hence the origins of the Mesolithic cultures – are still a matter of debate. A number of recent issues of *Mesolithic Miscellany*, for example, clearly show the variety of opinions and perspectives that have been put forward by a large number of researchers. Some authors have placed an emphasis on a chronological definition of the transition (Mellars 1981), others on adaptive processes towards sedentism (Lewthwaite and Rowley-Conwy 1980), still others on a substantial change in technology, such as increased microlithization (Rozoy 1984; see also Rozoy 1978) which implies a widespread use of the bow and arrow.

In Italy, as one of us tried to point out in a paper presented at the last Mesolithic Symposium (Bietti 1981), the situation is more complicated than that in northern Europe; the cultural processes probably differed locally. All regions were characterized, nevertheless, by a substantial increase in specialized activities.

Northern Italy including northern Tuscany, for example, seems to have been characterized by a series of cultural transformations of essentially 'middle European' type: a 'late Epi-Gravettian' in the final phase of Würm IV, followed by a 'Sauveterrian' facies in the Pre-Boreal and Boreal, and then by a 'Castelnovian' facies (e.g. Broglio 1973, 1980).

In other regions, such as the middle and southern Tyrrhenian zone, the local Epi-Gravettian tradition

seems to have continued through time;[1] thus sites dated to the late Boreal, such as Riparo Blanc in Latium (Taschini 1964, 1968) or level 1 of the Grotta della Madonna at Praia a Mare in Calabria (Cardini 1970), which are very rich in 'atypical' tools (denticulates and notches), may represent specialized adaptations (perhaps almost exclusively seasonal activities – e.g. Riparo Blanc) for rock marine mollusc gathering (Bietti 1981).

At this point, we believe that a more detailed discussion of the chronological sequences in the various regions – that is, the study of the 'antecedents' of the Mesolithic – is necessary and of paramount importance for a better understanding of the cultural processes involved.

As regards the north east of Italy, a local derivation of the Sauveterrian Pre-Boreal and Boreal Mesolithic from a late Epi-Gravettian cultural facies was first hypothesized by A. Broglio (1973). The same author has since appeared to take a more cautious view (Broglio 1980), although the hypothesis has been further emphasized by A. Guerreschi (1983). Of interest in this respect is the site of Isola Santa in northern Tuscany, which seems to show an evolution from a late Epi-Gravettian industry (level 5, dated to c. 10,800 BP) to Sauveterrian and then to an early Castelnovian industry (levels 4e–4a, c. 9300 to 7400 BP) (Biagi *et al.* 1980; Tozzi 1980).

This paper, however, will describe a possible Pleistocene 'antecedent' of Holocene complexes in the middle and southern Tyrrhenian region – the site of Riparo Salvini at Terracina (Latina province), near Monte Circeo in southern Latium. Systematic excavation of this site began only a few years ago. A radiocarbon determination for one square of the site is consistent with a Dryas II stadial date. The lithic industry belongs generally to the late Epi-Gravettian technocomplex, but contains a significant microlithic component with several geometric forms and microburins. Such tools are absent from later Holocene sites in the region, such as Riparo Blanc which is only 15 km away. From a traditional chronostratigraphic perspective, therefore, it seems that the

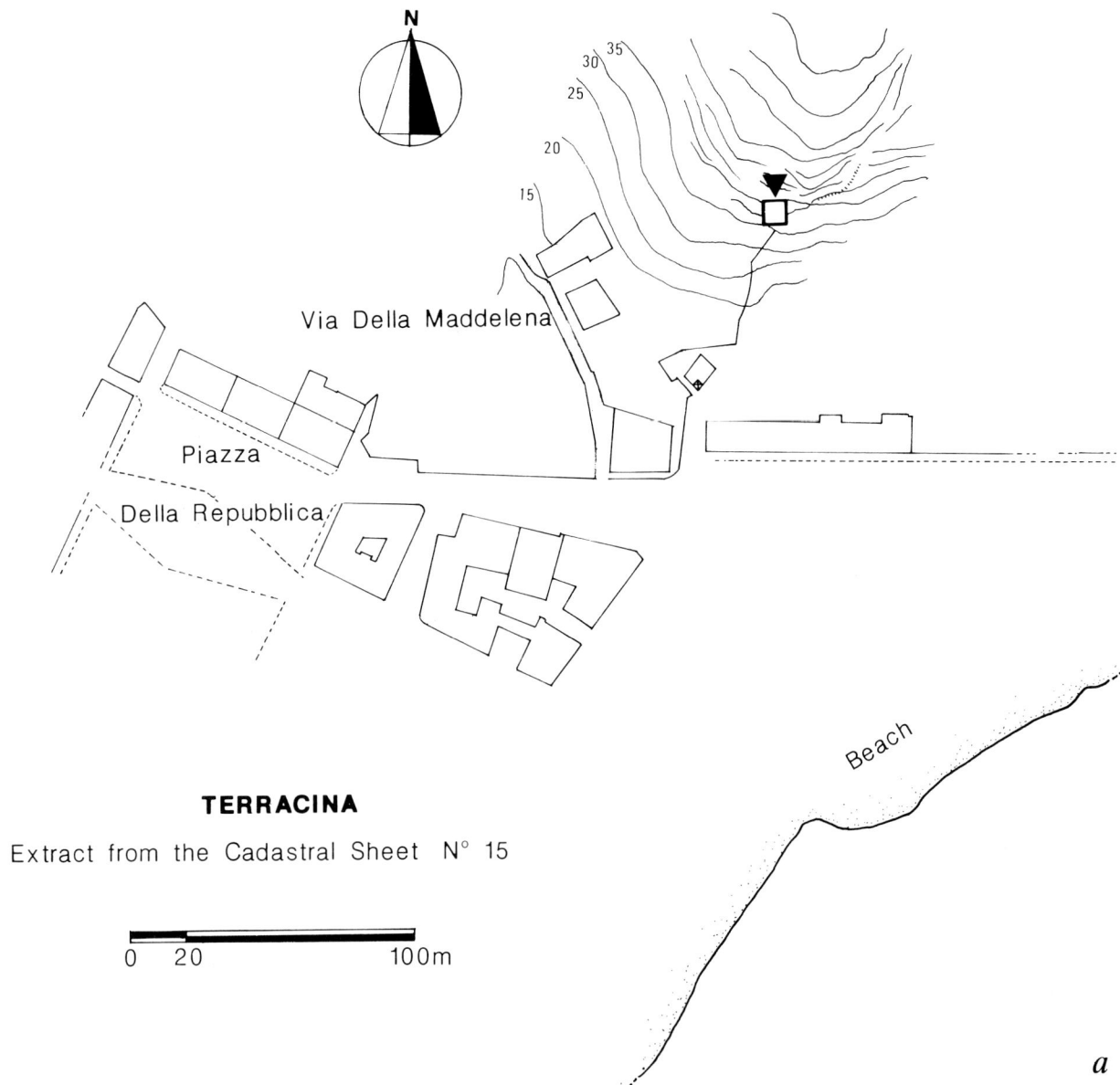

Figure 1a The location of Riparo Salvini in the town of Terracina (for enlargement of arrowed area — see *Fig. 1b*).

sequence of 'cultural facies' in southern Latium is essentially opposite to that at several north Italian sites, such as Isola Santa.

DESCRIPTION OF THE EXCAVATIONS AND OF THE STRATIGRAPHY

Riparo Salvini (named after the owner of the villa where it is situated) is a small (*c.* 35 m^2) rock-shelter in the town of Terracina, province of Latina. The shelter faces the Tyrrhenian sea in a south-south-west direction, at an average altitude of 35 metres. It is situated on a 'falaise' of Monte Giove, a middle to upper Cretaceous limestone formation formerly also called Monte Sant'Angelo – on the top of this hill there is also the Roman temple of Jupiter Anxur. On the same 'falaise' there are other caves, now empty, and some Roman burials excavated in the rock; one

of these burials, with an associated rock-carved inscription (*Fig. 1*), is very near to the shelter.

The presence of flint tools and fragments of bones was noticed by a local speleological group (the 'Anxur' group) around 1958–59 in a small vineyard in front of the shelter, and a short note was subsequently published (Chiappella *et al.* 1961). A test trench (2 x 1 m) was opened in May 1963 by L. Cardini. Below 30–40 cm of disturbed deposit, over a depth of *c.* 80 cm, a very abundant industry of Epi-Gravettian type was recovered, together with faunal remains consisting mostly of red deer, with some bones of aurochs and *Equus hydruntinus*. A broken pebble with an engraving of an animal's head was also found. In the following year (1964) a clandestine excavation was reported around Cardini's test trench and to the north west of it in the innermost part of the shelter.

517

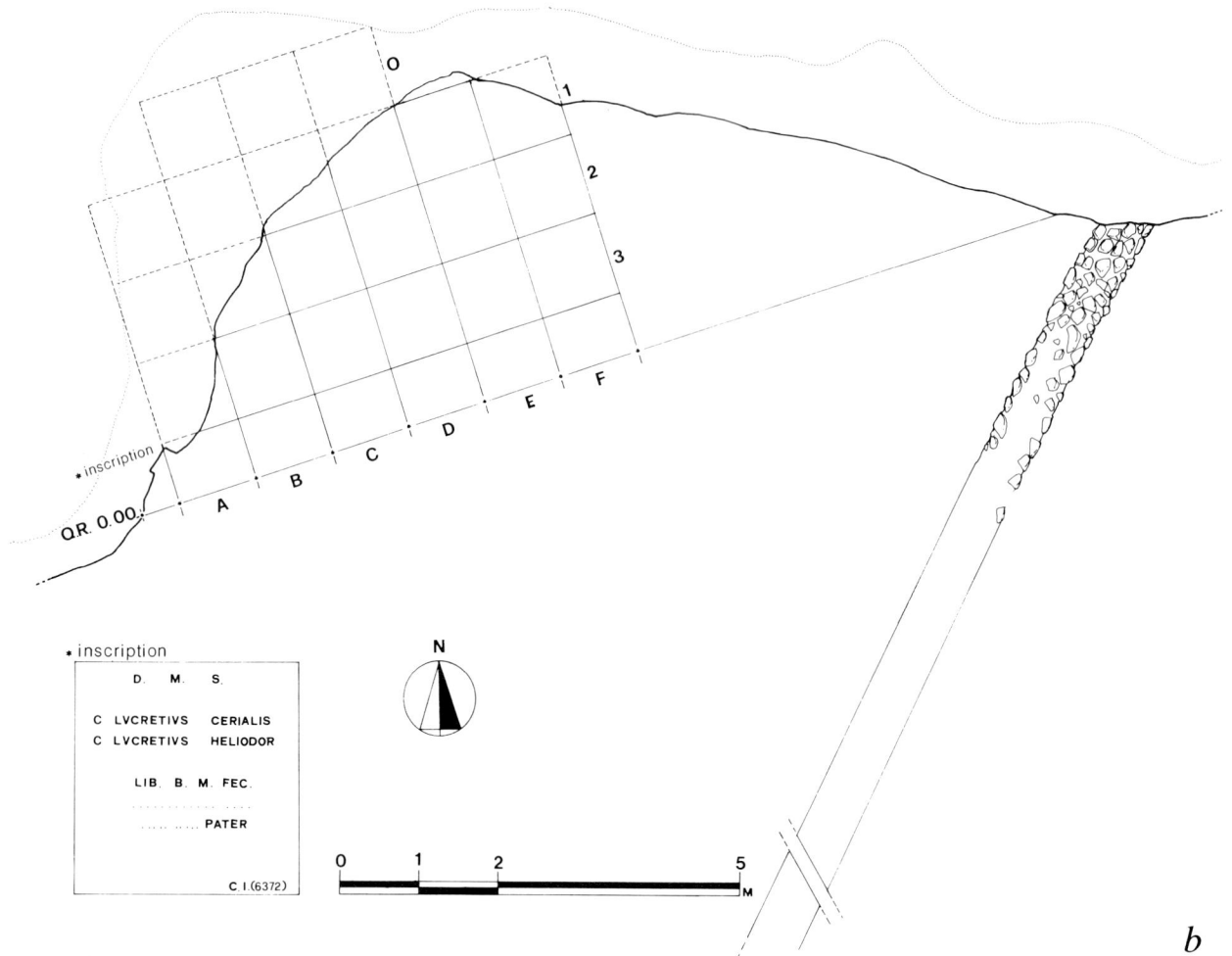

Figure 1b General map of the rock-shelter with the Roman funerary inscription on its left edge. The dashed contour indicates the innermost wall of the shelter.

It was not until fifteen years later, in May 1979, that a systematic excavation campaign was begun, with the financial support of the Faculty of Sciences of the University of Rome and the City Council of Terracina. The excavations are still in progress, and a preliminary report on the results obtained in 1979–80 has already been published (Bietti 1984a).

A grid of 1 × 1 m squares was established on the floor of the shelter (*Fig. 1b*). Initially, cleaning of the whole surface was undertaken for a depth of 20–40 cm, within which two pavements made of regularly-placed stones were discovered (*Fig. 2*), probably the remnants of a hut or small house built by local shepherds in recent times; the date, at least of the upper floor, should be later than 1890, since a coin of approximately this age was found. Two pictures, one dating from 1912 and one from 1925, clearly show a small house or hut where the shelter now stands.

Squares C3, C2 and D2 (see *Figs. 1 & 2*) were dug first in 1979, but the deposit was still disturbed to a considerable depth, as witnessed by several fragments of bricks mixed with the abundant Upper Palaeolithic industry and wild fauna. The same situation was found beneath the upper pavement (*Fig. 2*) in squares F1–F4, and the bedrock was

reached here at only 20–30 cm depth, without any trace of an *in situ* deposit. Moreover, in all these squares the extreme scarcity of pottery sherds of Roman times (in spite of the funerary inscription nearby) and the complete absence of any archaeological material of the Neolithic or Bronze Age is quite remarkable.

In 1980 it was decided to excavate more deeply in squares B1, B2 and C1, in the general area of Cardini's test trench. The excavation proceeded in arbitrary levels or 'spits'; after removing several 5–10 cm spits in the disturbed deposit, a slab of concrete approximately 80 x 70 x 5 cm (probably the base of a store built by the shepherds) was found in squares B1 and C1. This slab sealed a deposit of grey-black earth with a very rich flint industry, several bones, and without any trace of pottery sherds or fragments of bricks. Thus, this layer seemed to be *in situ*, and regular excavation was continued in square B1.

The stratigraphy in a section through squares B1–B2 is shown in *Fig. 3*:

A. lower pavement of the shepherds' hut, partly removed by L. Cardini's test trench and the clandestine excavations (spit 1).

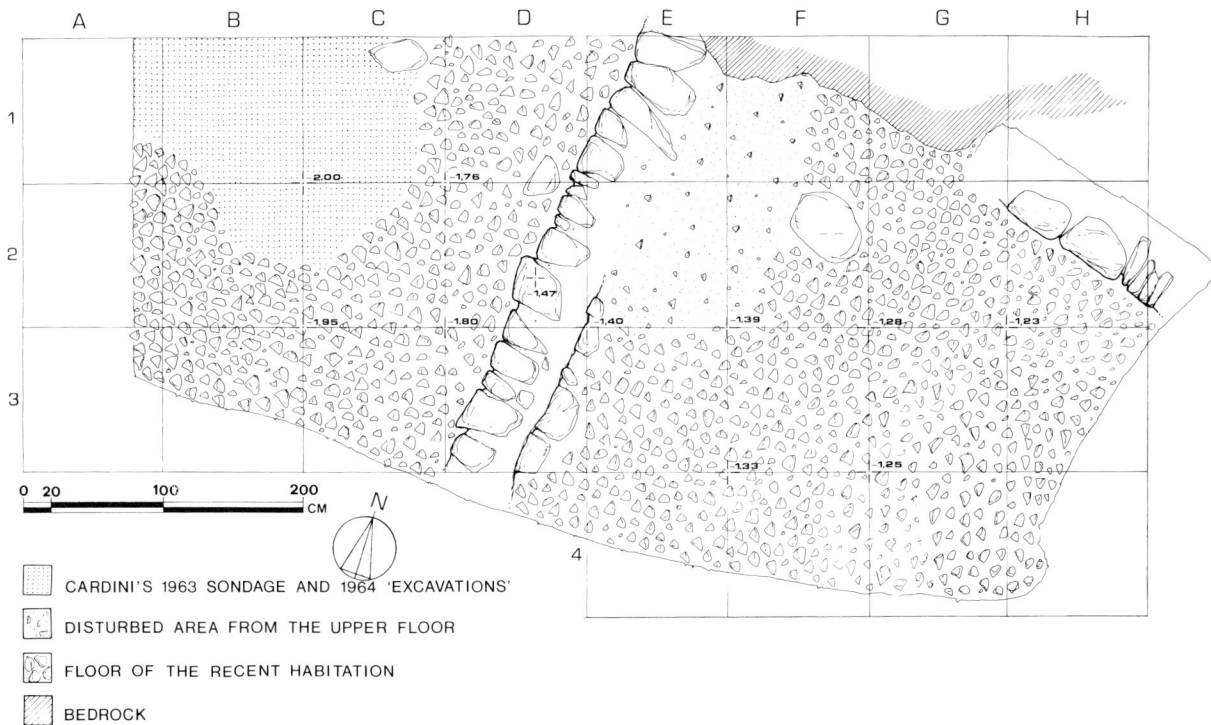

Figure 2 General plan of the excavation area at the beginning of the 1979 campaign. Spot levels are taken from the reference point Q.R. 0.00, shown in *Fig. 1b*

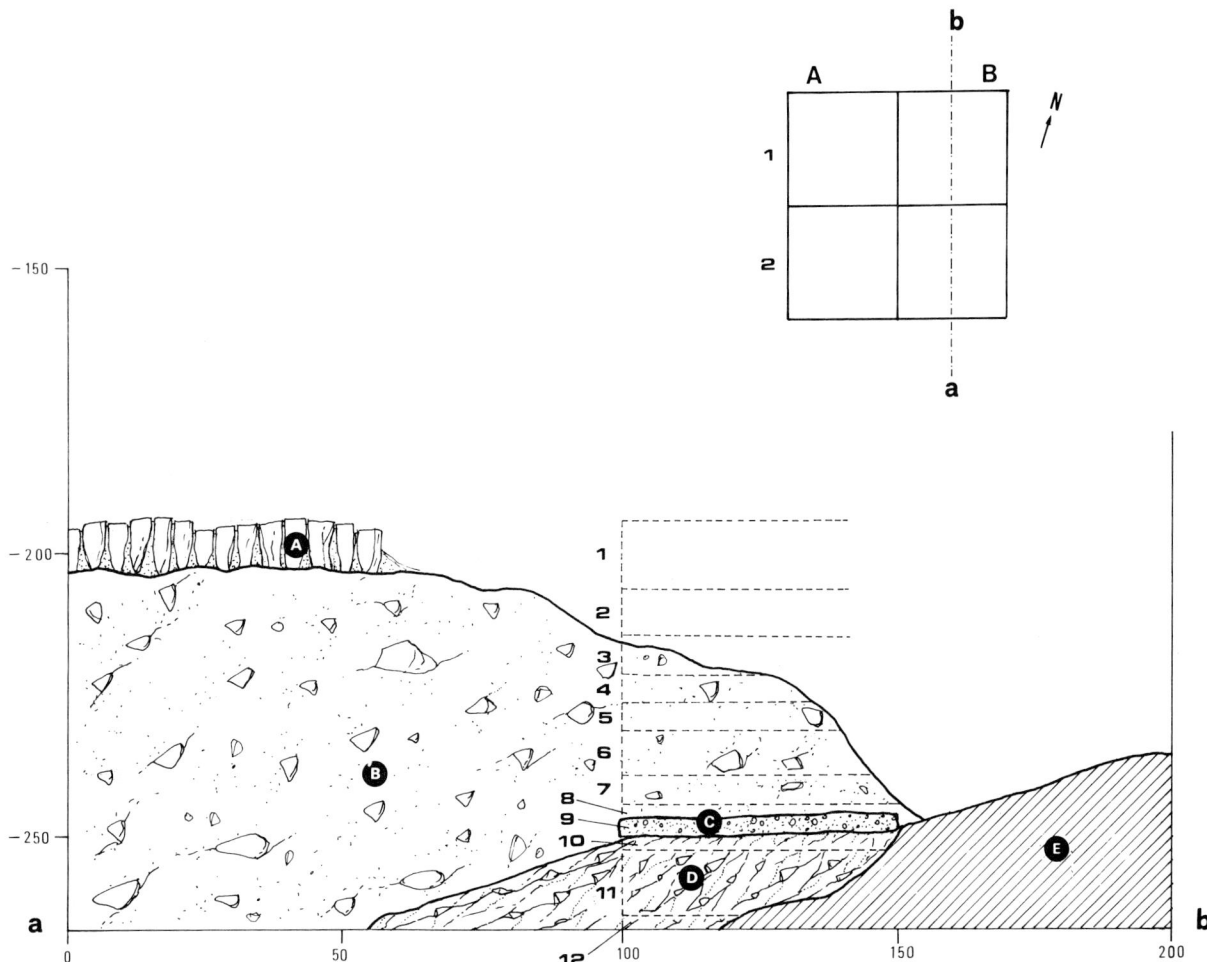

Figure 3 Stratigraphic section through squares B1–B2: A – shepherds' pavement; B – disturbed layer; C – concrete slab; D – *in situ* layer; E – bedrock. The numbers refer to the different spits; depths are measured from the reference point Q.R. 0.00, shown in *Fig. 1b*.

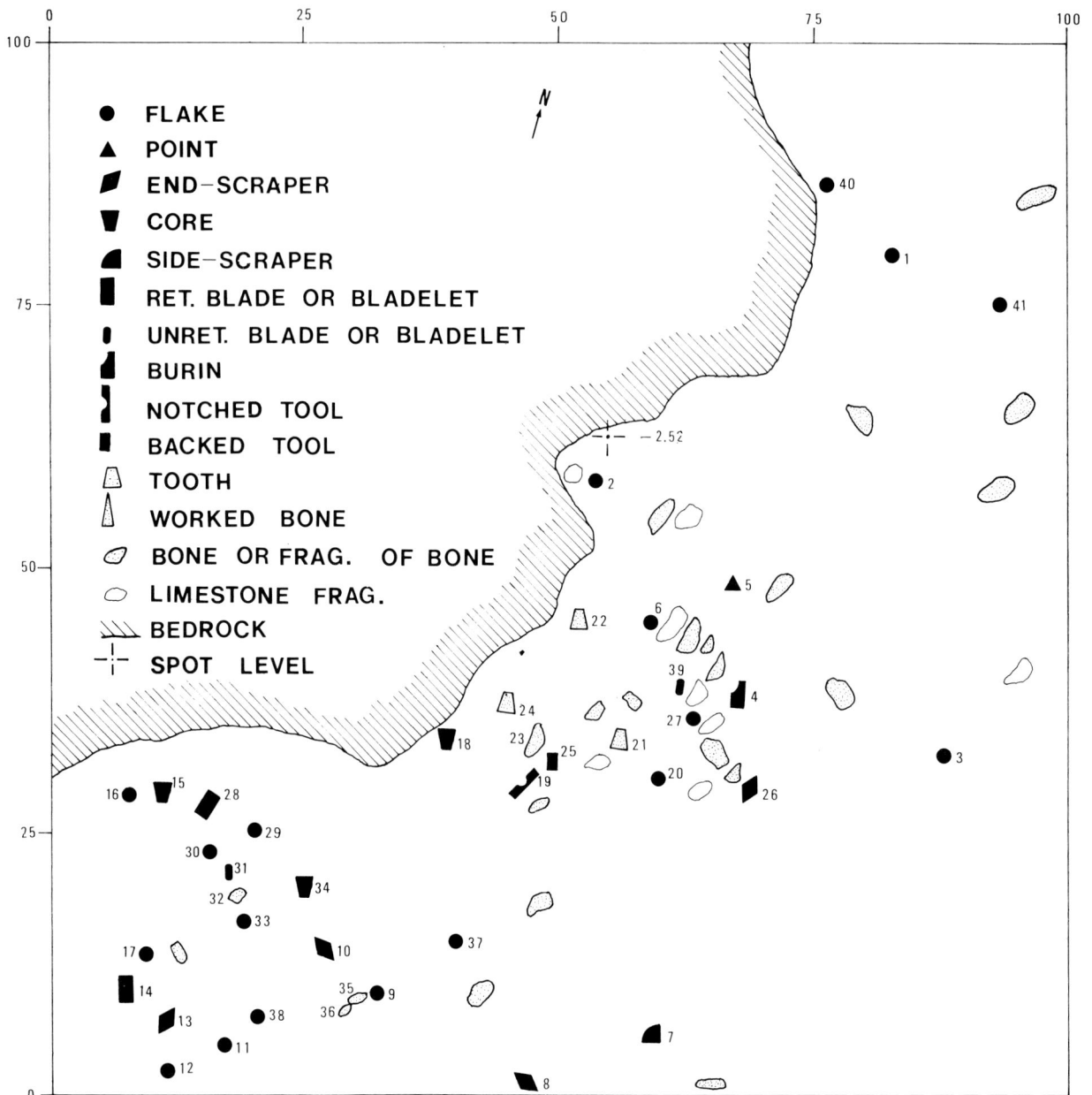

Figure 4 Horizontal distribution of the finds in square B1, spit 10.

B. disturbed layer with abundant faunal remains and an Upper Palaeolithic industry, sharp-edged limestone fragments, and some brick fragments and pottery sherds (spits 2–8).

C. slab of concrete (spit 9) – this slab is present only in squares B1–B2 and C1–C2.

D. layer of fine, grey-black earth with weathered limestone pebbles, and with an abundant fauna and Upper Palaeolithic industry *in situ* (spits 10–12).

E. limestone bedrock.

A sample of burnt bone fragments from spits 11 and 12 of layer D was submitted to the radiocarbon dating laboratory of Rome University; the result was a date of 12,400±170 BP (Alessio *et al.*, in press)

A series of plans of the horizontal distribution of the finds were made – one for spit 10, four for spit

11, and two for spit 12. The first map (spit 10) and the last map of spit 12 are presented in *Figs. 4* and *5*. As can be seen in *Fig. 5*, square B1 was almost completely excavated. The symbols for the tools and the bone fragments given in *Fig. 4* refer to the most common categories. A detailed analysis of the spatial correlations between bone fragments and flint implements is in progress but, as will become evident in the next section, there is no obvious correlation between the various items.

At the same time, excavation continued in squares E1–E3. In square E2, in particular, when the disturbed part of the deposit had been removed, the same layer of grey-black earth found in square B1 was encountered – again without any trace of pottery sherds or brick fragments. As will be discussed in more detail below, this part of layer D

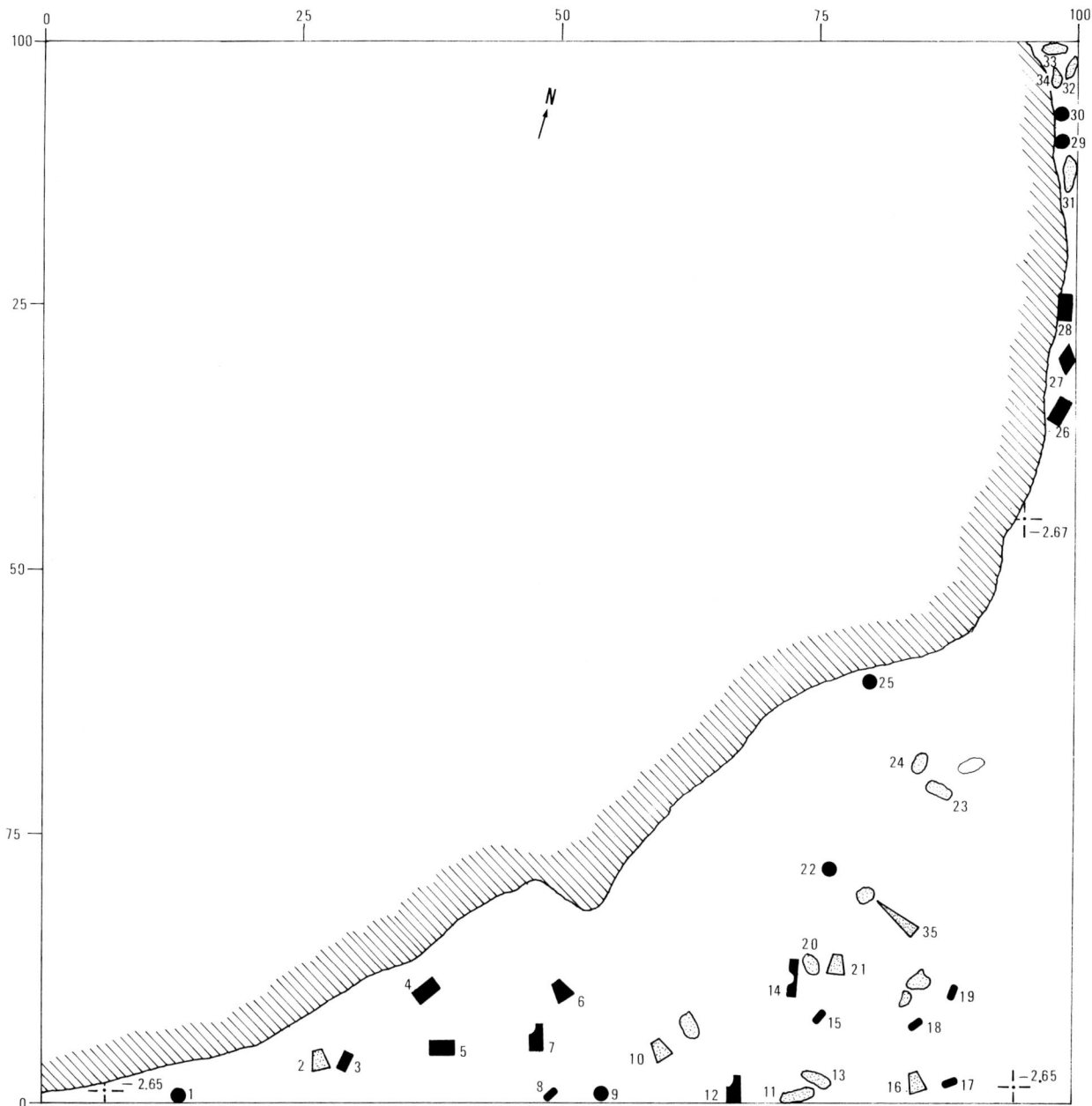

Figure 5   Horizontal distribution of the finds in square B1, base of spit 12. Symbols as in *Fig. 4*.

in square E2 differs considerably from its equivalent in square B1 in terms of its archaeological contents; there are a large number of · microburins and geometric tools in square E2 (very rare in square B1), with a very small quantity of faunal remains (very abundant in square B1).

In the 1981–84 seasons the excavated area was enlarged and the disturbed layer (B) was carefully cleared away. A general plan drawn at the end of the 1984 season is shown in *Fig. 6*. As can be seen, the area available for excavation is now much more restricted. This does not mean, however, that the *in situ* deposit is nearly exhausted, since the walls of the shelter plunge rather abruptly in all the squares where bedrock has been reached.

In *Fig. 7* is shown a complete stratigraphic section

through the '2' squares, essentially at right angles to the section shown in *Fig. 3*; it can be seen that in squares A2, B2 and C2 there is a large portion of the *in situ* deposit still to be excavated.

FAUNA AND INDUSTRIES

The fauna

Analysis of the faunal remains is in progress. P. Cassoli has analyzed the fauna from square B1 (layer D, spits 10–12). Red deer dominates the assemblage (*c.* 80% of the identifiable bones); *Equus hydruntinus* is present in all three spits, aurochs occurs in spits 10 and 11, while roe deer is present (a premolar) only in spit 12. More interesting is the presence of ibex (spits 10 and 11) and chamois (a

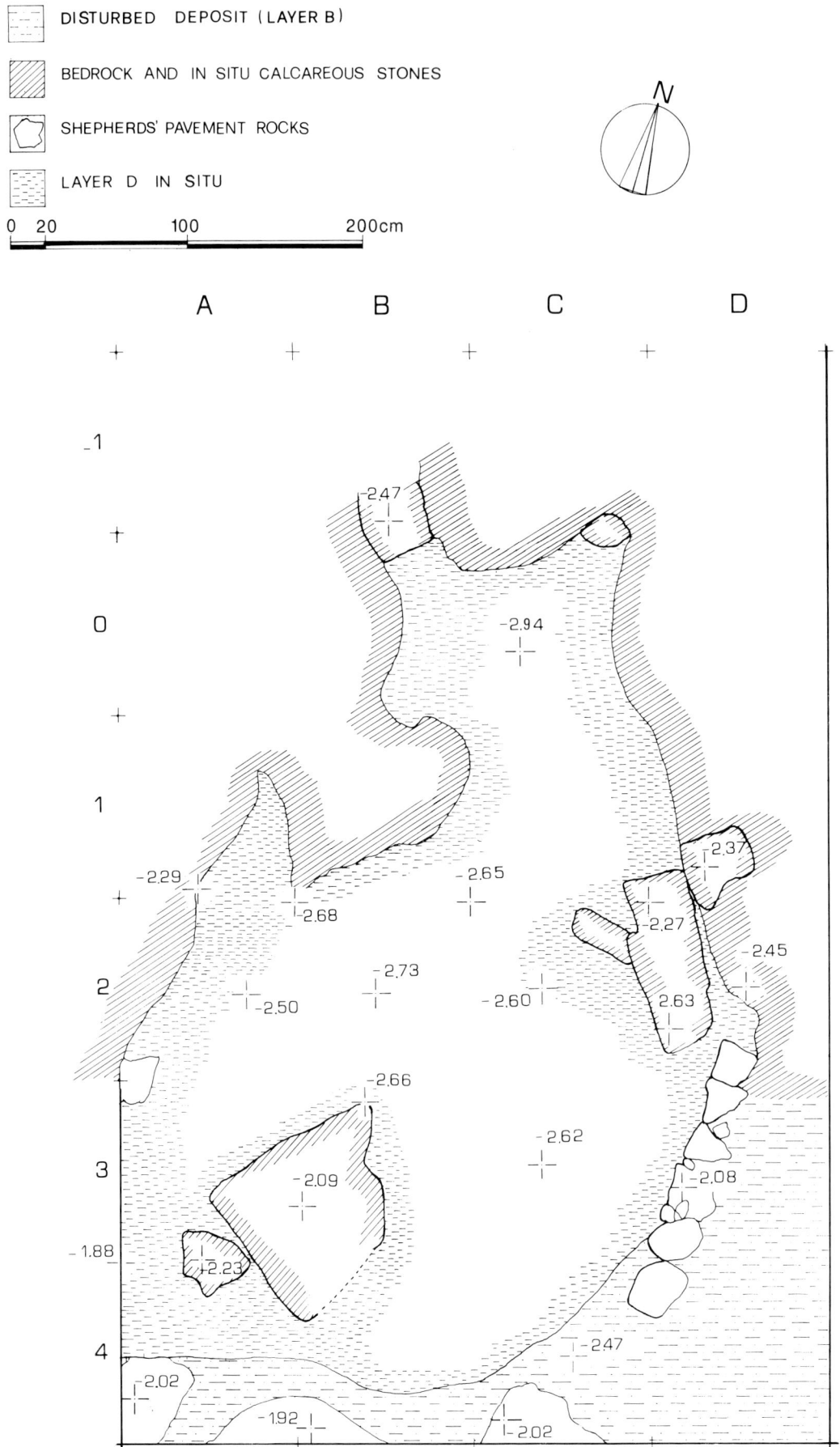

Figure 6 General plan of the excavation area at the end of the 1984 season.

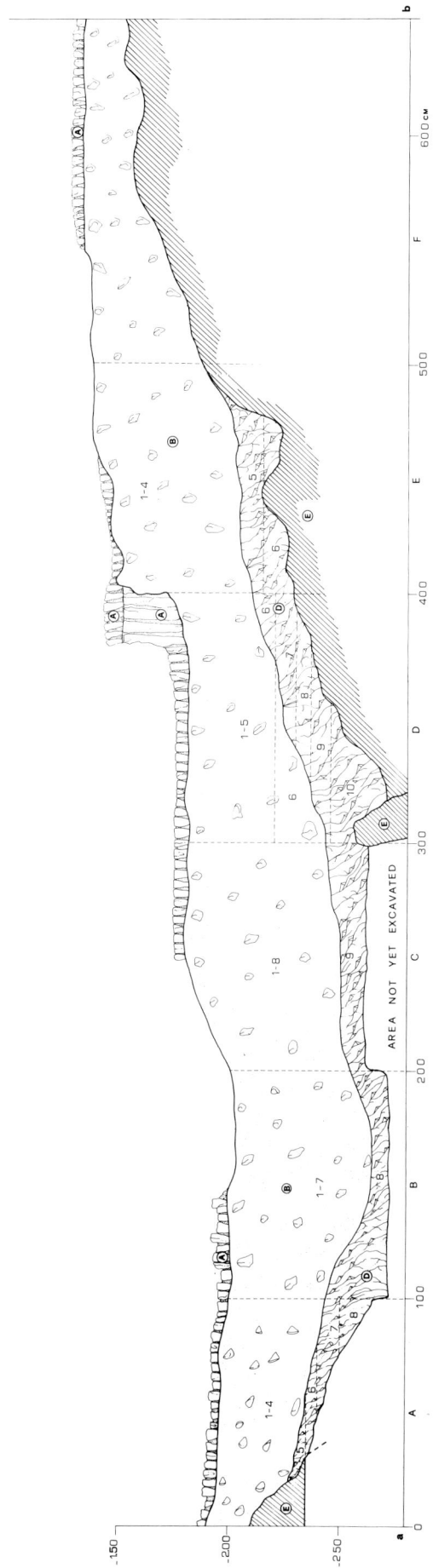

Figure 7 Stratigraphic section through squares A2–F2. Symbols as in *Fig. 3.*

523

phalange in spit 12), which is in agreement with the absolute date of 12,400±170 BP and consistent with the Dryas II stadial environment. The birds are not particularly diagnostic (*Anas platyrrhincus* and *Perdix perdix*); nor is the microfauna (a few fragments of *Lepus* sp. and *Arvicola*).

Representation of the different anatomical parts provides no clear evidence of deliberate selection. In fact, if we consider the most common species, red deer, almost all the anatomical parts are represented – skull (mostly teeth, but there are also some fragments of mandible, petrous bone, antlers), vertebrae, sternum (one fragment), ribs, long bones (humerus, ulna, radius, tibia), and extremities (mostly metapodials and phalanges).

Account also has to be taken of the fact that, as preliminary sedimentological and chemical analyses undertaken by A.M. Palmieri and A. Lentini in-

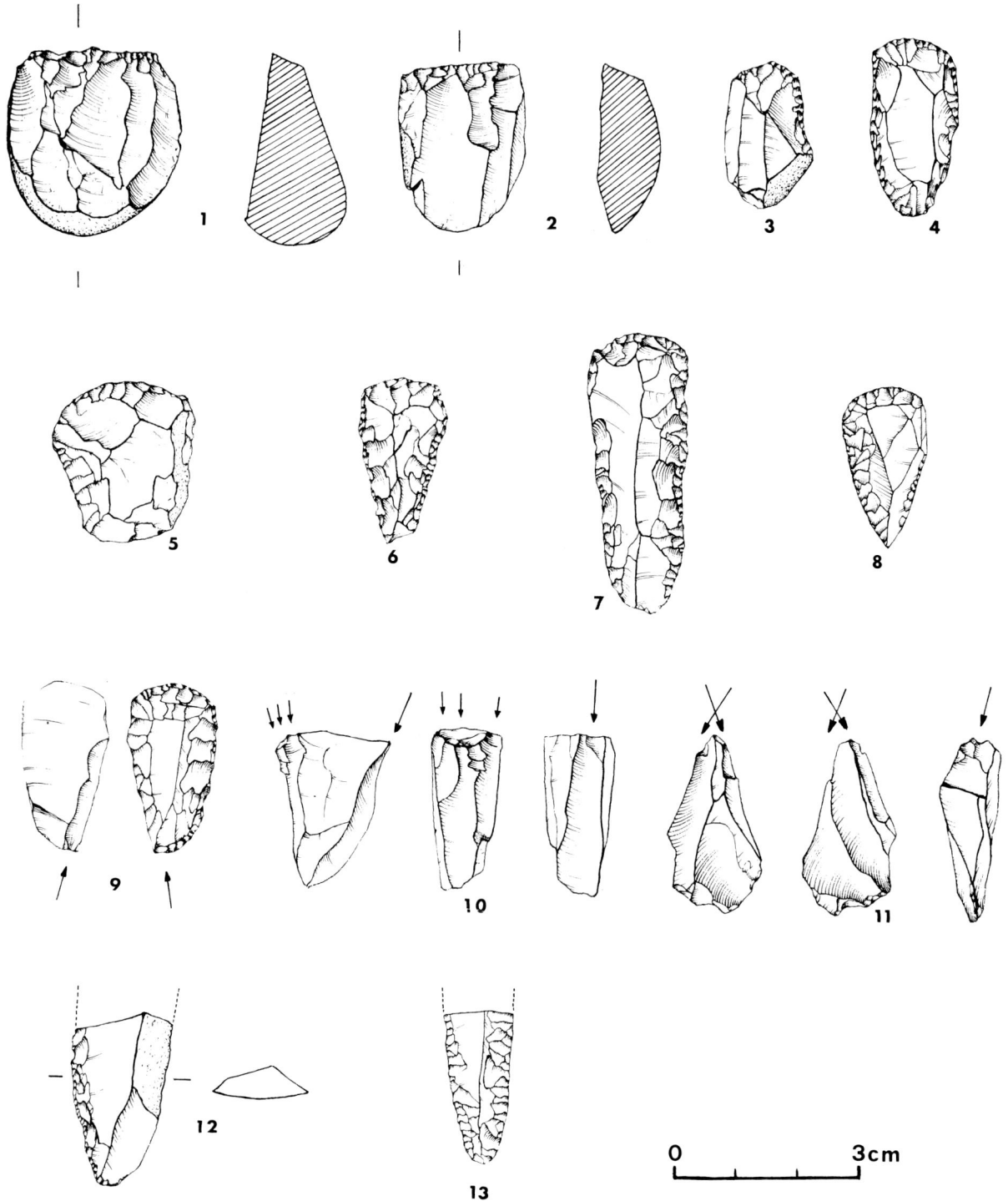

Figure 8 Industry from layer D of square B1, spits 10–12: cores with one striking platform (1, 2); end-scrapers on blades (3, 7); triangular end-scrapers (4, 6, 8); end-scraper on flake (5); combination tool, burin/end-scraper (9); burins (10, 11); retouched blades (12, 13).

dicate, the essentially acid character of layer D may have seriously affected the preservation of some bones. For example, two lower molars (M_1 and M_3) of *Equus hydruntinus* were found a few centimetres apart in spit 11, without any consistent trace of the mandible. Moreover, the collagen content of a *c.* 1 kg sample of unidentifiable fragments of long bones submitted for radiocarbon dating was insufficient for this purpose. Only the burnt bone fragments from spits 11 and 12, although much less in weight, provided a reasonable amount of collagen for dating.

Analysis of the faunal remains in layer D from the other squares is still in progress and is being done mainly by F. Guadagnoli. The preliminary results (F. Guadagnoli, pers. comm.) do not indicate substantial differences in species representation when compared to the results from square B1. In squares D1 and D2, for example, there is always a

clear majority of red deer remains, with a few aurochs fragments and, again, a fragment of phalange of chamois. On the other hand, there are important differences between the squares in terms of the *quantity* of faunal remains; in spits 10–12 of square B1 *c.* 2 kg of bones were collected, while in spit 10 of square D2 only 75 g of bones (*c.* 60 g of unidentifiable fragments) were recovered. This impression of intra-site quantitative variability is confirmed by the analysis of the artifacts (see below).

The industries

A preliminary description of the assemblages from spits 10–12 of square B1 (*Figs. 8 & 9a*) has already been published (Bietti 1984a). Among more than 220 tools there is a clear dominance of backed bladelets and fragments thereof (*c.* 33%) (*Fig. 9a*, nos. 1, 3, 4 and 6), with some truncated backed bladelets (*Fig. 9a*, no. 5) and end-scrapers (19%) –

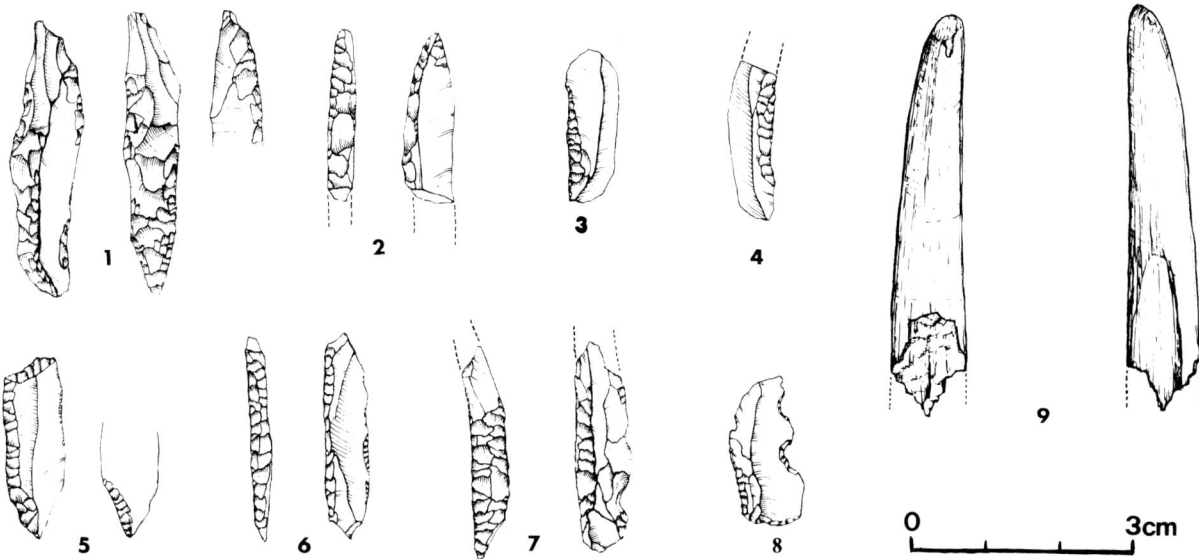

Figure 9a Industry from layer D of square B1, spits 10–12 – pointed backed bladelet (1); microgravette (2); partially-backed bladelet (3); fragment of backed microlith (4); truncated backed bladelet with inverse retouch (5); backed bladelet (6); notched backed bladelet (7); notched bladelet (8); fragment of bone point (9).

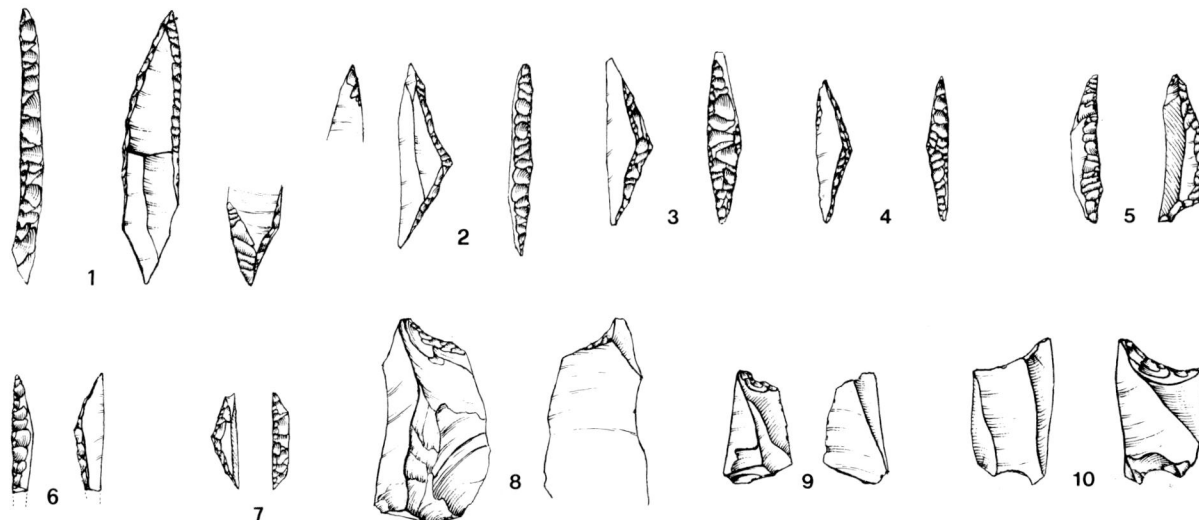

Figure 9b Industry from layer D of square E2, spits 5–6 – crescents (1, 5); triangles (2–4, 6, 7); single microburins (8, 9); double microburin (10).

primarily of the 'long' type (*Fig. 8*, nos. 3, 7) with some of 'triangular' type (*Fig. 8*, nos. 4, 6, 8) – while burins are rather rare (4%) (*Fig. 8*, nos. 10, 11). Retouched blades and fragments, as is usual in the Italian Epi-Gravettian, are well represented (*c.* 12%), as are notched bladelets (*c.* 5%) (*Fig. 9a*, no. 8). Geometric microliths are absent, and there are only two microburins and two notches with adjacent fracture. The industry on bone is represented by two fragments (e.g. *Fig. 9a*, no. 9).

This seems to be a typical final Epi-Gravettian industry of the Tyrrhenian coast – rare geometric microliths and microburins, with 'long' end-scrapers much more frequent than flake- or circular end-scrapers.

However, the situation changes radically when the assemblages from other squares are considered, especially the more recently excavated squares. Of a total of 183 retouched tools from spits 5–6 of square E2, for instance, only 1.6% are end-scrapers. In contrast, 7.1% are triangles (*Fig. 9b*, nos. 2–4, 6, 7) and 2.7% are crescents (*Fig. 9b*, nos. 1, 5 – no. 1 is a transitional form towards the microgravette). Correspondingly, there are 53 microburins (*Fig. 9b*, nos. 8, 9), a few of them double (*Fig. 9b*, no. 10), and 12 notches with adjacent fracture. The situation is similar for spit 10 of square D2 (149 retouched tools), as can be seen from *Table 1*.

The composition of the assemblages from layer D is summarized in *Table 1*. The types are classified according the type list of the Bordeaux school, with some modifications (for the basic classification and for the typology of the cores and definitions of the débitage, see Bietti 1977). The industry from spits 8 and 9 of squares B0–C0 (see *Fig. 6* and the stratigraphical section in *Fig. 10*) has been included in *Table 1* for comparison; it can be seen that this assemblage shows closer similarities with that from spits 10–12 of square B1.

Thus, as with the distribution of the faunal remains, the lithic assemblages show marked intra-site variability. We do not believe, however, that such variability indicates the presence of specialized activity areas within the deposit. In our opinion, layer D (or rather, what remains of it after the shepherds' disturbances), although spatially differentiated, represents an accumulation of archaeological materials which probably came from activity areas centred on the F and G squares (see *Figs. 1, 2 & 7*).

This point will be returned to in the next section, but it should be noted here that an analysis of three superimposed plans of square B1 – the plan of spit 10 (*Fig. 4*) and the next two plans of spit 11 – reveal no apparent clustering of tools and/or anatomical parts.

It can also be observed that the part of layer D which occurs in the D and E squares may be younger than that in the B and C squares, although the preliminary results of the sedimentological analyses seem to indicate substantial uniformity throughout the layer. Moreover, a sample of artifacts recovered from a sediment core taken from beneath spit 8 in the middle of square B2 (cf. *Fig. 7*) again contained some geometric tools and some fifteen microburins, in contrast to the adjacent square B1.

Some interesting observations concerning the reduction techniques used may be drawn from the quantitative analysis of the flint implements.

The industry is essentially microlithic; practically all the backed tools are on bladelets – the average width, on a sample of 88 pieces, is 0.67 cm (standard deviation, $s = 0.26$ cm). The truncations are mostly on bladelets (*Table 1*) and *c.* 56% of these bladelets show oblique truncation. The microliths are primarily double backed bladelets and points, as in many other sites of the local Epi-Gravettian (e.g. Bietti 1977).

The cores (*Fig. 8*, nos. 1 and 2) were exploited to the limit, owing to the scarcity of the raw material – viz. flint pebbles of small size which are available in the Pontinian plain. Of a sample of 59 cores, the average maximum dimension is $\bar{x} = 2.67$ cm ($s = 0.5$ cm), with no substantial differences amongst the different types; if one considers only the prismatic cores, the results are more or less the same ($\bar{x} = 2.65$, $s = 0.5$).

The blades and bladelets are substantially longer than the cores; measurements of the lengths of a sample of 109 complete blades and bladelets with retouch or partial retouch gave $\bar{L} = 3.13$ cm, $s = 0.7$ cm. The difference between the mean length of the blades and bladelets and the maximum dimension of the cores appears significant at a confidence limit of greater than 99% and suggests that the retouched blades/bladelets were detached at an early stage in the reduction process.

On the other hand, the mean length of the 'long' end-scrapers (*Table 1*, types 1, 8 and 9) is almost the same as the maximum dimension of the cores. A sample of 46 end-scrapers gave $\bar{L} = 2.64$ and $s = 0.5$, and the test of the difference between the means of the cores and the end-scrapers was significant only at a *c.* 50% level of confidence. This result suggests that the blanks used for the end-scrapers were detached at a late stage in the reduction process.

There also appears to be a difference between the retouched blades and bladelets and the unretouched examples among the débitage; measurements of the width gave $\bar{w} = 1.3$, $s = 0.5$ for the retouched examples ($n = 58$), and $\bar{w} = 0.76$, $s = 0.28$ for the unretouched examples ($n = 83$). The difference between the two means is significant at a confidence limit greater than 99%.

It seems, therefore, that the reduction process followed this hypothetical sequence: after suitable

Table 1: Retouched tools, cores and débitage for layer D in selected squares at Riparo Salvini (type list after Bietti 1977, pp. 203–214)

		B1 spits 10–12		B0–C0 spits 8–9		D2 spit 10		E2 spits 5–6	
		n	%	n	%	n	%	n	%
TOOLS:									
1.	Simple end-of-blade scrapers	12	5.3	3	1.32	1	0.67	1	0.55
2.	Double end-scrapers	–	–	4	1.76	–	–	–	–
3.	End-scrapers on flakes	6	2.6	5	2.2	–	–	–	–
5b.	End-scrapers on small flakes	2	0.88	5	2.2	–	–	–	–
6.	Thumb-nail end-scrapers	1	0.44	1	0.44	–	–	–	–
8.	Triangular end-scrapers	5	2.2	6	2.63	–	–	–	–
9.	End-scrapers on retouched blades	10	4.4	19	8.32	–	–	1	0.55
10b.	Fragments of end-scrapers	7	3.08	8	3.52	–	–	1	0.55
17.	Burin/End-scraper	3	1.32	2	0.88	–	–	1	0.55
18.	Truncation/End-scraper	–	–	–		1	0.67	–	–
23.	Borers	1	0.44	2	0.88	–	–	1	0.55
24.	Micro-borers	1	0.44	–	–	1	0.67	–	–
28.	Thorn (épine)	1	0.44	–	–	–	–	–	–
30.	Axial dihedral burins	2	0.88	2	0.88	1	0.67	1	0.55
31.	Angle dihedral burins	2	0.88	1	0.44	2	1.35	4	2.18
32.	Angle burins on fracture	2	0.88	–	–	–	–	–	–
36.	Multiple dihedral burins	2	0.88	–	–	–	–	–	–
37.	Axial burins on truncation	–	–	3	1.32	–	–	–	–
38.	Angle burins on truncation	–	–	1	0.44	–	–	–	–
41.	Transverse burins	–	–	–	–	1	0.67	–	–
42.	Multiple burins on truncation	–	–	1	0.44	–	–	–	–
48.	Backed tools and fragments	–	–	4	1.76	2	1.35	2	1.1
51.	Gravette points	–	–	1	0.44	–	–	–	–
52.	Microgravettes	1	0.88	4	1.76	–	–	–	–
57.	Straight truncated tools	–	–	–	–	1	0.67	1	0.65
58.	Obliquely truncated tools	–	–	1	0.44	2	1.35	–	–
59.	Partially truncated tools	–	–	–	–	–	–	1	0.55
61.	Retouched blades (one/both sides)	13	5.7	17	7.42	3	2.02	1	0.55
62.	Fragments of retouched blades	14	6.2	7	3.18	12	8.08	14	7.6
63.	Aurignacian blades	–	–	–	–	–	–	1	0.55
64.	Blades with large notches	–	–	–	–	1	0.67	–	–
72.	Notched tools	5	2.2	7	3.1	2	1.35	2	1.1
73.	Proximal or distal notched blade	2	0.88	–	–	10	6.7	4	2.18
74.	Denticulated	–	–	3	1.32	–	–	–	–
75.	Side-scrapers	5	2.2	11	4.8	2	1.35	2	1.1
76.	Raclettes	2	0.88	1	0.44	1	0.67	1	0.55
77.	Triangles	–	–	2	0.88	11	7.4	13	7.1
81.	Crescents	–	–	–	–	–	–	5	2.73
82.	Miscellaneous microliths	3	1.32	1	0.44	7	4.7	1	0.55
82b.	'à cran' microliths	–	–	1	0.88	2	1.35	–	–
83.	Truncated bladelets	8	3.5	9	3.95	6	4.03	9	4.9
84.	Pointed backed bladelets	3	1.32	8	3.52	10	6.7	9	4.9
85.	Backed bladelets	10	4.45	9	3.95	5	3.35	14	7.6
86.	Fragments of backed microliths	63	27.75	36	15.8	28	18.8	40	21.8
87.	Truncated backed bladelets	6	2.65	11	4.8	7	4.7	10	5.45
88.	Denticulated backed bladelets	1	0.44	–	–	–	–	–	–
90.	Denticulated bladelets	1	0.44	3	1.32	–	–	–	–
91.	Notched bladelets	11	4.85	4	1.76	15	10.3	22	12.1
94.	Bladelets with marginal direct retouch	11	4.85	11	4.8	11	7.4	14	7.6
95.	Inversely retouched bladelets	1	0.44	1	0.44	–	–	–	–
101.	Pointed blades	3	1.32	2	0.88	–	–	–	–
101b.	Pointed flakes	–	–	2	0.88	–	–	1	0.55
102.	Arenian points	–	–	2	0.88	–	–	–	–
103b.	Fragments of pointed tools	2	0.88	1	0.44	–	–	–	–
105.	Miscellaneous ('divers') tools	2	0.88	2	0.88	2	1.35	1	0.55
105b.	'Outils esquillés'	1	0.44	4	1.76	2	1.35	5	2.73
	Totals:	227		228		149		183	

preparation of the core, blades (as long as possible) were detached, then retouched and used. Subsequently, the production of bladelets started, mainly for backed, truncated and geometric tools. In between, some blades and flakes were detached for making into end-scrapers (the 'long' types often have cortex or are on ridged blades), burins, and other tools. The reduction process continued until the core was exhausted, and even involved the production of several flakes which were variously utilized. The proportions of the different types of cores (*Table 1*) gives a general idea of this roughly

Table 1 (cont'd): Retouched tools, cores and débitage for layer D in selected squares at Riparo Salvini (type list after Bietti 1977, pp. 203–214)

	B1 spits 10–12	B0–C0 spits 8–9	D2 spit 10	E2 spits 5–6
	n	*n*	*n*	*n*
DEBITAGE:				
Microburins	2	3	50	53
Notches with adjacent fractures	2	–	16	12
Burin spalls	19	19	38	38
Cores:				
a. prismatic with one platform	9	5	5	2
b. prismatic with two opposed platforms	5	8	2	2
c. prismatic with crossed platforms	4	3	3	2
d. globular cores	–	1	–	–
e. chopping tool type cores	1	–	–	–
f. shapeless cores and fragments	6	2	3	2
Ridged ('à crête') blades	3	2	1	4
Reflected blades	–	2	1	–
Overstepped blades	2	–	1	–
Blades with traces of retouch	7	4	2	2
Simple unretouched blades	2	2	6	3
Short fragments of blades	28	42	16	16
Reflected bladelets	4	11	3	10
Overstepped bladelets	2	3	1	2
Bladelets with traces of retouch	53	37	26	68
Simple unretouched bladelets	110	62	71	138
Short fragments of bladelets	166	77	158	202
Rejuvenation flakes	18	26	13	16
Flakes with traces of retouch	39	68	39	66
Simple unretouched flakes	109	63	39	44
Flakes with cortex ('calottes de galet')	62	45	11	25
Small waste fragments ('debris')	1108	263	606	1135

sketched exploitation process.

The reduction process outlined above is of general and 'global' character; in other words, it is a reconstruction of a set of technological operations which may have taken place at different sites. In the absence of more refined analyses of the provenance of the raw materials, it is not possible to establish that a complete operational sequence took place *at* Riparo Salvini. While it is reasonable to assume that the *débitage* of bladelets and the production of microliths and geometric tools was done at the shelter, as evidenced by the large quantity of microburins, it is possible that certain of the other tools (e.g. the retouched blades or the end-scrapers) were produced elsewhere and then brought to the site.

COMPARISONS WITH OTHER SITES: THE TRANSITION TO THE HOLOCENE

In this section the data from Riparo Salvini will be compared with those from other sites (all with absolute dates) in the middle–southern Tyrrhenian region, which range in age from Dryas II to the Boreal period.

In Latium there is the site of Grotta Polesini (Radmilli 1974) near Tivoli, about 30 km east of Rome, dated to Dryas III (*c.* 10,300 BP), the site of Peschio Ranaro (Biddittu 1973; see also Bietti 1984*b*) in an inland setting in southern Latium (province of Frosinone), dated to the early Pre-Boreal (9730±150 BP), and the site of Riparo Blanc (Taschini 1964, 1968) on the coast on the Circeo promontory, only about 15 km from Riparo Salvini, dated to the Boreal (8565±80 BP).

In Campania there is the coastal site of Grotta del Mezzogiorno in Salerno province (Tozzi 1976, in press) with dates ranging from Dryas III (layer 11: 10,780±450 BP) to the end of the Boreal (layer 4: 7540±135 BP). Further south in the province of Salerno, and also on the coast, is Grotta della Cala (Martini 1981), the upper layers of which range in age from Dryas II (layer H: 12,350±200 BP) to Dryas III (layer F: 10,390±80 BP).

In northern Calabria there is the important site of Grotta della Madonna, Praia a Mare, province of Cosenza (Cardini 1970) with dates ranging from Dryas II (lower part of layer L: 12,100±150 BP) to the Boreal (upper part of layer L: 8600±120 BP and layer I: 8735±80 BP).

In terms of its environmental framework and fauna, the situation at Grotta Polesini is similar to that at Riparo Salvini – the site is at the edge of a limestone formation (the Tiburtini mountains), with an overwhelming predominance of red deer, but with significant percentages of ibex and chamois. However, some cold climate species, such as *Gulo gulo* and *Lyrurus tetrix*, are present although in very small amounts. A comparison of the two sites also has to take account of statistical bias – the faunal assemblage from Grotta Polesini consists of several thousands of bones (Radmilli 1974).

The site of Peschio Ranaro is not yet fully published. Preliminary results (Biddittu 1973; see also Bietti 1984b) show a large quantity of cold climate species – including ibex, *Mustela nivalis* and *Marmota marmota* – consistent with the geographical position of this small inland cave at an altitude of *c*. 700 metres. The ibex is particularly important at this site; an analysis of the molars carried out by L. Cardini (1969; see also Bietti 1984b) indicates at least 30 individuals of this species.

The faunal assemblage from Riparo Blanc is exceptional (Taschini 1964); only a few bones of large mammals were found, while an enormous quantity of shells of marine molluscs (more than 32,000) was recovered. The interpretation of Riparo Blanc as a specialized site for the gathering of these molluscs is confirmed by the character of the industrial assemblage (Bietti 1981, 1984b).

The fauna of Grotta del Mezzogiorno in Campania has not been fully published, although it seems there was a mixed economy with red deer, wild boar, and with land molluscs in the majority in the lower layers and lagoonal marine molluscs (*Cardium*) in the upper layers (Tozzi 1976).

Layers H–F of Grotta della Cala again suggest a mixed economy (Bartolomei *et al.* 1976) with red deer in the majority, but also with roe deer, ibex and chamois. In addition, layer H produced a remarkable quantity of bird bones and shells of marine molluscs (Martini 1983).

The faunal remains from Grotta della Madonna, in Calabria, are also not fully published. Preliminary results (Cardini 1970; Cassoli, pers. comm.) suggest that the range of large mammals is similar to that found in the other coastal middle and southern Tyrrhenian sites – red deer, roe deer, wild boar (increasing in the upper levels), ibex and chamois, with a large quantity of small mammals and birds. In terms of the shellfish remains (Durante and Settepassi 1972) there is, as at Grotta del Mezzogiorno, a transition from land molluscs (*Helix* sp.) to marine molluscs (rock species, such as *Patella* and *Monodonta turbinata*) from the end of Dryas III to the Boreal. This is particularly evident in the upper part of layer L and in layer I.

Comparisons between the industrial assemblages from these sites are not easy, mainly because typological analyses have often been done by different methods. For example, the industry from Grotta della Cala was analyzed according to the scheme proposed by G. Laplace (1964). Moreover, in many cases, the cores and the débitage have not been included in the published data.

For the purposes of the present study, therefore, we have chosen general groups of tools, together with the microburins and the cores; the data from the different sites are presented in *Table 2* in terms of *absolute numbers* of artifacts in each category. The geometric tools have been grouped together – they consist mainly of triangles (in the majority) and crescents; there is only one trapeze at Peschio Ranaro, one at Grotta Polesini, and seven at Grotta della Madonna. For this last site, only the finds from layer L have been considered, and specifically only

Table 2:   Comparison of the Riparo Salvini industries with those from other sites

Assemblages	Total Retouched tools	End-scrapers and Burins	Retouched blades	Backed tools	Denticulates and Notches	Geometric tools	Microburins	Cores
RIPARO SALVINI								
Square B1, spits 10–12	227	54	27	88	19	–	4	25
Squares B0–C0, spits 8–9	228	61	24	75	17	2	2	19
Square D2, spit 10	149	6	16	61	27	11	66	13
Square E2, spits 5–6	183	9	15	76	28	18	65	10
GROTTA POLESINI	17,300	5400	2200	8200	190	24	20	1050
PESCHIO RANARO	319	84	52	140	26	4	13	25
RIPARO BLANC	255	23	10	6	135	–	–	44
GROTTA DEL MEZZOGIORNO								
Spits 14–11	263	108	11	70	6	–	3	?
Spits 9–7	402	156	19	120	8	–	2	?
Spits 6–4	79	26	4	22	4	1	10	?
GROTTA DELLA CALA								
Layer H	483	92	90	106	46	3	2	?
Layer G	191	31	32	33	17	1	1	?
GROTTA DELLA MADONNA								
Layer L, spits 65–60	413	53	101	115	36	1	–	47
Layer L, spits 59–53	560	71	105	301	40	8	–	67
Layer L, spits 52–47	266	56	44	59	41	22	8	53

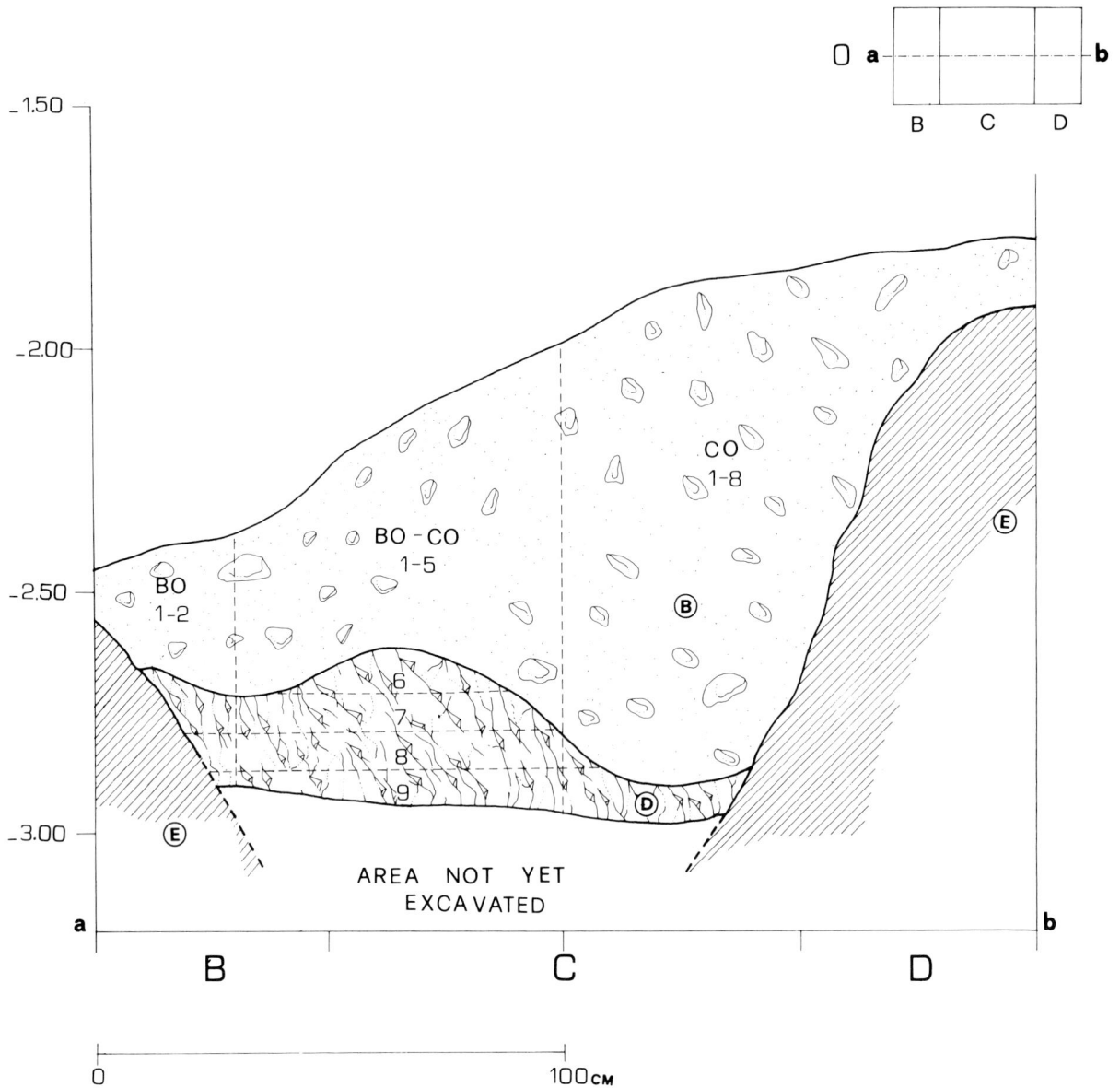

Figure 10 Stratigraphic section through squares B0–D0. Symbols as in *Fig. 3*.

those from levels between spit 65 (dated to Dryas III) and spit 47. The finds from the lower part of layer L (spits 73–70), dated to Dryas II, are too few to be incorporated into a quantitative comparison. For the same reason, layer F of Grotta della Cala, dated to the end of Dryas III, was not considered (only 16 retouched tools). Instead, in *Table 2* are shown the figures for layer G which should belong to Dryas III or to the Allerød, given the Dryas II dating of layer H.

As can be seen from *Table 2*, the discrepancies between squares D2 and E2 of Riparo Salvini and the other sites in terms of the geometric tools and especially the microburins are striking; these two squares alone produced more than twice the number of microburins as were recovered from all the other sites together!

Moving forward into Dryas III and the Pre-

Boreal, it can be seen from *Table 2* that the geometric microliths (with the exception perhaps of spits 52–47 of Grotta della Madonna) decrease. Similarly, at Grotta della Cala there are more geometric tools in layers P–M, dated to Dryas I (Martini 1978), than in layers H–F. Although the figures are probably affected by severe sampling bias (the difference between squares B0–C0, B1 and D2–E2 of Riparo Salvini provides the best example), and although for some sites (Peschio Ranaro, Grotta della Madonna) the data are largely unpublished and hence preliminary, it is nevertheless apparent from *Table 2* that the process of 'mesolithization' in the middle and southern Tyrrhenian region proceeded in a direction opposite to that indicated by the north Italian sequences.

The situation that has been presented here should therefore be taken as a warning for those researchers

530

who are inclined, in a typical chronostratigraphic perspective, to make simple generalizations about the transition processes between the Pleistocene and the Holocene. In our opinion, this transition should be analyzed at a more local scale, and the investigation of the *nature* of the sites should be given paramount importance. For example, the exceptional nature of Riparo Blanc is evident from *Table 2*; the overwhelming quantity of notched and denticulated tools is clearly functionally correlated with the great abundance of rock marine molluscs (Bietti 1981, 1984*b*), indicating a very specialized seasonal activity. The same correlation is present in the upper part of layer L of Grotta della Madonna (and even more so in layer I – see Bietti 1981), but not in a spectacular way as at Riparo Blanc; Grotta della Madonna consistently shows a mixed economy, with hunting an important activity.

Another case of specialized activity is represented, in our opinion, by Peschio Ranaro. Here, in the context of a strong Epi-Gravettian tradition, the large quantity of end-scrapers and backed tools, together with the abundant ibex remains, points towards a specialized site for the hunting of this species (Bietti 1981, 1984*b*).

We should like to conclude this paper with some speculative remarks on the interpretation of the *nature* of Riparo Salvini.

As has been stated above, the character of the deposit and, in particular, the profile of the bedrock (see *Figs. 6, 7 & 10*) suggest that layer D represents an accumulation of archaeological material derived from activities that most probably took place on the flatter, more even surface of the F, G and (perhaps) H squares. It is reasonable to suppose that the activity area for the geometric tools and the microburins was around squares F2 and G2. The large *in situ* rock between the C and D squares (see *Figs. 6 & 7*) acted like a natural barrier for material that slipped down from the activity area. The archaeological material would eventually have covered the top of this rock and some of it reached squares C2 and B2, at the bottom of which, in the core taken for sedimentological analysis, several microburins were found.

Subsequent human occupation, perhaps seasonal, with a different activity taking place in the same area, resulted in the deposition of different materials in the zone between the A and E squares – consistent with the situation found in spits 10–12 of square B1 (in the D and E squares this deposit was probably destroyed by the shepherds).

In order to confirm such a pattern in the deposition process, further excavation is needed, particularly in square C2, together with more radiocarbon dates (in process) and more detailed faunal analyses.

Was Riparo Salvini a residential unit? In our opinion, this possibility should be excluded; the surface of the shelter is too small (only *c.* 35 m^2). We are more inclined to think of it as a hunting stand, with repeated seasonal occupations over tens or even hundreds of years. Its position, moreover, at the interface between the Pontinian plain and the Fondi plain makes it a perfect point of observation of the animal herds passing in front of it.

These are, of course, merely speculative ideas. In order to place the interpretation of the nature of the site on a sounder basis, it will be necessary to analyze more thoroughly other sites which show clear intra-site variability (and not only in this region), and to try to perform inter-site correlation studies. We hope that in the not too distant future new, secure and precise data will be available to this end.

Note:

1. A sequence resembling that at sites in northern Italy may be present in a recently discovered site in Lucania (G. Cremonesi, pers. comm.). We look forward with interest to more detailed information about this site.

References

BARTOLOMEI, G., GAMBASSINI, P. and PALMA DI CESNOLA, A. (1976) Visita ai giacimenti del Poggio e della Cala a Marina di Camerota (Salerno). *Atti XVII Riunione Scientifica dell'Istituto Italiano di Preistoria e Protostoria*: 107–139.

BIAGI, P., CASTELLETTI, L., CREMASCHI, M., SALA, B. and TOZZI, C. (1980) Popolazione e territorio nell'Appennino Tosco-emiliano e nel tratto centrale del bacino del Po tra IX e il V millennio. *Emilia Preromana*, 8: 13–36.

BIDDITTU, I. (1973) Insediamenti del Paleolitico superiore. *Proposta per una Riserva Naturale dei Monti Ernici*. Frosinone, Club Alpino Italiano: 32–36.

BIETTI, A. (1977) Analysis and illustration of the Epigravettian industry collected during the 1955 excavation at Palidoro (Rome, Italy). *Quaternaria*, 19 (1976–1977): 197–387

BIETTI, A. (1981) The Mesolithic cultures in Italy: new activities in connection with Upper Paleolithic cultural traditions. In B. Gramsch (ed.), *Mesolithikum in Europa. 2. Internationales Symposium Potsdam, 3 bis 8 April 1978 Bericht* (Veröffentlichungen des Museums für Ur- und Frühgeschichte Potsdam, 14/15). Berlin, Deutscher Verlag der Wissenschaften: 33–50.

BIETTI, A. (1984a) Primi risultati dello scavo nel giacimento Epigravettiano finale di Riparo Salvini (Terracina, Latina). *Atti XXIV Riunione Scientifica dell'Istituto Italiano di Preistoria e Protostoria*: 195–205.

BIETTI, A. (1984b) Il Mesolitico nel Lazio. *Atti XXIV Riunione Scientifica dell'Istituto Italiano di Preistoria e Protostoria*: 79–102

BROGLIO, A. (1973) La preistoria della valle Padana dalla fine del Paleolitico agli inizi del Neolitico: cronologia, aspetti culturali e trasformazioni economiche. *Rivista di Scienze Preistoriche*, 28: 133–160.

BROGLIO, A. (1980) Culture e ambienti della fine del Paleolitico e del Mesolitico nell'Italia nord-orientale. *Preistoria Alpina*, 16: 7–29.

CARDINI, L. (1969) Lo scavo del 'Peschio Ranaro' a Collepardo (Frosinone). *Quaternaria*, 11: 284–285.

CARDINI, L. (1970) Praia a Mare. Relazione degli scavi 1957–1970 dell'Istituto Italiano di Paleontologia Umana. *Bullettino di Paletnologia Italiana*, 79: 31–59.

CHIAPPELLA, V.G., SILVESTRI, G. and SPEZZAFERRO, G. (1961) Scoperta di un nuovo giacimento paleolitico nella villa Salvini a Terracina. *Quaternaria*, 5 (1958–1961): 323.

DURANTE, S. and SETTEPASSI, F. (1972) I molluschi del giacimento quaternario della Grotta della Madonna a Praia a Mare (Calabria). *Quaternaria*, 16: 255–269.

GUERRESCHI, A. (1983) Tendenze evolutive in senso mesolitico dell'Epigravettiano italico finale dell'Italia nord-orientale. In *Il Popolamento delle Alpi in Età Mesolitica: VIII–V Millennio a.C.* (Preistoria Alpina, 19). Trento, Museo Tridentino di Scienze Naturali: 209–212.

LAPLACE, G. (1964) *Essai de Typologie Systématique*. Ferrara, Annali dell'Università di Ferrara 15, suppl. 2.

LEWTHWAITE, J. and ROWLEY-CONWY, P. (1980) The nature of hunter-gatherer adaptations. *Mesolithic Miscellany*, 1: 18–20.

MARTINI, F. (1978) L'Epigravettiano di Grotta della Cala a Marina di Camerota (Salerno). I. L'industria litica ed ossea e la cronologia assoluta dell'Epigravettiano evoluto. *Rivista di Scienze Preistoriche*, 33: 3–108.

MARTINI, F. (1981) L'Epigravettiano di Grotta della Cala a Marina di Cameronta (Salerno). II. L'industria litica e la cronologia assoluta dell'Epigravettiano finale. *Rivista di Scienze Preistoriche*, 36: 57–125.

MARTINI, F. (1983) Grotte de la Cala. In A. Bietti, F. Martini and C. Tozzi, L'Epigravettien évolué et final de la zone moyenne et basse Tyrrhénienne. *Colloque International: 'La position taxonomique et chronologique des industries à pointes à dos autour de la Méditerranée Européenne'. Rivista di Scienze Preistoriche*, 38: 319–349.

MELLARS, P. (1981) Towards a definition of the Mesolithic. *Mesolithic Miscellany*, 2(2): 13–16.

RADMILLI, A.M. (1974) Gli scavi nella Grotta Polesini a Ponte Lucano e la piu antica arte del Lazio. In *Origines*. Florence, Sansoni.

ROZOY, J-G. (1978) *Les Derniers Chasseurs. L'Epipaléolithique en France et en Belgique* (Bulletin de la Société archéologique champenoise, numéro spécial). Charleville, J-G. Rozoy.

ROZOY, J.G. (1984) The age of red deer or of bowmen. *Mesolithic Miscellany*, 5(2): 14–16.

TASCHINI, M. (1964) Il livello Mesolitico del Riparo Blanc al Monte Circeo. *Bullettino di Paletnologia Italiana*, 73: 65–88.

TASCHINI, M. (1968) La datation au C^{14} de l'abri Blanc (Mont Circé). Quelques observations sur le Mésolithique en Italie. *Quaternaria*, 10: 137–165.

TOZZI, C. (1976) Il Mesolitico della Campania. *Atti XVII Riunione Scientifica dell'Istituto Italiano di Preistoria e Protostoria*: 33–49.

TOZZI, C. (1980) Il Mesolitico dell'Appennino Tosco-emiliano. *La Toscana settentrionale dal Paleolitico all'Alto Medioevo*. Lucca, Nuova Grafica: 43–59.

TOZZI, C. (1983) Grotte du Mezzogiorno. In A. Bietti, F. Martini and C. Tozzi, L'Epigravettien évolué et final de la zone moyenne et basse Tyrrhénienne. *Colloque International: 'La position taxonomique et chronologique des industries à pointes à dos autour de la Méditerranée Européenne'. Rivista di Scienze Preistoriche*, 38: 319–349.

Liguria: 11,000–7000 BP

Paolo Biagi, Roberto Maggi and Renato Nisbet

Abstract

Research by local amateurs over the last two decades has led to the discovery of twelve Mesolithic sites in Liguria belonging both to the Sauveterrian and Castelnovian traditions. Most of them lie at high altitude in the eastern Apennine chain. Two of the Sauveterrian sites are very close to outcrops of dark red jasper, and have produced industries made largely from this local raw material. The Castelnovian encampments yielded assemblages made from both jasper and flint, the percentage of the latter increasing with distance from the jasper outcrops. In western Liguria the site of Pian del Re, close to a pass which connects the inner valleys with the sea, produced trapezes and notched blades almost exclusively chipped from a light-grey variety of quartzite available locally. No cave site has yet produced evidence of Mesolithic activity. Arma dello Stefanin and Arene Candide were both occupied during the final Epi-Gravettian and early Neolithic periods, but their stratigraphies show a gap in occupation corresponding to the Pre-Boreal, Boreal and early Atlantic climatic phases. The vegetational history of the region during the thirteenth to the seventh millennium BP is documented by a series of palynological cores and charcoal identifications, the most detailed of which are those from Arma dello Stefanin. Charcoal from the lowermost excavated layers of this cave is almost exclusively Scots Pine, while the layers above produced evidence of a marked increase in thermophilous vegetation culminating in the disappearance of the coniferae in the youngest final Epi-Gravettian layer. The stalagmite levels above should correspond to the entire Mesolithic period. A few charcoal fragments from these levels indicate more temperate climatic conditions with the first appearance of beech.

INTRODUCTION

In the beginning of the 1970s our knowledge of the Mesolithic of northern Italy was restricted to a few cave sites in the Trieste karst (Radmilli 1960). Some years later many sites were brought to light in the Adige valley (Broglio 1971) and in the north-eastern Alpine chain (Bagolini *et al.* 1983), as well as in the Tusco-Emilian Apennines (Biagi *et al.* 1980) and on the fluvial terraces of the central Po plain (Biagi 1981). The chronology of the north Italian Meso-lithic is now well known thanks to a good number of radiocarbon dates (Alessio *et al.* 1983). The Ligurian Mesolithic sites of the eastern Apennines were discovered a few years ago (Baffico *et al.* 1983; Biagi and Maggi 1983).

Mesolithic cave occupation had already been described by Cardini (1947) at the Arene Candide cave; while on the basis of a few radiocarbon dates (Alessio *et al.* 1967) some authors suggested that there were late Epi-Gravettian hunters in the region until the end of the ninth millennium BP (Palma di Cesnola 1974, 1983; Broglio 1981) (*Fig. 6A*). The excavation in progress at the Arma dello Stefanin in the Pennavaira valley (Biagi *et al.* 1987) and the re-examination of data collected during previous re-search (Biagi and Nisbet 1986) demonstrate that no Ligurian cave known so far was inhabited during the whole of the Mesolithic period. On the contrary, cave sites frequently show evidence of final Epi-Gravettian and early Neolithic Impressed Ware layers, always separated by sterile and/or stalagmite levels (Baissas 1974; Biagi and Maggi 1983).

THE MESOLITHIC ASSEMBLAGES

Fig. 3 shows the tool types characteristic of Ligurian Mesolithic assemblages. They can be put into chronological order with the help of the finds from the well-known sequences of the Adige valley and the Tusco-Emilian Apennines (Broglio 1971; Biagi *et al.* 1980; Broglio and Kozłowski 1983). The assemblage from Punta della Mortola at Villa Hanbury includes hyper-microlithic isosceles tri-angles, notched blades and microburins, mostly made from a type of flint which outcrops *c.* 100 m to the north west of the site (*Fig. 2*, site 1). Excavations at Punta della Mortola have revealed that the deposit is thoroughly disturbed and that the Pre-Boreal assemblage was probably redeposited during the 1930s (Baroni and Biagi, in press).

On the eastern Apennines at an altitude of some 700 m, the site of Nido del Merlo and the nearby site of Passo della Camilla (*Fig. 1*, sites 1, 2) are very close to outcrops of dark red jasper. They both produced a poor assemblage including microlithic scalene triangles and circular end-scrapers. A similar collection was found at Ferrada 3 (*Fig. 1*, site 10) on the left bank of the Lavagna river at an altitude of some 100 metres.

Prato Mollo (*Fig. 1*, site 6) lies on the southern slopes of Monte Aiona, 600 m south east of Passo della Spingarda (1549 m) and some 200 m north east of a large peat bog basin (1492 m) which is currently being studied by G.M. Macphail (in press). The Mesolithic assemblage comprises material belonging

T

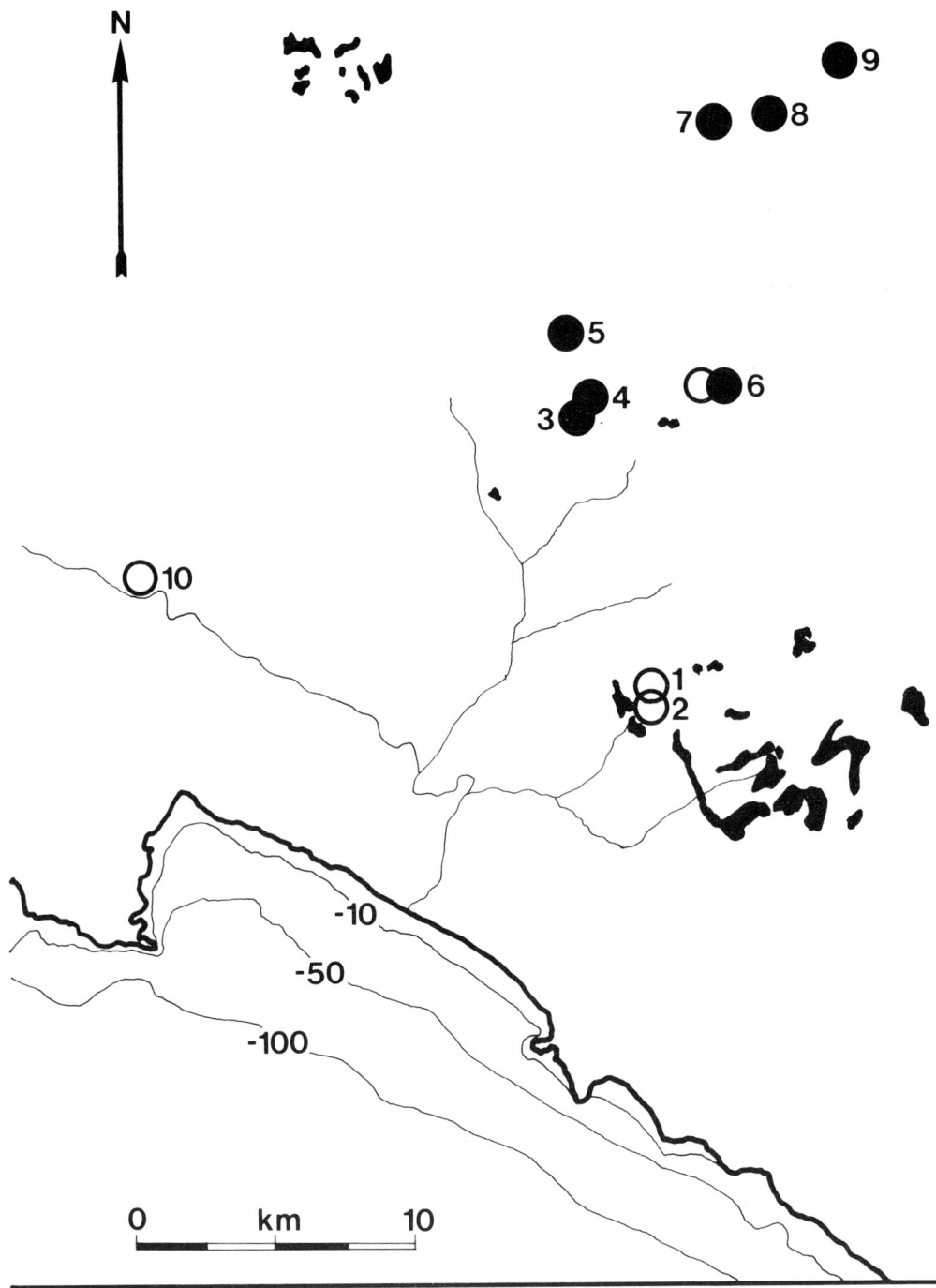

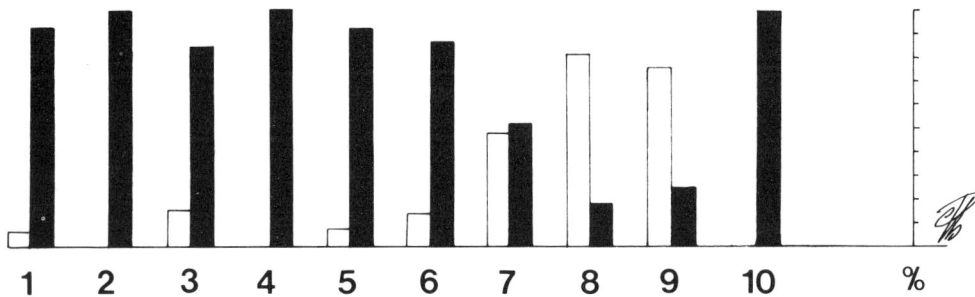

Figure 1   Mesolithic sites of eastern Liguria. *Key*: 1. Passo della Camilla; 2. Nido del Merlo; 3. Malga Perlezzi; 4. Colmo Rondio; 5. Bosco Lame; 6. Prato Mollo; 7. Groppo Rosso; 8. Prato della Cipolla; 9. Passo dello Zovallo; 10. Ferrada 3; areas shaded black indicate jasper outcrops. Histograms show the percentages of flint (unshaded) and jasper (shaded) for these sites. *Drawn by P. Biagi*

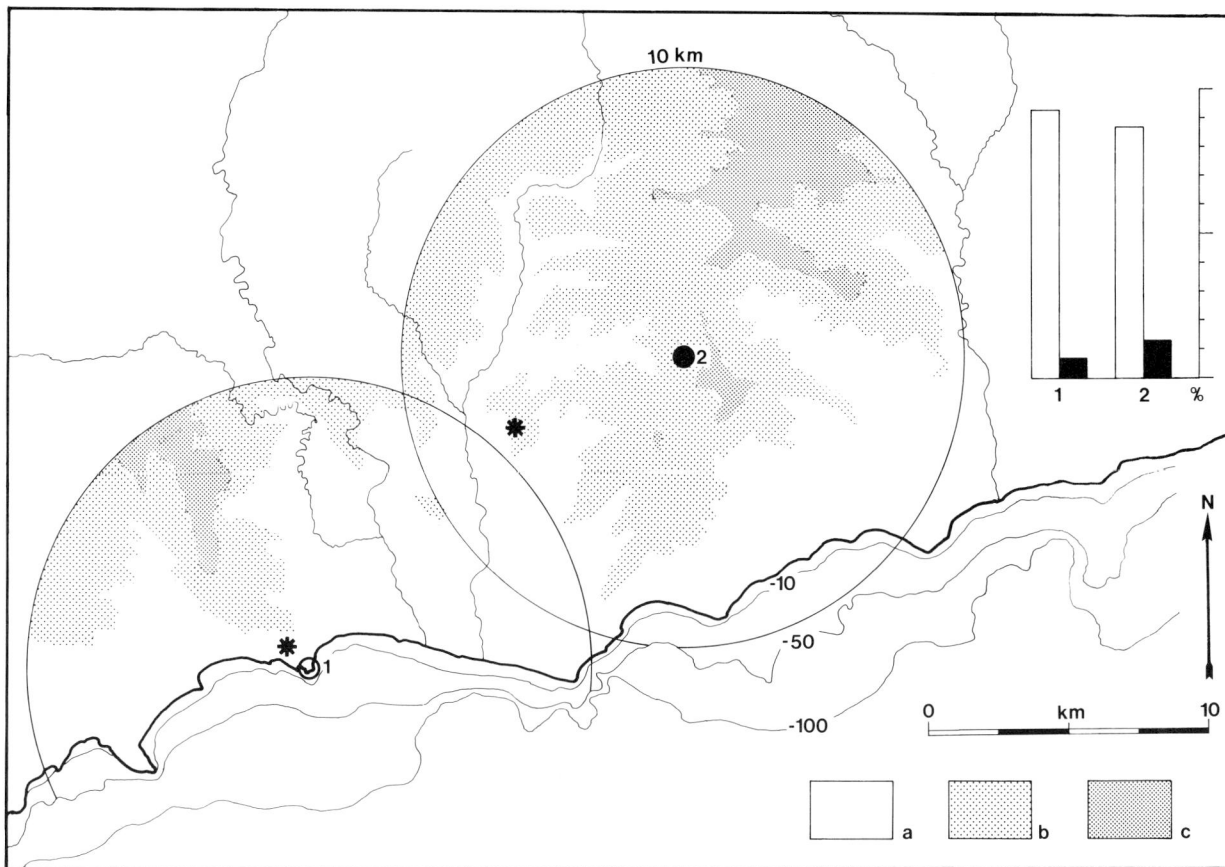

Figure 2 Mesolithic sites of western liguria. *Key*: 1. Punta della Mortola; 2. Pian del Re; *a*. land 0–500 m a.s.l.; *b*. land 500–1000 m a.s.l.; *c*. land over 1000 m a.s.l.; asterisks indicate raw material outcrops. Histograms show the percentages of locally available (unshaded) and imported (shaded) raw materials. *Drawn by P. Biagi*

both to the Sauveterrian and Castelnovian traditions.

Colmo Rondio (*Fig. 1*, site 4), in the Aiona mountains, produced surface finds with both microlithic bilaterally-backed points and trapezes and denticulated blades.

The industry from Malga Perlezzi (*Fig. 1*, site 3) is more difficult to define because of the scarcity of diagnostic implements.

All the other eastern Apennines sites can be attributed to the late Mesolithic Castelnovian culture (*Fig. 1*, sites 5, 7–9), including the western Apennine camp of Pian del Re at 850 m a.s.l. (*Fig. 2*, site 2). This site lies on the western slope of Monte Bignone, in an area of springs, very close to the pass of Colli Termini di Baiardo which connects the valleys of the interior to the Mediterranean sea, near Sanremo. The lithic assemblage is very specialized being composed of trapezes and notched blades, chipped from light-grey micro-crystalline quartzite, the nearest outcrop of which lies about 6.5 km west south west of the site.

THE VEGETATIONAL HISTORY

Data relating to the nature of the woodland cover of the Lateglacial and the beginning of the Holocene are very scarce and almost exclusively based on

charcoal identifications (Vernet 1970, 1974; Fancelli Galletti 1972) (*Fig. 6D*).

In this context, the stratigraphic sequence recently brought to light at the Arma dello Stefanin (*Fig. 4*) is of particular importance and has produced new data covering almost six millennia. Together with the Arene Candide succession, it provides the most important stratigraphy for Ligurian prehistory for the Lateglacial and Postglacial periods.

As mentioned already, no cave has yet produced evidence of Mesolithic activity. There is a gap in our knowledge covering the Pre-Boreal, Boreal and very early Atlantic climatic periods. In the high Apennines, the final phase of the Boreal seems to have been characterized by an expansion of the silver fir, recorded at Lake Agoraie (1300 m a.s.l.) and especially at Lajone near Pianpaludo (985 m a.s.l.) (Montanari *et al.* 1979). The reasons why the caves were not occupied during the Mesolithic are still difficult to understand. Climatic change with increased internal percolation can be seen as one cause; but the exploitation of, and adaptation to, new forms of environment cannot be excluded as contributory factors (Biagi and Maggi 1983; Biagi and Nisbet 1986).

Charcoal identifications from the uppermost layers of Arma dello Stefanin, as well as those from

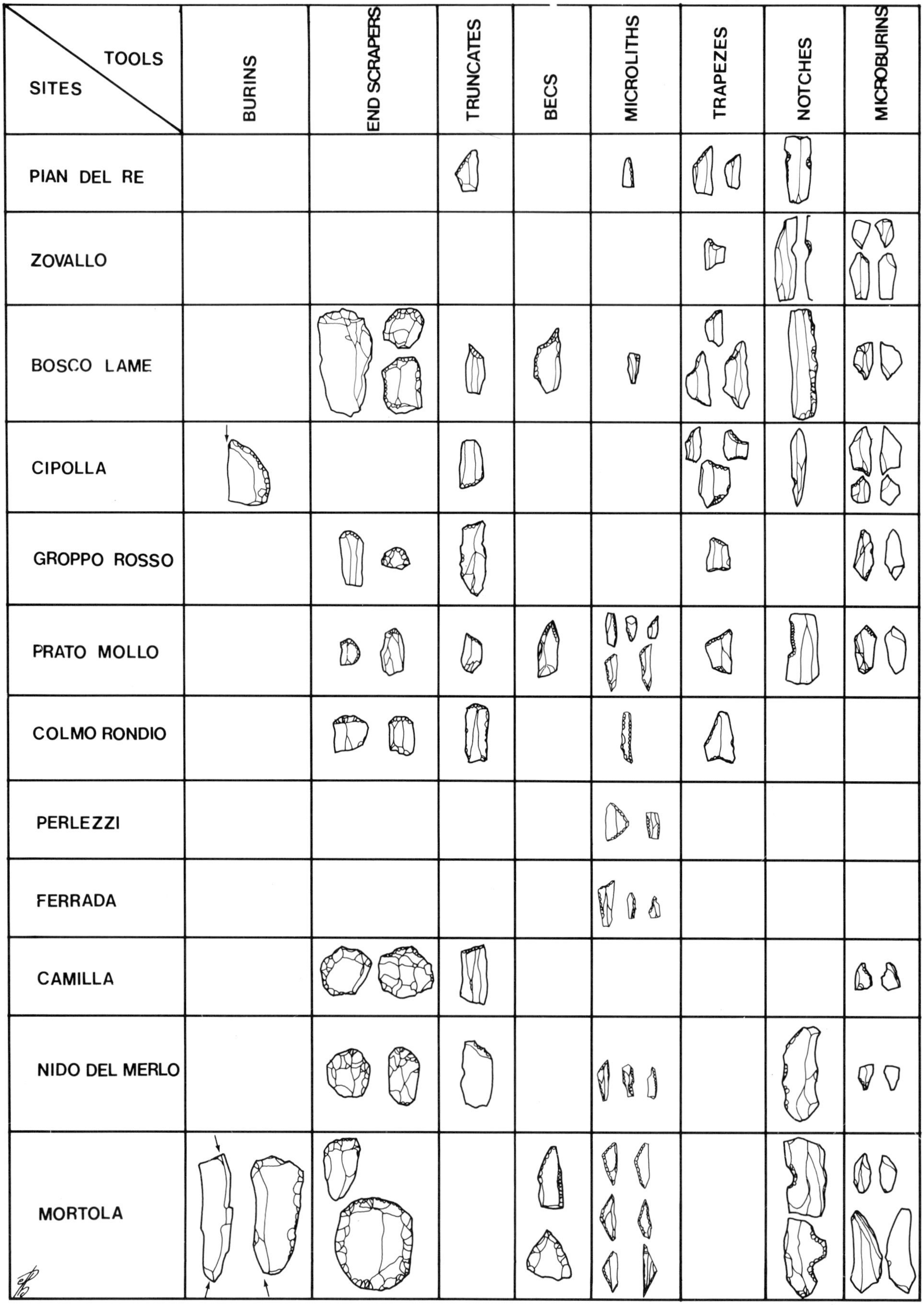

TOOLS SITES	BURINS	END SCRAPERS	TRUNCATES	BECS	MICROLITHS	TRAPEZES	NOTCHES	MICROBURINS
PIAN DEL RE								
ZOVALLO								
BOSCO LAME								
CIPOLLA								
GROPPO ROSSO								
PRATO MOLLO								
COLMO RONDIO								
PERLEZZI								
FERRADA								
CAMILLA								
NIDO DEL MERLO								
MORTOLA								

Figure 3 Typical chipped stone implements from Ligurian Mesolithic sites in chronological order (oldest site at the bottom). *Drawn by P. Biagi*

536

6610 ± 60 BP (Bln-3276)

12700 ± 300 BP (HAR-6915)

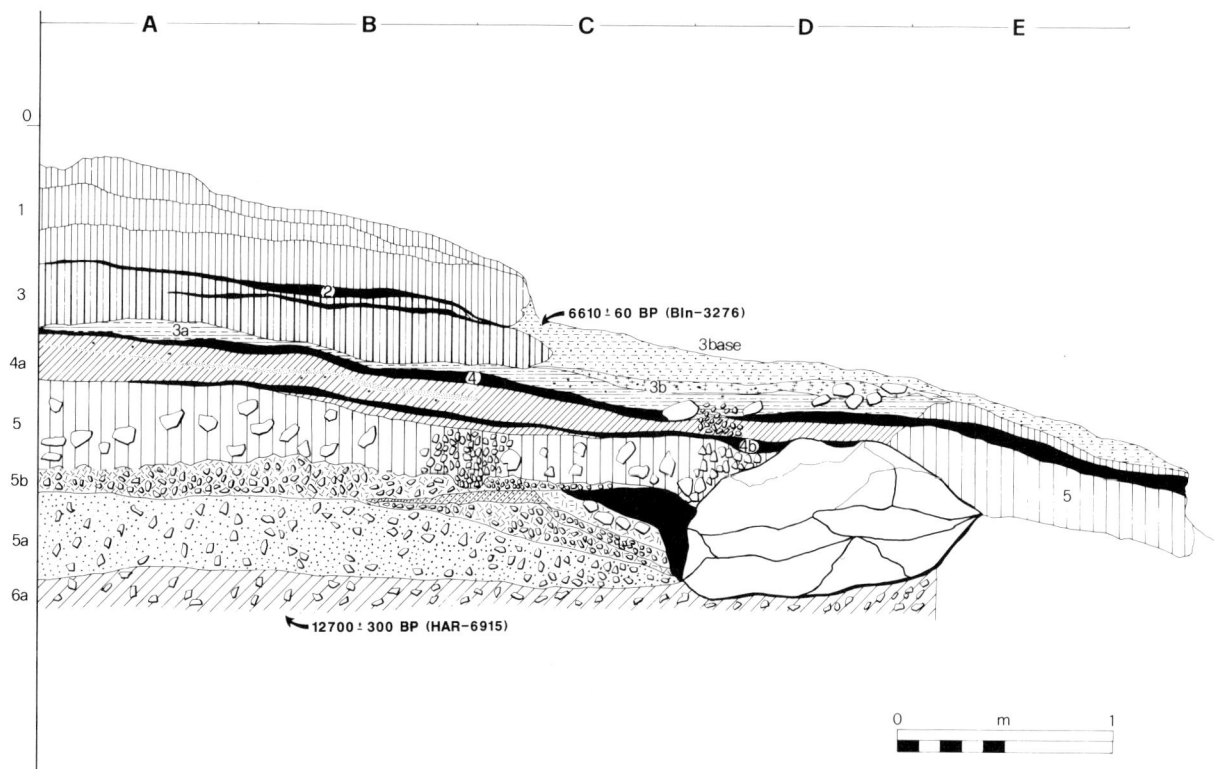

Figure 4   Stratigraphy of the Arma dello Stefanin (Pennavaria valley – Albenga). *Key*: 1. stalagmite; 2. early Neolithic; 3. stalagmite; 4. final Epi-Gravettian sequence. *Drawn by G. Marchesi*

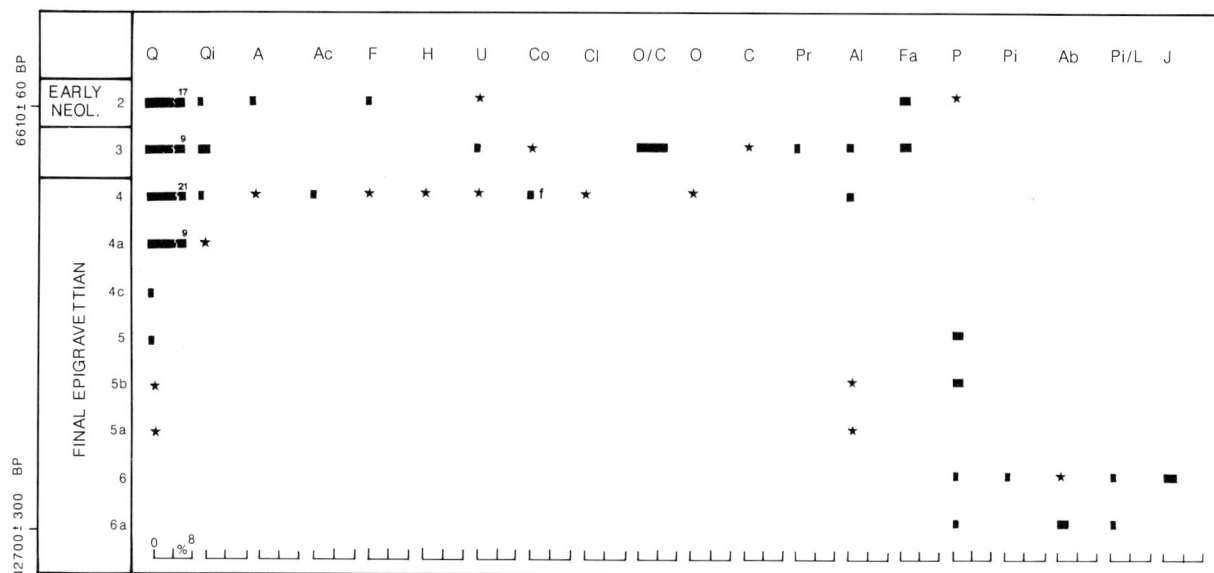

Figure 5   Charcoal identifications from Arma dello Stefanin. *Key*: Q – *Quercus pubescens*; Qi – *Quercus ilex*; A – *Acer pseudoplatanus*; Ac – *Acer campestre*; F – *Fraxinus*; H – *Hedera*; U – *Ulmus*; Co – *Corylus*; Cl – *Clematis*; O/C – *Ostrya* vel *Carpinus*; O – *Ostrya*; C – *Carpinus*; Pr – *Prunus*; Al – *Alnus*; Fa – *Fagus*; P – *Pinus sylvestris*; Pi – *Picea*; Ab – *Abies*; Pi/L – *Picea* vel *Larix*; J – *Juniperus*; ✳ – less than 5%. *Drawn by R. Nisbet*

Arene Candide cave, show that the final Palaeolithic flourished in an environment subject to rapid changes and that some of the temperate oscillations of the Lateglacial considerably changed the characteristic Würmian woodland cover composed mostly of coniferae. At Stefanin the lowermost layers excavated so far (layers 6 and 6a) produced charcoal almost exclusively of *Pinus* sub-genus *Diploxylon* (*Pinus* cf. *sylvestris*/Scots Pine) and *Juniperus*. A similar situation is known from layers 5a–5, but with a gradual increase in thermophilous vegetation with deciduous oak (*Quercus pubescens*) and alder (*Alnus*). This association might indicate a humid temperate episode preceding layer 4 which produced the youngest final Epi-Gravettian assemblage of the cave. In layer 4, itself, a vegetation composed of various thermophilous species makes its appearance while the coniferae disappear (?Allerød). If this

537

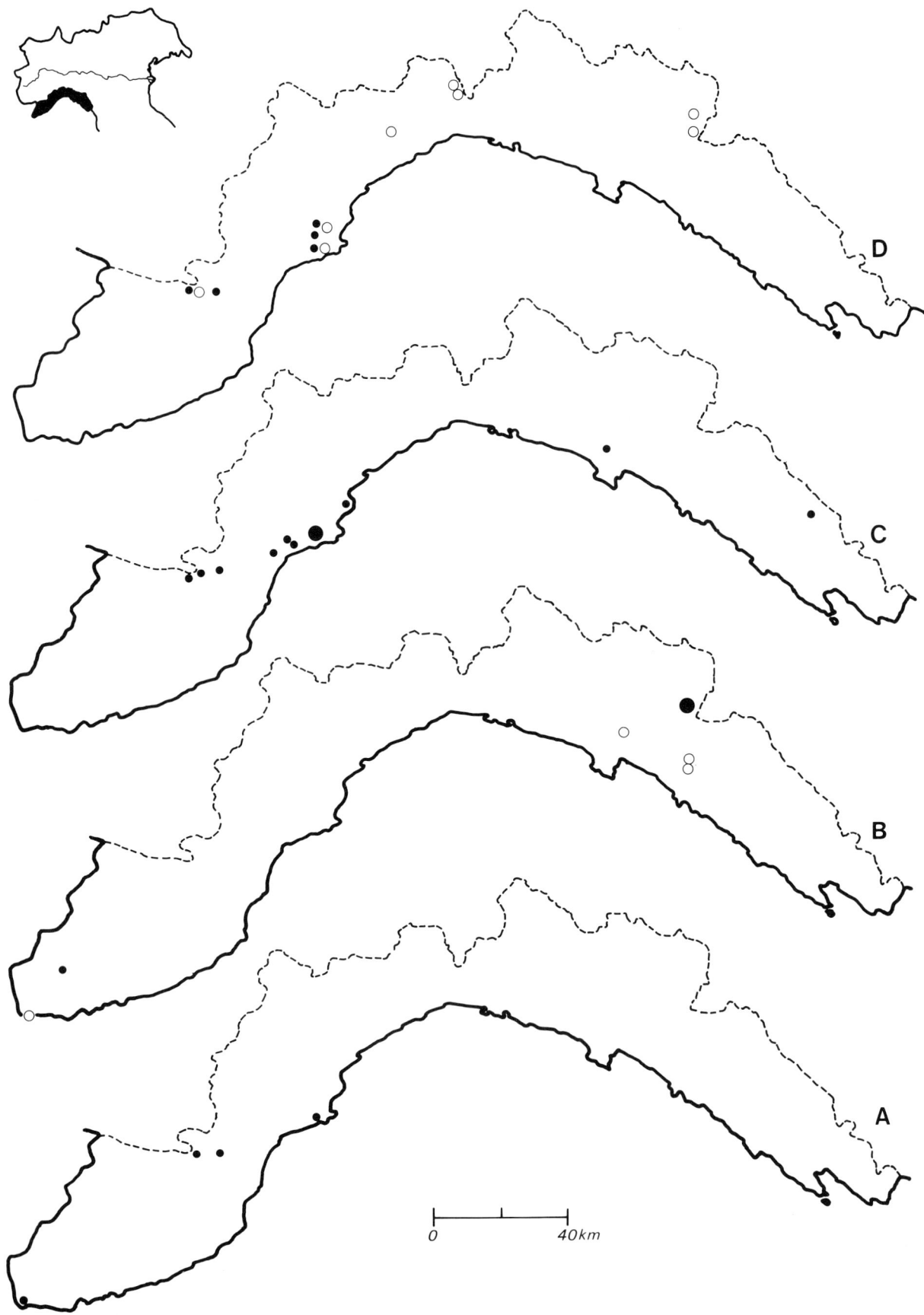

Figure 6   Liguria – site distributions: *A*. final Epi-Gravettian sites; *B*. Mesolithic Sauveterrian (circles) and Castelnovian (dots) sites; *C*. early Neolithic sites; *D*. sites with pollen (circles) and charcoal (dots) identifications. Large dots indicate concentrations of more than five sites. *Drawn by P. Biagi*

chronology is correct the thick stalagmite levels of layer 3 should belong to the Pre-Boreal and Boreal. It is interesting to observe that the charcoals from these levels indicate a temperate climate with pubescent oak (*Quercus* cf. *pubescens*) and hop-hornbeam (*Ostrya*) becomingly progressively humid with the first appearance of beech (*Fagus sylvatica*). At other caves like Arma dell'Aquila, a few kilometres from the sea, the late Palaeolithic layers are dominated by spruce/larch (*Picea/Larix*). Here, more than ten millennia later, the early and middle Neolithic occupations show evidence of maple (*Acer*), oak (*Quercus* cf. *pubescens*), juniper (*Juniperus*) and holm oak (*Quercus ilex*). The middle Atlantic is characterized by a forest with deciduous oak (*Quercus* cf. *pubescens*), ash (*Fraxinus*), hazel (*Corylus*) and alder (*Alnus*). Man's impact on the environment increased during this period with the first traces of agriculture at Arma dell'Aquila and the Arene Candide caves (Biagi and Nisbet 1986).

CONCLUSIONS

Liguria lies between two areas that are very important for their Mesolithic finds: the Tusco-Emilian Apennines to the east (Biagi *et al.* 1980; Tozzi 1980) and Provence to the west (Escalon de Fonton 1976a, 1976b). Significant differences can be observed in the site locations, tool types and supply of raw material for the three areas. The Sauveterrian encampments of eastern Liguria have produced assemblages made largely from dark red or pale green jasper from an outcrop very close to two of these sites. The Castelnovian stations have yielded collections with both jasper and flint artifacts. The percentage of flint tools seems to increase at those sites farther away from the jasper outcrops. An interesting phenomenon is the occurrence of many unretouched artifacts at several Castelnovian sites. At the very large site of Bosco delle Lame (*Fig. 1*, site 5), for instance, the collection comprises thousands of artifacts, mostly flakes, blades and some 200 cores to indicate that tools were produced locally. The two western sites of Punta della Mortola (*Fig. 2*, site 1) and Pian del Re (*Fig. 2*, site 2), located in a very different environment, have industries made largely from locally available material.

All the Ligurian Mesolithic camps are open-air sites, while in nearby Provence the best documented sequences are all from rock-shelters (Escalon de Fonton 1976b). A very different situation is that of the Tusco-Emilian Apennines where valley bottom 'base camps' have been excavated (Tozzi 1980). Many high altitude camps lying very close to passes have implements made of materials from various sources (Cremaschi 1978), mostly flint from the foot of the northern Apennines (Cremaschi *et al.* 1982).

It is still difficult to understand why no traces of

Mesolithic activity are documented in the Ligurian caves, while both Provence and Languedoc are rich in rock-shelters showing evidence of continuous occupation from the Lateglacial to the Atlantic period (Escalon de Fonton 1976b, 1976c).

Unfortunately, no Ligurian Mesolithic camp has produced faunal remains. The few data available for the final Epi-Gravettian show that the ibex was the commonest animal killed for meat at Arma dello Stefanin (Leale Anfossi 1972). Red deer and boar bones are very abundant at Arene Candide, a cave actually lying at 89 m a.s.l. with a steep drop to the Mediterranean sea, where the gathering of marine molluscs also played an important role in final Epi-Gravettian times (Emiliani *et al.* 1963).

A very different picture emerges at the beginning of the early Neolithic Impressed Ware culture (Bernabò Brea 1946, 1956). All the sites of this culture are concentrated in a very restricted zone of the Ponente (west) (*Fig. 6C*). They are all caves or rock-shelters often opening rather far from the coast (Biagi and Nisbet 1986). The only exceptions are the Levante (eastern) open settlements of Uscio and Suvero possibly belonging to the late seventh millennium BP (Maggi 1980; Biagi *et al.* 1987). It is probable that most of the coastal sites were destroyed during the Postglacial sea-level rise (Aloisi *et al.* 1978; Bazile 1987), as already observed in southern France (Mills 1982; Geddes *et al.* 1983). Thus, the origins of the Neolithic cannot be understood only through the study of the cave finds. In addition to the first pottery production, these sites also have other Neolithic elements, such as new flint types consisting of trapezes with flat retouch (*flèches tranchantes*) and imported obsidian pieces (Williams Thorpe *et al.* 1979). The early Neolithic economy at Arene Candide was based mainly on stock raising (Rowley-Conwy, in press) at the end of the eighth millennium BP (UB-2423: 6980±115 BP). According to the radiocarbon dates, at about the same period the Adige valley, the Po plain, the Trieste karst and the Tusco-Emilian Apennines still had a late Castelnovian way of life (R-1148: 6870±50 BP; R-892: 6930±60 BP; R-1043: 7050±60 BP; Birm-830: 6960±130 BP; Bln-3277: 6810±70 BP – Alessio *et al.* 1983; Accorsi *et al.* 1986).

References

ACCORSI, C.A., BANDINI MAZZANTI, M., BIAGI, P., CASTELLETTI, L., CREMASCHI, M., LEONI, L. and PAVARANI, M. (1986) Il sito mesolitico sopra Fienile Rossino sull'Altipiano di Cariàdeghe (Serle-Brescia). Aspetti pedostratigrafici, antracologici e palinologici. *Natura Bresciana*, 23: 239–292.

ALESSIO, M., ALLEGRI, L., BELLA, F., BROGLIO, A., CALDERONI, G., CORTESI, C., IMPROTA, S., PREITE MARTINEZ, M., PETRONE, V. and TURI, B. (1983) ^{14}C datings of three Mesolithic series of Trento Basin in the Adige valley (Vatte di Zambana, Pradestel, Romagnano) and comparisons with Mesolithic series of other regions. In *Il*

Popolamento delle Alpi in Età Mesolitica: VIII–V Millennio a.C. (Preistoria Alpina, 19). Trento, Museo Tridentino di Scienze Naturali: 245–254.

ALESSIO, M., BELLA, F., BACHECHI, F. and CORTESI, C. (1967) University of Rome carbon 14 dates V. *Radiocarbon*, 9: 346–367.

ALOISI, J-C., MONACO, A., PLANCHAIS, N., THOMMERET, J. and THOMMERET, Y. (1978) The Holocene transgression in the Golfe du Lion, southwestern France: palaeogeographic and palaeobotanical evolution. *Géographie Physique du Quaternaire*, 32: 145–162.

BAFFICO, O., BIAGI, P. and MAGGI, R. (1983) Il Mesolitico. In *Preistoria della Liguria Orientale*. Chiavari, Siri: 33–44.

BAGOLINI, B., BROGLIO, A. and LUNZ, R. (1983) Le Mésolithique des Dolomites. In *Il Popolamento delle Alpi in Età Mesolitica: VIII–V Millennio a.C.* (Preistoria Alpina, 19). Trento, Museo Tridentino di Scienze Naturali: 15–36.

BAISSAS, P. (1974) Les conditions sédimentologiques du passage Würm final–Holocène d'après les données de la grotte des Arene Candide. *Atti XVI Riunione dell'Istituto Italiano di Preistoria e Protoistoria*: 111–120.

BARONI, C. and BIAGI, P. (in press) Le ricerche archeologiche alla Punta della Mortola (Giardini di Villa Hanbury, Imperia): campagne 1985 e 1987. *Rivista Ingauna e Intemelia*, Nuova Serie A, 40.

BAZILE, F. (1987) Les lignes de rivage holocènes en Languedoc méditerranéen. In J. Guilaine, J. Courtin, J. Roudil and J-L. Vernet (eds), *Premières Communautés Paysannes en Méditerranée Occidentale*. Paris, Centre National de la Recherche Scientifique: 47–51.

BERNABÒ BREA, L. (1946) *Gli scavi nella Caverna delle Arene Candide. Parte I. Gli strati con ceramiche, 1.* Bordighera, Istituto di Studi Liguri.

BERNABÒ BREA, L. (1956) *Gli scavi nella Caverna delle Arene Candide. Parte I. Gli strati con ceramiche, 2.* Bordighera, Istituto di Studi Liguri.

BIAGI, P. (1981) Introduzione al Mesolitico della Lombardia. In *Atti I Convegno Archeologico Regionale*. Brescia, Geroldi: 55–76.

BIAGI, P., CASTELLETTI, L., CREMASCHI, M., SALA, B. and TOZZI, C. (1980) Popolazione e territorio nell'Appennino Tosco-emiliano e nel tratto centrale del bacino del Po tra il IX e il V millennio a.C. *Emilia Preromana*, 8: 13–36.

BIAGI, P. and MAGGI, R. (1983) Aspects of the Mesolithic age in Liguria. In *Il Popolamento delle Alpi in Età Mesolitica: VIII–V Millennio a.C.* (Preistoria Alpina, 19). Trento, Museo Tridentino di Scienze Naturali: 159–168.

BIAGI, P., MAGGI, R. and NISBET, R. (1987) Excavations at Arma dello Stefanin (Val Pennavaira, Albenga, northern Italy): 1982–1984. *Mesolithic Miscellany*, 8(1): 10–11.

BIAGI, P. and NISBET, R. (1986) Popolazione e territorio in Liguria tra il XII ed il IV millennio bc. In E.A. Arslan (ed.), *Scritti in Ricordo di G. Massari e di U. Tocchetti Pollini*. Milano, ET: 19–26.

BROGLIO, A. (1971) Risultati preliminari delle ricerche sui complessi epipaleolitici della Valle dell'Adige. *Preistoria Alpina*, 7: 135–241.

BROGLIO, A. (1981) De la fin du Paléolithique au commencement du Néolithique au sud des Alpes. *Archaeologia Interregionalis*, 1: 9–41.

BROGLIO, A. and KOZŁOWSKI, S.K. (1983) Tipologia ed evoluzione delle industrie mesolitiche di Romagnano III. In *Il Popolamento delle Alpi in Età Mesolitica: VIII–V Millennio a.C.* (Preistoria Alpina, 19). Trento, Museo Tridentino di Scienze Naturali: 93–148.

CARDINI, L. (1947) Gli strati mesolitici e paleolitici della Caverna delle Arene Candide. *Rivista di Studi Liguri*, 12: 3–11.

CREMASCHI, M. (1978) The source of the flint artefacts for the central Po plain and Apennine sites between the 7th and the 2nd millennium BC. In F. Engelen (ed.), *Third International Symposium on Flint* (Staringia, 6). Heerlen, Nederlandse Geologische Vereniging: 139–142.

CREMASCHI, M., BIAGI, P., ACCORSI, C.A., BANDINI MAZZANTI, M., RODOLFI, G., CASTELLETTI, L. and LEONI, L. (1982) Il sito Mesolitico di Monte Bagioletto (Appennino Reggiano) nel quadro delle variazioni ambientali oloceniche dell' Appennino Tosco-emiliano. *Emilia Preromana*, 9/10: 11–46.

EMILIANI, C., CARDINI, L., MAYEDA, T., McBURNEY, C.B.M. and TONGIORGI, E. (1963) Paleotemperature analysis of fossil shells of marine mollusks (food refuse) from the Arene Candide cave, Italy and the Haua Fteah cave, Cyrenaica. In H. Graig, S.L. Miller and G.J. Wasserberg (eds), *Isotopic and Cosmic Chemistry*. Amsterdam, North Holland Publishing Company: 133–156.

ESCALON DE FONTON, M. (1976a) La constitution de l'Epipaléolithique et du Mésolithique dans le Midi de la France. In S.K. Kozłowski (ed.), *Actes IX Congrès UISPP*, Colloque XIX. Paris, Centre National de la Recherche Scientifique: 53–70.

ESCALON DE FONTON, M. (1976b) Les civilisations de l'Epipaléolithique et du Mésolithique en Provence littorale. In H. de Lumley (ed.), *La Préhistoire Française*, tome 1. Paris, Centre National de la Recherche Scientifique: 1367–1378.

ESCALON DE FONTON, M. (1976c) Les civilisations de l'Epipaléolithique et du Mésolithique en Languedoc Oriental. In H. de Lumley (ed.), *La Préhistoire Française*, tome 1. Paris, Centre National de la Recherche Scientifique: 1382–1389.

FANCELLI GALLETTI, M.L. (1972) I carboni della Grotta delle Arene Candide e l'evoluzione forestale in Liguria dopo l'ultima glaciazione. *Atti della Società Toscana di Scienze Naturali*, Memorie, Serie A, 79: 206–211.

GEDDES, D.S., GUILAINE, J. and MONACO, A. (1983) Early Neolithic occupation on the submerged continental plateau of Roussillon (France). In P.M. Masters and N.C. Fleming (eds), *Quaternary Coastlines and Marine Archaeology*. London, Academic Press: 175–187.

GUERRI, M. (1976) Arene Candide. Livelli preceramici, scavo 1974. *Archeologia in Liguria*, 1: 157–158.

LEALE ANFOSSI, M. (1972) Il giacimento dell'Arma dello Stefanin (Val Pennavaira–Albenga). Scavi 1952–1962. *Rivista di Scienze Preistoriche*, 27(2): 249–322.

MACPHAIL, G.M. (in press) Palynological investigations in the Ligurian Apennines, northern Italy. *Archeologia in Liguria*, 3.

MAGGI, R. (1980) Appunti sulla preistoria della Riviera di Levante. *Annali del Museo Civico della Spezia*, 2 (1979–80): 169–191.

MILLS, N. (1982) The Neolithic of southern France. In C. Scarre (ed.), *Ancient France. Neolithic Societies and their Landscape 6000–2000 bc*. Edinburgh, University Press: 91–145.

MONTANARI, A., GUIDO, M. and BRAGGIO MORUCCHIO, G. (1979) Vicende paleoclimatiche del Postglaciale nell'Appennino ligure ricostruite attraverso l'esame dei diagrammi pollinici. In *Convegno di Meteorologia Appenninica*. Reggio Emilia, Amministrazione Provinciale: 1–9.

PALMA DI CESNOLA, A. (1974) Il Paleolitico superiore della Liguria alla luce delle recenti scoperte. *Atti XVI Riunione dell'Istituto Italiano di Preistoria e Protoistoria*: 23–36.

PALMA DI CESNOLA, A. (1983) L'Epigravettien évolué et final de la région haute-tyrrhénienne. *Rivista di Scienze Preistoriche*, 38: 301–318.

RADMILLI, A.M. (1960) Considerazioni sul Mesolitico Italiano. *Annali dell'Università di Ferrara*, NS, Sezione XV, 1: 133–141.

ROWLEY-CONWY, P.A. (in press) Faunal remains from Arene Candide. Preliminary report on the Neolithic and later material from the 1940–42 and 1948–50 excavations. *Archeologia in Liguria*, 3.

TOZZI, C. (1980) Il Mesolitico dell'Appennino Tosco-emiliano. In *La Toscana settentrionale dal Paleolitico all'Alto Medioevo*. Lucca, Nuova Grafica: 43–59.

VERNET, J-L. (1970) Analyse de charbon de bois de niveaux tardiglaciaires et postglaciaires de l'Arma du Stefanin (Savone, Italie). *Naturalia Monspelliensia*, 21: 243–246.

VERNET, J-L. (1974) Précisions sur l'évolution de la végétation dans la région méditerranéenne depuis le Tardiglaciaire d'après les charbon de bois de l'Arma du Nasino (Savone, Italie). *Bulletin de l'Association Française pour l'Etude du Quaternaire*, 39: 65–72.

WILLIAMS THORPE, O., WARREN, S.E. and BARFIELD, L.H. (1979) The sources and distribution of archaeological obsidian in northern Italy. *Preistoria Alpina*, 15: 73–92.

Isolating the Residuals: the Mesolithic Basis of Man–Animal Relationships on the Mediterranean Islands

J. Lewthwaite

Abstract

This paper examines the transition from foraging to food production within the Mediterranean basin. It accepts that the traditional 'diffusionist' model of the dispersion of fully-developed village-farming communities retains a certain validity in the eastern sector, particularly with regard to the settlement of Crete and Cyprus. On the other hand, such an explanation is inappropriate for the western basin, as many scholars have already concluded; but the alternative model of the progressive transformation of foragers into farmers through the gradual incorporation of first animal husbandry and then crop cultivation fails to explain certain anomalies when scrutinized in detail.

It is suggested that the western Mediterranean islands played a key role in mediating, indeed 'filtering' the dispersion of domesticates between the eastern village-farmers and the western advanced foragers. To this end the evidence for the Pre-Neolithic settlement of the Baleares, Corsica and Sardinia going back to 9000 BP (or even earlier) is summarized, with particular attention to faunal exploitation.

It is argued that the pattern of the dispersion of domesticates between Sicily and Spain is most elegantly explained in terms of the simultaneous operation of two axes: the one terrestrial or longshore, *via* the Maghreb as far as Andalusia; the other maritime, *via* the Tyrrhenian islands to Provence, this latter axis imposing a 'filter effect' on the dispersion of domesticates until bypassed.

It is postulated that the key to this phenomenon lies in the peculiar deficiency in terrestrial resources to which the western Mediterranean islands were subject after the isolation of the Pleistocene. It is suggested that the Pre-Neolithic populations were likely to have developed technological, economic and social responses which were pre-adaptive with respect to the rapid adoption and re-diffusion of elements of the Neolithic way of life which were comparable and complementary.

INTRODUCTION

Problem definition

This essay addresses the problem of the variation in the date and rate of the local transition from foraging to food production among the several regions of the Mediterranean basin. Older diffusionist models (Bernabò Brea 1950; Childe 1957) postulated a unitary phenomenon: following closely on the achievement of the Neolithic Revolution, communities of mixed farmers would have mastered the skills of seafaring in the coastlands of Anatolia and the Levant, enabling them to spread rapidly and uniformly with their crop plants, flocks and herds along the coasts and among the islands of the Mediterranean, their passage marked for the archaeologist by the distribution of polished stone tools and

ceramics, particularly those of the Impressed family. In the light of the research carried out over the last few decades, such a model no longer fits the facts; there is considerable variation between the eastern and western basins in respect of not only the definitive transition to food production but the very coherence of the various elements of the diffusionist model of the Neolithic – specifically the use of water craft, the husbandry of the various species of domestic animal, the practice of crop cultivation, the manufacture of ceramics, and permanent settlement in villages (*Fig. 1*; Lewthwaite 1981).

Mesolithic relevance

Could the environment of the western basin have been in some way less suitable for the Near Eastern-derived Neolithic farming system? The researches of palynologists, palaeobotanists and archaeologists, while handicapped by serious sampling deficiencies in spatial coverage, point rather towards the significance of latitude (i.e. towards a north–south rather than an east–west contrast) and altitude. Thus pine yields to deciduous oak in the course of the Holocene in Crete as in Catalunya or Corsica, while xerophile species of evergreen macchia such as wild olive and lentisk have been recorded in early Postglacial contexts from Alacant to the coast of the Argolid (*Fig. 2*; Hansen 1978; Bottema 1980; Reille, Triat-Laval and Vernet 1980; Van Zeist and Bottema 1982; Reille 1984; Vernet, Badal García, Grau Almero and Ros Mora 1984; Costantini, Piperno and Tusa 1987; Vernet, Badal García and Grau Almero 1987).

If the environment does not appear to be directly correlated with the observed variation, it is nonetheless possible that an indirect influence was exerted, in that (i) the western basin offered a greater potential for the development of a successful and stable foraging adaptation during the early Postglacial, which (ii) obstructed the diffusion of farming populations or technocomplexes. The analogy most frequently invoked is that of aboriginal California, where an advanced foraging population in an environment very similar to that of the Mediterranean

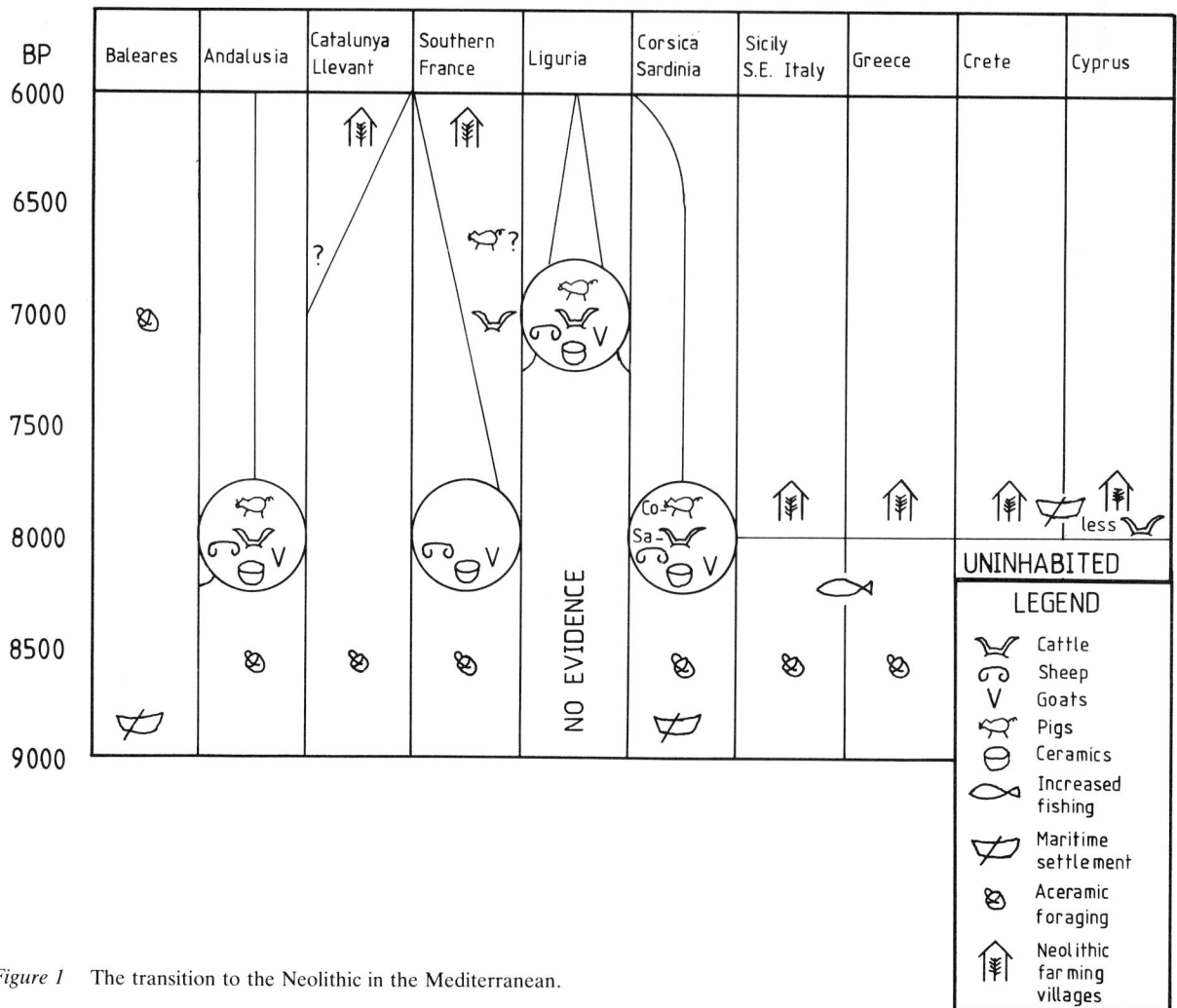

Figure 1 The transition to the Neolithic in the Mediterranean.

persisted in the exploitation of native resources (deer–salmon–acorns) despite the supposed availability of the Mesoamerican maize–beans–squash farming complex (e.g. Phillips 1975; *contra* Lewthwaite 1982). Paradoxically, this position is very close to that of proponents of an essentially autochthonous transition to food production and Neolithic culture among the several regions of the western and central Mediterranean through local processes of adaptation to Postglacial opportunities (e.g. Guilaine 1976, advocating a 'polygenic' model).

In effect, there is a convergence of opinion towards the proposition that the distinct patterns of development of the eastern and western basins must be due to the differential density of the Mesolithic presence in each region – from the whole of mainland Greece only two Mesolithic sites are known (Franchthi, in the Argolid, and Seidi, in Boeotia) besides Sidari on Corfu. Therefore, both the diffusionist and the autochthonist/polygenic models may deserve to be restricted rather than rejected *in toto*. Put at its simplest, a revised synthesis would propose that farming populations physically infiltrated a relatively vacant niche in the east whereas, in the west, indigenous Mesolithic

communities selectively adopted such elements of the Neolithic farming system as were compatible with, even complementary to, existing seasonality and scheduling, only much later being pushed over the threshold of equilibrium by some local circumstantial resource crisis. The latter model has recently been put forward in the context of the Mesolithic–Neolithic transition in Scandinavia by Zvelebil and Rowley-Conwy (1984).

The relevance of the islands

The fundamental contrasts between the developments in the western and eastern basins, essentially between the active and continuous process of change in the former compared with the dependency and stepwise growth of the latter, appear to be borne out by the researches into the pattern and process of island settlement conducted by Cherry (1981, 1984) whose conclusions may be summarized as follows:

1. In general, the pattern of settlement conforms to the predictions of models drawn from island biogeography, despite the active rather than passive nature of the underlying process.

2. Prior to and during the early Neolithic (9000–

542

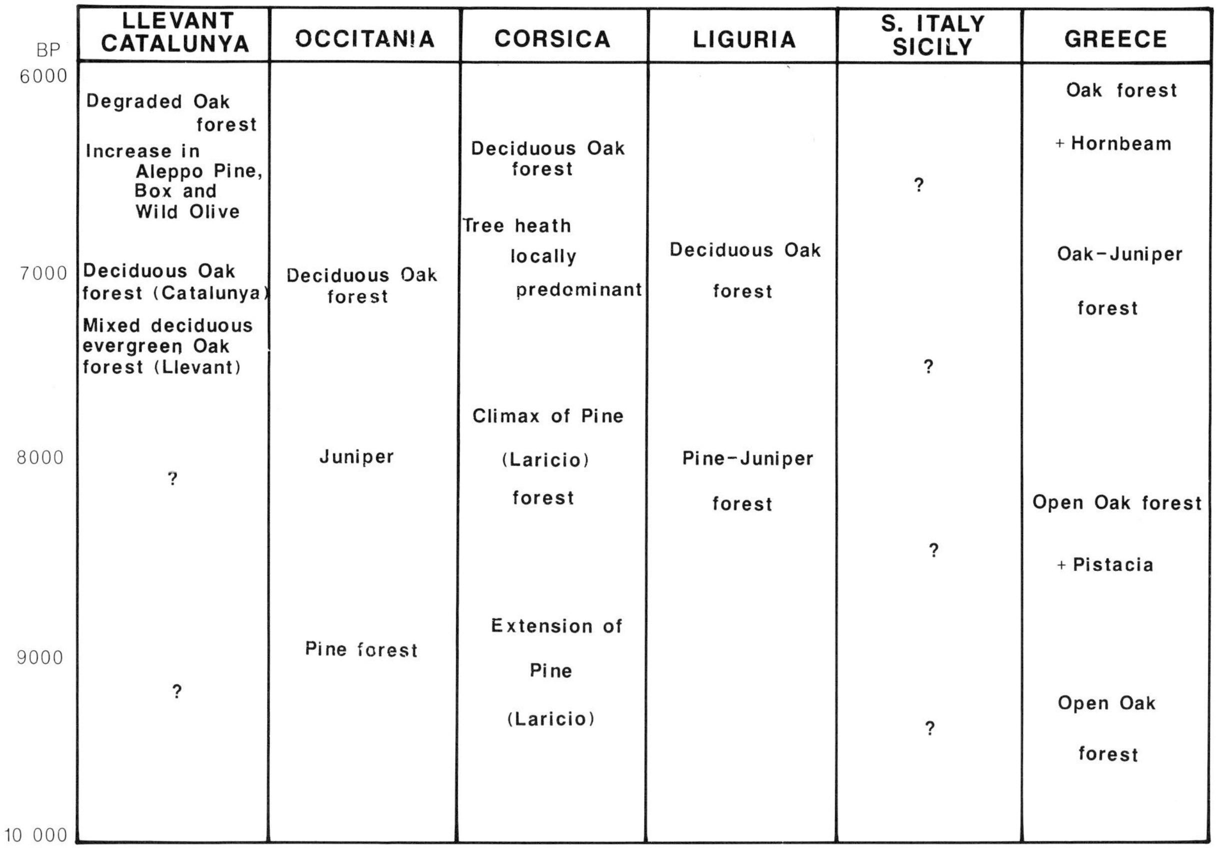

BP	LLEVANT CATALUNYA	OCCITANIA	CORSICA	LIGURIA	S. ITALY SICILY	GREECE
6000	Degraded Oak forest / Increase in Aleppo Pine, Box and Wild Olive	Deciduous Oak forest	Deciduous Oak forest / Tree heath locally predominant	Deciduous Oak forest	?	Oak forest + Hornbeam
7000	Deciduous Oak forest (Catalunya) / Mixed deciduous evergreen Oak forest (Llevant)					Oak–Juniper forest
					?	
8000	?	Juniper	Climax of Pine (Laricio) forest	Pine–Juniper forest		Open Oak forest + Pistacia
					?	
9000	?	Pine forest	Extension of Pine (Laricio)			Open Oak forest
					?	
10 000						

Figure 2   Early Postglacial Mediterranean vegetational dynamics.

6000 BP) the islands of the western basin were settled at a significantly faster rate than those of the east, probably on account of their larger mean size.

3. During the same period the islands of the western basin participated in the widespread and long-enduring interaction sphere of the Impressed Ware culture group, whereas the settlers of Crete and Cyprus appear to have become essentially isolated from their adjacent mainlands until the threshold of the Bronze Age.

It is tempting to suppose that these economic, demographic, social and cultural developments are correlated in some way. Bearing in mind Newell's (1984) model of the systemic changes among the variables wrought by population growth and increases in density, it is possible to envisage that the regional divergences occurred thus:

(i) The settlers of Crete and Cyprus, through their introduction of a developed mixed-farming system into vacant niches, were able to grow into viable populations within essentially closed systems – although it must be admitted that Stanley Price (1977a) has raised the possibility of a systemic collapse in the case of the Cypriot aceramic Neolithic.

(ii) The established Mesolithic (or Pre-Neolithic) communities of the western islands may have participated in an open system of biocultural interaction, which both expedited the initial selective adoption of

certain innovations (not limited to subsistence, as in the case of ceramic styles) and damped down the subsequent systemic change to a level compatible with the maintenance of such an open system for some two millennia (i.e. until the horizon of the inception of the regionally-differentiated middle Neolithic – cf. Mills 1987).

Such a scenario redirects attention towards the environmental peculiarities of the western islands, rather than the mainland, which might explain this paradox of their initial precocity and subsequent stability.

The filter model

Definition. This refers to the workings of a uni-directional innovation process within a system comprising a set of discrete regions with distinct behaviours linked in series, such that region $n+1$ depends upon region n for access to innovations which it in turn rediffuses to regions $n+2$, $n+3$, and so forth. The feature distinctive of this process is that the behaviour of any one region irreversibly predetermines the 'choices' made available to regions further down the line through the filtering-out of selected elements of an originally integrated system of innovations.

Application. It is proposed that the transmission of the West Asiatic farming complex to Cyprus, Crete,

543

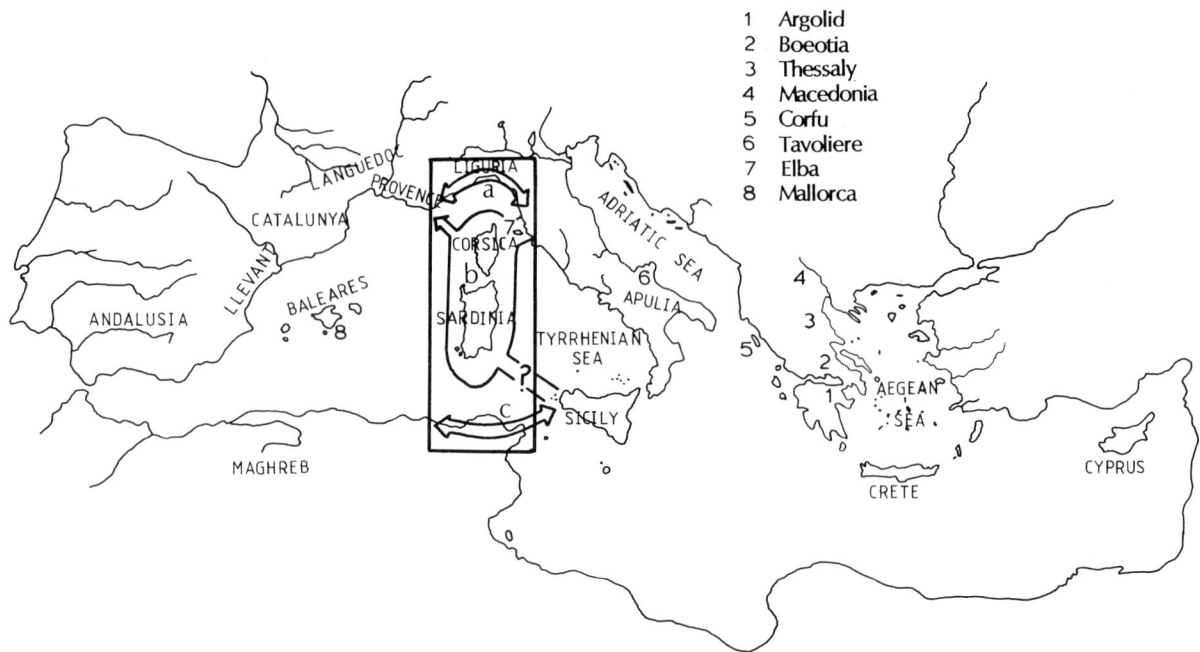

1 Argolid
2 Boeotia
3 Thessaly
4 Macedonia
5 Corfu
6 Tavoliere
7 Elba
8 Mallorca

Figure 3 Location of the regions and routeways of particular importance mentioned in the text.

mainland Greece, peninsular Italy and Sicily took place without any significant 'filtering', despite the successive water-crossings imposed by the Aegean and Adriatic seas, because of the relatively minor role played by indigenous Mesolithic communities. Three axes would be available for further onward transmission between the Tyrrhenian coasts of Italy and Sicily and the Mediterranean littoral of Iberia: (a) terrestrial, *via* Liguria; (b) maritime, *via* Elba, Corsica and Sardinia; (c) terrestrial, *via* the Mediterranean coast of the Maghreb (*Fig. 3*). Were (b) to have been the sole or major axis, it is predicted that insular Pre-Neolithic populations would have been in a position to 'filter' the farming system in the light of the requirements peculiar to the insular environments.

Falsification. For a model to be useful it is necessary that the criteria of its definitive falsification be specified in advance, since any poorness of fit can always be explained away as the consequence of poor and biased data or resolved through endless special pleading. Therefore, it is worth distinguishing clearly the several premises on which the model may rest from the model itself and, if the totality of the data cannot be tested in an essay of this length, justifying the selection of one variable rather than another as the key criterion.

The essence of the contrast between the developments in the eastern and western basins lies in the coherence, in the former case, of three variables which appear successively over two or more millennia in the latter, these being the husbandry of a wide range of domestic animals, the cultivation of crop plants, and the practice of sedentary settlement in permanent villages. The tardy appearance of the

villages in the west might be due to biases acting against their discovery – not so much the effects of the Postglacial transgression and subsequent developments in coastal morphology (*pace* Lewthwaite 1981), since this ought logically to affect eastern and western distributions alike, as the greater visibility of the *tells* of Thessaly and the rock- or *crosta*-cut ditches of the central Mediterranean compared with the scantier traces left by their western counterparts. Similarly, the apparent absence of on-site residues of agricultural activity from the Mediterranean prior to the mid-seventh millennium BP might be due to the failure to make flotation a standard practice. On the other hand, faunal analyses are sufficiently common, and the bones of domestic animals sufficiently familiar even to non-specialist excavators, for criteria of their presence or absence and, more significantly, of the presence or absence of certain species rather than others to be regarded as by far the most reliable of the several variables. Therefore, the filter model as presented here is very largely couched in terms of changes in man–animal relationships.

Would the model therefore be falsified if (i) crop cultivation and (ii) widespread sedentary village settlement were demonstrated at dates significantly in advance of those currently assumed? Neither question is easily answered.

In the case of crop cultivation, it must be borne in mind that the scheduling conflicts between foraging and the cultivation cycle in northern latitudes (Zvelebil and Rowley-Conwy 1984) would not have occurred (Clark Forbes 1976), and that small-scale cultivation might have been integrated with systems of residential as well as logistic mobility. Indeed, such an adoption of crop plants as a supplement and complement to native resources on the part of the western

544

Mesolithic groups would be predicted. Therefore, only cultivation on a scale permitting village settlement would constitute falsification.

It is just possible to envisage villages of affluent foragers in Mediterranean Mesolithic contexts of very high productivity, such as estuaries (Clarke 1976), which might subsequently have been erased from the archaeological record. However, proof of the existence of such villages on the western Mediterranean islands, held to be subject to more severe constraints, would require a major reformulation of the filter model if not its complete rejection.

The significance attributed to the first evidence of the presence of the domesticates in the Mediterranean rests on the premiss that domestication, at least as a primary phenomenon (i.e. excluding subsequent crossing with native boar and aurochs), did not occur locally and independently of Western Asiatic developments. The case for the introduction of the domestic sheep into the Mediterranean and for the feral origin of the island mouflon populations has been accepted by most specialists (Poplin 1979; Uerpmann 1979, 1987; Geddes 1985; Vigne 1984, 1987), while the morphological distinction between the domestic goat and the various forms of the European ibex precludes any derivation of the former from the latter. In the case of the pig, chromosomal evidence (Popescu, Quéré and Franceschi 1980) suggests an exotic origin for the domesticate and the (feral) island populations; inferences from the morphology of the earliest Neolithic examples are regarded as highly debatable by specialist archaeozoologists (Vigne 1984; Helmer 1987). Finally, in respect of cattle, Geddes is prepared to state that the earliest examples of domestic cattle in the Midi appear to have been introduced as such, rather than tamed locally (Geddes 1980).

DATA: THE ANTIQUITY OF HUMAN SETTLEMENT ON THE MEDITERRANEAN ISLANDS

Mallorca

The antiquity of human settlement has been pushed back over the last quarter-century from c. 4000 to c. 9000 BP:

1. In 1962 a handful of human bones and a few artifacts (flint flakes, bone needles) were found in association with examples of the now extinct endemic *Myotragus balearicus*, previously thought to have died out during the Pleistocene, in the limestone solution cave complex of So'n Muleta (Sóller) in a stratum yielding these dates: 5935±109 BP (KBN-640d), 7135±80 BP (KBN-640c), 8570±120 BP (UCLA-1704c) (Waldren 1982).

2. In 1968, excavations in the large (46×10×10/30 m) limestone shelter of So'n Matge (Valldemossa),

which is located in a more accessible and strategic position and which provides the key stratified sequence for Mallorcan prehistory, uncovered evidence of a relationship between man and *Myotragus* which was both more intensive and more credible. Two phases may be distinguished in the period of early settlement. In the first, which began some time before 6680±120 BP (QL-29) and which ceased at 5820±360 BP (CSIC-176), the relevant sector was used as a 'corral' and abattoir for *Myotragus*, as can be inferred from various pieces of evidence: an 125 cm accumulation of *Myotragus* coprolites, horn cores trimmed to prevent carcass damage from infighting, and butchery marks from flint tools on bones. In the second, which extended from 5750±115 BP (I-5516) down to the horizon of the introduction of domestic animals and ceramics at 4650±120 BP (QL-988), this sector was used for domestic purposes, the lenses of ash and charcoal which built up containing burned bones of *Myotragus* and a few artifacts (Waldren 1982).

3. A posthumous publication by Kopper (1984) reports the existence of apparently anthropogenic lenses of charcoal containing *Myotragus* bones which extend back at least as far as 9220±570 BP (P-2408) and possibly much earlier, while existing seventh millennium BP datings are confirmed by an overlying level dated to 6370±320 BP (Beta-6948). The site involved consists of another limestone solution cave complex at Ca'n Canet (Esporles).

4. Finally, Pons-Moyà and Coll Conesa (1984) claim that certain undated and unstratified assemblages discovered in the course of surface survey around Santanyí (sites of Rafal des Porcs, So'n Danus and Pont de la Plana) are typologically comparable with such continental Mesolithic assemblages as those of the Grotta della Madonna (Praia a Mare), the Baume de Fontbrégoua (Salernes), the Cauna d'Arques and the upper levels of El Filador (Tarragona), all dated to the period c. 9500–8500 BP.

Corsica

The antiquity of human settlement has again been pushed back to c. 9000 BP:

1. The discovery of the Pre-Neolithic of Corsica proceeded *pari passu* with that of the early Neolithic during the late 1960s. The small rock-shelter of Curacchiaghju (Livia), located at c. 700–800 m on a plateau in the southern interior of the island, yielded to the excavator (Lanfranchi 1967) not only an early Neolithic assemblage comparable to those uncovered at the abri D' of Filitosa (Suddacaro) and at Basi (Sarra di Farru) but an underlying basal level devoid of ceramics and 'typical' lithics, moreover lacking the finer imported raw materials such as flint and

obsidian which were a feature of early Neolithic assemblages (Weiss and Lanfranchi 1976). The acidic soil conditions induced by the granite composition of the shelter largely obliterated traces of the original faunal assemblage. This quantitative distinction was rapidly supplemented by a sequence of radiocarbon determinations, unexpectedly high but internally consistent: 8500±170 BP (Gif-795) for the Pre-Neolithic, 7300±160 BP (Gif-796) for the early Neolithic. The reliability of the Curacchiaghju stratigraphy has been undermined, however, by growing doubts concerning the homogeneity of the early Neolithic assemblage (Lewthwaite 1983, 1985; Lanfranchi 1987).

2. Subsequent excavations in the rock-shelter of Araguina-Sennola (Bonifaziu) at the southern end of the tip of the island yielded evidence of Pre-Neolithic occupation more reliable on account of the clear stratification of the much deeper body of the deposit which, being calcareous, preserved not only the faunal assemblages but burials from both the Pre-Neolithic and the early Neolithic levels. While the artifactual evidence was scanty, a radiocarbon determination from the upper part of the Pre-Neolithic stratum (XVIIIa) is strikingly in agreement with that from Curacchiaghju: 8520±150 BP (Gif-2705) (Lanfranchi and Weiss 1977). The question of the date of the introduction of domesticates is complicated by the presence of a handful of sheep and pig bones in level XVIIIa, sealed by a rockfall from any possibility of contamination by the overlying early Neolithic levels (Vigne 1983, 1987). In any case, even in the early Neolithic period, the overwhelming mass of the faunal evidence records the use of the site for hunting and trapping of the now extinct lagomorph *Prolagus sardus* (Vigne, Marinval-Vigne, Lanfranchi and Weiss 1981) minimally supplemented by aquatic and avian resources (Vigne 1984).

3. The previous concentration of research on the south of Corsica has been rectified in recent years by the researches of J. Magdeleine and J-C. Ottaviani in the north, particularly the Nebbiu region, rich in caves and favourable towards the preservation of faunal material on account of its calcareous composition. This programme has culminated in the discovery and excavation of the shelter of Strette (Barbaghju), intermittently washed by the stream which cuts through the *cuesta* landscape of the Nebbiu. Only preliminary accounts are available (Magdeleine 1980, 1985; Magdeleine and Ottaviani 1986) which have unfortunately been distorted in publication in résumé form (Bonifay 1983). The second sounding (Strette II) provides the key sequence and a series of radiocarbon determinations (Evin, Maréchal and Marien 1985: 437), as follows: a sterile layer (XXI) separates the early Neolithic (XX) from

the Pre-Neolithic, itself comprising one relatively rich level (XXII) and one somewhat poor level (XXIV), separated by another sterile layer (XXIII); the lower Pre-Neolithic level (XXIV) is dated to 9140±300 BP (Ly-2837). Once again, the food residues consist essentially of *Prolagus sardus* and shellfish, the lithics are made of poor quality local materials (although the larger Strette level XXII assemblage includes for the first time a few recognizable forms), while ceramics are entirely absent.

Sardinia

The question of the so-called 'Clactonian' assemblages of the Anglona region (Arca, Martini, Pitzalis, Tuveri and Ulzaga 1982) will not be discussed here (but *vide* Cherry 1984), since these do not in any case constitute proof of the continuity of settlement into the Holocene. However, such a continuity appears to have been discovered for the first time by a team with a primarily palaeontological orientation (Sondaar, De Boer, Sanges, Kotsakis and Esu 1984) in the three-level sequence of the Corbeddu cave (Olièna) in the east-centre of the island. Their findings may be summarized thus: (i) firstly, an upper level of Neolithic material and date, subdivided into level 1a, dated to 6260±180 BP (GrN-11433) and a level 1b, separated from the former by a stalagmite floor, assigned to 8040±100 BP (UT-C22-3568) – the Cardial assemblage associated with the latter is now therefore the oldest in the Tyrrhenian region, indeed as old as any in the Mediterranean basin; (ii) next, a middle level, dated to 9120±380 BP (GrN-11434), evincing less direct traces of human activity such as butchered and burned bones of *Prolagus sardus* and a well apparently dug into water-bearing layers at the back of the cave; (iii) finally, the third level incorporating bones of the now extinct deer *Megaceros cazioti* which appear to have been grouped into non-random patterns, worked and, in the case of some skulls, broken and polished. A determination of 13,590±140 BP was derived from the bone material of this level, which the excavators (Sondaar *et al.* 1984) interpret as a workshop rather than a ritual or butchery site.

Crete

Having reviewed the various strands of evidence alleged to demonstrate Pre-Neolithic, even Palaeolithic, settlement ('osteodontokeratic' artifacts, parietal art, possibly worked bones of the now extinct megacerine deer), Cherry (1981) concludes that there is no reliable attestation of human presence prior to 8000 BP. The earliest settlers of the knoll underlying Minoan Knossos brought with them cereals, legumes, sheep, goats, pigs and cattle, mud-brick architecture, but no ceramics, into an island apparently devoid of foragers. Radiocarbon determinations for this stratum (X) range from 8050±180 BP (BM-124) and 7910±140 BP (BM-278) to 7740±140 BP (BM-436) (Evans 1971). No other site is known from this earliest period.

Cyprus

The earliest settlers of Cyprus again appear to have been Neolithic farmers, distinguished by certain peculiar features in architecture and burial rite seemingly of Levantine origin. Dates for the sites now known from the aceramic Neolithic (more than a dozen) converge on a mid-eighth millennium BP inception, the earliest determination being 7655±160 BP (St-415) from Khirokitia, apart from two 'anomalous' ninth millennium BP dates from Kalavasos Tenta (Stanley Price 1977a, 1977b, 1979; Karageorghis 1982). For the purposes of this paper the fact of key importance is that these early mixed-farmers exploited cereals, legumes, sheep, goats and pigs, the Syrian fallow deer (*Dama mesopotamica*), but not cattle (Watson and Stanley Price 1977).

PATTERN: ISOLATING THE FILTERING EFFECT OF THE TYRRHENIAN ISLANDS

The dispersion of domesticates westward through the Mediterranean will be described in terms of two propositions: firstly, initial dispersion of all the species as far as Apulia and Sicily took the form of a unitary phenomenon; secondly, further dispersion as far as the Midi and Iberia occurred along two axes, a minor axis along the coast of the Maghreb as far as Andalusia which was free from filtering, and a major axis lying athwart the Tyrrhenian islands which can be identified precisely through its selectivity.

Verification of the former proposition

The simultaneous introduction of all domesticates into Crete and of all but cattle into Cyprus have been noted above. In the case of mainland Greece, the basal levels of several tells in Thessaly and Macedonia (e.g. Argissa, Otzaki, Achilleion and Nea Nikomedia), dated to the very beginning of the eighth millennium BP, have yielded remains of sheep, goats, pigs and cattle (Murray 1970; Halstead 1981). At Franchthi cave the faunal assemblage of the initial Neolithic levels, dated to 7794±140 BP (P-1392), is made up of ovicaprines to some 90%; as to the status of the scantier pig and cattle finds of this level, no definitive account is at present available (Payne 1975; Jacobsen 1981).

With respect to the Tavoliere, there is extreme confusion over the relationship between absolute dates (still rare) and the ceramic typological sequence established by Tinè (1983), which does not command universal acceptance. In effect, Tinè differentiates a welter of 'pure' styles, to each of which is allotted a unique time-slot, whereas Cipolloni Sampò, among others, argues on the basis of fieldwork that these styles overlap and interpenetrate – i.e. that they are of cultural, rather than chronological, significance (Cipolloni Sampò 1987). It is particularly regrettable that radiocarbon dated faunal analyses are not available from the village sites which are beginning to appear, such as those near Serracapriola beside the lower Fortore and Rendina I (Melfi) which contain ceramic assemblages attributable to the very earliest of Tinè's phases (Prato Don Michele), assigned to the period c. 8000–7500 BP (Cipolloni Sampò 1983; Whitehouse 1984). Bovines as well as ovicaprines have been identified by Geddes at the site of Torre Sabea (Gallipoli) near Lecce, in association with a ceramic assemblage which is archaic in appearance but as yet lacks absolute dates (Cremonesi and Guilaine 1987). Finally, the recently published faunal assemblage, within which Bökönyi has identified all four major species of domesticate, of Santa Tecchia near Foggia has yielded a radiocarbon date of as early as 7550±800 BP. However, the associated ceramics belong to a style (Masseria la Quercia) otherwise dated no earlier than 7000–6500 BP (Cassano and Manfredini 1983). The best that can be said is that there is no 'positive' evidence from a village site of a distinct priority of the introduction of ovicaprines relative to that of the other species, particularly bovines.

In the case of Sicily, the key site of the Grotta dell'Uzzo (Trapani) documents the simultaneous introduction of domestic sheep, goats, cattle and pigs in levels dated by a *terminus post quem* 8130±80 BP (P-2734) (Piperno, Scali and Tagliacozzo 1980; Costantini *et al.* 1987).

To sum up, despite the paucity of evidence, there is no demonstrable instance from the region extending from the Aegean to Sicily of a significant discrepancy between the date of the introduction of ovicaprines and that of the pig or cattle; on the contrary, there is every indication of their introduction as an integrated 'package'.

Verification of the latter hypothesis

It is paradoxically easiest to begin by defining the termini of the axes and horizons of dispersion in the relatively well-researched regions of Occitan France, Catalunya and the Levant, which form a cultural unity defined by the density of elaborate decoration based on cardial impressions (Coudrot 1976). With the acquisition of new dates from the classic sequence of the abri de la Font-des-Pigeons (Châteauneuf-les-Martigues), once held to be a hearth of indigenous Mesolithic sheep domestication, and with the recent rejection of early shell-derived determinations such as that of Cap Ragnon (Le Rove), the case for particularly precocious Provençal ovicaprine husbandry (c. 8000–7500 BP) has collapsed (Phillips 1975; Ducos 1977; Gascó and Gutherz 1983; Evin

1987). West of the Rhône, Geddes has concluded that the first domestic sheep were introduced into final Mesolithic or 'Proto-Neolithic' contexts c. 7500 BP, followed by cattle c. 7000 BP and the pig c. 6700 BP (Geddes 1983, 1985).

In the case of the Levant, controversy attends the attribution of the *terminus a quo* to one of two key sites.

On the one hand, the early Neolithic (Cardial) level of the Cova de l'Or (Beniarrés, Alacant) contains all the major domesticates, albeit with an overwhelming preponderance of ovicaprines and a very sparse representation of bovines; the earliest date for this level is 6740±380 BP (GANOP C-13) (Martí Oliver 1982, 1983). Such a date, faunal assemblage and cultural attribution accord with the orthodox model of the transmission of domesticates *via* Provence, Languedoc and Catalunya from a source further east, paralleling the derivation of Cardial forms and motifs from Guilaine's Tyrrhenian and ultimately Sicilian–south Italian facies within the Impressed Ware grouping (Guilaine 1980).

On the other hand, claims have been advanced for the presence of domesticates, including cattle, and indeed for the local domestication of ovicaprines at the site of the Cova Fosca (Ares del Maestrat, Castelló de la Plana – Olaría, Estévez Escalera and Yll 1982; Olaría and Gusí 1987). Domestic bovines would have been present at 7210±70 BP (CSIC-357) and sheep not only in the early Neolithic at 7640±160 BP (CSIC-353) but in the Mesolithic (Teledyne I-11313: 9460±160 BP and I-9868: 8880±200 BP).

Significantly, the ceramic assemblage has stronger affinities with contemporary sites farther south in Andalusia, anticipating by a millennium the spread of such motifs into the heartland of the classic Cardial culture as far as the Midi (Freises and Montjardin 1982; Arnal 1984). For this reason, some authors (Guilaine 1980; Aparicio Pérez 1982; Martí Oliver 1982) reject the dates, attributing the Cova Fosca to the Epi-Cardial period.

The present writer proposes an alternative interpretation – that domesticates were introduced into Iberia along two axes. One axis of dispersion, which may be traced back to a Sicilian–south Italian source *via* either mainland Italy or the Tyrrhenian islands, transmitted domesticates subject to the filter effect and the ceramic style out of which the Cardial tradition developed as far as the province of Alacant. The other, of which the Cova Fosca is but an outlier, reached Andalusia *via* the coast of the Maghreb. The concept of an 'outlier' is exemplified by the site of Peiro Signado (Portiragnes) in the Hérault which contains Lipariot obsidian and a ceramic assemblage quite distinct from that of the Cardial culture proper, pertaining rather to sites of Guilaine's

Tyrrhenian facies such as Caucade (Nice) and Basi in Corsica, indeed ultimately to the Stentinello culture of Sicily (Freises and Montjardin 1982; Grimal 1982; Roudil and Soulier 1984). This presupposes that Andalusian assemblages exist with the requisite properties of: (i) a full, 'unfiltered' range of domesticates; (ii) a ceramic tradition independent of the Tyrrhenian–Cardial ramage; and (iii) an antiquity equal to or greater than the sites of the Tyrrhenian–Occitan–Levantine axis. In fact, four sites in western Andalusia have yielded precisely such data, these being the caves of Nerja near Maro (Malaga), Parralejo (San José del Valle) and Dehesilla (Algar), both near Arcos de la Frontera (Cádiz), and Santiago Chica near Cazella de la Sierra (Seville) (Pellicer and Acosta 1982; Acosta 1987; Pellicer 1987). The series of determinations on which this hypothesis rests emanate from the University of Tokyo (Gakushuin) and are as follows: for Nerja the latest Epi-Palaeolithic determination is 7960±200 BP (GaK-8962), those for the level of contact 7890±170 BP (GaK-8974) and 7160±180 BP (GaK-8963), and those for the early Neolithic proper 7160±180 BP (GaK-8973), 7130±150 BP (GaK-8975) and 6480±180 BP (Gak-8959); for the early Neolithic of Dehesilla 7670±400 BP, 7120±200 BP, 7040±170 BP, and for that of Cueva Chica de Santiago 7890±180 BP and 7240±230 BP (Pellicer 1987: 643). It is only fair to point out, however, that recent determinations made by the University of Granada are much younger: for the inception of the Neolithic at Nerja 6200±100 BP (UGRA-261), at Dehesilla 6260±100 BP (UGRA-259), and at the Cueva Chica 6160±100 BP (UGRA-254) (González-Gómez, Sánchez-Sánchez and Villafranca-Sánchez 1987: 385). The first three sites have been subjected to the scrutiny of archaeozoologists; all the major domesticates, including pigs and cattle, were present (Boessneck and von den Driesch 1980). The derivation of the domestic fauna and of the impressed ceramics must be sought in the first instance along the Mediterranean coast of the Maghreb and ultimately further east, an area with which the present writer is, conveniently, quite unfamiliar. Comments by Camps, Olaría, Tinè and Tusa in the course of discussions at the 1983 Montpellier colloquium (published as *Premières Communautés en Méditerranée Occidentale* in 1987) suggest that the source of the Andalusian and Maghrebine impressed wares be sought in the pre-Stentinello culture identified at Monte Kronio and at the Uzzo cave.

The key question remains, therefore, that of explaining the introduction of domesticates and ceramic technology into Provence from a source among the village-farming communities of Sicily and the south-western provinces of peninsular Italy. Did this take place through deep-sea contacts mediated by Corsica and/or Sardinia, or along a continuous chain across land and longshore? It is important to recognize at the outset that the mere fact of the particularly strong resemblance obtaining between continental Italian assemblages, such as that of Pienza in Tuscany, and various sites of the early Neolithic of Corsica and Sardinia, specifically Su Carròppu di Sirri (Carbònia), Basi (Sarra di Farru), Strette (Barbaghju) and a cluster of sites around Aleria (Cateri) (Atzeni 1975; Camps 1978, 1979; Calvi Rezia 1980), is not in itself evidence of the direction of the initial innovation, since such formal similarities must be regarded in effect as a palimpsest compiled from perhaps a millennium of mutual interaction. The problem is not one of whether mainland innovations reached Corsica and Sardinia through the Elban archipelago from westernmost Sicily or, indeed, from any intermediate point on the Tyrrhenian coast of Italy, but rather one of whether such diffusion took place perpendicularly to the main axis of westward dispersion or not.

The fact that Geddes (1983, 1985) has detected a pattern of introduction of domesticates into the Midi, precisely in accordance with the prediction that a 'filter effect' operated during the eighth millennium BP, is one argument in favour of transmission *via* the islands rather than around the arc of the northern shore of the Ligurian Sea. Thus the absence of domestic cattle from eighth millennium BP contexts in southern France can be traced to a breakdown in transmission within the Tyrrhenian region. For, while domestic cattle have been identified from the very inception of the Neolithic (*c.* 8000 BP) in level 1b of Corbeddu cave (Olièna) on Sardinia (Sanges 1987), none have been found on Corsica until late in the seventh millennium BP (Vigne 1983, 1987); *a fortiori* none could have reached the Midi thence. Pig, on the other hand, reached Corsica, though passing no further, early in the eighth millennium BP, as evidenced by their presence at the site of Basi (Vigne 1983, 1987). A much more powerful argument, adduced by Biagi and Maggi (Baffico, Biagi and Maggi 1983; Biagi and Maggi 1983; Biagi and Nisbet 1986), is that Mesolithic settlement in Liguria lacked the continuity in space and time necessary for it to have functioned as a medium of transmission of domesticates. In effect, there appears to have been no visible activity in western Liguria between the final Epi-Gravettian levels at sites such as Riparo Mochi, Punta della Mortola, Arma di Nasino, Arma dello Stefanin and Arene Candide (dated at the latter site to 10,330±95 BP) and the inception of the Impressed Ware occupation at Pollera (MC-756: 6950±110 BP) and again at Arene Candide (UB-2423: 6980±115 BP and LJ-4143: 6910±110 BP). In eastern Liguria several sites have recently been discovered which document the pattern of evolution typical of the Po plain Mesolithic (final Epi-Gravettian–Sauveterrian–Tardenoisian–Castelnovian), but these appear to interact much more strongly with the latter than with the Tyrrhenian coast; indeed the latest sites are purely montane. Nor is it likely that a hypothetically continuous settlement distribution has simply been drowned by the Postglacial sea-level rise; some traces of human activity should surely have survived in the hinterland. On present evidence, therefore, Liguria appears to have functioned as a barrier rather than a bridge.

A consideration of the cultural classification of the Impressed Ware assemblages themselves points still more strongly towards the conclusion that the cementation of the eastern and western Ligurian facies into a single homogeneous region of continuous cultural contact took place at too late a date for the model of terrestrial or longshore transmission of the initial innovations (ovicaprines, ceramics). Whereas Guilaine lumps all the sites within the arc of coastline from Toulon to the Tiber together with the insular assemblages into his Tyrrhenian facies (Guilaine 1980), Biagi and Nisbet (1986) argue that only the eastern Ligurian sites (Pianaccia di Suvero, Castellaro di Uscio) really resemble Pienza and the insular examples, the western group representing rather an extension of the Provençal–Peiro Signado facies. In effect, the 'Ligurian lacuna' would have persisted into the seventh millennium BP, at least in terms of ceramic styles.

To conclude, it is only necessary to prove the greater antiquity of the beginning of the early Neolithic on Corsica and Sardinia. In the case of the former, the single radiocarbon determination from the Cardial level at Basi (Gif-1851: 7700±150 BP) fits the bill, even if some authors regard it as a few centuries too high. To this may be added, if the revised interpretation of the Curacchiaghju stratigraphy is accepted (Guilaine 1980; Lewthwaite 1983, 1985; Lanfranchi 1987), the 'Curasien' dates of 7300±160 BP (Gif-796), 7310±170 BP (Gif-1961), and 7600±180 BP (Gif-1962). As for Sardinia, an obsidian hydration determination for the Cardial assemblage of Su Carròppu suggests an initial occupation from *c.* 7550 to *c.* 6850 BP (Michels, Atzeni, Tsong and Smith 1984), further raised to *c.* 8000 BP by the Corbeddu cave (level 1b) date noted above (Sanges 1987).

Conclusion

Early in the eighth millennium BP ovicaprines and ceramic technology were introduced from southern Italy *via* Corsica into southern France and, thence, eastern Spain; domestic pigs reached Corsica, but passed no further; domestic cattle and, more surprisingly, red deer were transported to Sardinia (according to identifications made at both Su Carròppu and Corbeddu) but no further (Atzeni 1978; Sanges 1987). At the same time, the full range of

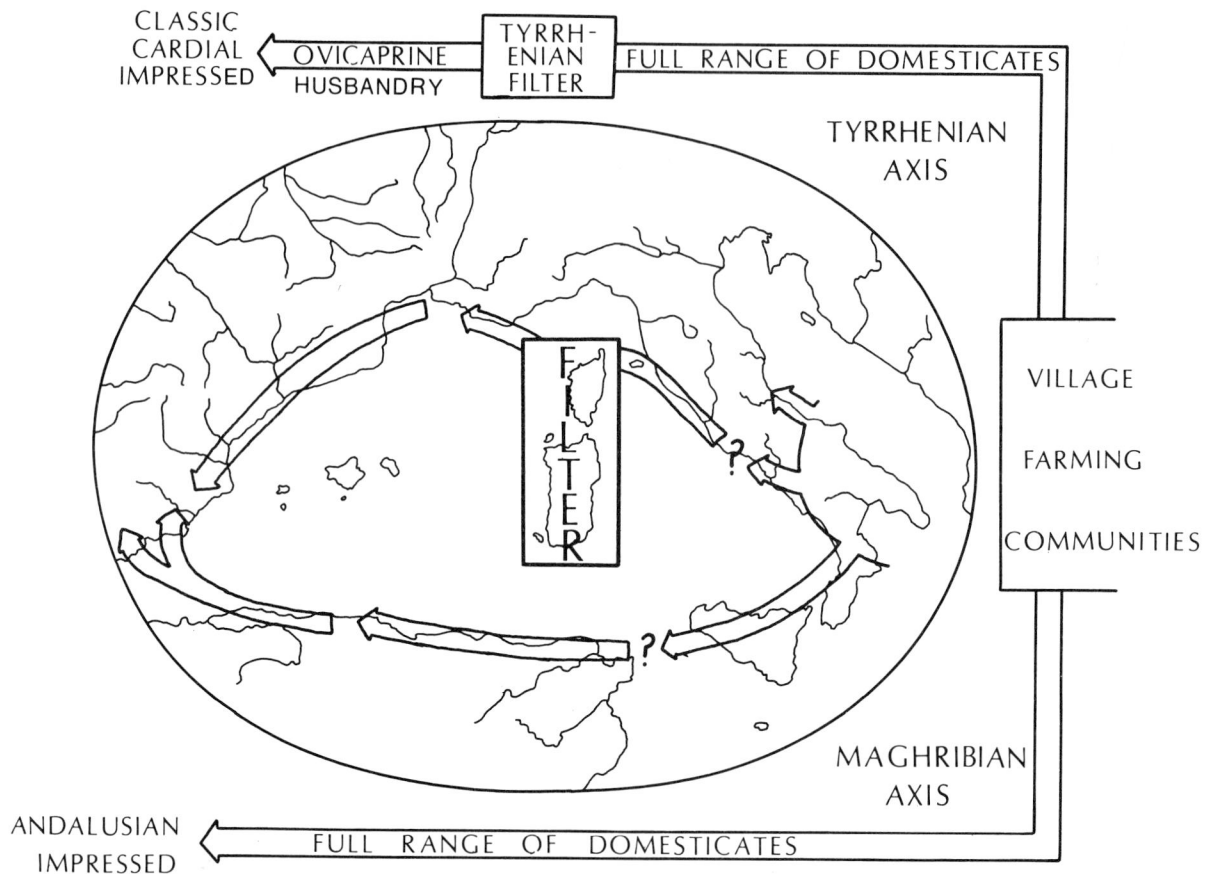

Figure 4 The early eighth millennium BP dispersion of domesticates.

domesticates, together with a slightly different ceramic industry, was introduced along the Mediterranean coast of the Maghreb into Andalusia (*Fig. 4*). Early in the seventh millennium BP the heartland of the classic Cardial culture acquired domestic cattle and pigs either from Andalusia, in company with the so-called 'Epi-Cardial' ceramic style, or from mainland Italy as the Ligurian gap was finally sparked, or from both simultaneously (*Fig. 5*).

PROCESS: PRE-NEOLITHIC PRE-ADAPTATIONS OF THE WESTERN ISLANDS

The burden of the preceding pages has been to isolate the insular factor as the residual variable which explains certain anomalies apparent in the mode of the transition from foraging to food production in the western Mediterranean. There is indeed growing evidence that the Tardenoisian/ Castelnovian populations of the arc of temperate forest stretching from Valencia to Venice were developing along a pathway which integrated coastal and riverine fishing, the hunting and trapping of game, the collection and perhaps (Vaquer and Barbaza 1987) the experimental cultivation of local plant resources, but, with the exception of the provocative but flawed proposal of Clarke (1976), no model predicting how and why this pathway should

terminate in the economic and cultural configuration of the Impressed Ware grouping (Lewthwaite 1981). It is proposed that the Pre-Neolithic population of the western Mediterranean islands, in coping with the extreme constraints of their environment, made certain adaptations which, in the case of the favourably-situated Tyrrhenian islands, enabled them to play a key role in the mediation of innovations between the village-farming communities of the south-central Mediterranean and the Mesolithic foragers of the continental west. Although no definite statement can yet be made, the possible nature of the pre-adaptations may be considered under three headings:

Technology

The most obviously relevant item of technology is the sea-going boat. To what extent can the physical difficulties of transporting minimal breeding units of the larger mammals account for the 'filter effect'? A 'minimal materialist model' would hold that during the eighth and seventh millennia BP the state of watercraft and seafaring skills was not sufficient to transport even sub-adult cattle across the Elban channel (Vigne 1983) and swine across the 175 km of open sea separating Calvi from St Tropez or Fréjus (Camps 1976), and that the 'filter effect' boils down to this. Two objections may have been raised against this view: firstly, that viable populations of cattle do

550

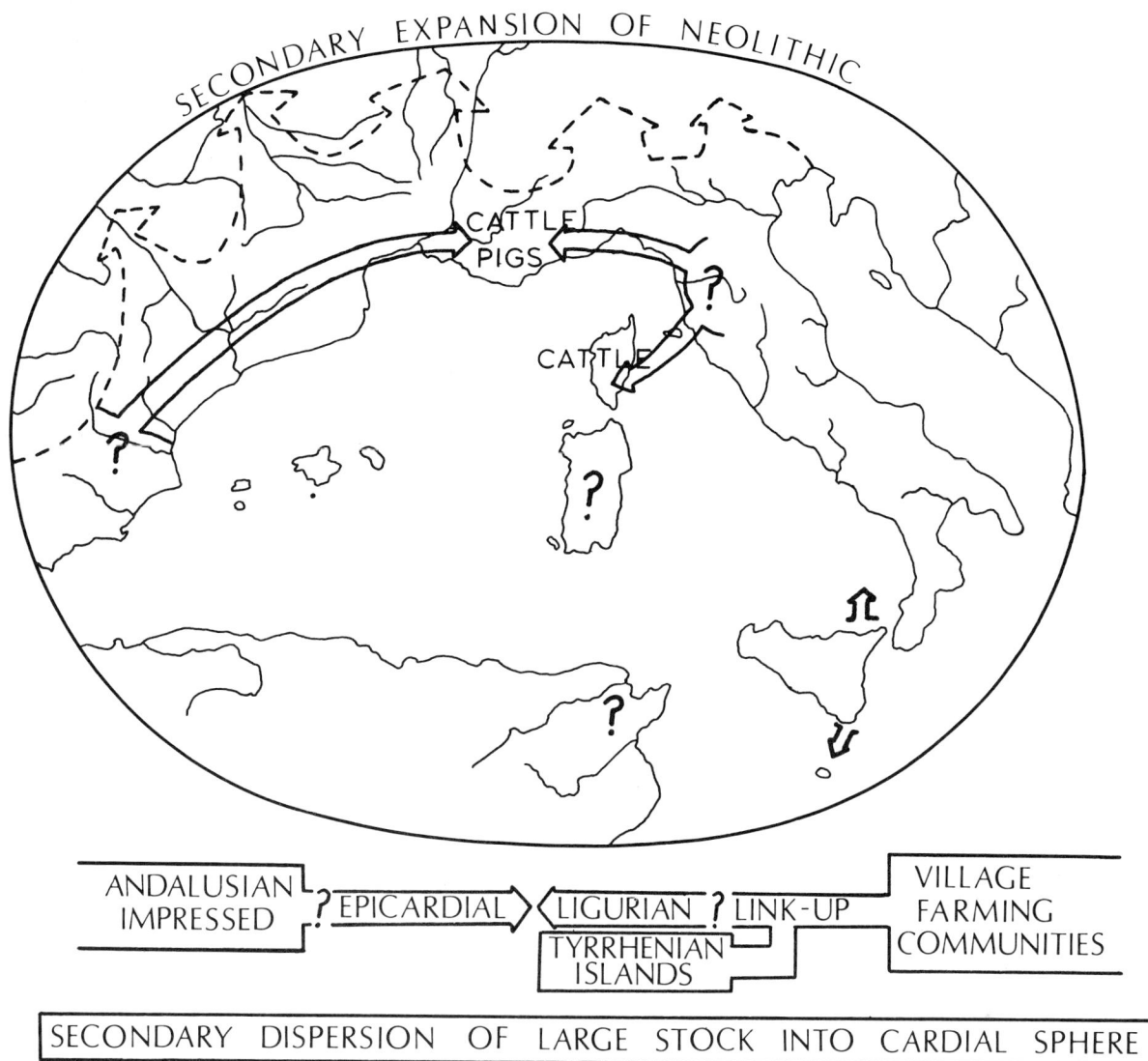

SECONDARY EXPANSION OF NEOLITHIC

CATTLE
PIGS

CATTLE

?

?

?

?

?

```
ANDALUSIAN     ?  EPICARDIAL  >  < LIGURIAN  ?  LINK-UP        VILLAGE
IMPRESSED                         TYRRHENIAN                   FARMING
                                  ISLANDS                      COMMUNITIES
```

SECONDARY DISPERSION OF LARGE STOCK INTO CARDIAL SPHERE

Figure 5 Seventh millennium BP internal networking and external expansion.

appear to have been transported across the south-eastern Aegean to Crete (probably *via* Karpathos) and across the lower Adriatic (Straits of Otranto?) to Apulia; secondly, that such mechanistic models detach such activities from their socio-economic context and ignore the active role of Mediterranean coastal populations in disseminating innovation at this juncture (Tusa 1985).

Subsistence and Settlement

The extant data appear to document a subsistence regime of appalling poverty, privation and precariousness. The Pre-Neolithic populations of the Tyrrhenian islands, once *Megaceros cazioti* had become extinct (at the very latest in the course of the ninth millennium BP, judging from the few phalanges found in the second level of Corbeddu – Sondaar *et al.* 1984), were reduced to a diet 99% of which consisted of *Prolagus sardus*, eked out with morsels of seal, fish, shellfish and seabirds (Vigne 1984), while their contemporaries on Mallorca consumed

Myotragus balearicus alone. Such an extreme dependence on single resources appears most implausible as a successful long-term strategy, and must reflect the gross sampling errors and biases which distort our impressions of the Pre-Neolithic. In an ideal world, the proportion of terrestrial and aquatic resources in the human diet could be resolved very efficiently through an analysis of the bones of the human population, as cogently argued by Price (this volume), but we are a very long way from any such eventuality. In the meantime, therefore, it is possible only to speculate on the contribution of the alternative resources – specifically plant foods and fish – and the reasons for their under-representation.

In the case of the plant produce, it must be recalled that during the period concerned (so-called Pre-Boreal–Boreal) the diversified and productive thermophile forest would only have been beginning its expansion from glacial confines at the expense of pines, juniper and steppic species, so that the abundance of nuts, fruits, roots, tubers and grains envisaged by Clarke (1976) would not be available till the Atlantic period, when they would in a sense be competing against cultigens. In the case of fish, it is easy to see the solution to terrestrial resource deficiencies in those species which are worthwhile prey in terms of individual size, propensity to school or predictability of seasonal migration, such as tunny and the giant grouper, mullet and sea bream; after all, a population able to reach the islands in the first place should have been able to exploit at least the coastal waters. Yet there is no trace of any serious exploitation of the seas comparable with the dense accumulation of fish, even of porpoises and other cetaceans which appear in contexts such as Franchthi cave (Payne 1975), the Grotta dell'Uzzo (Piperno 1985) or the cueva de Nerja (Boessneck and von den Driesch 1980). In the final analysis we may be dealing with a severely truncated and distorted site sample; even Araguina and So'n Matge do not share with the above the dual attributes of lateral extension and frontage onto an embayment.

Social organization

Perhaps the most important pre-adaptation of all would have been the maintenance of an extremely open social system, necessitated by the inability of island populations of extremely low density, dependent on precariously narrow resource bases, to maintain the minimal breeding units discussed by Newell (this volume) and Chapman (this volume). Once again, there is a dearth of empirical evidence to substantiate such an assumption; indeed, the extent of the dependence on coarse local rocks and on organic material such as bone (glimpsed in Mallorca and in the Corbeddu cave) when compared with the mobility of flint and obsidian in subsequent millennia, might even be held to prove the opposite. Perhaps future physical anthropological studies will be able to shed some light on the extent of gene flow or isolation ('founder effect', etc.). A second dimension of such 'openness' worthy of consideration is the possibility that the mechanisms providing 'social homeostasis' (i.e. the myth of egalitarianism among band level societies) might not have developed prior to the experience of contact with such potentially disequilibrating variables as early domesticates (Lewthwaite 1986, 1987), with the consequence that the social resistance to the crystallization of pastoral groupings might have been much weaker than in more favourably-endowed continental regions.

CONCLUSIONS

This essay clearly does not provide an answer commensurate with the problem on which it is focused. It may, however, serve some good in drawing attention to the existence of anomalies current in the field of the transition from foraging to food production in the western Mediterranean, which have not been resolved by the demise of naïve diffusionism and the acceptance of an equally naïve local processual explanation as the new orthodoxy. It is argued that the isolation of the peculiar circumstances affecting Pre-Neolithic populations on the western islands may provide the residual factor necessary to explain the pattern of the dispersion of domesticates beyond the radius of the first village-farming communities.

Acknowledgements: I gratefully acknowledge the many letters, offprints and books generously given by friends and colleagues, which made this article possible: E. Atzeni, P. Biagi, S. Bottema, J. Cherry, M. Cipolloni Sampò, L. Costantini, D. Geddes, P. Halstead, T. Jacobsen, F. de Lanfranchi, J. Magdeleine, R. Maggi, B. Martí Oliver, J. Michels, R. Nisbet, M. Piperno, F. Poplin, M. Reille, J-L. Roudil, P. Rowley-Conwy, J. Shackleton, S. Tusa, J. Vacquer, J-L. Vernet, J-D. Vigne, W. Waldren, M-C. Weiss, R. Whitehouse, and M. Zvelebil. Attendance at the Symposium was only made possible through the travel funds of the University of Bradford because of the kindness of Mr Arnold Aspinall, while the writer held an Honorary Research Assistantship in the School of Archaeological Sciences. Particular thanks are due to Ms Alison Cameron for typing the manuscript, to Mr Colin Merrony for drawing the illustrations, and to all those friends and colleagues who contributed to the one aspect of the Symposium which faithfully bore out its etymology.

References

ACOSTA, P. (1987) El Neolítico antiguo en el suroeste hispano: la cueva de la Dehesilla (Cádiz). In J. Guilaine, J. Courtin, J. Roudil and J-L. Vernet (eds), *Premières Communautés Paysannes en Méditerranée Occidentale*. Paris, Centre National de la Recherche Scientifique: 653–659.

APARICIO PÉREZ, J. (1982) La neolitización y el Neolítico en Valencia (España). In *Le Néolithique Ancien Méditerranéen*. Sète, Fédération Archéologique de l'Hérault: 81–96.

ARCA, M., MARTINI, F., PITZALIS, G., TUVERI, C. and ULZEGA, A. (1982) *Il Paleolitico dell'Anglona (Sardegna Settentrionale)* (Quaderni, 12). Sassari, Dessi.

ARNAL, G.B. (1984) Le Néolithique ancien du Languedoc. In W.H. Waldren, R. Chapman, J. Lewthwaite and R-C. Kennard (eds), *The Deya Conference of Prehistory. Early Settlement in the Western Mediterranean Islands and the Peripheral Areas*. Oxford, British Archaeological Reports (International Series) S229: 313–335.

ATZENI, E. (1975) *Nuovi Idoli della Sardegna Prenuragica*. Sassari, Gallizzi.

ATZENI, E. (1978) Documenti per la preistoria di Iglesias. *Iglesias. Storia e Società*. Iglesias, Rotary Club 208: 7–20.

BAFFICO, O., BIAGI, P. and MAGGI, R. (1983) Il Mesolitico. In R. Maggi (ed.), *Preistoria nella Liguria Orientale*. Chiavari, Renato Siri Editore: 33–44.

BERNABÒ BREA, L. (1950) Il Neolitico a ceramica impressa e la sua diffusione nel Mediterraneo. *Rivista Internazionale di Studi Liguri*, 16: 25–36.

BIAGI, P. and MAGGI, R. (1983) Aspects of the Mesolithic age in Liguria. In *Il Popolamento delle Alpi in Età Mesolitica: VIII–V Millennio a.C.* (Preistoria Alpina, 19). Trento, Museo Tridentino di Scienze Naturali: 159–168.

BIAGI, P. and NISBET, R. (1986) Popolazione e territorio in Liguria tra il XII ed il IV millennio bc. In E.A. Arslan (ed.), *Scritti in Ricordo di G. Massari e di U. Tocchetti Pollini*. Milan, ET: 19–26.

BOESSNECK, J. and VON DEN DRIESCH, A. (1980) Tierknochen-funde aus vier südspanischen Höhlen. In *Studien über frühe Tierknochenfunde von der iberischen Halbinsel*, 7. Munich, Universität and Madrid, Deutsches Archäologisches Institut: 1–83.

BONIFAY, E. (1983) Circonscription de la Corse. *Gallia Préhistoire*, 26(2): 511–525.

BOTTEMA, S. (1980) Palynological investigations on Crete. *Review of Palaeobotany and Palynology*, 31: 193–217.

CALVI REZIA, G. (1980) La ceramica impressa di Pienza (Toscana) e quella di Basi (Corsica). *Rivista di Scienze Preistoriche*, 35: 323–334.

CAMPS, G. (1976) La question des navigations préhistoriques dans le bassin occidental de la Méditerranée. In *Compte-Rendu de la Session du Congrès Préhistorique de France (Provence 1974)*, 20: 53–65.

CAMPS, G. (1978) Aperçu sur la préhistoire corse et ses problèmes. *Bulletin de la Société d'Etudes et de Recherches Préhistoriques* (Les Eyzies), 28: 22pp.

CAMPS, G. (1979) La préhistoire dans la région d'Aleria. *Archeologia Corsa*, 4: 5–21.

CASSANO, S.M. and MANFREDINI, A. (1983) *Studi sul Neolitico del Tavoliere della Puglia*. Oxford, British Archaeological Reports (International Series) S160.

CHERRY, J.F. (1981) Pattern and process in the earliest colonization of the Mediterranean islands. *Proceedings of the Prehistoric Society*, 47: 41–68.

CHERRY, J.F. (1984) The initial colonisation of the west Mediterranean islands in the light of island biogeography and palaeogeography. In W.H. Waldren, R. Chapman, J. Lewthwaite and R-C. Kennard (eds), *The Deya Conference of Prehistory. Early Settlement in the Western Mediterranean Islands and the Peripheral Areas*. Oxford, British Archaeological Reports (International Series) S229: 7–27.

CHILDE, V.G. (1957) *The Dawn of European Civilisation* (6th edition). London, Routledge and Kegan Paul.

CIPOLLONI SAMPÒ, M. (1983) Scavi nel villaggio neolitico di Rendina (1970–76). Relazione preliminare. *Origini*, 11 (1977–1982): 183–354.

CIPOLLONI SAMPÒ, M. (1987) Aspetti e problemi della cronologia del Neolitico antico in Italia meridionale: l'insediamento neolitico sull'Olivento (Valle dell'Ofanto-Basilicata). *Atti della Riunione Scientifica dell'Istituto Italiano di Preistoria e Protostoria*, 26(2): 697–705.

CLARKE, D.L. (1976) Mesolithic Europe: the economic basis. In G. de G. Sieveking, I.H. Longworth and K.E. Wilson (eds), *Problems in Economic and Social Archaeology*. London, Duckworth: 449–481.

CLARK FORBES, M.H. (1976) Farming and foraging in prehistoric Greece: a cultural ecological perspective. *Annals of the New York Academy of Sciences*, 268: 127–142.

COSTANTINI, L., PIPERNO, M. and TUSA, S. (1987) La néolithisation de la Sicile occidentale d'après les résultats des fouilles à la grotte de l'Uzzo (Trapani). In J. Guilaine, J. Courtin, J. Roudil and J-L. Vernet (eds), *Premières Communautés Paysannes en Méditerranée Occidentale*. Paris, Centre National de la Recherche Scientifique: 397–405.

COUDROT, J-L. (1976) Répartition de la céramique cardiale dans le bassin occidental de la Méditerranée. *Cahiers Archéologiques du Nord-Est*, 34: 1–108.

CREMONESI, G. and GUILAINE, J. (1987) L'habitat de Torre Sabea (Gallipoli, Puglia) dans le cadre du Néolithique ancien de l'Italie du sud-est. In J. Guilaine, J. Courtin, J. Roudil and J-L. Vernet (eds), *Premières Communautés Paysannes en Méditerranée Occidentale*. Paris, Centre National de la Recherche Scientifique: 377–385.

DUCOS, P. (1977) Le mouton de Châteauneuf-les-Martigues. In J-L. Miège (ed.), *L'Elévage en Méditerranée Occidentale*. Marseilles, Centre National de la Recherche Scientifique: 77–85.

EVANS, J.D. (1971) Neolithic Knossos; the growth of a settlement. *Proceedings of the Prehistoric Society*, 37(2): 95–117.

EVIN, J. (1987) Révision de la chronologie absolue des débuts du Néolithique en Provence et Languedoc. In J. Guilaine, J. Courtin, J. Roudil and J-L. Vernet (eds), *Premières Communautés Paysannes en Méditerranée Occidentale*. Paris, Centre National de la Recherche Scientifique: 27–36.

EVIN, J., MARÉCHAL, J. and MARIEN, G. (1985) Lyon natural radiocarbon measurements X. *Radiocarbon*, 27(2b): 386–454.

FREISES, A. and MONTJARDIN, R. (1982) Le Néolithique ancien côtier du Midi de la France. In *Le Néolithique Ancien Méditerranéen*. Sète, Fédération Archéologique de l'Hérault: 201–228.

GASCÓ, J. and GUTHERZ, X. (1983) *Premiers Paysans de la France Méditerranéenne*. Montpellier, Direction du Patrimoine.

GEDDES, D.S. (1980) *De la Chasse au Troupeau en Méditerranée Occidentale* (Archives d'Ecologie Préhistorique, 5). Montpellier, Ecole des Hautes Etudes en Sciences Sociales.

GEDDES, D.S. (1983) Neolithic transhumance in the Mediterranean Pyrenees. *World Archaeology*, 15(1): 51–66.

GEDDES, D.S. (1984) Settlement and subsistence during the Mesolithic and Neolithic in the Aude river valley (France). In W.H. Waldren, R. Chapman, J. Lewthwaite and R-C. Kennard (eds), *The Deya Conference of Prehistory. Early Settlement in the Western Mediterranean Islands and the Peripheral Areas*. Oxford, British Archaeological Reports (International Series) S229: 179–192.

GEDDES, D.S. (1985) Mesolithic domestic sheep in western Mediterranean Europe. *Journal of Archaeological Science*, 12: 25–48.

GONZÁLEZ-GÓMEZ, C., SÁNCHEZ-SÁNCHEZ, P. and VILLAFRANCA-SÁNCHEZ, E. (1987) University of Granada radiocarbon dates IV. *Radiocarbon*, 29(3): 381–388.

GRIMAL, J. (1982) Le Néolithique ancien de la plaine de l'Hérault. In *Le Néolithique Ancien Méditerranéen*. Sète, Fédération Archéologique de l'Hérault: 253–259.

GUILAINE, J. (1976) *Premiers Bergers et Paysans de l'Occident Méditerranéen*. Paris, Mouton.

GUILAINE, J. (1980) Problèmes actuels de la néolithisation et du Néolithique ancien en Méditerranée occidentale. In J.G.P. Best and N.M.W. de Vries (eds), *Interaction and Acculturation in the Mediterranean*, vol. 1. Amsterdam, B.K. Grüner: 3–22.

HALSTEAD, P.L.J. (1981) Counting sheep in Neolithic and Bronze Age Greece. In I. Hodder, G. Isaac and N. Hammond (eds), *Pattern of the Past*. Cambridge, University Press: 307–339.

HANSEN, J.M. (1978) The earliest seed remains from Greece: Palaeolithic through Neolithic at Franchthi cave. *Berichte der Deutsche Botanische Gesellschaft*, 91: 39–46.

HELMER, D. (1987) Les suidés du Cardial: sangliers ou cochons? In J. Guilaine, J. Courtin, J. Roudil and J-L. Vernet (eds), *Premières Communautés Paysannes en Méditerranée Occidentale*. Paris, Centre National de la Recherche Scientifique: 215–220.

JACOBSEN, T.W. (1981) Franchthi cave and the beginning of settled village life in Greece. *Hesperia*, 50(4): 303–319.

KARAGEORGHIS, V. (1982) *Cyprus from the Stone Age to the Romans*. London, Thames and Hudson.

KOPPER, J.S. (1984) Canet cave, Esporles, Mallorca. In W.H. Waldren, R. Chapman, J. Lewthwaite and R-C. Kennard, *The Deya Conference of Prehistory. Early Settlement in the Western Mediterranean Islands and the Peripheral Areas*. Oxford, British Archaeological Reports (International Series) S229: 61–69.

LANFRANCHI, F. DE (1967) La grotte sépulcrale de Curacchiaghju (Levie, Corse). *Bulletin de la Société Préhistorique Française*, 64: 587–612.

LANFRANCHI, F. DE (1987) Le Néolithique de Curacchiaghju. In J. Guilaine, J. Courtin, J. Roudil and J-L. Vernet (eds), *Premières Communautés Paysannes en Méditerranée Occidentale*. Paris, Centre National de la Recherche Scientifique: 433–442.

LANFRANCHI, F. DE and WEISS, M-C. (1977) *Araguina–Sennola* (Archeologia Corsa, 2). Ajaccio, Maison de la Culture de la Corse.

LEWTHWAITE, J.G. (1981) Ambiguous first impressions: a survey of recent work on the early Neolithic of the west Mediterranean. *Journal of Mediterranean Anthropology and Archaeology*, 1(2): 292–307.

LEWTHWAITE, J.G. (1982) Cardial disorder: ethnographic and archaeological comparisons for problems in the early prehistory of the west Mediterranean. In *Le Néolithique Ancien Méditerranéen*. Sète, Fédération Archéologique de l'Hérault: 311–318.

LEWTHWAITE, J.G. (1983) The Neolithic of Corsica. In C.J. Scarre (ed.), *Ancient France. Neolithic Societies and their Landscape 6000–2000 bc*. Edinburgh, University Press: 146–183.

LEWTHWAITE, J.G. (1985) From precocity to involution: the Neolithic of Corsica in its west Mediterranean and French contexts. *Oxford Journal of Archaeology*, 4(2): 47–68.

LEWTHWAITE, J.G. (1986) The transition to food production: a Mediterranean perspective. In M. Zvelebil (ed.), *Hunters in Transition: Mesolithic Societies of Temperate Eurasia and their Transition to Farming*. Cambridge, University Press: 53–66.

LEWTHWAITE, J.G. (1987) Essai dans le cadre du Néolithique ancien Méditerranéen pour extraire de sa coquille le 'facteur social'. In J. Guilaine, J. Courtin, J. Roudil and J-L. Vernet (eds), *Premières Communautés Paysannes en Méditerranée Occidentale*. Paris, Centre National de la Recherche Scientifique: 737–743.

MAGDELEINE, J. (1980) *Commune de Barbaghju (Haute Corse). Lieu-dit Strette. Rapport de Fouilles 1980*. Bastia, J. Magdeleine.

MAGDELEINE, J. (1985) Les premières occupations humaines de l'abri des Strette Barbaghju. *Archeologia Corsa*, 8–9 (1983–84): 30–50.

MAGDELEINE, J. and OTTAVIANI, J.C. (1986) L'abri préhistorique de Strette. *Bulletin de la Société des Sciences Historiques et Naturelles de la Corse*, 650: 81–90.

MARTÍ OLIVER, B. (1982) Neolitización y Neolítico antiguo en la zona oriental de la península Ibérica. In *Le Néolithique Ancien Méditerranéen*. Sète, Fédération Archéologique de l'Hérault: 97–106.

MARTÍ OLIVER, B. (1983) Cova de l'Or (Beniarrés, Alicante). Memoria de las campañas de excavación 1975–1979. *Noticiario Arqueológico Hispánico*, 16: 11–55.

MICHELS, J.W., ATZENI, E., TSONG, I.S.T. and SMITH, G.A. (1983) Obsidian hydration dating in Sardinia. In M.S. Balmuth and R.J. Rowland, Jr (eds), *Studies in Sardinian Archaeology*. Ann Arbor, University of Michigan Press: 83–113.

MILLS, N.T.W. (1987) Questions méthodologiques dans l'étude des premières communautés paysannes du Midi de la France. In J. Guilaine, J. Courtin, J. Roudil and J-L. Vernet (eds), *Premières Communautés en Méditerranée Occidentale*. Paris, Centre National de la Recherche Scientifique: 487–490.

MURRAY, J. (1970) *The First European Agriculture*. Edinburgh, University Press.

NEWELL, R. (1984) On the Mesolithic contribution to the social evolution of western European society. In J. Bintliff (ed.), *European Social Evolution*. Bradford, University of Bradford: 69–82.

OLARÍA, C., ESTÉVEZ ESCALERA, J. and YLL, E. (1982) Domesticación y paleoambiente de la Cova Fosca. In *Le Néolithique Ancien Méditerranéen*. Sète, Fédération Archéologique de l'Hérault: 107–120.

OLARÍA, C. and GUSI, F. (1987) Nouveaux aspects dans le problématique du Néolithique ancien dans la Méditerranée occidentale: Cova Fosca (Castellón, Espagne). In J. Guilaine, J. Courtin, J. Roudil and J-L. Vernet (eds), *Premières Communautés Paysannes en Méditerranée Occidentale*, Paris, Centre National de la Recherche Scientifique: 633–637.

PAYNE, S. (1975) Faunal change at Franchthi cave from 20,000 B.C. to 3,000 B.C. In A.T. Clason (ed.), *Archaeozoological Studies*. Amsterdam, North-Holland Publishing Company: 120–131.

PELLICER, M. (1987) El Neolítico de la cueva de Nerja (Málaga). In J. Guilaine, J. Courtin, J. Roudil and J-L. Vernet (eds), *Premières Communautés Paysannes en Méditerranée Occidentale*. Paris, Centre National de la Recherche Scientifique: 639–643.

PELLICER, M. and ACOSTA, P. (1982) El Neolítico antiguo en Andalucía occidental. In *Le Néolithique Ancien Méditerranéen*. Sète, Fédération Archéologique de l'Hérault: 49–60.

PHILLIPS, P. (1975) *Early Farmers of West Mediterranean Europe*. London, Hutchinson.

PIPERNO, M. (1985) Some ^{14}C dates for the palaeoeconomic evidence from the Holocene levels of Uzzo cave, Sicily. In C. Malone and S. Stoddart (eds), *Papers in Italian Archaeology IV The Cambridge Conference. Part ii: Prehistory*. Oxford, British Archaeological Reports (International Series) S244: 83–86.

PIPERNO, M., SCALI, S. and TAGIACOZZO, A. (1980) Mesolitico e Neolitico alla Grotta dell'Uzzo (Trapani). Prima dati per un'interpretazione paleoeconomica. *Quaternaria*, 22: 275–300.

PONS-MOYÀ, J. and COLL CONESA, J. (1984) Les industries litiques dels jaciments a l'aire lliure de la zona de Santanyí (Mallorca). In W.H. Waldren, R. Chapman, J. Lewthwaite and R-C. Kennard (eds), *The Deya Conference of Prehistory. Early Settlement in the Western Mediterranean Islands and the Peripheral Areas*. Oxford, British Archaeological Reports (International Series) S229: 841–857.

POPESCU, C.P., QUÉRÉ, J.P. and FRANCESCHI, P. (1980) Observations chromosomiques chez le sanglier français (*Sus scrofa scrofa*). *Annales de Génétique et Sélection Animales*, 12(4): 395–400.

POPLIN, F. (1979) Origine de Mouflon de Corse dans une nouvelle perspective paléontologique: par marronnage. *Annales de Génétique et Sélection Animales*, 11(2): 133–143.

REILLE, M. (1984) Origine de la végétation actuelle de la Corse sud-orientale: analyse pollinique de cinq marais côtiers. *Pollen et Spores*, 26(1): 43–60.

REILLE, M., TRIAT-LAVAL, H. and VERNET, J-L. (1980) Les témoignages des structures actuelles de végétation méditerranéenne durant le passé contemporain de l'action de l'homme. *Naturalia Monspeliensia*, numéro spécial hors série: 79–87.

ROUDIL, J-L. and SOULIER, M. (1984) Le gisement Néolithique ancien de Peiro Signado (Portiragnes-Hérault). Etude préliminaire. *Compte-Rendu de la Session du Congrès Préhistorique de France*, 21(2): 258–279.

SANGES, M. (1987) Gli strati del Neolitico antico e medio nella Grotta Corbeddu di Olièna (Nuoro). Nota preliminare. *Atti della Riunione Scientifica dell'Istituto Italiano di Preistoria e Protostoria*, 26(2): 825–830.

SONDAAR, P.Y., DE BOER, P.L., SANGES, M., KOTSAKIS, T. and ESU, D. (1984) First report on a Palaeolithic culture in Sardinia. In W.H. Waldren, R. Chapman, J. Lewthwaite and R-C. Kennard (eds), *The Deya Conference of Prehistory. Early Settlement in the Western Mediterranean Islands and the Peripheral Areas*. Oxford, British Archaeological Reports (International Series) S229: 29–59.

STANLEY PRICE, N.P. (1977a) Colonization and continuity in the early prehistory of Cyprus. *World Archaeology*, 9(1): 27–41.

STANLEY PRICE, N.P. (1977b) Khirokitia and the initial settlement of Cyprus. *Levant*, 9(1): 66–89.

STANLEY PRICE, N.P. (1979) *Early Prehistoric Settlement in Cyprus, 6500–3000 B.C.* Oxford, British Archaeological Reports (International Series) S65.

TINÈ, S. (1983) *Passo di Corvo e la Civiltà Neolitica del Tavoliere*. Genoa, Sagep.

TUSA, S. (1985) The beginning of farming communities in Sicily: the evidence of Uzzo cave. In C. Malone and S. Stoddart (eds), *Papers in Italian Archaeology IV The Cambridge Conference. Part ii: Prehistory*. Oxford, British Archaeological Reports (International Series) S244: 61–82.

UERPMANN, H-P. (1979) *Probleme der Neolithisierung des Mittelmeerraums* (Beihefte zum Tübinger Atlas des Vorderen Orient, B/28). Wiesbaden, Reichert.

UERPMANN, H-P. (1987) The origins and relations of Neolithic sheep and goats in the western Mediterranean. In J. Guilaine, J. Courtin, J. Roudil and J-L. Vernet (eds), *Premières Communautés Paysannes en Méditerranée Occidentale*. Paris, Centre National de la Recherche Scientifique: 175–179.

VAN ZEIST, W. and BOTTEMA, S. (1982) Vegetational history of the eastern Mediterranean and the Near East during the last 20,000 years. In J.L. Bintliff and W. van Zeist (eds), *Palaeoclimates, Palaeoenvironments and Human Communities in the Eastern Mediterranean Region in Later Prehistory*. Oxford, British Archaeological Reports (International Series) S133: 277–321.

VAQUER, J. and BARBAZA, M. (1987) Cueillette ou horticulture mésolithique: La Balma de l'Abeurador. In J. Guilaine, J. Courtin, J. Roudil and J-L. Vernet (eds), *Premières Communautés en Méditerranée Occidentale*. Paris, Centre National de la Recherche Scientifique: 231–242.

554

VERNET, J-L., BADAL GARCÍA, E., GRAU ALMERO, E. and ROS MORA, T. (1984) Charcoal analysis and the western Mediterranean prehistoric flora. In W.H. Waldren, R. Chapman, J. Lewthwaite and R-C. Kennard (eds), *The Deya Conference of Prehistory. Early Settlement in the Western Mediterranean Islands and the Peripheral Areas.* Oxford, British Archaeological Reports (International Series) 229: 165–177.

VERNET, J-L., BADAL GARCÍA, E. and GRAU ALMERO, E. (1987) L'Environnement végétal de l'homme au Néolithique du sud-est de l'Espagne (Valence, Alicante). Première synthèse d'après l'analyse anthracologique. In J. Guilaine, J. Courtin, J. Roudil and J-L. Vernet (eds), *Premières Communautés Paysannes en Méditerranée Occidentale.* Paris, Centre National de la Recherche Scientifique: 131–136.

VIGNE, J-D. (1983) *Les Mammifères Terrestres Non Volants du Post-Glaciaire de Corse et leurs Rapports avec l'Homme: L'Etude Paléo-Ethno-Zoologique Fondée sur les Ossements.* Thèse de 3e cycle. Paris, Université P. et M. Curie.

VIGNE, J-D. (1984) Premières données sur le début de l'élévage du mouton, de la chèvre et du porc dans le sud de la Corse (France). In J. Clutton-Brock and C. Grigson (eds), *Animals and Archaeology: 3. Early Herders and their Flocks.* Oxford, British Archaeological Reports (International Series) S202: 47–65.

VIGNE, J-D. (1987) L'exploitation des ressources alimentaires carnées en Corse du 7e au 4e millénaire B.C. In J. Guilaine, J. Courtin, J. Roudil and J-L. Vernet (eds), *Premières Communautés Paysannes en Méditerranée Occidentale.* Paris, Centre National de la Recherche Scientifique: 193–199.

VIGNE, J-D., MARINVAL-VIGNE, M.C., LANFRANCHI, F. DE and WEISS, M-C. (1981) Consommation du 'Lapin-rat' (*Prolagus sardus* Wagner) au Néolithique ancien Méditerranéen. Abri d'Araguina-Sennola (Bonifacio, Corse). *Bulletin de la Société Préhistorique Française,* 78(7): 222–224.

WALDREN, W.H. (1982) *Balearic Prehistoric Ecology and Culture.* Oxford, British Archaeological Reports (International Series) S149.

WATSON, J.P.N. and STANLEY PRICE, N.P. (1977) The vertebrate fauna from the 1972 sounding at Khirokitia. *Report of the Department of Antiquities, Cyprus,* 6: 232–260.

WEISS, M-C. and LANFRANCHI, F. DE (1976) Les civilisations néolithiques en Corse. In J. Guilaine (ed.), *La Préhistoire Française. Tome II: Les Civilisations Néolithiques et Proto-historiques.* Paris, Centre National de la Recherche Scientifique: 432–442.

WHITEHOUSE, R.D. (1984) Social organisation in the Neolithic of southeast Italy. In W.H. Waldren, R. Chapman, J. Lewthwaite and R-C. Kennard (eds), *The Deya Conference of Prehistory. Early Settlement in the Western Mediterranean Islands and the Peripheral Areas.* Oxford, British Archaeological Reports (International Series) S229: 1109–1137.

ZVELEBIL, M. and ROWLEY-CONWY, P. (1984) Transition to farming in northern Europe: a hunter-gatherer perspective. *Norwegian Archaeological Review,* 17(2): 104–125.

The Early Postglacial Period in the Pyrenees: Some Recent Work

Paul Bahn

Abstract

The Pyrenees were the region which first plugged the gap between the Palaeolithic and the Neolithic through Piette's pioneering work at Mas d'Azil in the 1880s. Until recently, however, little good information was available on the Mesolithic of either the French or the Spanish side of the chain. Work during the last couple of decades has begun to fill in the picture and restore the Pyrenees to a position of some importance in Mesolithic studies. After a brief account of early work, a review of some of the more important sites and results is presented, with emphasis on the central and eastern Spanish Pyrenees.

EARLY WORK

It is ironic that the Mesolithic should have been neglected in the Pyrenees, the region where the hiatus between the Old and New Stone Ages was first filled by Piette's discovery of the 'Azilian' and the 'Arisian' on the left bank of the grotte du Mas d'Azil in the 1880s. 'Azilian' material, including painted pebbles, had been found before, and Garrigou had interpreted flat, perforated harpoons as ear pendants in 1867 (Bahn 1984: 263); but it was Piette's pioneering work which revealed Epi-Palaeolithic and Mesolithic material in its stratigraphic context, sandwiched between the Magdalenian and the Neolithic. Subsequent work at the site, up to and including that by the Péquarts in the 1930s, merely confirmed his observations.

But Mesolithic material was poor stuff compared to the artwork of the Pyrenean Magdalenian; and apart from the Azilian, which had harpoons and painted pebbles to offer, the period was missed completely through poor excavation, or ignored in the haste to reach Magdalenian pay-dirt. For decades, therefore, very little was known of the Pyrenean archaeological record between the Azilian and the 'Neolithic', such as it was (see Bahn 1983). Even the Azilian material was little studied, and it is only recently that the painted pebbles have been analyzed (Couraud 1985) and many fakes weeded out (Couraud and Bahn 1982; Bahn and Couraud 1984).

CURRENT RESEARCH

The French Pyrenees

The situation began to improve with the important excavation by Laplace (1953) of the cave of Poey-maü (Arudy, Pyrénées-Atlantiques) which, unfortunately, remains almost totally unpublished. This work, together with the excavations resumed at the site in recent years, produced a detailed stratigraphy from Magdalenian to Eneolithic and a good series of radiocarbon dates. Analysis of the cultural and faunal material from the site will provide invaluable insights into this period in the western French Pyrenees. I have already argued (Bahn 1982a, 1982b, 1984) that the presence of millions of snail shells of a single species (and indeed a single phenotype) in the site is in large measure artificial and implies the existence of some form of Mesolithic 'snail farm'.

The early 1970s saw excavations by the Orliacs at the rock-shelter of La Tourasse (Haute-Garonne), a site which, for a while in the nineteenth century, rivalled the Mas d'Azil as a possible type-site for the Azilian. Here, too, a detailed stratification of Mesolithic layers was uncovered (Orliac 1975) from Azilian to Sauveterrian and a kind of Tardenoisian. Unfortunately, work at this important site ceased in 1976 (but resumed in 1985), and publication in depth is still awaited.

The 1970s and 1980s have also seen the pioneering excavations by Jean Guilaine and his team at several sites in the eastern Pyrenees and, most recently, Andorra, which have hugely increased all aspects of our knowledge of Mesolithic culture in this region, and of the cultural and economic transition to the Neolithic here (e.g. Guilaine *et al.* 1985; see also Bahn 1983, 1984; Geddes *et al.*, this volume).

The Spanish Pyrenees

Turning now to the Spanish side of the Pyrenees, excavations by Ignacio Barandiarán (see Barandiarán and Cava, this volume) at sites such as Berroberría and Zatoya are producing the first sound and extensive data on the period in the Basque area. In this paper, therefore, I would like to complete the picture with a brief summary of some recent work in the central and eastern Spanish Pyrenees, areas where the Mesolithic was almost unknown until a few years ago.

In fact, this region was thought to have a crude,

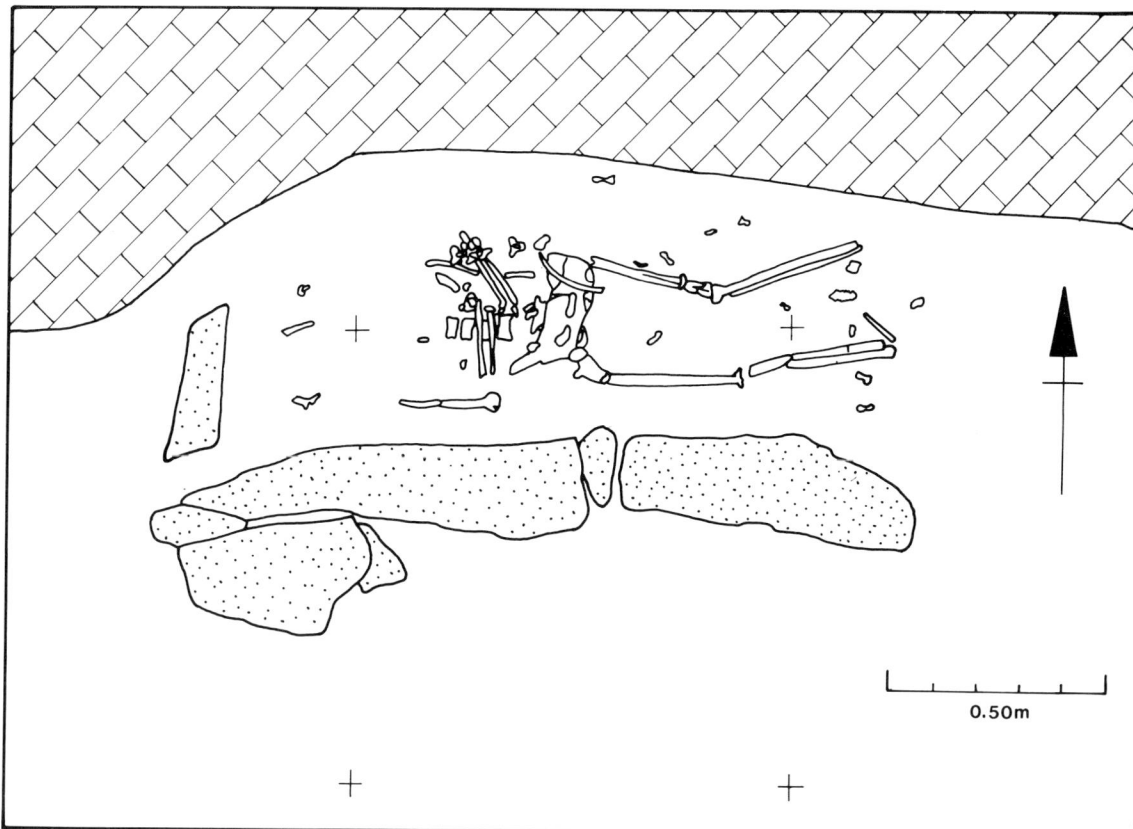

Figure 1   Roc del Migdia – 'megalithic' burial (after Yll *et al.* 1986).

macrolithic, 'Asturian' type of Mesolithic industry, at sites such as the Montgrí caves (Pericot 1965) and the cave of 'En Mollet' at Serinyá (Corominas 1948), but subsequent re-analysis, and particularly of the accompanying fauna, indicated that the tools represent early Würm and even pre-Würm occupation (Ripoll and de Lumley 1965).

In the east, primarily in the province of Girona, there are a number of sites comprising stone tools and little else. The lack of stratigraphy and of organic material means that dating is limited to assemblage typology, and is therefore somewhat uncertain. Almost identical microlithic industries have been found at the open site of Sant Benet (Soler 1977) and the site of Coma d'Infern, at the foot of a rock (Soler 1980); their high percentages of geometrics and microburins have led them to be attributed to the Epi-Palaeolithic, and they have been called Epi-Magdalenian. The distribution of sites of this period in Catalonia as a whole is very irregular, but this is clearly due to differential intensity of prospection.

One open-air site of great importance is that of Sota Palou (Carbonell *et al.* 1985), discovered in 1976 and excavated from 1979 to 1982. Located at 700 m altitude on a flat area in a wide valley, at the junction of mountain and plain, it is sheltered from cold northerly winds and receives a great deal of sunshine since it faces west. The site has produced two radiocarbon dates on charcoal: 8540±180 BP (UGRA-69 S.P.-803) and 9060±380 BP (UGRA-124 S.P.-814). Pollen analysis indicates that at this period the local climate was colder and drier than now, and the river closer to the camp. In view of all these factors it is not surprising that the excavators believe it was a warm-season site, chosen for its control of entries and exits in the valley of the River Freser. The 60 m² excavation showed evidence of three distinct activity zones: an area of stone-working, a domestic area where finished tools accumulated, and a hearth area. Two postholes were found, and there was good preservation of carbonized hazel-nuts, as is common in the European Mesolithic. Unfortunately, few bones survived; the handful found came from bison, boar, wild goat and rabbit.

A group of sites of great interest has been excavated in recent years near Vilanova de Sau; they comprise a series of rock-shelters along the foot of a cliff, near the only easy passage between the high plateau of Savassona and the low reaches of the valleys of the Riera Moran and the Ter. Castell Sa Sala was occupied in the Upper Palaeolithic by specialized exploiters of large herbivores (primarily horse), in the late winter and early spring. The Roc del Migdia, a long shelter, was occupied in the late Magdalenian (11,520±150 BP: UGRA-117 RM1a) and the Epi-Palaeolithic (Vila *et al.* 1982). Its lithic industry is dominated by quartz, and its fauna comprises red deer, ibex and boar. Other finds include acorns, hazel-nuts and snail shells. The site is particularly notable for a 'megalithic burial' (*Fig. 1*) – an individual burial in a rectangular structure of large slabs, surrounded by large hearths (Yll *et al.* 1986). A very similar burial was found some years ago in an Epi-Palaeolithic layer of the abri Cornille (Bouches-du-Rhône). It was located at the north end of the shelter (known as the abri Sulauze) against the back wall, enclosed by upright large stones (Escalon and Onoratini 1976: 222–224; Bouville *et al.* 1983).

Between Castell Sa Sala and Roc del Migdia, and only 100 m from the latter, is the small shelter of Cingle Vermell. Here a number of hearth structures have been excavated, mostly small ones ringed by two or three stones, as at Migdia. Unlike that site, the lithic industry of very small tools is primarily of flint. A radiocarbon date of 9760±160 BP (UGRA-68) has been obtained (Vila *et al.* 1985), and pollen indicates an optimal temperate and humid period. This fact, together with the area being the most humid part of Catalonia, accounts for the remarkable preservation in the site of plant material: not only acorns, walnuts and pine nuts but also seeds, cherry and plum stones, and even wood and leaves. The fauna comprises a great variety of species, about fifty in all, with the rabbit dominating in numbers, and the ibex dominating in terms of meat weight. Several types of freshwater fish are also represented.

It therefore appears (Yll *et al.* 1982) that the kinds of large animals exploited from Castell Sa Sala had gone by this period, and there was the usual Mesolithic concentration on smaller species and on a wider variety of resources, including fish and plants. It is still puzzling why the small group represented here (the site is 30 m² in area, and could not have held more than about 15 people) should have chosen this spot rather than the bigger shelters occupied earlier which shared its advantages: good access to raw materials (limestone, rock crystal, and outcrops of flint and quartz), easy ascent to the plateau, and excellent possibilities for control of animals migrating up the Ter valley, one of the most important natural lines of communication in Catalonia. Occupation of Cingle Vermell seems to have occurred repeatedly in the autumn and winter, and the excavators have speculated that the people of the area spent the warm season fishing on the banks of the Ter, and dispersed to rock-shelters in the winter.

The province of Huesca, in the central Spanish Pyrenees, has long been a blank on the distribution maps of most prehistoric periods, a blank made all the more noticeable by the more intense archaeological activity in the Basque and Catalan regions on either side. Much of the province is tough, arid country, and it was predictable that the blanks were due more to lack of exploration than to lack of material. Until recent times, the only possible traces of Mesolithic activity here were surface finds of macrolithic material – for example, those on the terraces of the Cinca at Fraga. Even now the picture is little

different where tools are concerned, though there is a possible geometric facies in the cave of Chaves, famous for its Cardial Neolithic (Utrilla 1980).

Rock art

Work in the region since the late 1970s by Vicente Baldellou and his team has produced a wide variety of unexpected finds, from the Cardial Neolithic mentioned above, far inland and in the uplands, to the first Palaeolithic decorated cave on the Spanish side of the Pyrenees, Fuente del Trucho. This cave is located in the wild canyons of the Río Vero, an area with hundreds of rock-shelters. Exploration of these is still in its early stages, but over 30 have already proved to be decorated; and while much of the decoration is schematic and assumed to be Bronze Age or later, some of it is in the classic style of the best Levantine art. In other words, Baldellou has found Levantine art farther north and farther inland than ever before, and, for the first time, in close proximity to Palaeolithic art, since the first such shelter found, Arpan L, is only a few hundred metres from Fuente del Trucho. Arpan L contains depictions of several stags, one of which is particularly fine (*Fig. 2*), as well as an archer. Located at 814 m altitude, and facing south, it is a shelter 10 m in length and 4.5 m deep; its soil has eroded away to bedrock, so that the paintings are now in quite a high position, 1.8 m above the ground (Dams 1984: 23).

Figure 2   Silhouette of a stag at Arpan L, length = *c.* 28 cm (after Baldellou 1984).

The site of Regacens, at 854 m altitude, faces south west and is 11 m long and 8 m high. It has depictions of six cervids, a wounded ibex, and three archers (Dams 1984). The small shelter of Litonares L has a

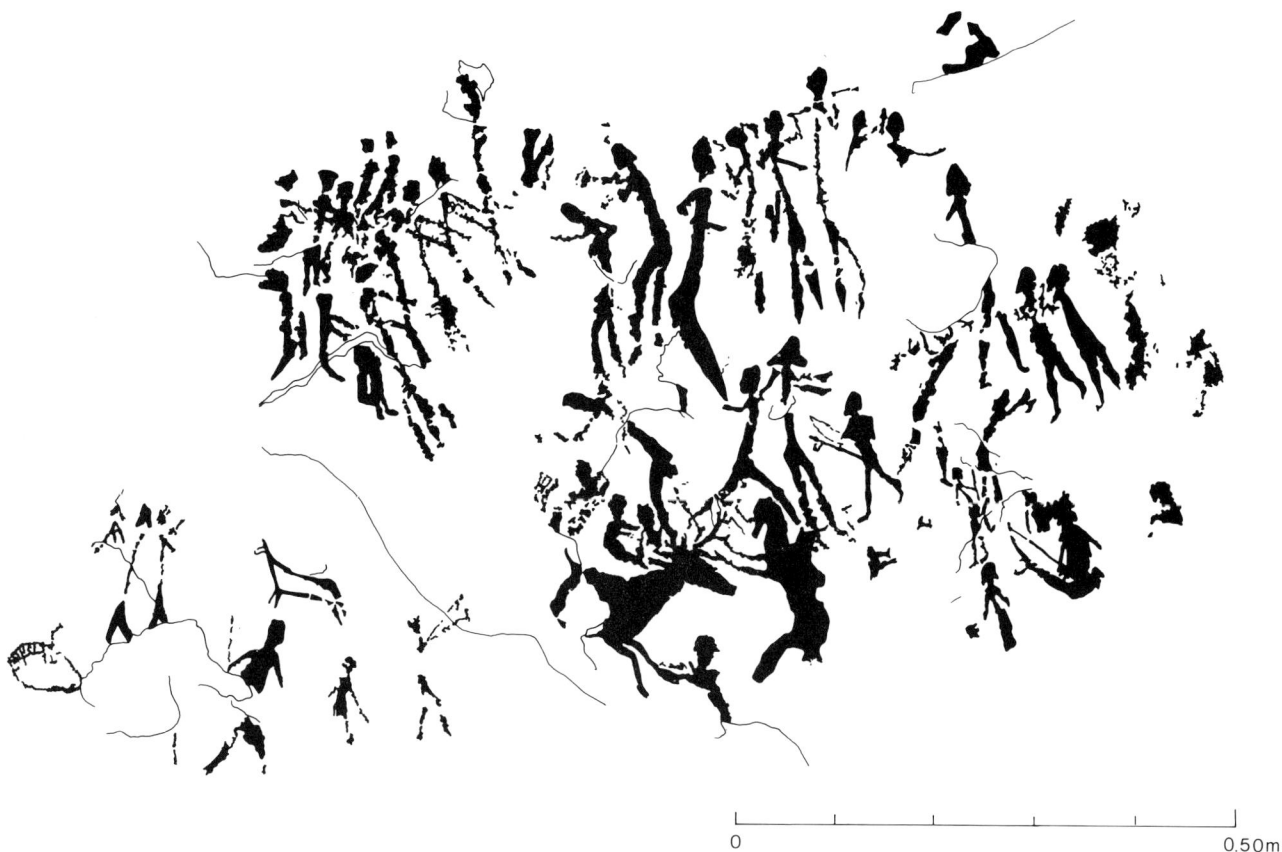

Figure 3   Panel 1 at Muriecho, showing scenes of humans with a stag (after Baldellou 1984).

cervid and a human, but barely visible (Baldellou 1984). The rock-shelter of Muriecho L, by way of contrast, has a magnificent scene of the capture of a stag, with numerous people depicted (*Fig. 3*). Other panels also depict cervids, and humans with weapons. Indeed Baldellou (1984: 139) has speculated that scenes like that of Muriecho imply an extreme and highly specialized control of deer by man at this period. Finally, the small shelter of Labarta L contains a few pictures, including a magnificent cervid. Certainly, this species dominates the art in those shelters found in Huesca, and is equally dominant in the schematic art – which itself may be Mesolithic in date, since recent discoveries in the Alicante–Valencia region of Spain suggest that some rock art (big 'idols', snakes, geometrics, etc.) which would normally be attributed to the Bronze Age, in fact *underlies* classic Levantine art.

It is clear that man was active in the Huesca area early in the Postglacial period, even if his living sites still elude us; he has left a rich legacy of art which we have barely begun to discover, and if some or all of the 'schematic' art must also now be assigned to the Mesolithic, then our entire conception of the quantity and styles of output in that period is going to have to alter quite radically. It is apt that the Pyrenees are returning to the foreground in Mesolithic studies through the kind of work outlined in this paper, and in view of the results achieved in the last few years one can confidently predict that the area has not yet yielded up its last surprise to the archaeologist.

Acknowledgments: I would like to thank V. Baldellou, J. Estévez, G. Laplace, M. Orliac, N. Soler and A. Vila for help and information on this topic. C. Meiklejohn and T.S. Constandse-Westermann kindly provided the abri Cornille references.

References

BAHN, P.G. (1982*a*) L'économie paléolithique et mésolithique du Béarn. *Revue de Pau et du Béarn*, 10: 127–140.

BAHN, P.G. (1982*b*) La néolithisation dans les Pyrénées atlantiques et centrales. In *Le Néolithique Ancien Méditerranéen*. Sète, Fédération Archéologique de l'Hérault: 191–199.

BAHN, P.G. (1983) The Neolithic of the French Pyrenees. In C.J. Scarre (ed.), *Ancient France 6000–2000 BC*. Edinburgh, University Press: 184–222.

BAHN, P.G. (1984) *Pyrenean Prehistory: a Palaeoeconomic Survey of the French Sites*. Warminster, Aris and Phillips.

BAHN, P.G. and COURAUD, C. (1984) Azilian pebbles: an unsolved mystery. *Endeavour*, 8: 156–158.

BALDELLOU, V. (1984) El arte levantino del Río Vero (Huesca). In *Juan Cabre Aguilo (1882–1982), encuentro de homenaje*. Zaragoza, Diputación Provincial: 133–139.

BOUVILLE, C., CONSTANDSE-WESTERMANN, T.S. and NEWELL, R.R. (1983) Les restes humains mésolithiques de l'abri Cornille, Istres (Bouches-du-Rhone). *Bulletin et Mémoires de la Société d'Anthropologie de Paris*, série XIII, 10: 89–110.

CARBONELL, E., CEBRIÀ, A., ESTEBAN, A., *et al.* (1985) *Sota Palou, Campdevànol. Un Centre d'Intervenció Prehistórica Postglaciar a l'aire Lliure*. Girona, Centre d'Investigacions Arqueològiques, Sèrie monogràfica no. 5.

COROMINAS, J-M. (1948) El mesolítico de la cueva 'd'En Mollet' de Seriñá. *Anales del Instituto de Estudiosos Gerundenses*, 3: 89–98.

COURAUD, C. (1985) *L'Art Azilien. Origine – Survivance* (XXe Supplément à Gallia Préhistoire). Paris, Centre National de la Recherche Scientifique.

COURAUD, C. and BAHN, P.G. (1982) Azilian pebbles in British collections: a re-examination. *Proceedings of the Prehistoric Society*, 48: 45–52.

DAMS, L. (1984) *Les Peintures Rupestres du Levant Espagnol.* Paris, Picard.

ESCALON DE FONTON, M. and ONORATINI, G. (1976) L'abri Cornille à Istres (Bouches-du-Rhone). *20ᵉ Congrès Préhistorique de France, Provence 1974*: 174–227.

GUILAINE, J., MARTZLUFF, M., COULAROU, J., *et al.* (1985) *Le Domaine Archéologique d'Andorre* (Histoire et Archéologie: les Dossiers, 96). Dijon.

LAPLACE, G. (1953) Les couches à escargots des cavernes pyrénéennes et le problème de l'Arisien de Piette. *Bulletin de la Société Préhistorique Française*, 50: 199–211.

ORLIAC, M. (1975) La grotte de la Tourasse. *Bulletin de l'Association Française pour l'Etude du Quaternaire*, 3–4: 189–190.

PERICOT, L. (1965) Sobre la industria arcaica del Montgrí. In *Homenaje a Jaime Vicens Vives*, vol. 1. Barcelona, Agusti Nuñez: 161–166.

RIPOLL, E. and LUMLEY, H. DE (1965) El paleolítico medio en Cataluña. *Ampurias*, 26–27: 1–70.

SOLER, N. (1977) El jaciment epipaleolític de Sant Benet (Sant Feliu de Guíxols, Girona). In, *Volum de la XX Assemblea Intercomarcal d'Estudiosos*, Sant Feliu de Guíxols: 295–312.

SOLER, N. (1980) El jaciment prehistòric de Coma d'Infern, a Les Encies (Les Planes, Girona). *Cypsela*, 3: 31–65.

UTRILLA, P. (1980) Epipaleolítico. In A. Beltran (ed.), *Atlas de Prehistoria y Arqueologia Aragonesas I.* Zaragoza, Diputación Provincial: 8–11.

VILA, A., ESTÉVEZ, J. and YLL, R. (1982) Sis millenaris de dinàmica econòmica abans del Neolític. *Ausa*, 10: 55–60.

VILA, A., YLL, R., ESTÉVEZ, J., ALCALDE, G., FARO, A., OLLER, J. and VILETTE, P. (1985) *El 'Cingle Vermell': Assentament de Caçadors-Recollectors del Xè Millenni BP* (Excavaciones Arqueològiques a Catalunya, no. 5). Barcelona, Departament de Cultura de la Generalitat de Catalunya.

YLL, E.I., ALCALDE, G., ESTÉVEZ, J. and VILA, A. (1982) La reconstrucción paleoecológica, El Cingle Vermell. In *Estat Actual de la Recerca Arqueològica a l'Istme Pirinenc*, 4rt Colloqui Internacional d'Arqueologia de Puigcerda, October 1980: 85–88.

YLL, E.I., WÜNSCH, G. and GUILLAMON, C. (1986) Metodologia instrumental per a l'estudi de sepultures mesolítiques (Roc del Migdia, Vilanova de Sau, Osona). *Cota Zero. Revista d'Arqueologia i Ciencia* (Vic), 2: 14–19.

Postglacial Environments, Settlement and Subsistence in the Pyrenees: the Balma Margineda, Andorra

David Geddes, Jean Guilaine, Jacques Coularou, Olivier Le Gall and Michel Martzluff

Abstract

A programme of prehistoric and palaeoecological research undertaken at the Balma Margineda (Principality of Andorra) has revealed a stratigraphy, well dated by human occupations, extending from the Upper Dryas to the middle of the Atlantic period (from the Epi-Palaeolithic to the Neolithic). Levels 8 and 7 contain a poorly defined (Azilian?) industry; sedimentological, palynological, anthracological and palaeontological studies suggest the existence of two broad phases. In levels 6, 5 and 4 the site lay at the transition between the montane and sub-alpine vegetation, under cold and dry conditions; the mammalian fauna is dominated consistently by the Pyrenean ibex, *Capra pyrenaïca*. In level 3 (Neolithic), the dense forest cover stabilizes the slopes; pines are dominant, but *Tilia, Quercus, Corylus, Alnus, Betula, Acer, Taxus,* and *Salix* are present; the site now lies at the lower limit of the montane vegetation; pollen and macrobotanic remains of domestic wheat and barley appear; domestic animals (sheep, goat, cattle, pig) appear alongside the wild fauna, still predominantly the ibex.

INTRODUCTION

The human conquest of the high mountain zone in the Pyrenees appears to begin at the end of the Pleistocene and the beginning of the Holocene, when the initial warming trend of the Bølling set in motion geomorphological and biological processes responsible for the creation of new mountain habitats. As part of a multi-disciplinary research programme examining Postglacial environments and prehistoric human adaptations in the eastern end of the Pyrenees, the Centre d'Anthropologie des Sociétés Rurales has investigated a series of Mesolithic occupation sites lying in the pre-Pyrenean uplands of France and Spain, and in the mountain zone in the Principality of Andorra (Guilaine *et al.* 1979, 1982, 1987). Human groups living along the base of the Pyrenean chain expanded into these new mountain habitats, modifying in the process certain aspects of their resource base, their subsistence practices, their seasonal cycle and settlement pattern, and most probably their social and economic organization as well. Abandoning the exploitation of gregarious herd animals (reindeer, horse, bison) which had been an important part of the Pleistocene landscape under the rigorous conditions of the Würm glacial episodes, late Magdalenian and Azilian groups began to regularly hunt other herbivorous mammals (red deer, roe deer, boar, aurochs) which had been

of limited importance up to this time. They adapted their subsistence and settlement strategies to gathering, collecting, fishing and hunting in closed, forested environments, and widened their resource base to include a diversity of plant, molluscan, bird and fish resources. Particular interest can be attached to the appearance of specialized sites for the seasonal hunting of ibex in mountainous zones, which were in all probability complementary to sites with a more diversified resource base lying at lower altitudes.

The Balma Margineda opens at an altitude of *c.* 1000 m in the valley of the Valira river, at the transition between the supra-mediterranean, *Quercus pubescens* vegetational stage which develops in the narrow, sheltered valley bottom, and the montane and sub-alpine associations of *Abies, Pinus sylvestris,* and *P. uncinata* which extend from 1000 m to *c.* 2500 m. Above the tree line, and in numerous exposed locations at lower altitudes where trees cannot grow, the coniferous forests give way to various types of alpine meadow. A geographic and ecological characteristic fundamental to the analysis of human exploitation of the Pyrenees is the penetration of temperate environments with mesophile and thermophile vegetation in sheltered valley bottoms right up to the bases of the highest Pyrenean massifs. In spite of the importance of the sheltered conditions in the valley bottom around the occupation site itself, the Balma Margineda lies at the entry to a vast, Pyrenean amphitheatre whose summits surpass 3000 m altitude, only 12 km north of a meso-mediterranean environment in the basin of Seo d'Urgell (*Fig. 1*).

STRATIGRAPHY, CHRONOLOGY AND CULTURAL SEQUENCES

Levels 10–7: early Epi-Palaeolithic

The lowermost archaeological unit examined so far, comprising levels 10, 9, 8 and 7, belongs to the extreme end of the Würm IV Stadial or the very beginning of the Postglacial period *c.* 11,000 BP, most probably lying in the Upper Dryas. The warming trend which began in the Pyrenees *c.* 13,000 BP was already producing visible effects on

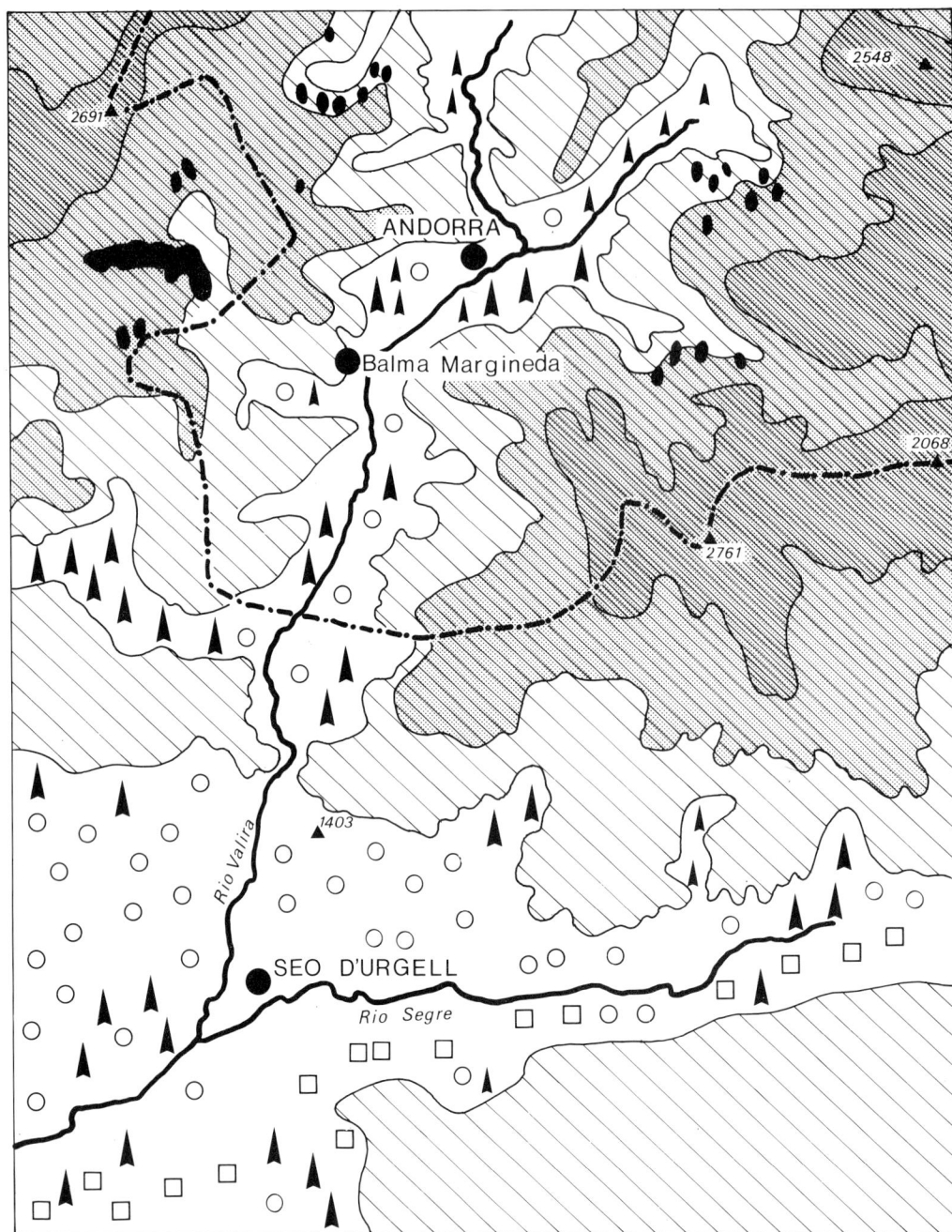

Quercus ilex ○

Quercus pubescens ▲

Pinus salzmanni □

Abies ●

Dry montane vegetation (**Pinus sylvestris** series), above 1000–1200m altitude

Sub-alpine vegetation (**Pinus uncinata** series), above 1800–2000m altitude

Alpine vegetation, above 2300–2500m altitude

Figure 1 Location of the Balma Margineda. *Drawing and copyright, J-L. Vernet*

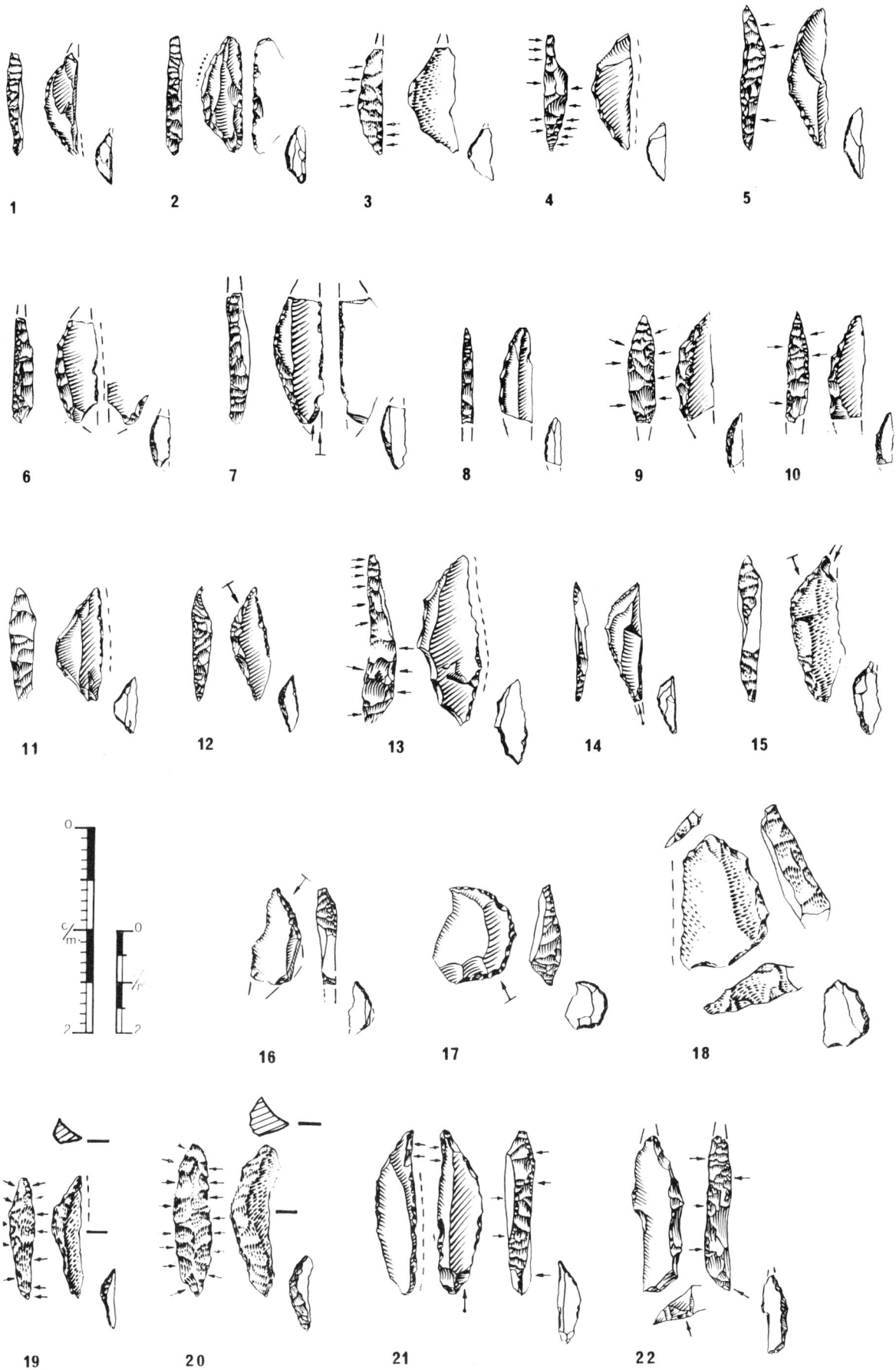

Figure 2   Geometric microliths and points from Balma Margineda level 6. *Drawing and copyright, Michel Martzluff*

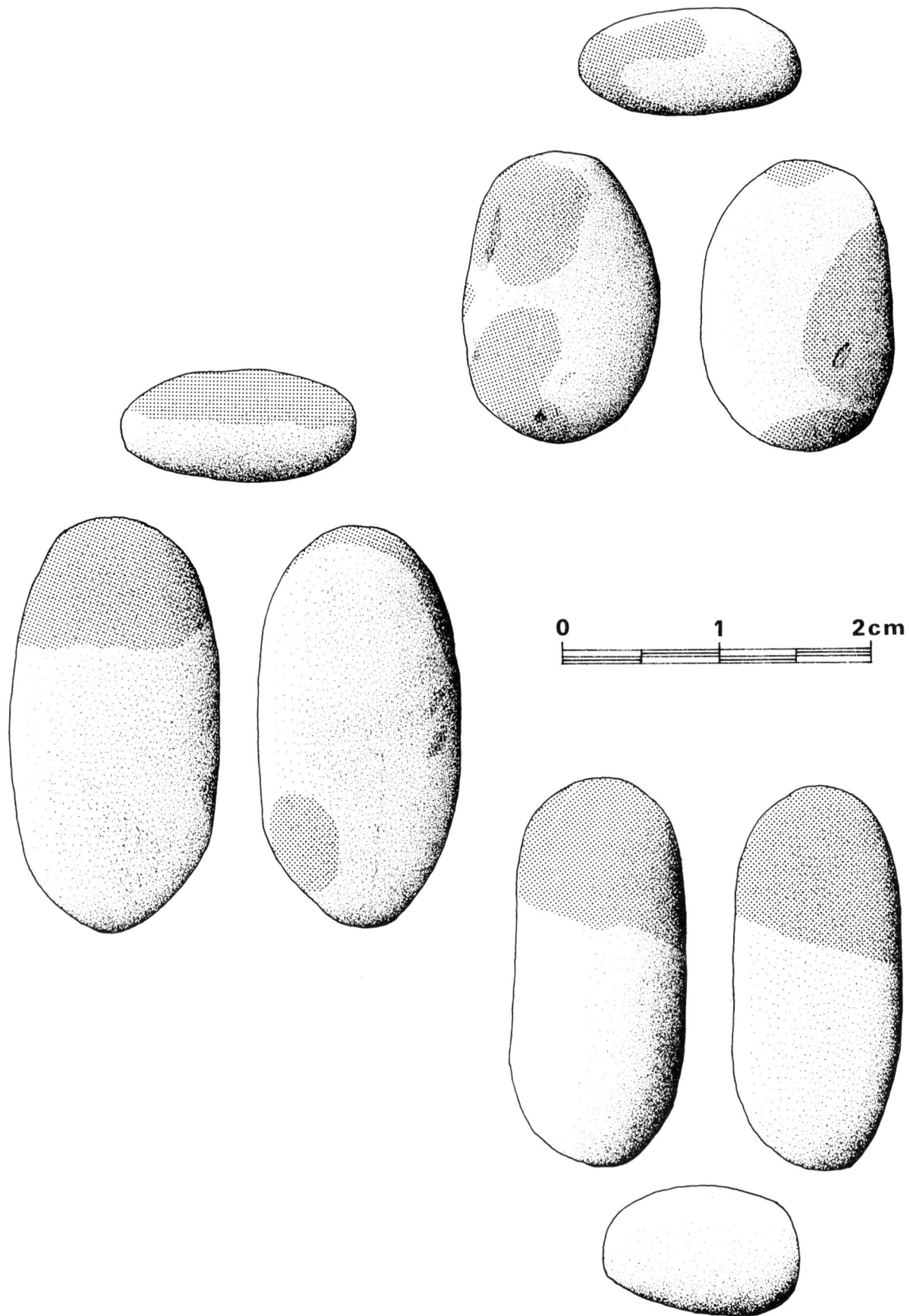

Figure 3   Red-painted pebbles from Balma Margineda levels 6 and 5. *Drawn by J. Coularou; copyright, C.A.S.R.*

the vegetation and the physical environment at this time (Jalut *et al.* 1982). A cooling phase has been shown at this time in the eastern and central Pyrenees (Jalut 1977; Jalut *et al.* 1982), and these authors estimate that mean temperatures in the Pyrenees would have been between 0 and 5 °C, *c.* 5–7 °C lower than those of today. Local conditions were acutely dependent upon conditions of exposure, shelter and insolation, and upon the natural processes of colonization and vegetational succession, on soil formation, and on the rise of temperature and, especially, humidity.

Levels 10 to 7 have so far yielded only a glimpse of the lithic assemblages dating to the very early Epi-Palaeolithic, and until excavations have progressed further we cannot consider our observations as definitive. Small backed points and backed bladelets generally less than 5 cm long, scrapers, some small points with curved backs (*pointes à dos courbé*), and débitage products are primarily made from local quartzite but, in some cases, from flint probably imported from the basin of Seo d'Urgell several kilometres to the south. No true microliths have been found.

Level 6: middle Azilian

The lowermost archaeological layer to be extensively excavated, level 6, can be placed at the end of the Upper Dryas and into the Pre-Boreal by radiocarbon dates of 10,640±260 BP (Ly-2843) and 9250±160 BP (Ly-2842) for the base and the middle of the level. The wood charcoal remains belong to species of the sub-alpine stage, principally *Pinus uncinata*, accompanied by *P. sylvestris* and *Juniperus* (Vernet and Krauss-Marguet 1985). No palynological results are yet available for this level.

The lithic industry of level 6 is based on flakes. Quartzite is again the most common raw material; however, the utilization of other finer-grained rocks (amorphous and hyaline quartz, radiolarite, rhyolite, muscovite, schist and flint) allowed the production of smaller flakes. The absence of local flint seems to have been accompanied by a maximum use of this valuable raw material. The abandoned flint cores resemble small cones or cylinders barely exceeding 2 cm in diameter.

Scrapers and backed bladelets are still present in this level, continuing from levels 10 to 7. Geometric microliths are now relatively abundant – numerous triangles in particular, but also crescents and points with curved backs (*pointes à dos courbé*) which are themselves very close typologically to the crescents. These miniscule geometric microliths, which rarely exceed 10 mm in length and 2 mm in width, were extracted from the ends of flakes and bladelets using the microburin technique (*Fig. 2*).

Among a handful of small white pebbles recovered in the upper part of level 6 and in level 5 which bear traces of red pigment, three pieces stand out. On one intact and one fragmentary specimen, a red band runs around the entire circumference of the pebble, and a second band runs down the medial line on each of the flatter faces (*Fig. 3*). A third river cobble bears a triangle engraved on one of its faces. Comparable painted pebbles were found at Mas d'Azil (cf. Couraud 1985).

Level 5

The fine yellow sediment of level 5, heavily charged with coarse *éboulis*, lies in the Pre-Boreal period, in the interval dated between *c.* 9200 BP (level 6) and 8500 BP (level 4). The pines are still very largely predominant both among the wood charcoal fragments, where *Pinus uncinata* outnumbers *P. sylvestris* by an increasing margin, and in the pollen sample (Leroyer 1985; Vernet and Krauss-Marguet 1985). Even though the pines produce a large number of pollen grains which readily disperse over long distances, the wood charcoal evidence suggests that the pine forest was well developed in the vicinity of the occupation site itself. The values of the Gramineae show that open zones persisted around the site, and it is the extent of the open vegetation which is certainly masked by the high pollen production of the pines.

Taking into account the high percentages of the Filicales, however, this cannot be taken to be an indication of a cool, dry interval. Rather, the local vegetation depends upon the natural processes of colonization, pedogenesis, temperature and humidity. The rising curve of fir (*Abies*) in the wood charcoal sample indicates warmer conditions, and marks the initial phases of the retreat of the pine forests to higher altitudes where conditions of temperature and humidity remain more favourable to them. The extension of *Abies* in Andorra before 8500 BP precedes its analogous development on the northern slopes of the Pyrenees, dated between 7500 and 7300 BP at the eastern end of the chain (Jalut 1977), and as late as 7000 BP in the central Pyrenees at Lourdes (Alimen *et al.* 1965). As is the case with *Abies*, the maximum of *Corylus* in level 5 at the Balma Margineda falls into the earlier part of the dated range observed elsewhere in the Pyrenees (cf. Jalut 1977). Elements of the supra-mediterranean, deciduous oak series begin to appear more frequently in this level – deciduous oaks (*Quercus* sp.), lime (*Tilia cordata*) and alder (*Alnus*). Overall, the time period covered by levels 6 and 5, covering perhaps as much as the two millennia between 10,500 and 8500 BP, stands out as one of the most important in the Postglacial environmental history of the Andorran Pyrenees. With few exceptions, and these may be in part a sampling problem, all the major trees were present at or near their modern altitudinal levels.

V

Figure 4 Triangles and trapezes from Balma Margineda level 4. *Drawing and copyright, Michel Martzluff*

Level 4: late Mesolithic

The gravel-laden sediments of level 4, which attain a thickness of 40 cm in places, can be subdivided into two parts which may reflect differing conditions of sedimentation (Brochier 1985). The basal sediments containing finer *éboulis*, generally *c.* 10 cm thick, give way to a fine, dark-grey sediment containing much coarser *éboulis*, generally *c.* 15 cm thick. The *éboulis* consists of coarse, heavily weathered fragments resulting from the mechanical erosion of the rock-shelter wall and the limited transport within the shelter itself. The slope of the base of level 4 is significantly shallower than that of the upper levels. This may point to a levelling of the natural sediments by the Mesolithic occupants, in order to construct a roughly horizontal living surface 2–3 m wide. Radiocarbon dates obtained for the base and the middle of level 4 – 8530±420 BP (Ly-2841) and 8390±150 BP (Ly-2840), respectively – place this late Mesolithic occupation in the Boreal period, but the total time-span represented by this thick level has not yet been determined.

Pines continue to dominate the pollen profile and, although their importance is certainly exaggerated to some extent by their high levels of pollen production, they still predominate among the wood charcoal fragments (Leroyer 1985; Vernet and Krauss-Marguet 1985). *Abies* develops slightly among the charcoal fragments, and the deciduous association broadens to include ash (*Fraxinus*), birch (*Betula*), maple (*Acer*) and wild cherry (*Prunus*), as well as the oaks (*Quercus* sp.), lime (*Tilia*) and alder (*Alnus*) observed in lower levels. The real importance of these taxa, and their relative values among the deciduous trees, are confused by the small sample size, differential pollen production and transport, and the discrepancies between the pollen and the wood charcoal data. The penetration of the supra-mediterranean, deciduous association into the upper valley of the Valira is nevertheless a good indicator of temperature conditions approaching those of today, and of increased humidity. Most notable, perhaps, is the abundance of *Tilia* pollen (23–29% of the total pollen count, 31% of the arboreal pollen), which has a particularly short transport distance. Even a more moderate frequency of *Tilia* pollen would attest to the importance of this taxon in the deciduous forest of this intermediate altitude zone, lying at the upper limit of the supra-mediterranean deciduous oak forest and the lower limit of the montane and sub-alpine coniferous forests. The development of the deciduous oak association signifies a more closed vegetal cover, and means as well the formation of loamy forest soils which, when cleared of their tree cover, will be favourable to the cultivation of cereals by the Neolithic, agricultural occupants of the site whose first presence has been dated to 6670±120 BP (Ly-2439).

The lithic assemblage of level 4 belongs to a complex of late and final Mesolithic industries identified in southern France and the Mediterranean facade of the Iberian Peninsula, characterized by small numbers of trapezes and large numbers of triangles (Barbaza, Guilaine and Vaquer 1986). In level 4 the average size of the geometric microliths nearly doubles, and their forms evolve from trapezes to isosceles and scalene triangles (*Fig. 4*). The microburin technique is absent.

The microlithic tool assemblage from the Balma Margineda level 4 resembles those from the final Mesolithic levels on the northern slopes of the Pyrenees at the abri de Dourgne and at the grotte Gazel, discussed by Guilaine (1973, 1979) and Barbaza *et al.* (1985), and certain Spanish late Mesolithic industries discussed by Fortea (1973). These final Mesolithic assemblages at the Balma Margineda stand out by their early date, in the second half of the ninth millennium BP. The comparable industries north of the Pyrenees date to the middle of the eighth millennium BP at the earliest, although this time period seems to have been one of erosion rather than deposition in the caves and rock-shelters of southern France, and the lithic industries dating between 8500 and 7500 BP are conspicuously rare.

SUBSISTENCE ECONOMY

Remains of the ibex, which can on biogeographic grounds probably be attributed to the Pyrenean form *Capra pyrenaïca*, constitute 90–99% of the faunal assemblage. During the cold, dry phases of the Pleistocene the habitat of *Capra ibex* and *C. pyrenaïca* expanded to include non-mountainous zones at low altitudes, where the relief was still sufficiently abrupt. In south-west France, for example, Delpech (1983) remarks that the ibex appears sporadically in the Lot (Roc de Combe), the Dordogne (La Ferrassie, Maldidier, Laugerie-Haute-Est, La Madeleine, La Gare de Couze) and the northern edge of the Pyrenees (Duruthy), yet seems to have been absent on the low topography of the plains and river valleys of the Aquitaine basin. Koby (1958) showed that the alpine species, *C. ibex*, is the principal form represented in the parietal and mobiliary art of the Dordogne. Delpech (1983) identified, at the site of Saint-Circq in the Dordogne, a cranium belonging to *C. ibex* with horn cores well developed and regularly curving rearward above the head. The Pyrenean ibex is known, however, since Würm III. It is depicted at Isturitz, first engraved on a calcareous fragment found in a Solutrean level, and later etched on bone fragments recovered in Magdalenian levels (Saint Perrier and Saint Perrier 1952). *Capra pyrenaïca* is also represented in the grotte d'Espeluges at Lourdes (Breuil 1937), the grotte d'Aurensan (Delporte 1974), Gargas (Clot

1973: 76, fig. 91) and Marsoulas (Brielle 1968) in the Pyrenees, and at Tito Bustillo, Ekain and Altexerri in the Cantabrian region of Spain (Altuna and Apellániz 1976, 1978; Moure 1980; Balbin and Moure 1981). At the grotte des Eglises, Delpech identified the horn core of a young *Capra pyrenaïca* which presents the beginning of the characteristic double bend and slight heteronym twist (Delpech and Le Gall 1983). Although profiles of ibex with regularly curving horns do seem to be represented in the Pyrenean zone at Isturitz, Bruniquel, Pair-non-Pair and Gargas (Leroi-Gourhan 1965: 357, figs. 205, 214, 248, 280, 282, 296–298, 313; Brielle 1968; Clot 1973: 73–77), we are confronted with the regional variability in the profile of the horn apparent in *Capra pyrenaïca* (Clouet 1979; Gonzales 1982: 181, fig. 2) on the one hand, and with a multitude of questions concerning the representation of anatomical details in Upper Palaeolithic art, on the other.

The rarity of the chamois (*Rupicapra rupicapra*), the other herbivore typical of the high mountain zone today, stands out conspicuously at the Balma Margineda as at other sites of the Pyrenees and the Cantabrian mountains. The chamois appears sporadically in Pleistocene and Holocene faunal assemblages of south-west France, Cantabria and the Pyrenees (Altuna 1972; Delpech 1983), but it is rare at those sites where it does appear. *Rupicapra* constitutes up to 5% of the faunal assemblage at La Ferrassie, Les Battuts, Laugerie-Haute-Est, Saint Eulalie and La Madelaine during different phases of Würm III and Würm IV (Delpech 1983). Comparison of these faunal assemblages reveals on the one hand several assemblages with very high frequencies of *Capra* and very low frequencies of *Rupicapra*, and on the other several sites where *Rupicapra* is relatively abundant, making up 5% to over 20% of the herbivores, but where the assemblage is dominated by the cervids. In the first case, *Capra* constitutes 99% of the fauna at the grotte des Eglises (Delpech and Le Gall 1983) and at the grotte de la Vache (Koby 1958); and in Cantabria dominates at Ermittía (84%), Ekain level VI (71%) and Rascaño (87–92%) (Altuna 1972, 1981; Altuna and Merino 1984). In the second case, on sites where *Rupicapra* is more abundant, the cervids (*Cervus elaphus*, *Capreolus capreolus* and *Rangifer tarandus*), singly or in combination, make up 47–67% of the faunal assemblage, generally followed in frequency by *Rupicapra* (9–25%) and then *Capra* (2–26%). This is the case at Aitzbitarte, Urtiaga, the grotte du Bois de Cantet and the grotte d'Aurensan. Altuna (1972), following Stehlin (Dubois and Stehlin 1932–33), discusses the possibility that the optimal habitat for the chamois lies in the piedmont under the cold conditions which prevailed during the Würm glaciations. Its retreat to the high mountains would constitute a secondary adaptation to a less favourable ecological zone. Alternatively, it is possible to speculate that the subsistence practices, settlement system, annual cycle and economic organization required for successful hunting of the ibex during the late Pleistocene and the Holocene effectively conflicted with the type of organization necessary for the exploitation of this second mountain herbivore.

From a climatic and ecological perspective, the quasi-exclusive presence of *Capra* cf. *pyrenaïca* in levels 10 to 6 at the Balma Margineda corresponds perfectly with the palaeoecological data which indicate that cold, relatively dry conditions prevailed at this altitude during the early Postglacial. The ibex is accompanied in these levels by rare specimens of *Rupicapra*, *Sus scrofa scrofa*, and *Cervus elaphus*. A slight increase in the relative frequency of *Sus* in level 5/6 marks the transition to the upper faunal ensemble. A second broad faunal grouping spans levels 5, 4 and 3. The ibex is still overwhelmingly predominant, making up 90% of the faunal remains, yet the deer and the boar now make up 10% of the faunal assemblage, reflecting their development in the deciduous forest which extends over the valley bottom.

The varying effects of the Postglacial amelioration according to altitude and the local environment of each site can be clearly seen through a comparison of the sequences at the Balma Margineda and the abri de Dourgne, a Mesolithic and Neolithic site located on the northern slopes of the Pyrenees (Geddes 1980, 1981). At Dourgne, a faunal association composed largely of ibex in the basal level gradually gives way during the Boreal to a series of mixed associations containing *Sus scrofa scrofa*, *Cervus elaphus*, *Capreolus capreolus* and *Capra pyrenaïca*. These faunal assemblages are dominated first by *Capra*, then by *Sus* plus the domestic ovicaprines. At the Balma Margineda, homogeneous associations of *Capra pyrenaïca*, spanning the period from the Upper Dryas to the Boreal, give way to a Neolithic faunal assemblage, poorly represented in the upper levels of the site, containing domestic ovicaprines.

A diversity of macrobotanic remains from autumn-ripening nuts and fruits have been recovered in all the Mesolithic and Neolithic levels, as a result of specific preservation conditions at the site and the recovery techniques implemented (Marinval 1985). The dry, powdery and extremely fine nature of the sediments eliminated the need for the type of wet-sieving procedures utilized at our other excavations. All macrobotanic remains could be recovered by sorting the residue left in fine-mesh sieves. The large number of carbonized hazel-nut shells stands out conspicuously at a site where *Corylus* is neither excessively common among the wood charcoal remains nor in the pollen profile. Seeds belonging to the genus *Valerianella*, which includes lamb's lettuce among other plants, have been recovered in Mesolithic levels at the Balma Margineda, the Balma Abeurador (Vaquer, Geddes, Barbaza and Erroux 1986), and Fontbrégoua (Courtin 1982). Remains of *Viburnum lantana*, *Pistacia*, *Crataegus* sp. (hawthorn), *Rubus fructicosus* (blackberry), *Prunus spinosa* (blackthorn) and *Rosa* sp. have also been identified.

The fish remains recovered from all levels belong to one species, the trout, *Salmo trutta fario* L., with the exception of one vertebra belonging to an eel, *Anguilla anguilla* L. The annual growth bands visible on the trout vertebrae indicate a distinct seasonality in the fishing activities undertaken at the Balma Margineda, and probably in the occupation of the site as a whole. Taking the 161 specimens studied from level 6 as an example, slightly more than one-third were captured at the beginning of the annual growth period, and more than a half at the very end of the growth period. These fall into the months of March to May and October to November under modern conditions, and correspond to very specific parts of the trout life cycle. In the autumn, trout move out of the main watercourses where they spend the warmer months of the year into smaller, fast-running and well-oxygenated affluents as the first stage in their annual migration upstream to their spawning areas. They remain in these small affluents until early December after reproduction is completed, and it is not uncommon for trout to remain near their spawning grounds until the first warming signs in late winter and early spring. The stream profile around the Balma Margineda suggests that the fish were captured on the same bank as the occupation site, about 300 m downstream from the site. It is interesting to draw comparisons with the grotte des Eglises, another specialized ibex-hunting site in the Pyrenees, where both trout and Atlantic salmon were captured during the late autumn and very early winter (Delpech and Le Gall 1983; Le Gall 1984).

CONCLUSION

The Balma Margineda fits into a complex of specialized ibex-hunting sites which appear at the end of the Würm and continue into the early Postglacial period in the Pyrenees – grotte des Eglises (Delpech and Le Gall 1985), abri de Dourgne (Geddes 1980); in Spain – Ermittía (Altuna 1972), Rascaño (Altuna 1981), Ekain (Altuna and Merino 1984), Erralla (Altuna and Mariezkurrena 1985), La Riera (Altuna 1986); and also in other mountainous areas of Europe.

The Lateglacial and Postglacial climatic amelioration, and the start of renewed biological activity in the mountains, opened up an environmental window of opportunity for the ibex. Before this time, habitat restriction limited the size and density of ibex populations. Subsequently, Neolithic agriculturalists expanded up into middle altitude zones of the Pyrenees at a remarkably early date, bringing domestic sheep and goat into direct ecological competition with the ibex for the use of mountain pastures, driving the chamois into higher mountain environments and competition with the ibex, and further depleting ibex herds by hunting. The occupation sequence at the Balma Margineda is capped by an early Neolithic level containing typical impressed pottery. Similarly, at the abri de Dourgne, a Mesolithic sequence containing relatively numerous ibex remains gives way to a Neolithic sequence characterized by the increasing importance of domestic ovicaprines.

The ibex-hunting sites of the Pyrenees and of Cantabrian Spain are associated with quite distinct lithic industries of the Magdalenian, Azilian, Sauveterrian, and Tardenoisian traditions. Toolkits composed of typologically and technologically different implements were equally effective for ibex-hunting and processing activities. Correspondingly, it does not seem possible to identify any distinctive components of the lithic assemblages present at ibex-hunting sites which would serve to differentiate them from contemporary and related deer- and boar-hunting sites at lower altitudes.

Initial examination of the Balma Margineda faunal remains demonstrated the abundance of remains of the lower limbs (carpals, tarsals, metapodials) and of the skull and dentition. This pattern of skeletal part representation typifies kill–butchery sites where whole animals are transported onto the site itself for skinning, evisceration, and disarticulation.

The extraordinary abundance of long bone shaft fragments and bone splinters, and the frequency of highly visible defleshing marks on the femoral and humeral shaft pieces together indicate that the butchering activities themselves were followed by meat processing. In level 6, for example, the highest minimum number of individuals resulted not from the metapodials or the teeth, but from the radius mid-shaft region containing the nutrient foramen and the proximal end of the articular surface for the ulna. The final processing techniques (smoking, drying, etc.) and ultimate destination of the meat thus obtained remains a matter of speculation.

Articular-end fragments themselves are nearly absent, and present a major interpretative problem. Two interpretations have been advanced recently to account for the differential destruction of articular ends – carnivore damage and bone-grease extraction (Binford 1978, 1981; Brain 1981). On the one hand, conventional evidence for bone destruction due to carnivores (pitting and scratching of bone surfaces, partially-gnawed articular ends, concave fractures) is negligible to absent; on the other hand, there is no direct evidence for bone-grease extraction, if it is not in the virtual absence of articular ends itself.

The fish vertebrae indicate occupation at the very end of the summer, during the autumn, and at the very beginning of the winter. The macrobotanic remains of autumn-ripening fruits and berries correspond with this seasonal data. The ibex remains, indicative of mixed herds of males and females, point to hunting during the autumn and early winter, when the ibex gather in mixed herds for the rut.

The Balma Margineda and other ibex-hunting sites repeatedly provide indications that they are specialized components of settlement–subsistence systems which draw upon a wider geographic zone throughout the annual cycle. Clark and Lerner's (1983) analysis of site catchment characteristics and faunal assemblages from Asturian sites in Cantabrian Spain points to the specificity of ibex-hunting sites. Three of the first four variables identified by their step-wise multiple regression relate to the exploitation of montane resources, and the ibex itself stands out as the single most significant variable. The variables related to the alpine zone are followed in the analysis principally by those related to exploitation of coastal and marine resources. In contrast, the vertebrate and invertebrate food remains that were presumably staples of the Asturian diet (red deer, limpets) were not valid diagnostic criteria among sites.

At the present stage of research, it is impossible to speculate whether we are dealing at the Balma Margineda with one of many more-or-less specialized logistic sites, located in differing ecological zones and utilized during different seasons, or with a specialized activity site attached to a single and relatively stable base camp. Resolution of this question depends on a combined programme of survey, palaeoenvironmental analysis and excavation undertaken at lower altitudes to the south, in and around the basin of Seo d'Urgell.

References

ALIMEN, H., FLORSCHÜTZ, F. and MENENDEZ-AMOR, J. (1965) Etude géologique et palynologique sur le Quaternaire des environs de Lourdes. In *Actes du IVᵉ Congrès International d'Etudes Pyrénéennes, Pau-Lourdes, 1962*, 1: 7–26.

ALTUNA, J. (1972) Fauna de mamíferos de los yacimientos prehistóricos de Guipúzcoa con catálogo de los mamíferos cuaternarios del Cantábrico y del Pirineo Occidental. *Munibe*, 24: 1–464.

ALTUNA, J. (1981) Restos óseos del yacimiento prehistórico del Rascaño. In J. González Echegaray and I. Barandiarán (eds), *El Paleolítico Superior de la Cueva del Rascaño (Santander)* (Monográfias del Centro de Investigación y Museo de Altamira, 3). Santander, Ministerio de Cultura: 223–269.

ALTUNA, J. (1986) The mammalian faunas from the prehistoric site of La Riera. In L.G. Straus and G.A. Clark (eds), *La Riera Cave: Stone Age Hunter-Gatherer Adaptations in Northern Spain*. Tempe, Arizona State University Anthropological Research Papers no. 36: 237–274.

ALTUNA, J. and APELLÁNIZ, J.M. (1976) Las figuras rupestres paleolíticas de la cueva de Altxerri (Guipúzcoa). *Munibe*, 28: 1–242.

ALTUNA, J. and APELLÁNIZ, J.M. (1978) Las figuras rupestres paleolíticas de la cueva de Ekain (Deba, Guipúzcoa). *Munibe*, 30: 1–151.

ALTUNA, J. and MARIEZKURRENA, K. (1984) Bases de subsistencia de origen animal de los pobladores de Ekain. In J. Altuna and J.M. Merino (eds), *El Yacimiento Prehistórico de la Cueva de Ekain (Deba, Guipúzcoa)*. San Sebastián, Sociedad de Estudios Vascos: 211–280.

ALTUNA, J. and MERINO, J.M. (1984) Relacion entre la faune cazada por los pobladores del yacimiento y las figuras representadas en el santuario. In J. Altuna and J.M. Merino (eds), *El Yacimiento Prehistórico de la Cueva de Ekain (Deba, Guipúzcoa)*. San Sebastián, Sociedad de Estudios Vascos: 281–351.

BALBIN, R. DE and MOURE, J. (1981) Las pinturas y grabados de la cueva de Tito Bustillo. El sector oriental. *Studia Archaeologica* (Valladolid), 66: 1–43.

BARBAZA, M., GUILAINE, J. and VAQUER, J. (1985) Fondaments chrono-culturels du Mésolithique en Languedoc occidental. *L'Anthropologie*, 88: 345–365.

BINFORD, L.R. (1978) *Nunamiut Ethnoarchaeology*. New York, Academic Press.

BINFORD, L.R. (1981) *Bones: Ancient Men and Modern Myths*. New York, Academic Press.

BRAIN, C.K. (1981) *The Hunters or the Hunted: an Introduction to African Cave Taphonomy*. Chicago, University Press.

BRIELLE, G. (1968) Les bouquetins dans l'art pariétal quaternaire pyrénéen. *Travaux de l'Institut d'Art Préhistorique de l'Université de Toulouse*, 10: 31–96.

BROCHIER, J-E. (1985) Ce que nous apprenne les sédiments. *Histoire et Archéologie: les Dossiers* (Dijon), 96: 16–18.

CLARK, G.A. and LERNER, S. (1983) Catchment analysis of Asturian sites. In G.A. Clark, *The Asturian of Cantabria: Early Holocene Hunter-Gatherers in Northern Spain* (Anthropological Papers of the University of Arizona, 41). Tucson, University of Arizona Press: 120–139.

CLOT, A. (1973) *L'Art Graphique Préhistorique des Hautes Pyrénées*. Morlaas (France), Editions P.G.P.: 73–77.

CLOT, A. (1982) Les bouquetins fossiles des Pyrénées occidentales et centrales. In C. Dendaleche (ed.), *Acta Biologica Montana* (Centre de Biologie des Ecosystèmes d'Altitude, University of Pau), 1: 251–267.

CLOUET, M. (1979) Note sur la systématique du bouquetin d'Espagne. *Bulletin de la Société d'Histoire Naturelle de Toulouse*, 115: 269–277.

COURAUD, C. (1985) *L'Art Azilien. Origine – Survivance* (XXᵉ supplément à Gallia Préhistoire). Paris, Centre National de la Recherche Scientifique.

COURTIN, J. (1982) Informations archéologiques. La grotte de Fontbregoua. *Gallia Préhistoire*, 25: 530.

DELPECH, F. (1983) *Les Faunes du Paléolithique Supérieur dans le Sud-Ouest de la France* (Cahiers du Quaternaire, 6). Paris, Centre National de la Recherche Scientifique.

DELPECH, F. and LE GALL, O. (1983) La faune magdalénienne de la grotte des Eglises (Ussat, Ariège). *Préhistoire Ariègeoise*, 38: 91–118.

DELPORTE, H. (1974) Le Magdalénien de la grotte d'Aurensan à Bagnères-de-Bigorre (Hautes-Pyrénées). *Antiquités Nationales*, 6: 10–25.

DUBOIS, A. and STEHLIN, H. (1932–33) La grotte de Cotencher, station moustérienne. *Mémoires de la Société Paléontologique Suisse*, 52: 1–178 and 53: 179–292.

FORTEA, J. (1973) *Los Complejos Microlaminares y Geométricos del Epipaleolítico Mediterráneo Español* (Memorias del Seminario de Prehistoria y Arqueología). Salamanca, Universidad de Salamanca.

GEDDES, D. (1980) *De la Chasse au Troupeau en Méditerranée Occidentale* (Archives d'Ecologie Préhistorique, 5). Toulouse, Ecole des Hautes Etudes en Sciences Sociales.

GEDDES, D. (1981) Les débuts de l'élevage dans la vallée de l'Aude. *Bulletin de la Société Préhistorique Française*, 78: 370–378.

GEDDES, D., BARBAZA, M., VAQUER, J. and GUILAINE, J. (1986) Tardiglacial and Postglacial in western Languedoc and the eastern Pyrenees (France). In L.G. Straus (ed.), *The End of the Palaeolithic in the Old World*. Oxford, British Archaeological Reports (International Series) S284: 63–80.

GONZALES, G. (1982) Eco-ethologie du bouquetin en Sierra de Gredos. In C. Dendaleche (ed.), *Acta Biologica Montana* (Centre de Biologie des Ecosystèmes d'Altitude, University of Pau), 1: 177–215.

GUILAINE, J. (1973) Pointes triangulaires du Mésolithique languedocien. In *Estudios Dedicados al Professor Dr Luis Pericot*. Barcelona, University of Barcelona: 77–83.

GUILAINE, J. (1975) Problèmes de la néolithisation en Méditerranée occidentale. In *L'Epipaléolithique Méditerranéen*. Paris, Centre National de la Recherche Scientifique: 189–196.

GUILAINE, J. et al. (1979) *L'Abri Jean Cros: Essai d'Approche d'un Communauté du Néolithique Ancien dans son Environnement*. Toulouse, Centre d'Anthropologie des Sociétés Rurales.

GUILAINE, J., BARBAZA, M., GASCO, J., GEDDES, D., JALUT, G., and VAQUER, J. (1987) L'abri du roc de Dourgne: écologie des cultures du Mésolithique et du Néolithique ancien dans une vallée montagnarde des Pyrénées de l'Est. In J. Guilaine, J. Courtin, J. Roudil and J-L. Vernet (eds), *Premières Communautés Paysannes en Méditerranée Occidentale*. Paris, Centre National de la Recherche Scientifique: 545–554.

GUILAINE, J., BARBAZA, M., GEDDES, D., VERNET, J-L., LLONGUERAS, M. and HOPF, M. (1982) Postglacial human adaptations in Catalonia (Spain). *Journal of Field Archaeology*, 9: 407–416.

JALUT, G. (1977) *Végétation et Climat des Pyrénées Méditerranéennes depuis Quinze Mille Ans* (Archives d'Ecologie Préhistorique, 2). Toulouse, Ecole des Hautes Etudes en Sciences Sociales.

JALUT, G., DELIBRIAS, G., DAGNAC, J., MARDONES, M. and BONHOURS, M. (1982) A paleoecological approach to the last 21,000 years in the Pyrenees: the peat bog of Freychinede (alt. 1350 m, Ariège, south France). *Paleogeography, Paleoclimatology, Paleobotany*, 40: 321–359.

KOBY, F. (1958) Le bouquetin dans la Préhistoire. *Actes de la Société Jurassienne d'Emulation*, 61: 29–64.

LE GALL, O. (1984) *Icthyofaune d'Eau Douce dans les Sites Préhistoriques* (Cahiers du Quaternaire, 8). Paris, Centre National de la Recherche Scientifique.

LEROI-GOURHAN, A. (1965) *Préhistoire de l'Art Occidental*. Paris, Mazenod.

LEROYER, C. (1985) Les Pollens. *Histoire et Archéologie: les Dossiers* (Dijon), 96: 22–23.

MARINVAL, P. (1985) Cueillette et Agriculture. *Histoire et Archéologie: les Dossiers* (Dijon), 96: 28–30.

MOURE, J.A. (1980) Las pinturas y grabados de la cueva de Tito Bustillo (Asturias). *Studia Archaeologica* (Valladolid), 61: 1–28.

SAINT PERRIER, R. DE and SAINT PERRIER, S. DE (1952) *La Grotte d'Isturitz. III. Les Solutréens, les Aurignaciens et les Moustériens*. Paris, Archives de l'Institut de Paléontologie Humaine, Mémoire 25.

VAQUER, J., GEDDES, D., BARBAZA, M. and ERROUX, J. (1986) Mesolithic plant exploitation at the Balma Margineda. *Oxford Journal of Archaeology*, 5: 1–18.

VERNET, J-L. and KRAUSS-MARGUET, I. (1985) Charbons de bois et végétation. *Histoire et Archéologie: les Dossiers* (Dijon), 96: 24–25.

571

The Evolution of the Mesolithic in the North East of the Iberian Peninsula

I. Barandiarán and A. Cava

Abstract

The results of excavations by the authors during the last fifteen years on settlement sites in Lower Aragon (Botiquería, Costalena), the Pyrenees (Zatoya, Berroberría) and the upper valley of the Ebro (La Peña) are outlined, with reference to other contemporary sites. The characteristic industries, radiocarbon dates, palaeobotanical and palaeozoological results are presented. An interpretation of these cultural groups in relation to landscape and subsistence is advanced which emphasizes the importance of migration from the end of the Lateglacial right through to the Boreal period.

The evolution of the Mesolithic in the Ebro basin can be divided into several 'periods': typical (or generic) Azilian, an early Epi-Palaeolithic ('Epi-Magdalenian' or 'Aziloid'), two facies of the Epi-Palaeolithic (micro-laminar or general, and geometric) as recognized by Fortea in the Spanish Levant, and a neolithized Epi-Palaeolithic or Mesolithic (with pottery).

INTRODUCTION

Most of the sites considered in this paper have been excavated by the authors over the last fifteen years. This statement is necessarily an interim one, since the analyses of the industries recovered and of the colonization and exploitation of the landscape have not been taken to the same stage, and complementary studies (palaeobotany, palaeozoology and isotopic dating) are still not complete.

The region under consideration lies in the northeast part of the Iberian Peninsula and is largely conterminous with the basin of the Ebro, an area of some 85,000 km². This is essentially a triangular depression, across which the river flows from north west to south east. The central part of the basin is, in Spanish terms, at moderate altitude, between 200 and 600 m above sea level. To the north lies the major chain of the Pyrenees, whilst the southern edge of the basin is defined by the Iberian mountains.

Various interpretative papers on the Mesolithic (Epi-Palaeolithic) of neighbouring regions have been published by M.R. González Morales (for the coastal area of Cantabria) and by J. Fortea (for the Spanish Levant).

The Ebro basin contains a variety of climatic zones and topographic units: in the north the climate is markedly oceanic, with high rainfall; on the mountain slopes it is sub-alpine in character; while in the central part of the basin it is of inland Mediterranean (or continental sub-arid) type.

It is our opinion that in early prehistory the Ebro valley was used as a route for migration or exchanges between other, better-known regions: on the one hand, between the northern flanks of the Pyrenees (from Aquitaine to Languedoc and adjacent areas) and the plateau of Castille; and on the other, between the coastal zones bordering the Atlantic and the Mediterranean. The strategic value of the Ebro as a linking route has been emphasized in the study of later periods – the Chalcolithic and the Iron Age.

THE SITES EXAMINED

Our working hypotheses are developed from our consideration of the following sites:

Covacho de Berroberría

The cave of Berroberría (Urdax, province of Navarra) was excavated by the Marquis de Loriana and Maluquer de Motes (beginning in 1959) and, more recently (1977–79), by Ignacio Barandiarán (Barandiarán 1979a). It contains 2.50 m of deposits which include important archaeological horizons spanning the transition from the final Palaeolithic to the Neolithic. There are several horizons overlying the final Magdalenian horizon: lower part of layer D (0.15 m) – typical Azilian; layer D (0.20–0.25 m) – post-Azilian Epi-Palaeolithic; layer C (0.25 m) – an Epi-Palaeolithic geometric industry in association with hearths; lower part of layer B (0.10 m) – developed Mesolithic or Neolithic with *Helix (Cepaea) nemoralis*; upper part of layer B (0.10–0.15 m) – Neolithic.

Cueva de Zatoya

In the cave of Zatoya (Abaurrea, province of Navarra) 2.50 m of deposits were examined in excavations undertaken by Ignacio Barandiarán and Ana Cava in 1975–76 and 1980 (Barandiarán 1977, 1979b, 1982). The basal layer (III) is probably attributable to the Allerød; the overlying layers contain material belonging to the various stages of the regional Epi-Palaeolithic: layer II (lower and middle) – ?Younger Dryas; layer II (upper) – Pre-Boreal; layer Ib – ?Boreal. These are covered by a stalagmite layer, 0.10 m thick, which in turn is overlain by layer I containing early Neolithic material. There are also some superficial finds attributable to the Chalcolithic and the Bronze Age.

Abrigo de La Peña

The rock-shelter of La Peña (Marañón, province of Navarra) was excavated in 1982–83 by M.A. Beguiristain and A. Cava. The deposits, which are up to 5.00 m deep, include a 0.95 m thick layer containing geometric Epi-Palaeolithic material; this is overlain by layers of variable thickness which span the Neolithic and Chalcolithic (Beguiristain and Cava 1985).

Abrigo de La Botiquería dels Moros

The sediments infilling the rock-shelter of La Botiquería dels Moros (Mazaleón, province of Teruel) varied between 1.00 m and 1.40 m in depth. Excavation by Ignacio Barandiarán in 1974 revealed four occupation horizons with hearths, separated by thinner layers corresponding to periods of abandonment (Barandiarán 1978; Barandiarán and Cava 1984). Of the layers containing archaeological mat-erial, two (layer 2, 0.50 m thick and dated by radiocarbon, and layer 4, 0.20 m thick) contained a geometric Epi-Palaeolithic industry; the upper two layers (layer 6, 0.10 m thick and layer 8, 0.20 m thick) belong to the Cardial/Impressed Ware Neo-lithic.

Abrigo de Costalena

The rock-shelter of Costalena (Maella, province of Zaragoza) was excavated in 1975 by I. Barandiarán and A. Cava (Barandiarán and Cava 1981, 1984). The deposits were 2.50 m deep and comprised six layers of differing thickness and density of occupation. Two of these may be ascribed to the geometric Epi-Palacolithic (laycr d, 70cm thick, 'carly' or gcneric Epi-Palaeolithic; layer c3, 30–60 cm thick, full Epi-Palaeolithic), two to the Cardial Neolithic (layers c2, c1), and two others to the Chalcolithic/Bronze Age (layers b, a).

In addition to these sites, we have studied the deposits in the Montico de Charratu rock-shelter (Albaina/Treviño, province of Burgos) and those in the Abauntz cave (Arraiz, province of Navarra). Other sites which can be drawn into discussion of these problems include: Arenaza I, Santimamiñe and Ekain on the Atlantic façade of the Basque area; Poeymaü, Bignalats, le Mas d'Azil or La Tourasse on the northern slopes of the Pyrenees; and Sant Gregori de Falset, L'Areny, Reclau Viver and Bora Gran on the Mediterranean coast (*Fig. 1*).

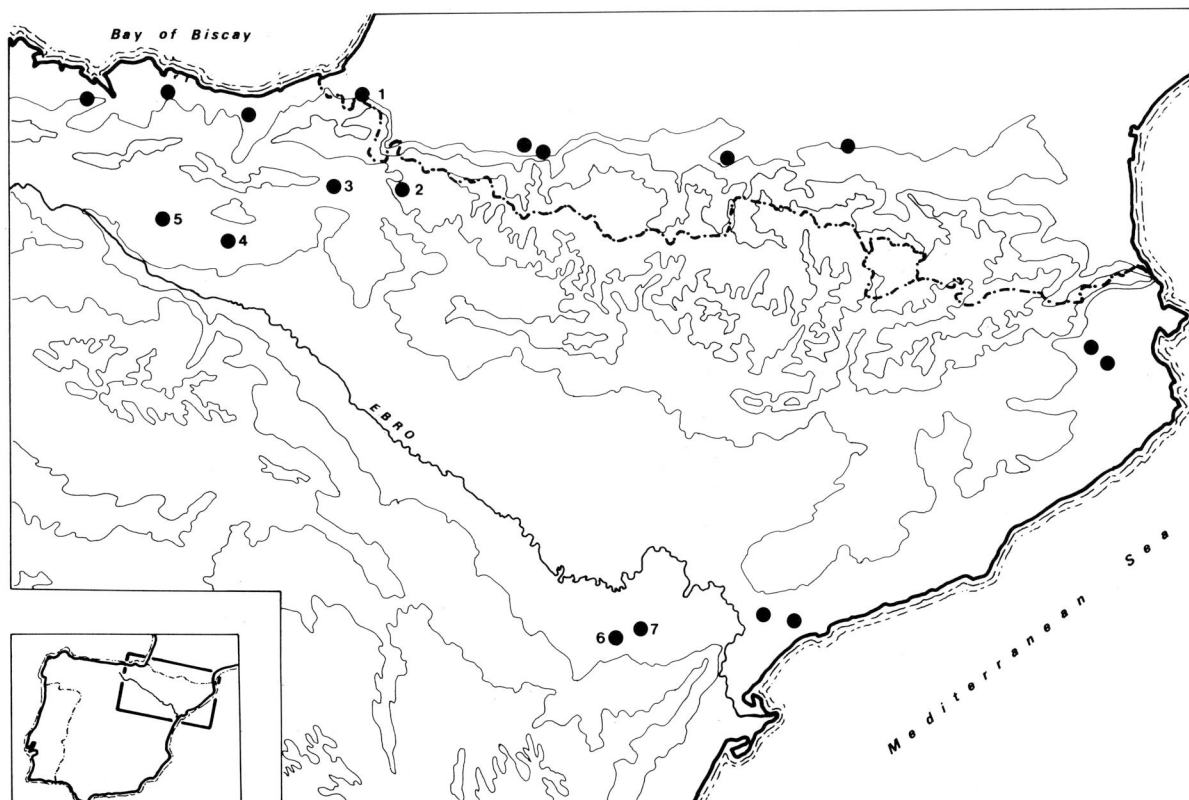

Figure 1 The Ebro basin showing the sites referred to in the text: 1 – Berroberría; 2 – Zatoya; 3 – Abauntz; 4 – La Peña; 5 – Montico de Charratu; 6 – Botiquería dels Moros; 7 – Costalena.

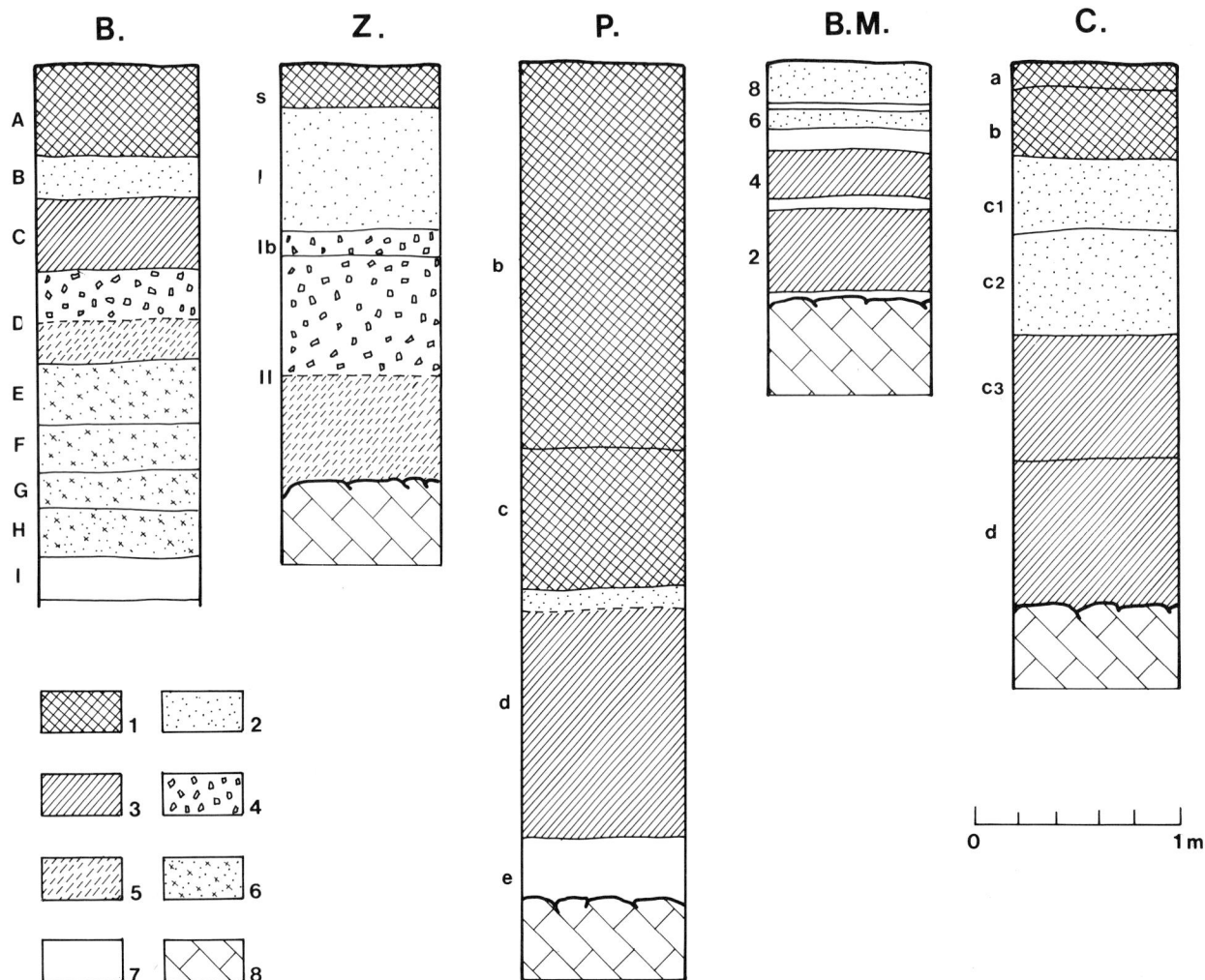

Figure 2 Schematic sections of Berroberría (B), Zatoya (Z), La Peña (P), Botiquería dels Moros (BM), and Costalena (C). *Key*: 1–Post-Neolithic; 2 – Neolithic; 3 – Geometric Epi-Palaeolithic; 4 – Micro-laminar Epi-Palaeolithic; 5 – Azilian; 6 – Lateglacial deposit; 7 – sterile layers; 8 – bedrock.

As yet, we have not found any open-air sites which display stratification.

It must be emphasized that most of these sites have been excavated in the last fifteen years; some are still being dug (Arenaza, Poeymaü), and for others final reports have not yet appeared (Zatoya, La Peña, Costalena).

THE ARCHAEOLOGICAL HORIZONS, THE SITES AND THEIR SETTINGS

Stratigraphic sequences

The superposition of the archaeological horizons identified so far follows the model presented in *Fig. 2*. In general, the initial occupation of the sites took place early in the Holocene. Thus, the Epi-Palaeolithic horizons are found established either directly on bedrock or on sterile basal deposits (La Peña, Zatoya, Botiquería, Costalena). The very high altitude of the sites and the severity of the climate – in brief, the interior location – made the Ebro basin a territory little utilized by Lateglacial human populations. Only the Berroberría cave on the Atlantic littoral and at an altitude of less than 100 m has produced an important assemblage of classic Magdalenian and Azilian material.

The Epi-Palaeolithic horizons are succeeded by Neolithic deposits; this later material, apart from the inclusion of a ceramic component, is not well defined. Only in the south part of the study area (Botiquería, Costalena) can these horizons be ascribed to the Cardial Neolithic. There is no indication of either animal domestication or agricultural activity before the seventh millennium BP.

It is possible to suggest various subdivisions within the Epi-Palaeolithic (or Mesolithic) of this region, on the basis of stratigraphy or typology. On present evidence, three broad subdivisions can be proposed. In theory, these represent chronologically successive stages, although this is not necessarily so everywhere. The first period is the early or generic Epi-Palaeolithic (non-geometric); the second is the geometric Epi-Palaeolithic; and the third includes a few indications of the beginnings of the Neolithic. Tentatively, they may be correlated with the early Epi-Palaeolithic, middle Epi-Palaeolithic and Mesolithic (Tardenoisian, Sauveterrian, etc.) as proposed by some prehistorians for southern France. Their correlation with the two *facies* of the Epi-Palaeolithic proposed by Fortea (1973) for the Spanish Levant is no more straightforward.

The archaeological horizons in the Ebro valley which are the subject of this paper have an overall time-range from the end of the Lateglacial (Younger Dryas), through the Pre-Boreal and Boreal, to end at the beginning of the Atlantic. In the Zatoya cave a thick stalagmite deposit may be noted between layer Ib (Boreal) and layer I (Atlantic). In the Botiquería rock-shelter it would appear that layers with evidence of fairly intensive occupation (layers 2, 4, 6, 8) are interstratified with others which contain much slighter indications of use or represent periods of abandonment (layers 3, 5, 7).

Absolute chronology

Available dates are few in number. Samples from Berroberría and La Peña are currently being processed by the British Museum laboratory. There are seven acceptable dates for the Zatoya cave. These fall into three series: for the early Epi-Palaeolithic (layer II, lower) – 11,840±240 BP (Ly-1400), 11,620±360 BP (Ly-1599), 11,480±270 BP (Ly-1399), and a fourth determination of 10,940 BP or earlier (Ly-1458); for an advanced stage of the Epi-Palaeolithic (layer Ib) – 8260±550 BP (Ly-1457) and 8150±220 BP (Ly-1398); and for the Neolithic with geometric traits (layer I) – 6320±280 BP (Ly-1397). The Abauntz cave has produced the following dates (Utrilla 1982): for the Lower Magdalenian horizon – 15,800±350 BP (Ly-1965); for layer d/c, Epi-Palaeolithic – 9530±300 BP (Ly-1964); for layer c, Neolithic – 6910±450 BP (I-11,537); for layer b4, middle/late Neolithic – 5390±120 BP (I-11,309); and for a funerary deposit attributable to the Chalcolithic – 4240±140 BP (Ly-1963). The geometric Epi-Palaeolithic level in the Botiquería rock-shelter has been dated to 7550±200 BP (Ly-1198).

In a recent paper the radiocarbon dates for Zatoya were correlated with isotopic dates for 21 sites spread along the Atlantic coast of Spain as far as the northern slopes of the Pyrenees (Barandiarán 1982*a*). However, the cultural stratification of each of these sites has sometimes been presented in such an ambiguous fashion that the Epi-Palaeolithic appears to extend over six millennia. The paucity of the assemblages recovered and their often atypical character, as well as the high proportion of basic tool types (i.e. those which tend to be culturally and chronologically undiagnostic), account for this rather unreliable diagnosis.

The character of the landscape

The known sites in the Ebro basin occur in widely differing circumstances with regard to altitude, relief, rainfall and vegetation, and hence can be characterized in terms of climate and landscape context. Zatoya is at 900 m, whereas Botiquería is at only 300 m; annual rainfall at Berroberría is 1800 mm, whereas at Botiquería hardly 300 mm falls.

The characteristics of the area thus allow us to assign the sites to a number of different climatic zones: oceanic (Berroberría, Ekain, Santimamiñe, Arenaza); sub-alpine with oceanic tendencies (Abauntz, Zatoya, Bignalats, Poeymaü, La Tourasse, le Mas d'Azil); oceanic–Mediterranean transition (Montico, La Peña); Mediterranean interior or continental (Botiquería, Costalena); and Mediterranean coastal (Sant Gregori, L'Areny, Reclau Viver, Bora Gran). All sites share a preference for locations with relatively easy access. From each of them, little effort was required to reach territories rich in a variety of resources (grassland, open spaces, woodland, and rocky areas). Each site is close to a perennial river with adequate fish stocks; not long ago there were still salmon around Berroberría, trout near La Peña and Abauntz, and other species at Costalena and Botiquería. Even in the most arid part of Lower Aragon, the Matarraña and Algas rivers (near to the sites of Costalena and Botiquería) continue to flow during the dry months – in an area with only 50 days of rain per year.

At the present day there are game reserves less than 50 km from some of the sites – for migratory birds (e.g. at Berroberría, close to the ring-dove (*Columba palumbus*) migration route from the Navarre Pyrenees) or for big game (as in Lower Aragon near the ibex reserve of Maestrazgo and Beceite; or Zatoya, near the central Pyrenees). The Atlantic coast is no more than two hours' walk from Berroberría, and the Mediterranean some two days from Costalena or Botiquería.

The only palynological studies available for the early Holocene in neighbouring areas are those for the Duruthy cave (Landes, France – studied by M.M. Paquereau), the Moura/Biarritz peat moss (Pyrénées Atlantiques – studied by F. Oldfield), the Poeymaü cave (Pyrénées Atlantiques – studied by F. Lévêque), and the Ekain cave (Guipúzcoa – studied by M. Dupré). Analyses for the caves at La Peña and Zatoya are currently being undertaken by P. López (Consejo Superior de Investigaciones Científicas) and A. Boyer-Klein (Musée de l'Homme), respectively. Samples from Botiquería and Costalena proved to be sterile.

A total of 3978 pollen grains and spores were counted by P. López from Abauntz. These comprised four series of samples reflecting the evolution of the landscape from the end of the Younger Dryas through the Pre-Boreal. An arboreal component initially dominated by conifers gave way to one in which these trees were accompanied by hazel (*Corylus*), some birch (*Betula*), alder (*Alnus*) and oak (*Quercus*); this latter assemblage was characteristic of the Epi-Palaeolithic. Amongst herbaceous plants, Cichoriae were more common than Gramineae, with

a rise in Carduaceae amongst the Compositae; these changes indicate a rise in both temperature and humidity.

At Berroberría, Boyer-Klein studied 8334 pollen grains and spores from 22 samples. Of these, four belonged to the lower part of layer D (Azilian), four to layer D ('evolved' Azilian), and two to layer C

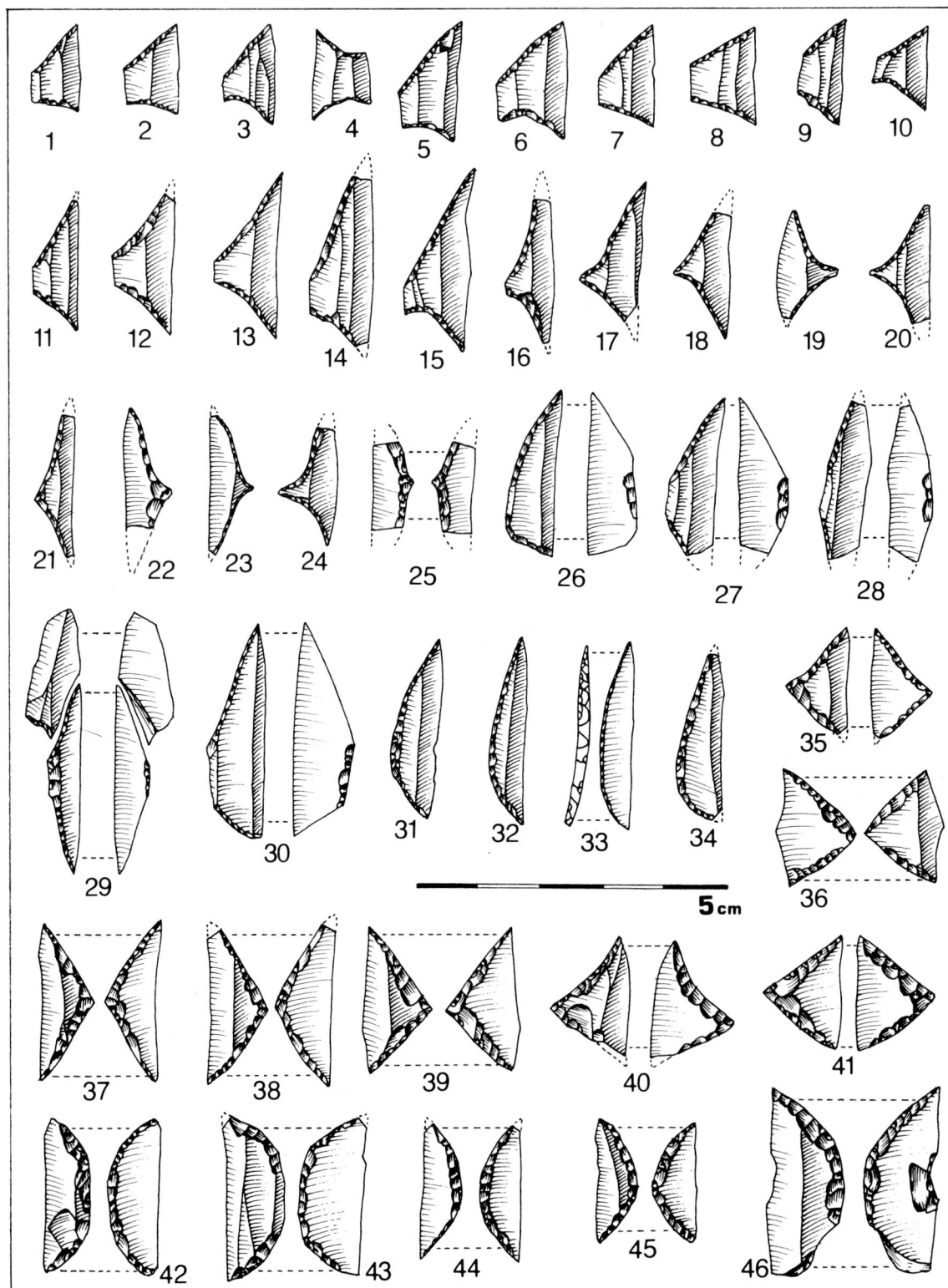

Figure 3   Selected geometric pieces from the Epi-Palaeolithic (nos. 1–12, 17–22, a6–32, 38) and Neolithic Cardial levels (nos. 23–35, 33–37, 39–46) at Botiquería (nos. 7–10, 12, 17, 21, 22, 35, 36, 38, 46) and Costalena (nos. 1–6, 11, 18–20, 23–34, 37, 39–45).

(geometric Epi-Palaeolithic). The series is completed by samples from the Neolithic (layers B, BA) and Chalcolithic/Bronze Age levels (layer A). Boyer-Klein's conclusions are that the lower part of layer D belongs to the Allerød interstadial (c. 11,800 BP) and is marked by a clear rise in the proportion of trees (and thus of humidity); whilst the upper part of layer D and the lower part of layer C indicate conditions of considerable wetness with a cold episode (layer D, upper) which may correspond to the Younger Dryas. The Pre-Boreal should be represented by the basal part of layer C.

The animal remains from layer d at Abauntz include amongst ungulates, red deer, a large bovid,

		E	P	B	BP	BB	D	T	G	mb	m		
B	D lr	.132 / 7	.057 / 3	.133 / 6	.075 / 4	.189 / 10	.170 / 9	0	0	0	.264 / 14	53	[1]
	D upr	.150 / 6	.025 / 1	.075 / 3	.100 / 4	.300 / 12	.125 / 5	0	.025 / 1	0	.200 / 8	40	[1]
Z	II	.207 / 135	.011 / 7	.089 / 58	.041 / 27	.434 / 283	.049 / 32	.021 / 14	.012 / 8	.005 / 3	.130 / 85	652	[1]
	Ib	.154 / 24	.032 / 5	.077 / 12	.071 / 11	.244 / 38	.179 / 28	.019 / 3	.026 / 4	.006 / 1	.192 / 30	156	[1]
	I	.149 / 52	.029 / 10	.066 / 23	.040 / 14	.083 / 29	.169 / 59	.032 / 11	.252 / 88	.046 / 16	.136 / 47	349	[1]
P	d	.085 / 11	.015 / 2	.023 / 3	.038 / 5	.031 / 4	.138 / 18	.015 / 2	.338 / 44	.231 / 30	.085 / 11	130	[1]
M	lr	090 / 6	0	.015 / 1	.164 / 11	.254 / 17	.075 / 5	0	0	0	.403 / 27	67	[1]
	upr	.200 / 11	0	.036 / 2	.073 / 4	.055 / 3	.236 / 13	.055 / 3	.164 / 9	.073 / 4	.109 / 6	55	[1]
A	d	.156 / 12	.026 / 2	.065 / 5	.065 / 5	.416 / 32	.104 / 8	.065 / 5	0	0	.104 / 8	77	[1]
BM	2	.082 / 24	.010 / 3	.017 / 5	.051 / 15	.065 / 19	.281 / 82	.062 / 18	.253 / 74	.099 / 29	.079 / 23	292	[1]
	4	.121 / 13	.028 / 3	0	.065 / 7	.112 / 12	.234 / 25	.037 / 4	.196 / 21	.103 / 11	.103 / 11	107	[1]
	6+8	.065 / 7	.056 / 6	0	.093 / 10	.037 / 4	.287 / 31	.046 / 5	.259 / 28	.009 / 1	.148 / 16	108	[1]
C	d	.125 / 9	.083 / 6	0	.042 / 3	.056 / 4	.222 / 16	.056 / 4	.042 / 3	.056 / 4	.319 / 23	72	[1]
	c3	.115 / 62	.026 / 14	.009 / 5	.026 / 14	.048 / 26	.237 / 128	.037 / 20	.187 / 101	.163 / 88	.150 / 81	539	[1]
	c2	.124 / 34	.029 / 8	.022 / 6	.033 / 9	.185 / 51	.193 / 53	.022 / 6	.200 / 55	.058 / 16	.135 / 37	275	[1]
		413	70	129	143	544	512	95	436	203	427	2972	

Figure 4 Typological composition of the lithic industries found at: Berroberría (B), Zatoya (Z), La Peña (P), Montico de Charratu (M), Abauntz (A), Botiquería dels Moros (B.M.) and Costalena (C). The types considered are: end-scrapers (E); piercers (P); burins (B); backed pieces (BP); backed bladelets (BB); denticulates (D); truncated pieces (T); geometric pieces (G); microburins (mb); and miscellaneous tools (M).

ibex and Pyrenean chamois; other mammals include bear, wild cat and marten. Analysis of the ages of the animals shows two clear cases where the kill was made between May and June – an ibex and a red deer fawn hunted during their first month of life. Wild boar were already present by the 'early' Neolithic.

Preliminary examination of the Zatoya faunal assemblage indicates the hunting of ungulates between April and September. At Botiquería and Costalena the most commonly hunted animals were red deer, wild boar and rabbit, while roe deer, chamois and horse were taken only occasionally. Species hunted at La Peña included wild boar, roe deer, ibex, Pyrenean chamois, rabbit and a large bovid; wild cat is also represented at this site.

THE STONE INDUSTRIES

The only archaeological remains which are sufficiently common to merit detailed study as an industry are those of flaked stone. Despite all the difficulties inherent in such an approach, typology is the sole means available by which to identify the essential cultural traits of the period and to achieve some chronological perspective. Much more difficult to achieve is the definition of points of contact and diffusion routes, as well as the frequency and intensity of exchanges.

Primary material

Chauchat (1973) has documented the transport of certain varieties of Cretaceous flint, from both the Labourd coastal area and the Bidache area, to inland Upper Palaeolithic sites. It is possible that the same sources of flint were exploited by the inhabitants of Berroberría.

Most of the worked pieces from Zatoya came from outcrops less than one kilometre's walk from the site.

Botiquería and Costalena display the use of different source materials according to the types of implement being produced. Small implements requiring carefully-executed retouch (geometric pieces and related forms, such as notched blades and microburins) were made from a fine-grained flint, perhaps imported to the site, whilst the heavier equipment was made from hard rocks available locally.

Certain sites (Abauntz, La Peña, Zatoya) were temporary, whilst others (Botiquería or Costalena, perhaps) were used for longer periods. In these two Lower Aragon sites a number of working areas could be identified, marked by the different stages of tool production and use through to the discard of worn tools.

Typology

Certain of the statistics presented in our previous publications were provisional, being based largely on inventories made at the time of excavation. One of us (Cava 1987) is presently completing a systematic revision of all assemblages, based on more uniform criteria of classification. This accounts for the differences between some of the totals shown in *Fig. 4* and those presented in publications between 1977 and 1984. *Fig. 4* displays the number of items in each typological group and their frequency in the various horizons under consideration. The general typological groupings follow those proposed by J. Fortea (1973).

The lithic industries from the different Epi-Palaeolithic horizons at Zatoya show a more or less constant percentage across the various archaeological layers of the 'basic' tool types – end-scrapers, piercers, burins, truncated pieces and miscellaneous pieces – although end-scrapers and burins tend to decline in significance in the upper layers of the sequence. The group which shows the most variation is backed bladelets. Although the proportion of backed flakes and blades remains more or less constant in all three layers, backed bladelets show a progressive decline in numbers; while they represent almost half the tools in layer II, they have declined to a quarter by layer Ib, and account for less than 10% in layer I. The notched and denticulated pieces are quite rare in layers Ib and I. Geometric pieces form an insignificant component of the layer II and Ib assemblages, but account for a quarter of all tools in layer I. Microburins follow the same pattern, although they are still not numerous in layer I.

Layer d in the rock-shelter of La Peña represents a transitional stage between the Epi-Palaeolithic and the Neolithic. In the upper part of this layer both pottery and geometric pieces with *double biseau* retouch appear. The industry is typical of the geometric Epi-Palaeolithic – geometric microliths (c. 33% of the total) and microburins (c. 25%) represent over half the tools. The notched and denticulated pieces (a group related directly to the manufacture of geometric pieces) are also well represented (almost 14% of the total). The other typological groups are quantitatively less important; end-scrapers and miscellaneous tools represent 8.5% and other categories less than 4% of the total.

At Montico de Charratu the six layers have been grouped into two series. The *lower series* (layers VI–IV) is characterized by an industry consisting of a small number of typological groups dominated by backed pieces (more than 40% of the tools) with an emphasis on small forms. These are associated with an interesting suite of large tools (*coins*[1], core-like end-scrapers, 'rabots'). The distinguishing characteristic of the *upper series* (layers III–I) is the heterogeneity shown by the assemblages from the different layers.

At Botiquería dels Moros there are four layers containing a geometric *facies* interstratified with sterile layers representing brief episodes when the shelter was not in use. The lithic industry is constant through all the levels – the most important components are the geometric pieces (microliths and microburins), and the notched and denticulated pieces; but the basic elements (end-scrapers, piercers, truncated pieces, and backed pieces) are always present, if only in small numbers. Burins are restricted to the earliest layer and even then occur only in limited numbers.

The Costalena sequence exhibits the same stages as at Botiquería, but with some distinctive features: (i) layer d belongs to an earlier stage of the full Epi-Palaeolithic than that represented by layer c3, with a small proportion of geometric items; (ii) layers c2 and c1, already fully Neolithic with impressed pots (some of Cardial type), are overlain by two other layers (layers b, a) attributable to the Chalcolithic, although the associated assemblages are very small. The proportions of the different typological groups at Costalena are similar to those at Botiquería, with a strong representation of geometric elements, as well as notched and denticulated pieces and a more or less constant percentage of basic elements (end-scrapers are relatively abundant and backed bladelets continue to form almost 20% of the tools, even in the Neolithic horizon – layer c2).

Analysis of the geometric tools in the Botiquería and Costalena sequences

The composition of the geometric component in the assemblages from these two sites is summarized in (*Fig. 5*).

	◢	◣	◺	◗	Totals
BM.2	57 •851	7 •104	3 •045		67 ¹
BM.4	8 •381	9 •429	4 •190		21 ¹
BM.8	6 •231	17 •654		3 •115	26 ¹
C.d	2	1			3 ¹
C.c3	80 •784	11 •108	11 •108		102 ¹
C.c2	14 •255	30 •545	6 •139	5 •091	55 ¹

	BM.2	BM.4	BM.6&8	Co.C3	Co.C2
Abrupt	73 •986	17 •810	9 •321	85 ¹	19 •396
Double biseau	1 •014	4 •190	19 •679	0	29 •604
Totals	74 ¹	21 ¹	28 ¹	86 ¹	48 ¹

Figure 5 Geometric pieces found at Botiquería in layers 2, 4 and 6/8, and at Costalena in layers d, c3 and c2.

Types represented

In the early horizons trapezes are numerically much more important than triangles. Towards the Neolithic, trapezes gradually become less important and triangles increase in number, attaining their maximum frequency in Cardial levels (layer c2 at Costalena; layers 6 and 8 at Botiquería). Segments are restricted to the Neolithic, whereas triangles with two concave sides and a central (lateral) spine (Muge- or Cocina-type triangles – cf. Brézillon 1971: 374) are present in both Epi-Palaeolithic and Neolithic contexts.

Types of retouch

It is necessary to distinguish between geometric pieces that have been shaped by abrupt retouch and those on which the retouch is non-abrupt and bifacial (retouch of Helwan or *double biseau* type).[2] In Epi-Palaeolithic horizons, the retouch is almost exclusively abrupt – 99% of geometric pieces in layer 2 and 81% of those in layer 4 at Botiquería, and 100% of those in layer c3 at Costalena. In the Neolithic levels *double biseau* retouch is predominant, although a significant proportion of the geometric pieces still have abrupt retouch. Thus, of those in layers 6 and 8 at Botiquería, 68% have *double biseau* retouch and 32% have abrupt retouch; in layer c2 at Costalena the figures are 60% and 40%, respectively.

There is some correlation between the type of retouch and the types of geometric tools found. In general, trapezes (the predominant type during the Epi-Palaeolithic) are shaped by abrupt retouch, whereas *double biseau* retouch is more frequent on triangles and true segments from Neolithic levels.

THE EVOLUTION OF THE REGIONAL EPI-PALAEOLITHIC/MESOLITHIC: FACIES AND DYNAMISM

In 1982 we proposed (Barandiarán 1982*b*) three main migration routes for the Basque Mesolithic/Epi-Palaeolithic populations in their search for localities with an adequate subsistence base (as seasonal settlements): (i) towards tidal zones along the coast to take advantage of the sea, inshore fishing and shellfish collecting on rocky shores; (ii) towards deciduous woodland and its margins where large herbivores were available for hunting, together with smaller animals and abundant plant food resources; and (iii) towards inland regions higher and further from the coast, both on the Mediterranean side and in the foothills of the Pyrenees. Thus Zatoya, Abauntz and Montico de Charratu are more than 50 km from the sea, and many sites are at altitudes above 450/500 metres. This altitudinal band was hardly ever exceeded during the Upper Palaeolithic.

We believe that this model of the process of expansion from the Basque area during the Holocene can be extended with equal validity to the populations of the Pyrenean region and of the Ebro basin. This dynamism may have produced more frequent opportunities for exchange and cultural contact than existed in the Upper Palaeolithic; solid evidence of this is provided by the 'exotic' items in the assemblages recovered in our excavations. Such mechanisms of contact could also account for the few typologically or technologically distinctive items amongst the lithic assemblages which do not seem to be of local origin. The same would apply to the pendants made from perforated shells of *Columbella rustica* of Mediterranean origin; these occur with geometric microlithic industries at three sites – Zatoya, Fuente Hoz and Padre Areso.

Any model of cultural dynamism in the Ebro basin ought, in our opinion, to be based on the following considerations:

1. This region was virtually uninhabited during the Lateglacial (and perhaps even throughout the Upper Palaeolithic). It is only with the climatic improvement of the Allerød and, more particularly, from the beginning of the Holocene that we see the large-scale arrival of populations from neighbouring areas – from both Atlantic and Mediterranean coasts undoubtedly and, less certainly, from the north side of the Pyrenees.

2. The cultural traditions of the incomers must have had to be adapted to the exploitation systems of the new areas, whilst at the same time maintaining the tradition of settlement in caves and rock-shelters. Thus basic economic strategies (which must inevitably have led to a gradual depletion of the natural resources) continued to develop; for the moment, there is no good evidence of any form of agriculture or stock-raising until quite an advanced stage of the regional Neolithic.

3. Thus, there was a continuum of local technology and subsistence; this 'residual' behaviour survived for three millennia, from *c.* 10,500/10,000 to *c.* 7500/7000 BP. It is for this reason that we prefer the term *Epi-Palaeolithic* to Mesolithic. In any case, Neolithic innovations in the study area are marked not by the appearance of a coherent cultural package but by the slow and sporadic appearance of introduced traits.

4. Consequently, in our opinion, only the flaked stone industry adequately reflects developments during this period.

Our French colleagues on the other side of the Pyrenees (e.g. Sacchi 1976) tend to divide the material from the Epi-Palaeolithic/Mesolithic into three successive blocs: Epi-Palaeolithic *sensu stricto*, including Azilian and Epi-Magdalenian; full Mesolithic or Sauveterrian; and late or evolved Mesolithic or even Proto-Neolithic ('Post-Sauveterrian', 'Tardenoisoid'). It is true that on the north side of the Pyrenees, as in the Ebro basin, detailed stratigraphical sequences in which this process can be documented with precision are not common – with the exception, perhaps, of those from Dourgne (Aude), La Tourasse (excavated long ago by the Orliacs), and Poeymaü (currently being excavated by G. Laplace and M. Livache). In any case, careful stratigraphical study throws up some ambiguous cultural situations at the end of the Lateglacial. We do not know whether these are instances of wider patterns of cultural evolution or are simply applicable to local circumstances; examples would include what have been called Magdalenian VIb or VII or Epi-Magdalenian (as studied in detail by Sacchi at the grotte de Gazel). The stratigraphy at Poeymaü also suggests the same sort of complexity for the Epi-Palaeolithic.

For the Ebro basin, we have proposed the following basic scheme for the evolution of the Epi-Palaeolithic/Mesolithic since 1977 (Barandiarán 1977):

I   Typical or generic Azilian (lower part of layer D at Berroberría, perhaps).
    Early Epi-Palaeolithic, 'Epi-Magdalenian' or 'Aziloid' (layer II at Zatoya and layer d at Abauntz).

II Micro-laminar or generic Epi-Palaeolithic (upper part of layer D at Berroberría, layer Ib at Zatoya, and the lower layers at Montico). An Epi-Palaeolithic of geometric *facies* (layer c3 at Costalena, layers 2 and 4 at Botiquería, layer C at Berroberría, and layer d at La Peña).

III Geometric Epi-Palaeolithic 'with pottery' ('Neolithic') (layer I at Zatoya, layers c2 and c1 at Costalena, and layers 6 and 8 at Botiquería).

Notes:

1. For a definition of this artifact type, see Brézillon 1971: 196–197. (Ed.)

2. This type of retouch, commonly known as 'Helwan' retouch, is also characteristic of geometric microliths found in Natufian contexts in the Near East; see also Brézillon 1971: 252. (Ed.)

Acknowledgements: The Editor is grateful to Ian Ralston (Department of Archaeology, University of Edinburgh) for producing the basic English translation of the original French manuscript, and to Brian Barron (Department of French, University of Edinburgh) for additional help with the English translation. Responsibility for any errors in translation rests with the Editor.

References

BARANDIARÁN, I. (1977) El proceso de transición Epipaleolítico–Neolítico en la cueva de Zatoya. *Príncipe de Viana*, 146–147: 5–46.

BARANDIARÁN, I. (1978) El abrigo de La Botiquería dels Moros. Mazaleón (Teruel). Excavaciones arqueológicas de 1974. *Cuaderno de Prehistoria y Arqueología Castellonense*, 5: 49–138.

BARANDIARÁN, I. (1979a) Excavaciones en el covacho de Berroberría (Urdax). Campaña de 1977. *Trabajos de Arqueología Navarra*, 1: 11–60.

BARANDIARÁN, I. (1979b) Azilien and post-Azilien dans le Pays Basque méridional. In D. de Sonneville-Bordes (ed.), *La Fin des Temps Glaciaires en Europe*. Paris, Centre National de la Recherche Scientifique.

BARANDIARÁN, I. (1982a) Datación por el C-14 de la cueva de Zatoya. *Trabajos de Arqueología Navarra*, 3: 43–57.

BARANDIARÁN, I. (1982b) Los comienzos del Holoceno en la Prehistoria vasca. *Cuaderno de Seccida Antropología. Prehistoria. Eusko–Ikaskuntza*, 1: 239–258.

BARANDIARÁN, I. and CAVA, A. (1981) Epipaleolítico y Neolítico en el abrigo de Costalena (Bajo Aragón). *Bajo Aragón. Prehistoria*, 3: 5–20.

BARANDIARÁN, I. and CAVA, A. (1984) Las industrias líticas del Epipaleolítico y del Neolítico en el Bajo Aragón. *Bajo Aragón. Prehistoria*, 5: 95–123.

BEGUIRISTAIN, M.A. and CAVA, A. (1985) Excavaciones en el abrigo de La Peña (Marañón, Navarra). Informe preliminar. *Trabajos de Arqueología Navarra*, 4: 7–18.

BRÉZILLON, M.N. (1971) *La Dénomination des Objets de Pierre Taillée* (2nd edition). Paris, Centre National de la Recherche Scientifique.

CAVA, A. (1987) La industria lítica de la Prehistoria reciente en la cuenca del Ebro. *Boletín del Museo de Zaragozà*, 5: 5–72.

CHAUCHAT, C. (1973) La grotte Lezia à Sare. *Bulletin du Musée Basque de Bayonne*, 61: 155–166.

FORTEA, J. (1973) *Los Complejos Microlaminares y Geométricos del Epipaleolítico Mediterráneo Español* (Memorias del Seminario de Prehistoria y Arqueología). Salamanca, Universidad de Salamanca.

SACCHI, D. (1976) Les civilisations de l'Epipaléolithique et du Mésolithique en Languedoc occidental (Bassin de l'Aude) et en Roussillon. In H. de Lumley (ed.), *La Préhistoire Française*, tome 1. Paris, Centre National de la Recherche Scientifique: 1390–1397.

UTRILLA, P. (1982) El yacimiento de la cueva de Abauntz (Arraiz, Navarra). *Trabajos de Arqueología Navarra*, 3: 203–345.

Thoughts on the Transition from the Magdalenian to the Azilian in Cantabria: Evidence from the Cueva de Los Azules, Asturias

Juan A. Fernández-Tresguerres Velasco

Abstract

Rich Azilian assemblages have been recovered from three levels within the cave of Los Azules (Cangas de Onis, Asturias, Spain), making it possible to trace certain aspects of the technological evolution of the Azilian during the eleventh and tenth millennia BP. An analysis of some of these aspects, such as the utilization of primary materials for the manufacture of tools, suggests that the Azilian reflects a trend towards technological simplification; it shows a marked pragmatism, linked to the appearance of the composite tool. Whilst marking the beginning of the process of transition from the Palaeolithic, the Azilian already shows characteristics typical of Epi-Palaeolithic industries.

INTRODUCTION

Several aspects of the evidence from the cueva de Los Azules – its location, industries and burial evidence – have been described in some detail in previous publications (Fernández-Tresguerres 1976, 1979, 1980); while elsewhere the present author has summarized the development of the Epi-Palaeolithic in the Cantabrian region (GTPC 1979; Fernández-Tresguerres 1983). In this paper it is proposed to document various trends which mark the transition from the Magdalenian to the Azilian, using the evidence from Los Azules. The conclusions can only be provisional, since the research is still in progress; nevertheless, certain facts stand out clearly.

Although relying here on the finds from a single site, these appear to confirm the conclusions reached on the basis of previous work on the Azilian in the provinces of Asturias and Santander (Fernández-Tresguerres 1980). Moreover, it should not be forgotten that these provinces, situated at the western extremity of the Franco-Cantabrian Palaeolithic region, show a marked similarity to the rest of the region from an industrial point of view, whilst retaining an identity of their own.

The excavations carried out at Los Azules during the summer of 1983 have contributed some important data which have provided a clearer insight into the process of the transition from the Magdalenian to the Azilian. It is this process which is the fundamental concern of this paper.

THE STRATIGRAPHY

The upper layers (1–4) have been described in previous publications, and will be referred to only briefly here:

Layer 1. This layer is archaeologically sterile; it consists of yellowish, clayey sediments which filled in the cave after the human occupations.

Layer 2. This is a reddish clay containing a sparse Azilian industry, and has possibly been derived from the remains of an occupation immediately outside the cave.

Layer 3. This layer is almost a metre thick and represents a long period of human occupation. It contains a very abundant Azilian industry, and has been divided into five sub-units.

Layer 4. The yellowish clay which forms layer 4 is archaeologically sterile. It decreases in thickness, and almost disappears, towards the rear of the entrance chamber of the cave.

Layer 5. This deposit was encountered during the 1983 excavations. The underlying Magdalenian level was channeled by a small stream, and the channel infilled by sediments containing remains of an Azilian occupation. Four horizons with hearths and spreads of ashes were identified in this layer, although the Azilian assemblages from the different levels form an essentially homogeneous industry.

Layer 6. This is composed of a reddish clay and contains a Magdalenian industry with harpoons.

Layer 7. This is a dark-reddish clay, containing a Magdalenian industry. Only the surface of the layer has been excavated so far, but on the basis of the lithic and bone artifacts recovered it would appear to belong to the Upper Magdalenian.

Thus, three layers containing Azilian industries have been found at Los Azules. The most recent corresponds to an occupation outside the cave, which was destroyed partly by erosion and partly as a result of human activities after the site was discovered. Very little survives of this occupation, which is represented by the few artifacts found in layer 2. These are insufficient to reveal the precise characteristics of the industry.

The characteristics of the industry from layer 3 can be determined in much greater detail, by virtue of the thickness of the deposit and the richness of its archaeological inventory. Although it shows considerable homogeneity, it is nevertheless possible to pick out certain details which are indicative of trends in the development of the Azilian industry (see Fernández-Tresguerres 1980).

Layer 5, like layer 4, was formed during a colder episode than that represented by layer 3. It is evident, therefore, that the Azilian appeared in the Cantabrian region when conditions were colder than those which obtained during the Pre-Boreal – that is, during the final stages of Dryas III. The industry from layer 5, although clearly Azilian, shows some striking differences from those in the overlying layers, which may be of significance for our understanding of the evolution of the Azilian.

Layer 6 (Magdalenian) is still under study and, although it is not yet possible to offer a detailed description of the composition of the assemblage, enough is known for it to be used as a point of reference. The most diagnostic elements are harpoons with a single row of barbs, characteristic of the final Magdalenian. Moreover, some of the harpoons and a few of the spear-points are decorated.

THE CHRONOLOGY

A series of radiocarbon dates are available for layer 3 (*Table 1*). Dates on samples from layers 5 and 6 are

Table 1: Radiocarbon dates for Azilian levels at Los Azules

Lab. No.	Layer	Date BP
CSIC-216	3a	9430±120
CSIC-260	3d	9540±120
BM-1879R	3cs	10,510±130
BM-1875R	3e1	10,480±210
BM-1876R	3e2	10,880±210
BM-1877R	3e3	11,320±360
BM-1878R	3f	10,910±290

still awaited from the British Museum radiocarbon laboratory. The dates produced by the British Museum laboratory for layer 3 at Los Azules are in agreement with those for the Cantabrian Azilian obtained from other Cantabrian and Pyrenean sites (*Table 2*).

The total of dates available for the Cantabrian Azilian is not very large, but the majority fall within the twelfth and eleventh millennia BP. It is possible that the lowermost Azilian levels of the cueva de Los Azules date to the beginning of the eleventh or the end of the twelfth millennium BP (the date of 11,320 BP for layer 3 of Los Azules seems too old).

From the climatic point of view the Azilian belongs to the later part of Dryas III and the Pre-Boreal, coinciding with the spread of forest vegetation which would have brought about some important changes in the behaviour of human groups.

THE INDUSTRY

The artifacts found in the Azilian levels at Los Azules are very abundant. The total number of tools recovered is more than 5000, while items of débitage exceed 500,000. Most of the material has been examined, but the analysis is still not complete. However, the main trends can be discerned; these are generally in accord with observations made elsewhere in the Cantabrian region.

The primary materials

The selection and mode of working of the primary materials are basic elements governing the character of an industry.

The study of the primary materials can provide a great deal of information about the character of a human group. It is often said that the Azilian is an impoverished culture compared to the Magdalenian; with a particular way of life already exhausted, the Azilian is regarded as lacking in originality and vitality – an expression of the general degeneration

Table 2: Radiocarbon dates for Azilian levels at sites in Cantabria and the Pyrenees

Site	Lab. No.	Layer	Date BP	Reference
CUEVA DE ZATOYA, Navarra	Ly-1399	II	11,480±270	Barandiarán 1982
	Ly-1599	II	11,620±360	
	Ly-1400	II	11,840±240	
CUEVA D'EKAIN, Guipúzcoa	CSIC-171	III	12,750±250	Altuna and Merino 1984
	CSIC-172	V	13,350±250	
	I-9239	IV	9420±185	
CUEVA D'URTIAGA, Guipúzcoa	CSIC-63	C	8700±100	Altuna 1972
	CSIC-64	C	10,280±190	
CUEVA DE RASCAÑO, Santander	BM-1448	1	10,558±90	Barandiarán and González Echegaray 1981
	BM-1449	1	10,480±244	
CUEVA DE LA RIERA, Asturias	BM-1494	27 Magd./Azil.	10,630±120	Straus et al. 1981

which followed the Magdalenian. This is one possible interpretation, even though it derives from a time when prehistorians were still fascinated by the sophistication of the technology and art of the Magdalenian, soon after its discovery. These preconceptions, however, do not entirely conform to reality.

The primary materials found at Los Azules are flint, quartzite, and quartz. All three can be found within a relatively short distance of the cave and·on the margins of the River Sella. Amongst the débitage recovered from the excavated levels there are a large number of flakes, cores and fragments of cores of the first two materials – flint and quartzite. The percentages are given in *Table 3*.

Table 3: Utilization of primary materials among the products of débitage at Los Azules

Layer	% Flint	% Quartzite	% Quartz
3	50.29	48.23	1.47
5	75.24	24.24	0.50
6	39.48	54.35	6.16
7	46.89	43.26	9.84

Flint and quartzite occur in roughly equal proportions in layer 3 (Azilian) and layer 7 (Magdalenian), although there is a significantly higher percentage of quartz in the Magdalenian layer. On the other hand, in layer 5 (Azilian) flint forms the highest percentage – the inverse of the situation found in layer 6 (Magdalenian). For the moment, little can be deduced from the distribution of the primary materials by layers, except that there is a progressive decrease in the proportion of quartz through the sequence.

An analysis of the distribution of these primary materials according to tool types yields a surprising result (*Table 4*). The balance between quartzite and

Table 4: Utilization of primary materials among the the major tool categories at Los Azules

	% Flint	% Quartzite	% Quartz
LAYER 3:			
Miscellaneous Pieces	55.00	40.43	2.00
End-scrapers	91.24	7.14	1.50
Tools on bladelets	98.14	1.84	–
LAYER 5:			
Miscellaneous pieces	85.41	14.58	–
End-scrapers	97.14	1.42	1.42
Tools on bladelets	98.81	1.18	–
LAYER 6:			
Miscellaneous pieces	48.38	48.38	3.22
End-scrapers	90.62	6.25	3.12
Tools on bladelets	100.00	–	–

flint breaks down, even in the layers in which the former is the most representative material amongst the débitage. The distribution of the materials across the three most important groups of tools found in the Azilian assemblages – miscellaneous pieces (notched, denticulated and splintered pieces), end-scrapers and tools on bladelets (especially backed bladelets and Azilian points) – highlights the imbalance in the percentages.

The distribution of the primary materials by layer for all the tool categories combined is shown in *Table 5*.

Table 5: Utilization of primary materials amongst the finished tools from Los Azules

Layer	% Flint	% Quartzite	% Quartz
3	89.82	9.29	0.82
5	97.14	2.64	0.80
6	85.18	12.59	2.22

Quartzite is important amongst the materials used for the miscellaneous tools, except in layer 5; amongst the other categories of tools, however, its utilization is sporadic – unlike the pattern revealed by the débitage. The raw material composition of layer 6 appears to be similar to that of layer 3, although this resemblance is misleading.

In order to understand the differences which exist between the raw material compositions of the various tool groups, it is necessary to take into consideration the quality of the different types of flint found in the various layers. Is the composition of layer 6 really identical to that of layer 3? Evidently it is not, if the quality of the material is taken into account. Small nodules of reddish radiolarian chert (flint) are available in large quantities in the vicinity of the cave. This is of very poor quality – full of faults and, hence, irregular in the way it fractures. The flakes struck from this flint are also irregular. On the other hand, flint of good quality is very rare in the vicinity of the cave. Both the Magdalenians and the Azilians would have found it easier to obtain the poorer quality material. Nonetheless, they exercised different preferences. The Azilians adopted the simpler solution, restricting themselves to what was immediately to hand. The reasons are uncertain, but the expansion of forests at the end of the Last Glaciation may have made it more difficult to locate the places where good quality flint is more abundant.

In the Magdalenian of layer 6 only 12.08% of the flint débitage is made up of the poor-quality, reddish, radiolarian flint. In layer 5 the percentage increases to 41.07%, and the proportion is greater still in layer 3 – as high as 70%.

This clearly affects the appearance of the industry. In the Magdalenian (layer 6) only 3.44% of the end-scrapers are made of the poor-quality flint and only 4.16% of the backed bladelets; none of the denticulated pieces, splintered pieces or notched pieces is made of this material. In layer 5 the proportion is higher: 30.85% of the end-scrapers, 24.39% of the miscellaneous pieces, and 29.12% of the tools on bladelets.

The significance of this has already been stated – the poor quality of the flint imprints the industry with a wholly distinctive character. The products of flaking are often very coarse and irregular. The result is an industry which is markedly atypical and irregular in terms of its tool morphology. The Azilian thus has the appearance of a very crude industry; from this point of view it is possible to speak of an Azilian degeneration. Regular flaking of a core and the technique of producing bladelets had almost been abandoned. This decline in bladelet technique shows up particularly in the analysis of the rest of the débitage, and it continues to decline towards the end of the Azilian at Los Azules. The frequency of unretouched bladelets in the different levels is shown in *Table 6*.

Table 6: Unretouched bladelets as a proportion of the tools found in the different levels at Los Azules

Layer	% Flint	% Quartzite
3	3.66	2.03
5	6.95	4.30
6	9.45	2.06

To understand the process better, it is necessary to take into account that the toolkit on bladelets increases during the Azilian. This is barely perceptible in *Table 4*. In the Magdalenian levels it is not only the number of bladelets which increases, but their quality and technical perfection; the bladelets are characteristically small, slender and finely curved. These are not found in the Azilian; at this level they become an exotic element. It could be that in the Azilian all the bladelets produced were made into tools, in contrast to what happens in the Magdalenian.

In short, with the appearance of the Azilian a certain pragmatism asserts itself. This is reflected in the apparent indifference shown towards the perfection of stone flaking; and this indifference may explain the more intensive exploitation of primary materials that are poorer in quality but available nearer to the cave, thus achieving a notable saving of time and effort without diminishing the effectiveness of the industry.

The tools

A general description of the lithic toolkit of the Cantabrian Azilian can be found in a previous publication (Fernández-Tresguerres 1980). The Azilian toolkit is characterized above all by small end-scrapers on flakes, backed bladelets and a few Azilian points, with notched, splintered and denticulated pieces present in smaller numbers; burins are rare. This standard description of an Azilian industry also applies to layer 5 of the cueva de Los Azules. Nevertheless, the layer 5 assemblage possesses characteristics which seem to offer modifications to the whole Azilian process, generally towards greater simplification in the use of retouch. A significant proportion (22.38%) of the bladelets from layer 5 have abrupt retouch on both lateral edges, either total or partial. In the upper part of layer 3 (final Azilian of Los Azules) this percentage is reduced to 4.57%. So far, the proportion of tools on bladelets in the Magdalenian horizon is only 3.5% (this contrasts with the 57.5% of layer 5); but in layer 6 there are many Dufour bladelets, which are rare in the Azilian layers. These differences might be explicable in terms of different activities, but the contrast is particularly striking.

The points form a fairly uniform group in all the Azilian levels, with more or less constant percentages (layer 5 = 8%; layer 3e = 8.9%; layer 3, upper level = 8%). Nevertheless, the figures are misleading to a certain extent. The small Azilian point, which is relatively short and wide (15 mm long × 6 mm wide) with a curved back (*Fig. 1*, e–h), is replaced in layer 5 by a kind of long, fine microgravette point (35 mm long × 6 mm wide) with a straight back; less typically these have a double backed edge – one of the two examples illustrated has deep bipolar retouch, while the other is more marginal (*Fig. 1*, a–d). The points with a double back are even more abundant in layer 5 than in layer 3.

Once again, it appears that the Azilian industry undergoes a process of simplification in respect of the flaking and retouch (and also a simplification of tool types). On the other hand, detailed analysis reveals a process of complexity, found throughout the Epi-Palaeolithic, in the production of the tools. The presence of small (and badly made) pieces can be misleading; to regard such pieces as tools in their own right (and to refer to them collectively as the 'toolkit') produces a false impression. It is more appropriate to think of them as components of which tools are made. The complexity of the Azilian industry thus acquires an unknown dimension, but one which can be surmised through the discoveries made at sites in northern Europe.

The bone industry and mobiliary art

The Azilian horizon of layer 3 is extremely rich in tools made of bone – awls/bodkins (*poinçons*), sharpened bones, rare spear-heads, spatulas and, above all, harpoons. All the harpoons are of typical Azilian type: flat, with a button-hole perforation and a single row of barbs (*Fig. 1*, nos. 1–10). It is also

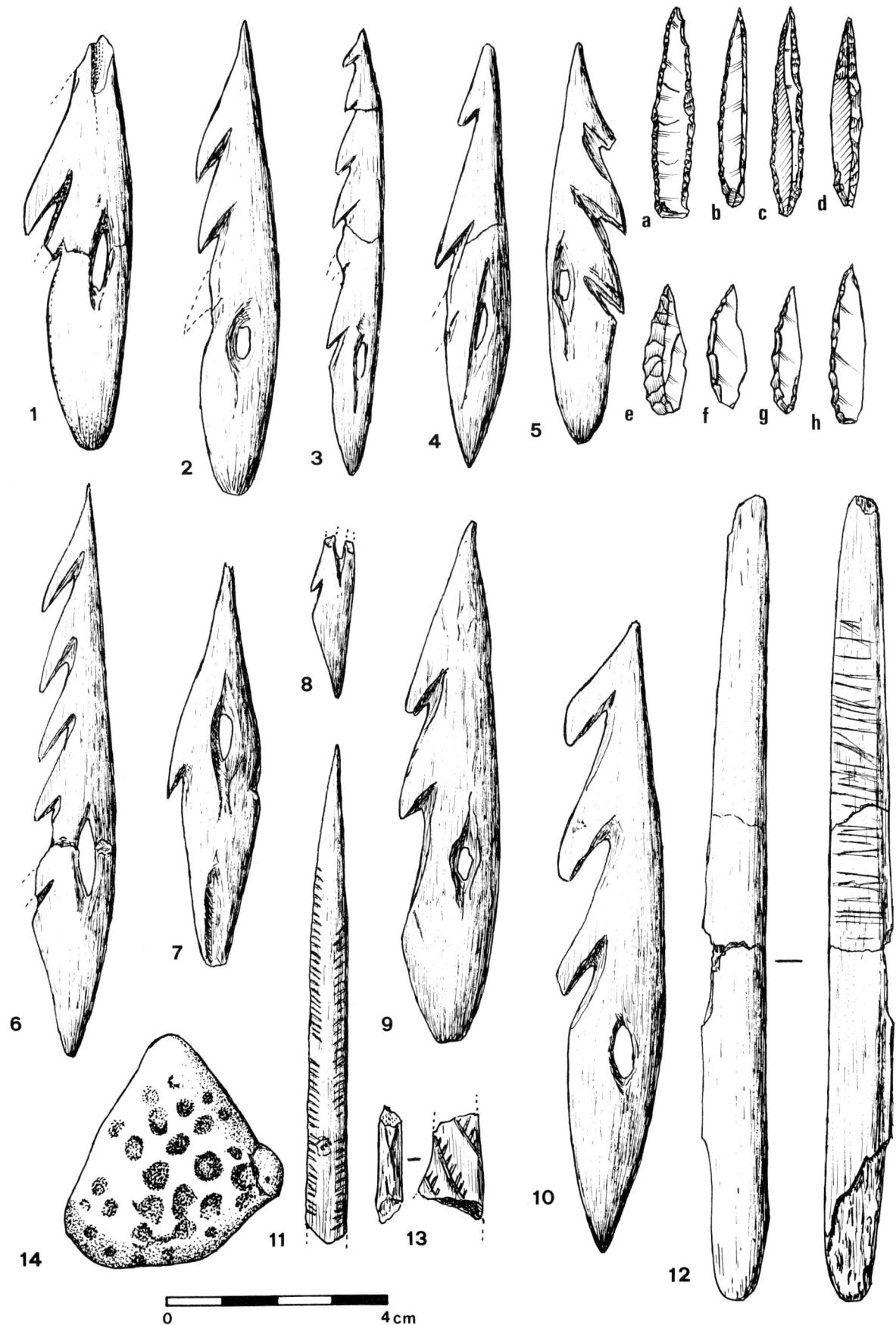

Figure 1 The bone and antler industries from the cueva de Los Azules.

notable that the oldest harpoons have the perforation located above the first barb, while the later harpoons have the perforation placed towards the base. No harpoons from this level are decorated. Among the artifacts from layer 3 decoration is found only on an awl (*Fig. 1*, no. 11) and on some of the spatulas (*Fig. 1*, no. 12); this is always limited to a motif of simple incisions, except in the case of a spatula with rows of incised dots.

Layer 5 is not rich in bone artifacts. To date, only a fragment of an Azilian harpoon (*Fig. 1*, no. 13) has been found; but this small fragment, which preserves a portion of a barb, is decorated – a unique find in the Cantabrian Azilian.[1] The decoration is very simple, consisting of incised lines crossed obliquely by series of shorter lines; this form of decoration is very similar to that found in the final Magdalenian and Azilian of the central and eastern parts of the province of Santander (González Sainz 1982). Another small fragment found in layer 5 shows similar decoration. It is interesting to note that this unique ornamented harpoon was found in the oldest Azilian layer, in contact with the Magdalenian level.

The contrast offered by layer 6 is striking. The surface of this Magdalenian level has been scraped over and it has already produced a fairly rich bone industry, including spear-heads and typical Magdalenian harpoons in which the decoration is much more abundant. Although only partially excavated, this level has yielded more mobiliary art than all the overlying Azilian levels together.

It is necessary to view these finds in a wider context. The Azilian bone industry, which appears badly made, contrasts with the *belles pièces* of the Magdalenian which were made with great care and sometimes extensively decorated. On the other hand, setting aside the aesthetic aspect of the question, pragmatism seems to have been the philosophy of the Azilian communities who followed the traditional hunter-gatherer way of life to which the human groups of western Europe remained tied for millennia.

In his review of the published papers of the Bordeaux symposium on 'La Fin des Temps Glaciaires en Europe', P.G. Bahn (1981) posed the question:

> What exactly *is* the Azilian? Is it a chronological period, a climatic phase, a cultural/economic stage, or just a flat harpoon, a painted pebble and a thumbnail scraper? (1981: 160)

It is not possible to give a precise answer, but we can begin to discern certain elements of the Azilian and the profound changes that occurred at the end of the Magdalenian. The disappearance of naturalistic art is an index, albeit a negative one, of this change; the purely abstract character of Azilian art (*Fig. 1*, no. 14) implies an important change in the vision of Palaeolithic man, irrespective of whether there were

other art forms on perishable materials. The small end-scraper, the near absence of the burin, the large number of small bladelets, a very distinctive bone industry – all demonstrate that the Azilian has a definite cultural personality, orientated towards the Epi-Palaeolithic. Yet these transformations took place before the climatic changes of the Pre-Boreal. The Azilian is characteristic of the final stages of the Last Glaciation, but it is strictly a cultural phenomenon; it seems pragmatic, with an evolved technical capacity, but is still fixed to traditional ways of life. It is heir to the great Palaeolithic tradition, but begins to deviate from it.

The cueva de Los Azules, although still in course of excavation, is beginning to open avenues to a better understanding of the significance of the Azilian.

Note:

1. Since this paper was submitted for publication, another decorated Azilian harpoon has been recovered in the excavations at Los Azules. This new find comes from layer 5a, and is a large (21 cm long), intact, uniserial harpoon with incised decoration on the upper surface; two 'periods' of decoration are evident on the piece, with one motif superimposed upon the other – see J. Fernández-Tresguerres 'Arpones decorados en el Aziliense Asturiano: cueva de Los Azules, Cangas de Onis', *Revista de Arqueologia*, 8, nº 78 (1987): 20–24. (Ed.)

Acknowledgements: This English translation of an original French text was produced by the Editor, with assistance from Brian Barron, Department of French, University of Edinburgh.

References

ALTUNA, J. (1972) Fauna de mamíferos de los yacimientos prehistóricos de Guipúzcoa con catálogo de los mamíferos cuaternarios del Cantábrico y del Pirineo occidental. *Munibe*, 24: 1–464.

ALTUNA, J. and MERINO, J.M. (eds) (1984) *El yacimiento prehistórico de la cueva de Ekain (Deba, Guipúzcoa)*. San Sebastián, Sociedad de Estudios Vascos.

BAHN, P.G. (1981) Review of D. de Sonneville-Bordes (ed.), 'La Fin des Temps Glaciaires en Europe'. *Antiquity*, 55: 159–160.

BARANDIARÁN, I. (1982) Datación por el C-14 de la cueva de Zatoya. *Trabajos de Arqueología Navarra*, 3: 43–57.

BARANDIARÁN, I. and GONZÁLEZ ECHEGARAY, J. (eds) (1981) *El Paleolítico Superior de la Cueva del Rascaño (Santander)*. (Monografías del Centro de Investigación y Museo de Altamira, 3). Santander, Ministerio de Cultura.

FERNÁNDEZ-TRESGUERRES, J.A. (1976) Azilian burial from Los Azules I, Asturias, Spain. *Current Anthropology*, 17: 769–770.

FERNÁNDEZ-TRESGUERRES, J.A. (1979) L'Azilien de la grotte de Los Azules I, Asturies (Espagne). In D. de Sonneville Bordes (ed.), *La Fin des Temps Glaciaires en Europe*. Paris, Centre National de la Recherche Scientifique: 745–752.

FERNÁNDEZ-TRESGUERRES, J.A. (1980) *El Aziliense en las Provincias de Asturias y Santander*. (Monografías del Centro de Investigación y Museo de Altamira, 2). Santander, Ministerio de Cultura.

FERNÁNDEZ-TRESGUERRES, J.A. (1983) Visión general del Epipaleolítico cantábrico. *Homenaje al Prof. Martín Almagro Basch*. Madrid, Ministerio de Cultura: 231–237.

González Sainz, C. (1982) Un colgante decorado de Cueva Morín (Santander). Reflexiones sobre un tema decorativo de finales del Paleolítico superior. *Ars Praehistorica*: 151–159.

Groupe de Travail de Préhistoire Cantabrique (GTPC) (1979) Chronostratigraphie et écologie des cultures du Paléolithique final en Espagne cantabrique. In D. de Sonneville-Bordes (ed.), *La Fin des Temps Glaciaires en Europe*. Paris, Centre National de la Recherche Scientifique: 713–719.

Straus, L.G., Altuna, J., Clark, G.A., González Morales, M.R., Laville, H., Leroi-Gourhan, A., Menéndez de la Hoz, M. and Ortea, J.A. (1981) Paleoecology at La Riera (Asturias, Spain). *Current Anthropology*, 22: 655–682.

Site Functional Complementarity in the Mesolithic of Northern Spain

G. A. Clark

Abstract

Since the mid-1970s evidence has accumulated that calls into question possible relationships among different kinds of Meso-lithic adaptations in Cantabrian Spain (e.g. Clarke 1976; Straus 1979; Clark 1983). Guided by a general west European tendency to juxtapose coastal shell middens and crude lithic industries, on the one hand, with inland Mesolithic stations and more complex assemblages, on the other, patterns of inter-assemblage variability in Cantabria have usually been 'explained' by recourse to a normative paradigm which equates assemblage differences with distinct and temporally-ordered 'cultures' (e.g. Azilian, Asturian). Since it can be shown that some of these Mesolithic assemblages are penecontemporaneous, the re-evaluation of the Cantabrian Mesolithic called for by Straus (1979) is attempted.

In this paper, I examine chronology, palaeoclimatic data, lithic and faunal assemblage composition, débitage and raw material characteristics, site sizes, numbers, distributions and settings for 58 Mesolithic sites assigned to Azilian and Asturian culture/ stratigraphic units. I assemble evidence which indicates functional complementarity for Azilian and Asturian sites, at least during the millennium (9500–8500 BP) when they overlap. Each assemblage is seen to pertain to one of two distinct generalized technologies which persist in Cantabria from c. 21,000 to c. 7000 BP, cross-cutting all of the classic culture/stratigraphic unit subdivisions found in that time interval. I conclude that functional explanations of Mesolithic assemblage variability which view culture as a complex adaptive system can be shown to be more tenable than those which depend upon variety-minimizing norm-ative paradigms.

INTRODUCTION

Since the mid-1970s, evidence has accumulated that calls into question possible relationships among different kinds of Mesolithic adaptations in northern Spain (e.g. Straus 1979; Fernández-Tresguerres 1980; González Morales 1982; Clark 1983a). As elsewhere in western Europe, a longstanding Spanish conven-tion contrasts coastally-situated shell midden sites and crude lithic industries (e.g. the Asturian) and inland Mesolithic stations with more complex micro-lithic assemblages (e.g. the Azilian). Patterns of inter-assemblage variability are then typically 'ex-plained' by recourse to a normative paradigm which equates assemblage differences with distinct and temporally-ordered 'cultures', thought to embody industrial traditions held in common and perpetuat-ed across generations by actual groups of people (e.g. Bordes 1968; Jordá 1977). While this perspec-tive, and the assumptions about human behaviour and the nature of the archaeological record that

underlie it, has been vigorously attacked in recent years (Binford 1982a; Binford and Sabloff 1982), it exhibits a remarkable tenacity as an explanatory framework despite repeated challenges based on epistemological considerations (Binford 1982b, 1983), new data (Straus et al. 1980, 1981; Clark and Straus 1983) and re-analyses of old sites, site contexts and collections (Straus 1983a; Clark 1983b).

Debates about the meaning of pattern in the archaeological record are not of course confined to the north Spanish Mesolithic, but the Spanish situation is nevertheless a classic one since it embodies all of the elements of this pan-disciplinary controversy. As Binford (1983b, 1983c) has pointed out, the debate centres on la méthode Bordes and how it is used by different investigators. Prac-tically all Spanish workers have adopted the Bord-esian approach to the extent that comparison of assemblages using standardized type lists and indices constitutes the basis for making inferences about resemblances among groups of collections. However, we often differ with respect to the meaning attached to pattern, depending ultimately on the assumptions made about what components contribute to observed differences and similarities in the archaeological record.

I believe that the overall character of an assemb-lage is determined by a small set of factors, although these factors can be related to one another in complex and intricate ways. Amongst the most general are: (i) the grain of an assemblage (its resolution and integrity – Binford 1981), and (ii) the typological systems imposed on artifacts, fauna, etc., by archaeologists as they seek to organize their data; in the case of artifacts, (iii) participation in a toolmaking tradition, (iv) idiosyncratic behaviour, and (v) variability in raw materials can all have important roles, as can (vi) the particular activity suites of which the artifacts were once a part. Sampling error and a component of random variation (or 'noise') in artifact form, frequency and context can also affect assessments of assemblage differences and similarities. It is the task of the archaeologist to attempt to untangle these interwoven strands of causality – to partition sources of observed variation across one or more of these commonly recognized causal vectors. If successful, this partitioning can result in the identification of differences amongst assemblages which can be more probably related to one or several factors than to others. Explanations achieved in this way become more tenable with the passage of time, as successive attempts to refute them fail.

THE NORTH SPANISH MESOLITHIC

In the context of the Vasco-Cantabrian Mesolithic, debates about pattern and what it might mean were brought into sharp focus recently with the publication of a speculative paper by Lawrence Straus (1979). Straus suggested, among other things, that since some Azilian and Asturian sites appeared to be contemporaneous (based on radiocarbon dates), a case might be made for considering the two assemblages to be functional complements of one another. He went on to develop some of the implications of contemporaneity by considering the nature of the formation processes at the two kinds of sites and by noting differences in site location, lithic and faunal inventories, and possible function. It is my intention in this essay to carry these provocative ideas one step further by examining chronology, palaeoclimatic data, lithic and faunal assemblage composition, débitage and raw material characteristics, site sizes, numbers, distributions and settings for 58 Mesolithic sites assigned to the Azilian and Asturian culture/stratigraphic units. While length limitations preclude exhaustive treatment, I show that functional explanations of Mesolithic assemblage variability which view culture as a complex adaptive system can in fact be applied in the Cantabrian case, and are more tenable than those which depend upon the variety-minimizing normative paradigms currently in use.

CHRONOLOGY

Since the argument for contemporaneity rests largely on the radiocarbon evidence, it is logical to begin with an evaluation of the ages of the two assemblage types in Cantabria. Both have a long history of investigation. Work at Azilian cave and rock-shelter sites was initiated by the French Institute of Human Palaeontology prior to World War I at Cueva del Valle and El Castillo, both in Santander (Breuil and Obermaier 1912). The five major Asturian sites (Penicial, Cueto de la Mina, La Riera, Balmori and Fonfría), all in the Llanes area of eastern Asturias, were excavated and published by the discoverer of the Asturian, the Count of Vega del Sella, between 1914 and 1923 (Vega del Sella 1923). Correcting an initial misconception about the age of the Asturian at the type site, Penicial (Vega del Sella 1914), the

Count subsequently recognized that the rudimentary quartzite lithic assemblages were in fact post-Pleistocene, 'pre-neolithic' phenomena (Vega del Sella 1915, 1916). In keeping with French chronological schemes being developed at the time in the Dordogne and in the Pyrenees, the Azilian of the Santander caves was assigned a terminal Pleistocene date. The Asturian, found stratified above the late Magdalenian and Azilian industries at some of the 'key' sites, was generally considered to be Holocene in age. This sequential ordering of the two assemblages, first proposed by Vega del Sella (1916) in the Cueto de la Mina site report, went unchallenged until the 1960s when Jordá (1959, 1963) and some other Spanish investigators tried to relegate the Asturian to the Lower or Middle Palaeolithic, emphasizing the crudeness of the lithic industry and supposed resemblances between it and Lower Pleistocene 'pebble tool' industries from the North African coast (e.g. Crusafont 1963). In the early 1970s the first Asturian radiocarbon assays became available, indicating a Boreal period age for Bricia, Coberizas, Penicial and La Riera (Clark 1976). Since then, 7 Asturian, 16 Azilian and 7 other Mesolithic levels in 15 sites have been dated (*Table 1*).

Radiocarbon evidence

Inspection of *Table 1* does in fact provide some support for the hypothesis of contemporaneity, although it is not evident in the grand mean dates for the two series, nor in their mean standard deviations. Except for the determinations from Mazaculos II level 3.3, a *terminus ante quem* date from the *base* of an Asturian *conchero*, and Urtiaga level C, an unreliable shell date from an Azilian cave deposit in Guipúzcoa, evidence for overlap only becomes apparent if *sample standard deviations for individual level dates* are taken into account. Straus (1979) had proposed, on the basis of a smaller series of determinations, that chronological overlap seemed to be indicated for the 9500–8500 BP interval. If we discount the Urtiaga shell date, and consider the sample standard deviations, a block of ten determinations falls in the millennium between 9500 and 8500 BP. The Asturian is represented by three samples – Penicial (upper cave), La Riera level 1B, base, Mazaculos II level 3.3, base; the Azilian by five – Cueva Oscura de Ania, Los Azules level 3a, Ekain level 4, Santimamiñe level 7, Los Azules level 3d; and there are two samples – Morín geological level 27, Arenaza I level 2 – which cannot be assigned to either culture or stratigraphic unit. Of some interest is the observation that all the 'late' Azilian sites are inland whereas *all* Asturian sites are coastal, which implies a bimodal pattern of site location for the period of overlap – possible evidence in support of the notion of functional complementarity (see below).

Table 1: Cantabrian Mesolithic radiocarbon dates

Site/Level	Cultural Assignment	Lab. No.	Age BP	Range	Substance dated	Reference
La Riera – Lev. B1 (top)	Asturian	GaK-3046	6500±200	6300–6700	charcoal	Clark & Straus 1983
Bricia – conchero	Asturian	GaK-2908	6800±160	6640–6960	charcoal	Clark 1976
Coberizas – Lev. B1	Asturian	GaK-2907	7100±170	6930–7270	charcoal	Clark 1976
Mazaculos II – Lev. 1.1	Asturian	GaK-8162	7280±220	7060–7500	charcoal	González Morales 1982
Zatoya – upper Lev. II	Post-Azilian ?	Ly-1398	8150±170	7980–8320	bone	Cava 1978
Penicial – upper cave	Asturian	GaK-2906	8650±180	8470–8830	charcoal	Clark 1976
La Riera – Lev. B1, base	Asturian	GaK-2909	8650±300	8350–8950	charcoal	Clark 1976
Urtiaga –Lev. C	Azilian	CSIC-63	8700±170	8530–8870	shell	Cava 1978
Morín – geol. stratum 27	Post-Azilian	I-5150	9000±150	8850–9150	travertine	Butzer 1973
Mazaculos II – Lev. 3.3, base	Asturian	GaK-6884	9290±400	8890–9690	charcoal	González Morales 1978
Cueva Oscura de Ania – Lev. ?	Azilian	?	9400±?	–	?	González Morales 1982
Los Azules – Lev. 3a	Azilian	CSIC-216	9430±120	9310–9550	charcoal	Fernández-Tresguerres 1976
Ekain – Lev. 4 (base)	Azilian	I-9239	9460±185	9275–9645	bone	Cava 1978
Santimamiñe – Lev. 7	Azilian	Gif-130	9470±400	9070–9870	charcoal	González Morales 1982
Los Azules – Lev. 3d	Azilian	CSIC-260	9540±120	9420–9660	charcoal	Fernández-Tresguerres 1976
Arenaza I – Lev. 2 (Bed D)	Azilian ?	CSIC-173	9600±180	9420–9780	charcoal	Cava 1978
Arenaza I – Lev. 3	Azilian ?	CSIC-174	10,300±180	10,120–10,480	bone	Cava 1978
Los Azules – Lev. 3e	Azilian	BM-1875R	10,480±210	10,270–10,690	bone	Burleigh *et al.* 1982
Los Azules – Lev. 3d (base)	Azilian	BM-1879R	10,510±130	10,380–10,640	bone	Burleigh *et al.* 1982
El Cierro – conchero	Azilian/ Upper Magdalenian	GaK-2548	10,400±500	9900–10,900	charcoal	Clark 1976
Rascaño – Lev. 1.3	Azilian	BM-1449	10,485± 90	10,395–10,575	bone	Barandiarán & González Echegaray 1981
Rascaño – Lev. 1.2	Azilian	BM-1448	10,560±245	10,315–10,805	bone	Barandiarán & González Echegaray 1981
La Riera – Lev. 27	Azilian/ Upper Magdalenian	BM-1494	10,630±120	10,510–10,750	bone	Clark & Straus 1983
Los Azules – Lev. 3e	Azilian	BM-1876R	10,880±210	10,670–11,090	bone	Burleigh *et al.* 1982
Los Azules – Lev. 3f	Azilian	BM-1878R	10,910±290	10,620–11,200	bone	Burleigh *et al.* 1982
Zatoya – Lev. III	Azilian	Ly-1458	≥10,940± ?	–	bone	Evin 1979
Los Azules – Lev. 3e	Azilian	BM-1877R	11,320±360	10,960–11,680	bone	Burleigh *et al.* 1982
Zatoya – lower Lev. II	Azilian	Ly-1399	11,480±270	11,210–11,750	bone	Cava 1978
Zatoya – lower Lev. II	Azilian	Ly-1599	11,620±360	11,260–11,980	bone	Evin 1979
Zatoya – Lev. III	Azilian	Ly-1400	11,840±240	11,600–12,080	bone	Cava 1978
SPANISH ASTURIAN	Mean of 7 dates from 5 sites		7817±223	7594–8040		
SPANISH AZILIAN	Mean of 16 dates from 7 sites		10,422±228	10,194–10,650		
FRENCH AZILIAN	Mean of 19 dates from 11 sites		10,508±300	10,208–10,808		Fernández-Tresguerres 1980: 171–172

CLIMATE

In terms of the standard western European Lateglacial and early Holocene climatic phases (see, e.g., Leroi-Gourhan and Girard 1979), the Azilian in Cantabria first appears in the relatively mild Allerød Oscillation (11,750–10,750 BP), although it is primarily a wet, cold, Dryas III phenomenon (10,750–10,150 BP). A few of the latest sites extend into the more temperate Pre-Boreal period (10,150–8650 BP), where they overlap with the earliest Asturian sites. Butzer (1981) places the Cantabrian Azilian in his phases 40–42, which run the gamut from cool and dry (40), to cold and unstable (41), to warming, drier and stable (42), although the resolution of his sedimentological approach is probably not adequate to detect changes with a periodicity or amplitude of less than two millennia.

Disagreements about the interpretation of palynological and sedimentological monitors of past climatic conditions, and preconceptions about what these phases should 'look like' in Cantabria (and their dating) make assignment of Azilian deposits to named climatic periods extremely problematical. At Morín, for example, the level 1 sediments indicate cold Dryas III climatic conditions (Butzer 1971a), whereas the pollen, with evidence of a slight warming trend, argues for a Dryas II/Allerød boundary date (Leroi-Gourhan 1971). At La Riera, the level 26 palaeoclimatic monitors both indicate de-

591

position under cold climatic conditions, but Leroi-Gourhan suggests a late Allerød date, while Laville (1986) favours Dryas III. Laville's analysis of level 27 sediments indicates a continuation of cold, wet Dryas III conditions, while the pollen spectra suggest a warming trend. Level 28, with a typical Azilian harpoon, has a thermophilous flora but the sediments indicate deposition under markedly cooler, wet conditions (for résumés of Azilian pollen and sediment data – see Fernández-Tresguerres 1980; GTPC 1979). What does seem clear is that there are *no systematic correlations* between kinds of Azilian industry and climatic phase assignments, nor are there any lineal time trends in either the archaeological or the faunal data (*contra* García Guinea 1975). In sharp contrast to south-west France, climatic change did not affect the composition of Upper and post-Paleolithic macrofaunal assemblages to any significant degree, despite evidence for marked changes in vegetation, moisture regime and temperature in both areas.

The Asturian begins in the Pre-Boreal period, but is principally a Boreal (8650–7350 BP) and early Atlantic period (7350–4950 BP) development (Butzer 1971b). Only Butzer (1981) indicates relatively cold initial conditions, placing it in his phases 41–44, characterized by cold unstable (41), followed by warm/dry (42) and warm/wet stable climates (43), and by warm/dry unstable conditions (44). In general, however, and regardless of time, pollen and sediment evidence indicate the temperate, humid conditions expected during these early to mid-Holocene intervals. The level 29 pollen sample from La Riera has a high incidence of trees, especially hazel (*Corylus avellana*) which accounts for 45% of the total pollen count, clearly indicating a warming Postglacial climate. Oak (*Quercus* sp.), elm (*Ulmus glabra*), alder (*Alnus glutinosa*), and birch (*Betula vulgaris*) are also represented. A dense undergrowth

of ferns (*Pteridium* spp.) suggests humid micro-environments in the vicinity of the cave mouth. Wet, temperate conditions with strong-to-moderate AP fractions and NAP spectra dominated by ferns and other humidity-tolerant species are also indicated in Asturian samples from Balmori, Coberizas and Cuartamentero (J.W. Gish, pers. comm.), as well as from the open site of Liencres (Clark and Menéndez Amor 1975) where the pollen evidence contrasts with the sedimentology (Butzer 1981).

THE INDUSTRIES

The contrast between the Asturian and the Azilian is nowhere more apparent than in the composition of their lithic industries. It is significant that, while they do not greatly resemble one another, each appears to pertain to one of the two generalized assemblage types which cross-cut these and other Cantabrian culture/stratigraphic units and which persist in time from the end of the Pleistocene to the Boreal/Atlantic boundary (Clark 1983c). The retouched tool components of 12 Azilian and 26 Asturian lithic collections classified according to the Sonneville-Bordes–Perrot typology are summarized in *Table 2* (see Clark 1975a, 1976, 1983a, 1983b; González Morales 1982 – for discussions of Asturian assemblages; Fernández-Tresguerres 1980; Straus 1985 – for the Azilian).

Small retouched tools

Table 2 reflects only morphological types recognized by the Bordesian scheme, which lacks a 'heavy-duty tool' component (see below). Moreover, sample representativeness is open to question since descriptions of all but 14 levels are based on analyses of (probably selected) museum collections from excavations in the 1900–1930 era. Exceptions in the Azilian series are Los Azules I levels 2, 3 (*capas*

Table 2: A summary of small tool group indices for 12 Azilian and 26 Asturian lithic collections

Unit	IG	IB	IBB	IP	IND	ISS	References
AZILIAN CAVE SITES (12 levels)	27.9	8.2	37.3	1.4	8.9	1.8	Martínez & Chapa 1980 Fernández-Tresguerres 1980 González Echegaray 1971, 1973 Cheynier & González Echegaray 1964 Straus *et al.* 1981 Clark & Straus 1983
ASTURIAN CAVE SITES (24 levels)	21.6	11.1	4.3	9.5	26.1	5.3	Clark 1975b, 1976, 1983 González Morales 1982
LIENCRES OPEN SITE (2 levels)	21.3	11.6	6.7	16.9	22.1	4.4	Clark 1975a, 1979

Key: IG=index of end-scrapers (types 1–16); IB=index of burins (types 27–44); IBB=index of backed bladelets (types 51, 85–87, 90, 91); IP=index of perforators (types 23, 24); IND=index of serrated pieces (notches, denticulates – types 74,75); ISS=index of side-scrapers (type 77)

superiores) and 3e (Fernández-Tresguerres 1980), La Riera levels 26–28 (Straus *et al.* 1981), and Morín level 1 (González Echegaray 1971, 1973); in the Asturian series La Riera cut B, level 1 (Clark and Richards 1978), Liencres surface, level 1 (Clark 1975*b*), Coberizas cut B, level 1 (Clark and Cartledge 1973), Balmori cut E, level 1 (Clark and Clark 1975), and Mazaculos II levels 1.1–3.3 (González Morales 1982). As is obvious from an inspection of the table, the principal differences are: (i) in the backed and retouched bladelet frequencies (absent or rare in the Asturian, relatively common in the Azilian); and (ii) in the incidence of serrated pieces (relatively common in the Asturian, rare in the Azilian).

While useful as summaries, these global indices mask a certain amount of variation, although they throw into sharp relief the major features of the retouched tool components in the two series. Liencres excepted, even the best Asturian collections are poor in small retouched tools, perhaps reflecting their possible function as bulk waste disposal areas or dumps (Straus 1979). The old Azilian collections from La Paloma have both the largest end-scraper (IG = 53.7) *and* the smallest backed bladelet components (IBB = 13.3), indicating possible sample selection during and/or after excavation (Hoyos *et al.* 1980). Among the 'good' Azilian samples, however, end-scraper indices range from 3.1 (Riera level 28) to 30.3 (Azules I level 2), backed bladelet frequencies from 33.2 (Azules I level 2) to 62.5 (Riera level 28) and notch/denticulates from 7.7 (Riera level 26) to 15.2 (Riera level 27). The fact that these extreme values tend to be found at coastally-situated La Riera and inland Los Azules, respectively, suggests that there may be some locational or topographical component to what appears to be a dichotomous pattern of assemblage variability. The 'good' Asturian samples exhibit much less internal variation, with the cave samples very similar statistically to one another although fairly distinct from Liencres, the single open-air site in the series (Clark 1983*a*).

The heavy-duty tool component

Not evident from *Table 2* is the nature of the heavy-duty tool (HDT) component in the two assemblage types. It is difficult to quantify these data for the Azilian because heavy-duty tools (picks, choppers, chopping tools, bifaces, etc.) are usually not distinguished as a separate category in the site reports and regional syntheses which serve as a basis for this discussion. However, they appear to be proportionately *much less common* in Azilian than in Asturian sites. If the latter is true, and it seems to be true on an impressionistic level, it is a point of real contrast between the two series. The HDT component in the Asturian cave collections makes up *c.* 69% of the

retouched tool total, but the Liencres sample (9.3%) is very different in this regard and much more like an Azilian site. The global incidence of HDTs in all Asturian collections combined is *c.* 53% (Clark 1975*b*). While I had tended to attribute this to selected (i.e. non-representative) samples, recent excavations at La Riera, Balmori, Liencres and Mazaculos II indicate that these distinctions are probably real. They suggest that very different combinations of activity and disposal behaviours contributed to the formation of the Azilian sites (and Liencres), on the one hand, and the Asturian cave sites, on the other.

Débitage characteristics

It could be argued that the character of the débitage fraction might emphasize functional distinctions among sites, since it is reasonable to suppose that the kinds and quantities of flaking debris might reflect different activities more faithfully than the sometimes scarce retouched tools. Débitage frequencies are clearly unreliable for the old collections, but usable information can be gleaned from some more recent site reports and from summaries of the characteristics of Asturian lithic industries.

In general, débitage was neither analyzed nor saved by the early excavators. Some idea of the distortion resulting from this kind of selection is given by the débitage:tool ratio for the Azilian collection from La Paloma, dug by E. Hernández Pacheco and P. Wernert in 1914–15 (Hernández Pacheco 1919). It is actually substantially less than one (0.53:1), whereas débitage:tool ratios from 26 strata at recently excavated La Riera average about twenty pieces of debris for every retouched tool (20.1:1). The enormous collections from Los Azules I (136,350 pieces in 1979), excavated by J. Fernández-Tresguerres since 1973, are all very heavily dominated by débitage: level 2 = 45.9:1; level 3cs = 35.6:1; level 3e = 86.5:1 (Fernández-Tresguerres 1980). The corresponding débitage fractions are 97.9%, 97.3% and 98.9%, respectively. At coastal La Riera, the global range of values extended from as few as eight pieces of débitage for every tool (levels 2, 3, 24) to as many as 40 (level 15). The ratios for Upper Magdalenian or Azilian levels 26 and 27, and Azilian level 28 are 23.9:1, 23:1 and 25:1, all rather close to the site average. The corresponding fractions are 96%, 95.9% and 96.2% (Straus and Clark 1986). The pattern at La Riera is thus one of relative consistency for the Azilian levels, whereas that at Los Azules I shows greater variability. A wide range of values probably indicates a wide disparity among the levels in the extent to which knapping was done *in situ* during the individual occupations (for further discussions of the interpretative potential of débitage, see Clark and Straus 1983; Straus *et al.* 1981).

The equivalent information for 25 Asturian cave sites and the open site of Liencres presents a very different picture. Débitage accounts for 79.7% of all Asturian lithic remains, including heavy-duty tools. The global débitage:tool ratios, made comparable to their Azilian counterparts by excluding the HDTs, are much lower – 7.4:1 (cave sites), 10.7:1 (Liencres) and 9.1:1 (all sites combined). Corresponding débitage fractions are 56.1%, 89.7% and 76.4% (HDTs included); 86.5%, 90.6% and 89% (HDTs excluded) (Clark 1975b). Data from Mazaculos II exhibit similar patterns. At this coastally situated rock-shelter site, three conchero samples give débitage:tool ratios of 4.2:1 (disturbed levels), 11:1 (level 1) and 4.1:1 (level 3). The corresponding débitage fractions (HDTs included) are 80.9%, 91.7% and 75.6%. The retouched components of these collections are dominated by picks, choppers and chopping tools, as underscored by the fact that the débitage:tool ratio increases to 34.7:1 (97.1%) in the disturbed levels if HDTs are excluded. The collections from levels 1–3 comprised heavy-duty tools only; no retouched flakes, blades or bladelets were recovered from these intact strata in this recently, carefully excavated site (González Morales 1982). While it might be tempting to discount the Asturian data because of selection in the old collections, full-scale, modern excavations at Liencres and Mazaculos II, and smaller tests at Coberizas, Balmori, La Riera and Penicial, were all conducted with the current emphasis on sample representativeness firmly in mind (Clark and Cartledge 1973; Clark and Clark 1975; Clark and Richards 1978; González Morales 1978, 1982; Clark 1979).

The most comprehensive attempt to deal with pattern in the débitage fraction is unfortunately site-specific. At La Riera, Straus and I divided flaking debris into primary (cores, plain and decortication flakes, blades, bladelets) and secondary (shatter and trimming flakes, burin spalls) categories in an effort to detect and control for stages in reduction sequences. The ratio of primary to secondary debris averaged across all levels was nearly one (0.96:1), but the range extended from 0.2:1 (level 10) to 2.1:1 (levels 21–23). Upper Magdalenian/Azilian levels 26–28 had primary:secondary debris ratios of 0.97:1, 1.65:1 and 1.68:1, respectively. Although level 26 is near the site average, levels 27 and 28 contain unusually high proportions of primary débitage, suggesting that basic core preparation and the production of flakes, blades and bladelets were relatively more important in these levels than in the rest of the sequence. The 1969 collection from the Asturian conchero (level 29) produced a primary:secondary debris ratio of 4.1:1; the ratio for the small 1976 collection was a similar 4.3:1, again indicating an emphasis on primary reduction (Straus and Clark 1986).

What emerges from these comparisons of débitage ratios in the two assemblages is: (i) a much higher incidence of (primarily flint) débitage in the Azilian collections, indicating more in situ knapping of flint than in the Asturian; (ii) much greater variability in the Azilian ratios, suggesting that a wider range of activities was responsible for the accumulation of these residues than was the case in the Asturian sites; (iii) very distinct retouched tool components dominated by HDTs in the case of the Asturian conchero sites, and by small tools in the case of Liencres and the Azilian cave sites; and (iv) at least at La Riera, some Mesolithic levels characterized by relatively evenly balanced primary:secondary debris ratios (level 26), and others with little evidence of secondary retouching (levels 27–29), suggesting in the latter case that finished tools made elsewhere were brought into and/or discarded in the cave mouth. At La Riera, levels with relatively little knapping debris tend to have more primary than secondary débitage, whereas levels with much debris, in general, tend to be heavily dominated by secondary débitage (Straus and Clark 1978). However, the distinction does not coincide with the Azilian (level 28)/Asturian (level 29) boundary. While we suspect that this pattern has credibility beyond the La Riera sequence, we cannot demonstrate it at present because of a lack of comparable data from other sites.

Raw material analyses

Information about lithic raw material variation in the two assemblage types is very uneven. Synthetic studies by Clark (1975b) and González Morales (1982) summarize raw material procurement patterns for the Asturian sites, but comparable data scarcely exist for the Azilian, being confined to isolated references in type lists from old collections (e.g. Martínez and Chapa 1980) and to more systematic investigations at a single site, La Riera (Straus et al. 1986). What information is available is given in Table 3.

Table 3 contains two kinds of data: relative frequencies of raw material types expressed as counts and as weights. Global count data from Asturian cave sites taken from Clark (1975b) and González Morales (1982) are in remarkable agreement, given that overlapping but different sets of collections were analyzed. The Asturian cave sites, with quartzite-dominated assemblages, are clearly very similar to one another so far as patterns of raw material procurement are concerned. A very different pattern is presented by the open coastal site of Liencres which, although it has produced the characteristic Asturian unifacial picks, has a lithic assemblage heavily dominated by flint (it is near a source). In this, it very strongly resembles the old Azilian collections from the inland cave site of La

Rock type	Counts expressed as percentages			
	Asturian: 29 levels in 26 cave sites (Clark 1975b)	Asturian: 21 levels in 15 cave sites (González Morales 1982)	Liencres Surface, Level 1 (Clark 1975b)	La Paloma Level 2, Azilian (Martínez & Chapa 1980)
quartzite	66.9	66.7	14.0	14.3
flint	24.9	24.3	85.4	80.8
quartz	5.8	3.6	0.1	2.7
limestone	1.6	1.6	<0.1	1.1
sandstone	0.7	3.5	–	1.1

Rock type	Weights expressed as percents (sandstone as % of total weight)			
	La Riera Lev. 26 (Up. Mag./Azilian)	La Riera Lev. 27 (Up. Mag./Azilian)	La Riera Lev. 28 (Azilian)	La Riera Lev. 29 (Asturian)
quartzite	68.6	65.6	64.1	64.4
flint	31.2	31.1	34.3	35.6
quartz	0.1	1.7	2.0	<0.1
limestone	–	1.8	<0.1	<0.1
schist	–	0.4	–	–
(sandstone)	(3.2)	(19.0)	(4.9)	–

Paloma, recently restudied by Martínez and Chapa (1980). While the sample from Liencres can probably be considered reliable, that from La Paloma is suspect because it consists mainly of retouched tools. Both collections have substantial numbers of small blades and bladelets, however, which are typically made of flint, so that the close correspondence in the flint and quartzite frequencies is probably not coincidental.

The La Riera weight data, from a sequence of two Upper Magdalenian/Azilian levels (26, 27), one Azilian level (28) and one Asturian level (29), all show similar percentages of quartzite and flint, indicating little basis to differentiate among these otherwise quite distinct occupations. Alone among Cantabrian collections, the La Riera stone artifacts were further classified on the basis of colour, texture and mineralogy into 28 morphologically distinct raw material categories (15 flints, 7 quartzites, 6 other rare rock types). On this more refined analytical level, levels 26–29 were once again virtually identical with about 50% Type I quartzite, 5–10% Type J quartzite, 15% Type A flint, and traces of other types (Straus *et al.* 1986). *Except in this case*, shifts in raw material procurement at La Riera generally coincide with breaks between culture/stratigraphic units, a phenomenon possibly related to changes in the settlement–subsistence systems within which lithic procurement strategies might have been 'embedded' (Binford 1979). That the Azilian and Asturian levels should have similar procurement patterns lends support to the hypothesis that these two kinds of assemblage might represent distinct activity and/or disposal facies *within a single settlement–subsistence system.*

When raw material is considered in relation to artifact types, there appears to be a strong general correlation between HDTs, notches, denticulates and side-scrapers, which are usually made of quartzite, and small tools made on flake and bladelet blanks (especially retouched bladelets) which are nearly always made of flint. Although documented most exhaustively at La Riera (Clark *et al.* 1986), the La Paloma collections show a virtually identical pattern (*Table 4*), as do the collections from Liencres and the Asturian cave sites. This contrast, which is also well documented in the Upper Palaeolithic sequence at La Riera, could be interpreted as evidence of a dichotomous pattern of assemblage variability which cross-cuts culture/stratigraphic unit boundaries. One kind of assemblage is characterized by a high incidence of quartzite HDTs, notches, denticulates and some other types, is typically associated with much knapping debris, and suggests an emphasis on 'expedient', even wasteful, *in situ* knapping of these abundant resources. The other, with many small flint tools and relatively little débitage, may indicate more economical 'curated' technologies made necessary because of the relative scarcity and small size of

Table 4: La Paloma – artifact types and raw materials

	% Quartzite	% Flint
Denticulates	80.0	20.0
Continuously retouched pieces	71.4	28.6
Side-scrapers	62.5	37.5
Backed bladelets	5.4	94.6
Azilian points	6.3	93.7
Flake end-scrapers	7.8	92.2

flint and chert nodules in the region (Binford 1979, 1980). Straus (1980) has shown that *local* procurement of lithic raw materials is typical of the Vasco-Cantabrian Upper Palaeolithic, so that long-distance exchange can effectively be ruled out as a factor contributing to the observed pattern (for a contrasting view of trade in exotic raw materials for the nearby French Pyrenees, see Bahn 1982).

ECONOMIC FAUNAS

The characteristics of Cantabrian Upper and post-Palaeolithic archaeological faunas have been described at length by a number of workers, and have been summarized in about a dozen recent publications (e.g. Altuna 1972, 1980; Freeman 1973; Straus 1977, 1983*b*, 1983*c*; Clark 1983*b*; Clark and Yi 1983). Both Clark (1983*b*) and González Morales (1982) make extremely strong cases for homogeneity in both the mammalian and molluscan components of Asturian faunas. Strongly correlated with sites located at low elevations on estuaries in the narrow coastal plain, Asturian economic faunas are uniformly dominated by red deer (*Cervus elaphus*), with smaller numbers of roe deer (*Capreolus capreolus*), boar (*Sus scrofa*), ibex (*Capra ibex*) and chamois (*Rupicapra rupicapra*) (from coastal alpine niches, if present in the site vicinity), and occasional horses (*Equus caballus*) and bovines (*Bos primigenius*). The fact that no Asturian fauna is dominated by ibex or chamois is probably due in part to site location. The only sites with caprid-dominated faunas are either inland alpine hunting stations, located in gorges and cliff faces in the Cantabrian mountains, or Basque Country coastal sites located in close proximity to alpine habitats (Straus 1977, 1983*a*). Shellfish collecting, which begins in earnest during the Solutrean, reaches its zenith in the Asturian with some 17 species recorded, although all collections are dominated numerically by two kinds of limpet (*Patella vulgata* and *P. intermedia*) and the thermophilous topshell (*Monodonta lineata*). An echinoderm (*Paracentrotus lividus*), two species of crab (*Cancer pagurus* and *Portunus puber*), three marine fish (*Labrus* sp., *Solea* sp., and unidentified sparids) and three anadromous salmonids (*Salmo salar*, *S. trutta trutta*, *S. trutta fario*) make up the remainder of the economic fauna.

The few Azilian faunas analyzed to date exhibit a bimodal pattern, with variation chiefly due to the above mentioned habitat preferences of the alpine caprines and the necessity or desirability of exploiting these animals from small hunting camps located purposefully in areas where they would normally be concentrated. Regardless of date and prevailing climate, Azilian sites situated in low-lying coastal plain environments (e.g. La Riera, Morín) tend to have red deer dominated faunas similar to those of the Asturian. Ibex and chamois are important in Azilian levels at Ermittía (Guipúzcoa) which, while near the sea, is located in rocky terrain on a cliff face at Rascaño (Santander) in the deeply incised gorge of the Río Miera, and at Collubíl high in the Cantabrian mountains on an upland tributary of the Sella (Asturias). These are all sites located in rocky, mountainous terrain where ibex (and to a lesser extent chamois) would have been prevalent in the landscape. Straus (1977, 1983*a*, 1983*b*) has convincingly argued that this bimodal pattern is a *general, Vasco-Cantabrian Upper Palaeolithic phenomenon*, citing evidence for ibex-dominated faunas at Bolinkoba (Gravettian, Solutrean), Rascaño (Upper Magdalenian), Collubíl (Upper Magdalenian), Chufín (Solutrean), and at a large number of other, similarly situated north Spanish sites. Such specialized hunting camps do not appear to be present in the inventory of Asturian sites which seem, by virtue of location, artifact and faunal content, to have been dumps accumulated by the residents of nearby base camps (Clark 1983*a*).

SITE LOCATIONAL DATA: IMPLICATIONS

The topographic settings of 58 of the more credible Azilian and Asturian cave and rock-shelter sites are summarized and compared in *Tables 5 & 6*. These sites were selected because they have produced the diagnostic artifact types used by convention to define these industries. It should be noted that there are many more claimed Mesolithic sites in northern Spain, including about 15 'Azilian' sites in the Basque provinces of Vizcaya and Guipúzcoa, and no less than 49 newly-discovered 'Asturian' *concheros* in Asturias and Santander (Barandiarán 1967; Gavelas 1980; González Morales 1982). Unambiguous assignment of these sites to named culture/stratigraphic units is impossible in default of their respective *fossiles directeurs* (Azilian harpoons, Asturian picks). In the case of the Asturian, identification of many of the new sites is based solely on the appearance of *concheros* characterized by small limpets and topshells. While such midden deposits are in fact highly correlated with the Boreal period and with Asturian industries, they often lack significant numbers of artifacts (Clark 1971).

A second group of sites has produced substantial microlith-dominated collections from known stratigraphic contexts but assignment of these materials is also problematical, since meaningful distinction between the late Magdalenian and Azilian industries in Cantabria is impossible if the characteristic harpoons are not recovered (Straus *et al.* 1981). Included here are collections from El Cierro, Collubíl, Sofoxó, Coberizas, La Chora, Camargo, Silibranka, Arenaza I, Kobeaga II, Bolinkoba, etc., which are usually categorized as 'Upper' or 'Final Magdalenian/

Table 5: Locational characteristics of 32 fairly credible Asturian sites

Site	Orientation	Lineal distance from sea (km)	Elevation above present sea level (m)	Size	Location	Drainage	Source
Aguila	S	1.5	50	S	coastal plain	Purón	Gavelas 1980; González Morales 1982
Allorú	W	1.6	30	S	coastal plain	(Calabres)	Clark 1976
Arenillas	S	0.2	5	L	coastal hills above beach	–	González Morales 1982
Arnero	NW	2.4	25–30	S	coastal plain	Bedón	Vega del Sella 1923
Balmori	SE	0.5	20–25	L	coastal plain	(Calabres)	Vega del Sella 1930
Bricia	S	1.6	25–30	S	coastal plain	Calabres	Jordá 1954
Camaleón	W	1.3	35	M	coastal plain	Felgaca (San Cecilio)	González Morales 1982
Cámara (Méré)	SW	6.9	110	S	interior valley	Cabras	González Morales 1982
Cáraba	N	1.1	50	L	coastal plain	(Purón)	González Morales 1982
Carmona	W	1.2	50	S	small cliff on coastal plain	Cerracín	González Morales 1982
Ceñil	NNE	3.0	80	M	cul-de-sac valley near estuary	Cueva–Sella	González Morales 1982
Coberizas	NW	1.6	55	M	hills near coast	Cabras–Bedón	Clark & Cartledge 1973
Collamosa (Acebal?)	NW	1.5	45	L	coastal plain	Carbocedo–Purón	González Morales 1982
Colomba	S, SE	1.8	40	L	coastal valley	San Cecilio	González Morales 1982
Colombres	SW	2.3	20	S	hills/edge of coastal plain	Cabra	Carballo 1960
Covariellas	S	2.7	90	S	valley on edge of coastal plain	Deva	González Morales 1982
Cuartamentero	SE, SW	1.0	30	M	coastal plain	Carbocedo	Clark 1976
Cueto de la Mina	S	1.5	25–30	L	coastal plain	Calabres	Vega del Sella 1916
Cuevas del Mar (4)	NW, SE	0.3–1.0	0–20	S, M	estuary	Nueva	Clark 1976
Elefante	S	0.2	40	S	top of coastal cliff	–	Clark 1976
Fonfría	N	0.4	35	S	coastal hill above estuary	Calabres	González Morales 1982
Juan de Covera	S	3.1	50	S	coastal valley	Dovedal–Purón	González Morales 1982
Leona (Llongar?)	S	0.7	25	S	coastal plain above estuary	(Calabres)	González Morales 1982
Mazaculos II (La Franca)	NW	0.3	35	L	hill above estuary	Cabra	González Morales 1982
Pendueles (Cuevona de)	S, SE	0.8–1.0	50	L, M	coastal plain	Novales	Gavelas 1980, González Morales 1982
Penicial	S	1.5	30–40	M	coastal plain	Nueva	Vega del Sella 1914
Pindal	N	0.2	10	M	coast	–	Jordá 1976
Puente de Puertas	S	1.4	10–20	S	coastal valley	Purón	González Morales 1982
Riera	W	1.5	25–30	M	coastal plain	Calabres	Clark & Richards 1978
Río (Lloseta)	SW	0.5	30–40	L	hills near coast	San Miguel–Sella	Moure & Cano 1976
Tres Calabres	S	1.8	25–30	S	coastal plain	Calabres	Jordá 1953
Vidiago (Cordoveganes?)	N	0.7	40	M	coastal plain	Purón	González Morales 1982

Azilian'. Some of these sites have been well published (e.g. La Chora, Coberizas, Sofoxó, Collubíl, Bolinkoba); others are known only as names in normative summaries of the regional prehistories (e.g. Silibranka, Camargo, Cobrantes). Sites with generally similar lithic industries, but which are believed to post-date the Azilian, include Liencres in Santander (Clark 1975a) and Marizulo cave in Guipúzcoa (Cava 1978). Reliance on archaeological index fossils only serves to underscore the arbitrary nature of the classic culture/stratigraphic unit designations.

Inspection of the Asturian data in *Table 5* shows the homogeneity with regard to site placement mentioned earlier (see also Clark and Lerner 1980; Clark 1983a). Asturian sites tend to be found in small (<36 m^2) and medium-sized (36–60 m^2) rock-shelters at low elevations ($\bar{x} = 36.5$ m) along

Table 6: Locational characteristics of 26 fairly credible Azilian sites

Site	Orientation	Lineal distance from sea (km)	Elevation above present sea level (m)	Size	Location	Drainage	Source
GUIPÚZCOA–VIZCAYA							
Aitzbitarte IV	WSW	8.0	220	L	coastal hills/gorgeside	Urumea	Straus 1975
Atxeta	N	6.5	20	S	plain near estuary	(Guernica)	Straus 1975
Ekain I	E	6.7	85	M	hills near estuary	Urola	Barandiarán & Altuna 1977
Ermittía	WNW	2.0	125	S	cliffside near coast	Deva	Straus 1983
Lumentxa	S	0.1	70	M	coastal mountainside	(Deva)	Aranzadi & Barandiarán 1935
Santimamiñe	S	5.0	150	L	coastal mountainside	(Guernica)	Straus 1975
Urtiaga	SW	1.8	130	S	hills near coast	Salbatoremendi (Urola)	Altuna & Apellániz 1978
SANTANDER–ASTURIAS							
Azules I	SW	27.5	150	S	interior mountainside	Güeña–Sella	Fernández Tresguerres 1976
Balmori	SE	0.5	20–25	L	coastal plain	Calabres	Clark & Clark 1975
Candamo	N	12.0	200	S	interior valley	Nalón	Hernández Pacheco 1919
Castillo	E	17.0	190	L	interior mountainside	Pas	Straus 1983
Cueto de la Mina	S	1.5	25–30	L	coastal plain	Calabres	Vega del Sella 1916
Meaza	SE	1.5	137	L	coastal plain	Curriña	Anderez 1953
Morín	NNW	7.0	65	M	coastal plain	Solia (Pas)	Vega del Sella 1921
Oscura (Ania)	?	33.0	150	?	interior valley	Andallón	Fernández Tresguerres 1980
Oscura (Perán/Perlora)	N	2.0	40–50	L	coastal hills	Espasa	Fernández & Mallo 1965
Otero	W	15.6	60	S	interior valley	Clarón	González Echegaray *et al.* 1963
Paloma	NW	30.0	156	L	interior valley	Soto	Hoyos *et al.* 1980
Pendo	S	8.0	80	L	coastal plain ridge	Pas	Straus 1975
Piélago'	W	20.0	225	S	hills/gorgeside	Miera	García Guinea 1975
Pindal	N	0.1	10	M	coast	–	Jordá 1976
Rascaño	SW	21.0	240	S	interior hills/gorgeside	Miera	Barandiarán & González Echegaray 1981
Riera	W	1.5	25–30	M	coastal plain	Calabres	Clark & Richards 1978
Río (Lloseta)	SW	0.5	12	L	hills near coast	San Miguel–Sella	Moure & Cano 1976
Salitre	W	27.5	500	L	interior mountains	Carcabal–Miera	Straus 1983
Valle	?	12.0	80	L	interior valley	Asón	Cheynier & González Echegaray 1964

estuaries, on the leeward (south) side of east–west trending coastal hill ranges and valleys, and in the heavily karstified limestone topography which is such a characteristic feature of eastern Asturias and western Santander. Even allowing for some minor northward displacement of the coast (for evidence of rising sea levels subsequent to Asturian midden formation, see González Morales 1982), it is clear that Asturian sites are never found very far inland nor at very great elevations. The mean distance to the present shoreline is a scant 1.4 km (ranging from 0.1 km at Pindal to 6.9 km at Cámara), with very little evidence for midden accumulation beyond 3 km inland.

Elsewhere, I have argued at length that the placement of Asturian sites makes sense in terms of maximizing access to key resources while minimizing the expenditure of energy in a 'logistical' type model (Binford 1980) in which *concheros* are the remains of dumps associated with base camps (Clark and Lerner 1980; Clark 1983a). Preference for this model takes into account the topography of the Cantabrian coastal plain, characterized by a lattice of short (10–30 km), swift, north–south trending, entrenched river valleys and altitudinally determined, north–south compression of environmental zones. Residential sites located near the coast are ideally situated: (i) to exploit forest and forest margin staples (red and roe deer, boar) and occasional, opportunistically acquired, high-yield parkland/grassland ungulates (horses, bovines); (ii) to take advantage of seasonally available alpine species (ibex, chamois) by means of hunting parties dispatched from such residential sites; and (iii) to exploit estuarine and coastal limpets and topshells, either as permanent dietary supplements and/or as 'emergency' foods in times or seasons of scarcity (see Bailey *et al.* 1983; Deith 1983 – for evidence of winter collection of shellfish in Asturian middens).

The Azilian data present a different picture (*Table 6*). On a global level, the mean distance to the present shoreline is 10.3 km and might have been as great as 15 km during the Dryas III interval, to which most Azilian sites are dated. Mean elevation is 122.2 m, indicating the existence of substantial numbers of sites located inland, in relatively high mountainous terrain (and in the Basque provinces, where a low-lying coastal plain is practically non-existent). Compared to the Asturian, Azilian site sizes are more bimodally distributed, with a tendency for the larger sites (>60 m²) to be found in coastal contexts (e.g. Balmori, Cueto de la Mina), although not necessarily at low elevations. Small sites (<36 m²) occur most often in high alpine gorges (e.g. Piélago, Rascaño) in terrain which is difficult of access. They tend to have ibex-dominated faunas, lending credence to a functional explanation of these sites as limited activity stations (what Binford calls 'transient, hunting camps') which owe their existence to monitoring, procurement and processing of these alpine caprines.

In considering the topography of northern Spain, where distinct micro-climates, vegetational associations and faunal communities are effectively 'stacked' vertically on top of one another along north–south trending river courses within a short distance of the sea, and given the near certainty of regular, cyclical, north–south movement by both men and animals within the confines of these entrenched valley systems, it is reasonable to expect that residential sites and limited activity stations might be identified which form persistent 'paired' elements within the 'logistical zone' (probably a single drainage catchment) of hunter-gatherer bands (Binford 1980, 1982a). Although there is very little evidence for such a bimodal distribution in the Asturian, Azilian site locational data indicate possible residential camp–hunting station dyads for Santimamiñe/Atxeta (Ría Guernica), Lumentxa/Ermittía (Deva), Ekain/Urtiaga (Urola), Morín/Piélago and Rascaño (Solia-Miera), Río/Azules (Sella), Valle/Mirón (Asón) and Candamo/Sofoxó (Nalón-Nora). While these elements in an Azilian settlement–subsistence system are not as distinct as might be desirable (due mainly to variation in the grain of the archaeological record and the way in which it is reported), it is significant that they form part of a general Upper Palaeolithic pattern in which such site functional relationships appear to be redundant and to persist over time (Straus 1983a). The fact that the Asturian configuration is quite distinct implies a fundamental re-articulation of the elements of the system at some point after c. 8500 BP, since there are few indications of inland occupation after that date.

CONCLUSIONS

The Mesolithic data presented here only begin to make sense when viewed from the larger perspective of patterns visible in the Cantabrian Upper Palaeolithic as a whole. Recent comparative evaluations of post-Aurignacian Upper Palaeolithic and Mesolithic assemblages by Straus (1983a, 1985) and Clark (1983c; Clark and Straus 1983) have determined the existence of two major Vasco-Cantabrian assemblage types which seem to persist and recur throughout the latter part of the Lateglacial and early Postglacial periods. These assemblage types are dominated on the one hand by quartzite notches and denticulates, side-scrapers and crude heavy-duty tools, and on the other by retouched (especially backed) bladelets with substantial numbers of small end-scrapers and burins made of flint. The Asturian is in general an example of the former; most Azilian collections (and probably Liencres) are examples of the latter. Work at La Riera has shown that collections assigned to many of the other conventionally defined culture/stratigraphic units can also be accommodated by this bimodal scheme. I believe that these assemblage types can most readily be explained in functional terms. They seem to represent two rather generalized and flexible technological subsystems which persist for about fifteen millennia (c. 21,000–7000 BP) and which probably reflect in some imperfect way two distinct, yet broadly defined, sets of activities or behaviours (*Table 7*).

In the case of the Asturian middens, which are typically the latest cultural deposits found in Cantabrian caves, that activity set probably involved the disposal of bulk garbage from nearby base camps, as Straus (1979) has recently proposed. The *concheros* are not themselves living surfaces (Mazaculos II level 3.3 excepted), but seem instead to be waste heaps piled in rock-shelters and in the mouths of caves after these had become so choked with deposits that they were no longer suitable living spaces. Of the associated residential sites themselves, however, we have no trace.

It is tempting to try to explain the Azilian-type configuration as the remains of technologies related to hunting, fishing and the procurement of plants. Many investigators do in fact tend to equate microlithic assemblages with the multi-component tools and weapons used in these activities (e.g. Clarke 1976). It is difficult to be more precise, however, since precise correlations with faunal remains, categories of débitage, and site locational data so far elude us. While there are clear-cut patterns in the faunal components and locational characteristics of Azilian sites, they are not correlated with differences in the lithic assemblages. It may be that only new and different kinds of data (e.g. micro-wear analy-

Table 7: Summary of evidence bearing on functional complementarity

Type of evidence	Comments:
Chronology	one-third of the dates indicate overlap for the 9500–8500 BP interval, although Azilian and Asturian grand means and mean standard deviations do not overlap.
Climate	wet, cold-to-very-cold conditions indicated for most Azilian sites; some (e.g. Cueva Morín) have very little evidence of arboreal vegetation. Pollen and sediment data from Asturian sites document temperate humid climates with high AP fractions.
Retouched tools	clear and striking differences with Azilian assemblages dominated by backed and retouched bladelets, Asturian assemblages by notches, denticulates and heavy-duty tools.
Débitage	débitage:tool ratios much higher, more variable for Azilian than for Asturian sites; débitage fractions generally higher for Azilian sites. More evidence for primary reduction in Asturian than in Azilian sites.
Raw materials	count data indicate marked and systematic differences with Azilian sites dominated by flint, Asturian sites by quartzite. weight data from La Riera indicate strong similarities across the Azilian/Asturian boundary. the flint-dominated Azilian assemblages are correlated with high small tool frequencies; the quartzite-dominated Asturian assemblages with large numbers of heavy-duty tools.
Economic faunas	undifferentiated except for the existence of Azilian ibex-hunting stations, apparently absent in the Asturian; Asturian faunas somewhat more diverse than Azilian ones (cf. Clark & Yi 1983).
Site location	Azilian residential camp–hunting station dyads indicated within drainage catchments; a unimodal pattern of coastal residential sites for the Asturian.

	Functional complementarity indicated?
Chronology	yes, for 9500–8500 BP interval.
Climate	evidence equivocal since Azilian pollen and sediment data neither always agree nor show a consistent pattern of disagreement; inadequate samples from sites dated independently to the period of overlap.
Retouched tools	yes
Débitage	yes – distinct activity/disposal facies indicated.
Raw materials	yes, similar procurement systems indicated for Azilian and Asturian by La Riera weight data; count data imply existence of two different technologies which are correlated with the ways the different raw materials were used.
Economic faunas	no, except insofar as this is evidence for a general pattern (cf. Straus 1977).
Site location	yes, for the 9500–8500 BP interval; no for post-8500 BP.

ses, improved information on seasonality) will allow for better resolution.

There are suggestions of periodicity in the occurrence of these technologies which hint at recurrent shifts in adaptation, perhaps coupled with changes in the distribution and availability of key resources. These changes have traditionally been explained by invoking changes in climate, with concomitant changes in sea level and in the extent of exposure of the continental shelf (cf. Bailey 1983*a*, 1983*b*). While the impact of climatic change on technology, human behaviour and resource distributions cannot be dismissed altogether for the north Spanish Upper Palaeolithic as a whole, it seems to have been of relatively minor importance from the more restricted perspective of the Pleistocene–Holocene boundary assemblages of interest here. The palaeoclimatic indicators document sometimes dramatic changes in the moisture and temperature regimes, and in climatic stability over the 12,000–6500 BP interval, but these appear to have had little effect on the nature of the resource base. To the extent that trends in the human food niche can be monitored over the long run (*c.* 45,000–2000 BP), patterns of increasing resource intensification and diversification seem to be documented, with the most diverse economic faunas occurring during the Asturian, and the most convincing examples of intensification corresponding to the established domestication economies of the Bronze and Iron Ages (see Clark and Yi 1983, for an expanded discussion of niche-width variation in Cantabrian archaeofaunas). In the absence of evidence to the contrary, Straus and I tend to explain these trends as due to subsistence pressure caused by imbalances between a growing regional population and its traditional resource base. As for the dichotomous pattern of assemblage variation noted here, it may be that the best single explanation is simply variation *in the ways in which sites were used through time*, or at least variation in the ways they are *perceived* to have been used, given the relatively coarse grain of the north Spanish archaeological record.

References

ALTUNA, J. (1972) Fauna de mamíferos de los yacimientos prehistóricos de Guipúzcoa con catálogo de los mamíferos cuaternarios del Cantábrico y del Pirineo occidental. *Munibe*, 24: 1–464.

ALTUNA, J. (1980) Historia de la domesticación animal en el País Vasco, desde sus origenes hasta la romanización. *Munibe*, 32: 1–163.

ALTUNA, J. and APELLÁNIZ, J. (1978) Las figuras rupestres paleolíticas de la cueva de Ekain. *Munibe*, 30: 1–151.

ANDEREZ, V. (1953) La cueva prehistórica de 'Meaza': estado actual de su exploración. *Miscelánea Comillas*, 19: 23–37.

ARANZADI, T. and BARANDIARÁN, J. (1935) *Santimamiñe y Lumentxa*. Bilbao, Diputación Provincial de Vizcaya.

BAHN, P.G. (1982) Intersite and interregional links during the Upper Palaeolithic: the Pyrenean evidence. *Oxford Journal of Archaeology*, 1: 247–267.

BAILEY, G. (1983a) Economic change in late Pleistocene Cantabria. In G. Bailey (ed.), *Hunter-Gatherer Economy in Prehistory*. Cambridge, University Press: 149–165.

BAILEY, G. (1983b) Problems of site formation and the interpretation of spatial and temporal discontinuities in the distribution of coastal middens. In P.M. Masters and N.C. Flemming (eds), *Quaternary Coastlines and Marine Archaeology*. London, Academic Press: 559–582.

BAILEY, G., DEITH, M. and SHACKLETON, N. (1983) Oxygen isotope analysis and seasonality determinations: limits and potential of a new technique. *American Antiquity*, 48: 390–399.

BARANDIARÁN, I. (1967) *El Paleomesolítico del Pirineo Occidental* (Seminario de Prehistoria y Protohistoria Monografías Arqueológicas, 3). Zaragoza, Universidad de Zaragoza.

BARANDIARÁN, I. and GONZÁLEZ ECHEGARAY, J. (eds) (1981) *El Paleolítico Superior de la Cueva del Rascaño* (Monografías del Centro de Investigación y Museo de Altamira, 3). Santander, Ministerio de Cultura.

BARANDIARÁN, J.M. DE and ALTUNA, J. (1977) Excavaciones en Ekain. *Munibe*, 29: 3–58.

BINFORD, L. (1979) Organization and formation processes: looking at curated technologies. *Journal of Anthropological Research*, 35: 255–273.

BINFORD, L. (1980) Willow smoke and dogs' tails: hunter-gatherer settlement systems and archaeological site formation. *American Antiquity*, 45: 4–20.

BINFORD, L. (1981) *Bones: Ancient Men and Modern Myths*. New York, Academic Press.

BINFORD, L. (1982a) The archaeology of place. *Journal of Anthropological Archaeology*, 1: 5–31.

BINFORD, L. (1982b) Objectivity – explanation – archaeology 1981. In C. Renfrew, M. Rowlands and B. Segraves (eds), *Theory and Explanation in Archaeology*. New York, Academic Press: 125–138.

BINFORD, L. (1983c) Working at archaeology: the generation gap – reactionary arguments and theory building. In L. Binford (ed.), *Working at Archaeology*. New York, Academic Press: 213–238.

BINFORD, L. and SABLOFF, J. (1982) Paradigms, systematics and archaeology. *Journal of Anthropological Research*, 38: 137–153.

BORDES, F. (1968) *The Old Stone Age*. New York, McGraw Hill.

BREUIL, H. and OBERMAIER, H. (1912) Les premiers travaux de l'Institut de Paléontologie Humaine. *L'Anthropologie*, 23: 1–27.

BURLEIGH, R., AMBERS, J. and MATTHEWS, K. (1982) British Museum natural radiocarbon measurements XV. *Radiocarbon*, 24: 262–290.

BUTZER, K.W. (1971a) Comunicación preliminar sobre la geología de Cueva Morín. In J. González Echegaray and L.G. Freeman (eds), *Cueva Morín: Excavaciones 1966–1968*. Santander, Patronato de las Cuevas Prehistóricas: 345–356.

BUTZER, K.W. (1971b) *Environment and Archaeology* (2nd edition). Chicago, Aldine.

BUTZER, K.W. (1973) Notas sobre la geomorfología regional de la parte occidental de la provincia de Santander y la estratigrafía de Cueva Morín. In J. González Echegaray and L.G. Freeman (eds), *Cueva Morín: Excavaciones 1969*. Santander, Patronato de las Cuevas Prehistóricas: 267–276.

BUTZER, K. (1981) Cave sediments, Upper Pleistocene stratigraphy and Mousterian facies in Cantabrian Spain. *Journal of Archaeological Science*, 8: 133–183.

CARBALLO, J. (1960) *Investigaciones Prehistóricas II*. Santander, Diputación Provincial.

CAVA, A. (1978) El depósito arqueológico en la cueva de Marizulo (Guipúzcoa). *Munibe*, 30: 155–172.

CHEYNIER, A. and GONZÁLEZ ECHEGARAY, J. (1964) La grotte de Valle. In E. Ripoll (ed.), *Miscelánea en Homenaje al Abate Henri Breuil*. Barcelona, Instituto de Prehistoria: 327–346.

CLARK, G.A. (1971) The Asturian of Cantabria: subsistence base and the evidence for post-Pleistocene climatic shifts. *American Anthropologist*, 73: 1244–1257.

CLARK, G.A. (1975a) Liencres: una estación al aire libre de estilo Asturiense cerca de Santander. *Cuadernos de Arqueología*, 3: 1–84.

CLARK, G.A. (1975b) El hombre y su ambiente a comienzos del Holoceno en la región cantábrica. *Boletín del Instituto de Estudios Asturianos*, 84–85: 363–387.

CLARK, G.A. (1976) *El Asturiense Cantábrico* (Bibliotheca Praehistorica Hispana, 13). Madrid, Consejo Superior de Investigaciones Científicas.

CLARK, G.A. (1979) Liencres: an open station of Asturian affinity near Santander, Spain. *Quaternaria*, 21: 249–286, 300–304.

CLARK, G.A. (1983a) Boreal phase settlement–subsistence models for Cantabrian Spain. In G. Bailey (ed.), *Hunter-Gatherer Economy in Prehistory*. Cambridge, University Press: 96–110.

CLARK, G.A. (1983b) *The Asturian of Cantabria: Early Holocene Hunter-Gatherers in Northern Spain* (Anthropological Papers of the University of Arizona, 41). Tucson, University of Arizona Press.

CLARK, G.A. (1983c) Una perspectiva funcionalista en la prehistoria de la región cantábrica. In A. Balíl *et al.* (eds), *Homenaje al Prof. Martín Almagro Basch*. Madrid, Ministerio de Cultura: 155–170.

CLARK, G.A. and CARTLEDGE, T. (1973) Recent excavations at the cave of Coberizas (Province of Asturias, Spain). *Quaternaria*, 17: 387–411.

CLARK, G.A. and CLARK, V. (1975) La cueva de Balmori (Asturias, España): nuevas aportaciones. *Trabajos de Prehistoria*, 32: 35–77.

CLARK, G.A. and LERNER, S. (1980) Prehistoric resource utilization in early Holocene Cantabrian Spain. *Anthropology UCLA*, 10: 53–96.

CLARK, G.A. and MENÉNDEZ AMOR, J. (1975) Apendice II: muestras de polen de Liencres, niveles 1 y 2. *Cuadernos de Arqueología*, 3: 67–70.

CLARK, G.A. and RICHARDS, L. (1978) Late and post-Pleistocene industries and fauna from the cave site of La Riera (Asturias, Spain). In L.G. Freeman (ed.), *Views of the Past*. The Hague, Mouton: 117–152.

CLARK, G.A. and STRAUS, L.G. (1983) Late Pleistocene hunter-gatherer adaptations in Cantabrian Spain. In G. Bailey (ed.), *Hunter-Gatherer Economy in Prehistory*. Cambridge, University Press: 131–148.

CLARK, G.A. and YI, S. (1983) Niche-width variation in Cantabrian archaeofaunas: a diachronic study. In J. Clutton-Brock and C. Grigson (eds), *Animals and Archaeology: 1. Hunters and their Prey*. Oxford, British Archaeological Reports (International Series) S163: 183–208.

CLARK, G.A., YOUNG, D., STRAUS, L.G. and JEWETT, R. (1986) Multivariate analysis of La Riera industries and fauna. In L.G. Straus and G.A. Clark (eds), *La Riera Cave: Stone Age Hunter-Gatherer Adaptations in Northern Spain*. Tempe, Arizona State University Anthropological Research Papers no. 36: 325–350.

CLARKE, D.L. (1976) Mesolithic Europe: the economic basis. In G. de G. Sieveking, I.H. Longworth and K.E. Wilson (eds), *Problems in Economic and Social Archaeology*. London, Duckworth: 449–481.

CRUSAFONT, M. (1963) ?Es la industria 'Asturiense' una evolucionada 'Pebble Culture'? *Spéléon*, 14: 77–88.

DEITH, M. (1983) Seasonality of shell collecting, determined by oxygen isotope analysis of marine shells from Asturian sites in Cantabria. In C. Grigson and J. Clutton-Brock (eds), *Animals and Archaeology: 2. Shell Middens, Fishes and Birds*. Oxford, British Archaeological Reports (International Series) S183: 67–76.

EVIN, J. (1979) Réflexions générales et données nouvelles sur la chronologie absolue ^{14}C des industries de la fin du Paléolithique supérieur et du début du Mésolithique. In D. de Sonneville-Bordes (ed.), *La Fin des Temps Glaciaires en Europe*. Paris, Centre National de Recherche Scientifique: 5–13.

FERNÁNDEZ, R. and MALLO, M. (1965) Primera cata de sondeo en Cueva Oscura. *Boletín del Instituto de Estudios Asturianos*, 54: 65–82.

FERNÁNDEZ-TRESGUERRES, J. (1976) Enterramiento aziliense de la cueva de Los Azules I (Cangas de Onis, Oviedo). *Boletín del Instituto de Estudios Asturianos*, 87: 273–288.

FERNÁNDEZ-TRESGUERRES, J. (1980) *El Aziliense en las Provincias de Asturias y Santander* (Monografías del Centro de Investigación y Museo de Altamira, 2). Santander, Ministerio de Cultura.

FREEMAN, L.G. (1973) The significance of mammalian faunas from Paleolithic occupations in Cantabrian Spain. *American Antiquity*, 38: 3–44.

GARCÍA GUINEA, M.A. (1975) El mesolítico en Cantabria. In M.A. García Guinea and M.A. Puente (eds), *La Prehistoria en la Cornisa Cantábrica*. Santander, Institución Cultural de Cantabria: 177–200.

GAVELAS, A. (1980) Sobre nuevos concheros asturienses en los concejos de Ribadesella y Llanes. *Boletín del Instituto de Estudios Asturianos*, 101: 675–703, 711–718.

GONZÁLEZ ECHEGARAY, J. (1971) El Paleolítico superior. In J. González Echegaray and L.G. Freeman (eds), *Cueva Morín: Excavaciones 1966–1968*. Santander, Patronato de las Cuevas Prehistóricas: 191–297.

GONZÁLEZ ECHEGARAY, J. (1973) Nuevas aportaciones al estudio del Paleolítico superior en Cueva Morín. In J. González Echegaray and L.G. Freeman (eds), *Cueva Morín: Excavaciones 1969*. Santander, Patronato de las Cuevas Prehistóricas: 165–216.

GONZÁLEZ ECHEGARAY, J., GARCÍA GUINEA, M.A., BEGÍNES, A. and MADARIAGA, B. (1963) *Cueva de la Chora*. Madrid, Excavaciones Arqueológicas en España 53.

GONZÁLEZ MORALES, M.R. (1978) Excavaciones en el conchero asturiense de la cueva de Mazaculos II (La Franca, Ribadedeva, Asturias). *Boletín del Instituto de Estudios Asturianos*, 93–94: 369–383.

GONZÁLEZ MORALES, M.R. (1982) *El Asturiense y Otras Culturas Locales* (Monografías del Centro de Investigación y Museo de Altamira, 7). Santander, Ministerio de Cultura.

GROUPE DE TRAVAIL DE PRÉHISTOIRE CANTABRIQUE (GTPC) (1979) Chronostratigraphie et écologie des cultures du Paléolithique final en Espagne cantabrique. In D. de Sonneville-Bordes (ed.), *La Fin des Temps Glaciaires en Europe*. Paris, Centre National de Recherche Scientifique: 713–719.

HERNÁNDEZ PACHECO, E. (1919) *La Cueva de la Peña de Candamo (Asturias)*. Madrid, Comisión de Investigaciones Paleontológicas y Prehistóricas Memoria 24.

HOYOS, M., MARTÍNEZ, M., CHAPA, T., CASTAÑOS, P. and SANCHIZ, F. (1980) *La Cueva de la Paloma, Soto de las Regueras (Asturias)*. Madrid, Excavaciones Arqueológicas en España 116.

JORDÁ, F. (1954) La cueva de Bricia (Asturias). *Boletín del Instituto de Estudios Asturianos*, 22: 169–195.

JORDÁ, F. (1959) Revisión de la cronología del Asturiense. *5º Congreso Arqueológico Nacional*. Zaragoza, Universidad de Zaragoza: 63–66.

JORDÁ, F. (1963) El Paleolítico superior cantábrica y sus industrias. *Saitabi*, 8: 3–22.

JORDÁ, F. (1975) El Paleolítico hispano; notas sobre el Asturiense. *Las Ciencias*, 40: 87–93.

JORDÁ, F. (1977) *Historia de Asturias: Prehistoria*. Oviedo, Ediciones Ayalga.

LAVILLE, H. (1986) Stratigraphy, sedimentology and chronology of the La Riera cave deposits. In L.G. Straus and G.A. Clark (eds), *La Riera Cave: Stone Age Hunter-Gatherer Adaptations in Northern Spain*. Tempe, Arizona State University Anthropological Research Papers no. 36: 25–56.

LEROI-GOURHAN, A. (1971) Análisis polínico de Cueva Morín. In J. González Echegaray and L.G. Freeman (eds), *Cueva Morín: Excavaciones 1966–1968*. Santander, Patronato de las Cuevas Prehistóricas: 359–365.

LEROI-GOURHAN, A. and GIRARD, M. (1979) Chronologie pollinique de quelques sites préhistoriques à la fin des temps glaciaires. In D. de Sonneville-Bordes (ed.), *La Fin des Temps Glaciaires en Europe*. Paris, Centre National de Recherche Scientifique: 49–52.

MARTÍNEZ, M. and CHAPA, T. (1980) La industria prehistórica de la cueva de la Paloma (Soto de las Regueras, Asturias). In M. Hoyos et al. (eds), *La Cueva de la Paloma (Soto de las Regueras, Asturias)*. Madrid, Excavaciones Arqueológicas en España 116: 115–204.

MOURE, J.A. and CANO, M. (1976) La cueva del Río de Ardines (Ribadesella, Asturias). *Boletín del Instituto de Estudios Asturianos*, 87: 260–271.

STRAUS, L.G. (1975) *A Study of the Solutrean in Vasco-Cantabrian Spain*. Unpublished Ph.D thesis, Department of Anthropology, University of Chicago.

STRAUS, L.G. (1977) Of deerslayers and mountain men: Paleolithic faunal exploitation in Cantabrian Spain. In L. Binford (ed.), *For Theory Building in Archaeology*. New York, Academic Press: 41–76.

STRAUS, L.G. (1979) Mesolithic adaptations along the northern coast of Spain. *Quaternaria*, 21: 305–327.

STRAUS, L.G. (1980) The role of raw materials in lithic assemblage variability. *Lithic Technology*, 9: 68–72.

STRAUS, L.G. (1983a) *El Solutrense Vasco-Cantábrico: una Nueva Perspectiva* (Monografías del Centro de Investigación y Museo de Altamira, 10). Madrid, Ministerio de Cultura.

STRAUS, L.G. (1983b) Terminal Pleistocene faunal exploitation in Cantabria and Gascony. In J. Clutton-Brock and C. Grigson (eds), *Animals and Archaeology: 1. Hunters and their Prey*. Oxford, British Archaeological Reports (International Series) S163: 209–225.

STRAUS, L.G. (1983c) From Mousterian to Magdalenian: cultural evolution viewed from Vasco-Cantabrian Spain and Pyrenean France. In E. Trinkaus (ed.), *The Mousterian Legacy: Human Biocultural Change in the Upper Pleistocene*. Oxford, British Archaeological Reports (International Series) S164: 73–111.

STRAUS, L.G. (1985) Chronostratigraphy of the Pleistocene/Holocene boundary: the Azilian problem in the Franco-Cantabrian region. *Palaeohistoria*, 27: 89–122.

STRAUS, L.G., ALTUNA, J., CLARK, G.A., GONZÁLEZ MORALES, M.R., LAVILLE, H., LEROI-GOURHAN, A., MENÉNDEZ DE LA HOZ, M. and ORTEA, J.A. (1981) Paleoecology at La Riera (Asturias, Spain). *Current Anthropology*, 22: 655–682.

STRAUS, L.G. and CLARK, G.A. (1978) Prehistoric investigations in Cantabrian Spain. *Journal of Field Archaeology*, 5: 287–317.

STRAUS, L.G. and CLARK, G.A. (1986) La Riera: archaeological remains – level content and characteristics. In L.G. Straus and G.A. Clark (eds), *La Riera Cave: Stone Age Hunter-Gatherer Adaptations in Northern Spain*. Tempe, Arizona State University Anthropological Research Papers no. 36: 75–188.

STRAUS, L.G., CLARK, G.A., ALTUNA, J. and ORTEA, J.A. (1980) Ice age subsistence in northern Spain. *Scientific American*, 242: 142–152.

STRAUS, L.G., CLARK, G.A., ORDAX, J., ESBERT, R. and SUAREZ, L. (1986) Patterns of lithic raw material variation at La Riera. In L.G. Straus and G.A. Clark (eds), *La Riera Cave: Stone Age Hunter-Gatherer Adaptations in Northern Spain*. Tempe, Arizona State University Anthropological Research Papers no. 36: 189–208.

VEGA DEL SELLA, CONDE DE LA (1914) *La Cueva del Penicial (Asturias)*. Madrid, Comisión de Investigaciones Paleontológicas y Prehistóricas Memoria 4.

VEGA DEL SELLA, CONDE DE LA (1915) Avance al estudio del Paleolítico superior en la región cantábrica. *Asociación Española para el Progreso de la Ciencias*: 139–160.

VEGA DEL SELLA, CONDE DE LA (1916) *El Paleolítico de Cueto de la Mina*. Madrid, Comisión de Investigaciones Paleontológicas y Prehistóricas Memoria 13.

VEGA DEL SELLA, CONDE DE LA (1921) *El Paleolítico de Cueva Morín (Santander) y Notas para la Climatología Cuaternaria*. Madrid, Comisión de Investigaciones Paleontológicas y Prehistóricas Memoria 29.

VEGA DEL SELLA, CONDE DE LA (1923) *El Asturiense: Nueva Industria Pre-neolítica*. Madrid, Comisión de Investigaciones Paleontológicas y Prehistóricas Memoria 32.

VEGA DEL SELLA, CONDE DE LA (1930) *Las Cuevas de la Riera y Balmori*. Madrid, Comisión de Investigaciones Paleontológicas y Prehistóricas Memoria 38.

Asturian Resource Exploitation: Recent Perspectives

M.R. González Morales

Abstract

In the last few years several studies devoted to the problem of Asturian subsistence patterns have been published. Some of these studies focus on catchment analysis or territorial approaches. However, certain of the data on which these studies rest seem to be inconsistent with that purpose, if not redundant. This paper uses the results of recent fieldwork to highlight the danger of making generalizations from an inadequate database, and of replacing the critical analysis of data by sophisticated 'methodological' developments.

INTRODUCTION

This paper is intended to be a historical and critical review of the models of subsistence patterns which have been proposed to date for the Asturian.

The excavation conducted by the Count of Vega del Sella in 1914 at the cave of El Penicial, on the eastern coast of the province of Asturias, was the beginning of systematic investigations of a regional Mesolithic culture known thereafter as *Asturian* (Vega del Sella 1914). The study of this phenomenon has always been controversial; the peculiarities of its lithic industry, the nature of the sites and their faunal composition were rather surprising elements, when compared with the Upper Palaeolithic and Epi-Palaeolithic cultures then known in western Europe.

In the first monograph study devoted to the definition and analysis of the Asturian (Vega del Sella 1923), the investigator carried out a rigorously scientific analysis of the available evidence, proposing a series of hypotheses, and then made field observations and trial excavations to verify them, limited, of course, by the methods of archaeology practised in those days. In this first study, and in later ones (Vega del Sella 1925, 1930), as well as defining the characteristics of the stone and bone industries and the stratigraphic position of Asturian deposits, Vega del Sella began to show a clear interest in the problem of subsistence. He discussed the faunal contents of the Asturian shell middens, relating them to impoverished hunting practices combined with shellfish collecting. This idea of 'economies of poverty' as typical of Mesolithic times was widely accepted at the time – and even today it has many advocates.

The development of ideas about the Asturian after Vega del Sella has been well summarized in the literature, especially by G.A. Clark (1976) and M.R. González Morales (1982). It seems unnecessary, therefore, to elaborate further on this topic here.

The renewed attention paid by G.A. Clark to the investigation of the Asturian since 1968, and the work done by G.N. Bailey on Asturian shell middens in 1971, drew attention once again to the problems of subsistence and resource exploitation during that period. In fact, the first explicit hypothesis of subsistence patterns – the possible seasonality of exploitation – and the first studies orientated toward site catchment analysis are found in the works of these investigators. Later, L.G. Straus offered his rather controversial view of the Asturian, including resource exploitation and subsistence patterns (Straus 1979); while the present author completed a revision of the 'Asturian question' and carried out several field seasons at the classic Asturian site of cueva de Mazaculos, and later at cueva de la Llana, in eastern Asturias (González Morales 1978; González Morales and Márquez Uría 1978; González Morales *et al.* 1980).

MODELS OF THE ASTURIAN

An analysis, necessarily short, of these recent contributions reveals a series of viewpoints that are not always coincident, and are often contradictory. This paper tries to shed some light on the kinds of problems we are facing now, and to suggest directions for future work.

A survey of the proposed patterns of Asturian resource exploitation reveals the following models.

Clark (1971, 1976, 1983) offered an interpretation of Asturian middens (*concheros*) as:

> trash heaps associated with base camps occupied by a local group or a major part thereof on a fairly continuous (perhaps even perennial) basis, and representing the residues from a wide variety of procurement, processing, maintenance and disposal activities (1983: 99).

According to Clark, the *concheros* were ideally located to facilitate exploitation of coastal, estuarine, forest and montane resources with a minimal expenditure of energy. He also invokes an admittedly weak piece of negative evidence to support his argument – the fact that no inland, montane Asturian sites are known to date. In this model, based on field observations made primarily during the 1969 field campaigns and on detailed research of Asturian materials in museums and those obtained from a test pit programme, the Asturians had an economy based on diversified resources, combining the hunting of open forest, forest and alpine species with intensive collecting of shellfish, in year-round settlements.

An alternative proposed by G.N. Bailey in 1973 viewed Asturian middens as the remains of seasonal sites, in a pattern of periodic migrations between the coast and the uplands. The basis for this proposal is the evidence of the great dependence of the Asturian economy on red deer as its primary meat source, given the fact that shellfish were of comparatively less importance in the total diet. The foundation for this last assumption was the calculation of the relative nutritional significance of the edible parts of red deer and shellfish, which revealed the very low calorific yield corresponding to quite spectacular quantities of shells (Bailey 1973).

Bailey's hypothesis implies that Asturian groups exploited shellfish during the winter and the spring as a complementary resource for seasonally impoverished hunting and that, during the summer and autumn, they followed the red deer herds to their montane grassland areas. The concentration of Asturian coastal sites in the estuaries of the main watercourses – considering these as routes from the coast to the mountains – is assumed to be supporting evidence for this hypothesis.

Several years later, Bailey proposed a more complex hypothesis of site exploitation territories on the Cantabrian coast from Upper Palaeolithic to Asturian times. In short, he considered that the 'unifying directive of the exploitation system' had been:

> the essentially stable relationship with the ungulate basis of the food supply, while the discontinuities arose from the differential spatial relationship between changes of sea level and a varied and generally restrictive landscape (1978: 60).

Following the same line of reasoning, Bailey stated in 1983 that:

> In the Cantabrian case, the main conclusion is that major, repeatedly used settlement sites tend to be located in accordance with the principles of terrestrial exploitation, particularly hunting of herd animals such as red deer (1983: 576).

That, of course, also includes Asturian sites.

Clark and Lerner have recently developed a complete study of Asturian resource exploitation, based on site catchment analysis techniques, proposing three main settlement/subsistence models, and complex verification procedures involving homogeneity tests, cluster analysis and discriminant function analysis, in order to accept or reject the models previously proposed. The results of all this work seem to support a model which postulates that 'Asturian sites are remains of base camps, situated amongst the hills and along the estuaries near the coast' (Clark and Lerner 1980: 88).

It is worth noting that, in 1979, L.G. Straus also proposed a kind of bipolar exploitation model for Mesolithic Cantabria, considering the Asturian as chronologically equivalent to the Azilian, and both of them as different functional or disposal facies of the same human groups. The subsistence strategies during this period might 'continue a trend towards subsistence diversification initiated at least in the Solutrean' (Straus 1979: 321).

DISCUSSION

Two observations may be drawn from the review presented above. First of all, there is a considerable amount of contradiction among all the hypotheses. Secondly, some of them have been tested even by means of sophisticated statistical techniques. However, when the results of some of the analyses are compared with the *archaeological record*, we find major inconsistencies.

For example, in cluster and discriminant function analyses (Clark and Lerner 1980: 84) it is surprising to find a cave located in two different clusters according to the results of the tests, which appears in the literature and old collections with two different names, but which several years ago was shown to be a single site (Mallo *et al.* 1980).

This use of references in old literature to sites dug at the beginning of the century leads to such inconsistent results; the phenomenon of considering a single site as two different ones because of different names in publications occurs repeatedly in the lists used for analyses (Sabina/Coberizas, El Río/La Lloseta). Furthermore, the site of Lledias, which was proven to be a fake several years ago, is still considered as an Asturian site. The inclusion of these errors can obviously distort factors such as distance to the sea, catchment areas, and so on.

In other cases, the inclusion of variables that are only present in *one* site, or in very few sites, has given rise to strange results. For example, in the variable entry sequence of a discriminant function analysis applied to Asturian sites (Clark and Lerner 1980: 88), of 30 variables considered and 15 used by the program, the otter (*Lutra lutra*) and the hare (*Lepus europaeus*) are ranked 6th and 8th, respectively, with greater discriminatory power than the percentage of woodland included in the territories, the average distance to the sea, woodland and alpine areas, or the heavy-duty tools (which are the major component of Asturian lithic industries).

When comparing such results with the archaeological record it becomes evident that the otter is cited only in a single reference, coming from the excavation of the shelter of Cueto de la Mina in 1916, and limited to a presence/absence statement, perhaps based on only one bone. The fate of *Lepus* is similar, being cited only once in each of three sites among the 28 sites considered.

In other example, a study of the distribution of sites along the Cantabrian coast (Bailey 1978) makes use of only *one-third*, or less, of the total number of sites known in the Asturian area at the present day (Gavelas 1980; González Morales 1982). The results of intensive survey work and publications during the last ten years are usually not considered, and several studies use data of very limited reliability – for instance, the reference to the shell midden of El Pendo as an example of a relatively inland Asturian settlement (Bailey 1978: 53–54). This assumption, the basis for the idea of the selection of inland sites for exploiting a wider terrestrial territory, is very hard to prove; as far as the present author is aware, this *conchero* is only cited in an old reference, and with hindsight it is not clear if El Pendo was an Asturian site at all.

The idea of Asturian shell middens as disposal areas and, by extension, the idea of the Asturian as a disposal or functional facies of the Azilian, seems very tempting. However, Asturian and Azilian dates *do not* overlap *sensu stricto*; most of them are clearly separated. In addition, at the cave of Mazaculos (La Franca, Spain) there are distinct occupation surfaces with hearths at the base of the Asturian midden, in which were also found typical Asturian picks and the same industry as in the rest of the midden. This is not coincidental. Mazaculos is the *only* large-scale Asturian *conchero* excavated in recent times, and the only one that is clearly stratified (González Morales 1978; González Morales and Márquez Uría 1978; González Morales *et al.* 1980).

At Mazaculos and several other caves, there is evidence of the contemporaneity of the late Asturian occupations with the first arrival of pottery in the region, perhaps after 5500 BP, and even with the first megalith builders, as shown by the presence of pottery of late Neolithic type in shell middens and by the discovery in 1924 of two Asturian picks in the chamber of one of the barrows located on Sierra Plana de Vidiago, close to the main Asturian concentration areas.

Thus, the present author believes that the gap between models and data can only be reduced by a very critical approach to the data, the use of statistical tests appropriate to the nature of the data and by a continuous, dialectic movement between models and data.

A fuller understanding of Asturian resource exploitation and subsistence patterns must be based on recent, large-scale excavations of Asturian sites and detailed field survey work, specialist analyses of faunal remains, and detailed estimations of potential resources for well-documented sites. Furthermore, old data and references must be used with a great deal of caution.

Acknowledgements: The author would like to thank Professor Edward Daley, Department of Philology, University of Cantabria, for reviewing and correcting the English of the final manuscript.

References

BAILEY, G.N. (1973) Concheros del Norte de España: una hipótesis preliminar. *Actas del XIIº Congreso Nacional de Arqueológico, Jaén 1971*. Zaragoza, Universidad de Zaragoza: 73–84.

BAILEY, G.N. (1978) Shell middens as indicators of Postglacial economies. In P.A. Mellars (ed.), *The Early Postglacial Settlement of Northern Europe*. London, Duckworth: 37–63.

BAILEY, G.N. (1983) Problems of site formation and the interpretation of spatial and temporal discontinuities in the distribution of coastal middens. In P.M. Masters and N.C. Flemming (eds), *Quaternary Coastlines and Marine Archaeology*. London, Academic Press: 559–582.

CLARK, G.A. (1971) The Asturian of Cantabria: subsistence base and the evidence for post-Pleistocene climatic shifts. *American Anthropologist*, 73: 1244–1257.

CLARK, G.A. (1976) *El Asturiense Cantábrico* (Bibliotheca Praehistorica Hispana, 13). Madrid, Consejo Superior de Investigaciones Científicas.

CLARK, G.A. (1983) Boreal phase settlement/subsistence models for Cantabrian Spain. In G. Bailey (ed.), *Hunter-Gatherer Economy in Prehistory. A European Perspective*. Cambridge, University Press: 96–110.

CLARK, G.A. and LERNER, S. (1980) Prehistoric resource utilization in early Holocene Cantabrian Spain. *Anthropology UCLA*, 10: 53–96.

GAVELAS, A. (1980) Sobre nuevos concheros asturienses en los concejos de Ribadesella y Llanes. *Boletín del Instituto de Estudios Asturianos*, 101: 675–703, 711–718.

GONZÁLEZ MORALES, M.R. (1978) Excavaciones en el conchero asturiense de la cueva de Mazaculos II (La Franca, Ribadedeva, Asturias). *Boletín del Instituto de Estudios Asturianos*, 93–94: 369–383.

GONZÁLEZ MORALES, M.R. (1982) *El Asturiense y Otras Culturas Locales*. (Monografías del Centro de Investigación y Museo de Altamira, 7). Santander, Ministerio de Cultura.

GONZÁLEZ MORALES, M.R. and MÁRQUEZ URÍA, M.C. (1978) The Asturian shell midden of cueva de Mazaculos II (La Franca, Asturias, Spain). *Current Anthropology*, 19(3): 614–615.

GONZÁLEZ MORALES, M.R., MÁRQUEZ URÍA, M.C., DIAZ, T.E., ORTEA, J.A. and VOLMAN, K. (1980) Informe preliminar de las excavaciones en el conchero asturiense de la cueva de Mazaculos II (La Franca, Asturias): campañas de 1976 a 1978. *Noticiario Arqueológico Hispánico*, 9: 35–62.

MALLO, M., CHAPA, T. and HOYOS, M. (1980) Identificación y estudio de la cueva del Río (Ribadesella, Asturias). *Zephyrus*, 30–31: 231–243.

STRAUS, L.G. (1979) Mesolithic adaptations along the northern coast of Spain. *Quaternaria*, 21: 305–327.

VEGA DEL SELLA, CONDE DE LA (1914) *La Cueva del Penicial (Asturias)*. Madrid, Comisión de Investigaciones Paleontológicas y Prehistóricas Memoria 4.

VEGA DEL SELLA, CONDE DE LA (1923) *El Asturiense. Nueva Industria Pre-neolítica*. Madrid, Comisión de Investigaciones Paleontológicas y Prehistóricas Memoria 32.

VEGA DEL SELLA, CONDE DE LA (1925) La transición al Neolítico en la costa Cantábrica. *Actas y Memorias de la Sociedad Española de Antropología, Etnografía y Prehistoria*, IV, Mem. XL, sec. 34: 165–172.

VEGA DEL SELLA, CONDE DE LA (1930) *Las Cuevas de la Riera y Balmori*. Madrid, Comision de Investigaciones Paleontológicas y Prehistóricas Memoria 38.

Spatial Organization in the Mesolithic Sites of Muge, Portugal

Jean Roche

Abstract

The excavations carried out between 1952 and 1973 in the Muge shell middens have made it possible, using various approaches, to analyze spatial organization in three sites: Moita do Sebastião, Cabeço da Amoreira, and Cabeço da Arruda.

At Moita do Sebastião an extensive 'décapage' of the basal level (*c.* 7350 BP) revealed the remains of a semi-circular hut surrounded by a zone that was fitted out for the needs of everyday life. The adult inhumations are arranged in two groups situated outside the residential zone. In contrast, the inhumations of young children are grouped inside this zone.

At Cabeço da Amoreira and Cabeço da Arruda careful study of the stratigraphy has established that there were, in addition to minor modifications during each occupation, major rearrangements of the sites – extensive levelling, excavation of deep ditches – corresponding to phases of renewed occupation. Cabeço da Amoreira witnessed three principal reoccupations, the oldest dated to *c.* 7030 BP and the latest to *c.* 6050 BP. The much more detailed stratigraphy of Cabeço da Arruda has provided a clearer insight into the history of the formation of this type of shell midden. Five periods of occupation can be discerned at this site; the oldest is dated to *c.* 6430 BP and the most recent to *c.* 5150 BP.

These periodic rearrangements of the sites raise the question of nomadism among the Mesolithic people of Muge.

INTRODUCTION

Excavations undertaken between 1952 and 1973 at the Muge shell middens were carried out on sites that were either in process of disappearing (Moita do Sebastião), or on sites of which the greater part of the fill had been removed in the course of previous excavations (Cabeço da Amoreira, Cabeço da Arruda). The methods of excavation therefore had to be adapted to suit each case (Roche 1972*b*; *Fig. 1*).

At Moita do Sebastião the shell midden had been levelled to make way for a building. Only the basal layer survived – an indurated deposit ('breccia'), which was continuous across the site.[1] A rescue excavation was undertaken; what remained of the midden was totally excavated, revealing the earliest structures that relate to human occupation of the site.

At Cabeço da Amoreira and Cabeço da Arruda it was deemed necessary to excavate in such a way as to preserve standing/control sections, the stratigraphic study of which would permit very detailed analysis of the sequence of occupations at the sites and would enable the successive rearrangements of the deposits by the Mesolithic occupants to be worked out.

MOITA DO SEBASTIÃO

The location of the shell midden (concheiro) of Moita do Sebastião was particularly favourable for a human occupation. Situated at the northern extremity of an elongated spur which rises some 15 m above the floodplain, the site permits effective surveillance of the valley and, with ravines on either side, its access is easily defended.

In common with the other Muge *concheiros*, Moita do Sebastião offered abundant resources for supporting a population which lived by hunting and gathering. In the eighth millennium BP the Muge region was situated at the interface between salt and fresh water, and a wide variety of fish and shellfish were available. As today, the marshlands would have attracted flocks of migratory birds. The scrub which covers the edges of the marsh shelters populations of bovids and deer, whose remains have been recovered from the middens (Roche 1975).

The presence of a habitation site was betrayed as early as the first season in 1952. The exploratory trench, with its axis north west–south east, cut through a patch of black, ashy soil, rich in organic matter. This feature was easily recognizable by its dark colour, which contrasted strongly with the much lighter colours of the surrounding sediments. It was bordered on the north west by a kind of miniwall made of river pebbles piled on top of one another. This concentration of stones is all the more striking as pebbles of this type are only found in a dispersed state over the rest of the site. The entire feature was excavated in 1953 and 1954. The black soil infilled a vast, roughly rectangular pit 11.60 m long and averaging 3.20 m wide, with its long axis orientated north east–south west. The mini-wall of river pebbles, up to 0.80 m thick in places, extended for a distance of 3.75 m along the south-west side of the pit.

At the base of the fill of the pit there was a bed of pebbles, irregularly laid out forming a rough pavement. Below this bed of pebbles were traces of holes

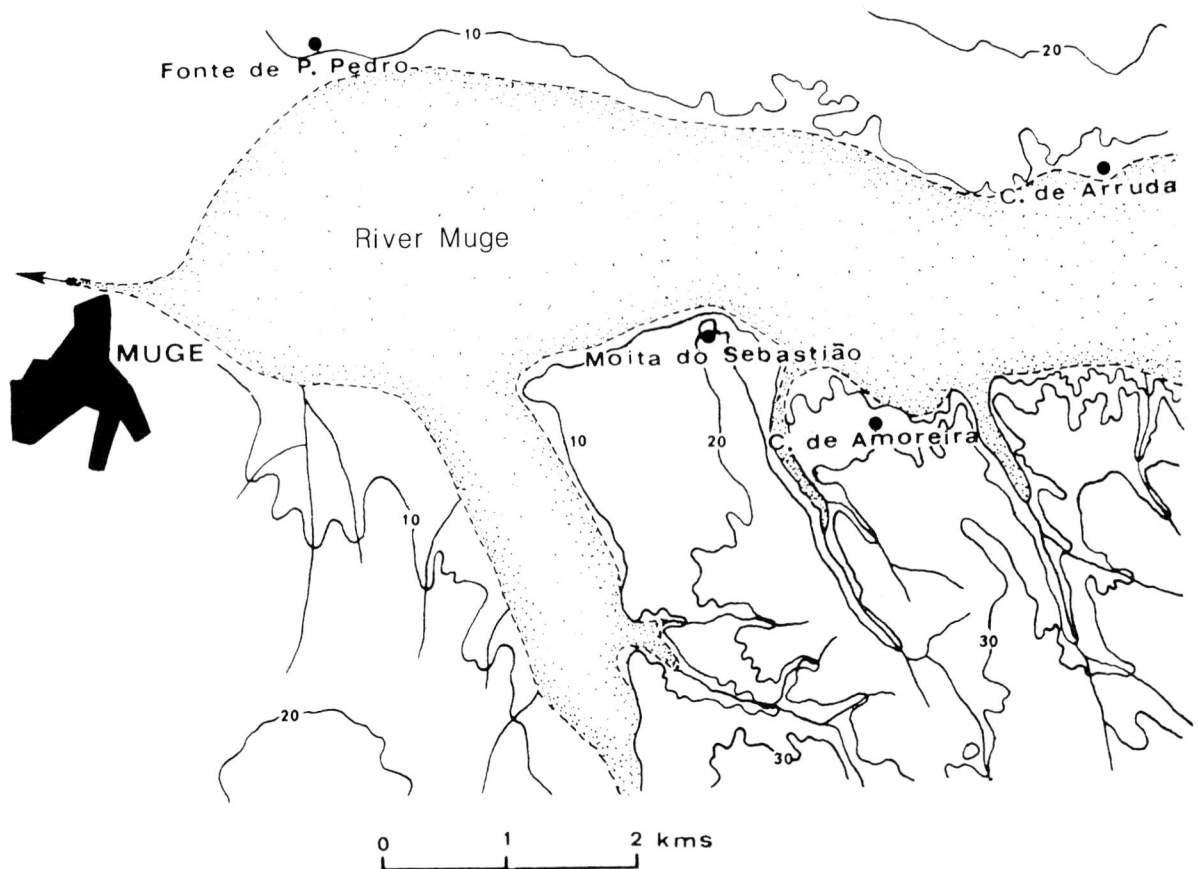

Figure 1 Location map of the Muge Mesolithic sites (the site of Fonte de Padre Pedro was destroyed at the beginning of this century).

excavated into the sand of the terrace which forms the sub-stratum of the site. Stripping of the area around the pit revealed other depressions excavated into the sand. Recognition of these holes and pits was facilitated by the contrast in colour between their fills and that of the sand.

By the end of the 1954 season, 94 holes and pits had been recorded, to which can be added two storage pits filled with shells of *Scrobicularia plana*. Analysis of these holes and pits, in most cases, provides an indication of their function.

Habitation hut

Sixty-one postholes were identified. These are characterized by their elongated profile and tapering base; the mean diameter is 0.20 m, and the mean depth is 0.55 metres. They are concentrated in a clearly-defined area (squares H–K.11–15), and are set out in a half-circle with the opening orientated towards the south. Such a concentration and arrangement is suggestive of a dwelling contemporary with the earliest occupation of the site. Artifacts are also particularly abundant and varied in this part of the site. This dwelling would have consisted of a semi-circular hut with a diameter of 7–8 m, open towards the south. This arrangement would give the occupants protection against north-westerly winds which blow in squalls during the winter months and against the heavy rains which accompany them. It

can be thought of as a light shelter placed directly in the sand of the terrace and constructed of a series of stakes, the largest of which were placed on either side of the entrance or on the periphery when the need arose. The framework was probably covered with branches, rushes or stems of Gramineae, and waterproofed with clay. This hypothesis is based on the presence around the dwelling of numerous fragments of clay bearing imprints of stems. This type of semi-circular hut, open on one side, was observed by Buckley at Badger Slacks in the Marsden area of the Pennines of northern England, associated with a 'Tardenoisian' (i.e. later Mesolithic) industry (cf. Clark and Rankine 1939: 104–105). Samples of charcoal from the basal layer of the site, taken close to the hut, have been dated by radiocarbon at two different laboratories: 7350±350 BP (Sa-16); 7080±130 BP (H-2119/1546).

Structures associated with the dwelling

Arranged around the hut and cut into the sand of the terrace were a number of associated features relating to a variety of domestic uses. These occupied a roughly oval area, measuring 13 m east to west and 9.50 m north to south. The hut is situated inside this zone but in an eccentric position, almost on the eastern edge, with the associated features extending a little way to the north east and south west of it. These features comprise:

608

Twelve shallow pits. These have steep sides and a flat or slightly concave base. They are roughly circular in shape; the mean diameter is 0.63 m, and the mean depth 0.46 metres. *Two* of them were cooking pits, the contents indicating that they had been used several times; the others appear to have served as rubbish pits.

Seven deep pits. These are distinguished by their semi-circular or U-shaped profiles and more elliptical plan; the mean diameter is 0.95 m, and the mean depth 0.63 metres. Their fill, which consists of greyish soil rich in small fragments of charcoal, suggests that they are the remains of hearths dug into the sand and, in some cases, cooking pits.

Two silos with shells. Their irregular form distinguishes them from the pits described above. Both are *c.* 2.50 m long; the maximum widths are 1.00 m and 1.50 m, and the depths 0.36 m and 0.27 m, respectively. They were filled with closed shells of *Scrobicularia plana*, implying that they had functioned as silos. One of these two silos abuts against the hut.

Three holes. These were intentionally dug into the sand, but there is nothing about the form or nature of the fill which indicates their function.

Four shallow hearths. These were situated directly on the sand without any preliminary preparation of the soil. Three of them had a roughly circular form, and produced struck flakes – one contained numerous carbonized shells of tiny Helicids (*Helix barbula*; *H. pisana*; *H. acuta*; *H. virgata*; *H. apicina*); the other two contained river pebbles shattered by the action of the fire. The diameters of these hearths are 0.75 m, 0.90 m and 1.50 m, and the mean thickness 0.12 metres. The fourth hearth consisted of a spread of ashes from around which a rich flint industry was recovered; its maximum diameter was 4.50 m, and the thickness at the centre 0.15 metres.

There are many problems posed by the existence of the trapezoidal pit (squares H–I.11–15) that remain unsolved:
1. Excavation has shown that the pit was established after the construction of the semi-circular hut and, probably, after its disappearance. The pebbles forming the paved floor of the pit covered over the traces of the stake-holes.
2. The trapezoidal pit is practically superimposed on the earlier semi-circular hut.
3. Its fill is homogeneous, does not seem to have been re-worked, and has produced a Mesolithic industry which is very similar to that observed in the semi-circular hut and the structures that surround it.
4. The true depth of this pit and the height of the low wall of pebbles which partly surrounds it could not be determined because of the levelling of the site.

What was the function of this pit? It was probably not a silo or a cooking pit. For it to be interpreted as a dwelling, it would have to be explained how and why the Mesolithic occupants of Moita do Sebastião constructed a dwelling of trapezoidal form and relatively large dimensions only a short time after having lived in a hut of semi-circular form and modest dimensions (*Fig. 2*).

Graves

A distinction can be made between the lay-out of the graves of adults and those of children.

Graves of adults

Twenty-six graves have been recovered at the base of the site yielding the remains of some 59 individuals (Ferembach 1974). They had been buried according to a definite funerary ritual (Roche 1972*a*). The bodies were laid out on the surface of the sand in slight natural depressions – except in five instances where the soil appeared to have been summarily arranged. The graves were arranged in two groups of unequal size and were always situated outside the dwelling zone. Twenty-one graves were clustered in an area of 75 m^2 contained in the rectangle formed by grid squares M–P.12–15 (*Fig. 2*). This group was situated close to the hut, 2–5 m to the south east of the entrance. Four graves were located in square K9 in an area of 6.25 m^2, some 3–4 m to the south west of the entrance of the hut. One isolated grave was found in square M16, 2.70 m to the north east of the hut.

Graves of young children

Eight graves have been recognized. The number of individuals could be not be determined, since the bones were often in a bad state of preservation owing to their extreme fragility; nor was it possible to observe the presence or absence of a funerary ritual. The remains were those of very young individuals, between 1 and 7 years old. They had been buried in a very restricted area (squares G–H.10), away from the graves of adults, and located inside the dwelling zone some 1.50 m to the west of the hut entrance. Unlike the adults, the bodies of the children were buried in 12 artificial depressions dug into the sand, adjacent to one another and arranged in a semi-circle with its opening orientated to the north west, opposite to that of the hut. The mean diameter of these pits is 0.85 m – an unusually large dimension which is explained by the encroachment of younger upon older graves. Their mean depth is 0.23 metres.

Summary

Thus, the first occupants of Moita do Sebastião organized their living space which they arranged in

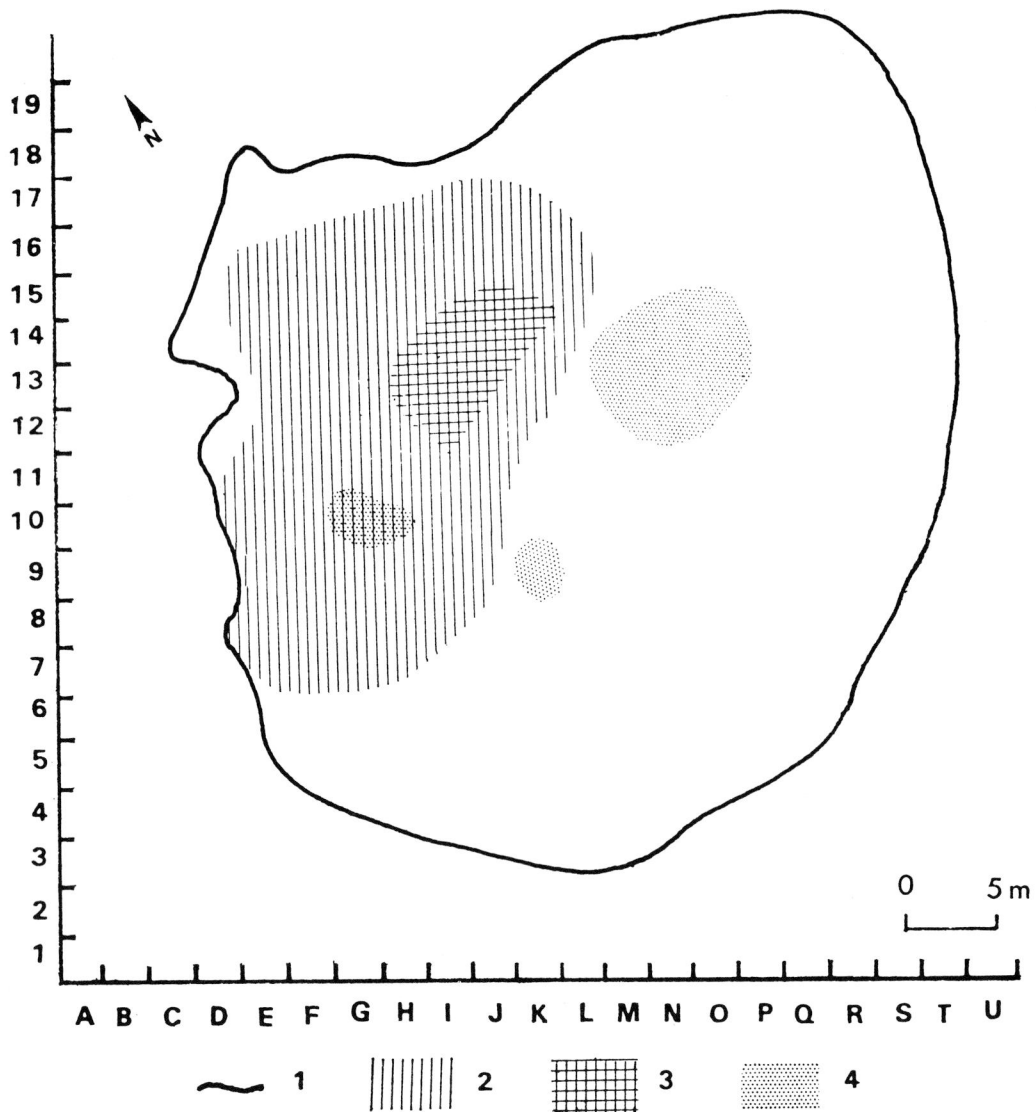

Figure 2 Moita do Sebastião – spatial organization during the earliest occupation of the site: 1 – limit of the shell midden; 2 – zone of rearrangement of the living space; 3 – hut emplacement; 4 – burial zones.

two principal zones: (i) a habitation zone – comprising a hut and other structures necessary for everyday life; and (ii) zones reserved for burials – the graves of adults were placed outside the living area but close by, while young children were buried in a clearly delimited place inside the living area, as if they had continued to participate in the life of the community.

The limited extent of these zones suggests that the first human group to install itself at Moita do Sebastião consisted of very few individuals – a single family, in the broad sense of the word.

CABEÇO DA AMOREIRA AND CABEÇO DA ARRUDA

The analysis of spatial organization at Cabeço da Amoreira and Cabeço da Arruda reveals a very different pattern. It was important to preserve standing/control sections in these two sites whose

deposits had already been extensively cut into by old excavations.

Thus, in the excavations at Cabeço da Amoreira (1958–1967) and at Cabeço da Arruda (1964–1965) it was not possible to undertake extensive 'décapage' which would have facilitated the study of spatial organization during the different stages in the formation of these shell middens. The most reasonable procedure was to excavate vertically in narrow strips, providing a clear perception of the stratigraphy. This method proved very fruitful, because it enabled a much better understanding of the chronology of the most important modifications made by the Mesolithic occupants to the deposits of these two sites. These deposits are naturally composite: layers of shells (often finely crushed, sometimes intact), ashy pockets and trails, black sediments rich in organic matter, bands of greyish-yellow sand sometimes hardened, lenses of light-yellow sand, and nodules of 'breccia'. The natural succession of the

610

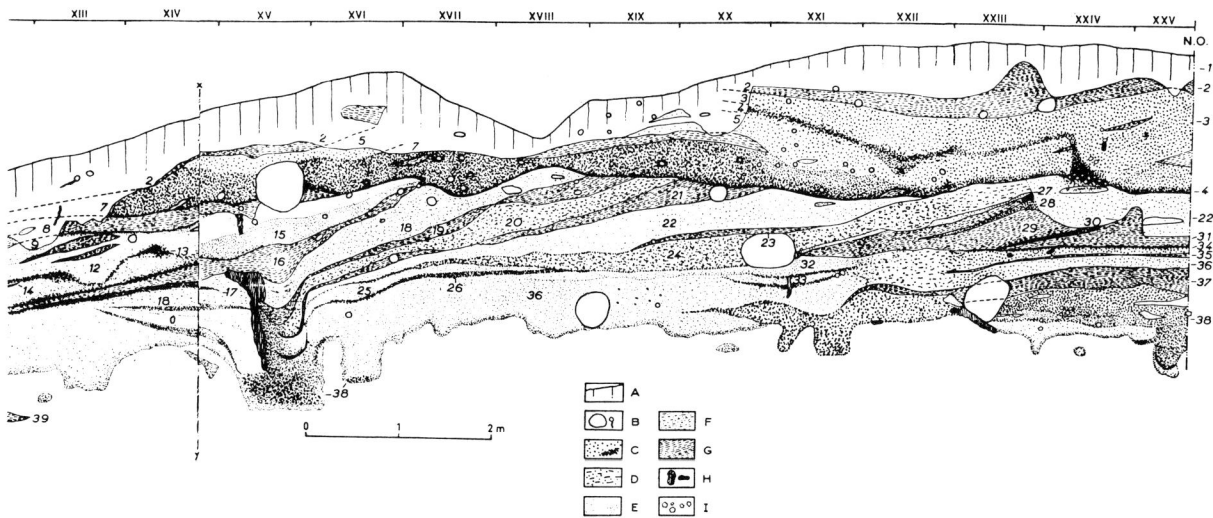

Figure 3   Cabeço da Amoreira – section in the north-west part of the longitudinal trench: xy – break of 30 cm; A – superficial or re-worked soil; B – krotovinas or root disturbance; C – black earth, hearths; D – mixture of black earth and crushed shells; E – sand; F – mixture of sand and crushed shells; G – shell beds; H – slabs and nodules of 'breccia'; I – pebbles.

layers was disturbed either by major modifications carried out by the occupants, or by frequent minor modifications (excavation of cooking pits, silos, rubbish pits, etc.). Modifications of the first kind provide the best evidence of spatial reorganization.

It is necessary to add that none of the Muge shell middens provides a stratigraphic sequence that can serve as a model for the analysis of the deposits of every site; rather the individual sites present partial, localized stratigraphies which to some extent can be inter-correlated.

To illustrate these observations, two stratigraphic sequences – one from Cabeço da Amoreira, the other from Cabeço da Arruda – will be discussed.

Cabeço da Amoreira

At this site a 25 m long trench, 3.20 m deep, revealed a sequence of 39 layers (Roche 1965). Major modifications of the deposits were noted, corresponding to three main periods in the history of occupation of the site (*Fig. 3*).

Layers 39–33. The earliest occupation of the site was characterized by discontinuous layers which dip at a shallow angle. People settled the terrace where a number of pits, some of them quite large, were dug. Layer 39 is dated to 7030±350 BP (Sa-195).

Layers 32–8. Settlement took place in the north-west part of the site and domestic rubbish was thrown out to the south east. This occupation led to the formation of a series of parallel layers with an average dip of 15–20° to the south east. They are formed of ashy soil, beds of crushed shells, and yellow sand. Locally, the order of these layers is disturbed by the excavation of pits.

Layers 7–2. At the beginning of the most recent occupation of the site by Mesolithic people, the

surface of the midden was flattened over a considerable length and the spoil thrown outwards, mainly towards the south east. This rearrangement of the site provided a more comfortable base for settlement than previously. The deposits of this occupation are formed of undulating layers of black and grey earth, rich in fragments of charcoal and organic matter. Here too, local disturbances were evident in the form of pits, some of them quite large. Layers 3–4 have been dated to 6050±300 BP (Sa-194).

The most recent deposits (layer 1) comprise sediments modified at various periods subsequent to the Mesolithic occupation.

Cabeço da Arruda

Re-excavation involved sinking a trench 9 m long and 5 m deep into the central part of the midden, aligned along its principal axis (Roche 1967). The section provided by this trench, because of its size and the complexity of the stratigraphy, has permitted a better understanding of the history of the formation of a *shell midden*. Eighty-eight layers were identified, relating to five main periods of occupation which resulted in major modifications of the site by its occupants (*Fig. 4*).

As was the case at Cabeço da Amoreira, there was also evidence of numerous minor modifications of much more limited extent.

Layers 88–54. These deposits are the remains of the first period of occupation. They extend along the full length of the trench directly overlying the sand of the fluviatile terrace. The earliest layers are initially almost horizontal, then suddenly dip to the south east and finally to the north west, which seems to imply successive displacements of the main occupation area. These early layers are generally formed of grey sand with yellow horizontal bands/bedding

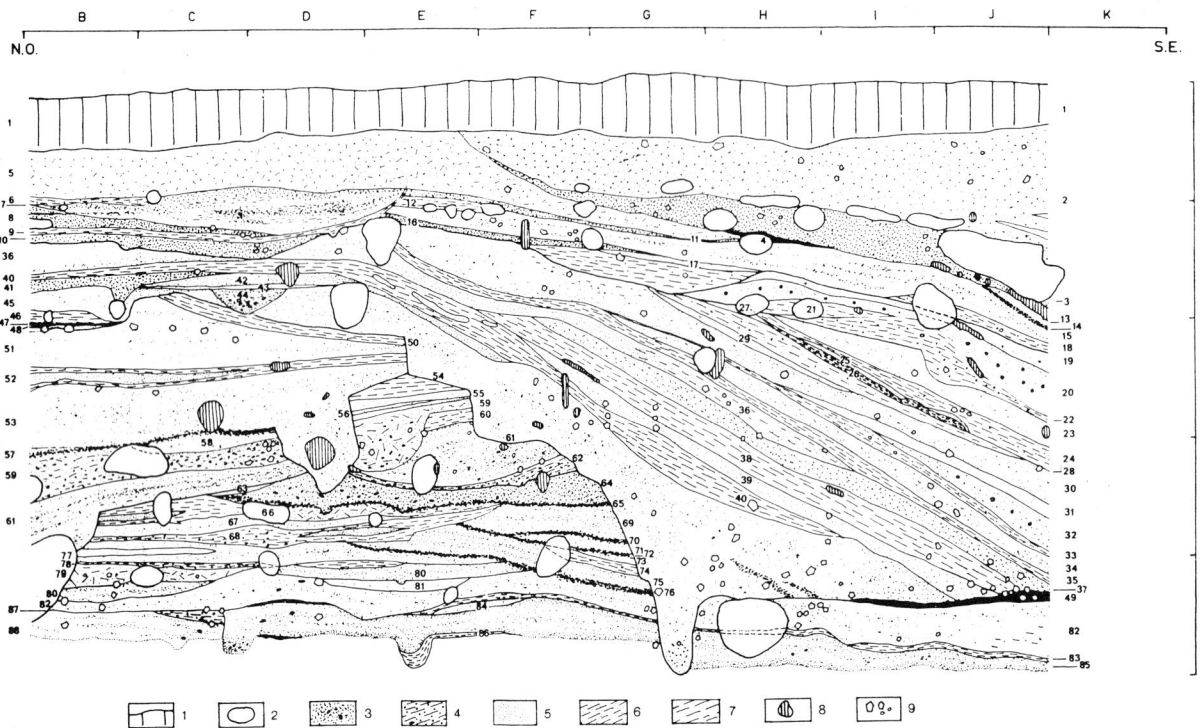

Figure 4 Cabeço da Arruda – NW–SE longitudinal section: 1 – superficial or re-worked soil; 2 – krotovinas; 3 – black earth, charcoal; 4 – mixture of black earth and crushed shells; 5 – grey-yellow earth; 6 – mixture of grey-yellow earth and shells; 7 – shell beds; 8 – nodules of 'breccia'; 9 – pebbles. Each division of the vertical and horizontal scales represents one metre.

planes intercalated with thin spreads of carbonaceous matter which are vestiges of soils and beds of shells, some of which are intact. There are also pits some of which, such as the rubbish pit in layer 59, are quite large. All of these early structures would have been mutilated by later occupations. Layer 83 has been dated to 6430±300 BP (Sa-197).

Layers 53–50. Little remains of this second phase, since the deposits were almost completely destroyed at the beginning of the third period of occupation. The deposits consist of a small series of layers with a very shallow dip – with the exception of layer 50 which dips at 15° to the north west. They are poor in charcoal but contain nodules of 'breccia', sometimes of large size. In the lower part of layer 53 a deep, narrow pit was recorded; the irregularity of the profile of this feature suggests the action of post-depositional deformation.

Layers 49–23. At the beginning of this third phase, there was a major rearrangement of the midden. The north-west part was levelled to facilitate settlement and a flat, elongated, shallow pit was dug. In contrast, in the south-east part of the midden the Mesolithic people cut an artificial slope into the earlier deposits; this took the form of a 'staircase' becoming gradually steeper and ending in a deep, narrow pit, and served to facilitate the throwing of rubbish away from the occupation area. This material accumulated as superposed spoil heaps, presenting a more or less constant 28° slope to the south east (layers 48–23).

Layers 22–19. At the beginning of the fourth phase of occupation, there was hurried removal of the mass of detritus and cooking remains that had accumulated during the previous phase. People abandoned the north-east zone to install themselves further to the south east. This new occupation led to the formation of a series of layers of shells (some of which are intact), of greyish earth mixed with shell fragments, and of yellowish earth. These layers dip at a shallow angle to the south east.

Layers 18–2. At the beginning of this fifth period of occupation, people proceeded to remove some of the former deposits, the material that was thrown out having a slope of 5° to the south east. The remains of the fourth period of occupation were almost completely destroyed by this process. Large pits were dug; these were infilled (especially in sections B–E) with alternating beds of broken shells, black earth, charcoal and yellow sand, which implies successive episodes of use. Layer 3 has been dated to 5150±300 BP (Sa-196).

CONCLUDING REMARKS

The major periodic modifications of the archaeological materials observed at Cabeço da Amoreira and Cabeço da Arruda are also likely to have occurred at Moita do Sebastião, and they raise the question of seasonal occupation of the sites. To what extent was the Mesolithic population of Muge a nomadic one?

One hypothesis argues for limited nomadism. A population of collectors and fishers would have found excellent opportunities for subsistence in this particular location. On the other hand, there were originally many more shell middens in the Muge region than have survived to the present day, as indicated by numerous archaeological remains. It may be supposed that, for reasons of convenience, there were temporary occupations of the sites, followed by reoccupations that resulted in rearrangements of the cultural residues.

The need to procure flint would in itself have fostered a tendency to a degree of nomadism, or at least to contacts between the Muge people and neighbouring populations. Flint is absent on the south bank of the River Tagus, but on the north bank it can be found in the limestone massifs of the Estremadra, 20 km away as the crow flies.

In 1953 a cache of flint in the form of a heap of ten large nodules which had undergone slight preparation was found at Moita do Sebastião (Roche 1972a: 73). The actual process of 'roughing out' the nodules had probably been undertaken at the place of collection, since no waste flakes were found around the cache.

Note:

1. The 'breccia' of Moita do Sebastião is an indurated deposit containing various archaeological materials (fragments of bone, pebbles, flints, charcoal, shells, etc.) bound together by a calcareous, crystalline cement. It was formed at the contact with the relatively impermeable clayey sands of the river terrace by percolation of rainwaters through the overlying layers of shells. It extended over the entire area of the site at the base of the midden and, because of its hardness, it has survived recent disturbances of the site. The same formation does not exist at Cabeço da Amoreira nor at Cabeço da Arruda, where the sands of the river terrace are permeable.

Acknowledgements: This English translation of an original French text was produced by the Editor, with assistance from Brian Barron, Department of French, University of Edinburgh.

References

CLARK, J.G.D. and RANKINE, W.F. (1939) Excavations at Farnham (Surrey), 1937–1938. The Horsham culture and the question of Mesolithic dwellings. *Proceedings of the Prehistoric Society*, 5: 61–118.

FEREMBACH, D. (1974) *Le Gisement Mésolithique de Moita do Sebastião, Muge, Portugal. II: Anthropologie*. Lisbon, Direcção Geral dos Assuntos Culturais.

ROCHE, J. (1965) Note sur la stratigraphie de l'amas coquillier mésolithique de Cabeço da Amoreira (Muge). *Comunicações dos Serviços Geológicos de Portugal*, 48 (1964–1965): 191–200.

ROCHE, J. (1967) Note sur la stratigraphie de l'amas coquillier mésolithique de Cabeço da Arruda (Muge). *Comunicações dos Serviços Geológicos de Portugal*, 52: 221–242.

ROCHE, J. (1972a) *Le Gisement Mésolithique de Moita do Sebastião, Muge, Portugal. I: Archéologie*. Lisbon, Instituto de Alta Cultura.

ROCHE, J. (1972b) Les amas coquilliers (*concheiros*) mésolithiques de Muge (Portugal). *Fundamenta*, A/7: 72–107.

ROCHE, J. (1975) Les amas coquilliers mésolithiques de Muge (Portugal). Chronologie, milieu naturel et leurs incidences sur le peuplement humain. *Approche Ecologique de l'Homme Fossile. Supplément au Bulletin de l'AFEQ*, 47: 353–359.

x

The Mesolithic Communities of the Sado Valley, Portugal, in their Ecological Setting

J.E. Morais Arnaud

Abstract

This paper presents a preliminary report on the Mesolithic shell middens of the Sado valley, Portugal. These were excavated mainly in the 1950s and 1960s by the staff of the National Museum of Archaeology and Ethnology, Lisbon. As a result of those excavations more than 200,000 artifacts and faunal remains, and about a hundred more or less complete skeletons were taken to the Museum where they have remained virtually unpublished.

In 1982 a long-term multidisciplinary research programme was initiated, with the objective of studying systematically the vast amount of material from the old excavations in the National Museum, and of re-locating and re-excavating some of the shell middens to obtain reliable chronological, stratigraphic, sedimentological, palaeoecological, and palaeoeconomic data. The accomplishment of such a vast task will take a few more years, but it has already been possible to achieve a better understanding of this important group of sites and to assess their potential contribution to the study of Postglacial 'adaptations' of the fisher-hunter-gatherers in this area of Europe, located at the interface between the Atlantic and the Mediterranean.

The radiocarbon dates already obtained show that this cluster of sites, like their better known counterparts of Muge in the Tagus valley, had been occupied over a period of at least 1000 years between the mid-eighth and the mid-seventh millennium BP, corresponding to the early Atlantic phase. The considerable inter-site variability in faunal remains and site size, in contrast to the apparent uniformity in the material culture and the burial rites, suggests that all of them belonged to the same settlement system. This probably included two base camps, occupied respectively during the autumn/winter with a greater emphasis on hunting activities, and the spring/summer with a greater emphasis on fishing activities, and several smaller sites connected with specialized economic activities which were occupied by only a part of the co-resident unit. Mollusc gathering was apparently a year-round activity, although it is not yet possible to quantify its contribution. Plants certainly made only a small contribution to the diet. Acorns, nowadays relatively abundant, are an important potential caloric source, but no archaeological evidence for their consumption has been recovered.

RESEARCH HISTORY

The Mesolithic communities of Portugal have been known mainly as a result of the work carried out at the Muge shell middens over the last hundred years by various scholars – viz. F.A. Pereira da Costa (1865), C. Ribeiro (1880), F. de P. Oliveira (1880, 1882), A.E. Mendes-Corrêa (1932, 1933, 1934), R. de Serpa-Pinto (1932), A. Athaide (1940) and, more recently, J. Roche (1954, 1960, 1965, 1972, and other works).

However, only 100 km to the south, another important cluster of Mesolithic shell middens was identified and partially excavated during the 1950s and 1960s. This is located in the lower Sado valley and, in spite of the many similarities which it presents in relation to the Muge valley, in both geographical setting and material culture, it also possesses some distinctive features (Morais Arnaud 1985).

The first two shell middens to be found in the Sado valley were identified in the 1930s by L. Antunes Barradas who, however, never carried out any systematic excavations and only published a short note on his findings (Antunes Barradas 1936). One of these shell middens, Portancho, had an estimated area of *c.* 100 m² and a depth of about 1 m, and was located in close proximity to the floodplain on the bottom of the terrace slope, only about 7 m above sea level and 2 m above the river. Recently, after a careful search of the area, this site was relocated but its state of preservation is very poor as a result of intensive cultivation. The other shell midden identified by Antunes Barradas, Quinta de Baixo (later renamed Cabeço do Pez), is the largest shell midden known in the area and the most extensively excavated (cf. *Table 2*).

Compared to their famous counterparts of Muge, the Sado shell middens did not attract much attention, and it was only twenty years after the publication of the short note by Antunes Barradas that a major programme of prospection and excavation was initiated in this area. This was undertaken under the supervision of the late Professor Manuel Heleno, who was Director of the Museu Nacional de Arquelogia e Etnologia in Lisbon (hereafter referred to as the 'National Museum') and Professor of Prehistory in the University of Lisbon from 1929 to 1966. As a result of this programme seven other shell middens were identified and partially excavated between 1955 and 1966, resulting in the accumulation of some 200,000 artifacts and faunal remains, as well as about a hundred more or less complete human skeletons. However, Heleno himself never published anything about these sites, or about hundreds of other sites of many different types and periods which had been detected and excavated by the staff of the National Museum during his long directorship. In 1966

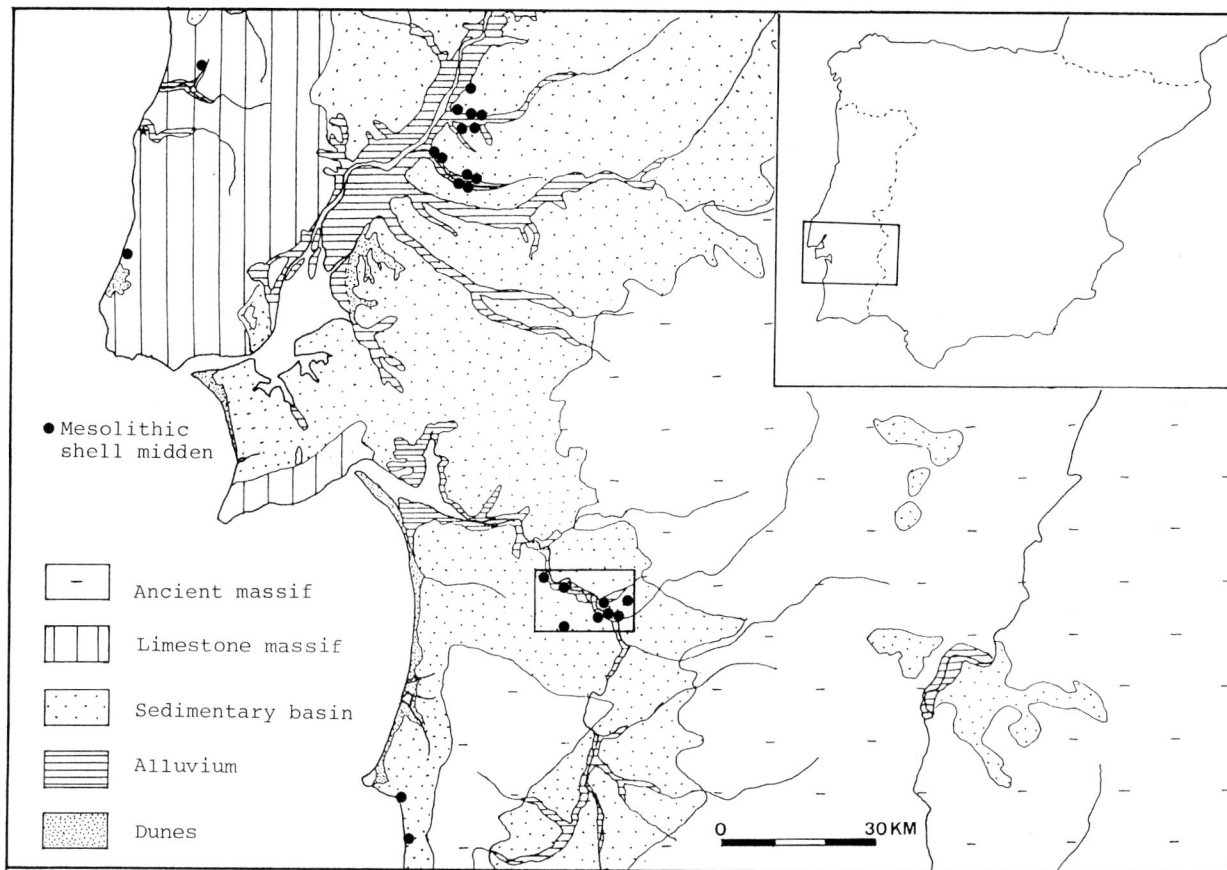

Figure 1 Simplified geological map of the Sado valley (based on *Carta Geologica de Portugal* 1:500,000 S.G.P., Lisbon 1972).

Heleno retired and, claiming that he was going to prepare the publication of all this material, he took with him all the field notes prepared by his foremen. Unfortunately, he died shortly afterwards without publishing anything, and his family claimed that he had not left any field notes. So, all that has remained are hundreds of boxes and packets full of artifacts, bones and shells, about a hundred large wooden 'coffins' containing human skeletal remains encased in massive blocks of paraffin wax, kept in the reserves of the National Museum, and a few plans of the excavations carried out in some of the shell middens, as well as detailed drawings of some of the human skeletons.

In 1967 and 1968 M. Farinha dos Santos, a former assistant of Professor Heleno, announced the identification of two other shell middens in the area (*Fig. 2*, sites 9, 11), but he has not yet done any excavation on them.

In spite of its great importance this entire assemblage of sites has remained virtually unstudied and unpublished. In fact, before 1981 the only publications about these sites, apart from the initial discovery note by Barradas (1936), were a description of most of the decorated pottery and a few artifacts from Cabeço do Pez (Farinha dos Santos *et al.* 1972), and a note on a few sherds of beaker pottery from the presumably Mesolithic shell midden of Barrada do Grilo (Farinha dos Santos *et al.* 1974).

Because of the great potential presented by all this material for achieving a better understanding of the Postglacial adaptations which occurred on the eve of the inception of agriculture in this southernmost part of Atlantic Europe, an interdisciplinary research programme was initiated in 1982. This is being undertaken in collaboration with specialists in other relevant disciplines, most of them connected with the National Museum and the Universities of Lisbon and Cambridge, with the objective of undertaking a systematic study of the Mesolithic settlement of this area in a palaeoecological and palaeoeconomic perspective. A presentation and discussion of the preliminary results of that programme is the main purpose of this paper.

The excavations of the Sado shell middens were undertaken by Mr Jaime Roldão, a former technician in the National Museum who retired a few years ago. He has been somewhat reserved about his work on these sites and was not available to help in their relocation, but examination of the material stored in the National Museum and of the few excavation plans available for some of the sites indicates a very consistent excavation and artifact recovery strategy. When a shell midden was located, as a result of information provided by local people, a series of very narrow cuttings 0.4–0.6 m in width and 5–20 m in length were dug to establish the exact limits of the site (*Fig. 3*). The Sado shell middens were difficult to

615

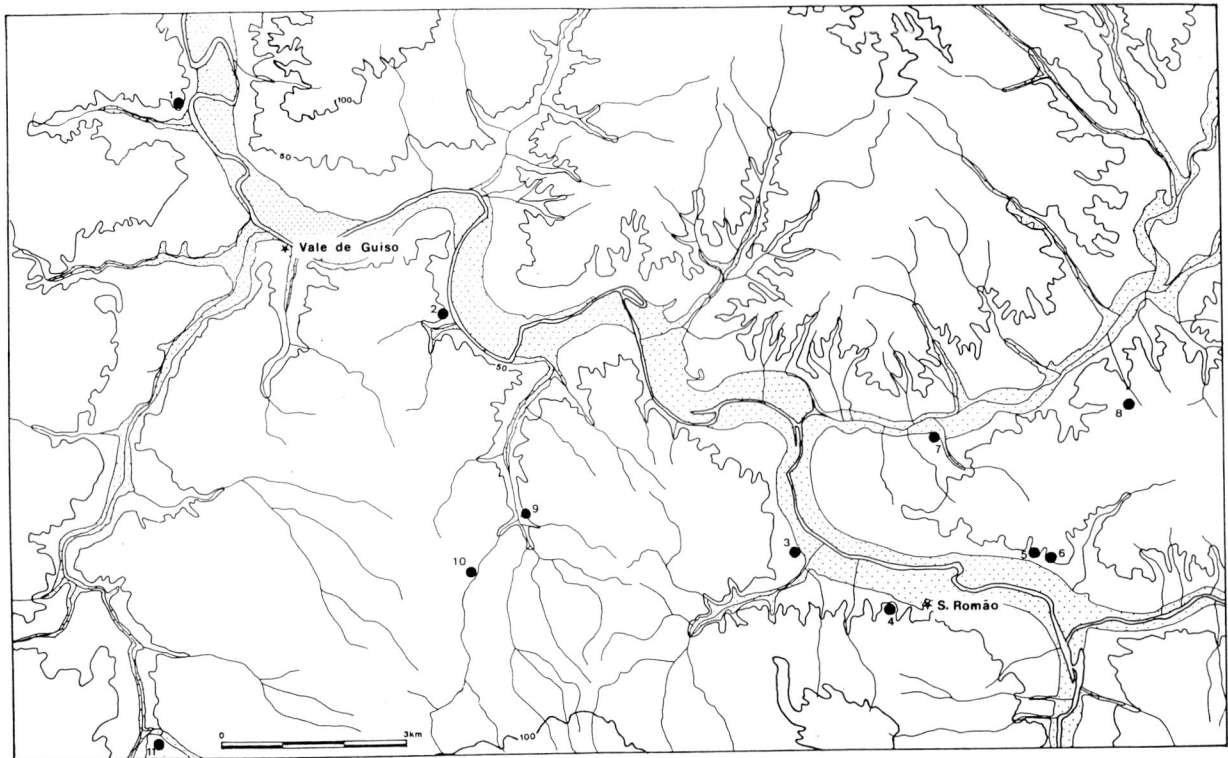

Figure 2 Topographical setting of the Sado shell middens. Stippled area indicates alluvial deposits at less than 10 m a.s.l. *Key*:
1 – Arapouco; 2 – Cabeço do Rebolador; 3 – Barrada das Vieiras; 4 – Amoreiras; 5 – Vale de Romeiras; 6 – Cabeço do Pez;
7 – Várzea da Mó; 8 – Barrada do Grilo; 9 – Fonte da Mina; 10 – Poças de São Bento; 11 – Barranco da Moura.

locate by surface observation because, unlike their counterparts in the Tagus valley which form mounds 3–5 m high, they are very shallow. In addition, in some cases the soil is not ploughed and, when it is, the shell remains tend to spread over a much larger area than that originally covered by the midden.

After a site was delimited, a much larger rectangular area was excavated, either in the central part of the midden or on its periphery, according to the topographic conditions. In the 1958 campaign at Cabeço do Pez three areas 7 × 7 m were subdivided into 3 m squares, separated by baulks 0.5 m wide. At other sites, however, each of the rectangular areas was divided into transects 1 m wide and excavated vertically. This certainly resulted in a much greater mixture of materials from different layers.

According to Mr Roldão, the material was separated according to arbitrary levels of 0.25 m, but on some of the finds boxes there is some information about the nature of the layer which produced the artifacts, such as 'black soil', 'shell layer', and so forth. This suggests that the natural stratigraphy was also taken into consideration to some extent.

As far as the recovery efficiency is concerned, it must be stressed that a large proportion of the flint and quartz flaking waste consists of very tiny splinters (<1 cm) and that some of the fish vertebrae and univalve shells collected are only 2 or 3 mm in diameter. This suggests that most, if not all, of the soil removed was sieved through a fine mesh and carefully scrutinized. On the other hand, the total

area excavated is considerable for what was a very small team (five or six workmen), but it must be taken into consideration that they worked in the area during a ten-year period, and that the average length of each season, according to Mr Roldão, was six months (usually from April/May until September/October).

In spite of the deficiencies which may have resulted from the lack of academic training of the excavators, the degree of recovery efficiency was remarkable for the standards practised in those days in Portugal. It should therefore be possible to assess the nature and extent of the biases and to introduce the necessary correcting factors in our appreciation of the material from the old excavations, by re-excavating reduced areas of each of these sites as exhaustively as possible and comparing the results – a procedure which has already started, but is not yet concluded.

GEOGRAPHICAL SETTING

These shell middens (*Fig. 1*) are located on the lower course of the Sado, a small river about 175 km long, which has its source on the massive schistic formation of the Carboniferous. It then flows northwards across the Tertiary sedimentary basin which is dominated by Miocene and Mio-Pliocene sandstones and marly limestones, but also includes sandy Pliocene deposits, especially on the left bank of the Sado basin where the remains of Pleistocene dune

616

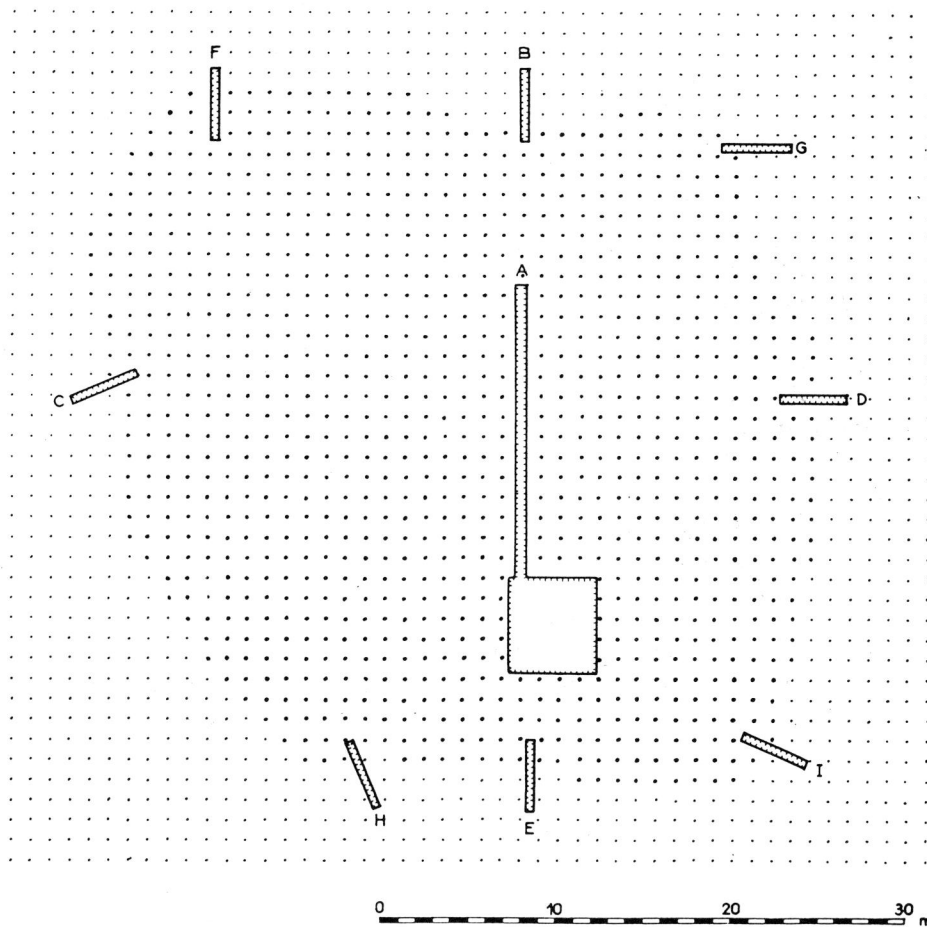

Figure 3 General plan of Amoreiras, with the areas excavated in 1958.

formations can also be observed in some areas.

Among the rivers originating in Portugal, the Sado is the one which offers the best navigability. It is still accessible to small boats up to 70 km from the mouth of the estuary, and during the early Holocene it would have provided an important means of communication in an area of relatively difficult terrain and dense vegetation.

In spite of the alluviation which has reduced its average width in the area of the shell middens from *c*. 0.7 km during the maximum of the Flandrian transgression to the present 30–60 m (*Fig. 2*), the tide can still penetrate up to 50 km from the estuary mouth during the summer high tides, when the influx of fresh water is substantially reduced. During most of the year, however, it does not penetrate more than 30 km upstream, about 20 km below the shell midden area.

This section of the valley is also characterized by a number of meanders, and before its present regularization, when the very extensive rice fields which

now completely cover the bottom of the valley were built, the river used to flood every winter. The influx of fresh water was also regularized by the building of a series of dams, but it still occasionally floods, covering the whole width of the valley.

In this section the valley is clearly entrenched and the erosion edge is very well marked, at just above 50 m (Brum Ferreira 1981). The shell middens tend to be located very close to that edge, with the exceptions of Várzea da Mó (*Fig. 2*, no. 7), located just a few metres above the valley of a small tributary of the Sado, and Poças de São Bento (*Fig. 2*, site 10), 3 km to the south of the valley at *c*. 80 m above sea level.

The location of a shell midden at such a distance from the river would have made the transport of shellfish to the site rather uneconomic, given their extremely low caloric value. This led us to consider the possibility of substantial geomorphological changes in this area since the beginning of the Atlantic phase. However, neither Dr Teresa Azevedo,

Y

a geomorphologist, nor João Cabral, an expert in neotectonics, have yet found in their preliminary surveys of the area any evidence suggesting the existence of shell beds closer to the site during the early Holocene.

The sites of Barrada do Grilo, Fonte da Mina and Barranco da Moura (*Fig. 2*, sites 8, 9, 11), although located close to small tributaries of the Sado, occupy similar positions to those facing the Sado itself.

Taking into consideration that most of these shell middens are located on the edge of a very steep slope some 40–50 m above the river bed, the need to transport the shells to the top of the slope, thus expending a considerable proportion of the caloric input provided by them, affords circumstantial evidence for the regular flooding of the entire river bed. In fact, the massive presence of shells of characteristically estuarine molluscs, such as *Cerastoderma edule* and *Scrobicularia plana*, in all these middens is proof of the regular penetration of the tides all year round up to the confluence with the Xarrama river, close to Cabeço do Pez, during the early Holocene. Both these mollusc species are characterized by a wide salinity tolerance, but they require a minimum of 12 and 5 ‰, respectively.

The soils of this area show a clear dominance of podzols and regosols, with very reduced agricultural capacity, and even with some limitations for forestry. The valleys of the Sado and its tributaries are nowadays characterized by hydromorphic soils of heavy texture, currently used for the cultivation of rice, but these were obviously formed a long time after the abandonment of the shell middens.

The modern vegetation of the area is characterized by a predominance of cork-oak groves which over large areas are sparse enough to allow the cultivation of cereals. In some areas there are also extensive pine woods. To what extent the present vegetation is the artifact of human action is difficult to assess, in the absence of a pollen diagram. Some peat deposits have been detected in the area, but are not deep enough to allow the construction of a continuous pollen diagram going as far back as the early Holocene. Recently, however, José Mateus has obtained a 9 m deep peat core going back to the eighth millennium BP from an ancient lagoon some 20 km to the west of São Romão, very close to the sea shore. In spite of the considerable differences between the two ecological niches, it is possible to use this diagram to establish a conjectural framework of the nature and extent of vegetation changes which occurred in this area between the end of the Boreal and the beginning of the Atlantic period.

According to Mateus (1985), the lowest part of the diagram, dated between *c.* 7500 and 6500 BP, is marked by a predominance of arboreal pollen, denoting the existence in the region of woodlands corresponding to three major phytogeographic zones:

(i) humid Mediterranean deciduous woods; (ii) sclerophyllous forests of eu-Mediterranean type; and (iii) littoral Mediterranean pine woods. The latter, probably formed of *Pinus pinea*, were especially abundant in the littoral during the Boreal, but by the beginning of the Atlantic period had declined sharply, possibly as a result of anthropogenic factors, never to recover their dominance.

Besides the pine woods, there is also evidence of vast areas of deciduous oak forest (*Quercus faginea*). This picture of the arboreal cover of the region was completed by incipient gallery groves of alder in the inner parts of the fluvial basins.

In the non-arboreal pollen, which constituted only 10–20% of the regional pollen during the late Boreal, the presence of the sclerophyllous elements of *Quercetalia ilicis* was detected. It is not clear whether these formed individualized maquis or just the arboreal substratum of the deciduous oak groves or even of the pine groves.

During the Atlantic period the pine woods suffered an irreversible decline (see above), while the deciduous oaks and the alder forest, on account of their 'climax' character, remained stable in the long term, but fluctuated markedly under the influence of anthropogenic factors and of the littoral ecosystem dynamics.

Further inland, in the shell midden area, it seems probable that a very similar vegetation mosaic existed during the Boreal and the early Atlantic periods, with a relative predominance of pine woods on the Plio-Pleistocene dune deposits. The holm-oak (*Quercus rotundifolia*), dominant today over considerable areas of the Alentejo uplands, was probably already present in the area integrated into the oak groves of *Quercus faginea*, along with the cork-oak (*Quercus suber*), now dominant on the lower Sado valley.

CHRONOMETRIC FRAMEWORK

Eight radiocarbon dates are already available for some of the Sado shell middens (*Table 1*).

With the exception of Q-2498, which is clearly anomalous, these dates show that the shell middens of the Sado valley were formed broadly during the same period as their Muge counterparts, which corresponds to the early Atlantic period of northern Europe.

It must, however, be stressed that these dates are still far from allowing the establishment of a sound chronometric framework for the Mesolithic settlement of this area. In fact, they do not cover all the layers of all the sites excavated and are mostly from shell samples. This limits to a certain extent their intrinsic value, at least until the research project currently underway at the Godwin Laboratory (Cambridge) on the reliability of shell samples for radiocarbon dating is concluded.

Table 1: Radiocarbon dates for the Sado shell middens

Site	Context	^{14}C age BP
Arapouco	shells from middle layers	7420±65 BP (Q−2492)
Poças de São Bento	shells from lower layer	7040±70 BP (Q−2493)
Poças de São Bento	shells from middle layers	6850±70 BP (Q−2495)
Poças de São Bento	charcoal from middle layers	6780±65 BP (Q−2494)
Cabeço do Pez	shells from middle layers	6730±75 BP (Q−2497)
Cabeço do Pez	shells from middle layers	6430±65 BP (Q−2496)
Cabeço do Pez	bones from upper layers	5535±130 BP (Q−2499)
Cabeço do Pez	conglomerate of shells and charcoal from lower layer	3565±50 BP (Q−2498)

As a result of these limitations, the apparent greater antiquity of Arapouco will need to be confirmed by other dates for that site and compared with dates for the earliest occupation layers of the remaining sites. For the moment, it seems wiser to consider these sites as broadly contemporaneous and as components of the same settlement system.

SITE AREA, MORPHOLOGY, DENSITY OF OCCUPATION AND STRATIGRAPHY

It is not yet possible to establish accurately the total area of some of these shell middens but, as shown in *Table 2*, they seem to be quite variable. At Cabeço do Pez (*Fig. 2*, site 6) the area excavations were concentrated on the western edge of the midden, and a series of narrow trenches were also opened on the eastern edge. The latter provided a variable number of artifacts, showing that the site had spread over at least 4000 m². However, two other trenches were opened some 50 m to the south east and still provided some material, suggesting that this site may have covered a much larger area, probably approaching 8000 m². It is not known whether this area was in fact continuous or not, but it can be concluded that this shell midden is the largest known so far in the area.

On the other side of a steep ravine from Cabeço do Pez is Vale de Romeiras (*Fig. 2*, site 5), by far the smallest shell midden (*c.* 54 m²) identified in the area and the only one which was apparently entirely excavated. Yet the excavations revealed the existence of at least 22 burials!

Table 2 shows that, apart from these two sites, the other sites which directly overlook the Sado valley tend to have similar areas – a little over 1000 m². On the other hand, the site of Poças de São Bento, 3 km to the south (*Fig. 2*, site 10), has a much larger area (3570 m²), comparable to the lower estimate made for Cabeço do Pez (4000 m²).

The stratigraphic sequence recorded in all the sites for which there is graphic documentation in the archives of the National Museum is very similar to that from Amoreiras (*Fig. 4*). Below a layer of brownish topsoil, 0.1–0.2 m deep, is a layer of black soil (0.2–0.8 m) which covers the main shell midden layer. The depth of the midden varies between 0.2 and 0.7 m, and its shape is rather irregular. Below the main shell midden layer there is always a layer of light-brown to whitish sandy soil, in which most of the human burials were made. This lies directly on relatively soft bedrock formed by the marly limestones of the Miocene. Preliminary sedimentological analysis of a stratigraphic sequence observed in a small cutting made in 1983 at Cabeço do Pez has shown (from bottom to top) a sequence of clayey silt, sand, silt, fine sand, silty clay, silt and fine sand, but the interpretation of this sequence in terms of the regime of occupation of the site will have to wait until more detailed analyses are completed. All these layers contain a certain amount of shell, but the considerable differences in density from layer to layer and from place to place make it very difficult to estimate the caloric value of the shellfish accumulated in these middens.

BURIALS

As shown in *Table 2*, burials have been found consistently at all the shell middens of the Sado valley, with the exception of Rebolador and Barrada do Grilo. However, in contrast to Moita do Sebastião,

Table 2: Comparative table of site areas and burial and artifact densities for the major shell middens of the Sado valley

Site	Area m²	Excavated area	Artifact density	Min. No. burials	Burial density
Arapouco	1174	135	32.10	17	0.125
Rebolador	(1000)	(30)	105.70	–	–
Amoreiras	1270	55	121.00	6	0.109
Romeiras	54	54	52.29	22	0.407
Cabeço do Pez	4000/8000	635	67.30	27	0.042
Poças de São Bento	3570	60	347.04	13	0.100

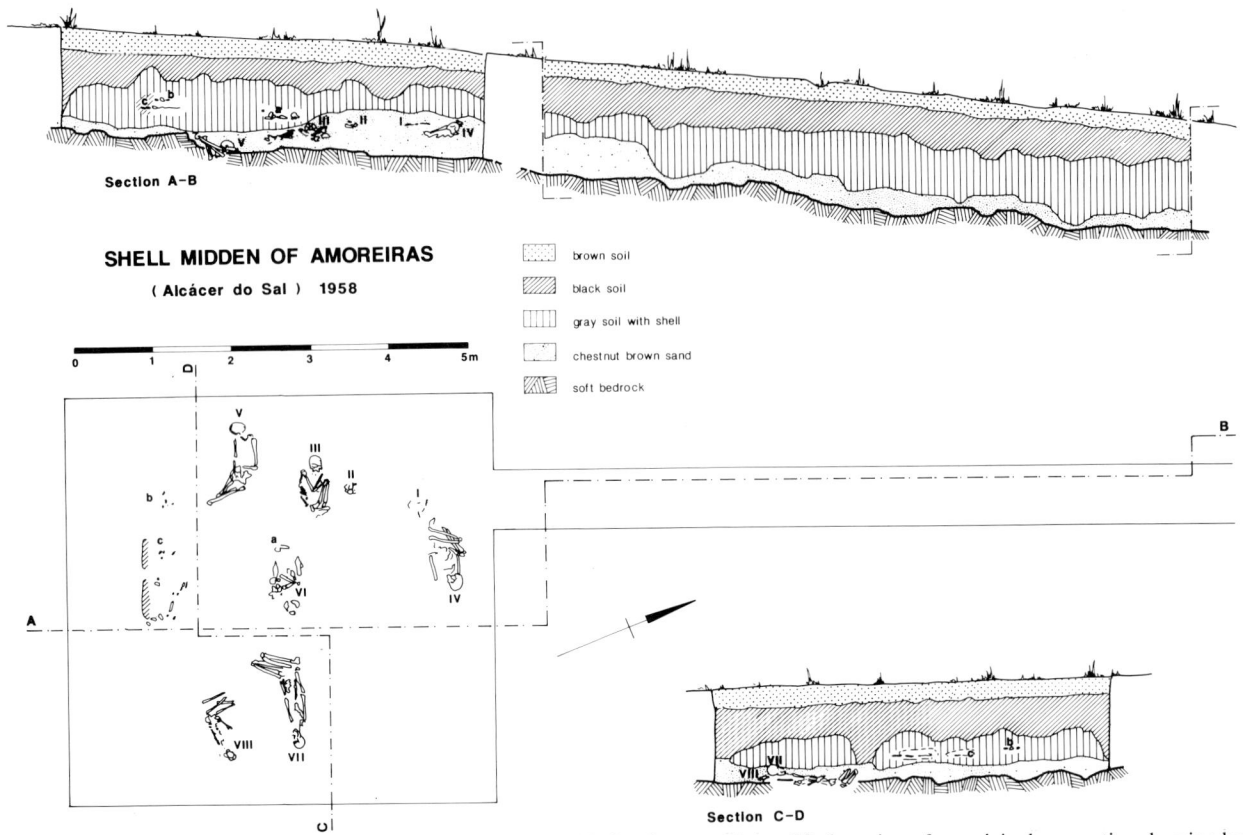

Section A-B

SHELL MIDDEN OF AMOREIRAS

(Alcácer do Sal) 1958

	brown soil
	black soil
	gray soil with shell
	chestnut brown sand
	soft bedrock

Section C-D

Figure 4   Amoreiras: detail of the main area excavated in 1958. Re-drawn and simplified version of an original excavation drawing by Mr Dario de Sousa, in the National Museum, Lisbon.

Cabeço das Amoreiras
Burial IV

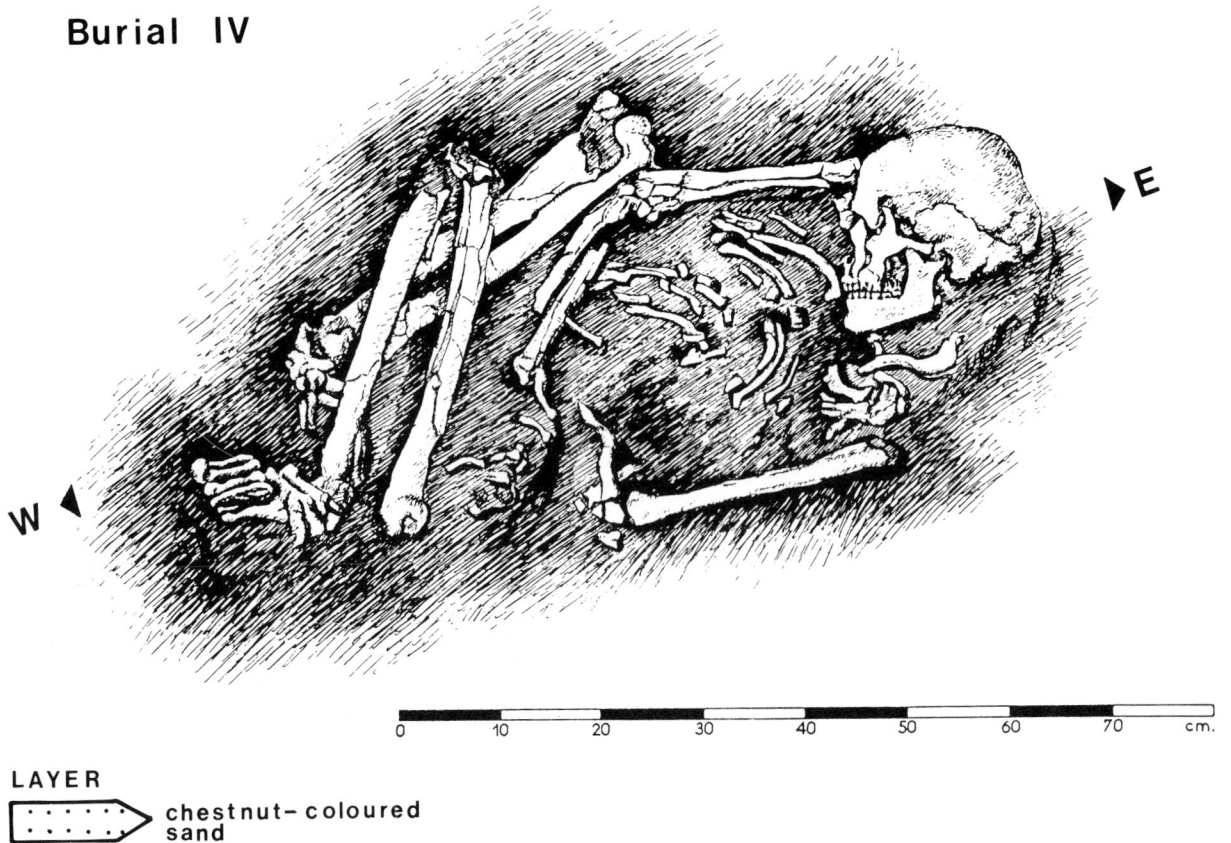

LAYER

chestnut-coloured sand

Figure 5   Amoreiras: detail of one of the burials excavated in 1958.

620

Muge, where burials in the supine position with the legs semi-contracted predominate (Roche 1960), on the Sado the hocker position was consistently used at all the shell middens, either fully contracted in the characteristic foetal position, or in a semi-contracted posture, the bodies lying either on their left or on their right sides (*Figs. 4 & 5*).

All the burials for which there is some documentation indicating their original location were found in the bottom layer, normally a light-brown sandy sediment, with no or few traces of occupation, underneath the main shell midden area. As the skeletons we̶ apparently placed in individual, or at least r̶ ̶ ̶ ̶burial pits, only occasionally was it p̶ ̶ ̶ ̶ any 'grave goods' indisputa̶ ̶ ̶ ̶al, but it was consiste̶ ̶ ̶ ̶ ̶ll beads were f̶ ̶ ̶ In sever̶ ̶h part̶ ̶ls, na̶ ̶hell b̶ ̶ ̶yers, ̶ ̶tween ̶rs. This ̶emeteries ̶ly Téviec ̶équart and ̶orethsen and ̶nd Skateholm ̶ ̶were found in ̶ ̶, but consistently c̶ VII and VIII) or west–c̶ São Bento both the disposition a̶ ̶ seem to be random. At Romeiras, how̶ ̶keletons of 22 individuals were placed radiall̶ ̶ a semi-circle with the aperture facing the river, suggesting close contemporaneity of these burials. In fact, in spite of the close proximity of all the burials, only one of the skeletons was superimposed on another one. Considering that Romeiras, the smallest shell midden identified so far, is located only about 300 m from what is by far the largest midden, it is tempting to consider the possibility that the former was used as the 'cemetery' of the latter, and that the apparently simultaneous burial of so many people was the result of some catastrophic event, such as the outbreak of an epidemic. Apart from this example, it seems plausible to suggest that most of the other burials took place gradually during the several hundred years of more or less regular occupation of these sites.

This close connection between the place of living and the place of burial has in recent times frequently been interpreted as the result of the need by descent groups to secure their access to crucial, but restricted, resources (e.g. Saxe 1970; Goldstein 1976; Renfrew

1976; Chapman 1981). Yet in few cases is the association of the burial place with a specific economic resource so clear as in the Mesolithic shell middens. Whether the molluscs were both 'crucial' and 'restricted' is, however, not yet clear.

The cleaning and restoring of this important assemblage of human skeletal remains is still in progress, but it will certainly make a major contribution to the knowledge of Mesolithic adaptations in this part of the world. In fact it is one of the largest in Europe, only superseded by the Muge assemblage (cf. Newell *et al.* 1979), and several recent collections of papers (Cohen and Armelagos 1984; Gilbert and Mielke 1985) have clearly shown the great potential offered by human skeletal remains for the study of the demographic, palaeopathologic, dietary and nutritional aspects of the Postglacial populations. This potential has also been demonstrated by the preliminary results of a thorough revision of the human skeletal remains of Muge (Meiklejohn *et al.* 1984; Lubell and Jackes 1985; Lubell *et al.*, this volume). As regards the Sado material, all that can be said for the moment is that both children and adults, and male and female persons were buried in the shell middens.

ARTIFACTS

Analysis of the lithic artifacts from the different sites is still too uneven to allow detailed inter-site comparisons, but some very general comments can be advanced.

The quality of the primary material is generally very poor at all the sites. This is reflected in the very low percentages of tools in relation to by-products (*Fig. 7*). In fact, the percentage of geometric microliths (the most common tools found at all the sites) varies from just 0.44% at Arapouco to 8.02% at Amoreiras, the average being 4.91%.

The most common materials are a series of poor siliceous rocks which can be loosely termed 'flint', but a small proportion of the tools are made of whitish or hialin quartz, or even of quartzite. The poor quality of the flint used in this area contrasts with that of the material used at Muge, suggesting that the catchment area of the Sado communities for this type of primary material was essentially local, not reaching the much better flint sources of the limestone massifs of the peninsulas of Setúbal and Lisbon.

Flint knapping is abundantly attested at all the sites but, apart from a few retouched bladelets and the occasional atypical scraper, the artifacts which can be considered as indisputably finished tools are mostly geometric microliths. Trapezes predominate at Arapouco and Vale de Romeiras, and crescents at Amoreiras and Poças de São Bento; triangles are always in a minority. Microburins are also present at

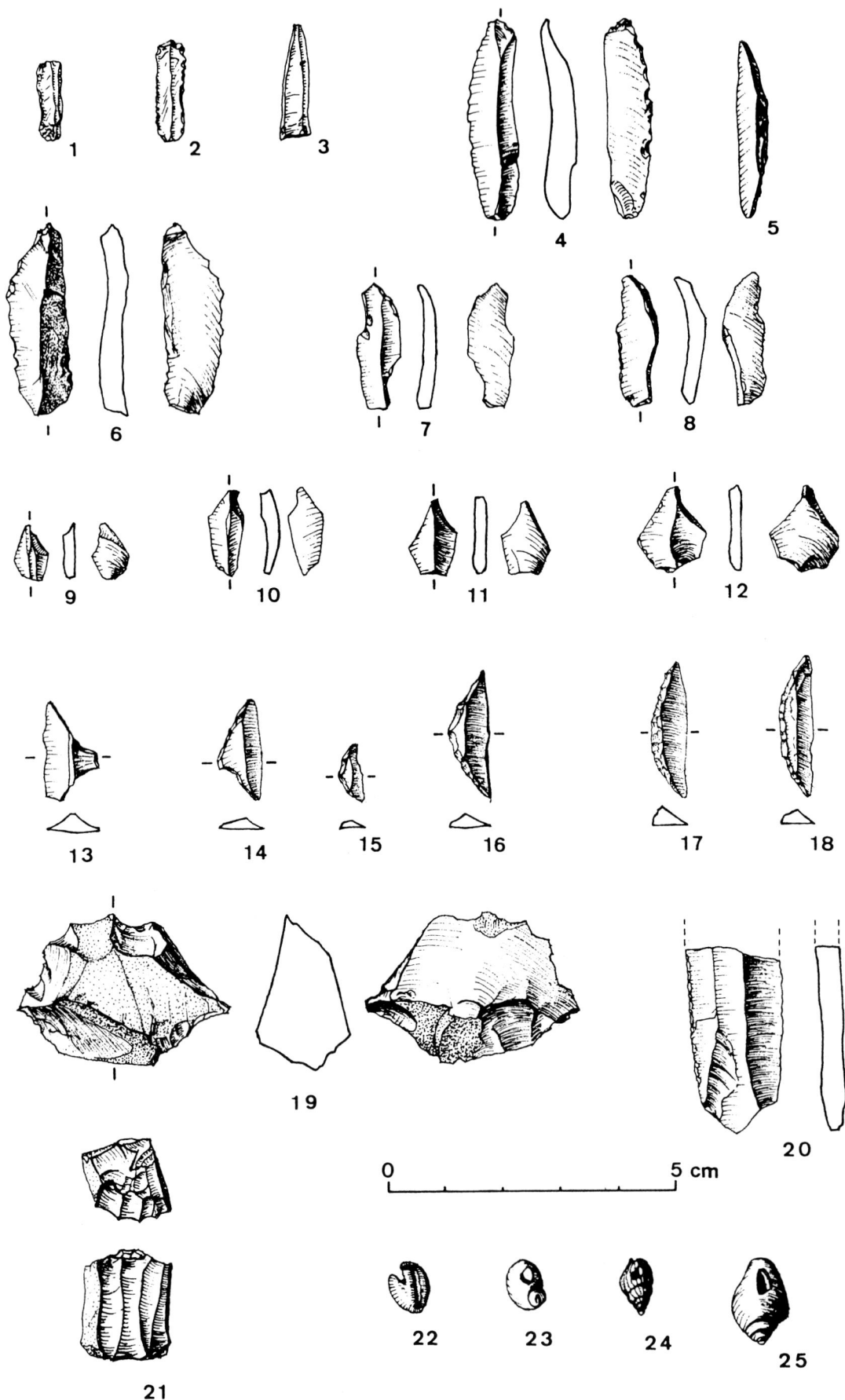

Figure 6 Amoreiras: a sample of the artifacts. Nos. 1–3 are in hialin quartz; nos. 4–21 are in flint; the shell-beads were made of *Trivia* sp. (no. 22), *Neritina fluviatilis* (no. 23), and *Hinia reticulata* (nos. 24 & 25 – no. 25 was thoroughly polished).

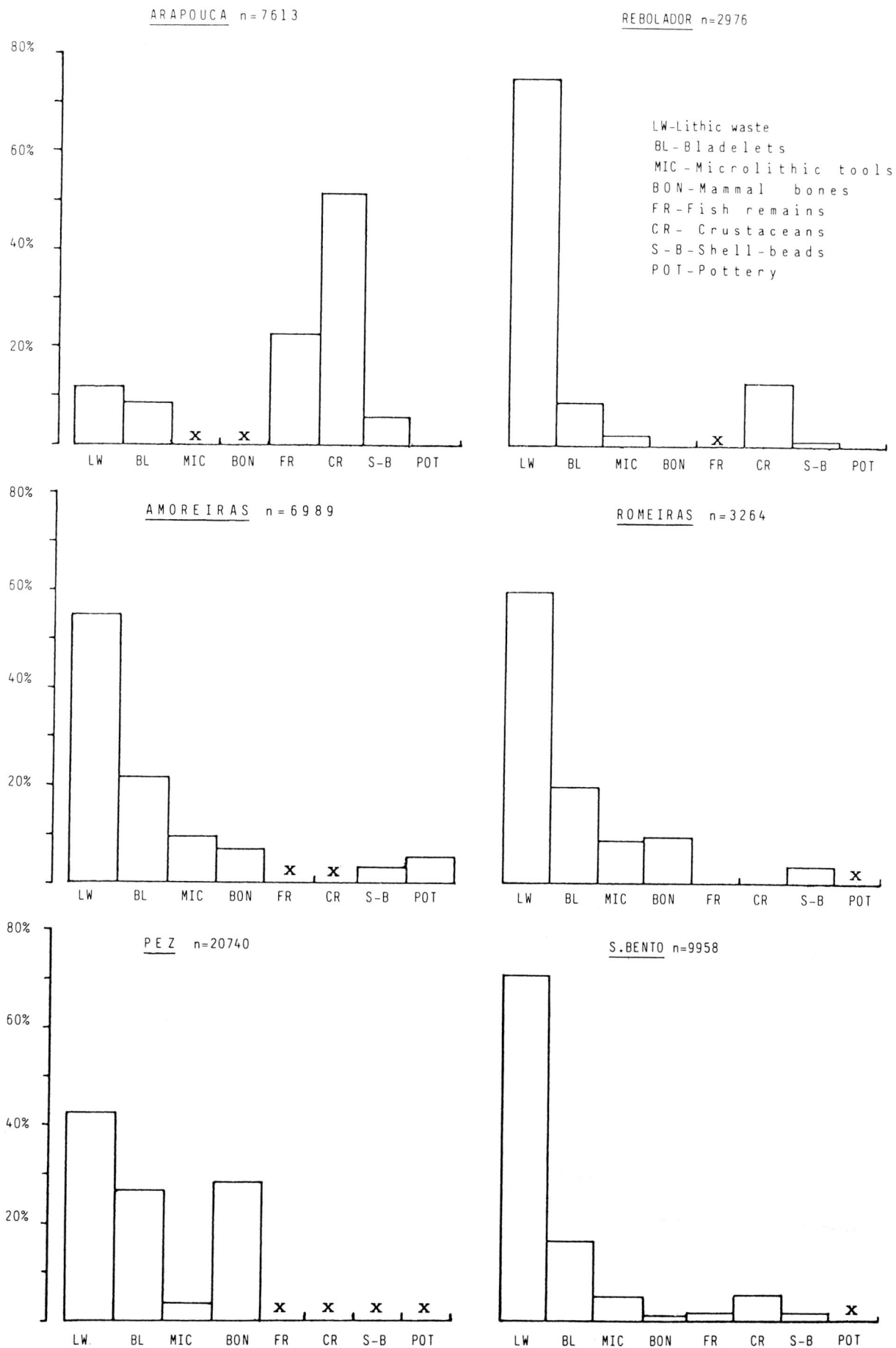

Figure 7 Comparative diagram of the major classes of artifacts and faunal remains of the six major shell middens of the Sado area.

623

all the sites, and at Cabeço do Rebolador they even outnumber geometrics. Considering that this site also has the largest percentage of waste products, this reinforces the common interpretation of micro-burins as by-products of the manufacture of geometric microliths rather than actual tools, and increases even further the disproportion between the number of finished tools and the various types of knapping by-products. It must be stressed, however, that many unretouched bladelets may have been *used*, as recent micro-wear analyses have suggested.

Apart from the 'flaked-stone' artifacts, mention must also be made of the occasional occurrence of other classes of artifacts. A few spatulae of bone and worked antler tips were recovered from Cabeço do Pez. Beads made of various univalve shells, common cockle shells and, less frequently, sectioned and perforated fish vertebrae were also found at most of the sites.

FAUNAL REMAINS

Molluscs

The most common molluscs represented at all the Sado shell middens, and the only ones which certainly made an appreciable caloric contribution to the diet of the Mesolithic communities, were the common cockle (*Cerastoderma edule*) and the peppery furrow-shell (*Scrobicularia plana*), in the proportion of about 2:1. At first sight cockle shells, which are much thicker and more resistant to breakage, seem overwhelmingly dominant but, when all the fragments of the two species are separated and weighed, the presence of furrow-shells, which are rarely found complete, becomes more conspicuous.

These two species live in considerably different habitats. The common cockle lives mostly in clean sandy deposits of the intertidal region, in the shallow waters of estuaries, lagoons and river banks; in some areas of the modern estuary of the Sado these molluscs reach very high densities (several thousand per m^2) but, as a result of their reduced commercial value, they are nowadays almost exclusively collected for use as bait by the local fishermen. Cockles have a considerable salinity tolerance (12–35 ‰) but, when salinity approaches the lower limits, the density tends to decrease.

Peppery furrow-shells live in a wide range of muddy sediments in the inner stagnant parts of estuaries, lagoons and river banks. They show a salinity tolerance even wider than that of the common cockle (6–30 ‰), but their overall density is much lower. Nowadays they are not so abundant on the Sado as on the Tagus estuary, but even in the latter a recent study recorded a maximum density of 124 individuals per m^2 (Rebelo and Guerreiro da Silva 1983). Moreover, furrow-shells are more difficult to catch since they tend to penetrate as deep in the muddy sediment as 25 cm, thanks to their very long siphons which can extend up to five or six times the length of the shell (Christensen and Dance 1980).

Mention must also be made of a few other mollusc species which were only very seldom found in the Sado shell middens, but which might occasionally have been used as food, such as oysters (*Crassostrea angulata*) which are relatively abundant at Cabeço do Rebolador and were also detected in other shell middens. After a period of great abundance and of prosperous commercial exploitation, oysters are nowadays extremely rare on the Sado estuary as a result of their great sensitivity to chemical pollution. Other molluscs which are very abundant on the Sado estuary but which were only very seldom collected from these sites are murices (*Murex brandaris*) and razor-shells (*Ensis siliqua*), only detected at Arapouco. The shells of the latter are extremely fragile and their rarity could be the result of taphonomic factors, but these could hardly have affected the former.

Finally, mention must be made of a series of univalvia which were systematically used to make shell beads at practically all the sites, as mentioned above. The species most commonly used for that purpose were, in decreasing order of frequency, *Neritina fluviatilis*, *Trivia* sp. and *Hinia reticulata*, all but the first species commonly found on the beaches of southern Portugal. At Arapouco were also found isolated examples of the following mollusc species: *Cypraea pyrum*, currently found only in the much warmer waters of Algarve, *Cerianthus*, *Dentalium*, characteristic of the sub-tidal zone, *Calyptraea chinensis*, *Gibbula magus* (topshell), and *Ocenebra edwardsi*.

Crustaceans

Crustaceans were also abundantly represented at Arapouco and at Cabeço do Rebolador by the extremities of their main claws, and have also occasionally occurred at the other shell middens of the area. Until now only one species was identified, *Carcinus maenas*, which is the most common crustacean on the modern estuary. These crabs have a very small amount of meat, hence their low economic value, but when trapped in the nets they are used mainly as bait. Thus, in spite of their abundance at those two sites, their contribution to the diet of the respective occupants was certainly very low indeed, although their presence may indicate a relative scarcity of other richer and more palatable foodstuffs, or of their use as bait, as today.

Fish

Fish remains were only collected in some abundance at Arapouco as well as (in smaller quantities) at

Rebolador and São Bento, but the occasional vertebra suggests that there was some fishing at several of the other sites. Given that all these sites are located in identical geological contexts and were excavated by the same team and according to the same methodology, it seems very likely that the material collected reflects to some extent the relative importance of fish in the activities and dietary habits of the occupants of the different shell middens, as well as differential resource availability. It must, however, be stressed that differential preservation may have strongly distorted the picture of fishing activities so far obtained.

Three main categories of fish remains have been identified: (i) vertebrae, by far the most abundant; (ii) otoliths, only abundantly found at Arapouco; and (iii) a few teeth. With few exceptions, however, each of these belongs to different fish families. Sciaenidae are the most abundant and are represented mainly by a large number of otoliths, attributed to at least two different species, one of which was already identified as meagre (*Argyrosomus regius*). These otoliths represent a large range of sizes and ages, and some of them may have come from individuals of 7–8 years, probably more than 1.5 m in length. However, only one large vertebra has been attributed to this solidly built bony fish family. On the other hand, most of the large vertebrae collected are attributable either to rays (Rajidae) or to sharks (Lamnidae), both families of cartilaginous fish which should not preserve better than the true bony ones. Some of the smaller vertebrae can be attributed to Mugilidae and to Sparidae. The most abundant teeth found were the characteristic ovoid molars of gilthead (*Sparus auratus*), although some others might have belonged to other Sparidae, namely to Couch's sea bream (*Sparus pagrus*) and to black sea bream (*Spondileosoma cantarus*). Also found at Arapouco, Rebolador and São Bento were a few teeth indisputably attributed to *Isurus oxyrinchus*, a large shark which may reach 3–4 m in length.

A comparison of the fish families and species represented at these shell middens with those which live in the modern estuary of the Sado will immediately demonstrate the enormous disparities and the strong effects of taphonomic processes. In fact, none of the species so far identified at these sites is characteristically estuarine and, if rays and different species of Sparidae are occasionally found in this estuary, others, like the Lamnidae, seem rare or have not been recorded there in recent times by the local fisherman (e.g. meagre). Yet meagre is represented at Arapouco alone by more than 100 individuals, of a wide range of sizes, and half of the otoliths collected were found in the same place. This suggests that they were systematically caught, occasionally in shoals of considerable size, probably with the aid of nets.

Meagre, a very much prized fish, is still relatively abundant around the coasts of Portugal and is mainly caught well offshore but, in the Mediterranean, 'it lives in shallow water over sandy bottoms, and the young especially can be found in estuaries and low salinity lagoons' (Wheeler 1978: 267). Their absence from the present Sado estuary may thus be the result of considerable ecological changes which have occurred in the estuary in recent times, mainly as a result of chemical pollution.

In fact, according to a detailed report on the fishing activities in Portugal at the end of the last century, meagre is still very abundant in the seas of southern Portugal and in the Tagus and Sado estuaries in which they used to spawn, but only between April and August, living well offshore during the rest of the year (Baldaque da Silva 1891). According to the same author, meagre used to live in shoals close to the bottom and were caught in the estuaries with enmeshing nets or by angling.

Sparidae are also not very abundant today and represent less than one percent of the total catch, by weight. The local fishermen, however, are very positive in their statement that they are only caught in the estuary between June and September.

Mammals

As shown in *Fig. 7*, the only sites in which mammal bones were found in appreciable quantities were Cabeço do Pez, Amoreiras and Romeiras, but a few were also collected at São Bento and Arapouco.

Most of these were studied in 1983 by Dr P. Rowley-Conwy and, as shown in *Table 3*, the only site in which there was enough material for a quantitative assessment of the relative importance of the various species is Cabeço do Pez. At this site there is a clear predominance of red deer (*Cervus elaphus*), followed by wild pig (*Sus scrofa ferus*). Of the remaining species only aurochs (*Bos primigenius*) was of some relevance in economic terms. Hare (*Lepus capensis*) and rabbit (*Oryctolagus cuniculus*) are also abundantly represented, but their contribution in caloric terms was quite small. However, their presence suggests that the landscape was relatively open. This is reinforced by the scarcity of roe deer (*Capreolus capreolus*) which normally shows a preference for dense woodlands (Rowley-Conwy 1983). The presence of horse (*Equus ferus*) is also interesting, because until now its presence had only been mentioned, but not confirmed, at one of the Muge sites, Cabeço da Arruda.

The only possibly domesticated species identified so far is the dog, but only one bone could be attributed to a definitely 'domestic' animal. Four other bones were attributable either to wolf or to large dog. In spite of the ambiguous nature of the

Table 3: List of mammal bones from the Sado shell middens classified in 1983 by P. Rowley-Conwy. 'Modified fragments' gives the number of articular ends of long bones, and the number of jaws and maxillae inferred from the teeth present. Long bone shaft fragments, antlers, lateral metapodials, phalanges, etc., are not counted. MNI is the raw count of the most common element; no pairing or extra calculations were made

	CABEÇO DO PEZ Modified Fragments		MNI		AMOREIRAS Fragments	MNI	ROMEIRAS Fragments	MNI	POÇAS DE SÃO BENTO Fragments	MNI
Red deer (*Cervus elaphus*)	657	69%	24	63%	23	2	33	1	16	2
Wild pig (*Sus scrofa*)	265	28%	9	24%	12	1	1	1	–	–
Aurochs (*Bos primigenius*)	27	3%	2	5%	12	1	1	1	3	1
Roe deer (*Capreolus capreolus*)	4	0.5%	2	5%	–	–	–	–	–	–
Horse (*Equus ferus*)	4	0.5%	1	3%	1	1	–	–	–	–
Rabbit (*Oryctolagus cuniculus*)	154		26		11	3	–	–	–	–
Hare (*Lepus capensis*)	125		14		1	1	1	1	–	–
Dog (*Canis familiaris*)	1		1		–	–	–	–	–	–
Dog/Wolf (*Canis* sp.)	4		1		1	1	–	–	–	–
Fox (*Vulpes vulpes*)	4		1		–	–	1	1	–	–
Wild cat (*Felis silvestris*)	2		1		–	–	–	–	–	–
Pardel lynx (*Felis pardina*)	4		2		–	–	–	–	–	–
Otter (*Lutra lutra*)	1		1		–	–	–	–	–	–
Hedgehog (*Erinaceous europeus*)	1		1		–	–	–	–	–	–

evidence available, the existence of dogs in this context seems perfectly acceptable in the light of growing evidence for the presence of domesticated dogs in several Mesolithic contexts in northern Europe. Skateholm I is particularly relevant here; seven dogs were buried with the same rites as human beings (Larsson 1984), showing that they were not just domesticated but had already established a very special relationship with the human beings, who probably used them as aids in hunting activities.

Among the remaining small animals, mention must be made of the presence of otter (*Lutra lutra*), a fish-eater which nowadays lives mainly along the margins of a few rivers in northern Portugal, but is also able to adapt to estuarine or coastal environments. Lynx (*Felis pardina*), nowadays found only in the Malcata mountain in central Portugal, is also represented by a few bones at Cabeço do Pez. All the others are still occasionally found in the Sado area.

Birds

In contrast to the abundance of mammal bones, bird bones are very scarce. In fact, only four have been identified so far, two of which are probably of an unspecified duck. It is, however, expected that the future use of fine-mesh dry-sieving and froth-flotation will reveal the presence of a few more bird bones, as well as other small-sized faunal remains not yet identified, which, even if dietarily unimportant, may offer some contribution towards the reconstruction of the environment.

SETTLEMENT PATTERN AND SUBSISTENCE STRATEGY

It has not yet been possible to complete the classification of more than a small part of the 200,000 artifacts and faunal remains collected during the 1950s and 1960s, and the radiocarbon dates already obtained are insufficient to establish a sound chronometric framework. Nor has it been possible to complete the series of small-scale control excavations planned for the shell middens still preserved in the area, or the systematic survey of this area. However, a consideration of the sparse evidence for seasonality of occupation already available for these sites, coupled with an analysis of the differences in site size, location and major classes of artifacts and food remains (*Table 2*; *Fig. 7*), seems at least sufficient to establish a provisional model for the settlement pattern and subsistence strategy of the Mesolithic communities of the area. This will have to be tested in the near-future by the systematic use of oxygen-isotope analysis or other reliable methods for the determination of the season or seasons of collection of the mollusc shells, since these are the only food remains which have been abundantly collected at all the sites.

Over the last decade there have been a number of studies of Mesolithic settlement systems and food procurement strategies in several areas of Europe, based on detailed quantification and seasonal scheduling of potential food resources (Jochim 1976; Paludan-Müller 1978; Price 1978, 1981a). However, given the almost complete lack of palaeo-environmental studies for the Sado valley or for ecologically comparable areas, such an approach would be impractical at present. It seems useful, nevertheless, to present in a very simplified diagram (*Fig. 8*) a seasonal schedule of both the *potential* food resources and those actually documented in the archaeological record.

The seasonal data for the four major species of mammals represented at most of the sites are based on Jochim (1976) and Price (1978, 1981a), in the absence of data for more meridional environments.

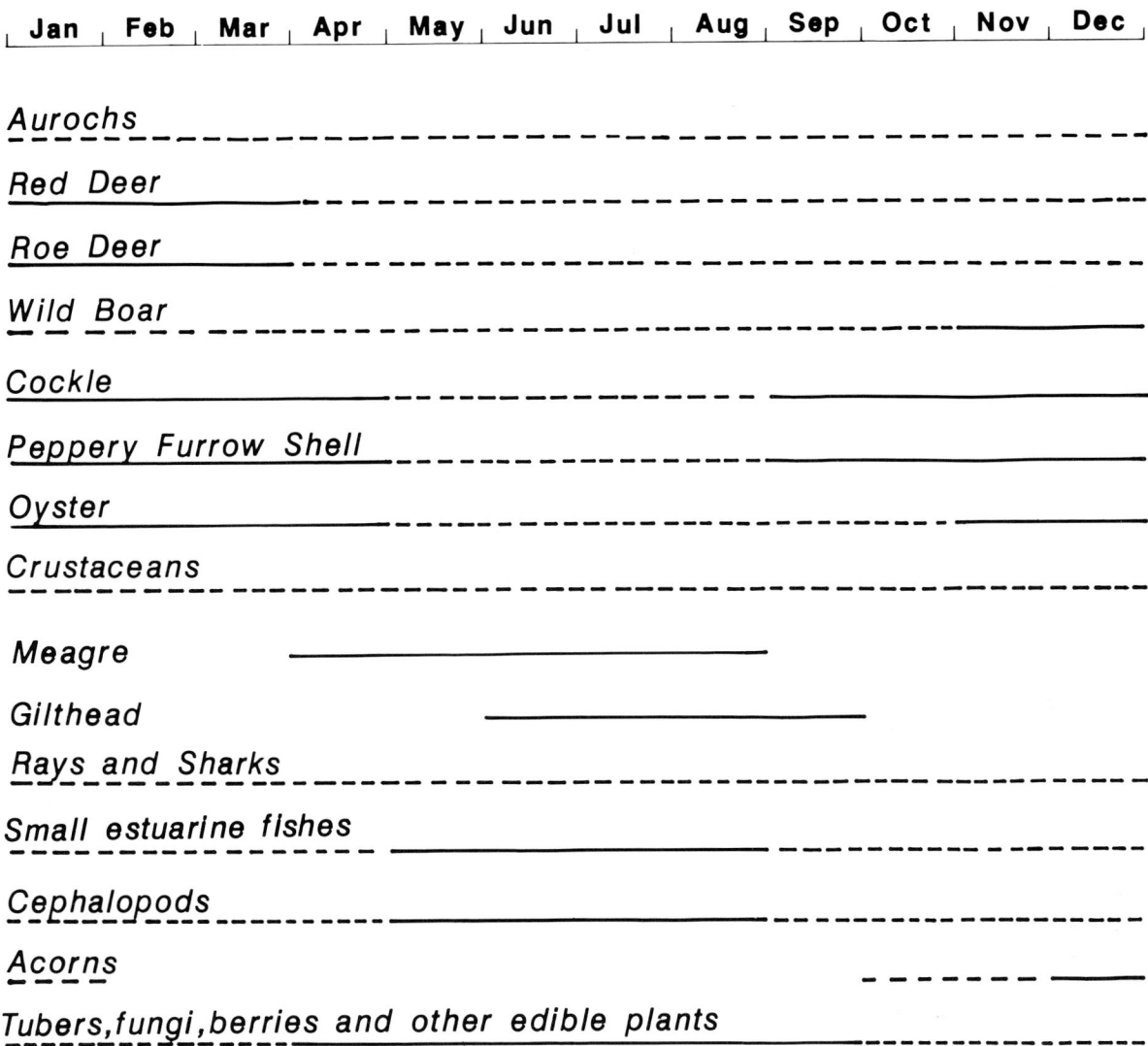

Jan	Feb	Mar	Apr	May	Jun	Jul	Aug	Sep	Oct	Nov	Dec

Aurochs ――――――――――――――――――――――――――――――――

Red Deer ―――――――――――――――――――――――――――――――

Roe Deer ――――――――――――――――――――――――――――――

Wild Boar ――――――――――――――――――――――――――――――

Cockle ――――――――――――――――――――――――――

Peppery Furrow Shell ――――――――――――――――――

Oyster ―――――――――――――――――――――――――

Crustaceans ――――――――――――――――――――――――――

Meagre ―――――――――――――――

Gilthead ――――――――――――

Rays and Sharks ――――――――――――――――――――――――

Small estuarine fishes ――――――――――――――――――――

* Cephalopods ―――――――――――――――――――――――

* Acorns ―――――――――

* Tubers, fungi, berries and other edible plants ―――――――――

―――― Optimum period

_ _ _ _ Availability period

(* indicates potential resources not yet documented archaeologically)

Figure 8 Seasonal schedule of the major potential food resources of the lower Sado valley.

Those for fish and shellfish are based on information from local fisherman and on official fisheries statistics; data for other resources are based on direct observation, unless otherwise stated in the text.

The molluscs and crustaceans which have been collected from the Sado shell middens are normally available in the estuary all year round, and so have no direct value as seasonal indicators. More meaningful in this respect are the fish remains. In fact, they were only found in abundance at Arapouco (*Fig. 7*), which is not surprising as this is the site located closest to the river mouth. As was emphasized above, the fish remains from Arapouco were certainly affected by taphonomic processes, but it seems very significant that the two main fish species which could be determined with accuracy, meagre (*Argyrosomus regius*) and gilthead (*Sparus aurata*), both show clear seasonal behaviour, only penetrating into the estuary during the spawning period – between April and August and between June and September, respectively. It can be suggested, then, that Arapouco was occupied at least during part of spring and summer.

Bone remains were only found abundantly, in both absolute and relative terms, at Cabeço do Pez, which is one of the sites located farther from the river mouth. The number of ageable jaws of wild pig already analyzed suggests an occupation of the site between August/September and January/February. The seasonal evidence available for red deer is more ambiguous; in fact, of the 14 determinable red deer antler fragments, seven were cast and seven were still attached to the skull, which could be interpreted as indicating a late spring/summer occupation. How-

627

ever, considering that antler was used at this site as a raw material, it could have been collected elsewhere and brought to the site at any time of year (Rowley-Conwy 1983).

If, on the other hand, all the species of mammals detected at Cabeço do Pez were living in the area all year round, it is nonetheless true that the optimum period for the hunting of those species which were more significant in economic terms, namely red deer and wild pig, is normally January to March and November to March, respectively. This circumstance reinforces the suggestion of an occupation of this site mainly during the autumn and winter. Today, Cabeço do Pez is located in a dense parkland of cork-oak and stone-pine. As mentioned above, it is not yet clear whether cork-oak was already firmly established in this area during the Boreal/Atlantic transition, but if that was the case, acorns might have contributed to the diet of the Mesolithic communities, either directly or indirectly, being a strong attraction at least to the wild pig populations of the area. Cork-oak acorns are available between October and January, reaching their optimum in terms of quantity and quality in December (Natividade 1950). Being more bitter than those of holm-oak, predominant further inland, it might be expected that they were parched or roasted to remove the tannic acid, thus increasing the probability of being preserved in carbonized form. Their apparent absence from the Sado shell middens can then be interpreted either as a result of their absence or scarcity in this area during the early Atlantic phase, or simply of their neglect for direct consumption.

Thus, the sharp contrast between the faunal remains from Arapouco and those from Cabeço do Pez can be interpreted as the result of seasonal occupation – during the spring/summer and during the autumn/winter, respectively. The evidence for seasonal occupation of the other sites of the area is less clear.

As shown in *Fig. 7*, the sites of Amoreiras and Romeiras show a marked similarity in the major classes of artifacts and faunal remains present, suggesting a similar regime of occupation and activities. Mammal bones are not as abundant as at Cabeço do Pez; even so they represent 7.13% and 9.28% of the total, respectively. Fish and crustacean remains are, however, very rare at Amoreiras and absent at Romeiras. This disproportion between the terrestrial and estuarine remains, together with the geographical proximity of these two sites to Cabeço do Pez, suggests an occupation during approximately the same period of the year, or in a transitional period between winter and spring when game was not so abundant as before. This would eventually be compensated for by vegetable food, such as berries, roots, tubers and fungi, as well as the many early

herbaceous spring greens which, according to Clarke (1976: 476), were widely available in the temperate forests and had a 'vital antiscorbutic value', although their dietary contribution in caloric terms was certainly very low.

Another common feature of the sites of Cabeço do Pez, Amoreiras and Romeiras is the presence of fragments of pottery, which at Amoreiras reached 4.57% of the total artifacts, suggesting a more permanent settlement. Its presence may, however, have purely chronological significance.

More difficult to explain in this respect are the assemblages from Rebolador and Poças de São Bento, in particular the latter. Rebolador is one of the smallest sites of the area and one of the few in which no human skeletal remains have yet been found. In spite of its proximity and the similarity of its topographical setting to Arapouco, the artifacts and faunal remains suggest a very different regime of occupation. In fact, the only point in common seems to be the relative abundance of crustacean remains, although these are much more abundant at Arapouco. However, while at this latter site fish remains are very abundant and mammal bones rare, at Rebolador fish remains are almost non-existent and mammal bones absent. The contrast between the artifacts is even clearer; at Arapouco the proportion of bladelets in relation to lithic waste is the highest so far recorded, while at Rebolador it is the lowest, reflecting the importance of flint knapping. Yet there is no particular abundance in the area of raw material suitable for that activity.

The establishment of the season of occupation at Rebolador is somewhat difficult, too. As mentioned above, crustaceans are available all year round, but at Rebolador a number of oysters were also found. These would have been available throughout the year, but should have reached their optimum period for consumption between November and April, that is, out of the reproduction period. An occupation during at least part of this period might explain the rarity of fish remains. The effects of differential preservation have certainly affected to a large extent the remains of the smaller fish species which normally live in the estuary during the whole year, and also the cephalopods which nowadays contribute about 25% to the total weight of the estuarine catches (cf. Peneda and Coelho 1978). It can be suggested that this site was a small late winter/early spring fishing camp that was occupied for a relatively short time by only a part of the co-resident group, in a transitional period when terrestrial resources were becoming scarce and marine resources were not yet plentiful.

The functional and seasonal interpretation of the site of Poças de São Bento and also, to some extent, of the sites of Fonte da Mina and Barranco da Moura (*Fig. 2*, sites 9, 10, 11) is more difficult. In fact, the site of Poças de São Bento shows some similarity with the sites of Amoreiras and Romeiras in terms of the artifacts, but there is a greater emphasis on fish and crustaceans than on mammals (*Fig. 7*). However, this site, which is located some 3 km from the River Sado or any of its tributaries, lies at an altitude of about 80 m a.s.l. and covers 3570 m². It is thus one of the largest shell middens of the area, comparable to Cabeço do Pez, although apparently with a considerably lower density of shells. Even though the tide might have penetrated 1.5 km into the narrow valley of the small stream which runs close to this site and Fonte da Mina (*Fig. 2*), the shellfish would have had to be carried over a distance of at least 1.5 km. The expenditure of energy involved would hardly have been compensated for by the caloric value of the meat obtained. On the other hand, and even more surprisingly, the low number of mammal bones collected suggests that hunting was not a particularly important activity, which might indicate a spring/summer occupation. In addition to these features, Poças do São Bento has produced by far the highest density of lithic waste of all the Sado sites – about five times that of Cabeço do Pez and ten times that of Arapouco (*Table 2*). Again, no sources of raw material have yet been found in the area.

Unfortunately, neither of the two other sites located at some distance from the Sado river was excavated, but the similarity of their location and size to Poças de São Bento would suggest a similar type of occupation. The similarity of setting between these three sites is reinforced by the fact that all of them are located close to the best natural water springs of the area, a resource of vital importance for a spring/summer occupation. This probably does not explain fully the establishment of the Mesolithic groups at such a distance from the river valley but, during the summer, the inner part of the estuary was certainly as insalubrious as it is nowadays. This is the result of the accumulation of stagnant waters in the parts of the valley not affected by the influence of the tide.

CONCLUSIONS

In spite of the limitations of the evidence available for some of the Sado sites, and assuming that all of them were broadly contemporary and components of the same settlement system, it may be suggested provisionally that each co-resident group would have been based on two large base camps occupied by most of the group during the autumn/winter season (e.g. Cabeço do Pez) and during the spring/summer season (e.g. Poças de São Bento), respectively. Each of these would have been associated with smaller temporary camps, connected with specialized economic activities. This very simplified model corresponds broadly to the concept of 'logistic

movement' used by Binford (1980) to distinguish the 'collectors' from the 'foragers'.

Confirmation and refinement of this model, or its invalidation and the elaboration of an alternative model, will depend on the exploration of various research avenues, namely:

1. The systematic determination of the season of occupation of these shell middens, based on the use of oxygen-isotope analyses of a vast number of cockle shells, selected by an adequate sampling strategy.

2. The exhaustive survey of the area, in order to detect other shell middens or other types of Mesolithic sites, and sources of raw material.

3. The excavation of small areas in all these shell middens in order to collect reliable samples of material, using froth-flotation, to obtain a more complete record of faunal and floral remains.

4. The refinement of the available chronometric framework by the dating of all the layers of occupation of all the shell middens of the area.

5. The restoration and exhaustive study of the human skeletal remains already excavated, with special emphasis on the nutritional status, the palaeopathology, and the genetic and demographic structure of this population.

6. The systematic coring of the edges of the Sado floodplain and its tributaries, to detect the location and extent of the ancient shell beds and peat deposits suitable for pollen analysis that would provide more detailed information on the late Boreal/Atlantic landscape and its transformation.

The potential contribution of this assemblage of sites for the study of the emergence of social complexity and the process of food procurement intensification which led to the inception of farming has already been emphasized (Morais Arnaud 1982), but it will be discussed in more detail elsewhere, in the light of recent developments in this field (Price 1981*b*; Price and Brown 1985).[1,2]

Note:

1. Many new data relating to the Sado sites have been collected since this paper was submitted for publication in September 1985.

2. For a comparison of the Sado shell middens with their counterparts of Muge, see Morais Arnaud (1987*a*), and for their interpretation in the light of current research in other areas of southern Portugal, see Morais Arnaud (1985, 1987*b*).

Acknowledgements: I wish to thank here to all those who have contributed to the Sado Project, namely the Director of the Museu Nacional de Arqueologia e Etnologia, Francisco Alves, for access to the material from the earlier excavations and for all the facilities provided for its study; Mr Jaime Roldão, who conducted most of those excavations and Mr Dario de Sousa, who drew the plans and sections, for information about the excavations; Dr Peter Rowley-Conwy (University of Cambridge), who has studied the bone remains; Dr Roy Switsur (Godwin Laboratory, University of Cambridge) for the radiocarbon dates; Dr Margaret Deith (Godwin Laboratory) for the oxygen-isotope analyses (in course) and for checking the text; Alwyne Wheeler (British Museum, Natural History) and Luis Fonseca (Oceanographic Laboratory, University of Lisbon) for the classification of the fish remains; Carlos Reis (Ocean Laboratory, University of Lisbon) for the classification of molluscs; José Mateus (Laboratory for Quaternary research, National Museum, Lisbon) for access to an early version of his pollen diagram; Fernando Real (Laboratory for Quaternary Research, National Museum, Lisbon) for sedimentological analyses in course; Dr Teresa Azevedo and João Cabral (Department of Geology, University of Lisbon) for geomorphological and neotectonic observations; Luis Oliveira, Maria José Pereira and many other students of the University of Lisbon who have helped me in the fieldwork and the classification of the artifacts; and Joaquim Franco who drew *Fig. 6*. Last but not least, I must express my gratitude to my wife, Teresa, for her constant encouragement and help throughout the development of the project.

Part of the fieldwork on the Sado area was subsidized by the Portuguese Ministry for Cultural Affairs. My participation in this Symposium was made possible by the generous financial support of the Calouste Gulbenkian Foundation.

References

ALBRETHSEN, S.E. and BRINCH PETERSEN, E. (1976) Excavation of a Mesolithic cemetery at Vedbæk, Denmark. *Acta Archaeologica*, 47: 1–28.

ATHAIDE, A. (1940) Novos esqueletos humanos dos concheiros mesoliticos de Muge. *I Congresso do Mundo Português*, vol. 1. Lisbon, Comissão Executiva dos Centenários: 630–651.

BALDAQUE DA SILVA, A.A. (1891) *Estado Actual das Pescas em Portugal*. Lisbon, Imprensa Nacional.

BARRADAS, L.A. (1936) Concheiros do Vale do Sado. *Anais da Faculdade de Ciencias do Porto*, 21(3): 175–179.

BINFORD, L.R. (1980) Willow smoke and dogs' tails: hunter-gatherer settlement systems and archaeological site formation. *American Antiquity*, 45: 4–20.

BRUM FERREIRA, D. DE (1981) *Carte Géomorphologique du Portugal*. Lisbon, Memórias do Centro de Estudos Geográficos no. 6.

CHAPMAN, R.W. (1981) The emergence of formal disposal areas and the 'problem' of megalithic tombs in prehistoric Europe. In R.W. Chapman, I.A. Kinnes and K. Randsborg (eds), *The Archaeology of Death*. Cambridge, University Press: 71–81.

CHRISTENSEN, J.M. and DANCE, S.P. (1980) *Seashells – Bivalves of the British and Northern European Seas*. Harmondsworth, Penguin Nature Guides.

COHEN, M.N. and ARMELAGOS, G.L. (eds) (1984) *Paleopathology at the Origins of Agriculture*. Orlando, Academic Press.

FARINHA DOS SANTOS, M., SOARES, J. and TAVARES DA SILVA, C. (1972) Campaniforme da Barrada do Grilo (Torrão-Vale do Sado). *O Arqueólogo Português*, (3ª Serie), 6: 163–192.

FARINHA DOS SANTOS, M., SOARES, J. and TAVARES DA SILVA, C. (1974) O concheiro epipaleolitico do Cabeço do Pez (Vale do Sado-Torrão). Primeira Noticia. *Actas do III Congresso Nacional de Arqueologia, Porto 1973*, vol. 1. Porto, Imprensa Portuguesa: 173–189.

GILBERT, R.I. and MIELKE, J.H. (eds) (1985) *The Analysis of Prehistoric Diets*. Orlando, Academic Press.

JOCHIM, M.A. (1976) *Hunter-Gatherer Subsistence and Settlement. A Predictive Model*. New York, Academic Press.

LARSSON, L. (1984) The Skateholm Project. A late Mesolithic settlement and cemetery complex at a southern Swedish bay. *Meddelanden från Lunds universitets historiska museum*, 1983–84: 5–38.

LUBELL, D. and JACKES, M. (1985) Mesolithic–Neolithic continuity: evidence from chronology and human biology. *Actas da I Reunião do Quaternario Iberico, Lisboa, 1985*, vol. 2. Lisbon, Comissão Organizadora da I Reunião do Quaternario Ibérico: 113–134.

MATEUS, J.E. (1985) The coastal lagoon region near Carvalhal during the Holocene; some geomorphological aspects derived from a palaeoecological study at Lagoa Travessa. *Actas da I Reunião do Quaternario Iberico, Lisboa, 1985*, vol. 2. Lisbon, Comissão Organizadora da I Reunião do Quaternario Ibérico: 237–249.

MEIKLEJOHN, C., SHENTAG, C., VENEMA, A. and KEY, P. (1984) Socioeconomic change and patterns of pathology and variation in the Mesolithic and Neolithic of western Europe: some suggestions. In M.N. Cohen and G. Armelagos (eds), *Paleopathology at the Origins of Agriculture*. Orlando, Academic Press: 75–100.

MENDES CORRÊA, A.E. (1933) Les nouvelles fouilles à Muge. *XV Congrès International d'Anthropologie et d'Archéologie Préhistoriques, Paris 1931*. Paris, Livrairie E. Nourry: 357–372.

MENDES CORRÊA, A.E. (1934) Novos elementos para a cronologia dos concheiros de Muge. *Anais da Faculdade de Ciencias do Porto*, 18: 154–159.

MORAIS ARNAUD, J.E. (1982) Le Néolithique ancien du Portugal et le processus de néolithisation. In *Le Néolithique Ancien Méditerranéen*. Sète, Fédération Archéologique de l'Hérault: 29–48.

MORAIS ARNAUD, J.E. (1985) Mesolithic in Portugal: a report on recent research. *Mesolithic Miscellany*, 6(2): 11–15.

MORAIS ARNAUD, J.E. (1987a) Os concheiros mesoliticos dos vales do Tejo e Sado: semelhancas e dissemelhancas. *Arqueologia* (Porto), 15: 53–64.

MORAIS ARNAUD, J.E. (1987b) Post-glacial adaptations in southern Portugal: a summary of the evidence. *Paper presented to the World Archaeological Congress, Southampton 1987*.

NEWELL, R.R., CONSTANDSE-WESTERMANN, T.S. and MEIKLEJOHN, C. (1979) The skeletal remains of Mesolithic man in western Europe: an evaluative catalogue. *Journal of Human Evolution*, 8: 1–28.

OLIVEIRA, F. DE P. (1880) Note sur les ossements humains qui se trouvent dans le Musée de la Section Géologique de Lisbonne. *IX Congrès International d'Anthropologie et d'Archéologie Préhistoriques*. Lisbon, Typographie de l'Academie Royale des Sciences: 291–303.

OLIVEIRA, F. DE P. (1892) Nouvelles fouilles faites dans les kjoekkenmoeddings de la vallée du Tage (mémoire posthume). *Comunicações da Comissão dos Trabalhos Geologicos* (Lisbon), 2: 57–81.

PALUDAN-MÜLLER, C. (1978) High Atlantic food gathering on northwestern Zealand, ecological conditions and spatial representation. In K. Kristiansen and C. Paludan-Müller (eds), *New Directions in Scandinavian Archaeology*. Copenhagen, National Museum of Denmark: 120–157.

PENEDA, M.C. and COELHO, A.T. (1978) *Valor e Potencialidades do Estuário do Rio Sado*. Lisbon, Serviço de Estudos do Ambiente (unpublished report).

PÉQUART, M., PÉQUART, ST-J., BOULE, M. and VALLOIS, H. (1937) *Téviec. Station-Nécropole Mésolithique du Morbihan*. (Archives de l'Institut de Paléontologie Humaine, mémoire 18). Paris, Masson.

PÉQUART, M. and PÉQUART, ST-J. (1954) *Hoëdic. Deuxième Station-Nécropole du Mésolithique Côtier Armoricain*. Anvers, de Sikkel.

PEREIRA DA COSTA, F.A. (1865) *Da existencia do Homem em epochas remotas no valle do Tejo. Primeiro opusculo: noticia sobre esqueletos humanos descobertos no Cabeço da Arruda*. Lisbon, Comissão Geologica de Portugal.

PRICE, T.D. (1978) Mesolithic settlement systems in the Netherlands. In P.A. Mellars (ed.), *The Early Postglacial Settlement of Northern Europe*. London, Duckworth: 81–113.

PRICE, T.D. (1981a) Regional approaches to human adaptation in the Mesolithic of the North European Plain. In B. Gramsch (ed.), *Mesolithikum in Europa. 2. Internationales Symposium Potsdam, 3 bis 8 April 1978 Bericht* (Veröffentlichungen des Museums für Ur- und Frügeschichte Potsdam, 14/15). Berlin, Deutscher Verlag der Wissenschaften: 217–234.

PRICE, T.D. (1981b) Complexity in 'non-complex' societies. In S.E. van der Leeuw (ed.), *Archaeological Approaches to the Study of Complexity*. Amsterdam, Instituut voor Prae- en Protohistorie: 53–97.

PRICE, T.D. and BROWN, J.A. (eds) (1985) *Prehistoric Hunter-Gatherers. The Emergence of Cultural Complexity*. Orlando, Academic Press.

REBELO, M.A.S. E S. and GUERREIRO DA SILVA, J.A. (1983) *Ciclo biologico de Scobicularia plana no estuário do Tejo*. Cascais, Laboratório Maritimo da Guia (unpublished report).

RENFREW, C. (1976) Megaliths, territories and populations. In S.J. De Laet (ed.), *Acculturation and Continuity in Atlantic Europe*. Ghent, Dissertationes Archaeologicae Gandenses 16: 198–220.

RIBEIRO, C. (1880) Les kjoekkenmoeddings de la vallée du Tage. *Comptes Rendues de la IXᵉ Session du Congrès International d'Anthropologie et d'Archéologie Préhistoriques*. Lisbon, Typographie de l'Academie Royale des Sciences: 279–290.

ROCHE, J. (1954) Résultats des dernières campagnes de fouilles exécutées à Moita do Sebastião (Muge). *Revista da Faculdade de Ciencias de Lisboa*, 2ᵉ série, C4: 179–186.

ROCHE, J. (1960) *Le Gisement mésolithique de Moita do Sebastião, Muge, Portugal. I: Archéologie*. Lisbon, Instituto de Alta Cultura.

ROCHE, J. (1965) Observations sur la stratigraphie et la chrono- logie des amas coquilliers mésolithiques de Muge (Portugal). *Bulletin de la Société Préhistorique Française*, 62: 130–139.

ROCHE, J. (1972) Les amas coquilliers (*concheiros*) mésolithiques de Muge (Portugal). *Fundamenta*, A/7: 72–107.

ROWLEY-CONWY, P. (1983) *The Faunal Remains from Cabeço do Pez*. Unpublished report.

SAXE, A. (1970) *Social Dimensions of Mortuary Practices*. Ann Arbor, University Microfilms.

SERPA PINTO, R. DE (1932) Notas sobre a indústria microlítica do Cabeço da Amoreira (Muge). *Associacion Española para el Progreso de las Ciencias* (Madrid): 46–54.

VIEIRA NATIVIDADE, J. (1950) *Subericultura*. Lisbon, Direccão Geral dos Serviços Florestais e Aquicolas.

WHEELER, A. (1978) *Key to the Fishes of Northern Europe*. London, Frederick Warne.

Archaeology and Human Biology of the Mesolithic–Neolithic Transition in Southern Portugal: a Preliminary Report

David Lubell, Mary Jackes and Christopher Meiklejohn

Abstract

We report here on research begun in June 1984, designed to test whether demographic change was a cause or consequence of the Mesolithic–Neolithic transition. We present data for human skeletons from the site of Moita do Sebastião which show that while dental pathologies were more common amongst older members of the population than is normally the case for Mesolithic Europeans, the population was nonetheless quite healthy. We also present archaeological and palaeoenvironmental data to show that: (i) during the mid-Holocene on the Atlantic coast south of Setúbal, forest cover was heavier than today, and habitats appropriate for *Cervus elaphus* and *Sus scrofa* were present; (ii) most molluscs in coastal sites could have been easily collected from the intertidal zone (e.g. *Mytilus*, *Patella*, *Cardium*), but large marine gastropods (e.g. *Thais haemastoma*) and fish (e.g. *Sparus auratus*) were probably obtained offshore, perhaps with nets; (iii) the Mesolithic economy, as elsewhere in Europe, may have included use of the domestic dog.

INTRODUCTION

What effect does a major change in the economy of a society have upon the health and demography of the people who compose it? What happened when 'Mesolithic' hunter-gatherers changed to being 'Neolithic' farmers and herders? And, why did they change at all?

We began to investigate these questions in Portugal during 1984, with two basic goals. One is to study the palaeopathology and palaeodemography of the larger collections of Mesolithic, Neolithic and post-Neolithic human skeletons that have already been excavated from Portugese sites (especially those near Muge), and thus test hypotheses proposed by others (e.g. Binford 1968; Hassan 1975; Cohen 1977; and see Cohen and Armelagos 1984) as to the effects upon human populations of the shift from foraging to agriculture. A second goal is to excavate and analyze Mesolithic and Neolithic sites from a range of environments (coastal, estuarine, inland, etc.) using an interdisciplinary methodology which while common elsewhere (e.g. in Spain – cf. Guilaine *et al*. 1982; Clark 1983; in the Maghreb – cf. Lubell, Sheppard and Jackes 1984, with references), has yet to be applied extensively in Portugal (see Morais-Arnaud 1982, and contribution to this volume). Eventually, we may request permission to re-excavate some of the sites from which skeletal samples we are studying derive.

In 1984, we inventoried the skeletal collections from Moita do Sebastião and Cabeço da Arruda housed at the Geological Survey in Lisbon, as well as making a preliminary inventory of Muge skeletal collections housed at the Mendes Correa Institute of Anthropology, University of Porto. A partial osteological study of the Lisbon collections from Moita do Sebastião was completed. In addition, we excavated a shell midden known as Medo Tojeiro (Zbyszweski and Penalva 1979) and tested another site called Samouqueira, said to be Mesolithic (Tavares da Silva and Soares 1981, 1982).

ARCHAEOLOGY

Medo Tojeiro

Medo Tojeiro (*Fig. 1*) is located on the Atlantic coast of Portugal, about 2 km south of the modern village of Almograve, which is 10 km south of Vila Nova do Milfontes. The site consists of two areas that are not necessarily closely related in time. One of these is a small remnant (*c.* 12 × 6 m) of a shell midden, overlooking the Atlantic from an elevation of 30 m a.s.l. It is disconformably underlain and overlain by dune sand. The other area is a blow-out within the dunes behind the midden, where there were several piles of apparently fire-cracked rock and about 300 large stone artifacts exposed on a deflated surface. The site was discovered by Carlos Penalva who collected the artifacts consisting primarily of several varieties of large chopper-like tools made of local coarse-grained quartzite or greywacke. They have been assigned to the Languedocian (or Mirensian) industry (Zbyszweski and Penalva 1979). This industry is probably equivalent to the Portuguese Asturian (defined by Maury 1977) and perhaps to the Asturian of Cantabria as well (but see discussion in Clark 1983). The assemblage is being re-studied by Sheppard.

Area 1, the midden

We excavated an area of *c.* 11 m² in the midden, using a combination of artificial (5 cm) and natural levels within one-metre squares. The maximum

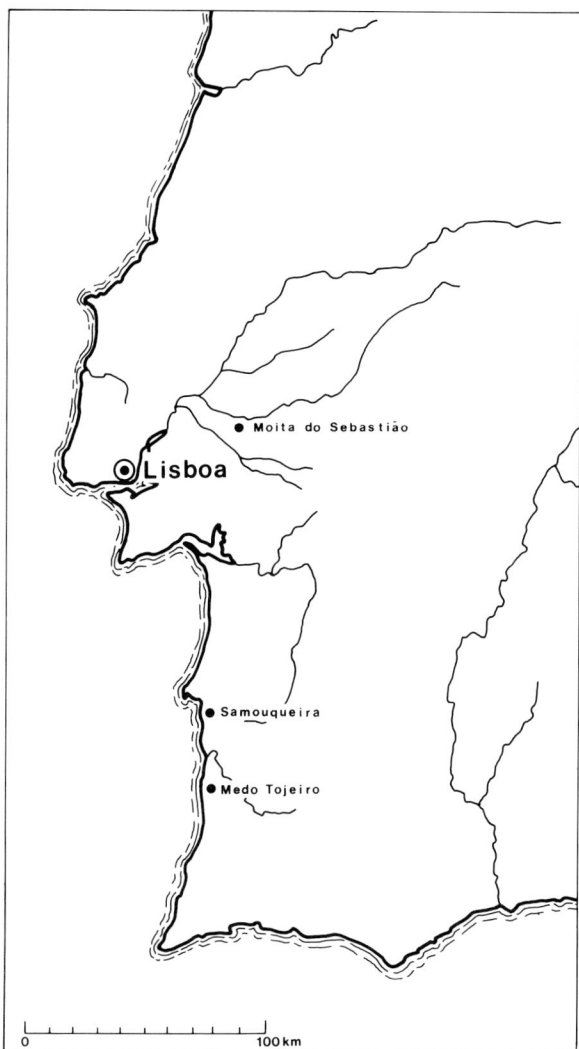

Figure 1   Location of key sites referred to in the text.

The only structural features noted during the excavation were several concentrations of fire-cracked rock that we interpret as hearths.

Artifacts were rare, consisting of a few pot sherds, several geometric microliths, one polished celt, one chopper, some chert bladelet fragments and a few greywacke flakes. These, according to Tavares da Silva, are all consistent with an assignment to the Older Neolithic and in accord with the date of 6570 ± 120 BP (BM–2275: calibrated range = 7189 [7108] 6929 BP, cf. Stuiver *et al.* 1986) obtained on a sample of marine shell collected in 1983 during our preliminary inspection of the site.

That sample probably came from couche 4, near the bottom of the midden. However, it was taken from the exposed western face in an area affected by chemical and physical weathering which obscured stratigraphic relationships and may have led to sample contamination. A second sample, of charcoal, was excavated from couche 4 within the midden in 1984. While so small as to require extended counting time, it has yielded an apparently reliable date (corrected for $\delta^{13}C$) of 5450 ± 160 BP (Beta–11723: calibrated range = 6406 [6282, 6222, 6208] 5989 BP, cf. Pearson *et al.* 1986). There is thus a difference of *c.* 900 radiocarbon years between the two samples. We are inclined to place more reliance on the charcoal date but admit that for now the best we can say is that the midden probably dates to between *c.* 7200 and *c.* 6200 BP.

No bone was recovered from our excavations. Fire-cracked rock was very common, forming up to 97% of the >2 mm fraction of the deposit by weight (means are given in *Table 1*). Couche 2 and couche 4 were especially rich in shell, as can be seen from the high values for shell in the <2 mm fraction and the low values for rock in the >2 mm fraction in *Table 1*.

While at least 20 species of marine invertebrates were found, probably only four (*Mytilus*, *Patella*, *Monodonta* and *Thais*) were major sources of food. Other species (*Cardium*, *Glycimeris*, *Ostrea*) were present but not common, and both barnacles and sea urchins appear to have been collected. *Thais*, a marine gastropod, is more frequent in upper levels than lower ones in some, but not all, excavated squares, while the limpet (*Patella*) tends to be more frequent in lower levels (*Table 2*). In addition, there

thickness of midden deposit was about 75 cm. In some places six levels (couches) could be discerned, but in general only four were observed. Distinctions between levels are based primarily on colour, shell content (both quantity and species observed), and texture. The top of the archaeological levels (couche 1) is a lag deposit composed almost entirely of fire-cracked rock. It grades into a deposit containing more shell which was sometimes called couche 1b. The main shell levels are couches 2 and 4 (*Table 1*).

Table 1:   Medo Tojeiro, 1984. Mean percentages, by weight, for shell and rock in the <2 mm and >2 mm fraction of 1 litre bulk samples

	<2 mm		>2 mm		
Couche	n	% shell	n	% rock	% shell
C.1	12	19.11	8	57.78	42.22
C.2	11	23.30	5	10.95	89.05
C.3	11	10.55	5	21.69	78.31
C.4	10	20.61	4	22.38	77.61
C.5	8	8.14	5	19.56	80.44
C.6	2	4.22	1	44.92	55.08

Table 2:   Medo Tojeiro, 1984. Mean percentage frequencies for major edible molluscs, calculated by weight of shell in the >2 mm fraction of 1 litre bulk samples

Couche	Patella	Monodonta	Thais	Mytilus
C.1	14.05	1.94	11.07	73.22
C.2	17.53	0.85	2.46	79.17
C.3	23.78	0.81	5.39	70.02
C.4	16.25	1.05	5.26	77.44
C.5	14.67	1.25	5.37	78.71
C.6	17.73	0.71	3.55	78.01

633

are quite distinctive frequency differences (shell *vs* stone, species represented) within the same level between adjacent squares (*Table 3*). This suggests

Table 3: Medo Tojeiro, 1984. Horizontal variability in composition of deposits in adjacent squares S3 and S4 as percentage frequencies by weight of 1 litre bulk samples

Couche	Shell				Mytilus		Patella	
	>2 mm		<2 mm					
	S3	S4	S3	S4	S3	S4	S3	S4
C.1	4.8	34.4	0.0	8.6	88.2	72.5	8.8	19.1
C.2	65.7	95.2	24.1	8.0	81.1	70.0	11.8	28.8
C.3	81.4	74.3	13.8	11.0	69.1	72.4	26.5	16.4
C.4	64.8	74.4	25.1	12.5	57.9	87.9	33.3	5.9
C.5	66.8	79.4	4.3	2.2	70.9	86.2	17.7	12.6

rapid accumulation of the deposits, resulting in a record of the collection and discard of individual 'catches' of shellfish, and/or other activities that are reflected in the different frequencies of stone and shell.

Area 2, the blow-out

This area was investigated under the supervision of Tavares da Silva and Soares. Several hearths, which appeared as deflated piles of angular rock fragments, were mapped and sectioned, and Soares discovered and excavated others not yet exposed by deflation. This hearth contained microlithic artifacts. Another, exposed on the surface, contained a greywacke flake amongst the fire-cracked rock (Tavares da Silva *et al.* 1985).

There is no indisputable connection between these hearths and the macrolithic industry found by Penalva on the surrounding deflated surface. Inspection of the surface of the blow-out revealed a mixture of cultural materials ranging in age from quite modern, to Mediaeval, to at least the Bronze Age (a mint condition Palmela point was found on the back slope of the blow-out near the hearths).

Thermoluminescence analyses conducted by Peter Sheppard and Lawrence Pavlish at the University of Toronto confirm that these features were hearths. Samples of greywacke and quartzite collected from modern beaches were compared with samples of the same rock types taken from the features. The results suggest that the rocks from the features were heated to 350–400 °C. The hearths could, of course, date from several widely separated periods.

The relationship between the two areas at Medo Tojeiro has yet to be determined. The radiocarbon dates from the blow-out may help, but stratigraphic continuity between the two areas will be almost impossible to establish. There were too few artifacts in the midden to undertake a comparative study with the materials collected by Penalva on the surface of the blow-out, and the artifacts found by Soares in the hearth are apparently neither sufficiently numerous nor diagnostic to warrant comparison with the scarce material from the midden. The geomorphological setting of Medo Tojeiro is complex and analyses are now underway (including palynology) to try and clarify the picture.

Samouqueira

Samouqueira is a very large site, covering an area of at least 120 × 140 metres. Our work there in 1984 was limited to four one-metre square test pits and an excavation of 7 × 2 m in one-metre squares using 5 cm artificial levels within thicker natural strata – all these in the part of the site thought to contain deposits dating to the Mesolithic. Because the site lies in what is now a ploughed field, there has been an undetermined amount of disturbance. The ground slopes up from the sea edge (a 10 m cliff) to an old beach about 200 m inland. There has been a good deal of overburden which reached >2 m at a distance of 40 m from the cliff edge. There were lithic artifacts scattered throughout the overburden, and there appear to be no remaining *in situ* deposits (Lubell and Jackes 1985).

In the main trench we recovered a rich assemblage of microlithic and macrolithic artifacts but no ceramics or ground stone artifacts. Marine shell (mostly *Mytilus* and *Patella* with some *Cardium*) was common (*Table 4*), and there were bones of *Cervus*

Table 4: Samouqueira, 1984. Percentages, by weight, of major species of edible molluscs

Couche	Patella	Mytilus	Cardium	Thais
surface	25.17	14.15	25.70	47.84
C.1b	31.90	20.00	+	54.76
C.2a	24.78	20.63	6.42	48.16
C.2b	35.86	16.67	9.83	39.60
C.3a	51.36	15.83	3.03	37.75
C.3b	48.64	11.73	+	44.32
C.3c	52.63	21.05	+	26.32
C.3d	78.36	+	+	18.86
C.3e	55.49	20.45	+	24.05

+ = present but not weighed

elaphus, Sus scrofa, Lepus capensis, Vulpes vulpes as well as birds, fish (*Sparus auratus*), and possibly dog (*?Canis lupus* f. *familiaris*).

Two partial human skeletons were excavated from the main trench, probably both males. Both showed evidence of pathological conditions: a healed fracture of the humerus with osteomyelitis, an infected foot, severe arthritis of one wrist. Both skeletons had been disturbed, probably by ploughing and then perhaps by subsequent downslope erosion. One may have been buried in full articulation; the other certainly was, probably as a flexed burial (after rigor mortis had relaxed) with the head to the west and the face to the north. In comparison with skeletal populations dated to the Portuguese Mesolithic (to be discussed later) these two Samouqueira individuals indicate rather elevated levels of pathology.

Two AMS radiocarbon dates are available for Samouqueira, and these suggest the deposits are so disturbed that further investigations are not warranted. Collagen from a bovid/cervid long bone fragment from the main excavation area is dated at 5060±130 BP (Beta 11722: calibrated range = 5949 [5887, 5816, 5767] 5652 BP, cf. Pearson et al. 1986). Human bone collagen from the same archaeological stratum is dated at 6370±70 BP (TO-130: calibrated range = 7324 [7274, 7200, 7199] 7188 BP, 20-year average of LSB, SKBF, KRBSMSB and LLDF – cf. Stuiver et al. 1986). The human remains are therefore certainly Mesolithic in age, but not all the associated archaeological material may be Mesolithic (Meiklejohn et al. 1986).

Artifact assemblage

A partial, and possibly not truly representative sample of the artifact assemblage was studied in the field by Sheppard. Additional studies of the entire excavated assemblage are now being undertaken by Soares. Sheppard's results show that the assemblage is predominantly microlithic and made on flint (Table 5), which is not locally available today.

Analyses of these finer grained materials using instrumental neutron activation analysis suggest that a wide range of raw materials, apparently coming from some distance, were employed in the manufacture of the microlithic component. We will attempt to locate sources during future field seasons and thus try to get some idea of the exploitation territory represented.

It is possible that greywacke débitage is systematically under-represented due to the difficulty of recognizing knapped greywacke. Experimental studies by Sheppard and Lello during the 1984 field season demonstrated that much of the débitage produced lacks any features diagnostic of human knapping.

Sheppard identified two separate technological patterns: one based on greywacke cobbles from the beach below the site, the other on a variety of fine-grained or crystalline rocks with good conchoidal fracture that we are, for now, lumping under the generic term flint.

The greywacke technology produced large primary flakes with minimal secondary retouch. Sheppard recognized only four cores. The greywacke artifacts were all made on fine-grained rock, and it therefore appears that only the finer grained were chosen from amongst the generally coarse-grained cobbles on the beach.

Flint seems to have been used almost exclusively for the manufacture of narrow bladelets with a mean width of 7.9±2.3 mm. These were struck from single platform cores (68%) on which there is only oc-

Table 5: Samouqueira, 1984. Frequencies of major artifact classes and raw materials

Artifact class	Flint		Greywacke		Quartzite		Crystal		Total	
	n	%	n	%	n	%	n	%	n	%
Trapeze concave	3	100.0	–	–	–	–	–	–	3	0.2
Trapeze straight	6	100.0	–	–	–	–	–	–	6	0.4
Trapeze conc./str.	1	50.0	–	–	1	50.0	–	–	2	0.1
Triangle straight	4	80.0	–	–	1	20.0	–	–	5	0.4
Segment	5	100.0	–	–	–	–	–	–	5	0.4
Microburin	8	66.7	–	–	4	33.3	–	–	12	0.9
Backed bladelet	7	100.0	–	–	–	–	–	–	7	0.5
Burin dihedral	1	100.0	–	–	–	–	–	–	1	0.1
Borer/bec	3	100.0	–	–	–	–	–	–	3	0.2
Truncation straight	1	100.0	–	–	–	–	–	–	1	0.1
Truncation oblique	1	100.0	–	–	–	–	–	–	1	0.1
Denticulate	–	–	–	–	1	100.0	–	–	1	0.1
Notch	7	46.7	7	46.7	1	6.7	–	–	15	1.1
Retouched piece	1	16.7	5	83.3	–	–	–	–	6	0.4
Utilized	–	–	1	50.0	1	50.0	–	–	2	0.1
Chopper	–	–	2	100.0	–	–	–	–	2	0.1
Core	21	67.7	4	12.9	5	16.1	1	3.2	31	2.3
Crested blade	1	100.0	–	–	–	–	–	–	1	0.1
Chunk	99	50.0	58	29.3	34	17.2	7	3.5	198	14.8
Flake	125	25.6	298	61.1	63	12.9	2	0.4	488	36.4
Bladelet	273	58.1	46	9.8	134	28.5	17	3.6	470	35.1
Blade	33	41.2	34	42.5	13	16.2	–	–	80	6.0
Total	600	44.8	455	34.0	258	19.3	27	2.0	1340	100.0

casional evidence for platform preparation (20%). Sheppard infers use of either direct percussion or simple indirect percussion. The bladelets were apparently intended primarily as blanks for the manufacture of both geometric and non-geometric microliths.

Discussion of archaeological data

These briefly summarized data raise several points of interest related to palaeoeconomies and settlement patterns.

Large marine gastropods occur at both sites but are more common at Samouqueira. Their presence requires some explanation since today they are apparently collected in nets offshore by fishermen using small boats. The implication that similar methods may have been used by the early and middle Holocene fishermen of this region is obvious.

Sheppard's analysis of artifacts suggests fairly wide-ranging catchment territories which is consistent with one of our working hypotheses – that the coastal sites represent seasonal occupations. Work is now underway on the isotopic composition of shell and bone which we hope will provide data to combine with palynological and palaeobotanical studies for an indication of the season of occupation.

We do not, as yet, have a very clear idea of the palaeoenvironmental conditions which obtained. Results of a preliminary analysis (C.T. Shay, *in litt.*, 15 March 1985) of charcoal recovered in some of the flotation samples from both Medo Tojeiro and Samouqueira are given in *Table 6*. Of 168 pieces so far identified, over 80% are conifer, 71% of them pine. About half are tentatively assigned to stone

pine (*Pinus* cf. *pinea*), groves of which are still common in this part of Portugal. The presence of this pine-nut-producing tree is nonetheless potentially important for our interpretation of subsistence and, perhaps, seasonality (since pine nuts would be a seasonal resource). The presence of both Juniper and Pistachio is also of interest.

Finally, marked human skeletal pathologies and the presence of possible domestic dog at Samouqueira may raise the crucial issue of how one defines Mesolithic as opposed to Neolithic. There is as yet no evidence that the inhabitants of either site were engaged in economies dependent upon domesticated plants and animals. For now, unfortunately, this issue must be left without discussion. We hope that future research will provide clarification.

PHYSICAL ANTHROPOLOGY

The major effort of this portion of the project, so far, has been the thorough study of the Moita do Sebastião collection housed at the Geological Survey in Lisbon. This entailed detailed examination and measurement of crania, dentition and post-cranial materials (including X-rays), as well as the removal of 9 mm diameter cores from all left femora. These cores are now being analyzed for osteon counts and several rib samples for stable isotopic ratios. Much of this research is still in progress.

Analyses of metrical data on femora and humeri demonstrate that the Moita population was smaller and less robust than modern Portuguese (the Coimbra sample: cf. Themido 1926; Tamagnini and Vieira de Campos 1949), but it is not yet clear whether Mesolithic Portuguese differed in size or robusticity from their contemporaries in other European sites. Bianchi *et al.* (1980) have compared early and middle Holocene Portuguese, Maghreb and Italian postcranials. It is evident that the Italian materials were more gracile than either the Portuguese or North Africans.

Studies now in progress, using vault measurements from Moita do Sebastião and other western Europe Mesolithic samples (as defined by Newell *et al.* 1979), suggest a north–south clinal distribution and the possibility that Moita male skulls are narrower and female skulls are shorter than those from other Mesolithic sites, especially those in Brittany and Scandinavia for which there are larger samples. Moita dentitions, on the other hand, may be larger than those of their northern contemporaries, but the significances have not been evaluated. Lefèvre (1973; see also Fléchier *et al.* 1976) has shown that while Muge teeth are larger than northern European Neolithic teeth, there are no clear differences between the Portuguese and Bretons of the Mesolithic. Only the premolars show fairly consistent differences but, in the absence of

Table 6: Charcoal from Samouqueira and Medo Tojeiro[a]

Taxa	Samouqueira (6 samples)		Medo Tojeiro (5 samples)	
	n	%	n	%
Conifers				
undifferentiated	13[b]	26.5	8	6.7
Pinus sp.	19[c]	38.8	9[d]	7.6
Pinus cf. *pinea*	10	20.4	81	68.1
Juniperus sp.			2	1.7
Hardwood				
undifferentiated	3	6.1	12	10.1
Pistacia sp.			3[e]	2.5
Unidentifiable	4	8.2	4	3.4
	49		119	

[a] Identifications by Janus Zwiazek; n = number of pieces; unidentifiable = pieces too small or too poorly preserved to identify

[b] Includes 3 uncharred conifer fragments and 2 uncharred cf. conifer fragments

[c] Includes 2 cf. *Pinus* sp.

[d] Includes 1 cf. *Pinus* sp.

[e] Includes 2 cf. *Pistacia*

published sample sizes, the significance of the differences cannot be evaluated.

The Portuguese skeletal size seems, on the slight evidence available, to have been unchanged into the Portuguese Neolithic and/or Chalcolithic. This is said on the basis of the robusticity of the female femur (Riquet 1972), and of pooled data on the humeral distal breadth (Spindler 1972).

Sexual dimorphism – expressed as (Male stature ÷ Female stature) × 100 – during the Mesolithic of Portugal was about 11.2%, little different from that of the modern Coimbra sample (11%) or the Visigothic dimorphism of 10.9% (Serra *et al.* 1952). There is no evidence on which to base a discussion of Neolithic sexual dimorphism.

Of 648 permanent teeth examined, 85 (13%) were carious, a level higher than any other reported for a Mesolithic European sample and higher than many Neolithic samples. The incidence of caries is clearly age-dependent. There are no deciduous teeth with caries, and the most carious teeth are, in general, from dentitions which show greater degrees of attrition. It is interesting that previous analyses of Moita dentition did not report such high caries rates (Ferembach 1972; Lefèvre 1973; Meiklejohn *et al.* 1984).

Linear enamel hypoplasia, which may be a marker of periodic nutritional or disease stress during childhood, is uncommon in deciduous teeth (3 of 46), but it is present in almost half the permanent teeth (148 of 515). It occurs with equivalent frequencies amongst males and females, but is more common in maxillary than mandibular teeth ($\chi^2:P = 0.0002$). As yet, we have no explanation for this anomaly.

Palaeodemographic investigations are being pursued from a number of directions using all available methods, so as to have a basis to compare their relative accuracy. Thus, we are counting osteons, using dental attrition (in the absence of a sufficient sample of pubic symphyses) and femoral X-rays to estimate adult ages of death. Dental attrition has been studied – using a modification of the Smith (1984) method for mandibular molars – by a seriation of mandibles. This indicates a very wide spread of adult ages but exact ages cannot yet be estimated and, in the demographic analysis, age class membership was assigned by grouping individuals at similar attrition levels.

The validity of our attrition stages (*Table 7*) is supported by the correlation (0.8) found between the stages and the height of the cemento-enamel

Table 7: Moita do Sebastião. Preliminary age breakdown of adults on the basis of mandibular attrition

M_1	M_2	M_3	Attrition stage	n	Guessed 'age'	Lost and carious molars / Observable molar sockets n	%
			1	2	15–20	1/4	25
			2	7	20–25	4/25	16
			3	7	25–30	5/28	18
			4	9	30–35	12/43	28
			5	9	35–40	±7/32	22
			6	3	40–45	4/14	29
			7	2	45–50	±4/8	50
			8	3	50–55	5/10	50
			9	3	55–60	±8/17	47
			10	2	60–65	±8/12	67
			11	3	65–70	±12/14	86

Table 8: Moita do Sebastião. Life table for collections at Lisbon and Porto, with male:female ratio adjusted to 1:1 by addition of 22.35 individuals, and with minimum infant adjustment assuming low mortality level

x	Dx	dx	lx	qx	Lx	Tx	ex	Cx	Mx
0	23.60	214.7	1000.0	0.215	4463.2	29712.5	29.7	150.2	0.0481
5	9.00	81.9	785.3	0.104	3721.8	25249.3	32.2	125.3	0.0220
10	1.00	9.1	703.4	0.013	3494.4	21527.5	30.6	117.6	0.0026
15	4.24	38.6	694.3	0.056	3375.2	18033.1	26.0	113.6	0.0114
20	8.48	77.1	655.7	0.118	3085.9	14657.9	22.4	103.9	0.0250
25-65	63.60	578.6	578.6	1.000	11572.1	11572.1	20.0	389.5	0.0500
	109.92								

Population size given 500 years = 56.5 (see Acsádi and Nemeskéri 1970: 65)
Crude death rate = 33.7
Juvenile:adult ratio = 0.139
Mean childhood mortality = 0.058 (mean of q5, q10, q15)

junction (CEJ) above the healthy, unbroken alveolar margin. Originally, we took six measurements per tooth for all teeth, but this soon became too time-consuming and the usefulness of so many measurements was dubious. Tests on the molars showed that midpoint measurements on M_1 gave the highest correlation with wear (0.86); so this tooth was chosen for the midpoint measurements. The second premolar (P_4) was measured as a control. While the results are still inconclusive, preliminary examination of the data seems to show that molar wear and M_1 CEJ height may, in combination, allow quite reasonable distributions of adults over postulated age categories.

Study of the Singh Index (Singh *et al.* 1972) with regard to age-related modifications of the trabecular patterns in all left femora, has suggested that the adult age spread is greater than indicated by the mandibular molar attrition seriation. The method, however, does not provide exact adult age estimates.

There are several major, and perhaps irresolvable, problems with the Moita sample, viz. underrepresentation of infants, juveniles and females. To date, we have been able only to estimate mortality, primarily on the basis of juvenile dentitions, a method which is complicated by the apparent loss of much of the juvenile material that had been housed in Porto. Our method of demographic analysis is based on life tables calculated for juveniles using age intervals of five years from birth to age 25, and pooling all individuals over age 25. This allows analysis in the absence of detailed age assessment. Our results must be considered very tentative. They show that life expectancy at birth was about 30 years and that almost one-third of the population died by age 20. If we assume Moita was used for a span of 500 years, we can use the palaeodemographic data to estimate the size of the group inhabiting the site as 57, with two deaths per year (*Table 8*). This is within the upper range of studied modern foraging populations (e.g. the !Kung San) living in less favoured environments than those which presumably existed in Portugal during the early and middle Holocene.

The Moita level of mortality, which we derive by studying ratios of juvenile (5–14 years) to adult (25+ years) deaths, is low by comparison with 30 other prehistoric samples from both the New and Old Worlds (Jackes and Lubell, n.d.). Thus, the high rate of enamel hypoplasia and the relatively high frequency of dental caries may be due to the fact that people of this population survived childhood stresses and lived longer than other Mesolithic populations. On the other hand, the abscessing and periodontal disease rates are not comparatively high, perhaps indicating good general health and nutrition.

Support for this comes from Nordin's femoral index (cf. Pfeiffer and King 1983) by which one estimates cortex thickness from radiographs of the mid-shaft of the femur. This is not necessarily a measure of great accuracy, but we used two analysts working over a period of several months so that we could average across three tests for a final result. The cortical thickness at the mid-shaft of the femur, the shape of the shaft and the form of the proximal trabecular structure as seen on radiographs (Singh's Index) are all related to a complex interplay of factors of which nutrition and individual age are probably the most important. We have not been able to demonstrate any correlations amongst the three sets of data, but we can say that the Moita distribution of the Nordin Index is very interesting and unusual in comparison with other published distributions (Pfeiffer and King 1983).

The Moita bone has great cortical thickness. The mean values for adult males and females at Moita are both high: males = 60.46 (*n* = 16, *s* = 4.2, *CV* = 7.0); females = 60.73 (*n* = 11, of which one is probably osteoporotic, *s* = 7.0, *CV* = 11.6); males and females pooled = 60.5 (*n* = 32, *s* = 5.3, *CV* = 8.7). This suggests that good nutrition did indeed underlie the postulated low mortality. Even the juvenile dead have high scores in general, though the dead of ages 5–7 seem all to have had reduced cortex.

Low mortality did not, apparently, equate with a life totally devoid of stress but the evidence is as yet ambiguous. The presence of linear enamel hypoplasia, suggesting some dietary stress, is in contrast to the apparent richness of the resources available. Moita do Sebastião was located on a tributary of the Muge estuary, and the published faunal materials (as well as unpublished collections from neighbouring sites) suggest a diet based upon a mixture of aquatic and terrestrial animals. We presume that plants were also an important element. Initial results of stable isotopic analyses of five human bone samples from Moita do Sebastião by Dr. H.P. Schwarcz (*in litt.*, 22 March 1985) show values for $\delta^{13}C$ (per mil with respect to PDB: –15.3 to –16.1, $\bar{x} = -16.4$, $s = 0.67$) and $\delta^{15}N$ (per mil with respect to atmosphere: 10.4 to 12.2, $\bar{x} = 11.8$, $s = 1.12$) which suggest that the human diet was equally divided between marine and terrestrial foods, since these values fall midway between terrestrial herbivores and marine carnivores.

It is, therefore, of some interest that social stress is also reflected in this sample. Amongst a relatively small collection of adults, there are two females with parry fractures and one male who had been shot in the foot. From this indication, slight though it is, pressures of increasing population or population density could be suggested – as was done, for example, with reference to the terminal Pleistocene Jebel Sahaba cemetery in the Nile valley (Wendorf 1968). The sample of the population buried at Moita may, however, be incomplete, so that at the moment it would be foolhardy to make guesses about the social structure. On the basis of the innominates, the group consisted of 41 individuals over 15 years of age; of these 29 were males and only 12 females. The study of the Mesolithic human biology requires information derived from our archaeological studies on the possibility of seasonal movement of groups and short-term occupations of particular sites. We need information on the representativeness of the buried sample.

We suspect that the Portuguese data may show little or no demographic change as a result of the shift to a Neolithic economy (whenever that occurred – the chronology is still uncertain). Mortality amongst the Mesolithic population at Moita do Sebastião was extremely low, due in large part to the very productive subsistence regime. Rather than a dramatic shift to the Neolithic, all indications are of continuity and a gradual transition. This has already been mentioned with reference to Samouqueira. Similarly, if we accept the Medo Tojeiro midden as Neolithic, we support the hypothesis that the Neolithic came in as a slow introduction of new elements into a basically strong and continuous Mesolithic economy. We reached similar conclusions, though not with reference to demographic data, for the Maghreb Epi-Palaeolithic, which has certain parallels to the Portuguese Mesolithic (Lubell 1984; Lubell, Sheppard and Jackes 1984). However, these interpretations of the Portuguese materials must not be seen as final. Far more, and more reliable, data need to be collected and analyzed.

Acknowledgements: Our research is funded by a grant from the Social Sciences and Humanities Research Council of Canada (Operating Grant 410–84–0030) to the authors who are principal co-investigators for archaeology and palaeoenvironments (DL) and human osteology (MJ, CJM). We thank the Director, Geological Survey of Portugal, Lisbon, for permission to study human skeletal collections in his care. The archaeological research done in 1984 and described here was undertaken in collaboration with C. Tavares da Silva and J. Soares (Museu de Arqueologia e Etnologia, Setúbal) and C. Penalva (Serviço Regional Arqueologia da Zona Zul, Evora) who have published a preliminary report (Tavares da Silva *et al.* 1985) on certain aspects of this research which utilizes earlier results of some of the work reported here. Additional archaeological fieldwork took place in 1986 at other sites, and osteological research in 1985–1986 continued on Mesolithic and Neolithic skeletal collections. Project personnel to date have included: Dr Peter Sheppard (Toronto, lithic technology and analysis), Dr Achilles Gautier (Gent, archaeozoology), Mr R. De Ceunynck (Gent, palynology), Dr C. Devereux (London, geomorphology), Dr C.T. Shay, Mr M. Kelly and Mr J. Zwiazek (Winnipeg, palaeobotany), Dr G. Weih (Victoria, osteology), and Dr H.P. Schwarcz (Hamilton, stable isotope studies). Student assistants have been Mr R. Lello and Mr J. Woollett (Edmonton, archaeology), Ms C. Hooey (Edmonton, geoarchaeology), Ms A. Lentacker (Gent, archaeozoology), Mrs E. Palmer (Edmonton, osteology) and Ms C. Schentag (Winnipeg, ostcology).

References

ACSÁDI, G. and NEMESKÉRI, J. (1970) *History of the Human Life Span and Mortality*. Budapest, Akadémiai Kiadó.

BIANCHI, F., BORGOGNINI TARLI, S.M., MARCHI, M. and PAOLI, G. (1980) An attempt of application of multivariate statistics to the problems of the Italian Mesolithic samples. *Homo*, 31: 153–166.

BINFORD, L.R. (1968) Post-Pleistocene adaptations. In L.R. Binford and S.R. Binford (eds), *New Perspectives in Archaeology*. Chicago, Aldine: 313–341.

CLARK, G.A. (1983) *The Asturian of Cantabria: Early Holocene Hunter-Gatherers in Northern Spain* (Anthropological Papers of the University of Arizona, 41). Tucson, University of Arizona Press.

COHEN, M.N. (1977) *The Food Crisis in Prehistory*. New Haven, Yale University Press.

COHEN, M. N. and ARMELAGOS, G.J. (eds) (1984) *Paleopathology at the Origins of Agriculture*. New York, Academic Press.

FLÉCHIER, J-P., LEFÈVRE, J. and VERDÈNE, J. (1976) Mensurations dentaires des hommes de Muge. *Bulletin et Mémoires de la Société d'Anthropologie de Paris*, 3, série XII: 147–164.

FEREMBACH, D. (1972) *Le Gisement Mésolithique de Moita do Sebastião, Muge, Portugal. II. Anthropologie*. Lisbon, Instituto de Alta Cultura.

GUILAINE, J., BARBAZA, M., GEDDES, D., VERNET, J-L., LLONGUERAS, M. and HOPF, M. (1982) Prehistoric human adaptations in Catalonia (Spain). *Journal of Field Archaeology*, 9: 407–416.

HASSAN, F.A. (1975) Determination of size, density, and growth rate of hunting-gathering populations. In S. Polgar (ed.), *Population, Ecology and Social Evolution*. The Hague, Mouton: 27–52.

JACKES, M.K. and LUBELL, D. (n.d.) *Where are the old folks?* Unpublished manuscript.

LEFÈVRE, J. (1973) Etude odontologique des hommes du Muge. *Bulletin et Mémoires de la Société d'Anthropologie de Paris*, 10, série XII: 301–333.

LUBELL, D. (1984) Palaeoenvironments and Epi-palaeolithic economies in the Maghreb (ca. 20,000 to 5000 B.P.). In J.D. Clark and S.A. Brandt (eds), *From Hunters to Farmers: the Causes and Consequences of Food Production in Africa*. Berkeley, University of California Press: 41–56.

LUBELL, D. and JACKES, M. (1985) Mesolithic–Neolithic continuity: evidence from chronology and human biology. In M. Ramos (ed.), *Actas, I Reunião do Quaternario Iberico*, Lisboa 1985. Lisbon, Instituto Nacional de Investigação Cientifica: 113–133.

LUBELL, D.P., SHEPPARD, P. and JACKES, M. (1984) Continuity in the Epipalaeolithic of Northern Africa with emphasis on the Maghreb. In F. Wendorf and A. Close (eds), *Advances in World Archaeology*, vol. 3. Orlando, Academic Press: 143–191.

MAURY, J. (1977) *Typologie et Préhistoire de l'Asturien du Portugal*. Oxford, British Archaeological Reports (International Series) S21.

MEIKLEJOHN, C., JACKES, M.K. and LUBELL, D. (1986) Radiocarbon dating of human skeletal material from two sites in Portugal. *Mesolithic Miscellany*. 7(2): 4–6.

MEIKLEJOHN, C., SCHENTAG, C., VENEMA, A. and KEY, P. (1984) Socio-economic change and patterns of pathology and variation in the Mesolithic and Neolithic of western Europe: some suggestions. In M.N. Cohen and G.J. Armelagos (eds), *Paleopathology at the Origins of Agriculture*: 75–100.

MORAIS-ARNAUD, J. (1982) Le Néolithique ancien et processus de néolithisation au Portugal. In J. Bousquet (ed.), *Le Néolithique Ancien Méditerranéen. Actes du Colloque International de Préhistoire, Montpellier, 1981*. Sète, Fédération Archéologique de l'Hérault: 29–48.

NEWELL, R.R., CONSTANDSE-WESTERMANN, T.S. and MEIKLEJOHN, C. (1979) The skeletal remains of Mesolithic man in western Europe: an evaluative catalogue. *Journal of Human Evolution*, 8(1): 1–233.

PEARSON, G.W., PILCHER, J.R., BAILLIE, M.G.L., CORBETT, D.M. and QUA, F. (1986) High-precision ^{14}C measurement of Irish oaks to show the natural ^{14}C variations from AD 1840–5210 BC. *Radiocarbon*, 28(2B): 911–934.

PFEIFFER, S. and KING, P. (1983) Cortical bone formation and diet among protohistoric Iroquoians. *American Journal of Physical Anthropology*, 60: 23–28.

RIQUET, R. (1972) Anthropologie de quelques néolithiques portugais. *Homo*, 23: 154–187.

SERRA, J.A., ALBUQUERQUE, R.M. and NETO, M.A.M. (1952) Caracteristicas da população da época visigótica de Silveirona (Estremoz). I – Estatura e Robustez dos ossos longos. *Contribuições para o Estuda da Antropologia Portuguesa* XXV, vol. 5, fasc. 4: 201–233.

SINGH, M., RIGGS, B.L., BEABOUT, J.W. and JOWSEY, J. (1972) Femoral trabecular-pattern index for evaluation of spinal osteoporosis. *Annals of Internal Medicine*, 77: 63–67.

SMITH, H. (1984) Patterns of molar wear in hunter-gatherers and agriculturalists. *American Journal of Physical Anthropology*, 63: 39–56.

SPINDLER, K. (1972) Ein krankes Ellenbogengelenk aus der Cova da Moura/Portugal. *Homo*, 23: 212–223.

STUIVER, M., PEARSON, G.W. and BRAZIUNAS, T.F. (1986) Radiocarbon age calibration of marine samples back to 9000 cal yr BP. *Radiocarbon*, 28(2B): 980–1021.

TAMAGNINI, E. and VIEIRA DE CAMPOS, D.S. (1949) O fémur português. *Contribuições para o Estuda da Antropologia Portuguesa* IV, vol. 2, fasc. 1: 1–69.

TAVARES DA SILVA, C. and SOARES, J. (1981) *Pré-Historia da Area de Sines*. Lisbon, Gabinet da Area de Sines.

TAVARES DA SILVA, C. and SOARES, J. (1982) Des structures d'habitat du Néolithique ancien au Portugal. In J. Bousquet (ed.), *Le Néolithique Ancien Méditerranéen. Actes du Colloque International de Préhistoire, Montpellier, 1981*. Sète, Fédération Archéologique de l'Hérault: 17–28.

TAVARES DA SILVA, C., SOARES, J. and PENALVA, C. (1985) Para o estudo das comunidades neoliticas do Alentejo litoral: o concheiro do Medo Tojeiro. *Arqueologia*, 11: 5–15.

THEMIDO, A.A. (1926) Sóbre alguns caracteres sexuais dos húmeros portugueses. *Contribuições para o Estuda da Antropologia Portuguesa* VII, vol. 2, fasc. 4: 103–173.

WENDORF, F. (1968) Site 117: a Nubian final Palaeolithic graveyard near Jebel Sahaba, Sudan. In F. Wendorf (ed.), *The Prehistory of Nubia*, vol. 2. Dallas, Southern Methodist University: 954–995.

ZBYSZWESKI, G. and PENALVA, C. (1979) A estação paleolítica do Medo Tojeiro (Baixo Alentejo). Contribução para o estudo do 'Languedocense' costiero. *Communicações dos Serviços Geológicos de Portugal*, 65: 231–237.

Site Index

Names of French and Spanish cave and rock-shelter sites are usually indexed under the second element, e.g. Dourgne (abri de), Los Azules (cueva de).

(g) indicates a *general* site locality, i.e. one containing a number of discrete sites or findspots.